The Law of
Judicial Precedent

The Law of Judicial Precedent

Bryan A. Garner
Carlos Bea
Rebecca White Berch
Neil M. Gorsuch
Harris L Hartz
Nathan L. Hecht
Brett M. Kavanaugh
Alex Kozinski
Sandra L. Lynch
William H. Pryor Jr.
Thomas M. Reavley
Jeffrey S. Sutton
Diane P. Wood

With a foreword by
Justice Stephen Breyer
Supreme Court of the United States

THOMSON
REUTERS®

Mat # 41648210

Bryan A. Garner is the author of more than 20 law-related books, including *Reading Law: The Interpretation of Legal Texts* (with the late Justice Antonin Scalia), and the editor in chief of *Black's Law Dictionary*. **Carlos Bea** is a judge on the U.S. Court of Appeals for the Ninth Circuit. **Rebecca White Berch** is a retired chief justice of the Supreme Court of Arizona. **Neil M. Gorsuch** is a judge on the U.S. Court of Appeals for the Tenth Circuit. **Harris L Hartz** is a judge on the U.S. Court of Appeals for the Tenth Circuit. **Nathan L. Hecht** is the chief justice of the Supreme Court of Texas. **Brett M. Kavanaugh** is a judge on the U.S. Court of Appeals for the District of Columbia Circuit. **Alex Kozinski** is a judge (formerly chief judge) on the U.S. Court of Appeals for the Ninth Circuit. **Sandra L. Lynch** is a judge (formerly chief judge) on the U.S. Court of Appeals for the First Circuit. **William H. Pryor Jr.** is a judge on the U.S. Court of Appeals for the Eleventh Circuit. **Thomas M. Reavley** is a senior judge on the U.S. Court of Appeals for the Fifth Circuit. **Jeffrey S. Sutton** is a judge on the U.S. Court of Appeals for the Sixth Circuit. **Diane P. Wood** is a judge (formerly chief judge) on the U.S. Court of Appeals for the Seventh Circuit.

Published by Thomson Reuters
610 Opperman Drive
P.O. Box 64526
St. Paul, MN 55164-0527
1-800-328-9352
ISBN 978-0-314-63420-7

Printed in the United States of America.

First printing

© 2016 by Bryan A. Garner. All rights reserved.

For authorization to reproduce any part of this book, contact Karolyne H.C. Garner, Esq., LawProse Inc. (kgarner@lawprose.org).

The publisher is not engaged in rendering legal or other professional advice, and this publication is not a substitute for a lawyer's advice. If you require legal or other expert advice, you should seek the services of a competent lawyer or other professional. The views expressed in this book are those of the authors as legal commentators. Nothing in this book prejudges any case that might come before any of the judicial authors.

THOMSON REUTERS

"It cannot be, there is no power in Venice
Can alter a decree established.
'Twill be recorded for a precedent,
And many an error by the same example
Will rush into the state. It cannot be."
—Shakespeare
(Portia, in *The Merchant of Venice*)

"Decided cases are
the anchors of the laws."
—Francis Bacon

"Respect for precedent is the necessary
foundation of judge-made law."
—A.V. Dicey

"The law must be stable,
yet it cannot stand still."
—Roscoe Pound

"Adherence to precedent must . . . be
the rule rather than the exception
if litigants are to have faith in
the even-handed administration
of justice in the courts."
—Benjamin N. Cardozo

To our independent judiciary,
past, present, and future

Short Table of Contents

Foreword by Justice Stephen Breyer..... xi

Preface............................ xiii

Table of Contents
with Blackletter Principles xv

Introduction 1

A. The Nature and Authority of Judicial Precedents
1. Treating Like Cases Alike 21
2. Vertical Precedents 27
3. Horizontal Precedents 35
4. Dicta vs. Holdings 44
5. Related Terminology................... 76
6. The Context for Extracting a Rule or Standard..................... 80
7. Substantially Similar Facts............. 92
8. Distinguishing Cases 97
9. Analogous Cases 105
10. Multiple Questions Decided........... 115
11. Narrow Cases 130
12. Hypothetical and Moot Cases.......... 133
13. Published vs. Unpublished Opinions.... 142
14. Syllabus and Headnotes 150

B. Weight of Decisions
15. Binding Decisions..................... 155
16. Nonbinding Decisions as Persuasive Authority 164
17. Leading Cases........................ 173
18. Ancient Decisions 176
19. Unanimous vs. Split Decisions.......... 182
20. Plurality Opinions 195
21. Per Curiam Opinions and Summary Dispositions................. 214
22. Equally Divided Opinions in Appellate Courts 220
23. Argument and Consideration.......... 226
24. Nonfinal Decisions 230
25. Approval, Acceptance, and Recognition......................... 233
26. Doubt, Criticism, and Disapproval...... 239
27. Status of Rendering Court............. 243
28. Judicial Reputations................... 248
29. Decisions of Inferior Courts........... 253
30. Decisions Pending Appeal............. 258
31. Decisions to Review or Not to Review........................ 260
32. Advisory Opinions.................... 269
33. Executive Opinions and Decisions 277
34. Legislative Interpretations............. 290

35. Lack of Precedents.................... 295
36. Choosing Between Discordant Decisions........................... 300
37. Overruled and Reversed Decisions: Retroactivity vs. Prospectivity 308

C. Some Practicalities of Stare Decisis
38. Stare Decisis with Statutes.............. 333
39. Statutory Reenactment 346
40. Stare Decisis with Constitutions........ 352
41. Practice and Procedure................ 370
42. Res Judicata Distinguished from Stare Decisis 373
43. Identical Sources of Dispute........... 378
44. Findings of Fact 382
45. Judicial Unity 385
46. Overruling a Decision................. 388
47. Reasons for Overruling................ 396
48. Reasons Against Overruling 404
49. Hardship in a Particular Case 411
50. Changes in Court's Organization or Personnel 415
51. Heightened Stare Decisis for Rules of Property 421

D. The Law of the Case
52. The Doctrine Generally................ 441
53. Final Rulings and Decisions 448
54. Incidental and Collateral Decisions...... 455
55. Cases Remanded to Trial Courts........ 459
56. Subsequent Appeals.................. 465
57. Transferred Decisions, Newly Assigned Judges, and Removed Actions.......... 472
58. Original-Jurisdiction Actions........... 478
59. Exceptions to Law of the Case.......... 480

E. Federal Doctrine and Practice
60. Law of the Circuit..................... 491
61. En Banc Review 495
62. Federal Courts of Coordinate Jurisdiction.......................... 509
63. Certworthiness....................... 517
64. Federal Courts Bound Only by Federal Precedents on Federal Questions 534
65. Jurisdiction and Powers of Federal Courts 551
66. Federal Common Law................. 558
67. Treaties and Interstate Compacts........ 562
68. Federal Law and International Law 565
69. Maritime Law 567

F. State Law in Federal Court
70. *Erie* Doctrine 571
71. Superseding State Decisions 589
72. Which State's Law Governs 593
73. Predicting State Law................... 598
74. Certified Questions.................... 617
75. Controlling State Precedents That Raise a Federal Question........... 646
76. Fictitious-Case and Test-Case Decisions............................ 651

G. State-Law Doctrine and Practice
77. Preeminence of State High Courts on State-Law Questions 655
78. Validity Under the State's Constitution 673
79. Federal Questions in State Courts 679
80. Inferior Federal Courts' Decisions in State Court 691
81. Reverse *Erie* Doctrine 694
82. State-Court Determinations Relating to Federalism................. 697
83. Interstate Uniformity of Decisions....... 702
84. Statutory Interpretation of Governing Out-of-State Laws 709

85. Borrowed-Statute Doctrine 716
86. Out-of-State Precedents as Persuasive Authority................... 724
87. Comity with Penal or Criminal Provisions.................... 729
88. Territorial Courts...................... 732

H. Foreign Precedents
89. Precedential Effect of English Common Law 737
90. Value of Foreign Precedents........... 751
91. Precedents in International Law......... 762

I. Arbitrations
92. The Use of Precedents in Arbitrations........................ 767
93. The Precedential Effect of Arbitral Awards....................... 773

Epilogue 781

Glossary............................ 785

Table of Cases 811

Bibliography........................ 845

Acknowledgments................... 861

Index 863

Foreword

"It is indispensable," Alexander Hamilton writes in *Federalist 78*, for courts to be "bound down by strict rules and precedents."[1] His maxim is not as simple as it sounds. How should courts identify the relevant precedents? Which parts of those precedents should be binding? And what if the governing precedent is wrong? Is respect for a misguided prior decision any better than the "foolish consistency" that Emerson calls "the hobgoblin of little minds"?[2]

These questions do not yield easy answers. Yet their difficulty is matched by their importance, leaving no choice but to ask them. The thirteen authors of this volume have done so with boldness and grace. It is hard to imagine a team better suited to untangle the intricacies of the topic than the fine group of appellate judges and the distinguished law professor who have collaborated to produce this book. Their thorough examination of how courts apply—and decline to apply—precedent offers an invaluable resource for lawyers, judges, and scholars.

Writing this foreword is nonetheless a sad task for me, because I do it in place of my late colleague and friend, Justice Antonin Scalia. He spent his life grappling with the questions this book addresses. I am confident that he would have enjoyed reading it.

I am equally confident that many others will find something to learn in its comprehensive explications. In studying them, we can strive to find a position that balances the need for stability with the need for adaptation, and achieves the kind of consistency that is not foolish, but enlightened.

Stephen Breyer
Associate Justice
Supreme Court of the United States
20 September 2016

---

[1] *The Federalist* No. 78, at 398–99 (Alexander Hamilton) (Garry Wills ed., 1982).
[2] Ralph Waldo Emerson, "Self-Reliance," in *Emerson's Essays* 45, 57 (Houghton, Mifflin & Co. 1980).

Preface

During the heyday of American legal treatises—about 1890 to 1940—several important works were produced in virtually every field of law. Single-volume treatises were known (as they still are) as "hornbooks," and the best ones contained blackletter statements of the law followed by illuminating commentary that elaborated the ideas contained in the blackletter. Among the most impressive hornbooks were those produced by Henry Campbell Black, who was most famous as the original author of *Black's Law Dictionary*, of which he produced two editions (1891 and 1910). But his treatises showed equal erudition and comprehensiveness. One of his best was a 1912 hornbook called *A Handbook on the Law of Judicial Precedent*. Since 1912, no one till now has attempted a hornbook-style treatment of the subject.

Understandably so. The task is a staggering one that involves all sorts of logistical and intellectual difficulties—not least of which is simply drawing together the variegated literature that has developed in a desultory and sporadic way, as well as multifarious caselaw that *always* develops that way. That's why the approach to writing this book was so very unconventional: I developed a working statement of the blackletter principles and then asked a dozen illustrious appellate judges to draft discrete sections of the book. That basic approach was much in line with the way I've written all my recent books: discern the major propositions first, and then write in support of them. The method brings focus to the work.

The drafts of most sections were written by my judicial coauthors. Meanwhile, I researched and wrote passages throughout the book and tried to ensure that the whole thing flowed and held together as a uniform piece. Once we had a complete draft, all the coauthors read the entire manuscript once or twice. Most had copious edits throughout, and many supplied more passages of their own where they thought amplification was needed. Or they suggested either consolidating sections or curtailing them when called for. The idea was to avoid "signed" sections and instead to make the entire book a fully coauthored work that each writer felt comfortable with. As you might imagine, all this took a great deal of time and effort. Nevertheless, it would be unrealistic for anyone to assume that all 13 coauthors stand by every single statement in the book.

That's a tricky point, since we tried to make the text read as if one author had written it. There is admittedly some degree of overlap between sections. Given the nature of the treatise, we thought a modicum of repetition to be not just tolerable but desirable. We've tried throughout to make the research uniformly thorough. But only you, the reader, can decide how well we've achieved our goals.

What we can collectively say is that producing the book has edified us individually on many points important to American jurisprudence. If we've also contributed something to the literature in the field, that's a boon. We hope you'll find the book edifying as well.

Bryan A. Garner
Dallas, Texas
20 September 2016

Table of Contents with Blackletter Principles

A. The Nature and Authority of Judicial Precedents

1. **Treating Like Cases Alike.** Like cases should be decided alike. Following established precedents helps keep the law settled, furthers the rule of law, and promotes both consistency and predictability. 21

2. **Vertical Precedents.** Lower courts must strictly follow vertical precedents—decisions of higher courts in the same jurisdiction. 27

3. **Horizontal Precedents.** A high court or intermediate appellate court generally adheres to horizontal precedents—namely, its own earlier decisions. But if there is a special justification to depart from or overrule precedent, a full court may overturn its own prior decision. Normally, federal three-judge panels are absolutely bound to follow precedents from the same court. 35

4. **Dicta vs. Holdings.** The *holding* of an appellate court constitutes the precedent, as a point necessarily decided. *Dicta* do not: they are merely remarks made in the course of a decision but not essential to the reasoning behind that decision. 44

5. **Related Terminology.** Allied to precedents, but distinct from them, are (1) opinions, (2) judgments, decrees, and mandates, (3) findings, (4) legal principles, (5) rules and standards, (6) judicial policies, and (7) modes of analysis. 76

6. **The Context for Extracting a Rule or Standard.** The language of a judicial decision must be interpreted with reference to the circumstances of the particular case and the question under consideration. Yet a general rule or standard may be extracted that is broader than that in the holding itself and broad enough to apply to a novel case. 80

7. **Substantially Similar Facts.** For one decision to be precedent for another, the facts in the two cases need not be identical. But they must be substantially similar, without material difference. 92

8. **Distinguishing Cases.** A court distinguishes a precedent by discerning material differences between it and the present dispute, thereby concluding that the precedent is either not entirely applicable or wholly inapplicable. 97

9. **Analogous Cases.** If there is no direct precedent, it is proper to argue by analogy and to apply legal principles extracted from cases that are analogous but not identical. But the analogy must be close. 105

10. **Multiple Questions Decided.** When the record presents several questions, and the court considers and deliberately decides each one, the case is precedential for them all. Both of two or more explicitly alternative holdings count as holdings—not as dicta. 115

11. **Narrow Cases.** On rare occasions, a case decided on its own special or peculiar circumstances, or only with a view to avoiding special hardship in the particular case, will not be relied on as an authority for any broad or general legal principle that might be derived from it. 130

12. **Hypothetical and Moot Cases.** A decision rendered on a purely hypothetical question has no precedential force. The same is generally true of moot questions—those on which no effective relief can be given—though the mootness doctrine has several important exceptions. If an amicable action or test case is genuinely contested and involves a question of law, the decision does have precedential force. 133

13. **Published vs. Unpublished Opinions.** An appellate court is bound only by decisions it has designated as binding—usually by publication—but it may find unpublished decisions persuasive. 142

14. **Syllabus and Headnotes.** The syllabus or headnote for a reported case summarizes, for the reader's convenience, the point or points decided. Whether prepared by the court itself or by an official or unofficial reporter, it is not normally part of the decision. 150

B. Weight of Decisions

15. **Binding Decisions.** Vertical precedents are absolutely binding. Not all horizontal precedents have the same value or carry the same weight. Various circumstances may strengthen or weaken the force of a horizontal precedent, including the court's expertise, the novelty of the issue, the extent of the analysis, and the degree to which the decision has been followed by later courts. 155

16. **Nonbinding Decisions as Persuasive Authority.** When an earlier decision is cited not as a binding precedent but as persuasive authority, its value is enhanced by sound, acute, and logical reasoning; by internal evidence that the case received the careful consideration of the court; and by the citation of pertinent authorities. Its value is diminished by the absence of any of these characteristics. 164

17. **Leading Cases.** A leading case is one that first definitely settled an important rule or legal principle and has since been consistently and frequently followed. Such cases are of the very highest authority. 173

18. **Ancient Decisions.** An ancient decision—one that has been long accepted as a correct exposition of the law or that has been repeatedly approved and followed—carries great weight as a precedent and will not be overruled or departed from except for the most cogent reasons. Unlike a statute, such a decision may become obsolete because of changed social or political conditions, or its authority may be gradually undermined by the drift of judicial doctrine away from the principles that it enunciated. 176

19. **Unanimous vs. Split Decisions.** A unanimous decision may have greater weight than a split decision—and often the closer the split, the weaker the precedent. 182

20. **Plurality Opinions.** A plurality opinion is an appellate opinion not having enough judges' votes to constitute a majority but receiving the greatest number of votes in support of the decision. With a plurality decision, the only opinion to be accorded precedential value is that which decides the case on the narrowest grounds. 195

21. **Per Curiam Opinions and Summary Dispositions.** A per curiam opinion—one handed down by an appellate court without identifying the writing judge—is binding on lower courts. Although a short per curiam that offers little reasoning and resembles a summary order is not entitled to much precedential value, a per curiam that details the court's reasoning and analysis of precedents is entitled to the same precedential weight as a signed opinion. 214

22. **Equally Divided Opinions in Appellate Courts.** If appellate judges divide equally in a case, the lower court's judgment will be affirmed. The affirmance is conclusive of the litigants' rights in the particular lawsuit, but it settles no question of law and does not have precedential force in similar cases in the same or any other court. 220

23. **Argument and Consideration.** The authority of a precedent is greatly increased by the fact that the case was exhaustively argued by counsel and fully and maturely considered by the court. It is diminished by the fact that the case was submitted without argument, or on scanty or insufficient argument, or that it did not receive the court's attentive consideration. 226

24. **Nonfinal Decisions.** Decisions rendered ex parte or in preliminary or interlocutory proceedings do not have as much force or value as contested ones that have been handed down with a final disposition. 230

25. **Approval, Acceptance, and Recognition.** Another court's approval of a decision can bolster its credibility and increase its value as precedent. The absence of approval or affirmation through citation or reference can leave an opinion vulnerable to attack. 233

26. **Doubt, Criticism, and Disapproval.** The value of a decision as precedent diminishes when the court issuing it expresses doubt and hesitation or when it has been criticized or disapproved by the same court, by other courts of learning and ability, by well-regarded legal scholars, or by the legal profession generally. 239

27. **Status of Rendering Court.** A court's rank and standing are important in considering a precedent's weight. Great deference is paid to those courts possessing an acknowledged reputation for learning and ability or a special and intimate familiarity with the branch of the law to which the decision in question relates. 243

28. **Judicial Reputations.** A decision's authority may be magnified by the eminence of the judge who wrote the opinion. 248

29. **Decisions of Inferior Courts.** Opinions of trial and other inferior courts generally rank low on the scale of authority but may be followed by higher courts or courts of another jurisdiction when no precedent exists or for other special reasons. 253

30. **Decisions Pending Appeal.** A decision from which an appeal is pending in a higher court should be followed, on the principle of stare decisis, until it is reversed. But the grant of a rehearing in an appellate court suspends all the force of the original decision as an authority until the final conclusion is announced. 258

31. **Decisions to Review or Not to Review.** An appellate court's grant of discretionary review weakens the authority of a nonfinal decision; the court's refusal to grant review in no way implies approval or disapproval of the decision and final judgment of the court below. 260

32. **Advisory Opinions.** An advisory opinion by a state high court, given in response to a question propounded to it by the executive or legislative department, is merely persuasive authority. 269

33. **Executive Opinions and Decisions.** Decisions or opinions of special tribunals, quasi-judicial bodies, attorneys general, and administrative tribunals are not precedents in court. But they are treated with respect and may be allowed to have considerable influence. 277

34. **Legislative Interpretations.** A legislative interpretation of a constitution, statute, or treaty does not control a court's judgment and is not a direct precedent. But in doubtful cases, it may merit some weight and consideration. 290

35. **Lack of Precedents.** If no binding precedent exists for determining a particular case, and the decisions in other jurisdictions on the question involved are in irreconcilable conflict, the court will adopt a rule that appears to be founded on the better rationale. A state may also adopt the rule of another state that has a substantially similar law. 295

36. **Choosing Between Discordant Decisions.** If two decisions of equal authority are irreconcilable, the choice of which one to follow depends on the circumstances. 300

37. **Overruled and Reversed Decisions: Retroactivity vs. Prospectivity.** A decision that has been overruled by the court that rendered it, or been reversed on appeal, should no longer be cited as a precedent in any court within the same system. With only a few exceptions of great importance (collateral review and vested rights), a decision of a high court overruling its former decision is retroactive and restores the legal rule or principle that was in force before the overruled decision was made. The former decision remains conclusive for the litigants in that case. 308

C. Some Practicalities of Stare Decisis

38. **Stare Decisis with Statutes.** Stare decisis applies with special force to questions of statutory construction. Although courts have power to overrule their decisions and change their interpretations, they do so only for the most compelling reasons—but almost never when the previous decision has been repeatedly followed, has long been acquiesced in, or has become a rule of property. 333

39. **Statutory Reenactment.** A statute reenacting (or substantially reenacting) a prior statute whose words have received a judicial interpretation must be regarded as having been adopted with knowledge of that interpretation. 346

40. **Stare Decisis with Constitutions.** The doctrine of stare decisis applies less rigidly in constitutional cases than it does in statutory cases because the correction of an erroneous constitutional decision by the legislature is well-nigh impossible. Yet stare decisis should and does play a significant role in constitutional adjudication. 352

41. **Practice and Procedure.** Stare decisis applies less strongly to decisions on matters of practice and procedure than to those involving property and contract rights. 370

42. **Res Judicata Distinguished from Stare Decisis.** A judgment is binding and conclusive as res judicata only on the parties to the particular lawsuit and those in privity with them: it creates estoppel for disputed matters of fact and law. By contrast, stare decisis is conclusive on questions of law, not of fact, and a judicial precedent is applied to a similar state of facts later arising, no matter who the parties are. 373

43. **Identical Sources of Dispute.** Once fully considered and decided by an appellate court, a question of law will not be reexamined in a later controversy when the claim or defense arises from the same or identical instrument, transaction, or occurrence, even if the later lawsuit is entirely independent of the first and the parties are not the same. 378

44. **Findings of Fact.** A precedent is valuable and authoritative only as establishing a legal rule or principle. Stare decisis does not apply to findings of fact and has only limited application to cases that turn on the admissibility or weight of evidence or on the application of a settled legal principle to the facts established in the particular controversy. 382

45. **Judicial Unity.** Judges sitting in the same appellate court should not make contradictory or conflicting rulings in the same case or on the same subject. Each should defer to and accept decisions already made. 385

46. **Overruling a Decision.** Stare decisis does not prevent a court from overruling a horizontal precedent that on reconsideration it finds to be plainly and palpably wrong. But the court must first decide whether overruling the precedent would result in more harm than continuing to follow the erroneous decision. 388

47. **Reasons for Overruling.** A court may decide to overrule a horizontal precedent if there are sound and necessary reasons to do so. 396

48. **Reasons Against Overruling.** A court may decide against overruling an established horizontal precedent, even if it is now considered erroneous or open to grave doubts. 404

49. **Hardship in a Particular Case.** The fact that applying a well-settled legal rule will work hardship in a particular case is not reason for overruling an earlier decision or even departing from it. 411

50. **Changes in Court's Organization or Personnel.** A change in the court's organization or in judicial personnel should not throw former decisions open to reconsideration or justify their reversal except on grounds that would have warranted such a course if the makeup of the court had remained the same. ... 415

51. **Heightened Stare Decisis for Rules of Property.** A precedent that creates a rule of property—a widely relied-on legal principle established by a judicial decision or series of decisions relating to title to real, personal, or intellectual property—is generally treated as inviolable. 421

D. The Law of the Case

52. **The Doctrine Generally.** When a point or question arising in the course of litigation has been finally decided, the legal rule or principle announced as applicable to the facts presented becomes the law of that case in all its later stages or developments. It is binding on the parties, their privies, and the courts. 441

53. **Final Rulings and Decisions.** For a ruling or decision to become the law of the case, it must issue from a court with jurisdiction over the dispute and be final as to the matters involved—and it must be part of the same case. 448

54. **Incidental and Collateral Decisions.** The law-of-the-case doctrine applies to decisions necessary to resolve the dispute as opposed to decisions collateral or incidental to its resolution. The doctrine requires a holding on the relevant issue before it can be closed to its further consideration. 455

55. **Cases Remanded to Trial Courts.** When a case has been heard and determined by an appellate court, the legal rules and principles laid down as applicable to it bind the trial court in all further proceedings in the same lawsuit. They cannot be reviewed, ignored, or departed from. 459

56. **Subsequent Appeals.** When an appellate court decides a case that later returns there by appeal or writ of error, only questions that were not determined in the previous decision will be considered. A point of law already adjudicated becomes the law of the case and may not be reversed or departed from at any later stage without a relevant exception to the doctrine. 465

57. **Transferred Decisions, Newly Assigned Judges, and Removed Actions.** When a case has been transferred from one venue to another in the same court system, reassigned to new judges within the same court system, or removed from one court system to another, the rulings and decisions previously made by the prior court and judges are generally binding on the later court and judges—except on questions of law within the special expertise of the transferee court. 472

58. **Original-Jurisdiction Actions.** The law-of-the-case doctrine is relaxed in original actions before the U.S. Supreme Court. 478

59. **Exceptions to Law of the Case.** A court may reconsider legal questions previously decided during the same case if materially new facts are presented at a later stage of the case, if controlling legal authority has changed significantly since the prior decision, or if reconsideration is necessary to prevent a miscarriage of justice. 480

E. Federal Doctrine and Practice

60. **Law of the Circuit.** A federal district court or (with rare exceptions) a circuit panel must follow decisions of the court of appeals in the same circuit in preference to the decisions of all other courts, state or national, unless there is a contrary decision by the U.S. Supreme Court. 491

61. **En Banc Review.** Although a decision of a three-judge panel of a federal circuit is binding precedent within the circuit, a circuit court may hear or rehear a case en banc to consider an issue of exceptional importance, to resolve a conflict in the court's precedents, or to ensure that the court's decisions conform to Supreme Court precedent. An en banc decision is especially authoritative. 495

62. **Federal Courts of Coordinate Jurisdiction.** Although ordinarily a decision of a coordinate court has no stare decisis effect, a federal court will treat a decision of a federal court of equal rank respectfully and may be persuaded by it. A federal court may decide to treat as binding the decisions of its parent court issued before the court's own creation. On appeal from a federal district court, the Federal Circuit will follow the law of the district court's regional circuit on matters outside its specific statutory jurisdiction. 509

63. **Certworthiness.** A federal circuit-court or state high-court decision is considered certworthy—that is, a serious candidate for U.S. Supreme Court review—if it (1) involves a federal question that has split the federal circuits or state high courts, or (2) has great practical significance or importance to federal jurisprudence. 517

64. **Federal Courts Bound Only by Federal Precedents on Federal Questions.** In interpreting and applying the U.S. Constitution, a treaty, or a federal statute, federal courts are not bound to follow the decisions of any state court—only relevant federal decisions. State-court precedents construing federal law are persuasive only. 534

65. **Jurisdiction and Powers of Federal Courts.** Questions concerning the jurisdiction and powers of federal courts are to be decided exclusively by those courts. The statutes and judicial decisions of a state are not controlling authority. 551

66. **Federal Common Law.** Although there is no general federal common law, federal courts fashion common law in limited circumstances and sometimes borrow state law to supply a legal rule. 558

67. **Treaties and Interstate Compacts.** Because treaties and interstate compacts are federal law, federal courts are not bound by state-court interpretations of them. 562

68. **Federal Law and International Law.** Questions of international law and international comity, like those arising under treaties with foreign nations, are decided by federal courts in the exercise of their independent judgment. The decisions of the state courts are not controlling. 565

69. **Maritime Law.** In exercising their jurisdiction in admiralty and maritime cases, federal courts are governed by federal statutes and the general principles of maritime law. In some instances, however, federal courts may borrow state rules or allow state law to supplement general maritime law. 567

F. State Law in Federal Court

70. *Erie* **Doctrine.** Common-law claims that came to the federal courts under diversity jurisdiction were once typically decided as matters of federal law. But in *Erie Railroad v. Tompkins* (1938), the U.S. Supreme Court overruled a century of precedent to hold that such claims must be decided under state law. Even so, federal procedural rules apply in federal litigation. 571

71. **Superseding State Decisions.** When a state-law question has been decided by a federal court in the preliminary stages of a lawsuit, and a contrary ruling is made by the state's high court on the same question before the federal court finally disposes of the case, the federal court will reverse its decision and conform to the judgment of the state court. 589

72. **Which State's Law Governs.** A federal court in a diversity case must follow the conflict-of-laws doctrine of the forum state to determine which state's substantive law applies to a state-law issue in the case. The same rule applies to a state-law claim before the federal court under supplemental jurisdiction. There is no clear rule, however, to determine which state's laws should govern when a state-law question comes before the federal court under its federal-question jurisdiction. 593

73. **Predicting State Law.** When a question of state law must be resolved by a federal court, and there is no decision by the highest state court, the federal court must predict how the high court would decide the issue, relying on the same clues that would be used by the state's lower courts and following decisions of the state's intermediate appellate courts unless there is good reason to believe that the high court would not agree. 598

74. **Certified Questions.** If a federal court must rule on a question of unclear state law, and the state has a procedure in place for ruling on certified questions received from federal courts, the federal court has the option of certifying the question directly to the state high court. 617

75. **Controlling State Precedents That Raise a Federal Question.** In a federal-question case, a federal court is ordinarily bound to follow the precedents established by state-court decisions on the interpretation of the state constitution and state statutes. 646

76. **Fictitious-Case and Test-Case Decisions.** A federal court will not entertain a suggestion that a decision of a state's high court was rendered in a fictitious or test case—and is therefore not binding—unless the facts underlying the decision show that it was made solely for the purpose of anticipating and influencing the judgment of the federal court in an already-pending action. 651

G. State-Law Doctrine and Practice

77. **Preeminence of State High Courts on State-Law Questions.** Whether construing a state's constitution, statutes, or regulations, or for that matter developing common law, the state high court has the final say—and thus final authority—over the interpretation of its own state's laws. 655

78. **Validity Under the State's Constitution.** A federal court should be reluctant to adjudge a state statute as consistent with or conflicting with the state constitution if the state courts have not addressed the statute's validity. Yet exceptional circumstances may arise in which the federal court may have to rule on a state statute's validity under the state constitution. 673

79. **Federal Questions in State Courts.** With a federal question—that is, one arising under the Constitution, statutes, or treaties of the United States—state courts must follow any applicable U.S. Supreme Court decisions, overruling if necessary their own previous decisions to the contrary. 679

80. **Inferior Federal Courts' Decisions in State Court.** Though entitled to respectful consideration in the state courts, the decisions of inferior federal courts are not controlling authority in state court unless their judgments operate by way of estoppel. 691

81. **Reverse *Erie* Doctrine.** When state law is preempted by federal law, or federal law controls, state courts are bound by U.S. Supreme Court precedent. 694

82. **State-Court Determinations Relating to Federalism.** On a question relating to the jurisdiction, powers, and procedures of the various federal courts, the decisions of the U.S. Supreme Court are binding and conclusive on the state courts, and decisions of lower federal courts merit careful consideration. 697

83. **Interstate Uniformity of Decisions.** For the sake of uniformity, as well as out of respect for authority, a state's high court deciding a new question should consider the general or current trend of judicial decisions in other states if unanimity is apparent and widely extended. If the matter is important and the general prevalence of the same legal rule is desirable, the state court may pursue this course even though doing so requires overruling one or more horizontal precedents. 702

84. **Statutory Interpretation of Governing Out-of-State Laws.** When a pending issue is governed by the law of another state, or by some law other than that of the forum state, and authoritative expositions of the other state's law can be found from that state's courts, they will generally be accepted and followed as binding precedents. 709

85. **Borrowed-Statute Doctrine.** When one state enacts another state's statutory language that has a settled judicial interpretation, it is sometimes presumed that the settled interpretation is adopted with the statute. But this overstates the matter: properly viewed, the decisions of the source state's high court on a point concerning the statute are merely persuasive precedents and are not binding on the courts of the borrowing state. 716

86. **Out-of-State Precedents as Persuasive Authority.** On a question of general jurisprudence or the interpretation of a domestic statute, a decision made in a similar legal system is not binding as precedent. Yet it may be cited as persuasive authority, respected for its reasoning and judgment, and followed if approved. 724

87. **Comity with Penal or Criminal Provisions.** A state trial court will determine for itself, not necessarily following another state's decisions, whether a sister state's legislation is penal or criminal, and therefore unenforceable in the state where the lawsuit is filed, or whether it is either contrary to the laws and policy of that state or injurious to its own citizens. 729

88. **Territorial Courts.** The courts of a territory will follow the decisions of the U.S. Supreme Court, and of the U.S. circuit court having appellate jurisdiction, on all questions of law with one exception: on questions about the interpretation of a statute adopted from a state, they will follow the decisions of that state's courts. 732

H. Foreign Precedents

89. **Precedential Effect of English Common Law.** Most states have adopted English common law antedating the American Revolution as binding judicial precedent as long as it is not repugnant to the laws of those states or the laws of the United States. States often treat later English precedents as persuasive authority. 737

90. **Value of Foreign Precedents.** The value of a foreign precedent is increased by its relevance to the issue at hand, but is diminished to the extent that it is based on conditions—geographic, climatic, social, economic, or political—peculiar to the foreign state or country. U.S. courts generally do not apply the law of a foreign country unless it gives rise to the claim or applies through choice-of-law principles. But a U.S. court will apply foreign law when the litigants' rights depend on it and the circumstances favor keeping the case in an American forum. 751

91. **Precedents in International Law.** In international law, precedents are never treated as binding; they are often considered persuasive, sometimes highly so. 762

I. Arbitrations

92. **The Use of Precedents in Arbitrations.** Ordinary principles of stare decisis generally do not apply in arbitration proceedings, or in court review and enforcement of arbitration awards. 767

93. **The Precedential Effect of Arbitral Awards.** Although arbitral awards have no binding precedential value, they may be considered persuasive. 773

Introduction

One might be tempted to say, after long and hard study, that the law of judicial precedent amounts to no more than this: all tribunals look at decisional precursors; all have at least some discretion in deciding whether to follow those precursors (or to distinguish them); and the higher the court, the greater its discretion. That's about it.

But that's gross reductionism. There's actually much more to it than that. There are nuances and complications. It takes patience and acuity to work through them. It's fair to say that "[l]ay people—and, for that matter, more than a few lawyers and judges—have more misunderstandings about the nature and role of precedents than about any other aspect of legal reasoning."[1] So let's start at the very beginning.

Judicial precedents are one of the two main sources of law in the Anglo-American legal system. Constitutions and statutes make up the other. Traditionally, statutes and precedents were considered to be very different types of law. Statutes have always been thought of as "written law." Because they are written, their text tends to be analyzed very closely.

Precedents contained in judicial opinions have traditionally been considered "unwritten law" because long ago judges simply read or announced their decisions from the bench, without writing them down.[2] In fact, some English judges still do that.

---

[1] Lief H. Carter, "Legal Reasoning," in 2 *Encyclopedia of the American Judicial System* 875, 879 (Robert J. Janosik ed., 1987); *cf.* W.W. Buckland & Arnold D. McNair, *Roman Law and Common Law* 8 (F.H. Lawson ed., 2d ed. 1952) (noting that "some of the dislike of the [common-law] doctrine expressed by foreign lawyers is probably due to some misconception of its nature"); Francis Lieber, *On Civil Liberty and Self-Government* 209 (Theodore D. Woolsey ed., 3d ed. 1883) (noting even more pertly that "[t]he continental lawyers have a great fear of precedent, but . . . they do not comprehend the nature of precedent").

[2] Timothy Walker, *Introduction to American Law* § 18, at 53 (Clement Bates ed., 10th ed. 1895) (stating that *common law* "is said to be unwritten because there is no record of its formal enactment").

It used to be widely thought—until about the end of the 19th century—that judicial precedents were merely *evidence* of the law, as opposed to a *source* of it. No serious legal thinker now believes this. Today, precedents are understood to make up part of the law: "A judicial precedent speaks . . . with authority; it is not merely evidence of the law but a source of it; and the courts are bound to follow the law that is so established."[3]

Because all American appellate judges produce written opinions today, few commentators now refer to caselaw as unwritten law. Yet although judicial opinions are now written, reading caselaw differs fundamentally from reading statutes. Judges often say that they *construe* or *interpret* a statute, which means they try to determine the meaning of its language. By contrast, judges and lawyers often say that they *analyze* a judicial precedent. Although analyzing an opinion involves delving into the judge's words, you must go beyond the judge's words—which in themselves are of no great significance, as opposed to what they denote.[4] You must also understand the opinion's legal background, the facts of the case, and the relationship between those facts and the outcome.

In other words, with caselaw you can't just interpret its language; you must also engage in legal reasoning to find what we call the case's *holding*—the rule or principle necessary to justify or explain the outcome. When lawyers and judges analyze a precedent, they're usually trying to determine just what its holding is. They're also trying to gauge how broadly or narrowly the holding sweeps—that is, how it will apply to future cases that present a similar issue but with different facts.

You begin the task of analyzing a precedent with the thought in mind that readers—yourself included—may find its meaning

---

[3] John Salmond, *Jurisprudence* § 56, at 176 (Glanville L. Williams ed., 10th ed. 1947); *see* Burke Shartel, *Our Legal System and How It Operates* 416–17 (1951) ("Judicial lawmaking and the following of precedent are correlative acts. They are like the proposal and acceptance of marriage. The judges who lay down a precedent offer it as a guide for subsequent decision; the judges who follow the precedent accept it as a guide.").

[4] *See* A.W.B. Simpson, "The *Ratio Decidendi* of a Case and the Doctrine of Binding Precedent," in *Oxford Essays in Jurisprudence* 148, 166 (A.G. Guest ed., 1961) ("[T]he formulation of the rule by the judge is not, and cannot be, treated as precisely the same as a statutory rule, where every word is sacred.").

uncertain. Opinion-writing isn't an exact science or a precise art. A judge might not reach a perfect understanding of the basis for the judgment. And even a judge who clearly grasps that basis might not be able to articulate it in ways that others will understand. That's why reading an opinion calls for careful thought and at times a tolerance for frustration. Different readers may come away from the same opinion with quite different versions of its meaning. And different meanings are even more likely to be found when different readers take various approaches to the analysis.

Finding the right approach depends partly on your purpose. Are you arguing an appeal from the opinion? Urging a lower court that its decision is or isn't controlled by a higher court's decision? Relying on the opinion—or distinguishing it—before the court that delivered it? Planning a transaction and hoping to find a secure basis for the deal? Offering general advice to a client who needs to plan how to act despite a set of legal principles that are still developing? Sitting as a judge and weighing the opinion's importance to your own decision? You may be looking for different things in each of these situations. At times a narrowly technical approach may be called for. Other occasions may demand a broader approach, one that relies more heavily on sensitivity, seasoned judgment, even intuition.

Whatever your purpose, you'll begin by trying to identify a holding that expresses a legal rule. Doing that requires you to master the facts and pay attention to the procedural context that frames the question. You might not need to go any further—the decision may reconfirm a well-settled proposition, or you may conclude that greater refinement is inappropriate for other reasons. But more often you'll need to draw on sophisticated analytic tools and various doctrines related to understanding precedent.

Entrenched ideas

Let's consider some instances. Does major-league baseball engage in "interstate commerce" so that it must obey federal antitrust laws like other businesses operating across state lines? Should a farmer feel confident that he doesn't "take" wildlife in violation of the Endangered Species Act when he plows a field, even if in the process he unintentionally disturbs birds that have settled there? You might think the answer to these questions is yes. Surely professional baseball is a form of commerce—an interstate one at that. And it may seem odd to think of a farmer's "taking" wildlife by plowing a field. But in both cases your intuitions would be entirely wrong—legally speaking. And the reason they're wrong has to do with the nature of judicial precedent.

On behalf of the U.S. Supreme Court, Holmes J. wrote nearly a century ago that "giving exhibitions of baseball" doesn't involve interstate commerce.[5] In the years since then, the Supreme Court has reconsidered that decision, even admitting doubts about its soundness, but has adhered to it all the same.[6] As for our farmer, the Court has more recently upheld regulations interpreting the statutory term *take* to apply to him.[7] This despite the intuition that "taking" requires an act aimed at killing or capturing wildlife, an intuition that one dissenting judge expressed this way: "[I]f I were intent on taking a rabbit, a squirrel, or a deer, as the term 'take' is used in common English parlance, I would go forth with my dogs or my guns or my snares and proceed to 'harass, . . . pursue, hunt, shoot, wound, kill, trap, capture, or collect' one of the target species."[8]

A judicial precedent does its most strenuous work when a later court thinks it's wrong. Let's assume it's pretty obvious that "exhibitions of baseball" do involve interstate commerce. If we lacked a system of precedent, courts faced with the issue would have to decide it on the merits in every case, and presumably they would get the outcome right more often than not. But in a system

---

5   *Federal Baseball Club of Baltimore v. National League of Prof'l Baseball Clubs*, 259 U.S. 200, 208 (1922).

6   See *Flood v. Kuhn*, 407 U.S. 258 (1972); *United States v. Shubert*, 348 U.S. 222, 230 (1955); *Toolson v. New York Yankees, Inc.*, 346 U.S. 356 (1953) (per curiam). See 15 U.S.C. § 26b (codifying in significant measure baseball's exemption from the antitrust laws).

7   *Babbitt v. Sweet Home Chapter of Cmtys. for a Great Or.*, 515 U.S. 687, 690 (1995).

8   *Sweet Home Chapter of Cmtys. for a Great Or. v. Babbitt*, 1 F.3d 1, 12 (D.C. Cir. 1993) (Sentelle J. dissenting) (quoting 16 U.S.C. § 1532(19)), *opinion modified on reh'g*, 17 F.3d 1463 (D.C. Cir. 1994), *rev'd*, 515 U.S. 687 (1995).

respectful of precedent, if an authoritative court holds that baseball isn't engaged in interstate commerce, later courts may be obliged to get the answer wrong in every case that follows. The power of precedent includes, then, the power to enshrine wrong decisions.[9]

It's this very aspect of precedent that has proved such a rich source of material for the satirist. Take Jeremy Bentham, who called the art of judicial decision-making "the art of being methodically ignorant of what everyone knows."[10] Or the inimitable Jonathan Swift: "It is a maxim among these lawyers that whatever hath been done before may legally be done again: and therefore they take special care to record all the decisions formerly made against common justice and the general reason of mankind."[11] Bentham and Swift were describing precedent at its worst; at its best it amounts to a prudent guide for future decisions.

The legal doctrine commanding deference to precedent derives its shorthand Latin name, *stare decisis*, from the maxim *stare decisis et non quieta movere*—"to stand by things decided and not disturb settled points."[12] Under stare decisis, in short, a court must either follow or distinguish the controlling decisions of its predecessor

---

9 See Clarence Morris, *How Lawyers Think* 25–26 (1938) ("Past experience is not only a source of suggestions for the solution of new problems: it is also a source of perpetuation of error."). *See also* W.J.V. Windeyer, *Lectures on Legal History* 97 (2d ed. 1949) ("Judges will hold themselves bound by decisions of which they disapprove.").

10 Rupert Cross & J.W. Harris, *Precedent in English Law* 1 (4th ed. 1991) (attributing this aphorism to Jeremy Bentham).

11 Jonathan Swift, *Gulliver's Travels and Other Writings* 274 (1726; repr. 1962).

12 *Garner's Dictionary of Legal Usage* 841 (3d ed. 2011); *see also In re Osborne*, 76 F.3d 306, 309 (9th Cir. 1996) ("Stare decisis is the policy of the court to stand by precedent; the term is but an abbreviation of *stare decisis et non quieta movere*— 'to stand by and adhere to decisions and not disturb what is settled.'"); *Planned Parenthood of SE Pa. v. Casey*, 505 U.S. 833, 954 (1992) (Rehnquist C.J. concurring in the judgment in part and dissenting in part) ("*Stare decisis* is defined in *Black's Law Dictionary* as meaning 'to abide by, or adhere to, decided cases.'") (citation omitted); *see further Bonner v. City of Prichard*, 661 F.2d 1206, 1211 (11th Cir. 1981) (en banc) ("The full phrase is *stare decisis et non quieta movere*—'to adhere to precedents and *not to unsettle things which are established*.'") (emphasis in original); Laurence H. Tribe, *The Invisible Constitution* 208 (2008) (defining *stare decisis* as "the principle that carefully considered constitutional interpretations issued by the organs of government should not be revisited absent circumstances more compelling than a mere change in the identity of the individuals who authored the interpretations in question").

court on a question of law. For stare decisis to apply, a decision must have been rendered by a majority of the voting judges of the hearing court; must involve an issue of law, not of fact; and usually must be in a published opinion.[13] Most important, the court must have decided the issue for which the precedent is claimed; it cannot merely have discussed it in dictum, ignored it, or assumed the point without ruling on it.[14]

Despite the age of the Latin phrase, stare decisis isn't well understood. To the contrary, the application of stare decisis remains remarkably uncertain.[15] Perhaps that's because it's not so much a doctrine as a *method*: "As applied in the United States, the rule of stare decisis is a matter of technique. In whatever way courts reach their conclusion, they are expected to place the situation they are judging within the generalized class of some existing decision."[16]

The legal basis for the doctrine

The Constitution does not mention the doctrine of precedent or stare decisis. Sometimes courts (including the U.S. Supreme Court) refer to stare decisis as a mere "judicial policy."[17]

But can that be right? Not infrequently the Supreme Court reaffirms debatable decisions on the ground that they warrant

---

13 *But see* Fed. R. App. P. 32.1 (preventing courts from restricting the citation of unpublished opinions issued on or after 1 January 2007); Fed. R. App. P. 32.1 Committee Note (stating that the rule "says nothing about what effect a court must give to one of its unpublished opinions or to the unpublished opinions of another court"). See § 13.

14 *Webster v. Fall*, 266 U.S. 507, 511 (1925) ("Questions which merely lurk in the record, neither brought to the attention of the court nor ruled upon, are not to be considered as having been so decided as to constitute precedents.").

15 *See, e.g.*, Randy E. Barnett, *Trumping Precedent with Original Meaning: Not as Radical as It Sounds*, 22 Const. Comment. 257, 261 (2005) ("How and when precedent should be rejected remains one of the great unresolved controversies of jurisprudence.").

16 Max Radin, "Case Law and Stare Decisis: Concerning *Präjudizienrecht in Amerika*," in *Essays on Jurisprudence from the Columbia Law Review* 3, 16 (1963) (italics omitted).

17 *See, e.g., Agostini v. Felton*, 521 U.S. 203, 235 (1997) (quoting *Payne v. Tennessee*, 501 U.S. 808, 828 (1991)); *Seminole Tribe of Fla. v. Florida*, 517 U.S. 44, 63 (1996).

deference as precedent.[18] But by what power might judges favor a mere policy of their own hand over what (they are convinced) the Constitution commands or the legislature requires? And if precedent lacks constitutional grounding, might Congress have the power to compel courts to disregard it, to decide cases without reference to precedent? Could courts even choose to disregard precedents and abandon stare decisis?

Perhaps some degree of respect for precedent may be required for federal courts to exercise the "judicial Power" endowed by Article III, or to comply with other constitutional commands like due process.[19] By the time of the founding, William Blackstone reported that it was "an established rule" that English courts should "abide by former precedents."[20] In *The Federalist*, Alexander Hamilton emphasized that "[t]o avoid an arbitrary discretion in the courts, it is indispensable that they should be bound down by strict rules and precedents."[21] And Story J. maintained in his

---

18 See *Michigan v. Bay Mills Indian Cmty.*, 134 S.Ct. 2024, 2031 (2014) (reaffirming *Kiowa Tribe of Okla. v. Manufacturing Techs., Inc.*, 523 U.S. 751 (1998)); *Dickerson v. United States*, 530 U.S. 428, 432 (2000) (reaffirming *Miranda v. Arizona*, 384 U.S. 436 (1966)).

19 Gary Lawson, *Stare Decisis and Constitutional Meaning: Panel II—The Constitutional Case Against Precedent*, 17 Harv J.L. & Pub. Pol'y 23, 28–29 (1994). For interesting discussions of the constitutional status of stare decisis from varying perspectives, see Jonathan F. Mitchell, *Stare Decisis and Constitutional Text*, 110 Mich. L. Rev. 1 (2011); John O. McGinnis & Michael B. Rappaport, *Reconciling Originalism and Precedent*, 103 Nw. U. L. Rev. 803 (2009); Daniel A. Farber, *The Rule of Law and the Law of Precedents*, 90 Minn. L. Rev. 1173 (2006); Randy E. Barnett, *It's a Bird, It's a Plane, No, It's Super Precedent: A Response to Farber and Gerhardt*, 90 Minn. L. Rev. 1232 (2006); Richard H. Fallon Jr., *Stare Decisis and the Constitution: An Essay on Constitutional Methodology*, 76 N.Y.U. L. Rev. 570 (2001); Michael Stokes Paulsen, *Abrogating Stare Decisis by Statute: May Congress Remove the Precedential Effect of* Roe *and* Casey*?*, 109 Yale L.J. 1535 (2000).

20 1 William Blackstone, *Commentaries on the Laws of England* 69 (4th ed. 1770); see *id.* at 70; see also Emily Kadens, *Justice Blackstone's Common Law Orthodoxy*, 103 Nw. U. L. Rev. 1553, 1558 (2009) (noting Blackstone's conviction that "the judge was obligated by his oath to obey the precedent set in the authoritative sources"). For a fascinating evaluation of Blackstone's later treatment of precedent as a justice of the Court of Common Pleas, see *id.* at 1589–92; *cf.* 1 Henry de Bracton, *De Legibus et Consuetudinibus Angliæ* 9 (ca. 1250; Sir Travers Twiss ed., 1878) ("If, however, any new and unaccustomed cases shall emerge, and such as have not been usual in the realm, if, indeed any like cases should have occurred, let them be judged after a similar case, for it is a good occasion to proceed from like to like.").

21 *The Federalist* No. 78, at 471 (Alexander Hamilton) (Clinton Rossiter ed., 1961).

Commentaries on the Constitution that the "conclusive effect of judicial adjudications, was in the full view of the framers."[22]

In fact, it was in the founding era that the modern concept crystallized.[23] In his celebrated *Commentaries on American Law*, Kent traced the doctrine of precedent to the formative years of American law: "The inviolability of precedents was . . . inculcated at a period which we have been accustomed to regard as the infancy of our law, with as much zeal and decision as at any subsequent period."[24] Today, the Supreme Court's occasional references to stare decisis as a "judicial policy" rather than an "inexorable command" should be read as suggesting not that the doctrine lacks constitutional provenance but that the doctrine doesn't demand obedience to precedent without exception. It leaves room for courts to distinguish and overrule. But even if that's true, other intriguing questions remain—not least how much respect for precedent the Constitution requires or, put differently, how far courts may go in distinguishing and overruling precedent consistently with the Constitution[25] or in declaring what counts as precedent and what doesn't.

---

22 1 Joseph Story, *Commentaries on the Constitution of the United States* § 378, at 350 (2d ed. 1858).

23 *See* 12 William Holdsworth, *A History of English Law* 146 (2d ed. 1938) ("The modern theory as to the authority of decided cases was reached substantially by the second half of the eighteenth century."); *but see* G.W. Keeton, *The Elementary Principles of Jurisprudence* 97 (2d ed. 1949) ("The doctrine of judicial precedent is of modern growth, and was unknown in the Middle Ages. Its growth has coincided with the development of a modern system of law reporting, the origins of which are discoverable in later Tudor times."). *Contra* Alf Ross, *On Law and Justice* 85 (1959) ("As early as the thirteenth century it became common to cite precedents, and in his famous *Note Book* Bracton made a collection of 2,000 legal cases, almost certainly for practical use.").

24 1 James Kent, *Commentaries on American Law* *477 (Charles M. Barnes ed., 13th ed. 1884).

25 *See, e.g., Anastasoff v. United States*, 223 F.3d 898, 899–905 (8th Cir. 2000) ("8th Circuit Rule 28A(i), insofar as it would allow us to avoid the precedential effect of our prior decisions, purports to expand the judicial power beyond the bounds of Article III, and is therefore unconstitutional."), *vacated as moot on reh'g en banc*, 235 F.3d 1054 (8th Cir. 2000); Fallon, *Stare Decisis and the Constitution*, 76 N.Y.U. L. Rev. at 591–97; Paulsen, *Abrogating Stare Decisis by Statute*, 109 Yale L.J. at 1578–82. *But see Hart v. Massanari*, 266 F.3d 1155 (9th Cir. 2001) (examining historical views about binding and persuasive precedent and reporting of cases, finding that judicial opinions were usually not binding

The practical justifications for the doctrine

Why do we bother with precedent? How is it that a system devoted in part to preserving *wrong* decisions has proved so durable in Anglo-American law and come to be thought of by many as central to our conception of justice?

Five discrete arguments are frequently advanced here. Some depend on the consequences associated with respecting precedent. Other arguments are rule-based, grounded on the conviction that a just judicial system requires at least some degree of deference to precedent. And some suggest that it's simply better than all the alternatives.[26] Let's consider each of the five practical arguments in defense of our system of precedent.

First, the past can teach valuable lessons inherently worthy of our respect. Precedent is a way of accumulating and passing down the learning of past generations, a font of established wisdom richer than what can be found in any single judge or panel of judges: "The stock of precedents is produced by generations of judges wrestling with hard questions. . . . Precedent . . . allows each judge to build on the wisdom of others."[27] Sometimes it is also said that past cases are worthy of consideration by virtue of the very fact that they *are* our past: "We must respect the past because the world of culture that we inherit from it makes us who we are."[28] Or to put it negatively, a judge who departs from a precedent without rationally distinguishing it is necessarily, though perhaps only implicitly, criticizing it.[29] Hewing to past decisions

---

precedent, and concluding that Constitution's framers didn't oppose issuance of nonprecedential opinions).

26 Richard A. Wasserstrom, *The Judicial Decision: Toward a Theory of Legal Justification* 56 (1961) ("Although the thought of following rules blindly and inexorably may appear to some an absurdity from the outset, the conception of a legal system in which rules are not followed has been characterized by others as an even greater monstrosity.").

27 Frank H. Easterbrook, *Stability and Reliability in Judicial Decisions*, 73 Cornell L. Rev. 422, 422–23 (1988); *see also Burnet v. Coronado Oil & Gas Co.*, 285 U.S. 393, 406 (1932) (Brandeis J. dissenting); *cf.* Edmund Burke, *Reflections on the Revolution in France* 95 (1790; L.G. Mitchell ed., 1993) (making much the same point).

28 Anthony T. Kronman, *Precedent and Tradition*, 99 Yale L.J. 1029, 1066 (1990).

29 B.A. Wortley, *Jurisprudence* 66 (1967).

isn't just a matter of inertia. It's also a matter of professional honor and fealty.

Second, cases are decided one at a time, and rules often take shape only slowly and from the accumulation of case-specific decisions pointing in the same direction. Our system deals with questions of law by increment, by degree, and on specific facts litigated from the bottom up.[30] This system allows for a greater degree of fine-tuning and refinement—and constant improvement.[31]

Third, efficiency benefits are often claimed for precedent.[32] Just as citizens benefit from having some idea what law will apply to their cases, so too courts, litigants, and the public at large gain something from a system that doesn't require each case to be litigated anew and instead allows resort to rules already at hand.[33] As Cardozo J. put it: "[T]he labor of judges would be increased almost to the breaking point if every past decision could be reopened in every case, and one could not lay one's own course of bricks on the secure foundation of the courses laid by others who had gone before him."[34]

Fourth, by seeking to ensure some consistency in outcomes among decision-makers, the doctrine of precedent may simultaneously promote respect for the judiciary as a neutral source.[35] In this way, the doctrine might be thought to be thoroughly utilitarian.[36]

---

30 Joseph Raz, *The Authority of Law: Essays on Law and Morality* 196 (2d ed. 2009) ("Judicial law-making tends to be by the way of piecemeal reform. The ability of the courts radically to reshape a substantial area of the law by a single decision is very limited."); Easterbrook, *Stability and Reliability in Judicial Decisions*, 73 Cornell L. Rev. at 423.

31 *See* Francis Lieber, *On Civil Liberty and Self-Government* 213 (Theodore D. Woolsey ed., 3d ed. 1883) ("The common law is at all time expanding and improving.").

32 *Id.* (noting that stare decisis "expedites the work of the courts by preventing the constant reconsideration of settled questions").

33 *See* Lief H. Carter & Thomas F. Burke, *Reason in Law* 24 (6th ed. 2002) (noting that although precedents never provide complete certainty, they "help narrow the range of legal choices judges face when they justify a decision").

34 Benjamin N. Cardozo, *The Nature of the Judicial Process* 149 (1921; repr. 1991).

35 *See, e.g.*, Cass R. Sunstein, *On Analogical Reasoning*, 106 Harv. L. Rev. 741, 782 (1993).

36 Robert von Moschzisker, *Stare Decisis in Courts of Last Resort*, 37 Harv. L. Rev. 409, 410 (1924) ("It must be remembered constantly . . . that the rule of stare

The somewhat negative cast on this score is that for those unhappy with the new decision, we spread the blame: "By citing a precedent, we at once become followers and cease to be leaders; our responsibility, therefore, seems to be divided, or at any rate it is shared by some one else."[37]

Fifth, a respect for precedent is said to advance notice and reliance interests. To a society aspiring to live under the rule of law, it's no small thing to ensure that citizens can determine in advance what the law will require of them and have the chance to conform their conduct to it.[38] As Holmes J. put it, "People want to know under what circumstances and how far they will run the risk of coming against what is so much stronger than themselves, and hence it becomes a business to find out when this danger is to be feared."[39]

In this enterprise, then, the right answer to a legal question is sometimes less important than a clear one.[40] Does it matter

---

decisis is not a contrivance to hamper the judge in administering justice, but is intended to advance the general usefulness of the law and thus benefit the greatest number.").

37 Francis Lieber, *Legal and Political Hermeneutics* 185 (William G. Hammond ed., 3d ed. 1880).

38 *See, e.g., Hubbard v. United States*, 514 U.S. 695, 716 (1995) ("The doctrine of stare decisis protects the legitimate expectations of those who live under the law.") (Scalia J. concurring in part & concurring in the judgment); Frederick Schauer, *Precedent*, 39 Stan. L. Rev. 571, 597 (1987) ("When a decisionmaker must decide this case in the same way as the last, parties will be better able to anticipate the future. The ability to predict what a decisionmaker will do helps us plan our lives, have some degree of repose, and avoid the paralysis of foreseeing only the unknown."); *Helvering v. Hallock*, 309 U.S. 106, 119 (1940) ("[S]tare decisis embodies an important social policy. It represents an element of continuity in law[] and is rooted in the psychologic need to satisfy reasonable expectations.").

39 Oliver Wendell Holmes, *The Path of the Law*, 10 Harv. L. Rev. 457, 457 (1897).

40 *See Di Santo v. Pennsylvania*, 273 U.S. 34, 42 (1927), *overruled in part by California v. Thompson*, 313 U.S. 109 (1941) (Brandeis J. dissenting) ("It is usually more important that a rule of law be settled, than that it be settled right."); *see also Hubbard*, 514 U.S. at 724 (Rehnquist C.J. dissenting) ("This, then, is clearly a case where it is better that the matter be decided than that it be decided right."); *cf. Gilman v. Philadelphia*, 70 U.S. (3 Wall.) 713, 724 (1865) (per Swayne J.) ("It is almost as important that the law should be settled permanently, as that it should be settled correctly.") (a much less bold statement); *see also* Henry Finch, *Law, or, A Discourse Thereof* 40 (1759) ("Common error goeth for a law. An acquittance made by a mayor in his own name only (where the

more which side of the road the law says we should drive on, or that everyone follows the same rule? To facilitate social coordination, the answer we choose may be less important than that an answer simply be chosen and be clear. A system of precedent—the promise that future cases will be decided as similar past cases were decided—helps ensure that people can know what the law will be when applied to them, their actions, and their enterprises. Productive social coordination stands strong on the basis of (relatively) ascertainable ground rules.

The con arguments

To be sure, our system of precedent, perhaps like anything else constructed by imperfect humans, guarantees costs along with its benefits. One we've already seen: deference to precedent can wind up ensconcing not just wise decisions but wrong ones. In the name of obedience to precedent, judges may pass judgment without giving much thought to the merits of the case at hand, inviting a sort of "judicial somnambulism."[41]

Holmes J. expressed this risk shortly before becoming a judge: "It is revolting to have no better reason for a rule of law than that so it was laid down in the time of Henry IV. It is still more revolting if the grounds upon which it was laid down have vanished long since, and the rule simply persists from blind imitation of the past."[42] But 18 years later, as Chief Justice of Massachusetts, he seemed more cautious: "[P]recisely because I believe that the world would be just as well off if it lived under laws that differed from ours in many ways, and because I believe that the claim of our especial code to respect is simply that it exists, that it is the one to which we have become accustomed, and not that it represents an eternal principle, I am slow to consent to overruling a precedent."[43]

---

town is incorporate by the name of the mayor, sheriff and burgesses) shall be allowed for good, if there be an hundred precedents and more of like acquittances; and that is for common quietness.").

41   Jerome Frank, *Law and the Modern Mind* 171 (1930; repr. 1963).

42   Oliver Wendell Holmes, *The Common Law* 469 (1881).

43   Oliver Wendell Holmes, *Law in Science and Science in Law*, 12 Harv. L. Rev. 443, 460 (1899).

Respect for precedent may also create abiding injustice as the cost of ensuring consistency and predictability more systemically.[44] In the words of Jerome Frank, courts may "feel obligated to consecrate their blunders."[45] A precedent may yield not just wrong results (as with the baseball holding) but gravely wrong ones (as with *Dred Scott*—the infamous pre-Civil War case in which the U.S. Supreme Court held that no black person, enslaved or free, could be a citizen of the United States, nor of any individual state, and therefore had no standing in federal court[46]). While unjust judicial decisions can be overruled, that change can come slowly—very slowly. Radical system-wide reform by way of legislation can be more difficult in an incremental case-or-controversy process respectful of precedent.[47]

One can question, too, how well precedent ever fulfills the goals it is said to serve. Take, for example, the goal of predictability. Looking up precedents has never been easy or cheap. At one time, precedents were accessible only in expensive and rare lawbooks. Now precedents are ubiquitous—easy to produce and store, thanks to the computer. Yet that very ubiquity can make it more difficult than ever to know what the controlling law is—a sort of information overload.[48] The accelerating speed with which cases have filled the *Federal Reporter* illustrates the problem. The *Reporter*'s first series, which contained but 300 volumes, spanned 1880 to mid-1924—meaning that on average it covered a year's

---

44 *See* Francis Lieber, *Legal and Political Hermeneutics* 191 (William G. Hammond ed., 3d ed. 1880) ("Precedents, like every other thing, may be sadly misapplied. The most absurd as well as the most criminal political acts, are propped with precedents."); *but see* Paul Vinogradoff, *Common-Sense in Law* 177 (1925) ("[I]t has been said with some exaggeration that in law certainty is more important than justice."); Note, *Stare Decisis*, 34 Harv. L. Rev. 74, 74 (1920) ("The doctrine of stare decisis is based upon the principle that certainty in law is preferable to reason and correct legal principles.").

45 Jerome Frank, *Courts on Trial* 267 (1950).

46 *Dred Scott v. Sandford*, 60 U.S. (19 How.) 393 (1856).

47 *See* Joseph Raz, *The Authority of Law: Essays on Law and Morality* 196–97 (2d ed. 2009) ("Nothing [about judges' training] prepares them to rethink radically the fundamental assumptions on which the law is based.").

48 *See* Peter W. Martin, *Reconfiguring Law Reports and the Concept of Precedent for a Digital Age*, 53 Vill. L. Rev. 1, 43–44 (2008); Jerome Frank, *Law and the Modern Mind* 207–08 (1930) (discussing problems of legal complexity).

worth of opinions in just shy of seven volumes. The second series contained 999 volumes covering mid-1924 to mid-1993—over 14 volumes a year. The current third series has taken well over 600 volumes to cover just the time between mid-1993 and the present day—a pace approaching 30 volumes a year. Lawyers have a hard time staying abreast of developments even in specialized fields. Nonlawyers have little chance.

But weighty as such criticisms are, our system doesn't lack counterbalances to them. The American judiciary doesn't treat precedent as an ironclad edict. Not every decision offered by one court binds every other court. By dividing our courts into parallel systems (federal and state) and even limiting precedential effect horizontally within those parallel systems (federal circuits, for example, generally aren't bound by one another's decisions), we have achieved a significant degree of flexibility in the system. Nor, as we have seen, is every word in every judicial opinion binding even on those courts generally obliged to follow the source's dictates. And to be sure, most courts have the power to overrule their own precedents.

Like most other social arrangements, a system of precedent can hope to achieve only some roughly workable accommodation between competing goals—in our case between interests like predictability and equality on one hand, and adaptability and individual justice on the other. It has been well said that "[t]he doctrine of precedent entails both constraint and creativity. If precedents bound absolutely, . . . judges would have very little capacity and opportunity to develop the common law; but if judges could ignore precedents completely, the doctrine would not exist in any meaningful sense."[49]

Unsurprisingly, even as harsh a critic of the doctrine of precedent as Jerome Frank conceded that "no sensible person suggests that stare decisis be abandoned."[50]

---

49 Neil Duxbury, *The Nature and Authority of Precedent* 27 (2008); *see also* Frank H. Easterbrook, *Stability and Reliability in Judicial Decisions*, 73 Cornell L. Rev. 422, 523 (1988) (stating that a system of precedent "ought to be unstable" to a degree).

50 Jerome Frank, *Courts on Trial* 286 (1950).

The two major legal systems

Of course, our system isn't universal. Although the common-law doctrine of precedent is firmly established, civil-law systems traditionally reject any such doctrine. In fact, perhaps the key feature distinguishing the two major types is the common-law system's reliance on judicial precedent as a source of law.[51]

The common law has its origins in 12th-century England.[52] It serves as the foundation of private law in 49 American states, 9 Canadian provinces, England, Wales, Ireland, and most of the former British Commonwealth. The common law was uncodified; no comprehensive set of legal rules or statutes existed. Although statutes governed a few scattered areas of law, the common law consisted mainly of precedents found in recorded judicial pronouncements. Judges therefore played an enormous role in shaping the law in common-law systems.

Anglo-American lawyers have long described their devotion to precedent as if it were always and everywhere immanent in human nature. The doctrine is often said to be deeply rooted in the human psyche's sense of fairness and regularity—founded in what one commentator called "the imitative faculty in man."[53] Holmes J. seemed to think the idea to be a human inevitability: "[I]mitation of the past, until we have a clear reason for change, no more needs justification than appetite. It is a form of the inevitable

---

[51] See Henri Lévy-Ullmann, *The English Legal Tradition: Its Sources and History* 56 (M. Mitchell trans., Frederic M. Goadby ed., 1935) (calling the authoritativeness of precedent "the cornerstone of the modern legal system of England and of all Anglo-Saxon countries").

[52] See David Ibbetson, "Common Law," in 2 *The Oxford International Encyclopedia of Legal History* 80, 80 (Stanley N. Katz ed., 2009).

[53] Frederic R. Coudert, *Certainty and Justice* 3 (1914); see John Chipman Gray, *The Nature and Sources of the Law* 198 (Roland Gray ed., 2d ed. 1921) ("[T]he weight attached to precedents in every department of life is closely connected with the force of habit, and has its roots deep in human nature."); G.W. Keeton, *The Elementary Principles of Jurisprudence* 96 (2d ed. 1949) ("Respect for what has been decided by persons of repute is not peculiar to the law. It is a characteristic of social intercourse, its origin being attributable to some extent to conservatism, to self-distrust in the individual, to mental laziness, or simply to the necessity of accepting a rule, and the predisposition of the human mind to accept one which has been framed by a person entitled to respect.").

to be accepted until we have a clear vision of what different things we want."[54]

Even so, as it pertains to law, this notion of precedent has been largely peculiar to the English-speaking peoples. It is said to be "[t]he most distinctive characteristic of English law and American law."[55] Roman law had no system of legal precedent[56]—nor have its civil-law offshoots anything as systematic as the Anglo-American approach.[57] So any attempt to suggest that our system of legal precedents is a universal manifestation of human nature fails, however cogent and irrefutable the arguments might seem to be. The origin of the difference between Anglo-American law and the civil-law systems of the world, when it comes to the treatment of precedents, has been considered one of the great unsolved problems of comparative jurisprudence.[58] If there is a solution to this paradox, it seems to lie in the strong doctrinal commitment within civil-law jurisdictions to the idea that judicial opinions can never be a valid source of law—a commitment rooted in history.

Civil law has its origins in Roman law. Continental Europe, Latin America, Quebec, and Louisiana, as well as China, Korea,

---

54 Oliver Wendell Holmes, "Holdsworth's English Law," in *Collected Legal Papers* 285, 290 (1920).

55 Edwin W. Patterson, *Jurisprudence: Men and Ideas of the Law* 300 (1953).

56 W.W. Buckland, *A Text-book of Roman Law from Augustus to Justinian* 638 (Peter Stein ed., 3d ed. 1963) ("Roman law had no system of precedent."); see H.F. Jolowicz, *Historical Introduction to the Study of Roman Law* 569 (1952) ("Justinian definitely forbade the use of precedents.").

57 See Alf Ross, *On Law and Justice* 85 (1959) ("Justinian forbade to decide according to precedent . . . . Similar prohibitions are to be found in the Prussian Code . . . of 1794. And in Denmark after the introduction of the *Danish Code* (1683) the advocates were forbidden to cite precedents in the Supreme Court. The prohibition was rescinded in 1771. Such drastic prohibitions proved to be ineffective."); Thomas Erskine Holland, *The Elements of Jurisprudence* 59–60 (7th ed. 1895) ("The Codes of Prussia and Austria expressly provide that judgments shall not have the force of law, and although the Codes of France, Italy and Belgium are silent on the point, the rule in all these countries is substantially the same, viz. that previous decisions are instructive, but not authoritative.") (footnotes omitted).

58 John Chipman Gray, *The Nature and Sources of the Law* 212 (Roland Gray ed., 2d ed. 1921) ("The cause of this distinction between the English and the Continental Law is one of the unsolved problems of Comparative Jurisprudence. Is it due to a difference in race, or in political organization, or to the presence on the Continent of the systematic body of the Roman Law?").

and Japan, follow civil law based on codified Roman law (including the Napoleonic Code), whereas Scotland and South Africa rely on civil law derived from uncodified Roman law. Unlike countries with common-law systems, those with civil-law systems are governed by putatively comprehensive legal codes. These codes exist for all areas of law and provide not only the applicable legal rules but also the appropriate punishments and remedies. The judge's role is thus limited to finding the facts of the case and applying code provisions to those facts. Although the universe of legal codes is continually updated, the drafting is left to legislators and legal scholars, not judges.[59] The codes are the sole source of law, which is meant to be "judge-proof."[60]

Interestingly, one commentator in 1904 predicted that stare decisis would be abolished in the United States and replaced by the civil-law method "within the lifetime of men who are already admitted to the practice of the legal profession."[61] That prognostication proved to be quite wrong. And yet there has been a palpable convergence of techniques within both systems.

The civil-law world has moved toward common-law methods—still not referring much to binding precedents but instead relying a great deal on statements of abstract principle in caselaw.[62] In effect, the world has given rise to hybrid systems: civil-law systems behave much like common-law systems, though without an explicit acknowledgment of the fact.[63] Perhaps the best-known

---

59 *See* Rupert Cross & J.W. Harris, *Precedent in English Law* 10–11 (4th ed. 1991) (noting that judicial decisions in France, a civil-law country, aren't considered a source of law and stating that "it would be possible for a French appellate court to set aside a ruling founded exclusively on a past decision on the ground that the ruling lacked an adequate legal basis").

60 John Henry Merryman, *The Civil Law Tradition* 50 (1969) ("Judges are prohibited from making law in the interest of certainty. . . . [T]he emphasis on certainty is an expression of a desire to make the law judge-proof.").

61 Edward B. Whitney, *The Doctrine of Stare Decisis*, 3 Mich. L. Rev. 89, 106 (1904).

62 Albert A. Ehrenzweig, *Psychoanalytic Jurisprudence* § 109, at 133 (1971).

63 *See id.* at 132–33; Robert Alexy, *A Theory of Legal Argumentation* 274 (Ruth Adler & Neil MacCormick trans., 2011) ("Nowadays, even in continental European law, the importance—at least the de facto importance—of precedent is acknowledged on all sides.").

example of a hybrid system today is the European Court of Justice, the highest court in the European Union. Although EU law reflects the civil-law background of most of its Member States, the Court of Justice renders decisions that are precedential.

Meanwhile, the common-law world has moved as well: the "statutorification" of the common law proceeds apace.[64] The judge's job today is more and more a matter of interpreting and applying codes.[65]

The mission of this book

We don't purport to offer a grand unifying theory of precedent. Any such theory is probably impossible.[66] Nor do we seek to trace every historical development.[67] We aim instead at a much more modest target, a conventional description of contemporary practice useful to the working lawyer and judge.

Even in that, however, our purpose is limited. Although we inherited many ideas from England, that country and other common-law countries have since evolved in slightly different

---

64 *See* James Willard Hurst, *Law and Social Order in the United States* 36–37 (1977) ("From the 1880's, but most markedly from the take-off decade of 1905–1915, the regulatory component of statute law became much more prominent and added considerably to the volume of legislation . . . . [T]he curve of statute law continues to mount; the long-term course of public policy has been to make legislation the framework and principal body of the law."). *See generally* Guido Calabresi, *A Common Law for the Age of Statutes* (1982) (coining the term *statutorification*).

65 *See* W.W. Buckland & Arnold D. McNair, *Roman Law and Common Law* 9 (F.H. Lawson ed., 2d ed. 1952) (likening the 20th-century American lawyer's approach to caselaw to that of French and German lawyers).

66 *See* Easterbrook, *Stability and Reliability in Judicial Decisions*, 73 Cornell L. Rev. at 423 ("[W]e do not have—never can have—a comprehensive theory of precedent."); John Chipman Gray, *The Nature and Sources of the Law* 198 (Roland Gray ed., 2d ed. 1921) ("[P]recedents . . . are to be generally but not always followed, and . . . no rules have been, or apparently ever can be, laid down to determine the matter precisely."); *see also* Aristotle, *Nicomachean Ethics* § 1.3, at 4 (Terence Irwin trans., 1985) ("[T]he educated person seeks exactness in each area to the extent that the nature of the subject allows; for apparently it is just as mistaken to demand demonstrations from a rhetorician as to accept [merely] persuasive arguments from a mathematician.") (bracketed interpolation in original).

67 For a good account of competing schools of thought in American legal history, see Charles W. Collier, *Precedent and Legal Authority: A Critical History*, 1988 Wis. L. Rev. 771.

directions. We don't presume to offer any extensive treatment of how other countries treat precedent.[68] Our focus is on the American system.

We seek here to elucidate a constellation of doctrines that are sorely in need of elucidation. After all, common-law lawyers and judges habitually behave as if precedents govern their work[69]—though they may not have closely examined how and why this is so.[70] As the legal philosopher Francis Lieber observed in the 19th century, "It is very necessary . . . that we should ascertain what precedents have binding power, and how far they have it."[71]

---

68 *See* Rupert Cross & J.W. Harris, *Precedent in English Law* 22–24 (4th ed. 1991) (comparing the treatment of precedent in Commonwealth countries as opposed to England); *see also* Giacomo A.M. Ponzetto & Patricio A. Fernandez, *Case Law Versus Statute Law: An Evolutionary Comparison*, 37 J. Legal Stud. 379 (2008); Vincy Fon & Francesco Parisi, *Judicial Precedents in Civil Law Systems: A Dynamic Analysis*, 26 Int'l Rev. L. & Econ. 519 (2007).

69 Edwin W. Patterson, *Jurisprudence: Men and Ideas of the Law* 300 (1953) ("The briefs of lawyers are ordinarily based on the assumption that the court will be bound by and will apply previously established law, and the opinions of courts ordinarily purport to justify their decisions as applications of previously established law.").

70 *See* John Dickinson, *Legal Rules: Their Function in the Process of Decision*, 79 U. Penn. L. Rev. 833, 833–34 (1931) ("Lawyers are seldom philosophers enough to formulate or even be fully aware of . . . deeply basic presuppositions of their thought.").

71 Francis Lieber, *Legal and Political Hermeneutics* 192 (William G. Hammond ed., 3d ed. 1880).

A. The Nature and Authority of Judicial Precedents

1. Treating Like Cases Alike

Like cases should be decided alike. Following established precedents helps keep the law settled, furthers the rule of law, and promotes both consistency and predictability.

Our system of precedent seeks consistency to ensure that recurrent legal problems will be dealt with similarly—will be treated equally. Hard questions arise when it comes to deciding what it means for two cases to be "alike."[1] A system of precedent doesn't guarantee that past and future cases will be treated alike: the powers to distinguish and overrule (powers we will examine at some length) preclude any such ironclad promise. But whether or not it's essential to the aspiration of ensuring equal treatment under law—fundamental fairness—a system of precedent is often defended on the ground that it at least goes some way to realizing the hope.[2] In a democracy, citizens and litigants must have confidence in the judiciary and in the rule of law, which requires that a judge's decisions must not be—and must not seem to be—arbitrary, based on personal preference, or unbounded.[3]

---

[1] See H.L.A. Hart, *The Concept of Law* 159–67 (2d ed. 1994).

[2] *See generally* Alfonso Ruiz Miguel, *Equality Before the Law and Precedent*, 10 Ratio Juris 372 (1997); Ruggero J. Aldisert, *Precedent: What It Is and What It Isn't; When Do We Kiss It and When Do We Kill It?*, 17 Pepp. L. Rev. 605 (1990). *But see* Christopher J. Peters, *Foolish Consistency: On Equality, Integrity, and Justice in Stare Decisis*, 105 Yale L.J. 2031 (1996).

[3] *See, e.g., Planned Parenthood of SE Pa. v. Casey*, 505 U.S. 833, 854 (1992) (noting that "the very concept of the rule of law underlying our own Constitution requires such continuity over time that a respect for precedent is, by definition, indispensable"); *Patterson v. McLean Credit Union*, 491 U.S. 164, 172 (1989) (calling stare decisis "a basic self-governing principle within the Judicial Branch, which is entrusted with the sensitive and difficult task of fashioning and preserving a jurisprudential system that is not based upon 'an arbitrary discretion'") (quoting *The Federalist* No. 78, at 490 (Alexander Hamilton) (H. Lodge ed., 1888)); Lewis F. Powell Jr., *Stare Decisis and Judicial Restraint*, 47 Wash. & Lee L. Rev. 281, 288 (1990) (commenting that to eliminate constitutional stare decisis would undermine the rule of law by "represent[ing] an explicit endorsement of the idea that the Constitution is nothing more than what five Justices say it is").

In common usage, a precedent is a former happening that guides later decisions in similar circumstances. That's not a uniquely legal concept. It's part of life in general. Think of a child's established expectation of an allowance if the child keeps a clean room, or anyone's expectation, after years of habituation, that the family will eat dinner at 7:30 p.m. sharp. More challengingly, think of trying to argue your way out of a parking ticket because you've parked at the questionable spot many times with impunity. Reliance on past actions to inform present ones pervades many aspects of our everyday lives.

The legal meaning of *precedent* aligns with the everyday sense. *Black's Law Dictionary* defines it as a "decided case that furnishes a basis for determining later cases involving similar facts or issues."[4] Put another way, precedents are "prior decisions that might be deemed to have some positive utility in deciding later cases."[5] As in common usage, an appeal to judicial precedent is an argument that the present action isn't an innovation.[6] The core of what judges do involves locating relevant precedent, determining the extent to which it binds them, and applying it to the facts of a given dispute.

But again, just how similar is similar? That is, if no two cases are truly identical—and factually, they cannot be—then which facts that actually matter are close enough to make the two cases alike enough (i.e., apart from nonessential factual divergences) to be subjected to the same rule? That question merits extensive treatment, and much of this book is devoted to it.

---

[4] *Black's Law Dictionary* 1366 (Bryan A. Garner ed., 10th ed. 2014); *cf.* Francis Lieber, *On Civil Liberty and Self-Government* 208 (Theodore D. Woolsey ed., 3d ed. 1883) ("A precedent in law is an ascertained principle applied to a new class of cases, which in the variety of practical life has offered itself."); 1 Kent, *Commentaries on American Law* at *473 (observing that "[a]djudged cases become precedents for future cases resting upon analogous facts, and brought within the same reason").

[5] Jeffrey C. Dobbins, *Structure and Precedent*, 108 Mich. L. Rev. 1453, 1460 (2010).

[6] Henry Campbell Black, *Handbook on the Law of Judicial Precedents* § 1, at 2 (1912).

Syllogistic reasoning

Let's first set forth a basic idea: every decided case can be thought of as representing either a positive or a negative syllogism. A positive syllogism runs this way:

    Major premise: Under specified circumstances, the rights of certain parties are X and Y.
    Minor premise: In this particular case, the parties are of the kind contemplated by the rule in the major premise and the circumstances are as specified—all other facts being immaterial.
    Conclusion: The rights of the parties in this case are X and Y.

A negative syllogism runs this way:

    Major premise: Only under specified circumstances are the rights of certain parties X and Y.
    Minor premise: In this particular case, the material circumstances aren't as specified in the rule in the major premise.
    Conclusion: The rights of the parties in this case aren't X and Y.

The "specified circumstances" of the major premise usually derive from either of the two most common sources of law today: a governing text (such as a statute or contract) or one or more precedents. We are concerned here with the latter source, precedents—including precedents about the proper reading of a statute, contract, or other legal instrument.

Of course, not all precedent is created equal: there is a hierarchy. Chief among the differences between precedents is that some bind future courts, while others merely persuade. Binding precedent is "very powerful medicine."[7] If it's on point, it "*is* the law" and "cannot be considered and cast aside," even if a later court disagrees with it—unless and until it is overruled.[8] All other precedent is merely persuasive or conditional. Lacking the coercive authority of binding precedent, it draws its power mainly from its coherence and logical force. Hence even with persuasive precedent,

---

7   *Hart v. Massanari*, 266 F.3d 1155, 1171 (9th Cir. 2001).
8   *Id.* at 1170.

there's a pecking order, based (as we will see) on the precedent's age, source, novelty, acuity, and prevalence.

Back to the dictionary

Let's consider again the definition of *precedent* in *Black's Law Dictionary*: "a decided case that furnishes a basis for determining later cases involving similar facts or issues."[9] Although the definition (necessarily) simplifies, it bears an important insight. In America, judges don't decide disputes one after another willy-nilly, without reference to what came before. They take account of lessons from past cases. So once the highest court within a jurisdiction decides a question, it is resolved as far as future lower courts are concerned. And when future cases present similar but different questions, the earlier decisions may help guide the later courts.

As the definition suggests, the judicial use of precedent bears a kinship to analogical reasoning.[10] (See § 9.) In daily life we often say, "X worked well; Y is like X, but Z isn't; therefore, we should choose Y over Z." But while the kinship with reasoning by analogy can't be denied, neither should it be overstated. After all, when we reason by analogy, don't we often mean to suggest the goodness (or badness) of a particular choice on its merits? Don't we mean to suggest that someone should choose Y because of the goodness of X: X worked out well, and so should Y? By contrast, when we apply precedent, we don't necessarily vouch for its quality. In ruling that current case Y is like former case X and should be decided like X, we may mean simply to say that X is authoritative, not to imply that it's necessarily good or right.[11]

Let's consider further just what *furnish* means in the definition. What is it to "furnish" a basis for deciding a later case? The formulation is a little mysterious. For our purposes, at least two principal meanings are worth noting.

---

9 *Black's Law Dictionary* at 1366.
10 *See generally* Frederick Schauer, "Precedent," in *The Routledge Companion to Philosophy of Law* 123, 126–27 (Andrei Marmor ed., 2012).
11 *See id.*

Sometimes a precedent "furnishes" simply a historical example or data point—which can be especially helpful to a trial judge in a gray area in which the judge has considerable discretion. Courts may look to a decided case from one area as a source of wisdom and learning when faced with the challenge of deciding a new case in another area. The precedent may not dispose of the new case—it may not be a sufficient basis for the later decision—but it represents a source of experience, insight, and learning that courts may find helpful. So for example, the Supreme Court has found that earlier separation-of-powers cases contain valuable lessons about the scope of federalism.[12] It has found First Amendment and federalism precedents informative when seeking to derive a statute's meaning.[13] The list might go on and on.

But precedent is often said to "furnish" a basis for decision in another, more powerful sense. Courts sometimes say that the abstract principle (*ratio decidendi*) for which the earlier case stands must be respected—it must "control"—in later cases to the extent the principle remains applicable, even if the factual setting differs. So, for example, if the principle in an earlier plowing case applies with equal force to the current harvesting dispute, it should yield the same result.

At its best, judicial decision-making isn't about peremptory ukases but about justifying outcomes with reasons. Indeed, judicial opinions are usually full of analytical discussions. These reasonings have a gravitational force of their own. They are often inspected by later courts and respected when they are thought to apply to the dispute at hand. The Supreme Court often considers one case's reasoning to "compel" or "dictate" a later case's result.[14]

---

12   See, e.g., *New York v. United States*, 505 U.S. 144, 182 (1992).
13   See, e.g., *Eastern R.R. Presidents Conference v. Noerr Motor Freight, Inc.*, 365 U.S. 127, 132 n.6 (1961); *Parker v. Brown*, 317 U.S. 341 (1943).
14   See, e.g., *Salazar v. Ramah Navajo Chapter*, 132 S.Ct. 2181, 2190 (2012) ("The principles underlying *Cherokee Nation [of Oklahoma v. Leavitt*, 543 U.S. 631 (2005),] and *Ferris [v. United States*, 27 Ct. Cl. 542 (1892),] dictate the result in this case."); *Miller v. Johnson*, 515 U.S. 900, 913 (1995) ("Our reasoning in *Shaw [v. Reno*, 509 U.S. 630 (1993),] compels this conclusion."); *Blount v. Rizzi*, 400 U.S. 410, 417 (1971) ("[O]ur decision in *Freedman v. Maryland*, 380 U.S. 51 (1965), compels this conclusion.").

So an earlier decision can furnish a basis for ruling on a similar case in two ways. It can dictate the outcome if the precedent is binding, or it can weigh in favor of one outcome over another if it is not binding. What makes an earlier case binding, and on whom, is the topic of the next two sections.

2. Vertical Precedents

Lower courts must strictly follow vertical precedents—decisions of higher courts in the same jurisdiction.

Judicial precedents come in two flavors: vertical and horizontal. Federal and state courts are absolutely bound by vertical precedents—those delivered by higher courts within the same jurisdiction.[1] This binding tie is often said to be a matter of "owing obedience."[2] The rule is that courts must adhere not just to the result but also to any reasoning necessary to that result.[3]

Not until the early 1980s did scholarly commentators first use the antonyms *horizontal* and *vertical* in reference to precedents. Before that time, the phrase *stare decisis* was often ambiguous. It could refer to a court's standing by its own earlier decisions or to a court's following or distinguishing the precedent of a higher court. The vertical/horizontal terminology promotes clearer thinking by avoiding the ambiguity.

---

1   *See Hutto v. Davis*, 454 U.S. 370, 375 (1982) (per curiam) ("[U]nless we wish anarchy to prevail within the federal judicial system, a precedent of this Court must be followed by the lower federal courts no matter how misguided the judges of those courts may think it to be."); *see also* Basil Jones, "Stare Decisis," in 26 *The American and English Encyclopaedia of Law* 158, 170 (David S. Garland & Lucius P. McGehee eds., 2d ed. 1904) ("An inferior court cannot decide adversely to a decision of a court of last resort and send the case up to that court again upon the ground that in the former decision of the court of last resort certain points were not sufficiently argued or noticed by the justice delivering the opinion there."); Frederick Pollock, *A First Book of Jurisprudence for Students of the Common Law* 309 (1896) ("Decisions of an appellate court of last resort are binding on all courts from which an appeal lies to it, and, of course, on all tribunals inferior to them.").

2   *See, e.g.*, 18 James W. Moore et al., *Moore's Federal Practice* § 134.02[2], at 134-26.2 n.24 (3d ed. 2015) ("Stare decisis applies to courts owing obedience to rendering court."); *Gately v. Massachusetts*, 2 F.3d 1221, 1226 (1st Cir. 1993) ("The doctrine of stare decisis renders the ruling of *law* in a case binding in future cases before the same court or other courts owing obedience to the decision.") (emphasis in original).

3   *See Seminole Tribe of Fla. v. Florida*, 517 U.S. 44, 67 (1996).

Vertical precedents in federal courts

The power of vertical precedents in the federal courts is rooted in the Constitution. Under Article III, the "judicial Power of the United States, shall be vested in one supreme Court, and in such inferior Courts as the Congress may from time to time ordain and establish."[4] The lower federal courts are thus "inferior" to the Supreme Court and must strictly adhere to the Supreme Court's decisions—as a result creating a great degree of national uniformity.[5] As Jackson J. said, humbly but firmly, of the Supreme Court: "We are not final because we are infallible, but we are infallible only because we are final."[6]

Vertical precedents follow "the path of appellate review."[7] As a result, a federal district court must follow the decisions of the federal circuit court in the same jurisdiction, as well as Supreme Court precedent. The federal circuit courts are likewise bound by the Supreme Court's decisions.

The Supreme Court has emphasized that "unless we wish anarchy to prevail within the federal judicial system, a precedent of this Court must be followed by the lower federal courts no matter how misguided the judges of those courts may think it to be."[8] In the same vein, the Eighth Circuit has said that federal courts "cannot for even a moment entertain" a litigant's theory that the Supreme Court erred.[9] Instead, if a Supreme Court decision "is to be modified, overruled or disregarded, that will have to be done by the Supreme Court."[10] Some judges, however, may choose to

---

4   U.S. Const. art. III, § 1, cl. 1.

5   *See* Thomas G. Walker, "Precedent," in *The Oxford Companion to the Supreme Court of the United States* 769, 769 (Kermit L. Hall ed., 2d ed. 2005) ("Decisions by the Supreme Court are not only binding on the future decisions of the justices themselves [with exceptions], but also on every inferior court in the land. This imposes a degree of national uniformity.").

6   *Brown v. Allen*, 344 U.S. 443 (1953).

7   Evan H. Caminker, *Why Must Inferior Courts Obey Superior Court Precedents?*, 46 Stan. L. Rev. 817, 825 (1994).

8   *Hutto*, 454 U.S. at 375.

9   *United States v. Pate*, 754 F.3d 550, 554 (8th Cir. 2014) (internal quotation marks omitted).

10   *Id.* (quoting *Bakewell v. United States*, 110 F.2d 564, 564 (8th Cir. 1940) (per curiam)).

discuss their misgivings about a Supreme Court decision while still following it faithfully.[11]

Lower courts are bound even by old and crumbling high-court precedent—until the high court itself changes direction. In the 1953 case of *Wilko v. Swan*,[12] the Supreme Court held invalid an agreement to arbitrate a claim under § 12(2) of the Securities Exchange Act. Thirty-five years later, the Fifth Circuit, deciding that the *Wilko* decision was obsolescent, held that those claims were arbitrable.[13] The Supreme Court then affirmed the court of appeals' judgment but criticized it for not following Supreme Court precedent: "If a precedent of this Court has direct application in a case, yet appears to rest on reasons rejected in some other line of decisions, the Court of Appeals should follow the case which directly controls, leaving to this Court the prerogative of overruling its own decisions."[14] In dissent, Stevens J., who would have stayed with the original *Wilko* rule, said that the circuit court had "engaged in an indefensible brand of judicial activism" by refusing to follow the controlling precedent of the Supreme Court.[15]

The Supreme Court has often reiterated this position.[16] By a per curiam opinion in *Thurston Motor Lines, Inc. v. Jordan K. Rand, Ltd.*,[17] the Ninth Circuit was told: "Needless to say, only this Court may overrule one of its precedents. Until that occurs

---

11 See, e.g., *Lyons v. City of Xenia*, 417 F.3d 565, 582–84 (6th Cir. 2005) (Sutton J. concurring); see also *Pearson v. Callahan*, 555 U.S. 223, 234–36 (2009) (noting *City of Xenia* and adopting a new rule consistent with the Sixth Circuit's reasoning); *Khan v. State Oil Co.*, 93 F.3d 1358, 1363–64 (7th Cir. 1996) (relying on *Albrecht v. Herald Co.*, 390 U.S. 145 (1968), despite its "increasingly wobbly, moth-eaten foundations" because the Supreme Court had not expressly overruled it). See infra pp. 302–03.

12 346 U.S. 427 (1953).

13 *Rodriguez de Quijas v. Shearson/Lehman Bros., Inc.*, 845 F.2d 1296, 1299 (5th Cir. 1988).

14 *Rodriguez de Quijas v. Shearson/Am. Express, Inc.*, 490 U.S. 477, 484 (1989).

15 *Id.* at 486 (Stevens J. dissenting).

16 See, e.g., *Agostini v. Felton*, 521 U.S. 203, 237 (1997) (repeating the statement accompanying note 14 *supra*).

17 460 U.S. 533 (1983) (per curiam).

Rice is the law, and the decision below cannot be reconciled with it."[18]

That rejection of circuit-court action by the Supreme Court has been criticized in some quarters.[19] One commentator calls it a display of the "autocratic view of the force and immutability of its own precedents."[20] Another commentator would allow circuit courts to predict Supreme Court rulings under narrow circumstances.[21] Still others suggest that Congress should legislate on the precedential effect of judicial decisions.[22] We believe, however, that the bright-line rule established by the Court is both wise and necessary: it promotes consistency and predictability while discouraging adventurous second-guessing by widely dispersed subaltern judges.

Premonitions of a high-court overruling

Sometimes the Supreme Court appears poised to overturn its own precedent. But even then, as long as the precedent is still "good law," federal courts must follow it. A good example of this principle is the federal courts' treatment of the Supreme Court's decisions in *Almendarez-Torres v. United States*[23] and *Apprendi v. New Jersey*.[24] In 1998, the Supreme Court held in *Almendarez-Torres* that a prosecutor isn't required to submit the fact of a defendant's prior conviction to the jury, even if that fact leads to a higher statutory maximum penalty.[25] Two years later, the Supreme Court held in *Apprendi* that the Sixth and Fourteenth Amendments

---

18   *Id.* at 535.
19   C. Steven Bradford, *Following Dead Precedent: The Supreme Court's Ill-Advised Rejection of Anticipatory Overruling*, 59 Fordham L. Rev. 39 (1990).
20   Ashutosh Bhagwat, *Separate but Equal? The Supreme Court, the Lower Federal Courts, and the Nature of the "Judicial Power,"* 80 B.U. L. Rev. 967, 1014 (2000).
21   Evan H. Caminker, *Precedent and Prediction: The Forward-Looking Aspects of Inferior Court Decisionmaking*, 73 Tex. L. Rev. 1 (1994).
22   Caminker, *Why Must Inferior Courts Obey Superior Court Precedents?*, 46 Stan. L. Rev. 817; Jeffrey C. Dobbins, *Structure and Precedent*, 108 Mich. L. Rev. 1453 (2010).
23   523 U.S. 224 (1998).
24   530 U.S. 466 (2000).
25   *Almendarez-Torres*, 523 U.S. at 239–47.

required prosecutors to prove to the jury beyond a reasonable doubt any fact that leads to a higher statutory maximum penalty (unless the fact is admitted by the defendant).[26] Despite that holding, the Supreme Court declined to overturn *Almendarez-Torres*. In *Apprendi*, the Supreme Court explained that "[e]ven though it is arguable that *Almendarez-Torres* was incorrectly decided, and that a logical application of our reasoning today should apply," the defendant "does not contest the decision's validity, and we need not revisit it for purposes of our decision today to treat the [*Almendarez-Torres*] case as a narrow exception to the general rule."[27] Even if a later federal judge were to believe that a Supreme Court precedent seems wrong, the court must still apply it.

A variation on this issue occasionally poses difficulties for lower courts. What happens when the Supreme Court overturns the standard that it had previously used to resolve a particular class of cases? Are the results reached under the old standard still binding precedent? The answer is no.[28] Instead, federal courts must apply the new standard and reach the result dictated under that new standard. Suppose, for example, that the Supreme Court applied a rational-basis test to gender-based classifications for several years. Then suppose the Supreme Court holds that intermediate scrutiny applies to all gender-based classifications. Are lower courts still bound by the outcome reached by the Supreme Court when it evaluated a specific gender-based classification under the rational-basis test? No. Otherwise, the Supreme Court would have to rethink all its horizontal precedents decided under the old standard in order to implement its new legal standard.[29] In that situation, however, the lower court must carefully assess the new Supreme Court precedent to be certain that the lower court isn't jumping ahead of the Supreme Court.

---

26 *Apprendi*, 530 U.S. at 469, 490.
27 *Id.* at 489–90; *see also Alleyne v. United States*, 133 S.Ct. 2151, 2160 n.1 (2013) (declining to rethink *Almendarez-Torres*).
28 *See Seminole Tribe of Fla. v. Florida*, 517 U.S. 44, 66–67 (1996); *Planned Parenthood of SE Pa. v. Casey*, 947 F.2d 682, 691–93 (3d Cir. 1991).
29 *See Casey*, 947 F.2d at 692.

Although it's inappropriate to do so, federal courts have sometimes explicitly declined to follow Supreme Court precedent. In a notorious case,[30] the District Court for the Southern District of Alabama refused to follow Supreme Court precedent in a school-prayer case. The court ruled against the plaintiffs, declaring that the district court's "independent review of the relevant historical documents and its reading of the scholarly analysis convinces it that the United States Supreme Court has erred in its reading of history."[31] The court recognized the likely futility of its ruling, expressing that "[p]erhaps this opinion will be no more than a voice crying in the wilderness and this attempt to right that which this Court is persuaded is a misreading of history will come to nothing more than blowing in the hurricane."[32]

The district court was right to predict the futility of its approach. The losing plaintiffs there applied to the Supreme Court for a stay of the district court's judgment, which Powell J. granted.[33] In the stay order, Powell J. wrote that "[u]nless and until this Court reconsiders" its precedents, "they appear to control this case. In my view, the District Court was obligated to follow them."[34] On appeal, the Eleventh Circuit reversed the district court's decision in relevant part, noting that under "our form of government and long established law and custom, the Supreme Court is the ultimate authority on the interpretation of our Constitution and laws; its interpretations may not be disregarded."[35] The lesson is this: to the extent that a lower court disagrees with Supreme Court precedent, the judge may say as much, but the judge still must follow the precedent.

On occasion, the Supreme Court has sternly reminded lower courts of their obligation to follow Supreme Court precedent. In both qualified-immunity cases and cases under the Antiterrorism and Effective Death Penalty Act of 1996 (AEDPA), the Supreme

---

30   *Jaffree v. Board of Sch. Comm'rs*, 554 F. Supp. 1104 (S.D. Ala. 1983).
31   *Id.* at 1128.
32   *Id.*
33   *Jaffree v. Board of Sch. Comm'rs*, 459 U.S. 1314 (1983).
34   *Id.*
35   *Jaffree v. Wallace*, 705 F.2d 1526, 1532, 1537 (11th Cir. 1983).

Court has repeatedly chided lower courts for failing to apply Supreme Court standards faithfully. For example, in *Al-Kidd v. Ashcroft*, the Ninth Circuit veered off the Supreme Court's charted course in a qualified-immunity case.[36] In reversing, the Supreme Court emphasized that it had "repeatedly told courts—and the Ninth Circuit in particular"—to apply the qualified-immunity standard articulated by the Supreme Court.[37]

In sum, federal courts owe unflinching fealty to Supreme Court precedents. That is true even if the court believes that the precedent was wrongly decided or is likely to be soon overturned by the Supreme Court itself.

Vertical precedents in state courts

The principles of vertical and horizontal precedent are much the same in state courts. The decisions of a state's high court furnish binding precedents to guide all the courts over which it exercises appellate jurisdiction. The judges of all the inferior courts are bound to accept and follow those precedents completely, without regard to their own previous decisions or their independent views of the law. It is firmly established law that a state's high court is "unquestionably 'the ultimate exposito[r] of state law.'"[38] (See § 77.)

An intermediate appellate court must accept and follow the rulings of the high court whenever applicable precedents are found, without reexamining the questions involved, and must overrule its own previous decisions to the contrary if necessary. It isn't the place of intermediate appellate courts to "attempt to overrule decisions of a higher court."[39] As in the federal court system, a state's intermediate appellate courts owe allegiance to the state's high court.

---

36 *Al-Kidd v. Ashcroft*, 580 F.3d 949 (9th Cir. 2009).

37 *Ashcroft v. al-Kidd*, 563 U.S. 731, 742 (2011); *see also Carroll v. Carman*, 135 S.Ct. 348, 350–52 (2014) (per curiam); *Stanton v. Sims*, 134 S.Ct. 3, 4–6 (2013) (per curiam).

38 *Riley v. Kennedy*, 553 U.S. 406, 425 (2008) (quoting *Mullaney v. Wilbur*, 421 U.S. 684, 691 (1975)).

39 *Auto Equity Sales, Inc. v. Superior Court of Santa Clara Cnty.*, 369 P.2d 937, 940 (Cal. 1962) (in bank).

The lower courts within a jurisdiction must follow a decision of an intermediate appellate court until the high court either reverses that decision or announces a contrary doctrine. If there are several such intermediate courts in the state, and their decisions on the same question of law are in conflict, a trial court should follow the rulings of the appellate court in the same district, division, or department where it sits. Yet if that appellate court hasn't spoken on the issue, then the trial court will often follow the decisions of the state's other appellate courts.[40]

Decisions of inferior state courts aren't binding on courts of equal rank and coordinate jurisdiction. But they may be respected for their reasoning and may be followed for the sake of uniformity and comity.

Because state courts are bound by vertical precedents, both the U.S. Supreme Court and state appellate courts can create binding precedent for lower state courts. Hence state intermediate and trial courts may at times owe obedience to two masters.

The Supremacy Clause of the U.S. Constitution provides that the Constitution and federal law "shall be the supreme Law of the Land; and the Judges in every State shall be bound thereby."[41] With the U.S. Supreme Court rests the ultimate authority to interpret both the Constitution and federal law, and its decisions in exercise of that authority are binding on state courts.[42] But despite the supremacy of federal law, the role of federal precedent in state courts isn't always clear, and many of the complications that can arise are addressed in later sections (see §§ 77–82).

---

40   See, e.g., id. at 939–40; *Mountain View Coach Lines, Inc. v. Storms*, 476 N.Y.S.2d 918, 919–20 (App. Div. 1984); *People v. Foote*, 432 N.E.2d 1254, 1257 (Ill. App. Ct. 1982); *Chapman v. Pinellas Cnty.*, 423 So. 2d 578, 580 (Fla. Dist. Ct. App. 1982); *State v. Hayes*, 333 So. 2d 51, 52–53 (Fla. Dist. Ct. App. 1976).

41   U.S. Const. art. VI, cl. 2.

42   See *McCulloch v. Maryland*, 17 U.S. (4 Wheat.) 316, 400–01 (1819); see also *Cooper v. Aaron*, 358 U.S. 1, 18–20 (1958).

3. Horizontal Precedents

A high court or intermediate appellate court generally adheres to horizontal precedents—namely, its own earlier decisions. But if there is a special justification to depart from or overrule precedent, a full court may overturn its own prior decision. Normally, federal three-judge panels are absolutely bound to follow precedents from the same court.

With horizontal precedents—past decisions of the same court—nothing about stare decisis is absolute. Adherence to precedent is "the preferred course because it promotes the evenhanded, predictable, and consistent development of legal principles, fosters reliance on judicial decisions, and contributes to the actual and perceived integrity of the judicial process."[1] But unlike the absolutist doctrine that prevailed in England from the late 19th century through 1966,[2] American-style horizontal stare decisis isn't a rigid, inflexible rule.[3] Rather, a court will depart from its own

---

1   *Payne v. Tennessee*, 501 U.S. 808, 827 (1991).

2   *See London St. Tramways Ltd. v. London City Council* [1898] A.C. 375, 381 (per Lord Halsbury) ("[A] decision of this House [the House of Lords] once given upon a point of law is conclusive upon this House afterwards."); Note, *Stare Decisis*, 34 Harv. L. Rev. 74, 74 (1920) ("[T]he House of Lords and the Court of Appeal hold that they have no power to reverse themselves on a proposition of law, no matter how erroneous their previous decision may have been."); John Salmond, *Jurisprudence* 181–82 (Glanville L. Williams ed., 10th ed. 1947) (citing *London St. Tramways*) ("The House of Lords is absolutely bound by its own decisions."); *cf.* A.W.B. Simpson, "The *Ratio Decidendi* of a Case and the Doctrine of Binding Precedent," in *Oxford Essays in Jurisprudence* 148, 152 (A.G. Guest ed., 1961) ("[H]ow can the House put itself under a legal obligation by simply saying that it is under a legal obligation?"). *But see* Louis Blom-Cooper, "1966 and All That: The Story of the Practice Statement," in *The Judicial House of Lords 1876–2009* 128, 128 (Louis Blom-Cooper et al. eds., 2009) ("[T]hat day [26 July 1966], . . . [the law lords] dropped a pebble into the judicial pool that produced not merely a few ripples but also a seismic wave in English juridical thinking."); J.H. Baker, *An Introduction to English Legal History* 200–01 (4th ed. 2002) ("The House of Lords in 1966 freed itself from the self-imposed fetter.") (citing *Practice Note* [1966] 3 All E.R. 77).

3   *Payne*, 501 U.S. at 828; *see also Seminole Tribe of Fla. v. Florida*, 517 U.S. 44, 63 (1996) (noting that "we always have treated stare decisis as a 'principle of policy,' and not as an 'inexorable command'") (internal citations omitted); *see also* George Whitecross Paton, *A Textbook of Jurisprudence* § 45, at 209 (G.W. Paton & David P. Perham eds., 4th ed. 1972) ("Even in America, where the common law system was inherited, the doctrine of precedent is more liberal."); Frederick Pollock,

precedent when the departure is "supported by some special justification."[4] Notably, some of the most important Supreme Court decisions in U.S. history were those in which the Court overruled or departed from one of its precedents—cases such as *Brown v. Board of Education*,[5] *West Virginia State Board of Education v. Barnette*,[6] *Mapp v. Ohio*,[7] and *Lawrence v. Texas*.[8]

Why has the American version of this Anglo-American principle historically been more fluid than the English version? Six reasons have been posited:

- the sheer deluge of American decisions;
- the difficulty of amending the Constitution, and the relative abundance of constitutional questions in American litigation (see § 40);
- the supposed American need for flexibility in legal development because of rapid social and economic changes;
- the casebook method used in American legal pedagogy—in which teacher and student labor to extract the "best" rule;
- the American Law Institute's restatements of the law, which offer state courts substitutes for and criticism of their own precedents; and

---

A First Book of Jurisprudence for Students of the Common Law 300 (1896) ("Usage differs on the point whether . . . a court [of last resort] shall treat itself as bound by its own decisions. The House of Lords has gone farthest in this direction; the Supreme Court of the United States, on the other hand, has more than once openly reversed its own previous doctrine."); *and see also id.* at 311–18.

4   *Dickerson v. United States*, 530 U.S. 428, 443 (2000) (internal quotation marks and citation omitted); *see also Citizens United v. Federal Election Comm'n*, 558 U.S. 310, 362 (2010) ("Our precedent is to be respected unless the most convincing of reasons demonstrates that adherence to it puts us on a course that is sure error."); *Planned Parenthood of SE Pa. v. Casey*, 505 U.S. 833, 864 (1992) (noting that "a decision to overrule should rest on some special reason over and above the belief that a prior case was wrongly decided").

5   347 U.S. 483 (1954).
6   319 U.S. 624 (1943).
7   367 U.S. 643 (1961).
8   539 U.S. 558 (2003).

- the habit of citing other states' precedents as persuasive authorities.⁹

Each one of these contributing factors remains a plausible partial explanation of why American habits have tended as they have.

Horizontal precedents in federal circuit courts

Below the Supreme Court, the federal circuit courts must consider how to apply horizontal stare decisis to their own published decisions (they normally don't treat their unpublished opinions as binding).¹⁰ That decision depends on whether the en banc court of appeals or a three-judge panel is considering its own precedent.

As an initial matter, federal courts aren't generally bound by opinions of federal courts of appeals outside their own circuit.¹¹ Rather, each of the 13 federal circuit courts follows only its own precedent.

Within each circuit, the rules for three-judge panels are generally strict. Traditionally speaking, three-judge panels are absolutely bound by prior decisions of the en banc court. They are also strictly bound by the decisions of prior panels under the "law-of-the-circuit" rule (see § 60). Under that rule, only the Supreme

---

9   Edwin W. Patterson, *Jurisprudence: Men and Ideas of the Law* 304 (1953) (relying in large measure on Arthur L. Goodhart, "Case Law in England and America," in *Essays in Jurisprudence and the Common Law* 65–71 (1931)).

10 *See, e.g., United States v. Townsend*, 762 F.3d 641, 646 (7th Cir. 2014) ("[U]npublished decisions are not binding on subsequent panels."); *Minor v. Bostwick Labs., Inc.*, 669 F.3d 428, 433 n.6 (4th Cir. 2012) ("Unpublished decisions are also not binding upon us."); *United States v. Master*, 614 F.3d 236, 239 n.2 (6th Cir. 2010) ("[I]t is 'well-established law in this circuit that unpublished cases are not binding precedent.'") (quoting *Bell v. Johnson*, 308 F.3d 594, 611 (6th Cir. 2002)); *United States v. Sauseda*, 596 F.3d 279, 282 (5th Cir. 2010) (per curiam); *Moore v. Barnhart*, 405 F.3d 1208, 1211 n.3 (11th Cir. 2005) (per curiam); *United States v. Goff*, 314 F.3d 1248, 1250 (10th Cir. 2003); *Hart v. Massanari*, 266 F.3d 1155, 1180 (9th Cir. 2001).

11 *See, e.g., Helmerich & Payne Int'l Drilling Co. v. Bolivarian Republic of Venezuela*, 784 F.3d 804, 813 (D.C. Cir. 2015) ("[W]e are not *bound* by the decisions of other circuits.") (internal quotation marks and citation omitted); *United States v. Sykes*, 598 F.3d 334, 337 (7th Cir. 2010) ("[W]hile we carefully and respectfully consider the opinions of our sister circuits, we certainly do not defer to them.") (quoting *Atchison, Topeka & Santa Fe Ry. v. Pena*, 44 F.3d 437, 443 (7th Cir. 1994)) (internal quotation marks omitted).

Court or the court of appeals sitting en banc may overrule a prior panel's decision.[12]

The law-of-the-circuit rule has one obvious and commonsense caveat: a panel may depart from or overrule an earlier panel's decision when it has been repudiated or undermined by later controlling authority, such as a statute, an intervening Supreme Court decision, or en banc decision.[13] In those circumstances, the vertical obligation trumps the horizontal obligation. The First Circuit also recognizes a somewhat more expansive principle: one panel may "overrule another in 'those relatively rare instances in which authority that postdates the original decision, although not directly controlling, nevertheless offers a sound reason for believing that the former panel, in light of fresh developments, would change its collective mind.'"[14]

When sitting en banc, a circuit court follows the principle of horizontal precedents issued in prior en banc decisions in the same

---

12 See, e.g., *United States v. White*, 782 F.3d 1118, 1126–27 (10th Cir. 2015) ("[O]ne panel of this court cannot overrule the judgment of another panel absent en banc consideration or an intervening Supreme Court decision.") (internal quotation marks and alteration omitted); *United States v. Franz*, 772 F.3d 134, 144 n.8 (3d Cir. 2014); *Allaithi v. Rumsfeld*, 753 F.3d 1327, 1330–31 (D.C. Cir. 2014); *United States v. Martinez*, 606 F.3d 1303, 1305 (11th Cir. 2010); *Rutherford v. Columbia Gas*, 575 F.3d 616, 619 (6th Cir. 2009); *United States v. Snyder*, 511 F.3d 813, 818 (8th Cir. 2008); *United States v. Rodriguez-Pacheco*, 475 F.3d 434, 441 (1st Cir. 2007); *McMellon v. United States*, 387 F.3d 329, 332 (4th Cir. 2004) (en banc); *Gelman v. Ashcroft*, 372 F.3d 495, 499 (2d Cir. 2004); *In re Watts*, 298 F.3d 1077, 1083–84 (9th Cir. 2002) (O'Scannlain J. concurring in judgment); *Gochicoa v. Johnson*, 238 F.3d 278, 286 n.11 (5th Cir. 2000).

13 See, e.g., *Rendon v. Holder*, 782 F.3d 466, 472 n.4 (9th Cir. 2015) (one three-judge panel can overrule another three-judge panel if "intervening higher authority 'is clearly irreconcilable with our prior circuit authority'") (citation omitted); *Chester ex rel. NLRB v. Grane Healthcare Co.*, 666 F.3d 87, 94 (3d Cir. 2011) ("a panel of our Court may decline to follow a prior decision of our Court without the necessity of an en banc decision when the prior decision conflicts with a Supreme Court decision") (internal quotation marks omitted); *Rodriguez-Pacheco*, 475 F.3d at 441 (exception to law-of-the-circuit rule "applies when 'an existing panel decision is undermined by controlling authority, subsequently announced, such as an opinion of the Supreme Court'") (internal citation and alterations omitted); *Gelman*, 372 F.3d at 499 ("We do, however, recognize an exception" to the law-of-the-circuit rule "where there has been an intervening Supreme Court decision that casts doubt on our controlling precedent.") (internal quotation marks and citation omitted).

14 *Rodriguez-Pacheco*, 475 F.3d at 442 (citation omitted).

way that the U.S. Supreme Court does regarding its prior decisions. Like the Supreme Court, an en banc court of appeals may depart from or overrule prior en banc precedent if there is a special justification for doing so.[15]

When an en banc court decides whether to depart from or overrule en banc precedent, it considers the same factors weighed by the Supreme Court. In a concurring opinion in a 2013 case,[16] Smith J. of the Third Circuit explained that "even sitting en banc, we do not conduct a plenary re-examination of our prior decisions; we instead remain constrained by our precedent to the degree counseled by principles of stare decisis."[17] After reviewing the relevant factors set forth by the Supreme Court, Smith J. pointed out that the "other courts of appeals have concluded" that the "same considerations should guide our own stare decisis analysis" when an en banc court of appeals reconsiders its precedent.[18]

But what weight must the en banc court give to an older three-judge panel decision? Rule 35 of the Federal Rules of Appellate Procedure speaks to this issue indirectly. It says that a court of appeals should proceed en banc only when necessary to ensure uniformity—that is, when the circuit's own precedents conflict—or when the case is exceptionally important.[19] (See § 61.)

---

15   See, e.g., Deckers Corp. v. United States, 752 F.3d 949, 965 (Fed. Cir. 2014); Morrow v. Balaski, 719 F.3d 160, 179 (3d Cir. 2013) (en banc) (Smith J. concurring); Minn-Chem, Inc. v. Agrium, Inc., 683 F.3d 845, 848 (7th Cir. 2012) (en banc); United States v. Bowling, No. 08-6184, 2009 WL 6854970, at *1 n. (10th Cir. 23 Dec. 2009) (en banc); Ross v. Reed, 704 F.2d 705, 707 (4th Cir. 1983); Bonner v. City of Prichard, 661 F.2d 1206, 1212 (11th Cir. 1981) (en banc).

16   Morrow v. Balaski, 719 F.3d 160 (3d Cir. 2013) (en banc).

17   Id. at 179 (Smith J. concurring) (internal quotation marks and citation omitted).

18   Id. at 180 (collecting en banc cases from other circuits applying the Supreme Court's factors); see also, e.g., Al-Sharif v. U.S. Citizenship & Immigration Servs., 734 F.3d 207, 212 (3d Cir. 2013) (en banc); United States v. Heredia, 483 F.3d 913, 918–19 (9th Cir. 2007) (en banc); Critical Mass Energy Project v. NRC, 975 F.2d 871, 875–76 (D.C. Cir. 1992) (en banc); cf. Tate v. Showboat Marina Casino P'ship, 431 F.3d 580, 583 (7th Cir. 2005) ("[T]he Supreme Court has specified considerations that a court should weigh in deciding whether to follow or to overrule a previous decision.").

19   See Fed. R. App. P. 35(a). For an en banc court's authority to consider an issue decided in a prior appeal in the same litigation, see, e.g., Cottier v. City of Martin, 604 F.3d 553, 557 (8th Cir. 2010) (en banc) (collecting cases); Irving v. United States, 162 F.3d 154, 161 (1st Cir. 1998) (en banc); Watkins v. U.S. Army, 875

Horizontal precedents, unlike vertical precedents, don't control in the federal district courts. District-court judges aren't bound by the decisions of other district-court judges, or even by their own decisions.[20] As the Third Circuit said in a 1991 case,[21] "there is no such thing as 'the law of the district.'"[22] Even when the facts of an earlier district-court case are identical with those in a later case, if "a second judge believes that a different result may obtain, independent analysis is appropriate."[23]

A principle of policy

The Supreme Court has established that because following horizontal precedent is a "principle of policy" and "the preferred course," it is inherently flexible.[24] That doctrine may be peculiar

---

F.2d 699, 704 n.8 (9th Cir. 1989) (en banc); *Shimman v. International Union of Operating Eng'rs, Local 18*, 744 F.2d 1226, 1229 n.3 (6th Cir. 1984) (en banc); *Van Gemert v. Boeing Co.*, 590 F.2d 433, 436 n.9 (2d Cir. 1978) (en banc); *In re Central R.R. of N.J.*, 485 F.2d 208, 210–11 (3d Cir. 1973) (en banc).

For an en banc court's authority to overrule a panel's decision in an earlier case, see, e.g., *Cyr v. Reliance Standard Life Ins. Co.*, 642 F.3d 1202, 1203–04 (9th Cir. 2011) (en banc); *United States v. Padilla*, 415 F.3d 211, 215 (1st Cir. 2005) (en banc); *United States v. Palmer*, 380 F.3d 395, 396 (8th Cir. 2004) (en banc).

20 See, e.g., *Camreta v. Greene*, 563 U.S. 692, 709 n.7 (2011) ("A decision of a federal district court judge is not binding precedent in either a different judicial district, the same judicial district, or even upon the same judge in a different case.") (quoting 18 James W. Moore et al., *Moore's Federal Practice* § 134.02[1][d], at 134-26 (3d ed. 2011)).

21 *Threadgill v. Armstrong World Indus., Inc.*, 928 F.2d 1366 (3d Cir. 1991).

22 *Id.* at 1371 & n.7 (collecting cases from other circuits for "similar statements of the law"); see also, e.g., *ATSI Commc'ns, Inc. v. Shaar Fund, Ltd.*, 547 F.3d 109, 112 n.4 (2d Cir. 2008); *Garcia v. Tyson Foods, Inc.*, 534 F.3d 1320, 1329 (10th Cir. 2008); *Midlock v. Apple Vacations W., Inc.*, 406 F.3d 453, 457 (7th Cir. 2005); *Fishman & Tobin, Inc. v. Tropical Shipping & Constr. Co.*, 240 F.3d 956, 965 (11th Cir. 2001); *In re Exec. Office of President*, 215 F.3d 20, 24 (D.C. Cir. 2000) (per curiam).

23 *Threadgill*, 928 F.2d at 1371. See, e.g., *Garcia v. Tyson Foods, Inc.*, 534 F.3d 1320, 1329 (10th Cir. 2008) ("[D]istrict court decisions cannot be treated as authoritative on issues of law. The reasoning of district judges is of course entitled to respect, but the decision of a district judge cannot be a controlling precedent.") (quoting *Bank of Am., N.A. v. Moglia*, 330 F.3d 942, 949 (7th Cir. 2003)); see also *In re Ford*, 415 B.R. 51, 60 (Bankr. N.D.N.Y. 2009) (commenting that "there is no 'law of the district' mandated for district judges to follow, [and] bankruptcy judges are likewise not bound by decisions of a single district court judge").

24 *Payne v. Tennessee*, 501 U.S. 808, 827–30 (1991) (overruling two precedents about the inadmissibility of victim-impact evidence and related prosecutorial

to a high court: "[W]hen governing decisions are unworkable or are badly reasoned, 'this Court has never felt constrained to follow precedent.'"[25] The Court has also suggested that stare decisis is weak when its own previous decision has become outdated,[26] when the reliance interests at stake aren't strong, or when "the most convincing of reasons demonstrates that adherence to [stare decisis] puts us on a course that is sure error."[27]

Because stare decisis is a "principle of policy," often its underlying policy considerations compete: the need for confidence that the judiciary is getting cases right, for example, might compete with considerations of stability and finality, and a court must simultaneously "seek principles of change no less than principles of stability."[28] Hence when a court does choose to overrule its own

---

argument at a capital sentencing hearing as established in two earlier cases that were "decided by the narrowest of margins," "questioned by Members of the Court in later decisions," and "wrongly decided").

25   *Id.* at 827 (citation omitted); *cf.* Rupert Cross & J.W. Harris, *Precedent in English Law* 5 (4th ed. 1991) (noting that "[u]nder the practice prevailing [in the United Kingdom's House of Lords] between 1898 and 1966, the House considered itself absolutely bound by its past decisions"—a straitjacket that was considerably relaxed by a 1966 Practice Statement that allowed the House to depart from a past decision "when it thought right to do so").

26   *See Runyon v. McCrary*, 427 U.S. 160, 191 (1976) ("[W]hen a rule, after it has been duly tested by experience, has been found to be inconsistent with the sense of justice or with the social welfare, there should be less hesitation in frank avowal and full abandonment. . . . If judges have woefully misinterpreted the *mores* of their day, or if the *mores* of their day are no longer those of ours, they ought not to tie, in helpless submission, the hands of their successors.") (Stevens J. concurring) (quoting Benjamin N. Cardozo, *The Nature of the Judicial Process* 149 (1921)).

27   *Citizens United v. Federal Election Comm'n*, 558 U.S. 310, 362–63 (2010) ("Beyond workability, the relevant factors in deciding whether to adhere to the principle of stare decisis include the antiquity of the precedent, the reliance interests at stake, and of course whether the decision was well reasoned.") (citing *Montejo v. Louisiana*, 556 U.S. 778, 792 (2009)); *Halliburton Co. v. Erica P. John Fund, Inc.*, 134 S.Ct. 2398, 2425 (2014) (Thomas J. concurring in the judgment) (The Court has "not hesitated to overrule decisions . . . when 'the theoretical underpinnings of those decisions are called into serious question,' . . . when the decisions have become 'irreconcilable' with intervening developments in 'competing legal doctrines or policies,' . . . or when they are otherwise 'a positive detriment to coherence and consistency in the law[.'] Just one of these circumstances can justify our correction of bad precedent.") (internal citations omitted).

28   Roscoe Pound, *Interpretations of Legal History* 1 (1923).

precedents, it should do so carefully, with moderation, and with due regard for all the important considerations that undergird the doctrine.

To strike that balance, a court must carefully read the previous decision and determine what was actually decided, and what were mere dicta or snippets of language. The court must consider how that earlier decision has been applied over the years, whether it has been modified by interpretation in the interim, and whether some intervening statute or other higher authority has abrogated it. Only then can a court ask whether the decision should be followed or whether the decision has become "unworkable," was "badly reasoned,"[29] or no longer constitutes the correct course in light of experience.[30] Even then, the U.S. Supreme Court has counseled caution: "[A] decision to overrule should rest on some special reason over and above the belief that a prior case was wrongly decided."[31]

A summary of vertical and horizontal precedents

Four statements can sum up the principles of vertical and horizontal precedents discussed in § 2 and in this § 3:

(1) If an applicable precedent issued from a court hierarchically superior to the one deciding a new case, then the decision *must* follow the vertical precedent.

(2) If an applicable precedent issued from the very court deciding a new case, then the court *should* follow it, but in certain circumstances may depart from it.

(3) If a seemingly applicable precedent issued from a court hierarchically inferior to the one deciding a new case, then

---

29 *See Pearson v. Callahan*, 555 U.S. 223, 234 (2009) (derogating the rigid and inefficient two-step sequential procedure previously required to determine the existence of officials' qualified immunity by *Saucier v. Katz*, 533 U.S. 194 (2001)).

30 *Id.* at 233–34 (stating that the "experience" standard is correct when evaluating an evidentiary or procedural standard that upsets no settled expectations).

31 *Planned Parenthood of SE Pa. v. Casey*, 505 U.S. 833, 864 (1992); *see also Halliburton*, 134 S.Ct. at 2407 ("Before overturning a long-settled precedent . . . we require 'special justification,' not just an argument that the precedent was wrongly decided.") (per Roberts C.J.) (internal citations omitted).

the decision *need not* (but may) adopt the reasoning and decision.

(4) If a seemingly applicable precedent issued from a court outside the jurisdiction, and there is no hierarchical relationship to the deciding court, it *may* be considered persuasive if it is cogently reasoned—but never binding.[32]

---

[32] With acknowledgments to William Twining & David Miers, *How to Do Things with Rules* § 4.1, at 315 (4th ed. 1999).

4. Dicta vs. Holdings

The *holding* of an appellate court constitutes the precedent, as a point necessarily decided. *Dicta* do not: they are merely remarks made in the course of a decision but not essential to the reasoning behind that decision.

Not all text within a judicial decision serves as precedent. That's a role generally reserved only for holdings: the parts of a decision that focus on the legal questions actually presented to and decided by the court. A holding consists of the "court's determination of a matter of law pivotal to its decision."[1] Everything else amounts to dicta—what Francis Bacon in 1617 called the "vapours and fumes of law."[2] A witty opening paragraph, the background information on how the law developed, the digressions speculating on how similar hypothetical cases might be resolved—none of those things bind future courts. They are entitled to little deference because they are essentially ultra vires pronouncements about the law.[3] They are not law per se.[4]

So the line between holding and dictum—a distinction that arose in legal literature during the late 18th century—matters. The process of sorting holding from dictum has been said to go "to the heart of the business of judging."[5] Although older authorities often presented the distinction as clear-cut,[6] the dividing line

---

1 *Black's Law Dictionary* 849 (Bryan A. Garner ed., 10th ed. 2014).

2 Francis Bacon, "The Lord Keeper's Speech in the Exchequer" (1617), in 2 *The Works of Francis Bacon* 477, 478 (Basil Montagu ed., 1887).

3 A.W.B. Simpson, "The *Ratio Decidendi* of a Case and the Doctrine of Binding Precedent," in *Oxford Essays in Jurisprudence* 148, 161 (A.G. Guest ed., 1961); *see* 2 John Austin, *Lectures on Jurisprudence* 622 (Robert Campbell ed., 5th ed. 1885) ("Such general propositions, occurring in the course of a decision, as have not this implication with the specific peculiarities of the case, are commonly styled extra-judicial, and commonly have no authority.").

4 *See* Steven J. Burton, *An Introduction to Law and Legal Reasoning* 38–39 (2d ed. 1995) ("[T]he holding of a case has the privileged status of 'the law.' Dicta forecast, in a vague and less reliable way, what the law is likely to become.").

5 Michael Abramowicz & Maxwell Stearns, *Defining Dicta*, 57 Stan. L. Rev. 953, 958 (2005).

6 *See, e.g.*, Walter Denton Smith, *A Manual of Elementary Law* 81 (1896) ("If the rule stated by the judge tends directly to decide th[e] issue, it forms part of the

sometimes isn't a bright one, but a swath of gray—one that is subject to much scholarly debate and judicial disagreement.[7]

Part of the problem is that commentators and judges don't uniformly define what counts as a holding. At times, judges say that the holding consists of only those legal propositions absolutely necessary to the result.[8] At other times, courts give *holding* a more capacious meaning, including within it all the legal propositions that were actually found applicable to a decision, that were based on the case-specific facts, and that led to the result—whether or not they were strictly necessary.[9] This latter view permits a single decision to stand as precedent for alternative rationales.

Whichever level of breadth one gives to *holding*, its ascertainment normally involves inductive reasoning, as the legal philosopher John Austin noted: "Looking at the *general reasons* alleged by the Court for its decisions, and *abstracting those reasons from the modifications which were suggested by the peculiarities of the cases*, we arrive at a *ground* or *principle* of decision."[10] It is this principle that "will apply universally to cases of a class, and which, like a statute law, may serve as a rule of conduct."[11] But again, this process of abstracting may result in a narrower or a broader proposition.

---

doctrine of the case; if not, it is ordinarily obiter dictum.").

[7] *Compare United States v. Johnson*, 256 F.3d 895, 914–15 (9th Cir. 2001) (per Kozinski J.), *with id.* at 919–20 (Tashima J. concurring) (debating the proper definition of *dictum*).

[8] *Seminole Tribe of Fla. v. Florida*, 517 U.S. 44, 67 (1996); *see* Ruggero J. Aldisert, *Precedent: What It Is and What It Isn't; When Do We Kiss It and When Do We Kill It?*, 17 Pepp. L. Rev. 605, 609 (1990).

[9] *See Johnson*, 256 F.3d at 914 (per Kozinski J.) (stating the Ninth Circuit's "well-reasoned dictum" rule: "We hold . . . that where a panel confronts an issue germane to the eventual resolution of the case, and resolves it after reasoned consideration in a published opinion, that ruling becomes the law of the circuit, regardless of whether doing so is necessary in some strict logical sense.").

[10] 2 John Austin, *Lectures on Jurisprudence* 622 (Robert Campbell ed., 5th ed. 1885) (italics in original). *See* John C. Townes, *Law Books and How to Use Them* 49 (1909) ("[I]n almost every case the principle on which the decision rests is broader than the decision and hence there is more uncertainty as to the exact doctrine announced and a resulting fear on the part of counsel and the courts especially the latter, lest the precedent be extended too far.").

[11] Austin, *Lectures on Jurisprudence* at 622.

A near-synonym for *holding* is the fuzzy Latinism *ratio decidendi*[12]—often shortened to *ratio*. The Latin phrase literally means "reason for deciding." (The plural is *rationes decidendi*.) Whereas *holding* might be thought to equate more nearly with the court's determination of the concrete problem before it, *ratio decidendi* is normally seen as a genus-proposition of which the concrete holding is one species or instance. So the *ratio decidendi* is a more generalized statement of the holding—more generalized, typically, than one finds in the decision or opinion itself. The distinction is a fine one for those who observe it. Many authorities don't: they define *ratio decidendi* as if it were perfectly synonymous with *holding*. One commentator lists four essential elements of a *ratio decidendi*: (1) it must be a ruling on a point of law; (2) it must be expressly or impliedly given by a judge; (3) it must relate to an issue raised in the litigation; and (4) it must be necessary as a justification for the decision reached.[13] This four-part test neatly states what most American lawyers would term the *holding*. In the remainder of this text (apart from quotations of others' work), we rarely use the phrase *ratio decidendi*. But the literature using the phrase is so vast that we think it important for readers both to be familiar with it and to understand why we avoid it.

As the definitions of *holding* and *ratio* have varied, so has that of *dictum*. Generally, a *dictum* is a statement in a judicial opinion that is unnecessary to the case's resolution.[14] It's a statement that "does not explain why the court's judgment goes in favor of the winner."[15] In the words of Posner J., it is "a statement in a judicial opinion that could have been deleted without seriously impairing

---

12 See Julio C. Cueto-Rua, *Judicial Methods of Interpretation of the Law* 60 n.41 (1981) ("It is an acknowledged fact that 'ratio decidendi' and 'principle' are very ambiguous expressions."); *see also Garner's Dictionary of Legal Usage* 751 (3d ed. 2011) (calling *ratio decidendi* "more than a little ambiguous"); Jerome Frank, *Courts on Trial* 279 (1950) (referring sarcastically to the "delightful vagueness" of *ratio decidendi*).

13 John Bell, "Precedent," in *The New Oxford Companion to Law* 923 (Peter Cane & Joanne Conaghan eds., 2008).

14 *Johnson*, 256 F.3d at 920 (Tashima J. concurring); *see Garner's Dictionary of Legal Usage* at 275 (defining *dictum* as "a nonbinding, incidental opinion given by a judge in the course of a written opinion delivered in support of a judgment").

15 Pierre N. Leval, *Judging Under the Constitution: Dicta About Dicta*, 81 N.Y.U. L. Rev. 1249, 1256 (2006).

the analytical foundations of the holding."[16] Because it is an incidental remark, it "may not have received the full and careful consideration of the court that uttered it."[17]

One view posits that to identify dictum, "it is useful to turn the questioned proposition around to assert its opposite."[18] If such a change wouldn't require alteration of "the court's judgment or the reasoning that supports it, then the proposition is dictum."[19] It amounts, in short, to a superfluity.

Perhaps it's easier simply to define *dicta* more narrowly as just statements untethered to the facts of the case and not presented for adjudication.[20] After all, the traditional view (assuming that the jurisdiction bans advisory opinions) is that no court has the power to establish a legal rule on facts not before it.[21] One of the age-old maxims of organic law is that "[w]hat is not judicially presented cannot be judicially considered, decided, or adjudged."[22]

Viewed as a whole, positions on the holding/dictum dichotomy range from the quasi-scientific to the more resolutely skeptical.[23]

---

16   *Sarnoff v. American Home Prods. Corp.*, 798 F.2d 1075, 1084 (7th Cir. 1986).

17   *Id.*

18   Leval, *Judging Under the Constitution*, 81 N.Y.U. L. Rev. at 1257.

19   *Id.*

20   *See, e.g., Weinberger v. Salfi*, 422 U.S. 749, 787 n.3 (1975) (Brennan J. dissenting) ("[S]ince the Court reverses on the merits, the *source* of the District Court's jurisdiction is immaterial . . . . The Court's decision on the latter question . . . can only be characterized as dictum."); *Stein v. New York*, 346 U.S. 156, 189 (1953) ("It is clear, however, that these statements were dicta about a proposition not essential to the result."); *Carpentier v. Montgomery*, 80 U.S. (13 Wall.) 480, 488–89 (1871) ("In that case . . . the point was not material in the case . . . ; so that the intimation was nothing but an obiter dictum of the judge who delivered the opinion.") (italics omitted); *Travieso v. Travieso*, 474 So. 2d 1184, 1185 (Fla. 1985) (calling testimony of attorney-experts in another court "[n]ot material to its holding, and therefore dicta").

21   George Whitecross Paton, *A Textbook of Jurisprudence* 214 (G.W. Paton & David P. Derham eds., 4th ed. 1972).

22   William T. Hughes, *The Law Restated: The Roots of the Law* 21 (1915) (translating *De non apparentibus et non existentibus eadem est ratio*); cf. *Black's Law Dictionary* 1910 (Bryan A. Garner ed., 10th ed. 2014) (defining the Latin maxim more literally: "The rule is the same respecting things that do not appear and things that do not exist").

23   *See* Neil Duxbury, *The Nature and Authority of Precedent* 76–90 (2008) (cataloguing various commentators' approaches to defining and divining the *ratio* [we would say *holding*]).

Some authorities not only suggest that there is a reliable way to distinguish between dictum and holding—and a way to determine a holding's applicability to a current dispute—but also purport to describe the process in nearly scientific terms.[24]

Others say that the holding of an earlier case can often be explained in various ways—and that its applicability to a current dispute is sometimes indeterminate—but see these tasks as being guided by meaningful constraints.[25] Still others see the enterprise as hopeless, suggesting that judges manipulate the language of former decisions and declare so much or so little of those former decisions' holdings as suits their personal preferences in resolving the case at hand—perhaps lending a false sense of inevitability to their decisions.[26]

In practice, however, the distinction is often straightforward. It's often possible to identify the parts of an opinion with lucidity and relative ease. Let's consider two cases that demonstrate the usual lack of blurriness.

---

24 *See, e.g.*, Michael Sinclair, *Precedent, Super-Precedent*, 14 Geo. Mason L. Rev. 363, 380–85 (2007) (describing the "quasiscientific scholasticism" of Christopher Columbus Langdell); Charles W. Collier, *Precedent and Legal Authority: A Critical History*, 1988 Wis. L. Rev. 771, 787–89 (1988) (recounting Sir Fredrick Pollock's "general paradigm of legal method based on inductive science"); Arthur L. Goodhart, *Determining the* Ratio Decidendi *of a Case*, 40 Yale L.J. 161, 181–82 (1930) (laying down five rules for identifying the "principle" of a case and ten rules for cleaving out material facts from immaterial ones).

25 *See, e.g.*, Joseph Raz, *The Authority of Law: Essays on Law and Morality* 184 (2d ed. 2009) ("Sometimes these rules for determining the *ratio* [i.e., holding] may yield indeterminate results: it may be impossible to say what the *ratio* is or to say there is none.... In the main, however, the identification of the *ratio* of a case is reasonably straightforward."); H.L.A. Hart, *The Concept of Law* 134 (3d ed. 2012) ("[T]here is no single method of determining the rule for which a given authoritative precedent is an authority. Notwithstanding this, in the vast majority of decided cases there is very little doubt."); *see also* Cass R. Sunstein, *On Analogical Reasoning*, 106 Harv. L. Rev. 741, 780–81 (1993) ("The process of reasoning by analogy is not science, and it cannot be anchored in anything other than what human beings actually believe. But surely this does not disqualify it as a mode of reasoning. It may even be said to be the central feature of the common law method.").

26 *Cf.* Jerome Frank, *Law and the Modern Mind* 159 (1930).

First, consider a rather short example from a simpler era—a Texas Supreme Court case decided in 1872–1873. Here is the full opinion, with a few annotations:

WALKER, J. It does not appear from the statement of the facts in this case, except by inference, who shot the mules of the appellee [Deaton]; but it appears to be conceded by attorneys that they were shot by one or both of the appellant's [Chandler's] sons, who were minors at the time of the shooting. As a general rule of law, minors are liable for their own torts. The father is not liable in this action as the case is presented to us. There is no presumption growing out of the domestic relation of parent and child, which would hold the father responsible for a crime or tort committed by his minor child, unless it be shown that the father is himself in some way implicated as principal or accessory; and there is no proof of anything of this kind in this case. Had it been shown on the trial that Chandler counseled or abetted his sons in shooting Deaton's mules, he might have been held responsible for the act; or, if he concealed the offense, knowing it to have been committed, he might be liable in a criminal prosecution; and there may be some doubt whether concealing a knowledge of the act might not be so far regarded as approbating and adopting the act of his sons as to make him liable in damages. This question, however, does not arise in the case on the record before us, and we will not be understood as deciding it. The judgment of the District Court is reversed, and the cause remanded.

Reversed and remanded.*

> Facts—from which we infer that Deaton sued Chandler in tort for damages resulting from the shooting of his mules. Deaton succeeded in the trial court. Chandler has appealed, insisting that he is not responsible for Deaton's damages.

> A statement of law that is dictum. The minors weren't sued, so the question wasn't presented.

> This is dictum: although the facts doubtless describe a crime as well as a tort, it's a civil suit: the holding bears on tort only.

> The reason for the decision, though imprecisely put. The writer probably meant *obligation* rather than *presumption*.

> The decision or holding—from which we infer that a parent is not responsible to the owner of personal property for damage to that property committed by a minor child, at least not merely on account of the parent–child relationship.

> Dicta in the form of hypotheticals not actually presented.

> Disclaimer of any holding on dicta.

> The disposition or statement of the mandate.

> The mandate. See pp. 76–77.

Chandler v. Deaton, 37 Tex. 406, 406–07 (1872–1873) (with acknowledgments to John C. Townes, *Law Books and How to Use Them* 51–52 (1909) for this example).

This example shows that if one is to discern the various parts of a judicial opinion, one must have some experience in reading opinions. Without that experience, the reader would never draw the inferences noted. One inference not noted on the preceding page is the unstated *ratio decidendi* for which the holding in the case represents but one instance: a person isn't responsible for another person's tort, and the parent–child relationship presents no exception to this rule. We gather this point from the statement of the rationale, beginning with "There is no presumption that." The holding ("The father is not liable . . ."), though couched in father–son terms, should be understood to embrace parents and their children generally—not just male parents and male children. The dicta noted in the left-hand sidebars are readily identifiable as such, at least to someone with a modicum of legal training.

Not always, however, is the question so plain. Let's take a second example—dealing with one of the earliest known statements of the *ejusdem generis* rule, which posits that broad words at the end of a list of specifics are limited by the types of specifics mentioned. In the 1774 case of *Moore v. Magrath*,[27] the eminent Lord Mansfield (1705–1793) made this general statement about a deed provision ending with broad catchall words (essentially *and all my other property in the kingdom of Ireland*): "It is very common to put in a sweeping clause; and the use and object of it in general is, to guard against any accidental omission: but in such cases, it is meant to refer to estates or things of the same nature and description with those that have been already mentioned."[28]

One learned commentator has called this statement dictum.[29] Is it, though? It certainly seems so at first. But the following sentence, just three words later, contains a telltale *therefore*: "I am therefore of opinion from the words of the preamble, that the donor did not intend to include his paternal estate [different in kind from the specifics preceding the broad words]: and it is more

---

27 98 Eng. Rep. 939, 941, 1 Cowper 9, 12 (K.B. 1774).
28 *Id.*
29 Glanville L. Williams, *The Origin and Logical Implications of the* Ejusdem Generis *Rule*, 7 Conv. & Prop. Law. 119, 122 (1943).

than probable that the drawer by mistake omitted inserting the two counties before the words 'in the kingdom of Ireland.'"[30]

This type of reasoning is called an "enthymeme"—a syllogism in which one of the premises has been suppressed.[31] In Lord Mansfield's reasoning, the minor premise of the syllogism has been omitted:

Major premise:

Although drafters commonly insert a "sweeping clause" (broad words) at the end of a list, they mean only to guard against accidental omissions—not to broaden coverage to things unlike the listed items.

[Tacit minor premise:

The drafter of the deed at issue used just such a sweeping clause.]

Conclusion:

The sweeping clause in the deed doesn't cover interests in properties unlike those listed before.

So is the major premise dictum? It's necessary to the holding, which might be fairly stated this way: if a clause in a deed lists specific types of property but then uses the broad words *or any other property* at the end of the list, the broad words do not include types of property different in kind from the specific types listed. The word *therefore* shows that Lord Mansfield was reasoning from the major premise. And it was hardly untethered from the facts.

The distinction between a holding and a dictum doesn't depend on whether the point was argued by counsel and deliberately considered by the court (see § 23), but instead on whether the solution of the particular point was more or less necessary to determining the issues involved in the case. Whether a statement is a holding or dictum isn't always settled within an opinion. Litigants and later courts may dispute what parts of an opinion were in fact

---

30 *Moore*, 98 Eng. Rep. at 941, 1 Cowper at 12–13 (italics in original).

31 *See* Bryan A. Garner, *The Winning Brief* 128–31 (3d ed. 2014) (explaining enthymemes in legal reasoning in some detail); *see also* A.G. Guest, "Logic in the Law," in *Oxford Essays in Jurisprudence* 176, 182 (1961) ("In most cases, of course, the main argument will turn upon the meaning of the major premiss [BrE spelling], or upon the truth of the minor.").

essential to the precise ruling.[32] To prevent mischaracterization of their holdings, courts often expressly state that a given conclusion is the holding of a case.[33] But as we have just seen and will see again, explicitness or inexplicitness isn't always determinative.

Some practical difficulties

The very fact that we're dealing with written opinions complicates the technique of applying the holding/dictum dichotomy for a simple reason: some judges write lucidly, while others write obscurely. Not all writers have the skill of clear expression. The more opaque the opinion—the more rambling, verbose, ill-structured, and vague—the greater the challenge to all readers. At its nadir in American legal history, from about 1880 to about 1920, judicial writing was often obscure. Today the primary source of obscurity is sheer length: judicial opinions have become longer and longer with each succeeding generation. Hence many opinions demand great effort from the reader to grasp their nuances. We must recognize this challenging fact.[34]

The first step in ascertaining the holding in an appellate-court opinion is to determine the precise action taken by the trial court. This requires analyzing, if the material is available, the particular

---

32   See, e.g., *Cohen v. Alliant Enters., Inc.*, 60 S.W.3d 536, 540 (Ky. 2001) (Johnstone J. dissenting) ("To answer [the question before the court] in the affirmative, the majority ignores precedent or characterizes holdings as mere dicta."); *State v. Sanders*, 737 N.W.2d 44, 54 (Wis. Ct. App. 2007) (Brown J. concurring) ("The term 'dicta,' in my view, is often too broadly defined, usually by a lawyer who is searching for a way not to be bound by a prior published decision.").

33   *Breaux v. Diamond M. Drilling Co.*, 850 F.2d 239, 241 (5th Cir. 1988) (reiterating the relevant standard and the basis for the decision "to avoid any suggestion that our conclusion is dicta").

34   See Neil MacCormick, *Legal Reasoning and Legal Theory* 84–85 (1978) ("[T]here is a possibility that some precedents contain relatively clear rulings on fairly sharply defined points of law, and that others contain implicit rulings of similar, but perhaps less, relative clarity. Yet others because of judicial disagreement or simple confusion contain none. It is only a dogmatic fiction that the third class has anything which could reasonably be called a *ratio* [i.e., holding] at all."); *see also* Karl Llewellyn, *Jurisprudence: Realism in Theory and Practice* 124 (1962) ("Where . . . all you have is precedents . . . with the reasons obscure, then one lawyer can build a letter-perfect case on the language, or some language, announced in the process of actual decision; the opposing lawyer can show the language to be distinguishable stuff, and can bring other language.").

civil or criminal procedure used by the trial court to reach its result, noting how the trial court erred (according to the appellant's claims), and analyzing whether the appellate court made its decision based on the claimed errors or on grounds other than those raised by the litigants. Then we can glean what the appellate court actually decided and determine which aspects of the appellate court's written opinion were necessary to its ultimate decision, thereby rendering those parts of the opinion its holdings.

To determine whether a particular point of law is necessary to the court's ultimate decision, some courts ask whether the point of law in question could be deleted from the opinion without seriously impairing the basis of the decision.[35] This line of thought suggests that alternative reasoning may or may not constitute a holding because a court could still reach the same ultimate decision even if one of the alternative routes of reasoning were omitted.[36] Some courts are therefore reluctant to consider alternative reasonings to be holdings because they are inferred, not express.[37] But most courts consider alternative holdings to be binding precedent.[38] (See generally § 10.)

While the line between holding and dictum is theoretically stark, it can get blurry in practice: "The distinction between . . . dicta and the elusive *ratio decidendi* [i.e., holding] is in essence a distinction between relevance and irrelevance, and much of the

---

35 See *International Truck & Engine Corp. v. Bray*, 372 F.3d 717, 721 (5th Cir. 2004) (stating that "[a] statement is dictum if it 'could have been deleted without seriously impairing the analytical foundations of the holding,'" while "[a] statement is not dictum if it is necessary to the result or constitutes an explication of the governing rules of law") (quoting *Gochicoa v. Johnson*, 238 F.3d 278, 286 n.11 (5th Cir. 2000)).

36 See Michael Abramowicz & Maxwell Stearns, *Defining Dicta*, 57 Stan. L. Rev. 953, 1056 (noting that the requirement that a holding be "necessary" to a court's ultimate decision is inconsistent with the judicial practice of according precedential status to alternative justifications).

37 *In re Hearn*, 376 F.3d 447, 453 n.5 (5th Cir. 2004).

38 See *Woods v. Interstate Realty Co.*, 337 U.S. 535, 537 (1949) ("[W]here a decision rests on two or more grounds, none can be relegated to the category of *obiter dictum*."); *Hearn*, 376 F.3d at 453 n.5 ("It is well-established that alternative holdings of this Court are binding on future panels."); *Whetsel v. Network Prop. Servs., LLC*, 246 F.3d 897, 903 (7th Cir. 2001) (stating that "alternative holdings . . . are entitled to precedential weight").

difficulty in elucidating the conception of the *ratio decidendi* arises from attempts to give a precise meaning to relevance in this context."[39] Relevance isn't exactly in the eye of the beholder, for there are often objective ways to judge it. But in borderline cases many will disagree on where the delineation lies.[40]

Although some commentators suggest that this line is "almost entirely malleable,"[41] they may be confusing deference to persuasive authority with following binding authority. Courts routinely defer to aspects of earlier opinions extending well beyond the narrow application of a legal principle to a discrete set of facts. The result is an "*inclusive* paradigm of precedent in which binding effect attaches to a vast array of judicial propositions."[42]

Take, for example, the U.S. Supreme Court's decision in *Kappos v. Hyatt*.[43] There, the Court characterized a part of another Supreme Court case as "not strictly necessary to [that case's] holding," but nonetheless believed the discussion was worthy of deference because it was "not the kind of ill-considered dicta that we are inclined to ignore."[44] The Court explained that the discussion deserved deference because it was well reasoned and had been reiterated in several later cases.[45] Essentially, the Court invoked the concept of "judicial dictum," which is stronger than ordinary dictum (*see infra* pp. 62–65).

This more expansive view of precedent isn't confined to the Supreme Court. An empirical study of lower courts confirms the

---

39 A.W.B. Simpson, "The *Ratio Decidendi* of a Case and the Doctrine of Binding Precedent," in *Oxford Essays in Jurisprudence* 148, 161 (A.G. Guest ed., 1961); *cf.* Dennis Lloyd, *Introduction to Jurisprudence* 378 (rev. ed. 1965) ("the whole process [of determining the *ratio decidendi*—or we would say *holding*] is too indeterminate to be reduced to specific rules").

40 John H. Farrar & Anthony M. Dugdale, *Introduction to Legal Method* 89 (2d ed. 1984) ("[R]*atio decidendi* is a flexible notion which is 'fuzzy at the edges' and purposely left so by the courts for policy reasons because *it itself* is not so much a rule as *an analogical technique used to create a rule*.") (emphasis in original).

41 Michael C. Dorf, *Dicta and Article III*, 142 U. Pa. L. Rev. 1997, 2005 (1994).

42 Randy J. Kozel, *The Scope of Precedent*, 113 Mich. L. Rev. 179, 183 (2014).

43 132 S.Ct. 1690 (2012).

44 *Id.* at 1699 (discussing *Butterworth v. United States ex rel. Hoe*, 112 U.S. 50 (1884)).

45 *Id.*

prevalence of "abid[ing] by statements from higher courts even though they are recognized as dicta."[46] So not all dicta are created equal. Those in vertical precedents carry added weight. And sometimes, as we'll see in the discussion of judicial dictum, a dictum may functionally take on precedential force because it is particularly well-considered.[47]

A 2005 Fourth Circuit case serves as a good example of the power of dictum in vertical precedents.[48] The court considered a challenge to a school's requirement that students recite the Pledge of Allegiance. The plaintiff asserted that because the pledge contains the phrase "under God," students were indirectly coerced into adopting a religious message in violation of the Establishment Clause.[49] The Supreme Court had recently considered a similar challenge.[50] It discussed the purposes of having schoolchildren recite the Pledge of Allegiance but didn't reach the merits of the issue before dismissing the case on standing grounds.[51] Nonetheless, the Fourth Circuit's reasoning relied in part on dicta from that Supreme Court decision: "'The very purpose of a national flag is to serve as a symbol of our country....'"[52] Further: "Pledging allegiance to that flag is 'a common public acknowledgment of the ideals that our flag symbolizes. Its recitation is a patriotic exercise designed to foster national unity and pride in those principles.'"[53] The court rejected the challenge, concluding

---

46 *See* David E. Klein & Neal Devins, *Dicta, Schmicta: Theory Versus Practice in Lower Court Decision Making*, 54 Wm. & Mary L. Rev. 2021, 2044 (2013).

47 *See* Pierre N. Leval, *Judging Under the Constitution: Dicta About Dicta*, 81 N.Y.U. L. Rev. 1249, 1250 (2006).

48 *Myers v. Loudoun Cnty. Pub. Schs.*, 418 F.3d 395 (4th Cir. 2005); *see also Nichol v. Pullman Standard, Inc.*, 889 F.2d 115, 120 n.8 (7th Cir. 1989); *Coeur d'Alene Tribe of Idaho v. Hammond*, 384 F.3d 674, 683 (9th Cir. 2004); Leval, *Judging Under the Constitution: Dicta About Dicta*, 81 N.Y.U. L. Rev. at 1252.

49 *Myers*, 418 F.3d at 399.

50 *See Elk Grove Unified Sch. Dist. v. Newdow*, 542 U.S. 1 (2004).

51 *Id.* at 6–7, 17–18.

52 *Myers*, 418 F.3d at 407 (quoting *Texas v. Johnson*, 491 U.S. 397, 405 (1989)); *see Elk Grove Unified Sch. Dist.*, 542 U.S. at 6 (same).

53 *Myers*, 418 F.3d at 407 (quoting *Elk Grove Unified Sch. Dist.*, 542 U.S. at 6).

that "the Pledge is by its nature a patriotic exercise, not a religious exercise."[54]

Courts sometimes narrowly cabin precedential holdings, particularly when faced with holdings that prove inconvenient or disagreeable. The Supreme Court's decision in *United States v. Alvarez*[55] exemplifies that sort of reasoning. Alvarez falsely stated that he had been awarded the Congressional Medal of Honor. He did so intentionally, but only in an effort to win respect—not with any intent to gain financial benefit, employment, or privileges extended to soldiers who have earned the medal.[56] He was convicted of violating the Stolen Valor Act of 2005, which criminalizes making false statements about earning military decorations or medals, especially the Medal of Honor.[57] The government argued that the First Amendment gives no protection to false statements and quoted language from several Supreme Court precedents.[58] For example, the Court has said:

- "the knowingly false statement and the false statement made with reckless disregard of the truth do not enjoy constitutional protection";[59]
- "false statements of fact are particularly valueless because they interfere with the truth-seeking function of the marketplace of ideas"[60] and have "no constitutional value";[61] and

---

54   *Id.* at 408. *Accord Newdow v. Rio Linda Union Sch. Dist.*, 597 F.3d 1007, 1037 (9th Cir. 2010) ("[B]oth the purpose and effect of the Pledge are that of a predominantly patriotic, not a religious, exercise.").

55   132 S.Ct. 2537 (2012).

56   *Id.* at 2542.

57   18 U.S.C. § 704 (2012); *see* 132 S.Ct. at 2542–43.

58   *Alvarez*, 132 S.Ct. at 2544–45.

59   *Id.* at 2545 (citing *Garrison v. Louisiana*, 379 U.S. 64, 75 (1964)).

60   *Id.* (citing *Hustler Magazine, Inc. v. Falwell*, 485 U.S. 46, 52 (1988)).

61   *Id.* (citing *Gertz v. Robert Welch, Inc.*, 418 U.S. 323, 340 (1974)).

- "[u]ntruthful speech . . . has never been protected for its own sake"[62] because "[s]preading false information in and of itself carries no First Amendment credentials."[63]

The government noted that the Court has also said that false statements "are not protected by the First Amendment *in the same manner* as truthful statements."[64]

Yet the government didn't acknowledge the suggestion that *some* protection does exist, and the Court rejected the government's proposed categorical rule "that false statements receive no First Amendment protection."[65] The cited cases involved fraud, defamation, and other offenses. None concerned a statute like the Stolen Valor Act, which expressly punishes false speech and doesn't require proof of a legally cognizable harm associated with a false statement.[66] So because the falsity of the statements in the cited cases wasn't determinative, the quotations from the previous decisions were considered dicta not binding on the Court.[67] The Court declared that if it had agreed with the government that an interest in truth was by itself enough to uphold a ban on false statements that weren't made to gain a material advantage, it would give the government a broad power of censorship and infringe the First Amendment.[68] Note, too, that this was an instance of dicta within horizontal precedents—a weaker type than that found in vertical precedents (see § 3).

Gauging breadth

Sometimes a holding isn't stated outright. While ascertaining the holding might seem fairly straightforward, doing so can be quite difficult when it isn't stated expressly. The problem is that a holding can often be stated many ways, from very narrowly to

---

62   *Id.* (citing *Virginia State Bd. of Pharmacy v. Virginia Citizens Consumer Council, Inc.*, 425 U.S. 748, 771 (1976)).

63   *Id.* (citing *Herbert v. Lando*, 441 U.S. 153, 171 (1979)).

64   *Id.* (citing *Brown v. Hartlage*, 456 U.S. 45, 60–61 (1982) (emphasis added)).

65   *Id.*

66   *Id.*

67   *Id.*

68   *Id.* at 2547–48.

very broadly. How it's most sensibly stated determines how useful or harmful it may be as precedent in later cases.

As for explicit statements, the general ones in an opinion have less precedential value than the specific ones. No judge can write opinions with mathematical precision. The meaning of the opinion, even the holding, must be read in context, with due regard for the difficulty—the impossibility, really—of the court's anticipating every circumstance in which the language could be applied. Marshall C.J. expressed this principle almost two centuries ago: "It is a maxim not to be disregarded, that general expressions, in every opinion, are to be taken in connection with the case in which those expressions are used."[69] Outside that context, the value of the holding as principle ceases to be binding, though it may still be persuasive. Or, as Marshall wrote: "If they go beyond the case, they may be respected, but ought not to control the judgment in a subsequent suit when the very point is presented for decision."[70] Marshall further explained the "obvious" reasoning behind the maxim: "The question actually before the Court is investigated with care, and considered in its full extent. Other principles which may serve to illustrate it, are considered in their relation to the case decided, but their possible bearing on all other cases is seldom completely investigated."[71]

The maxim hasn't weakened with time. In 1935 the Supreme Court wrote: "In the course of the [prior] opinion of the court, expressions occur which tend to sustain the government's contention, but these are beyond the point involved and, therefore, do not come within the rule of stare decisis."[72] Lower courts have also recognized the force of the maxim.[73]

---

69   *Cohens v. Virginia*, 19 U.S. (6 Wheat.) 264, 399 (1821).

70   *Id.*; *cf.* Dennis Lloyd, *Introduction to Jurisprudence* 374 (rev. ed. 1965) (stating that "no illustration is needed to prove the point that judges, however cautious they may be by training and disposition, sometimes state rules in terms wider than needed for the disposal of the matter at hand").

71   *Cohens*, 19 U.S. at 399–400.

72   *Humphrey's Executor v. United States*, 295 U.S. 602, 626 (1935).

73   See *Irwin v. Simmons*, 140 F.2d 558, 563 (2d Cir. 1944) ("Generalizations found in the opinions in the foregoing cases must be read in the light of the specific issues there before the court; 'asides' in an opinion are not to be taken as

Even so, when the court itself tries to make its holding explicit, we should pay close attention to how it formulates that holding. The court might state at the end of an opinion: "We hold that Sylvester, the testator's cat, cannot inherit the $10,000 bequeathed to him." Is this really the holding of the case? Although necessary to the outcome, it seems too narrow a statement of the issue and answer. It's hard to think of any good reason why Sylvester should be treated differently from any other cat. More important, it doesn't sound much like a principle or legal rule that could apply to later cases, which is what the doctrine of precedent is all about. The moral is that while the court's statement of the holding is important, it doesn't necessarily decide the matter. One must still determine how to formulate the holding exactly.

Let's try a somewhat broader statement of the holding: "cats cannot inherit money under a will." This is a definite improvement. It's beginning to sound like a more general rule or principle that courts could use to decide the outcomes of future cases. But it still seems too narrow. Why just cats? All the reasons the court gives for not allowing cats to inherit seem as if they should apply to other animals as well.

So we take another stab at formulating the holding of the case: "animals cannot inherit money under a will." This statement is a plausible legal rule. It would be a perfectly reasonable description of the holding of the case—although it isn't the only possible way to formulate the holding. Whether the holding is declared explicitly by a judge or inferred by someone analyzing an inexplicit opinion, it can be stated broadly or narrowly. As an early-20th-century commentator put it, "there stretches up and away from every single case in the books not one possible gradation of widening generalizations, but many."[74]

---

authoritative."); *Heinlein v. Stefan*, 759 A.2d 1180, 1186 (Md. Ct. Spec. App. 2000) ("What we are trying to communicate is that in a context where it makes no apparent critical difference at that moment, an opinion writer's choice of words may be more a matter of art than a considered legal judgment and is, therefore, not precedential authority for anything.").

74 Herman Oliphant, *A Return to Stare Decisis*, 14 ABA J. 71, 73 (1928).

Let's state the holding even more broadly. Should the holding be that animals cannot inherit *any* type of property under a will? Or that animals cannot own property, period? Or that animals have no rights at all? One might state the *issue* this broadly, but doing so would expand the holding beyond reason. It probably wouldn't be supported by the court's discussion.

What if the court had stated that the result might be different if someone had promised the testator to use the money to take care of Sylvester? Should we consider this to be part of the holding? We might then state the holding as follows: "an animal may not inherit money under a will unless a human being has promised to use the money to take care of the animal."

This statement may sound like a reasonable rule, but there's a problem with it. Specifically, the part about the promise might not be necessary to the outcome of the case. What if the facts don't mention a promise at all? The court's offhand comment that the outcome might have been different if someone had made such a promise would be dictum, so it can't form any part of the holding.

Lower courts may wonder how finely they should slice the reasoning of a higher court. This question is especially important when the precedent being evaluated comes from the U.S. Supreme Court. When a court picks through a menu of 8,000 to 9,000 cases, chooses the 75 or 80 that seem to be most significant, and devotes its full resources to the proper disposition of that tiny number of cases, it seems likely that the Court expects lower courts to respect its considered expressions of law.

In a 1998 case,[75] for example, the Seventh Circuit considered the question whether a theory of criminal liability is a "count" for purposes of the statute giving the government the right to take an interlocutory appeal from an order dismissing an indictment or information "as to any one or more counts."[76] A dissenting judge

---

75 *United States v. Bloom*, 149 F.3d 649 (7th Cir. 1998), *overruled on other grounds by Skilling v. United States*, 561 U.S. 358 (2010) (rejecting the theory, accepted in *Bloom*, that mail fraud could be proved by a deprivation of an intangible right to honest services, and holding instead that bribery, kickbacks, or something closely analogous had to be shown).

76 *Bloom*, 149 F.3d at 652.

had labeled as dictum the language from an earlier case indicating that a theory would suffice. The Seventh Circuit panel, however, had this to say—Easterbrook J. writing for the court:

> Even if the passage could be called dictum, it is not an aside unrelated to the subject of the case. The question had been briefed by the parties, so the statement was informed rather than casual; it is a considered expression by the Court supported by earlier cases . . . that supply more extensive analysis and is not incompatible with any decision before or since. . . . It would ill serve the interests of litigants and the judicial system as a whole to row against the tide of such statements. . . . The Supreme Court often articulates positions through language that an unsympathetic audience might dismiss as dictum—consider the catalog of rules in *Miranda v. Arizona* . . . —and it expects these formulations to be followed. See *Baxter v. Palmigiano* . . . (disapproving, with some asperity, a court's decision to alter one of the guidelines announced, arguably in dictum, in *Wolff v. McDonnell* . . .). The Court can hear only a small portion of all litigated disputes; it uses considered dicta to influence others for which there is no room on the docket. Appellate courts that dismiss these expressions and strike off on their own increase the disparity among tribunals (for other judges are likely to follow the Supreme Court's marching orders) and frustrate the evenhanded administration of justice by giving the litigants an outcome other than the one the Supreme Court would be likely to reach were the case heard there.[77]

This passage underscores the degree of judgment that goes into classifying a court's reasoning as holding or dictum. When the Supreme Court is plainly going in a certain direction—for instance, in habeas corpus cases from state-court convictions, the Court has repeatedly stressed the high degree of deference that is required—a lower court would risk summary reversal if it tried to confine an earlier Supreme Court decision to only that case's facts. On the other hand, in developing areas of the law it is sometimes reasonable to proceed cautiously, to make sure that one isn't overreading the Supreme Court's decision. This is particularly true if the decision in question was narrowly divided or elicited a number

---

77   *Id.* at 653 (citations omitted).

of separate opinions concurring, concurring in the judgment, or dissenting (see § 19).

Obiter dictum vs. judicial dictum

Our discussion of dictum so far has mostly been about only one type—the major one—called in full *obiter dictum*. It is in the nature of a peripheral, off-the-cuff judicial remark. Obiter dictum historically differs from *judicial dictum*, which is "an opinion by a court on a question that is directly involved, briefed, and argued by counsel, and even passed on by the court, but that is not essential to the decision and therefore not binding even if it may later be accorded some weight."[78] The dichotomy between the two lies in both their nature and their consequential uses.[79] Obiter dictum is seldom considered precedential—though it is sometimes persuasive—and it isn't binding under the doctrine of stare decisis.[80] Judicial dictum, on the other hand, is said to carry more weight

---

78   *Black's Law Dictionary* 549 (Bryan A. Garner ed., 10th ed. 2014); *see* 14 Ill. Law & Prac. *Courts* § 72 (2015) ("'Judicial dictum' refers to a remark or opinion upon a point argued by counsel and deliberately passed upon by the court, though not essential to the disposition of the case. It involves an issue briefed and argued by the parties. Judicial dictum, unlike obiter dictum, is generally entitled to weight and should be followed unless found to be erroneous."); 12A Fla. Jur. 2d *Courts and Judges* § 192 (2015) ("In distinction from obiter dicta, 'judicial dicta' are comments in a judicial opinion that are unnecessary to the disposition of the case but involve an issue briefed and argued by the parties. Judicial dicta have the force of a determination by a reviewing court and should receive dispositive weight in an inferior court.").

79   *Garner's Dictionary of Legal Usage* 275 (3d ed. 2011); *see also Black's Law Dictionary* at 549 (s.v. *judicial dictum*); *Wolf v. Meister-Neiberg, Inc.*, 551 N.E.2d 353, 355 (Ill. App. Ct. 1990) (explaining the two types of dicta), *aff'd*, 570 N.E.2d 327 (Ill. 1991).

80   *See, e.g., Central Green Co. v. United States*, 531 U.S. 425, 431 (2001) (citing *Humphrey's Executor v. United States*, 295 U.S. 602, 627 (1935), for the proposition that "dicta [based on isolated comments] 'may be followed if sufficiently persuasive' but are not binding"); *United States v. Johnson*, 256 F.3d 895, 915 (9th Cir. 2001) (en banc) (per Kozinski J.) ("Where it is clear that a statement is made casually and without analysis, where the statement is uttered in passing without due consideration of the alternatives, or where it is merely a prelude to another legal issue that commands the panel's full attention, it may be appropriate to re-visit the issue in a later case."); *see also* 18 James W. Moore et al., *Moore's Federal Practice* § 134.03[2], at 134-30 to 134-36.1 (3d ed. 2015) (listing cases).

and has been held by some courts to be binding precedent[81] in the absence of contrary higher authority.

The Ninth Circuit recognized binding judicial dictum in a 2001 case.[82] While apprehending a suspect, Washington state officers broke into defendant Johnson's fenced-in yard without a warrant and smelled marijuana in a detached shed on Johnson's property. After obtaining a search warrant, they found marijuana inside the shed. At trial, Johnson moved to suppress the evidence on the ground that it had been seized illegally. The district court denied the motion, finding the initial search of Johnson's property justified under the hot-pursuit exception to the Fourth Amendment's warrant requirement. Having decided that, the court didn't address the officers' argument that the search was also justified under the open-fields doctrine.[83]

On appeal, a three-judge panel of the Ninth Circuit assumed without deciding that the shed was located on Johnson's curtilage,[84] because whether the search took place within the curtilage was a question for the district court to decide.[85] The panel affirmed the district court's decision, agreeing that the search met the requirements of the hot-pursuit exception.[86]

But on rehearing en banc, a majority of the court held that the curtilage question must be reviewed de novo on appeal. Although one judge declared that deciding the standard of review was merely dictum "unnecessary to [the] disposition of the case,"[87] the majority held that when a panel's published opinion contains a reasoned consideration of and ruling on an issue germane to the resolution of the case, "that ruling becomes the law of the circuit, regardless of whether [the ruling] is necessary in some

---

81 See *Johnson*, 256 F.3d at 914 (per Kozinski J.) (stating the Ninth Circuit's "well-reasoned dictum" rule).
82 *United States v. Johnson*, 256 F.3d 895 (9th Cir. 2001) (en banc).
83 *Id.* at 898.
84 *United States v. Johnson*, 207 F.3d 538, 543–44 (9th Cir. 2000).
85 256 F.3d at 898.
86 207 F.3d at 548–50.
87 256 F.3d at 919–20 (Tashima J. concurring).

strict logical sense."[88] The majority reasoned that panels are often presented with multiple issues, any of which could be dispositive. To provide guidance for future cases, and especially to prevent a lower court from repeating an error when a case is remanded, an appellate panel may find it appropriate to rule on several issues.[89] Johnson had fairly presented and argued an issue about the standard of review for curtilage determinations, which the court had carefully analyzed, rather than making "a casual, off-hand remark or a broad statement of principle."[90] So the en banc panel's holding that a curtilage determination must be reviewed de novo superseded the panel's decision, which would otherwise have been the law of the circuit.[91]

In addition to the Ninth Circuit, the Second Circuit has agreed that some judicial dicta can serve as binding precedent, stating that "in some contexts expressions of views by an appellate court must be regarded as the law of the circuit, even though not an announcement of a holding or even of a necessary step in the reasoning leading to a holding."[92] But other circuits appear not to have adopted this rule. Further, federal courts generally give greater deference to the "considered dicta" of state courts when it comes to interpreting state law.[93]

---

88   *Id.* at 914.

89   *Id.*

90   *Id.* at 915–16.

91   *Id.*

92   *United States v. Oshatz*, 912 F.2d 534, 540 (2d Cir. 1990) (noting the particular applicability of this principle in the context of a "clear statement of an approved or disapproved aspect of trial court procedure"). *But see United States v. Bell*, 524 F.2d 202, 206 (2d Cir. 1975) (distinguishing obiter dictum from judicial dictum and stating that while judicial dictum "is not binding upon us, it must be given considerable weight and cannot be ignored in the resolution of [a] close question we have to decide").

93   *See, e.g., Peerless Indem. Ins. Co. v. Frost*, 723 F.3d 12, 20 (1st Cir. 2013) (citing *Dibella v. Hopkins*, 403 F.3d 102, 113 (2d Cir. 2005), for the proposition that "statements by state's lower courts, even if dicta, can be helpful indicators of state law") (internal quotation marks omitted); *Covington v. Continental Gen. Tire, Inc.*, 381 F.3d 216, 218 (3d Cir. 2004) (stating that in a diversity case in which a federal court must predict how a state court would rule on a particular point of law, the federal court "must consider relevant state precedents, analogous decisions, *considered dicta*, scholarly works, and any other reliable data tending convincingly to show how the highest court in the state would decide

Some might say that all this slicing and dicing of dicta into subtypes is unhelpful—the basic holding/dictum distinction being difficult enough itself. Labeling something *judicial dictum* may simply be a way of saying that it's particularly persuasive. We do not, by including this subsection, endorse the obiter/judicial dichotomy; rather, we simply note its existence in the literature. On the whole, we think it might be more beneficial not to engage in minute divisions of dictum at all.

The (limited) utility of dicta

To recognize that dicta bear less binding force than a holding isn't to suggest that dicta are useless.[94] Far from it. If that were true, it would make no sense for courts to go out of their way so often "to ingraft on . . . decisions statements of the law that have no direct application to the matter in controversy."[95] Dicta may afford litigants the benefit of a fuller understanding of the court's decisional path or related areas of concern. Dicta can be a source of advice to successors, sometimes thoughtful advice that ought to be heeded.

Consider a 1994 Seventh Circuit case[96] in which the court's holding—that under ERISA, a nonfiduciary cannot be held liable for knowing participation in a fiduciary's breach of duty—was premised on Supreme Court dicta from a year before in

---

the issue at hand") (internal quotation marks omitted) (emphasis added); 20 Charles Alan Wright & Mary Kay Kane, *Federal Practice and Procedure* § 61, at 498 (2d ed. 2011) (noting that when federal courts interpret state law, "[m]ere obiter [dicta from a state court] may be entitled to little weight, while a carefully considered statement by the state court, though technically dictum, must carry great weight, and may even, in the absence of any conflicting indication of the law of the state, be regarded as conclusive").

94 *See* Neil MacCormick, *Rhetoric and the Rule of Law: A Theory of Legal Reasoning* 160 (2005) ("[O]*biter dicta* are not to be dismissed merely because they are not binding. These after all include judges' discussion of the inherent values of the law, their weighing of principles, and indeed their attempts to formulate principles hitherto more implicit than explicit in the law. Much legal argument concerns matters such as these, and the absence of strictly binding force in such dicta is irrelevant to their broader value as an element in legal discourse.").

95 *Brief Making and the Use of Law Books* 378 (Roger W. Cooley ed., 5th ed. 1926).

96 *Reich v. Continental Cas. Co.*, 33 F.3d 754 (7th Cir. 1994).

Mertens v. Hewitt Associates.[97] The Seventh Circuit opined that the Supreme Court's explicit dicta mustn't be gainsaid because the majority opinion in that decision "goes out of its way to throw cold water on the idea of an implied liability of non-fiduciaries for knowing participation in fiduciaries' misconduct."[98] Acknowledging that the comment is dictum, the majority added that "it is *considered* dictum. If we thought the Court had overlooked some point that might have altered its view, we would be less reluctant to buck the dictum. But it appears not to have."[99]

Given the lack of a bright-line distinction, one might ask: why bother with the *dictum* and *holding* labels? Posner J. of the Seventh Circuit explains the importance of the dichotomy in this way:

> What is at stake in distinguishing holding from dictum is that a dictum is not authoritative. It is the part of an opinion that a later court, even if it is an inferior court, is free to reject. So instead of asking what the word "dictum" means we can ask what reasons there are against a court's giving weight to a passage found in a previous opinion. There are many. One is that the passage was unnecessary to the outcome of the earlier case and therefore perhaps not as fully considered as it would have been if it were essential to the outcome. A closely related reason is that the passage was not an integral part of the earlier opinion—it can be sloughed off without damaging the analytical structure of the opinion, and so it was a redundant part of that opinion and, again, may not have been fully considered. Still another reason is that the passage was not grounded in the facts of the case and the judges may therefore have lacked an adequate experiential basis for it; another, that the issue addressed in the passage was not presented as an issue, hence was not refined by the fires of adversary presentation. All these are reasons for thinking that a particular passage was not a fully measured judicial pronouncement, that it was not likely to be relied on by readers, and indeed that it may not have been part

---

97   508 U.S. 248 (1993).
98   *Reich*, 33 F.3d at 757.
99   *Id.* (emphasis added).

of the decision that resolved the case or controversy on which the court's jurisdiction depended (if a federal court).[100]

Another possible (and traditional) response proceeds along these lines. The availability of something denominated *dictum*—the capacity of a court to offer views that do not bind—may serve a useful function, allowing judges a chance to influence the direction of decisions in future cases, and in hopes that they will persuade other judges to decide future cases a certain way.[101] But it is tentative, not definitive.

Meanwhile, the practice of giving binding effect to the holdings in an earlier decision promotes predictability and reliance interests in the law.[102] Here, then, we see the underlying—and, yes, competing—goals of our system of precedent at play in doctrinal guise. While seeking to ensure that like cases are treated alike and to streamline the adjudication of future disputes, the American system of precedent remains more than a little wary about the fallibility of judges, the inability of anyone to foretell the future, and the danger of a dead hand's weighing down future cases with rules that must be slavishly obeyed. So if we must bind the future to gain the benefits associated with precedent, let us bind it only so far.

The U.S. Supreme Court has declared (apparently in dictum) that dicta "may be followed if sufficiently persuasive but are not binding."[103] In *Central Green Co. v. United States*,[104] the owner of

---

100 *United States v. Crawley*, 837 F.2d 291, 292–93 (7th Cir. 1988).

101 *See* Karl Llewellyn, *The Case Law System in America* 14–15 (Paul Gewirtz ed., 1989) (explaining that dictum can be "a pertinent expression of opinion—like that, for example, of a legal scholar—which may meet with later approval, thanks to the esteem enjoyed by the opinion writer or to the excellence of its conception or reasoning").

102 *See, e.g.*, Michael C. Dorf, *Dicta and Article III*, 142 U. Pa. L. Rev. 1997, 2028 (1994) ("Private citizens, legislators, government agents, judges, and others making decisions and ordering their affairs rely on the knowledge that their actions will have predictable legal consequences. But, no less than they rely on outcomes of cases, these actors may rely on rationales. Thus, one could argue, reliance interests counsel in favor of a rationale-oriented distinction.").

103 *See, e.g., Central Green Co.*, 531 U.S. 425, 431 (2001) (citing *Humphrey's Executor*, 295 U.S. at 627).

104 *Id.* at 427–28.

a pistachio farm sued the United States under the Federal Tort Claims Act for damages allegedly caused by flooding from a federally owned canal that could be used to control floods. The government argued that it was immune from suit under the Flood Control Act of 1928, which stated: "No liability of any kind shall attach to or rest upon the United States for any damage from or by floods or flood waters at any place."[105] After the district court dismissed the complaint, the Ninth Circuit affirmed, finding that immunity attached even though the federally owned canal "serve[d] no flood control purpose."[106] The Supreme Court reversed, finding that whether the waters in the flood-control channel were "flood waters" depended on the character of the waters, not the channel.[107] The Court concluded that courts should determine the scope of the immunity conferred based on the character of the water and the purpose behind its release, not the character of the federal project or its purposes.[108]

The Court distinguished dictum from the earlier case of *United States v. James*,[109] in which the Court had said that "the terms 'flood' and 'flood waters' [in the statute] apply to all waters contained in or carried through a federal flood control project for purposes of or related to flood control, as well as to waters that such projects cannot control."[110] But that statement wasn't necessary to the decision because the fact that the damage was caused by floodwaters wasn't disputed. The question was whether the Flood Control Act's use of the word *damage* included personal injuries.[111] Because the answer in *Central Green* didn't rely on interpreting the phrase *floods or flood waters*, the Court noted that the "isolated comment" on the meaning in *James* was "unquestionably dictum

---

105 33 U.S.C. § 702(c) (1934).
106 *Central Green Co. v. United States*, 177 F.3d 834, 839 (9th Cir. 1999).
107 531 U.S. at 434.
108 *Id.*
109 478 U.S. 597 (1986).
110 *Id.* at 605.
111 *Id.* at 604–05; *see* Antonin Scalia & Bryan A. Garner, *Reading Law: The Interpretation of Legal Texts* 1–3, 44–46 (2012) (maintaining that the Supreme Court's decision in *James* was textually flawed—and disconcertingly so).

because it was not essential to [the Court's] disposition of any of the issues contested."[112]

Dictum should never be taken as determining an issue of law when it conflicts with a holding on point, even if the dictum is more recent. But if there is no precedential holding on a legal issue, dictum may be as persuasive as an unpublished opinion[113] (see § 13). When dictum is the product of the research, deliberation, and editing by judges and their staffs, it may be accorded a greater value of objectivity than secondary sources such as law-review articles and the litigants' briefs, even though some courts equate dicta with secondary sources.[114]

Vertical dicta

Again, not all dicta are created equal. Intermediate courts typically treat higher courts' dicta—those in vertical precedents—with greater respect than their own, not only because of the position of the higher court, but also because today's dicta are an indication

---

[112] *Central Green*, 531 U.S. at 430–31.

[113] *See, e.g.*, Ninth Circuit Rule 36-3(a) ("Unpublished dispositions and orders of this Court are not precedent, except when relevant under the doctrine of law of the case or rules of claim preclusion or issue preclusion."); *United States v. Austin*, 426 F.3d 1266, 1274 (10th Cir. 2005) ("[U]npublished orders are not binding precedent. . . . and we have generally determined that citation to unpublished opinions is not favored. However, if an unpublished opinion or order and judgment has persuasive value with respect to a material issue in a case and would assist the court in its disposition, we allow citation to that decision.") (internal citation omitted).

[114] *See Ex parte Rathmell*, 717 S.W.2d 33, 37 (Tex. Crim. App. 1986) (en banc) (Teague J. concurring and dissenting) ("[p]ractice commentaries, like obiter dicta, may prove persuasive, but are not binding authority") (internal citations omitted); *Kurczi v. Eli Lilly & Co.*, 113 F.3d 1426, 1429 (6th Cir. 1997) (noting that persuasive data "include the state's supreme court dicta, restatements of law, law review commentaries, and the majority rule among other states"); *see also McDonald's Corp. v. Robertson*, 147 F.3d 1301, 1315 (11th Cir. 1998) (Carnes J. specially concurring) ("Somewhat like statements in a law review article written by a judge, or a judge's comments in a lecture, dicta can be used as a vehicle for offering to the bench and bar that judge's views on an issue, for whatever those views are worth. The persuasiveness of the rationale given can increase the weight accorded those views, but the fact that the views are formed and put forward in a context of a case in which they do not matter will always subtract from the weight given them.").

of what may well be tomorrow's binding precedent.[115] All federal courts place significant weight on the dicta of the U.S. Supreme Court.[116] For instance, when a particular exception to a general rule has been mentioned and developed by the Court, but found unnecessary to a decision because of another ground, the Court's treatment of that issue in dictum can suggest what the Court would hold if the issue were necessary for determination.[117] But when Supreme Court dictum conflicts with the holding of a circuit court, the latter is "bound to follow [its] own binding precedent rather than Supreme Court dicta."[118]

Many courts go further. In the Sixth Circuit, "[l]ower courts are obligated to follow Supreme Court dict[um], particularly where there is not substantial reason for disregarding it, such as

---

115 *See In re Cavalry Constr., Inc.*, 496 B.R. 106, 115 (S.D.N.Y. 2013) (stating that even if a statement made by an appellate court were "dictum in some sense, as a general principle, a federal district court is required to give great weight to the pronouncements of its Court of Appeals, even though those pronouncements appear by way of dictum") (internal quotation marks omitted); *see also* 18 James W. Moore et al., *Moore's Federal Practice* § 134.03[2], at 134-30 to 134-36.1 (3d ed. 2015).

116 *See Newdow v. Peterson*, 753 F.3d 105, 108 n.3 (2d Cir. 2014) (per curiam) (noting that circuit courts "have an obligation to accord great deference to Supreme Court *dicta*, absent a change in the legal landscape") (internal quotation marks omitted); *Valladolid v. Pacific Operations Offshore, LLP*, 604 F.3d 1126, 1131 (9th Cir. 2010) (noting that while courts "treat the considered dicta of the Supreme Court with greater weight and deference as prophecy of what that Court might hold," courts "do not blindly . . . follow an unconsidered statement simply because it was uttered by the Supreme Court") (internal quotation marks omitted); *McCoy v. Massachusetts Inst. of Tech.*, 950 F.2d 13, 19 (1st Cir. 1991) (commenting that "federal appellate courts are bound by the Supreme Court's considered dicta almost as firmly as by the Court's outright holdings, particularly when . . . a [Supreme Court] dictum is of recent vintage and not enfeebled by any subsequent statement"); *see also* 18 Moore et al., *Moore's Federal Practice* § 134.03[2], at 134-34 n.11.1 (listing cases).

117 *See Valladolid*, 604 F.3d at 1131; Michael C. Dorf, *Dicta and Article III*, 142 U. Pa. L. Rev. 1997, 2026 (1994) (A "lower court might view [a] higher court's dicta as a fairly reliable prediction of what the higher court would do if it actually had to decide the question previously addressed only in dictum. Because the higher court can reverse the lower court for the latter's failure to predict the former's legal views, the prudent lower court may choose to follow dicta as a way to avoid being overruled.").

118 *Martinez v. City of Oxnard*, 270 F.3d 852, 857 n.3 (9th Cir. 2001), *rev'd sub nom. Chavez v. Martinez*, 538 U.S. 760 (2003).

age or subsequent statements undermining its rationale."[119] Other courts of appeals follow similar rules.[120] But the Supreme Court itself isn't "bound to follow [its own] dicta in a prior case in which the point . . . at issue was not fully debated."[121] In *Central Virginia Community College v. Katz*,[122] the Court considered whether Congress could constitutionally abrogate state sovereign immunity through its exercise of bankruptcy-clause powers, after a company in Chapter 11 proceedings sued state institutions to recover preferential transfers.[123] In dicta in an earlier case, the Court had made statements that assumed that limits on congressional power to abrogate state sovereign immunity would apply to Congress's bankruptcy powers.[124] In *Katz*, though, the Court held that its previous assumption was incorrect, that its statements in dicta

---

119   *ACLU of Ky. v. McCreary Cnty.*, 607 F.3d 439, 447 (6th Cir. 2010).

120   *See, e.g.*, *Newdow*, 753 F.3d at 108 n.3 (remarking on court's obligation); *United States v. Quinn*, 728 F.3d 243, 256 (3d Cir. 2013) (en banc) (The court "cannot lightly ignore the force of Supreme Court dicta. . . . The Supreme Court uses dicta to help control and influence the many issues it cannot decide because of its limited docket. . . . Appellate courts that dismiss these expressions . . . increase the disparity among tribunals . . . and frustrate the evenhanded administration of justice.") (internal quotation marks and citations omitted); *United States v. Fareed*, 296 F.3d 243, 247 (4th Cir. 2002) (adopting rule of 10th Cir. in *Gaylor*); *Acosta v. Master Maint. & Constr. Inc.*, 452 F.3d 373, 377 (5th Cir. 2006) (discussing the use of Supreme Court dicta, in conjunction with a phrase's plain meaning and congressional use, to determine meaning of statutory text); *Wisconsin Right to Life, Inc. v. Barland*, 751 F.3d 804, 836 (7th Cir. 2014) (noting that "the Supreme court's dicta must be respected") (internal citations omitted); *Harpole v. Arkansas Dep't of Human Servs.*, 820 F.2d 923, 927 (8th Cir. 1987) ("As an appellate court, we should not rely solely on dicta, even Supreme Court dicta, when making decisions with constitutional implications."); *Blake v. Baker*, 745 F.3d 977, 982 n.3 (9th Cir. 2014) (noting that "Supreme Court dicta have a weight that is greater than ordinary judicial dicta as prophecy of what that Court might hold") (internal quotations omitted); *Gaylor v. United States*, 74 F.3d 214, 217 (10th Cir. 1996) (commenting that courts in the circuit are "bound by Supreme Court dicta almost as firmly as by the Court's outright holdings"); *Kehoe v. Fidelity Fed. Bank & Trust*, 421 F.3d 1209, 1214 (11th Cir. 2005) (observing that when a specific Supreme Court case doesn't control, the court may nonetheless be "guided by the Supreme Court's dicta in that decision").

121   *Central Va. Cmty. Coll. v. Katz*, 546 U.S. 356, 363 (2006).

122   *Id.*

123   *Id.* at 360–61.

124   *Id.* at 363 (citing *Seminole Tribe of Fla. v. Florida*, 517 U.S 44 (1996)).

were not binding, and that Congress had the power to treat state entities like other creditors.[125]

The enterprise of deciding how much of a past case will be said to control in a future case might be described as involving a dialogue between the writer and the reader, between the earlier court and the later court. On the whole, the later court has the power to determine the extent of the earlier court's holding.[126]

But in this dialogue, the earlier (or writing) court can do much to shape how its opinion will be read by those who come later. It can, for example, demarcate what it believes to be its holding. This is perhaps much more typical today than it once was. In the days when common-law appellate courts spoke not as a collective but through seriatim opinions, readers had to pore over each judge's opinion, looking for unifying and common threads of analysis. The task was made all the more difficult by the fact that those opinions were often orally delivered and transcribed by others, exhibiting the freer and less deliberate structure that often attends oral remarks. Today, American appellate courts typically speak through a unified opinion, one delivered in writing and only after many rounds of editing, and one that often highlights in the first paragraph which litigant wins and the essential reasons for that outcome.

Divining reasoning when none is given

When a writing court remains silent about its reasons for decision, it can do much to imperil the precedential value of the decision: later courts may try to reconstruct the essential reasoning that led to the outcome, but sometimes they won't succeed in the effort—or perhaps even bother making it.[127]

---

125 *Id.* at 378–79.

126 *See* Elizabeth Mertz, *The Language of Law School* 63 (2007) ("What a case means emerges only as it is interpreted as precedent in subsequent cases.").

127 *See, e.g., Hagans v. Lavine*, 415 U.S. 528, 533 n.5 (1974) (noting that when jurisdictional issues have been tacitly passed on in earlier decisions, the Supreme Court has never held itself bound by those tacit holdings when a later case properly presents the jurisdictional issues).

Yet if the process of deciding what is and isn't controlling amounts to a dialogue between courts over time, the later court always gets the last word. Like any other author, the writing court can do only so much to control what readers will take away from its handiwork. Like any other written document, a court's writing may later be understood in ways its authors didn't anticipate. But interpretation is the second court's starting point: the court seeks to determine fairly what was essential to the decision in the earlier case.[128] As with almost any other document, a precedent may be susceptible of more than one plausible interpretation, and disputes may arise over which one gives truest voice to its meaning.

Meanwhile, given that interpretation is a familiar judicial function, not every case *will* prove difficult: often identifying the holding of a case "is reasonably straightforward."[129] When it isn't, though, one sympathizes with the tolerant view that "judges do not and are never likely to tie themselves rigidly to any precise method of elucidating the [holding] of a case."[130] Or as another commentator puts it: "There may indeed be as many ways of finding the *ratio* [i.e., holding] of a case as there are ways of finding a lost cat; certainly the *ratio* of some cases seems as elusive."[131]

---

128 Neil Duxbury, *The Nature and Authority of Precedent* 75 (2008) ("[T]he *ratio* [i.e., holding] can be determined as much by the interpreter as by the speaker, and . . . when judges excavate *rationes* [i.e., holdings] from past decisions they are likely to influence if not determine how that precedent is conceived as authority in the future."); Michael Abramowicz & Maxwell Stearns, *Defining Dicta*, 57 Stan. L. Rev. 953, 1050 (2005).

129 Joseph Raz, *The Authority of Law: Essays on Law and Morality* 184 (2d ed. 2009); *see also* Duxbury, *The Nature and Authority of Precedent* at 74 ("The difficulty of the issue can easily be exaggerated; the *ratio decidendi* [i.e., holding] of a case is often not so much interpreted as repeated, for one need look no further than the headnote of most cases to know that the case yields a *ratio* which will be unambiguous to any later court.").

130 Dennis Lloyd, *Introduction to Jurisprudence* 377 (rev. ed. 1965) (substituting *holding* for *ratio*).

131 A.W.B. Simpson, "The *Ratio Decidendi* of a Case and the Doctrine of Binding Precedent," in *Oxford Essays in Jurisprudence* 148, 159 (A.G. Guest ed., 1961).

A cynical view rejected

Although the jurisprudential holding/dictum distinction isn't always straightforward, we have aligned ourselves with the orthodox view that "ascertaining . . . the proposition of law for which a decision is authority is one of the most important investigations that can be undertaken regarding a reported case."[132] But there is another view—a jaded, cynical view developed by some jurisprudents—that the distinction is merely "a device employed by subsequent courts for the adoption or rejection of doctrine expressed in previous cases, according to the inclinations of the subsequent court."[133] This view attributes to judges a kind of hypocrisy, trickery, or psychological lack of self-awareness whereby a judge follows this ploy: "The rule is quite simple, if you agree with the other bloke you say it is part of the *ratio* [i.e., holding]; if you don't you say it is *obiter dictum*, with the implication that he is a congenital idiot."[134]

If this position is to be taken seriously, judges aren't being candid when they say they are "constrained" or "compelled" by precedent. On this view, all judges are willful—eager to impose their own will in cases regardless of what the law seems to require—but some cloak their willfulness in sham legal doctrine by which they hope to remove the appearance of their own subjectivity from the decision-making equation. The proponents of this view, we believe, seek to convince people that all judges are political, that all judges are willful, and that we therefore ought to *allow* them to be overtly willful in their decision-making.

---

132 Eugene Wambaugh, *The Study of Cases* § 4, at 8 (2d ed. 1894); *see* Norman Dorsen, *The Embattled Constitution* 141 (2013) ("What is problematic is not the utterance of dicta, but the failure to distinguish between holding and dictum."); Lackland H. Bloom Jr., *Interpretive Issues in* Seminole *and* Alden, 55 SMU L. Rev. 377, 382 (2002) ("Perhaps no question is closer to the heart of common law adjudication, as well as the use of precedent in constitutional law, [than] the ability to distinguish dicta from the holding of a case.").

133 R.W.M. Dias & G.B.J. Hughes, *Jurisprudence* 81 (1957).

134 Rupert Cross & J.W. Harris, *Precedent in English Law* 50 (4th ed. 1991) (reporting a quip related by Lord Asquith in 1 J. Soc'y Pub. Teachers of L. 359 (new series 1950)).

We reject and explicitly disapprove any position that elevates the individual judge over the law. Ours is a system dependent on laws. We believe that most judges who serve in our system of justice sincerely believe that they are following rules that constrain them—and earnestly seek to follow these rules. We also reject the view that all judges are political and thus should be encouraged to further their own policy preferences. Instead, we believe that good judges often decide cases in ways antithetical to their own policy preferences—when the law so requires.

When it comes to statutory construction, a judge should take the words of statutes seriously regardless of whether the judge personally favors the policies enshrined in those statutes. And when it comes to precedent, the judge should work hard to sort holdings from dicta, with integrity, and to discern just how much constraint a given ruling imposes. Good judging entails more than a fair degree of self-abnegation not just out of respect for other judges who have already decided the issue, but as a result of the doctrine that is the subject of this book.

5. Related Terminology

Allied to precedents, but distinct from them, are (1) opinions, (2) judgments, decrees, and mandates, (3) findings, (4) legal principles, (5) rules and standards, (6) judicial policies, and (7) modes of analysis.

As we work through the profusion of doctrines relating to precedent, we must attend to matters of vocabulary. Many terms besides *holding, dictum, vertical precedent, horizontal precedent,* and *stare decisis* have roles to play.

The *opinion* of the court is the entire essay written by a judge to explain the outcome, including (normally) the factual recitation, the application of law to the facts, the analysis of the litigants' arguments, and the statement of the result. Although *decision* is sometimes used synonymously with *opinion*, the word typically refers more narrowly to the yea-or-nay outcome: who wins, and to what extent.

Judgment is also used in this latter sense, though it is more widely considered a term of art meaning "the judicial determination or sentence of the court in a cause within its jurisdiction."[1] Normally appearing at the end of an opinion, the judgment declares the outcome. It might state, for example, that "the judgment of the trial court is affirmed." Or it might just say "affirmed." Often the court's judgment is printed in italic type. In British English, by contrast, *judgment* refers to an entire judicial opinion: while Americans write of Justice Holmes's opinion, the British write of Lord Denning's judgment. Here, of course, we follow American usage, in which *judgment* refers specifically to the dispositive statement of winner vs. loser. Most often it refers to such a statement that is final—at least final as to the court making it.[2] A venerated treatise on the law of judgments notes that "[w]hile the

---

[1] A.C. Freeman, *A Treatise of the Law of Judgments* § 2, at 4 (Edward W. Tuttle ed., 5th ed. 1925); *see* 1 Henry Campbell Black, *A Treatise on the Law of Judgments* § 1, at 2 (2d ed. 1902) (stating that a judgment "is always a declaration that a liability, recognized as within the jural sphere, does or does not exist").

[2] Freeman, *A Treatise of the Law of Judgments* § 2, at 5.

two may be [usually are] combined in one instrument, the opinion forms no part of the judgment."[3] A close synonym of *judgment* in American legal usage is *mandate*.

A *decree* is traditionally a judgment issued by a court of equity, as opposed to a court of law.[4] But since the administration of law and that of equity were merged in most American courts by the early 20th century, the distinction has become less one of substance than of idiom. We normally refer to *consent decrees*, *custody decrees*, and *divorce decrees* but to *court judgments* generally and to *declaratory judgments*, *default judgments*, and *summary judgments* in particular. These are largely matters of linguistic custom.

Different still from all these terms is *finding*, which typically denotes a trial court's determination of fact, whether by jury or judge as fact-finder.

Legal principles, by contrast, are those background ideas that courts sometimes rely on when deciding cases. They take the form of broad-stroke prescriptions, like the general preference for access to justice or the maxim that "nobody should profit from his or her own wrong."[5] Legal principles "evolve rather like a custom and are binding only if they have considerable authoritative support in a line of judgments."[6] Unlike legal *rules*, which have a "canonical, algorithmic form" and are often outcome-determinative, legal principles are "always applicable but never outcome-determinative just because they are applicable."[7] They "incline a decision toward

---

3   *Id.* § 3, at 6.
4   1 Black, *A Treatise on the Law of Judgments* § 1, at 3–4.
5   *See, e.g., Riggs v. Palmer*, 22 N.E. 188, 190 (N.Y. 1889) ("No one shall be permitted to profit by his own fraud, or to take advantage of his own wrong . . . . These maxims are dictated by public policy, have their foundation in universal law administered in all civilized countries, and have nowhere been superseded by statutes."); *Barker v. Kallash*, 468 N.E.2d 39, 43 (N.Y. 1984) (stating that the maxim rests "upon the public policy consideration that the courts should not lend assistance to one who seeks compensation under the law for injuries resulting from his own acts when they involve a substantial violation of the law").
6   Joseph Raz, *Legal Principles and the Limits of Law*, 81 Yale L.J. 823, 848 (1972).
7   *See* Larry Alexander, *The Objectivity of Morality, Rules, and Law: A Conceptual Map*, 65 Ala. L. Rev. 501, 509 (2013).

a particular outcome but do not necessitate that outcome."[8] And since their strength comes from their persuasive force alone, they might be outweighed in specific cases.

Despite their inability to determine outcomes directly, legal principles play a significant role in shaping judicial decisions. First, they guide interpretation of precedent since courts will often read precedent with background legal principles in mind. They also help courts intuit the correct outcome when they find themselves without clear precedent.[9]

Related to principles but distinct from them are *rules* and *standards*, which denote different levels of specificity for norms. A *rule* is a specific norm with a clear delineation (e.g., "at a speed no greater than 70 miles per hour," or "a wage of $12 per hour"). A *standard* is a more open-ended norm (e.g., "at a safe speed," or "a fair wage"). "Beyond a reasonable doubt," and other norms that incorporate the word *reasonable*, create standards. Enforcing a rule involves significantly less discretion than enforcing a standard.[10] A judicial holding, like a piece of legislation, may establish either a rule or a standard—most commonly the latter.

Judicial policies also inform judicial decision-making. These policies aren't precedent; they don't bind courts and aren't authoritative in any formal way. Rather, they're applied judge by judge and opinion by opinion, in accordance with judges' conceptions of what is appropriate in a particular case and what a judge's role should be more generally.[11] Yet they manage to have tangible effects on how precedent is created and interpreted. One of the most pervasive judicial policies is that of self-restraint—a self-imposed practice by judges to limit the exercise of their own power. This policy encourages judges to avoid wading into the domains of the other

---

8   *Id.*
9   Raz, *Legal Principles and the Limits of Law*, 81 Yale L.J. at 841.
10 *See* Maurice Finkelstein, *Judicial Self-Limitation*, 37 Harv. L. Rev. 338, 345 (1924) ("[C]ourts are not always well equipped for the handling of standards. But human conduct cannot be regulated by hard and fast rules. The resort to legal standards in such cases has always proved inevitable.").
11 Richard A. Posner, *The Meaning of Judicial Self-Restraint*, 59 Ind. L.J. 1, 18 (1983).

branches of government. The doctrine of constitutional avoidance is an offshoot of this policy, urging courts to steer clear of constitutional questions whenever possible.[12] Judges often exercise restraint by writing narrow opinions limited to the facts of the case before them. Other policies, like comity with state courts and the decision whether to publish an opinion, impose similar non-precedential limitations.

Last, the *modes of analysis* that courts use in analyzing statutes or legal decisions influence judicial decision-making. Modes of analysis aren't binding on future courts in the same way as legal rules are. Although they won't often be part of a court's holding, they still have strong effect. The canons of statutory construction are one particularly influential mode of analysis.[13] They play a minor role in cases where binding precedent rules the day. But if there's a dearth of precedent, they help fill the gaps. Take, for example, a 2014 Fifth Circuit case[14] in which the court had to decide whether a forklift was a "motor vehicle" for purposes of a Louisiana motorist-insurance statute.[15] Finding no binding Louisiana law on point and no definition of *motor vehicle* in the statute, the court turned to canons of statutory interpretation. It looked to the dictionary definition of *motor vehicle* (employing the ordinary-meaning canon) and to the use of *motor vehicle* in similar statutes (employing the related-statutes canon).[16] With the help of those canons, it concluded that the term *motor vehicle* includes forklifts. Even a court without on-point precedent can use the canons as a framework for its analysis, rather than starting from scratch.

---

12 See *Ashwander v. Tennessee Valley Auth.*, 297 U.S. 288, 347 (1936) (Brandeis J. concurring).
13 See Antonin Scalia & Bryan A. Garner, *Reading Law: The Interpretation of Legal Texts* 9, 51 (2012).
14 *Boyett v. Redland Ins. Co.*, 741 F.3d 604 (5th Cir. 2014).
15 *Id.* at 612.
16 *Id.* at 615.

6. The Context for Extracting a Rule or Standard

The language of a judicial decision must be interpreted with reference to the circumstances of the particular case and the question under consideration. Yet a general rule or standard may be extracted that is broader than that in the holding itself and broad enough to apply to a novel case.

With caselaw, a general rule or standard must be extracted from an individual concrete decision. This norm then becomes applicable to similar cases in the future. Analytically, we begin with facts. Most judicial opinions contain a recital of the facts, usually toward the beginning. Yet we must remember: "The discovery of what facts are material in any decision is by no means easy."[1] One must be wary of taking the recital of facts as necessarily complete and dispositive. The court presents those facts that it thinks relevant to explain its decision. Ideally, these are the facts that have played a role in the court's arrival at its holding. Sometimes the facts may also show the court's sense of fairness or justice in reaching its decision. Poignant facts that "shock the court's conscience," to use that classic phrase from the courts of equity, may even lead to a decision that is broader and more general than was really needed to decide the particular case. Sometimes when that happens, as the old saying goes, "bad facts make bad law."

Analyzing the facts involves more than just reading the court's recital. The discussion—the part of the opinion that explains the court's reasoning—usually concentrates on some of the facts initially recited and seems to ignore others. One must understand why a court might do this. Here are three possible explanations. First, the decision may really have been influenced by all the facts recited, despite their omission from the discussion. Second, the court may have been writing cautiously, setting out even those facts that it didn't consider critical as a way to leave the door open for others to draw possible distinctions in the future. Third, the court may simply have thought that the case presented a story that would be interesting to lawyers or even to the general public.

---

1   G.W. Keeton, *The Elementary Principles of Jurisprudence* 107 (2d ed. 1949).

The difficulty in weighing the relative importance of facts is aggravated by the reality that most appellate cases are decided by panels of three or more judges. The writing judge may include facts that no other judge thinks are relevant. Or another judge may insist that the opinion include or exclude certain facts, contrary to the instincts of the author or other judges on the panel. Usually the reader has no way of knowing how the facts were selected. But these explanations may help explain why some fact—even one highlighted in the opinion—seems irrelevant to the result.

This difficulty is aggravated still further when a court doesn't lay out all the facts it took into account in reaching its decision. Anyone not involved in the particular litigation will be hard put to guess what those facts might have been. Even if the record is complete, the full facts aren't likely to be much help when the court hasn't left any evidence that the missing facts played a role in its decision. Although this kind of guesswork may be interesting, it's not much help in crafting a persuasive legal argument or extracting a rule or standard.

Most cases combine law and fact in ways that emphasize the central role of the facts. These are cases that require application of a legal standard to specific facts, and in these cases it's not likely that a dispositive fact will be omitted.

Negligence cases provide a good illustration. The law adopts a standard of reasonable care because it's impossible to provide specific rules to guide all the behavior that is governed by the negligence standard. A ruling that specific facts do or do not amount to negligence is by its very nature narrowly limited. For the most part, you'll need to find a lot of decisions on similar facts to develop much sense of what the cases mean when taken together. But some generic fact situations may occur so often that they provide a good working sense of the law. Even if the jurisdiction's high court never states an explicit rule about, for example, the circumstances that support a finding of negligence when a customer slips on a supermarket floor, experienced lawyers may be able to define a clear local rule that is much more precise than the general negligence standard.

Although it's often easy to cherry-pick a sentence from a case to support an argument, the sentence has no precedential force unless it is relevant "to those points of law which are raised by the record, considered by the court, and necessary to a decision."[2] Over the years, courts have repeatedly asserted this principle.[3] The premise is that a court is primarily concerned with adjudicating the case before it. So a decision based on a certain set of facts should not control the outcome of a later case with a factual context that the court adjudicating the earlier case had no opportunity to consider.

But this principle is hard to reconcile with the courts' practice of establishing doctrinal frameworks, which by their very nature extend beyond the facts of a given case. A rigid view of precedent would counsel against applying a doctrinal framework to any set of facts not before the court at the time it applied the framework. But courts seldom refuse to apply doctrinal frameworks on this rationale, and instead have been generally willing to export them to different sets of facts.

We see this tendency, for example, in cases applying the Commerce Clause's doctrinal framework of whether economic activity substantially affects commerce, in numerous administrative disputes governed by the two-step inquiry established by *Chevron, U.S.A. v. Natural Resources Defense Council*,[4] and in

---

2 Henry Campbell Black, *Handbook on the Law of Judicial Precedents* § 11, at 49 (1912).

3 *See, e.g., German Alliance Ins. Co. v. Home Water Supply Co.*, 226 U.S. 220, 234 (1912) ("What was said in the opinion must be limited, under well-known rules, to the facts and issues involved in the particular record under investigation."); *Armour & Co. v. Wantock*, 323 U.S. 126, 133 (1944) ("words of our opinions are to be read in the light of the facts of the case under discussion"); *Cohens v. Virginia*, 19 U.S. (6 Wheat.) 264, 399–400 (1821) ("general expressions, in every opinion, are to be taken in connection with the case in which those expressions are used"); *cf. Quinn v. Leathem* [1901] A.C. 495, 506 (per Lord Halsbury) ("Every judgment must be read as applicable to the particular facts proved or assumed to be proved, since the generality of the expressions which may be found there are not intended to be expositions of the whole law but are governed and qualified by the particular facts of the case in which such expressions are to be found.").

4 467 U.S. 837 (1984).

equal-protection and due-process challenges necessitating the application of discrete levels of scrutiny.[5]

This isn't to say that courts haven't tried to confine the application of doctrinal frameworks to a particular set of facts. The U.S. Supreme Court's decision in *Burwell v. Hobby Lobby Stores, Inc.*[6] is a good example. There, the Court held that Hobby Lobby was entitled to protection under the Religious Freedom Restoration Act, which provides "a claim or defense to persons whose religious exercise is substantially burdened by government" and institutes a strict-scrutiny standard.[7] The Court explained that the Act was intended to apply broadly, and that "[w]hen rights, whether constitutional or statutory, are extended to corporations, the purpose is to protect the rights of . . . people [associated with a corporation]."[8] But it was careful to note that it had "no occasion . . . to consider" the Act's applicability to publicly held corporations; rather, it was considering the Act's applicability to "closely held corporations, each owned and controlled by members of a single family, [where] no one has disputed the sincerity of their religious beliefs."[9] The Court therefore made it clear that *Hobby Lobby* should not be cited for the proposition that the Act applies to all corporations—only closely held ones such as the one for which the case is known.

Lawyers might nevertheless argue that the rationale underlying *Hobby Lobby*'s conclusion justifies extending the Act's protection to publicly held corporations. After all, the rationale that carries the force of precedent is that "without which the judgment in the case could not have been given," and not the reasoning articulated by the court.[10]

It isn't uncommon for courts to narrow their holdings artificially in an effort to achieve a desirable result without establishing

---

5   Randy J. Kozel, *The Scope of Precedent*, 113 Mich. L. Rev. 179, 193–94 (2014).
6   134 S.Ct. 2751 (2014).
7   *See* 42 U.S.C. § 2000bb(b) (2012) (enacted in 1993); *Hobby Lobby*, 134 S.Ct. at 2767–68.
8   *Hobby Lobby*, 134 S.Ct. at 2768.
9   *Id.* at 2774.
10   Henry Campbell Black, *Handbook on the Law of Judicial Precedents* § 7, at 40 (1912).

prospectively binding rules.[11] Rehnquist C.J. famously criticized this practice as akin to issuing "a restricted railroad ticket, good for this day and train only."[12]

Courts are constantly grappling with how broadly or narrowly their opinions should be interpreted. A perceptive commentator sums it up nicely: "One might say that there is a point on every train trip when it comes time to disembark. The trick is catching the right stop."[13]

Assumptions underlying court decisions

Judicial opinions are always premised on a series of assumptions about what the law is. Yet those assumptions—whether implicit or explicit—aren't generally considered precedential. A decision's authority as precedent is limited to the points of law raised by the record, considered by the court, and determined by the outcome. The assumptions a court uses to reach a particular result do not themselves create new precedent or strengthen existing precedent.

Take the example of *City of Los Angeles v. Lyons*.[14] In that 1983 case, the U.S. Supreme Court held that a plaintiff had no standing to bring a claim for injunctive relief against the City of Los Angeles based on the LAPD's practice of placing suspects in chokeholds during arrest: the plaintiff couldn't show that he was reasonably likely to be subject to an arrest (and therefore subject to a chokehold) again.[15] The Court in *Lyons* explicitly assumed that the city might be liable for damages, even if injunctive relief was

---

11   *See* Richard M. Re, *On "A Ticket Good for One Day Only*," 16 Green Bag 2d 155, 161 (2013).

12   *County of Washington v. Gunther*, 452 U.S. 161, 183 (1981) (Rehnquist J. dissenting) (quoting *Smith v. Allwright*, 321 U.S. 649, 669 (1944) (Roberts J. dissenting) (internal quotation marks omitted)); *see also Elk Grove Unified Sch. Dist. v. Newdow*, 542 U.S. 1, 25 (2004) (Rehnquist C.J. concurring in the judgment) ("Although the court may have succeeded in confining this novel principle almost narrowly enough to be, like the proverbial excursion ticket—good for this day only—our doctrine of prudential standing should be governed by general principles, rather than ad hoc improvisations.").

13   Re, *On "A Ticket Good for One Day Only*," 16 Green Bag 2d at 166.

14   461 U.S. 95 (1983).

15   *Id.* at 111–12.

unavailable. But that part of the opinion isn't precedential. An opinion is precedential only for the points of law argued by the litigants and adjudicated by the court—even if the court bases its holding in part on the truth or falsity of a background assumption. For example, the Court in *Lyons* held that the case didn't fall into the category of "capable of repetition yet evading review"— an exception to the mootness doctrine—because the policy was reviewable through lawsuits for damages.[16] This doesn't mean that *Lyons* can be cited as precedent for the proposition that a damage claim would lie in a similar case. For example, if a defendant asserted that a city isn't liable for the informal practices of its employees, a plaintiff wouldn't be able to cite *Lyons* as binding precedent in support of the proposition that such suits for damages are authorized. Certainly, the *Lyons* Court's assumption would constitute persuasive authority, but because the matter had not been raised by the litigants and wasn't adjudicated by the Court, *Lyons* would not be binding. This is so even though the availability of a damages remedy is arguably essential in the chain of reasoning that led to the result in *Lyons*.

Or take a 2014 example: the Supreme Court's *Hobby Lobby* decision.[17] In that case, the Court held that requiring certain employers to provide their female employees with no-cost access to contraception violates the employers' rights under the Religious Freedom Restoration Act. A crucial part of the Court's reasoning was that there were more narrowly tailored ways of achieving the government's compelling interest in female reproductive health— in particular, a mechanism provided in the Affordable Care Act by which certain religious nonprofit organizations could opt out of the requirement, compelling an insurer to pick up the cost of contraception instead.[18] The Court's reliance on the availability of the opt-out provision, however, isn't precedent for that provision's legality. The precedential value of *Hobby Lobby* is limited to the claims raised by the litigants and adjudicated by the Court, in

---

16   *Id.* at 109.
17   *Burwell v. Hobby Lobby Stores, Inc.*, 134 S.Ct. 2751 (2014).
18   *Id.* at 2782.

this case the consistency of the compulsory requirement with the Religious Freedom Restoration Act. In future litigation, the opt-out provision might still be open to challenge, despite the Court's statement in *Hobby Lobby*. That's because, as in *Lyons*, the Court cannot be read to have rendered a binding precedent on a hypothetical legal question, even when its reasoning rests in part on assuming that the hypothetical question will be resolved a certain way.[19]

But if tacitly assumed rules or principles are so essentially involved in the decision that the particular judgment couldn't logically have been given without recognizing and applying them, they do become authoritative. Determining these "implicit holdings" requires reading between the lines. A reader must ask whether, in light of the questions involved in a case and the decision reached, a particular opinion necessarily recognized and applied a given rule or principle. In those instances, the decision might (silently) serve as persuasive authority for that proposition.

Consider *Braden v. 30th Judicial City Court of Kentucky*.[20] The U.S. Supreme Court held that a habeas petitioner doesn't need to be present within a district court's territorial jurisdiction to seek habeas relief from that court. In light of that holding, a petitioner imprisoned in Alabama was allowed to litigate his habeas petition in a Kentucky federal district court. The Court supported its holding by noting that it had previously adjudicated habeas claims from petitioners outside a district court's territorial jurisdiction without imposing a jurisdictional bar—most notably, in cases involving petitioners outside the country.[21] Those cases implicitly held that absence from the district does not jurisdictionally bar the petitioners' claim.[22] The Court's use of those implicit holdings shows there is some vitality to assumed rules or principles.

---

19 *See Zubik v. Burwell*, 136 S.Ct. 1557, 1560–61 (2016) (per curiam) (same).
20 410 U.S. 484 (1973).
21 *See, e.g., Burns v. Wilson*, 346 U.S. 137, 138 (1953).
22 *Braden*, 410 U.S. at 498.

Similarly, in a 1967 case,[23] the Third Circuit wrote: "It is settled too, that matters pertinent to an issue before a court and which were clearly presented to it, by brief or appendix thereto, are to be taken as covered by the court's decision though not mentioned in the opinion."[24] The issue in that case was whether the Pennsylvania Supreme Court had ruled that racial discrimination in admissions by a private college didn't violate the Pennsylvania Public Accommodations Act. The Third Circuit held that the state court had so ruled in an opinion denying relief to members of a minority rejected for admission even though the court's opinion had not mentioned the state law. The issue had been fully and aggressively briefed in state court.

Accepting or rejecting assumed rules

Whether this idea of assumed rules gets accepted or rejected depends on context. Courts sometimes say that answers to questions "merely lurk[ing] in the record, neither brought to the attention of the court nor ruled upon, are not to be considered as having been so decided as to constitute precedents."[25] For example, courts routinely reject claims that plaintiffs have Article III standing based on the fact that prior similarly situated plaintiffs received a ruling on the merits, even though such a ruling must have implicitly held that the prior plaintiff did have standing.[26] The Supreme Court has explained that "[w]hen a potential jurisdictional defect is neither noted nor discussed in a federal decision, the decision does not stand for the proposition that no defect existed."[27]

What leads to this inconsistent treatment of assumed rules and principles? On the one hand, relying on them has its benefits,

---

23 *Pennsylvania v. Brown*, 373 F.2d 771 (3d Cir. 1967).
24 *Id.* at 777 (citing *Bingham v. United States*, 296 U.S. 211, 218–19 (1935)).
25 *Webster v. Fall*, 266 U.S. 507, 511 (1925).
26 *See, e.g., Indian Oasis-Baboquivari Unified Sch. Dist. No. 40 v. Kirk*, 91 F.3d 1240, 1243–44 (9th Cir. 1996).
27 *Arizona Christian Sch. Tuition Org. v. Winn*, 563 U.S. 125, 144 (2011); *see also Hagans v. Lavine*, 415 U.S. 528, 533 n.5 (1974) (explaining that "when questions of jurisdiction have been passed on in prior decisions *sub silentio*, this Court has never considered itself bound when a subsequent case finally brings the jurisdictional issue before us").

such as encouraging consistent adjudication for similarly situated parties and respect for prior decisions. On the other hand, because assumed rules and principles aren't necessarily fully vetted, they don't have the same logical strength as precedent. Rules and principles that are implicit in a court's ruling might have resulted merely from a lawyer's poor briefing or a judge's oversight.

These conflicting concerns leave the proper role of assumed rules and principles in limbo. An advocate can buttress a position by claiming, for instance, that a given rule was assumed in past judicial decisions, and at the margin this approach might have some appeal. The court's assumption might suggest custom though not a binding norm. That will be particularly effective if case after case assumes a given rule: the assumed rule looks more volitional than accidental. Still, reliance on an assumed rule or principle doesn't make a strong centerpiece for an argument, and many courts will reject this line of argument outright. So in most cases, other analytical approaches will meet with more success.

The scope of a rule

It's normally thought to be within the court's discretion to decide the scope of a rule or standard: as long as it forms the basis of the holding, it's precedential. The Court in *Miranda v. Arizona*,[28] for example, need not have set forth in detail a specific set of warnings to resolve the question presented; nonetheless, it chose to do so, and the full set of warnings is generally viewed as part of the holding. Similarly, in *McDonnell Douglas Corp. v. Green*,[29] the Court need not have set forth a three-step analysis for adjudicating claims of intentional discrimination. But the Court was empowered to resolve the question before it however broadly it wished. And as future courts have understood, *McDonnell Douglas*'s three-step framework is precedential.

How are future courts to know how broadly to read a newly established legal norm? Take *Lyons*[30] as an example again (see

---

28   384 U.S. 436 (1966).
29   411 U.S. 792 (1973).
30   *City of Los Angeles v. Lyons*, 461 U.S. 95 (1983).

pp. 84–85). The Court could have held that plaintiffs *in Fourth Amendment challenges* must establish that they are likely to be subject to the challenged conduct again. Or the Court could have held that *under § 1983* a plaintiff must show that the challenged conduct is likely to recur. Instead, the decision holds far more broadly that a plaintiff generally lacks standing to raise a claim for injunctive relief when the plaintiff cannot show that he or she is reasonably likely to be subject to the challenged conduct again.

It might seem natural to divine an opinion's intended scope by its language. Unfortunately, language can be misleading. A holding can be poorly articulated, or certain language could be purely descriptive and not intended to be part of the holding. And sometimes the language of an opinion may purport to hold something when that language is in fact dictum. As Friendly J. of the Second Circuit put it, "A judge's power to bind is limited to the issue that is before him; he cannot transmute dictum into decision by waving a wand and uttering the word 'hold.'"[31]

Courts must therefore deduce legal rules not only from the language of opinions, but from their underlying logic as well. In *Lyons*, the Court explained that Lyons's "standing to seek the injunction requested depend[s] on whether he [is] likely to suffer future injury from the use of the chokeholds by police officers."[32] That explanation is logically unrelated to a particular claim or a particular constitutional violation. Lyons couldn't get relief for a much more fundamental reason: because a court lacks the power to enjoin a defendant based on a plaintiff's speculation that a future unlawful act may be committed against the plaintiff. That's why *Lyons* could be cited as the relevant precedent in *Honig v. Doe*,[33] a case involving a statutory challenge to a school's expulsion of a disabled child. Although the facts of the case, the relevant claim, and the asserted violation couldn't be further afield from *Lyons*, the plaintiff was still obliged, under *Lyons*, to show that the school district was likely to subject him to the challenged conduct again.

---

31 *United States v. Rubin*, 609 F.2d 51, 69 n.2 (2d Cir. 1979) (Friendly J. concurring).
32 *Lyons*, 461 U.S. at 105.
33 484 U.S. 305, 320–23 (1988).

But courts must be mindful of the limitations on even broad legal standards. For example, *Lyons* doesn't provide any metric for deciding whether a particular practice is reasonably likely to recur. A future court isn't necessarily compelled to extrapolate reasonableness from whatever the empirical likelihood of recurrence may have been in *Lyons*. Even if, for example, an academic study conducted after *Lyons* proved that there was a 10% chance that Lyons would have been subjected again to a chokehold, a lower court in a different case would be free to independently assess what probability of recurrence is required to confer standing. It would have been a closer question if the evidence before the Court in *Lyons* had been that there was a 10% chance of recurrence. While a lower court would not be bound by that figure, it would have significant persuasive force in determining the meaning of "reasonable likelihood." And if the Court in *Lyons* had specifically stated that there was a 10% chance of recurrence, the figure would have become an established legal rule and would therefore bind lower courts.

The line is inevitably blurry when a court incorporates a particular probability into a norm—and when it intends a probability to be purely descriptive. For example, in *Cardoza-Fonseca*, the Supreme Court approvingly quoted an international-law treatise stating that the ordinary meaning of "well-founded fear of persecution" would encapsulate someone fleeing from a country in which "every tenth adult male person is either put to death or sent to some remote labor camp."[34] Later in the opinion, the Court also stated, "There is simply no room in the United Nations' definition for concluding that because an applicant only has a 10% chance of being shot, tortured, or otherwise persecuted, that he or she has no 'well-founded fear' of the event happening."[35] Lower courts have largely interpreted these statements to mean that a 10% chance of persecution gives rise to a well-founded fear,[36] even though it isn't clear that the Court intended to establish such a specific rule.

---

34   *INS v. Cardoza-Fonseca*, 480 U.S. 421, 431 (1987) (internal quotation marks omitted).
35   *Id.* at 440.
36   *See, e.g., Al-Harbi v. INS*, 242 F.3d 882, 888 (9th Cir. 2001).

There's no hard-and-fast formula for interpreting the scope of a legal norm. That's why the boundaries of newly established norms are so frequently litigated. Each such norm requires careful and individualized scrutiny of the scope intended by the authoring court.

7. Substantially Similar Facts

For one decision to be precedent for another, the facts in the two cases need not be identical. But they must be substantially similar, without material difference.

In 1933, the legal philosopher Felix S. Cohen wrote that a common-law judge deciding a case is typically presented with this question: "Granted that there are differences between the cited precedent and the case at Bar, and assuming that the decision in the earlier case was a desirable one, is it desirable to attach legal weight to any of the factual differences between the instant case and the earlier case?"[1] If not, the earlier case will be followed or its holding simply applied. But the preliminary decision is whether the factual differences between the cases should matter. This point is almost always the subject of contention.[2]

So context matters a great deal. Holmes J. emphasized this point while sitting on the Massachusetts Supreme Judicial Court: "Upon questions of construction when no arbitrary rule is involved, it is always more important to consider the words and the circumstances than even strong analogies in earlier decisions."[3] His next words got to the nub of a problem: "The successive neglect of a series of small distinctions, in the effort to follow precedent, is very liable to end in perverting instruments from their plain meaning."[4]

In short, rules are transmogrified over time as similarities or dissimilarities are amplified in judges' opinions, or else diminished. Critics of the doctrine of precedent warn that judges must

---

1 Felix S. Cohen, *Ethical Systems and Legal Ideals* 38 (1933; repr. 1976); *see* Glanville L. Williams, *Learning the Law* 93 (A.T.H. Smith ed., 14th ed. 2010) ("We know that in the flux of life all the facts of a case will never recur; but the legally material facts may recur and it is with these that the doctrine [of precedent] is concerned.").

2 *See* Stephen M. Feldman, "History and Law," in *The Oxford Companion to American Law* 361, 361 (Kermit L. Hall ed., 2002) ("[T]he similarity or dissimilarity between a prior case (or precedent) and a current case is almost always disputable.").

3 *Merrill v. Preston*, 135 Mass. 451, 455 (1883) (per Holmes J.).

4 *Id.*

be alert and reflective: "[S]ome of the greatest errors of thinking have arisen from the mechanical, unreflective application of old formulations . . . to new situations that are sufficiently discrepant from the old so that the emphasis on likenesses is misleading and the neglect of differences leads to unfortunate or foolish consequences."[5] Which is merely to say that acuteness of mind is required to avoid the abuse of precedents.

An illustration is in order. Consider a line of cases in which a rule was extended incrementally until it was tacitly transformed in its application. The Arkansas Supreme Court announced a clear rule in 1894 for determining whether a railroad company could be held responsible for negligently setting fire to flammable property adjacent to the railroad line. In the late 19th century and for decades after, locomotives burned coal or oil and were prone to sporadically dropping bits of burning fuel. Steel wheels and tracks also threw off sparks.

In that 1894 case,[6] cotton stacked on a depot platform near the tracks caught fire within 10 or 15 minutes after a train had stopped, stood for 10 to 15 minutes, and then departed. Although no witnesses had seen sparks thrown by the train, there was no other positive evidence of how the fire had started. The fire soon destroyed the depot and a nearby warehouse and its contents. The court held: "These were facts from which the jury might have inferred that the fire originated in sparks from the engine of the train which had just passed, there being no evidence to explain its origin upon any other theory."[7] The important facts of this case were that a fire began shortly after a train had passed, and the railroad couldn't identify an alternative possible cause.

That 1894 rule was cited in many similar cases. Although there were small factual differences in each case, the common, important facts were the recent passage of a train that might have thrown sparks and the railroad's inability to identify any other

---

5   Jerome Frank, *Courts on Trial* 276 (1950).
6   *St. Louis & San Francisco Ry. v. Dodd*, 27 S.W. 227 (Ark. 1894).
7   *Id.* at 229.

possible cause of the fire. For instance, in 1905[8] a locked, unattended warehouse full of hay standing about 34 feet from the railroad tracks was discovered burning about 10 to 20 minutes after a train had passed. Even though an expert opined that the train probably couldn't have cast a spark 35 feet, there was no evidence that anything else had started the fire.[9] The court ruled that the jury had properly inferred that the railroad was liable.[10] Similarly in 1910, a fire was spotted in grassland adjoining railroad tracks soon after a train had passed.[11] The wind spread the fire, which destroyed a peach orchard.[12] Again, there was no alternative explanation for the fire other than sparks from the train, and the jury's finding that the railroad was responsible was upheld.[13] And in 1921,[14] a sawmill near a railroad track caught fire minutes after a train on a nearby spur track passed by. Again, no one saw sparks, but witnesses said that the wind was blowing from the direction of the tracks toward the mill; it was inferable that flammable material such as wood or sawdust lay outside the mill and that a spark could have reached it.[15] The court stated: "Under repeated decisions of this court, circumstances similar to those narrated by witnesses in the present case warrant the inference that the fire was set out by a passing engine."[16]

A 1944 case,[17] however, had a substantial factual difference. There, two trains passed the plaintiff's property about 30 minutes apart.[18] The grass alongside the railroad tracks was seen burning shortly afterward. Witnesses said the wind was blowing toward

---

8   *St. Louis, Iron Mountain & Southern Ry. v. Coombs*, 88 S.W. 595 (Ark. 1905).
9   *Id.* at 596.
10 *Id.* at 597.
11 *Missouri & North Arkansas R.R. v. Phillips*, 133 S.W. 191, 191 (Ark. 1910).
12 *Id.*
13 *Id.*
14 *Chicago, Rock Island & Pac. Ry. v. Cobbs*, 235 S.W. 995 (Ark. 1921).
15 *Id.* at 996.
16 *Id.* at 996–97.
17 *Missouri Pac. R.R. v. Campbell*, 177 S.W.2d 174 (Ark. 1944).
18 *Id.* at 176.

the plaintiff's home and spread the fire to the house.[19] Unlike in earlier cases, though, this time the railroad adduced evidence that large fires had been burning under washtubs at the house just before the fire started. That could have caused the fire, the railroad's counsel argued.[20] But the court stated: "We have laid down the rule, and have adhered to it, that in the absence of direct and positive testimony as to the origin of the fire which consumes [flammable] property situated near a railroad track soon after the passing of a locomotive, the inference might be drawn that the fire originated from sparks from the passing locomotive."[21]

Notice that the court didn't cite the remainder of the rule, "there being no evidence to explain its origin upon any other theory."[22] Instead, it relied on its own dictum (though calling it a holding): "We have held that in order to be able to draw that inference it is not essential that the evidence should exclude all possibility of another origin of the fire or that the evidence be undisputed, but it is sufficient 'if all the facts and circumstances in evidence fairly warrant the conclusion that the fire did not originate from some other cause.'"[23] But in the cited case, there was no evidence or argument of any other cause for the fire.[24] Here there was. Two years later the same court returned to the full rule announced in 1894, but cited only the 1944 case, which had truncated the rule.[25]

The 1894 rule has long since been replaced by a 1955 statute that holds railroad operators responsible for fires negligently caused by employees or equipment.[26] The statute doesn't state that the railroad is inferentially negligent if no other cause for a

---

19 Id.
20 Id.
21 Id. (citing *Chicago, Rock Island & Pac. Ry. v. National Fire Ins. Co.*, 235 S.W. 1006, 1007 (Ark. 1921)).
22 *St. Louis & San Francisco Ry. v. Dodd*, 27 S.W. 227, 229 (Ark. 1894).
23 *Campbell*, 177 S.W.2d at 176 (citing *St. Louis, Iron Mountain & Southern Ry. v. Dawson*, 92 S.W. 27, 27 (Ark. 1906)).
24 *St. Louis, Iron Mountain & Southern Ry.*, 92 S.W. at 27.
25 *Missouri & Arkansas Ry. v. Treece*, 194 S.W.2d 203 (Ark. 1946).
26 Ark. Code § 23-12-913.

fire can be found. But in a 1965 case,[27] the court cited the statute and explained that the 1894 rule remained good.[28] Two small fires were discovered by foresters shortly after a train had climbed a hill through a forest; the fires spread and destroyed acres of property.[29] The court found the railroad responsible.[30] No other possible cause was mentioned, but the court glossed over the fact that the foresters had put out another small fire nearby before the train arrived.[31] It looks as if the 1944 rule holds firm—its predecessor by half a century having been elongated despite the repetition of the same words.

---

27   *Kansas City Southern Ry. v. Beaty*, 388 S.W.2d 79 (Ark. 1965).
28   *Id.* at 81.
29   *Id.* at 82.
30   *Id.*
31   *Id.*

8. Distinguishing Cases

A court distinguishes a precedent by discerning material differences between it and the present dispute, thereby concluding that the precedent is either not entirely applicable or wholly inapplicable.

After identifying what it believes to be the essential reasons on which an earlier court founded its decision, a later court must determine whether that principle should apply to the pending case. If the new case is dissimilar to the pending case in ways that seem important, the court will "distinguish" it and reach a result different from what the precedent would otherwise suggest or even dictate. In common parlance, either the precedent or the pending case may be said to be "distinguished" from the other.

How does distinguishing take place? Typically, courts identify conditions to the reasoning that were in the former case but are not present in the current dispute. So, for example, if the reasoning in a former case might once have appeared to be "if A, B, C, then X," a later court may provide that the rule should now be "if A, B, C, *and D*, then X," with the new modification (D) found in the former case but not present in the current case. In this way, the former decision might be said to be "rerationalized."[1] Any student of history, Holmes J. remarked, is familiar with the "common phenomenon" of rerationalizing precedent to fit a contemporary problem. Through primitive customs, beliefs, or necessity, a rule or formula is established. Over the years and centuries, the underlying reason for having the rule fades away, but the rule itself persists. How to account for the rule then? "Some ground of policy is thought of, which seems to explain it and to reconcile it with the present state of things; and then the rule adapts itself to

---

1   Joseph Raz, *The Authority of Law* 186 (1979); *see also* Neil Duxbury, *The Nature and Authority of Precedent* 115 (2008) ("When a court distinguishes between cases it is not repealing the *ratio* [i.e., holding] of a precedent but amending it so that the later case falls outside its scope."); Michael C. Dorf, *Dicta and Article III*, 142 U. Pa. L. Rev. 1997, 2035 (1994) ("[T]he common law evolves through a process of rerationalization.") (citing Oliver Wendell Holmes, *The Common Law* 5 (1881)).

the new reasons which have been found for it, and enters on a new career," Holmes said.[2] The old rule is given a new content, and "in time even the form modifies itself to fit the meaning which it has received."[3]

Even here, however, the discipline of distinguishing imposes some limits on the second court's creative capacity. A court may (because of changes in technology, say) hold a former rule or line of reasoning inapplicable to a current case. But to do so it must identify a significant condition (D) that is present in the earlier case but not present in the current one, or present in the new case but absent from the earlier one.[4] Another possibility is that the first court acknowledged that D was a background fact but didn't acknowledge D as necessary for the decision. In any event, not just any difference will do: "the distinction must be such that it provides a sufficiently convincing reason for declining to follow a previous decision."[5] The power to distinguish, then, usually enables a later court to depart from an earlier decision only so far as that prior decision can be preserved consistently with the positing of sound reasons.[6] As Karl Llewellyn described the process: "It is common to see a later narrowing of a [holding] that, in the heat of the moment and of the argument, was too broadly phrased. The original judge, later courts will say, did not have the other possible sorts of cases in mind."[7] Once a case arises that undermines the holding, Llewellyn said, "we must reconsider

---

2   Holmes, *The Common Law* at 8–9.

3   *Id.*

4   *See* Raz, *The Authority of Law* at 188; *see also* Duxbury, *The Nature and Authority of Precedent* at 75 ("[T]he selection of the *ratio* [i.e., holding] is unlikely to be an act of unconstrained discretion. Judges invariably feel compelled to provide cogent reasons for the constructions they place on past decisions, and may well consider themselves bound by particular rules of practice; and in any event, the available range of *rationes* in an earlier case will be limited.").

5   Duxbury, *The Nature and Authority of Precedent* at 114.

6   *Id.* at 115–16; *see also id.* at 92 ("*Rationes*, we might say, beget *rationes*: the fact that an earlier decision provides reasons for deciding in a particular way on particular facts means that a court which does not follow that decision will recognize the importance of providing its own reasons for deciding differently.").

7   Karl Llewellyn, *The Case Law System in America* 15 (Paul Gewirtz ed., 1989) (substituting *holding* for *ratio*).

the overbroad wording [the judge] employed; in the case actually before him, the following narrower version would have been perfectly adequate, and so on."[8] Joseph Raz frames distinguishing as a "very restricted form of law-making" requiring the presence of two critical conditions:

> (1) The modified rule must be the rule laid down in the precedent restricted by the addition of a further condition for its application.
> (2) The modified rule must be such as to justify the order made in the precedent.[9]

Take an example, the now-discredited case of *Buck v. Bell*.[10] There, Holmes J. reasoned that prior decisions permitting (among other things) compelled vaccines meant that the government could also sterilize the "feeble-minded."[11] But there were surely ways to distinguish those former cases. Holmes J. seemingly conceptualized the holding of the vaccine cases as permitting states to impose compelled medical action on individuals. But he might have just as easily said that those cases also involved efforts to save life—a condition important on its own terms and present in the former cases but not in the forced-sterilization project.[12] To distinguish, then, a court will usually articulate a new condition, justified on its own terms, one that preserves the former rule while separating it from the current case. The old decision is retained (unlike in the process of overruling) but separated from (and so deemed not to control) the current case.

---

8   *Id.*; *see* Wolfgang Friedmann, *Legal Theory* 468 (5th ed. 1967) ("The distinction of precedent . . . takes three main forms: (a) the distinction of facts; (b) the relegation of objectionable judicial opinions to the position of *obiter dicta*; [and] (c) the reliance on one or the other judgment where the authority of a precedent rests on a concurrence of judgments which arrive at the same result for different reasons.").

9   Raz, *The Authority of Law* at 186.

10 274 U.S. 200 (1927).

11 *Id.* at 207 (citing *Jacobson v. Massachusetts*, 197 U.S. 11 (1905)).

12 *See* Cass R. Sunstein, *On Analogical Reasoning*, 106 Harv. L. Rev. 741, 757 (1993) (arguing that Holmes J. failed to "explore the many possibly relevant similarities and differences" between Virginia's sterilization statute and the forced-vaccination and conscription programs upheld in prior cases).

That's not to say that in distinguishing a precedent, courts will always be able to offer a persuasive distinction. Sometimes courts will even acknowledge that a precedent's holding cannot be fairly rerationalized but decline to follow it anyway. Again, baseball. The Supreme Court has declined repeated invitations to extend baseball's antitrust exemption to other activities involving "local exhibitions"—boxing, football, even theater—all while acknowledging that the reasoning of its baseball decision would seem to control. The Court has done so even while explaining that the reasoning of the baseball decision isn't persuasive and shouldn't be extended to other analogous contexts.[13] Other times courts say so much as a prelude to overruling the disfavored decision. Sometimes (as with baseball) courts decline to overrule the original decision because of the reliance interests that have developed around it, but cordon off its holding and prevent it from spreading anywhere else. Precedents of this stripe come to occupy a sort of doctrinal no-man's land: outliers never overruled but also never harmonized with later decisions. They still do some work, but a very narrow sort: controlling those cases arising on identical facts (and especially reliance interests) but nothing more.

However accomplished, the process of distinguishing serves one of precedent's competing purposes—permitting some room for change and adaptation. As a result, it's rare that a lawyer or judge has to go very far back in volumes of law reports when searching the law, although the higher the court, the more likely it is that older cases remain important sources of law. What remains vital from the past is adapted to today's problems and brought forward in the caselaw; what no longer remains pertinent is sloughed off or atrophies along the way. Precedents, then, have a sort of natural life span, remaining durable only as long as persuasive analogies can still be made to them. Perhaps this is why few take much of *Buck v. Bell* or the baseball decision seriously today: though yet to

---

13   See, e.g., *United States v. Shubert*, 348 U.S. 222, 229–30 (1955); *United States v. International Boxing Club of N.Y.*, 348 U.S. 236, 240–41 (1955); *Radovich v. National Football League*, 352 U.S. 445, 452 (1957). See generally Dorf, *Dicta and Article III*, 142 U. Pa. L. Rev. at 1997 (discussing a "facts-and-outcome" approach to precedent that reflects this sort of treatment of precedent).

be formally overruled, in time both have become highly "distinguished" (in the sense "quarantined," not "esteemed").[14]

Essentially, distinguishing is a way of limiting horizontal precedents later thought to be unwise—and doing so one exception at a time—or it's a way for a later court to clarify the intended scope of a horizontal precedent. With the benefit of hindsight, the later court "refin[es] away a wrong decision by the usual process of exceptions, which in the course of time eats up the rule itself."[15] If it's a vertical precedent that's being distinguished, the lower court is essentially saying that the case it is now ruling on does not fit within the scope of the vertical precedent and instead presents a case of first impression.

Cases that get distinguished often enough are commonly said to die—or at least to suffer near-death experiences. Douglas J. said that "[t]hey slowly become mere ghosts of their former selves, barely clinging to existence."[16] Black J. suggested that they're buried as anonymous paupers: "Their interment is tactfully accomplished, without ceremony, eulogy, or report of their demise. The ground beneath them has been deftly excavated by a soothing process which limits them to their facts, their precise facts, their 'plain requirements.'"[17]

The question still remains: when will a court choose whether to follow or to distinguish a precedent? Let's say a realistic route to distinction exists but the option to follow the precedent exists, too. How does a court decide which way to go? In a similar vein, what happens when a precedent is patently distinguishable and furnishes only an example, a lesson, but not a sufficient reason

---

14   See, e.g., *Skinner v. Oklahoma ex rel. Williamson*, 316 U.S. 535 (1942) (striking down on equal-protection grounds an Oklahoma statute providing for involuntary sterilization of "habitual criminals"); *Brewer v. Valk*, 167 S.E. 638 (N.C. 1933) (declaring that a state sterilization statute failed to provide adequate procedural due process); *In re Opinion of the Justices*, 162 So. 123 (Ala. 1935) (same); *In re Hendrickson*, 123 P.2d 322 (Wash. 1942) (en banc) (same); *McKinney v. McKinney*, 805 S.W.2d 66 (Ark. 1991) (same).

15   John F. Dillon, *The Laws and Jurisprudence of England and America* 237 (1894).

16   William O. Douglas, *We the Judges* 199 (1956).

17   *H.P. Hood & Sons, Inc. v. Du Mond*, 336 U.S. 525, 555 (1949) (Black J. dissenting).

for decision by itself? How much force will a later court give the precedent?

Doubts about the force to give an earlier decision are most heavily influenced by the later court's impression about the strength of its reasoning: "as Justice Samuel F. Miller remarked, 'the convincing power of the opinion or decision in a reported case must depend very largely on the force of the reasoning by which it is supported, and of this every lawyer and every court must of necessity be his and its own judge.'"[18] That is the central consideration.

Susceptibility to distinguishing

Although a decision with a broader rationale might seem to bear greater precedential effect, it may also prove easier to distinguish or be more subject to the claim that parts of it are dicta (see § 4).

Take, for example, *McDaniel v. Sanchez*,[19] in which the Supreme Court decided that it wasn't bound to follow a particular footnote from an earlier case.[20] In *East Carroll Parish School Board v. Marshall*,[21] the Court's per curiam opinion included a footnote addressing the scope of the Voting Rights Act.[22] In it, the *East Carroll* Court stated (even though the parties hadn't litigated the issue) that court-ordered reapportionment plans aren't controlled by the preclearance requirement in the Act.[23] Burger C.J. flagged the footnote as dictum in a brief concurrence.[24] When the Court later decided *McDaniel*, it held—contrary to the footnote in *East Carroll*—that a court-ordered reapportionment plan *is* subject to the preclearance requirement when the plan is proposed by a

---

18 Charles W. Collier, *Precedent and Legal Authority: A Critical History*, 1988 Wis. L. Rev. 771, 780, 787–89 (1988); *see also* Neil Duxbury, *The Nature and Authority of Precedent* 151–52 (2008).
19 452 U.S. 130 (1981).
20 *Id.* at 141–42.
21 424 U.S. 636 (1976) (per curiam).
22 *Id.* at 638 n.6.
23 *Id.*
24 *Id.* at 648 (Burger C.J. concurring).

legislative body: "The discussion of § 5 in *East Carroll* was dictum unnecessary to the decision in that case. It is, therefore, not controlling in this case, in which the impact of § 5 is directly placed in issue."[25]

The broader the ground of decision, the more apt it can be to miss or fail to anticipate something important—thereby marking itself as a potential candidate for future narrowing or even overturning. Consider *Saucier v. Katz*.[26] There, the Court enunciated a broad new procedural standard that wasn't necessary to resolve the dispute at hand. In holding that the defendant law-enforcement officer was entitled to qualified immunity, the Court prescribed a mandatory two-step process for federal courts addressing any government official's qualified-immunity claim: only after asking (1) whether "the facts alleged show the officer's conduct violated a constitutional right" could the trial court ask (2) whether the right was "clearly established."[27] Before *Saucier*, this two-step approach had been favored, but not required. *Saucier* made it mandatory. Just eight years later, following a spate of criticism from commentators and jurists who assailed *Saucier* as unduly rigid and confusing, the Court fell back to its earlier position—that the two-step procedure, while "often appropriate," wasn't required.[28] (See § 41.)

A writing court may sometimes indicate its belief that two or more alternative grounds for decision were *all* essential to its holding, a choice that later courts will usually respect, giving effect to the various alternative grounds for decision rather than picking between them (see § 10). The Supreme Court has long held that alternative bases for decisions are entitled to precedential effect: "Of course, where there are two grounds, upon either of which the judgment of the trial court can be rested, and the appellate court sustains both, the ruling on neither is obiter, but each is the judgment of the court and of equal validity with the other."[29]

---

25 *McDaniel*, 452 U.S. at 141.
26 533 U.S. 194 (2001).
27 *Id.* at 201.
28 *Pearson v. Callahan*, 555 U.S. 223, 236 (2009).
29 *See Union Pac. R.R. v. Mason City & Ft. Dodge R.R.*, 199 U.S. 160, 166 (1905).

Some may see tension here with the notion—also endorsed by the Court—that a holding must be necessary to a decision, for one might claim the broader of two alternative grounds for a decision to be unnecessary.[30] Courts sometimes argue that an earlier panel that gave two alternative reasons for its decision considered both necessary to that decision.[31]

---

30 See, e.g., Kastigar v. United States, 406 U.S. 441, 454–55 (1972) (discussing broad language that petitioners cited for precedential authority and characterizing it as "unnecessary to the Court's decision" and hence dictum that "cannot be considered binding authority") (referring to Counselman v. Hitchcock, 142 U.S. 547 (1892)).

31 See, e.g., Miranda B. v. Kitzhaber, 328 F.3d 1181, 1186 (9th Cir. 2003) (per curiam); United States v. Johnson, 256 F.3d 895, 914 (9th Cir. 2001) (en banc) (per Kozinski J.); see also Michael Abramowicz & Maxwell Stearns, Defining Dicta, 57 Stan. L. Rev. 953, 1056–60 (2005).

9. Analogous Cases

If there is no direct precedent, it is proper to argue by analogy and to apply legal principles extracted from cases that are analogous but not identical. But the analogy must be close.

Analogical reasoning—an "ever-present feature of daily life"[1]—is as old as the common law. Bracton, a judge of the Court of King's Bench and of Assize, is credited with using it in his landmark *De Legibus et Consuetudinibus Angliae* (ca. 1250): "Following the Italian glossator Azo, the author of the treatise known as *Bracton* pointed to the legal technique of proceeding *a similibus ad similia*, from similar case to similar case, underlining this by using cases that had been decided by English judges as the basis of his statements of legal rules and analogies drawn from them."[2] For early common-law judges, analogizing was especially pervasive because so little law had yet been made. But because novel situations constantly arise, analogizing is still a necessity.

All courts, and particularly high courts, commonly face issues for which no direct precedent exists. One of the critical functions of a high court is to resolve "important question[s] of . . . law that [have] not been, but should be, settled" by that court.[3]

In the absence of controlling precedent, the litigants are entitled to rely on a legal rule that governed a case analogous in its pertinent features: "The advantage of a proper use of analogy is that it enables the new situation to be dealt with by a rule which can be placed in a coherent relation with rules that are already established. It is thus assumed that the law is a consistent body of principles and every attempt is made to keep it as such."[4]

Analogical reasoning takes either of two possible forms: either the court concludes that factual similarities between the precedent

---

1 Douglas Lind, *Logic and Legal Reasoning* § 2.2, at 10 (2001).
2 David Ibbetson, "Doctrine of Precedent," in 4 *The Oxford International Encyclopedia of Legal History* 377, 377 (Stanley N. Katz ed., 2009).
3 U.S. Sup. Ct. Rule 10(c).
4 George Whitecross Paton, *A Textbook of Jurisprudence* 228 (G.W. Paton & David P. Derham eds., 4th ed. 1972).

and the pending case are great enough to warrant the same outcome, or else the court spots enough factual differences to conclude that a different outcome is warranted (see § 8). Sometimes a finding of great similarity arises as an a fortiori argument—that is, the precedent was based on facts even more tenuous than the facts in the pending case: the new case presents an even stronger case for the same result.[5]

The practice of reasoning by analogy is undergirded by the basic principle that like cases should be decided alike (see § 1)— just as in cases that arise under the Equal Protection Clause of the U.S. Constitution the court must first find that the plaintiff has been treated differently from a comparable litigant (either someone outside the plaintiff's class or, in the rare class-of-one cases, others who are also subject to the law or regulation under attack).

Examples of this principle abound in American appellate courts. (Trial-court decisions are regarded as nonprecedential.[6]) In a 2014 case[7] turning on the scope of a phrase in a statute governing securities lawsuits, the U.S. Supreme Court looked first at the statute's basic focus, second at the natural meaning of the language, and third at earlier decisions to support its interpretation.[8] In another case the same year, involving the right of an indicted defendant to challenge a grand jury's probable-cause determination in a pretrial asset-forfeiture hearing—no such right being found—the Court began by saying that it has "twice considered

---

5   *See* Larry Alexander & Emily Sherwin, *Demystifying Legal Reasoning* 67 (2008).

6   *E.g., Howard v. Wal-Mart Stores, Inc.*, 160 F.3d 358, 359 (7th Cir. 1998); *Fishman & Tobin, Inc. v. Tropical Shipping & Constr. Co.*, 240 F.3d 956, 965 (11th Cir. 2001); *Hart v. Massanari*, 266 F.3d 1155, 1163 (9th Cir. 2001) ("[M]ost decisions of the federal courts are not viewed as binding precedent. No trial court decisions are; almost four-fifths of the merits decisions of courts of appeals are not."). *But see United States v. Auginash*, 266 F.3d 781, 784 (8th Cir. 2001) ("Certainly we may accord precedential weight to the opinion of a district court, either within this circuit or from another circuit, and indeed sometimes do so.").

7   *Chadbourne & Parke LLP v. Troice*, 134 S.Ct. 1058 (2014).

8   *Id.* at 1066.

claims, similar to the [defendants'],"relevant to the merits of the new case.[9]

Sometimes the Court rejects the proposed analogy, as it did in *Carey v. Musladin*.[10] That case presented the question whether buttons displaying the victim's image worn by family members in a courtroom were prejudicial enough to deny the defendant a fair trial.[11] The Court rejected a proposed analogy to an earlier courtroom-practice decision, *Estelle v. Williams*,[12] which had found such prejudice when an accused was forced to appear in prison garb.[13] It distinguished *Estelle* as a case concerning a government-sponsored practice; the state court in *Carey* didn't rule unreasonably when it concluded that a different rule should apply to spectator behavior.[14]

Federal circuit courts have likewise looked to precedent and reasoning by analogy.[15] Just as with the Supreme Court, sometimes the courts of appeals refuse to accept a proffered analogy. For example, the Ninth Circuit rejected a petitioner's attempt to analogize Special Agricultural Applicant status to advance-parole status in an immigration case because the facts were fundamentally different.[16] And the First Circuit said it couldn't use an earlier, inapplicable statute to reason by analogy in deciding whether a bank's agent had acted inappropriately.[17]

---

9   *Kaley v. United States*, 134 S.Ct. 1090, 1096 (2014).
10 549 U.S. 70 (2006).
11 *Id.* at 72–74.
12 425 U.S. 501 (1976).
13 *Carey*, 549 U.S. at 76–77.
14 *Id.*
15 See, e.g., *Workman v. United Methodist Comm. on Relief of Gen. Bd. of Global Ministries of United Methodist Church*, 320 F.3d 259, 262 (D.C. Cir. 2003) (in applying District of Columbia law, which didn't specifically speak to the issue at hand, court was "left to reason by analogy from D.C. cases"); *La Reunion Francaise SA v. Barnes*, 247 F.3d 1022, 1024 (9th Cir. 2001) ("There is no clear test for whether the subject matter of a contract is maritime. Instead, we look to precedent and reason by analogy.").
16 *De Herrera v. Gonzales*, 234 F. App'x 764, 765 (9th Cir. 2007).
17 *Jewett v. United States*, 100 F. 832, 840 (1st Cir. 1900) ("The position was created after section 5209 was enacted, and so it is impossible to reason by analogy from one to the other.").

The essential maneuver is to isolate the features making it appropriate to apply the rule from an earlier case that is similar in critical respects. In employment-discrimination cases, the court is often searching for comparator-employees who are similarly situated to the plaintiff. In a 2012 case,[18] the Seventh Circuit took a "flexible, common-sense, and factual" approach to the question of comparability, asking "essentially, are there enough common features between the individuals to allow a meaningful comparison?"[19] This requires the court to identify and assess the key variables, which include in that field such facts as the existence of common job responsibilities, a common supervisor, comparable disciplinary records, comparable educational and experiential backgrounds, and so on. The need to distill the critical holding of an earlier decision, and then to decide whether it applies to a later case, can sometimes give rise to significant disagreements among judges.[20]

Qualified-immunity cases provide a good example of this doctrine in operation. In *Harlow v. Fitzgerald*,[21] the Supreme Court held that "government officials performing discretionary functions generally are shielded from liability for civil damages insofar as their conduct does not violate clearly established statutory or constitutional rights of which a reasonable person would have known."[22] To decide whether this form of immunity is proper, courts must consider whether the plaintiff has alleged the violation of a constitutional right—and, if so, whether the right was "clearly established" at the time of the defendant's alleged

---

18 *Coleman v. Donahoe*, 667 F.3d 835 (7th Cir. 2012).

19 *Id.* at 841.

20 *Compare Gasperini v. Center for Humanities, Inc.*, 518 U.S. 415 (1996) (holding that a state policy for ensuring that jury verdicts aren't excessive had to be adapted to federal procedure, under which the Seventh Amendment made it impossible for the federal court to handle the matter in exactly the same way as the state court did), *with Shady Grove Orthopedic Assocs., P.A. v. Allstate Ins. Co.*, 559 U.S. 393 (2010) (holding that a state law prohibiting class actions in suits seeking penalties or statutory minimum damages couldn't be adapted for use in federal court, because the state law conflicted with Fed. R. Civ. P. 23, a rule that is valid under the Rules Enabling Act).

21 457 U.S. 800 (1982).

22 *Id.* at 818.

misconduct.[23] The search for "clearly established" law is a search for closely analogous cases.[24]

What level of generality?

The Supreme Court has cautioned against evaluating analogies at too high a level of generality. As it said in 1987, "the contours of the right must be sufficiently clear that a reasonable official would understand that what he is doing violates that right."[25] On the other hand, the Court said, "This is not to say that an official action is protected by qualified immunity unless the very action in question has previously been held unlawful, . . . but it is to say that in the light of preexisting law the unlawfulness must be apparent."[26] Yet the Court has also cautioned against too rigid a search for similarity: in one case, it rejected a lower court's insistence that the facts of the earlier cases be "materially similar" to the situation at hand.[27] Instead, the analogous cases need only

---

23   *Pearson v. Callahan*, 555 U.S. 223 (2009).
24   *See, e.g., Findlay v. Lendermon*, 722 F.3d 895, 900 (7th Cir. 2013); *Burns v. Pennsylvania Dep't of Corr.*, 642 F.3d 163, 177 (3d Cir. 2011) (describing the clearly-established-law analysis as one in which the court must "inquire into the general legal principles governing analogous factual situations . . . and . . . determine whether the official should have related this established law to the instant situation") (citation and brackets omitted); *Griffin Indus., Inc. v. Irvin*, 496 F.3d 1189, 1209 (11th Cir. 2007) (labeling the search for analogous cases as the "most common" way to determine whether law is clearly established); *Veneklase v. City of Fargo*, 78 F.3d 1264, 1267 (8th Cir. 1996); *Trigalet v. Young*, 54 F.3d 645, 648 (10th Cir. 1995) (reversing district court's denial of qualified immunity on the grounds that the plaintiffs "cited no case, nor have we found one, that is sufficiently analogous to the facts here to persuade us that the law became clearly established"); *cf. Ohio Civil Serv. Emps. Ass'n v. Seiter*, 858 F.2d 1171, 1176 (6th Cir. 1988) ("While no two cases are completely analogous, there must be limitations upon the extent to which a court may rely on holdings in contexts other than the one being considered to demonstrate that a principle has been clearly established."). *But see Karl v. City of Mountlake Terrace*, 678 F.3d 1062, 1073 (9th Cir. 2012) (holding that an official wasn't entitled to qualified immunity when a reasonable official would have known his actions would violate a subordinate's constitutional rights, even though the case presented a new set of facts, because "closely analogous preexisting case law is not required to show that a right was clearly established") (citation omitted).
25   *Anderson v. Creighton*, 483 U.S. 635, 640 (1987); *see also Ashcroft v. al-Kidd*, 563 U.S. 731, 741, 742 (2011).
26   *Anderson*, 483 U.S. at 640.
27   *Hope v. Pelzer*, 536 U.S. 730, 739 (2002).

provide "fair warning" to the public official whose actions might be found unconstitutional.[28]

Because analogical reasoning doesn't have the force of deduction, a sound analogy must be close. If differences in material circumstances would bring the case under a different rule or principle of law, the analogy isn't close enough.[29]

The cases are legion in which courts say they are following a previous decision because its facts are analogous.[30] For example, in a 2000 case,[31] a designer and manufacturer of children's clothing sued Wal-Mart for selling knockoffs of the designer's outfits. The plaintiff alleged that Wal-Mart had infringed on an unregistered trade dress under the Lanham Act. The Supreme Court had to decide whether the product's design was distinctive and therefore protectable under the Lanham Act. The Court looked to the facts and its decision in *Qualitex Co. v. Jacobson Products*.[32] In that case, a manufacturer and seller of green-gold dry-cleaning press pads alleged that another seller of similarly colored pads was infringing under the Lanham Act. The Court held that a color alone couldn't be protected as a trademark—but that it could be protected upon a showing of secondary meaning (that is, that the mark's primary significance is to identify the source of the product rather than the product itself). In *Wal-Mart Stores*, the U.S. Supreme Court analogized: "It seems to us that design, like color, is not inherently

---

28 *Id.* at 741.
29 1 James Kent, *Commentaries on American Law* *478 (Charles M. Barnes ed., 13th ed. 1884) ("If the analogy be imperfect, the application may be erroneous.").
30 *See, e.g., Evans v. Commonwealth*, 204 S.E.2d 413, 414 (Va. 1974) (per curiam) ("No case directly in point has been cited to us, and we have found none. We look to decisions in analogous cases in other jurisdictions."); *Philadelphia Trust, Safe Deposit & Ins. Co. v. Allison*, 80 A. 833, 835 (Me. 1911) ("We know of no case where the facts are like those in the case at bar. But the cases we have cited, all involving the right of personal election, are so closely analogous in principle to this one that they may be regarded as authorities on the question."); *McDonald v. Brown*, 51 A. 213, 214 (R.I. 1902) ("While no case has been cited by counsel, nor have we been able to find any, in which the particular question here raised was involved, we have found several which are closely analogous, and which strongly confirm us in the view which we have taken of the statute aforesaid.").
31 *Wal-Mart Stores, Inc. v. Samara Bros., Inc.*, 529 U.S. 205 (2000).
32 514 U.S. 159 (1995).

distinctive. . . . In the case of product design, as in the case of color, we think consumer predisposition to equate the feature with the source does not exist."[33]

Meanwhile, as we saw in § 8, courts distinguish earlier cases based on dissimilar circumstances.[34] Take, for example, the 2010 case of *Skilling v. United States*.[35] Enron Corporation, which had appeared to be a financially sound company, suddenly collapsed four months after Skilling, its chief executive officer, resigned. There was widespread media coverage of the collapse and the government investigation that led to Skilling's being charged

---

33   *Wal-Mart Stores*, 529 U.S. at 212–13.
34   *See, e.g., Wyoming v. Oklahoma*, 502 U.S. 437, 448 (1992) ("[The Master] concluded, however, that none of these cases was analogous to this one because none of them involved a direct injury in the form of a loss of specific tax revenues—an undisputed fact here. In our view, the Master's conclusion about Wyoming's standing is sound.") (citation omitted); *United States v. Dow*, 357 U.S. 17, 27 (1958) ("Dow relies on *Danforth v. United States* . . . and *United States v. Dickinson*, . . . but neither case is in point on the issue before us. In *Danforth* the Court rejected the landowner's claim for interest on the ground, inter alia, that the construction of a set-back levee near his land did not amount to a 'taking' because the Government by such action had not yet appropriated the property to its use. The expressly limited holding in *Dickinson* was that the statute of limitations did not bar an action under the Tucker Act for a taking by flooding when it was uncertain at what stage in the flooding operation the land had become appropriated to public use. In the present case there is no dispute over the fact that the United States appropriated Parcel 1 on the date that it entered into physical possession entered under order of the District Court."); *Waldrop v. State*, 48 So. 609, 609 (Miss. 1909) ("The *De Silva Case* . . . is not analogous to this case. In that case Mrs. De Silva was the party charged with the assault and battery, and at that time Mrs. De Silva had in her hands some insulting postal cards, which she charged the prosecutrix with sending to her daughter. At the time sharp words ensued between the parties, followed by the assault. The court said, under these circumstances, and because the cards were the cause of trouble at the very time, and were in the hands of Mrs. De Silva, they should have been admitted when Mrs. De Silva was being prosecuted. But the facts of this case are quite different. Waldrop is the person accused of sending the letters, and he had denied to the husband that he had done so. Since Waldrop was accused of sending the letters, there was no reason why this should have caused him to assault Seillier."); *MacFee v. Horan*, 41 N.W. 239, 239 (Minn. 1889) ("That agreement was valid. There was nothing in it immoral or contrary to public policy. The case is therefore not analogous to that in *Oscanyan v. Arms Co.*, 103 U.S. 261, . . . for in that case the contract sued on was a corrupt one, forbidden by morality and public policy. Here what is relied on to defeat a recovery is alleged conduct or acts of plaintiffs independent of the contract, and not affecting its validity.").
35   561 U.S. 358 (2010).

with conspiracy, securities fraud, making false representations to auditors, and insider trading.

Skilling sought a change of venue on grounds that the extensive pretrial publicity and local hostility made it impossible to seat an impartial jury in Houston. As evidence, he produced hundreds of detailed news reports about Enron's downfall and affidavits from experts who had compared local perceptions of the case with those of people in other venues.[36] The district court denied the motion, observing that the media coverage had been unemotional and objective, the facts of the case were not sensational or heinous, and voir dire would reveal a juror's prejudice.[37]

After his conviction, Skilling argued on appeal that he had not gotten a fair trial because the drumbeat of negative media coverage meant the jurors couldn't be impartial.[38] He cited the 1961 case of *Irvin v. Dowd*[39] as support. The Supreme Court readily distinguished this case on the facts.

Irvin lived in a small, rural community when he was accused of a robbery spree and multiple murders. Pretrial media coverage included reports that he had confessed to the crimes, had had numerous run-ins with the law beginning as a juvenile, and had confessed to 24 burglaries. Many more highly prejudicial facts or allegations about the crimes were also publicized.[40] Only 30,000 people lived in the area, and some 95% were constantly bombarded with newspaper and broadcast stories openly discussing Irvin's guilt and bad character. Some 90% of the veniremembers admitted that they believed he was guilty, including eight of the twelve jurors seated. Although the jurors said they could be impartial, the Supreme Court held that because a man's life was at stake, he couldn't get a fair trial in a place consumed by "a wave of public passion" and a jury that was plainly biased.[41]

---

36 *Id.* at 369–70.
37 *Id.* at 370.
38 *Id.* at 375.
39 366 U.S. 717 (1961).
40 *Skilling*, 561 U.S. at 392–93.
41 *Id.* at 393–94 (quoting *Irvin*, 366 U.S. at 728).

Skilling's circumstances had no resemblance to Irvin's. The objective, unemotional news stories about Enron and Skilling's role in its collapse didn't resemble the biased, horrifying reports about Irvin. The population of Houston, a huge metropolis, actually had much less media exposure to Skilling's case than Irvin's rural community had to his. And the jurors seated in Skilling's trial didn't have any opinions about Skilling before the trial, unlike those in Irvin's. There was little or no reason for the district court in Skilling's trial to disbelieve the jurors' promises to be impartial.[42]

To supply a relevant legal principle, courts often draw on analogous, though not identical, cases. The difficulty lies with determining how closely a case must conform to the present circumstances in order for it to be useful. There is an extensive literature on the use of analogies,[43] but many of the articles focus

---

42 Id. at 394.
43 See Randy Beck, *Transtemporal Separation of Powers in the Law of Precedent*, 87 Notre Dame L. Rev. 1405, 1409–10 (2012) ("Judges often possess a degree of leeway in determining how narrowly or broadly a previous opinion should be read. Circumstances may also influence the precedential weight accorded a prior holding. The strength of the presumption that an earlier legal conclusion should be followed in later litigation can vary with the conditions under which it was announced."); Scott Brewer, *Exemplary Reasoning: Semantics, Pragmatics, and the Rational Force of Legal Argument by Analogy*, 109 Harv. L. Rev. 923 (1996) (developing a philosophical explanation of analogical reasoning in the common-law system); Dan Hunter, *Reason Is Too Large: Analogy and Precedent in Law*, 50 Emory L.J. 1197 (2001) (explaining features of cognitive-science theories of analogy, particularly the multiple-constraint model); Francis Lieber, *Legal and Political Hermeneutics, or Principles of Interpretation and Construction in Law and Politics, with Remarks on Precedents and Authorities*, 16 Cardozo L. Rev. 2079 (1995) (summary of the history of analogical reasoning, including thinkers such as Cicero and Grotius); Linda Meyer, *"Nothing We Say Matters": Teague and New Rules*, 61 U. Chi. L. Rev. 423 (1994) (discussing analogies in the context of new constitutional rules); Emily Sherwin, *A Defense of Analogical Reasoning in Law*, 66 U. Chi. L. Rev. 1179 (1999) (defending the use of analogical reasoning because "it produces a wealth of data for decision-making; it represents the collaborative effort of a number of judges over time; it tends to correct biases that might lead judges to discount the force of prior decisions; and it exerts a conservative force in law, holding the development of law to a gradual pace"); Cass R. Sunstein, *On Analogical Reasoning*, 106 Harv. L. Rev. 741 (1993) (noting that there has been little academic work on analogies, attempting "to offer an account of analogical reasoning and to suggest that, at least for law, it has distinctive advantages over forms of thought that seem to be far superior," and proposing rules for appropriate analogies).

on formal cognitive models that are of limited use to courts.[44] As Cass Sunstein has noted, the subject of analogies "receives little attention in the most influential works in Anglo-American jurisprudence and legal theory."[45] Sunstein nonetheless supports reasoning by analogy. He offers four characteristics that he sees as necessary for sound analogizing: "a requirement of principled consistency, a focus on concrete particulars, incompletely theorized judgments, and the creation and testing of principles having a low or intermediate level of generality."[46]

---

44   *See* Diane P. Wood, *Legal Scholarship for Judges*, 124 Yale L.J. 2592 (2015).
45   Sunstein, *On Analogical Reasoning*, 106 Harv. L. Rev. at 741.
46   *Id.* at 790; *cf.* James DeWitt Andrews, "Jurisprudence and Legal Institutions," 13 *American Law and Procedure* 1, 348–49 (1950) (positing a different four characteristics for safe application of analogies in legal reasoning: "unchanged principles, unchanged policies, unchanged conditions of society or trade, and undistinguishable elemental facts involved in both the precedent and the case at bar").

10. Multiple Questions Decided

When the record presents several questions, and the court considers and deliberately decides each one, the case is precedential for them all. Both of two or more explicitly alternative holdings count as holdings—not as dicta.

Because a dispute before an appellate court often raises more than one question to be decided, the court may deliver several distinct holdings. This tendency is particularly manifest in intermediate appellate courts, which may not know which of several grounds will prove persuasive to the high court. The decisions in such cases will be considered an "authority" on each of the points decided—but not, as we have seen, an authority on the dicta.[1] This much is uncontroversial.

Complications may arise, however, when a court, in the course of resolving an issue, states several legal propositions that influence the resolution of that issue in some way or another. Are all the propositions thus stated holdings in the case? The answer has us revert once again to how we determine the scope of a holding.[2] (See §§ 4, 6.) But here we address specifically the situation in which a decision contains several statements of the law, so that one must determine which of those statements are within the case's authority as precedent. The issue whether a precedential holding is broad enough to encompass a question now under consideration is distinct from the issue whether a concededly applicable holding should be followed.[3]

---

[1] *See, e.g., United States v. Zhang*, 789 F.3d 214 (1st Cir. 2015) (establishing binding circuit precedent on two questions: whether the United States qualifies as a victim under the Mandatory Victims Restitution Act and whether a defendant's restitution obligation to a government agency may be offset by funds forfeited to the Attorney General); *Welk v. GMAC Mortg., LLC*, 850 F. Supp. 2d 976, 984 (D. Minn. 2012) (noting that an earlier Minnesota Supreme Court case "contain[ed] numerous holdings regarding Minnesota law that are binding on both lower state courts and on federal courts applying Minnesota law").

[2] *See generally* Michael Abramowicz & Maxwell Stearns, *Defining Dicta*, 57 Stan. L. Rev. 953 (2005).

[3] *See, e.g., Kimble v. Marvel Entm't, LLC*, 135 S.Ct. 2401, 2405–06 (2015) (addressing whether to adhere to a precedent when all parties agreed that the

For example, courts often confront threshold questions of law before reaching the merits of a dispute.[4] Or a defendant may present multiple claims of error on appeal, each of which could be dispositive.[5] When a court resolves several issues, each sufficient itself to dispose of the case, which of its rulings have controlling weight? Does a ruling have the force of precedent even though it could have been omitted from the opinion without changing the result?

Predictably enough, jurists differ on this point. To some, a decision on any question that's fully argued to and adjudicated by a court is binding authority.[6] This is the so-called loose doctrine of precedent.[7] To others, a decision that wasn't logically necessary to reach a final conclusion is dicta and thus has no authoritative force.[8] This is often referred to as the "strict" or "orthodox" doctrine of precedent.[9] Still others adopt a happy medium, concluding that both the strict and the loose doctrines are valid interpretive methods that lawyers and judges may apply at their convenience.[10]

---

precedent, if valid, controlled the outcome of the case). That doctrine is discussed in detail later in this book.

[4] *See, e.g., Arizona State Legislature v. Arizona Indep. Redistricting Comm'n*, 135 S.Ct. 2652, 2663–66 (2015); *United States v. Windsor*, 133 S.Ct. 2675, 2684–89 (2013); *Monsanto Co. v. Geertson Seed Farms*, 561 U.S. 139, 149–56 (2010).

[5] *See, e.g., United States v. Macias*, 789 F.3d 1011 (9th Cir. 2015); *United States v. Si*, 343 F.3d 1116, 1120 (9th Cir. 2003).

[6] *See United States v. Johnson*, 256 F.3d 895, 914 (9th Cir. 2001) (en banc) (per Kozinski J.) ("[W]here a panel confronts an issue germane to the eventual resolution of the case, and resolves it after reasoned consideration in a published opinion, that ruling becomes the law of the circuit."); *see further Barapind v. Enomoto*, 400 F.3d 744, 751 & n.8 (9th Cir. 2005) (en banc) (per curiam) (adopting the view of Kozinski J. as law of the circuit).

[7] *See* Karl Llewellyn, *The Bramble Bush* 67–68 (6th ed. 1977) ("[The loose view] is the view that a court has decided, and decided authoritatively, *any* point or all points on which it chose to rest a case, or on which it chose, after due argument, to pass.").

[8] *See Johnson*, 256 F.3d at 919–20 (Tashima J. concurring) (concluding that statements that weren't necessary to the decision "have no binding or precedential impact") (quoting *Export Grp. v. Reef Indus., Inc.*, 54 F.3d 1466, 1472 (9th Cir. 1995)).

[9] *See* Llewellyn, *The Bramble Bush* at 66–67.

[10] *See id.* at 66–68.

Also unsurprisingly, these doctrines are different with horizontal precedent and with vertical precedent.

Courts construing horizontal precedent (for example, a high court interpreting its own earlier decisions) haven't been entirely consistent in resolving whether all the propositions that influence a decision constitute holdings. Many cases have applied some version of a test under which "all that is necessary for a decision to be authoritative is to show application of the judicial mind to the subject."[11] According to this test, if an appellate court expressly addressed and decided a "question germane to, though not necessarily decisive of, the controversy," the decision would be considered a holding, not mere dictum.[12] One can see strains of this mode of analysis in recent cases that, in determining whether to treat a statement in an earlier case as authoritative, consider how closely reasoned the underlying analysis was—whether the judicial mind was truly applied to the question.[13]

---

11 *E.g., City of Detroit v. Public Utils. Comm'n*, 286 N.W. 368, 379 (Mich. 1939); accord *Schmidt v. Prince George's Hosp.*, 784 A.2d 1112, 1121 (Md. 2001) (quoting *Carstairs v. Cochran*, 52 A. 601, 601 (Md. 1902)).

12 *City of Detroit*, 286 N.W. at 379 (quoting *Chase v. American Cartage Co.*, 186 N.W. 598, 599 (Wis. 1922)); *see also Luhman v. Beecher*, 424 N.W.2d 753, 755 (Wis. Ct. App. 1988) ("[M]atters not decisive to the primary issue presented but germane to that issue are not dicta, but binding decisions of the court."); *In re Moody's Estate*, 83 S.W.2d 141, 142 (Mo. Ct. App. 1935) ("[W]here the record properly presents a question, a decision thereon is not obiter dictum, though, perhaps, the decision of some other point determines the affirmation or reversal of the judgment in that case.") (quoting *State ex rel. Weast v. Moore*, 147 S.W. 551, 552 (Mo. Ct. App. 1912)); *cf. District of Columbia v. Beretta, U.S.A., Corp.*, 872 A.2d 633, 639–41 (D.C. 2005) (en banc) (treating earlier opinion answering a certified question about strict liability for manufacturers and distributors of "Saturday Night Specials" as binding on the issue whether the manufacturers and distributors could be liable under a negligence theory, reasoning that the court was permitted to "expand[] [its] inquiry ... to render an informed decision on the reach of established theories of tort law in the District of Columbia") (internal quotation marks and citations omitted).

13 *See, e.g., Schuette v. Coalition to Defend Affirmative Action*, 134 S.Ct. 1623, 1645 (2014) (Scalia J. concurring) (stating that the Court "should not design [its] jurisprudence to conform to dictum in a footnote in a four-Justice opinion" (referring to *United States v. Carolene Prods.*, 304 U.S. 144, 152–53 n.4 (1938) (plurality opinion))); *see also Robinson v. Ariyoshi*, 658 P.2d 287, 298 (Haw. 1982) ("To hold that an opinion is a *dictum* is not equivalent to holding either that the court in the particular case acted unwisely in giving it or that no respect should be shown it. There are all shades.... An opinion expressed after full argument and due consideration upon a doubtful point closely connected with,

Other courts have applied a similar test but have formulated it differently, asking whether the statement in question was on an issue sufficiently "interrelated with the determinative issues in the case."[14] The Hawaii Supreme Court considers a higher court's statement—even dictum—binding on lower courts when it (1) "was passed upon by the court with as great care and deliberation as if it had been necessary to decide it," (2) "was closely connected with the question upon which the case was decided," and (3) "was expressed with a view to settling a question that would in all probability have to be decided before the litigation was ended."[15]

The Idaho Supreme Court's decision in a 1928 case[16] provides a helpful illustration of this approach. There, the court considered whether a statute requiring auto-transportation companies to insure vehicles they operated applied to a private "carrier of the property of others for compensation."[17] In an earlier case, the court had held that the statute didn't apply to private carriers. But the plaintiff contended that the earlier case wasn't dispositive because the private carrier there was carrying only his own property, rather than that of others.[18] The court found the earlier case dispositive. It concluded: "The question of whether private carriers of either kind, even though . . . there is a distinction to be made, were amenable to the [statute], was a question which appears to have been fairly within the issues presented, and was considered and deliberately decided therein."[19]

---

or apparently though not necessarily involved in a case, should perhaps, on principle, be given greater weight than an actual decision rendered upon little argument and consideration. It should at least be given greater weight than an opinion expressed merely by the way.") (quoting *Nobrega v. Nobrega*, 14 Haw. 152, 153–54 (1902)).

14   *Board of Educ. of Louisville v. County Bd. of Educ. for Jefferson Cnty.*, 97 S.W.2d 11, 11 (Ky. 1936); *see also Burns v. Lukens*, 269 P. 596, 597 (Idaho 1928) (characterizing a statement in an earlier case as a holding because it was "fairly within the issues presented, and was considered and deliberately decided therein").

15   *Robinson*, 658 P.2d at 298 (quoting *Nobrega*, 14 Haw. at 155).

16   *Burns*, 269 P. 596.

17   *Id.* at 596.

18   *Id.* (citing *Smallwood v. Jeter*, 244 P. 149 (Idaho 1926)).

19   *Id.* at 597.

Other cases have applied a more stringent test, asking whether the statement in question was strictly *necessary* to the result of the earlier case.[20] Judge Ferren of the District of Columbia Court of Appeals stated this formulation of the rule as follows: "[F]or purposes of binding precedent, a holding is a narrow concept, a statement of the outcome accompanied by one or more legal steps or conclusions along the way that ... are 'necessary' to explain the outcome; other observations are dicta."[21]

For an example of the necessary-to-the-result test, consider *Arkansas Game & Fish Commission v. United States*.[22] There, the U.S. Supreme Court considered whether a temporary flood that was government-induced could qualify as a taking under the Takings Clause. The government had argued that it couldn't, relying on an earlier Takings Clause case, *Sanguinetti v. United States*,[23] which in the course of holding that "there was no taking on the[ ] facts"[24] stated that "in order to create an enforceable liability against the Government, it is, at least, necessary that the overflow be the direct result of the structure, and constitute an actual, *permanent* invasion of the land."[25] The Court in *Arkansas Game & Fish* declined to read *Sanguinetti* as requiring that flooding be permanent in order to constitute a taking, noting that the

---

20 *See, e.g., Seminole Tribe of Fla. v. Florida*, 517 U.S. 44, 67 (1996) ("When an opinion issues for the Court, it is not only the result but also those portions of the opinion necessary to that result by which we are bound."); *NLRB v. Hendricks Cnty. Rural Elec. Membership Corp.*, 454 U.S. 170, 186–88 (1981) (declining to follow statement from earlier case because it was "[o]bviously ... unnecessary to the ... question decided in" the earlier case); *Rossiter v. Potter*, 357 F.3d 26, 31 (1st Cir. 2004) ("[W]hen a statement in a judicial decision is essential to the result reached in the case, it becomes part of the court's holding."); *see also United States v. Rubin*, 609 F.2d 51, 69 n.2 (2d Cir. 1979) (Friendly J. concurring) (quoted *supra* on p. 89 in one of his hallmark utterances about how the word *hold* possesses no magical power to transform what would otherwise be dictum).

21 *Parker v. K&L Gates, LLP*, 76 A.3d 859, 873 (D.C. 2013) (Ferren J. concurring); *but see id.* at 877–78 (McLeese J. concurring) ("[I]t is not accurate to say that only rulings essential to the outcome can constitute holdings.").

22 133 S.Ct. 511 (2012).

23 264 U.S. 146 (1924).

24 *Arkansas Game & Fish*, 133 S.Ct. at 520.

25 *Id.* (emphasis added) (quoting *Sanguinetti*, 264 U.S. at 149).

reference to *permanent* "appear[ed] in a nondispositive sentence in *Sanguinetti.*"[26] The Court noted Marshall C.J.'s "sage observation that 'general expressions, in every opinion, are to be taken in connection with the case in which those expressions are used. If they go beyond the case, they may be respected, but ought not to control the judgment in a subsequent suit when the very point is presented for decision.'"[27]

Implicit holdings

As we have seen, the holding of a case encompasses *at least* all the statements in the opinion that were strictly necessary to the result. This rule obtains for unstated propositions as well. That is, if a proposition's validity is logically necessary to the result of a given case, the case will generally be treated as standing for that proposition even if the point wasn't explicitly stated by the court. These propositions are often termed "implicit holdings."[28] (See § 10.)

For example, in *United States v. Asad*,[29] a prisoner filed a habeas petition alleging that he had received ineffective assistance of counsel because his attorney failed to appeal as the defendant had requested—this despite the defendant's having earlier explicitly waived his right to appeal or to bring a collateral challenge to

---

26 *Id.*

27 *Id.* (quoting *Cohens v. Virginia*, 19 U.S. (6 Wheat.) 264, 399 (1821)); *see also Ohio v. Clark*, 135 S.Ct. 2173, 2183–85 (2015) (Scalia J. concurring in the judgment) (agreeing with the result reached by the majority but criticizing various statements in the majority opinion as dicta because they were not "necessary to decide the case" and thus not part of the holding); *Zivotofsky ex rel. Zivotofsky v. Kerry*, 135 S.Ct. 2076, 2089–90 (2015) (qualifying broad statement in earlier opinion that "described the President as 'the sole organ of the federal government in the field of international relations'" because it was "not necessary to the holding of" the case and inconsistent with the structure of the Constitution) (quoting *United States v. Curtiss-Wright Exp. Corp.*, 299 U.S. 304, 320 (1936)); *Kastigar v. United States*, 406 U.S. 441, 449–55 (1972) (retreating from statement in earlier opinion that was broader than necessary to resolve the question presented).

28 *See, e.g., United States v. Caro-Muñiz*, 406 F.3d 22, 26–27 (1st Cir. 2005) (deriving an "implicit holding" from an earlier decision and explicitly adopting that holding as circuit precedent).

29 No. 12-127, 2014 WL 1329937 (E.D. La. 2 Apr. 2014).

his plea agreement.[30] Under the Supreme Court's decision in *Roe v. Flores-Ortega*,[31] an attorney's failure to file a notice of appeal at the client's request is typically ineffective assistance of counsel. So the *Asad* court was required to decide two questions: "First, does the rule of *Flores-Ortega* still apply even though Asad waived his right to appeal? And second, even if it does apply, does Asad's waiver of his collateral challenge rights bar him from bringing a collateral challenge based on *Flores-Ortega* in the first place?"[32]

Fifth Circuit precedent dictated an affirmative answer to the first question. In *United States v. Tapp*,[33] the Fifth Circuit had held that "a failure to file a requested notice of appeal is *per se* ineffective assistance of counsel even if the defendant has waived his right to appeal in a plea agreement."[34] There was no explicit vertical precedent on the second question, but the *Asad* court concluded that *Tapp* implicitly held that the answer to that question was no. Although the *Tapp* court never directly addressed whether the waiver precluded a collateral challenge, it did go on to focus on the merits of whether the appeal waiver precluded a *Flores-Ortega* claim. The *Asad* court stated: "[G]iven that the Fifth Circuit reached the merits of the motion (and resolved them in favor of the defendant), this Court must assume that it answered the antecedent question in the negative."[35]

The rule concerning implicit holdings generally doesn't extend to jurisdictional questions. The Supreme Court has "repeatedly held that the existence of unaddressed jurisdictional defects has no precedential effect."[36] That is, a ruling on the merits of a case in which the court's jurisdiction wasn't challenged or assumed doesn't constitute precedent on the question whether the court has jurisdiction over such a case.[37]

---

30 *Id.* at *1.
31 528 U.S. 470 (2000).
32 *Asad*, 2014 WL 1329937, at *3.
33 491 F.3d 263 (5th Cir. 2007).
34 *Asad*, 2014 WL 1329937, at *3 (citing *Tapp*, 491 F.3d at 265–66).
35 *Id.* at *4.
36 *Lewis v. Casey*, 518 U.S. 343, 352 n.2 (1996).
37 *See, e.g., Steel Co. v. Citizens for a Better Env't*, 523 U.S. 83, 91 (1998).

In sum, a decision containing multiple statements of the law is considered authority for at least those statements that were strictly necessary to the case's outcome. The authority of other statements in the decision is determined on a sliding scale: the more closely related the statement to the determinative issues in the case, and the more cogently reasoned the analysis leading to the statement, the more likely the statement is to be considered authoritative. A court's analysis of what a given case stands for as precedent may also be intertwined with an assessment of how meritorious or unmeritorious that case's reasoning was.[38] To ensure that a case's authority encompasses only those questions that have been carefully considered by the rendering court, a strict approach, closer to the necessary-to-the-result end of the scale, is best. This approach leads to greater clarity of the law.

But a "looser" rule of precedent obtains for courts construing vertical precedent. As we've seen, a lower court will generally follow a higher court's dictum even when the statement in question was undeniably not part of the higher court's holding. As the First Circuit has said: "[F]ederal appellate courts are bound by the Supreme Court's considered dicta almost as firmly as by the Court's outright holdings, particularly when . . . a dictum is of recent vintage and not enfeebled by any subsequent statement."[39]

Alternative holdings

Alternative holdings are a distinct issue from multiple holdings. It is blackletter law that "where a decision rests on two or more grounds, none can be relegated to the category of obiter dictum."[40] That is, alternative holdings are still holdings, even though

---

[38] *See, e.g., Parker v. K&L Gates, LLP*, 76 A.3d 859, 880 (D.C. 2013) (McLeese J. concurring) (declining to follow an earlier statement that could have been characterized as a holding because a later case that had gone the other way "seem[ed] . . . clearly correct as an original matter").

[39] *Cuevas v. United States*, 778 F.3d 267, 272–73 (1st Cir. 2015) (quoting *McCoy v. Massachusetts Inst. of Tech.*, 950 F.2d 13, 19 (1st Cir. 1991)); *see also Yanez-Marquez v. Lynch*, 789 F.3d 434, 450 (4th Cir. 2015); *Schwab v. Crosby*, 451 F.3d 1308, 1325–26 (11th Cir. 2006) (collecting cases).

[40] *Woods v. Interstate Realty Co.*, 337 U.S. 535, 537 (1949); *accord United States v. Title Ins. & Trust Co.*, 265 U.S. 472, 486 (1924); *United States v. Rodriguez*, 406 F.3d 1261, 1276 n.5 (11th Cir. 2005) (Carnes J. concurring in the denial of reh'g

they aren't logically necessary to the case's disposition. This is true even when one of the holdings was "more dwelt upon and perhaps ... more fully argued and considered" than the other.[41] Of the argument to the contrary—that alternative holdings are dicta—it has been said: "The argument is plausible, but specious, and it does not represent the view that lawyers take."[42]

Consider, for example, a case in which a criminal defendant raises claims of error both in his conviction and in his sentence.[43] If the court of appeals considers both claims and finds no error in either of them, each of the court's conclusions is precedential. Under a strict doctrine, every "no error" conclusion is necessary to affirm the judgment below. And under the loose approach, the court has deliberately and carefully addressed each issue presented, so each of its rulings is precedential.

Now consider the same conundrum—but this time assume that the court decides to reverse based on one of the defendant's claims of error related to his conviction. Also assume that the court considers the other claims and finds that none have merit. Are the "no error" conclusions now merely dicta because they made no difference to the outcome? Under the strict view of precedent, they would be. But under the loose doctrine, each ruling

---

en banc); *Mutual Benefit Health & Accident Ass'n v. Cohen*, 194 F.2d 232, 239 (8th Cir. 1952); *Local No. 6167, United Mine Workers of Am. v. Jewell Ridge Coal Corp.*, 145 F.2d 10, 12–13 (4th Cir. 1944); *Parsons v. Federal Realty Corp.*, 143 So. 912, 920 (Fla. 1931) (en banc); *Swiss Oil Corp. v. Shanks*, 270 S.W. 478, 478–80 (Ky. 1925), *aff'd*, 273 U.S. 407 (1927); *see also* Basil Jones, "Stare Decisis," in 26 *The American and English Encyclopaedia of Law* 158, 171 (David S. Garland & Lucius P. McGehee eds., 2d ed. 1904) ("Where the record presents two or more points, any one of which, if sustained, would determine the case, and the court decides them all, the decision upon any one of the points cannot be regarded as obiter [i.e., dictum]."); *cf. Camreta v. Greene*, 563 U.S. 692, 705–09 (2011) (concluding that a court's determination that a government official violated the law was reviewable and "[n]o mere dictum," even though the court found that the official was entitled to qualified immunity, because otherwise it would be too difficult for the courts to "clarify constitutional rights without undue delay") (quoting *Bunting v. Mellen*, 541 U.S. 1019, 1024 (2004) (Scalia J. dissenting from denial of certiorari)).

41 *Richmond Screw Anchor Co. v. United States*, 275 U.S. 331, 340 (1928).

42 *Brief Making and the Use of Law Books* 373 (Roger W. Cooley ed., 5th ed. 1926).

43 *See, e.g., United States v. Brooks*, 610 F.3d 1186, 1193 (9th Cir. 2010); *United States v. Si*, 343 F.3d 1116, 1120 (9th Cir. 2003).

would be precedential because it was disputed by the litigants and resolved by the court in a reasoned decision. Each ruling would be binding on remand. Professor Edmund Morgan addressed this very puzzle in his classic text *Introduction to the Study of Law*.[44] He viewed each of the rulings as authoritative because each was "distinctly presented and deliberately considered."[45] Morgan rejected the "hypercritical" approach that only one "of the several propositions enunciated by the court constitutes decision" and the remainder "must be classed as dicta."[46]

Suppose the reviewing court studies the case carefully and concludes that the trial court erred on each and every claim raised by the defendant. If the court of appeals rules on more than one of these points, then, under the strict rule, the entire opinion becomes nonbinding dicta. This is logical because none of the individual points resolved was *necessary* to decide the case; the same result could have been reached by relying on any one of them and omitting all the others.[47] Or the reviewing court could have avoided this pitfall by limiting its ruling to a single point raised by the defendant and reversing on that point alone. But that would be inefficient and wasteful, and it might jeopardize the chance of affirmance by a higher court. Without the benefit of the reviewing court's ruling on the other points raised in the appeal, the trial court would be likely to make the same errors on remand. This dilemma is similar to that raised by multiple causation in torts, in which a plaintiff who suffers numerous injuries might not be able to prove that any one of them is the but-for cause of the ultimate harm.[48] The Supreme Court has criticized this paradox,[49] indeed for a time even *requiring* lower courts to resolve unnecessary

---

44 Edmund M. Morgan, *Introduction to the Study of Law* 107–10 (1926).

45 *Id.* at 110.

46 *Id.* at 109–10.

47 *See id.* at 110.

48 *See* Ken Kress, *Legal Indeterminacy*, 77 Cal. L. Rev. 283, 298 n.54 (1989).

49 *See Woods v. Interstate Realty Co.*, 337 U.S. 535, 537 (1949) ("But where a decision rests on two or more grounds, none can be relegated to the category of *obiter dictum*.").

claims in certain circumstances.[50] The Court later retreated from that "rigid order of battle" and permitted courts to resolve similar matters on a single prong if appropriate.[51] So courts have largely abandoned defining precedent using the strict doctrine in favor of the more pragmatic loose doctrine.

Applying the strict doctrine faithfully can assuredly lead to absurd results. But this isn't the only reason to consider authoritative all questions that a court decides after thorough deliberation. Doing so also advances the goals of giving guidance to lower courts and to lawyers. By reviewing multiple claims of error that are briefed by the litigants, a court of appeals can more easily develop several areas of substantive law in a single case.[52]

Take, for example, a criminal case in which the defendant claims that certain evidence introduced by the prosecution at trial was seized unlawfully, but also argues that there is insufficient evidence to support the conviction, even if the disputed evidence is considered. A reviewing court might take up the sufficiency-of-the-evidence question first. If it takes into account the disputed evidence and still determines that the verdict cannot stand, it can reverse without addressing the suppression question. But the suppression question, being fully briefed and argued, may provide a vehicle for elucidating an important point of law. If the case is reversed for insufficient evidence, there can be no retrial, so the suppression issue will be lost forever. Yet the search-and-seizure question may be far more important than the fact-specific sufficiency question when it comes to developing the law.

---

50 See, e.g., Saucier v. Katz, 533 U.S. 194, 201 (2001) (establishing a mandatory two-pronged test for determining whether an officer is shielded by qualified immunity—see supra p. 103); see also Thomas Healy, The Rise of Unnecessary Constitutional Rulings, 83 N.C. L. Rev. 847, 871, 889–95 (2005) (identifying areas "in which the Court has authorized unnecessary constitutional rulings").

51 Pearson v. Callahan, 555 U.S. 223, 234–36 (2009) (also involving questions of qualified immunity) (internal quotation marks omitted).

52 See Morgan, Introduction to the Study of Law at 110.

Close calls on alternative holdings vs. dicta

One difficulty, however, is that it's not always clear whether a given proposition is an alternative holding or merely dictum.[53] For an interesting example of a disagreement over this very point, consider a 2002 Eleventh Circuit case[54] in which the court had to decide whether a federal prisoner's habeas petition was timely under 28 U.S.C. § 2255. Congress had amended § 2255 in 1996 to impose a one-year statute of limitations on habeas petitions that ran from "the date on which the facts supporting the claim or claims presented could have been discovered through the exercise of due diligence."[55]

Aron's conviction had become final in September 1994, and he filed a § 2255 motion in July 1998, arguing that his appellate counsel had been constitutionally deficient. He contended that his motion was timely because he had not been able to discover the facts underlying his ineffective-assistance-of-counsel claim until less than a year before he filed the § 2255 motion.

The majority of the panel first stated that the one-year limitations period should run from the date of the 1996 amendment, not the date the petitioner's conviction became final, meaning that Aron wasn't required to show due diligence before that date.[56] The court then held that Aron had made sufficient due-diligence allegations that he was entitled to an evidentiary hearing on whether he had complied with the statute of limitations.[57] The majority characterized the former statement as a holding: "The fact that either error would be sufficient to warrant reversal does not mean that future panels are free to treat one of these two findings as dicta, nor does it mean that the district court on remand may

---

53 *Compare, e.g., Operating Eng'rs Pension Trust v. Charles Minor Equip. Rental*, 766 F.2d 1301, 1304 (9th Cir. 1985) (characterizing earlier statement as an alternative holding), *with id.* at 1306–07 (Fletcher J. dissenting) (arguing that the statement was "merely advisory, and ha[d] no binding or precedential impact," *id.* at 1307).

54 *Aron v. United States*, 291 F.3d 708 (11th Cir. 2002).

55 *Id.* at 711 (quoting 28 U.S.C. § 2255(4)).

56 *Id.* at 713.

57 *Id.* at 714–15.

disregard one in favor of the other."[58] Specifically, the majority added, "The fact that Aron claims to have exercised due diligence from the time his conviction became final does not make this portion of the opinion dicta."[59]

Although Carnes J. concurred in the majority's conclusion that Aron should have been afforded an evidentiary hearing, he did "not join the dicta . . . concerning what would happen if a petitioner exercised due diligence to ascertain the facts relating to his claims after, but not before" the amendments to § 2255.[60] Carnes J. viewed the majority's statements on that score as dicta rather than a holding because "the facts of this case, as established for purposes of this appeal by the sworn pleadings of petitioner Aron in the district court, [were] that he demonstrated due diligence throughout the period before as well as after" the amendments, and "[t]he holding of a case on appeal can extend no further than the facts presented in that case at the time of the appeal."[61]

A 2002 Ninth Circuit case[62] provides yet another useful illustration of the sometimes-slippery line between an alternative holding and dictum. The court considered whether the term *unpaid losses* in § 816 of the Internal Revenue Code included accrued unpaid losses. In a 1967 precedent,[63] the court had held that the term, as used in a different provision, § 806, did include accrued unpaid losses.[64] The 1967 precedent had "looked to" the predecessor of § 816 (styled § 801),[65] noting the parties' agreement that "the term as used in [§ 801] should have the same meaning as it has in section 806."[66] The court concluded that *unpaid losses* included accrued unpaid losses in § 801, noting that this "interpretation of

---

58   *Id.* at 713 n.4 (citations omitted).
59   *Id.*
60   *Id.* at 716 (Carnes J. concurring).
61   *Id.*
62   *Best Life Assurance Co. v. Commissioner*, 281 F.3d 828 (9th Cir. 2002).
63   *United States v. Occidental Life Ins. Co.*, 385 F.2d 1 (9th Cir. 1967).
64   *Best Life*, 281 F.3d at 831 (citing *Occidental Life*, 385 F.2d at 1–2, 4–7).
65   *Id.* (quoting *Occidental Life*, 385 F.2d at 5–6).
66   *Occidental Life*, 385 F.2d at 5.

section 801 [was] . . . persuasive in support of the result which [it] reach[ed]."[67]

Faced with the argument that the 1967 case controlled the outcome because it had issued an "alternative holding" regarding the proper construction of § 801, the Ninth Circuit characterized the precedent's analysis of § 801 as dictum rather than an alternative holding and declined to follow it.[68] The court explained that in the earlier case, "our statements regarding the scope of § 801 were used to support our holding with regard to § 806—we did not make an alternative holding under § 801 itself."[69] In the earlier case, the court had noted that "an examination of section 801 along these comparative lines is not required for a conclusion as to the meaning of 'unpaid losses' in section 806,"[70] so the court's interpretation of § 801 was simply "persuasive in support of the result."[71]

One could argue that this result is clearly correct: because the meaning of *unpaid losses* under § 801 wasn't at issue in the 1967 precedent, it wasn't possible for that case to have rested its decision, even in the alternative, on an analysis of § 801. On the other hand, given the parties' agreement in 1967 that §§ 801 and 806 should be construed identically regarding the meaning of *unpaid losses*, one could view the court's construction of § 801 as an alternative way to reach the holding about § 806. The chain of logic would go as follows: (1) *Unpaid losses* as used in § 801 includes accrued unpaid losses. (2) The parties agree that the term *unpaid losses* should be construed the same in §§ 801 and 806. (3) Therefore, *unpaid losses* as used in § 806 includes accrued unpaid losses. Under that line of reasoning, the statement regarding § 801 is necessary to the result.

A final point: although alternative holdings or rationales of an appellate court are binding, it's improper for a later court to

---

67   *Id.* at 5–6.
68   *Best Life*, 281 F.3d at 833–34.
69   *Id.* at 834.
70   *Occidental Life*, 385 F.2d at 5–6.
71   *Id.*

infer an alternative holding or rationale where none is sufficiently expressed in the precedent.[72]

The rule that alternative holdings qualify as binding precedent is clear in theory and usually easy to apply in practice. But as the preceding cases show, sometimes the line between an alternative holding and a statement of dictum gets blurry. Hence courts that embrace the loose definition of precedent may settle questions that don't, strictly speaking, require answers.

This approach is a concern to those who believe that allowing courts to opine on abstract legal issues results in decisions rife with ill-considered statements of law.[73] But dismissing all "unnecessary" statements as dicta isn't the only way to guard against careless lawmaking. After all, even a court that adheres to the loose doctrine of precedent need not accept as binding a determination "made casually and without analysis," or a statement "uttered in passing without due consideration of the alternatives."[74]

Under the looser doctrine of precedent, if each of a court's well-reasoned conclusions is considered precedential, lawyers can avoid the uncertainty of parsing an opinion to determine which points were "necessary" to the holding. This is particularly important given that even "judges often disagree about what is and is not necessary to the resolution of a case."[75]

The modern doctrine of precedent allows courts to resolve all questions that the litigants brief and argue—even those not logically necessary to the case's outcome. While some lawyers and judges view these determinations as "judicial dicta,"[76] the better view is that such decisions serve as fully binding precedent.

---

72 *In re Hearn*, 376 F.3d 447, 453 n.5 (5th Cir. 2004).

73 See *United States v. Crawley*, 837 F.2d 291, 292–93 (7th Cir. 1988) (per Posner J.) (observing that peripheral conclusions "may not have received the full and careful consideration of the court that uttered [them]" or may not have been refined by the "fires of adversary presentation") (internal quotation marks omitted).

74 *United States v. Johnson*, 256 F.3d 895, 915 (9th Cir. 2001) (en banc) (per Kozinski J.).

75 *Id.* at 914.

76 See Karl Llewellyn, *The Bramble Bush* 42 (6th ed. 1977).

11. Narrow Cases

On rare occasions, a case decided on its own special or peculiar circumstances, or only with a view to avoiding special hardship in the particular case, will not be relied on as an authority for any broad or general legal principle that might be derived from it.

Courts and individual judges, especially those writing separately, sometimes urge that because an earlier case (or the present majority opinion) is a limited holding, it should not be extended to new situations.[1] A judge who is uncertain about how broadly a judicially announced rule should apply will try to straiten the rationale with statements that tie it to the specific facts before the court.

The Fourth Amendment offers a good example of this tendency. The Supreme Court requires lower courts to evaluate the

---

1 *Mahan v. Howell*, 410 U.S. 315, 334, *modified*, 411 U.S. 922 (1973) (Brennan J. concurring in part and dissenting in part) ("Since every reapportionment case presents as its factual predicate a unique combination of circumstances, decisions upholding or invalidating a legislative plan cannot normally have great precedential significance."); *Town of Bloomfield v. Charter Oak Nat'l Bank*, 121 U.S. 121, 133–34 (1887) ("The case [*New Haven, Middletown & Willimantic R.R. v. Town of Chatham*] is an exceptional one, depending on its peculiar circumstances."); *Mooney v. Edwards*, 17 A. 973, 975 (N.J. 1889) ("[A]s the reasoning of the case [*Boston Tpk. Co. v. Town of Pomfret*, 20 Conn. 590 (1850)] is not a whit more convincing than this authority, it must stand as having been decided upon the hardship of the individual case."); *Rosenzweig v. Thompson*, 8 A. 659, 660 (Md. 1887) ("[T]he authority of that case, as sustaining the broad general proposition contended for, . . . has been thoroughly discredited by the more recent decisions. . . . '[T]here were special circumstances which induced Sir JOHN LEACH to come to the conclusion he did in that case, and that the decision was far from establishing the general proposition . . . .'") (quoting *Davies v. Davies*, 2 Keen, 539); *see also Taylor v. Kentucky*, 436 U.S. 478, 490 (1978) ("We hold that on the facts of this case the trial court's refusal to give petitioner's requested instruction on the presumption of innocence resulted in a violation of his right to a fair trial."); *Kentucky v. Whorton*, 441 U.S. 786, 789 (1979) (per curiam) ("[T]he Court's holding was expressly limited to the facts . . . . This explicitly limited holding . . . belie[s] any intention to create a rule that an instruction on the presumption of innocence is constitutionally required in every case."); *Toyosaburo Korematsu v. United States*, 323 U.S. 214, 219–20 (1944) ("Compulsory exclusion of large groups of citizens from their homes, *except under circumstances of direst emergency and peril*, is inconsistent with our basic governmental institutions.") (emphasis added).

"totality of the circumstances."[2] This test makes it difficult to take a case in which the trunk of someone's car was searched and apply it to a vacation home, a container on top of the car, a friend's apartment, or a jacket. Occasionally courts will face genuinely unusual cases, because they involve obscure statutes,[3] or bizarre behavior,[4] or an odd setting.[5] Even in those cases, however, modern search tools enable judges to see the broader principles on which those cases rely, and to the extent those principles are ascertainable, the judge will see no legitimate reason to discount the importance of the ruling. The fair application of precedent is always an important constraint on the power of the judiciary.[6]

It's even harder to find modern courts noting that because an earlier decision was based on a peculiar hardship, it should not be followed. To the contrary, many decisions say that it's improper to decide a case based on specific circumstances or individual hardships rather than a neutral application of the law.[7] These

---

2   See, e.g., *Ohio v. Robinette*, 519 U.S. 33, 39 (1996); *Florida v. Royer*, 460 U.S. 491, 506 (1983) (rejecting a "litmus-paper test" for compliance with the Fourth Amendment in light of the "endless variations in the facts and circumstances").

3   E.g., *United States v. Winnie*, 97 F.3d 975 (1996).

4   E.g., *Zygowski v. Erie Morning Telegram, Inc.*, 298 F.2d 639, 641 (3d Cir. 1962) (finding that plaintiff wasn't an employee because of the highly unusual circumstances surrounding his employment, including the fact that he was married to his nominal employer); *Carlson v. McLyman*, 74 A.2d 853, 856 (R.I. 1950) (allowing for review by the Supreme Court because of the "extraordinary and peculiar circumstances in the case").

5   E.g., *Attorney Gen. of U.S. v. Covington & Burling*, 430 F. Supp. 1117, 1120 (D.D.C. 1977) (pointing to the "unusual setting" and "peculiar way in which the question of privilege has arisen"); *State v. Lewis*, 468 So. 2d 557, 561 (La. 1985) (Calogero J. dissenting) (noting that the defendant's criminal appeal was "unlike any other case in this Court in recent memory" because the defendant's ineffective-assistance-of-counsel application had been disposed of before appellate review); *Strawn v. State Tax Comm'n*, 388 P.2d 286, 289 (Or. 1964) (en banc) (stating, in case involving valuation of skeleton log cars used in logging, that "[t]his has been a case dependent upon analysis of facts unlike any other case we have found").

6   See Erica S. Weisgerber, *Unpublished Opinions: A Convenient Means to an Unconstitutional End*, 97 Geo. L.J. 621, 637 (2009) ("Madison viewed that precedent would confine the decisions of judges in almost every case that came before them, with exceptions falling only within 'extraordinary and peculiar circumstances.'").

7   *Peralta v. United States*, 70 U.S. (3 Wall.) 434, 439 (1865) ("There will sometimes, in applying those rules to the various affairs of life, be cases of individual

statements imply that decisions based on hardship rather than the law deserve no precedential effect. Even so, a ruling based on the particular circumstances of the litigants is sometimes appropriate.

Certain administrative tribunals that issue expressly nonprecedential opinions meant to apply only to the litigants then before the tribunal may see little need to justify their rulings by reference to earlier cases. For example, the notion of "extreme hardship," which allows for relief from removal in some immigration cases, seems to lend itself particularly well to determinations based on individual circumstances that would not necessarily require citation of previous cases.[8] Further, the outcomes of cases falling within categories traditionally covered by equity are designed by definition to strike a balance that depends on special or peculiar circumstances. The equity courts weren't originally bound by the principle of stare decisis; as time went on, that distinction largely slipped away.[9]

Finally, we should recognize that a court cannot really spay its decision so that it will forever have no progeny. That decision is left to successor courts. As Holmes J. noted in 1906: "[A] court, by announcing that its decision is confined to the facts before it, does not decide in advance that logic will not drive it further when new facts arise."[10]

---

hardship; but this does not prove that the rules are unwise . . . . The right of property, as every other valuable right, depends in a great measure for its security on the stability of judicial decisions."); *Wilson v. Simpson*, 50 U.S. (9 How.) 109, 116 (1850) ("The question of individual hardship cannot control the settlement of great legal questions."). *See generally* 12A Fla. Jur. 2d *Courts and Judges* § 190 (2015) (stating that "[t]he courts are bound to follow the law as it exists even though its application in isolated cases may work a hardship" and noting several rationales for the rule).

8   *See* 8 U.S.C. § 1182 (2015).

9   *See* John R. Kroger, *Supreme Court Equity, 1789–1835, and the History of American Judging*, 34 Hous. L. Rev. 1425, 1434 (1998) ("[T]raditional equity eschewed use of precedents."); H. Brent McKnight, *How Shall We Then Reason? The Historical Setting of Equity*, 45 Mercer L. Rev. 919, 924 (1994) (Even before the Revolutionary War, equity had become "as rigid and precedent bound as the common law.").

10   *Haddock v. Haddock*, 201 U.S. 562, 631 (1906) (Holmes J. dissenting).

12. Hypothetical and Moot Cases

A decision rendered on a purely hypothetical question has no precedential force. The same is generally true of moot questions—those on which no effective relief can be given—though the mootness doctrine has several important exceptions. If an amicable action or test case is genuinely contested and involves a question of law, the decision does have precedential force.

The orthodox view of justiciability has long been that a court's dealing with something other than an actual case or controversy will be considered "extrajudicial, ultra vires, not binding upon the very court or upon any other."[1] Courts are thought to be more liable to imprudent decisions when nothing real is at stake.[2] A question is hypothetical if it's based on pretense; it's moot if the court cannot possibly grant effective relief or issue an order that will have any effect on the litigants.[3] The proposition that a decision rendered on such a question carries no precedential weight is pretty uncontroversial.[4] Article III of the Constitution forbids

---

1 *Brief Making and the Use of Law Books* 368 (Roger W. Cooley ed., 5th ed 1926).
2 13B Charles Alan Wright, Arthur R. Miller et al., *Federal Practice and Procedure* § 3533.1, at 731 (2008).
3 *Know v. Service Emps.*, 132 S.Ct. 2277, 2278 (2012) (noting that a case "becomes moot only when it is impossible for a court to grant any effectual relief whatever to the prevailing party") (internal citations omitted); *Mills v. Green*, 159 U.S. 651, 653 (1895) ("[W]hen, pending an appeal from the judgment of a lower court, and without any fault of the defendant, an event occurs which renders it impossible for this court, if it should decide the case in favor of the plaintiff, to grant him any effectual relief whatever, the court will not proceed to a formal judgment, but will dismiss the appeal.").
4 *Genesis Healthcare Corp. v. Symczyk*, 133 S.Ct. 1523, 1528 (2013) ("If an intervening circumstance deprives the plaintiff of a 'personal stake in the outcome of the lawsuit,' at any point during litigation, the action can no longer proceed and must be dismissed as moot.") (citation omitted); *Brownlow v. Schwartz*, 261 U.S. 216, 217 (1923) ("It thus appears that there is now no actual controversy between the parties—no issue on the merits which this court can properly decide. The case has become moot.... This court will not proceed to a determination when its judgment would be wholly ineffectual for want of a subject matter on which it could operate."); *California v. San Pablo & T.R. Co.*, 149 U.S. 308, 314 (1893) ("But the court is not empowered to decide moot questions or abstract propositions, or to declare, for the government of future cases,

federal courts to decide this kind of case or issue.[5] The authority of state courts to render such decisions varies, although most are subject to restrictions comparable to those on the federal courts—and they generally refuse to issue advisory opinions (see § 32).[6] This

---

principles or rules of law which cannot affect the result as to the thing in issue in the case before it."); *United States v. Barton*, 633 F.3d 168, 172 (3d Cir. 2011) ("[T]he Supreme Court's discussion in *Heller* of the categorical exceptions to the Second Amendment wasn't abstract and hypothetical; it was outcome-determinative. [Hence] we are bound by it."); *In re Adoption of L.O.*, 282 P.3d 977, 980 (Utah 2012) ("Generally, we will not decide a case that is moot. . . . An appeal is moot if during the pendency of the appeal circumstances change so that the controversy is eliminated, thereby rendering the relief requested impossible or of no legal effect.") (internal quotation marks omitted); *Burr v. Boone*, 477 So. 2d 692 (La. 1985) (per curiam) ("Unlike the hypothetical situation described by this court in dicta in *Dillon v. Medellin*, 409 So. 2d 570 (La. 1982), a prima facie case supporting the exercise of jurisdiction has been established."); *Freeman v. Board of Med. Exam'rs for S. Dist. of Indian Territory*, 95 P. 229, 230 (Okla. 1908) ("The Supreme Court will not decide abstract or hypothetical cases disconnected from the granting of actual relief, or from the determination of which no practical relief can follow. . . . [A]ny declaration of principle set out in the decree [for a mere hypothetical case] would be entitled to, and would receive, no more consideration than mere dicta.") (internal quotation marks omitted).

5   See, e.g., *Singer Mfg. Co. v. Wright*, 141 U.S. 696, 700 (1891) ("The taxes being paid, the further prosecution of this suit to enjoin their collection would present only a moot question, upon which we have neither the right nor the inclination to express an opinion."); *National Advert. Co. v. City of Miami*, 402 F.3d 1329, 1332 (11th Cir. 2005) (per curiam) ("[F]ederal courts lack jurisdiction to hear and decide cases where changes in the law have rendered the case moot."); *Walling v. Shenandoah-Dives Mining Co.*, 134 F.2d 395, 396–97 (10th Cir. 1943) ("When in the course of a trial the matter in controversy comes to an end, either by an act of one or both of the parties or by operation of law, the question becomes moot and the court is without further jurisdiction in the matter."); *California Canning Peach Growers v. Myers*, 78 F.2d 194, 195 (9th Cir. 1935) (per curiam) (dismissing case because "[t]he questions arising upon this appeal have become moot").

6   See, e.g., *State ex rel. Morrison v. Sebelius*, 179 P.3d 366, 383 (Kan. 2008); *Not in Montana: Citizens Against CI-97 v. State ex rel. McGrath*, 147 P.3d 174, 176 (Mont. 2006); *Baker v. Town of Goshen*, 730 A.2d 592, 596–97 (Vt. 1999); *Church Point Wholesale Beverage Co. v. Tarver*, 614 So. 2d 697, 702 (La. 1993); *Richland Cnty. Water Res. Bd. v. Pribbernow*, 442 N.W.2d 916, 918–19 (N.D. 1989). *But see Advisory Op. to Governor re Judicial Vacancy Due to Mandatory Ret.*, 940 So. 2d 1090, 1090 (Fla. 2006) (citing Fla. Const. art. IV, which allows "[t]he governor [to] request in writing the opinion of the justices of the supreme court as to the interpretation of any portion of this constitution upon any question affecting the governor's executive powers and duties"); *Answer of the Justices to the Governor*, 829 N.E.2d 1111 (Mass. 2005) (citing Mass. Const. pt. 2, ch. III, art. II, which provides that "[e]ach branch of the legislature, as well as the governor or the council, shall have authority to require the opinions of the justices of

prohibition eliminates any question about a decision's precedential effect because there ought not to be any decision in the first place as a result of justiciability doctrines such as standing, ripeness, and mootness. But if a court were nonetheless to decide a hypothetical or moot question in the course of an otherwise appropriate decision, then the principle here stated has some teeth: reasoning not material to the decision can be disregarded as dictum.[7]

Mootness most commonly comes in two circumstances: (1) when the plaintiff stops seeking relief or obtains relief by settling,[8] and (2) when events occurring after the filing of suit

---

the supreme judicial court, upon important questions of law, and upon solemn occasions"); *In re Advisory Op. to the Governor*, 732 A.2d 55, 59 (R.I. 1999) (citing R.I. Const. art. X, § 3, which provides that "[t]he judges of the supreme court shall give their written opinion upon any question of law whenever requested by the governor or by either house of the general assembly"); *Opinion of the Justices*, 384 So. 2d 1056, 1058 (Ala. 1980) (citing Ala. Code § 12-2-10, which allows "[t]he Governor, by a request in writing, or either house of the Legislature, by a resolution of such house, [to] obtain a written opinion of the justices of the Supreme Court of Alabama or a majority thereof on important constitutional questions"); *State v. Warmington*, 403 P.2d 849, 850 (Nev. 1965) ("Our appellate jurisdiction in criminal cases does not embrace the resolution of mere moot questions."); *Siefferman v. Johnson*, 94 N.E.2d 317, 319 (Ill. 1950) ("[W]here a reviewing court has notice of facts which show that only moot questions or mere abstract propositions are involved it will dismiss the appeal or writ of error."); *Warhurst v. Morgan*, 140 P.2d 236, 236 (Okla. 1943) (per curiam) ("[T]he Supreme Court will not attempt to determine abstract, hypothetical or moot questions."); *Campbell v. Reynolds*, 29 P.2d 941, 941 (Okla. 1934) (per curiam) ("This court has universally held that where the controversy between the plaintiff in error and defendant in error has ended and the question has become moot, the proceedings will not be retained by this court to determine an abstract, hypothetical, or moot question.").

7   *See* Michael Abramowicz & Maxwell Stearns, *Defining Dicta*, 57 Stan. L. Rev. 953, 1037 (2005) (examining the difficulties of using hypotheticals in court decisions); Ryan S. Killian, *Dicta and the Rule of Law*, 2013 Pepp. L. Rev. 1, 9 n.58 (2013) (discussing the relationship between dicta and advisory opinions); Judith M. Stinson, *Why Dicta Becomes Holding and Why It Matters*, 76 Brook. L. Rev. 219, 225–27 (2010) ("Even when a court has thoroughly considered the issue, if the statement has no impact on the merits, a court is more likely to be wrong. In these instances, the court has less incentive to ensure the 'correct' decision because it is not binding on the parties before the court, much less future litigants. This result is not unique to dicta; courts similarly cannot rule, and therefore cannot create binding precedent, in cases absent standing or when the decision is moot.").

8   13B Charles Alan Wright, Arthur R. Miller et al., *Federal Practice and Procedure* § 3533.2, at 763 (2008) ("The easiest [mootness] cases are those in which

make the relief sought no longer possible or useful.[9] More often, a court that agrees to decide a moot or apparently moot case has found that an exception to the mootness doctrine applies.[10] The decisions in these cases do have precedential value.

At the federal level, there are five important exceptions to the mootness doctrine. The first two are far and away the most common. First is the "capable-of-repetition-yet-evading-review exception,"[11] which applies when "(1) the challenged action was in its duration too short to be fully litigated prior to its cessation or expiration, and (2) there was a reasonable expectation that the same complaining party would be subjected to the same action again."[12] Second, the "involuntary-cessation exception" covers a defendant's attempt to render a case moot by discontinuing the complained-of conduct.[13] When the defendant remains capable of resuming the wrongful behavior, the court may invoke the exception.[14]

---

the plaintiff simply withdraws, or agrees to settlement of all issues.").

9   *Id.* § 3533, at 718.
10 *Butler v. WinCo Foods, LLC*, 613 Fed. App'x 584, 585–86 (9th Cir. 2015).
11 *See, e.g., Southern Pac. Terminal Co. v. ICC*, 219 U.S. 498, 515 (1911); *Roe v. Wade*, 410 U.S. 113, 124 (1974).
12 *Wisconsin Dep't of Indus. v. Gould, Inc.*, 475 U.S. 282, 285 n.3 (1986) (expiration of three-year order debarring plaintiff from contracting with the state did not moot appeal); *SEC v. Sloan*, 436 U.S. 103, 108–10 (1978) (expiration of SEC orders suspending trading of corporation's common stock did not moot case); *Weinstein v. Bradford*, 423 U.S. 147, 149 (1975); *SEC v. Okin*, 132 F.2d 784, 787 (2d Cir. 1943) (applying exception to actions of an officer of a private company); *People for the Ethical Treatment of Animals, Inc. v. Gittens*, 396 F.3d 416, 422 (D.C. Cir. 2005) ("Later cases speak not of orders, but of repetition of the 'controversy.'"); *Cerro Wire & Cable Co. v. FERC*, 677 F.2d 124, 127 n.2 (D.C. Cir. 1982) (expiration of certificates to transport natural gas issued by Federal Energy Regulatory Commission did not moot claim); *see also* 13A Charles Alan Wright et al., *Federal Practice and Procedure* § 3533.8 (2d ed. 1984 & Supp. 2008) ("Courts confronting discontinued or expired official acts frequently deny mootness on the ground that the acts are 'capable of repetition, yet evading review.'"); 15 James W. Moore et al., *Moore's Federal Practice* § 101.99[1], at 101-408.4 (3d ed. 2016) ("an exception to the mootness doctrine will be found if the defendant's conduct is capable of repetition, yet will evade review").
13 Moore et al., *Moore's Federal Practice* § 101.99[2], at 101-424.
14 *United States v. W.T. Grant Co.*, 345 U.S. 629, 632 (1953); *see also Friends of the Earth v. Laidlaw Envtl. Servs. (TOC), Inc.*, 528 U.S. 167, 174 (2000) ("A

The last three exceptions apply in specific circumstances. The "collateral-consequences exception" applies when a court finds that the events giving rise to the suit not only caused direct harm but will lead to related, ongoing harm.[15] This exception originally applied to criminal cases in which the appellant had already served the sentence. Such a case is not moot because the conviction will have continuing effects on the appellant, such as hindering obtaining employment or housing, and if the court finds the conviction wrongful, the defendant directly benefits from the decision.[16] Civil cases that fall under the exception are less common in federal courts than in state courts. Where a litigant has suffered an injury that has potential future repercussions, as when a person has been involuntarily committed to and then released from a mental hospital, the case will not be moot.[17]

The fourth and fifth exceptions apply to class actions. The "inherently-transitory exception" saves a case from becoming moot when it is uncertain or unlikely that all the class members' claims

---

defendant's voluntary cessation of allegedly unlawful conduct ordinarily does not suffice to moot a case.").

[15] *See Spencer v. Kemna*, 523 U.S. 1, 10–11 (1998); *Sibron v. New York*, 392 U.S. 40, 55–56 (1968).

[16] *See, e.g., Fiswick v. United States*, 329 U.S. 211, 222 (1946) (holding that where collateral consequences exist, the defendant "has a substantial stake in the judgment of conviction which survives the satisfaction of the sentence imposed on him"); *see also Sibron*, 392 U.S. at 51 (holding that review was appropriate even after defendant had served his sentence because "there was a good chance that there would be 'ample opportunity to review' the question presented on the merits in a future proceeding") (citing *St. Pierre v. United States*, 319 U.S. 41, 43 (1943)).

[17] *In re Surrick*, 338 F.3d 224, 230 (3d Cir. 2003) (attorney's suspension, although expired, was not moot because continuing stigma associated with the suspension constituted possible collateral consequences); *New England Health Care Emps. Union, Dist. 1199, SEIU AFL-CIO v. Mt. Sinai Hosp.*, 65 F.3d 1024, 1029 (9th Cir. 1995) (repeal of applicable statute did not moot future consequences arising from statute's effects while in force); *see also In re Alfred H.H.*, 910 N.E.2d 74 (Ill. 2009) ("Though the appellate court is correct that the mere reversal of an adjudication will not, in itself, purge a respondent's mental health records of any mention of the admission or treatment, that is not the same as saying that there is no effect whatsoever. In fact, there are a host of potential legal benefits to such a reversal."); *see also, e.g., In re Cummings*, 13 S.W.3d 472, 475 (Tex. 2000) ("[B]eing the subject of a protective order does carry a stigma. Not only does a protective order carry a social stigma, but there are also legal repercussions.").

will be satisfied before a case is litigated.[18] And the "picking-off exception" discourages a defendant from settling with the named plaintiffs before the class is certified in an attempt to render the class action moot.[19]

Some other exceptions are recognized, usually by state courts, such as the "public-interest exception," under which a court may decide to settle a question of law that is likely to recur and is of great public interest.[20] Some lower federal courts seem to have

---

18 See, e.g., *Gawry v. Countrywide Home Loans*, 395 Fed. App'x 152, 158–59 (6th Cir. 2010) ("[T]he crux of the 'inherently transitory' exception is the uncertainty about the length of time a claim will remain alive.") (internal citation omitted); *Robidoux v. Celani*, 987 F.2d 931, 939 (2d Cir. 1993) (class action challenging delays in processing various public assistance applications was not moot even though the named plaintiffs received their benefits before the class could be certified because "[a]ppellants' claims are inherently transitory since the Department will almost always be able to process a delayed application before a plaintiff can obtain relief through litigation"); *Thorpe v. District of Columbia*, 916 F. Supp. 2d 65, 67 (D.D.C. 2013) (holding that the inherently transitory exception applied to claims of nursing home inhabitants as "[t]he length of any individual's stay in a nursing facility is impossible to predict, so even though there are certainly individuals whose claims will not expire within the time it would take to litigate their claims, there is no way for plaintiffs to ensure that the Named Plaintiffs will be those individuals").

19 See *Chen v. Allstate Ins. Co.*, 819 F.3d 1136, 1147 (9th Cir. 2016) ("[W]hen a defendant consents to judgment affording complete relief on a named plaintiff's individual claims before certification, but fails to offer complete relief on the plaintiff's class claims, a court should not enter judgment on the individual claims, over the plaintiff's objection, before the plaintiff has had a fair opportunity to move for class certification."); *id.* ("*Campbell–Ewald* clearly suggests it would be inappropriate to enter judgment under these circumstances. As *Campbell–Ewald* explained, '[w]hile a class lacks independent status until certified, *a would-be class representative with a live claim of her own must be accorded a fair opportunity to show that certification is warranted*'") (quoting *Campbell–Ewald Co. v. Gomez*, 136 S.Ct. 663, 672 (2016) (holding that an unaccepted settlement offer or offer of judgment does not moot a complaint)); *see also Wilson v. Gordon*, 822 F.3d 934, 949–50 (6th Cir. 2016) ("Though *Campbell–Ewald* sheds little light on the 'picking off' exception, the Court did observe that allowing an unaccepted offer to moot a case would place defendants like Campbell–Ewald 'in the driver's seat,' enabling them to avoid significant class-based liability.").

20 See *In re Shelby R.*, 955 N.E.2d 990, 994 (Ill. 2013) ("Application of this exception, which is narrowly construed, requires a clear showing of each of the following criteria: (1) the question presented is of a public nature; (2) an authoritative determination of the question is desirable for the future guidance of public officers; and (3) the question is likely to recur."); *Burkett v. Schwendiman*, 773 P.2d 42, 44 (Utah 1989) ("On occasion, we invoke an exception to the mootness doctrine, as when the case presents an issue that affects the public interest, is

adopted a form of the public-interest exception,[21] although the Supreme Court has refused to decide a moot question on the sole ground of public importance.[22]

Courts sometimes apply a mootness exception without expressly naming it. For example, in a 1968 case,[23] the Supreme Court considered whether an expired ten-day injunction constraining the petitioners' right of free speech had been validly imposed. The Court found that the injunction's apparent validity had been the basis for later restrictions on the petitioners' rights by local officials. Therefore, the original injunction still had a substantial effect on the petitioner's First Amendment rights.[24] Although the collateral-consequences exception is never mentioned in the decision, it seems to have been a factor in finding that the case was not truly moot.

Amicable actions or test cases are often intended to test a law's reach or its constitutionality. Federal courts don't bar them when there is a genuine controversy. In the 1850 case of *Lord v. Veazie*,[25] Taney C.J. explained that amicable actions are "approved and

---

likely to recur, and because of the brief time that any one litigant is affected, is capable of evading review."); *Norma Fay Pyles Lynch Family Purpose LLC v. Putnam Cnty.*, 301 S.W.3d 196, 210–11 (Tenn. 2009) ("To guide their discretion, the courts should first address the following threshold considerations: (1) the public interest exception should not be invoked in cases affecting only private rights and claims personal to the parties; (2) the public interest exception should be invoked only with regard to 'issues of great importance to the public and the administration of justice'; (3) the public interest exception should not be invoked if the issue is unlikely to arise in the future; and (4) the public interest exception should not be invoked if the record is inadequate or if the issue has not been effectively addressed in the earlier proceedings.") (internal citations omitted).

21 *See, e.g., Dyer v. SEC*, 266 F.2d 33, 47 (8th Cir. 1959) (agreeing to clarify securities law because "there also is a recognized right of judicial discretion, in the public interest, to deal with the validity or propriety of administrative regulations and actions, where they have justiciably been brought into court, even though they may perhaps have ceased thereafter to have a direct significance in the particular situation").

22 *See Street Emps. Div. 998 v. Wisconsin Emp't Relations Bd.*, 340 U.S. 416, 418 (1951).

23 *Carroll v. President & Comm'rs of Princess Anne*, 393 U.S. 175 (1968).

24 *Id.* at 178.

25 49 U.S. (8 How.) 251 (1850).

encouraged, because they facilitate greatly the administration of justice."[26] In other words, litigants may agree to bring an amicable action or test case to court when they agree on the facts but disagree about how the law applies to them.[27] But the Court in *Veazie* refused to entertain the case because the plaintiff's interests and the defendant's interests were aligned and were in conflict only with third parties.[28]

The earliest amicable action in a federal court, *United States v. Yale Todd*,[29] was brought before the Supreme Court in 1794 ostensibly to settle a matter of veterans' pension rights but also to settle a question of constitutional powers.[30] The Court's minutes reflect that it was docketed as an "amicable action."[31] And in *Pennington v. Coxe*,[32] Marshall C.J. said at the outset of his opinion: "This was a feigned issue, between Tench Coxe a citizen of the state of Pennsylvania, and Edward Pennington a citizen of the state of New York, to try the question, whether sugar actually refined, but not sold and sent out of the manufactory, before the 1st of July 1802, is liable to any duty to the United States, upon being sent out after that day."[33] In these cases, despite the fiction in the issues presented, a true legal controversy existed, so the Court's opinions were not merely advisory and became precedents.

---

26 *Id.* at 254.
27 James E. Pfander & Daniel D. Birk, *Article III Judicial Power, The Adverse-Party Requirement, and Non-Contentious Jurisdiction*, 124 Yale L.J. 1346, 1435 (2015).
28 49 U.S. at 255.
29 *United States v. Yale Todd* (1794), reported in *United States v. Ferreira*, 54 U.S. (1 How.) 40 (1851).
30 *Id.* at 52 (Note by the Chief Justice).
31 *See* "Extract from the Minutes of the Supreme Court, February 17, 1794," in 6 *The Documentary History of the Supreme Court of the United States* 380–81 (Maeva Marcus ed., 1998).
32 6 U.S. (3 Cranch) 33 (1796).
33 *Id.* at 34.

In state courts, amicable actions were commonly identified as such in the 19th century and in the early 20th.[34] But they had largely fallen out of favor by 1950 and had almost vanished by 1970.

Today, on the whole, amicable actions are rarities. Few litigants with true adversity, it seems, want to conduct lawsuits in which they "will not embarrass each other with unnecessary forms or technicalities, and will mutually admit facts which they know to be true, and without requiring proof, and will bring the point in dispute before the court for decision, without subjecting each other to unnecessary expense or delay."[35]

---

34 *See, e.g., State v. McCullough*, 18 P. 756, 757 (Nev. 1888) ("[T]here must be an actual controversy and adverse interests. The amity consists in the manner in which it is brought to issue before the court."); *Martin v. Francis*, 13 Kan. 220, 220 (1874) ("This was an amicable action, instituted in June, 1874, at the instance and under the direction of Ed. Russell, state superintendent of insurance, as a test case. Martin was only a nominal plaintiff."); *Petway v. Hoover*, 12 Tenn. App. 618, 623 (1931) ("[A]n amicable action is not fictitious within the meaning of the rule.").

35 *Veazie*, 49 U.S. at 255.

13. Published vs. Unpublished Opinions

An appellate court is bound only by decisions it has designated as binding—usually by publication—but it may find unpublished decisions persuasive.

In most state and federal jurisdictions, only the more important opinions are officially published. Even though an opinion is released as a slip copy, printed in a book, or otherwise reported, it may remain unofficial if it hasn't been designated for official publication. The judges themselves usually decide whether to have an opinion published. Most appellate judges write dozens of opinions each year, and many of these don't concern an important or novel legal issue. Judges normally won't have those opinions officially published. The printed volume of reports usually show whether the cases it contains have been designated for publication.

By local rule in most jurisdictions, only opinions that have been so designated may serve as precedents.[1] Cases that aren't officially published are only persuasive authority. In some state and federal courts, unpublished cases have no authority at all, and lawyers in those jurisdictions have sometimes been forbidden by rule to even cite an unpublished case. Those rules have been defended on the ground that they prevent giving an unfair advantage to large organizations capable of obtaining and maintaining such opinions. But today most courts explicitly permit citing unpublished opinions without according them binding effect.[2] It's important to know the rules governing publication in a given jurisdiction.

---

[1] *See, e.g., Minor v. Bostwick Labs., Inc.*, 669 F.3d 428, 433 n.6 (4th Cir. 2012) ("Unpublished decisions are . . . not binding upon us."); *Crump v. Lafler*, 657 F.3d 393, 405 (6th Cir. 2011) ("Unpublished decisions in the Sixth Circuit are, of course, not binding precedent on subsequent panels but their reasoning may be instructive or helpful.") (internal quotation marks and citation omitted); *Valentine v. Francis*, 270 F.3d 1032, 1035 (6th Cir. 2001) ("[E]n banc consideration is required to overrule a published opinion of the court.") (quoting 6th Cir. R. 206(c)).

[2] *See* Fed. R. App. P. 32.1 (effective 2007) *and* Committee Notes (noting that an unpublished federal opinion may be cited in federal court "for its persuasive value").

The convention of giving precedential effect only to published opinions arose in part as a matter of practicality: before the digital age, only published decisions were generally accessible, either in libraries or in bound sets. Unpublished opinions were known only by the litigants involved or through privately made copies. Therefore, repeat players and large organizations such as governments or large law firms, which had the means to obtain and maintain such files, enjoyed an advantage because of their greater access to those opinions. But in today's era of electronic storage and availability, virtually all opinions, published or unpublished, are readily available.[3]

In days past, one knew that a case was published because it appeared in the official reports. That is, most courts in the United States once had an official set of reports. Meanwhile, their decisions were published in other places. This is still true of the U.S. Supreme Court: the Court has its reporter of decisions, and its official reports are the bound-in-buckram *United States Reports*. But the Court's decisions are widely available elsewhere: they appear in West Publishing's *Supreme Court Reporter* (both in print and through the online Westlaw service) and the *Lawyer's Edition* reports, now owned by LexisNexis (and also available in print and online). Unless there is a discrepancy between the "official" *U.S. Report* and the version that appears in the West or LexisNexis report, however, one gains nothing by citing the case as it appears in one or the other source. Discrepancies are rare, though they can arise if, for example, the private parties use the Court's Preliminary Prints in their bound volumes instead of waiting for the final edited version of the decision that is in the bound volume of the *U.S. Reports*.

Budgetary pressures, as well as the increasing availability of opinions both through the official websites of the issuing courts and through commercial online services, have led most state courts and the lower federal courts to abandon the practice of

---

3   Kirt Shuldberg, *Digital Influence: Technology and Unpublished Opinions in the Federal Courts of Appeals*, 85 Cal. L. Rev. 541, 544 (1997) ("[O]pinions that are not published in print are nevertheless made available to the public in digital format.").

issuing "official reports." Anyone interested in immediate access to an appellate court's decisions can find them on the court's own website, and it usually takes only a few days for the commercial services to pick them up.

"Unpublished" vs. "nonprecedential" opinions

This issue should not be confused with the distinct question of the status of the so-called unpublished opinion or order. A more accurate term for this group of opinions is *nonprecedential*. Since 2001, West has published the *Federal Appendix*, which provides the full text of these nonprecedential dispositions.[4] They are also available on the court websites, so to call them "unpublished" is to ignore reality. Until 2006, rules in many federal circuit courts forbade lawyers to cite "unpublished" opinions either in briefs or at oral argument. That year, however, the Federal Rules of Appellate Procedure were amended to add Rule 32.1, which states that "[a] court may not prohibit or restrict the citation of federal judicial opinions, orders, judgments, or other written dispositions that have been: (i) designated as 'unpublished,' 'not for publication,' 'nonprecedential,' 'not precedent,' or the like; and (ii) issued on or after January 1, 2007." The Committee Notes to the new rule stress its limited scope. It neither requires nor forbids any court to *use* the "unpublished" format. Nor, importantly, does it say anything about "what effect a court must give to one of its unpublished opinions or to the unpublished opinions of another court."[5]

The Seventh Circuit has implemented Rule 32.1 through a local rule that provides as follows:

> **(b) Publication.** The court may dispose of an appeal by an opinion or an order. Opinions, which may be signed or

---

[4] See Thomson Reuters, *Federal Appendix* (National Reporter System), http://legalsolutions.thomsonreuters.com/law-products/Reporters/Federal-Appendix-National-Reporter-System/p/100000796 (last visited 28 May 2015).

[5] Committee Note to Fed. R. App. P. 32.1, ¶ 2; *see* Amy E. Sloan, *The Dog That Didn't Bark: Stealth Procedures and the Erosion of Stare Decisis in the Federal Courts of Appeals*, 78 Fordham L. Rev. 713, 720–21 (2009) (noting commonalities and variations in circuit courts' rules on precedential effect of prior decisions).

per curiam, are released in printed form, are published in the Federal Reporter, and constitute the law of the circuit. Orders, which are unsigned, are released in photocopied form, are not published in the Federal Reporter, and are not treated as precedents. Every order bears the legend: "Nonprecedential disposition. To be cited only in accordance with Fed. R. App. P. 32.1."

A future court gives whatever effect the issuing court prescribes for its own unpublished opinions.

Other circuits have their own variations on this rule. In the Tenth Circuit, "[t]he citation of unpublished decisions is permitted to the full extent of the authority found in Fed. R. App. P. 32.1," including all unpublished dispositions before 2007; further, "[u]npublished decisions are not precedential, but may be cited for their persuasive value."[6] In the First Circuit, "[a]n unpublished judicial opinion, order, judgment or other written disposition of this court may be cited regardless of the date of issuance. The court will consider such dispositions for their persuasive value but not as binding precedent."[7] The Sixth Circuit simply says that litigants may cite any unpublished opinion, and that Federal Appellate Rule 32.1(a) doesn't apply.[8] The District of Columbia Circuit permits citations to nonprecedential opinions of its own making before 2002 only "when the binding (i.e., the res judicata or law of the case) or preclusive effect of the disposition, rather than its quality as precedent, is relevant."[9] Nonprecedential decisions after that date, however, "may be cited as precedent."[10]

Reporting in our digital age

It used to be said that the value of a precedent could be weakened or even destroyed by the fact that the report of it is meager, obscure, or imperfect, or that two or more reports of the same case differ about the facts involved or the principles laid down by the

---

6   10th Cir. R. 32.1(A).
7   1st Cir. R. 32.1.0(a).
8   6th Cir. R. 32.1(a).
9   D.C. Cir. R. 32.1(b)(1)(A).
10   *Id.*; *see also* 8th Cir. R. 32.1A (similar rule).

court. The job of reporting judicial decisions has evolved over the centuries from a rather haphazard enterprise undertaken by volunteer notetakers to a fully digital, perfectly accurate undertaking. Hence the problem of an inaccurate account of what a court has actually done isn't likely to arise today in any court of record. This issue began to fade with the universal adoption of written opinions; it came close to extinction with the rise of West's National Reporter System and a general push to publish opinions without any editorial discretion on the part of the reporter. Today, when most opinions are posted on the court's own website in digital form, and that same digital file is transmitted to West and other publishers, it has ceased to exist. It is no longer true, as it was in 1912, that "there are many . . . reports of the decisions of most of the courts of last resort" and that it is "usually possible to find several entirely independent reports of any novel or specially important decision."[11]

It is therefore no longer possible to imagine situations such as those that arose in the cases that Henry Campbell Black cited for the proposition that courts have found that their own written opinions "contradict the testimony of the official report."[12] The legal profession is no longer forced to consult "[s]canty, incomplete, or partial reports of cases" whose value must be sharply discounted because "it is not possible adequately to determine what the precedent precisely was."[13] Even as of 1912, when Black was writing, the problem of incomplete or inconsistent reports was becoming rare, given judges' then-developing tendency to provide "detailed recital[s] of the facts" and also "the more important of the precedents cited by counsel."[14] Full reports of cases almost never appear in newspapers anymore either, as was apparently sometimes still the case in Black's time.[15]

---

[11] Henry Campbell Black, *Handbook on the Law of Judicial Precedents* §§ 45–47, at 140–41 (1912). *See generally* William D. Popkin, *Evolution of the Judicial Opinion* (2007).

[12] Black, *Handbook on the Law of Judicial Precedents*, at 141.

[13] *Id.* at 142.

[14] *Id.* at 143–44.

[15] *See id.* at 144–45.

A shrinking number of state courts retain their own reporters and their own style. The remainder have scuttled their official reports, leaving websites or West as the sole reporters of those state courts' decisions.[16] The exact text (which is in the public domain from the standpoint of copyright) shows up more or less instantly on Westlaw, Lexis, and Google Books. This leaves almost no room (as there was in 1912) for two reports of the same case to differ, for example, "in the comparative fullness or brevity of the statement of the facts."[17]

Affirmance without opinion

A new problem has arisen, however, in the wake of surging caseloads and courts' efforts to find efficiencies within the judicial system. For nearly 50 years, for example, the Fifth Circuit has by local rule authorized the practice of "affirmance without opinion."[18] In such a case, the rule states, "the court may, in its discretion, enter either of the following orders (using all-caps as presented here): 'AFFIRMED. See 5th Cir. R. 47.6,' or 'ENFORCED. See 5th Cir. R. 47.6.'" Other circuits have summary-disposition rules, though labeled in various ways.[19] The Ninth Circuit distinguishes among opinions, memoranda, and orders as follows: "A written, reasoned disposition of a case or motion which is designated as an opinion under Circuit Rule 36-2 is an OPINION of the Court. It may be an authored opinion or a per curiam opinion. A written, reasoned disposition of a case or motion which isn't intended for publication under Circuit Rule 36-2 is a MEMORANDUM. Any

---

16   Popkin, *Evolution of the Judicial Opinion* at 104–05.
17   Black, *Handbook on the Law of Judicial Precedents*, at 141.
18   *See* 5th Cir. R. 47.6.
19   *See, e.g.*, 1st Cir. R. 27.0(c) (motion for summary disposition must be "promptly filed when the occasion appears"); 2d Cir. R. 32.1.1 (summary orders); 3d Cir. R. 27.4 (laying out use of summary action); 4th Cir. R. 27(f) ("The Court may also sua sponte summarily dispose of any appeal at any time."); 8th Cir. R. 47A; 10th Cir. R. 27.2 (summary disposition); 11th Cir. R. 42-4 (empowering court to dismiss any appeal that is "frivolous and entirely without merit"). *But see United States v. Fortner*, 455 F.3d 752, 754 (7th Cir. 2006) ("Motions for summary affirmance generally should be confined to certain limited circumstances."). *See generally* 28 U.S.C. § 2106 (2005) (authorizing federal circuit courts to issue rulings "as may be just under the circumstances").

other disposition of a matter before the Court is an ORDER."[20] This implies strongly, and practice verifies, that an order does not reveal the court's reasoning, even if the order has the effect of disposing of the appeal. Commentary in response to Federal Rule of Appellate Procedure 32.1, which forbids courts to restrict the citation of anything the court issues, makes it clear that many courts of appeals regard dispositions that are unaccompanied by a reasoned explanation as nonprecedential.[21] These are decisions rendered with little if any explanation. Hence they aren't regarded by the issuing courts as worthy of precedential status—even though counsel are entitled to refer to them, and they can be important in giving rise to claim or issue preclusion.

The modern situation

The traditional view that unpublished opinions lack authoritative value and should not even be cited by counsel—a sort of "see no evil, cite no evil"—has softened considerably. Now in the federal system, unpublished opinions are generally citable "for their persuasive value."[22] In declining to publish, the court (once again) may be sending various signals—perhaps "this one is very easy and routine and doesn't require much analysis," but also quite possibly "we're not sure about this one." As a result and as with summary decisions, a later court may be leery of giving much weight to unpublished opinions.[23] But in this realm, conventions haven't settled into a fully established pattern.

---

20 *See* 9th Cir. R. 36-1.

21 *See, e.g.*, 1st Cir. R. 32.1.0(a) ("The court will consider such dispositions for their persuasive value but not as binding precedent."); 2d Cir. R. 32.1.1 (detailing the use and nonprecedential effect of summary orders); 7th Cir. R. 32.1(b) ("Orders, which are unsigned, are released in photocopied form, are not published in the Federal Reporter, and are not treated as precedents.").

22 Fed. R. App. P. 32.1 advisory committee's note to 2006 amendment.

23 *Compare Anastasoff v. United States*, 223 F.3d 898, 899 (8th Cir. 2000) (holding a local rule that unpublished opinions aren't precedential to be unconstitutional), *opinion vacated as moot on reh'g en banc*, 235 F.3d 1054 (8th Cir. 2000), *with Hart v. Massanari*, 266 F.3d 1155 (9th Cir. 2001) (upholding as constitutional a local rule that unpublished opinions aren't precedential); *see also* Lauren K. Robel, *The Myth of the Disposable Opinion: Unpublished Opinions and Government Litigants in the United States Courts of Appeals*, 87 Mich. L. Rev. 940, 946-55 (1989); William L. Reynolds & William M. Richman, *The*

Remember, though, that there's an interesting disagreement about whether federal courts may legitimately issue "unpublished" decisions at all. The practice has been severely criticized[24] and, in one case, declared unconstitutional.[25] (That holding was vacated by the en banc Eighth Circuit and the case then dismissed as moot.) As things stand today, no case has suggested that the practice is unconstitutional or that courts cannot follow their own rules and precedents on the matter.

Non-Precedential Precedent—Limited Publication and No-Citation Rules in the United States Courts of Appeals, 78 Colum. L. Rev. 1167 (1978).

24 *National Classification Comm. v. United States*, 765 F.2d 164, 173 n.2 (D.C. Cir. 1985) (statement of Wald J.); Martha J. Dragich, *Will the Federal Courts of Appeals Perish if They Publish? Or Does the Declining Use of Opinions to Explain and Justify Judicial Decisions Pose a Greater Threat?*, 44 Am. U. L. Rev. 757, 802 (1995) ("The courts of appeals' admittedly legitimate concerns with increasing caseloads do not warrant practices that threaten the development of a coherent body of law and fundamentally alter our appellate traditions."); Lawrence J. Fox, *Those Unpublished Opinions: An Appropriate Expedience or an Abdication of Responsibility*, 32 Hofstra L. Rev. 1215 (2004) (asking "whether judges are acting ethically when they write opinions that they then designate as unciteable"); *Plumley v. Austin*, 135 S.Ct. 828, 831 (2015) (Thomas J. dissenting from denial of cert.) ("It is hard to imagine a reason that the Court of Appeals would not have published this opinion except to avoid creating binding law for the Circuit.").

25 *Anastasoff*, 223 F.3d at 899 (nonpublication "expands the judicial power beyond the limits set by Article III by allowing us complete discretion to determine which judicial decisions will bind us and which will not"). *But see Hart*, 266 F.3d at 1175 ("*Anastasoff* erred in holding that, as a constitutional matter, courts of appeal may not decide which of their opinions will be deemed binding on themselves and the courts below them.").

14. Syllabus and Headnotes

The syllabus or headnote for a reported case summarizes, for the reader's convenience, the point or points decided. Whether prepared by the court itself or by an official or unofficial reporter, it is not normally part of the decision.

Rarely today is a reported judicial opinion not accompanied by editorial enhancements. Attorneys and law students are almost always greeted by the familiar sight of a syllabus and headnotes preceding the text of an opinion.

A syllabus is a synopsis of the opinion written by a court clerk, by an editor at a commercial publisher, or less often by the writing judge.[1] The syllabus typically contains a distillation of the material facts, the points decided, and the legal reasoning underlying those conclusions.[2] Some publishers cap their summaries at a single paragraph, while others devote a paragraph to each topic discussed in the opinion. The *United States Reports*, the official publication of all U.S. Supreme Court decisions, specifically marks the summary as a syllabus, whereas most commercial reporters provide an unlabeled summary set apart from the opinion.

Reading the syllabus is a good way to preview the issues and conclusions that will be covered in greater depth in the opinion. Yet the syllabus is generally not considered part of the law. It is only an interpretation of the statements made in the opinion and cannot alter the scope of the decision. As Frankfurter J. pointedly wrote in 1955: "[C]ases hold only what they decide, not what slipshod or ignorant headnote writers state them to decide; . . . decisions are one thing, gratuitous remarks another."[3]

---

1 William A. Hilyerd, *Using the Law Library: A Guide for Educators Part VI: Working with Judicial Opinions and Other Primary Sources*, 35 J.L. & Educ. 67, 69–70 (2006).

2 Henry Campbell Black, *Handbook on the Law of Judicial Precedents* § 14, at 53–54, 58–60 (1912).

3 *Bisso v. Inland Waterways Corp.*, 349 U.S. 85, 100 (1955) (Frankfurter J. dissenting); *see Law Books and Their Use* 27 (3d ed. 1925) ("The headnotes are ordinarily the work of the reporter . . . . The headnote is no part of the decision, and is not to be taken as authoritative.").

Courts have consistently rebuffed litigants' attempts to ascribe precedential value to statements in the syllabus. The leading case on the issue is *United States v. Detroit Timber & Lumber Co.*[4] There, the Supreme Court dismissed counsel's argument that the issue in the case was definitively settled by an assertion from the syllabus of an earlier Supreme Court case: "[T]he headnote is not the work of the court, nor does it state its decision.... It is simply the work of the reporter, [it] gives his understanding of the decision, and [it] is prepared for the convenience of the profession in the examination of the reports."[5] *Detroit Timber* has since become one of the most frequently cited Supreme Court cases, since it appears as a note at the beginning of every Supreme Court case: "The syllabus constitutes no part of the opinion of the Court but has been prepared by the Reporter of Decisions for the convenience of the reader. See *United States v. Detroit Timber & Lumber Co.*, 200 U.S. 321, 337 (1906)."

Contrarian stances

On the other hand, a few states have adopted the position that the syllabus *should* maintain some semblance of precedent. A Kansas statute requires a judge delivering a court's opinion to prepare a syllabus discussing "points of law arising from the facts in the case, that have been determined by the court."[6] The statute continues: "[T]he syllabus shall be submitted to the judges concurring therein for revisal before publication thereof; and it shall be inserted in the book of reports without alteration, unless by consent of the judges concurring therein."[7] The Kansas Supreme Court treats those syllabi as binding—indeed, as articulating holdings.[8]

---

4 200 U.S. 321 (1906).
5 *Id.* at 337.
6 Kan. Stat. Ann. § 20-203.
7 *Id.*
8 See *Bonanza, Inc. v. McLean*, 747 P.2d 792, 800 (Kan. 1987) ("In *Sykes v. Perry*, ... it was held in Syllabus ¶ 2 that the provisions not specifically mentioned in a written contract but which are essential in carrying out its purposes may be implied and, when properly implied, are as binding as if written therein.") (internal citation omitted).

Ohio, West Virginia, and Minnesota have similar rules.[9] Ohio is the most extreme example. Ohio state law requires that any legal points decided in an Ohio Supreme Court case must be found in a syllabus.[10] It is the syllabus, and not the whole opinion, that carries precedential weight. West Virginia takes a similar, though less drastic, approach. There, the syllabus is a constitutional obligation.[11] It typically sets forth the important points of law, leaving discussion of factual issues to the opinion.[12] In West Virginia, both the syllabus and the opinion carry precedential authority, and litigants are free to cite either.[13]

There is even a small contingent who believe that the syllabus should be the *only* part of a case that has precedential authority. One commentator jocosely argues that such an approach would make the practice of law more efficient and give the average citizen a better understanding of legal issues.[14]

Although the vast majority of courts still maintain that syllabi lack the force of precedent, they serve as a valuable resource for lawyers and nonlawyers alike.

The sequelae

Following the syllabus or summary are usually headnotes, anywhere from one or two to several dozen. The headnotes can serve a bit like an index by helping readers find the part of the opinion relevant to their purpose. Typically, the headnotes are numbered, and the editor or publisher adds corresponding numbers in the opinion at the beginning of the paragraph where each

---

9 See Peter W. Martin, *Reconfiguring Law Reports and the Concept of Precedent for a Digital Age*, 53 Vill. L. Rev. 1, 12 n.62 (2008).

10 See *State v. Wilson*, 388 N.E.2d 745, 751 (Ohio 1979); *Smith v. Klem*, 450 N.E.2d 1171, 1173 (Ohio 1983).

11 See W. Va. Const. art. VIII, § 4 ("[I]t shall be the duty of the court to prepare a syllabus of the points adjudicated in each case in which an opinion is written and in which a majority of the justices thereof concurred, which shall be prefixed to the published report of the case.").

12 See *Koonce v. Doolittle*, 37 S.E. 644, 645 (W. Va. 1900).

13 See *State v. McKinley*, 764 S.E.2d 303, 309–13 (W. Va. 2014) (explaining history and current law of precedential value of opinions and syllabi from West Virginia courts).

14 Gil Grantmore [pseudonym], *The Headnote*, 5 Green Bag 2d 157, 162 (2002).

point is discussed. Especially in a long opinion, where only part of the legal discussion is relevant to your research, headnotes can be very useful locating tools. But once again, they are no substitute for reading the opinion.

Nor are they considered primary authority. As a popular treatise said in the early 20th century: "It is obvious that headnotes cannot as a rule have any binding authority, for this is inherent only in the decision itself."[15] Even when the judge responsible for the opinion has written the headnote, it is not considered law.[16] A central problem with headnotes is that they tend to be "overloaded with dicta" and underloaded with holdings.[17]

In older cases the headnotes are followed by argument of counsel. A reader of these cases must be careful to distinguish those arguments from the opinion of the court. Obviously, an argument has no precedential value. But sometimes it may give some insight into the background of the case and help convey a better understanding of the court's decision. In a few older English cases, the report consists of almost nothing but the argument of counsel. A famous example is the contracts case *Raffles v. Wichelhaus*,[18] in which the court abruptly stops an arguing lawyer and declares—without any explanation—that there must be judgment for the defendants. Although almost all modern case reports have an opinion, they usually omit the arguments of the lawyers and simply list their names. Casebooks usually cut out all references to the lawyers and their arguments.

In many older cases a separate statement of facts written by the reporter—not the court—comes next. If the statement of facts wasn't written by the court, it must be viewed cautiously. One illustration is another famous contracts case, *Hadley v. Baxendale*,[19] which concerns the rule for consequential damages. A critical issue in *Hadley* was whether the defendant shipping company's

---

15   *Brief Making and the Use of Law Books* 31 (Roger W. Cooley ed., 5th ed 1926).
16   *Id.* at 356.
17   *Id.* at 357.
18   [1864] 159 Eng. Rep. 375; 2 H.&C. 906 (Ex.).
19   [1854] 156 Eng. Rep. 145; 9 Ex. 341.

employee knew that the plaintiff's mill was stopped because of a broken crankshaft. According to the reporter's recitation of the facts, the plaintiffs told the shipper's employee that it was stopped. But the writing judge seems to have assumed that the shipper's employee didn't know that the mill was stopped. The lesson here is to be careful with facts that are not part of the opinion itself.

B. Weight of Decisions

15. Binding Decisions

Vertical precedents are absolutely binding. Not all horizontal precedents have the same value or carry the same weight. Various circumstances may strengthen or weaken the force of a horizontal precedent, including the court's expertise, the novelty of the issue, the extent of the analysis, and the degree to which the decision has been followed by later courts.

The weight that a court is to place on a particular precedent is, in the 19th-century words of Miller J. of the U.S. Supreme Court, "often a question of no little anxiety."[1] As always, much depends on context. The most influential cases, of course, are those that establish the law in the court's jurisdiction. A decision rendered by an appellate court is normally binding on future panels of that court (unless it is a high court) and on all lower courts within the appellate court's jurisdiction. Judges are obliged to follow vertical precedents even when they disagree with the reasoning. When a court is presented with a case that can be resolved by a legal rule established in an earlier binding case, the only question is how to apply that rule to the facts of the current case. And even when no earlier court has addressed the precise legal question presented, earlier cases erect the legal architecture under which the new question must be resolved.

When dealing with binding vertical precedent, a court has no room to decide how much weight or value to give each case. Normally, all binding precedent is due equal respect. For example, a federal circuit court presented with two seemingly conflicting U.S. Supreme Court precedents has a duty to reconcile them (see § 36). The lower court isn't authorized to simply pick the more persuasive rationale, or defer to the older or newer case. Instead, it must seek a legal rule that gives effect to both holdings.

---

[1] Letter of Justice Samuel F. Miller to John F. Dillon, 16 Nov. 1885, *reproduced in* John F. Dillon, *The Laws and Jurisprudence of England and America* 261, 261 (1894).

Some have argued that opinions rendered under certain procedural postures should be accorded less weight even if they would otherwise constitute binding vertical precedent.[2] For example, it is sometimes asserted that legal rulings rendered when a case is in an interlocutory posture are of less precedential weight than those made on final judgment.[3] While it is true that "the findings of fact and conclusions of law made by a court granting a preliminary injunction are not binding at trial on the merits,"[4] there is little if any reason to believe that questions of pure law resolved in an appeal from the grant or denial of a preliminary injunction don't have any precedential effect. Indeed, the Supreme Court has sometimes cited legal conclusions rendered in interlocutory appeals without ever suggesting that they are due less weight.[5]

The question is especially complicated when dealing with horizontal precedent. For high courts and intermediate appellate courts sitting en banc, stare decisis isn't a procrustean bed. They are free to reconsider their precedents and determine whether they are still good law. The factors that courts consider when they contemplate overruling a prior holding include whether the precedent has proved unworkable as a practical matter, whether the precedent has generated significant reliance interests, whether intervening changes in doctrine have undermined the prior rule, and whether changes in fact (or understandings of fact) have eroded the prior rule's assumptions.

Sometimes a judicial opinion deserves more than just a close reading. Sometimes, if the stakes are high or if you're not quite sure about what the opinion really means, you may want to question just how binding this precedent should be. While many cases are technically binding, they can nonetheless carry greater or lesser authority—and one with greater authority will probably

---

2   *See* Henry Campbell Black, *Handbook on the Law of Judicial Precedents* § 25, at 83–85 (1912).

3   *Id.*

4   *University of Tex. v. Camenisch*, 451 U.S. 390, 395 (1981).

5   *See, e.g., Burwell v. Hobby Lobby Stores, Inc.*, 134 S.Ct. 2751, 2779 (2014) (relying on the analysis regarding the scope of the Religious Freedom Restoration Act in *Gonzales v. O Centro Espirita Beneficente Uniao do Vegetal*, 546 U.S. 418, 430–31 (2006), even though *Gonzales* was an appeal from a preliminary injunction).

stand well into the future, while a weak one may be overruled or distinguished in later opinions until it becomes more an exception than a rule.

The first thing to do is to go outside the opinion itself. Check the authorities that the court invoked in the opinion—the cases and statutes cited and the secondary sources quoted. Do these authorities relied on really stand for the propositions attributed to them? Does the court fairly distinguish the authorities it finds not controlling? Are there any relevant authorities that the court didn't discuss?

If you find that the court has treated prior authority fairly, you can be more confident about the meaning and precedential value of its present decision.

The task is harder when the court's treatment of authority seems disingenuous or worse. What then? What was the court trying to do? Did it mean to introduce a new principle that would erode existing law? Did it mean to maintain the general course of the law but find a way to reach a particular outcome in this case? Or did it just not know what it was doing? It's not a trivial question because you need to know the answer in order to predict how the precedent will affect the outcome of future cases. Unfortunately, there are no sure guides.

Time and again you'll find that studying the authorities cited in an opinion leaves you less confident of the court's treatment. But that's not always a bad thing. Those doubts are fair ground for arguing the opinion's meaning—and especially its breadth—both to the court that rendered it and to other courts.

Other things can affect the precedential value of a holding as well. A plenary decision is more likely, other things being equal, to bear greater persuasive force than a summary disposition. That's not to say that summary dispositions never win admirers. Sometimes a line of reasoning can be teased from a summary disposition and appear persuasive, even obvious. But there's no guarantee that future lawyers and courts will undertake the work, and even if they do they might well hesitate to give the decision much weight: the unwillingness of the writing court to say much may signal a tentativeness about the conclusion that the later court may take as a cue for caution. Burger C.J. explained the Supreme Court's practice with respect to summary dispositions in an oft-cited concurrence: "When we summarily affirm, without opinion, the judgment of a three-judge District Court we affirm the judgment but not necessarily the reasoning by which it was reached."[6] That settles the case at hand, but it doesn't necessarily signal any change in the applicable law, Burger warned: "Indeed, upon fuller consideration of an issue under plenary review, the Court has not hesitated to discard a rule which a line of summary affirmances may appear to have established."[7] (See §§ 21, 46.)

An opinion is stronger authority for a point of decision that is fully explained. The more thoroughly an opinion explains its holding, the less likely it should be overruled or distinguished on the ground that its holding was not thoroughly considered. Judges aren't likely to contradict a precedent just because they disagree with its reasoning. They are much more willing to do so if they think the prior court simply failed to consider the point that persuades them. As the West Virginia Supreme Court has observed, "a precedent-creating opinion that contains no extensive analysis of an important issue is more vulnerable to being overruled than an opinion which demonstrates that the court was aware of conflicting decisions and gave at least some persuasive discussion as to why the old law must be changed."[8] Other jurisdictions have expressed similar views.[9]

---

6   *Fusari v. Steinberg*, 419 U.S. 379, 391 (1975) (Burger C.J. concurring).

7   *Id.* (citing, for example, *Reynolds v. Sims*, 377 U.S. 533 (1964)).

8   *State v. Guthrie*, 461 S.E.2d 163, 185 n.28 (W. Va. 1995).

9   See *Brower v. State*, 969 P.2d 42, 59 (Wash. 1998) (en banc) ("Overruling a prior decision should not be undertaken lightly. This is especially true where the precedential case is recent and the varying views on the issue were thoroughly explored in the case.") (citation omitted); *Santow v. Ullman*, 166 A.2d 135, 140 (Del. 1960) ("We are quite aware that the exception to the general rule has stood, almost unchallenged, for a very long time. But we cannot find that any real examination of the logic of the rule was ever made in any of our decisions."); *State v. California Co.*, 56 N.W.2d 762, 763 (N.D. 1953) ("Only one inference can be drawn from a review of the former decisions announced by this court, and that inference is that they were arrived at after thorough deliberation. The decisions heretofore rendered by this court were reasoned conclusions backed by authority and considered with care. No cogent reason has been

Precedential holdings in their infancy

A legal decision striking out on new terrain is like a newborn animal: alive and full of promise, but potentially shaky on its legs and susceptible to predation. That is, a fledgling decision on a novel question often has less precedential potency than a more aged one. When a decision has just been issued, its reasoning hasn't been assessed by other courts, and the ramifications of its holding haven't been felt. Unlike decisions entrenched over time, a decision just rendered won't have created many reliance interests, so a higher court might be less hesitant to snuff it out. That's exactly what happened with *National League of Cities v. Usery*.[10] There, the U.S. Supreme Court held that the Commerce Clause didn't authorize Congress to enforce the minimum-wage and overtime provisions of the Fair Labor Standards Act against the states in areas of traditional government functions.[11] That ruling left certain state employees unprotected by the FLSA. But the Court reversed course a mere nine years later.[12] In doing so, it directly attacked *Usery* for its novelty. It observed that in the years following *Usery*, the distinction between traditional and nontraditional government employees had proved unworkable and led to inconsistent results.[13] So in part because of its novelty, this precedent found itself struck down before it gained much force or was thoroughly examined by lower courts.

Not all novel decisions are so fragile. Indeed, if an opinion's reasoning is powerful and its analysis cogent, it may be compelling from birth—think Athena, born fully armed from the head of Zeus. *Strickland v. Washington*[14] provides a famous example. In *Strickland*, the Court held that defense counsel in a criminal case may be ineffective for failing to provide reasonably competent

---

presented sustaining the plaintiffs' conclusion that the former decisions were erroneous.").

10   426 U.S. 833 (1976).
11   *Id.* at 853–55.
12   *Garcia v. San Antonio Metro. Transit Auth.*, 469 U.S. 528, 546–47 (1985).
13   *Id.*; *see also United States v. Scott*, 437 U.S. 82 (1978) (overruling *United States v. Jenkins*, 420 U.S. 358 (1975)).
14   466 U.S. 668 (1984).

representation and provided a framework for analyzing attorney competence.[15] That commodious view of the Sixth Amendment right to counsel was certainly novel, so *Strickland* broke new ground. Yet it immediately took hold as a powerful precedent, surviving to this day substantially unaltered. In the 20 years since, it has been cited over 200,000 times. Novelty isn't always a bad thing.

These examples demonstrate that not all novel cases can be treated alike. Each must be evaluated, perhaps more closely than a more entrenched case, for its logical coherence and likely strength. That's particularly true because courts, too, will take that approach in assessing a novel precedent.

Outlier cases

A single or isolated decision on any given point of law isn't regarded as possessing the same authority or conclusive effect as a series of decisions on that point, unless it has long been acquiesced in or stood unchallenged. Much as a leading case gains persuasive force by virtue of being widely followed, a solitary decision earns less respect because of its status as a historical anomaly. It might be solitary because it stated a legal principle so elementary and fundamental that the question has never been litigated again. Generally speaking, when a case is never (or rarely) followed, there's cause to be suspicious.

That's not always so. *Marbury v. Madison*[16] was in a sense a "solitary decision" as well as being the archetype of a "leading case." But almost universally when presented with a solitary case, a court will give it less weight.

For example, the U.S. Supreme Court in *Jones v. Alfred H. Mayer Co.*[17] held for the first time that Congress can use its enforcement power under the Thirteenth Amendment to prohibit private racial discrimination in the sale of property—a holding in deep tension with its previous decision in *Hodges v. United States*.[18]

---

15   *Id.* at 686–87.
16   5 U.S. (1 Cranch) 137 (1803).
17   392 U.S. 409 (1968).
18   203 U.S. 1 (1906).

Yet *Hodges* was overruled cursorily, in a footnote, without any discussion of stare decisis at all.[19] That's because *Hodges* had rarely been followed in the 60 years since being decided. So the case hadn't created significant reliance interests, hadn't garnered the acquiescence of the political branches, and hadn't been tested in the crucible of the adversarial process.

An opinion that has in fact induced considerable reliance interests will often receive more respect than one that hasn't. Sometimes, as we have said, having a settled answer to a particular social-coordination problem is more important than the nuances of whether it is "correct." Sometimes the degree of reliance interests generated by a decision correlates to its subject matter. For example, contract law often creates high reliance interests (e.g., Is this standard contract language enforceable? How will it be interpreted?). Meanwhile, evidence law may induce reliance less often (e.g., the admissibility of hearsay in court proceedings years after the fact isn't likely to alter a speaker's behavior).[20] The more it can be said that a precedent serves the reliance goals underlying the doctrine, the more gravitational pull it is likely to exert (see § 51).

Sometimes an outlier case is anomalous only because it involves a seldom-tested theory. In the Fifth Circuit case of *Rodrigue v. Rodrigue*,[21] the noted painter George Rodrigue claimed that under federal copyright law, Louisiana family law couldn't transfer half his copyright interests in his paintings to his soon-to-be ex-wife. That is, the paintings he created during his marriage shouldn't have been treated as community property because of § 201(e) of the Copyright Act. That provision restricts the government's power to transfer rights under a copyright:

> When an individual author's ownership of a copyright, or of any of the exclusive rights under a copyright, has not previously been transferred voluntarily by that individual author,

---

19 *Jones*, 392 U.S. at 443 n.78.
20 *Payne v. Tennessee*, 501 U.S. 808, 828 (1991) (noting that stare decisis is at its pinnacle of importance when proprietary and contractual rights are involved, together with their attendant reliance interests—the opposite being true in cases where only procedural and evidentiary rules are involved).
21 218 F.3d 432 (5th Cir. 2000).

> no action by any governmental body or other official or organization purporting to seize, expropriate, transfer, or exercise rights of ownership with respect to the copyright, or any of the exclusive rights under a copyright, shall be given effect under this title....[22]

Even so, the court held that the copyright interests were nevertheless community property on this rather abstract reasoning: "George's... contention does not persuade us that allowing differing state laws—in particular, community property laws that differ from state to state among the eight that presently have some version of such marital property regimes—to apply just to the economic benefit derived from copyrights will somehow damage the federal interests in predictability and uniformity."[23] The decision has been criticized by many commentators and seriously questioned by a Supreme Court Justice.[24] Yet the proposition for which the case stands appears never again to have been tested in any federal case. It has been cited only once, in a district-court opinion, where it wasn't substantively discussed.[25] So it remains a solitary case.

To be sure, an outlier is sometimes right. Courts aren't immune from groupthink. Consider *Lexecon Inc. v. Milberg Weiss Bershad Hynes & Lerach*.[26] Every circuit to interpret the federal statute authorizing the transfer of cases for coordinated *pretrial* proceedings read the law to allow the receiving court to hold on to the case *through trial*. Only one judge in dissent[27] hewed to the contrary view before the Supreme Court took up the matter and enforced the statute's plain meaning. Still, when courts repeatedly arrive at the same destination by means of their own independent judgment, that tends to command attention. Indeed, a decision

---

22 17 U.S.C. § 201(e).

23 *Rodrigue*, 218 F.3d at 441 (footnote omitted).

24 *See* Antonin Scalia & Bryan A. Garner, *Making Your Case: The Art of Persuading Judges* 47–51 (2008).

25 *Dagel v. Resident News, LLC*, No. 3:11-CV-663-L, 2012 WL 2068727, at *7 (N.D. Tex. 8 June 2012).

26 523 U.S. 26 (1998).

27 *See In re American Cont'l Corp./Lincoln Sav. & Loan Sec. Litig.*, 102 F.3d 1524, 1540 (9th Cir. 1996) (Kozinski J. dissenting).

tested over time and found to be sound by successive courts may even come to stand for a proposition or doctrine broader than the initial decision X, and sometimes discussed in shorthand as the doctrine of X. To name just a few, *Erie Railroad v. Tompkins*,[28] *Chevron, U.S.A. v. Natural Resources Defense Council*,[29] and *Teague v. Lane*[30] each spawned entire areas of law invariably referred to by the original case's name.

---

28   304 U.S. 64 (1938).
29   467 U.S. 837 (1984).
30   489 U.S. 288 (1989).

16. Nonbinding Decisions as Persuasive Authority

When an earlier decision is cited not as a binding precedent but as persuasive authority, its value is enhanced by sound, acute, and logical reasoning; by internal evidence that the case received the careful consideration of the court; and by the citation of pertinent authorities. Its value is diminished by the absence of any of these characteristics.

Persuasive, nonbinding authority may help convince a court to adopt a particular position. It may come in the form not only of cases, but also of topical law-review articles, relevant treatises, or Restatements. Not all authority, caselaw or otherwise, carries equal weight in the case-deciding function. Courts may perceive authority as being compelling (or not) depending on many factors. Most significantly, its relevance and sound reasoning will affect the weight it receives, but so too may the reputation of the author or issuing court, the extent to which the authority has been cited and followed elsewhere, and the extent to which the authority is founded on solid principles, whether scientific, legal, or other. The degree to which the court agreed on the reasoning and the result may also affect a case's practical significance.[1]

While binding caselaw must be followed,[2] persuasive caselaw is "not binding on a court but is nonetheless entitled to respect and careful consideration."[3] A well-reasoned relevant case from a neighboring jurisdiction—or even dicta from cases within the jurisdiction—might provide persuasive authority. Persuasive authority may influence or guide an outcome. Even though a court

---

[1] *Maloney v. Conroy*, 545 A.2d 1059, 1060–61 (Conn. 1988) (declining to follow *Dillon v. Legg*, 441 P.2d 912 (Cal. 1968), in medical malpractice context, noting that "a bare majority" of the court recognized claim for emotional distress to a bystander not in danger), *overruled by Clohessy v. Bachelor*, 675 A.2d 852, 860 (Conn. 1996), *as recognized in Squeo v. Norwalk Hosp. Ass'n*, 113 A.3d 932, 940 (Conn. 2015); *see also* Frederick Schauer, *Authority and Authorities*, 94 Va. L. Rev. 1931, 1945–46 (2008) (commenting on the persuasive value of consensus).

[2] *Black's Law Dictionary* 1366 (Bryan A. Garner ed., 10th ed. 2014). *See generally* Schauer, *Authority and Authorities*, 94 Va. L. Rev. at 1940–41.

[3] *Black's Law Dictionary* at 1367.

needn't follow it, the court may choose to do so if the case is well reasoned and seems to achieve a just result.

Although courts often follow persuasive authority when the litigants cite nonbinding materials, they are just as likely to do so on their own initiative. Courts don't typically take the legal analysis in the litigants' briefs as the last word on the subject but as a starting point for their own legal research. The reasons courts offer for doing this vary widely. At times (perhaps more commonly in the past than now) the court invokes the expertise of a specialized tribunal (see § 27) or of a particular judge (see § 28).[4] Even though such on-the-record praise of the judge or court that rendered a persuasive decision still occurs,[5] courts today are more likely to point to less subjective, more tangible rationales. For example, one state high court may adopt another state high court's analysis of the latter state's own statute if it is "substantially similar" to the first state's law.[6] Lower state courts also look to the decisions of the other states' high courts when examining similar statutes.[7] The same holds when another state high court has examined similar

---

4   *See, e.g., Fulmer v. Southern Ry.*, 45 S.E. 196, 201 (S.C. 1903) (in banc) ("[W]hile, of course, it has no binding force here as an authority, it is persuasive because of the learning and ability of the court which rendered it, and because of the force of the reasons given in support of it."); *see also* American Law Institute and Am. Bar Ass'n Continuing Legal Educ., *Eminent Domain and Land Valuation Litigation Appellate Practice*, C709 ALI-ABA 149, 187 (1992) (recommending that appellate attorneys provide persuasive authority when discussing a new question in the jurisdiction and that when doing so they "rely[] primarily on case law from the courts with the weightiest reputations").

5   *See, e.g., People v. Thoro Prods. Co.*, 70 P.3d 1188, 1208–09 (Colo. 2003) (en banc) ("The *Harmon* case is persuasive because its author is an administrative law judge who specializes in environmental cases.").

6   *See, e.g., Beneficial Consumer Disc. Co. v. Vukman*, 77 A.3d 547, 552 (Pa. 2013) ("While the New Jersey Court's decision is not binding, it is persuasive because the pre-foreclosure notice statute at issue in *Guillaume* is substantially similar to Act 91.").

7   *See, e.g., Smith & Spidahl Enters., Inc. v. Lee*, 557 N.W.2d 865, 869 (Wis. Ct. App. 1996) ("The reasoning of the Iowa court in *Creston* is persuasive because the Iowa statutes are identical to the Wisconsin statutes relating to the perfection of security interests through financing statements."); *Hollywood Television Serv., Inc. v. Picture Waves, Inc.*, 136 N.E.2d 617, 619 (Ohio Ct. App. 1954) (per curiam) ("The opinion in *Drake v. National Bank of Commerce*, 168 Va. 230, 190 S.E. 302, 109 A.L.R. 1517, is persuasive because of the soundness with which the statute there involved is discussed as it relates to an interpretation of the word 'creditors' as found in the Act.").

facts.[8] Federal courts similarly draw from the decisions of other federal courts outside their own circuit when there are factual similarities between a cited case and the case at hand,[9] or similar legal approaches taken by two different circuits. They may even go further than that and refer to decisions of tribunals outside the United States.[10]

Courts aren't limited to these rationales, of course; they might follow another court's decision simply because it makes sense[11] or convincingly interprets higher authority.[12] Courts may also point to the logic that can be gleaned from a group of cases in labeling them persuasive authority.[13] Courts may be particularly likely

---

8   *See, e.g., Ingram v. State*, 50 A.3d 1127, 1134–35 (Md. 2012) ("The analysis in *Grillot v. State*, 353 Ark. 294, 107 S.W.3d 136 (2003), although an opinion of a sister state's high court, is persuasive because the case presents a similar scenario to Ingram's and provides additional, sound guidance for the proper exercise of discretion in similar contexts.").

9   *See, e.g., Catudal v. Browne*, No. 2:12-cv-00197, 2012 WL 1068530, at *4 (S.D. Ohio 29 Mar. 2012) ("[V]arious federal courts have held that guardians ad litem are not state actors for the purposes of § 1983. Such authority is persuasive because, similar to a private attorney's duty to his or her client, a guardian ad litem owes his or her undivided loyalty to the minor, not the state.") (internal quotation marks and citations omitted).

10 *See, e.g., Roper v. Simmons*, 543 U.S. 551, 575–78 (2005); *Olympic Airways v. Husain*, 540 U.S. 644, 658 (2004) (Scalia J. dissenting). *See generally* Rex D. Glensy, *Which Countries Count?*: Lawrence v. Texas *and the Selection of Foreign Persuasive Authority*, 45 Va. J. Int'l L. 357 (2005), for an overview of this practice.

11 *See United States v. Jones*, 260 B.R. 415, 419 (E.D. Mich. 2000) ("This decision is persuasive, because it rests on principles that make sense—bankruptcy courts are to administer bankruptcy estates, not property which lies outside the estate.").

12 *See, e.g., Schrader v. Hamilton*, 959 F. Supp. 1205, 1211 (C.D. Cal. 1997) (finding Fifth Circuit's analysis "persuasive because it simply tailors the 'zone of interests' test articulated in *Association of Data Processing Serv. Org. v. Camp*, 397 U.S. 150, 153, 90 S.Ct. 827, 829, 25 L.Ed.2d 184 (1970), to the ERISA context"); *see also* Chad Flanders, *Toward a Theory of Persuasive Authority*, 62 Okla. L. Rev. 55 (2009) (examining the rather straightforward idea that the "bindingness" of persuasive sources lies in their ability to persuade); Clyde H. Hamilton, *Effective Appellate Brief Writing*, 50 S.C. L. Rev. 581, 588 (1999) (advising appellate attorneys to use persuasive authority "that contains a particularly scholarly discourse upon the issue").

13 *See, e.g., United Egg Producers v. Standard Brands, Inc.*, 44 F.3d 940, 943 (11th Cir. 1995).

to cite persuasive sources when confronting a novel or difficult issue.[14]

Sometimes a federal circuit court must take sides in a circuit split—or even create one. Although a circuit court often expresses hesitation in creating a split,[15] sometimes there is no hand-wringing.[16] In choosing sides, the deciding court will typically state on the record that such a split exists and then explain its decision. The court might take the time to outline how its own earlier decisions accord with those of the courts with which it is siding.[17] Or it might help justify its decision by noting that most other circuits

---

[14] *See* James Leonard, *An Analysis of Citations to Authority in Ohio Appellate Decisions Published in 1990*, 86 Law Libr. J. 129, 152 (1994) (showing that Ohio Supreme Court was more likely to cite nonbinding opinions in difficult cases or cases involving novel questions of law).

[15] *See, e.g., United States v. Philip Morris USA Inc.*, 396 F.3d 1190, 1201 (D.C. Cir. 2005) (noting that "we avoid creating circuit splits when possible"); *United States v. Alexander*, 287 F.3d 811, 820 (9th Cir. 2002) ("[A]bsent a strong reason to do so, we will not create a direct conflict with other circuits.") (internal quotation marks omitted); *Chrysler Credit Corp. v. Country Chrysler, Inc.*, 928 F.2d 1509, 1521 (10th Cir. 1991) ("Splitting the circuits always is something we approach with trepidation."); *see also United States v. Games-Perez*, 695 F.3d 1104, 1115 (10th Cir. 2012) (Murphy J. concurring in denial of rehearing en banc) ("[T]he circuits have historically been loath to create a split where none exists. . . . The avoidance of unnecessary circuit splits furthers the legitimacy of the judiciary and reduces friction flowing from the application of different rules to similarly situated individuals based solely on their geographic location."). The Seventh Circuit has a local rule designed to ensure that circuit splits (or a split with a state high court) will be created only with the approval of the full en banc court. *See* 7th Cir. R. 40(e).

[16] *See, e.g., Muniz v. Sabol*, 517 F.3d 29, 31 (1st Cir. 2008) ("[F]our circuit courts of appeal that have considered the issue have determined that the BOP lacks such authority. Each of the circuit opinions has been accompanied by a dissent. While we are loath to create a circuit split, we respectfully side with the dissenters.") (footnote omitted); *Woods v. Carey*, 722 F.3d 1177, 1183 n.8 (9th Cir. 2013) ("[A]lthough a circuit split is not desirable, we are not required to follow the initial circuit to decide an issue if our own careful analysis of the legal question leads us to conclude that Congress intended the contrary result.").

[17] *See, e.g., Khan v. Attorney Gen.*, 691 F.3d 488, 493 (3d Cir. 2012) (following Second Circuit on question whether a premature petition for review can ripen upon a final decision of the Board of Immigration Appeals); *Dorosh v. Ashcroft*, 398 F.3d 379, 382 (6th Cir. 2004) (rejecting Ninth Circuit's decision to reject the Board of Immigration Appeals' corroboration rule and joining two circuits holding the opposite because "this Court has repeatedly emphasized the importance of corroborating evidence").

to take a position are on a particular side of the split,[18] or else that the most recent decisions by other circuits have been on one side of a split.[19] But the court will typically also provide specific reasons for its choice, such as its view of the proper way to interpret a statute,[20] its understanding of legislative meaning,[21] or a lack of precedential support for one side.[22] At other times, a court of appeals will identify the split but decline to join the fray, announcing that the facts of the case at hand do not require aligning itself with either side.[23]

---

18   See, e.g., *United States v. Rentz*, 777 F.3d 1105, 1114 (10th Cir. 2015) (en banc) ("Most other circuits to have come this way before us have reached the same destination we do."); *Union Asset Mgmt. Holding A.G. v. Dell, Inc.*, 669 F.3d 632, 644 (5th Cir. 2012) ("We join the majority of circuits in allowing our district courts the flexibility to choose between the percentage and lodestar methods in common fund cases."). *But see United States v. Tisdale*, 248 F.3d 964, 977 (10th Cir. 2001) ("We side with the minority of the circuit courts which have held that note 6's language [in U.S. Sentencing Guideline § 5G1.3] is *permissive*.").

19   See, e.g., *Acute Care Specialists II v. United States*, 727 F.3d 802, 810–11 (7th Cir. 2013) ("We are mindful of the fact that this holding places us in tension with the Second Circuit . . . . The recent trend among our sister circuits, however, has been to treat these claims as at least partially attributable to partnership items, and thus within the purview of § 7422(h).").

20   See, e.g., *Service Emps. Int'l, Inc. v. Director, Office of Workers' Comp. Program*, 595 F.3d 447, 453 (2d Cir. 2010) ("We recognize that some of our sister circuits find no ambiguity in the unamended provision for judicial review under the DBA. . . . We disagree.").

21   See, e.g., *AES Corp. v. Dow Chem. Co.*, 325 F.3d 174, 183 (3d Cir. 2003) (siding with First Circuit and rejecting the Second Circuit's view based on Congress's decision to limit private negotiations under the Exchange Act).

22   See, e.g., *Walker v. Astrue*, 593 F.3d 274, 279 (3d Cir. 2010) (rejecting Tenth Circuit's approach to Rule 54(d)(2) question because it "finds little support in the law," since it relied on a case that is "not good law under the amended Federal Rules of Civil Procedure"); *United States v. Davenport*, 484 F.3d 321, 329 (5th Cir. 2007) (stating that although "we have the utmost respect for the Tenth Circuit, we decline to follow its decision" because it offered little "insight into its conclusion" in the form of prior precedents or any actual explanation).

23   See, e.g., *Lopez-Fernandez v. Holder*, 735 F.3d 1043, 1046 (8th Cir. 2013) ("We need not decide today whether to join other circuits in holding that an egregious Fourth Amendment violation affirmatively compels exclusion in a removal proceeding because the Petitioners have not alleged an egregious violation."); *United States v. Lara-Unzueta*, 735 F.3d 954, 961 (7th Cir. 2013); *United States v. Magnesium Corp. of Am.*, 616 F.3d 1129, 1140 (10th Cir. 2010) ("Though U.S. Magnesium spends considerable energy encouraging us to join the circuits that have adopted *Alaska Hunters*, and invites us to conclude that

Taking the road less traveled

Yet courts often decide not to follow the rules and decisions of their counterparts in other jurisdictions and aren't shy about charting their own course. The reason may simply be that the facts of the case at hand and those of a case decided elsewhere are dissimilar.[24] Or it may be that important legal rules in the home forum and the foreign forum conflict.[25] It may also be that the local rules for the deciding court differ enough from those of another forum that any realistic possibility of extracting persuasive value from that forum's decisions is foreclosed.[26] At other times courts will decline to follow the decision of another court because of a perceived flaw in the decision. For example, the other court may have failed to consider a relevant federal statute.[27] It may have

---

those circuits have the better view of administrative law, we have no need to wade into such deep waters to decide the appeal before us.").

24 *See, e.g., Vantrease v. Commissioner of Soc. Sec.*, No. 1:13-cv-861, 2015 WL 1401316, at *8 n.8 (W.D. Mich. 26 Mar. 2015) ("*Nazzaro* is not persuasive authority because the facts of that case are not remotely analogous."); *Kortyna v. Lafayette Coll.*, 47 F. Supp. 3d 225, 237 n.33 (E.D. Pa. 2014) ("The plaintiff also offers precedent from other circuits to support this argument. None of these cases is persuasive because none involve parties with established employer–employee relationships."); *Cardon v. Cotton Lane Holdings, Inc.*, 841 P.2d 198, 201–02 (Ariz. 1992) ("*Bell* is not persuasive authority because it involved an action to enforce an executory agreement for the sale of real property; it did not involve a deed of trust given as security for a loan.").

25 *See, e.g., In re Fretter, Inc.*, 219 B.R. 769, 779 n.7 (Bankr. N.D. Ohio 1998) ("*In re Crivello* is not persuasive authority because it is directly contrary to the *Federated* decision, which is the law of this Circuit."); *State v. Harris*, 327 P.3d 1276, 1279–80 (Wash. Ct. App. 2014) ("*Schuette* is not persuasive authority because in Florida, the test for causation is two-pronged. The State must not only prove 'but-for' causation but also must show that the loss bears 'a significant relationship' to the offense of conviction.").

26 *See, e.g., Priesmeyer v. Pacific SW Bank, F.S.B.*, 917 S.W.2d 937, 940 (Tex. App.—Austin 1996, no writ) (per curiam) ("We are also unpersuaded by *Resolution Trust Corp. v. Camp*, 965 F.2d 25 (5th Cir. 1992) . . . . *Camp* is not persuasive authority because federal summary judgment practice differs widely from Texas summary judgment practice.").

27 *Alonso v. Blackstone Fin. Grp. LLC*, 962 F. Supp. 2d 1188, 1198 (E.D. Cal. 2013) ("Since the *Moritz* court did not consider the intent of the FDCPA in deciding whether a payment made due to a violation of the statute was actual damages, the court does not consider it persuasive authority in this instance.").

failed to make a crucial part of its holding particularly clear.[28] Or it may have relied on a test that the deciding court has explicitly rejected.[29]

An authority derives its persuasive power from its ability to convince others to go along with it.[30] Persuasiveness usually derives from sound reasoning, logical structure, authoritative support, evidence that the case received the careful consideration of the court, and citation of pertinent authorities.[31]

The 1968 California Supreme Court case of *Dillon v. Legg*[32] has been cited countless times as an example of what can make a nonbinding authority particularly persuasive. In *Dillon*, the court abandoned the traditional rule that a third-party bystander could recover for emotional distress only if the bystander was within the "zone of danger" when the event occurred. The trial court had granted summary judgment dismissing a mother's claim for emotional distress arising from watching the defendant's vehicle roll over and kill her two-year-old daughter. Under the traditional rule, the mother had no valid legal claim because she wasn't in the "zone of danger"—that is, there was no chance that she could have suffered physical impact.[33] The California Supreme Court reversed, reasoning in part that allowing the claim to proceed in this case was a logical extension of established tort law.[34] In a cleanly written, persuasive opinion, the court broke with tradition and held that a parent who watched, even from safety, as a car ran

---

28 *See, e.g., Commonwealth v. Jordan*, 785 N.E.2d 368, 379 n.13 (Mass. 2003) ("[I]n *State v. Chapman*, 317 S.C. 302, 306, 454 S.E.2d 317 (1995), the Supreme Court of South Carolina did state that 'race and/or gender based discrimination' was unlawful. It did not make clear, however, that it was recognizing mixed race-gender groups. We therefore do not consider it persuasive authority.").

29 *American Nat'l Prop. & Cas. Co. v. Julie R.*, 90 Cal. Rptr. 2d 119, 126 (Ct. App. 1999) ("*Hartford* is not persuasive authority because its causal analysis approximates the 'any cause in fact' test that we have rejected in favor of the substantial factor test.").

30 Frederick Schauer, *Authority and Authorities*, 94 Va. L. Rev. 1931, 1941–44 (2008).

31 *See generally id.* at 1931.

32 441 P.2d 912 (Cal. 1968).

33 *Id.* at 915.

34 *Id.* at 924–25.

over and killed his or her young child presented a valid prima facie case and so could pursue a claim for emotional distress.[35]

At the time, *Dillon* was viewed as a groundbreaking extension of recognized tort law, and it has since been cited as authority in nearly a thousand cases across 48 states and the District of Columbia as courts across the nation have reshaped the tort of emotional distress.[36] *Dillon*'s persuasiveness stemmed not only from the emotional impact of the facts, but also from the court's logical, creative citation of cases, treatises, and law-review articles. It comprehensively reviewed the law of duty beginning in feudal times and discussed in some depth why the court should not deny a claim through fear of fraudulent claims.[37] The court also relied on analogy, finding it incongruous that the decedent's older sister could recover because she may have been in the zone of danger, but the decedent's mother couldn't even though she watched helplessly as her baby was killed by the defendant's vehicle.[38] Although the voluminous citations to *Dillon* resulted in part from its departure from settled law, the courts citing it also doubtless relied on the force of its reasoning to influence the course of the law.

The *Dillon* opinion exhibits the hallmarks of persuasiveness that made it a seminal opinion in bystander tort recovery, despite later evolutions in the law. The court's reasoning was comprehensive and persuasive.[39] Interestingly, the court's best-known member, Roger Traynor, didn't write the opinion. Instead, he dissented.[40]

---

35 *Id.* at 925.

36 *Compare Trombetta v. Conkling*, 626 N.E.2d 653, 655 (N.Y. 1993) (declining to adopt *Dillon*), *with Leong v. Takasaki*, 520 P.2d 758, 765–66 (Haw. 1974) (agreeing with *Dillon*).

37 *Dillon*, 441 P.2d at 916–19; *see also Howard Frank, M.D., P.C. v. Superior Court*, 722 P.2d 955, 960–61 (Ariz. 1986) (in banc) (citing *Dillon* to support the proposition that the fear of increased litigation is not a legitimate reason to deny an otherwise valid claim because it is the court's duty to address claims on their merits and the system will weed out meritless ones).

38 *Dillon*, 441 P.2d at 915.

39 *Id.* at 916–21 ("We cannot let the difficulties of adjudication frustrate the principle that there be a remedy for every substantial wrong.").

40 *Id.* at 925 (Traynor J. dissenting).

Although not typically mentioned as a factor influencing an authority's persuasiveness, a compelling set of facts underlies many a groundbreaking case. *Dillon* exemplifies the point.[41] Similarly, opinions resolving a new circumstance or dealing logically and convincingly with a new technology are apt to be persuasive. The advent of the automobile once required rethinking product liability[42] and concepts of personal jurisdiction,[43] spawning cogent opinions that came to be oft-cited. In recent years, the Internet has spawned similar cutting-edge cases.[44] A well-reasoned opinion in a groundbreaking case involving personal jurisdiction or e-discovery and their intersection with the Internet will likely serve as compelling authority for future courts.

The absence of the noted characteristics diminishes a case's value as precedent. Hence an opinion that states a legal rule but doesn't explain how that rule applies to the case before the court is unlikely to persuade later courts that aren't bound by the decision. The same is true of cases that aren't well reasoned, logically organized, well written, or adequately supported.

In sum, it's useful for courts to consult the holdings of sister tribunals, if only to learn whether the rules that govern them enjoy a broad consensus or whether the court has become an outlier. Perhaps it will decide to remain an outlier if it is convinced that its rule is the correct one. But at least the decision will be made consciously, and, if it is a lower court, the issue will be sharpened for possible high-court attention.

---

41 *See id.* at 914.

42 *See MacPherson v. Buick Motor Co.*, 111 N.E. 1050 (N.Y. 1916).

43 *See Hess v. Pawloski*, 274 U.S. 352 (1927) (moving from concepts of actual consent and personal service to implied consent).

44 *See generally Boschetto v. Hansing*, 539 F.3d 1011 (9th Cir. 2008) (holding that Internet sale of vehicle through eBay didn't provide sufficient minimum contacts with buyer's forum state to impose personal jurisdiction over nonresident seller); *Zubulake v. UBS Warburg LLC*, 220 F.R.D. 212 (S.D.N.Y. 2003) (addressing a litigant's duty to preserve electronic evidence).

17. Leading Cases

A leading case is one that first definitely settled an important rule or legal principle and has since been consistently and frequently followed. Such cases are of the very highest authority.

Virtually all important legal rules have beneath them a case in which they were first established—a leading case to which later courts show respect and even obeisance.[1] *Marbury v. Madison*[2] is the quintessential leading case because it settled beyond doubt a then-uncertain but extremely important question: whether courts may subject legislative and executive actions to judicial review for their constitutionality.

A leading case is an especially powerful precedent. A brief today arguing that *Marbury* should be overturned would be laughed out of court. But why? What is it about leading cases that entitle them to greater respect? For starters, a leader isn't a leader without followers. To be a leading case, an opinion must be cited and followed in later cases. No case—regardless of its importance to the litigants or to society more broadly—can be a leading case if it's widely ignored in later opinions or remains a historical outlier among the surrounding jurisprudence.

But that explanation just invites a new question: What features of a case persuade other courts to follow it? Three things.

First, the case must definitively settle the question before the court. An opinion whose contours are unclear or one that bypasses

---

[1] See *Black's Law Dictionary* 1023 (Bryan A. Garner ed., 10th ed. 2014) (defining *leading case* as a "judicial decision that first definitively settled an important legal rule or principle and that has since been often and consistently followed"); *see also* Paul Vinogradoff, *Common-Sense in Law* 189 (1925) ("When a new principle has been formulated by the judges, their decision on the case assumes authority, and if this authority is followed on subsequent occasions the case is called a leading case."); 1 John William Smith, *A Selection of Leading Cases on Various Branches of the Law* vi (Thomas Willes Chitty et al. eds., 11th ed. 1903) (defining *leading case* as one that "involves, and is usually cited to establish, some point or principle of real practical importance").

[2] 5 U.S. (1 Cranch) 137 (1803).

key aspects of the issue presented cannot constitute a leading case. That's because if an opinion contains ambiguities that are susceptible to diverse interpretations, its scope will continue to be litigated and future courts will likely disagree about its application. Often ambiguity is a deliberate choice on the court's part. An opinion might leave a question unresolved to allow the issue to percolate more in the lower courts, or to give the court time to find a future case in which the issue might be more sharply presented. Such opinions are unlikely to be remembered as leading cases.

Second, the case must have wide applicability. A case narrowly confined to peculiar facts can't lead future courts. Hence leading cases must establish a governing legal framework applicable to a wide variety of factual situations. For example, *Katz v. United States*[3] is a leading case because it creates a framework for assessing Fourth Amendment challenges. By contrast, *Florida v. Jardines*,[4] which settles a significant doctrinal question regarding when and where police-dog sniffs are permissible, is unlikely to become a leading case because its applicability is narrow.

Third, a leading case typically addresses a question of significant legal or societal importance, often affecting the substantial rights of a great many people. That doesn't necessarily mean that the opinion deals with major issues of public policy or constitutional design: *Palsgraf v. Long Island Railroad*,[5] for example, is a leading case because it established principles applicable to thousands of garden-variety tort actions.

While leading cases are often relatively old, age isn't a defining feature of whether a case is leading. For example, *Wal-Mart Stores, Inc. v. Dukes*,[6] decided in 2011, could already be described as a (if not *the*) leading case in the area of class certification. *Gideon v. Wainwright*[7] and *Miranda v. Arizona*[8] were considered leading

---

[3] 389 U.S. 347 (1967).
[4] 133 S.Ct. 1409 (2013).
[5] 162 N.E. 99 (N.Y. 1928).
[6] 564 U.S. 338 (2011).
[7] 372 U.S. 335 (1963).
[8] 384 U.S. 436 (1966).

cases soon after publication. Such examples underscore the point that when an opinion settles a question of wide-ranging applicability and significance, it is likely to be a leading case irrespective of its age.

The concept of a leading case is especially important when dealing with state common law. Because state common-law rulings aren't subject to binding pronouncement at the national level, the relative uniformity of state common-law adjudication is maintained largely by leading cases. These cases establish principles that have attained a kind of unassailable status, even though they aren't technically binding. *Palsgraf*, for example, has helped establish the law of tort duties across the country.[9] A leading case can therefore become tantamount to a statute: people conform their behavior to its holding based on the reasonable expectation that it will remain the governing law. In the shifting landscape of the common law, leading cases serve as essential guideposts to help courts find their way.

---

[9] *But see, e.g., Behrendt v. Gulf Underwriters Ins. Co.*, 768 N.W.2d 568, 574 (Wis. 2009) (noting that Wisconsin has "long followed the minority view of duty as set forth in the dissent of *Palsgraf*").

18. Ancient Decisions

An ancient decision—one that has been long accepted as a correct exposition of the law or that has been repeatedly approved and followed—carries great weight as a precedent and will not be overruled or departed from except for the most cogent reasons. Unlike a statute, such a decision may become obsolete because of changed social or political conditions, or its authority may be gradually undermined by the drift of judicial doctrine away from the principles that it enunciated.

An ancient case is one that has long remained good law. There doesn't appear to be a consensus about just how long, but the term is now typically applied to cases from the 19th century or earlier. In the 19th century, by contrast, the dividing line was thought to be 1688—the year of the Glorious Revolution in England.[1] Today those cases might be thought antediluvian.

Designating a case "ancient" is more descriptive than normative; unlike a leading case, an ancient case isn't always an especially powerful precedent. Instead, its persuasiveness depends on the degree to which its underlying principles have been buttressed or weakened by later cases and events. The fact that a case remains an accurate statement of the law through many generations often shows that it should be afforded special respect for much the same reason as a leading case.[2]

---

[1] 1 James Kent, *Commentaries on American Law* *479 (Charles M. Barnes ed., 13th ed. 1884) ("The division line between the ancient and the modern English reports may, for the sake of convenient arrangement, be placed at the revolution in the year 1688.").

[2] *See* Henry J. Abraham, *The Judicial Process* 325 (6th ed. 1993) (noting that "a good many judges generally seem to accord considerably more sanctity to very old and hallowed 'precedents,' such as most of Chief Justice John Marshall's decisions, than to those of relatively recent vintage"); John Salmond, *Jurisprudence* § 60, at 184 (Glanville L. Williams ed., 10th ed. 1947) ("[O]ther things being equal, a precedent acquires added authority from the lapse of time. The longer it has stood unquestioned and unreversed, the more harm in the way of uncertainty and the disappointment of reasonable expectations will result from its reversal. A decision which might be lawfully overruled without hesitation while yet new, may after the lapse of a number of years acquire such increased strength as to be practically of absolute and no longer of merely

There is much overlap between leading and ancient cases. Yet an ancient case is defined by its age alone, whereas a leading case is the product of a wider set of factors, age not necessarily included. Leading cases need not be old; conversely, ancient cases need not be the first to settle an important and widely applicable question.

Nor do ancient cases need to contain the most cogent statement of a given doctrine. An ancient case can actually be less persuasive than a more recent precedent when the ancient case hasn't been consistently followed, depends on assumptions that have been empirically disproved, or contradicts the logic of later cases. Hence no clear inference can be drawn from a case's ancient status alone. Instead, an analysis of the case's reasoning becomes necessary to ensure that time hasn't enfeebled its underlying rationale.

For example, in *Brown v. Board of Education*,[3] the U.S. Supreme Court declined to apply the on-point precedent of *Plessy v. Ferguson*,[4] partly because *Plessy*'s premises had proved wrong in the intervening years. The Court declined to "turn the clock back . . . to 1896 when [*Plessy*] was written . . . [and instead] consider[ed] public education in the light of its full development and its present place in American life."[5]

Ancient cases are especially probative when addressing a question in which legal rights depend on the recognition of those rights in the early common law. For example, in addressing the scope of immunity under 42 U.S.C. § 1983, courts look to ancient cases to define the traditional immunities enjoyed by public officials at common law.[6] Similarly, ancient cases are important in deciding which federal claims confer a right to a jury trial under the Seventh Amendment: the right attaches only to claims analogous to those

---

conditional authority. This effect of lapse of time has repeatedly received judicial recognition.").

3   347 U.S. 483 (1954).
4   163 U.S. 537 (1896).
5   *Brown*, 347 U.S. at 492.
6   See *Rehberg v. Paulk*, 132 S.Ct. 1497, 1502 (2012).

for which a jury trial was required at common law.[7] The importance of ancient cases in these contexts is based not on their persuasiveness, but rather on the historical status of particular rights.

Although a decision's antiquity tends to favor the application of stare decisis, the age of full maturity is debatable. In *Montejo v. Louisiana*,[8] Scalia J. wrote that the fact that the Court's prior decision[9] was "only two decades old" argued in favor of abandoning the precedent.[10] In dissent, Stevens J. wrote: "[A]lthough the Court acknowledges that 'antiquity' is a factor that counsels in favor of retaining precedent, it concludes that the fact *Jackson* is 'only two decades old' cuts in favor of abandoning the rule it established. I would have thought that the 23-year existence of a simple bright-line rule would be a factor that cuts in the other direction."[11] Alito J., concurring, countered: "I can only assume that the dissent thinks that our constitutional precedents are like certain wines, which are most treasured when they are neither too young nor too old."[12]

Because law often pays heed to history, ancient cases will often be powerful precedent. But their relative strength always depends on the context in which they are deployed.

Obsoleteness

Although the same isn't true of statutes,[13] precedents become obsolete if the conditions or facts that existed when they were rendered are different or no longer exist, or if the underlying rationale is no longer sound. Obsolescent opinions generally have little precedential value, and an opinion's full obsoleteness is a traditional reason for overruling it. Yet obsolete opinions sometimes

---

7   See *City of Monterey v. Del Monte Dunes at Monterey, Ltd.*, 526 U.S. 687, 708–09 (1999).
8   556 U.S. 778 (2009).
9   *Michigan v. Jackson*, 475 U.S. 625 (1986).
10 *Montejo*, 556 U.S. at 793.
11 *Id.* at 809–10 (Stevens J. dissenting).
12 *Id.* at 801 (Alito J. concurring).
13 Antonin Scalia & Bryan A. Garner, *Reading Law: The Interpretation of Legal Texts* 336–39 (2012).

retain their precedential value if other stare decisis considerations weigh in favor of adhering to the outmoded precedent.

Every opinion is rendered under a specific set of conditions, and when those conditions change or no longer exist, the precedent can become obsolete and run the risk of being overturned.[14] As Cardozo J. wrote in 1916, while on the New York Court of Appeals: "Precedents drawn from the days of travel by stage coach do not fit the conditions of travel today."[15]

In addition to a change in conditions, other factors might render an opinion obsolete. If the facts that underpin an opinion change or are later shown to be false in a way that calls the case's holding into question, the earlier case may be considered obsolete.[16] A precedent may also become obsolete if the reasons underlying it no longer exist.[17]

Among the prime examples are opinions establishing tort immunity for charities. By 1938, courts in most states had adopted a rule that charities were immune from tort liability based on various conditions and policy considerations.[18] By 1985, however,

---

14 *Rotemi Realty, Inc. v. Act Realty Co.*, 911 So. 2d 1181, 1188 (Fla. 2005) (noting that "stare decisis counsels us to follow our precedents unless there has been a significant change in circumstances after the adoption of the legal rule") (internal quotation marks omitted); *In re Estate of McFarland*, 167 S.W.3d 299, 306 (Tenn. 2005) (noting that in general, "well-settled rules of law will be overturned . . . when . . . changes in conditions . . . render the precedent obsolete"); *see also* 21 C.J.S. *Courts* § 202 (2014).

15 *MacPherson v. Buick Motor Co.*, 111 N.E. 1050, 217 N.Y. 382, 391 (1916).

16 *See Planned Parenthood of SE Pa. v. Casey*, 505 U.S. 833, 860 (1992) (commenting that "no change in [the] factual underpinning [of *Roe v. Wade*, 410 U.S. 113 (1973)] has left its central holding obsolete").

17 *See Flagiello v. Pennsylvania Hosp.*, 208 A.2d 193, 206 (Pa. 1965) (observing that in most cases, "when a court decides to . . . abandon a court-made rule . . . , it starts out by saying that the reason for the rule no longer exists") (internal quotation marks omitted); *see also Carroll v. Kittle*, 457 P.2d 21, 28 (Kan. 1969), *superseded by statute*, Kan. Stat. Ann. § 46-901 et seq. (1970), *as recognized in Commerce Bank of St. Joseph, N.A. v. State*, 833 P.2d 996, 1001 (Kan. 1992) (observing that "when the reason for a rule no longer exists, the rule itself should be abandoned").

18 Daniel A. Barfield, Note, *Better to Give Than to Receive: Should Nonprofit Corporations and Charities Pay Punitive Damages?*, 29 Val. U. L. Rev. 1193, 1194 (1995).

most states had abolished the charitable-immunity rule.[19] Many abolished the rule through the courts, often by reason of obsoleteness. For example, in a 1966 case,[20] the Idaho Supreme Court abandoned cases applying the charitable-immunity rule because the rule's three justifications were no longer sound.[21] Given that the reasons for the rule no longer existed, the horizontal precedent wasn't followed and the court abrogated the obsolete rule "in toto."[22]

The conditions present when the charitable-immunity rule was established have also ceased to exist, at least with respect to charitable hospitals. The rule was originally adopted when "[l]iability insurance was not yet readily available, and most hospitals were, indeed, strictly, charitable institutions subsisting mainly on donations."[23] Since the rule was adopted, however, insurance has become widely available, and charitable donations haven't depended on whether a state allows tort actions against charities.[24] Based in part on these changed conditions, courts began to abandon the obsolete charitable-immunity rule.[25]

Yet an obsolete precedent might retain its precedential value if a court finds that stare decisis considerations so dictate. For example, before overruling an opinion, the Michigan Supreme Court considers "whether the previous decision has become so embedded, so accepted, so fundamental, to everyone's expectations that to change it would produce not just readjustments, but practical real-world dislocations."[26] Under these circumstances, even if the court "wrongly decided" a case, the court might still adhere to the

---

19 Paul T. O'Neill, *Charitable Immunity: The Time to End Laissez-Faire Health Care in Massachusetts Has Come*, 82 Mass. L. Rev. 223, 230 (1997).
20 *Bell v. Presbytery of Boise*, 421 P.2d 745 (Idaho 1966).
21 *Id.* at 746–47.
22 *Id.* at 747.
23 O'Neill, *Charitable Immunity*, 82 Mass. L. Rev. at 228.
24 *President of Georgetown Coll. v. Hughes*, 130 F.2d 810, 823–24 (D.C. Cir. 1942).
25 *See, e.g., id.* at 827–28; *see also* Barfield, *Better to Give*, 29 Val. U. L. Rev. at 1195.
26 *Robinson v. City of Detroit*, 613 N.W.2d 307, 321 (Mich. 2000).

decision.[27] Hence even if an opinion is completely obsolete, it still might retain its precedential value if "overruling [the] precedent would cause chaos."[28]

---

27 *Id.* at 320–21.
28 *Westfield Ins. Co. v. Galatis*, 797 N.E.2d 1256, 1270 (Ohio 2003).

19. Unanimous vs. Split Decisions

A unanimous decision may have greater weight than a split decision—and often the closer the split, the weaker the precedent.

A unanimous decision is one in which all the members of a multijudge panel agree. When everyone sitting on a case agrees on the outcome of an issue or case, the panel speaks with one voice. The decision carries the full weight of the panel's authority. By contrast, a split decision is inherently weaker because at least one voice of equal authority has declared the decision to be flawed in either reasoning or result.

Other things being equal, courts will usually consider a precedent that speaks for a unanimous court as more authoritative than one that speaks for a split panel.[1] But things aren't always equal. Some dissents or concurrences powerfully explain legal thinking and ultimately prove canonical.[2] Some split decisions are honed and improved by virtue of the challenge presented by dissenting colleagues. And some unanimous opinions skimp on persuasive reasoning because they lack a dissenting challenge.

When a tribunal comprises two or more judges, "the concurrence of a majority of the judges sitting is necessary or sufficient"[3] to decide the case. Typically, one judge drafts the opinion of the court, which "speaks ostensibly for all who do not dissent or are not indicated as not taking any part in the decision."[4] A judge who doesn't agree with the majority opinion may file a dissenting opinion to explain his or her vote in the case.[5] Likewise, a judge may concur in the judgment to express disagreement with the majority's reasoning or write a "simple concurrence," in which

---

1 Neil Duxbury, *The Nature and Authority of Precedent* 62 (2008).
2 *See, e.g.*, *Katz v. United States*, 389 U.S. 347, 360 (1967) (Harlan J. concurring), *Lochner v. New York*, 198 U.S. 45, 65 (1905) (Holmes J. dissenting), and *Plessy v. Ferguson*, 163 U.S. 537, 552 (1896) (Harlan J. dissenting).
3 21 C.J.S. *Courts* § 192, at 186 (2006).
4 Emlin McClain, *Dissenting Opinions*, 14 Yale L.J. 191, 196 (1905).
5 *Id.*

the judge agrees with both the reasoning and result of the majority opinion but wishes to write separately to make some other point.[6] Although a minority opinion doesn't bind the litigants and has no precedential value,[7] it may have some persuasive value.

In traditional English practice, all the judges announced their views in seriatim opinions.[8] In this way, each judge contributed to the understanding of the result, making "plain the view of the court as a deliberative body, and the legal conclusion reached by it, to serve as a precedent in other cases."[9] Although seriatim opinions were common in U.S. courts at the time of the nation's founding, they came to be thought of as "weak and divided" opinions that were "unable to assert any real authority."[10] At the turn of the 19th century, Marshall C.J. persuaded his U.S. Supreme Court colleagues to abandon the practice of issuing seriatim opinions in favor of a single "opinion of the Court" that would speak for all the Justices in one voice.[11] Since that time, Chief Justices from Taft to Roberts have encouraged unanimous opinions as a means to promote stability in the law and the legitimacy of the Court.[12]

Unanimity in a high court may come about for several different reasons. Sometimes the result in the lower court may appear to the judges to be so obviously incorrect in light of the governing law that a per curiam reversal is the disposition of choice.[13]

---

6 Igor Kirman, *Standing Apart to Be a Part: The Precedential Value of Supreme Court Concurring Opinions*, 95 Colum. L. Rev. 2083, 2084 (1995).

7 20 Am. Jur. 2d *Courts* § 134, at 537 (2015).

8 Kirman, *Standing Apart*, 95 Colum. L. Rev. at 2085–86.

9 McClain, *Dissenting Opinions*, 14 Yale L.J. at 195.

10 M. Todd Henderson, *From Seriatim to Consensus and Back Again: A Theory of Dissent*, 2007 Sup. Ct. Rev. 283, 308 (2007).

11 *Id.* at 313; *see* Bryan A. Garner, "Opinions, Style of," in *The Oxford Companion to the Supreme Court of the United States* 706, 707 (Kermit Hall ed., 2d ed. 2005); Karl M. ZoBell, *Division of Opinion in the Supreme Court: A History of Judicial Disintegration*, 44 Cornell L.Q. 186, 192–93 (1959).

12 *See* Sandra Day O'Connor, *William Howard Taft and the Importance of Unanimity*, 28 J. Sup. Ct. History 157 (2003); Mark Sherman, *Roberts Touts Unanimity on Supreme Court*, Washington Post (17 Nov. 2006), http://www.washingtonpost.com/wp-dyn/content/article/2006/11/17/AR2006111700999.html.

13 *See, e.g., Johnson v. City of Shelby*, 135 S.Ct. 346, 346 (2014) (per curiam); *Hinton v. Alabama*, 134 S.Ct. 1081, 1083 (2014) (per curiam); *Coleman v. Johnson*, 132

An opinion may be unanimous because it concerns a straightforward question of statutory interpretation that the judges regard as clear. Or a decision may be unanimous if all members of the court agree that an earlier decision should apply to a new situation. Consider the 1977 case of *Connally v. Georgia*.[14] A law provided that a magistrate would be paid $5 for every warrant issued, but nothing if the magistrate chose not to issue the requested warrant.[15] The Supreme Court's unanimous per curiam opinion concluded that this case was governed by the Court's 1927 decision in *Tumey v. Ohio*,[16] which invalidated as a violation of due process a law providing that a decision-maker in a municipal tribunal would be compensated by a portion of the fines he imposed.[17]

Unanimity that conveys a moral stance

An opinion may be unanimous because all the judges regard the case as one of great importance—one in which the value of a lockstep pronouncement is high. This type of case best illustrates the blackletter rule: unanimity produces a clear and forceful resolution of the case. It signals that the Justices stand shoulder to shoulder, thereby signaling to those in society who disagree with the decision that there is little hope trying to avoid, reconsider, or limit the decision.

Sometimes unanimity confers moral authority. In the years leading up to *Brown v. Board of Education*,[18] Warren C.J. was very much concerned with maintaining unanimity within the Court on the sensitive topic of eliminating state-sponsored racial segregation.[19] As an astute politician, he realized that the demise

---

S.Ct. 2060, 2062 (2012) (per curiam); *Nitro-Lift Techs., LLC v. Howard*, 133 S.Ct. 500, 503–04 (2012) (per curiam).

14   429 U.S. 245 (1977) (per curiam).
15   Ga. Code Ann. § 24-1601 (1971).
16   273 U.S. 510 (1927).
17   *Connally*, 429 U.S. at 247–50.
18   347 U.S. 483 (1954).
19   *See* Dennis J. Hutchinson, *Unanimity and Desegregation: Decisionmaking in the Supreme Court, 1948–1958*, 68 Geo. L.J. 1 (1979) (a thorough account of how the *Brown* decision came to be unanimous, and how the Court remained unanimous for the first four years afterward).

of the separate-but-equal doctrine would be deeply unpopular in the southern states. He was also aware that judicial opinions are enforceable in the final analysis either because the public (especially the losing side) accepts them or because the President, Congress, or preferably both are persuaded to stand behind the Court's ruling. Had there been any ambivalence, Congress might have exploited it. The necessary message of finality in the Court's decision would have been diluted, perhaps fatally so. But Warren J. succeeded in his mission, and the Court carried on speaking in a single voice even as the southern states mounted their campaign of massive resistance and interposition. Not until 1958, when violence broke out in Little Rock and the President had to call in the National Guard, did that pattern break. But it broke in a way that in certain ways actually underscored its unanimity: all nine Justices individually signed the Court's opinion.

Frankfurter J. not only signed the Court's opinion; he also wrote a separate concurrence in *Cooper v. Aaron*.[20] That made *Cooper* the first case after *Brown* to reveal any individual views of the Justices. Today, the Court considers a unanimous opinion to be either a decision in which there are no separate opinions or a decision in which any separate opinion is a concurrence, rather than one that explicitly concurs only in the judgment. The latter kind of opinion destroys unanimity; the former doesn't.

For many years, the Court continued to enforce *Brown* with unanimous or near-unanimous opinions. In 1971, for example, in an opinion for a unanimous Court by Burger C.J., it upheld busing as a proper remedy to undo the effects of state-sponsored racial segregation.[21]

It was plain to the entire country that the question of the constitutionality of racial segregation in public facilities was of the highest importance. The same was true in the early 1970s, when the Watergate scandal was on the front page of all newspapers, and the special prosecutor was trying to compel the President to turn over the secret tapes that the White House had created. There

---

20   358 U.S. 1 (1958).
21   *Swann v. Charlotte-Mecklenburg Bd. of Educ.*, 402 U.S. 1 (1971).

seemed little doubt that the tapes might reveal information pertinent to the criminal investigations that the special prosecutor was pursuing. Yet it was also clear that an order purporting to compel the President to turn over confidential materials might impair his ability to carry out his duties. When the President invoked executive privilege in response to a subpoena for the tapes (and associated documents) from the grand jury, litigation quickly followed. The district court denied the President's motion to quash. In a highly unusual move, the Supreme Court granted a petition for certiorari before judgment in the court of appeals "because of the importance of the issues presented and the need for their prompt resolution."[22]

Writing for a unanimous Court (Rehnquist J. having recused himself), Burger C.J. rejected the President's formal objections to the litigation, which were based on an alleged lack of finality and an alleged lack of jurisdiction to adjudicate a dispute between two branches of the federal government. The Court held that ultimately it had before it a judicial proceeding brought in the name of the United States, though by the special prosecutor, and that the issues were, if not commonplace, certainly of a type that courts ordinarily consider. It found that the special prosecutor had sufficiently demonstrated the relevance, admissibility, and specificity of the materials he sought and that no privilege protected them from production. On that basis, it affirmed the judgment of the district court.[23] The fact that the Court's opinion was unanimous added an extra measure of force to its statement at a time when the integrity of a branch of the government had come under intense scrutiny.

In *Clinton v. Jones*,[24] the Court once again adjudicated a matter of great sensitivity for interbranch relations. This time it wasn't a criminal proceeding that implicated the President and his closest advisers. Rather, it was a civil lawsuit brought by a private party who sought civil damages for conduct that the President

---

22 *United States v. Nixon*, 418 U.S. 683, 687 (1974).
23 *Id.* at 714.
24 520 U.S. 681 (1997).

had allegedly undertaken before he took office. The President didn't seek to avoid the litigation altogether, but he did argue that "in all but the most exceptional cases the Constitution requires the federal courts to defer such litigation until his term ends and that, in any event, respect for the office warrants such a stay."[25] Emphatically acknowledging the importance of the case,[26] the Court was unmoved by the President's arguments on the merits. It rejected in particular his argument that the need to participate in the civil litigation would burden him in his official duties. Notably, this opinion missed unanimity by one vote: Breyer J., while agreeing with the outcome, concurred only in the judgment. In his view, the stay that the President requested should have been denied, but on the narrow basis that he had failed to show why it was essential (and that showing could include considerations of the unique needs that accompany the office of the President), not on the broader ground adopted by the majority.

If a unanimous precedent is almost always a strong one, does that mean that a precedent based on a split decision is almost always weak? Not necessarily. Many 5–4 opinions, however controversial they may be, have established what seem to be durable rules. Recent examples of such splits are:

- *National Federation of Independent Business v. Sebelius* (2012);[27]
- *Citizens United v. Federal Election Commission* (2010);[28]
- *Ashcroft v. Iqbal* (2009);[29]
- *Boumediene v. Bush* (2008);[30]
- *Parents Involved in Community Schools v. Seattle School District No. 1* (2007);[31] and
- *Gonzales v. Carhart* (2007).[32]

---

25 *Id.* at 684.
26 *Id.* at 689.
27 132 S.Ct. 2566 (2012).
28 558 U.S. 310 (2010).
29 556 U.S. 662 (2009).
30 553 U.S. 723 (2008).
31 551 U.S. 701 (2007).
32 550 U.S. 124 (2007).

When there is no formal majority opinion, but instead either a plurality or a completely splintered Court, the *Marks* rule[33] comes into play, meaning that the opinion representing the narrowest ground to which a majority of the Justices subscribed becomes the rule of decision (see § 20).

Supreme Court unanimity today

The modern Supreme Court has continued its tradition of frequent unanimity.[34] While the Justices often write separately when they can't agree, the Court has in recent years issued unanimous decisions in about 40% of its cases.[35] Decisional harmony is still more common in the federal appellate courts, most of which decide more than 90% of cases unanimously.[36] Examining the decision-making of the Supreme Court, one study identified five factors that correlate with unanimous decisions: "[1] cases in which less time is spent by the Justices between oral argument and the decision date; [2] routine or less important cases; [3] cases in which the ideological direction of the decision is liberal; [4] cases involving federal action; and [5] cases that do not contain civil liberties issues."[37]

Unanimity isn't always possible, however, and dissenting opinions may affect the weight of the decision's authority. When a court cannot speak with one voice, and one or more judges dissent, the judgment of the majority binds the litigants before it: "[F]or the purposes of the case, the final judgment announced by the majority of a divided court is as conclusive and effectual as

---

33 *Marks v. United States*, 430 U.S. 188 (1977).

34 Thomas R. Hensley & Scott P. Johnson, *Unanimity on the Rehnquist Court*, 31 Akron L. Rev. 387, 388 (1998); *see also id.* at 387 (explaining that "nearly one-half of the Court's decisions were unanimous during the 1996–1997 term") (internal footnote omitted).

35 *See* Pamela C. Corley et al., *The Puzzle of Unanimity: Consensus on the United States Supreme Court* 96 (2013).

36 *See* Christopher A. Cotropia, *Determining Uniformity Within the Federal Circuit by Measuring Dissent and En Banc Review*, 43 Loy. L.A. L. Rev. 801, 815 (2010).

37 Hensley & Johnson, *Unanimity on the Rehnquist Court*, 31 Akron L. Rev. at 396–97.

though the judges had been unanimous."[38] The majority opinion of a divided court also settles the law for all those courts subject to its appellate jurisdiction.[39] The presence of a dissenting opinion doesn't detract from the binding effect of the higher court's majority opinion,[40] even if the composition of the court so changes that current judges might be expected to reach a different result.[41]

As for the court that issued the decision, the principle of stare decisis requires that the majority opinion be considered controlling precedent unless and until it is overruled.[42] The fact that

---

38 Emlin McClain, *Dissenting Opinions*, 14 Yale L.J. 191, 192 (1905).

39 Henry Campbell Black, *Handbook on the Law of Judicial Precedents* § 43, at 131–32 (1912).

40 *See, e.g.*, *Moulton Niguel Water Dist. v. Colombo*, 4 Cal. Rptr. 3d 519, 523 (Ct. App. 2003) ("[W]hether there are dissents or not, we are required to follow the precedents set by the decisions of our Supreme Court."); *State v. Niemeyer*, 740 A.2d 416, 422 (Conn. App. Ct. 1999), *rev'd on other grounds*, 782 A.2d 658 (Conn. 2001) ("It is axiomatic . . . that we cannot rule in accordance with a dissent that is contrary to a controlling majority opinion of our Supreme Court."); *Marlin v. State*, 993 A.2d 1141, 1151 (Md. Ct. Spec. App. 2010) ("[O]pinions assented to by a majority of the Court [of Appeals], unless subsequently overruled in another case or by statute, are the law, and must be followed by this Court. Therefore, despite appellant's preference for the dissent in *Bedford*, it does not constitute a binding precedent upon this Court."); *Lake Valley Assocs., LLC v. Township of Pemberton*, 987 A.2d 623, 628 (N.J. Super. Ct. App. Div. 2010) (per curiam) ("Because we are an intermediate appellate court, we are bound to follow the law as it has been expressed by a majority of the members of our Supreme Court. We therefore decline plaintiff's invitation to apply in this case the reasoning set forth in Judge Conford's dissent, which the Supreme Court has failed to embrace in the three ensuing decades.") (internal citation omitted); *State v. Brooks*, 236 P.3d 250, 253 (Wash. Ct. App. 2010) ("[W]e reject Brooks's contention that *Walls* is not settled because one judge dissented. A majority opinion is settled law.").

41 *Hertz v. Industrial Comm'n*, 72 N.E.2d 755, 756 (Ohio Ct. App. 1942) ("It might be said that prospectively the law as announced in this case is *in nubibus*, inasmuch as the Supreme Court, as now constituted, has but one member who concurred in the majority opinion and one member who noted dissent. However, until that Court has by its own formal action reversed the [prior] case we are bound to follow it.").

42 *See, e.g.*, *Newton v. Mann*, 137 P.2d 776, 777 (Colo. 1943) (en banc) ("A dissenting opinion shows that the case has been thoroughly considered. The opinions of the majority govern. When that question arises in future cases, the dissenting justice is as much bound by the decision of the majority as is the justice who wrote the prevailing opinion. Admitting the excellence of the dissenting opinion in the previous case we see no reason to disturb the authority.") (internal quotation marks and citations omitted); *Lanvale Props., LLC v. County of Cabarrus*, 731 S.E.2d 800, 811 (N.C. 2012) ("[T]he dissent attempts to brush

the court was divided over the decision, however, may leave the decision more vulnerable to challenge and more likely to be overruled. Although the Supreme Court hasn't listed the number of Justices agreeing with the decision as a factor to consider when determining whether a decision should be overruled,[43] the Court often mentions that the decisions it overrules were decided by a narrow margin.[44] State courts also frequently consider whether

---

aside our decision in *Smith Chapel* by referring to the dissenting opinion in that case. . . . But the existence of a dissenting opinion in our decisions does not undermine the decision's status as binding precedent. . . . As a result, *Smith Chapel* governs this case no matter how much the dissent wishes otherwise."); *Deutsche Bank Nat'l Trust Co. v. Matthews*, 273 P.3d 43, 46 n.1 (Okla. 2012) ("The dissenting opinion in this matter relies upon Justice Opala's concurring opinion in *Toxic Waste Impact Grp., Inc. v. Leavitt* for the proposition that standing is not a jurisdictional question. Justice Opala's concurring opinion was not the majority opinion of this Court and as such . . . has no binding, precedential value.") (internal quotation marks and citations omitted).

43 See *Planned Parenthood of SE Pa. v. Casey*, 505 U.S. 833, 854–55 (1992) ("[W]hen this Court reexamines a prior holding, its judgment is customarily informed by a series of prudential and pragmatic considerations designed to test the consistency of overruling a prior decision with the ideal of the rule of law, and to gauge the respective costs of reaffirming and overruling a prior case. Thus, for example, we may ask whether the rule has proven to be intolerable simply in defying practical workability; whether the rule is subject to a kind of reliance that would lend a special hardship to the consequences of overruling and add inequity to the cost of repudiation; whether related principles of law have so far developed as to have left the old rule no more than a remnant of abandoned doctrine; or whether facts have so changed, or come to be seen so differently, as to have robbed the old rule of significant application or justification.") (citations omitted).

44 See, e.g., *Roper v. Simmons*, 543 U.S. 551, 562 (2005) (overruling *Stanford v. Kentucky*, 492 U.S. 361 (1989), in which four Justices dissented); *Lawrence v. Texas*, 539 U.S. 558, 566 (2003) (overruling *Bowers v. Hardwick*, 478 U.S. 186 (1986), in which "an opinion by Justice White[] sustained the Georgia law," "Chief Justice Burger and Justice Powell joined the opinion of the Court and filed separate, concurring opinions," and "[f]our Justices dissented"); *Seminole Tribe of Fla. v. Florida*, 517 U.S. 44, 59–60 (1996) (overruling *Pennsylvania v. Union Gas Co.*, 491 U.S. 1 (1989), in which the decision was rendered by a plurality of the Court plus a fifth Justice who wrote separately because he didn't agree with the plurality's reasoning); *Payne v. Tennessee*, 501 U.S. 808, 828–30 (1991) (overruling *Booth v. Maryland*, 482 U.S. 496 (1987), and *South Carolina v. Gathers*, 490 U.S. 805 (1989), which were decided by "the narrowest of margins"); *Garcia v. San Antonio Metro. Transit Auth.*, 469 U.S. 528, 530 (1985) (overruling *National League of Cities v. Usery*, 426 U.S. 833 (1976), which was decided by "a sharply divided vote"—see § 40); *Katz v. United States*, 389 U.S. 347, 353 (1967) (overruling *Olmstead v. United States*, 277 U.S. 438 (1928), which was decided by "a closely divided Court"); *Afroyim v. Rusk*, 387 U.S. 253, 255–56 (1967) (overruling

the court divided over a former opinion when determining its binding effect.[45]

Courts citing cases from other jurisdictions as persuasive authority typically consider whether a decision was unanimous or divided. A well-reasoned dissent may prompt the court to decline to adopt the other jurisdiction's reasoning.[46]

What's the worth of a separate opinion? Although a concurrence or dissent is nothing to count on by itself, often it must be reckoned with. A concurrence that addresses an issue explicitly put aside by the court presents little difficulty: you know the inclinations of as many judges as join the opinion. A dissent that directly disagrees with the majority is similar. But if the majority barely outnumbered the dissenters, you'll be left wondering whether the dissenters will try again the next time the issue comes up, or instead will surrender to the force of precedent.

More confusion arises from a separate opinion that purports to "explain" the court's opinion, particularly if the author also joins

---

Perez v. Brownell, 356 U.S. 44 (1958), which was decided 5–4); *Gideon v. Wainwright*, 372 U.S. 335, 337–38 (1963) (overruling *Betts v. Brady*, 316 U.S. 455 (1942), which was decided by a "divided Court"); *United States v. Darby*, 312 U.S. 100, 115–17 (1941) (overruling *Hammer v. Dagenhart*, 247 U.S. 251 (1918), which was decided by "a bare majority of the Court over the powerful and now classic dissent of Mr. Justice Holmes").

45 See, e.g., *State v. Jones*, 107 P.2d 324, 325 (N.M. 1940) (overruling *City of Roswell v. Jones*, 67 P.2d 286 (N.M. 1937), which was "a divided opinion in the court"); *Cook v. State*, 841 P.2d 1345, 1353 (Wyo. 1992) (overruling *Birr v. State*, 744 P.2d 1117 (Wyo. 1987), which was "decided on a narrow margin over spirited dissent").

46 *Schlaefer v. Schlaefer*, 112 F.2d 177, 186 n.10 (D.C. Cir. 1940) (citing *Schooley v. Schooley*, 169 N.W. 56, 57 (Iowa 1917), but noting that the court was divided 4–3 and noting that the case "is greatly weakened by the strong dissent of Salinger, J."); *Scibilia v. City of Philadelphia*, 124 A. 273, 278 (Pa. 1924) ("The case on which plaintiff chiefly relies is *Missano v. New York City*, . . . where recovery was allowed; but a divided court, and a strong dissenting opinion, serve to weaken it materially as an authority."); *City of Corsicana v. Wren*, 317 S.W.2d 516, 520 (Tex. 1958) ("*Van Gilder v. City of Morgantown* . . . is to the same effect, although conceding it to be somewhat weakened as authority here by the number of the dissents."); *Schultze v. Alamo Ice & Brewing Co.*, 21 S.W. 160, 162 (Tex. Civ. App.—Austin 1893, no pet.) ("The cases of *Hayes v. Fessenden* . . . and *Bank v. Fellowes* . . . are in line with the case of *Howard v. Veazie*; but [*Fellowes*] is weakened by the dissent of two judges of the five composing the court.").

the court's opinion. As unofficial as it is, the separate explanation may take root in the future, suggesting a line of argument that may yet succeed.

Dissents

Dissents can be important, so it's dangerous to say that they're legally irrelevant and that you can safely skip them. As a legal analyst, you must pay attention to dissents, especially those that are well reasoned.

One important reason to read dissenting opinions is that they may clarify what the majority is doing. For instance, the majority may essentially be overruling one of the court's earlier precedents, but might not want to draw a lot of attention to that. The majority may write a footnote that says something like this: "In light of our opinion today, we doubt that *Flom v. Baumgartner* is still good law." Or the majority might not mention the precedent at all. A dissenting judge might blow the whistle on them with something like this: "The majority opinion has effectively overruled a well-established precedent in this jurisdiction, *Flom v. Baumgartner*."

Dissenting opinions can also suggest where the law is headed. If the dissenting judges make a strong enough case for their position, they may be laying the groundwork for a change in the law. The judges in the majority may rethink their positions, or there may be a change in personnel that shifts the balance of power on the court. A strong dissent (for example, in an appellate court) may also cause the highest court of that jurisdiction to take notice and review the case, raising the possibility that the majority's opinion might be reversed. All these are reasons to pay attention to dissents.[47]

What effects can multiple opinions have? Plurality opinions, concurrences, and dissents, like once-common seriatim opinions, can complicate the reading and analysis of an opinion and make it much harder to know its exact holdings.

---

47   *See* Diane P. Wood, *When to Hold, When to Fold, and When to Reshuffle*, 100 Cal. L. Rev. 1445 (2012) (canvassing the reasons why appellate judges, at both the intermediate and high-court levels, write separate opinions).

Sometimes it can be hard even to figure out how the judges voted. You'll sometimes find a summary of the votes in the preliminary materials. Here's an example from a Supreme Court syllabus:

> White, J., delivered the opinion of the court, in which Burger, C.J., and Blackmun, Powell, Rehnquist, Stevens, and O'Connor, JJ., joined. Burger, C.J., filed a concurring opinion. Marshall, J., filed a dissenting opinion, in which Brennan, J., joined.

Notice that in this case, Burger C.J. not only joined in the majority opinion but also filed a concurrence to refine his position.

It can matter a lot whether you are reading the majority's opinion or a plurality or a concurrence or a dissent. Many reports identify the author of the opinion at the top of the page, which is helpful in tracking which opinion you are reading. You should also pay close attention to how the judges use key words such as "conclude" or "hold." When you read "we hold" or "we conclude," you can be fairly sure that the judge is speaking on behalf of the majority. On the other hand, phrases such as "we *would* hold" signal that whoever wrote those words didn't have the support of a majority on the court. Likewise, use of the singular pronoun "I" in an opinion should caution you that the judge probably doesn't have substantial support (unless there is only one judge, of course).

Unfortunately, judges don't always make it easy for readers. Consider the U.S. Supreme Court, which has nine Justices. With annoying frequency, they will decide a case without producing a majority opinion. In other words, a majority of five or more Justices agree on the outcome, but aren't all willing to join in a single opinion. What happens then is that one of the Justices will write what is called a *plurality opinion* (see § 20). This opinion explains the outcome agreed on by the majority and has obtained the most votes from majority members. Other Justices who agree on the plurality opinion's outcome but don't want to sign on to the opinion will write one or more concurring opinions. Hence the case might have a plurality opinion that speaks for three Justices and a concurring opinion that speaks for two more. The other four Justices may sign on to a dissent.

When there isn't a majority opinion, readers must reconcile the plurality and concurring opinions. In cases like these the concurring Justices have a lot of power. But because only those statements, rules, or principles that have the support of a majority of the judges can bind lower courts, in general these split decisions make weak precedents. That brings us to the next section.

20. Plurality Opinions

A plurality opinion is an appellate opinion not having enough judges' votes to constitute a majority but receiving the greatest number of votes in support of the decision. With a plurality decision, the only opinion to be accorded precedential value is that which decides the case on the narrowest grounds.

A plurality opinion is one that doesn't garner enough appellate judges' votes to constitute a majority, "but ha[s] received the greatest number of votes of any of the opinions filed,"[1] among those opinions supporting the mandate.[2] A plurality opinion results when a majority of the sitting court agrees on the ultimate result but not on "a single rationale to support the result."[3] Other opinions consonant with the result but differing in the underlying reasons are concurrences.[4] Meanwhile, opinions disagreeing with the result are dissents. Unlike other opinions in which a majority agrees on both the result and reasoning set forth in the court's opinion, no true "opinion of the court" exists in the case of a plurality opinion.[5] Hence these opinions are sometimes referred to as "no-clear-majority decisions."[6]

To illustrate, in a situation in which nine Justices hear a case, three Justices (A, B, and C) may concur in one opinion and find that the opinion of the lower court should be affirmed; a fourth Justice (D) may write a separate opinion, in which another Justice (E) joins, also voting to affirm the lower court's ruling, but based on different reasoning. The remaining four Justices (F, G, H, and I) may dissent, either together or separately, finding that the lower-court ruling should be reversed. In such a situation, the result is to affirm the lower court because five Justices (A, B, C, D,

---

1 *Garner's Dictionary of Legal Usage* 683 (3d ed. 2011).
2 James F. Spriggs II & David R. Stras, *Explaining Plurality Decisions*, 99 Geo. L.J. 515, 519 (2011).
3 Linda Novak, Note, *The Precedential Value of Supreme Court Plurality Decisions*, 80 Colum. L. Rev. 756, 756 n.1 (1980).
4 *Id.*
5 *Id.*
6 *Id.*

and E) agree on that result. But only three of the five "majority" Justices agreed on one rationale to support the result, while two others supported a separate rationale, neither rationale garnering enough votes to form a majority of the sitting Court. The opinion in which Justices A, B, and C concur is the plurality opinion because, of those supporting the result, it has accumulated the most votes. The ABC opinion isn't necessarily the opinion entitled to precedential effect, however. Instead, the opinion that lower courts follow is the one decided on the narrowest grounds.[7] So if the D–E opinion provides a narrower rule, it is the only opinion that will be considered precedential. Yet dissents, however narrow, will not be entitled to precedential effect, even if the reasoning in those opinions may be persuasive.

For a good example of a plurality opinion, consider *Pennsylvania v. Delaware Valley Citizens' Council for Clean Air*.[8] In that case, White J. wrote an opinion in which Rehnquist C.J. and Powell and Scalia JJ. joined, to reverse the judgment of the lower court. O'Connor J. wrote separately, concurring in part and in the judgment. The remaining four Justices dissented. White J.'s opinion is considered the plurality opinion, but lower courts have considered O'Connor J.'s opinion—in which no other Justice joined—as the holding of *Delaware Valley*.[9]

In perhaps the Court's most famous plurality opinion, *Regents of University of California v. Bakke*, Powell J. wrote the Court's opinion.[10] Three Justices joined the opinion in part, but five Justices wrote separately.[11] In all, eight Justices concurred and dissented in part. Despite the Court's fractured decision, educational institutions relied on Powell J.'s opinion in *Bakke* for 25 years.[12] Yet district courts remained uncertain about its precedential value.[13]

---

[7] *Marks v. United States*, 430 U.S. 188, 193 (1977).
[8] 483 U.S. 711 (1987).
[9] Mark Alan Thurmon, Note, *When the Court Divides: Reconsidering the Precedential Value of Supreme Court Plurality Decisions*, 42 Duke L.J. 419, 434 (1992).
[10] *Regents of Univ. of Cal. v. Bakke*, 438 U.S. 265, 269 (1978).
[11] *See id.* at 269, 324, 379, 387, 402, 408.
[12] *See Grutter v. Bollinger*, 539 U.S. 306, 323 (2003).
[13] *See id.* at 325.

Near the end of *Bakke*'s reign, the Sixth Circuit in *Grutter v. Bollinger* overruled the court below and held that Powell J.'s opinion was valid precedent.[14] The Sixth Circuit applied the *Marks* rule, which dictates that the narrowest rationale that a majority of the Court concurred in is binding precedent.[15] Even so, the Supreme Court had long recognized that applying *Marks* to *Bakke* "baffled and divided lower courts."[16] When *Grutter* was appealed from the Sixth Circuit, the Court clarified the law by adopting Powell J.'s views from *Bakke* into its holding.[17]

The practice of issuing plurality opinions is rooted in courts' increased resort to concurring opinions to advance an analysis or reasoning that differs from that of the majority. As we saw in § 19, in the early 1800s Marshall C.J. encouraged the Supreme Court to abandon the practice of issuing seriatim opinions and to embrace a new practice: adopting the decision of the majority as the opinion "of the Court."[18] He believed that seriatim opinions were "confusing and diminished the precedential value of the Court's decisions."[19]

Implementing a majority-rule system engendered the lower-court practice of identifying what rule the majority had adopted.[20] From the time of the Marshall Court and throughout the first half of the 20th century, identifying the majority rule was rarely difficult because few concurring opinions were issued.[21] But during the 1930s, Frankfurter J. began encouraging Justices to write

---

14　*See id.* at 321; *Grutter v. Bollinger*, 288 F.3d 732, 739 (6th Cir. 2002) (en banc); *see also Grutter v. Bollinger*, 137 F. Supp. 2d 821, 847 (E.D. Mich. 2001) (finding that the concurring opinions in *Bakke* were so "fundamentally different" from one another that there was no discernible holding).

15　*Grutter*, 288 F.3d at 739; *see also Marks*, 430 U.S. at 193.

16　*Grutter*, 539 U.S. at 325 (quoting *Nichols v. United States*, 511 U.S. 738, 745 (1994)).

17　*See id.*

18　M. Todd Henderson, *From Seriatim to Consensus and Back Again: A Theory of Dissent*, 2007 Sup. Ct. Rev. 283, 313 (2007); Linas E. Ledebur, Comment, *Plurality Rule: Concurring Opinions and a Divided Supreme Court*, 113 Penn St. L. Rev. 899, 901–02 (2009).

19　*See* Ledebur, *Plurality Rule*, 113 Penn St. L. Rev. at 901–02.

20　*Id.* at 902.

21　*Id.* at 903.

concurring opinions, embracing the practice himself.[22] In *Graves v. New York ex rel. O'Keefe*, Frankfurter J. wrote: "The volume of the Court's business has long since made impossible the early healthy practice whereby the Justices gave expression to individual opinions. But the old tradition still has relevance . . . ."[23] Although the following decade witnessed only the rare concurrence, in the latter half of the century and into the 21st century, concurring opinions accompanied more than half the Court's opinions.[24] The increase in concurrences in turn led to an increase in plurality opinions.[25]

Finding the precedential parts

The existence of plurality opinions has prompted discussion of their proper treatment as precedents. Because a plurality opinion lacks a true "opinion of the court"—that is, one in which a majority of judges agree to the reason and result—lower courts and practitioners may have difficulty ascertaining the legal rule that emanates from the opinion.[26] Although the U.S. Supreme Court has issued some guidance on how lower courts should interpret plurality opinions, debate still exists about what should be considered the holding of any particular plurality opinion and how courts should determine that holding.[27]

Some have questioned how much weight to accord plurality opinions, which create rules for future cases on the basis of reasoning not endorsed by a clear majority of the court. Such a point arose in 1972, when the Arizona Supreme Court chose to ignore

---

22 *Id.*

23 306 U.S. 466, 487 (1939) (Frankfurter J. concurring) (internal footnote omitted).

24 Ledebur, *Plurality Rule*, 113 Penn St. L. Rev. at 903–04 (noting that in the 1936–1937 term, only one out of 149 opinions had a concurring opinion, whereas during the 2007–2008 term, more than half of the Court's opinions contained concurrences).

25 *Id.*

26 *See, e.g., Unity Real Estate Co. v. Hudson*, 178 F.3d 649, 658 (3d Cir. 1999) ("The splintered nature of the Court makes it difficult to distill a guiding principle.").

27 *See, e.g.*, Ledebur, *Plurality Rule*, 113 Penn St. L. Rev. at 910–14 (discussing different solutions to deal with plurality opinions).

the U.S. Supreme Court's 4–3 opinion in *Fuentes v. Shevin*,[28] noting as follows: "When, however, we have doubts that once the full court hears the case that the opinion will stand, we are reluctant to declare unconstitutional Arizona statutes based upon a decision by less than a clear majority."[29] The Arizona court's disrespectful behavior was rewarded.[30] The Supreme Court reversed course in *Mitchell v. W.T. Grant Co.*[31] and *North Georgia Finishing, Inc. v. Di-Chem, Inc.*[32] Technically, however, the *Fuentes* opinion wasn't a plurality: it was "a four-justice majority of a seven-justice shorthanded Court."[33]

The rationale supporting a court's decision affects the precedential value of an opinion by shaping future conduct, articulating the legal principles underlying a decision, and guarding against "judicial bias and arbitrariness."[34] In the absence of a unified rationale to support a decision, its precedential value may be called into question and, in the view of some, is substantially diminished. Yet "the lack of a supporting majority rationale impairs neither the effect of the judgment in the particular case nor its precedential value in identical cases."[35]

The Marks *rule*

The prevailing approach for determining the rule that emerges from a plurality decision was established in the 1977 case of *Marks v. United States*.[36] Under the *Marks* rule, lower courts must follow the position taken by the Justices who concurred in the judgment on the narrowest grounds. The *Marks* Court did not elaborate on

---

28   407 U.S. 67 (1972).
29   *Roofing Wholesale Co. v. Palmer*, 502 P.2d 1327, 1329–30 (Ariz. 1972) (in banc).
30   *See* Michael A. Berch et al., *Introduction to Legal Method and Process: Cases and Materials* 246, 266 (5th ed. 2010) (discussing the Arizona Supreme Court's reaction to *Fuentes*).
31   416 U.S. 600 (1974).
32   419 U.S. 601 (1975).
33   *Id.* at 617 (Blackmun J. dissenting) (describing *Fuentes*).
34   Linda Novak, Note, *The Precedential Value of Supreme Court Plurality Decisions*, 80 Colum. L. Rev. 756, 757–58 (1980).
35   *Id.* at 758.
36   430 U.S. 188, 193 (1977).

how to identify the narrowest grounds. But the prevailing view is that the narrowest grounds are those that, when applied to other cases, would consistently produce results that a majority of the Justices supporting the result in the governing precedent would have reached. The narrowest grounds may be thought of as a common-denominator standard.

In *Marks*, the Supreme Court addressed the precedential value of an earlier Supreme Court obscenity decision, *Memoirs v. Massachusetts*.[37] *Memoirs* produced no majority opinion, but a plurality opinion joined by three Justices held that a book couldn't be banned as obscene unless it was "utterly without redeeming social value."[38] Black and Douglas JJ. wrote separately, concurring in the outcome but taking the view that a book could *never* be banned as obscene.[39] Three Justices dissented and would have allowed the ban.[40]

Confronted with the question how to interpret the splintered opinion in *Memoirs*, the Supreme Court in *Marks* held that when "a fragmented Court decides a case and no single rationale explaining the result enjoys the assent of five Justices, the holding of the Court may be viewed as that position taken by those Members who concurred in the judgments on the narrowest grounds."[41] The Court in *Marks* noted that the narrowest

---

37 A Book Named "John Cleland's Memoirs of a Woman of Pleasure" v. Attorney Gen. of Mass., 383 U.S. 413 (1966) (plurality opinion of Brennan J., joined by Warren C.J. and Fortas J.).

38 *Id.* at 419 (plurality opinion).

39 *See id.* at 421 (Black J. concurring in the judgment) (citing *Ginzburg v. United States*, 383 U.S. 463, 476, 497 (1966) (Black J. dissenting)); *id.* at 424–26 (Douglas J. concurring in the judgment); *id.* at 421 (Stewart J. concurring in the judgment on separate grounds) (citing *Ginzburg*, 383 U.S. at 499 (Stewart J. dissenting)).

40 *Id.* at 441 (Clark J. dissenting); *id.* at 455 (Harlan J. dissenting); *id.* at 460 (White J. dissenting).

41 *Marks*, 430 U.S. at 193 (quoting *Gregg v. Georgia*, 428 U.S. 153, 169 n.15 (1976)); *see also United States v. Santos*, 553 U.S. 507, 523 (2008) (plurality opinion) (identifying narrowest ground of decision between plurality and concurrence that serves as holding under *Marks* rule); *Panetti v. Quarterman*, 551 U.S. 930, 949 (2007) ("When there is no majority opinion, the narrower holding controls."); *United States v. Williams*, 435 F.3d 1148, 1157 (9th Cir. 2006) ("We need not find a legal opinion which a majority joined, but merely a legal standard which,

position in *Memoirs* was that of the three-Justice plurality. The *Marks* Court thus concluded that under the precedent established by *Memoirs*, a book couldn't be banned as obscene unless it was utterly without redeeming social value.

The Supreme Court's approach in *Marks* was commonsensical. As the D.C. Circuit has explained, because "Justices Black and Douglas had to agree, as a logical consequence of their own position, with the plurality's view that anything with redeeming social value is not obscene, the plurality of three in effect spoke for five Justices: *Marks*'s narrowest-grounds approach yielded a logical result."[42] The D.C. Circuit explained that "*Marks* is workable—one opinion can be meaningfully regarded as 'narrower' than another—only when one opinion is a logical subset of other, broader opinions. In essence, the narrowest opinion must represent a common denominator of the Court's reasoning; it must embody a position implicitly approved by at least five Justices to support the judgment."[43]

The other federal circuits follow this reasoning.[44] For example, the Third Circuit has said that when there are multiple opinions written in a decision, "the idea is to locate the opinion of the Justice or Justices who concurred on the narrowest grounds *necessary to secure a majority*. In other words, a lower court should not follow an opinion that, though part of the majority in that case,

---

when applied, will necessarily produce results with which a majority of the Court from that case would agree.") (quoting *Planned Parenthood of SE Pa. v. Casey*, 947 F.2d 682, 693 (3d Cir. 1991)).

42 *King v. Palmer*, 950 F.2d 771, 781 (D.C. Cir. 1991) (en banc) (internal quotation marks omitted).

43 *Id.*

44 *United States v. Johnson*, 467 F.3d 56, 64 (1st Cir. 2006); *United States v. Alcan Aluminum Corp.*, 315 F.3d 179, 189 (2d Cir. 2003); *Anker Energy Corp. v. Consolidation Coal Co.*, 177 F.3d 161, 170 (3d Cir. 1999); *A.T. Massey Coal Co., Inc. v. Massanari*, 305 F.3d 226, 236 (4th Cir. 2002); *United States v. Duron-Caldera*, 737 F.3d 988, 994 n. 4 (5th Cir. 2013); *United States v. Kratt*, 579 F.3d 558, 562 (6th Cir. 2009); *Gibson v. American Cyanamid Co.*, 760 F.3d 600, 619 (7th Cir. 2014); *United States v. Bailey*, 571 F.3d 791, 798 (8th Cir. 2009); *Lair v. Bullock*, 697 F.3d 1200, 1205 (9th Cir. 2012); *United States v. Carrizales-Toledo*, 454 F.3d 1142, 1151 (10th Cir. 2006); *United States v. Robison*, 521 F.3d 1319, 1323 (11th Cir. 2008) (Mem.).

was unnecessary to secure a five-Justice majority."[45] For example, the court continued, "if three Justices issue the broadest opinion, two Justices concur on narrower grounds, and one Justice concurs on still-narrower grounds, the two-Justice opinion is binding because that was the narrowest of the opinions necessary to secure a majority."[46] This statement differs from strict *Marks* analysis, under which the one-Justice opinion would control as the narrowest. The mathematical element ("necessary to secure a majority") appears to be a Third Circuit gloss. Among the other circuits, only the Ninth Circuit has expressly cited the Third Circuit's reasoning,[47] but neither adheres to it exclusively.[48]

The *Marks* rule is somewhat less important for the Supreme Court itself than it is for the lower courts. The Supreme Court—applying horizontal precedent—has flexibility to interpret, clarify, or refashion its precedents, not to mention overturn them.[49] (See §§ 3, 46–48.) By contrast, vertical precedent is absolute, making it important that lower courts properly understand and apply this essential rule.[50] With this in mind, it follows that the primary purpose of the *Marks* rule is to keep the law stable and predictable: "This objective requires that, whenever possible, there be a single legal standard for the lower courts to apply in similar cases and that this standard, when properly applied, produce results with which a majority of the Justices in the case articulating the standard would agree."[51] The "binding opinion from a splintered decision is as authoritative for lower courts as a nine-Justice opinion. While the opinion's symbolic and perceived authority, as well

---

45 *Casey*, 947 F.2d at 694 n.7.
46 *Id.*
47 *Jackson v. Danberg*, 594 F.3d 210, 220 (3d Cir. 2010); *Dickens v. Brewer*, 631 F.3d 1139, 1145 (9th Cir. 2011).
48 *Rappa v. New Castle Cnty.*, 18 F.3d 1043, 1057–58 (3d Cir. 1994) (citing *King*, 950 F.2d at 781; *Casey*, 947 F.2d at 781); *United States v. Williams*, 435 F.3d 1148, 1157 n.9 (9th Cir. 2006).
49 *See Grutter v. Bollinger*, 539 U.S. 306, 325 (2003) (reexamining precedent rather than applying *Marks* rule); *Nichols v. United States*, 511 U.S. 738, 745–46 (1994) (same).
50 *United States v. Duvall*, 740 F.3d 604, 611 (D.C. Cir. 2013) (Kavanaugh J. concurring in the denial of rehearing en banc).
51 *Casey*, 947 F.2d at 693.

as its duration, may be less, that makes no difference for a lower court."[52]

The *Marks* rule admits of straightforward application when two of the opinions reach the same result but one does so for narrower reasons, meaning that the narrower opinion would require the result in a subset of the cases in which the broader opinion would require that result.[53] In such a case, the narrower opinion is controlling. For example, in a 2014 case,[54] the First Circuit was required to apply the Supreme Court's holding in *National Federation of Independent Business v. Sebelius*[55] that the Affordable Care Act's Medicaid expansion was unconstitutional under the Spending Clause. A three-Justice plurality in *Sebelius* had found the provision unconstitutional because it (1) placed a condition on the receipt of funds that didn't govern the use of those funds and (2) was unduly coercive.[56] A separate opinion, joined by four Justices, found the provision unconstitutional "based on a finding of coercion alone."[57] The First Circuit found the plurality's opinion to be controlling under the *Marks* test because it would find a constitutional violation in a narrower set of cases than would the four-Justice opinion.[58]

Another example of how the *Marks* rule works in practice is the federal circuit courts' treatment of the Supreme Court's splintered opinion in *Freeman v. United States*.[59] In that case, a federal statute permitted district courts to reduce a criminal defendant's sentence under three conditions. First, the defendant must have accepted a Rule 11(c)(1)(C) plea agreement. In that kind of plea agreement, a defendant typically pleads guilty and agrees to a specific sentencing range under the federal sentencing guidelines. Second, the district court must have sentenced the defendant

---

52 *Id.* at 694.
53 *See Johnson*, 467 F.3d at 62–64.
54 *Mayhew v. Burwell*, 772 F.3d 80 (1st Cir. 2014).
55 132 S.Ct. 2566 (2012).
56 *Mayhew*, 772 F.3d at 86–88 (analyzing *Sebelius*).
57 *Id.* at 88.
58 *Id.* at 88–89.
59 564 U.S. 522 (2011).

"based on" the guidelines range.[60] And third, the federal sentencing guidelines must have been retroactively amended to reduce the guidelines range for the defendant's offense.

Kennedy J.'s plurality opinion in *Freeman*, which was joined by three other Justices, held that a Rule 11(c)(1)(C) plea agreement is always "based on" the guidelines range, and that a defendant who agrees to such a plea agreement is therefore eligible for resentencing if the guidelines range is retroactively reduced.[61] A four-Justice dissent, by contrast, held that a Rule 11(c)(1)(C) plea agreement is always "based on" the plea agreement, not the guidelines range, and that a defendant who agrees to such a plea agreement isn't eligible for resentencing.[62] In a concurring opinion, Sotomayor J. chose a middle ground. She concluded that a Rule 11(c)(1)(C) plea agreement is "based on" a guidelines range only when the plea agreement makes it clear that the sentence is based on that range.[63] Her concurrence wasn't joined by any other Justice.

Almost every federal circuit court to consider the *Marks* issue in *Freeman* has held that Sotomayor J.'s opinion is controlling.[64] The First Circuit, for example, concluded in 2011 that although the "gap between the plurality and the concurrence is wide," it "is still possible to tease out a common denominator."[65] In the view

60   18 U.S.C. § 3582(c)(2).
61   *See Freeman*, 564 U.S. at 529–31 (plurality opinion of Kennedy J.).
62   *See id.* at 544–51 (Roberts C.J. dissenting).
63   *See id.* at 534 (Sotomayor J. concurring).
64   *See, e.g., United States v. Rivera-Martínez*, 665 F.3d 344, 347–48 (1st Cir. 2011); *United States v. White*, 429 F. App'x 43, 47 (2d Cir. 2011) (unpublished); *United States v. Thompson*, 682 F.3d 285, 289–90 (3d Cir. 2012); *United States v. Brown*, 653 F.3d 337, 340 & n.1 (4th Cir. 2011); *United States v. Banks*, 770 F.3d 346, 351 n.4 (5th Cir. 2014) (per curiam) (noting that Sotomayor J.'s concurrence "is widely considered to express the holding in *Freeman*" without explicitly accepting Sotomayor J.'s opinion as controlling); *United States v. Rocha*, 587 F. App'x 199, 200 (5th Cir. 2014) (unpublished) (relying on Sotomayor J.'s concurrence); *United States v. Smith*, 658 F.3d 608, 611 (6th Cir. 2011); *United States v. Dixon*, 687 F.3d 356, 359–60 (7th Cir. 2012); *United States v. Browne*, 698 F.3d 1042, 1045 (8th Cir. 2012); *United States v. Austin*, 676 F.3d 924, 927 (9th Cir. 2012); *United States v. Graham*, 704 F.3d 1275, 1278 (10th Cir. 2013); *United States v. Lawson*, 686 F.3d 1317, 1321 n.2 (11th Cir. 2012) (per curiam). *But see United States v. Epps*, 707 F.3d 337, 350–51 (D.C. Cir. 2013) (holding that Sotomayor J.'s opinion wasn't controlling).
65   *Rivera-Martínez*, 665 F.3d at 348.

of the First Circuit, in those situations in which Sotomayor J.'s opinion would permit resentencing, Kennedy J.'s four-vote plurality opinion "would surely agree."[66] The Third Circuit similarly concluded that because Sotomayor J.'s opinion is "narrower" than Kennedy J.'s plurality opinion, Sotomayor J.'s opinion "expresses the holding of the Court."[67]

Yet the D.C. Circuit held in 2013 that Sotomayor J.'s opinion *wasn't* controlling.[68] According to that court, "there is no controlling opinion in *Freeman* because the plurality and concurring opinions do not share common reasoning whereby one analysis is a logical subset of the other."[69] And three years later, the Ninth Circuit agreed. It applied the D.C. Circuit's approach that "the concurrence posits a narrow test to which the plurality must necessarily agree as a logical consequence of its own, broader position."[70] The court found no common denominator between Justice Sotomayor's and the plurality's rationale. Instead, the court determined that the *Freeman* plurality had explicitly rejected Justice Sotomayor's reasoning, which fundamentally diverged from theirs,[71] and hence Sotomayor J.'s opinion could not be considered controlling. The court instead applied the Third Circuit's approach, which "looks to results rather than reasoning" and looked for the narrowest grounds that would necessarily produce results that the majority of the Justices would agree on.[72] Finding that this approach makes the most sense, the Ninth Circuit stated its impact on vertical precedents: "A fractured Supreme Court decision should only bind the federal courts of appeal when a majority of the Justices agree upon a single underlying rationale

---

66 *Id.*

67 *Thompson*, 682 F.3d at 289–90.

68 *See Epps*, 707 F.3d at 350–51.

69 *Id.* at 350 (citations and internal quotation marks omitted). *But see Duvall*, 740 F.3d at 612–17 (Kavanaugh J. concurring in the denial of rehearing en banc) (disagreeing with the reasoning in *Epps*).

70 *United States v. Davis*, 825 F.3d 1014, 1020 (9th Cir. 2016) (en banc) (quoting *Epps* at 348 (emphasis omitted) and *King*, 950 F.2d at 782).

71 *Id.*

72 *Id.* (quoting *Planned Parenthood of SE Pa. v. Casey*, 947 F.2d 682, 693 (3d Cir. 1991)).

and one opinion can reasonably be described as a logical subset of the other. When no single rationale commands a majority of the Court, only the specific result is binding on lower federal courts."[73]

The Supreme Court has said that the *Marks* "test is more easily stated than applied."[74] That is true. But in the vast majority of situations, it is possible to ascertain the common-denominator or middle-ground principle and to apply that principle as binding vertical precedent in future cases.

Beyond Marks

In rare cases, there may be no single narrowest ground or common-denominator opinion in a Supreme Court precedent.[75] For example, a four-Justice plurality and a one-Justice concurrence may reach the same result but rely on different rationales, neither of which can be definitively characterized as the middle ground or common denominator for purposes of future cases. As we've seen, *Freeman* is one example of this. *Marks* didn't address that scenario. But under our system of vertical precedent, there is a commonsense answer: lower courts should "run the facts and circumstances of the current case through the tests articulated in the Justices' various opinions in the binding case and adopt the result that a majority of the Supreme Court would have reached."[76]

By taking this approach, lower courts will reach the result with which a majority of the Justices who decided the relevant precedent would necessarily agree. This approach doesn't attempt to predict what a *future* Supreme Court would do. Rather, it seeks to determine the correct result in the lower court under the tests or standards applied by a majority of the Justices who decided the precedent in question.

To further complicate matters, in some plurality decisions a majority agreement exists only among both concurring and

---

73 *Id.*; *see also Lair v. Bullock*, 697 F.3d 1200, 1205 (9th Cir. 2012).
74 *Nichols*, 511 U.S. at 745.
75 *See id.* at 743–45 (describing the splintered decision in *Baldasar v. Illinois*, 446 U.S. 222 (1980), *overruled by Nichols v. United States*, 511 U.S. 738 (1994)).
76 *Duvall*, 740 F.3d at 611 (Kavanaugh J. concurring in the denial of rehearing en banc); *see also Johnson*, 467 F.3d at 64–65.

dissenting Justices.[77] And whether such "dual majorities" (as they are called) actually have precedential effect is a subject of debate among both judges and legal scholars. One commentator frames the crucial question this way: "Can a [dual] majority—a majority depending on the aggregation of both concurring and dissenting Justices' votes for support—create the law?"[78]

There are sound arguments on both sides. On the one hand, "common sense suggests that a legal proposition becomes law whenever majority support among Supreme Court Justices is certain. Some scholars . . . believe that five aligned votes create a binding precedent regardless of the opinion from which those votes are derived."[79] On the other hand, as one commentator put it, "[t]raditional conceptions of the *ratio decidendi* [i.e., holding] preclude use of any proposition taken by dissenting Justices to form a majority. This view has been attributed to the requirement that the *ratio decidendi* be the most narrow proposition necessary to reach the result."[80] Since a dissenting opinion can't be considered

---

77 Michael L. Eber, Comment, *When the Dissent Creates the Law: Cross-Cutting Majorities and the Prediction Model of Precedent*, 58 Emory L.J. 207, 208 (2008) ("Beyond the difficulties associated with applying this 'narrowest grounds' test, the *Marks* rule suffers from an underappreciated defect. Some plurality decisions involve majority agreement that is not between 'those Members who concurred in the judgments.'") (quoting *Marks*, 430 U.S. at 193); *see also* Ken Kimura, Note, *A Legitimacy Model for the Interpretation of Plurality Decisions*, 77 Cornell L. Rev. 1593, 1604–05 (1992) ("For a dual-majority to exist, there must be agreement between at least one coalition of concurring Justices and one coalition of dissenting Justices. It is only those plurality decisions in which a dual-majority exists that a numerical majority of Justices explicitly advocates a single rule of law.").

78 Eber, *When the Dissent Creates the Law* at 210 (footnotes omitted) (referring to such majorities as "cross-cutting majorities," even though *dual majority* is the predominant term in the scholarship).

79 *Id.* at 210 (footnotes and internal quotation marks omitted); *see also* Kimura, *A Legitimacy Model for the Interpretation of Plurality Decisions*, 77 Cornell L. Rev. at 1624 ("Courts should attribute persuasive authority to a legal rule that a numerical majority of Justices support."); Linda Novak, Note, *The Precedential Value of Supreme Court Plurality Decisions*, 80 Colum. L. Rev. 756, 767–69 (1980) ("[T]he technical alignment of the Justices is irrelevant; what is important is the presence of agreement by an actual majority of the Court.").

80 Mark Alan Thurmon, Note, *When the Court Divides: Reconsidering the Precedential Value of Supreme Court Plurality Decisions*, 42 Duke L.J. 419, 453 (1992); *see also* Eber, *When the Dissent Creates the Law*, 58 Emory L.J. at 209–20 ("If a dissent created the law, it would not be styled as a dissent. . . . [D]issents have

necessary to the outcome, this argument goes, it can't be characterized as necessary to the result and therefore can't establish the court's holding.[81]

The issue remains unsettled in part because it hasn't been authoritatively addressed in the caselaw, and courts have come down on different sides.[82] Courts dismissing the concept of dual majorities typically find it to be inconsistent with the language of *Marks*.[83] Articulating this reasoning in a 2014 case, the Seventh Circuit said: "*Marks* itself instructs that 'the holding is the narrowest position taken by those members who *concurred* in the judgment.'"[84] By disagreeing with the outcome, dissenters have by definition disagreed with the reasoning behind that outcome, this argument continues, so "if the dissenters disagree with the outcome of the case, then lower courts and (more importantly) litigants will not have a clear idea on the contours of the standard

---

no legally binding force and are necessarily dicta. Under this analysis, the very concept of a [dual] majority is at odds with basic rule of law values.").

[81] Thurmon, *When the Court Divides*, 42 Duke L.J. at 453.

[82] *Compare King*, 950 F.2d at 783 ("[W]e do not think we are free to combine a dissent with a concurrence to form a *Marks* majority."), *with Johnson*, 467 F.3d at 65 ("[W]e do not share the reservations of the D.C. Circuit [in *King*] about combining a dissent with a concurrence to find the ground of decision embraced by a majority of the Justices.").

[83] *See, e.g., United States v. Freedman Farms, Inc.*, 786 F. Supp. 2d 1016, 1021 (E.D.N.C. 2011) ("[T]he plain wording of *Marks* does not contemplate considering the position of dissenting Justices. To the contrary, *Marks* directs lower courts that '[w]hen a fragmented [Supreme] Court decides a case and no single rationale explaining the result enjoys the assent of five Justices, the holding . . . may be viewed as that position taken by those Members *who concurred in the judgment* on the narrowest grounds.'") (emphasis in original) (quoting *Marks*, 430 U.S. at 193).

[84] *Gibson v. American Cyanamid Co.*, 760 F.3d 600, 620 (7th Cir. 2014) (emphasis in original) (citations omitted) (quoting *Marks*, 40 U.S. at 193); *cert. denied*, 135 S. Ct. 2311 (2015); *see also State v. Griep*, 863 N.W.2d 567, 579 n.16 (Wis. 2015) ("Under *Marks*, the positions of the justices who dissented from the judgment are not counted in examining the divided opinions for holdings.") (citing *Marks*, 430 U.S. at 193), *cert. denied*, 136 S.Ct. 793 (2016); *Roark v. Macoupin Creek Drainage Dist.*, 738 N.E.2d 574, 583 (Ill. App. Ct. 2000) ("The mere ability to construct, from various concurring and dissenting opinions, a common denominator of probable outcome on an issue addressed in only one of those opinions does not make for a majority holding.") (quoting 5 Am. Jur. 2d *Appellate Review* § 602, at 298 (1995)).

and how to apply it in future cases. This is not the way to make binding precedent."[85]

But as the D.C. Circuit has noted, the *Marks* rule "does not apply unless the narrowest opinion represents a 'common denominator of the Court's reasoning' and 'embod[ies] a position implicitly approved by at least five Justices who support the judgment.'"[86] Indeed, the rule is considerably less useful when the rationale of one opinion doesn't lead to the same result in a strict subset of cases in which the other opinion would lead to that result.[87] In such cases, most courts have endeavored to "find common ground shared by" a majority of the higher court.[88]

For example, in a 2006 case[89] the First Circuit applied the Supreme Court's fragmented decision in *Rapanos v. United States*,[90] which considered the jurisdictional reach of the Clean Water Act. A four-Justice plurality set forth one method of analysis for deciding that question, a solitary concurrence by Kennedy J. set forth another, and a four-Justice dissent a third. But neither the plurality nor the concurrence was "narrower" than the other in the sense used in *Marks*. So noting that the four dissenting Justices would have found jurisdiction in any case in which the test espoused by the plurality *or* the test espoused by the concurrence were satisfied, the First Circuit held that jurisdiction would be proper if the requirements of either the plurality's test or Kennedy J.'s test were met.[91] And the Environmental Protection

---

85 *Gibson*, 760 F.3d at 620.
86 *Association of Bituminous Contractors, Inc. v. Apfel*, 156 F.3d 1246, 1254 (D.C. Cir. 1998) (quoting *King*, 950 F.2d at 781).
87 See *Johnson*, 467 F.3d at 64.
88 *E.g., id.* at 65 (endorsing "combining a dissent with a concurrence to find the ground of decision embraced by a majority of the Justices"); *Tyler v. Bethlehem Steel Corp.*, 958 F.2d 1176, 1182 (2d Cir. 1992) ("In essence, what we must do is find common ground shared by five or more justices."); *United States v. Davis*, 825 F.3d 1014, 1016 (9th Cir. 2016) (en banc) ("[W]e hold that where we can identify no rationale common to a majority of the Justices, we are bound only by the result.").
89 *Johnson*, 467 F.3d 56.
90 547 U.S. 715 (2006).
91 See *Johnson*, 467 F.3d at 64–66.

Agency, the Department of Justice, and several other courts have agreed.[92]

But other courts have interpreted *Rapanos* differently,[93] illustrating the uncertainty surrounding dual majorities' precedential weight. Yet in the gray area left by *Marks*, many courts have embraced dual majorities in interpreting splintered decisions.[94]

Indeed, the Supreme Court has repeatedly done so in interpreting its own precedents.[95] In *Moses H. Cone Memorial Hospital*

---

[92] Eber, *When the Dissent Creates the Law*, 58 Emory L.J. at 209; *see, e.g., United States v. Donovan*, 661 F.3d 174, 182 (3d Cir. 2011) ("We agree with the conclusion of the First Circuit Court of Appeals that neither the plurality's test nor Justice Kennedy's can be viewed as relying on narrower grounds than the other, and that, therefore, a strict application of *Marks* is not a workable framework for determining the governing standard established by *Rapanos*. We also agree with its conclusion that each of the plurality's test and Justice Kennedy's test should be used to determine the Corps' jurisdiction under the CWA."); *United States v. Bailey*, 571 F.3d 791, 799 (8th Cir. 2009) ("We find Judge Lipez's reasoning in *Johnson* to be persuasive, and thus we join the First Circuit in holding that the Corps has jurisdiction over wetlands that satisfy either the plurality or Justice Kennedy's test.").

[93] *See, e.g., United States v. Robison*, 505 F.3d 1208, 1221 (11th Cir. 2007) ("It would be inconsistent with *Marks* to allow the dissenting *Rapanos* Justices to carry the day and impose an 'either/or' test . . . . The fact that the dissenting Justices would uphold CWA jurisdiction under both Justice Scalia's test and Justice Kennedy's test is of no moment under *Marks*. . . . Thus, pursuant to *Marks*, we are left to determine which of the positions taken by the *Rapanos* Justices *concurring in the judgment* is the 'narrowest,' i.e., the least 'far-reaching.'") (emphasis in original) (citations omitted) (citing *Rapanos*, 547 U.S. at 810 (Stevens J. dissenting); *Marks*, 430 U.S. at 193); *United States v. Gerke Excavating, Inc.*, 464 F.3d 723, 724 (7th Cir. 2006) (per curiam) ("There was, however, no majority opinion in *Rapanos*. . . . When a majority of the Supreme Court agrees only on the outcome of a case and not on the ground for that outcome, lower-court judges are to follow the narrowest ground to which a majority of the Justices would have assented if forced to choose. In *Rapanos*, that is Justice Kennedy's ground.") (citation omitted) (citing *Marks*, 430 U.S. at 193).

[94] *See, e.g., Student Pub. Interest Research Grp. of N.J., Inc. v. AT&T Bell Labs.*, 842 F.2d 1436, 1451 (3d Cir. 1988) ("Because the four dissenters would allow contingency multipliers in all cases in which Justice O'Connor would allow them, her position commands a majority of the court.") (citing *Pennsylvania v. Delaware Valley Citizens' Council for Clean Air*, 483 U.S. 711 (1987)); *State v. Constantine*, 330 P.3d 226, 233 n.4 (Wash. Ct. App. 2014) ("Precedent includes a majority of justices, even a majority that is comprised of [sic] concurring and dissenting opinions.").

[95] *See, e.g., Alexander v. Choate*, 469 U.S. 287, 294 n.11 (1985) (implying that dissenting Justices can be counted towards a majority by counting the three dissenting Justices in *Guardians Ass'n v. Civil Serv. Comm'n of the City of N.Y.*,

v. Mercury Construction Corp.,[96] for example, the hospital sued the contractor in North Carolina state court, seeking to preclude arbitration over unpaid construction costs. The contractor then filed a diversity-of-citizenship action in federal district court, seeking to compel arbitration under the Federal Arbitration Act. The federal court stayed that action because of the parallel state action, citing *Colorado River Water Conservation District v. United States*.[97] Finding that the stay order did not meet *Colorado River's* extraordinary-circumstances test, the Fourth Circuit reversed the order and remanded the case to the district court with instructions to enter an order to arbitrate. The hospital appealed to the Supreme Court, arguing in part that the Court's later decision in *Will v. Calvert Fire Insurance Co.*[98] undermined the *Colorado River* test and that therefore, the district court's stay order was proper. The Supreme Court instead found that a dual majority in *Calvert* had in fact reaffirmed the *Colorado River* test:

> The Hospital relies on the opinion of Justice Rehnquist, announcing the judgment of the Court. The Hospital argues that Justice Rehnquist's opinion, if not expressly overruling *Colorado River*, at least modifies its holding substantially. But

---

463 U.S. 582 (1983), along with the three Justices signing the plurality opinion and the one concurring Justice as "seven Justices [who held the] view that a majority of the Court in *University of California Regents v. Bakke* had already concluded that Title VI reached only intentional discrimination") (citations omitted); *United States v. Jacobsen*, 466 U.S. 109, 117 n.12 (1984) ("For present purposes, the disagreement between the majority and the dissenters in that case with respect to the comparison between the private search and the official search is less significant than the agreement on the standard to be applied in evaluating the relationship between the two searches.") (citing *Walter v. United States*, 447 U.S. 649 (1980)); *Moses H. Cone Mem'l Hosp. v. Mercury Constr. Corp.*, 460 U.S. 1, 17 (1983) ("[T]he Court of Appeals correctly recognized that the four dissenting Justices and Justice Blackmun [concurring] formed a majority."). *But cf. United States v. Duvall*, 740 F.3d 604, 611 n.2 (D.C. Cir. 2013) (Kavanaugh J. concurring in the denial of rehearing en banc) ("When the Supreme Court itself applies *Marks*, it is not bound in the same way that lower courts are . . . to strictly follow the narrowest opinion from a prior splintered Supreme Court decision. That's because the Supreme Court is free to reconsider or refine or tweak its own precedents—including splintered precedents—and it does so in appropriate cases.").

96   460 U.S. 1 (1983).
97   424 U.S. 800 (1976).
98   437 U.S. 655 (1978).

it is clear that a majority of the Court reaffirmed the *Colorado River* test in *Calvert*. Justice Rehnquist's opinion commanded only four votes. It was opposed by the dissenting opinion, in which four Justices concluded that the *Calvert* District Court's stay was impermissible under *Colorado River*. Justice Blackmun, although concurring in the judgment, agreed with the dissent that *Colorado River*'s exceptional-circumstances test was controlling . . . . On remand, *the Court of Appeals correctly recognized that the four dissenting Justices and Justice Blackmun formed a majority* to require application of the *Colorado River* test.[99]

Scholarly arguments for according precedential weight to dual majorities have typically appeared as elements of proposed alternatives to the *Marks rule*,[100] proponents acknowledging that "[u]nder the traditional view, dissenting votes may not contribute to the majority consensus required for imperative authority."[101] But the consensus among these commentators is that, while not technically binding under *Marks*,[102] dual-majority alignments should be given significant persuasive authority—particularly where decisions are so fragmented as to render the *Marks* framework

---

[99] *Moses H. Cone*, 460 U.S. at 17 (emphasis added) (citations omitted).

[100] *See, e.g.*, Eber, *When the Dissent Creates the Law*, 58 Emory L.J. 207 (proposing the "prediction model"); Kimura, *A Legitimacy Model for the Interpretation of Plurality Decisions*, 77 Cornell L. Rev. 1593 (proposing the "legitimacy model"); Thurmon, *When the Court Divides*, 42 Duke L.J. 419 (proposing the "hybrid approach").

[101] Thurmon, *When the Court Divides*, 42 Duke L.J. at 466 n.a.; *see also* Kimura, *A Legitimacy Model for the Interpretation of Plurality Decisions*, 77 Cornell L. Rev. at 1614 ("The absence [in a dual-majority plurality decision] of an internal rule [that coherently justifies the particular outcome of the case] frustrates efforts to attribute binding precedential effect.").

[102] *See* Eber, *When the Dissent Creates the Law*, 58 Emory L.J. at 218 ("[T]he *Marks* rule . . . bars counting dissenting opinions . . . toward the 'narrowest grounds' of a decision.").

inapplicable.[103] On balance, and considering the Supreme Court's reliance on dual majorities in such cases as *Moses H. Cone*,[104] we agree.

---

103 *See id.* at 212 ("[L]ower courts should treat [dual] majorities as maximally persuasive, albeit nonbinding, authority."); Kimura, *A Legitimacy Model for the Interpretation of Plurality Decisions*, 77 Cornell L. Rev. at 1614–16 ("The presence . . . of a majority rule [in a dual-majority plurality decision] places persuasive limits on the lower courts' use of alternative rules. . . . The *identified rule* should be given precedential value because the presence of a numerical majority of Justices who concur justifies that rule (or no other rule is proper).") (emphasis in original); Thurmon, *When the Court Divides*, 42 Duke L.J. at 466 n.a. ("[S]uch alignments, which occur in dual majority cases, should receive maximum persuasive authority."); *see also Johnson*, 467 F.3d at 65 ("Since *Marks*, several members of the Court have indicated that whenever a decision is fragmented such that no single opinion has the support of five Justices, lower courts should examine the plurality, concurring and dissenting opinions to extract the principles that a majority has embraced.").

104 460 U.S. at 17; *see also League of United Latin Am. Citizens v. Perry*, 548 U.S. 399, 414 (2006) (finding that agreement among one concurring and four dissenting Justices in *Vieth v. Jubelirer*, 541 U.S. 267 (2004), establishes majority support for a proposition); *Alexander v. Sandoval*, 532 U.S. 275, 281–82 (2001) (finding agreement between plurality, concurring, and dissenting opinions in *Guardians*, 463 U.S. 582, to support two legal propositions); *Waters v. Churchill*, 511 U.S. 661, 685 (1994) (Souter J. concurring) (analyzing agreements between plurality, concurring, and dissenting opinions to determine what test lower courts should apply).

21. Per Curiam Opinions and Summary Dispositions

A per curiam opinion—one handed down by an appellate court without identifying the writing judge—is binding on lower courts. Although a short per curiam that offers little reasoning and resembles a summary order is not entitled to much precedential value, a per curiam that details the court's reasoning and analysis of precedents is entitled to the same precedential weight as a signed opinion.

A per curiam opinion resolves the immediate case before a court by an unsigned opinion of the court.[1] Although all the judges' names are listed, no authoring judge is identified. The degree of precedential value depends on the nature of the opinion, its context,[2] and the jurisdiction.[3] Some per curiam opinions resemble mere orders and are very short—sometimes only a single sentence—not an opinion in the usual sense.[4] Even such an opinion can be precedential in that it sets forth the court's view regarding the applicable legal principles.[5] A short per curiam opinion that summarily affirms or reverses a lower court's judgment is entitled to less precedential weight than a signed opinion. It is

---

1   Stephen L. Wasby et al., *The Per Curiam Opinion: Its Nature and Functions*, 76 Judicature 29, 29–30 (1992).

2   *See Walker v. Doe*, 558 S.E.2d 290, 295 (W. Va. 2001) ("[T]he 'value of any per curiam opinion . . . is in large measure a function of the quality of the opinion's legal reasoning.'") (quoting Steven C. Sparling, Note, *Cutting the Gordian Knot: Resolution of the Sentencing Dispute Over Dismissed Charges After* United States v. Watts, 6 Geo. Mason L. Rev. 1079, 1093–94 (1998)).

3   *See, e.g., Walker*, 558 S.E.2d at 296 (overruling caselaw in West Virginia that had stated that "per curiam opinions are not legal precedent").

4   *Rosengrant v. Havard*, 273 U.S. 664, 664 (1927) (per curiam) ("Affirmed on the authority of *Grant Smith-Porter Ship Company v. Herman F. Rohde*, 257 U.S. 469, 42 S.Ct. 157, 65 L. Ed. 321, 25 A.L.R. 1008 [(1927)], and *Millers' Indemnity Underwriters v. Braud*, 270 U.S. 59, 46 S.Ct. 194, 70 L. Ed. 470 [(1926)].").

5   *See, e.g., Nebraska Press Ass'n v. Stuart*, 427 U.S. 539, 558 (1976) (relying on the Supreme Court's per curiam decision in *New York Times Co. v. United States*, 403 U.S. 713 (1971), in finding that the Court had "accepted the *Near* and *Keefe* condemnation of prior restraint as presumptively unconstitutional") (quoting *Pittsburgh Press Co. v. Pittsburgh Comm'n on Human Relations*, 413 U.S. 376, 396 (1973)).

sometimes ignored altogether.[6] Other per curiam opinions, however, explain the court's reasoning and analysis in some detail.[7] Such an opinion merits the same precedential weight as a signed opinion because it reflects the agreed reasoning of a majority.[8]

The use of per curiams, together with their corresponding precedential value, has evolved over time. Per curiams have their "roots in that period of English law when opinions were not only anonymous, but also sometimes represented the feelings of only a majority of the court, with no dissent permitted."[9] In early United States law, the per curiam was mostly used to resolve cases with "'indisputably clear' substantive law"—that is, cases in which the law was unmistakable and the result so obvious that the court could dispose of the case unanimously with minimal effort.[10] The earliest per curiams dismissed appeals that were moot or that lacked federal jurisdiction.[11] Later, courts issued per curiams for cases decided on the merits, but only in cases that were "so easily decided that they did not require the more elaborate presentation of a signed opinion."[12] These early, typically short per curiams

---

[6] *Compare John Baizley Iron Works v. Span*, 281 U.S. 222, 228–32 (1930) (failing to cite or consider the Court's one-sentence per curiam opinion in *Rosengrant*, 273 U.S. at 664), *with id.* at 232 (Stone J. dissenting) (finding that the per curiam *Rosengrant* was on point and called for a result opposite of what the majority reached).

[7] *See, e.g., Buckley v. Valeo*, 424 U.S. 1 (1976) (per curiam opinion containing 139 pages of reasoning before reaching the Court's conclusion).

[8] *See, e.g., id.* (per curiam opinion relied on as authority in more than 100 Supreme Court decisions and 600 lower-court decisions).

[9] Richard Lowell Nygaard, *The Maligned Per Curiam: A Fresh Look at an Old Colleague*, 5 Scribes J. Legal Writing 41, 43–44 (1996).

[10] Stephen L. Wasby et al., *The Per Curiam Opinion: Its Nature and Functions*, 76 Judicature 29, 29–30 (1992); *see also* Laura Krugman Ray, *The History of the Per Curiam Opinion: Consensus and Individual Expression on the Supreme Court*, 27 J. Sup. Ct. Hist. 176, 177 (2002) ("The subtext of a per curiam was clear: this case is so easily resolvable, so lacking in complexity or disagreement among the Justices, that it requires only a brief, forthright opinion that any member of the Court could draft and that no member of the Court need sign.").

[11] Wasby et al., *The Per Curiam Opinion*, 76 Judicature at 29–30.

[12] Ray, *The History of the Per Curiam Opinion*, 27 J. Sup. Ct. Hist. at 178.

have precedential value because they apply well-settled legal principles to unique facts.[13]

The notion that per curiams resolved only obvious cases supported by the entire court began to erode when judges started dissenting.[14] In the U.S. Supreme Court, Holmes J., who came to bear the moniker "the Great Dissenter," was the first Justice to dissent from a per curiam opinion—in 1909.[15] Two more decades passed before another Supreme Court Justice wrote separately after a per curiam,[16] but eventually the practice grew.[17]

As separate opinions became more common, the per curiam as a tool to dispose of clear and easy cases evolved into "an opinion form useful precisely because it permitted the widest possible display of divergent opinions."[18] For example, in two Supreme Court cases in the 1970s, the court disposed of each case in a per curiam opinion that was accompanied by nine separate opinions. In *Furman v. Georgia*, the Court considered whether the death penalty violated the Eighth Amendment's prohibition against cruel and unusual punishment.[19] It issued a one-paragraph per curiam opinion finding the death penalty as then applied unconstitutional.[20] Each Justice then wrote a separate opinion either concurring in or dissenting from the per curiam.[21] Similarly, the

---

13   *See* Wasby et al., *The Per Curiam Opinion*, 76 Judicature at 29–30, 36; *see also* 21 C.J.S. *Courts* § 240 (2014) ("A 'per curiam opinion' is an opinion of the court in a case in which the judges are all of one mind, and which is so clear that it is not considered necessary to provide an extended discussion.").

14   Ray, *The History of the Per Curiam Opinion*, 27 J. Sup. Ct. Hist. at 178–80.

15   *See Chicago, Burlington & Quincy Ry. v. Williams*, 214 U.S. 492, 495–96 (1909) (per curiam) (Holmes J. dissenting); *see also* Laura Krugman Ray, *The Road to Bush v. Gore: The History of the Supreme Court's Use of the Per Curiam Opinion*, 79 Neb. L. Rev. 517, 524 (2000).

16   Ray, *The History of the Per Curiam Opinion*, 27 J. Sup. Ct. Hist. at 180 (citing *Broad River Power Co. v. South Carolina ex rel. Daniel*, 282 U.S. 187, 187 (1930), in which the Court produced two separate opinions following a short per curiam, with each opinion gaining the support of four Justices, all of whom supported the per curiam's result but for different reasons).

17   *Id.* at 180–82.

18   *Id.* at 185.

19   408 U.S. 238, 239 (1972) (per curiam).

20   *Id.* at 239–40.

21   *Id.* at 240–470.

Court decided the First Amendment issue in *New York Times Co. v. United States* with a per curiam after which each Justice wrote separately.[22] In both cases, the wide-ranging opinions demonstrate the shift of per curiam opinions from deciding obvious cases to disposing of cases when the majority agrees on the result but not the reasoning.

In addition to the continued use of the per curiam to resolve unchallenging cases,[23] a court may use it to decide a case in which time is of the essence, even if there is disagreement among a court's members.[24] For example, the Supreme Court decided *Bush v. Gore* in a substantial per curiam opinion, followed by one concurrence and four dissents.[25] The opinions reflected the disagreement among the Justices.[26] But unlike the opinions in *Furman* and *New York Times*, in which the Court issued a one-page per curiam opinion with individual opinions following, the per curiam opinion in *Bush v. Gore* was detailed: it provided thorough reasoning in support of the Court's decision.[27]

Dismissals and summary affirmances

Summary dispositions by a high court, such as traditional per curiam opinions, have binding effect. The Court has written that "[v]otes to affirm summarily, and to dismiss for want of a substantial federal question, it hardly needs comment, are votes on the merits of a case . . . . [T]he lower courts are bound by summary decisions by this Court until such time as the Court informs

---

22 403 U.S. 713, 714–63 (1971).
23 *See, e.g., Nitro-Lift Techs., LLC v. Howard*, 133 S.Ct. 500 (2012) (short, four-page per curiam opinion reversing Oklahoma Supreme Court because it ignored binding Supreme Court precedent); *Williams v. Johnson*, 134 S.Ct. 2659 (2014) (per curiam) (granting the petition for certiorari, vacating the Ninth Circuit's decision, and remanding in light of the new Sixth Amendment standards set forth in 28 U.S.C. § 2254(d)).
24 *See, e.g., Bush v. Gore*, 531 U.S. 98 (2000).
25 *Id.* at 100–58.
26 Laura Krugman Ray, *The Road to* Bush v. Gore*: The History of the Supreme Court's Use of the Per Curiam Opinion*, 79 Neb. L. Rev. 517, 568–69 (2000).
27 *Bush*, 531 U.S. at 100–11.

[them] that [they] are not."[28] Although the Court itself may feel somewhat more free to modify or set aside an earlier summary disposition,[29] most lower federal courts do not regard themselves as having that luxury. The Sixth Circuit made this point in its same-sex-marriage decision: "From the perspective of a lower court, summary dispositions remain 'controlling precedent, unless and until reexamined by [the Supreme] Court.' And the Court has told us to treat the two types of decisions, whether summary dispositions or full-merits decisions, the same . . . ."[30] Once again, each state appears to have established its own rule on this point.[31]

---

28 *Hicks v. Miranda*, 422 U.S. 332, 344–45 (1975) (internal quotation marks omitted).

29 *See Illinois State Bd. of Elections v. Socialist Workers Party*, 440 U.S. 173, 180–83 (1979) ("[S]ummary affirmances have considerably less precedential value than an opinion on the merits. . . . [T]he precedential effect of a summary affirmance can extend no farther than the precise issues presented and necessarily decided by those actions. A summary disposition affirms only the judgment of the court below, and no more may be read into our action than was essential to sustain that judgment. Questions which merely lurk in the record are not resolved, and no resolution of them may be inferred.") (internal quotations and citations omitted); *see also Wisconsin Dep't of Revenue v. William Wrigley Jr., Co.*, 505 U.S. 214, 224 n.2 (1992) ("[O]ur summary disposition affirmed only the judgment below, and cannot be taken as adopting the reasoning of the lower court.").

30 *DeBoer v. Snyder*, 772 F.3d 388, 401 (6th Cir. 2014) (quoting *Tully v. Griffin, Inc.*, 429 U.S. 68, 74 (1976)) (citations omitted), *rev'd sub nom. Obergefell v. Hodges*, 135 S.Ct. 2584 (2015); *see also Windsor v. United States*, 699 F.3d 169, 193–94 (2d Cir. 2012) (Straub J. dissenting) (discussing binding nature of summary dispositions, specifically *Baker v. Nelson*, 409 U.S. 810 (1972), *overruled by Obergefell*, 135 S.Ct. 2584, which Straub J. believed foreclosed plaintiff Windsor's claim).

31 *See* Ala. R. App. P. 53(d) ("An order of affirmance issued by the Supreme Court or the Court of Civil Appeals by which a judgment or order is affirmed without an opinion, pursuant to section (a), shall have no precedential value and shall not be cited in arguments or briefs and shall not be used by any court within this state, except for the purpose of establishing the application of the doctrine of law of the case, res judicata, collateral estoppel, double jeopardy, or procedural bar."); Ariz. Sup. Ct. R. 111(c) ("(1) Memorandum decisions of Arizona state courts are not precedential and such a decision may be cited only: (A) to establish claim preclusion, issue preclusion, or law of the case; (B) to assist the appellate court in deciding whether to issue a published opinion, grant a motion for reconsideration, or grant a petition for review; or (C) for persuasive value, but only if it was issued on or after January 1, 2015, no opinion adequately addresses the issue before the court, and the citation is not to a depublished opinion or a depublished portion of an opinion."); Ill. Sup. Ct. R. 23 ("(c) In any case in which the panel unanimously determines that any

Although the one-line orders embodied in summary affirmances bind lower courts, the same isn't true of another type of one-line order: denials of writs of certiorari. This action—in truth a kind of inaction—"imports no expression of opinion upon the merits of the case, as the bar has been told many times."[32] Unlike a summary disposition, a refusal to hear a case says nothing about the merits. It says only that, for any number of possible reasons, the Court didn't want to review the lower-court ruling: "The 'variety of considerations [that] underlie denials of the writ' counsels against according denials of certiorari any precedential value."[33] A decision not to decide doesn't tell the bench or bar whether the Court approved of the lower-court decision, thought the case presented a poor vehicle for reviewing the issue presented, sought to wait for a division of authority on the issue among the courts of appeals, or preferred to see further development in the lower courts over how to address the issue, whether on one side of the debate or the other.

A contrary rule would wreak havoc. A nine-member Court is in no position to assess the merits of the 9,000 or so certiorari petitions filed each year. And in some areas, such review would have destructive consequences. If the Court's denials of certiorari amounted to precedential decisions, that would undermine every habeas corpus and § 2255 petition filed after the criminal defendant had petitioned for direct review by certiorari. That isn't the law. The denial of a certiorari petition that a criminal defendant files after direct review of the state-court conviction doesn't affect the merits of a later habeas corpus petition filed by the defendant.[34]

---

one or more of the following dispositive circumstances exist, the decision of the court may be made by summary order. . . . (e) (1) An order entered under subpart (b) or (c) of this rule is not precedential and may not be cited by any party except to support contentions of double jeopardy, *res judicata*, collateral estoppel or law of the case."); *see also Williams v. State*, 45 So. 3d 14, 17 (Fla. Dist. Ct. App. 2010) (per curiam) (Webster J. concurring in the result) ("A per curiam decision with no written opinion has no precedential value.").

32   *United States v. Carver*, 260 U.S. 482, 490 (1923).
33   *Teague v. Lane*, 489 U.S. 288, 296 (1989) (internal citation omitted).
34   *See Brown v. Allen*, 344 U.S. 443, 456 (1953).

22. Equally Divided Opinions in Appellate Courts

If appellate judges divide equally in a case, the lower court's judgment will be affirmed. The affirmance is conclusive of the litigants' rights in the particular lawsuit, but it settles no question of law and does not have precedential force in similar cases in the same or any other court.

An equally divided opinion occurs when the same number of judges vote for either of two different results.[1] This situation might arise, for example, after the recusal of one judge among five or seven or nine, leaving an even number of judges to decide the case—which in turn creates the risk of an even split. It might also occur when a judge dies and isn't replaced for some time, as happened when Scalia J. died in February 2016—leaving eight justices on the U.S. Supreme Court to decide cases for the rest of the term.

As a general rule, when appellate judges are equally divided the result is to affirm the decision below,[2] to bind the litigants

---

[1] *See* Ryan Black & Lee Epstein, *Recusals and the "Problem" of an Equally Divided Supreme Court*, 7 J. App. Prac. & Process 75, 76–77 (2005) (noting that "the justices enjoy the unreviewable power to determine individually whether and when to disqualify themselves from cases in which their impartiality could reasonably be questioned").

[2] *See, e.g., Durant v. Essex Co.*, 74 U.S. (7 Wall.) 107, 109 (1868) ("Where the judges of the Supreme Court . . . are equally divided in opinion, . . . the judgment of affirmance . . . is as conclusive and binding in every respect upon the parties as if rendered upon the concurrence of all the judges upon every question involved in the case."); *Pierce v. Pierce*, 767 P.2d 292, 292 (Kan. 1989) (per curiam) ("The general rule in this jurisdiction, and elsewhere, is that when one of the justices is disqualified to participate in a decision of issues raised in an appeal and the remaining six justices are equally divided in their conclusions, the judgment of the trial court must stand.") (internal quotation marks and citation omitted); *Doll v. Major Muffler Ctrs., Inc.*, 687 P.2d 48, 51 (Mont. 1984) ("This Court previously has concluded that where the judges are equally divided, the judgment appealed from stands affirmed."); *Moore v. City of Creedmoor*, 481 S.E.2d 14, 24 (N.C. 1997) ("Justice Whichard recused and took no part in the consideration or decision of this case. The remaining members of the Court are equally divided on this issue, with three members voting to affirm and three members voting to reverse the decision of the Court of Appeals. Therefore, as to this issue, the decision of the Court of Appeals is left undisturbed and stands without precedential value."); *Thomas Phillips Co. v. Dover Mach. Prods.*, 94 N.E.2d 701, 701 (Ohio 1950) (per curiam) ("It appearing that the judges of the court are equally divided in opinion as to the merits of this case (one judge not participating) and are for that reason unable

under the principle of res judicata, and to be without precedential weight.[3]

This rule is an application of a broad principle governing multi-member bodies acting by majority rule—including legislative bodies—that "the body cannot take any affirmative action based on a tie."[4] For example, a tie in the House of Representatives results in the defeat of the motion or bill. The same holds true in the Senate, unless the Vice President breaks the tie, in which case the vote would no longer be equally divided.[5]

The U.S. Supreme Court has applied this rule of affirmance since its earliest days and has held to it whether the tie results from a recusal, absence, or vacancy, or from the court's size.[6] For example, in the 1825 opinion of *The Antelope*, the Court squarely

---

to agree upon a judgment, and the entry of that fact constituting an affirmance of the judgment of the Court of Appeals, that judgment is hereby affirmed."); *League of Or. Cities v. State*, 87 P.3d 672, 673 (Or. 2004) (per curiam) ("[W]e align ourselves with the United States Supreme Court, which has held that an equally divided court cannot act to grant affirmative relief."); *Commonwealth v. Nole*, 485 A.2d 766, 767 (Pa. 1984) (per curiam) ("The Court being equally divided, the Order of the Superior Court is affirmed."); *Croton Chem. Corp. v. Birkenwald, Inc.*, 307 P.2d 881, 881 (Wash. 1957) (en banc) (per curiam) ("One of the judges of this court being incapacitated and absent on account of illness, this case was argued to the remaining eight judges sitting *En Banc*. These eight judges are divided in their opinions and there is no majority for affirmance or for reversal. Therefore the judgment of the lower court stands affirmed."); *Hornback v. Archdiocese of Milwaukee*, 752 N.W.2d 862, 878 (Wis. 2008) ("This court is equally divided on whether to affirm or reverse the decision of the court of appeals dismissing the plaintiffs' complaint against the Archdiocese of Milwaukee. Consequently, we affirm the court of appeals' decision to affirm the circuit court's dismissal of the plaintiffs' claims against the Archdiocese of Milwaukee, without further analysis of that issue."); 5 Am. Jur. 2d *Appellate Review* § 779 (2014).

3   Black & Epstein, *Recusals and the "Problem" of an Equally Divided Supreme Court*, 7 J. App. Prac. & Process at 81 (internal footnotes omitted).

4   Edward A. Hartnett, *Ties in the Supreme Court of the United States*, 44 Wm. & Mary L. Rev. 643, 652 (2002); *see, e.g., Durant*, 74 U.S. at 109 ("It has long been the doctrine in this country and in England, where courts consist of several members, that no affirmative action can be had in a cause where the judges are equally divided in opinion as to the judgment to be rendered or order to be made.").

5   Hartnett, *Ties in the Supreme Court of the United States*, 44 Wm. & Mary L. Rev. at 655.

6   *Id.* at 646; *see, e.g., Durant*, 74 U.S. at 112; *Etting v. Bank of the U.S.*, 24 U.S. (11 Wheat.) 59, 78 (1826).

stated that "[w]here the Court is equally divided, the decree of the Court below is of course affirmed, so far as the point of division goes."[7] Just one year later, the Court once again divided equally, affirming the judgment below and declining to analyze the law at issue:

> In the very elaborate arguments which have been made at the bar, several cases have been cited which have been attentively considered. No attempt will be made to analyze them, or to decide on their application to the case before us, because the Judges are divided respecting it. Consequently, the principles of law which have been argued cannot be settled; but the judgment is affirmed, the Court being divided in opinion upon it.[8]

When an appellate court exercising original jurisdiction is faced with an even split between the judges, it may be required to determine which result constitutes affirmative judicial action.[9] For example, in 1952 the Supreme Court ordered a lawyer to show good cause why he shouldn't be disbarred from practice in the Court after his disbarment in New Jersey.[10] Clark J. didn't participate in the decision, and the remaining eight Justices were evenly divided on the question whether the attorney had met his burden to show that he should not be disbarred.[11] Despite the even split, the Court disbarred the attorney, suggesting that the Justices reached "an understanding that affirmative action would be required to displace the prior order."[12]

By contrast, when a court is exercising appellate jurisdiction, it is much more obvious what constitutes affirmative judicial

---

7   23 U.S. (10 Wheat.) 66, 67 (1825).
8   *Etting*, 24 U.S. at 77–78.
9   Hartnett, *Ties in the Supreme Court of the United States*, 44 Wm. & Mary L. Rev. at 646.
10 *In re Isserman*, 345 U.S. 286, 287 (1953), *vacated*, 348 U.S. 1 (1954) (per curiam).
11 *Id*. at 286–94.
12 Hartnett, *Ties in the Supreme Court of the United States*, 44 Wm. & Mary L. Rev. at 657 ("The Supreme Court later flipped the default position by amending its rules to provide that 'no order of disbarment will be entered except with the concurrence of a majority of the justices participating,' granted Isserman's petition for rehearing, set aside the disbarment, and discharged the rule to show cause.").

action.[13] As Field J. explained in 1868: "In cases of appeal or writ of error in this court, the appellant or plaintiff in error is always the moving party. It is affirmative action which he asks. The question presented is, shall the judgment, or decree, be reversed?"[14] If the judges' vote is deadlocked, the Justice wrote, "the reversal cannot be had, for no order can be made."[15]

When an appellate court agrees to reconsider a case en banc but stands evenly divided after rehearing, the district court's opinion will be affirmed.[16] The appellate court's grant of a rehearing vacates the earlier panel's opinion.[17] Because the en banc court reviews the lower court's judgment, not the vacated panel decision, an equally divided court reinstates the lower court's judgment, not the earlier panel opinion.[18] When an equally divided appellate

---

13 *Id.*
14 *Durant v. Essex Co.*, 74 U.S. at 112.
15 *Id.*
16 *See, e.g., Castañeda v. Souza*, 810 F.3d 15, 17 (1st Cir. 2015) (en banc) (stating in a case evenly divided by a vote of three to three: "The judgments entered in the district courts are affirmed by an equally divided en banc court."); *Compucredit Holdings Corp. v. Akanthos Capital Mgmt., LLC*, 698 F.3d 1348, 1349 (11th Cir. 2012) ("The decision of the district court is affirmed by an evenly divided court. The opinion of the panel remains vacated."); *Baker v. Pataki*, 85 F.3d 919, 921 (2d Cir. 1996) ("The ten remaining judges are evenly divided as to the merits of this case. The order of the district court is therefore affirmed . . . ."); *Stupak-Thrall v. United States*, 89 F.3d 1269, 1269 (6th Cir. 1996) (en banc) ("The en banc court is equally divided in this case. . . . Hence, as is customary under such circumstances, the judgment of the District Court is affirmed by an equally divided vote."); *Wells v. Davis*, 198 So. 838, 840 (Fla. 1940) (per curiam) ("When members of the Supreme Court, sitting six members in a body, and after full consultation, it appears that the members of the court are permanently and equally divided in opinion as to whether the judgment of the Supreme Court should be adhered to on rehearing, and there is no prospect of an immediate change in the personnel of the court, the previous judgment of the Supreme Court should not be disturbed."); *Jones v. Head*, 196 S.E. 725, 730 (Ga. 1937) ("[O]n rehearing the court stands evenly divided as to whether the former judgment of affirmance should be adhered to, or whether it should be vacated and the judgment of the trial court reversed. . . . The judgment of affirmance is therefore adhered to by operation of law.").
17 *See, e.g.*, 4th Cir. R. 35(c) ("Granting of rehearing en banc vacates the previous panel judgment and opinion; the rehearing is a review of the judgment or decision from which review is sought and not a review of the judgment of the panel.").
18 *Henderson v. Fort Worth Indep. Sch. Dist.*, 584 F.2d 115, 116 (5th Cir. 1978) (en banc) (per curiam) ("A petition for rehearing en banc was granted, which

court affirms a lower court's decision, the affirmance binds the litigants in the particular lawsuit but has no precedential weight in the future.[19] The lower court's decision is also stripped of precedential value.[20] The opinions of the divided appellate court may

---

effectively vacates the panel opinion as a citable precedent. With the panel opinion vacated, the en banc court has reached an even division as to the issues raised on appeal. Thus, the district court is affirmed by operation of law, and the decision of the court of appeals has no precedential value."); *Peoples v. CCA Detention Ctrs.*, 449 F.3d 1097, 1099 (10th Cir. 2006) (en banc) (per curiam) ("Because there is no majority on the en banc panel, the district court's ruling . . . is affirmed by an equally divided court. . . . That portion of the original panel opinion addressing this issue is, therefore, vacated and lacks precedential value.") (citing *Zuni Pub. Sch. Dist. No. 89 v. United States Dep't of Educ.*, 437 F.3d 1289 (10th Cir. 2006) (en banc) (per curiam); *United States v. Rivera*, 874 F.2d 754 (10th Cir. 1989) (en banc) (per curiam)); *Dasher v. Stripling*, 714 F.2d 1084, 1084 (11th Cir. 1983) (en banc) (per curiam) ("This Court took the case en banc, which resulted in the panel opinion being vacated. The judges of the en banc court are equally divided on the proper disposition of this case. Therefore, the judgment of the district court is affirmed as a matter of law, and this decision of the Court of Appeals has no precedential value.").

[19] *Neil v. Biggers*, 409 U.S. 188, 192 (1972) ("Nor is an affirmance by an equally divided Court entitled to precedential weight."); *Ohio ex rel. Eaton v. Price*, 364 U.S. 263, 263–64 (1960) (per curiam) ("The judgment of the Ohio Supreme Court in this case is being affirmed ex necessitate, by an equally divided Court. Four of the Justices participating are of the opinion that the judgment should be affirmed, while we four think it should be reversed. Accordingly, the judgment is without force as precedent."); *United States v. Garcia*, 604 F.3d 186, 190 n.2 (5th Cir. 2010) ("Decisions by an equally divided en banc court are not binding precedent but only affirm the judgment by operation of law."); *L.D.G., Inc. v. Brown*, 211 P.3d 1110, 1130 (Alaska 2009) ("An evenly divided decision by this court results in an affirmance, but that decision is not binding in future cases."); *In re Godoshian's Estate*, 312 N.W.2d 209, 210 (Mich. Ct. App. 1981) ("The appellate courts of this state have on two prior occasions considered the arguments advanced by appellant. In *In re DeWaters' Estate*, the Supreme Court affirmed a judgment of the circuit court holding that such bonds were not taxable. However, this decision was rendered by an equally divided court. Thus, it had no precedential value outside of the specific case under consideration.") (citation omitted); *Bailey v. Lewis Farm, Inc.*, 171 P.3d 336, 338 n.1 (Or. 2007) ("The Court of Appeals decision affirming the trial court's judgment by an evenly divided vote allowed that judgment to stand but does not have any precedential effect."); *Weiley v. Albert Einstein Med. Ctr.*, 51 A.3d 202, 217 n.16 (Pa. Super. Ct. 2012) ("Since the [Supreme] Court was divided evenly, this opinion does not have precedential value, although it has persuasive value."); *see also* 20 Am. Jur. 2d *Courts* § 134, at 537–38 (2015).

[20] *See, e.g.*, *United Food & Commercial Workers Union, Local 72 v. Borough of Dunmore*, 40 F. Supp. 2d 576, 586 (M.D. Pa. 1999) ("Where, as here, the Pennsylvania Supreme Court is evenly split on an issue, the lower court judgment is affirmed, but is deprived of precedential value. In other words, the issue remains unsettled and neither the lower court opinion nor the opinions of

nevertheless be instructive and offer guidance to lower courts deciding a similar issue.[21] Some commentators have characterized these opinions as "inefficient" and a "waste [of] time and energy,"[22] and have accused the Supreme Court, when the Justices divide equally on an issue, of "leav[ing] a legal area murkier than before the justices entered it."[23] But because courts rarely issue equally divided opinions, those opinions haven't been especially troublesome for the law's development.[24]

---

the divided appellate court judges can be invoked as stare decisis.") (citations omitted).
[21] *Id.*; *see also Weiley*, 51 A.3d at 217 n.16.
[22] Ryan Black & Lee Epstein, *Recusals and the "Problem" of an Equally Divided Supreme Court*, 7 J. App. Prac. & Process 75, 83 (2005).
[23] *Id.*
[24] *Id.* at 84–85.

23. Argument and Consideration

The authority of a precedent is greatly increased by the fact that the case was exhaustively argued by counsel and fully and maturely considered by the court. It is diminished by the fact that the case was submitted without argument, or on scanty or insufficient argument, or that it did not receive the court's attentive consideration.

The precedential sway of a case is directly related to the care and reasoning reflected in the court's opinion. That's part of why the adversary system is a cornerstone of our jurisprudence. In the words of a leading 19th-century commentator, "the doctrine of judicial precedent implies that the point to the decision whereof such force is attributed should have been argued by opposing counsel."[1]

True, there are exceptions that prove the rule. *Erie Railroad v. Tompkins*, for example, famously begins with the sentence, "The question for decision is whether the oft-challenged doctrine of *Swift v. Tyson* shall now be disapproved."[2] Few decisions of the U.S. Supreme Court have had greater precedential impact (see § 70), but the reason for that has nothing to do with how exhaustively counsel argued the point. There was no argument at all: counsel had not asked that *Swift* be overruled. The Court decided the issue on its own.

But generally speaking, the quality of counsel's argument has an indelible effect on a decision. Still, it is rare to see a court acknowledging this fact. To the contrary, courts are more often faced with the challenge of giving each side's position an equal hearing, even if counsel for one litigant possesses much more skill than counsel for the other.

The adversary system pushes courts toward the formal view that all cases fully briefed and orally argued by counsel are, by definition, fully and maturely considered by the court. Statements

---

[1] John F. Dillon, *The Laws and Jurisprudence of England and America* 233 (1894).
[2] *Erie R.R. v. Tompkins*, 304 U.S. 64, 69 (1938) (referring to *Swift v. Tyson*, 41 U.S. (16 Pet.) 1 (1842)).

supporting the related proposition—that a case submitted without sufficient argument has less precedential value—are also uncommon, although they do occasionally occur. One appears in the U.S. Supreme Court's 2014 decision in *McCutcheon v. Federal Election Commission*.[3] In that case, the Court dismissed *Buckley v. Valeo*[4] as lacking precedential weight on a certain issue because the opinion in that case was "written without the benefit of full briefing or argument on the issue."[5] The Court wrote: "We are confronted with a different statute and different legal arguments, at a different point in the development of campaign finance regulation. Appellants' substantial First Amendment challenge to the system of aggregate limits currently in place thus merits our plenary consideration."[6] *McCutcheon* offered other examples as well for the proposition that the Court believes that it need not adhere to an earlier decision on an issue that the earlier case didn't fully consider.[7]

The Supreme Court doesn't always sharply distinguish between this rule and the rule recognizing that cases resolved by summary affirmance are entitled to less precedential weight for purposes of horizontal stare decisis.[8] Because it invokes the rule relating to the quality of reasoning only sporadically, it is hard to describe precisely when it does and doesn't apply.

---

3   134 S.Ct. 1434, 1447 (2014).
4   424 U.S. 1 (1976).
5   134 S.Ct. at 1447.
6   *Id.* (citations and footnote omitted).
7   *See, e.g., Toucey v. New York Life Ins. Co.*, 314 U.S. 118, 139–40 (1941) (departing from "[l]oose language and a sporadic, ill-considered decision" when asked to resolve a question "with our eyes wide open and in the light of full consideration"); *Hohn v. United States*, 524 U.S. 236, 251 (1998) (describing this rule as an exception to stare decisis: "We have recognized, however, that stare decisis is a 'principle of policy' rather than 'an inexorable command.' For example, we have felt less constrained to follow precedent where, as here, the opinion was rendered without full briefing or argument.") (citing *Gray v. Mississippi*, 481 U.S. 648, 651 n.1 (1987), which in turn questioned the precedential value of *Davis v. Georgia*, 429 U.S. 122 (1976) (per curiam)).
8   *See, e.g., Edelman v. Jordan*, 415 U.S. 651, 671 (1974) (summary affirmances "are not of the same precedential value as would be an opinion of this Court treating the question on the merits").

The Massachusetts Supreme Judicial Court has suggested a more concrete approach: it will consider "significant issues in moot cases . . . [only] where the issue has been 'fully argued on both sides, where the question was certain, or at least very likely, to arise again in similar factual circumstances, and especially where appellate review could not be obtained before the recurring question would again be moot.'"[9]

If one or more litigants bring an issue to the court's attention, but the court chooses not to address it, then the decision isn't authority for any implicit position that the court might be assumed to have taken in ruling.[10] Courts often decline to address arguments: many opinions conclude by saying something like "we have considered the other arguments and find them to be without merit."[11] Yet if the court decides to raise a legal point on its own initiative, then the weight of its decision will be the same as if it were responding to a litigant's argument. The point will be authoritative unless it qualifies as dictum.

This formulation leaves room for a court to make precedential decisions on issues it chooses to write about though not expressly raised by the litigants. Within this set of cases, jurisdictional issues deserve special mention both because they arise frequently and because they involve the court's power to render a binding decision. Most courts hold that if a court has previously made a decision on the merits on a particular issue without considering whether it had jurisdiction to do so, the earlier case doesn't

---

9   *Martin v. Commonwealth*, 897 N.E.2d 991, 991–92 (Mass. 2008) (citing *Lockhart v. Attorney Gen.*, 459 N.E.2d 813, 815 (Mass. 1984)).

10 *See Central Va. Cmty. Coll. v. Katz*, 546 U.S. 356, 363 (2006) ("[W]e are not bound to follow our dicta in a prior case in which the point now at issue was not fully debated."); *United States v. Bennett*, 100 F.3d 1105, 1110 (3d Cir. 1996) ("Neither party had briefed or argued the issue of whether Pennsylvania's burglary statute is generic. A court's statement concerning an issue not raised on appeal is dicta."); *United States v. Crawley*, 837 F.2d 291, 293 (7th Cir. 1988) ("that the issue addressed in the passage was not presented as an issue" is a factor in determining that passage was dictum); *State v. Mueller*, 549 N.W.2d 455, 461 n.5 (Wis. Ct. App. 1996) ("A statement by a court regarding an issue never briefed is not a holding.").

11 *See, e.g., Clark v. United States*, 289 U.S. 1, 20 (1933); *National Carbide Corp. v. Commissioner*, 336 U.S. 422, 439 (1949); *Barnhart v. Thomas*, 540 U.S. 20, 29 (2003); *MCI Commc'ns Corp. v. AT&T Co.*, 708 F.2d 1081, 1174 (7th Cir. 1983).

stand for the proposition that jurisdiction was in fact proper.[12] This principle has been extended to other types of issues that were not presented and thus not squarely decided by a court.[13] These extensions may be nothing more than special applications of the rule that a court won't normally accept as binding precedent a point that was passed by in silence, either because the litigants never brought it up or because the court found no need to discuss it.

---

12 See *Ayrshire Collieries Corp. v. United States*, 331 U.S. 132, 137 n.2 (1947) ("The mere fact that the case was entertained by this Court is no basis for considering it as authoritative on the jurisdictional issue, it being the firm policy of this Court not to recognize the exercise of jurisdiction as precedent where the issue was ignored."); *United States v. Los Angeles Tucker Truck Lines, Inc.*, 344 U.S. 33, 37–38 (1952) ("The effect of the omission was not there raised in briefs or argument nor discussed in the opinion of the Court. Therefore, the case is not a binding precedent on this point."); *United States v. More*, 7 U.S. (3 Cranch) 159, 172 (1805) (from the opinion's accompanying description of oral argument: "But this court has exercised appellate jurisdiction in a criminal case [in *United States v. Simms*].... No question was made, in that case, as to the jurisdiction. It passed *sub silentio*, and the court does not consider itself as bound by that case.").

13 *Legal Servs. Corp. v. Velazquez*, 531 U.S. 533, 557 (2001) (Scalia J. dissenting) ("Judicial decisions do not stand as binding 'precedent' for points that were not raised, not argued, and hence not analyzed."); *Webster v. Fall*, 266 U.S. 507, 511 (1925) ("We do not stop to inquire whether all or any of them [the cases] can be differentiated from the case now under consideration, since in none of them was the point here at issue suggested or decided. The most that can be said is that the point was in the cases if any one had seen fit to raise it. Questions which merely lurk in the record, neither brought to the attention of the court nor ruled upon, are not to be considered as having been so decided as to constitute precedents."); *Boyd v. Alabama*, 94 U.S. 645, 648 (1876) ("Courts seldom undertake, in any case, to pass upon the validity of legislation, where the question is not made by the parties. Their habit is to meet questions of that kind when they are raised, but not to anticipate them.... The fact that acts may in this way have been often before the court is never deemed a reason for not subsequently considering their validity when that question is presented."); *Massey v. Fulks*, 376 S.W.3d 389, 394 (Ark. 2011) ("No argument was raised in *Dodson* that the non-claim period was extended based on the lack of notice. Our practice is to limit our opinions to the issues that are presented to us, and we are not bound by matters that are passed upon *sub silentio*."); *Heaney v. Northeast Park Dist. of Evanston*, 195 N.E. 649, 651 (Ill. 1935) ("The questions which we have considered in this case were neither presented, considered, nor decided in that one, and it is not an authority upon any point now being examined. A decision by a court of review is not an authority upon a question neither considered nor decided by it.").

24. Nonfinal Decisions

Decisions rendered ex parte or in preliminary or interlocutory proceedings do not have as much force or value as contested ones that have been handed down with a final disposition.

A nonfinal decision doesn't conclusively dispose of an issue or claim. Examples are interlocutory orders,[1] ex parte decisions,[2] temporary restraining orders, and preliminary injunctions. Such decisions often only tentatively resolve evidentiary, discovery, and attorney–client-privilege issues arising during the course of litigation.

Nonfinal decisions differ from decisions on the merits in several ways.[3] Generally speaking, they serve a narrow purpose and are "less formal" and "less complete."[4] They are "by . . . nature interlocutory, tentative, and impermanent."[5]

---

1   *See Black's Law Dictionary* 1271 (Bryan A. Garner ed., 10th ed. 2014) (defining an *interlocutory order* as "relat[ing] to some intermediate matter in [a] case"); *see also* 56 Am. Jur. 2d *Motions, Rules, and Orders* § 43, at 69 (2014) (explaining that interlocutory orders "leave[] something further to be determined or adjudicated in disposing of the parties and their rights").

2   *See Black's Law Dictionary* at 1271 (defining an *ex parte order* as "[a]n order made by the court upon the application of one party to an action without notice to the other").

3   *Valdez v. Applegate*, 616 F.2d 570, 572 (10th Cir. 1980) ("The determination of a motion for a preliminary injunction and a decision on the merits are different.").

4   *See University of Tex. v. Camenisch*, 451 U.S. 390, 395 (1981) ("The purpose of a preliminary injunction is merely to preserve the relative positions of the parties until a trial on the merits can be held. Given this limited purpose, and given the haste that is often necessary if those positions are to be preserved, a preliminary injunction is customarily granted on the basis of procedures that are less formal and evidence that is less complete than in a trial on the merits.").

5   *See Madison Square Garden Boxing, Inc. v. Shavers*, 562 F.2d 141, 144 (2d Cir. 1977) (describing a preliminary injunction); *see also Hamilton Watch Co. v. Benrus Watch Co.*, 206 F.2d 738, 742 (2d Cir. 1953) ("[A] preliminary injunction—as indicated by the numerous more or less synonymous adjectives used to label it—is, by its very nature, interlocutory, tentative, provisional, ad interim, impermanent, mutable, not fixed or final or conclusive, characterized by its for-the-time-beingness. It serves as an equitable policing measure to prevent the parties from harming one another during the litigation; to keep the parties, while the suit goes on, as far as possible in the respective positions they occupied when the suit began.").

In many ways, the difference between a dispositive and a nonfinal decision parallels the difference between a judgment and an order. A judgment encompasses "the court's official and final consideration and determination of the respective rights and obligations of the parties."[6] An order, by contrast, is a "determination by a court or judge [that] is intermediate in nature."[7] So orders are generally nondispositive and judgments are generally dispositive. Yet the designation *order* or *judgment* doesn't conclusively determine whether the decision is final. For example, a final order sometimes falls "within the scope of the term 'judgment.'"[8] Even decisions on certain motions, such as a motion to dismiss or a motion for summary judgment, can conclusively dispose of an issue or claim or, sometimes, a case.[9]

The key distinguishing factor between a nondispositive order and a dispositive judgment isn't nomenclature but finality: "whether [the action] is a final adjudication of the cause, or a ruling on a motion, preliminary or collateral to the final adjudication."[10] Final orders are "conclusive as to the parties and must be obeyed until . . . reversed, modified, or set aside," whereas nonfinal orders generally aren't binding on the court until the culmination of the controversy. Hence interlocutory orders may be reconsidered and modified.[11]

A nonfinal decision cannot become the law of the case. Under the law-of-the-case doctrine, a court's decision on the applicable legal rule "should continue to govern the same issue in subsequent

---

6   56 Am. Jur. 2d *Motions, Rules, and Orders* § 42, at 68 (2014).

7   *Id.*

8   *Id.*

9   Ruby J. Krajick, *Making Motions and Opposing Motions* 1 (2010), http://www.nysd.uscourts.gov/file/forms_instructions/motion-opposition-to-motion-and-reply (explaining that a decision on some motions may be "dispositive" in that "the entire case[] could end" and others could be "non-dispositive" in "that the decision on the motion will not directly end a claim or a party's involvement in the case").

10 56 Am. Jur. 2d *Motions, Rules, and Orders* § 42, at 68–69 (2014); *see also* 18B Charles Alan Wright, Arthur R. Miller et al., *Federal Practice and Procedure* § 4478.5, at 791 (2d ed. 2002 & Supp. 2015).

11 *See* 56 Am. Jur. 2d *Motions, Rules, and Orders* § 55, at 89–90 (2010).

stages of the same case."[12] Although the doctrine has been called "an amorphous concept,"[13] at its core it "merely expresses the practice of courts generally to refuse to reopen what has been decided."[14] Only final decisions—binding adjudications or final judgments—may become the law of the case.[15] So "[p]reliminary or tentative rulings do not establish law of the case."[16] And a decision that doesn't bind the court that issued it or the litigants cannot bind nonparties.

For more on the law-of-the-case doctrine, see §§ 52–59.

---

12 21 C.J.S. *Courts* § 237, at 233 (2014).

13 *Arizona v. California*, 460 U.S. 605, 618 (1983), *decision supplemented*, 466 U.S. 144 (1984).

14 *Messigner v. Anderson*, 225 U.S. 436, 444 (1912).

15 *United States v. Bettenhausen*, 499 F.2d 1223, 1230 (10th Cir. 1974) (citing *United States v. United States Smelting Ref. & Mining Co.*, 339 U.S. 186, 198–99 (1950)); *see also* 18B Wright et al., *Federal Practice and Procedure* § 4478.5, at 791.

16 18B Wright et al., *Federal Practice and Procedure* § 4478.5, at 791; *see also* 21 C.J.S. *Courts* § 239 (2014) ("The law of the case doctrine generally applies to final determinations after a hearing on the merits, although there is some question whether it applies to interlocutory rulings."); *id.* ("[T]here is . . . some authority that the law of the case does apply to interlocutory orders."). *See, e.g.*, *In re Evangeline Ref. Co.*, 890 F.2d 1312, 1322 (5th Cir. 1989) ("Interim fee awards are not final determinations . . . . Rather, they are interlocutory and reviewable . . . . Thus, we conclude that the law of the case doctrine does not apply to interim fee awards.").

25. Approval, Acceptance, and Recognition

Another court's approval of a decision can bolster its credibility and increase its value as precedent. The absence of approval or affirmation through citation or reference can leave an opinion vulnerable to attack.

To justify reliance on a case, a court may note that other courts have cited it approvingly.[1] The impulse to call attention to approbation is especially strong when there is some reason to doubt an opinion's validity. For example, approval might rejuvenate an opinion that courts could otherwise consider obsolete.[2] Approval by a higher court can enhance the authority of an opinion that probably wouldn't otherwise be followed, such as an opinion issued by a lower court[3] or a court in another state,[4] or even an opinion that simply appears weak in its reasoning.

The effect of approval on a precedent is amplified when it is repeated, and courts often cite repeated approval to convey the

---

1   See, e.g., *Stowik v. Sirker*, 522 So. 2d 106, 107 (Fla. Dist. Ct. App. 1988); *State v. Smith*, 35 S.E. 615, 616 (N.C. 1900); *Massie v. Enyart*, 32 Ark. 251, 256 (1877) (noting that "[t]he decision has been approved by several of our later decisions"); *Sanchez v. Forster*, 65 P. 1077, 1078 (Cal. 1901) (referring to an 1886 case that was "approved by this court in [a recent] case [from 1899]"); *Pendleton v. Pendleton*, 6 N.C. 82, 83 (1811) (noting that "[t]he principle of [a supporting] decision has been approved in [several cases]").

2   See, e.g., *White v. White*, 326 P.2d 306, 311 (Kan. 1958) (relying on rule established in cases from 1914 and 1917 and explaining that "[t]he rule of the foregoing decisions has been approved, stated and applied in many of our more recent decisions"); *Schumann v. Fisher*, 164 N.E.2d 759, 761 (Ohio Ct. App. 1959) (noting that a 1938 "decision has been approved and followed in a long line of decisions by the Supreme Court, the most recent decision being [a 1956 case]"); *Barland v. Eau Claire Cnty.*, 575 N.W.2d 691, 704 n.23 (Wis. 1998) (observing that a relevant case "is not the most recent proclamation of law" but "has been routinely cited and discussed in our decisions").

3   See, e.g., *Jackson v. King*, 63 P. 297, 297 (Kan. Ct. App. 1900) (per curiam) (discussing court-of-appeals decision that was "approved by the supreme court . . . in the same case"); see also *Hayes v. Hayes*, 135 N.Y.S. 225, 226 (App. Div. 1912) (deciding that, between two irreconcilable cases, the earlier ought to be followed because that "decision has been approved by the Court of Appeals, in the very words of the opinion").

4   See, e.g., *In re Jones' Estate*, 2 P.2d 483, 485 (Cal. Ct. App. 1931) (explaining that the relevant rule "ha[d] been approved by the Supreme Court of this state" and therefore should be followed).

strength of the precedent while bolstering their own opinion relying on it.[5] Repeated approval decreases the probability that later courts will overrule the decision[6] because "opinions that have been reconsidered and reaffirmed are more likely to be correct on the merits."[7] A precedent that has never been cited or affirmed—or that has not been recently cited—is vulnerable to doubt.[8]

Like approval, acceptance of a rule or decision by courts, lawmakers, litigants, and the public can fortify a precedent's value. When courts in a particular jurisdiction have accepted a principle as sound, the likelihood increases that it will withstand future challenge. In determining what the correct law is, a court would be remiss to ignore such a well-accepted position. Most courts

---

5 See, e.g., *Los Angeles Title Ins. Co. v. City of Los Angeles*, 198 P. 1001, 1003 (Cal. Dist. Ct. App. 1921) ("This decision has been approved in many later cases...."); *Septer v. Boyles*, 5 P.2d 785, 786 (Kan. 1931) ("This decision has been approved and followed numerous times."); *Herring v. Warwick*, 71 S.E. 462, 463 (N.C. 1911) ("This decision has been approved in several cases...."); *Albers v. Great Cent. Transp. Corp.*, 59 N.E.2d 389, 390 (Ohio Ct. App. 1944) ("[T]he decision has been approved and followed without exception in all subsequent cases.").

6 See *Randall v. Sorrell*, 548 U.S. 230, 244 (2006) ("[T]he rule of law demands that adhering to our prior case law be the norm. Departure from precedent is exceptional, and requires 'special justification.' This is especially true where, as here, the principle has become settled through iteration and reiteration over a long period of time.") (internal citation omitted); *see also Erie R.R. v. Tompkins*, 304 U.S. 64, 84 (1938) (Butler J. dissenting) (rejecting the majority's decision to overrule *Swift v. Tyson*, 41 U.S. (16 Pet.) 1 (1842), and explaining that its "doctrine ... has been followed by this Court in an unbroken line of decisions [and] ... was not questioned until more than 50 years later, and then by a single judge").

7 Randy J. Kozel, *Stare Decisis as Judicial Doctrine*, 67 Wash. & Lee L. Rev. 411, 432 (2010).

8 See, e.g., *Gilstrap v. Amtrak*, 998 F.2d 559, 562 (8th Cir. 1993) ("[W]e agree ... that the age of the decision and the absence of recent citation to it suggest that the Washington Supreme Court might well reconsider its former ruling were an appropriate opportunity to arise."); *Fluor W., Inc. v. G & H Offshore Towing Co.*, 447 F.2d 35, 37 (5th Cir. 1971) (per curiam) ("[T]he age of that decision would cause its continuing precedential value to be questionable in [the] absence of reaffirmation by later cases."); *Newport Beach Country Club, Inc. v. Founding Members of the Newport Beach Country Club*, 45 Cal. Rptr. 3d 207, 213–14 (Ct. App. 2006) (finding that another case "has not withstood the test of time" and that "[t]he Supreme Court has never confirmed [the case]").

respond to a strong convergence of opinion on a particular issue by following the majority rule, even when not obliged to do so.[9]

Superprecedents

Oft-cited decisions that have achieved general acceptance represent stable precedents that are "practically immune to reconsideration and reversal."[10] Scholars have referred to the most stable of these as "superprecedents."[11] Many such precedents address concepts fundamental to our way of life or the judicial system. For example, in *Marbury v. Madison*,[12] the U.S. Supreme Court recognized the power of judicial review, which has since become a cornerstone of government and legal jurisprudence.[13] Its strength as a precedent results not just from frequent citation and the absence of criticism, but from acceptance of the decision's correctness. Every instance of judicial review, whether the reviewing court refers to *Marbury* or not, is further validation of the hallowed decision.

Another example of a superprecedent—one that we all encounter every day even though few even realize it—is the decision in the *Legal Tender Cases*,[14] upholding the constitutionality of paper money. As one scholar points out, "[t]he possibility of . . . returning to a world without legal tender . . . is simply

---

9   *See, e.g.*, *Etcheverry v. Tri-Ag Serv., Inc.*, 993 P.2d 366, 368 (Cal. 2000) ("[W]here the decisions of the lower federal courts on a federal question are both numerous and consistent, we should hesitate to reject their authority.") (internal quotation marks omitted).

10 Michael J. Gerhardt, *Super Precedent*, 90 Minn. L. Rev. 1204, 1206, 1213–17 (2006) (discussing superprecedents such as landmark opinions addressing issues of constitutional law); *see Black's Law Dictionary* 1367 (Bryan A. Garner ed., 10th ed. 2014) (providing two senses of *superprecedent*: (1) "[a] precedent that defines the law and its requirements so effectively that it prevents divergent holdings in later legal decisions on similar facts or induces disputants to settle their claims without litigation," and (2) "[a] precedent that has become so well established in the law by a long line of reaffirmations that it is very difficult to overturn"—sense 2 being the one referred to in the text).

11 *E.g.*, Gerhardt, *Super Precedent*, 90 Minn. L. Rev. at 1205–06.

12 5 U.S. (1 Cranch) 137 (1803).

13 *See* Gerhardt, *Super Precedent*, 90 Minn. L. Rev. at 1208–09 (opining that overruling *Marbury* is "unimaginable").

14 79 U.S. (12 Wall.) 457, 553–54 (1870), *abrogated on other grounds by Pennsylvania Coal Co. v. Mahon*, 260 U.S. 393, 414–15 (1922).

unthinkable," and "no one—not even scholars who believe the case was wrongly decided—seriously believes the decision ought to be revisited."[15] Hence although the *Legal Tender Cases* (*Knox v. Lee* and *Parker v. Davis*) aren't well known by name or commonly cited as precedents, they are virtually impervious to challenge.

Even opinions that once stood on shaky ground can achieve superprecedent status. For example, *Miranda v. Arizona*,[16] which requires law-enforcement authorities to warn criminal defendants of enumerated rights before the defendants' statements can be used in court, has been the subject of criticism, challenged by Congress,[17] and called "a derelict on the waters of the law."[18] But its reaffirmation by the Supreme Court in the 2000 case of *Dickerson v. United States*,[19] repeated application of the core *Miranda* requirements, and public awareness of *Miranda* rights have together given the opinion superprecedent status.[20] Although the Court could overrule *Miranda*, its long-standing approval and reapplication over the years would make the task burdensome—requiring considerable justification and backpedaling—and therefore unlikely.

The age of maturity

A related factor affecting the value of a precedent is its age.[21] Unlike approval or acceptance, however, the effect of age on a precedent isn't entirely predictable. That is, whether a court addresses an opinion's recent issuance or its antiquity, the court may construe

---

15 Gerhardt, *Super Precedent*, 90 Minn. L. Rev. at 1214.

16 384 U.S. 436 (1966).

17 Kit Kinports, *The Supreme Court's Love–Hate Relationship with* Miranda, 101 J. Crim L. & Criminology 375, 377 (2011) (pointing out that "Congress enacted the 1968 Crime Control Bill aimed at overturning" *Miranda*).

18 Office of Legal Policy, U.S. Dep't of Justice, Report to the Attorney General on the Law of Pretrial Interrogation (1986).

19 530 U.S. 428, 432 (2000).

20 *See* Gerhardt, *Super Precedent*, 90 Minn. L. Rev. at 1217–18 (pointing to factors weighing in favor of categorizing *Miranda v. Arizona* as a superprecedent).

21 *See Montejo v. Louisiana*, 556 U.S. 778, 792 (2009) (listing "antiquity" among factors affecting the Court's decision whether to overrule an opinion).

the age of the opinion positively or negatively[22]—though we generally espouse the view that age enhances weight. Even when the court expresses a preference for long-standing decisions, it may disagree about whether the opinion is sufficiently old to warrant respect for its antiquity.[23]

One reason courts may accord an older opinion more respect is that its venerability may have led courts, litigants, and the public to rely on it.[24] Dissenting in *South Carolina v. Gathers*, Scalia J. expressed the classical view of ancient decisions: "I had thought that the respect accorded prior decisions increases, rather than decreases, with their antiquity, as the society adjusts itself to their existence, and the surrounding law becomes premised upon their validity."[25] On the other hand, the weight that tends to grow with

---

22 *Compare Harmelin v. Michigan*, 501 U.S. 957, 996 (1991) (Kennedy J. concurring) (arguing that "stare decisis counsels our adherence to the narrow proportionality principle that has existed in our Eighth Amendment jurisprudence for 80 years"), *and United States v. Madden*, 733 F.3d 1314, 1319 (11th Cir. 2013) (stating that the court of appeals "follow[s its] oldest precedent"), *with People ex rel. Daley v. Strayhorn*, 521 N.E.2d 864, 873 (Ill. 1988) (Clark J. specially concurring) ("Changing times and circumstances may convince us, in appropriate cases, to overrule past precedent. I cannot in good conscience, however, argue for the overruling of a case written in ink which is not yet dry."). *See* Charles N.W. Keckler, *The Hazards of Precedent: A Parameterization of Legal Change*, 80 Miss. L.J. 105, 174 (2010) (finding that the court seems to have "reversed the value it at one time accorded to the age of precedents"); Randy J. Kozel, *Stare Decisis as Judicial Doctrine*, 67 Wash. & Lee L. Rev. 411, 430 (2010) ("The Court sometimes instructs that older opinions are entitled to more deference than newer ones. Interestingly enough, it occasionally takes the opposite position, explaining that recent opinions receive the greatest deference.").

23 *Compare Montejo*, 556 U.S. at 792 ("[T]he opinion is only two decades old, and eliminating it would not upset expectations."), *with id.* at 809–10 (Stevens J. dissenting) ("[A]lthough the Court acknowledges that 'antiquity' is a factor that counsels in favor of retaining precedent, it concludes that the fact [that *Michigan v. Jackson*, 475 U.S. 625 (1986)] is 'only two decades old' cuts 'in favor of abandoning' the rule it established. . . . I would have thought that the 23-year existence of a simple bright-line rule would be a factor that cuts in the other direction."). *See id.* at 801 (Alito J. concurring) ("The dissent . . . invokes *Jackson*'s antiquity, stating that 'the 23-year existence of a simple bright-line rule' should weigh in favor of its retention. . . . But in [*Arizona v. Gant*, 556 U.S. 332 (2009)], the Court had no compunction about casting aside a 28-year-old bright-line rule.").

24 Kozel, *Stare Decisis*, 67 Wash. & Lee L. Rev. at 431.

25 490 U.S. 805, 824 (1989) (Scalia J. dissenting), *overruled by Payne v. Tennessee*, 501 U.S. 808 (1991).

age also gives courts some incentive to be sure the precedent is correct. Scalia J. added: "The freshness of error not only deprives it of the respect to which long-established practice is entitled, but also counsels that the opportunity of correction be seized at once, before state and federal laws and practices have been adjusted to embody it."[26]

But the level of reliance correlates not just to the age of a precedent but also to its subject matter, reasoning, persuasiveness, publicity, among other factors.[27] As one scholar points out, "the authority of a decision may increase with its age since the fact that it has not been tampered with by subsequent judges shows that they tend to regard themselves as bound by it."[28] For more on the value of antiquity, see § 18.

---

26   *Gathers*, 490 U.S. at 824.
27   *See* Kozel, *Stare Decisis*, 67 Wash. & Lee L. Rev. at 431.
28   David Vong, *Binding Precedent and English Judicial Law-Making*, 21 Jura Falconis 318, 337 n.102 (1985), https://www.law.kuleuven.be/jura/art/21n3/vong.pdf.

26. Doubt, Criticism, and Disapproval

The value of a decision as precedent diminishes when the court issuing it expresses doubt and hesitation or when it has been criticized or disapproved by the same court, by other courts of learning and ability, by well-regarded legal scholars, or by the legal profession generally.

Differences among judges about the outcome or rationale of an opinion may diminish its worth as a precedent.[1] Differences among judges deciding cases are inevitable, since every judge has a unique background and independent concerns about any given issue. But judges "may suppress some disagreements with each other because they believe disagreement and dissent are detrimental to the law or to their court."[2] So they may strive for consensus[3] or even suppress disagreement to shore up a decision's full value as a precedent (see § 19).

The most effective way for a judge to depart from the court's opinion is to write separately. While concurrences represent "disagree[ment] with the majority's rationale"[4] but agreement with the outcome, dissents oppose the outcome. A telling dissent or concurrence may detract from the weight of a precedent by questioning the proper reasoning or outcome of the case.[5] A dissenting opinion may state that the law requires a different result or advocate a change in the law.[6] Judges who advocate change often

---

[1] See Charles N.W. Keckler, *The Hazards of Precedent: A Parameterization of Legal Change*, 80 Miss. L.J. 105, 143 (2010) ("One obvious source or indicator of a flawed opinion is its accompaniment by a dissenting opinion[, which] . . . indicat[es] it has failed the quality test of at least one inspector—the dissenting judge or judges.").

[2] Jeffrey A. Lefstin, *The Measure of the Doubt: Dissent, Indeterminacy, and Interpretation at the Federal Circuit*, 58 Hastings L.J. 1025, 1033 (2007).

[3] See id.

[4] Gerald Lebovits, *Technique: A Legal Method to the Madness*, N.Y. St. B. Ass'n J., June 2003, at 64, 60.

[5] See Lefstin, *Measure of Doubt*, 58 Hastings L.J. at 1031.

[6] Sylvia H. Walbolt & Stephanie C. Zimmerman, *"I Must Dissent." Why?*, Fla. B.J., Nov. 2008, at 36, 36; see also Lefstin, *Measure of Doubt*, 58 Hastings L.J. at 1046.

set forth their alternative vision. They sometimes outright encourage a higher court or the legislature to correct the law or what the judge perceives to be its erroneous application.[7]

Like internal disagreement and doubt about the correctness of a court's decision, external disagreement or disapproval can undermine a precedent for the obvious reason that courts hesitate to rely on decisions they have reason to doubt.[8] Disagreeing with or disapproving precedent is one method a court may employ to avoid the result or the reasoning set forth in a particular case.[9] Lower courts' questioning of a case can indicate to higher courts that the precedent may need to be overruled.[10] Courts may sometimes even "mock[] a precedent for being outside the mainstream of law."[11] In *United States v. Dixon*, the Supreme Court wrote of its own opinion: "We would mock stare decisis and only add chaos

---

7   See Walbolt & Zimmerman, *"I Must Dissent,"* Fla. B.J. at 39–40; *see also LeGendre v. Monroe Cnty.*, 600 N.W.2d 78, 80 (Mich. Ct. App. 1999) (per curiam) (noting that on one issue, the court "disagree[s] with, but must follow [mandatory precedent], . . . and therefore affirm"); *Ross v. Policemen's Relief & Pension Fund of Pittsburgh*, 871 A.2d 277, 278 n.1 (Pa. Commw. Ct. 2005) (pointing out that one of this court's opinions "was *disagreed with* by [their] Superior Court," which also declined to extend another of their decisions, and stating that "[o]ur Supreme Court has not addressed the issue but we look forward to the day that it has the opportunity to reconcile this division between our Courts").

8   See Timothy Schwarz, Comment, *Cases Time Forgot: Why Judges Can Sometimes Ignore Controlling Precedent*, 56 Emory L.J. 1475, 1484 (2007) ("Judges attempt to avoid precedent when they believe the results suggested by the precedent do not correctly decide the case being adjudicated."); *cf. In re McKinney*, 341 B.R. 892, 894–95 & n.1 (Bankr. C.D. Ill. 2006) (summarizing chronological progression of law at issue, and pointing out that one relevant case was later disagreed with).

9   See Schwarz, *Cases Time Forgot*, 56 Emory L.J. at 1483; *see also Pritchard v. State*, 788 P.2d 1178, 1183 (Ariz. 1990) (in banc) (noting that "[t]he state . . . bases its argument on several pre-1984 cases" and explaining that "these cases do not justify their holdings in light of the statute's purposes and policies"); *El Paso Pipe & Supply Co. v. Mountain States Leasing, Inc.*, 617 S.W.2d 189, 190 (Tex. 1981) (per curiam) (pointing to several cases erroneously relied on by the lower court in reaching their decision, and explaining that one "was not appealed to this court, and we disapprove that opinion").

10 See Michael H. LeRoy, *Overruling Precedent: "A Derelict in the Stream of the Law,"* 66 SMU L. Rev. 711, 721 (2013).

11 *Id.*

to our double jeopardy jurisprudence by pretending that *Grady* [*v. Corbin*] survives when it does not."[12]

Yet the precise effect of disapproval or criticism depends on both the strength and the source of the disapproval. For example, if a high court or appellate court disapproves a lower court's decision, the disapproval may render the lower court's opinion virtually worthless, sometimes even expressly stating that the opinion represents bad law.[13] In other cases, the court citing the past opinion may be more hesitant about its disapproval, permitting the decision reviewed to retain some value as a precedent as long as it doesn't conflict with a newly established principle.[14]

Often, a reviewing court will explicitly state what part of the opinion is disapproved.[15] But in other cases, especially when the disapproved opinion isn't directly before the court, the court may state more generally that any parts of the opinion that conflict

---

12   509 U.S. 688, 712 (1993) (citing *Grady v. Corbin*, 495 U.S. 508 (1990)).

13   See, e.g., *Pattisson v. Cavanagh*, 64 P.2d 945, 945 (Cal. 1937) (in bank) (per curiam) (resolving lower-court conflict by disapproving one of the decisions); *State v. Varner*, 616 So. 2d 988, 989 (Fla. 1993) (resolving a conflict between lower courts and stating that it "disapprove[s] the opinions in *Williams, Walker,* and *Bannerman* to the extent they are inconsistent with our views here"); *State v. Hall*, 534 So. 2d 1144, 1144 (Fla. 1988) (noting that in a contemporaneous case issued by the court, it disapproved a lower-court opinion, "predicated as it was on the rationale of our original opinion, . . . which was withdrawn on rehearing").

14   See, e.g., *Goodwin v. State*, 634 So. 2d 157, 157 (Fla. 1994) (per curiam) ("We disapprove the opinion in *Murphy v. State*, 578 So. 2d 410 (Fla. Dist. Ct. App. 1991), to the extent it is inconsistent with this opinion."); *Davis v. Zoning Bd. of Adjustment*, 865 S.W.2d 941, 942 n.3 (Tex. 1993) (per curiam) (disapproving lower-court opinion "to the extent it holds that a trial court's jurisdiction under § 211.011 depends upon service and return of the writ of certiorari"); *Halsell v. Dehoyos*, 810 S.W.2d 371, 372 n.1 (Tex. 1991) (high court disapproving a previous opinion of the court of appeals "to the extent that it is inconsistent with [the high court's] holding"); *Vallandigham v. Clover Park Sch. Dist. No. 400*, 109 P.3d 805, 810, 814 (Wash. 2005) (en banc) (addressing conflict between lower courts and disapproving of one that "at least to some extent, adopted [an incorrect] standard").

15   See, e.g., *Babcock v. Whatmore*, 707 So. 2d 702, 705 (Fla. 1998) ("[W]e approve the result in *Whatmore* as explained herein, but we disapprove the following language: [quoting appellate court]."); *Paul v. State*, 129 So. 3d 1058, 1059 (Fla. 2013) (resolving certified conflict between courts of appeals and stating that "[w]e approve the Fourth District's decision below . . . [and] [w]e disapprove the opinion in the conflicting case").

with a particular point of law are disapproved, leaving future courts and litigants to determine what parts of the opinion remain good law and what parts do not.[16]

The court may also choose not to explicitly overrule a decision to avoid determining whether that decision was incorrectly decided at the time it was written, seeking only to limit its future usefulness.[17]

If a court overexercises its power to disapprove or disagree with earlier opinions, the state of the law may become more confusing.[18] Yet disagreement, both internal and external, is an effective method of disregarding, distinguishing, or diminishing the weight of a precedent. Although it may sometimes result in confusing jurisprudence, it also provides an avenue for courts to clarify that certain opinions, while not directly on review, have depreciated in value.

---

16 *See, e.g., Zheng v. Ashcroft*, 332 F.3d 1186, 1196 (9th Cir. 2003) ("To the extent that [listed decisions] require actual knowledge and 'willful[] accept[ance]'— contrary to clear congressional intent to require only awareness—we disapprove of those decisions."); *Coito v. Superior Court*, 278 P.3d 860, 872 (Cal. 2012) (disapproving of a number of cases "to the extent they suggest that a witness statement taken by an attorney does not, as a matter of law, constitute work product").

17 *See, e.g., United States v. One Assortment of 89 Firearms*, 465 U.S. 354, 361 (1984) ("Whatever the validity of *Coffey* on its facts, its ambiguous reasoning seems to have been a source of confusion for some time. . . . The time has come to clarify [this issue]. To the extent that *Coffey v. United States* [116 U.S. 436 (1886)] suggests otherwise, it is hereby disapproved.").

18 *Nored v. City of Tempe*, 614 F. Supp. 2d 991, 994 n.3 (D. Ariz. 2008) (noting that "[t]he Arizona state courts' decisions on point have not been entirely consistent with regard to whether failure to comply with the statute deprives the court of jurisdiction over the claim" and summarizing a number of opinions on point, including several that have been disagreed with, disapproved, or rejected).

27. Status of Rendering Court

A court's rank and standing are important in considering a precedent's weight. Great deference is paid to those courts possessing an acknowledged reputation for learning and ability or a special and intimate familiarity with the branch of the law to which the decision in question relates.

The value of a precedent depends in large measure on the deciding court's position within the judicial hierarchy.[1] This dependence results from the nature of horizontal precedent (for courts of the same rank) and vertical precedent.[2] The decisions of lower courts, of course, can never bind courts of superior rank.[3] (See § 2.) Whether the decision of a panel or a division of an appellate court binds other panels or divisions of that court differs from one jurisdiction to the next.[4]

---

[1] *Cf. McCarthy v. Olin Corp.*, 119 F.3d 148, 153 (2d Cir. 1997) (In determining the substantive law of a state, a federal court "afford[s] the greatest weight to decisions of the [high court of the state]."); *In re Barakat*, 173 B.R. 672, 677 (Bankr. C.D. Cal. 1994) ("Stare decisis maintains a hierarchical dimension which is believed to be crucial to the efficient operation of the judicial system.").

[2] 20 Am. Jur. 2d *Courts* § 138, at 542–44 (2015); *see Barakat*, 173 B.R. at 677 (stating that "stare decisis . . . not only binds lower courts within a circuit to a court of appeals decision from that circuit, but also binds the court of appeals to its own rulings"); *Owen v. Jim Allee Imps., Inc.*, 380 S.W.3d 276, 284 (Tex. App.—Dallas 2012, no pet.) (appellate court "is bound by decisions of the United States Supreme Court, the Texas Supreme Court, *and* prior decisions of this Court").

[3] 20 Am. Jur. 2d *Courts* § 138, at 542–44 (2015). *See, e.g., Midway Airlines, Inc. v. Department of Revenue*, 602 N.E.2d 13, 16 (Ill. App. Ct. 1992) (reviewing court "not bound to accept the reasons given by the lower court in ruling upon the correctness of that judgment"); *Commonwealth ex rel. Berman v. Berman*, 432 A.2d 1066, 1067 (Pa. Super. Ct. 1981) (court "not bound by [the lower court's] inferences or deductions") (quoting *In re Custody of Hernandez*, 376 A.2d 648, 656 (Pa. Super. Ct. 1977)).

[4] *See In re Muskin, Inc.*, 151 B.R. 252, 254 (Bankr. N.D. Cal. 1993) ("[T]he case law as to the binding nature of Appellate Panel decision[s] is wildly inconsistent."). *Compare Hart v. Massanari*, 266 F.3d 1155, 1171 (9th Cir. 2001) ("Circuit law . . . binds all courts within a particular circuit, including the court of appeals itself. Thus, the first panel to consider an issue sets the law not only for all the inferior courts in the circuit, but also future panels of the court of appeals."), *Tebo v. Havlik*, 343 N.W.2d 181, 185 (Mich. 1984) ("A decision by any panel of the Court of Appeals is, therefore, controlling statewide until contradicted by another panel of the Court of Appeals."), *and Renn v. Utah*

A rendering court's rank is most significant within a jurisdiction, although it's not irrelevant for nonbinding authority from outside the jurisdiction. The decisions of a court of one state, even that of its high court, would not bind courts of any level in another state applying its own law.[5] A New York superior court stated that even dicta from its high court, the Court of Appeals, should be given greater weight than holdings of courts from other jurisdictions.[6] Within a jurisdiction, rank plays so great a role in the weight of a precedent that dicta of the high court of a state may carry greater weight than holdings of the lower courts,[7] though the lower courts "are not bound to follow a higher court's dictum."[8]

In the same manner, federal district courts are bound by circuit courts' decisions, and both district courts and circuit courts are bound by opinions of the U.S. Supreme Court.[9] Indeed, on

---

State Bd. of Pardons, 904 P.2d 677, 681 (Utah 1995) (holding that appellate panel decision "had the binding effect of stare decisis on other panels of the Court of Appeals, including the panel that decided the instant case and all lower courts"), *with Bonner v. City of Prichard*, 661 F.2d 1206, 1209 (11th Cir. 1981) (en banc) ("[D]ecisions of the court of appeals for one circuit are not binding upon the courts of appeals for other circuits."), *and In re Selden*, 121 B.R. 59, 62 (Bankr. D. Or. 1990) ("[Bankruptcy Appellate Panel] decisions arising from another district in the circuit are not binding on this bankruptcy court.").

5 See, e.g., *Stone v. Mellon Mortg. Co.*, 771 So. 2d 451, 456 n.1 (Ala. 2000) ("No opinion from another state court is binding on the courts of Alabama, but we often cite such an opinion as persuasive authority."); *New York Life Ins. Co. v. Ware*, 157 So. 894, 895 (Miss. 1934) (explaining that decisions of other states aren't binding precedent and that "stare decisis is properly applicable only as between the several courts composing the same judicial system").

6 See, e.g., *People v. Bneses*, 398 N.Y.S.2d 507, 510 (Sup. Ct. 1977) (stating that "lower courts must be bound by rulings of their highest courts of whatever vintage" and that dicta from a higher court within the jurisdiction "clearly must carry greater weight than the holdings of courts in other jurisdictions").

7 *Travelers Indem. Co. v. DiBartolo*, 131 F.3d 343, 352 (3d Cir. 1997) (listing the order of priority in caselaw of a state as "the decisional law of the highest state court in analogous cases; the dicta of that court; and to a lesser degree, the decisional law of lower state courts" and explaining that "[d]ecisions of lower state courts should be accorded proper regard, but not conclusive effect in interpreting state law, especially when the highest court has already addressed the issue in dicta").

8 *In re Swanson*, 289 B.R. 372, 374 (Bankr. C.D. Ill. 2003).

9 *In re Barakat*, 173 B.R. 672, 677 (Bankr. C.D. Cal. 1994) ("No one contests that all inferior courts are bound by Supreme Court decisions. When no Supreme Court decision has been issued, the decisions of the court of appeals for a particular circuit are binding on all lower courts within that circuit. Even if the

federal or constitutional issues, all courts, state and federal, are bound by U.S. Supreme Court decisions.[10] On federal issues, states aren't similarly bound by lower federal-court decisions.[11] But even in cases dealing with state-law issues, courts will sometimes look to federal jurisprudence for guidance on the matter, particularly when federal law mirrors state law.[12] So although the rank of a court will not conclusively indicate how other courts treat its decisions, rank certainly bears on the weight of its decision, especially when both the deciding and referencing courts are part of the same jurisdiction.

Beyond rank, several other factors bear on the value accorded to a court's opinion. In particular, the reputation of the judges on the court[13] and of the court itself[14] can affect the persuasive value of an opinion. Additionally, the opinion of a court that has decided many cases dealing with a particular subject will often be considered more reliable on that subject. For example, the Second Circuit, headquartered in New York City, is considered the "Mother Court" of securities regulation,[15] and the D.C. Circuit,

---

circuits are split and the lower court disagrees with its own circuit, the lower court must still follow its court of appeals.") (citation omitted).

[10] *Hall v. Pennsylvania Bd. of Prob. & Parole*, 851 A.2d 859, 863 (Pa. 2004) ("It is beyond cavil that this Court is bound by the determinations of the United States Supreme Court on issues of federal law, including the construction and interpretation of the federal constitution.").

[11] *See, e.g., Krentz v. Consolidated Rail Corp.*, 910 A.2d 20, 34 n.16 (Pa. 2006) ("Although this Court is not bound by the decisions of the United States District Courts or the Courts of Appeals as to the interpretation of federal statutes, we may look to them for guidance.").

[12] *See, e.g., Peschel v. City of Missoula*, 664 F. Supp. 2d 1149, 1161 (D. Mont. 2009) ("The Montana Supreme Court has found it proper to rely on federal jurisprudence as persuasive authority for construing a provision of the Montana Constitution which is similar to a provision of the federal constitution.") (internal quotation marks omitted).

[13] Michael E. Solimine, *Judicial Stratification and the Reputations of the United States Courts of Appeals*, 32 Fla. St. U. L. Rev. 1331, 1342 (2005) ("[T]he Second Circuit's reputation is closely aligned with that of the well-known judges that served on it—starting with Learned Hand, who served from 1924 to 1961, but also including Charles Clark, Jerome Frank, Augustus Hand, and Henry Friendly, among others.") (footnotes omitted).

[14] *See id.* at 1341–42 (discussing the Second and D.C. Circuits).

[15] Margaret V. Sachs, *Judge Friendly and the Law of Securities Regulation: The Creation of a Judicial Reputation*, 50 SMU L. Rev. 777, 782 (1997) ("Second Circuit

headquartered in Washington, D.C., is influential when it comes to administrative law.[16]

Another measure of a court's reliability is its rate of affirmance or reversal on appeal.[17] This assessment has been applied in particular to circuit courts, whose decisions are reviewed by the Supreme Court.[18] The opinion of a court that is often reversed by the Supreme Court won't be as persuasive to other courts that aren't bound by that court's decisions, especially if the right result is obscure or disputable. The court's reputation may be marred by large reversal numbers even if the court has a larger caseload and its reversal percentage is comparable to that of other courts.

Still, a court that has been reviewed often and found to be correct in its analysis and conclusions will likely be perceived by other courts as generally more worthy of respect[19] because its opinions not only have been tested, but have withstood scrutiny. Yet even if a court's opinions aren't accepted for review, the higher court's refusal to review the opinion may be perceived favorably.[20]

---

opinions accounted for up to seventy percent of the federal appeals court opinions appearing as principal cases in securities regulation casebooks.").

16   See, e.g., Solimine, *Judicial Stratification*, 32 Fla. St. U. L. Rev. at 1344 n.69 (noting that the judges of the D.C. Circuit, which is well respected, "have all developed an expertise in administrative and regulatory law") (quoting 2 *Almanac of the Federal Judiciary*, at D.C. Cir. 1 (2005)).

17   See id. at 1343, 1347.

18   *Id.* at 1347 (suggesting that "the circuit's relationship with the Supreme Court . . . may be a barometer of reputation" and that "[t]he number of cases reviewed from a circuit might be considered to be some indication of the importance of the cases decided by that circuit").

19   *Id.* at 1343 (pointing to the findings of another researcher that "the Second Circuit was reviewed the most but reversed the second least; both [are] . . . indicia of the circuit's prestige and influence"); see also id. at 1347 (pointing to the "rate of affirmance by the Supreme Court" as a measure of reputation). *But see id.* at 1347 n.90 (recognizing that the accuracy of this measure is uncertain, especially because the Supreme Court weighs a number of factors in determining whether to grant review).

20   *Id.* at 1341 (pointing to another scholar's determination that the D.C. Circuit's reputation stems from its jurisdiction over key federal regulatory agencies "and the fact that few such cases are reviewed by the Supreme Court").

This perception persists even though several factors may influence a court's decision to grant or deny review of a lower court's decision.[21]

Ultimately, the status of a court rendering a decision bears heavily on the weight accorded to that decision by other courts. As we've seen, several factors influencing the court's reputation can also affect the weight of its precedent. The effect of these factors may fluctuate from one court to the next, depending on that court's view of the deciding court's reputation.

---

21 *See id.* at 1347 n.90; *see also* Jeff Bleich, *The Reversed Circuit*, 57 Or. St. B. Bull. 17, 18, 21 (1997) (discussing the frequency with which the Ninth Circuit is reviewed and reversed as compared to other circuit courts, and evaluating the court's reputation as one of many possible factors that might affect its reversal rate); *cf.* Sup. Ct. R. 10 (providing an official list of reasons that the U.S. Supreme Court may grant certiorari, but noting that the list is "neither controlling nor fully measuring the Court's discretion").

28. Judicial Reputations

A decision's authority may be magnified by the eminence of the judge who wrote the opinion.

A revered judge's opinion often commands greater persuasive value than the same opinion would if it had been signed by a different judge. Distinction within the legal profession emerges perhaps primarily from four factors: (1) acknowledged legal erudition, (2) fair-minded judge-craft, (3) a long career, and (4) a commitment to both intellectual rigor and fidelity to the law.[1]

These four factors are sometimes divided even further into such judicial attributes as "leadership on the Court, writing ability, judicial restraint, judicial activism, enhancement of the Court's power, protection of individual rights, length of service, impact on the law, impact on society, intellectual and legal ability,[2] protection of societal rights, dissent behavior, and personal attributes."[3] As an early-20th-century commentator put it, "When the Declaration of Independence asserts that all men are created equal, it is not speaking of judges."[4]

So within a given jurisdiction, the identity of an authoring judge can influence how appellate judges and other readers perceive the opinion. If the judge has become particularly renowned,

---

1 See William Lucy, "Judges, Distinguished," in *The New Oxford Companion to Law* 649, 650 (Peter Cane & Joanne Conaghan eds., 2008).

2 William G. Ross, *The Ratings Game: Factors That Influence Judicial Reputation*, 79 Marq. L. Rev. 401, 414 (1996) ("Intellectual vigor is virtually a pre-requisite for judicial greatness. . . . Three of the top fourteen justices on the 1970 and 1993 Blaustein-Mersky lists—Story, Holmes, and Cardozo—made original contributions to legal thought before serving on the Court. Two others, Frankfurter and Stone, were longtime law school professors and at least two more—Brandeis and Black—were serious legal thinkers."); see Bernard Schwartz, *Supreme Court Superstars: The Ten Greatest Justices*, 31 Tulsa L.J. 93, 98 (1995) (calling Story J. "the most learned scholar ever to sit on the Supreme Court").

3 Ross, *The Ratings Game*, 79 Marq. L. Rev. at 403. See John C. Townes, *Law Books and How to Use Them* 67 (1909) ("[T]he reputation of the judge delivering an opinion frequently enters largely into its value. The known capacity, learning, care and righteousness of the judge must give character to his decisions.").

4 Townes, *Law Books and How to Use Them* at 67.

even courts outside the jurisdiction may look to that judge's opinions for guidance in deciding difficult questions, questions of first impression, or questions falling within a particular area of that judge's expertise. By writing several highly respected opinions on a particular subject, a judge may begin to establish a reputation as an authority in that field, thereby increasing the precedential value of the judge's opinions.

In a letter written in 1885, Miller J. of the U.S. Supreme Court exemplified the point: "[A] decision often has a merit apart from the standing of the court in which it is made, owing to the high character of the judges of the court, or of the judge who delivered the opinion. Opinions delivered by such judges as Marshall, Taney, Kent, and Shaw, have a value apart from the courts in which they were delivered."[5] He went so far as to venture that "[e]ven the dissenting opinions of these men and their *obiter dicta* have weight in the minds of lawyers who have a just estimate of their character, which they cannot give to many courts of last resort of acknowledged ability."[6] Yet he cautioned against being overawed by reputation. Critical thinking is always crucial: "[T]he convincing power of an opinion or decision in a reported case must depend very largely on the force of the reasoning by which it is supported, and of this every lawyer and every court must of necessity be his and its own judge."[7]

Courts sometimes explicitly mention authoring judges by name and refer to their intellect or experience. Illustrations abound. For example, in 1848 an Alabama court wrote that "the well deserved reputation of Judge St. George Tucker, both as a man and a jurist, induces us to think that the practical interpretation of the statute referred to, has conformed to what he supposed should be its legal

---

5   Letter of Justice Samuel F. Miller to John F. Dillon, 16 Nov. 1885, *reproduced in* John F. Dillon, *The Laws and Jurisprudence of England and America* 261, 263 (1894) (referring to Chief Justice John Marshall, Chief Justice Roger Taney, Chancellor James Kent of New York, and Massachusetts Supreme Judicial Court Chief Justice Lemuel Shaw of Boston). We don't endorse Miller J.'s inclusion of Taney C.J. alongside the others.

6   *Id.*

7   *Id.*

construction."[8] Similarly, in 1893 an Arizona court stated: "The great reputation of Judge Moses Hallett for erudition, especially in questions involving mining rights, gives rise to much diffidence upon our part in attempting to criticise his decision in that case."[9] In 1988, the Texas Supreme Court recognized the reputation that Cardozo C.J. had built for himself on New York's highest court: "Because the author of the majority opinion ... was a man of preeminent reputation, [his] holding in *Palsgraf*[10] was almost immediately incorporated into the Restatement of Torts, and thus has since become firmly entrenched in the law."[11]

A court in the Northern District of New York approved of an opinion by Learned Hand J. of the Second Circuit, noting that he was "the most eminent jurist in this Circuit."[12] More often, however, courts acknowledge a judge's reputation subtly, by simply invoking the judge's name as the author of an opinion or originator of an idea.[13]

More recently, authors of an article providing advice to litigants noted: "The reputation of the authoring judge will undoubtedly affect the likelihood that a court will overturn an earlier decision."[14] After serving on an appellate court for some time, the authors contend, judges develop a sense of how well the trial judges in their jurisdiction do their job. "In most appellate jurisdictions, there are a few trial judges whose rulings come to the appellate court almost with a presumption of error, and a larger number whose decisions are very difficult to overturn because of a well-deserved reputation for excellence."[15] So the reputation of the

---

8 *Logan v. Logan*, 13 Ala. 653, 658 (1848).
9 *Watervale Mining Co. v. Leach*, 33 P. 418, 423 (Ariz. 1893).
10 *Palsgraf v. Long Island R.R.*, 162 N.E. 99 (N.Y. 1928).
11 *Brown v. Edwards Transfer Co.*, 764 S.W.2d 220, 225 (Tex. 1988).
12 *United States v. One 1959 Buick 4-Door Sedan*, 188 F. Supp. 155, 157 (N.D.N.Y. 1960).
13 See, e.g., *Keystone Bituminous Coal Ass'n v. DeBenedictis*, 480 U.S. 470, 473, 483–91 (1987) (discussing an opinion written by Holmes J. and relying on various points made in that opinion with repeated reference to Holmes J.).
14 James C. Schroeder & Robert M. Dow Jr., *Arguing for Changes in the Law*, 25 No. 2 Litig. 37, 41 (1999).
15 *Id.*

authoring judge may influence how carefully an appellate court scrutinizes the reasoning set forth in an opinion or how receptive the court is to allegations of error on the part of that judge.

But a judge's reputation isn't just relevant to appellate courts reviewing an opinion by that judge—it may be recognized[16] even in jurisdictions in which the judge doesn't sit.[17] This is especially true when a court deals with subject matter on which the judge is considered preeminent. For example, Friendly J.'s Second Circuit opinions on the subject of securities law were given great weight because of his meaningful contributions to that field.[18] In one instance, the Alaska Supreme Court stated that substantial authority existed to require an awareness of wrongdoing in securities crimes and relied principally on reasoning from Friendly J.[19] Likewise, opinions of highly regarded judges may be relied on even by courts of superior authority.[20]

When faced with a difficult decision, a court will often defer or give greater weight to the position advanced by a well-respected judge. For example, in 1957 the Arkansas Supreme Court had to choose between two positions on a workers'-compensation claim, both with strong support in the law.[21] The court reviewed both

---

16　See Michael E. Solimine, *Judicial Stratification and the Reputations of the United States Courts of Appeals*, 32 Fla. St. U. L. Rev. 1331, 1348 (2005) (explaining that reference to a judge by name "reflects the greater authoritative weight that the Court wishes to give to the lower court opinion being referenced").

17　Id. at 1346; see David E. Klein, *Making Law in the United States Courts of Appeals* 94 (2002).

18　Margaret V. Sachs, *Judge Friendly and the Law of Securities Regulation: The Creation of a Judicial Reputation*, 50 SMU L. Rev. 777, 780–81 (1997) ("Judge Friendly is said to have done 'more to shape the law of securities regulation than any [other] judge in the country.' The author of eighty majority opinions in the area, he tackled everything from Rule 10b-5 and the proxy rules to extraterritoriality, criminality, and tender offers.") (footnote omitted) (quoting Bruce A. Ackerman et al., *In Memoriam: Henry J. Friendly*, 99 Harv. L. Rev. 1709, 1723 (1986)); see also Solimine, *Judicial Stratification*, 32 Fla. St. U. L. Rev. at 1343 n.61.

19　*Hentzner v. State*, 613 P.2d 821, 827 (Alaska 1980).

20　See, e.g., *Sosa v. Alvarez-Machain*, 542 U.S. 692, 712 (2004) (referring to a statement of Friendly J.); *F. Hoffmann-La Roche Ltd. v. Empagran S.A.*, 542 U.S. 155, 165 (2004) (citing opinion of Learned Hand J. and naming him as the writing judge).

21　*Martin v. Lavender Radio & Supply, Inc.*, 305 S.W.2d 845, 847–48 (Ark. 1957).

and adopted the position set forth by Cardozo C.J. in a 1929 New York Court of Appeals case.[22] In doing so, the court mentioned Justice Cardozo by name three times, in the end determining that "[t]he reasoning set forth by Justice Cardozo seems to us to be entirely logical and persuasive, and worthy of adoption."[23]

A court that decides to follow a position expressed in a dissent by a highly regarded judge may similarly invoke the name of the dissenting writer to add credibility to its opinion. In one instance, the D.C. Court of Appeals noted that Cardozo J.'s dissenting opinion in *Landress v. Phoenix Mutual Life Insurance Co.*[24] "has several times been quoted, adopted and followed by other courts."[25] The court recalled another scholar's evaluation that "[t]he dissenting opinion of Justice Cardozo presents one of the most brilliantly reasoned opinions in the field of insurance law."[26]

The presence of esteemed judges on a court improves the reputation of the court itself, making its opinions more valuable and leading other courts to rely on them.[27] Hence one scholar pointed out that Cardozo C.J.'s "judicial contribution was made on the New York court, where he spent fifteen years, most of his judicial career."[28] He continued: "During the Cardozo years, that court was recognized as the strongest in the country, and its judgments had a decisive influence on American law."[29]

---

22   *Id.* at 849.

23   *Id.* at 849.

24   291 U.S. 491 (1934).

25   *Raley v. Life & Cas. Ins. Co. of Tenn.*, 117 A.2d 110, 112 (D.C. 1955).

26   *Id.* at 113 (quoting 1 John Alan Appleman, *Insurance Law and Practice* § 447, at 555).

27   *See* Mitu Gulati & Veronica Sanchez, *Giants in a World of Pygmies? Testing the Superstar Hypothesis with Judicial Opinions in Casebooks*, 87 Iowa L. Rev. 1141, 1180–81 (2002) (noting that the Seventh Circuit's reputation improved substantially after the appointments of Posner J. and Easterbrook J., having previously been considered "an unremarkable circuit").

28   Bernard Schwartz, *Supreme Court Superstars: The Ten Greatest Justices*, 31 Tulsa L.J. 93, 151 (1995).

29   *Id.*

29. Decisions of Inferior Courts

Opinions of trial and other inferior courts generally rank low on the scale of authority but may be followed by higher courts or courts of another jurisdiction when no precedent exists or for other special reasons.

"Inferior" or lower courts are subordinate to at least one other court in a judicial hierarchy. They are bound to follow the precedent of a higher court and are subject to its review.[1] (See § 2.) Hence every court that isn't a high court is a lower, or inferior, court within the hierarchy. The characterization of a court as "inferior" or "superior" isn't absolute but may depend on the issues before the court: in some instances the court may be subject to review, while in others it may have final authority.[2]

Within the federal system, lower courts consist of circuit courts of appeals, district courts, bankruptcy courts, and several courts of special jurisdiction—including the U.S. Tax Court, the U.S. Court of Appeals for Veterans Claims, the U.S. Court of International Trade, the U.S. Court of Appeals for the Armed Forces, and the U.S. Court of Federal Claims.[3] State judiciaries generally have two levels of lower courts—trial courts and intermediate appellate courts. States also often have several other courts with limited or specialized jurisdiction. These may serve a particular city, district, precinct, or county, or may have limited jurisdiction. For example, some may handle civil claims up to a particular amount, while others may deal exclusively with traffic violations, domestic relations, juvenile offenses, probate issues, or

---

[1] Martha J. Dragich, *Uniformity, Inferiority, and the Law of the Circuit Doctrine,* 56 Loy. L. Rev. 535, 577 (2010).

[2] *See, e.g., State ex rel. Walker v. Harrington,* 27 A.2d 67, 73–74 (Del. 1942) (explaining that "[t]he words 'inferior tribunal' have more than one meaning," and that "[t]he Superior Court is a court of general common law jurisdiction, and in that sense it is not an 'inferior tribunal,'" but finding that the Supreme Court doesn't "lack jurisdiction to issue writs of mandamus" to that court, even though it "sits as a court of last resort" for appeals from the Orphans' Court), *superseded by constitutional amendment,* Del. Const. art V.

[3] *Court Role and Structure,* United States Courts, http://www.uscourts.gov/about-federal-courts/court-role-and-structure (last visited 4 Oct. 2015).

other areas of law. The decisions of these courts are sometimes subject to appellate review by general-jurisdiction trial courts. Arizona's court structure, for example, allows superior courts to review decisions originating in justice-of-the-peace courts and municipal courts.[4]

All federal courts except the U.S. Supreme Court are inferior courts because they are subject to review and supervision by the Supreme Court.[5] On issues of federal law and federal constitutional law, state high courts are similarly inferior to the Supreme Court, which is endowed with oversight and supervisory power.[6] But on issues of state law, state high courts have final authority.[7] Often they also supervise lower courts by controlling their budgets, by establishing court rules, and by issuing administrative orders.

The concepts of inferiority and superiority have long been a part of the legal system. In England, "the common law presumed that all inferior courts and tribunals were subject to review in the Court of King's Bench; the common law or supervisory writs carried this presumption into effect."[8] Unlike appellate jurisdiction, which predominantly affected the litigants, the supervisory writs affected the inferior courts specifically, "threatening the inferior [court] judge with contempt if he or she failed to comply with the

---

4   Ariz. Super. Ct. R. App. Proc. Civ. 1(a).

5   James E. Pfander, *Federal Supremacy, State Court Inferiority, and the Constitutionality of Jurisdiction-Stripping Legislation*, 101 Nw. U. L. Rev. 191, 212 (2007); *see also* Dragich, *Uniformity*, 56 Loy. L. Rev. at 568–69 (explaining that the U.S. Constitution established "one supreme Court" and that therefore any courts created by Congress must be inferior courts).

6   Pfander, *Federal Supremacy*, 101 Nw. U. L. Rev. at 212 (explaining that supervision may be exercised through writs of certiorari, mandamus, prohibition, and habeas corpus).

7   *See, e.g., Kopp v. Fair Political Practices Comm'n*, 905 P.2d 1248, 1259 (Cal. 1995) (in bank) ("Our sovereign duty as a court of last resort . . . requires that we not automatically accept the federal court's ruling on this important state law issue, but . . . question afresh ourselves and reach a different conclusion if state law leads us to that result.") (citation omitted); *State v. Gore*, 681 P.2d 227, 231 (Wash. 1984) (en banc) ("While the Supreme Court's interpretation of a similar federal statute is persuasive authority, it is not controlling in our interpretation of a state statute. Further, once this court has decided an issue of state law, that interpretation is binding on all lower courts until it is overruled by this court.") (citations omitted).

8   Pfander, *Federal Supremacy*, 101 Nw. U. L. Rev. at 213.

superior court's orders."[9] Similarly, early on in the United States, "the Supreme Court . . . insisted that state courts give effect to the rules of federal law as the Court pronounce[d] them."[10]

Inferior-court decisions have less precedential worth because courts superior in rank aren't bound by them[11] and may overrule, vacate, reverse, or depublish[12] them. Likewise, in some jurisdictions, intermediate courts aren't bound by earlier intermediate-court decisions.[13] And trial courts aren't bound at all by other trial-court decisions, or even their own decisions, though trial judges may follow them at their discretion.[14] In fact, some trial-court decisions are so bereft of precedential value that they don't bind even courts lower in rank.

For example, in South Carolina the courts of common pleas are the civil-trial courts.[15] Yet the U.S. Supreme Court remarked that such a court "does not appear to have such importance and competence . . . that its decisions should be taken as authoritative expositions of that State's 'law.' . . . [A] Common Pleas decision does not exact conformity from either the same court or lesser courts within its territorial jurisdiction,"[16] adding that it also "may apparently be ignored by other Courts of Common Pleas."[17]

---

9   *Id.* at 214.

10 *Id.* at 214 & n.92 (citing *Martin v. Hunter's Lessee*, 14 U.S. (1 Wheat.) 304, 305–06, 313 (1816), which rejected a Virginia appellate court's determination that "the appellate power of the supreme court of the United States does not extend to this court").

11 20 Am. Jur. 2d *Courts* § 138, at 542–44 (2015).

12 *Cf.* Michael A. Berch, *Analysis of Arizona's Depublication Rule and Practice*, 32 Ariz. St. L.J. 175, 176–79 (2000) (criticizing the practice of depublishing opinions).

13 20 Am. Jur. 2d *Courts* § 138, at 542–44 (2015).

14 *See, e.g., Scott v. State*, 822 A.2d 472, 475 (Md. Ct. Spec. App. 2003) (explaining that "trial court ruling[s] may stand as the law of the case when no appeal is taken from it" but that they are "inapplicable between courts of coordinate jurisdiction before entry of a final judgment") (internal quotation marks omitted); *see also* 20 Am. Jur. 2d *Courts* § 137, at 541 (2015) (stating that "[a] court's decision to follow a prior decision of another court of equal and concurrent jurisdiction generally involves the exercise of discretion on some level").

15 *King v. Order of United Commercial Travelers*, 333 U.S. 154, 159 (1948).

16 *Id.* at 161.

17 *Id.*

Because the law set forth in lower-court decisions might not survive appellate review, out-of-state courts naturally hesitate to rely on the decisions of trial courts when attempting to ascertain the law of the state where those courts sit. For example, the Pennsylvania Supreme Court, interpreting a New York statute, looked to the interpretation of a similar New Jersey statute by the New Jersey Supreme Court, despite the existence of contrary decisions from lower courts in New York.[18] The court explained that "[the] decisions of the lower courts of New York, holding a contrary view, are not binding upon us in the absence of a decision of the court of last resort of that state."[19] Instead, the court declared that "the construction of a statute of a state by its highest tribunal will ordinarily be received as conclusive in the courts of other states."[20] (See §§ 77, 84.)

Yet in the absence of a high-court decision, the federal court "may use the decisional law of the state's lower courts" among other sources to determine the law of the state;[21] in fact, "where jurisdiction rests on diversity of citizenship, federal courts . . . must follow the decisions of intermediate state courts in the absence of convincing evidence that the highest court of the state would decide differently."[22]

One reason why lower-court decisions are often unsuited to establish precedent is the nature of the decisional process itself. Generally, lower-court decisions are shorter than published opinions of higher courts and contain less reasoning because those courts' primary job is to rule on cases then pending, not to shape the law. The prevailing view on the role of inferior courts is that they should decide cases according to what the law is and not what it may become.[23] Because lower-court cases are usually decided

---

18   *Schmaltz v. York Mfg. Co.*, 53 A. 522, 528 (Pa. 1902).
19   *Id.*
20   *Id.*
21   *Meridian Mut. Ins. Co. v. Kellman*, 197 F.3d 1178, 1181 (6th Cir. 1999).
22   *Stoner v. New York Life Ins. Co.*, 311 U.S. 464, 467 (1940).
23   *See* Evan H. Caminker, *Precedent and Prediction: The Forward-Looking Aspects of Inferior Court Decisionmaking*, 73 Tex. L. Rev. 1, 1–22 (1994) (noting that some scholars believe that inferior courts should not only apply the law as it

expeditiously by one judge, a decision might not receive the same consideration and scrutiny as one issued by a high court. Trial courts also generally have much larger caseloads than high courts, which often have discretion to accept or deny review of lower-court decisions. In states that provide a right of first appeal, intermediate appellate courts may likewise have heavy caseloads. So intermediate appellate courts, or courts with mandatory appellate jurisdiction, don't have as much time or as many resources to devote to resolving a case as high courts with discretionary jurisdiction. The press of judicial business may result in opinions that aren't so thoroughly researched and closely reasoned. They may therefore prove less valuable as precedent.

Although inferior-court decisions have diminished value as legal precedent, they have practical and immediate value to the litigants because they resolve conflicts between them, unless and until the decisions are appealed. Within a jurisdiction, the law expounded by lower courts, particularly intermediate appellate courts, often serves as a starting point for high courts to interpret the law. When no decision has been issued by a state's high court, it may review lower-court decisions to see how courts have applied the law, evaluate conflicting analyses among the lower courts,[24] and perhaps even rely on the reasoning and conclusion of a lower court to reach its own result.[25]

---

exists but also consider how appellate courts will react to their decisions—a view that is essentially an invitation to willful judging).

24   *See, e.g., Vega v. Morris*, 910 P.2d 6, 7–10 (Ariz. 1996) (in banc) (granting review to resolve a conflict between courts of appeals and discussing the analyses in those cases).

25   *See, e.g., State v. Rascon*, 519 P.2d 37, 38 (Ariz. 1974) (in banc) (relying on and approving of a prior "well considered" court-of-appeals opinion on the constitutionality of a state statute).

30. Decisions Pending Appeal

A decision from which an appeal is pending in a higher court should be followed, on the principle of stare decisis, until it is reversed. But the grant of a rehearing in an appellate court suspends all the force of the original decision as an authority until the final conclusion is announced.

Once a court is finished with the case, the decision is normally final for purposes of claim and issue preclusion, enforcement, and sometimes stare decisis[1]—even if an appeal to a higher court is pending.[2] There is a distinction between an appeal to a higher court and actions taken within one court (such as an intermediate appellate court) to reconsider a decision. The latter actions, which may be a decision by a panel to rehear a case or a decision by the full court to hear a case en banc, have the effect of vacating the court's initial decision (normally a panel decision) and keeping the case under consideration until the result upon rehearing is

---

[1] *See, e.g., People v. Bing*, 558 N.E.2d 1011, 1014 (N.Y. 1990) ("The doctrine of stare decisis provides that once a court has decided a legal issue, subsequent appeals presenting similar facts should be decided in conformity with the earlier decision."); *see also* Joseph Mead, *Stare Decisis in the Inferior Courts of the United States*, 12 Nev. L.J. 787, 794–804 (2012) (examining stare decisis in federal district courts). *Contra Rantz v. Kaufman*, 109 P.3d 132, 141 (Colo. 2005) (en banc) (stating that "for the purposes of issue preclusion, a judgment that is still pending on appeal is not final").

[2] *See, e.g.*, Mich. Ct. R. 7.215(C)(2) ("A published opinion of the Court of Appeals has precedential effect under the rule of stare decisis. The filing of an application for leave to appeal to the Supreme Court or a Supreme Court order granting leave to appeal does not diminish the precedential effect of a published opinion of the Court of Appeals."); *Starzenski v. City of Elkhart*, 87 F.3d 872, 878 (7th Cir. 1996) ("Indiana law provides that a pending appeal does not undermine the force of a judgment."); *Rhoten v. Dickson*, 223 P.3d 786, 798 (Kan. 2010) ("Both federal and Kansas courts have held a pending appeal does not suspend the finality of the lower court's judgment for claim preclusion purposes."); *Mansfield State Bank v. Cohn*, 407 N.Y.S.2d 373, 376 (Sup. Ct. 1977) ("The fact that the default judgment is under appeal does not detract from its validity, nor render it less conclusive while it remains in full force and effect.") (citation omitted); *State ex rel. Utils. Comm'n v. Thornburg*, 417 S.E.2d 73, 74 (N.C. 1992) ("Pending further orders of this Court, the writ of supersedeas issued by the Court of Appeals shall remain in full force and effect.").

announced.[3] The first part of the rule is reflected in Federal Rule of Civil Procedure 62 and Federal Rule of Appellate Procedure 8, both of which address the topic of a stay or injunction pending appeal. Civil Rule 62 provides for an automatic stay of the district court's judgment for 14 days after its entry, but after that the winning party may begin proceedings to execute on the judgment. A litigant may ask the district court to stay execution of the judgment pending certain posttrial motions (including a motion for new trial or a motion for judgment as a matter of law), or pending appeal. The district court is authorized to grant such a stay, but a stay will commonly be conditioned on the losing party's posting an appropriate bond. If the district court refuses a request to stay its decision, Appellate Rule 8 permits the party to submit the same request to the court of appeals. That court too may stay the effect of the district court's judgment, either with or without conditions.

---

3   Kan. Sup. Ct. R. 7.05(c), 7.06(c) ("If a motion for rehearing is granted, the order suspends the effect of the original decision until the matter is decided on rehearing."); *Miller v. Burley*, 187 S.E.2d 803, 813 (W. Va. 1972) ("As a general rule, when a rehearing is granted, the status of the case is the same as though no hearing had occurred. The granting of a rehearing withdraws an opinion previously rendered and destroys its force and effect unless it is subsequently adopted by the same tribunal."); 2 Am. Jur. Pleading and Practice Forms Annotated *Appeal and Error* § 800 (2016) ("While the denial of a petition or motion for rehearing leaves the judgment in full force as of the time of its rendition, where a rehearing is granted, the case stands as if no previous hearing had been had, suspending, but not vacating the original judgment.").

31. Decisions to Review or Not to Review

An appellate court's grant of discretionary review weakens the authority of a nonfinal decision; the court's refusal to grant review in no way implies approval or disapproval of the decision and final judgment of the court below.

If an appellate court with discretionary review—such as the U.S. Supreme Court or the high court in a state—grants review in a case, the authority of the decision under review is weakened. Such a decision is typically not final in the sense that there can be no further review, and for that reason alone it would have limited precedential value.[1] But because more cases on discretionary review are reversed than are affirmed,[2] the higher court's decision to grant review may suggest to the bench and bar that the lower court's decision will likely not stand as good law for long. That's true even if the judgment is affirmed, because the higher court's opinion will displace the lower court's as the authoritative law on the issues under review (though the lower-court decision may remain good law for points not raised before or addressed by the higher court). Such opinions bear little authority, since courts are unlikely to place much reliance on them.

But then neither are litigants themselves. Because of the uncertainty engendered by a grant of appellate review, litigants in lower courts often seek a stay when review is granted in another case whose dispositive issue is the same as in their own case.

---

[1] See *Linkletter v. Walker*, 381 U.S. 618, 622 n.5 (1965) (noting that a case becomes "final" when the availability of appeal has been exhausted or has lapsed, and the time to petition for certiorari has passed); *State Farm Ins. Co. v. Edwards*, 339 S.W.3d 456, 458 n.2 (Ky. 2011) ("[C]learly there can be no precedential value to a holding that is still being considered."); *cf. State v. Smith*, 308 P.3d 135, 136 n.1 (N.M. Ct. App. 2013) (stating that "a formal Court of Appeals opinion has controlling authority in this Court, even when our Supreme Court has granted certiorari in the case").

[2] See Lee Epstein et al., *The Supreme Court Compendium: Data, Decisions, and Developments* 270–71 (5th ed. 2012) (showing the "proportion in which the petitioning party received a favorable disposition" for each term from 1946 to 2009, ranging from 44.4% in 1993 to 76.5% in 2008); Theodore Eisenberg & Geoffrey P. Miller, *Reversal, Dissent, and Variability in State Supreme Courts: The Centrality of Jurisdictional Source*, 89 B.U. L. Rev. 1451, 1470–80 (2009).

Intermediate and lower courts may find themselves caught between binding precedent and the implications of a grant of review when earlier decisions have addressed an issue later taken up by the high court. In this situation, the earlier vertical precedent may be binding on lower courts even though the grant of review in a later case raising the same issue calls this precedent into question. For instance, in a 2007 California case,[3] a criminal defendant challenged the constitutionality of aspects of the state's sentencing scheme. Binding California precedent upheld the scheme,[4] but the U.S. Supreme Court had granted certiorari in a separate case challenging the scheme.[5] The state appellate court correctly followed the binding vertical precedent from the California Supreme Court.[6] Yet because the U.S. Supreme Court decided its case while the California case was on rehearing, the state court had to vacate its decision and apply the new precedent.[7]

While granting discretionary review weakens a lower court's decision, denying review should have no effect at all. The denial of discretionary review neither approves nor disapproves the decision below. That "the denial of a writ of certiorari imports no expression of opinion upon the merits of the case" has been confirmed repeatedly.[8] In *Maryland v. Baltimore Radio Show*,[9] Frankfurter J. set out perhaps the most thorough explanation for this rule.[10] The denial of a petition for certiorari, he explained,

> simply means that fewer than four members of the Court deemed it desirable to review a decision of the lower court as a matter "of sound judicial discretion." A variety of considerations underlie denials of the writ, and as to the same

---

3   *People v. Lammers*, No. H030091, 2007 WL 64850 (Cal. Ct. App. 11 Jan. 2007), *vacated* 2007 WL 987900 (Cal. Ct. App. 3 Apr. 2007).
4   *See People v. Black*, 113 P.3d 534 (Cal. 2005), *vacated as moot*, 549 U.S. 1190 (2007).
5   *Cunningham v. California*, 549 U.S. 270 (2007).
6   *Lammers*, 2007 WL 64850.
7   *Lammers*, 2007 WL 987900.
8   *See, e.g., Teague v. Lane*, 489 U.S. 288, 296 (1989) (quoting *United States v. Carver*, 260 U.S. 482, 490 (1923)).
9   338 U.S. 912 (1950).
10 *Id.* at 917–18.

petition different reasons may lead different Justices to the same result.... Narrowly technical reasons may lead to denials. Review may be sought too late; the judgment of the lower court may not be final; it may not be the judgment of a State court of last resort; the decision may be supportable as a matter of State law, not subject to review by this Court, even though the State court also passed on issues of federal law. A decision may satisfy all these technical requirements and yet may commend itself for review to fewer than four members of the Court. Pertinent considerations of judicial policy here come into play. A case may raise an important question but the record may be cloudy. It may be desirable to have different aspects of an issue further illumined by the lower courts. Wise adjudication has its own time for ripening.[11]

Another Justice has emphasized that "[t]here is a critical difference between a judgment of affirmance and an order denying a petition for a writ of certiorari. The former determines the rights of the litigants; the latter expresses no opinion on the merits of the case."[12]

The same rule has been applied in state courts with discretionary review.[13] When the state's high court has discretion to review a case, its decision not to do so cannot be read to imply approval or adoption of the lower court's judgment or opinion. Courts correctly reject any implication from the denial of review. In one case,[14] for example, a state intermediate court of appeals was considering an issue that had been addressed by a sister court of appeals, but not by the state high court.[15] The appellant urged the court to follow the earlier intermediate court's reasoning,

---

11 *Id.* (Frankfurter J. opinion respecting the denial of petition for certiorari).

12 *Schiro v. Indiana*, 493 U.S. 910 (1989) (Stevens J. on the denial of petition for certiorari).

13 *See, e.g., Potvin v. Lincoln Serv. & Equip. Co.*, 6 A.3d 60, 79–80 (Conn. 2010); *State v. Williams*, 800 So. 2d 790, 803 (La. 2001); *Commonwealth v. LeClair*, 840 N.E.2d 510, 514 (Mass. 2006); *Powell v. Anderson*, 660 N.W.2d 107, 123 (Minn. 2003) (en banc); *State v. Williams*, 686 S.E.2d 493, 505 n.1 (N.C. 2009); *Heartland Bank v. National City Bank*, 869 N.E.2d 746, 753 (Ohio Ct. App. 2007); *Loram Maint. of Way, Inc. v. Ianni*, 210 S.W.3d 593, 596 (Tex. 2006); *Morgan v. Carillon Invs., Inc.*, 88 P.3d 1159, 1162 n.1 (Ariz. Ct. App. 2004).

14 *Heartland Bank*, 869 N.E.2d 746.

15 *Id.* at 753 (citing *First Merit Bank v. Angelini*, 823 N.E.2d 485 (Ohio Ct. App. 2004)).

arguing that "the Supreme Court's decision not to accept the case for review implies that it concurred with the resolution of the case."[16] The court correctly rejected this argument, explaining that "a decision by the Supreme Court of Ohio not to accept an appeal is not a determination on the merits of the case."[17]

Signaling a higher court's approval

Some state courts have a procedure by which the high court *can* indicate its approval of a lower court's opinion. For instance, the Supreme Court of Pennsylvania may issue a per curiam affirmance not only of the intermediate court's judgment but also of its opinion.[18] If the court affirms the opinion as well as the judgment, it has approved the lower court's rationale as well as its judgment.[19] Similarly, if the Supreme Court of Texas "refuses" a petition for review, rather than "denying" it, the decision below is given precedential value as if it were a decision of the Supreme Court itself.[20]

A 2007 Texas intermediate appellate decision[21] illustrates the rule's application in such a state. At issue was the duty owed by one participant to others in a sporting event. The plaintiff and defendant were softball coaches. The plaintiff was injured when a bat flew out of the defendant's hand during practice and hit the plaintiff in the face. The court recognized that several other intermediate courts of appeals had addressed the question of duty and concluded that sports participants owe no negligence duty whatsoever to one another.[22] Several cases had been appealed for

---

16   *Id.*
17   *Id.*
18   See *In re Stevenson*, 40 A.3d 1212, 1216 (Pa. 2012).
19   See *Commonwealth v. Tilghman*, 673 A.2d 898, 904 (Pa. 1996).
20   See Tex. R. App. P. 56.1(c) ("Petition Refused. If the Supreme Court determines—after a response has been filed or requested—that the court of appeals' judgment is correct and that the legal principles announced in the opinion are likewise correct, the Court will refuse the petition with the notation 'Refused.' The court of appeals' opinion in the case has the same precedential value as an opinion of the Supreme Court."); *Hyundai Motor Co. v. Vasquez*, 189 S.W.3d 743, 754 n.52 (Tex. 2006).
21   *Chrismon v. Brown*, 246 S.W.3d 102 (Tex. App.—Houston [14th Dist.] 2007, no pet.).
22   *Id.* at 111.

discretionary review by the Supreme Court of Texas, but review had been denied each time, leaving the issue open.[23] In one such case,[24] two justices dissented from the denial of review, stating their view that Texas courts should apply a different limited-duty rule: "a defendant does not owe a duty to protect a participant from risks inherent in the sport or activity in which the participant has chosen to take part."[25] This rule, the justices urged, would satisfy two competing public-policy interests. On one hand, it would "enabl[e] participants to play within the normal customs of their chosen sport without incurring liability," and on the other it would allow that "when a defendant creates a risk separate and apart from those that arise from the nature of the sport, a defendant is subject to the ordinary rules of negligence for determining liability."[26]

The intermediate appellate court in the 2007 case agreed with this standard, which had already been adopted in several other states and seemed, in the court's judgment, to best balance the competing policy issues.[27] Although a dissenting justice contended that the Texas Supreme Court had "affirmatively declined to adopt" the standard in the earlier cases,[28] the majority was correct to reject this characterization of the Texas Supreme Court's actions. The court explained that the refusal of discretionary

---

23 *Id.* (citing *Phi Delta Theta Co. v. Moore*, 10 S.W.3d 658, 659–63 (Tex. 1999) (Enoch J. dissenting from denial of petition after court dismissed petition as improvidently granted); *Davis v. Greer*, 940 S.W.2d 582 (Tex. 1996) (Gonzalez J. dissenting from denial of petition for writ of error)).

24 *Phi Delta Theta Co.*, 10 S.W.3d 658.

25 *Id.* at 661 (Enoch J. dissenting from denial of petition for writ of error).

26 *Id.* at 662; *see Davis*, 940 S.W.2d at 582–83 (Gonzalez J. dissenting from denial of petition for writ of error) ("By voluntarily participating in a competitive sport, a participant is deemed to have consented to and assumed the risk of all harmful contacts and foreseeable injuries that are inherent to that particular sport. This more accurately reflects the understanding of sports participants. This is very similar to the standard that courts in Texas and throughout the country have utilized. However, it would prevent cases such as the one now before us from proceeding to trial merely because a plaintiff alleges that the defendant acted recklessly or intentionally when it is clear that the injury resulted from a risk that was an obvious and foreseeable part of the game.").

27 *Chrismon*, 246 S.W.3d at 111–12.

28 *Id.* at 119 (Edelman J. dissenting).

review indicated the high court's dissatisfaction that "the opinions in those cases declared the law correctly in all respects but was of the opinion that the application for writ of error (or petition for review) presented no error of law which required reversal or which was of such importance to Texas jurisprudence as to require correction."[29]

The rule that a denial of discretionary review implies neither approval nor disapproval of the decision below applies even within the same case. In other words, a higher court's decision not to grant review doesn't give the lower court's decision status as law of the case vis-à-vis the higher court, which can later review the issues on the merits if they come up again on appeal. In one case,[30] the Supreme Court of Texas addressed the question whether its denial of discretionary review in an interlocutory appeal taken earlier in the case precluded it from addressing the issues raised in the appeal from final judgment after trial.[31] An employee under the influence of methamphetamines had injured a police officer who was protecting the employee's wife from her husband, who had threatened her with a gun.[32] Having been shot and injured, the officer sued the employer for negligent supervision.[33] Although the officer didn't allege that the employee was acting within the scope of his employment, he did allege that the employer was liable for the employee's conduct because it was aware that he was under the influence of drugs and nevertheless transported him to the worksite and "loosed" him "on an unsuspecting public."[34] The employer in turn argued that it owed no duty to the officer because its employee was off duty when he shot the officer, even though he

---

29 *Id.* at 112 n.11 (adumbrating that because Texas has a procedure by which the Supreme Court may adopt a lower court's opinion as its own, its not having done so in the earlier cases made it particularly clear that the denial of review didn't indicate approval of the merits of the lower-court decisions).

30 *Loram Maint. of Way, Inc. v. Ianni*, 210 S.W.3d 593 (Tex. 2006).

31 *Id.* at 595–96.

32 *Id.* at 595.

33 *Id.*

34 *Ianni v. Loram Maint. of Way, Inc.*, 16 S.W.3d 508, 512 (Tex. App.—El Paso 2000, pet. denied).

was staying at a company-provided motel.[35] Under Texas law, an employer may owe a duty of care to those potentially harmed by a drunk or otherwise incapacitated employee if it takes affirmative action to control the employee.[36] The trial court granted summary judgment for the employer, and the officer appealed.[37]

On appeal, the intermediate court of appeals reversed and remanded for trial, finding that the officer had raised a genuine dispute of material fact about whether the employer had affirmatively controlled its employee when it allowed him to use methamphetamine on the job and ignored reports that the employee was out of control.[38] The high court denied the employer's petition for review. At trial, the jury found for the officer, and the intermediate court of appeals affirmed, concluding that the employer owed the officer a duty of care and that sufficient evidence supported the verdict.[39] The court concluded that the employer had taken action to protect a coworker's wife when the employee threatened her, but took no further action to protect other individuals.[40]

When the employer again petitioned for review at the Supreme Court of Texas, the court granted the petition. The officer argued that the duty-of-care issue couldn't be addressed because it was the law of the case.[41] The court rejected that argument because its decision not to review a case was "not evidence that the Court agree[d] with the law as decided by the court of appeals."[42] The court was correct to reject the officer's law-of-the-case argument, since its earlier decision not to review the first appeal had no precedential significance and didn't give the court of appeals' decision greater authority than it would have on its own.

---

35 *Loram Maint. of Way, Inc.*, 210 S.W.3d at 595; *Ianni*, 16 S.W.3d at 512.
36 *See Otis Eng'g Corp. v. Clark*, 668 S.W.2d 307, 311 (Tex. 1983).
37 *Ianni*, 16 S.W.3d at 511.
38 *Id.* at 520–23.
39 *Loram Maint. of Way, Inc. v. Ianni*, 141 S.W.3d 722 (Tex. App.—El Paso 2004), rev'd, 210 S.W.3d 593 (Tex. 2006).
40 *Loram Maint. of Way, Inc.*, 141 S.W.3d at 728–29.
41 *Loram Maint. of Way, Inc.*, 210 S.W.3d at 595–96.
42 *Id.* at 596.

High courts' administrative role

The supervisory authority that high courts often have over the lower courts within their jurisdiction is exercised through writs of mandamus or other procedures. The Supreme Court of Illinois, for example, with constitutional and common-law authority to supervise all lower courts,[43] will issue a supervisory order if a lower court acts "in excess of its authority" or "as an abuse of its discretionary authority."[44] Supervisory orders are usually limited to situations in which the normal appellate process wouldn't afford adequate relief and "the dispute involves a matter important to the administration of justice or intervention is necessary to keep an inferior tribunal from acting beyond the scope of its authority."[45] The same rule that applies to the denial of discretionary review applies with full force to such collateral forms of review; indeed, because such orders are typically recognized to be extraordinary remedies, a court's declination to issue one cannot be said to indicate approval of the decision below.[46] One Illinois court has explained that such a denial doesn't even affect the litigants in the case at issue: "a supreme court's denial of a motion for a supervisory order does not have the effect of a ruling on any issue, nor does it support the decision of the lower court."[47] The litigants may therefore pursue the same issues again on direct appeal.

Dissentals

Despite the long-standing rule that a denial of review says nothing about the opinion below, justices occasionally write opinions commenting on the denial. These opinions are often called "dissentals," that is, dissents from the denial in which the justice

---

43 *See* Ill. Const. art. VI, § 16; Ill. Sup. Ct. R. 383.
44 *People ex rel. Daley v. Suria*, 490 N.E.2d 1288, 1293 (Ill. 1986).
45 *People ex rel. Birkett v. Bakilis*, 752 N.E.2d 1107, 1109 (Ill. 2001) (citation omitted).
46 *See Chambers v. O'Quinn*, 242 S.W.3d 30, 32 (Tex. 2007) (per curiam) ("The writ of mandamus is a discretionary writ, and its denial, without comment on the merits, cannot deprive another appellate court from considering the matter in a subsequent appeal.").
47 *People ex rel. Madigan v. Illinois Commerce Comm'n*, 941 N.E.2d 947, 956–57 (Ill. App. Ct. 2010).

(or justices) explains why the case merited review and should have been granted. Occasionally, a justice will write to emphasize that the denial of review should not be read to imply approval of the opinion below. For example, Alito J. issued one such opinion in a case in which the petition for certiorari involved what he described as "a highly unusual practice" in class-action certification: "insist[ing] that class counsel 'ensure that the lawyers staffed on the case fairly reflect the class composition in terms of relevant race and gender metrics.'"[48] Although he agreed that certiorari should be denied, he wrote to emphasize the potential constitutional problems with such a requirement.[49]

Objecting to the modern practice of writing opinions regarding the denial of certiorari, Stevens J. has argued that opinions dissenting from the denial of certiorari are "totally unnecessary" and "potentially misleading."[50] True, a denial of certiorari implies nothing favorable or unfavorable, and a published dissent from denial generally carries little weight. Dissentals are used by individual Justices to explain their views on why the case merits review. They might serve to inform the bar of the Court's potential interest in certain issues that the case raises. It is therefore understandable that modern Supreme Court Justices—including Stevens J. himself[51]—have issued such opinions.[52]

---

48 *Martin v. Blessing*, 134 S.Ct. 402 (2013) (Alito J. statement respecting the denial of petition for certiorari).

49 *Id.* at 402–03.

50 *Singleton v. Commissioner*, 439 U.S. 940, 944–45 (1978) (Stevens J. opinion respecting the denial of petition for certiorari); *see* Daniel McGowan, *Judicial Writing and the Ethics of the Judicial Office*, 14 Geo. J. Legal Ethics 509, 516 (2001) (discussing dissents to denials of rehearing en banc in circuit courts).

51 *See, e.g., Smith v. North Carolina*, 459 U.S. 1056 (1982) (Stevens J. opinion respecting the denial of petitions for certiorari).

52 For more on this subject, see Alex Kozinski & James Burnham, *I Say Dissental, You Say Concurral*, 121 Yale L.J. Online 601 (2012), http://yalelawjournal.org/forum/i-say-dissental-you-say-concurral. *See also infra* p. 533.

32. Advisory Opinions

An advisory opinion by a state high court, given in response to a question propounded to it by the executive or legislative department, is merely persuasive authority.

Courts are generally considered to have authority to decide only cases actually presented to them, not others. The orthodox jurisprudential view is that "[j]udicial declaration, unaccompanied by judicial application, is of no authority."[1] As one influential commentator long ago noted: "No court can refuse to decide an actual case over which it has jurisdiction; and no court can decide a wholly imaginary case."[2] Hence in 1793, when President George Washington asked the U.S. Supreme Court to deliver an opinion on the construction of the 1778 treaty with France, the Justices declined to comply.[3] Although this policy has been both praised[4] and dispraised,[5] it has long held firm. Before being appointed to the U.S. Supreme Court, Frankfurter J. wrote: "It must be remembered that advisory opinions are not merely advisory opinions. They are ghosts that slay."[6]

Yet as we will see, in some states a constitutional provision allows the governor or the legislature to procure from the state's high court an opinion on an important question of law—especially

---

[1] John Salmond, *Jurisprudence* § 62, at 192 (Glanville L. Williams ed., 10th ed. 1947).

[2] Eugene Wambaugh, *The Study of Cases* § 5, at 8 (2d ed. 1894).

[3] 13 Charles Alan Wright, Arthur R. Miller et al., *Federal Practice and Procedure* § 3529.1, at 641–42 (3d ed. 2008 & Supp. 2015); *see* Joan R. Gunderson, *Advisory Opinions*, in *The Oxford Companion to the Supreme Court of the United States* 21, 21 (Kermit L. Hall ed., 2d ed. 2005).

[4] *See* Alexis de Tocqueville, *Democracy in America* 192 (1840; Eduardo Nolla ed., 2012).

[5] James Bryce, *The American Commonwealth* 234–35 (1888; Liberty Fund Inc. ed., 1995).

[6] Felix Frankfurter, *A Note on Advisory Opinions*, 37 Harv. L. Rev. 1002, 1008 (1924); *see id.* at 1005 (warning that "[t]he advisory opinion deprives constitutional interpretation of the judgment of the legislature upon facts, of the legal defence of legislation as an application of settled legal principles to new situations, and of the means of securing new facts through the process of legislation within allowable limits of trial and error").

the constitutionality of a contemplated statute. Although this procedure has been called "wholly foreign to the general theory of judicial duty,"[7] today decisions on such points are often accepted as advisory opinions—opinions that answer questions of law submitted to a court, usually by another branch of government or another court.[8]

In English courts, the common-law power to issue advisory opinions was undisputed. The practice derived from a function of the King's Bench, which was composed of legally trained judges who provided opinions to the King, his Council, and the House of Lords.[9] The English practice was firmly established early on, and the English government continued to rely on advisory opinions throughout the following centuries. Between 1827 and 1899, English judges issued 125 advisory opinions to the House of Lords, which were adopted by the majority in all but five cases.[10] From this system emerged several "of the most canonical contributions to British and American common law."[11]

But the convention wasn't generally accepted in the United States. In 1789, the delegates of the Constitutional Convention refused to approve a proposal giving the legislature and the executive authority to require an opinion of the Supreme Court Justices.[12] Four years later came the Supreme Court's declination of President Washington to construe the Franco-American treaty.[13] Later that year, the Supreme Court Justices refused to respond to questions from Secretary of State Thomas Jefferson,

---

7 Wambaugh, *Study of Cases* § 5, at 12.

8 *Black's Law Dictionary* 1265 (Bryan A. Garner ed., 10th ed. 2014); Note, *Advisory Opinions on the Constitutionality of Statutes*, 69 Harv. L. Rev. 1302, 1302 (1956).

9 Pascal F. Calogero Jr., *Advisory Opinions: A Wise Change for Louisiana and Its Judiciary?*, 38 Loy. L. Rev. 329, 335 (1992).

10 Jonathan D. Persky, Note, *"Ghosts That Slay": A Contemporary Look at State Advisory Opinions*, 37 Conn. L. Rev. 1155, 1162–63 (2005).

11 *Id.* (citing *Wright v. Tatham* [1837] 112 Eng. Rep. 488 (K.B.); *Cox v. Hickman* [1860] 11 Eng. Rep. 431 (H.L.); and *M'Naghten's Case* [1843] 8 Eng. Rep. 718 (H.L.)).

12 Calogero, *Advisory Opinions*, 38 Loy. L. Rev. at 333 (citing 2 *The Records of the Federal Convention of 1787* 341 (Max Farrand ed., rev. ed. 1937)).

13 See the first paragraph of this section.

citing the case-and-controversy requirement and separation-of-powers concerns.[14] Since that time, the federal prohibition on advisory opinions has been indisputable.[15]

Although advisory opinions are disallowed in the federal system because federal courts' jurisdiction is limited by the Constitution,[16] state courts aren't similarly prohibited.[17] At one time, the courts of North Carolina issued advisory opinions without express constitutional or statutory authority,[18] but later ended this practice.[19] Several states followed English practice and enacted provisions granting their highest courts the authority to issue advisory opinions. Massachusetts enacted the first such provision in the 18th century[20] (establishing the model for other states) and then issued the earliest reported advisory opinion in

---

14 See Stewart Jay, *Most Humble Servants: The Advisory Role of Early Judges* 57–65, 179–80 (1997) (citing Letter from the Supreme Court Justices to Thomas Jefferson (8 Aug. 1793)).

15 See *DaimlerChrysler Corp. v. Cuno*, 547 U.S. 332, 341 (2006) ("[N]o principle is more fundamental to the judiciary's proper role in our system of government than the constitutional limitation of federal-court jurisdiction to actual cases or controversies.") (quoting *Raines v. Byrd*, 521 U.S. 811, 818 (1997)) (internal quotation marks omitted); see also 13 Charles Alan Wright, Arthur R. Miller et al., *Federal Practice and Procedure* § 3529, at 611–17 (3d ed. 2008 & Supp. 2015)

16 U.S. Const. art. III, § 2 (extending jurisdiction to cases and controversies); *Alvarez v. Smith*, 558 U.S. 87, 92 (2009) ("The Constitution permits this Court to decide legal questions only in the context of actual 'Cases' or 'Controversies.'"); *DaimlerChrysler Corp. v. Cuno*, 547 U.S. 332, 341 (2006) ("Determining that a matter before the federal courts is a proper case or controversy under Article III therefore assumes particular importance in ensuring that the Federal Judiciary respects the proper—and properly limited—role of the courts in a democratic society.") (internal quotation marks omitted).

17 See Mel A. Topf, *State Supreme Court Advisory Opinions as Illegitimate Judicial Review*, 2001 Mich. St. L. Rev. 101, 101 n.1 (noting that only ten states allowed advisory opinions at the time of writing).

18 See *id.* (explaining that the North Carolina justices began rendering advisory opinions, without authority, in 1776). For an example of such an opinion, see *In re Advisory Op. to the Governor*, 61 S.E.2d 529, 531 (N.C. 1950).

19 Jonathan D. Persky, *"Ghosts That Slay": A Contemporary Look at State Advisory Opinions*, 37 Conn. L. Rev. 1155, 1170 (2005) (explaining that the court abandoned this practice in 1985).

20 Calogero, *Advisory Opinions*, 38 Loy. L. Rev. at 336; see Mass. Const. pt. 2, ch. III, art. II.

the United States, in 1781.[21] Most states having authorized the issuance of advisory opinions have done so through constitutional provisions.[22] Two others convey authority by statute.[23] Even so, with state constitutional prohibitions some state high courts have held statutes providing for advisory opinions unconstitutional.[24] For example, the Texas legislature passed a statute that allowed the state's courts to advise on "the constitutionality of any law or any order, rule or regulation . . . which may be involved in any case pending but undetermined in a trial court."[25] A trial court certified a question regarding the constitutionality of a statute at issue in a suit before it to the Texas Court of Civil Appeals, which then certified the question to the Texas Supreme Court.[26] The court reviewed the statute granting it authority to issue an advisory opinion and determined that the statute conflicted with the court's limited jurisdiction—extending only to original and appellate jurisdiction—as set forth in the Texas Constitution.[27] As a result, the court declared the statute void.[28]

Most states allow their highest courts to issue advisory opinions only in response to certified questions of law from a federal court (see § 74).

---

21 Topf, *Illegitimate Judicial Review*, 2001 Mich. St. L. Rev. at 103–04; *see Opinions of the Justices*, 126 Mass. 547, 547 (1879) (decided in 1781 but published in 1879) (settling a disagreement between the House of Representatives and the Senate on the meaning of a constitutional provision); *see also* Manley O. Hudson, *Advisory Opinions of National and International Courts*, 37 Harv. L. Rev. 970, 977 (1924) (discussing the post-1780 Massachusetts experience).

22 Topf, *Illegitimate Judicial Review*, 2001 Mich. St. L. Rev. at 101 n.1 (explaining that eight states have constitutional provisions and listing them: Colo. Const. art. VI, § 3 (since 1886); Fla. Const. art. IV, § 1(c) (since 1868); Me. Const. art. VI, § 3 (since 1820); Mass. Const. pt. 2, ch. III, art. II (since 1780); Mich. Const. art. III, § 8 (since 1963); N.H. Const. pt. 2, art. 74 (since 1784); R.I. Const. art. X, § 3 (since 1842); S.D. Const. art. V, § 5 (since 1889)).

23 *See* Ala. Code § 12-2-10 (1940) (since 1923); Del. Code Ann. tit. 10, § 141(a) (1995) (since 1852).

24 Note, *Advisory Opinions on the Constitutionality of Statutes*, 69 Harv. L. Rev. at 1305.

25 Tex. Rev. Civ. Stat. Ann. art. 1851a, § 1 (1933).

26 *Morrow v. Corbin*, 62 S.W.2d 641, 643 (Tex. 1933).

27 *Id.* at 645–46.

28 *Id.* at 651.

Restrictions on advisory opinions

The provisions allowing advisory opinions usually contain restrictions on who may request an opinion,[29] on what types of issues the justices may opine on,[30] and in what circumstances the justices may issue such opinions.[31]

If no constitutional authority requires courts to render advisory opinions, courts have generally refused such requests from the legislative and executive branches.[32] Even when advisory opinions are sanctioned by express authority, justices have expressed doubt about rendering such advice.[33] Particularly, justices have been

---

29 *See, e.g.*, Mass. Const. pt. 2, ch. III, art. II (giving "[e]ach branch of the legislature, as well as the governor and council, . . . authority to require the opinions of the justices"); Fla. Const. art. IV, § 1(c); S.D. Const. art. V, § 5; Del. Code Ann. tit. 10, § 141 (1995) (each allowing only the governor to request an advisory opinion).

30 *See, e.g.*, R.I. Const. art. X, § 3 (justices must answer "any question of law"); Ala. Code § 12-2-10 (1940) (authorizing advisory opinions only on constitutional questions).

31 *See, e.g.*, *Opinion of the Justices*, 815 A.2d 791, 794 (Me. 2002) (stating that the initial inquiry, in accordance with the Maine Constitution, is to determine whether a solemn occasion warrants the justices' giving advice).

32 *See, e.g.*, *National Educ. Ass'n Topeka, Inc. v. USD 501*, 608 P.2d 920, 923 (Kan. 1980) (finding that the "court is without constitutional authority to render advisory opinions" because those opinions "would go beyond the limits of determining an actual case or controversy and would violate the doctrine of separation of powers"); *People v. Campbell*, 589 P.2d 1360, 1361 (Colo. 1978) (en banc) (stating that the Colorado Supreme Court "do[es] not render advisory opinions on hypothetical fact situations"); *Rosnick v. Zoning Comm'n of Southbury*, 374 A.2d 245, 308–09 (Conn. 1977) (per curiam) (refusing to decide moot issue because the "court does not sit to advise on abstract principles"); *Smith v. Alabama Dry Dock & Shipbuilding Co.*, 309 So. 2d 424, 427 (Ala. 1975) (noting that "[t]here must be a bona fide existing controversy of a justiciable character or the court is without jurisdiction"); *United Servs. Life Ins. Co. v. Delaney*, 396 S.W.2d 855, 856, 859 (Tex. 1965); *In re Workmen's Comp. Fund*, 119 N.E. 1027, 1028 (N.Y. 1918) (Cardozo J.) (stating that courts "do not give advisory opinions . . . [because that] is not the exercise of the judicial function").

33 *See, e.g.*, *Answer of the Justices to the Governor*, 829 N.E.2d 1111, 1115 (Mass. 2005) (stating that "[p]eriodically, we cast aside our doubts as to the existence of a solemn occasion and give advisory opinions despite our doubts") (internal quotation marks omitted); *Department of Revenue v. Kuhnlein*, 646 So. 2d 717, 720–21 (Fla. 1994) (noting that Florida has general standing requirements and that "parties must not . . . request[] an advisory opinion, except in those rare instances in which advisory opinions are authorized by the Constitution") (citation omitted); *In re Opinions of the Justices*, 96 So. 487, 489 (Ala. 1923) (calling the practice of issuing advisory opinions "preservative and conservative");

cautious about rendering opinions that would affect the rights of individuals. For example, the Florida justices, in response to a question about a proposed order and a set of jurisdictional facts, explained that "[a]n answer [to such a question would] affect directly the rights of individuals . . . . An opinion without their participation would deny to them a traditional aspect of due process—the right to be heard."[34]

Courts have generally accorded advisory opinions little to no precedential value. Justices issuing such opinions have held that the opinions "bind no one whatsoever"[35] and cannot be considered judicial precedent.[36] Typical is this statement of the Delaware Supreme Court: "Since the giving of the opinion fixes no legal rights and entails no legal consequences, it involves no exertion of power over any person; it is merely the performance of an advisory function."[37] Courts provide various justifications for this view, among them the need to issue the opinions quickly,[38] the absence of argument to illuminate the nuances of the issues at hand,[39]

---

see also In re Request for Advisory Op. from Governor, 812 A.2d 789, 790 (R.I. 2002) (declining to make factual findings although the Rhode Island advisory mandate has been construed broadly, and "despite [the justices'] constitutional duty to respond," because fact-finding "inheres in the Court as the judicial branch").

34 *Advisory Op. to the Governor*, 196 So. 2d 737, 739 (Fla. 1967) (per curiam).

35 *Opinion of the Justices*, 198 So. 2d 269, 280 (Ala. 1967) (quoting *In re Opinions of the Justices*, 96 So. 487, 489 (Ala. 1923)); *see also Opinion of the Justices to the Senate*, 366 N.E.2d 733, 736 (Mass. 1977) (advisory opinions "not binding in subsequent litigation"); *Opinion of the Justices*, 25 N.H. 537, 538 (1852) ("[W]hatever opinions we might express . . . must be regarded as impressions by which we should not feel ourselves bound . . . .").

36 *Opinion of the Justices*, 413 A.2d 1245, 1248 (Del. 1980) (because "advisory opinions do not decide a case, do not adjudicate a dispute and are not judicial rulings in any sense[,] . . . they are not binding on any court and do not carry precedential effect").

37 *In re Opinions of the Justices*, 88 A.2d 128, 136 (Del. 1952) (per curiam).

38 *In re Opinion of the Justices*, 16 Me. 479, 479–80 (1840) (noting that an advisory-opinion request "cannot be allowed the time for that extensive research and patient examination and reflection, which the importance of the questions . . . may demand").

39 *Opinion to the Governor*, 178 A. 433, 440 (R.I. 1935) (stating that an advisory opinion, "given, as it must be, without the aid which the court derives, in adversary cases, from able and experienced counsel, . . . can have no weight as a precedent").

and the court's compromised decision-making ability due to the scarcity of facts.[40] Courts similarly hold that advisory opinions are merely the "opinion of the individual [j]ustices"[41] and "not the opinions of the [court] itself,"[42] and therefore are "not binding precedent."[43]

Two states differ only under limited circumstances. The South Dakota Constitution expressly states: "The Governor has authority to require opinions of the Supreme Court upon important questions of law involved in the exercise of his executive power and upon solemn occasions."[44] And the Colorado Constitution directs: "The supreme court shall give its opinion upon important questions upon solemn occasions when required by the governor, the senate, or the house of representatives; and all such opinions shall be published in connection with the reported decision of said court."[45] Colorado's high court thoroughly examined this provision and concluded that its advisory opinions "have all the force and effect of judicial precedents."[46]

Although courts issuing opinions in the regular course of review aren't bound by a prior advisory opinion, they have determined that they are bound by a prior nonadvisory decision.[47]

---

40 *See* Felix Frankfurter, *A Note on Advisory Opinions*, 37 Harv. L. Rev. 1002, 1003 (1924) (stating that advisory opinions are "bound to result in sterile conclusions unrelated to actualities").

41 *Opinion of the Justices*, 907 So. 2d 1022, 1025 (Ala. 2005); *see also Opinion of the Justices*, 840 A.2d 637, 638 (Del. 2003) ("Such opinions are the individual, personal views of the individual [j]ustices . . . .").

42 *Opinion of the Justices*, 840 A.2d at 638.

43 *Id.*; *Opinion of the Justices*, 907 So. 2d at 1025; *see* Note, *Advisory Opinions on the Constitutionality of Statutes*, 69 Harv. L. Rev. 1302, 1302–04 (1956) (explaining that one reason for courts' determinations that advisory opinions aren't precedential is that they are the product of an extrajudicial act).

44 S.D. Const. art. V, § 5; *see also* Topf, *Illegitimate Judicial Review*, 2001 Mich. St. L. Rev. at 108 n.32 (explaining that the South Dakota Constitution originally allowed the governor to require opinions "of the judges of the Supreme Court," but that the phrase "the judges of" was deleted in 1972 because opinions from the court—rather than individual judges—were considered binding).

45 Colo. Const. art. VI, § 3.

46 *In re Senate Resolution Relating to Senate Bill No. 65*, 21 P. 478, 467–69 (Colo. 1889).

47 *See, e.g., In re Opinion of the Justices*, 115 N.E. 978, 979 (Mass. 1917).

Further, courts have held that despite their freedom to disregard an advisory opinion, they won't generally rethink questions previously answered.[48] And while recognizing that they aren't bound by these decisions, courts have suggested that advisory opinions do bear some degree of precedential force.[49]

So while courts are generally free to ignore even their own advisory opinions, the practical effect of these legal determinations is much weightier. As some justices have recognized, advisory opinions are "what one would expect the [j]ustices to say if the issue had been presented to them in litigation,"[50] are "read by the public, the profession, the Governor and the Senate as ... definitive expression[s] of [the justices'] views,"[51] and are arguably "taken as binding by virtually everyone[,] including at times the advising justices."[52]

For state judicial opinions issued in response to a federal court's certified question—a widespread phenomenon since the mid-20th century—see § 74.

---

48 See, e.g., Barley v. South Fla. Water Mgmt. Dist., 823 So. 2d 73, 82 (Fla. 2002) (per curiam) ("[A]lthough our advisory opinions are not strictly binding precedent in the most technical sense, only under *extraordinary* circumstances will we revisit an issue decided in our earlier advisory opinions.") (quoting Ray v. Mortham, 742 So. 2d 1276, 1285 (Fla. 1999) (per curiam)).

49 See Lee v. Dowda, 19 So. 2d 570, 572 (Fla. 1944) (en banc) ("While advisory opinions to the Governor are not binding judicial precedents, they are frequently very persuasive and usually adhered to."); Barley, 823 So. 2d at 82 (quoting Lee v. Dowda for same proposition); In re Opinion of the Justices, 121 A. 902, 904 (Me. 1923) (noting that "although [an advisory opinion] does not have the binding force of a judgment, [it] may yet be regarded as detrimental to the interests of those to whom it is adverse").

50 Opinion of the Justices, 413 A.2d 1245, 1248 (Del. 1980).

51 Advisory Ops. re Constitutionality of 1972 PA 294, 208 N.W.2d 469, 483 (Mich. 1973) (Levin J. concurring).

52 Topf, *Illegitimate Judicial Review*, 2001 Mich. St. L. Rev. at 129.

33. Executive Opinions and Decisions

Decisions or opinions of special tribunals, quasi-judicial bodies, attorneys general, and administrative tribunals are not precedents in court. But they are treated with respect and may be allowed to have considerable influence.

Nonjudicial decisions—those rendered by special tribunals or quasi-judicial bodies—may offer interpretations of constitutions, statutes, and treaties. But American courts don't consider them legal precedents, and in no sense are they recognized to be controlling authority of the same character as binding judicial decisions. Even so, courts from many jurisdictions cite them as persuasive authority and treat them respectfully.

A common example of a decision from an entity considered to be quasi-judicial in nature is an opinion from the attorney general. An attorney-general opinion is sometimes regarded as quasi-judicial because of the close relationship between the office and the corresponding state or federal government and the nature of the duties of the office, which may involve prosecuting in the name of the governmental entity and giving legal advice to officers and agencies.[1] Attorneys general are often required by statute to issue formal opinions on questions submitted by the legislature and other government officers.[2] Most courts recognize that such opinions should be accorded some influential value. Federal courts

---

[1] See, e.g., *People ex rel. Breuning v. Berry*, 304 P.2d 818, 822 (Cal. Dist. Ct. App. 1956) ("Although the opinions of the [AG] are not of controlling authority, yet in view of their relation to the general government and the nature of their duties, they are to be regarded as having a quasi-judicial character and entitled to great respect.").

[2] See, e.g., *LaFountain v. Attorney Gen.*, 503 N.W.2d 739, 740 (Mich. Ct. App. 1993) (state statute requires AG "to give his opinion upon all questions of law submitted to him by the legislature . . . or any other state officer."); *Saefke v. Stenehjem*, 673 N.W.2d 41, 45 (N.D. 2003) ("The [AG] has the statutory duty to issue opinions to state officers and public entities and to consult with and advise the several state's attorneys in matters relating to the duties of their office."); *see also* Robert L. Larson, *Importance and Value of Attorney General Opinions*, 41 Iowa L. Rev. 351 (1955); Erwin C. Surrency, *Legal Opinions of the Attorney General of the United States: Their Application in the Courts*, 29 Temple L.Q. 26 (1955).

generally accord respect to federal attorney-general opinions.[3] As we will see, most state courts do the same (with some significant variations) for state-attorney-general opinions.[4] Courts may take

---

[3] See *United States v. Falk & Brother*, 204 U.S. 143, 150 (1907) ("[T]he [AG]'s opinion cannot be overlooked."); see also *McElroy v. United States ex rel. Guagliardo*, 361 U.S. 281, 285–86 (1960); *Roberts v. United States*, 320 U.S. 264, 270–72 (1943); *United States v. Page*, 137 U.S. 673 (1891).

[4] See, e.g., *Alabama–Tenn. Nat. Gas Co. v. Southern Nat. Gas Co.*, 694 So. 2d 1344, 1346 (Ala. 1997) (Alabama courts treat AG opinions as advisory and persuasive authority); *State v. Kenaitze Indian Tribe*, 83 P.3d 1060, 1066 n.22 (Alaska 2004) (Alaska courts give "some deference" to AG opinions, but doing so is largely discretionary); *Logan v. Forever Living Prods. Int'l, Inc.*, 52 P.3d 760, 763 n.4 (Ariz. 2002) (Arizona courts treat AG opinions as advisory and with due respect); *Gray v. Mitchell*, 285 S.W.3d 222, 231 n.5 (Ark. 2008) (Arkansas courts treat AG opinions as nonbinding authority); *Planned Parenthood Affiliates of Cal. v. Van de Kamp*, 226 Cal. Rptr. 361, 368 (Ct. App. 1986) (California courts accord AG opinions "great respect" and give "great weight" to them); *Colorado Ass'n of Pub. Emps. v. Lamm*, 677 P.2d 1350, 1360 (Colo. 1984) (en banc) (Colorado courts regard AG opinions as having "some significance"); *Velez v. Commissioner of Corr.*, 738 A.2d 604, 610 (Conn. 1999) (Connecticut courts regard AG opinions with "careful consideration and . . . as highly persuasive"); *Council 81 v. State*, 288 A.2d 453, 455 (Del. Ch. 1972) (Delaware courts treat AG opinions as advisory but helpful); *Beverly v. Division of Beverage of Dep't of Bus. Regulation*, 282 So. 2d 657, 660 (Fla. Dist. Ct. App. 1973) (per curiam) (Florida courts afford "great weight" to AG opinions); *Moore v. Ray*, 499 S.E.2d 636, 637 (Ga. 1998) (Georgia courts consider AG opinions as persuasive authority); *Taniguchi v. Association of Apartment Owners of King Manor, Inc.*, 155 P.3d 1138, 1147 n.12 (Haw. 2007) (Hawaii courts regard AG opinions as "highly instructive"); *Holly Care Ctr. v. State, Dep't of Emp't*, 714 P.2d 45, 51 (Idaho 1986) (Idaho courts treat AG opinions as advisory but give them deference); *Burris v. White*, 901 N.E.2d 895, 899 (Ill. 2009) (Illinois courts accord AG opinions "considerable weight" when they are well reasoned); *Miller Brewing Co. v. Bartholemew Cnty. Beverage Co.*, 674 N.E.2d 193, 203 (Ind. Ct. App. 1996) (Indiana courts find official AG opinions "helpful on occasion"); *Bradley v. Iowa Dep't of Pers.*, 596 N.W.2d 526, 530 (Iowa 1999) (Iowa courts give "respectful consideration" to AG opinions); *Data Tree, LLC v. Meek*, 109 P.3d 1226, 1234 (Kan. 2005) (Kansas courts treat AG opinions as persuasive authority); *Carter v. Smith*, 366 S.W.3d 414, 420 n.2 (Ky. 2012) (Kentucky courts treat AG opinions as "highly persuasive" and accord them "great weight"); *Holley v. Plum Creek Timber Co.*, 877 So. 2d 284, 291 (La. Ct. App. 2004) (Louisiana courts treat AG opinions as persuasive authority); *Dodds v. Shamer*, 663 A.2d 1318, 1326 (Md. 1995) (Maryland courts consider AG opinions for their persuasive value); *Williams v. City of Rochester Hills*, 625 N.W.2d 64, 74 (Mich. Ct. App. 2000) (per curiam) (Michigan courts treat AG opinions as persuasive authority); *Billigmeier v. County of Hennepin*, 428 N.W.2d 79, 82 (Minn. 1988) (Minnesota courts give "careful consideration" to AG opinions); *Blackwell v. Mississippi Bd. of Animal Health*, 784 So. 2d 996, 1000 (Miss. Ct. App. 2001) (Mississippi courts treat AG opinions with "careful consideration" and regard them as persuasive); *Mesker Bros. Indus., Inc. v. Leachman*, 529 S.W.2d 153, 158 (Mo. 1975) (Missouri courts treat AG opinions as persuasive authority); *State ex rel. Jenkins v. Carisch*

judicial notice of attorney-general opinions either at the request of a litigant or on their own initiative.[5]

For this purpose, and for the guidance of the bar generally, most attorneys general have established an opinions committee devoted solely to issuing considered pronouncements on the meaning or effect of statutes within the jurisdiction. These are collected into accessible formats for the use of practitioners and others who may have need of them.

Theatres, Inc., 564 P.2d 1316, 1319 (Mont. 1977) (Montana courts treat AG opinions as persuasive authority and will uphold them if not erroneous); *Bonn v. City of Omaha*, 814 N.W.2d 114, 120 (Neb. Ct. App. 2012) (Nebraska courts give "substantial weight" and respectful consideration to AG opinions); *Blackjack Bonding v. City of Las Vegas Mun. Court*, 14 P.3d 1275, 1279 (Nev. 2000) (Nevada courts treat AG opinions as nonbinding authority); *Quarto v. Adams*, 929 A.2d 1111, 1117 (N.J. Super. Ct. App. Div. 2007) (New Jersey courts treat AG opinions with "a degree of deference"); *First Thrift & Loan Ass'n v. State ex rel. Robinson*, 304 P.2d 582, 588 (N.M. 1956) (New Mexico courts give as much weight to AG opinions as the courts "deem they merit"); *Nelson v. New York State Civil Serv. Comm'n*, 469 N.Y.S.2d 224, 226 (App. Div. 1983) (New York courts treat AG opinions with "great deference"); *Delconte v. State*, 329 S.E.2d 636, 639 n.3 (N.C. 1985) (North Carolina courts give "some weight" to AG opinions); *Riemers v. City of Grand Forks*, 723 N.W.2d 518, 522 (N.D. 2006) (North Dakota courts treat AG opinions with respect and follow them if they are persuasive); *State ex rel. North Olmsted Fire Fighters Ass'n v. City of North Olmsted*, 597 N.E.2d 136, 139 (Ohio 1992) (per curiam) (Ohio courts treat AG opinions as persuasive authority); *State ex rel. Clifton v. Reeser*, 543 P.2d 1379, 1384 (Okla. 1975) (Oklahoma courts treat AG opinions with "great respect"); *Alexander v. Gladden*, 288 P.2d 219, 223 (Or. 1955) (Oregon gives "earnest consideration" to AG opinions); *Commonwealth ex rel. Pappert v. Coy*, 860 A.2d 1201, 1208 (Pa. Commw. Ct. 2004) (Pennsylvania courts afford "great weight" to AG opinions); *Charleston Cnty. Sch. Dist. v. Harrell*, 713 S.E.2d 604, 609 (S.C. 2011) (South Carolina courts treat AG opinions as persuasive authority); *Stumes v. Delano*, 508 N.W.2d 366, 372 (S.D. 1993) (South Dakota courts treat AG opinions as nonbinding authority); *Scott v. Ashland Healthcare Ctr., Inc.*, 49 S.W.3d 281, 287 (Tenn. 2001) (Tennessee courts treat AG opinions as nonbinding authority); *Holmes v. Morales*, 924 S.W.2d 920, 924 (Tex. 1996) (Texas courts treat AG opinions as persuasive authority); *In re Dixon*, 183 A.2d 522, 524 (Vt. 1962) (Vermont courts afford AG opinions persuasive weight); *Beck v. Shelton*, 593 S.E.2d 195, 200 (Va. 2004) (Virginia courts give "due consideration" to AG opinions); *Thurston Cnty. ex rel. Bd. of Cnty. Comm'rs v. City of Olympia*, 86 P.3d 151, 154 (Wash. 2004) (en banc) (Washington courts accord AG opinions "great weight"); *Hoover v. Blankenship*, 487 S.E.2d 328, 332 (W. Va. 1997) (West Virginia courts treat AG opinions as nonbinding authority); *Schill v. Wisconsin Rapids Sch. Dist.*, 786 N.W.2d 177, 205 (Wis. 2010) (Wisconsin courts treat well-reasoned AG opinions as persuasive authority); *Galesburg Constr. Co. v. Board of Trs. of Mem'l Hosp.*, 641 P.2d 745, 750 n.9 (Wyo. 1982) (Wyoming courts accord AG opinions some weight).

5   *See* Fed. R. Evid. 201(c); *KVUE, Inc. v. Moore*, 709 F.2d 922, 929 (5th Cir. 1983).

Although attorney-general opinions aren't controlling,[6] they are often accorded great weight.[7] Courts will follow the attorney-general's opinion if it is persuasive and doesn't conflict with the plain language of the statute.[8] In some states, an attorney-general

---

[6] *Water Works & Sewer Bd. of Talladega v. Consolidated Publ'g, Inc.*, 892 So. 2d 859, 866 n.5 (Ala. 2004) ("While an opinion of the [AG] is not binding, it can constitute persuasive authority.") (internal quotation marks omitted); *City of Prescott v. Town of Chino Valley*, 803 P.2d 891, 894 n.2 (Ariz. 1990) (in banc) ("[AG]'s opinions are not binding on this court."); *In re Lietz Constr. Co.*, 47 P.3d 1275, 1285 (Kan. 2002) ("While an opinion of the [AG] is neither conclusive nor binding on this court, an [AG] opinion may be persuasive authority."); *Danse Corp. v. City of Madison Heights*, 644 N.W.2d 721, 726 n.6 (Mich. 2002) (per curiam) ("[O]pinions of the [AG] are not binding on courts as precedent."); *Gershman Inv. Corp. v. Danforth*, 517 S.W.2d 33, 35 (Mo. 1974) (en banc) ("An [AG] is a member of the Executive Department. He has no judicial power and may not declare the law. His opinions may be persuasive to some and not to others. In any event, the judicial power of the state is vested in the courts designated in Mo. Const. art. V, § 1. The courts declare the law.") (citation omitted); *State ex rel. Van Dyke v. Public Emps. Ret. Bd.*, 793 N.E.2d 438, 445 (Ohio 2003) (per curiam) ("[AG] opinions are not binding on courts; at best, they are persuasive authority."); *Green Bay Educ. Ass'n v. State Dep't of Pub. Instruction*, 453 N.W.2d 915, 918–19 (Wis. Ct. App. 1990) ("[A]ttorney general opinions are merely persuasive, nonbinding authority upon a reviewing court.").

[7] *Cedar Shake & Shingle Bureau v. City of Los Angeles*, 997 F.2d 620, 625 (9th Cir. 1993) ("That the [AG] has issued a reasonable opinion on the question, however, is not dispositive. Although opinions of the state [AG] are generally regarded as highly persuasive, we are not bound by them.") (internal quotation marks and citations omitted); *Ennabe v. Manosa*, 319 P.3d 201, 213 n.14 (Cal. 2014) ("As we have explained, absent controlling authority, the [AG]'s opinion is persuasive because we presume that the Legislature was cognizant of the [AG]'s construction of [the statute] and would have taken corrective action if it disagreed with that construction.") (internal quotation marks and citations omitted); *Commonwealth ex rel. Pappert v. Coy*, 860 A.2d 1201, 1208 (Pa. Commw. Ct. 2004) ("[A]lthough opinions of the [AG] are not binding on the Court, the courts customarily afford great weight to official opinions of the [AG]."); *City of Dallas v. Abbott*, 304 S.W.3d 380, 384 (Tex. 2010) ("While the [AG]'s interpretation of the Act may be persuasive, it is not controlling."); *Kruzel v. Podell*, 226 N.W.2d 458, 462 (Wis. 1975) ("While the opinions of the [AG] are not authoritative sources of the law, they are in some cases highly persuasive; and, of course, in cases where an [AG]'s opinion has been followed by consistent administrative practices, those opinions may well become authoritative as a practical construction of a statute.").

[8] *Northland Family Planning Clinic, Inc. v. Cox*, 487 F.3d 323, 338 (6th Cir. 2007) ("The state finally contends that the [AG]'s Opinion should have been granted a greater degree of deference by the district court as a persuasive authority for interpreting Michigan law. . . . [T]his Court's case law makes clear that we are not to give the [AG]'s interpretative views controlling weight . . . . [E]ven were we to grant the [AG]'s views 'substantial weight,' we still have to reject

opinion is binding on public officials unless it is overturned by a court.[9]

Courts take many factors into account when determining how much persuasive weight an attorney-general opinion should be given. They may consider whether it has been challenged since being rendered or whether the legislature leaves the statute intact after an attorney-general opinion interprets a statute in a particular way or questions its constitutionality. Leaving a statute unchanged after such an interpretation is traditionally viewed as implicit approval.[10] A statute that has remained unchanged for many years

---

his interpretation, for it conflicts with the statutory language.") (internal quotation marks and citations omitted); *Billigmeier v. County of Hennepin*, 428 N.W.2d 79, 82 (Minn. 1988) ("When appropriate, opinions of the [AG] are entitled to careful consideration by appellate courts, particularly where they are of long standing."); *Riemers v. City of Grand Forks*, 723 N.W.2d 518, 521–22 (N.D. 2006) ("An [AG]'s opinion is not binding authority upon the courts; however, opinions of the [AG] are entitled to respect, and courts should follow them if they are persuasive.") (internal quotation marks omitted).

9 *State ex rel. Fent v. State ex rel. Okla. Water Res. Bd.*, 66 P.3d 432, 441 (Okla. 2003) ("As the state's chief law officer, the [AG] has been entrusted with the duty of providing legal guidance to public officers and of advising them on questions of law which relate to their official duties. With the exception of an [AG]'s opinion that an act of the legislature is unconstitutional, an [AG]'s opinion is binding upon the state officials whom it affects. Public officers have the duty to follow [AG] opinions until they are judicially relieved of compliance.") (footnotes omitted); *City of Brainerd v. Brainerd Inv. P'ship*, 812 N.W.2d 885, 891 (Minn. Ct. App. 2012) ("When appropriate, opinions of the [AG] are entitled to careful consideration by appellate courts, particularly where they are of long standing. In fact, in some limited and carefully delineated situations, the legislature has by statute expressly given [AG]'s opinions the force of law unless and until a court of competent jurisdiction overrules them. For example, Minn. Stat. § 8.07 (2010) grants [AG]'s opinions the force of law regarding the regulation of certain school matters. Nonetheless, it is also well settled that opinions of the [AG] are not binding on the court.") (internal quotation marks and citations omitted).

10 *Napa Valley Educators Ass'n v. Napa Valley Unified Sch. Dist.*, 239 Cal. Rptr. 395, 399 (Ct. App. 1987) ("In the absence of controlling authority, these opinions are persuasive 'since the Legislature is presumed to be cognizant of that construction of the statute.'") (quoting *Henderson v. Los Angeles City Bd. of Educ.*, 144 Cal. Rptr. 568, 573 (Ct. App. 1978)); *Meyer v. Board of Trs. of San Dieguito Union High Sch. Dist.*, 15 Cal. Rptr. 717, 724 (Dist. Ct. App. 1961) ("It must be presumed that the aforesaid interpretation has come to the attention of the Legislature, and if it were contrary to the legislative intent that some corrective measure would have been adopted in the course of the many enactments on the subject in the meantime."); *Gottschalk v. Sueppel*, 140 N.W.2d 866, 873 (Iowa 1966) (noting that the interpretation was made immediately after the Act that

since the issuance of a negative opinion may afford the opinion even greater weight.[11] Similarly, if the legislature has taken steps to amend the statute after the attorney general rendered its decision but has left the section as so interpreted untouched, courts may also afford the decision greater weight.[12] Members of the government and other citizens may come to rely on such long-standing attorney-general opinions to guide their actions,[13] and some courts

---

it was interpreting was passed and the opinion wasn't disturbed by legislature); *Terry v. Edgin*, 561 P.2d 60, 65 (Okla. 1977) ("[W]e have held that silence by the legislature may be regarded as acquiescence or approval of the interpretation placed upon statutory provisions by the [AG]."); *Browning-Ferris, Inc. v. Commonwealth*, 300 S.E.2d 603, 605–06 (Va. 1983) ("The legislature is presumed to have had knowledge of the [AG]'s interpretation of the statutes, and its failure to make corrective amendments evinces legislative acquiescence in the [AG]'s view."); *In re Dixon*, 183 A.2d 522, 524 (Vt. 1962) ("The legislature has not seen fit to change the law since this opinion was issued. The fact that it has not done so tends to confirm the propriety of the [AG]'s opinion.").

[11] *See, e.g., Smith v. Municipal Court of Glendale Judicial Dist.*, 334 P.2d 931, 935 (Cal. Dist. Ct. App. 1959) (AG opinion entitled to "great weight" because 18 years had passed with no challenge); *Billigmeier v. County of Hennepin*, 428 N.W.2d 79, 82 (Minn. 1988) ("When appropriate, opinions of the [AG] are entitled to careful consideration by appellate courts, particularly where they are of long standing."); *Beck v. Shelton*, 593 S.E.2d 195, 200 (Va. 2004) (AG opinion is particularly "entitled to due consideration . . . when the General Assembly has known of the [decision], in this case for five years, and has done nothing to change it."); *Galesburg Constr. Co. v. Board of Trs. of Mem'l Hosp.*, 641 P.2d 745, 750 n.9 (Wyo. 1982) (when a construction has stood for nearly 20 years, the AG opinion is particularly entitled to weight because it has "been weathered by time[,] and when the legislature has failed over a long period to make any change in a statute following its interpretation by the [AG][, s]uch acquiescence is worthy of careful consideration in an inquiry into the intent of that body").

[12] *See, e.g., Schill v. Wisconsin Rapids Sch. Dist.*, 786 N.W.2d 177, 205 (Wis. 2010) ("Furthermore, a statutory interpretation by the [AG] 'is accorded even greater weight, and is regarded as presumptively correct, when the legislature later amends the statute but makes no changes in response to the [AG]'s opinion.'") (quoting *Staples ex rel. Staples v. Glienke*, 416 N.W.2d 920, 924 (Wis. Ct. App. 1987)).

[13] *See, e.g., Hemphill v. Montgomery*, 548 N.W.2d 579, 581 (Iowa 1996) (noting that although AG opinions aren't binding, state officials had consistently "rel[ied] on those opinions for approximately fifty years"); *Murfreesboro Bank & Trust Co. v. Evans*, 241 S.W.2d 862, 864 (Tenn. 1951) (if an AG opinion has been "consistently followed by the Department [for nearly a decade, it] should be given persuasive weight by the Court"), *overruled by Pierce v. Woods*, 597 S.W.2d 295 (Tenn. 1980); *Gaynor Constr. Co. v. Board of Trs., Ector Cnty. Indep. Sch. Dist.*, 233 S.W.2d 472, 478 (Tex. Civ. App.—El Paso 1950, writ ref'd) ("Especially is this so since we judicially know that these opinions have served

show much greater respect for a decision when there is evidence of reliance.[14]

If there are conflicting attorney-general opinions on a given issue, courts will understandably accord those opinions less weight than they would if they had been uniform.[15] On the other hand, if opinions by two or more succeeding attorneys general come to a consistent conclusion, courts will consider those opinions as having greater significance.[16]

The practical approach that courts take in analyzing attorney-general opinions is similar to the method by which they evaluate the persuasiveness of nonbinding judicial opinions. Some courts will perform a wholly independent analysis of the issue before them and cite attorney-general opinions only summarily as further

---

as guides to the Trustees of Independent school districts throughout this state in the administration of their duties relating to contracting for the construction of such buildings for a number of years.").

14 *See, e.g., Star Tribune Co. v. University of Minn. Bd. of Regents*, 683 N.W.2d 274, 289 (Minn. 2004) (en banc) ("We have stated that opinions of the [AG] are entitled to careful consideration when they are of long standing, but have typically coupled this factor with administrative reliance on the opinion."); *In re Bartell v. State*, 284 N.W.2d 834, 838 (Minn. 1979) (en banc) ("While we have stated that we will carefully consider such constructions when they are of long standing and accompanied by administrative reliance, in this case we are unable to determine prior agency practice from the record.").

15 *See, e.g., Harris Cnty. Comm'rs Court v. Moore*, 420 U.S. 77, 87 n.10 (1975) ("The [AG opinion], however, may be given close scrutiny by the state courts, as it appears to be in direct conflict with several earlier opinions of the [AG]."); *Alexander v. Gladden*, 288 P.2d 219, 223 (Or. 1955) ("We give earnest consideration to opinions of the [AG], but we are not bound by them, especially when the present [AG] expresses views contrary to those expressed by his predecessor."); *City of Fort Worth v. Abbott*, 258 S.W.3d 320, 326 (Tex. App.—Austin 2008, no pet.) ("[W]e are not bound to follow them—especially in a situation, as here, where the [AG] has issued conflicting opinions on the same issue.").

16 *See, e.g., Beverly v. Division of Beverage of Dep't of Bus. Regulation*, 282 So. 2d 657, 660 (Fla. Dist. Ct. App. 1973) (per curiam) ("While the official opinions of the [AG] of the State of Florida are not legally binding upon the courts of this State, they are entitled to great weight in construing the law of this State. The fact that two different [AG]s have reached the same conclusion with respect to the exact issue now before us lends considerable persuasive influence to their opinions and weighs heavily in favor of our conclusion herein."); *Tennessee Bd. of Dispensing Opticians v. Eyear Corp.*, 400 S.W.2d 734, 739 (Tenn. 1966) ("Where a consistent interpretation has been given such should be given persuasive weight by this Court.").

support for the court's holding.[17] Others may discuss the decisions and their reasoning in much greater detail. The court may then either agree with an opinion's reasoning[18] or distinguish the opinion and find that it doesn't squarely apply to the facts in the case to be decided.[19] Even if the opinion isn't directly on point, the court may glean general principles or guidelines from it to apply to the facts before the court.[20] Some courts may find that even though the attorney-general opinion is on point and applies directly to the case at hand, its reasoning isn't cogent and compelling, or else its outcome isn't well supported.[21] Other courts may simply refuse

---

17 *See, e.g., Bonito Partners, LLC v. City of Flagstaff*, 270 P.3d 902, 907 n.5 (Ariz. Ct. App. 2012); *DuPree v. Carroll*, 967 So. 2d 27, 31 (Miss. 2007); *Adams Outdoor Advert., L.P. v. County of Dane*, 811 N.W.2d 421, 428 n.4 (Wis. Ct. App. 2012).

18 *See, e.g., Ex parte Jim Walter Res., Inc.*, 91 So. 3d 50, 54 (Ala. 2012); *Browning v. Florida Prosecuting Attorneys Ass'n*, 56 So. 3d 873, 876–77 (Fla. Dist. Ct. App. 2011); *Burris v. White*, 901 N.E.2d 895, 899 (Ill. 2009); *Bocanegra v. City of Chicago Electoral Bd.*, 954 N.E.2d 859, 865–66 (Ill. App. Ct. 2011); *Wibben v. Iowa Dep't of Transp., Motor Vehicle Div.*, 409 N.W.2d 475, 477 (Iowa 1987); *Louisville Metro Dep't of Corr. v. Commonwealth*, 258 S.W.3d 419, 421–22 (Ky. Ct. App. 2007); *Attorney Gen. v. PowerPick Club of Mich.*, 783 N.W.2d 515, 526–27 (Mich. Ct. App. 2010); *State v. Brown*, 771 N.W.2d 267, 274–75 (N.D. 2009); *General Dynamics Land Sys., Inc. v. Tracy*, 700 N.E.2d 1242, 1244–45 (Ohio 1998); *In re Texas Dep't of State Health Servs.*, 278 S.W.3d 1, 5 (Tex. App.—Austin 2008, no pet.).

19 *See, e.g., Dupree v. Hiraga*, 219 P.3d 1084, 1110 n.32 (Haw. 2009) ("Thus, the opinion addresses a factual situation distinct from that here, and the [AG's] opinion's comment about the importance of intent must be considered in light of that factual context."); *State ex rel. Data Trace Info. Servs., LLC v. Cuyahoga Cnty. Fiscal Officer*, 963 N.E.2d 1288, 1300–01 (Ohio 2012) (per curiam); *CAO Holdings, Inc. v. Trost*, 333 S.W.3d 73, 85 (Tenn. 2010) ("In addition, the factual circumstances addressed by the [AG] differ substantively from the facts of this case."); *Standley v. Sansom*, 367 S.W.3d 343, 350–51 (Tex. App.—San Antonio 2012, pet. denied) ("Moreover, the [AG] opinions are necessarily limited to the particular facts and circumstances presented in each case.").

20 *See, e.g., In re Barnwell Cnty. Hosp.*, 471 B.R. 849, 862–63 (Bankr. D.S.C. 2012).

21 *See, e.g., United States v. Bibbins*, 637 F.3d 1087, 1095 (9th Cir. 2011) (finding a Nevada AG opinion from 1969 to be unpersuasive because of the "scant reasoning to support its conclusion"); *Alabama Dep't of Pub. Safety v. Barbour*, 5 So. 3d 601, 610–11 (Ala. Civ. App. 2008) (disagreeing with AG opinion's reliance on certain cases); *Hofman Ranch v. Yuba Cnty. Local Agency Formation Comm'n*, 91 Cal. Rptr. 3d 458, 463 (Ct. App. 2009) (disagreeing with AG opinion that draws its conclusion "without authority"); *Leddy v. Cornell*, 120 P. 153, 155–56 (Colo. 1912) (en banc) ("Respecting that [AG] opinion, it is sufficient to say that, while it is persuasive, it is neither conclusive nor binding, and since it seems to be without authoritative legal support, it should not be approved

to address the opinions, perhaps noting that they aren't binding precedent in any event.[22]

Agency interpretations

Courts also consider how administrative agencies have glossed statutes. With the rise of the administrative state during the 20th century, an extensive body of administrative law and procedure has developed in order to limit and review legislative delegations of authority to executive agencies.[23] With respect to administrative interpretations of statutes, the courts have ranged between two extremes, which one commentator calls independent judgment versus deference: "At one pole, courts ignore the administrative view. When operating in this 'independent judgment' mode, a court employs traditional tools of statutory interpretation . . . to arrive at what it regards as the best interpretation of the statute."[24] In the other "mode," a court asks whether the administrative interpretation is "one that a reasonable interpreter might embrace. . . . The task of the court is viewed not as discovering the best interpretation, but rather as [ensuring] that the executive view

---

or followed."); *Edney v. State*, 3 So. 3d 1281, 1283–84 (Fla. Dist. Ct. App. 2009) (finding AG's views not persuasive); *Greenwood v. Estes*, 504 P.2d 206, 211 (Kan. 1972) (declining to follow AG opinion because it was "without authoritative legal support").

22 *Arkansas Prof'l Bail Bondsman Licensing Bd. v. Oudin*, 69 S.W.3d 855, 862–63 (Ark. 2002) ("We need not address the effect of that opinion, however, other than to note that [AG]'s opinions are not binding precedent."); *State ex rel. Citizens for Responsible Dev. v. City of Milton*, 731 N.W.2d 640, 643 n.4 (Wis. Ct. App. 2007) ("We decline to address the parties' arguments over the various [AG] opinions . . . . Such opinions are not controlling precedent, and we do not find them persuasive here.").

23 *See* 2 Am. Jur. 2d *Administrative Law* §§ 1, 14, 18 (2014). *See generally* Daniel R. Schuckers & Kyle Appelgate, *The Rise of Pennsylvania's Administrative Agencies and Legislative and Judicial Attempts to Constrain Them*, 81 Pa. B. Ass'n Q. 124 (2010); Jonathan T. Molot, *The Judicial Perspective in the Administrative State: Reconciling Modern Doctrines of Deference with the Judiciary's Structural Role*, 53 Stan. L. Rev. 1 (2000); Richard B. Stewart, *The Reformation of American Administrative Law*, 88 Harv. L. Rev. 1669 (1975).

24 Thomas W. Merrill, *Judicial Deference to Executive Precedent*, 101 Yale L.J. 969, 971 (1992).

does not contradict the statute and otherwise furthers legitimate objectives."[25]

In the 1944 case of *Skidmore v. Swift & Co.*,[26] the U.S. Supreme Court announced a rule that agency interpretations do not bind courts but "do constitute a body of experience and informed judgment to which courts and litigants may properly resort for guidance."[27] The Court explained that the weight of the guidance in a particular case "will depend upon the thoroughness evident in [the agency's] consideration, the validity of its reasoning, its consistency with earlier and later pronouncements, and all those factors which give it power to persuade."[28] In addition to these factors, courts applying *Skidmore* "considered a number of factors favoring heightened scrutiny of agency rules."[29] For example, when "an agency's rule 'flatly contradicted' its prior rule, was of recent vintage, or concerned a nontechnical area within the court's expertise, courts were less apt to defer to the rule."[30] The consideration of all these factors allowed the court "to determine the relative expertise of courts and agencies, the potential for agency bias, and the capacity of courts to familiarize themselves with the factual circumstances of the subject of agency regulations."[31] Hence courts had a fair amount of discretion in choosing whether to follow an agency's interpretation of a statute.

In 1984, however, the Supreme Court swung the pendulum toward deference with its decision in *Chevron, U.S.A. v. Natural Resources Defense Council*,[32] which set forth a new two-step standard for judicial review of agency rules that interpret statutes that the agency administers and that Congress has empowered the agency to interpret: "First, always, is the question whether

---

25 *Id.*
26 323 U.S. 134 (1944).
27 *Id.* at 140.
28 *Id.*
29 David M. Hasen, *The Ambiguous Basis of Judicial Deference to Administrative Rules*, 17 Yale J. on Reg. 327, 334 (2000).
30 *Id.*
31 *Id.* at 334–35.
32 467 U.S. 837 (1984).

Congress has directly spoken to the precise question at issue. If the intent of Congress is clear, that is the end of the matter."[33] If Congress has not spoken on the question, "the court does not simply impose its own construction on the statute.... [Instead,] the question for the court is whether the agency's answer is based on a permissible construction of the statute."[34]

Yet the Court hasn't always deferred to reasonable agency interpretations of law. In 2000[35] and 2001,[36] the Court refused to apply *Chevron* deference to informal agency actions.[37] In the second of those cases, the Court explained that "administrative implementation of a particular statutory provision qualifies for *Chevron* deference when it appears that Congress delegated authority to the agency generally to make rules carrying the force of law," and the agency's interpretation was issued in the exercise of that authority.[38]

---

33 *Id.* at 842.
34 *Id.* at 843 (footnotes omitted).
35 *Christensen v. Harris Cnty.*, 529 U.S. 576 (2000).
36 *United States v. Mead Corp.*, 533 U.S. 218 (2001); *see* Michael A. Berch et al., *Introduction to Legal Method and Process: Cases and Materials* 436 (Jesse H. Choper et al. eds., 4th ed. 2006).
37 *See* Kristin E. Hickman & Matthew D. Krueger, *In Search of the Modern* Skidmore *Standard*, 107 Colum. L. Rev. 1235, 1245–46 (2007); Eric R. Womack, *Into the Third Era of Administrative Law: An Empirical Study of the Supreme Court's Retreat from* Chevron *Principles in* United States v. Mead, 107 Dick. L. Rev. 289, 304 (2002).
38 *Mead*, 533 U.S. at 226–27.

State courts generally accord some deference to agency interpretations of statutes. But perhaps with the intuitive or even empirically based knowledge that agency rule-writers often take their interpretations of statutes to an extreme,[39] many state courts don't follow the federal *Chevron/Skidmore* model.[40] They tend to

---

[39] See Christopher J. Walker, *Inside Agency Statutory Interpretation*, 67 Stan. L. Rev. 999, 1063 (2015) (noting empirically that 80% of agency rule-drafters are inclined to say that an agency "is more aggressive in its interpretive efforts if it is confident that *Chevron* deference . . . applies.").

[40] *Robbins v. Arizona Dep't of Econ. Sec.*, 300 P.3d 556, 558 (Ariz. Ct. App. 2013) ("We accord deference to agencies' interpretations of legislation they are charged with implementing. However, the agency's interpretation is not infallible, and courts must remain the final authority on critical questions of statutory construction.") (internal quotation marks and citations omitted); *Florida Dep't of Revenue v. Florida Mun. Power Agency*, 789 So. 2d 320, 323 (Fla. 2001) ("The Department's interpretation of a statute which it is charged with enforcing is entitled to great deference and will not be overturned unless it is clearly erroneous or contrary to legislative intent."); *Fishburn v. Indiana Pub. Ret. Sys.*, 2 N.E.3d 814, 824 (Ind. Ct. App. 2014) ("[A]n interpretation of a statute by an administrative agency charged with the duty of enforcing the statute is entitled to great weight, unless this interpretation would be inconsistent with the statute itself.") (internal quotation marks omitted); *Jones Cnty. Sch. Dist. v. Department of Revenue*, 111 So. 3d 588, 597–98 (Miss. 2013) (en banc) ("[E]ven though an agency's interpretation is an important factor that usually warrants strong consideration, the Court does not defer to an agency's interpretation in the sense that it yields judgment or opinion. Further, no deference is due if the agency's interpretation is contrary to the unambiguous terms or best reading of a statute.") (internal quotation marks and citations omitted); *GE Solid State, Inc. v. Director, Div. of Taxation*, 625 A.2d 468, 472 (N.J. 1993) ("Generally, courts accord substantial deference to the interpretation an agency gives to a statute that the agency is charged with enforcing."); *State ex rel. Clayburgh v. American W. Cmty. Promotions, Inc.*, 645 N.W.2d 196, 200 (N.D. 2002) ("The Commissioner's interpretation of a statute is entitled to some deference if it does not contradict clear and unambiguous statutory language. . . . [But] an administrative agency's construction of a statute is accorded much less weight when the only issue to be resolved by a court is a nontechnical question of law.") (internal quotation marks and citations omitted); *Berry v. Labor & Indus. Review Comm'n*, 570 N.W.2d 610, 612–13 (Wis. Ct. App. 1997) ("We are not bound by the [agency's] legal conclusions . . . . In certain situations, however, we defer to the [agency's] interpretation of a statute. We will accord the [agency's] interpretation great weight once we have determined: (1) that the agency was charged by the legislature with the duty of administering the statute; (2) that the interpretation of the agency is one of long-standing; (3) that the agency employed its expertise or specialized knowledge in forming the interpretation; and (4) that the agency's interpretation will provide uniformity and consistency in the application of the statute.") (internal quotation marks and citations omitted). *But see Northwest Youth Servs., Inc. v. Commonwealth Dep't of Pub. Welfare*, 66 A.3d 301, 311 (Pa. 2013) ("Pennsylvania courts' treatment of deference to administrative agency rules has followed the United

be chary of transfers of interpretive power to administrative agencies beyond what is explicitly or implicitly revealed by a fair reading of the statute at issue.

Other types of nonjudicial decisions include those rendered by state ethics boards and state-bar committees. These are similar to attorney-general opinions because they are merely advisory even if they're informed.[41] Like attorney-general opinions, they are normally thought of as potentially persuasive but not binding.[42]

States Supreme Court's lead, at least to an interim developmental stage."); *West Virginia Health Care Cost Review Auth. v. Boone Mem'l Hosp.*, 472 S.E.2d 411, 419 (W. Va. 1996) ("[O]ur standard of review analysis begins with a nod in the direction of [*Chevron*]. The rule of deference traditionally applies when an agency's interpretation is a product of delegated authority for rulemaking.") (internal quotation marks and citations omitted).

41 *See, e.g., Louisiana Bd. of Ethics v. Holden*, 121 So. 3d 113, 117 n.7 (La. Ct. App. 2013) ("Like [AG] opinions, the advisory opinions of a board or commission have been recognized as persuasive authority, and the court has discretion to review them as such.").

42 *See, e.g., Bruzas v. Richardson*, 945 N.E.2d 1208, 1213 (Ill. App. Ct. 2011) ("[W]e note that bar association opinions, formal or informal, are not binding precedent, although courts may look to them as a guide."); *Elane v. St. Bernard Hosp.*, 672 N.E.2d 820, 825 (Ill. App. Ct. 1996) (finding Chicago Bar Association Professional Responsibility Committee and Illinois Judicial Ethics Committee opinions not precedent, but soundly analyzed); *Reed v. Breton*, 756 N.W.2d 89, 92 (Mich. Ct. App. 2008) (State Bar Ethics Committee opinions are not binding but "instructive" and may provide some guidance); *People v. MacShane*, 847 N.Y.S.2d 338, 340 (App. Div. 2007) (opinion of Advisory Committee on Judicial Ethics "provide[s] important guidance to courts"); *Royston, Rayzor, Vickery & Williams, LLP v. Lopez*, 443 S.W.3d 196 (Tex. App.—Corpus Christi 2013), *rev'd*, 467 S.W.3d 494 (Tex. 2015) (Texas Ethics Commission opinions are advisory rather than binding); *Burke v. Lewis*, 122 P.3d 533, 541 n.6 (Utah 2005) (while not bound by opinions issued by the Ethics Advisory Committee, "the analyses contained in the committee's opinions provide a rich vein of material worthy of examination").

34. Legislative Interpretations

A legislative interpretation of a constitution, statute, or treaty does not control a court's judgment and is not a direct precedent. But in doubtful cases, it may merit some weight and consideration.

In their lawmaking, legislatures often express their understandings of the meaning and purpose of the laws in development. These interpretations may be found within committee reports, committee minutes, and legislative fact sheets. Likewise, legal interpretations are found in presidential signing statements, governor veto statements, and attorney-general opinions. Meanwhile, agencies typically interpret the statutes they are charged with enforcing. Courts often look to these interpretations for guidance when the meaning of a law isn't plain.

One view is that these sources of "authority" are hardly equal—that legislative history is of little if any value and that any resort to it represents retrograde public policy and promotes bad lawmaking, since legislatures are empowered to speak officially only through statutes.[1] This view represents the traditional "no-recourse rule," which held sway for centuries: courts aren't to consider what has been said in preenactment proceedings. Even on this view, agency interpretations, which occur postenactment, may be given some consideration.

Another view is that when legislatures develop legislation in the modern era, they go to great lengths to produce legislative history—hence it is only respectful for courts to pore over it in addition to whatever words have been duly enacted.[2] This view was more popular in the mid- to late 20th century than it is today, but it remains prominent. Even those who encourage judges not to delve into legislative history acknowledge that advocates must use arguments based on it.[3]

---

[1] *See* Antonin Scalia & Bryan A. Garner, *Reading Law: The Interpretation of Legal Texts* 369–90 (2012).

[2] Robert A. Katzmann, *Judging Statutes* 29–54 (2014).

[3] *See* Antonin Scalia & Bryan A. Garner, *Making Your Case* 48–51 (2008).

For courts that entertain legislative history, the traditional view is that when a constitution,[4] treaty,[5] or statute[6] is clear and

---

[4] *Taomae v. Lingle*, 118 P.3d 1188, 1194 (Haw. 2005) ("In interpreting constitutional provisions, the general rule is that, if the words used in a constitutional provision ... are clear and unambiguous, they are to be construed as they are written.") (internal quotation marks omitted); *State ex rel. Gardner v. Holm*, 62 N.W.2d 52, 55 (Minn. 1954) ("In construing a provision of our constitution, however, we are governed by certain well-established rules. Foremost among these is the rule that, where the language used is clear, explicit, and unambiguous, the language of the provision itself is the best evidence of the intention of the framers of the constitution. If the language is free from obscurity, the courts must give it the ordinary meaning of the words used."); *Hines v. Winters*, 320 P.2d 1114, 1118 (Okla. 1957) ("The object of construction, applied to a constitution, is to give effect to the intent of its framers, and of the people adopting it. This intent is to be found in the instrument itself; and when the text of a constitutional provision is not ambiguous, the courts, in giving construction thereto, are not at liberty to search for its meaning beyond the instrument.") (internal quotation marks omitted); *Management Council of Wyo. Legislature v. Geringer*, 953 P.2d 839, 843 (Wyo. 1998) ("If the constitutional language is clear and unambiguous, we must accept and apply the plain meaning of that language.").

[5] *United States v. Duarte-Acero*, 208 F.3d 1282, 1285 (11th Cir. 2000) ("If the language of the treaty is clear and unambiguous, as with any exercise in statutory construction, our analysis ends there and we apply the words of the treaty as written."); *Marquez-Ramos v. Reno*, 69 F.3d 477, 480 (10th Cir. 1995) ("[W]e start with the text of the treaty and the context in which the written words are used. Where the text is clear, we interpret it as written.") (internal quotation marks and citations omitted); *Herrera v. United States*, 39 Fed. Cl. 419, 421 (1997) ("Where the terms of a treaty are unambiguous, they must be given their plain meaning.").

[6] *Barnhart v. Sigmon Coal Co.*, 534 U.S. 438, 450 (2002) ("As in all statutory construction cases, we begin with the language of the statute. The first step is to determine whether the language at issue has a plain and unambiguous meaning with regard to the particular dispute in the case. The inquiry ceases if the statutory language is unambiguous and the statutory scheme is coherent and consistent.") (internal quotation marks and citations omitted); *United States v. Husted*, 545 F.3d 1240, 1245 (10th Cir. 2008) ("When a statute is unambiguous, however, we must apply its plain meaning except in the rarest of cases; after all, there can be no greater statement of legislative intent than an unambiguious statute itself."); *United States v. Abuagla*, 336 F.3d 277, 278 (4th Cir. 2003) ("We must first determine whether the language at issue has a plain and unambiguous meaning with regard to the particular dispute in the case. Our inquiry must cease if the statutory language is unambiguous and the statutory scheme is coherent and consistent.") (internal quotation marks and citations omitted); *McMillan v. Live Nation Entm't, Inc.*, 401 S.W.3d 473, 476 (Ark. 2012) ("When the language of the statute is plain and unambiguous, and conveys a clear and definite meaning, there is no need to resort to rules of statutory interpretation."); *Lincoln Cnty. Fiscal Court v. Department of Pub. Advocacy*, 794 S.W.2d 162, 163 (Ky. 1990) ("Where the words of the statute are clear and unambiguous and express the legislative intent, there is no room for

unambiguous, courts will apply it as written without further investigating whether there might be some doubt about its meaning. For "courts must presume that a legislature says in a statute what it means and means in a statute what it says there."[7]

If text is truly ambiguous, then courts often look to other sources to determine its meaning.[8] When interpreting an ambiguous statute, the court's primary goal is to determine the meaning of the legislature's words.[9] The court may consider, among other indications, the legislature's practical construction given to a statute,[10] statements made during legislative deliberations[11] (but

---

construction or interpretation and the statute must be given its effect as written."); *In re Certified Question from U.S. Ct. App. for the Sixth Cir.*, 659 N.W.2d 597, 600 (Mich. 2003) ("A fundamental principle of statutory construction is that a clear and unambiguous statute leaves no room for judicial construction or interpretation.") (internal quotation marks omitted).

7   *Connecticut Nat'l Bank v. Germain*, 503 U.S. 249, 253–54 (1992).

8   16 Am. Jur. 2d *Constitutional Law* § 64, at 418 (2014); 74 Am. Jur. 2d *Treaties* § 18, at 904 (2014); 73 Am. Jur. 2d *Statutes* § 104, at 342 (2012).

9   73 Am. Jur. 2d *Statutes* § 59, at 294 (2012) (using the term *intent* as opposed to *meaning*); see Antonin Scalia & Bryan A. Garner, *Reading Law: The Interpretation of Legal Texts* 391–96 (2012) (explaining that when it comes to statutory construction, *intent* is best understood as a synonym of *meaning*).

10   See *Niagara Falls Urban Renewal Agency v. O'Hara*, 394 N.Y.S.2d 951 (App. Div. 1977) (considering an official form that the legislature drafted because the form defined terms from a related statute); *Commonwealth v. Highhawk*, 687 A.2d 1123, 1126 (Pa. Super. Ct. 1996) ("[I]n construing legislative intent, the Court may look to the following factors: . . . (8) Legislative and administrative interpretations of such statute.").

11   See, e.g., *People v. Collins*, 824 N.E.2d 262, 266 (Ill. 2005) ("Where statutory language is ambiguous, however, we may consider other extrinsic aids for construction, such as legislative history and transcripts of legislative debates, to resolve the ambiguity."); *Schultz v. Harrison Radiator Div. Gen. Motors Corp.*, 683 N.E.2d 307, 310 (N.Y. 1997) ("While the statements of legislators made during legislative debates are not dispositive of legislative intent, such statements may be accorded some weight in the absence of more definitive manifestations of legislative purpose.") (citation omitted). *But see Phillips v. Larry's Drive-In Pharmacy, Inc.*, 647 S.E.2d 920, 925 (W. Va. 2007) ("A court should also recognize that the understanding of one or a few members of the Legislature is not necessarily determinative of legislative intent. No guarantee can issue that those who supported a legislator's proposal shared his view of its compass.") (internal quotation marks and citation omitted); 73 Am. Jur. 2d *Statutes* § 82, at 319 (2012) ("The opinions of individual legislators, or the testimony of a member of the legislature as to the intention of the legislature in enacting a statute, may not be given consideration. It is ultimately provisions of laws, rather than principal concerns of legislators, which govern.") (footnotes omitted); *id.* § 85,

not those made postenactment),[12] and the legislature's response to judicial interpretations of a statute.[13] When a law has been passed

---

at 324 ("[T]he general rule is that the statements and opinions of legislators uttered in a legislature are not appropriate sources of information from which to discover the meaning of the language of a statute passed by such body."); see id. § 87, at 325–26 (weight of committee reports); id. § 88, at 326–27 (weight of statements of authors or sponsors of a bill). *Contra* Antonin Scalia & Bryan A. Garner, *Reading Law: The Interpretation of Legal Texts* 369–90 (2012) (arguing against any uses of legislative history except to establish linguistic usage or to refute application of the absurdity canon).

[12] *Graham Cnty. Soil & Water Conservation Dist. v. United States ex rel. Wilson*, 559 U.S. 280, 297–98 (2010) ("There is, in fact, only one item in the legislative record that squarely corroborates respondent's reading of the statute: a letter sent by the primary sponsors of the 1986 amendments to the [AG] in 1999. Needless to say, this letter does not qualify as legislative 'history,' given that it was written 13 years after the amendments were enacted. It is consequently of scant or no value for our purposes.") (citation omitted); *Phillips*, 647 S.E.2d at 925 ("Ordinarily a court cannot consider the individual views of members of the Legislature or city council which are offered to prove the intent and meaning of a statute or ordinance after its passage and after litigation has arisen over its meaning and intent. Post-enactment statements by an individual legislator are suggestive of the Legislature's intent, and certainly might be considered when the statements are consistent with the statutory language and legislative history. Still, courts should not be placed in the position of passing upon the credibility of legislators and ex-legislators.") (internal quotation marks and citations omitted).

[13] *People v. Bonnetta*, 205 P.3d 279, 285 (Cal. 2009) ("Although the absence of legislative response to a judicial construction of a statute will not be deemed an implied ratification of that construction, when a statute has been construed by the courts and the Legislature thereafter reenacts the statute without changing the interpreted language, a presumption is raised that the Legislature was aware of and has acquiesced in that construction."); *Frank M. Hall & Co. v. Newsom*, 125 P.3d 444, 451 (Colo. 2005) (en banc) ("Subsequent legislative acts certainly cannot dispositively interpret earlier ones for the courts, but subsequent clarification of ambiguous legislation is one accepted aid to the discovery of legislative intent."); *Blount v. Stroud*, 904 N.E.2d 1, 15 (Ill. 2009) ("Where the legislature chooses not to amend a statute after a judicial construction, it will be presumed that it has acquiesced in the court's statement of the legislative intent. This presumption, however, is merely a jurisprudential principle; it is not a rule of law.") (internal quotation marks and citations omitted); *Bakala v. Town of Stonington*, 647 A.2d 85, 87 (Me. 1994) ("When prior legislative terminology is ambiguous, however, enactments by a later Legislature may be helpful in ascertaining legislative intent."); *State ex rel. Howard Elec. Coop. v. Riney*, 490 S.W.2d 1, 9 (Mo. 1973) (per curiam) ("[W]here a judicial construction has been placed upon the language of a statute for a long period of time, so that there has been abundant opportunity for the lawmaking power to give further expression to its will, the failure to do so amounts to legislative approval and ratification of the construction placed upon the statute by the courts, and that such construction should generally be adhered to, leaving

by the people through the process of initiative or referendum, the court sometimes determines meaning by considering the language of a voter pamphlet.[14] The court must not consider, however, the postenactment statement of a drafter of a voter initiative[15] or the after-the-fact testimony of a legislator who voted on an act.[16]

---

it to the legislature to amend the law should a change be deemed necessary.") (quoting 50 Am. Jur. *Statutes* § 326); *In re Gerling*, 303 S.W.2d 915, 920 (Mo. 1957) ("It is not disputed that predecessors of the present [AG] several times ruled that the statute in question does not extend to joint tenancies. We judicially notice that at the session of the 69th General Assembly, just closed, a bill (S.B. 243) was introduced and passed the Senate, which would have brought Missouri in line with most of the states and the federal government by making specific provision with respect to joint tenancies. That bill, however, did not pass the other house. These facts buttress our view that it is not within the intendment of the present statute that joint tenancies be included."); *Roberts v. Tishman Speyer Props., L.P.*, 918 N.E.2d 900, 907 (N.Y. 2009) (per curiam) ("It is true that, where the practical construction of a statute is well known, the Legislature may be charged with knowledge of that construction and its failure to act may be deemed an acceptance."); *Moncrief v. Wyoming State Bd. of Equalization*, 856 P.2d 440, 444–45 (Wyo. 1993) ("[W]here the legislature, by subsequent amendment or legislation in the same act or on the same subject, enacts language which clarifies previously ambiguous language, the subsequent language gives meaning to the previously ambiguous expression."); *see also* 73 Am. Jur. 2d *Statutes* § 82, at 318–19 (2012).

14 *Robert L. v. Superior Court*, 69 P.3d 951, 955 (Cal. 2003) ("When the language is ambiguous, we refer to other indicia of the voters' intent, particularly the analyses and arguments contained in the official ballot pamphlet.") (internal quotation marks omitted); *Pierce Cnty. v. State*, 78 P.3d 640, 646 (Wash. 2003) (en banc) ("A court interpreting an initiative measure must ascertain the voters' intent in approving the measure. Where the language of the initiative is clear and unambiguous, a court may not look beyond the text of the measure; however, if the initiative is susceptible to more than one reasonable interpretation, a court may determine the voters' intent by applying canons of statutory construction or by examining the statements in the voters pamphlet.") (internal quotation marks omitted).

15 *Arizona Citizens Clean Elections Comm'n v. Brain*, 322 P.3d 139, 142 (Ariz. 2014) ("[J]ust as a legislator, lobbyist, or other interested party lacks competence to testify about legislative intent in passing a law, the drafter of a voter initiative is not competent to testify about the voters' intent in passing that initiative.") (citations omitted).

16 *See* Antonin Scalia & Bryan A. Garner, *Reading Law: The Interpretation of Legal Texts* 135 (2012).

35. Lack of Precedents

If no binding precedent exists for determining a particular case, and the decisions in other jurisdictions on the question involved are in irreconcilable conflict, the court will adopt a rule that appears to be founded on the better rationale. A state may also adopt the rule of another state that has a substantially similar law.

State courts often face open questions on matters of state law—that is, cases of first impression. The court may ultimately decide to follow a sister state's precedent (see §§ 83–87). But out-of-state decisions often amount to a potpourri. As the Arizona Supreme Court has observed, authorities may be so scattered that "the quest for uniformity is a fruitless endeavor."[1] In the end, the court must determine on its own which, if any, rules to espouse.

The court may decide the case by following a prevailing trend in authority. If the gap between conflicting sister-state decisions is temporal, a court is likely to follow the rule established in more recent decisions: changed circumstances may have rendered the older rule obsolescent or even obsolete, or else the newer preference may be motivated by an interest in uniformity.[2]

A court may also elect to adopt a majority rule—one that more sister states have adopted than some other rule less widely followed[3]—especially if the question is one in which uniformity is particularly desirable. This consideration comes to the fore particularly when the point involves interstate matters.

But a court considering an open question is also bound to apply its independent judgment. If the preponderance of authority or a

---

[1] *Orca Commc'ns Unlimited, LLC v. Noder*, 337 P.3d 545, 549 (Ariz. 2014).

[2] *See, e.g., Frisk v. Superior Court*, 132 Cal. Rptr. 3d 602, 609 (Ct. App. 2011), *as modified on denial of reh'g* (23 Nov. 2011) ("[T]he authority of an older case may be as effectively dissipated by a later trend of decision as by a statement expressly overruling it.").

[3] *See, e.g., Owens v. Milwaukee Ins. Co.*, 123 N.E.2d 645, 646 (Ind. App. 1955) (in banc) (question of first impression "ought to be decided in harmony with the weight of authority elsewhere"); *Soehnlein v. Soehnlein*, 131 N.W. 739, 743 (Wis. 1911).

recent trend seems to be founded on poor reasoning or is inconsistent with existing state law, the court might not hesitate to embark on an uncharted route. As the Montana Supreme Court explained this duty: "[T]his court is not bound to follow [foreign] authorities and where the case is of first import in this court, it should follow that view which it feels is best expressed in the law."[4] In that case, the Montana Supreme Court adopted a minority position on the interpretation of an insurance provision.[5]

Both logic and history bear on the analysis. In 2002, a New Jersey appellate court announced its criterion for deciding such matters: "The weight of authority is not to be measured by the quantity of decisions reaching a particular result, but rather by the logical force of the decisions reached."[6] Historical circumstances may lead a court to hew closely to the decisions of a particular sister state. For instance, West Virginia courts may follow Virginia precedent that was in place before the two states separated.[7] And the borrowed-statute doctrine, though it is generally a weak canon of construction (see § 85), may result in State A's court applying State B's court decisions that interpret a statute that State A adopted from State B—applying them, in other words, as if they were near-binding precedent.

Courts may also give special weight to constitutional interpretations by the courts of a state whose constitution served as a model for their own state's constitution. For example, in a 2002 case,[8] the New Hampshire Supreme Court relied on the Massachusetts high court's interpretation of that state's constitutional provision protecting the rights of the accused.[9] At issue

---

4   *Holmstrom v. Mutual Benefit Health & Accident Ass'n*, 364 P.2d 1065, 1067 (Mont. 1961).

5   *Id.*

6   *Union Ink Co. v. AT&T Corp.*, 801 A.2d 361, 374 (N.J. Super. Ct. App. Div. 2002).

7   *Mills v. Woods*, 57 S.E.2d 713, 715 (W. Va. 1950) ("[H]aving been decided before the formation of this State, [a Virginia decision] is binding precedent in this jurisdiction the same as though it had been decided by this Court there being no West Virginia case to the contrary.").

8   *State v. Roache*, 803 A.2d 572 (N.H. 2002).

9   *Id.* at 577.

was whether to adopt a federal constitutional decision, *Moran v. Burbine*, in which the U.S. Supreme Court had held that a suspect's waiver of his Fifth Amendment privileges against self-incrimination—specifically his rights to silence and to counsel—was valid despite the police department's failure to inform the suspect that an attorney retained for him had telephoned.[10] The Massachusetts court had interpreted its constitution's protections to be broader than the Fifth Amendment's, holding that state protections are violated whenever a suspect isn't informed of his rights before waiving them.[11] The New Hampshire court observed that the Massachusetts Constitution antedates the U.S. Constitution and that New Hampshire had adopted its privilege against self-incrimination just four years later (in 1784).[12] The court concluded that the New Hampshire Constitution included the same broader protections recognized in Massachusetts precedent, observing: "Given that the language of the privilege is identical, and given the shared history of our state constitutions, we give weight to the Massachusetts Supreme Judicial Court's interpretation."[13]

A decision of an inferior court in another state is ordinarily entitled to little consideration as an authority on general principles of law. (See § 73, at pp. 607–10.) Such a decision isn't a conclusive pronouncement of state law. Courts are correct not to consider such decisions as binding precedent in that state or as an authoritative statement of its law, since they would not be binding on appellate courts within the state.

Yet the decisions of inferior courts are often cited for their sound reasoning and persuasive value.[14] The courts of other states are particularly likely to consider lower-court decisions when called on to determine how the high court of that state would

---

10 475 U.S. 412, 421–22 (1986).
11 *See Roache*, 803 A.2d at 577 (citing *Commonwealth v. Mavredakis*, 725 N.E.2d 169 (Mass. 2000)).
12 *Id.*
13 *Id.*
14 *See, e.g., Martinez v. Enterprise Rent-A-Car Co.*, 13 Cal. Rptr. 3d 857, 862 (Ct. App. 2004) (discussing a Michigan Court of Appeals decision interpreting similar statutory language as support for its interpretation of a California statute).

rule on a question.[15] That is particularly so when the rule is long-standing or has been unanimously recognized by the state's inferior courts. After all, the state's high court is more likely to adopt a rule that has been uniformly announced by lower-court judges familiar with the law of the state—judges who have considered the various arguments for and against the rule.

When a lower-court ruling seems to have been undermined by changed circumstances or other developments in the law of the state, it is particularly unlikely to be followed. In a 2000 case,[16] a New Jersey court was called on to determine the New York rule governing the interpretation of an insurance-policy provision covering the "collapse" of a structure.[17] The court determined that the majority rule was that such a policy covered situations in which there is "any serious impairment of structural integrity that connotes imminent collapse" and didn't require that the building have fully collapsed.[18] The insurer cited two decisions of New York intermediate appellate courts, both over 30 years old, in which the court had concluded that coverage was limited to "an actual falling-in or near total destruction."[19] Observing that these cases reflected a minority view and were inconsistent with more recent New York decisions construing coverage under the broader majority view, the New Jersey court declined to follow them. The court predicted that the New York high court would, if faced with the question, adopt the majority position.[20]

If no precedent can be found to support maintaining a particular lawsuit, awarding particular relief, or imposing a particular liability or penalty, the court may well conclude that the law

---

15 *See, e.g., Ehrenzweig v. Ehrenzweig*, 390 N.Y.S.2d 976, 980 (Sup. Ct. 1977) (considering Connecticut intermediate-appellate-court decisions in construing Connecticut law, but noting that such decisions aren't controlling statements of Connecticut law).

16 *Fantis Foods, Inc. v. North River Ins. Co.*, 753 A.2d 176 (N.J. Super. Ct. App. Div. 2000).

17 *Id.* at 177–78.

18 *Id.* at 183.

19 *Id.* (citing *Graffeo v. U.S. Fid. & Guar. Co.*, 246 N.Y.S.2d 258, 260 (App. Div. 1964); *Weiss v. Home Ins. Co.*, 189 N.Y.S.2d 355, 357 (App. Div. 1959)).

20 *Id.* at 184–85.

doesn't sanction doing so. The lack of precedent may persuade the court that the claim is an empty one.

36. Choosing Between Discordant Decisions

If two decisions of equal authority are irreconcilable, the choice of which one to follow depends on the circumstances.

Oscar Wilde provided himself an excuse when he noted that "consistency is the last refuge of the unimaginative."[1] But you can't use this excuse when a precedent you believe to be correct is based on a decision from which the same court has later deviated. Nor does it excuse a court that speaks from both sides of its mouth. This does happen—often enough, in fact, that under Federal Rule of Appellate Procedure 35(b)(1)(A), an intracircuit split is grounds for granting a petition for rehearing en banc[2] (see § 61).

A court considering discordant decisions must first determine whether the perceived conflict between them is real. If at all possible, the opinions should be harmonized. The optimal situation, of course, is to try to prevent the emergence of conflicting or contradictory decisions. Many jurisdictions have rules to prevent courts from issuing decisions that needlessly depart from existing caselaw. But despite all due care, conflicts sometimes arise.

No general rule accurately accounts for all situations. The approach to resolving the problem of discordant decisions depends on which court handed down which decision and which court is trying to choose between them. We present five scenarios here.

When a high court finds discordant opinions among its own (horizontal) precedents

A court of last resort generally follows its decision in the most recent case, which must have tacitly overruled any truly inconsistent holding. Yet as the court with the final say, it does have

---

[1] Oscar Wilde, "The Relation of Dress to Art," in *Pall Mall Gaz.* (28 Feb. 1885), *reprinted in Aristotle at Afternoon Tea: The Rare Oscar Wilde* 52 (John Wyse Jackson ed., 1991).

[2] Fed. R. App. P. 35 (b)(1)(A); *see United States v. Hogan*, 986 F.2d 1364, 1369 (11th Cir. 1993) ("Ideally, the phrase 'intracircuit split of authority' should be oxymoronic, because it is the firmly established rule of this Circuit that each succeeding panel is bound by the holding of the first panel to address an issue of law, unless and until that holding is overruled en banc, or by the Supreme Court.").

authority to revert to an earlier precedent and, ultimately, to "adopt and follow the line of opinions that announces what [it] conceive[s] to be the sounder reasoning, and . . . is therefore the correct one."[3]

Sometimes a state's legislature or constitution will direct how courts should resolve a conflict. A 1910 Georgia statute provided that if the Georgia Supreme Court handed down conflicting decisions, then that court and the appellate courts were "bound by the oldest unanimous decision of the Supreme Court . . . unless and until that case is overruled, modified, distinguished, or declared obiter."[4] Because most opinions are not unanimous, this full-bench rule proved hard to administer and was implicitly nullified in 1945[5] (though it was again applied as late as 1979[6]). The Georgia Supreme Court now follows the most-recent-opinion rule for horizontal precedents.[7]

When a lower court finds discordant opinions within vertical precedents

Lower courts almost uniformly adhere to the rule that the most recent opinion of the high court within the jurisdiction is to be followed.[8] The lower court will examine whether the later case overruled all or part of an earlier case. If the overruling was express, then its task is easy. If the overruling was thought to be tacit, things get more difficult. Before a lower court makes the

---

3   *Meade v. Commonwealth*, 282 S.W. 781, 783 (Ky. 1926).
4   *Fidelity-Phenix Ins. Co. v. Mauldin*, 179 S.E.2d 525, 527 (Ga. Ct. App. 1970) (citing 1933 Georgia Code § 6-1611).
5   *See Hall v. Hopper*, 216 S.E.2d 839, 843 (Ga. 1975).
6   *Department of Transp. v. Kendricks*, 56 S.E.2d 610, 612 (Ga. Ct. App. 1979).
7   *Massey v. Butts Cnty.*, 637 S.E.2d 385, 387 n.2 (Ga. 2006); *see Houston v. Lowes of Savannah, Inc.*, 219 S.E.2d 115, 116 (Ga. 1975).
8   *See, e.g., State v. Williams*, 9 S.W.3d 3, 12 (Mo. Ct. App. 1999); *Luhman v. Beecher*, 424 N.W.2d 753, 755 (Wis. Ct. App. 1988); *Treme v. Thomas*, 161 S.W.2d 124, 132 (Tex. Civ. App.—Beaumont 1942, writ ref'd w.o.m.); *Jolley v. Clemens*, 82 P.2d 51, 60 (Cal. Ct. App. 1938); *State ex rel. Dep't of Fin. Insts. of Ind. v. Sonntag*, 195 N.E. 601, 606 (Ind. App. 1935) (in banc); *Smith v. Overstreet's Adm'r*, 81 S.W.2d 571, 572 (Ky. 1935); *Bruner v. Automobile Ins. Co. of Hartford*, 164 S.E. 134, 135 (S.C. 1932); *Parker v. Plympton*, 273 P. 1030, 1034 (Colo. 1928); *Hornsby v. State*, 163 N.E. 923, 924 (Ohio Ct. App. 1928); *Fox v. State*, 87 So. 621, 622 (Ala. Ct. App. 1920).

assumption of a tacit overruling, it will want to exhaust all possibilities of reconciling the two decisions—perhaps even assuming that the highest court may not adopt just one of the decisions if confronted with the question but may instead reconcile the decisions by thoughtfully distinguishing them. Yet once the lower court has analyzed how far the later decision goes (and thus how much of the earlier decision is overruled), it is simply doing its job as a part of a vertical hierarchy when it follows the later case.

Even so, an appellate court may rationally choose to follow an earlier decision that directly controls even though the more recent precedent, though seemingly applicable, rests on reasons that have later been rejected by the high court.[9] By not presuming that the high court has by implication overruled an earlier precedent, that court's prerogative to overrule its own decisions is preserved.[10]

In *Khan v. State Oil Co.*,[11] an antitrust case, the Seventh Circuit was asked to reject a key Supreme Court precedent that controlled the question whether "resale price fixing is illegal per se regardless of the competitive position of the price fixer or whether the price fixed is a floor or a ceiling."[12] The court sympathized with State Oil's argument that *Albrecht v. Herald Co.*[13] was inconsistent with the Supreme Court's line of decisions establishing that the plaintiff in an antitrust suit must prove that the defendant's conduct produced the kind of injury that the antitrust laws were intended to protect against.[14] It even stated that the argument "may well portend the doom of *Albrecht*."[15] But it could not disregard the

---

9   *Agostini v. Felton*, 521 U.S. 203, 237 (1997) (quoting *Rodriguez de Quias v. Shearson/Am. Express, Inc.*, 490 U.S. 477, 484 (1989)). *See, e.g., United States v. Santiago*, 268 F.3d 151, 154–55 (2d Cir. 2001); *United States v. Singletary*, 268 F.3d 196, 200–03 (3d Cir. 2001) (explaining reliance on test established in earlier opinion); *United States v. Leija-Sanchez*, 602 F.3d 797, 799 (7th Cir. 2010); *Evans v. Secretary, Fla. Dep't of Corrections*, 699 F.3d 1249, 1263 (11th Cir. 2012); *State ex rel. Dep't of Fin. Insts. of Ind. v. Sonntag*, 195 N.E. 601, 606 (Ind. App. 1935) (in banc); *Wright v. General Elec. Co.*, 242 S.W.3d 674, 679 (Ky. Ct. App. 2007).

10 *Agostini*, 521 U.S. 203, 237 (1997).

11 93 F.3d 1358 (7th Cir. 1996), *vacated*, 522 U.S. 3 (1997).

12 *Id.* at 1362.

13 390 U.S. 145 (1968).

14 *Khan v. State Oil Co.*, 93 F.3d at 1362–63.

15 *Id.* at 1363.

precedent: "[D]espite all its infirmities, its increasingly wobbly, moth-eaten foundations, *Albrecht* has not been *expressly* overruled . . . . And the Supreme Court has told the lower federal courts . . . not to anticipate an overruling of a decision by the Court; we are to leave the overruling to the Court itself."[16] On appeal, the Supreme Court did overrule *Albrecht* and commented favorably on the Seventh Circuit's restraint.[17]

American law has diverged from English law on this point, as on so many others. English courts have long been known to say that a later decision reached in ignorance of an earlier one by the same court, or in ignorance of a governing statute, was given *per incuriam* (by oversight).[18] Hence a judge might "refuse to follow [a] past decision if . . . the court giving the decision had omitted to consider some relevant Act of Parliament or some decision which was binding on it."[19] The (intermediate) Court of Appeal may also choose between the earlier decision and the later one[20]—even if the conflict is between two Supreme Court decisions: "[W]hen there are conflicting decisions of . . . the Supreme Court, and the later judgment has been delivered without any reference to the former, the Court of Appeal is at liberty to say that it prefers the earlier reasoning."[21] This course of action isn't available to American trial and intermediate courts.

When an intermediate appellate court finds discordant opinions among its own precedents

With an intermediate appellate court, an earlier horizontal precedent nearly always controls.[22] This doctrine is based on the "general rule" that "one panel may not overrule the decision of a

---

16 *Id.* (emphasis in original).
17 *State Oil Co. v. Khan*, 522 U.S. 3, 20 (1997).
18 *See* W.F. Frank, *The General Principles of English Law* 24 (3d ed. 1964).
19 *Id.*
20 Glanville L. Williams, *Learning the Law* 114–15 (A.T.H. Smith ed., 15th ed. 2013).
21 *Id.*
22 *See McMellon v. United States*, 387 F.3d 329, 333 (4th Cir. 2004) (en banc) ("Most of the other circuits agree and follow the earlier of conflicting panel opinions.").

prior panel."[23] The federal appellate courts in particular apply this solution to resolve a conflict between different panels and hold that the earlier opinion controls later panels and also the district courts in the circuit.[24]

An exception arises when there is sound reason for a later panel to overrule the prior panel, as when:

- the later panel determines that the decision was clearly contrary to a then-standing vertical precedent;[25]
- an intervening vertical precedent effectively overrules the earlier panel's decision;[26]
- the court is applying a statute that has been amended in the interim;[27] or
- (with a federal circuit court applying state law) the state courts have expressly said they disagree with a previous panel decision and would have decided the matter differently.[28]

Some federal circuit courts have additional rules.

The First Circuit has a narrow exception to stare decisis in "relatively rare instances [when] authority that postdates the original decision, although not directly controlling, nevertheless offers a sound reason for believing that the former panel, in light of fresh developments, would change its collective mind" because "recent Supreme Court precedent calls into legitimate question a prior

---

23 *Billiot v. Puckett*, 135 F.3d 311, 316 (5th Cir. 1998).
24 *United States v. Madden*, 733 F.3d 1314, 1319 (11th Cir. 2013); *In re Grant*, 635 F.3d 1227, 1232 (D.C. Cir. 2011); *Rios v. City of Del Rio*, 444 F.3d 417, 458 m.8 (5th Cir. 2006); *Kyocera Corp. v. Prudential-Bache Trade Servs., Inc.*, 341 F.3d 987, 995 (9th Cir. 2003) (en banc); *Haynes v. Williams*, 88 F.3d 898, 900 n.4 (10th Cir. 1996).
25 *Mennen Co. v. Atlantic Mut. Ins. Co.*, 147 F.3d 287, 294 n.9 (3d Cir. 1998).
26 *Miller v. Gammie*, 335 F.3d 889, 892–93 (9th Cir. 2003) (en banc).
27 *Babb v. Lozowsky*, 719 F.3d 1019, 1029 (9th Cir. 2013), *overruled on other grounds by Moore v. Helling*, 763 F.3d 1011 (9th Cir. 2014); *Bennett v. MIS Corp.*, 607 F.3d 1076, 1098 (6th Cir. 2010).
28 *Bennett*, 607 F.3d at 1098.

opinion of an inferior court."[29] Such instances, the court has cautioned, may fairly be described as "hen's-teeth rare."[30]

In the Seventh Circuit, a rule provides for a rehearing sua sponte if a panel decision would overrule a prior decision—or even create a conflict with another circuit court's decision. The panel's proposed opinion must be circulated to all the circuit's active members, who vote on whether to rehear the case en banc. If a majority votes not to, then the panel's opinion may be issued.[31]

The Eighth Circuit once had a unique rule under which a panel was free to choose which line of precedent to follow.[32] The court definitively abrogated the rule in a 2011 en banc decision, stating: "in accordance with the almost universal practice in other federal circuits, . . . when faced with conflicting panel opinions, the earliest opinion must be followed 'as it should have controlled the subsequent panels that created the conflict.'"[33]

When an intermediate appellate court perceives discord between a recent vertical precedent and its own precedents

When actual discord exists, the higher court obviously governs. But there is no bright line for determining discord. When a higher court's decision does not plainly or expressly overrule a lower court's holding, the Fifth Circuit has held that "[a] Supreme Court decision must be more than merely illuminating . . . because a panel . . . can only overrule a prior panel decision if such overruling is unequivocally directed by controlling Supreme Court precedent."[34] The Ninth Circuit agrees: "It is not enough for there to be 'some tension' between the intervening higher authority and

---

29 *Igartua v. United States*, 626 F.3d 592, 604 (1st Cir. 2010) (internal quotation marks, citations, and emphasis omitted).

30 *Id.* (internal quotation marks, citations, and emphasis omitted).

31 7th Cir. R. 40(e).

32 *Mader v. United States*, 654 F.3d 794, 800 (8th Cir. 2011) (en banc) (quoting *Meyer v. Schnucks Mkts., Inc.*, 163 F.3d 1048, 1051 (8th Cir. 1998)).

33 *Mader*, 654 F.3d at 800 (quoting *T.L. ex rel. Ingram v. United States*, 443 F.3d 956, 960 (8th Cir. 2006)).

34 *In re Texas Grand Prarie Hotel Realty, L.L.C.*, 710 F.3d 324, 331 (5th Cir. 2013) (internal quotation marks omitted); *see Miller v. Gammie*, 335 F.3d 889, 892–93 (9th Cir. 2003) (en banc).

prior circuit precedent, or for the intervening higher authority to 'cast doubt' on the prior circuit precedent. . . . The intervening higher precedent must be 'clearly inconsistent' with the prior circuit precedent."[35] Further, it has considered "the sometimes very difficult question of when a three-judge panel may reexamine normally controlling precedent in the face of an intervening United State Supreme Court decision"[36] and determined that a later panel should follow the Supreme Court precedent when the circuit court and Supreme Court cases are closely on point and "the reasoning or theory of our prior circuit authority is clearly irreconcilable with the reasoning or theory of intervening higher authority."[37]

When a trial court encounters discordant opinions among intermediate appellate courts that have no obligation to uniformity, and the lower court is not bound by any particular appellate division, circuit, or district

In some jurisdictions, such as California and Arizona, the appellate courts are divided into departments within a division. The Arizona Supreme Court has recognized that each lower court of appeal must treat the decisions of coordinate courts as "highly persuasive and binding" unless the court determines that the other court's decision is clearly erroneous or intervening changes in the law make a prior decision inapplicable.[38] When two decisions are applicable but conflicting, a trial court has the "discretion to adopt the decision that most persuasively interprets the law, regardless of the division to which the department making the decision belongs or within which the trial court sits."[39] In effect, neither opinion is binding at all; both are treated merely as persuasive.[40] The Arizona rule is premised on rejection of a proposed rule that

---

35 *Lair v. Bullock*, 697 F.3d 1200, 1207 (9th Cir. 2012).
36 *Miller*, 335 F.3d at 892.
37 *Id.* at 893.
38 *Scappaticci v. Southwest Sav. & Loan Ass'n*, 662 P.2d 131, 136 (Ariz. 1983) (in banc); *see Castillo v. Industrial Comm'n*, 520 P.2d 1142, 1148 (Ariz. Ct. App. 1974) (articulating rule).
39 *State v. Patterson*, 218 P.3d 1031, 1037 (Ariz. Ct. App. 2009).
40 *See id.*

"a trial court must follow the decision of the department in the division in which the trial court is located."[41]

As for California, the state high court has declared that a court-of-appeal decision "stands . . . as a decision of a court of last resort in this state, until and unless disapproved by this court or until change of the law by legislative action."[42] The rule of stare decisis underlies that declaration.[43] But stare decisis does not control when "there is more than one appellate court decision, and such appellate decisions are in conflict. . . . [T]he court exercising inferior jurisdiction can and must make a choice between the conflicting decisions."[44] Even so, as a practical matter, a superior court will ordinarily follow an appellate opinion issued within its own district even if it isn't bound to do so.[45]

---

41   *See id.* at 1035.
42   *Cole v. Rush*, 289 P.2d 450, 453 (Cal. 1955) (in bank), *overruled on other grounds by Vesely v. Sager*, 486 P.2d 151 (Cal. 1971).
43   *Auto Equity Sales, Inc. v. Superior Court of Santa Clara Cnty.*, 369 P.2d 937, 940 (Cal. 1962) (in bank).
44   *Id.*
45   *McCallum v. McCallum*, 190 Cal. App. 3d 308, 316 (Ct. App. 1987).

37. Overruled and Reversed Decisions: Retroactivity vs. Prospectivity

A decision that has been overruled by the court that rendered it, or been reversed on appeal, should no longer be cited as a precedent in any court within the same system. With only a few exceptions of great importance (collateral review and vested rights), a decision of a high court overruling its former decision is retroactive and restores the legal rule or principle that was in force before the overruled decision was made. The former decision remains conclusive for the litigants in that case.

When an appellate court reverses a lower court's judgment, it nullifies whatever precedential effect the lower court's judgment bore. And when a court overrules its own earlier decision, the law expressed in the opinion supporting that earlier decision is no longer either good law or binding precedent.[1] In both these situations, the earlier opinion explaining the reversed or overruled judgment can't any longer be cited as good authority in courts of the same jurisdiction. But a decision that a court has "overruled in part" or "reversed in part" maintains precedential value to the extent that the earlier opinion doesn't conflict with the overruling or reversing opinion.[2]

"[F]or near a thousand years" (in the words of Holmes J.), when courts have overruled a precedent or established a "new" rule, their holdings have applied to litigants "regardless of when

---

[1] *Hohn v. United States*, 524 U.S. 236, 252–53 (1998) (noting that the Court's "decisions remain binding precedent until we see fit to reconsider them, regardless of whether subsequent cases have raised doubts about their continuing vitality"); *see also United States v. Gallo*, 195 F.3d 1278, 1284 (11th Cir. 1999) (noting that a court's precedent is "no longer binding once it has been substantially undermined or overruled by either a change in statutory law or Supreme Court jurisprudence or if it is in conflict with existing Supreme Court precedent").

[2] *See, e.g., Burns Mfg. Co. v. Boehm*, 356 A.2d 763, 767 n.5 (Pa. 1976) (noting that a decision "was overruled in part by" a later case); *Children's Hosp. of Birmingham, Inc. v. Kelley*, 537 So. 2d 921, 921 (Ala. Civ. App. 1988) (affirming in part and reversing in part lower-court judgment).

the transaction litigated took place."³ As William Blackstone explained in the 18th century, "[a]t common law there was no authority for the proposition that judicial decisions made law only for the future."⁴ The retroactive application of new rules springs directly from the age-old understanding that judges do not "pronounce a new law, but . . . maintain and expound the old one."⁵ On this view, when a court overrules a decision, it doesn't make new law but instead restates and applies the preexisting legal rule. Henry Campbell Black explained this point in his 1912 treatise on precedent: "The theory is, not that the overruled decision made law, which is changed by the later decision, but that the earlier decision, being a mistake, never was the law, but that the law is and always has been as expounded in the later decision."⁶

In the United States, the retroactivity of judicial decisions is sometimes said to inhere in the very structure of the Constitution.⁷ The Founders divided the legislative and judicial powers and invested them in separate bodies with separate functions.⁸ Congress was to make forward-looking laws of general applicability but was generally forbidden to act retroactively.⁹ Judges on the other hand, were to look backward, resolving specific cases and controversies and pronouncing what the law *is*.¹⁰ From the beginning, "[f]ully retroactive decisionmaking was considered

---

3 *Kuhn v. Fairmont Coal Co.*, 215 U.S. 349, 372 (1910) (Holmes J. dissenting).
4 *Linkletter v. Walker*, 381 U.S. 618, 622 (1965).
5 1 William Blackstone, *Commentaries on the Laws of England* 69 (4th ed. 1770); *see* Paul Vinogradoff, *Common-Sense in Law* 207 (1925) ("[T]he common law . . . stands or falls with the admission of legal principles obtained not by command, but by retrospective estimates of right and justice.").
6 Henry Campbell Black, *Handbook on the Law of Judicial Precedents* § 212, at 689 (1912).
7 *See* Neil M. Gorsuch, *Of Lions and Bears, Judges and Legislators, and the Legacy of Justice Scalia*, 66 Case W. Res. L. Rev. 905, 909–10 (2016); *see also De Niz Robles v. Lynch*, 803 F.3d 1165, 1170 (10th Cir. 2015) (suggesting that "the presumption of retroactivity attaching to judicial decisions was anticipated by the Constitution and inheres in its separation of powers").
8 *See* U.S. Const. art. I.
9 *See, e.g., Landgraf v. USI Film Prods.*, 511 U.S. 244, 265 (1994).
10 *See Marbury v. Madison*, 5 U.S. (1 Cranch) 137, 177 (1803); *The Federalist* No. 44 (James Madison), Nos. 78, 81 (Alexander Hamilton).

a principal distinction between the judicial and the legislative power: '[I]t is said that that which distinguishes a judicial from a legislative act is, that the one is a determination of what the existing law is in relation to some existing thing already done or happened, while the other is a predetermination of what the law shall be for the regulation of all future cases.'"[11] For most of our history, the Supreme Court followed the common-law tradition and the Founders' guidance, largely keeping to "a general rule of retrospective effect for . . . constitutional decisions."[12]

For a period during the 20th century, however, the Supreme Court departed from the traditional view of retroactivity. Early in the century, the Court began to question the blanket approach to retroactivity. In a 1932 case called *Sunburst Oil*,[13] the Court considered the validity of a state court's refusal to give retroactive effect to its ruling.[14] It concluded that states could choose whether to apply their decisions retroactively or prospectively, explaining that a state "in defining the limits of adherence to precedent may make a choice for itself between the principle of forward operation and that of relation backward. It may say that decisions of its highest court, though later overruled, are law none the less for intermediate transactions."[15] Or, at its discretion, the state court may "hold to the ancient dogma that the law declared by its courts had a Platonic or ideal existence before the act of declaration, in which event the discredited declaration will be viewed as if it had never been, and the reconsidered declaration as law from the beginning."[16] Since the Court's decision in *Sunburst Oil*, a few courts have referred to applying a new decisional rule only prospectively as "sunbursting" the law.[17]

---

11 *Harper v. Virginia Dep't of Taxation*, 509 U.S. 86, 107 (1993) (Scalia J. concurring) (quoting Thomas Cooley, *Constitutional Limitations* *91).

12 *Robinson v. Neil*, 409 U.S. 505, 507 (1973).

13 *Great Northern Ry. v. Sunburst Oil & Ref. Co.*, 287 U.S. 358 (1932).

14 *Id.* at 364.

15 *Id.*

16 *Id.* at 365.

17 *See, e.g., Heritage Farms, Inc. v. Markel Ins. Co.*, 810 N.W.2d 465, 479–80 (Wis. 2012) (explaining that it will "sunburst" a new legal rule to avoid inequities resulting from the change in law and justifiable reliance on the old law).

In criminal cases, the 20th-century Supreme Court adopted a multifactor balancing test that gave different types of decisions different degrees of retroactivity.[18] Indeed, some decisions announcing new constitutional rules were deemed to have no retroactive effect at all—even to the litigants before the Court itself.[19] Supporters lauded this approach because it made judicial lawmaking (and the overruling of precedent) less disruptive and more palatable.[20]

Yet this new approach not only proved practically unworkable but also created serious constitutional problems (as dissenters hastened to point out).[21] For one thing, nonretroactivity undermined the separation of powers: giving new rules only prospective effect made the Court's "constitutional function . . . not one of adjudication but in effect of legislation."[22] Nonretroactivity also raised obvious equal-protection concerns by treating similarly situated defendants differently: often the Court would apply a new rule only to the defendant lucky enough to have appealed his case to the Court at just the right moment.[23] Defendants who had been arrested before the Court pronounced its new rule—even those with a trial or appeal pending—would not be provided relief.

The tide finally turned in the 1982 case of *United States v. Johnson*,[24] in which a majority of the Court criticized nonretroactivity and acknowledged that its recent jurisprudence "must be rethought."[25] Soon after *Johnson*, the Court ruled in *Griffith*

---

18 *Desist v. United States*, 394 U.S. 244, 249 (1969).
19 *Morrissey v. Brewer*, 408 U.S. 471, 490 (1972).
20 Beryl Harold Levy, *Realist Jurisprudence and Prospective Overruling*, 109 U. Pa. L. Rev. 1 (1960).
21 *See, e.g., Desist*, 394 U.S. at 258 (Harlan J. dissenting); *Mackey v. United States*, 401 U.S. 667, 678–79 (1971) (Harlan J. concurring in part and dissenting in part).
22 *Desist*, 394 U.S. at 258 (Harlan J. dissenting) (quoting *Mackey v. United States*, 401 U.S. 667, 679 (1971) (Harlan J. concurring in judgment)).
23 *See id.*; *Mackey*, 401 U.S. at 678–79 (Harlan J. concurring in part and dissenting in part).
24 457 U.S. 537 (1982).
25 *Id.* at 548.

v. Kentucky[26] that the integrity of judicial review requires courts to apply newly declared constitutional rules of procedure retroactively to all criminal cases pending on direct review.[27] The Court acknowledged that doing otherwise "violates basic norms of constitutional adjudication."[28]

The history of retroactivity in the civil context largely mirrors that of retroactivity in the criminal context. In the 1971 case of *Chevron Oil Co. v. Huson*,[29] the Court departed from "near a thousand years"[30] of retroactivity and adopted a balancing test that considered reliance interests and equities when determining whether a ruling should be given retroactive effect. Just as in the criminal context, *Chevron Oil* created confusion and inconsistent results, and 20 years later it was overruled.[31] The overruling decision was *Harper v. Virginia Department of Taxation*,[32] in which the Court held that when an opinion does not "expressly reserve" the question of retroactivity in the adoption of a new rule, that decision must be "given full retroactive effect in all cases still open on direct review."[33] Although *Harper* signaled a return to traditional retroactivity analysis in civil cases, the express-reservation exception has allowed lower courts to occasionally use *Chevron Oil* to make across-the-board nonretroactivity determinations in decisions that actually announce a new rule.[34] Even so, *Harper* means that new rules in civil cases are now almost always applied retroactively.

Although retroactivity arguably inheres in the structure of the Constitution and is largely the rule at the federal level, our system

---

26 479 U.S. 314 (1987).
27 *Id.* at 323.
28 *Id.* at 322.
29 404 U.S. 97 (1971).
30 *Kuhn*, 215 U.S. at 372 (Holmes J. dissenting).
31 *See, e.g., James B. Beam Distilling Co. v. Georgia*, 501 U.S. 529 (1991).
32 509 U.S. 86 (1993).
33 *Id.* at 97.
34 *See, e.g., In re Mersmann*, 505 F.3d 1033, 1052 (10th Cir. 2007).

of dual sovereignty permits state courts to craft their own rules on the subject.[35] Most states have adopted the orthodox view.[36]

Collateral review of criminal judgments

As for federal collateral review, new constitutional rules of criminal procedure—that is, decisions in which "the result was not *dictated* by precedent existing at the time the defendant's conviction became final" on direct review[37]—generally don't apply retroactively. Although an exception to the general rule, nonretroactivity on federal collateral review does not generate the structural and equal-protection problems created by the Court's broad experiment with nonretroactivity in the mid-20th century. Federal collateral review, after all, is a "constitutionally gratuitous"[38] procedure that has little connection to the common-law judicial function. It generally examines only whether state courts have followed "established constitutional standards" in a defendant's trial, and reviewing courts considering finality must take into account comity and states' interests.[39] Because federal collateral review aims to police state courts rather than determine what the law *is*, there would be little reason to apply new rules retroactively. Doing so would undermine the finality of judgments and the deterrent effect of the criminal law while providing no incentive for states to follow established constitutional procedures.[40]

Of course, nonretroactivity on federal collateral review has its own exceptions. In *Teague v. Lane*,[41] the Court defined two circumstances in which new constitutional rules are applied retroactively on collateral review. First, a new rule will "be applied retroactively if it places 'certain kinds of primary, private individual

---

35 *Danforth v. Minnesota*, 552 U.S. 264 (2008).
36 See, e.g., *DiCenzo v. A-Best Prods. Co.*, 897 N.E.2d 132, 137 (Ohio 2008); *County of Los Angeles v. Faus*, 312 P.2d 680, 685–86 (Cal. 1957) (in bank).
37 *Teague v. Lane*, 489 U.S. 288, 301 (1989).
38 Richard H. Fallon Jr. & Daniel J. Meltzer, *New Law, Non-Retroactivity, and Constitutional Remedies*, 104 Harv. L. Rev. 1731, 1813 (1991).
39 *Teague*, 489 U.S. at 306, 308.
40 *Id.* at 309–10.
41 489 U.S. 288 (1989).

conduct beyond the power of the criminal lawmaking authority to proscribe.'"[42] This exception is most often invoked with writs of habeas corpus.

Second, a new rule will also be applied retroactively if it represents a "watershed" rule of procedure that "implicate[s] the fundamental fairness of the trial"[43]—a rule without which the likelihood of an accurate conviction would be seriously diminished.[44] The exception for watershed rules of criminal procedure is extremely narrow. Perhaps no such rules will ever emerge other than the rule announced by the Supreme Court in *Gideon v. Wainwright*.[45] In *Schriro v. Summerlin*,[46] for example, the Court rejected an argument that it had created a watershed rule of procedure in *Ring v. Arizona*.[47] In that case, the newly announced procedural rule required that a jury, not a judge, decide aggravating factors for capital punishment.[48] The *Schriro* Court held that the rule in *Ring* wasn't a watershed rule because judicial fact-finding didn't diminish the accuracy of a decision so much that it would create an impermissibly great risk of punishing conduct not covered by the law.[49] The Supreme Court has never declared any new rule of procedure a watershed rule fully retroactive on collateral review. For example, the landmark 2004 decision in *Crawford v. Washington*[50] redefined whether certain hearsay statements violate the Sixth Amendment's Confrontation Clause, but it is decidedly *not* a watershed rule of criminal procedure warranting full retroactive effect. In 2007, the Court explained that *Crawford* didn't change the required magnitude for the accuracy of convictions and wasn't

---

42   *Id.* at 311 (quoting *Mackey*, 401 U.S. at 692 (Harlan J. concurring in judgment)).
43   *Id.* at 312–13.
44   *Id.*
45   372 U.S. 335 (1963); *see Whorton v. Bockting*, 549 U.S. 406, 419 (2007) (looking to *Gideon* for paradigm of watershed rule).
46   542 U.S. 348 (2004).
47   536 U.S. 584 (2002).
48   *Id.* at 603–09.
49   *Schriro*, 542 U.S. at 355–57.
50   541 U.S. 36 (2004).

a rule that altered the Court's "understanding of the bedrock procedural elements essential to the fairness of a proceeding."[51]

State courts may retroactively apply new constitutional rules of criminal procedure beyond these two exceptions even if the federal courts wouldn't.[52] In *Danforth v. Minnesota*,[53] the Supreme Court clarified that a state high court was free to apply the new rule announced in *Crawford v. Washington* retroactively even though the Supreme Court had instructed the federal courts not to do so.[54] The majority in *Danforth* rejected the minority's contention that the concerns with uniformity in *Teague v. Lane*[55] trump state interests: "This interest in uniformity . . . does not outweigh the general principle that States are independent sovereigns with plenary authority to make and enforce their own laws as long as they do not infringe on federal constitutional guarantees. . . . Nonuniformity is, in fact, an unavoidable reality in a federalist system of government."[56] Even so, as the Court noted in 2016, "when a new substantive rule of constitutional law controls the outcome of a case, the Constitution requires state collateral-review courts to give retroactive effect to that rule."[57] The Supreme Court has distinguished *Danforth* as holding "only that *Teague*'s general rule of nonretroactivity . . . does not prevent states from providing greater relief in their own collateral courts."[58]

---

51   *Whorton v. Bockting*, 549 U.S. 406, 418–21 (2007) (quoting *Sawyer v. Smith*, 497 U.S. 227, 242 (1990)).

52   *Danforth*, 552 U.S. at 282; *see, e.g.*, *People v. Maxson*, 759 N.W.2d 817, 821–25 (Mich. 2008) (applying state law to determine w hether a decision requiring appointment of appellate counsel in certain circumstances was retroactive); *see also, e.g.*, *Siers v. Weber*, 851 N.W.2d 731, 742 (S.D. 2014) (adopting, in light of *Danforth*, the *Teague* exceptions for retroactivity while acknowledging that the state high court's previous "retroactivity analysis ha[d] largely ignored *Teague* altogether").

53   552 U.S. 264 (2004).

54   *Id.* at 277–82.

55   489 U.S. 288 (1989).

56   *Danforth*, 552 U.S. at 280.

57   *Montgomery v. Louisiana*, 136 S.Ct. 718, 729 (2016) (hyphen added in phrasal adjective).

58   *Id.*

No retroactive destruction of vested rights or contracts

When rights of property have accrued and contracts have been made in reliance on the law as interpreted by a decision of the high court, and when the rights or contracts were valid at the time of their inception under the decision, a later decision overruling the earlier decision and reversing the legal rule it established generally doesn't destroy those vested rights or invalidate those contracts. The California Supreme Court has described vested rights and contracts as a "well-recognized exception" to the general rule that overruling decisions operate retroactively:

> [W]here a constitutional provision or statute has received a given construction by a court of last resort and contracts have been made or property rights acquired under and in accordance with its decision, such contracts will not be invalidated nor will vested rights acquired under the decision be impaired by a change of construction adopted in a subsequent decision. Under those circumstances it has been the rule to give prospective, and not retrospective, effect to the later decision.[59]

Ohio courts recognize the exception, too: in a 1994 case,[60] the Ohio Supreme Court ruled that its decision declaring a mortmain statute unconstitutional couldn't be applied retroactively to invalidate property rights vested in several grandchildren upon the death of a testator.[61] Likewise, in a 1926 case,[62] the North Carolina Supreme Court held that an overruling decision about registration of deeds couldn't invalidate a title recorded under an earlier judicial rule.[63] And 54 years later, the same high court ruled that its decision abrogating sovereign immunity applied prospectively in an action for breach of an employment contract terminated years before the judicial decision.[64]

The exception to the rule that decisions apply retroactively operates only when the old rule was established by a high court.

---

59 *County of Los Angeles v. Faus*, 312 P.2d 680, 686 (Cal. 1957) (in bank).
60 *Wendell v. Ameritrust Co.*, 630 N.E.2d 368 (Ohio 1994).
61 *Id.* at 371.
62 *Wilkinson v. Wallace*, 134 S.E. 401 (N.C. 1926).
63 *Id.* at 402.
64 *MacDonald v. University of N.C.*, 263 S.E.2d 578, 582 (N.C. 1980).

As Henry Campbell Black explained a century ago, "The judgment of an inferior court, even if it is not appealed, is in no sense binding on the higher court; and anyone who relies on it as a basis for a contract or a title, does so at his peril."[65] For example, in a 1983 decision known as *Guelfi*, an intermediate appellate court in California interpreted the meaning of "compensation earnable"—on which California employees' pensions are based—and ruled that overtime payments and others didn't constitute compensation earnable.[66] Fourteen years later, the California Supreme Court abrogated that interpretation and held that overtime payments and others must be included as compensation earnable for purposes of calculating employees' retirement benefits.[67] It declined, however, to consider whether that decision should be applied retroactively.[68] For the next 20 years, the retirement boards of several counties relied on the interpretation in *Guelfi* to calculate pensions and then argued in litigation that retroactivity should not apply.[69] The California appellate court rejected that argument because it wasn't based on "the ruling of a court of last resort, but . . . the construction of a statute by a Court of Appeal."[70] The California Supreme Court's interpretation nullifying *Guelfi* applied retroactively for the benefit of the employees.[71]

Similarly, in a suit brought in federal court based on diversity of citizenship, a federal district court, applying Pennsylvania law, ruled that an employer's insurance carrier was immune from a worker's suit based on a decision of the Pennsylvania Supreme Court despite an earlier precedent of the Third Circuit standing for the contrary proposition.[72] Again, Henry Campbell Black: "If

---

65 Henry Campbell Black, *Handbook on the Law of Judicial Precedents* § 214, at 695 (1912).
66 *Guelfi v. Marin Cnty. Emps. Ret. Ass'n*, 193 Cal. Rptr. 343, 349 (Ct. App. 1983).
67 *Ventura Cnty. Deputy Sheriffs' Ass'n v. Board of Ret.*, 940 P.2d 891, 893 (Cal. 1997) (overruling *Guelfi*).
68 *In re Retirement Cases*, 1 Cal. Rptr. 3d 790, 796 (Ct. App. 2003).
69 *Id.* at 796–97.
70 *Id.* at 809.
71 *Id.* at 796–97, 808–09 & n.13.
72 *DeMartino v. Zurich Ins. Co.*, 307 F. Supp. 571, 572, 574 (W.D. Pa. 1969).

the court of last resort afterwards lays down a contrary rule, the inferior courts will be bound to adopt and follow it, and a party so situated cannot claim that an exception shall be made in his favor."[73]

Nor does the exception apply to the retroactive operation of new procedural rules. In a 1984 Georgia case,[74] the plaintiff relied on an old rule that would have allowed him to reinstate a lawsuit he had voluntarily dismissed by simply paying costs in the earlier dismissed action.[75] Even though the Georgia Supreme Court had overruled the precedent that the plaintiff had relied on, the plaintiff argued that the new rule didn't have retroactive effect because "he had a vested right to reinstate his [lawsuit] by paying costs in the [earlier] action, so long as this was done within six months after the latter decision."[76] The Georgia Supreme Court rejected that argument on the ground that "there are no vested rights in any course of procedure."[77] And in a 1983 case,[78] the Ohio Court of Appeals held that an overruling decision by the Ohio Supreme Court, which adopted a date-of-discovery rule for the statute of limitations in suits for medical malpractice, applied retroactively.[79] The court explained: "Although the new rule has the potential of exposing doctors (and their insurance companies) to liability for greater periods of time than did the old rule, it is a procedural change and does not entail the disruption of any contractual or vested right."[80]

Overruling of tax precedents

A decision of the high court overruling the grant of a tax exemption may apply only prospectively, protecting the taxpayer from later assessment and collection of taxes for the time when the

---

73   Black, *Handbook on the Law of Judicial Precedents* § 214, at 695.
74   *Foster v. Bowen*, 315 S.E.2d 656 (Ga. 1984).
75   *Id.* at 657.
76   *Id.*
77   *Id.*
78   *Obral v. Fairview Gen. Hosp.*, 468 N.E.2d 141 (Ohio Ct. App. 1983).
79   *Id.* at 144.
80   *Id.*

earlier decision was the law of the jurisdiction. But an overruling decision may operate retroactively if the taxpayer's reliance on the earlier decision was unjustified.

Although caselaw varies concerning the effect of a decision overruling a tax precedent, some courts haven't applied the overruling decision retroactively if it nullifies a tax exemption on which the taxpayer has justifiably relied. For example, in a 1948 case,[81] the Kentucky Court of Appeals acknowledged that it had ruled more than 40 years earlier that a gymnastics association, an educational institution, was exempt from property taxes assessed by the city.[82] When the court overruled that decades-old decision, it declared its ruling prospective from the date of its decision in a later suit between the same litigants.[83] The court reasoned that "the Association being a non-profit organization, and classed under this Court's ruling in 1904 as an educational institution, was entitled to make its plans accordingly."[84] And in a 1947 case,[85] the Oklahoma Supreme Court applied only prospectively its decision overruling a precedent declaring the estates of Native Americans exempt from state taxes.[86] The court reasoned that because many estates had been administered in reliance on the earlier precedent, the titles vested by the closing of those estates should not be disturbed because

> many estates have been administered upon and closed and titles vested with no thought that any such tax liability existed and without any demand for or effort to collect such a tax; and ... the stability of titles might be grievously affected unless we set at rest, or permit to remain at rest, any question as to the liability of any such estates for any such tax.[87]

---

81 *German Gymnastic Ass'n v. City of Louisville*, 209 S.W.2d 75 (Ky. 1948).
82 *Id.* at 75–76 (discussing *German Gymnastic Ass'n v. City of Louisville*, 80 S.W. 201 (Ky. 1904)).
83 *Id.* at 76.
84 *Id.*
85 *Yarbrough v. Oklahoma Tax Comm'n*, 193 P.2d 1017 (Okla. 1947).
86 *Id.* at 1019–22.
87 *Id.* at 1021.

Even when a court applies a new decision retroactively, it may nevertheless decide that the taxpayer cannot be subjected to criminal prosecution or civil penalty for relying on the overruled precedent. In *James v. United States*, for example, the U.S. Supreme Court overruled a decision that embezzled funds were not to be included in the gross income of an embezzler,[88] but the Court ordered the dismissal of an indictment of an embezzler who could have relied on the overruled precedent and not willfully failed to pay taxes owed.[89] Such an embezzler couldn't have "willfully" evaded tax obligations, as the criminal law required for conviction.[90] And in a 1949 case,[91] the Mississippi Supreme Court retroactively applied its overruling decision to tax an oil-and-gas lessee's interest,[92] but it refrained from imposing a "penalty" because the taxpayer had "acted in good faith and in full reliance" on the earlier precedent.[93]

But when the taxpayer cannot establish any reliance on the overruled precedent, courts readily apply new rules retroactively. In a 1974 Fourth Circuit case,[94] the taxpayer argued that its expenses for the dissolution and liquidation of a corporation should have been considered deductible under a binding precedent of the Fourth Circuit, but that court, sitting en banc, overruled its precedent and applied its new rule retroactively.[95] The Fourth Circuit reasoned "that the taxpayer was not influenced in any action taken by it by our decision,"[96] and the taxpayer "should have known that [the earlier precedent] had not been acquiesced

---

88 366 U.S. 213 (1961).

89 *Id.* at 221–22.

90 *Id.* (holding that willfulness couldn't be proved in a criminal prosecution for "failing to include embezzled funds in gross income in the year of misappropriation so long as the statute contained the gloss placed upon it by [the overruled precedent] at the time the alleged crime was committed").

91 *Bailey v. Federal Land Bank*, 40 So. 2d 173 (Miss. 1949) (en banc).

92 *Id.*

93 *Id.* at 176.

94 *Of Course, Inc. v. Commissioner*, 499 F.2d 754 (4th Cir. 1974) (en banc).

95 *Id.* at 757–60.

96 *Id.* at 759.

in by the Commissioner and was contrary to the majority of the Circuits."[97]

Nor will a taxpayer benefit from an overruled precedent when seeking a refund for the overpayment of taxes. In a 1955 Ohio case,[98] taxpayers challenged the tax commissioner's refusal to award certificates of abatement for their overpayments of franchise taxes, hoping to benefit from an earlier decision since overruled by the Ohio Supreme Court.[99] But the court ruled that the commissioner had acted properly in refusing their abatement, basing its ruling on the high court's new, overruling decision.[100] The court applied the general rule that judicial decisions operate retroactively and reasoned that the exception for vested or contractual rights didn't apply.[101]

Other courts have retroactively applied new rules about taxation because the tax collector was no longer bound to defer to earlier precedent, including (1) suits involving the *federal* Internal Revenue Service and new rules under *state* law, and (2) suits involving *state* collectors and new rules announced by the U.S. Supreme Court. Three cases are illustrative.

First, in a 1961 Tenth Circuit case,[102] a husband and wife, before his death, agreed to own their business ventures as tenants in common.[103] But their agreement was considered invalid under governing state precedents, which treated their ventures as community property.[104] When the New Mexico Supreme Court later overruled those precedents and held that married couples could hold their property as tenants in common, the Internal Revenue Service applied that ruling retroactively and sought deficiencies in income taxes from the surviving spouse.[105] The Tenth Circuit

---

97 *Id.* at 760.
98 *Peerless Elec. Co. v. Bowers*, 129 N.E.2d 467 (Ohio 1955) (per curiam).
99 *Id.* at 468.
100 *Id.*
101 *Id.*
102 *Massaglia v. Commissioner*, 286 F.2d 258 (10th Cir. 1961).
103 *Id.* at 260.
104 *Id.*
105 *Id.* at 261.

ruled that the Commissioner could "change his position with respect to the taxable incidences of property based upon a change of controlling state decisional law."[106] The court found that the Commissioner had not acted inequitably: "This inconsistency was not brought about by the Commissioner's own doing. He has done no more than follow the vicissitudes of controlling state law in which he had no voice and which he was bound to follow."[107]

Second, in a 1952 case,[108] the Oklahoma Supreme Court refused to award a refund of state taxes paid under protest after the U.S. Supreme Court overruled Oklahoma law that certain lessees of lands were federal instrumentalities exempt from state taxes.[109] The Oklahoma Supreme Court gave that ruling full retroactive effect and concluded that the new rule made clear that taxes "were rightfully due the State" and that the funds "could well be used by it in the exercise of its governmental functions."[110]

Third, in a 1934 New York case,[111] a taxpayer paid state taxes on royalties from copyrights until the U.S. Supreme Court ruled, in *Long v. Rockwood*,[112] that a state couldn't tax income from royalties for the use of federal patents.[113] When the Supreme Court four years later overruled *Long*,[114] state authorities successfully sought back taxes for the period during which the authorities had respected the earlier, now overruled, precedent. The state court reasoned that the hardship to the taxpayer was "no greater . . . than was that suffered by the state."[115] The overruled decision "deprived the state of revenue to which it was justly entitled."[116]

---

106 *Id.* at 262.
107 *Id.*
108 *Texas Co. v. Oklahoma Tax Comm'n*, 249 P.2d 985 (Okla. 1952).
109 *Id.* at 989.
110 *Id.*
111 *People ex rel. Rice v. Graves*, 273 N.Y.S. 582 (App. Div. 1934).
112 277 U.S. 142 (1928).
113 *Graves*, 273 N.Y.S. at 585–86.
114 *See Fox Film Corp. v. Doyal*, 286 U.S. 123 (1932).
115 *Graves*, 273 N.Y.S. at 591.
116 *Id.*

The question of supersession

In addition to the question of the proper application of the overruling opinion, the question arises to what degree it supersedes the overruled decision. The extent to which an overruling decision impairs the value of a past decision is affected by the manner in which the past decision is overruled. A court may explicitly overrule a past decision, as when the Supreme Court specifically rejected the "separate but equal" doctrine[117] or held the doctrine of *Swift v. Tyson*[118] unconstitutional[119] (see § 70). When the court takes such direct action, the state of the law is clear.

On the other hand, a court may overrule a decision implicitly or tacitly when it "directly contradicts the earlier rule of law"[120] or "undercut[s] the theory or reasoning underlying the . . . precedent in such a way that the cases are clearly irreconcilable" but doesn't explicitly declare the prior decision overruled.[121] The Supreme Court has cautioned against finding its decisions implicitly overruled. In *State Oil Co. v. Khan*,[122] as we saw in § 37, the Supreme Court reviewed the decision of the Seventh Circuit Court of Appeals that relied on a Supreme Court precedent, *Albrecht v. Herald Co.*,[123] despite the circuit court's determination that the case was "unsound when decided" and "inconsistent with later decisions."[124] On review, the Supreme Court expressly overruled *Albrecht*[125] but approved the court of appeals' reliance on it, explaining that "it is this Court's prerogative alone to overrule one of its precedents."[126]

---

117 *Brown v. Board of Educ.*, 347 U.S. 483, 490–91, 494–95 (1954), *overruling Plessy v. Ferguson*, 163 U.S. 537 (1896).
118 41 U.S. (16 Pet.) 1 (1842).
119 *Erie R.R. v. Tompkins*, 304 U.S. 64, 77–80 (1938).
120 *Lunsford v. Saberhagen Holdings, Inc.*, 208 P.3d 1092, 1100 (Wash. 2009) (en banc).
121 *Miller v. Gammie*, 335 F.3d 889, 900 (9th Cir. 2003) (en banc).
122 522 U.S. 3 (1997).
123 390 U.S. 145 (1968).
124 *Khan v. State Oil Co.*, 93 F.3d 1358, 1363–64 (7th Cir. 1996).
125 *State Oil Co. v. Khan*, 522 U.S. 3, 22 (1997).
126 *Id.* at 20.

State courts have expressed similar hesitation to recognize the implicit overruling of a past decision.[127] As for the effect of a tacit overruling, the Missouri Supreme Court explained that "the implicit nature of a *sub silentio* holding has no stare decisis effect and is not binding on future decisions of th[e] Court."[128] Although not all courts deal with implicit overrulings in the same manner, it is evident that an implicit overruling doesn't impale a prior decision as mortally as one that is expressly overruled.

Finally, although a decision that has been overruled or reversed is no longer good law in the jurisdiction that rendered it, it may be cited as persuasive authority in another jurisdiction. Other jurisdictions may find that the overruled case is better reasoned than the decision overruling it or that it better comports with the law or policy of their state.

Conclusive effect of an overruled decision on litigants

Although a decision may be overruled with respect to the abstract rule or legal principle announced, the overruling impairs neither its conclusive effect as a judgment in the particular case nor its effect on the litigants. But if an appeal from the judgment is pending, it will be decided in accordance with the latest decision of the court having final appellate jurisdiction. Likewise, if the action remains pending, whether in the appellate courts or not, the law-of-the-case doctrine typically won't prevent accounting for the new decision.

Once a court has issued a final judgment and once all appellate rights, whether exercised or not, have come to an end, that judgment generally binds the litigants, even if the principle of law at issue is later overruled in a separate case. Finality is the reason. At some point, the risks associated with the law's delays must cease so that the litigants may structure their affairs based on a final

---

127 *See, e.g., Puryear v. State*, 810 So. 2d 901, 905 (Fla. 2002) ("[T]his Court does not intentionally overrule itself sub silentio."); *State v. Honeycutt*, 421 S.W.3d 410, 422 (Mo. 2013) (en banc), *as modified* (24 Dec. 2013) ("Generally, this Court presumes, absent a contrary showing, that an opinion of this Court has not been overruled *sub silentio*.").

128 *Honeycutt*, 421 S.W.3d at 422.

judgment. As we've seen, it's often more important to resolve disputes finally than it is to entertain more litigation in the hope of a better answer—even the correct answer. There are few limitations on the power of a final judgment over the litigants in a case.

Federated Department Stores v. Moitie[129] offers one example. An assortment of claimants filed seven different antitrust lawsuits. A federal district court consolidated the lawsuits and dismissed them all under Civil Rule 12(b)(6), on the ground that the plaintiffs had failed to allege an injury to their business or property, as required under the Clayton Act. The plaintiffs in five of the lawsuits appealed, and the Ninth Circuit eventually reversed. For reasons of their own, the plaintiffs in the other two lawsuits didn't appeal but instead refiled similar lawsuits in state court. The defendants removed the state-court lawsuits to federal court and successfully moved to dismiss on res judicata grounds. The plaintiffs in those two lawsuits appealed.[130]

At issue before the Supreme Court was whether the plaintiffs in the other two actions could benefit from the Ninth Circuit's ruling. No, the Supreme Court answered: "A final judgment on the merits of an action," it reasoned, "precludes the parties or their privies from relitigating issues that were or could have been raised in that action."[131] "Nor," it added, "are the res judicata consequences of a final, unappealed judgment on the merits altered by the fact that the judgment may have been wrong or rested on a legal principle subsequently overruled in another case."[132] A judgment can't be challenged in a collateral action because—"merely" because, said the Court—it was "based upon an erroneous view of the law."[133] It may be corrected only by direct review and not by suing again on the same claim."[134] Any other approach, the Court observed, would undermine the purpose of res judicata by

---

129 452 U.S. 394 (1981).
130 *See id.* at 396–98.
131 *Id.* at 398.
132 *Id.*
133 *Id.*
134 *Id.*

"creating elements of uncertainty and confusion" and by "undermining the conclusive character of judgments."[135]

Another Supreme Court decision illustrates how long this rule has been with us and how forceful it can be. At stake in the 1932 case of *Reed v. Allen*[136] were rights to real property left in a will—possession of the property and rents from it—claimed by two different litigants. Party A filed an interpleader lawsuit against party B for rents from the property—and won. While the appeal from that action was pending, party A filed a separate ejectment lawsuit against party B to obtain possession of the property. Relying on the decision in the interpleader action, the trial court granted relief to party A and ejected party B from the property. Party B didn't appeal the ejectment-action decision and, as fortune would have it, managed to prevail on appeal in the interpleader action. Oddly enough, that left party B with rents from the property and party A in possession of the same property.[137] No matter, the Supreme Court concluded: "The judgment in the ejectment action was final and not open to assault collaterally, but subject to impeachment only through some form of direct attack"—a "course [that party B] neglected to follow."[138]

So when a final judgment is rendered by a court with competent jurisdiction, and the time to appeal has run out, claim preclusion prevents relitigation of issues that were or could have been raised in the course of litigation.[139] That's true even if there has been a change in the relevant law and the legal rule or principle on which the judgment rested is determined to be erroneous or wrongly applied to the facts of the case. The rule is an old one, as *Reed* demonstrates, and it is followed in federal and state courts, as other sources confirm.[140]

---

135 *Id.* at 398–99.
136 286 U.S. 191 (1932).
137 *See id.* at 196–97.
138 *Id.* at 198.
139 *Moitie*, 452 U.S. at 398.
140 *See, e.g.*, Henry Campbell Black, *Handbook on the Law of Judicial Precedents* § 213, at 691 (1912); *Medvick v. City of Univ. City*, 995 F.2d 857, 858 (8th Cir. 1993); *Precision Air Parts, Inc. v. Avco Corp.*, 736 F.2d 1499, 1503 (11th Cir. 1984);

Although one might assume that the same rule would apply to collateral estoppel or issue preclusion, that's not generally so. Claim preclusion normally precludes relitigating claims after final judgment, yet issue preclusion alone usually doesn't bar resurrecting a claim when "a substantial change in the legal climate" has occurred.[141] Here's how the Restatement of Judgments puts the point: "Although an issue is actually litigated and determined by a valid and final judgment, and the determination is essential to the judgment, relitigation of the issue in a subsequent action between the parties is not precluded" if "[t]he issue is one of law and (a) the two actions involve claims that are substantially unrelated, or (b) a new determination is warranted in order to take account of an intervening change in the applicable legal context or otherwise to avoid inequitable administration of the laws."[142]

Courts are particularly apt to apply the new rule in two overlapping settings. One occurs when a litigant is a governmental agency responsible for implementing a change of law and for doing so consistently for many individuals and entities.[143] The other is constitutional litigation, which will invariably involve governmental actors. "Unreflective invocation of collateral estoppel against parties with an ongoing interest in constitutional issues," the Supreme Court has warned, "could freeze doctrine in areas of the law where responsiveness to changing patterns of conduct or social mores is critical."[144]

These issues may emerge not only when two parties participate in two distinct actions, but also in the same action when the losing party seeks to alter a previously entered judgment. Most of the doctrine in this area has been codified in two subsections of Federal Civil Rule 60(b): "On motion and just terms, the court

---

State v. Ketterer, 18 N.E.3d 1199, 1201 (Ohio 2014); *Wright v. Cordesville Pentecostal Holiness Church*, 426 S.E.2d 772, 773 (S.C. 1993).

141   See, e.g., *Coors Brewing Co. v. Méndez-Torres*, 562 F.3d 3, 11 (1st Cir. 2009), abrogated on other grounds by *Levin v. Commerce Energy, Inc.*, 560 U.S. 413 (2010); Restatement (Second) of Judgments § 28(2).

142   Restatement (Second) of Judgments § 28.

143   *Id.* cmt. c.

144   *Montana v. United States*, 440 U.S. 147, 162–63 (1979).

may relieve a party or its legal representative from a final judgment, order, or proceeding for the following reasons: . . . (5) the judgment has been satisfied, released, or discharged; it is based on an earlier judgment that has been reversed or vacated; or applying it prospectively is no longer equitable; or (6) any other reason that justifies relief."[145] Most states have similar rules.[146]

What might seem to be a wide-ranging invitation for changing previously entered judgments turns out to be severely cabined. For one thing, "[r]elief under Rule 60(b) is an extraordinary remedy," and as a result trial courts do not grant it lightly.[147] For another, a Rule 60(b) motion isn't a substitute for an appeal. To benefit from a change in law that postdates a trial court's decision, the losing party, generally speaking, must appeal. If the change in law occurs after the trial court's decision and during appeal, the losing side may benefit from the new decision. That is because "a court is to apply the law in effect at the time it renders its decision,"[148] even if the law changes between the time when the lower court ruled and the time when the appellate court rules.[149]

But if a litigant decides not to appeal, the trial court's decision "becomes the law of the case as to the parties."[150] And if, instead of appealing, the losing party later files a Rule 60(b) motion in the trial court to try to benefit from the change in law, the party is likely to lose based on the "well settled principle of law that a Rule 60(b) motion seeking relief from a final judgment is not a substitute for a timely and proper appeal."[151] As the Supreme Court has explained, a Rule 60(b) motion cannot excuse "a considered choice not to appeal. . . . There must be an end to litigation

---

145 *See* 11 Charles Alan Wright, Arthur R. Miller et al., *Federal Practice and Procedure* §§ 2863–2864, at 448–528 (3d ed. 2012).

146 *See, e.g.*, Mass. R. Civ. P. 60; Ohio Civ. R. 60.

147 *Design Classics, Inc. v. Westphal*, 788 F.2d 1384, 1386 (8th Cir. 1986).

148 *Kaiser Aluminum & Chem. Corp. v. Bonjorno*, 494 U.S. 827, 836–37 (1990) (quoting *Bradley v. Richmond Sch. Bd.*, 416 U.S. 696, 711 (1974)).

149 *Id.* at 837.

150 *Design Classics, Inc.*, 788 F.2d at 1386.

151 *Dowell v. State Farm Fire & Cas. Auto. Ins. Co.*, 993 F.2d 46, 48 (4th Cir. 1993).

someday, and free, calculated, deliberate choices"[152] that a litigant has made should not provide that litigant with grounds for later relief.[153] Indefatigable feuding is discouraged: "Finality is an institutional value that transcends the litigants' parochial interests."[154]

As to relief under Rule 60(b)(5) more specifically, the provision doesn't apply merely because a precedent on which the trial or appellate court relied was later overruled. The second ground for relief under the subsection—that "a prior judgment upon which [the court's] decision is based has been reversed or otherwise vacated"—refers to judgments grounded on claim or issue preclusion, not judgments grounded on precedents later overruled.[155] "The 'prior judgment' clause of Rule 60(b)(5) does not contemplate relief based merely upon precedential evolution."[156] As the First Circuit has explained: "[T]o come within [this category], the prior judgment must be directly related to the purportedly reversing decision by, for example, giving rise to the cause of action or being part of the same proceeding. In the absence of such a direct connection, a change in applicable law does not provide sufficient basis for relief."[157]

The third category of Rule 60(b)(5) relief—that "applying [the prior judgment] prospectively is no longer equitable"—permits a district court to alter a judgment based solely on a change in controlling law in some circumstances, particularly with respect

---

152 *Ackerman v. United States*, 340 U.S. 193, 198 (1950).

153 *Id.*

154 *Comfort v. Lynn Sch. Comm.*, 560 F.3d 22, 26 (1st Cir. 2009) (internal quotation marks omitted).

155 *Wright v. Cordesville Pentecostal Holiness Church*, 426 S.E.2d 772, 773 (S.C. 1993).

156 *Harris v. Martin*, 834 F.2d 361, 364 (3d Cir. 1987) (internal quotation marks omitted).

157 *Comfort*, 560 F.3d at 27 (internal quotation marks and citations omitted); *see also Butler v. Eaton*, 141 U.S. 240, 242–44 (1891) (allowing relitigation after a precedential case with the same parties and issues was overturned); 11 Charles Alan Wright, Arthur R. Miller et al., *Federal Practice and Procedure* § 2863 (3d ed. 2012) (explaining that reliance on overruled precedent isn't enough—the two judgments must be related "in the sense of claim or issue preclusion").

to an injunction that requires long-term supervision.[158] But here, too, the courts' institutional interests in finality will often defeat such motions.[159] Two examples show the kinds of unusual circumstances required to invoke the motion successfully. In one, the Supreme Court modified a federal-court injunction applied to a county prison based on an intervening change in law and the significant costs to the government of complying with the original injunction.[160] In the other, the Court modified a federal-court injunction that had barred governmental aid to local parochial schools based on changes in the Court's Establishment Clause jurisprudence after the injunction's entry.[161]

What of Rule 60(b)(6)? Courts may grant such motions for "any other reason that justifies relief." Despite the broad swath of settings potentially covered by this inviting language, the courts haven't liberally granted such motions. Altering a judgment under Rule 60(b)(6) requires unusual circumstances, and it isn't a substitute for a failure to file a timely appeal, whether in federal court[162] or state court.[163] Such relief is rarely granted based on a change in law alone.[164] The state courts also hold to the view that a change in the law by itself will not suffice to overturn a judgment antedating the change.[165]

---

158 *See Comfort*, 560 F.3d at 28 (citing *Allen v. McCurry*, 449 U.S. 90, 94 (1980)); *Paul Revere Variable Annuity Ins. Co. v. Zang*, 248 F.3d 1, 7 (1st Cir. 2001); *see also Harris v. Martin*, 834 F.2d 361, 365 (3d Cir. 1987) (holding that change in the law alone doesn't give grounds for granting a Rule 60(b)(5) motion).

159 *See Comfort*, 560 F.3d at 24–25 (declining to modify school-desegregation order based on change in precedent).

160 *See Rufo v. Inmates of Suffolk Cnty. Jail*, 502 U.S. 367, 393 (1992).

161 *See Agostini v. Felton*, 521 U.S. 203, 237–40 (1997).

162 *See, e.g., Hunter v. Underwood*, 362 F.3d 468, 475 (8th Cir. 2004) (citing *Kocher v. Dow Chem. Co.*, 132 F.3d 1225, 1229 (8th Cir. 1997)).

163 *See, e.g., Patterson v. Hays*, 623 So. 2d 1142, 1145 (Ala. 1993).

164 *Agostini*, 521 U.S. at 239 ("Intervening developments in the law by themselves rarely constitute the extraordinary circumstances required for relief under Rule 60(b)(6) . . . .").

165 *See, e.g., Regan v. S. Cent. Reg'l Med. Ctr.*, 47 So. 3d 651, 656 (Miss. 2010); *see also Rollins Envtl. Servs., Inc. v. Superior Court*, 330 N.E.2d 814, 817–18 (Mass. 1975) (holding that Massachusetts courts will adopt the construction of the federal rules when interpreting their state rules because they are "substantially the same").

One exceptional circumstance that justifies relief is the "common-accident exception." Consider *Gondeck v. Pan Am. World Airways, Inc.*,[166] in which the same accident led to the death of two men. The Fifth Circuit set aside an award to one set of survivors by the Department of Labor under the Longshoreman's and Harbor Workers' Compensation Act, and the Supreme Court denied a petition for a writ of certiorari. In a separate action, the Fourth Circuit upheld an award to the other set of survivors. After the Fourth Circuit decision, the survivors of the first action returned to the Supreme Court with a petition for rehearing three years after the original certiorari petition had been denied. In granting relief, the Court reasoned that because, "of those eligible for compensation from the accident, this petitioner stands alone in not receiving it, the interests of justice would make unfair the strict application of our rules."[167] The Tenth Circuit reached a similar result in affirming a grant of Rule 60(b)(6) relief after "the same vehicular accident . . . produced divergent results in federal and state courts."[168] State courts have granted relief under similar circumstances.[169]

Exception for injunctions

When an injunction issues to give effect to a particular law and that law later changes, a different rule governs. A party may move to modify that injunction, even when entered by consent, if changes in law make clear that the enjoined conduct is no longer impermissible.[170] In the 1943 case of *Coca-Cola Co. v. Standard Bottling Co.*,[171] for example, the litigants had consented to a decree in 1925 that enjoined Standard Bottling from selling any beverages described as *cola*, except for the product Coca-Cola. But in 1941, the district court modified the decree after "numerous decisions in

---

166 382 U.S. 25 (1965).
167 *Id.* at 27 (internal quotation marks omitted).
168 *Pierce v. Cook & Co.*, 518 F.2d 720, 721, 723–24 (10th Cir. 1975).
169 *See, e.g.*, *Norman v. Nichiro Gyogyo Kaisha, Ltd.*, 761 P.2d 713, 715 (Alaska 1988).
170 *See Agostini v. Felton*, 521 U.S. 203, 215 (1997) ("A court errs when it refuses to modify an injunction or consent decree in light of such changes.").
171 138 F.2d 788, 788–89 (10th Cir. 1943).

many courts"[172] ruled that Coca-Cola lacked "any exclusive right to the word 'cola,' except its own trademark of 'Coca-Cola.'"[173] The Tenth Circuit properly affirmed that modification.

Similarly, in *Pasadena City Board of Education v. Spangler*,[174] the Supreme Court vacated a lower court's refusal to modify a consent decree governing the desegregation of schools when a later decision of the Supreme Court[175] made clear that the district court lacked the equitable authority to require certain desegregation remedies.[176]

The same rule applies to the modification of injunctions based on later changes in the underlying statutory law.[177] In the seminal case of *System Federation No. 91 Railway Employees v. Wright*,[178] for example, the litigants' consent decree initially prohibited discrimination against nonunion employees, but later changes to the Railway Labor Act allowed what was disallowed under the consent decree.[179] Modification of that decree was not only permitted but even encouraged by the Supreme Court.[180]

This rule has its limits: as the Court has made clear, "a decision that *clarifies* the law will not, in and of itself, provide a basis for modifying a decree," but "it could constitute a change in circumstances that would support modification if the parties had based their agreement on a misunderstanding of the governing law."[181]

---

172 *Id.* at 790.
173 *Id.* at 789.
174 427 U.S. 424 (1976).
175 *Swann v. Charlotte–Mecklenburg Bd. of Educ.*, 402 U.S. 1 (1971).
176 *Spangler*, 427 U.S. at 435.
177 *System Fed'n No. 91 Ry. Emps. v. Wright*, 364 U.S. 642, 647–48 (1961) ("Nevertheless the court cannot be required to disregard significant changes in law or facts if it is 'satisfied that what it has been doing has been turned through changing circumstances into an instrument of wrong.'") (quoting *United States v. Swift & Co.*, 286 U.S. 106, 114–15 (1932)).
178 *Id.*
179 *Id.* at 651.
180 *Id.*
181 *Rufo v. Inmates of Suffolk Cnty. Jail*, 502 U.S. 367, 390 (1992) (emphasis added).

C. Some Practicalities of Stare Decisis

38. Stare Decisis with Statutes

Stare decisis applies with special force to questions of statutory construction. Although courts have power to overrule their decisions and change their interpretations, they do so only for the most compelling reasons—but almost never when the previous decision has been repeatedly followed, has long been acquiesced in, or has become a rule of property.

Jurisprudential writers distinguish between judicial precedents that interpret and apply a preexisting rule, such as one found in a statute, and those that create law from a void, as with the common law: "A *declaratory* precedent is one which is merely the application of an already existing rule of law; an *original* precedent is one which creates and applies a new rule."[1] When the law is already sufficiently well stated, as when it is embodied in a statute or set forth fully and clearly in some comparatively modern case, declaratory precedents become the norm.[2]

The traditional Anglo-American view is that an authoritative interpretation of the written law (legislation) acquires the power of law and becomes part of the statute itself.[3] The old maxim is *legis interpretatio legis vim obtinet*[4]—that is, "the interpretation of law obtains the force of law."[5] Hence "in England and in the United States a reported case may be cited with almost as much confidence as an Act of Parliament [or other legislative enactment]."[6] As some courts have expressly noted, declaratory precedents interpreting

---

1 John Salmond, *Jurisprudence* § 57, at 177 (Glanville L. Williams ed., 10th ed. 1947).
2 *See* Thomas Erskine Holland, *The Elements of Jurisprudence* 66 (7th ed. 1895) ("Legislation tends with advancing civilisation to become the nearly exclusive source of new law.").
3 Henry Campbell Black, *Handbook on the Construction and Interpretation of the Laws* § 183, at 616 (2d ed. 1911).
4 Thomas Branch, *Principia Legis et Aequitatis* 53 (1753).
5 *Black's Law Dictionary* 1926 (Bryan A. Garner ed., 10th ed. 2014).
6 Holland, *The Elements of Jurisprudence* at 59.

statutes deserve more deference than original (common-law) precedents.[7] The Supreme Court itself has repeatedly stated that stare decisis "has special force in respect to statutory interpretation because Congress remains free to alter what we have done."[8]

But the Court hasn't explained how the "special force" of stare decisis in statutory decisions relates to stare decisis in original (common-law) cases, so the application of stare decisis there remains remarkably uncertain.[9] Perhaps that's because it's not so much a doctrine as a method.[10] In his 2014 *Bay Mills* dissent, Thomas J. pointed out this problem when he rejected "the majority's intimation that stare decisis applies as strongly to common-law decisions as to those involving statutory interpretation." The Justice noted that the Court has given stare decisis less force when interpreting a common-law statute such as the Sherman Act. He went on to say: "Surely no higher standard of stare decisis can apply when dealing with common law proper, which Congress certainly expects the Court to shape in the absence of legislative action."[11]

The American method may be most accurately characterized as a three-tiered approach to stare decisis. The U.S. Supreme Court gives strong effect to statutory precedents, medium effect

---

7   See, e.g., *Froud v. Celotex Corp.*, 456 N.E.2d 131, 137 (Ill. 1983) (noting that "[c]onsiderations of stare decisis weigh more heavily in the area of statutory construction" than in the area of the common law).

8   *Halliburton Co. v. Erica P. John Fund, Inc.*, 134 S.Ct. 2398, 2411 (2014) (quoting *John R. Sand & Gravel Co. v. United States*, 552 U.S. 130, 139 (2008)).

9   See, e.g., Randy E. Barnett, *Trumping Precedent with Original Meaning: Not as Radical as It Sounds*, 22 Const. Comment. 257, 261 (2005) ("How and when precedent should be rejected remains one of the great unresolved controversies of jurisprudence.").

10 Max Radin, "Case Law and Stare Decisis: Concerning *Präjudizienrecht in Amerika*," in *Essays on Jurisprudence from the Columbia Law Review* 3, 16 (1963) ("[A]s applied in the United States, the rule of stare decisis is a matter of technique. In whatever way courts reach their conclusion, they are expected to place the situation they are judging within the generalized class of some existing decision.").

11 *Michigan v. Bay Mills Indian Cmty.*, 134 S.Ct. 2024, 2053 n.6 (2014) (Thomas J. dissenting); see also Lawrence C. Marshall, *"Let Congress Do It": The Case for an Absolute Rule of Statutory Stare Decisis*, 88 Mich. L. Rev. 177, 182–83 (1989) (discussing the endurance of the principle even though the Court occasionally departs from it).

to common-law precedents, and weaker effect to constitutional precedents.[12] With statutory interpretation, unlike (for practical purposes) constitutional interpretation, the legislature can alter an erroneous statutory holding.[13] Hence courts generally won't depart from a settled judicial interpretation of a statute even if the earlier holding is of questionable validity.[14]

Some prominent examples of the heightened strength of statutory precedents

Consider the case we mentioned in the introduction on page 4: the U.S. Supreme Court's holding[15] that the baseball industry is exempt from the reach of the federal antitrust law, the Sherman Act.[16] This holding has been called "one of federal law's most enduring anomalies."[17] The Court held that the Sherman Act didn't apply to the "business [of] giving exhibitions of baseball" because such exhibitions were "purely state affairs."[18] Thirty years later, in a one-paragraph per curiam opinion in a case called *Toolson v. New York Yankees*,[19] the Court reaffirmed *Federal Baseball* insofar as it exempted the baseball business from the strictures of the Sherman Act, reasoning that Congress had been aware of the

---

12 See Earl Maltz, *The Nature of Precedent*, 66 N.C. L. Rev. 367, 388 (1988); *see also* Frank H. Easterbrook, *Stability and Reliability in Judicial Decisions*, 73 Cornell L. Rev. 422, 426 n.16 (1988) (observing that "[o]ne of the most famous overruling decisions also contains a strong statement of the special durability of the construction of a statute") (citing *Erie R.R. v. Tompkins*, 304 U.S. 64, 77–78 (1938)).

13 See *John R. Sand & Gravel Co. v. United States*, 552 U.S. 130, 139 (2008).

14 See, e.g., *Illinois Brick Co. v. Illinois*, 431 U.S. 720, 736–37 (1977) (noting that because "considerations of stare decisis weigh heavily in the area of statutory construction, where Congress is free to change th[e] Court's interpretation of its legislation," the Court would adhere to its prior interpretation of the Clayton Act "even if [it] were persuaded" that the earlier decision was wrong); *Hill v. Atlantic & N.C. R.R.*, 55 S.E. 854, 868 (N.C. 1906) ("[A]n authoritative judicial construction put upon a statute has the force of law by becoming, as it were, a part of the statute itself.").

15 *Federal Baseball Club of Baltimore v. National League of Prof'l Baseball Clubs*, 259 U.S. 200, 208 (1922).

16 15 U.S.C. § 1 (prohibiting unreasonable restraints of trade).

17 *City of San Jose v. Commissioner of Baseball*, 776 F.3d 686, 687 (9th Cir. 2015).

18 *Federal Baseball*, 259 U.S. at 208.

19 346 U.S. 356 (1953) (per curiam).

Federal Baseball holding "but ha[d] not seen fit to bring such business under these laws.... The business has thus been left for thirty years to develop, on the understanding that it was not subject to existing antitrust legislation."[20] The Court concluded that "if there are evils in this field which now warrant application to it of the antitrust laws it should be by legislation."[21] Two Justices dissented on grounds that *Federal Baseball*'s holding that the Sherman Act didn't reach the baseball industry was based on an indefensibly outmoded interpretation of the Commerce Clause.[22]

Twenty years after *Toolson*, in *Flood v. Kuhn*,[23] the Court frankly acknowledged that "[p]rofessional baseball is a business and it is engaged in interstate commerce" and that the holdings of *Federal Baseball* and *Toolson* that baseball was exempt from the Sherman Act were "aberration[s]."[24] But, the Court said, "the aberration is an established one . . . fully entitled to the benefit of stare decisis," particularly because baseball "ha[d] been allowed to develop and to expand unhindered by federal legislative action" and because of "the confusion and retroactivity problems that inevitably would result with a judicial overturning of *Federal Baseball*."[25] The Court conceded that some errors become enshrined by the passage of time: "If there is any inconsistency or illogic in all this, it is an inconsistency and illogic of long standing that is to be remedied by the Congress and not by this Court."[26]

Another representative example is *John R. Sand & Gravel v. United States*.[27] There, the Supreme Court reaffirmed century-old precedent that the time limits in the Tucker Act (allowing certain claims against the federal government) are jurisdictional.[28] The Court acknowledged that if it were interpreting the statute for the

---

20   *Id.* at 357.
21   *Id.*
22   *Id.* at 357–60 (Burton J. dissenting).
23   407 U.S. 258 (1972).
24   *Id.* at 282.
25   *Id.* at 282–83.
26   *Id.* at 284.
27   552 U.S. 130 (2008).
28   *Id.* at 139.

first time under the modern doctrine concerning whether statutes permit equitable tolling, it might reach a different result. But then the Court concluded that "[a]ny anomaly" created by the old precedent and the new doctrine was "not critical" and adhered to the precedent on stare decisis grounds.[29]

Finally, consider the Supreme Court's 2015 landmark decision in *Kimble v. Marvel Entertainment*.[30] There, the Court addressed whether it should overrule the 1964 case of *Brulotte v. Thys Co.*,[31] which "held that a patent holder cannot charge royalties for the use of his invention after its patent term has expired."[32] The Court declined to overrule *Brulotte*, noting that the decision implicated a "superpowered form of stare decisis" because it was based on an interpretation of a statute and lay "at the intersection of two areas of law[:] property (patents) and contracts (licensing agreements)." Reliance interests are especially important in both areas.[33] The Court found no "super-special justification" to reconsider the decision, explaining that its "statutory and doctrinal underpinnings have not eroded over time" and that the decision had not "proved unworkable."[34]

Three Justices dissented. In their view, the decision didn't implicate reliance interests—to the contrary, it "most often functions to upset the parties' expectations."[35]

The pros and cons of overruling

Decisions overturning a statutory precedent are uncommon. But sometimes a court will determine that an earlier interpretation of a statute was so wrongheaded or has had such calamitous

---

29   *Id.* at 136–39; *see also United States v. Kwai Fun Wong*, 135 S.Ct. 1625, 1635 (2015) (reiterating that *John R. Sand*'s holding rested on stare decisis grounds and suggesting that the result might well have been different had the Court been writing on a clean slate).

30   135 S.Ct. 2401 (2015).

31   379 U.S. 29 (1964).

32   *Kimble*, 135 S.Ct. at 2405.

33   *Id.* at 2410.

34   *Id.* at 2411.

35   *Id.* at 2417.

consequences—while earning meager reliance—that it should not be retained. While each case turns on its own facts, courts are generally reluctant to overrule a statutory holding unless both (1) the judges are certain or nearly certain that the earlier decision was wrong and (2) there hasn't been significant reliance on the earlier decision.

The Supreme Court's decision in *Leegin Creative Leather Products v. PSKS*[36] is an excellent (and controversial) example that is usefully contrasted with *Kimble*. In *Leegin*, the Court considered the continuing vitality of its nearly 100-year-old precedent known as *Dr. Miles*,[37] which made minimum-price agreements between a manufacturer and a distributor illegal per se under the Sherman Act. The *Leegin* majority, surveying the antitrust caselaw and economic literature of the past century, determined that later doctrinal and academic developments had "rejected the rationales on which *Dr. Miles* was based."[38] Those developments, the Court said, made clear that vertical minimum-price restrictions were not so obviously anticompetitive as to warrant per se treatment.[39] The Court thus turned to the question whether stare decisis concerns required retaining *Dr. Miles*.

The majority acknowledged that "concerns about maintaining settled law are strong when the question is one of statutory interpretation."[40] But the majority also noted that the Court had long treated the Sherman Act as a "common-law statute" because of its open-ended prohibition of "restraint[s] of trade," the interpretation of which could "evolve to meet the dynamics of present economic conditions."[41] So the normal rule concerning statutory stare decisis wasn't entirely apt here. Further, the Court argued, later doctrinal developments, as well as commentators and federal antitrust regulators, had "called into serious question" the holding of *Dr. Miles*.[42]

---

36 551 U.S. 877 (2007).
37 *Dr. Miles Med. Co. v. John D. Park & Sons Co.*, 220 U.S. 373 (1911).
38 *Leegin*, 551 U.S. at 887.
39 *Id.* at 894.
40 *Id.* at 899.
41 *Id.* (alteration in original).
42 *Id.* at 900 (quoting *State Oil Co. v. Khan*, 522 U.S. 3, 21 (1997)).

The majority rejected the argument that by making vertical price restraints legal in certain contexts and then repealing those enactments, Congress had "ratified" the rule of *Dr. Miles*. Rather, Congress "intended § 1 to give courts the ability 'to develop governing principles of law' in the common-law tradition."[43] It likewise rejected the proposition that reliance interests required adherence to *Dr. Miles*, noting that the rule established by that case was "narrow[]" and that in any event "reliance interests . . . cannot justify an inefficient rule."[44]

In dissent, Breyer J. attacked the majority's stare decisis analysis. His analysis provides a useful catalogue of the various considerations that the Supreme Court generally takes into account when it determines whether to overrule an earlier case:

- *Whether the decision was constitutional or statutory.* As noted, courts "appl[y] stare decisis more 'rigidly' in statutory than in constitutional cases."[45] *Dr. Miles* was a statutory holding.[46]
- *Length of time since prior decision.* Breyer J. suggested that courts should be more reluctant to overrule older decisions like *Dr. Miles*.[47]
- *Whether the prior decision is "unworkable."* "[T]he fact that a decision creates an 'unworkable' legal regime argues in favor of overruling," Breyer J. explained.[48] But the per se rule had "proved practical over the course of the last century."[49]
- *Whether the prior decision "unsettled" the law.* Breyer J. noted that the per se prohibition on vertical minimum-price

---

43   *Id.* at 905 (quoting *Texas Indus., Inc. v. Radcliff Materials, Inc.*, 451 U.S. 630, 643 (1981)).
44   *Id.* at 906.
45   *Id.* at 923 (Breyer J. dissenting).
46   *Id.* at 924.
47   *Id.*
48   *Id.*
49   *Id.*

agreements was itself settled law, and that the majority's change here would "unsettle that law."[50]

- *Whether the case involves property or contract rights.* Because cases involving property and contract rights implicate substantial reliance interests, Breyer J. explained, courts should hesitate to overrule precedents involving those rights.[51] Here, he said, both Congress and corporations had placed "considerable reliance upon the *per se* rule."[52]

- *Whether the rule of the prior cases "has become 'embedded' in our 'national culture.'"*[53] In Breyer J.'s view, "[t]he *per se* rule forbidding minimum resale price maintenance agreements ha[d] long been 'embedded' in the law of antitrust."[54]

Reasonable minds can disagree about whether the majority or dissent in *Leegin* had the better of the stare decisis argument. But the warring opinions provide an excellent example of the various arguments that can be made in support of retaining or overruling a statutory precedent and how those arguments may be deployed. They also illustrate more broadly how judges' views of their institutional role—often vis-à-vis the legislature—inform their approach to stare decisis questions. The *Leegin* majority appeared much more comfortable than the dissent with divining from the economic literature a consensus about the competitive effects of vertical minimum price fixing, and hence more comfortable setting down a rule to govern such agreements in common-law fashion. The dissent thought the economic issue was so complicated as to be ill-suited for judicial resolution—that it would have been more prudent to leave in place an almost century-old precedent and let Congress make any changes necessary in light of advancements in economic thought. Similar concerns were at play in *Kimble*, but there the position that the proper rule was for Congress to decide won the day.

---

50   *Id.*
51   *Id.* at 925.
52   *Id.*
53   *Id.* at 926 (quoting *Dickerson v. United States*, 530 U.S. 428, 443–44 (2000)).
54   *Id.*

For another example of the Supreme Court's casting aside an earlier statutory precedent, consider the 1995 case of *Hubbard v. United States*.[55] There, the Court confronted the question whether to overrule its 40-year-old holding in *United States v. Bramblett*[56] that the federal false-statement statute[57] applies to false statements made in judicial proceedings. The *Hubbard* majority concluded that *Bramblett*'s statutory analysis was "seriously flawed."[58] It also noted that lower courts, in "an obvious attempt to impose limits on *Bramblett*[]," had crafted a "judicial function" exception, unmoored to the statutory text, under which the statute applied only to "administrative" or "housekeeping" functions of a court.[59] The Court acknowledged that reconsideration of a statutory precedent was appropriate "only in the rarest circumstances."[60] But Stevens J., speaking for a plurality of the Court, concluded that such reconsideration was appropriate "because of the absence of significant reliance interests in adhering to *Bramblett*"—there was in fact evidence that prosecutors didn't often use § 1001 to "deter[] and punish[] litigation-related misconduct"—and because the development of the judicial-function exception was a "highly unusual 'intervening development of the law.'"[61]

Scalia J., joined by Kennedy J., concurred in part and concurred in the judgment, noting that they did "not regard the Courts of Appeals' attempts to limit *Bramblett* as an 'intervening development of the law.'"[62] Scalia J. would have overruled *Bramblett* simply because it was an erroneous decision on which little reliance had been placed.

Rehnquist C.J., joined by two other Justices, dissented. Like Scalia J., he rejected the proposition that a body of law developed

---

55 514 U.S. 695 (1995).
56 348 U.S. 503 (1955).
57 18 U.S.C. § 1001.
58 *Hubbard*, 514 U.S. at 702.
59 *Id.* at 708–09, 713 (plurality opinion) (quoting *Morgan v. United States*, 309 F.2d 234, 237 (D.C. Cir. 1962)).
60 514 U.S. at 713.
61 *Id.* (quoting *Patterson v. McLean Credit Union*, 491 U.S. 164, 173 (1989)).
62 514 U.S. at 716 (Scalia J. concurring in part & concurring in the judgment).

in the lower courts could be treated as an "intervening development of the law" that formed the basis for overruling a prior Supreme Court decision.[63] He also found the claim that there had been little reliance on *Bramblett* to be unpersuasive,[64] and closed by emphasizing the institutional-legitimacy goals that stare decisis is designed to serve: "The opinion of one Justice that another's view of a statute was wrong, even really wrong, does not overcome the institutional advantages conferred by adherence to stare decisis in cases where the wrong is fully redressable by a coordinate branch of government."[65] The decision to overrule, Rehnquist J. said, "disregard[s] the respect due a unanimous decision rendered by six Justices who took the same oath of office sworn by the six Justices who overrule *Bramblett* today."[66] The principle of stare decisis "presumes to reinforce the notion that justice is dispensed according to law and not to serve the proclivities of individuals."[67]

Finally, Rehnquist J. harked back to Brandeis J.: "This, then, is clearly a case where it is better that the matter be decided than that it be decided right. *Bramblett* governs this case, and if the rule of that case is to be overturned it should be at the hands of Congress, and not of this Court."[68]

In a small but perhaps increasing number of cases, courts display a willingness to overturn earlier statutory rulings merely on the grounds that they were "clearly erroneous," even if other stare decisis considerations might militate in favor of retaining them.

State courts pretty much mirror the federal approach. In a 2000 case,[69] the Iowa Supreme Court overruled its earlier holding that an owned-but-not-insured exclusion in a liability-insurance policy was contrary to Iowa's uninsured-motorist statute and hence unenforceable.[70] The court explained that the earlier decision had

---

63 *Id.* at 718–19 (Rehnquist J. dissenting).
64 *Id.* at 722–23.
65 *Id.* at 724.
66 *Id.* at 723.
67 *Id.* at 723–24.
68 *Id.* at 724 (internal quotation marks and citations omitted).
69 *Miller v. Westfield Ins. Co.*, 606 N.W.2d 301 (Iowa 2000) (en banc).
70 *Lindahl v. Howe*, 345 N.W.2d 548 (Iowa 1984) (en banc).

"proceed[ed] upon a wrong principle, [was] built upon a false premise, and arriv[ed] at an erroneous conclusion."[71] It concluded that although "the insurance industry and the public may have relied on [the earlier] decision in considering their insurance sales and purchases," stare decisis didn't prevent the court from reconsidering the "manifest" statutory error committed by the predecessor court.[72]

One important thing to remember is that stare decisis doesn't apply to statutory interpretation unless the statute being interpreted is the same one that was being interpreted in the earlier case. A statute merely similar in its tenor isn't enough to bind a later court. In two cases, the U.S. Supreme Court held that the doctrine cannot be invoked in favor of decisions on former statutes that weren't identical to the one under review.

In *Pollock v. Farmers' Loan & Trust Co.*,[73] Pollock and others were shareholders in Farmers' Loan & Trust Co., which was required under an 1894 federal income-tax statute to withhold taxes on its income.[74] Much of that income came from investments in real estate.[75] The shareholders argued that the statute was unconstitutional on grounds that taxing the rents and other income produced by the real estate imposed a direct tax on the land. They asserted that the Supreme Court's tax-law decisions under income-tax statutes passed in the 1860s (and later repealed) were binding on the present case.[76] Before beginning its analysis, the Court warned that stare decisis applies only when a prior decision is directly on point.[77] It examined several cases in which it had decided that taxes on land or on landowners are direct taxes.[78]

---

71 *Miller*, 606 N.W.2d at 306 (alterations in original) (quoting *Stuart v. Pilgrim*, 74 N.W.2d 212, 216 (Iowa 1956)).
72 Id.
73 157 U.S. 429 (1895).
74 Id. at 429.
75 Id.
76 Id. at 574.
77 Id.
78 Id. at 579.

It explained that under stare decisis none of those decisions applied because the statutes of the 1860s had imposed taxes directly on land and the Court had not addressed whether under those statutes taxes on income from land were taxes on land.[79] Instead, the Court found that income from land is an incident of ownership and a tax on the land would not be distinguishable from one on the income.[80] To this extent, it held the tax statute invalid.[81]

Likewise, in *McDaid v. Oklahoma ex rel. Smith*,[82] the Supreme Court was urged to rely on previous decisions under statutes similar to the one in issue. Under an 1890 federal statute, the Secretary of the Interior appointed several trustees for a town site in Oklahoma and authorized them to execute deeds for lots.[83] Several parties had a dispute about who had the earliest claim to certain lots.[84] The trustees settled the dispute, and the losers appealed to the Commissioner of the General Land Office, who ordered the trustees to grant them deeds.[85] The trustees refused, claiming that the United States had passed title to the lots to them and freed them from the control and authority of the land office.[86] In support of their position, the trustees cited several of the Court's decisions under similar statutes that had passed the right to control the title or to decide on the right to the title from the land office after Congress granted authority over the land to another.[87] The Court declined to rely on the cited precedents and proceeded to construe the current statute.[88] The Court held that

---

79 *Id.*
80 *Id.* at 580–81.
81 *Id.* at 584.
82 150 U.S. 209 (1893).
83 *Id.* at 209–10.
84 *Id.* at 210.
85 *Id.*
86 *Id.* at 210–11, 217.
87 *Id.* at 217.
88 *Id.*

the statute did not transfer any title to the trustees and control of the title remained with the land office.[89]

---

89 *Id.* at 220.

39. Statutory Reenactment

A statute reenacting (or substantially reenacting) a prior statute whose words have received a judicial interpretation must be regarded as having been adopted with knowledge of that interpretation.

When a legislature reenacts a statute that a court has previously interpreted a particular way, courts generally presume that the legislature concomitantly adopts that interpretation in the reenacted statute. This is sometimes referred to as the "reenactment canon."[1] As the Supreme Court wrote in one case, "We find the long and well-settled construction of the Act *plus reenactment of the [relevant] provision without change of the established interpretation* most persuasive indications that the rule of the [previous] cases has become part of the warp and woof of the legislation."[2]

A related principle holds that when a legislature incorporates provisions of an older law into a new law, the legislature is presumed to have intended that those provisions receive the same interpretation in the new law as they did in the old. This is sometimes called the "prior-construction canon."[3] The Supreme Court defined this canon as "the rule that, when 'judicial interpretations have settled the meaning of an existing statutory provision, repetition of the same language in a new statute' is presumed to incorporate that interpretation."[4]

A prime example of the prior-construction canon is the U.S. Supreme Court's 1978 decision in *Lorillard v. Pons*.[5] In that case, the Court considered the question whether there is a right to a jury trial in a private suit for lost wages under the Age Discrimination in Employment Act of 1967. The Court held that there is,

---

[1] *Black's Law Dictionary* 1469 (Bryan A. Garner ed., 10th ed. 2014).

[2] *Francis v. Southern Pac. Co.*, 333 U.S. 445, 450 (1948) (emphasis added).

[3] *Armstrong v. Exceptional Child Ctr., Inc.*, 135 S.Ct. 1378, 1386 (2015). *See generally* Antonin Scalia & Bryan A. Garner, *Reading Law: The Interpretation of Legal Texts* § 54, at 322–26 (2012).

[4] *Armstrong*, 135 S.Ct. at 1386 (quoting *Bragdon v. Abbott*, 524 U.S. 624, 645 (1998)).

[5] 434 U.S. 575 (1978).

reasoning that the Act incorporated the procedures of the Fair Labor Standards Act, and that courts had long held that there is such a right in private actions brought under that older statute.[6]

But the prior-construction canon merely articulates a presumption, and that presumption can be overcome. In *United States v. Kwai Fun Wong*,[7] the Supreme Court considered whether the Federal Tort Claims Act, which provides that tort actions against the United States "shall be forever barred" unless they complied with certain time limits, allowed for equitable tolling.[8] The government argued that the statute didn't permit equitable tolling, noting that the FTCA had been enacted after the Court concluded that a different statute, the Tucker Act, with the same "shall be forever barred" language, didn't permit equitable tolling.[9] But the Court rejected this argument, explaining that under modern caselaw there is another rebuttable presumption—that time-bars in suits against the government *may* be equitably tolled. The fact that the Tucker Act's similarly worded language had been construed to prohibit equitable tolling, the Court ruled, wasn't sufficient to overcome that presumption for the FTCA.[10]

It's important to distinguish the reenactment canon—which covers a situation in which the legislature has actually *reenacted* the statute that has received a particular interpretation—from a situation in which the legislature has simply *failed to overturn* a prior interpretation of a statute. Courts generally don't "draw inferences of approval from the unexplained inaction of [the legislature]."[11] For example, in *Boys Markets v. Retail Clerks Union*,[12] the Supreme Court considered whether to overrule its holding in *Sinclair Refining v. Atkinson*.[13] That ruling interpreted the Norris–LaGuardia Act to prohibit a federal district court from enjoining

---

6   *Id.* at 580–81.
7   135 S.Ct. 1625 (2015).
8   *Id.* at 1629 (quoting 28 U.S.C. § 2401(b)).
9   *Id.* at 1634.
10 *Id.* at 1636–38.
11 *United States v. Board of Comm'rs of Sheffield*, 435 U.S. 110, 135 (1978).
12 398 U.S. 235 (1970).
13 370 U.S. 195 (1962).

a strike that breaches the union's no-strike obligation under a collective-bargaining agreement that requires arbitration of the underlying labor dispute.[14] The Court declined to infer congressional approval of *Sinclair* from Congress's failure to legislatively abrogate the Court's decision, reasoning that "[i]t is at best treacherous to find in congressional silence alone the adoption of a controlling rule of law,"[15] and so decided to reconsider the decision's correctness. The Court ultimately overruled *Sinclair*.[16]

Despite the rule that silence doesn't signal legislative approval, courts will generally not overturn an earlier interpretation of a statute in the absence of exceptional circumstances (see § 38).

Consider the application of the reenactment canon to a situation in which the legislature has amended parts of the law in question, but not the provision under consideration. Should a court infer ratification of prior constructions of that provision on the theory that the legislature took a fresh look at the law as a whole and affirmatively decided not to change the provision at issue? Or is this merely an example of legislative silence, from which no inference of approval should be drawn? The courts haven't been consistent in their approach to this question.

For example, in *Forest Grove School District v. T.A.*,[17] the Supreme Court considered the meaning of a provision in the Individuals with Disabilities Education Act. The provision had previously been interpreted to allow courts to reimburse parents for the cost of private special education under certain conditions. The Court, noting that the provision had been left unchanged in recent amendments to the Act, determined that the provision continued to allow for those reimbursements under the reenactment canon.[18]

---

14 *Boys Mkts.*, 398 U.S. at 237–38.
15 *Id.* at 241–42 (alteration in original) (quoting *Girouard v. United States*, 328 U.S. 61, 69 (1946)).
16 *Id.* at 238.
17 557 U.S. 230 (2009).
18 *Id.* at 239–40.

By contrast, in *Central Bank of Denver v. First Interstate Bank of Denver*,[19] the Court considered whether civil liability under § 10(b) of the Securities Exchange Act of 1934 extends to individuals who aid and abet violations of the Act. There, the Court declined to draw an inference of legislative approval from Congress's failure to legislatively overrule court holdings that § 10(b) covered aiding and abetting, even though Congress had amended the securities laws many times after those holdings.[20] The Court explained that "[i]t is impossible to assert with any degree of assurance that congressional failure to act represents affirmative congressional approval of the [courts'] statutory interpretation."[21] The Court also noted that while lower courts had held that § 10(b) allowed for aiding-and-abetting liability, the Supreme Court had expressly reserved the issue.[22] This suggests that when Congress fails to effectively overrule a lower-court interpretation of a statute, that's less of a sign of congressional approval than its apparent acquiescence in a Supreme Court interpretation of the same statute would be.

The tension between the reenactment canon and the rule that legislative silence isn't equivalent to legislative approval was brought into sharp relief in *Kimble v. Marvel Entertainment*.[23] In that 2015 case, the Supreme Court considered whether to overrule *Brulotte v. Thys Co.*,[24] which had interpreted a provision of the patent laws to mean that "a patent holder cannot charge royalties for the use of his invention after its patent term has expired."[25] The Court decided to adhere to *Brulotte*. In the course of its analysis, the majority noted that "Congress ha[d] spurned multiple opportunities to reverse *Brulotte*" for more than 50 years: "During that time, Congress has repeatedly amended the patent laws, including the specific provision . . . on which *Brulotte*

---

19   511 U.S. 164 (1994).
20   *Id.* at 185–86.
21   *Id.* at 186 (second alteration in original) (internal quotation marks and citation omitted).
22   *Id.*
23   *Kimble v. Marvel Entm't, LLC*, 135 S.Ct. 2401 (2015).
24   379 U.S. 29 (1964).
25   *Kimble*, 135 S.Ct. at 2405.

rested. *Brulotte* survived every such change. Indeed, Congress has rebuffed bills that would have replaced *Brulotte*'s per se rule with the same antitrust-style analysis [petitioner] now urges."[26] That history of frequent changes in patent laws—but never the *Brulotte* rule—"further supports leaving the decision in place," the majority concluded.[27]

Moreover, the Court said, Congress had many chances to overrule *Brulotte* by statute but declined to do so.[28] The Court found no "superspecial justification" to reconsider the decision, explaining that its "statutory and doctrinal underpinnings have not eroded over time" and that the decision had not "proved unworkable."[29] Interestingly, the majority made no attempt to defend the merits of the *Brulotte* rule, conceding that it had been harshly criticized as inefficient.[30] But those arguments, the Court said, were properly addressed to Congress, not the Supreme Court.

Three Justices dissented, calling *Brulotte* a "bald act of policymaking" that didn't represent an actual interpretation of the Patent Act and pointing out that the case's "reasoning has been soundly refuted."[31] The dissent criticized the majority for relying too heavily on Congress's failure to overturn *Brulotte*, calling it "at best treacherous to find in congressional silence alone the adoption of a controlling rule of law."[32] In the dissent's view, because *Brulotte* was a "judge-made rule" rather than the language of the statute, it was up to the Court, not Congress, to correct the mistake.[33]

The dissenters thought that given the difficulty of passing legislation in Congress, the Court couldn't confidently infer from

---

26   *Id.* at 2409–10 (citations omitted).
27   *Id.*
28   *Id.*
29   *Id.* at 2411.
30   *Id.* at 2406 n.3, 2412–13.
31   *Id.* at 2415 (Alito J. dissenting).
32   *Id.* at 2418 (Alito J. dissenting) (quoting *Girouard v. United States*, 328 U.S. 61, 69 (1946)).
33   *Id.* at 2417.

Congress's failure to legislatively overrule *Brulotte* that it approved of the decision.[34]

The *Kimble* decision provides guidance to all courts on the importance of the reenactment canon. It confirms the majority en banc opinion in a 2009 case[35] in which a statute had been amended seven times without overturning unanimous precedents interpreting it.[36] The six dissenters wanted to reach a new interpretation that would have created an intercircuit conflict—and wanted to do so because they thought they had found a "better" interpretation.[37]

---

34 *Id.* at 2418–19.
35 *Wheeler v. Pilgrim's Pride Corp.*, 591 F.3d 355 (5th Cir. 2009).
36 *Id.* at 361.
37 *Id.* at 371–85 (Garza J. dissenting, with five others joining).

40. Stare Decisis with Constitutions

The doctrine of stare decisis applies less rigidly in constitutional cases than it does in statutory cases because the correction of an erroneous constitutional decision by the legislature is well-nigh impossible. Yet stare decisis should and does play a significant role in constitutional adjudication.

Although the idea may seem counterintuitive, constitutional precedents are somewhat more protean and mutable than others.[1] Once a constitutional ruling has been handed down, there are only two ways to change it: the high court itself can reject the principle of stare decisis and modify or overrule its earlier ruling, or the Constitution can be amended. At the federal level, the latter process has produced only 27 amendments—or 17 if we discount the Bill of Rights, whose 10 amendments were passed immediately in response to many of the ratification conventions.

Stare decisis is flexible in constitutional cases because "correction through legislative action is practically impossible."[2] Hence stare decisis as a policy principle may be stronger or weaker in any given case depending on the policy considerations involved in its application: in constitutional cases, the value of correct reasoning may trump stability given the difficulty of making changes to a constitutional precedent, while stability may trump perfect correctness in property-rights cases given the importance of preserving settled expectations. The state high courts take the same approach when they are construing their own constitutions.[3]

---

[1] *See* Kenneth L. Karst, "Precedent," in 3 *Encyclopedia of the American Constitution* 1436, 1437 (Leonard W. Levy et al. eds., 1986) ("Supreme Court Justices themselves . . . give precedent a force that is weaker in constitutional cases than in other areas of the law.").

[2] *Payne v. Tennessee*, 501 U.S. 808, 828 (1991) (internal quotation marks omitted); *see also Alleyne v. United States*, 133 S.Ct. 2151, 2163 n.5 (2013) ("The force of stare decisis is at its nadir in cases concerning procedural rules that implicate fundamental constitutional protections.").

[3] *See, e.g.*, *Diggins v. Jackson*, 164 P.3d 647, 649 (Alaska 2007) (per curiam) ("Stare decisis is at its strongest in cases involving the interpretation of statutes. Unlike cases involving the constitution, the legislature may override an incorrect statutory interpretation. There is thus less justification in such cases for a court to overturn its own rulings.").

As Brandeis J. put it in a gloss on his famous quotation about its being more important that a legal rule be settled than that it be right: "But in cases involving the Federal Constitution, where correction through legislative action is practically impossible, this Court has often overruled its earlier decisions. The Court bows to the lessons of experience and the force of better reasoning, recognizing that the process of trial and error, so fruitful in the physical sciences, is appropriate also in the judicial function."[4]

Yet there are famous exceptions to this apparent willingness to reconsider constitutional rulings. Perhaps in the end all the Court can say is what it did in *Citizens United*: "When considering whether to reexamine a prior erroneous holding, we must balance the importance of having constitutional questions *decided* against the importance of having them *decided right*."[5] If at least five members of the Court are sufficiently convinced that the law has gone gravely wrong, then the Court will exercise its prerogative to overrule the earlier case and put things aright.

The Supreme Court has overruled its constitutional precedents infrequently, but the cases in which it has done so are among the Court's most significant decisions:

- *Erie Railroad v. Tompkins*,[6] overruling *Swift v. Tyson*;[7]
- *Brown v. Board of Education*,[8] overruling *Plessy v. Ferguson*;[9]
- *Lawrence v. Texas*,[10] overruling *Bowers v. Hardwick*;[11]

---

[4] *Burnet v. Coronado Oil & Gas Co.*, 285 U.S. 393, 406–08 (1932) (Brandeis J. dissenting) (footnotes omitted). See *Edelman v. Jordan*, 415 U.S. 651, 694 (1974) ("Since we deal with a constitutional question, we are less constrained by the principle of stare decisis than we are in other areas of the law.") (citing Brandeis J.'s *Burnet* dissent).

[5] *Citizens United v. Federal Election Comm'n*, 558 U.S. 310, 378 (2010) (Roberts C.J. concurring).

[6] 304 U.S. 64 (1938).

[7] 41 U.S. (16 Pet.) 1 (1842).

[8] 347 U.S. 483 (1954).

[9] 163 U.S. 537 (1896).

[10] 539 U.S. 558 (2003).

[11] 478 U.S. 186 (1986).

- *Citizens United v. Federal Election Commission*,[12] overruling *Austin v. Michigan Chamber of Commerce*[13] and *McConnell v. Federal Election Commission*,[14] and
- *Obergefell v. Hodges*,[15] overruling *Baker v. Nelson*.[16]

Douglas J.'s rationale for weakened stare decisis with high courts' constitutional decisions

In a 1949 speech, Douglas J. argued that stare decisis should exert less power on judges who sit on high courts when the issues are constitutional, calling the role of the doctrine in constitutional law "tenuous."[17] A judge facing a constitutional decision, Douglas said, "may have compulsions to revere past history and accept what was once written. But he remembers above all else that it is the Constitution which he swore to support and defend, not the gloss which his predecessors may have put on it."[18] Douglas pointed to 8 constitutional overrulings by the U.S. Supreme Court from 1860 to 1890 and another 21 from 1937 to March 1949.[19] Of the 1937–1949 cases, the "great majority," he said, had been decided within the preceding 20 years.[20]

---

12   558 U.S. 310 (2010).
13   494 U.S. 652 (1990).
14   540 U.S. 93 (2003).
15   135 S.Ct. 2584 (2015).
16   409 U.S. 810 (1972).
17   William O. Douglas, "Stare Decisis" (1949), in *Essays on Jurisprudence from the Columbia Law Review* 18, 19 (1963). *See also* William O. Douglas, *We the Judges* 429 (1956) ("Stare decisis has . . . little place in American constitutional law.").
18   Douglas, "Stare Decisis" at 19. *Contra* Henry Campbell Black, *Handbook of American Constitutional Law* § 69, at 90 (4th ed. 1927) (asserting as blackletter, but without supporting text, that "stare decisis applies with special force to the construction of constitutions, and an interpretation once deliberately put upon the provisions of such an instrument should not be departed from without grave reasons"). *But see* Frank H. Easterbrook, *Stability and Reliability in Judicial Decisions*, 73 Cornell L. Rev. 422, 427–31 (1988) (offering an interesting rejoinder to Douglas J.'s view).
19   Douglas, "Stare Decisis" at 22–23, 26; *cf.* Louis Blom-Cooper, "1966 and All That: The Story of the Practice Statement," in *The Judicial House of Lords 1876–2009* 128, 137 (Louis Blom-Cooper et al. eds., 2009) (noting that in the first 40 years after the House of Lords declared (in 1966) that it could overrule its own previous decisions, it overtly overruled 21 precedents).
20   Douglas, "Stare Decisis" at 26.

Cure through textual amendment

The only remedy for an erroneous constitutional decision within the authority of the political branches is a constitutional amendment, and it is an all-but-Sisyphean task to propose and ratify a federal constitutional amendment. Hence a high-court judge who determines that an earlier view on the interpretation of a particular provision of a constitution was in error may well confess the error and adopt a different view in a later case—despite the doctrine of stare decisis. Accompanied by many such judicial mea culpas are the memorable (and oft-quoted) words of Frankfurter J.: "Wisdom too often never comes, and so one ought not to reject it merely because it comes late."[21]

Is there a point at which a precedent has gathered so much weight—or age—that it's unlikely to be scuttled? One study in the late 1950s found that since its first term the Supreme Court had overruled only three decisions that were over 95 years old.[22] A 1995 survey found in reviewing 154 of the Supreme Court's overruled decisions that the most frequently overruled cases were no more than ten years old (26.6%).[23] Those from 11 to 20 years old made up 23.4% of the overruled cases, whereas just 6.4% of them were over 90 years old.[24] Finally, another study found that precedents that are later overruled last an average of 29.11 years with a median of 20 years, and that 51% of overrulings have occurred within 20 years.[25]

---

21 E.g., *Ring v. Arizona*, 536 U.S. 584, 614 (2002) (Breyer J. concurring in the judgment) (quoting *Henslee v. Union Planters Nat'l Bank & Trust Co.*, 335 U.S. 595, 600 (1949) (Frankfurter J. dissenting) (agreeing with the Court's holding that the Eighth Amendment doesn't permit a judge to impose a death sentence and stating that his earlier contrary view was incorrect)); *see also Boys Mkts., Inc. v. Retail Clerks Union, Local 770*, 398 U.S. 235, 255 (1970) (Stewart J. concurring) (using the same quote to explain his change of heart in a statutory case); *Self v. Bennett*, 474 So. 2d 673, 679 (Ala. 1985) (Embry J. dissenting) (same).

22 S. Sidney Ulmer, *An Empirical Analysis of Selected Aspects of Lawmaking of the United States Supreme Court*, 8 J. Pub. L. 414, 424 (1959).

23 Saul Brenner & Harold J. Spaeth, *Stare Indecisis: The Alteration of Precedent on the Supreme Court, 1946–1992* 29 (1995).

24 *Id.*

25 Michael H. LeRoy, *Death of a Precedent: Should Justices Rethink Their Consensus Norms?*, 43 Hofstra L. Rev. 377, 395 (2014).

For example, in *Garcia v. San Antonio Metropolitan Transit Authority*,[26] the Supreme Court overruled its nine-year-old decision in *National League of Cities v. Usery*[27] that "the Commerce Clause does not empower Congress to enforce the minimum-wage and overtime provisions of the Fair Labor Standards Act . . . against the States 'in areas of traditional governmental functions.'"[28] The Court explained that the *National League of Cities* rule, which had required "a judicial appraisal of whether a particular governmental function is 'integral' or 'traditional,'" had proved "unsound in principle and unworkable in practice."[29]

As important as the landmark decisions overruling constitutional precedent have been, it can be nearly as startling to see the Court later affirm, or at least decline to dismantle, a recent major constitutional decision. The Supreme Court has done this in several ways. There are occasions when the Court makes clear that its recent game-changing constitutional precedent is here to stay, as in the strong endorsement of *Citizens United* that the Court provided in *McCutcheon v. Federal Election Commission*.[30] The same could be said of the Court's one-two punch in *District of Columbia v. Heller*[31] and *McDonald v. City of Chicago*.[32] But in the aftermath of *Brown*, the Court took a quieter tack, expanding the reach of desegregation to several areas of civic life, such as public beaches[33] and golf courses,[34] using perfunctory and short per curiam opinions.

The Court nevertheless regards the overruling of a constitutional decision as a highly serious matter, and for good reason. Along with the responsibility to "say what the law is"—a

---

26   469 U.S. 528 (1985).
27   426 U.S. 833 (1976).
28   *Garcia*, 469 U.S. at 530 (quoting *National League of Cities*, 426 U.S. at 852).
29   *Id.* at 546–47.
30   134 S.Ct. 1434 (2014).
31   554 U.S. 570 (2008).
32   561 U.S. 742 (2010).
33   *Mayor & City Council of Baltimore v. Dawson*, 350 U.S. 877 (1955) (per curiam).
34   *Holmes v. City of Atlanta*, 350 U.S. 879 (1955) (per curiam).

prerogative the Court has claimed since *Marbury v. Madison*[35]—comes the duty to render stable decisions that respect the constitutional text and provide the foundation on which the other two branches of the federal government, the states, and the people can build the legal system. It is sometimes not clear, however, how best to achieve that goal.

Two strains of thought about age

One school of thought holds that the older a decision is, the less willing the Court should be to overrule it (see § 18). This approach emphasizes the reliance interests that build up around accepted constitutional doctrine, as well as the stability that stare decisis bestows. More recent decisions can be overruled more readily, as part of the process of fine-tuning the Court's understanding of an area of law.

Another school of thought takes the opposite approach: the oldest decisions should be subject to more searching reconsideration because facts change, times change, and the country should not be saddled with rules of law whose relevance disappeared decades if not centuries ago. More recent decisions, this group argues, deserve a chance to be left alone to see whether they are correct.

The Barnette *decision*

One of the most famous and dramatic judicial about-faces occurred in 1943 in *West Virginia State Board of Education v. Barnette*,[36] in which the U.S. Supreme Court held that the First Amendment forbids a public school from requiring students to salute the flag. Only three years before *Barnette*, the Court had reached the opposite conclusion in an 8–1 decision in *Minersville School District v. Gobitis*.[37] Two years after *Gobitis*, in *Jones v. City*

---

35   5 U.S. (1 Cranch) 137 (1803).
36   319 U.S. 624 (1943). *See* Jeffrey S. Sutton, *Barnette, Frankfurter, and Judicial Review*, 96 Marq. L. Rev. 133, 141 (2012); G.L. Peterson et al., *Recollections of* West Virginia State Board of Education v. Barnette, 81 St. John's L. Rev. 755, 763–64 (2007).
37   310 U.S. 586 (1940).

of Opelika,³⁸ three Justices who had voted with the *Gobitis* majority in that case stated that their views had changed, explaining that "our democratic form of government functioning under the historic Bill of Rights has a high responsibility to accommodate itself to the religious views of minorities however unpopular and unorthodox those views may be."³⁹ Finally, in *Barnette*, Jackson J., a new appointee, joined by fellow new appointee Rutledge J., the three dissenters in *Jones*, and Stone C.J., the lone dissenter in *Gobitis*, overruled *Gobitis*, concluding with one of the more memorable passages in all of American constitutional law:

> If there is any fixed star in our constitutional constellation, it is that no official, high or petty, can prescribe what shall be orthodox in politics, nationalism, religion, or other matters of opinion or force citizens to confess by word or act their faith therein. If there are any circumstances which permit an exception, they do not now occur to us.⁴⁰

Black and Douglas JJ. wrote a separate opinion to provide "a brief statement of reasons for [their] change in view."⁴¹ They reasoned that while the *Gobitis* decision rested on the "sound" principle that the Constitution should not be "a rigid bar against state regulation of conduct thought inimical to the public welfare," the Court had erred in applying that principle in *Gobitis* itself:⁴² "Neither our domestic tranquillity in peace nor our martial effort in war depend on compelling little children to participate in a ceremony which ends in nothing for them but a fear of spiritual condemnation. If . . . their fears are groundless, time and reason are the proper antidotes for their errors."⁴³ Instead, Black and Douglas saw a darker intent behind the rule: "The ceremonial, when enforced against conscientious objectors, more likely to defeat than to serve its high purpose, is a handy implement for disguised religious

---

38   316 U.S. 584 (1942), *vacated*, 319 U.S. 103 (1943) (per curiam).
39   *Id.* at 624 (Black, Douglas & Murphy JJ. dissenting).
40   *Barnette*, 319 U.S. at 642.
41   *Id.* at 643 (Black & Douglas JJ. concurring).
42   *Id.* at 644.
43   *Id.*

persecution. As such, it is inconsistent with our Constitution's plan and purpose."[44]

While rare, such instances of judges' changing their minds on momentous constitutional questions are by no means unheard of. Brennan J. changed his views on the constitutionality of legislative prayer,[45] and Thomas J. changed his mind concerning whether the Sixth Amendment allows a judge to find the fact of a prior conviction in order to enhance a defendant's sentence.[46] Blackmun J. memorably decided, late in his tenure, that the Court's efforts to develop procedural and substantive rules that would allow the death penalty to be constitutionally administered—efforts that he had joined—had failed.[47] Blackmun J. declared his belief that the punishment couldn't be administered in accordance with the Constitution, stating that "[f]rom this day forward, I no longer shall tinker with the machinery of death."[48] More recently, Ginsburg J. admitted overlooking relevant precedent concerning the First Amendment's Free Exercise Clause in joining an earlier opinion, but recalled Jackson J.'s "sage comment: 'I see no reason why I should be consciously wrong today because I was unconsciously wrong yesterday.'"[49]

---

44 *Id.*

45 See *Marsh v. Chambers*, 463 U.S. 783, 795–96 & n.2 (1983) (Brennan J. dissenting) (explaining that "after much reflection," he had determined that he was wrong in suggesting in a previous opinion that legislative prayer is permissible under the First Amendment).

46 See *Apprendi v. New Jersey*, 530 U.S. 466, 520–21 & n.10 (2000) (Thomas J. concurring) (stating that his decision to vote with the majority in *Almendarez-Torres v. United States*, which held that the fact of a prior conviction isn't an element of an offense that need be proved to a jury beyond a reasonable doubt, was erroneous).

47 *Callins v. Collins*, 510 U.S. 1141, 1145–46 & n.2 (1994) (Blackmun J. dissenting from denial of certiorari).

48 *Id.* at 1145; *see also Victor v. Nebraska*, 511 U.S. 1, 38 (1994) (Blackmun J. concurring in part and dissenting in part) (adhering to this view).

49 *Burwell v. Hobby Lobby Stores, Inc.*, 134 S.Ct. 2751, 2793 n.11 (2014) (Ginsburg J. dissenting) (quoting *Massachusetts v. United States*, 333 U.S. 611, 639–40 (1948) (Jackson J. dissenting)).

Factors at play in reconsidering constitutional precedents

Perhaps the most famous recent example of the application of stare decisis in constitutional interpretation is the Supreme Court's 1992 plurality decision in *Planned Parenthood of Southeastern Pennsylvania v. Casey*.[50] There, the Court addressed the continuing validity of the "essential holding" of *Roe v. Wade*[51] that the Fourteenth Amendment to the United States Constitution prohibits the state from unduly interfering with a woman's right to choose to have an abortion before viability.[52] In a discussion of stare decisis principles, the Court explained that its determination whether to overrule a prior decision "is customarily informed by a series of prudential and pragmatic considerations designed to test the consistency of overruling [the] decision with the ideal rule of law, and to gauge the respective costs of reaffirming and overruling [the decision]."[53] The Court cited four examples of these considerations: (1) whether the rule has proved to be "intolerable simply in defying practical workability," (2) "whether the rule is subject to a kind of reliance that would lend a special hardship to the consequences of overruling and add inequity to the cost of repudiation," (3) "whether related principles of law have so far developed as to have left the old rule no more than a remnant of abandoned doctrine," and (4) "whether facts have so changed, or come to be seen so differently, as to have robbed the old rule of significant application or justification."[54]

Applying these considerations to *Roe*, the Court determined that the decision met all these criteria and deserved adherence:

> While [*Roe*] has engendered disapproval, it has not been unworkable. An entire generation has come of age free to assume *Roe*'s concept of liberty in defining the capacity of women to act in society, and to make reproductive decisions; no erosion of principle going to liberty or personal autonomy has left *Roe*'s central holding a doctrinal remnant; *Roe* portends no

---

50   505 U.S. 833, 846 (1992) (plurality opinion).
51   410 U.S. 113 (1973).
52   *Casey*, 505 U.S. at 846, 878.
53   *Id.* at 854.
54   *Id.* at 854–55.

developments at odds with other precedent for the analysis of personal liberty; and no changes of fact have rendered viability more or less appropriate as the point at which the balance of interests tips.[55]

The Court also emphasized that its legitimacy as the ultimate arbiter of the meaning of the Constitution and "lesser sources of legal principle" would be undermined by the Court's being too willing to overturn precedents, like *Roe*, concerning "intensely divisive controvers[ies]."[56] This loss of legitimacy would result from the inevitable perception that the later decision was "a surrender to political pressure."[57]

The doctrine of stare decisis doesn't compel inflexible adherence anyway, but that is especially true in the realm of constitutional interpretation.[58] Cases involving constitutional interpretation in which the Court hasn't adhered to stare decisis are discussed in § 40.

The U.S. Supreme Court's decision in *Dickerson v. United States*,[59] which reaffirmed the Court's 1966 decision in *Miranda v. Arizona*[60] on stare decisis grounds, is also instructive. *Miranda* "held that certain warnings must be given before a suspect's statement made during custodial interrogation could be admitted in evidence."[61] After *Miranda* was decided, Congress enacted a statute providing that confessions are admissible in evidence as long as they are voluntarily given, with voluntariness to be assessed based on the totality of the circumstances.[62] The statute thus purported to overrule *Miranda*.

The Supreme Court in *Dickerson* first determined that *Miranda* was a constitutional decision, rather than an announcement of a

---

55   *Id.* at 860–61; *but cf. id.* at 873 (rejecting *Roe*'s "rigid trimester framework," which the Court did "not consider to be part of the essential holding of *Roe*").
56   *Id.* at 865–66.
57   *Id.* at 867.
58   *Id.* at 854 (internal quotation marks and citation omitted).
59   530 U.S. 428 (2000).
60   384 U.S. 436 (1966).
61   *Dickerson*, 530 U.S. at 431–32.
62   *See* 18 U.S.C. 3501.

"prophylactic" procedure that wasn't itself constitutionally mandated.[63] Hence the Court was forced to choose between overruling *Miranda* and striking down the congressional statute as unconstitutional.

The Court declined to rethink *Miranda*, stating that "[w]hether or not we would agree with *Miranda*'s reasoning and its resulting rule, were we addressing the issue in the first instance, the principles of stare decisis weigh heavily against overruling it now."[64] In fact, the author of the *Dickerson* opinion, Rehnquist J., had been highly critical of the *Miranda* decision in the past and had taken steps to limit its reach.[65] But he believed that the holding itself deserved adherence: the *Miranda* warnings, explained the Court, had "become embedded in routine police practice to the point where [they] ha[d] become part of our national culture."[66] And cases refining *Miranda*, far from undermining the case's "doctrinal underpinnings," had in fact "reduced the impact of the *Miranda* rule on legitimate law enforcement while reaffirming the decision's core ruling that unwarned statements may not be used as evidence in the prosecution's case in chief."[67] Thus, in the majority's view, all three of the considerations motivating the doctrine of stare decisis weighed in favor of retaining the *Miranda* rule.[68]

The Court wasn't unanimous in its view that *Miranda* retained vitality. In dissent, Scalia J. condemned the majority's analysis of post-*Miranda* doctrinal developments, opining that more recent caselaw had "stripp[ed] [*Miranda*'s] holding of its only constitutionally legitimate support."[69]

---

63 *Dickerson*, 530 U.S. at 438.
64 *Id.* at 443.
65 *See generally, e.g., New York v. Quarles*, 467 U.S. 649 (1984).
66 *Dickerson*, 530 U.S. at 443.
67 *Id.* at 443–44.
68 *See also, e.g., United States v. Maine*, 420 U.S. 515, 524–27 (1975) (reaffirming earlier holdings that "paramount rights to the offshore seabed inhere in the Federal Government as an incident of national sovereignty" because Congress had passed legislation based on that premise and "a great deal of public and private business ha[d] been transacted in accordance with those decisions").
69 *Dickerson*, 530 U.S. at 461–62 (Scalia J. dissenting).

Gideon v. Wainwright[70] illustrates an instance in which stare decisis considerations didn't favor retaining an old constitutional rule.[71] There, the Supreme Court considered whether to overrule its holding in *Betts v. Brady*[72] that the Fourteenth Amendment doesn't categorically require the appointment of counsel to indigent criminal defendants in state court. The Court determined that *Betts* should be overruled, concluding that the case was in fact inconsistent with the Court's earlier precedents regarding the constitutional right to counsel and relying on the "obvious truth" that "in our adversary system of criminal justice, any person haled into court, who is too poor to hire a lawyer, cannot be assured a fair trial unless counsel is provided for him."[73] Hence in the Court's view, retaining the *Betts* rule would not have maintained continuity of the law or ensured the integrity of the judiciary—quite the contrary, in fact. The Court didn't explicitly discuss reliance interests, but it is fair to assume that it thought little reliance had been placed on a 19-year-old decision that was, in the Court's view, out of step with previous constitutional doctrine.

In a concurring opinion, Harlan J. disputed the Court's contention that *Betts* constituted an "abrupt break" with precedent.[74] He thought that the law had gradually evolved to an understanding that "the mere existence of a serious criminal charge constitute[s] in itself special circumstances requiring the services of counsel at trial," meaning that the rule of *Betts* was "no longer a reality."[75] So Harlan J. also thought that overruling *Betts* would promote consistency in the law, although for slightly different reasons than did the majority.

Similar considerations prompted the Supreme Court to overrule its holding in a five-year-old decision, *Pennsylvania v. Union*

---

70   372 U.S. 335 (1963).
71   *See also, e.g., Erie R.R. v. Tompkins*, 304 U.S. 64 (1938) (holding that there is no general federal common law and overruling *Swift v. Tyson*, 41 U.S. (16 Pet.) 1 (1842)).
72   316 U.S. 455 (1942).
73   *Gideon*, 372 U.S. at 344.
74   *Id.* at 349 (Harlan J. concurring).
75   *Id.* at 351.

Gas Co.,[76] that Congress can abrogate states' sovereign immunity through its commerce power. In *Seminole Tribe of Florida v. Florida*,[77] the Court called *Union Gas* "a solitary departure from established law."[78] It was a plurality opinion, meaning that no "expressed rationale [was] agreed upon by a majority of the Court" (indeed, "a majority of the Court expressly disagreed with the rationale of the plurality,"[79] rendering it a "questionable precedential value"[80]). Further, the *Seminole Tribe* Court said, the decision had "created confusion among the lower courts that ha[d] sought to understand and apply the deeply fractured decision."[81] Finally, the *Union Gas* plurality's rationale "deviated sharply from [the Court's] established federalism jurisprudence and essentially eviscerated [its] decision in" *Hans v. Louisiana*,[82] which had held that states enjoy sovereign immunity in certain cases beyond those described in the text of the Eleventh Amendment.[83] As the Court concluded, "none of the policies underlying stare decisis require our continuing adherence" to *Union Gas*.[84] Since it involved a constitutional question, the only alternative to overturning was a constitutional amendment, the Court noted. "Finally, both the result in *Union Gas* and the plurality's rationale depart from our established understanding of the Eleventh Amendment and undermine the accepted function of Article III. . . . *Union Gas* was wrongly decided and . . . is . . . overruled."[85]

For an interesting example of an argument in which changes in factual circumstances have rendered an old constitutional precedent obsolete, consider Kennedy J.'s 2015 concurring opinion

---

76   491 U.S. 1 (1989).
77   517 U.S. 44 (1996).
78   *Id.* at 66.
79   *Id.* at 63.
80   *Id.* at 66.
81   *Id.*
82   134 U.S. 1 (1890).
83   *Seminole Tribe*, 517 U.S. at 63–64.
84   *Id.* at 66.
85   *Id.* (citations omitted).

in *Direct Marketing Association v. Brohl*.[86] Kennedy J. advocated overruling the Court's 1967 decision in *National Bellas Hess v. Department of Revenue of Illinois*,[87] which held that under the Commerce Clause, states cannot require a business to collect use taxes if the business doesn't have a physical location in the state. The reasoning was that the business doesn't have a sufficient nexus with the state to justify imposition of the tax-collecting duty. In *Brohl*, Kennedy J. explained that "in view of the dramatic technological and social changes that ha[ve] taken place in our increasingly interconnected economy," "[t]here is a powerful case to be made that a retailer doing extensive business within a State has a sufficiently 'substantial nexus' to justify imposing some minor tax-collection duty, even if that business is done through mail or the Internet."[88]

Constitutional reconsideration in intermediate courts

Intermediate appellate courts won't generally overrule their earlier constitutional interpretations in the absence of intervening controlling authority. But in rare cases, intervening persuasive authority and other legal developments may convince a court that the former panel would change its mind in light of these developments.[89] For example, in a 1992 case[90] the First Circuit held that the Dormant Commerce Clause applies to Puerto Rico, abrogating its earlier contrary holding that dated from 1947.[91] The court explained that in light of intervening persuasive authority applying the Dormant Commerce Clause to territorial governments (including that of Puerto Rico), as well as the increased autonomy

---

86 135 S.Ct. 1124 (2015).
87 386 U.S. 753 (1967), *overruled by Quill Corp. v. North Dakota*, 504 U.S. 298 (1992).
88 *Brohl*, 135 S.Ct. at 1135 (Kennedy J. concurring).
89 *See United States v. Rodriguez-Pacheco*, 475 F.3d 434, 442 (1st Cir. 2007) (quoting *Williams v. Ashland Eng'g Co.*, 45 F.3d 588, 592 (1st Cir. 1995)).
90 *Trailer Marine Transp. Corp. v. Rivera Vazquez*, 977 F.2d 1 (1st Cir. 1992).
91 *Buscaglia v. Ballester*, 162 F.2d 805 (1st Cir. 1947).

of Puerto Rico, the reasoning in the earlier case had been "sapped" and was no longer controlling.[92]

As a matter of practice, courts generally avoid readjudicating the constitutionality of statutes. This has long been the usual practice both in lower courts[93] and in high courts.[94] For example, in a 2014 case[95] a federal appellate court declined to reconsider an earlier decision upholding a statute[96] outlawing the possession of a firearm by any person who has been convicted of a "misdemeanor crime of domestic violence" against a Second Amendment challenge.[97] The court explained that the defendant's argument that the statute was an unconstitutional abridgment of his right to bear arms was "squarely foreclosed" by circuit precedent.[98]

Four exceptional circumstances

Four exceptions to the general rule about constitutional reliance merit mention.

First, the rejection of a facial challenge to the constitutionality of a statute doesn't require the later rejection of an as-applied challenge.[99] The reasons for this exception stem from the distinction between facial challenges and as-applied challenges: the usual rule is that the former require the litigant to show that the statute is invalid in all or almost all applications, whereas the latter require

---

92 *Trailer Marine Transp.*, 977 F.2d at 9.
93 *See, e.g., Gregory Constr. Co. v. Blanchard*, No. 88-1938, 1989 WL 78201, at *4 (6th Cir. 17 July 1989) (holding that earlier panel decision that a statute was unconstitutional precluded readjudication of the question); *United States v. Hawes*, 529 F.2d 472, 476–77 (5th Cir. 1976) (holding that earlier panel decision that a statute was constitutional precluded readjudication of the question).
94 *See, e.g., Verba v. Ghaphery*, 552 S.E.2d 406, 410 (W. Va. 2001) (per curiam) (rejecting, on stare decisis grounds, constitutional challenge to statutory cap on noneconomic damages recoverable in medical malpractice actions); *Multnomah Cnty. v. Sliker*, 10 Or. 65, 66 (1881) (holding that "unless error is plainly shown to exist," earlier decision on the constitutionality of a statute is binding under the doctrine of stare decisis).
95 *United States v. Carter*, 752 F.3d 8 (1st Cir. 2014) (en banc).
96 18 U.S.C. § 922(g)(9).
97 *Carter*, 752 F.3d at 13 (citing *United States v. Booker*, 644 F.3d 12, 25–26 (1st Cir. 2011)).
98 *Id.*; accord *United States v. Voisine*, 778 F.3d 176, 186 (1st Cir. 2015).
99 *See, e.g., Ward v. Utah*, 398 F.3d 1239, 1246 n.2 (10th Cir. 2005).

only that the litigant show that the statute is invalid in his or her particular case.[100] For similar reasons, a decision regarding a statute's constitutionality as applied to one litigant isn't necessarily binding with respect to a decision on the statute's constitutionality as applied to a different litigant.[101]

Second, a court may reconsider horizontal precedent on the constitutionality of a statute when it is convinced that its earlier decision rested on a dated or incorrect view of the facts or law and that the issue is important enough that the interest in resolving the question correctly outweighs the concerns that generally support the doctrine of stare decisis. In *West Coast Hotel Co. v. Parrish*,[102] one example of this exception, the Supreme Court considered the constitutional validity of a Washington minimum-wage law.[103] The Court had previously held in *Adkins v. Children's Hospital*[104] that a similar law was invalid under the Fifth Amendment's Due Process Clause. But it determined that a reexamination of *Adkins* was "not only appropriate, but . . . imperative," given "[t]he importance of the question, in which many states having similar laws are concerned, the close division by which the decision in the *Adkins* Case was reached, and the economic conditions which have supervened."[105] The Court ultimately overruled *Adkins* and upheld the validity of the Washington law, signaling the end of the oft-criticized *Lochner*[106] era of jurisprudence.

Third, stare decisis considerations may have less weight when a litigant argues that a statute is unconstitutionally vague. Earlier holdings that the statute was constitutional do not preclude a later finding of invalidity on vagueness grounds. That's because "[u]nlike other judicial mistakes that need correction, the error of having rejected a vagueness challenge manifests itself precisely

---

100 See *Gonzales v. Carhart*, 550 U.S. 124, 168 (2007).
101 See, e.g., *Kansas City Southern Ry. v. Anderson*, 233 U.S. 325, 329–30 (1914); *Helvering v. Proctor*, 140 F.2d 87, 91 (2d Cir. 1944) (Frank J. dissenting).
102 300 U.S. 379 (1937).
103 *Id.* at 386.
104 261 U.S. 525 (1923).
105 *Parrish*, 300 U.S. at 390.
106 *Lochner v. New York*, 198 U.S. 45 (1905).

in subsequent judicial decisions: the inability of later opinions to impart the predictability that the earlier opinion forecast."[107] So if a statute proves incapable of judicial administration, stare decisis concerns must yield.[108]

For example, in *Johnson v. United States*,[109] the Supreme Court held that the residual clause of the Armed Career Criminal Act was unconstitutionally vague in violation of the Due Process Clause.[110] The Court explained that its earlier cases to the contrary didn't deserve adherence because the clause had proved itself "a judicial morass that defies systemic solution."[111] The Court also noted that those earlier cases "opined about vagueness without full briefing or argument on that issue—a circumstance that le[ft it] 'less constrained to follow precedent.'"[112] In dissent, Alito J. criticized the majority for "brushing aside stare decisis," arguing that there was no "good reason[] for overruling" the earlier cases.[113]

Finally, a lower court may reconsider an earlier decision on the constitutionality of a statute based on intervening developments in a higher court's caselaw. For example, in a 2004 case,[114] the First Circuit considered a constitutional challenge to a Maine statute providing that sectarian schools weren't eligible for receipt of public funds. The court had previously upheld the statute's constitutionality, and the district court had dismissed the case on the basis of that precedent.[115] The appellate court determined that it wasn't bound by the prior panel opinion because recent Supreme Court cases had "provide[d] more focused direction" in the area of the law in question, and so the court "reject[ed] a rote application

---

107 *Johnson v. United States*, 135 S.Ct. 2551 (2015).
108 *See id.*; *see also Payne v. Tennessee*, 501 U.S. 808, 827 (1991) (noting that the Court need not follow precedent "when governing decisions are unworkable").
109 135 S.Ct. at 2551.
110 *Id.* at 2563.
111 *Id.* at 2562 (internal quotation marks and citation omitted).
112 *Id.* at 2562–63 (quoting *Hohn v. United States*, 524 U.S. 236, 251 (1998)).
113 *Id.* at 2573, 2576 (Alito J. dissenting).
114 *Eulitt ex rel. Eulitt v. Maine Dep't of Educ.*, 386 F.3d 344 (1st Cir. 2004).
115 *Id.* at 347 (citing *Strout v. Albanese*, 178 F.3d 57 (1st Cir. 1999)).

of stare decisis" and "undert[ook] a fresh analysis."[116] In the end, however, the court ultimately upheld the statute's constitutionality.

---

116 *Id.* at 350.

41. Practice and Procedure

Stare decisis applies less strongly to decisions on matters of practice and procedure than to those involving property and contract rights.

While the doctrine of stare decisis is at its zenith when the overturning of a precedent would upset important settled expectations—especially those relating to property and contract rights (see § 51)[1]—it is at its nadir in cases involving procedural and evidentiary rules.[2] After all, procedural rules don't usually dictate the parties' real-world actions or upset their expectations. Before a case arises, litigants-to-be don't generally consider how a court's later procedural rule might affect its decision about the case. As the U.S. Supreme Court has put it: "Revisiting precedent is particularly appropriate where . . . a departure would not upset expectations, the precedent consists of a judge-made rule that was recently adopted to improve the operation of the courts, and experience has pointed up the precedent's shortcomings."[3]

---

[1] *See, e.g., Michigan v. Bay Mills Indian Cmty.*, 134 S.Ct. 2024, 2036 (2014) (reaffirming the Court's precedent holding that Congress can decide how and whether to grant Indian tribes immunity from suit relating to gaming activity on Indian land and noting that "tribes across the country, as well as entities and individuals doing business with them, have for many years relied on [the precedent] (along with its forebears and progeny), negotiating their contracts and structuring their transactions against a backdrop of tribal immunity," and that "in . . . cases involving contract and property rights, concerns of stare decisis are . . . 'at their acme'") (citations omitted); *Minnesota Mining Co. v. National Mining Co.*, 70 U.S. (3 Wall.) 332, 334 (1865) ("Where questions arise which affect titles to land it is of great importance to the public that when they are once decided they should no longer be considered open. Such decisions become rules of property, and many titles may be injuriously affected by their change. Legislatures may alter or change their laws, without injury, as they affect the future only; but where courts vacillate and overrule their own decisions on the construction of statutes affecting the title to real property, their decisions are retrospective and may affect titles purchased on the faith of their stability. Doubtful questions on subjects of this nature, when once decided, should be considered no longer doubtful or subject to change.").

[2] *Payne v. Tennessee*, 501 U.S. 808, 828 (1991) (holding that the Eighth Amendment doesn't bar a state prosecutor's introduction into evidence of victim-impact statements to a jury during sentencing, and overruling two previous decisions of the Court to the contrary).

[3] *Pearson v. Callahan*, 555 U.S. 223, 233 (2009).

The case in which the Court made that statement, *Pearson v. Callahan*,[4] illustrates how and why a procedural rule is more apt to be abandoned than one whose abandonment would upset settled expectations. Eight years earlier, in *Saucier v. Katz*,[5] the Court had used a two-step analysis to determine whether a police officer had qualified immunity: by first considering whether the officer's conduct violated a constitutional right and only then by considering whether the right was a clearly established one. This procedure drew harsh criticism because it forced the lower courts to engage in an abstract analysis about whether a constitutional right even existed in cases that could be easily dismissed because any such theoretical right wasn't in fact clearly established. As the Supreme Court dryly put it, the lower courts had had "much firsthand experience bearing on [*Saucier*'s] advantages and disadvantages."[6] The Court noted that because the *Saucier* precedent was merely procedural, its overturning "would not upset settled expectations on anyone's part"—as overturning property or contract precedent certainly would.[7] Nor did any constitutional or statutory precedent require the decision to have been "badly reasoned" or "unworkable" to overturn it.[8] Instead, the Court merely found it "sufficient that we now have a considerable body of new experience to consider regarding the consequences of requiring adherence to this inflexible procedure" and determined that *Saucier*'s rule "should not be retained."[9]

Stare decisis doesn't apply in the same way to all precedents about procedural matters: the ones that create reliance interests

---

4   *Id.*
5   533 U.S. 194, 201 (2001).
6   *Pearson*, 555 U.S. at 231.
7   *Id.* at 233.
8   *Id.* at 234.
9   *Id.*; *see also Hohn v. United States*, 524 U.S. 236, 251–52 (1998) (overruling 53-year-old precedent that had held that the Court lacked statutory certiorari jurisdiction to review refusals to issue certificates of probable cause: "The role of stare decisis, furthermore, is 'somewhat reduced . . . in the case of a procedural rule . . . which does not serve as a guide to lawful behavior.' . . . Here we have a rule of procedure that does not alter primary conduct.") (quoting *United States v. Gaudin*, 515 U.S. 506, 521 (1995)).

are more likely to be respected under stare decisis than those that don't. It is more likely, for example, that litigants will come to rely on a court's precedential interpretation of a statute of limitations[10] than that they will behave so as to satisfy a precedent's standing requirements.[11] So stare decisis tends to preserve the former decisions more rigidly than the latter.

---

10   *See, e.g., Morris v. Stifel, Nicolaus & Co.*, 600 F.2d 139, 145 (8th Cir. 1979) (noting "the importance of stare decisis to the extent that what statute of limitations applies should be relatively fixed and ascertainable. Parties rely on the limitations period.").

11   *See, e.g., Hein v. Freedom from Religion Found., Inc.*, 551 U.S. 587, 637 (2007) (Scalia J. concurring in the judgment) ("[O]ne does not arrange his affairs with an eye to standing."); *Lansing Sch. Educ. Ass'n v. Lansing Bd. of Educ.*, 792 N.W.2d 686, 698 (Mich. 2010) (stating in overruling a questioned standing doctrine, "[I]t seems unlikely that potential future defendants, including the government, have been violating laws on the basis of the assumption it could not be challenged because no party would have standing under [a questioned precedent] to do so. To the extent that such interests exist, they are not the type of reliance interests that this Court seeks to protect.").

42. Res Judicata Distinguished from Stare Decisis

A judgment is binding and conclusive as res judicata only on the parties to the particular lawsuit and those in privity with them: it creates estoppel for disputed matters of fact and law. By contrast, stare decisis is conclusive on questions of law, not of fact, and a judicial precedent is applied to a similar state of facts later arising, no matter who the parties are.

Res judicata and stare decisis are similar in some ways. Under each doctrine, a later court will decline to reexamine an issue that has already been adjudicated. But the doctrines aren't coterminous: they differ in their coverage of issues, litigants, and jurisdictions.

At its highest level of generalization, res judicata takes in two concepts that modern courts call *claim preclusion* and *issue preclusion*.[1] Claim preclusion prevents a litigant from bringing a claim if a court that had jurisdiction has already rendered a final judgment on the merits of that claim in a previous action involving the same litigants or their privies.[2] Issue preclusion prevents the same parties from relitigating issues of ultimate fact that they had already litigated in earlier suits.[3] A nonparty to the first action can use issue preclusion offensively against the party who lost the issue decided in the first case, within certain limits.[4] Stare decisis may determine which of these two concepts of res judicata applies in a particular jurisdiction.

Although the term *res judicata* is sometimes used to refer only to claim preclusion, it is also often used to refer to preclusion doctrine generally, a convention that this section will

---

[1] *Migra v. Warren City Sch. Dist. Bd. of Educ.*, 465 U.S. 75, 77 n.1 (1984) (stating that res judicata consists "of two preclusion concepts: 'issue preclusion' and 'claim preclusion'").

[2] *In re International Nutronics, Inc.*, 28 F.3d 965, 969 (9th Cir. 1994).

[3] *Schiro v. Farley*, 510 U.S. 222, 232 (1994) (noting that issue preclusion "means simply that when an issue of ultimate fact has once been determined by a valid and final judgment, that issue cannot again be litigated between the same parties in any future lawsuit") (internal quotation marks omitted).

[4] *Allen v. McCurry*, 449 U.S. 90, 94–95 (1980); *Parklane Hosiery Co. v. Shore*, 439 U.S. 322, 329–31 (1979) (setting forth requirements for and limitations on the doctrine of nonmutual offensive issue preclusion).

follow. Stare decisis and issue preclusion are similar in that both doctrines change the weight accorded to particular findings or statements in the earlier opinion depending on how extensively they were considered and litigated. For a determination to have issue-preclusive effect, the issue decided in the earlier case must have been extensively and well litigated in the first action.[5]

The doctrine of res judicata applies to disputed facts as well as to disputed mixed questions of fact and law, such as whether the defendant drove the car negligently or whether the plaintiff received adequate notice of the rejection of a claim so as to start the running of the statute of limitations. By contrast, stare decisis applies only to questions of law.[6] In other words, stare decisis dictates which legal principle should apply, while res judicata involves a judgment that results from a particular application of a legal principle to particular facts.[7]

Stare decisis also differs from res judicata in who is bound. Res judicata binds only the litigants involved and others in privity with them, while stare decisis binds all litigants involved in any relevant lawsuit within the given jurisdiction.[8] As the First

---

5   See *Synanon Church v. United States*, 820 F.2d 421, 426–27 (D.C. Cir. 1987).

6   *State ex rel. Dep't of Nat. Res. & Envtl. Control v. Phillips*, 400 A.2d 299, 308 (Del. Ch. 1979), aff'd, 449 A.2d 250 (Del. 1982) ("Stare Decisis is applicable only to questions of law, unlike res judicata, which is applicable to questions of both law and fact."); *Board of Educ. Lands & Funds v. Gillett*, 64 N.W.2d 105, 110 (Neb. 1954) ("Res judicata and stare decisis are distinguishable in that the former may relate to both law and facts whereas the latter relates to legal principles only.") (internal quotation marks omitted); *State Hosp. for Criminal Insane v. Consolidated Water Supply Co.*, 110 A. 281, 284 (Pa. 1920) ("[Stare decisis has] to do with the binding effect of legal principles, and [res judicata] with the conclusiveness of prior judicial findings based upon the same facts as those involved in a pending controversy.").

7   *Scott v. Gossett*, 158 P.2d 804, 807 (Idaho 1945) ("The rule of stare decisis (to stand by decided principle) is not to be confused with res adjudicata or law of the case.... The doctrine of stare decisis ... is based upon the legal principle or rule involved and not upon the judgment which results therefrom. In this particular stare decisis differs from res judicata, which is based upon the judgment.") (internal punctuation, quotation marks, and citation omitted); *Winston Bros. Co. v. Galloway*, 121 P.2d 457, 459 (Or. 1942) (in banc) ("The doctrine of res judicata is not to be confused with that of stare decisis as the two are based upon wholly different principles.").

8   *Peregoy v. Amoco Prod. Co.*, 742 F. Supp. 372, 374 (E.D. Tex. 1990) ("Stare decisis gives force of law to precedent, and is broader than the doctrines of res judicata

Circuit framed the distinction: "Stare decisis, unlike the doctrines of res judicata and collateral estoppel, is not narrowly confined to parties and privies, and it does not draw its force from the policy protecting final judgments."[9] Instead, when stare decisis applies, "the doctrine is broad in impact, reaching strangers to the earlier litigation."[10] Put another way, although res judicata generally won't bind those who aren't in privity with the original litigants, stare decisis will.[11]

The two doctrines also differ in jurisdictional scope. Res judicata applies across jurisdictions.[12] Indeed, the Constitution requires that states recognize the judgments of sister states.[13] Stare decisis, on the other hand, applies only within the jurisdiction that created it.[14]

---

and collateral estoppel. Stare decisis does not require commonality or privity among the parties to the present or prior litigation."), *aff'd*, 929 F.2d 196 (5th Cir. 1991) (per curiam); *Gillett*, 64 N.W.2d at 110 ("Res judicata and stare decisis are distinguishable in that . . . the former binds parties and privies, whereas the latter governs a decision on the same question between strangers to the record.") (internal quotation marks omitted).

9   *EEOC v. Trabucco*, 791 F.2d 1, 2 (1st Cir. 1986).
10 *Id.*
11 *College Sports Council v. Department of Educ.*, 465 F.3d 20, 22–23 (D.C. Cir. 2006) (per curiam) ("There are no material differences between the complaint in [the earlier case] and the complaint in this case . . . . Therefore, the jurisdictional holding in [the earlier case] is *res judicata* here as to the five parties who appeared in [the earlier case]. In addition, all parties here are bound by the stare decisis effect of this court's decisions.") (citation omitted).
12 *Underwriters Nat'l Assurance Co. v. North Carolina Life & Accident & Health Ins. Guar. Ass'n*, 455 U.S. 691, 704 (1982) (stating that the Full Faith and Credit Clause of the Constitution requires states to recognize the judgments of other states); *Sutton v. Leib*, 342 U.S. 402, 406 (1952) (same); *Semtek Int'l Inc. v. Lockheed Martin Corp.*, 531 U.S. 497, 507 (2001) (holding that under federal common law, state courts must recognize federal-court judgments); *Migra*, 465 U.S. at 81 (federal courts must recognize the judgments of states).
13 U.S. Const. art. IV, § 1, cl. 1 ("Full Faith and Credit shall be given in each State to the public Acts, Records, and judicial Proceedings of every other State."); *see* 28 U.S.C. § 1738 ("The records and judicial proceedings of any court of any such State . . . shall have the same full faith and credit in every court within the United States . . . as they have by law or usage in the courts of such State . . . from which they are taken.").
14 *See, e.g., Balmer v. Elan Corp.*, 599 S.E.2d 158, 161 (Ga. 2004) ("[T]he appellate courts of this state are not bound by decisions of other states or federal courts except the United States Supreme Court.") (internal quotation marks omitted).

Further, the two doctrines differ in hierarchical effect. Under stare decisis, only cases decided by a higher court or by the same court have precedential effect on later courts; lower-court precedents cannot bind higher courts.[15] But a lower-court ruling *can* have res judicata effect on a higher court.

Similarly, a judgment by one federal district judge may have res judicata effect on another, but one federal district court's decision isn't precedential for another—even if they're in the same district.[16] As the Seventh Circuit has stated: "[D]istrict judges . . . must not treat decisions by other district judges[,] in this and a fortiori in other circuits, as controlling, unless of course the doctrine of res judicata or of collateral estoppel applies. Such decisions will normally be entitled to no more weight than their intrinsic persuasiveness merits."[17]

Stare decisis also differs from res judicata in the elements of a prior decision that are binding on a later court. At least with claim preclusion, res judicata bars litigation of any claims of law or facts that *could* have been raised in the earlier litigation, even if they weren't.[18] By contrast, stare decisis applies only to legal issues that were *actually* raised and decided by the precedential decision.[19]

---

15 *Catalina Mktg. Sales Corp. v. Department of Treasury*, 678 N.W.2d 619, 625 (Mich. 2004) (stating that the Michigan Supreme Court "is not bound by Court of Appeals decisions"); *State ex rel. Martinez v. City of Las Vegas*, 89 P.3d 47, 54 (N.M. 2004) ("[T]he Court of Appeals remains bound by Supreme Court precedent.") (internal punctuation omitted); *State Bd. of Equalization v. Courtesy Motors, Inc.*, 362 P.2d 134, 135 (Wyo. 1961) ("[T]he judgments of district courts are not precedents and are valuable only to the extent that any sound view is worthy of consideration.") (footnote omitted).

16 *United States v. Articles of Drug Consisting of 203 Paper Bags*, 818 F.2d 569, 572 (7th Cir. 1987) ("A single district court decision . . . has little precedential effect. It is not binding on . . . other district judges in the same district.").

17 *Colby v. J.C. Penney Co.*, 811 F.2d 1119, 1124 (7th Cir. 1987) (emphasis omitted).

18 *Brown v. Felsen*, 442 U.S. 127, 131 (1979) ("Res judicata prevents litigation of all grounds for, or defenses to, recovery that were previously available to the parties, regardless of whether they were asserted or determined in the prior proceeding.").

19 *Beacon Oil Co. v. O'Leary*, 71 F.3d 391, 395 (Fed. Cir. 1995) ("Stare decisis applies only to legal issues that were actually decided in a prior action."); *State v. Honeycutt*, 421 S.W.3d 410, 422 (Mo. 2013), *as modified* (24 Dec. 2013) ("[S]tare decisis applies only to decisions on points arising and decided in causes and

Finally, the two doctrines differ in the degree to which they bind later courts. Courts aren't at liberty to decline to follow res judicata just because they think the earlier decision was erroneous.[20] They have more leeway, though, to decline to follow an erroneous precedent under the doctrine of stare decisis.[21] Further, stare decisis may become inapplicable because of later enactments, decisions, and analyses that have undermined the earlier decision or its reasoning. But courts cannot question the wisdom of a determination that has res judicata effect, regardless of any later changes of law.[22]

Despite these differences, both stare decisis and res judicata promote a similar goal: stability in the law. Res judicata stands for the idea that once an issue has been decided for particular litigants, it should not be undone by a later lawsuit. This doctrine lets parties rest assured that they need not relitigate issues in the future: they can live without a cloud of uncertain future litigation perpetually hovering. Similarly, stare decisis promotes the fundamental notion emphasized throughout this book: that like cases will be decided alike.

---

does not extend to mere implications from issues actually decided.") (internal quotation marks omitted).

[20] *People v. Kidd*, 75 N.E.2d 851, 854 (Ill. 1947) ("[A] judgment does not lose its effectiveness as res judicata from the mere fact that it is irregular or erroneous. The doctrine of res judicata is not dependent upon the correctness of the judgment, or of the verdict or finding on which it is based.").

[21] *Trabucco*, 791 F.2d at 2 (noting that stare decisis, as distinguished from res judicata, "leaves some room for judgment as to its preclusive power, and it stems from the principles of stability and equal treatment underlying the orderly development of legal doctrine"); *J.E. Bernard & Co. v. United States*, 324 F. Supp. 496, 500 n.9 (Cust. Ct. 1971) ("In contrast to stare decisis, the doctrines of res judicata and collateral estoppel bar further litigation even if the first judgment is erroneous. This is to say that unlike stare decisis, a fact, question or right distinctly adjudged in the original action cannot be disputed in a subsequent action, even though the determination was reached upon an erroneous view or by an erroneous application of the law.") (internal quotation marks omitted).

[22] See *LaBarbera v. Batsch*, 227 N.E.2d 55, 60 (Ohio 1967) ("The principle that an erroneous but existing and final judgment is judicata has been adhered to in the face of subsequent changes of law by higher courts in other actions.").

43. Identical Sources of Dispute

Once fully considered and decided by an appellate court, a question of law will not be reexamined in a later controversy when the claim or defense arises from the same or identical instrument, transaction, or occurrence, even if the later lawsuit is entirely independent of the first and the parties are not the same.

When an appellate court decides a legal question fully, an equal or lower court in the same jurisdiction will not reexamine it if (1) the claim or defense grows out of the identical instrument, transaction, or occurrence, and (2) the party opposed to the previous decision has failed to prove a material change to law or fact.[1] This is true even if the second lawsuit is entirely independent of the first and the litigants are different. So unlike preclusion doctrine (see § 42), stare decisis may be applied when a later lawsuit doesn't involve the same litigants as the precedent.[2]

For example, in *United States v. Maine*, the United States government sued 13 states bordering the Atlantic to establish that it had exclusive sovereign rights over the seabed, extending three miles from the coast.[3] The states contested federal ownership because of the disputed area's rich yield of oil, natural gas, sulfur, and salt.[4] The U.S. Supreme Court determined that three previous cases on the same issue[5] had "completely dispose[d]" of the

---

[1] *Perez v. Volvo Car Corp.*, 247 F.3d 303, 313 (1st Cir. 2001) (holding that the court was bound under the principles of stare decisis by a previous case regarding the same facts of the same allegedly fraudulent scheme of a car manufacturer but still examining additional evidence that the plaintiffs submitted); *EEOC v. Trabucco*, 791 F.2d 1, 5 (1st Cir. 1986) (finding that appellant had not overcome the "heavy presumption" that "accompanies a ruling on the precise issue in a prior case").

[2] *See McDuffie v. Estelle*, 935 F.2d 682, 686 n.7 (5th Cir. 1991) (holding that even if collateral estoppel didn't foreclose the Texas prison system from relitigating a constitutional issue, "straightforward application of stare decisis would preclude reconsideration of the constitutionality" of the issue).

[3] 420 U.S. 515, 516–17 (1975).

[4] *Id.* at 527.

[5] *United States v. Louisiana*, 339 U.S. 699 (1950); *United States v. Texas*, 339 U.S. 707 (1950); *United States v. California*, 332 U.S. 19 (1947).

states' ownership claims,[6] noting that although the states being sued were not litigants in these previous cases, and therefore not estopped by res judicata from raising the same issues in the current lawsuit, "the doctrine of stare decisis is still a powerful force in our jurisprudence; and although on occasion the Court has declared—and acted accordingly—that constitutional decisions are open to reexamination, we are convinced that the doctrine has peculiar force and relevance in the present context."[7]

Other illuminating examples:

- In a dispute over whether the municipality or private landowners were responsible for maintaining a road, the First Circuit held that "[t]echnically, the doctrine of collateral estoppel, or issue preclusion, does not apply here because these landowners were not parties to the [earlier] proceedings," but "in this setting we think that the doctrine of stare decisis should be invoked to give our resolution of the . . . issue in that case precedential value."[8]

- In a patent-infringement case in which the Seventh Circuit had previously held the relevant patent valid, the court held that "once there has been a judicial determination of validity, the party challenging validity in a later action in the same court has the burden of presenting 'persuasive new evidence' of invalidity and demonstrating that there is a 'material distinction' between the cases."[9] The court explained: "This is but an application of the doctrine of stare decisis."[10]

---

6   *Maine*, 420 U.S. at 522.

7   *Id.* at 527.

8   *United States v. 177.51 Acres of Land*, 716 F.2d 78, 81 (1st Cir. 1983) (citing 18 Charles Alan Wright, Arthur R. Miller et al., *Federal Practice and Procedure* § 4449, at 417 (1981)).

9   *Illinois Tool Works, Inc. v. Foster Grant Co.*, 547 F.2d 1300, 1302 (7th Cir. 1976).

10 *Id.* at 1303 (noting that stare decisis effectively strengthened the statutory presumption arising out of a determination of validity by the Patent and Trademark Office) (citing 35 U.S.C. § 282); *see also American Home Prods. Corp. v. Lockwood Mfg. Co.*, 483 F.2d 1120, 1125 (6th Cir. 1973) ("[T]he normal statutory presumption of validity accorded to a patent (35 U.S.C. § 282) is greatly enhanced when it has been held valid in a prior decision. A prior adjudication of [a patent's] validity should be followed 'unless the court is convinced of a

- In a criminal case, the Seventh Circuit had previously held that the admission of tapes as evidence wasn't erroneous. In an appeal by different members of the same criminal gang regarding the same tapes, the Seventh Circuit held that it would be "inappropriate" for the later panel to offer an "independent view" and rejected the claims on the basis of stare decisis.[11]
- In a contract case in which the Fifth Circuit had previously interpreted a provision in the *same* contract, the Eleventh Circuit (created when the Fifth Circuit was split in 1981) held that it "need not determine whether this would be a proper use of offensive collateral estoppel, since it is certain that we are bound by the [previous Fifth Circuit] decision under the doctrine of stare decisis, absent a countervailing decision by the Supreme Court or by this Court sitting en banc. We are not at liberty to reconsider this issue."[12]
- In two bankruptcy appeals regarding the same issue and identical and nearly identical security instruments that were the subject of litigation in earlier Ninth Circuit cases, the Ninth Circuit held that it was still bound by those earlier cases.[13]
- In a tax appeal in which a statute had been previously interpreted by the District of Columbia Circuit, the same court held that its previous interpretation controlled under the doctrine of stare decisis because there were no legal changes "to relieve [the court] of [its] obligation to follow a recent and well-considered decision of this court."[14]

---

very palpable error in law or fact.'") (quoting *Cold Metal Process Co. v. Republic Steel Corp.*, 233 F.2d 828, 837 (6th Cir. 1956)).

11 *United States v. Hoover*, 246 F.3d 1054, 1057 (7th Cir. 2001); *see also* 1 *Criminal Procedure Checklists 5th Amendment* § 11:20, Westlaw (database updated Sept. 2015).

12 *Ransom v. S&S Food Ctr., Inc.*, 700 F.2d 670, 674 (11th Cir. 1983), *overruled by Turner v. Beneficial Corp.*, 242 F.3d 1023 (11th Cir. 2001) (en banc).

13 *In re Staff Mortg. & Inv. Corp.*, 655 F.2d 967, 969 (9th Cir. 1981); *In re Staff Mortg. & Inv. Corp.*, 625 F.2d 281, 283 (9th Cir. 1980).

14 *Brewster v. Commissioner*, 607 F.2d 1369, 1373–74 (D.C. Cir. 1979) (per curiam).

IDENTICAL SOURCES OF DISPUTE

- In a criminal case in which the First Circuit had previously found that pretrial publicity didn't deprive eight codefendants of a fair trial and the district court didn't err in admitting certain evidence, the same court held in another codefendant's appeal that "the doctrine of stare decisis bars relitigation" of the issues and that "[i]f order and fairness are to attend the legal process, that point can be resolved no differently" for the defendant "than for his identically situated codefendants."[15]

Because of the rules of vertical precedent, a litigant cannot use stare decisis to argue that another jurisdiction's ruling is binding, even if the applicable law is the same.[16]

Some courts have found that the application of stare decisis to claims adjudicated without the defendants' participation could cause "an injustice of precisely the sort that due process seeks to avoid."[17] A contrary view is that there is no due-process problem because the Constitution allows a court to bar a defendant from raising already-litigated defenses. This means a fortiori that a court may give at least prima facie effect to already-litigated matters. The court observed that "under the prima facie rule a defendant may present additional evidence with respect to questions previously litigated, while under res judicata he is completely bound by the former litigation."[18]

---

15 *United States v. Reveron Martinez*, 836 F.2d 684, 687 (1st Cir. 1988).

16 *See, e.g., SGC Land, LLC v. Louisiana Midstream Gas Servs.*, 939 F. Supp. 2d 612, 624 (W.D. La. 2013), *amended on reconsideration in part* (3 Aug. 2013) (reexamining a previous decision as to the meaning of an Easement and Right of Way Agreement); *Texas Instruments, Inc. v. Linear Techs. Corp.*, 182 F. Supp. 2d 580, 589 (E.D. Tex. 2002) (stating that stare decisis doesn't bind a district-court judge to follow another district-court judge's decision, even if the cases involve identical legal questions and facts).

17 *Texas Instruments, Inc.*, 182 F. Supp. 2d at 589–90.

18 *Michigan v. Morton Salt Co.*, 259 F. Supp. 35, 62 (D. Minn. 1966), *aff'd sub nom. Hardy Salt Co. v. Illinois*, 377 F.2d 768 (8th Cir. 1967).

44. Findings of Fact

A precedent is valuable and authoritative only as establishing a legal rule or principle. Stare decisis does not apply to findings of fact and has only limited application to cases that turn on the admissibility or weight of evidence or on the application of a settled legal principle to the facts established in the particular controversy.

Precedents wield authority and power only to the extent that they establish or reinforce a legal rule or principle.[1] Stare decisis has no application to findings of fact[2] or to mixed questions of fact and law,[3] and it applies quite narrowly to certain types of cases.

Take for example a case in which a previous defendant was found guilty of reckless driving for driving 30 m.p.h. over the speed limit as measured by police radar. This holding—that driving 30 m.p.h. over the speed limit as measured by police radar was reckless—doesn't have stare decisis effect on a different defendant

---

1 See *Black's Law Dictionary* 1626 (Bryan A. Garner ed., 10th ed. 2014) (s.v. *stare decisis*).

2 See *United States v. Reveron Martinez*, 836 F.2d 684, 691 (1st Cir. 1988) (holding that stare decisis "deals only with law"); *In re Tug Helen B. Moran, Inc.*, 607 F.2d 1029, 1031 (2d Cir. 1979) (same); *United States v. Brown*, 631 F.3d 638, 643 (3d Cir. 2011) (stating that stare decisis regards legal determinations; factual findings are binding on only the parties before the court); *Seay v. Hutto*, 483 F. App'x 900, 903 (5th Cir. 2012) (per curiam) (noting that "stare decisis means that like facts will receive like treatment in a court of law"); *Lawton v. Commissioner*, 164 F.2d 380, 384 (6th Cir. 1947) (noting that under stare decisis, courts consider past adjudicated law); *Spector v. United States*, 193 F.2d 1002, 1006 (9th Cir. 1952) (stating that "no principle of stare decisis or res judicata makes a finding of fact applicable to persons not parties to the action in which the finding is made"); *Meredith v. Beech Aircraft Corp.*, 18 F.3d 890, 895 (10th Cir. 1994) (stating that stare decisis is the policy of courts to adhere to precedent regarding points of *law*, not specific factual issues); *Cable Holdings of Ga., Inc. v. McNeil Real Estate Fund VI, Ltd.*, 988 F.2d 1071, 1081 (11th Cir. 1993) (Tjoflat J. dissenting from denial of rehearing en banc) (stare decisis provides a stable body of *law*); *Mahoney v. Babbitt*, 113 F.3d 219, 224 (D.C. Cir. 1997) (only principles of law have stare decisis effect); *Deckers Corp. v. United States*, 752 F.3d 949, 956 (Fed. Cir. 2014) (noting that stare decisis "is limited to only the legal determinations made" and doesn't apply to issues of fact).

3 *Wyatt v. Pennsylvania R.R.*, 158 F. Supp. 502, 504 (D. Del. 1958) (stare decisis has no application to mixed questions of law and fact); *Union Trust Co. v. Williamson Cnty. Bd. of Zoning Appeals*, 500 S.W.2d 608, 615 (Tenn. 1973) (same).

accused of driving at the same speed. The second driver might have been escaping from a maniac intent on killing him, might have stronger evidence invalidating the accuracy of the officer's speed radar, or might have convinced the jury through his testimony that he wasn't going 30 m.p.h. over the speed limit and that the police officer had a vendetta against him.

This principle was applied in a 1993 Michigan case[4] in which the plaintiffs sued for medical malpractice, and the trial court granted partial summary judgment to the defendants.[5] The trial court held that defendant Oakwood Hospital was entitled to charitable immunity under Michigan law because a case decided 30 years earlier had held that the same hospital was entitled to charitable immunity.[6] The appellate court reversed, holding that the issue whether a defendant is a charitable institution depended on fact findings, and that stare decisis establishes "stability [only] in the law" and "does not control findings of fact."[7] The 30-year-old decision didn't dictate the outcome of the case on appeal, which could have different facts and evidence. Hence the appellate court remanded the case for the trial court to assess the facts.[8] (For more, see § 43 on identical sources for dispute, as when the same written contract or other document governs.)

Nor does stare decisis apply to the admissibility of evidence. In a 2011 Illinois case,[9] the trial court concluded that stare decisis mandated the admission of a letter based on a previous case.[10] The appellate court reversed, holding that the question of admissibility "must be governed by the facts of each individual case."[11]

---

4   *Guardiola v. Oakwood Hosp.*, 504 N.W.2d 701 (Mich. Ct. App. 1993).
5   *Id.* at 702.
6   *Id.*
7   *Id.* at 704 (internal quotation marks and citations omitted).
8   *Id.*; *see Smith v. Russo Asiatic Bank*, 290 N.Y.S. 471, 474–75 (Sup. Ct. 1936) (whether the plaintiff was a "creditor" couldn't be decided by the parties' citation of other cases deciding issue of law because "the doctrine of stare decisis relates to legal principles, not to facts") (quoting *In re People, by Beha*, 175 N.E. 118, 119 (N.Y. 1931)).
9   *In re J.Y.*, 962 N.E.2d 1 (Ill. App. Ct. 2011).
10   *Id.* at 5.
11   *Id.*

The court concluded that the state had not called any witnesses to testify about how the letter was prepared or to lay any other foundation for a business or medical record.[12] Instead, the trial court had admitted the letter because similar letters had been admitted in past juvenile proceedings.[13] The appellate court therefore concluded that "the trial court's reliance on stare decisis was misguided."[14]

Courts have also found that the doctrine of stare decisis doesn't apply when determining negligence,[15] gross negligence,[16] conclusions such as seaworthiness,[17] whether a jury error occurred,[18] whether a defendant could obtain a fair and impartial jury,[19] or sufficiency of the evidence.[20]

---

12   *Id.*

13   *Id.*

14   *Id.* at 6.

15   *Sandell v. Des Moines City Ry.*, 168 N.W. 226, 228 (Iowa 1918) (holding that no decision of a fact question in a previous negligence case is stare decisis).

16   *Ake v. Birnbaum*, 25 So. 2d 213, 215 (Fla. 1945) (en banc).

17   *Partos v. Pacific Coast S.S. (The Diamond Cement)*, 95 F.2d 738, 742 (9th Cir. 1938).

18   *Gross Coal Co. v. City of Milwaukee*, 175 N.W. 793, 794 (Wis. 1920).

19   *State v. Means*, 268 N.W.2d 802, 811 (S.D. 1978).

20   *Turner v. Elliott*, 206 P.2d 48, 49 (Cal. Dist. Ct. App. 1949), *disapproved on other grounds by Turner v. Mellon*, 257 P.2d 15, 17 (Cal. 1953) (in bank).

45. Judicial Unity

Judges sitting in the same appellate court should not make contradictory or conflicting rulings in the same case or on the same subject. Each should defer to and accept decisions already made.

As a matter of judicial administration, judges on the same court generally strive for harmony with the rulings of colleagues and predecessors.[1] Sometimes trial judges in a given jurisdiction will differ in their attitudes toward granting continuances for trials, for example, or toward imposing severe criminal sentences. The trial judges will exercise their discretion differently from each other. These differences will inevitably induce counsel to engage in forum-shopping to whatever extent they can. That practice can give rise to perceptions of uneven justice, especially in jurisdictions where a civil or criminal litigant has a right to move to disqualify the trial judge.[2] Although this procedure is nothing like a peremptory challenge to a juror of the kind challenged in *Batson v. Kentucky*,[3] in theory it may have similar equal-protection implications.

Leadership by the presiding judge, judicial-education programs, and moral suasion by colleagues seem the only avenues toward promoting judicial unity at the trial-court level because one trial judge's decision doesn't bind another trial court.[4] The resulting lack of unity is legally acceptable, as the Seventh Circuit

---

[1] *Texas Instruments, Inc. v. Linear Techs. Corp.*, 182 F. Supp. 2d 580, 589 (E.D. Tex. 2002) ("[O]rdinarily in federal practice, judges of coordinate jurisdiction, sitting in cases involving identical legal questions under the same facts and circumstances, should not reconsider the decisions of each other.") (citing *United States v. Koenig*, 290 F.2d 166, 172 (5th Cir. 1961); *Prack v. Weissinger*, 276 F.2d 446, 450 (4th Cir. 1960)).

[2] *See, e.g.*, Alaska Stat. § 22.20.022; Ariz. R. Crim. P. 10.2; Cal. Civ. Proc. Code § 170.6; Minn. R. Crim. P. 26.03 subd. 14; Mont. Code § 3-1-804; Nev. Sup. Ct. R. 48.1; N.M. R. Civ. P. 1-088.1; N.D. Cent. Code § 20-15-21; Tex. R. Civ. P. 18b.

[3] 476 U.S. 79 (1986).

[4] *TMF Tool Co. v. Muller*, 913 F.2d 1185, 1191 (7th Cir. 1990) ("[F]or a variety of quite valid reasons, including consistency of result, it is an entirely proper practice for district judges to give deference to persuasive opinions by their

has explained: "[T]he responsibility for maintaining the law's uniformity is a responsibility of appellate rather than trial judges and because the Supreme Court does not assume the burden of resolving conflicts between district judges whether in the same or different circuits."[5]

In appellate courts, judicial unity is usually enforced by rule (see, e.g., § 60). In the Ninth Circuit, the court's jurisprudence prohibits a three-judge panel from overruling the decision of a previous three-judge or en banc panel.[6] Hence stare decisis promotes judicial unity. This is the prevailing federal approach.[7] Some

---

    colleagues on the same court. But while this is a laudable and worthwhile practice, it does not convert district court decisions into binding precedent.").

[5] *Id.* (internal quotation marks, citations, and emphasis omitted).

[6] *Miller v. Gammie*, 335 F.3d 889, 899 (9th Cir. 2003) (en banc); *Federal Appellate Practice Guide: Ninth Circuit 2d* § 8:19 ("The principal way the Ninth Circuit avoids having these shifting three-judge panels issue conflicting decisions is to follow a rule of intracircuit stare decisis: panel decisions bind subsequent panels except in certain narrow situations discussed below [that the first decision was clearly erroneous, its enforcement would work a manifest injustice, or other changed circumstances exist, including new Supreme Court precedent] or unless overruled by the court en banc.").

[7] *See San Juan Cable LLC v. Puerto Rico Tel. Co.*, 612 F.3d 25, 33 (1st Cir. 2010) ("[T]he 'law of the circuit' rule is a subset of stare decisis. It is one of the building blocks on which the federal judicial system rests. Under the rule, newly constituted panels in a multi-panel circuit court are bound by prior panel decisions that are closely on point."); *United States v. Wilkerson*, 361 F.3d 717, 732 (2d Cir. 2004) (later panels are bound by the decisions of prior panels until they are overruled by an en banc panel of the Second Circuit or the Supreme Court); *Reich v. D.M. Sabia Co.*, 90 F.3d 854, 858 (3d Cir. 1996) (same); *McMellon v. United States*, 387 F.3d 329, 332 (4th Cir. 2004) (en banc) (one panel cannot overrule a decision issued by another panel); *United States v. Short*, 181 F.3d 620, 624 (5th Cir. 1999) (panel bound "by the precedent of previous panels absent an intervening Supreme Court case explicitly or implicitly overruling that prior precedent"); *Bennett v. MIS Corp.*, 607 F.3d 1076, 1095 (6th Cir. 2010) (a panel of the court cannot overrule a prior panel without en banc review or "an intervening and binding change in the state of the law"); *Jesinoski v. Countrywide Home Loans, Inc.*, 729 F.3d 1092, 1093 (8th Cir. 2013) (per curiam) (calling it a "cardinal rule" in the Eighth Circuit that "one panel is bound by the decision of a prior panel"), *rev'd*, 135 S.Ct. 790 (2015); *United States v. Meyers*, 200 F.3d 715, 720 (10th Cir. 2000) (calling itself "bound by the precedent of prior panels absent *en banc* reconsideration or a superseding contrary decision by the Supreme Court"); *Smith v. GTE Corp.*, 236 F.3d 1292, 1302 (11th Cir. 2001) (noting that a panel must follow prior panel precedent even if the later panel is convinced that the precedent is wrong); *Ranger Cellular v. FCC*, 348 F.3d 1044, 1049–50 (D.C. Cir. 2003) ("Once a panel of this court has decided a matter, subsequent panels are bound by that decision unless and until it is changed by

circuits allow a three-judge panel to overrule a previous three-judge panel, but only in highly unusual circumstances.[8] (See § 60.)

In California, the state's intermediate appellate courts may adopt rulings that conflict with the rulings of other intermediate appellate courts sitting in different geographic districts.[9] When those conflicts arise (as they sometimes do), the California Supreme Court often grants a petition for review to eliminate them in much the same way that the U.S. Supreme Court grants certiorari in cases in which the federal circuits are split. The same is true in both New York[10] and Texas.[11] Yet a decision in a case on point from a sister court may be followed as persuasive authority.[12]

---

the court en banc."); *Tunik v. Merit Sys. Prots. Bd.*, 407 F.3d 1326, 1338 (Fed. Cir. 2005) (noting that panels in its circuit "are bound by prior panel decisions").

8   *United States v. Williams*, 184 F.3d 666, 671 (7th Cir. 1999) (later panel will "give fair consideration to any substantial argument" that it should overrule previous panel decisions, but overruling circuit precedent requires "compelling reasons").

9   *People v. Yeats*, 136 Cal. Rptr. 243, 245 (Ct. App. 1977) (declining to follow a court-of-appeal decision from another district); *Sarti v. Salt Creek Ltd.*, 85 Cal. Rptr. 3d 506, 510 (Ct. App. 2008) ("Unlike at least some federal intermediate appellate courts, though, there is no horizontal stare decisis in the California Court of Appeal."); *Black's Law Dictionary* 1626 (Bryan A. Garner ed., 10th ed. 2014) (defining *horizontal stare decisis* as "[t]he doctrine that a court, esp. an appellate court, must adhere to its own prior decisions, unless it finds compelling reasons to overrule itself"); 9 B.E. Witkin, *California Procedure* § 498, at 558 (5th ed. 2008) (state court-of-appeal decisions not binding on other courts of appeals).

10   *Vanderhoef v. Silver*, 978 N.Y.S.2d 379, 379 (App. Div. 2013) (citing *Mountain View Coach Lines, Inc. v. Storms*, 476 N.Y.S.2d 918, 919 (App. Div. 1984) (declining to follow two cases from another intermediate appellate court: "While we should accept the decisions of sister departments as persuasive, we are free to reach a contrary result.")).

11   *See also Shook v. State*, 244 S.W.2d 220, 221 (Tex. Crim. App. 1951) (stating that courts are not bound by the decisions of other courts of equal jurisdiction); *Entergy Gulf States, Inc. v. Traxler*, 320 S.W.3d 553, 557 (Tex. App.—Beaumont 2010) (stating that "the opinions of a sister court of appeals are not binding precedent in other courts of appeals"), *rev'd*, 376 S.W.3d 742 (Tex. 2012); *Public, Inc. v. County of Galveston*, 264 S.W.3d 338, 344 (Tex. App.—Houston [14th District] 2008, no pet.) (pointing out that civil case decided by another Texas court of appeals was not binding).

12   *See, e.g., Jankowiak v. Allstate Prop. & Cas. Ins. Co.*, 201 S.W.3d 200, 208 (Tex. App.—Houston [14th District] 2006, no pet.).

46. Overruling a Decision

Stare decisis does not prevent a court from overruling a horizontal precedent that on reconsideration it finds to be plainly and palpably wrong. But the court must first decide whether overruling the precedent would result in more harm than continuing to follow the erroneous decision.

As we've already seen, stare decisis isn't an ineluctable doctrine to be applied with procrustean rigor. As Doe J. of New Hampshire, a celebrated judge of the late 19th century, said in 1870: "The maxim which, taken literally, requires courts to follow decided cases, is shown by the thousands of overruled decisions, to be a figurative expression requiring only a reasonable respect for decided cases."[1] Sometimes it is necessary for the judge to identify the rare occasion "when it is necessary to say that what judges have put together they can also put asunder."[2]

Courts aren't bound to follow an erroneous horizontal precedent when doing so would result in more harm than overturning the prior decision would cause: this weighing of alternative harms is the normal assessment in deciding whether to overrule precedent. But harm to an individual litigant as a result of overruling a decision is a thin reed to grasp as a basis for avoiding the step. A judicial decision, naturally, will always favor some and disfavor others. Injury to the loser should not be a reason to withhold benefit from the winner. After all, moments before the decision was overruled, the now-loser was benefiting from a precedent that injured the now-winner.

It also makes good sense as a matter of judicial policy to consider whether overruling a precedent and adopting its opposite would cause more harm than good.[3] But before weighing this

---

[1] *Lisbon v. Lyman*, 49 N.H. 553, 602 (1870) (per Doe J.).
[2] Patrick Devlin, *The Judge* 201 (1979).
[3] *See, e.g., McElroy v. State*, 703 N.W.2d 385, 395 (Iowa 2005) ("When a rule, after it has been duly tested by experience, has been found to be inconsistent with the sense of justice or with the social welfare, there should be less hesitation in frank avowal and full abandonment.") (brackets omitted) (quoting Benjamin N. Cardozo, *The Nature of the Judicial Process* 150 (1921)).

question, the judges should also consider whether they are acting within the law or displacing the legislature. When the old rule has been the subject of legislative regulation, a court's capacity to overrule its precedent should be more restricted than when the rule derives from the common law.[4]

Some courts have noted that stare decisis should exert less force for common-law decisions than for cases interpreting statutes (see § 38). As the Pennsylvania Supreme Court reasoned in 1981: "It is the essence of common law courts today as in earlier times to view the body of the law as a living and developing legal system designed to serve societal needs in elevating the life and utility of the law rather than as a static set of rules."[5] The aspiration, the court said, is to balance precedent, which looks to the past, with pubic policy, which looks to the present and future. "The goal which we seek is a blend which takes into account in due proportion the wisdom of the past and the needs of the present."[6]

Courts generally recognize the "fundamental jurisprudential policy that prior applicable precedent usually must be followed even though the case, if considered anew, might be decided differently by the current justices."[7] Courts justify applying precedent and treating like cases alike "based on the assumption that certainty, predictability and stability in the law are the major objectives of the legal system; i.e., that parties should be able to regulate

---

4   See *Chamberlin v. State Farm Mut. Auto. Ins. Co.*, 36 S.W.3d 281, 284 (Ark. 2001) (citing its own precedent for the proposition that "the field of common law is not primarily the legislature's province but the court's and that the court is free to amend the common law and [is] not bound to adhere to outmoded holdings pending legislative action," and that alternatively, when "the rights at issue are governed by statute and not common law," the court will accord greater weight to legislative inaction).

5   *Hack v. Hack*, 433 A.2d 859, 868 (Pa. 1981) (internal quotation marks omitted); *cf. O'Connor v. City of Rutland*, 772 A.2d 551, 552–53 (Vt. 2001) (declining to overturn precedent because the "doctrine was for the Legislature and not the courts, partly because the Legislature's fact-finding and problem-solving process is better suited for the task in this area of the law") (internal quotation marks and citation omitted).

6   *Hack*, 433 A.2d at 868.

7   *Trope v. Katz*, 902 P.2d 259, 269 (Cal. 1995) (in bank) (internal punctuation omitted).

their conduct and enter into relationships with reasonable assurance of the governing rules of law."[8]

So stare decisis is neither absolutely binding nor inescapable,[9] and courts do have the power to overrule their own prior decisions. As the U.S. Supreme Court has put it, although stare decisis promotes valuable social policies, such as continuity in law and stability in reasonable expectations, "stare decisis is a principle of policy and not a mechanical formula of adherence to the latest decision, however recent and questionable, when such adherence involves collision with a prior doctrine more embracing in its scope, intrinsically sounder, and verified by experience."[10]

Holmes J., writing extrajudicially while an associate justice on the Massachusetts high court, famously mocked blind adherence to past cases: "It is revolting to have no better reason for a rule of law than that so it was laid down in the time of Henry IV."[11] He went further: "It is still more revolting if the grounds upon which it was laid down have vanished long since, and the rule simply persists from blind imitation of the past."[12]

Indeed, as some courts have put it, true respect for prior caselaw requires reexamining horizontal precedent to ensure that it has been and continues to be correct.[13] Hence courts consider the doctrine of stare decisis to be a principle of policy and weigh factors for and against overruling prior erroneous precedent.[14]

---

8   *Id.*

9   *State Oil Co. v. Khan*, 522 U.S. 3, 20 (1997).

10 *Helvering v. Hallock*, 309 U.S. 106, 119 (1940); *see Riverisland Cold Storage, Inc. v. Fresno-Madera Prod. Credit Ass'n*, 291 P.3d 316, 322 n.9 (Cal. 2013) (same); *People v. Petrenko*, 931 N.E.2d 1198, 1212 (Ill. 2010) (same); *People v. Bing*, 558 N.E.2d 1011, 1014 (N.Y. 1990) (same).

11 Oliver Wendell Holmes, *The Path of the Law*, 10 Harv. L. Rev. 457, 469 (1897).

12 *Id.*

13 *See Matheney v. Commonwealth*, 191 S.W.3d 599, 604 (Ky. 2006) ("While we recognize this Court should decide cases with a respect for precedent, this respect does not require blind imitation of the past or unquestioned acceptance ad infinitum. Rather, in many ways, respect for precedent *demands* proper reconsideration when we find sound legal reasons to question the correctness of our prior analysis.") (internal quotation marks omitted).

14 *See Higby v. Mahoney*, 396 N.E.2d 183, 184 (N.Y. 1979) (per curiam) ("The doctrine of Stare decisis does not, of course, demand unyielding resignation to

But the mere erroneousness of a prior line of precedent is generally not sufficient to overturn it. Instead there must be other reasons for reversing course.[15] In the words of the U.S. Supreme Court, "in most matters it is more important that the applicable rule of law be settled than that it be settled right."[16]

Further, judicial consistency promotes the rule of law, while frequent changes in the law undermine public confidence in judges. As the Wisconsin Supreme Court observed in 2005, failing to abide by stare decisis raises serious concerns about whether the court is in fact "implementing principles founded in the law rather than in the proclivities of individuals."[17]

Still, when a court has determined that a prior decision was wrongly decided, it may balance the negative impact of the rule as it stands against the negative impact of overruling the precedent. As the Washington Supreme Court has stated, the alternative may just amount to evading the court's responsibility: "Reluctant as we are to depart from former decisions we cannot yield to them, if, in yielding, we perpetuate error and sacrifice principle. We have thought it wisest to overrule outright rather than to evade, as is often done, by an attempt to distinguish where distinction there is none."[18]

---

even recent precedent. Policy considerations are inherent in the prudent, considered application of the doctrine.") (citation omitted).

15   *Halliburton Co. v. Erica P. John Fund, Inc.*, 134 S.Ct. 2398, 2407 (2014) ("Before overturning a long-settled precedent, however, we require 'special justification,' not just an argument that the precedent was wrongly decided.") (quoting *Dickerson v. United States*, 530 U.S. 428, 443 (2000)); *State v. Hickman*, 68 P.3d 418, 426 (Ariz. 2003) (stating that overturning precedent "require[s] more than that a prior case was wrongly decided"); *State ex rel. Moore v. Molpus*, 578 So. 2d 624, 635 (Miss. 1991) (en banc) ("In stare decisis generally, we look for error, but, finding that, we look for more.").

16   *Agostini v. Felton*, 521 U.S. 203, 235 (1997) (internal quotation marks omitted). *But see Barden v. Northern Pac. R.R.*, 154 U.S. 288, 322 (1894) ("It is more important that the court should be right upon later and more elaborate consideration of the cases than consistent with previous declarations.").

17   *Progressive N. Ins. Co. v. Romanshek*, 697 N.W.2d 417, 429 (Wis. 2005) (internal punctuation omitted).

18   *DeElche v. Jacobsen*, 622 P.2d 835, 840–41 (Wash. 1980) (en banc) (internal quotation marks omitted); *see State v. Miranda*, 878 A.2d 1118, 1122 (Conn. 2005) (per curiam) ("When a previous decision clearly creates injustice, the court should seriously consider whether the goals of stare decisis are outweighed,

392   SOME PRACTICALITIES OF STARE DECISIS

Once a precedent has been overruled, it "is definitely and formally deprived of all authority."[19] (For more on the effects of overrulings, see § 37.) Meanwhile, the overruling decision has been established as a new precedent.[20]

The bane of overruling good horizontal precedent

As long as the prior construction is working well and has been relied on by all affected, a high court is expected to give a statute a consistent meaning (see § 38). What happens when a high court fails to adhere to this principle and reverses a better-reasoned horizontal precedent? Let's consider one such case[21] that reversed a 12-year-old precedent construing a state statute.

In the first case, a 1975 Texas decision,[22] a man had married a woman with a son from a previous relationship. Although the man promised to adopt the boy, he never did.[23] The couple later had a son together.[24] The husband had taken out four life-insurance policies that named his wife as primary beneficiary.[25] Two policies named the wife's first son—described as the insured's "stepson"—and the insured's "children born of the marriage" as the contingent beneficiaries.[26] A third named only his "child or children" as contingent beneficiaries. The fourth and last named

---

   rather than dictated, by the prudential and pragmatic considerations that inform the doctrine to enforce a clearly erroneous decision. The court must weigh the benefits of stare decisis against its burdens in deciding whether to overturn a precedent it thinks is unjust.") (internal punctuation omitted); *Thompson v. Sanford*, 663 S.W.2d 932, 935 (Ark. 1984) ("[I]t is necessary, as a matter of public policy, to uphold prior decisions unless a great injury or injustice would result.").

19 John Salmond, *Jurisprudence* § 61, at 189 (Glanville L. Williams ed., 10th ed. 1947).

20 Francis Lieber, *On Civil Liberty and Self-Government* 209 (Theodore D. Woolsey ed., 3d ed. 1883) ("that which upsets the precedent cannot otherwise then become, in the independent life of the law, precedent in turn").

21 *Crawford v. Coleman ex rel. Shoaf*, 726 S.W.2d 9 (Tex. 1987).

22 *Deveroex v. Nelson*, 529 S.W.2d 510, 511 (Tex. 1975).

23 Id.

24 Id.

25 Id.

26 Id.

only his wife's son—described as the insured's "son."[27] Each policy provided that the contingent beneficiary would receive the proceeds if the primary beneficiary wasn't living; it didn't provide for that beneficiary's disqualification.[28]

The wife became disqualified under a "slayer statute," which stated:

> The interest of a beneficiary in a life insurance policy or contract heretofore or hereafter issued shall be forfeited when the beneficiary is the principal or an accomplice in willfully bringing about the death of the insured. When such is the case, the nearest relative of the insured shall receive said insurance.[29]

The natural son's guardian argued that since the wife was still alive, though disqualified, her son couldn't claim the insurance proceeds.[30] Further, the guardian argued that the insured's natural son should receive all the proceeds of each policy because he was the only true relative of the insured.[31]

The essential question was whether the second sentence took effect upon the disqualification of only one beneficiary—or whether it took effect upon a lapse of all beneficiaries.

The probate court found that the stepson had been adopted by estoppel,[32] so he was entitled to proceeds from each of the policies. The guardian appealed, arguing in both the district court and then in the court of appeals that the stepson had not been adopted and that the natural son was the only one entitled to all the insurance proceeds.[33] Both courts affirmed the constructive adoption.[34] The district court decided that both sons should share the proceeds of all four policies equally.[35] The court of appeals generally agreed but modified the judgment to give the proceeds of the final policy only

---

27 *Id.* at 511–12.
28 *Id.* at 513.
29 Tex. Ins. Code art. 21.23 (repealed 2003).
30 *Deveroex*, 529 S.W.2d at 513.
31 *Id.* at 512.
32 *Id.*
33 *Id.*
34 *Id.*
35 *Id.*

to the wife's first son—he was, after all, expressly named as the sole contingent beneficiary.[36] It examined the language of the statute and found no legislative intent to deprive an innocent named beneficiary of the insurance proceeds.[37]

The Texas Supreme Court affirmed, agreeing with the appellate court's reasoning that the statute required the proceeds to be distributed to the insured's nearest relative only if all the beneficiaries, primary and contingent, were disqualified from receiving them.[38] It also adopted that reasoning in an analogous case decided by another court of appeals. In that case, the language of the policy was silent about the payment of proceeds when a living primary beneficiary was disqualified. The court of appeals held that the named contingent beneficiary was entitled to the proceeds according to the insured's intent as expressed in the policy.[39]

Twelve years later, in 1987, a similar case was presented to the Texas Supreme Court.[40] A husband had killed his wife, whose life-insurance policy contained preprinted language stating that the beneficiaries were, in order, the insured's spouse, then the insured's children, and finally the insured's parents.[41] It defined *children* as including stepchildren and didn't permit the insured to name beneficiaries specifically.[42] The wife's parents sought the proceeds from this policy under the same statute. The trial court awarded the proceeds to the stepson, and the court of appeals affirmed, citing the 1975 case as authority because the stepson wasn't disqualified as a beneficiary under the statute.[43]

---

36 *Deveroex v. Nelson*, 517 S.W.2d 658, 664 (Tex. Civ. App.—Houston [14th Dist.] 1974), *aff'd*, 529 S.W.2d 510 (Tex. 1975).

37 *Id.*

38 529 S.W.2d at 513–14; *see* 517 S.W.2d at 664.

39 *Williams v. Williams*, 262 S.W.2d 111 (Tex. Civ. App.—Galveston 1953, no writ).

40 *Crawford*, 726 S.W.2d at 9.

41 *Id.* at 9–10.

42 *Id.* at 9.

43 *Crawford v. Coleman ex rel. Shoaf*, 701 S.W.2d 79, 80 (Tex. App.—Fort Worth 1985), *rev'd*, 726 S.W.2d 9 (Tex. 1987).

This time the Texas Supreme Court reversed.[44] Instead of following its precedent, it chose to interpret the statutory language anew to find that it preempted the beneficiary provisions of the policy.[45] The insureds in both cases presumably didn't imagine they would be killed, so the court declared that focusing on the insured's intent when choosing the beneficiaries was improper.[46] In other words, the later court supposed that if the testators had considered the possibility that their spouses would kill them, they might have wanted to exclude their stepchildren. The court overruled the 1975 holding[47] and awarded the insurance proceeds to the insured's parents.[48]

What might happen, though, if the named contingent beneficiaries weren't stepchildren but instead were close friends who had nothing to do with the slayer? Would they, too, be disinherited under the reading that if the primary beneficiary is a slayer, the second sentence of the statute automatically kicks in? Far from settling the law, the overruling case created more doubts about it.

The next two sections will consider factors for and against overruling horizontal precedents: courts weigh them in deciding whether the doctrine of stare decisis can be overcome.

---

44 *Crawford*, 726 S.W.2d at 9, 11.
45 *Id.* at 11.
46 *Id.*
47 *Id.* at 10.
48 *Id.* at 11.

47. Reasons for Overruling

A court may decide to overrule a horizontal precedent if there are sound and necessary reasons to do so.

Courts must consider many factors when deciding whether to overrule an earlier decision, most saliently these:

(A) the decision is contrary to plain principles of law;

(B) the decision is isolated and hasn't been followed or acquiesced in;

(C) a divided court's decision on a matter of great importance is now seriously doubted;

(D) the decision has been met with general dissatisfaction, protest, or severe criticism;

(E) no serious reliance interests have built up around the decision; and

(F) although some private rights may be injured by overruling the decision, it was wrong in the first place, it produces general injustice, and less harm will result from overruling the decision than from allowing it to stand.[1]

Although these factors are numerous, some commentators have argued that they all are actually proxies for a single factor: reliance interests.[2] Indeed, courts often discuss reliance interests in general as a crucial factor in deciding whether to overrule horizontal precedent.[3] But we think it's useful to discuss the factors individually.

---

[1] *Cf.* Robert E. Keeton, *Venturing to Do Justice: Reforming Private Law* 14 (1969) (listing four of the six items listed in the text but phrasing them differently: "changing a rule long questioned and only fluctuatingly applied; overruling a decision that is in irreconcilable conflict with another; changing a rule that has caused great confusion; and overruling when the court is convinced that the reason for the precedent no longer exists, that 'modern circumstances and justice combine' to justify the change, and that 'no one's present personal rights or vested property interests will be injured' by it") (quoting *Restifo v. McDonald*, 230 A.2d 199, 203–04 (Pa. 1967) (Bell C.J. dissenting)).

[2] *See, e.g.*, Randy J. Kozel, *Stare Decisis as Judicial Doctrine*, 67 Wash. & Lee L. Rev. 411 (2010).

[3] *See, e.g.*, *Haynie v. State*, 664 N.W.2d 129, 136 (Mich. 2003) ("[Courts] must examine whether the previous decision has become so embedded, so accepted, so fundamental, to everyone's expectations that to change it would produce

(A) *The decision is contrary to plain principles of law.*

The primary and most important factor to weigh in considering whether to overrule an earlier decision is its correctness. Courts are more willing to overrule a horizontal precedent that they determine to be obviously incorrect or ill reasoned.[4] As the Florida Supreme Court stated: "The doctrine of stare decisis bends where ... there has been an error in legal analysis. ... Intellectual honesty continues to demand that precedent be followed unless there has been a clear showing that the earlier decision was factually or legally erroneous or has not proven acceptable in actual practice."[5]

(B) *The decision is isolated and hasn't been followed or acquiesced in.*

Courts consider whether a particular precedential rule is supported by a single, isolated case or by a series of cases. Courts generally give less precedential weight to decisions that are isolated and haven't been followed (or acquiesced in) than to a line of precedent.[6] For instance, the Iowa Supreme Court declined to follow a solitary 71-year-old precedent that had found a conclusive presumption against admitting to bail a defendant indicted upon a capital offense.[7] Similarly, when related principles of law have

---

not just readjustments, but practical real-world dislocations. . . . [T]o have reliance, the knowledge must be of the sort that causes a person or entity to attempt to conform his conduct to a certain norm before the triggering event.") (internal quotation marks omitted).

[4] *Montejo v. Louisiana*, 556 U.S. 778, 793 (2009); *see* Francis Lieber, *On Civil Liberty and Self-Government* 211 (Theodore D. Woolsey ed., 3d ed. 1883) ("If the precedent is bad, let it be overruled by all means, or let the legislature regulate the matter by statute.").

[5] *Puryear v. State*, 810 So. 2d 901, 905 (Fla. 2002) (citations omitted).

[6] *State v. Surma*, 57 N.W.2d 370, 373 (Wis. 1953) ("[C]ourts are more prone not to apply the doctrine of stare decisis to a single decision as distinguished from a line of decisions adhering to the same principle."); *Stein Enters., Inc. v. Golla*, 426 A.2d 1129, 1133 (Pa. 1981) ("[T]he doctrine of stare decisis does not prevent us from departing from this solitary, stale precedent.").

[7] *Ford v. Dilley*, 156 N.W. 513, 519 (Iowa 1916) ("It is significant, too, that in the 71 years since Hight's Case was decided it has never been referred to in this jurisdiction."); *see Heyert v. Orange & Rockland Utils., Inc.*, 218 N.E.2d 263, 268 (N.Y. 1966) ("[I]t is the duty of the court to reexamine the question if justice demands it especially where, as in that instance, there was only one prior precedent in the jurisdiction decided by a sharply divided court.").

so changed as to leave a particular precedent outdated, courts are more likely to be amenable to overruling the precedent.[8] When a particular precedent stands alone or is at odds with related legal doctrine, it's often a sign that the particular case was poorly reasoned or incorrect. How isolated a particular precedent is, therefore, matters when courts decide whether to overrule it.

(C) *A divided court's decision on a matter of great importance is now seriously doubted.*

Courts sometimes justify overturning precedent based on sharp divisions and vigorous dissents in the deciding case. In *Payne v. Tennessee*,[9] for example, the U.S. Supreme Court overruled two recently decided cases, *Booth v. Maryland*[10] and *South Carolina v. Gathers*.[11] Both had held that at capital-sentencing hearings, the Eighth Amendment bars evidence of the effect that the victim's death had on the victim's family. Both *Booth* and *Gathers* were 5–4 decisions, and both included more than one dissenting opinion. *Payne* overruled both precedents, holding that the Eighth Amendment doesn't render victim-impact evidence inadmissible at a capital-sentencing hearing.[12] In overruling them, the *Payne* Court noted that "*Booth* and *Gathers* were decided by the narrowest of margins, over spirited dissents challenging the basic underpinnings of those decisions," adding: "They have been questioned by Members of the Supreme Court in later decisions and have defied consistent application by the lower courts."[13]

---

8   See *Patterson v. McLean Credit Union*, 491 U.S. 164, 173–74 (1989) (stating that one factor courts consider in deciding whether to overrule precedent is whether similar law has so developed as to have left the old rule irreconcilable with modern doctrine); *State v. Quintero*, 34 A.3d 612, 616 (N.H. 2011) (same); *Herrera v. Quality Pontiac*, 73 P.3d 181, 188 (N.M. 2003) (same); *State v. Outagamie Cnty. Bd. of Adjustment*, 628 N.W.2d 376, 383 (Wis. 2001) (same).

9   501 U.S. 808 (1991).

10 482 U.S. 496 (1987).

11 490 U.S. 805 (1989).

12 *Payne*, 501 U.S. at 827.

13 *Id.* at 828–29; see *Legal Tender Cases*, 79 U.S. (12 Wall.) 457, 553–54 (1870) (overruling *Hepburn v. Griswold*, 75 U.S. (8 Wall.) 603 (1869), and stating that *Hepburn* "was decided by a divided court, and by a court having a less number of judges than the law then in existence provided this court shall have"); *id.* at

At other times, though, judges have noted that a divided court and a vigorous dissent signal that all the issues were carefully considered in the prior case.[14] As the Court noted in the 5–4 decision *Patterson v. McLean Credit Union*,[15] a precedential case that was sharply divided with vigorous dissents should be accorded *more* deference because it shows that all the issues were considered. As the *Patterson* majority stated in declining to overrule that precedent, "It was recognized at the time [of the precedential decision] that a strong case could be made for the [opposing view], but that view did not prevail."[16] In general, though, the fact that a court has been divided on a question is not as important as the strength of the reason for the division, as reflected in a dissenting or concurring opinion, which may be expressly adopted by a later court in overruling the prior opinion.[17]

(D) *The decision has been met with general dissatisfaction, protest, or severe criticism.*

Courts justifiably consider the degree of rancor that a precedent creates. When a legal rule has proved difficult or confusing to apply, this difficulty or confusion is "itself a reason for

---

570 (Bradley J. concurring) ("Where the decision is recent, and is only made by a bare majority of the court, and during a time of public excitement on the subject, when the question has largely entered into the political discussions of the day, I consider it our right and duty to subject it to a further examination, if a majority of the court are dissatisfied with the former decision."); *Ex parte Lewis*, 219 S.W.3d 335, 376 (Tex. Crim. App. 2007) (citing this passage in *Payne* to justify overturning its own precedent).

14 See, e.g., *Citizens United v. Federal Election Comm'n*, 558 U.S. 310, 385 (2010) (Roberts C.J. concurring) ("We have ... had the benefit of a comprehensive dissent that has helped ensure that the Court has considered all the relevant issues.").

15 491 U.S. 164 (1989), *superseded by statute*, Civil Rights Act of 1991, 42 U.S.C. § 101.

16 *Id.* at 171–72 (citations omitted).

17 See, e.g., *City of North Wildwood v. Board of Comm'rs*, 365 A.2d 465, 466 (N.J. 1976) (per curiam) (overruling precedent, *In re Glen Rock*, 135 A.2d 506 (N.J. 1957), which held that certain water rates to users outside a municipality were not subject to the regulatory power of the public-utility board and observing that one of the justices had filed a "vigorous dissent" in *In re Glen Rock*. The court ultimately overruled *Glen Rock* "for the reasons expressed by Justice Francis in his dissent" and because "neither reason nor policy justifie[d] [its] viability").

reexamining that decision."[18] If a particular legal rule has shown itself to be unreasonable, courts consider this a factor in support of overruling the precedent.[19] Similarly, courts consider whether there has been a significant change in circumstances since the legal rule was promulgated.[20] Further, courts will often consider whether a particular line of precedent has proved unworkable.[21] In *Michigan v. Jackson*,[22] for example, the Supreme Court established the rule that police cannot interrogate a criminal defendant once the defendant has invoked the right to counsel at an arraignment or similar proceeding. But it later held this rule unworkable because more than half the states appoint counsel without a defendant's request.[23] In the later case, the Court called unworkability "a traditional ground for overruling" precedent.[24]

Further, courts will consider sustained criticism by courts and commentators as a reason to overrule earlier decisions. When deciding to change from a contributory-negligence to a comparative-negligence regime, for instance, some state courts noted that courts both within and outside their own jurisdictions,

---

18 *Nichols v. United States*, 511 U.S. 738, 746 (1994).

19 *Haney v. City of Lexington*, 386 S.W.2d 738, 739 (Ky. 1964) ("If its worth has been proven by extended experience, we can be content with that theory. But when a theory supporting a rule of law is not grounded upon sound logic, is not just, and has been discredited by actual experience, it should be discarded, and with it, the rule it supports."); *Dini v. Naiditch*, 170 N.E.2d 881, 885 (Ill. 1960) ("[A]n illogical anachronism, originating in a vastly different social order, and pock-marked by judicial refinements, . . . should not be perpetuated in the name of 'stare decisis.'").

20 *Puryear v. State*, 810 So. 2d 901, 905 (Fla. 2002) ("The doctrine of stare decisis bends where there has been a significant change in circumstances since the adoption of the legal rule.").

21 *See Herrera v. Quality Pontiac*, 73 P.3d 181, 188 (N.M. 2003) ("Particular questions must be considered before overturning precedent[, including] whether the precedent is so unworkable as to be intolerable."); *State Commercial Fisheries Entry Comm'n v. Carlson*, 65 P.3d 851, 859 (Alaska 2003); *People v. Hernandez*, 896 N.E.2d 297, 304 (Ill. 2008).

22 475 U.S. 625 (1986).

23 *Montejo v. Louisiana*, 556 U.S. 778, 785 (2009).

24 *Id.* at 779 (overruling *Michigan v. Jackson*, 475 U.S. 625 (1986)).

as well as many scholars, had criticized the old rule for its harshness and inequity.[25]

(E) *No serious reliance interests have built up around the decision.*

Some legal decisions engender no kind of reliance at all: think of the judicial interpretation of a statute providing for disbarment in the event of a felony conviction.[26] Courts have been less reluctant to overturn precedent when no reliance interests are at stake—especially when the precedent has proved to be injurious to public entities. This has long been the case. In 1909, the Arkansas Supreme Court wrote that when no rule of property is at stake, and "the dignity and sovereignty of the state is involved," the court has a "duty to correct the mistake of the court as speedily as possible by overruling a former decision which we become thoroughly satisfied is erroneous and contrary to the recognized rules established by the other courts of the country."[27] When the Arkansas court made that statement, it overturned a precedent that held a lawsuit to stop a state officer from violating a contract with the state to be a suit against the officer, not against the state. Instead, the court concluded, such a suit *is* in fact a suit against the state and therefore prohibited by the Arkansas Constitution.

(F) *Although some private rights may be injured by overruling the decision, it was wrong in the first place, it produces general injustice, and less harm will result from overruling the decision than from allowing it to stand.*

Courts must sometimes consider whether a legal rule results in injustice generally.[28] In a dissenting opinion, Stone C.J. stated the principle well: "Before overruling a precedent in any case it

---

25   *See, e.g., Hoffman v. Jones*, 280 So. 2d 431, 435 (Fla. 1973); *Li v. Yellow Cab Co.*, 532 P.2d 1226, 1230 (Cal. 1975).
26   *See* Note, *Stare Decisis*, 34 Harv. L. Rev. 74, 75 (1920) (providing this very example).
27   *Pitcock v. State*, 121 S.W. 742, 747 (Ark. 1909).
28   *State ex rel. Moore v. Molpus*, 578 So. 2d 624, 635 (Miss. 1991) ("One accepted ground for judicial overruling of a demonstrably erroneous prior constitutional interpretation is that, across the years, it has produced great and sustained harm.").

is the duty of the Court to make certain that more harm will not be done in rejecting than in retaining a rule of even dubious validity."[29]

The Illinois Supreme Court, for example, has stated that "when a rule of law has once been settled, . . . such rule ought to be followed unless it can be shown that serious detriment is thereby likely to arise prejudicial to public interests."[30] Although some private rights may be injured by overruling a decision, courts are more willing to overturn it if (1) it was wrong when decided, (2) it produces general inconvenience or injustice, and (3) less harm will result from overruling the decision than from allowing it to stand.[31] As the Michigan Supreme Court said in a 2002 case:[32] "[B]efore this court overrules a decision deliberately made, it should be convinced not merely that the case was wrongly decided, but also that less injury will result from overruling than from following it."[33] There, the defendant pleaded nolo contendere but mentally ill to second-degree murder and felony possession of a firearm.[34] At sentencing, the defendant's attorney allocuted on behalf of the defendant. The trial court didn't directly ask the defendant whether she had anything to say.[35] The defendant appealed, arguing that under Michigan court rules, the court was expressly required to ask her whether she had anything to say on her own behalf.[36] The Michigan Court of Appeals denied leave to appeal, but the Michigan Supreme Court granted it. An earlier Michigan case had held that the trial court was specifically

---

29 *United States v. South-Eastern Underwriters Ass'n*, 322 U.S. 533, 580 (1944) (Stone C.J. dissenting).

30 *Vitro v. Mihelcic*, 806 N.E.2d 632, 635 (Ill. 2004) (internal quotation marks omitted).

31 See *Thomas v. Anchorage Equal Rights Comm'n*, 102 P.3d 937, 943 (Alaska 2004) ("We will overrule a prior decision only when clearly convinced that the rule was originally erroneous or is no longer sound because of changed conditions, and that more good than harm would result from a departure from precedent.").

32 *People v. Petit*, 648 N.W.2d 193 (Mich. 2002).

33 *Id.* at 199 (internal quotation marks omitted).

34 *Id.* at 195.

35 *Id.*

36 *Id.* at 197.

required to ask the defendant during its sentencing colloquy whether she had anything to add.[37] The Michigan Supreme Court affirmed the defendant's conviction and sentence and overruled the precedent, concluding that overruling the decision "will create no practical real-world dislocations" because defendants' primary behavior would not be affected.[38]

---

37 *Id.*
38 *Id.* at 199.

48. Reasons Against Overruling

A court may decide against overruling an established horizontal precedent, even if it is now considered erroneous or open to grave doubts.

Many factors also militate against overruling horizontal precedent, among them these:

(A) The decision has stood unchallenged for many years.

(B) The same or other courts have approved and followed the decision in many later decisions.

(C) The decision has been universally accepted, acted on, and acquiesced in by courts, the legal profession, and the general public.

(D) The decision has become a rule of property.

(E) Reliance has been placed on the prior decision: contracts have been made, business transacted, and rights adjusted in reliance on the decision for a long time or to a great extent.

(F) The prior decision involved interpreting a statute.

Although courts aren't straitjacketed into applying horizontal precedents and can overrule prior cases for the reasons cited in the preceding section, they generally abide by the doctrine of stare decisis. In addition to the factors that support overturning precedent, courts also consider several reasons for not overturning, most of them being proxies for the degree to which the public has relied on a particular precedent.[1] As one distinguished commentator has noted, although "[a] practice of consistently and rigidly adhering to precedent eventually produces an accumulation of outmoded rules,"[2] yet "[r]estraint in exercising the power to overrule precedent is essential to the stability of the law."[3]

---

[1] *See* Randy J. Kozel, *Stare Decisis as Judicial Doctrine*, 67 Wash. & Lee L. Rev. 411, 414 (2010).

[2] Robert E. Keeton, *Venturing to Do Justice: Reforming Private Law* 15 (1969).

[3] *Id.*

(A) *The decision has stood unchallenged for many years.*

One factor that courts consider is how old a particular line of precedent is. The antiquity of a decision is a relevant factor that courts must consider when deciding whether to overrule horizontal precedent (see § 18). As the Oregon Supreme Court put it: "Courts do not lightly overturn precedent, especially when the precedent has been followed for a long time."[4] Yet the recent vintage of precedent will not necessarily militate in favor of reconsideration. The Georgia Supreme Court, when considering whether to overrule a case holding that the state can require an accused to be tried by a jury even when the accused would rather be tried by a judge,[5] noted that its precedent was less than eight years old:[6] "When we consider whether an earlier decision ought to be reexamined, we consider a number of factors, including the age of the precedent, the reliance interests involved, the workability of the prior decision, and most importantly, the soundness of its reasoning."[7]

Even though the prior case was "decided not long ago, it was based on principles that have been a settled part of our law for decades."[8] The Georgia Supreme Court affirmed the jury-tried conviction and declined to overrule its recent precedent.

---

4   *Keltner v. Washington Cnty.*, 800 P.2d 752, 754 (Or. 1990) (declining to reconsider the Oregon rule preventing a plaintiff in an action for breach of contract from recovering damages for purely mental distress); *see State ex rel. Foster v. Naftalin*, 74 N.W.2d 249, 267–68 (Minn. 1956) (stating that "[when] decisions have stood unchallenged for many years they should not be lightly overruled," and declining to overturn the rule of nonseverability, under which a material variance between a bill passed by the legislature and that approved by the governor renders the entire law void); *Public Serv. Ry. v. Matteucci*, 143 A. 221, 222 (N.J. 1928) ("[H]aving stood unchallenged for more than half a century, [a case] should not now be overthrown by judicial decision.").

5   *Zigan v. State*, 638 S.E.2d 322 (Ga. 2006).

6   *Smith v. State*, 757 S.E.2d 865, 866 (Ga. 2014).

7   *Id.* at 867 (internal quotation marks and citations omitted).

8   *Id.*

(B) *The same or other courts have approved and followed the decision in many later decisions.*

When considering whether to rethink a particular doctrine, courts consider not only the antiquity of a case, but also whether it has been followed in later cases. Whereas isolated cases are afforded less stare decisis weight, a court is more reluctant to overturn a horizontal line of precedent that many later decisions have approved of and followed. As the U.S. Supreme Court has stated, it generally will not rethink a prior decision when "unanimous interpretation of a statute has been accepted as settled law for several decades."[9]

(C) *The decision has been universally accepted, acted on, and acquiesced in by courts, the legal profession, and the general public.*

Further, courts consider not only the degree to which a case has been accepted in its own jurisdiction, but also whether the rule has been accepted, acted on, and acquiesced in by other courts, the legal profession, and the public generally. As the Supreme Judicial Court of Maine recently reiterated, a doctrine may be "too often recognized by courts of the highest respectability to be questioned now."[10]

---

[9] *IBP, Inc. v. Alvarez*, 546 U.S. 21, 32 (2005) (declining to overturn precedent construing the Fair Labor Standards Act).

[10] *Godbout v. WLB Holding, Inc.*, 997 A.2d 92, 94 (Me. 2010); *see Jansen v. City of Atchison*, 16 Kan. 358, 382 (1876) (finding that a "doctrine generally recognized in the courts of other states, generally approved by eminent jurists, [and] hitherto followed by this court" will not be revisited).

(D) *The decision has become a rule of property.*

Courts are particularly reluctant to overrule horizontal precedent affecting property rights, as the Supreme Court has noted: "Considerations in favor of stare decisis are at their acme in cases involving property and contract rights, where reliance interests are involved."[11] The Court recognized this doctrine as early as 1865: "Where questions arise which affect titles to land it is of great importance to the public that when they are once decided they should no longer be considered open. Such decisions become rules of property, and many titles may be injuriously affected by their change."[12] It's one thing when a new law affects future rules of property only, the court reasoned, "but where courts vacillate and overrule their own decisions on the construction of statutes affecting the title to real property, their decisions are retrospective and may affect titles purchased on the faith of their stability."[13] In this field, stability trumps correctness for strictly practical reasons: "Doubtful questions on subjects of this nature, when once decided, should be considered no longer doubtful or subject to change. Parties should not be encouraged to speculate on a change of the law when the administrators of it is changed."[14]

Another example: in *Michigan v. Bay Mills Indian Community*,[15] Michigan sued the Bay Mills Indian Community in federal

---

11   *Payne v. Tennessee*, 501 U.S. 808, 828 (1991); *see Oregon ex rel. State Land Bd. v. Corvallis Sand & Gravel Co.*, 429 U.S. 363, 381 (1977) ("Substantive rules governing the law of real property are peculiarly subject to the principle of stare decisis."); *Citizens United v. Federal Election Comm'n*, 558 U.S. 310, 365 (2010) (stating that "reliance interests are important considerations in property and contract cases, where parties may have acted in conformance with existing legal rules in order to conduct transactions," but finding no reliance interests in that case).

12   *Minnesota Mining Co. v. National Mining Co.*, 70 U.S. (3 Wall.) 332, 334 (1865); *see The Genesee Chief*, 53 U.S. (12 How.) 443, 458 (1851) (holding that in cases involving contracts and property rights, "stare decisis is the safe and established rule of judicial policy, and should always be adhered to," and declining to overturn a prior case that had settled the ownership of a particular title); *United States v. Title Ins. & Trust Co.*, 265 U.S. 472, 486 (1924) ("[T]o disturb [a rule of property] now would be fraught with many injurious results.").

13   70 U.S. at 334.

14   *Id.*

15   134 S.Ct. 2024 (2014).

court to enjoin operation of a casino outside tribal lands, and the district court granted relief.[16] The Sixth Circuit reversed, holding that sovereign immunity barred the suit.[17] The Supreme Court affirmed, declining to overrule a prior case that had held the doctrine of tribal sovereign immunity not to include exceptions for off-reservation conduct or commercial activity.[18] The Court recognized that entities and individuals had negotiated contracts and structured transactions against a backdrop of tribal immunity, and that "[a]s in other cases involving contract and property rights, concerns of stare decisis are thus at their acme."[19]

For more on rules of property, see § 51.

(E) *Reliance has been placed on the prior decision: contracts have been made, business transacted, and rights adjusted in reliance on the decision for a long time or to a great extent.*

Courts are particularly reluctant to overturn horizontal precedent when the public has relied on a legal rule enunciated in a particular line of cases. For the Supreme Court, for instance, strong "reliance interests" are a particularly influential reason not to overturn horizontal precedent.[20] Indeed, one reason that the doctrine of stare decisis exists is to "foster[] reliance on judicial decisions."[21] The assumption is that people shape their lives according to the rule of law, which should not be subject to flux:

---

16 *Id.* at 2029.
17 *Id.*
18 *Id.* at 2036.
19 *Id.* (internal citations omitted).
20 *Planned Parenthood of SE Pa. v. Casey*, 505 U.S. 833, 855 (1992) (stating as one factor in considering overturning precedent whether parties justifiably relied on the precedent so that reversing it would create an undue hardship, but concluding that "the classic case for weighing reliance heavily in favor of following the earlier rule occurs in the commercial context"); *Higby v. Mahoney*, 396 N.E.2d 183, 184 (N.Y. 1979) (per curiam) ("Whether it is appropriate for the courts to overturn judicial precedent must depend on several factors. Among them will be . . . the extent and degree to which action may justifiably have been taken in reliance on the precedent.").
21 *State Oil Co. v. Khan*, 522 U.S. 3, 20 (1997).

"Stability in the law allows individuals to plan their affairs and to safely judge of their legal rights."[22]

Similarly, courts are particularly deferential to horizontal precedent in the field of commercial law, in which the "prior precedent is more likely to have guided numerous people in their conduct."[23] As the Wisconsin Supreme Court has stated, "stare decisis is particularly controlling where the legal rule impacts contractual relationships and has been relied upon by industry."[24] Further, stare decisis is particularly strong in the field of trust law.[25]

(F) *The prior decision involved interpreting a statute.*

As we have seen, courts are also less willing to overturn precedent that interprets a statute than they are to overturn constitutional precedent. As the Supreme Court has stated, "considerations of stare decisis weigh heavily in the area of statutory construction, where Congress is free to change this Court's interpretation of its legislation."[26] Similarly, the New York high court has stated that horizontal precedents based on statutory interpretation are "entitled" to stability because "in such cases courts are

---

22   *In re Estate of McFarland*, 167 S.W.3d 299, 306 (Tenn. 2005) (internal quotation marks omitted).

23   *Heyert v. Orange & Rockland Utils., Inc.*, 218 N.E.2d 263, 268–69 (N.Y. 1966) (stating that "[a]lthough courts are not compelled to follow so-called rules of property, the doctrine of stare decisis is more strictly followed where property rights, especially rights in real property, are concerned and where rights have become vested in reliance on the precedents," and declining to overturn precedent that held that a town's easement for highway purposes didn't include the right to grant rights to lay gas mains in the street to private utility corporations) (internal quotation marks omitted).

24   *Progressive N. Ins. Co. v. Romanshek*, 697 N.W.2d 417, 429 (Wis. 2005) (citation omitted) (declining to overrule precedent requiring that a hit-and-run involve physical contact in an accident involving an unknown vehicle); *see Heyert*, 218 N.E.2d at 268 ("In the field of commercial law the courts have been slower in deviating from precedent. The prior precedent is more likely to have guided numerous people in their conduct.") (citation omitted).

25   *Johnson v. Chicago, Burlington & Quincy R.R.*, 66 N.W.2d 763, 770 (Minn. 1954) (overturning precedent that had eliminated the forum non conveniens doctrine from Federal Employers Liability Act cases).

26   *Pearson v. Callahan*, 555 U.S. 223, 233 (2009) (internal quotation marks omitted); *see IBP*, 546 U.S. at 32 ("Considerations of stare decisis are particularly forceful in the area of statutory construction, especially when a unanimous interpretation of a statute has been accepted as settled law for several decades.").

interpreting legislative intention and a sequential contradiction is a grossly arrogated legislative power. Moreover, if the precedent or precedents have misinterpreted the legislative intention, the Legislature's competency to correct the misinterpretation is readily at hand."[27]

When a court has construed a particular statute and the legislature has failed to amend that statute to negate the court's ruling, courts have interpreted this failure to act as "legislative acceptance or approval of the construction rendered in the earlier case."[28] But legislative "inaction" isn't dispositive.[29]

In constitutional cases, by contrast, high courts are more willing to reconsider doctrine than in statutory-interpretation cases "because in such cases correction through legislative action is practically impossible."[30] (See § 40.) But in the context of a constitutional rule, lower courts and high courts will avoid reexamining even constitutional precedent if they are able to decide the case on narrower grounds: "[I]t is a well-established principle governing the prudent exercise of this Court's jurisdiction that normally the Court will not decide a constitutional question if there is some other ground upon which to dispose of the case."[31]

---

27 *Higby*, 396 N.E.2d at 184–85 (internal quotation marks and citations omitted).

28 *Johnson v. State*, 91 So. 2d 185, 187 (Fla. 1956) (en banc).

29 *Wenke v. Gehl Co.*, 682 N.W.2d 405, 417 (Wis. 2004) ("[P]roper invocation of the doctrine of legislative acquiescence requires more than merely noting that the legislature has not amended a statute to 'correct' a prior judicial construction. The doctrine of legislative acquiescence is merely a presumption to aid in statutory construction."). *But see Johnson v. Transportation Agency, Santa Clara Cnty.*, 480 U.S. 616, 672 (1987) (Scalia J. dissenting) (referring to the "legislative inaction" rule as a "canard" because a later Congress's inaction should not be used to interpret the statute of an earlier Congress).

30 *Seminole Tribe of Fla. v. Florida*, 517 U.S. 44, 63 (1996) (internal quotation marks omitted).

31 *Bond v. United States*, 134 S.Ct. 2077, 2087 (2014) (internal quotation marks omitted); *see Ashwander v. Tennessee Valley Auth.*, 297 U.S. 288, 347 (1936) (Brandeis J. concurring).

49. Hardship in a Particular Case

The fact that applying a well-settled legal rule will work hardship in a particular case is not reason for overruling an earlier decision or even departing from it.

Although applying precedent may work a hardship in a particular case, judges are traditionally exhorted to keep the law stable. As the Georgia Supreme Court wrote in 1879, hardship "is no reason for melting down the law. For the sake of fixedness and uniformity, law must be treated as a solid, not as a fluid."[1] The metaphor continued. Law, the court said, "must have, and always retain, a certain degree of hardness, to keep its outlines firm and constant. Water changes shape with every vessel into which it is poured; and a liquid law would vary with the mental conformation of judges, and become a synonym for vagueness and instability."[2] Courts are supposed to understand and withstand the temptations of short-term expediencies: "Stability and certainty in the law are of the very first importance. Hardship may sometimes result from a stern adherence to general rules. This is unavoidable under any system of jurisprudence."[3]

In the 1853 Ohio case in which the latter pronouncement had been delivered,[4] the claimant sought to enforce a mortgage that had been executed and certified by a justice of the peace before only one witness rather than the two required by statute. As a result, the claimant's interest was defeated by a later judgment lien. The court refused to overrule precedent, holding that a mortgage has no effect before due execution and delivery for recordation despite the hardship to the would-be mortgagee who had relied on the imperfect certification.

When a court is asked to overrule a horizontal precedent, it will consider factors that apply in general to circumstances similar

---

[1] *Southern Star Lightning Rod Co. v. Duvall*, 64 Ga. 262, 268 (1879) (per Bleckley J.).
[2] *Id.*
[3] *White v. Denman*, 1 Ohio St. 110, 114–15 (1853).
[4] *Id.*

to the case at hand such as whether the prior case defies practical workability, whether reliance interests would work an undue hardship if the case were overruled, and whether changes in the law and facts no longer justify the decision in the prior case.[5] Other authorities identify factors such as the plausibility of the existing interpretation of a statute, the extent to which that interpretation has been woven into the fabric of the law, and the strength of the arguments for changing the interpretation.[6] Whether applying the precedent in a particular case will work a hardship isn't one of the factors that a court will consider, because "not only would the principle of stare decisis have to be ignored, but it would have a tendency to cause decisions of courts to be regarded as unstable and vacillating."[7]

In some jurisdictions, a prerequisite to overruling a horizontal precedent is that, without the overruling, a "great injury or injustice would result."[8] In a 1984 Arkansas case,[9] multiple litigants attacked an earlier case that had held certain state political subdivisions to be self-insurers if those subdivisions failed to carry motor-vehicle insurance.[10] The court declined to overrule the precedent,[11] observing that although the litigants had argued that applying precedent was harmful, "[n]one of the parties have given us any convincing authority or reasons why [precedent] should not be followed."[12]

But no authority suggests that injury or injustice in a particular case, rather than cases in general, is a reason to overrule horizontal precedent. There is a strong presumption of the validity of earlier decisions.[13] Considering the effect of the law in a particular case is tantamount to disregarding the law: "In determining a case the

---

5 *Paige v. City of Sterling Heights*, 720 N.W.2d 219, 227 (Mich. 2006).
6 20 Am. Jur. 2d *Courts* § 128, at 529 (2015).
7 *McGraw v. Merryman*, 104 A. 540, 545 (Md. 1918).
8 *Thompson v. Sanford*, 663 S.W.2d 932, 935 (Ark. 1984).
9 *Id.*
10 *Id.* at 934.
11 *Id.* at 933.
12 *Id.* at 935.
13 *Id.*

court is not concerned with what the law ought to be, but its sole function is to declare what the law, applicable to the facts of the case, is."[14] This principle particularly guides trial courts. No recognized principle allows a court "to depart from an established rule of law to meet a particular case of supposed hardship."[15]

Courts should disregard not only any hardship occasioned by applying precedent, but also whatever hardship would be occasioned in a particular case by the decision to overrule horizontal precedent. Courts will consider the hardship to *reliance* interests that would be worked by overruling precedent, but not the hardship to the particular parties.[16]

Consider a 2006 case from the Michigan Supreme Court.[17] The plaintiff sought workers'-compensation death-dependency benefits after his father's death.[18] The workers'-compensation agency awarded benefits to the plaintiff based on a prior Michigan case, which held that the phrase *proximate cause* in the workers'-compensation statute regarding benefits to dependents didn't mean the sole proximate cause of death but rather required that the work-related injury be a substantial factor in the employee's death.[19]

The Michigan Supreme Court reversed, holding that as a matter of statutory interpretation the controlling precedent had been wrongly decided because other Michigan statutes referred to *a proximate cause* to mean "a substantial factor," but used the language *the proximate cause* to mean "the sole proximate cause."[20] The court held that the prior case must be overruled.[21] Over a dissent

---

14 *Cayuga Indian Nation v. Cuomo*, 771 F. Supp. 19, 23 n.7 (N.D.N.Y. 1991) (citing 21 C.J.S. *Courts* § 187 (1940)) (refusing to disregard precedent holding that laches is not a valid defense to Indian land claims, though the equities in the case favored recognizing laches as a defense).

15 *Id.*

16 *See* Randy J. Kozel, *Stare Decisis as Judicial Doctrine*, 67 Wash. & Lee L. Rev. 411, 414 (2010).

17 *Paige v. City of Sterling Heights*, 720 N.W.2d 219 (Mich. 2006).

18 *Id.* at 222.

19 *Id.* at 223.

20 *Id.*

21 *Id.*

that argued that the court didn't sufficiently consider "whether reliance interests would be misplaced and cause an undue hardship if established precedent were overruled," and that the reliance of the workers'-compensation bar sufficed to establish the reliance of workers and employers,[22] the court held that no reliance interests counseled against overruling precedent.[23] The court noted that the decedent had not "positioned himself in reliance" on the precedent, but the court didn't address the possible hardship created by the decision on the plaintiff who had brought the action and who had been awarded benefits below based on the precedent.[24] The hardship in the particular case wasn't addressed by the court.

Hardship created for particular parties in a case isn't a consideration weighing for or against overruling precedent. Courts consider hardship only insofar as it affects reliance interests, and the hardship occasioned by reliance interests is a factor weighed in *favor* of stare decisis.

---

22   *Id.* at 238 (Cavanaugh J. dissenting).
23   *Id.* at 228.
24   *Id.* at 229.

50. Changes in Court's Organization or Personnel

A change in the court's organization or in judicial personnel should not throw former decisions open to reconsideration or justify their reversal except on grounds that would have warranted such a course if the makeup of the court had remained the same.

Commentators often adumbrate or even assert outright that the composition of a court might affect the outcome of a case and even lead to the overruling of an earlier decision. Some have even gone so far as to say that the only difference between an overruled case and the new decision is the court's membership.[1] Yet stare decisis dictates that a precedent shouldn't be overruled simply because new judges populate the court.[2] It wouldn't carry much persuasive power to argue that *Marbury v. Madison* should be overruled because Marshall C.J. no longer sits on the U.S. Supreme Court. Indeed, as one of his colleagues wrote in 1831 (dissenting from one of Marshall's opinions): "We must respect the solemn decisions of our predecessors and associates, as we may wish that those who succeed us should respect ours, or [else] the supreme law of the land, so far as depends on judicial interpretation, will change with the change of judges."[3] That would make a hash out of the doctrine of stare decisis, since most precedents

---

1   *See, e.g., Newdow v. Rio Linda Union Sch. Dist.*, 597 F.3d 1007, 1075 n.55 (9th Cir. 2010) (Reinhardt J. dissenting) ("In truth, the only reason this case is being decided differently today than it was seven years ago is that a random lottery drew the members of *this* panel to decide the issue.").

2   *See, e.g.,* Basil Jones, "Stare Decisis," in 26 *The American and English Encyclopaedia of Law* 168 (David S. Garland & Lucius P. McGehee eds., 2d ed. 1904) ("A change in the personnel or organization of the court affords no ground for the reopening of a question which has been once settled authoritatively by it.").

3   *Ex parte Crane*, 30 U.S. (5 Pet.) 190, 202–03 (1831) (Baldwin J. dissenting); *cf. Pollock v. Farmers' Loan & Trust Co.*, 157 U.S. 429, 650–51 (1895) ("The conservation and orderly development of our institutions rest on our acceptance of the results of the past, and their use as lights to guide our steps in the future. . . . In the discharge of its function of interpreting the Constitution, this court exercises an august power. . . . If the permanency of its conclusions is to depend upon the personal opinions of those who, from time to time, may make up its membership, it will inevitably become a theater of political strife.").

cited are from panels of judges who no longer sit on the court that established them.

The authority of precedent derives not from the wisdom or authority of particular judges who render a decision but from the fact that it is a judgment of the court whose jurisdiction hasn't changed.[4] Hence a change in the composition of court personnel is a "type of 'circumstance' that does not rise to the level necessary to overturn the doctrine of stare decisis."[5] This rule is so because "we may be confident in the assumption that a precedent may *not* properly be overruled simply because a majority of the Court believes it to be error," as the Texas Court of Criminal Appeals said in a 1993 case.[6] "If the rule were otherwise," the court wrote, "then no precedent would be safe and our law could change after every change in Court personnel."[7] The court cited Cardozo J. for this proposition: "The situation would . . . be intolerable if the [periodic] changes in the composition of the court were accompanied by changes in its rulings. In such circumstances there is nothing to do except to stand by the errors of our brethren of the [time] before, whether we relish them or not."[8]

So a court on which certain judges have come to determine that a prior case was wrongly decided, or a court that has had a change of personnel and can now muster the necessary votes to overrule a prior case, cannot properly overrule the prior case without considering both the doctrine of stare decisis and the factors that it requires: "The concepts of stare decisis and judicial restraint are too vital to our system of jurisprudence to accommodate simple changes of heart or court personnel."[9]

This principle is no less true in jurisdictions where court personnel change frequently through elections. The authority of

---

4   *Olcott v. Tioga R.R.*, 26 Barb. 147 (N.Y. Gen. Term 1857).
5   *People v. Barrow*, 749 N.E.2d 892, 915 (Ill. 2001) (Freeman J. concurring).
6   *Garrett v. State*, 851 S.W.2d 853, 862 (Tex. Crim. App. 1993) (en banc) (Campbell J. dissenting) (quoting Benjamin N. Cardozo, *The Nature of the Judicial Process* 150 (1921)).
7   851 S.W.2d at 862–63.
8   *Id.* at 863.
9   *Thomas v. State*, 326 So. 2d 413, 418 n.9 (Fla. 1975) (England J. dissenting).

precedent comes from its having been rendered by the court, not the elected officials on the court, as has long been recognized. As the Court for the Correction of Errors of New York, formerly the high court in that state, opined in 1833: "Especially in this court, where nearly one-fourth of its members are annually changed, and by popular election, the maxim that it is best to adhere to our decisions, and not to disturb questions which have once been put at rest here, should be permitted to have its full effect."[10]

Similarly, an organizational change to a court that doesn't affect its jurisdiction isn't a reason to disrupt stare decisis. A new court invested with a previous court's jurisdiction, succeeding it in duty and function, is bound by the decision of the court that preceded by the terms of stare decisis.[11] A prime example occurred in 1980, when Congress created the Eleventh Circuit Court of Appeals, made up of districts formerly in the Fifth Circuit.[12] In the very first case heard by the newly constituted Court of Appeals for the Eleventh Circuit, the en banc court adopted all precedents of the Fifth Circuit. Its reasoning is instructive:

> [T]his court could decide to proceed with its duties without any precedent, deciding each legal principle anew, and relying upon decisions of the former Fifth Circuit and other circuit and district courts as only persuasive authority and not binding. This court, the trial courts, the bar and the public are entitled to a better result than to be cast adrift among the differing precedents of other jurisdictions, required to examine afresh every legal principle that eventually arises in the Eleventh Circuit.... We tend to think of stare decisis as only "it is decided." The full phrase is *stare decisis et non quieta movere*—"to adhere to precedents and not to unsettle things which are established." The prospect of decades of writing on a clean slate in pursuit of the possibility that in some case or cases we might find a rule we like better (or even conclude that an old Fifth Circuit decision is wrong) is at best unappealing, at worst catastrophic.[13]

---

10   *Driggs v. Rockwell*, 11 Wend. 504, 507 (N.Y. 1833).
11   Henry Campbell Black, *Handbook on the Law of Judicial Precedents* § 60, at 190 (1912).
12   Fifth Circuit Court of Appeals Reorganization Act of 1980, Pub. L. No. 96-452, 94 Stat. 1994 (codified as amended at 28 U.S.C. §§ 41, 44(a), 48).
13   *Bonner v. City of Prichard*, 661 F.2d 1206, 1211 (11th Cir. 1981) (en banc).

In later cases, the Eleventh Circuit has observed that it is bound by the horizontal precedent of the Fifth Circuit and hasn't considered the reorganization of the court as grounds for ignoring the doctrine of stare decisis.[14]

Some counterexamples

Neither a change in the composition of a court's members nor a change in its organization supplies a sufficient reason to disturb the doctrine of stare decisis. A court with new members, or newly constituted, will examine the factors that guide stare decisis when deciding whether to overrule horizontal precedent[15] (see §§ 47–49).

Yet there are curious outlier instances. In the early 1940s, for example, the U.S. Supreme Court decided a 5–4 case[16] that within a year was reheard and reversed—also 5–4.[17] *Jones v. City of Opelika* was a consolidation of three cases in which persons were convicted of selling books or pamphlets of a religious nature without a peddler's license, even though they were primarily engaged in proselytizing.[18] The petitioners contended that the licensing ordinances interfered with their constitutional rights to freedom of religion, speech, and a free press.[19] In 1942, the Court decided that the ordinances were not aimed at interfering with any of those rights and were proper exercises of control over sales activities.[20] Byrnes J., who had voted with the majority, resigned later in 1942. That same year, the Superior Court of Pennsylvania cited *Jones* in a very similar case.[21] The Supreme Court consolidated Murdock's

---

14   *McMahon v. Presidential Airways, Inc.*, 502 F.3d 1331, 1341 n.10 (11th Cir. 2007); *Brooks v. Central Bank of Birmingham*, 717 F.2d 1340, 1343 (11th Cir. 1983) (per curiam) ("Of greater significance, however, is our uncompromising adherence to the rule of stare decisis and our binding obligation to follow the precedential decisions of this circuit.") (referring to Fifth Circuit case *White v. United States Pipe & Foundry Co.*, 646 F.2d 203 (5th Cir. Unit B May 1981)).

15   Henry Campbell Black, *Handbook on the Law of Judicial Precedents* § 60, at 189–91 (1912).

16   *Jones v. City of Opelika*, 316 U.S. 584 (1942).

17   *Jones v. City of Opelika*, 319 U.S. 103 (1943) (mem.).

18   316 U.S. at 586–91.

19   *Id.* at 593.

20   *Id.* at 597–98.

21   *Commonwealth v. Murdock*, 27 A.2d 666, 669 (Pa. Super. Ct. 1942).

appeal with the early 1943 rehearing of *Jones v. City of Opelika*.[22] This time the Court decided that the petitioners were practicing their religion and that the sales of printed materials were merely incidental.[23] Hence the licensing ordinances restricted religious practices and couldn't be upheld.[24] The previous case was expressly vacated.[25] Eight of the Justices maintained the same positions in both cases. But Byrnes's replacement, Rutledge J., voted with the members who had previously constituted the minority, thus bringing about the reversal. Their position accorded with a dissenting opinion that Rutledge had delivered on the circuit bench in 1942.[26] Perhaps the very fact that the case was on rehearing mollifies the appearance of the decision's having been attributable only to a change in personnel.

Another tale on this score was a litigious saga that played out from 1850 to 1860 in Pennsylvania: *Hole v. Rittenhouse*.[27] The case began when Rittenhouse and two others claimed they had acquired a 400-acre tract of land by adverse possession and sought to eject Hole, who asserted superior ownership. They won a jury verdict in 1851,[28] which Hole appealed to the Pennsylvania Supreme Court. A year later, in a 3–2 decision, the court found for Rittenhouse. Black C.J. wrote for the majority that a rule articulated by the court in 1847 in *Waggoner v. Hastings*,[29] and repeated as recently as 1851, dictated that a person who had actual possession of part of a tract under color of title had constructive possession of the whole.[30] But because Rittenhouse's claim hadn't been fully proved, the court reversed and remanded for a new trial.[31] One concurring justice, Lowrie J., wobbled in his separate opinion, opining that

---

22   *Murdock v. Pennsylvania*, 319 U.S. 105 (1943); *Jones v. City of Opelika*, 319 U.S. 103 (1943) (mem.).
23   *Murdock*, 319 U.S. at 110–12.
24   *Id.* at 113–15.
25   *Id.* at 117.
26   *Busey v. District of Columbia*, 129 F.2d 24, 28 (D.C. Cir. 1942).
27   37 Pa. 116 (1860).
28   *Id.* at 116.
29   5 Pa. 300 (1847).
30   *Hole v. Rittenhouse*, 19 Pa. 305, 307 (1852) (citing *Waggoner*, 5 Pa. 300).
31   *Id.* at 311.

the rule in *Waggoner* was too broad because it would unreasonably permit a person who possessed a few acres of a hundred-acre tract to claim possession of the whole tract.[32] In 1855, having lost again at trial, Hole petitioned the court and won another reversal and new trial.[33] This time, the decision was 4–1, and the court overruled *Waggoner* and its progeny.[34] One of the justices who had heard the case in 1852 and voted in Rittenhouse's favor had since died and been replaced. His replacement joined the majority in favor of Hole. Black J. wrote a stinging dissent in which he noted that it takes about nine years for the court's majority to change personnel. "If each new set of Judges shall consider themselves at liberty to overthrow the doctrines of their predecessors, our system of jurisprudence (if system it can be called) would be the most fickle, uncertain, and vicious that the civilized world ever saw."[35] Only stare decisis stands in the way of that "great calamity," Black said, so of the current court's predecessors, "I would stand by their decisions, because they have passed into the law and become a part of it—have been relied and acted on—and rights have grown up under them which it is unjust and cruel to take away."[36]

Black J. resigned from the court in 1857.[37] The jury in Hole's third trial found in favor of Rittenhouse in 1858, and Hole again appealed to the Pennsylvania Supreme Court.[38] The court's opinion in Hole's favor was unanimous, and the lower court's judgment reversed again, but this time no new trial was ordered.[39] In essence, the court declared: "We have spoken three times, and thrice is enough."[40] After ten years, Rittenhouse and the other adverse claimants were finally ousted from the land.

---

32 *Id.* (Lowrie J. concurring).
33 *Hole v. Rittenhouse*, 25 Pa. 491, 502 (1855).
34 *Id.* at 498–501; *see Hole v. Rittenhouse*, 37 Pa. 116, 119 (1860).
35 *Hole v. Rittenhouse*, 2 Phila. Rep. 411, 417 (Pa. 1855) (per Black J.). Reproduced in full in R.E. Megarry, *A Second Miscellany-at-Law* 141–43 (1973).
36 *Id.*
37 27 Pa. iii (1858).
38 *Hole*, 37 Pa. at 116.
39 *Id.* at 121.
40 Megarry, *A Second Miscellany-at-Law* at 143.

51. Heightened Stare Decisis for Rules of Property

A precedent that creates a rule of property—a widely relied-on legal principle established by a judicial decision or series of decisions relating to title to real, personal, or intellectual property—is generally treated as inviolable.

A venerable legal principle stresses the importance of reliance interests when dealing with property rights. Bushrod Washington J. put the point well in an 1806 decision of the U.S. Supreme Court: "[I]n questions which respect the rights of property, it is better to adhere to principles once fixed ... than to unsettle the law in order to render it more consistent with the dictates of sound reason."[1] Later in the 19th century, Chancellor James Kent of New York traced this view to the most famous English judge of the preceding century: "Lord Mansfield frequently observed that the certainty of a rule was often of much more importance in mercantile cases than the reason of it, and that a settled rule ought to be observed for the sake of property."[2]

The rule-of-property doctrine embodies reliance principles for precedents affecting property, including its creation, ownership, transfer, and devolution.[3] The doctrine holds that stare decisis applies with "peculiar force and strictness" to decisions governing real property, vested rights, and, in some circumstances, "matters of general commercial importance which tend to influence future business transactions."[4] Stability in rules governing property

---

1 *Marine Ins. Co. of Alexandria v. Tucker*, 7 U.S. (3 Cranch) 357, 388 (1806) (per Washington J.).
2 1 James Kent, *Commentaries on American Law* *477 (Charles M. Barnes ed., 13th ed. 1884).
3 *Union Trust Co. v. Williamson Cnty. Bd. of Zoning Appeals*, 500 S.W.2d 608, 615–16 (Tenn. 1973); *see also City of Memphis v. Overton*, 392 S.W.2d 98, 101 (Tenn. 1965).
4 *Abbott v. City of Los Angeles*, 326 P.2d 484, 494–95 (Cal. 1958) (in bank) (quoting 14 Am. Jur. *Carriage of Persons* § 65, at 286; *id.* § 126 at 343); *see* Frederick Pollock, *A First Book of Jurisprudence for Students of the Common Law* 306–07 (1896) ("Where a decision, or still more a series of decisions to the same effect, has been accepted for law and acted upon by many persons, and especially where a rule thus arrived at has become a guide to lawyers and their clients in their dealings with property, the Courts, even Courts of Appeal, are slow

interests is particularly important because those rules create unusually strong reliance interests: individuals rely on rules governing their entitlements in entering into other commercial transactions.[5] Judicial decisions overruling rules of property almost always interfere with those established interests,[6] and may even implicate due-process concerns.[7] As the Supreme Court explained in a mid-19th-century case:[8] "Where questions arise which affect titles to land it is of great importance to the public that when they are once decided they should no longer be considered open. Such decisions become rules of property, and many titles may be injuriously affected by their change."[9] That's not the case when a legislature changes laws that apply only to future interests and events, the court noted. "[B]ut where courts vacillate and overrule their own decisions on the construction of statutes affecting the title to real property, their decisions are retrospective and may affect titles purchased on the faith of their stability." Once decided, then, issues that affect property rights "should be considered no longer doubtful or subject to change."[10]

The phrase *rule of property* may be either a doctrinal term of art or a generic descriptor. For example, some courts have followed

---

    to interfere with the rule, and it may perhaps be upheld although modern research has shown that it was originally founded on a mistake; for the reversal of a rule that has been commonly acted upon might well produce an amount of inconvenience greater than any advantage that could be expected from the restoration or establishment of a rule more correct in itself."); *cf. Kimble v. Marvel Entm't, LLC*, 135 S.Ct. 2401, 2404 (2015) (recognizing that stare decisis considerations are "at their acme" in cases involving property and contractual rights) (quoting *Payne v. Tennessee*, 501 U.S. 808, 828 (1991)).

5   *Bogle Farms, Inc. v. Baca*, 925 P.2d 1184, 1192–93 (N.M. 1996) (collecting cases).
6   See *Heyert v. Orange & Rockland Utils., Inc.*, 218 N.E.2d 263, 269 (N.Y. 1966) (adhering to "a rule of property which [could not] be changed retrospectively without altering the substance of prior land grants").
7   See *United States v. Standard Oil Co.*, 20 F. Supp. 427, 455 & n.9 (S.D. Cal. 1937) (citing *Great Northern Ry. v. Sunburst Oil & Ref. Co.*, 287 U.S. 358, 362–63 (1932) (Cardozo J.)); *see also Stop the Beach Renourishment, Inc. v. Florida Dep't of Envtl. Prot.*, 560 U.S 702, 713–17 (2010) (plurality opinion); Barton H. Thompson Jr., *Judicial Takings*, 76 Va. L. Rev. 1449, 1463–72 (1990).
8   *Minnesota Mining Co. v. National Mining Co.*, 70 U.S. (3 Wall.) 332, 334 (1865).
9   *Id.*
10 *Id.*

Black's Law Dictionary, which (in its fourth edition) defined a rule of property as "[a] settled rule or principle, resting usually on precedents or a course of decisions, regulating the ownership or devolution of property."[11] Other courts use the phrase *rule of property* to refer to any rule affecting property but not necessarily title. That elicits a further, separate inquiry into the stare decisis weight suggested by the doctrine.[12] We will follow the former sense of the phrase because it appears to be the majority usage. But in either case, a court must decide whether the rule governing the property issue at stake is sufficiently settled to be entitled the weight accorded a true rule of property under the doctrine.

A classic example applying the rule-of-property doctrine came in a 1966 New York case.[13] The petitioner, Heyert, held title to land that extended underneath the town road running over her property. She had presumptively granted the town an easement under the relevant highway law. When the town authorized a utility company to install gas pipes under the street, Heyert brought a takings claim, arguing that the town's easement for highway purposes didn't include the right to install gas mains. The court first observed that a series of past decisions had held that easements for highway purposes were only "reservation[s] of a mere 'right of way'" and so, without more, "included only the right of passage over the surface of the land" and such improvements as directly or indirectly pertained to that right, such as street lighting and drainage sewers.[14] Although the use of public streets had evolved,[15] "thousands of deeds conveying rights of way . . . ha[d] been made on this rule, which ha[d] existed since the common law began in [New York]," and which had just recently received

---

11 *City of Memphis*, 392 S.W.2d at 101 (quoting *Black's Law Dictionary* 1497 (4th ed. 1951)); *Abbott*, 326 P.2d at 494 (same).

12 *See, e.g., Bogle Farms*, 925 P.2d at 1192–93 (collecting cases) ("Insofar as [a previous judicial decision] pronounced a rule that affects title to real estate, it did adopt a 'rule of property.' Whether we should adhere to [that decision] as a matter of stare decisis, however, involves more than mere talismanic invocation of a phrase.").

13 *Heyert*, 218 N.E.2d 263.

14 *Id.* at 266–67 (collecting cases).

15 *See id.* at 270–71 (Keating J. concurring).

yet another unequivocal expression by the high court.[16] This "long succession of decisions . . . fits the classic definition of a rule of property," the court said.[17] Declining to overrule all that horizontal precedent, the court held that Heyert was entitled to recover for the appropriation of her land for the gas mains.[18]

Achieving inviolability

For a rule affecting property to acquire the status of inviolability, it must meet a high standard: "[B]efore setting up a judicial declaration as a rule of property, we should require, at least, that it be fixed, long-continued, and relied upon by persons acquiring property, so that its repudiation would amount to a denial of due process."[19] Reliance is usually presumed once a rule of property has been recognized.

In general, only decisions of the highest court in the relevant jurisdiction may establish a rule of property.[20] After all, decisions of lower state courts or federal district courts, though "entitled to great weight, . . . are subject to appeal and reversal."[21] Reviewing courts have consistently declined to respect even those decisions of lower courts that have stood unchallenged for many years.[22] This may be attributable in part to the relationship between the doctrine of the rule of property and vertical precedents: as the Delaware Supreme Court has explained in holding that a longstanding decision of a lower court wasn't a rule of property, "stare decisis has little application to a case in which an appellate court is examining a decision of a lower court."[23] So usually only a high

---

16 *Id.* at 269.

17 *Id.*

18 *Id.* at 270.

19 *United States v. Standard Oil Co.*, 20 F. Supp. 427, 458 (S.D. Cal. 1937) (citing *Fleming v. Fleming*, 264 U.S. 29, 31 (1924)).

20 *See Calaf v. Gonzalez*, 127 F.2d 934, 938 (1st Cir. 1942).

21 *Id.*

22 *See, e.g., Santow v. Ullman*, 166 A.2d 135, 140 (Del. 1960).

23 *Id.*

court's decisions create rules that are sufficiently stable to become rules of property.[24]

Although high-court decisions are capable of establishing a rule of property, a single decision, standing alone, may fail to do so. Or it may establish only a limited rule of property.[25] While a series of judgments that have been "commonly acquiesced in as settled law" may demonstrate that a principle has become sufficiently "settled, fixed, [and] stable," a single decision may fail to place a principle "beyond contention and dispute" in the manner necessary to be considered a rule of property.[26] Indeed, the rule of property governing the scope of highway easements, introduced earlier, was a classic example precisely because of the "long succession of decisions on th[e] subject."[27] And to the extent that long-standing rules of an executive department may establish rules of property, they do so only "in the clearest of instances of long and continued promulgation and reliance."[28] The preference for a series of decisions instead of regulations is similar to the requirement that a rule of property be issued by a high court, so that it's no longer subject to appeal or reversal but is beyond dispute.

There remains the scope of the rule established. A rule of property is generally confined in scope to the actual issues adjudicated.[29] For this reason, some courts have observed that "dictum alone will not support a rule of property."[30] But when dicta are later relied on by the general public or in later decisions, a "rule stated by way of dicta . . . [may] become a rule of property."[31] For

---

24 *Calaf*, 127 F.2d at 938 (rejecting argument that a series of district-court decisions had established a rule of property because "[t]he district court is in no sense a court of last resort").

25 See *Bogle Farms, Inc. v. Baca*, 925 P.2d 1184, 1193 (N.M. 1996) (citing *Hart v. Burnett*, 15 Cal. 530, 609 (1860)).

26 *Id.*

27 *Heyert v. Orange & Rockland Utils., Inc.*, 218 N.E.2d 263, 266–69 (N.Y. 1966).

28 *Standard Oil*, 20 F. Supp. at 458.

29 See, e.g., *Union Trust Co. v. Williamson Cnty. Bd. of Zoning Appeals*, 500 S.W.2d 608, 615–16 (Tenn. 1973).

30 *Id.* at 616.

31 *Liberto v. Steele*, 221 S.W.2d 701, 704 (Tenn. 1949) (collecting cases) (recognizing that a distinction made in dictum had so evolved).

example, in the old Tennessee case of *Erck v. Church*,[32] Erck sued to recover possession of a disputed parcel of land along his boundary. His neighbor, Warner, had built a fence that enclosed the disputed land, not realizing that the parcel belonged to Erck. Warner had occupied the land for more than seven years (the limitations period for the state's adverse-possession law) and then deeded his lot to Church. But the deed to Church didn't include the disputed land, and "there [was] no evidence that Warner undertook to transfer to Church his possessory right to it." Hence the court held that Church's occupation of the disputed parcel began a new period of limitations, and so Erck could sue to recover.[33]

In its ruling, though, the Tennessee Supreme Court stated in dictum that "[t]he right of action accrues when one takes possession as his own, *whether by mistake or otherwise*, and the right of recovery is barred in seven years from such entry, if the possession be unbroken."[34] The implication that adverse possession may occur by mistake conflicted with earlier authority that accidental possession couldn't be considered adverse. Even though the implication came in dictum, the Tennessee Supreme Court nevertheless relied on it in a case 25 years later because "such dicta in '*Erck v. Church* has been recognized as a ruling case upon its facts since the date of its decision.'"[35] That is, in reaffirming *Erck v. Church*, the Tennessee Supreme Court had found that "the rule stated by way of dicta . . . had become a rule of property in Tennessee."[36]

Strict application of these judicial policies disfavoring lower-court decisions, administrative regulations, and dictum might

---

32   11 S.W. 794 (Tenn. 1889).

33   *Id.* at 794–95.

34   *Id.* at 794 (emphasis added).

35   *Liberto*, 221 S.W.2d at 704 (quoting *Williams v. Hewitt*, 164 S.W. 1198, 1199 (Tenn. 1914)).

36   *Id.*; *see also Williams*, 164 S.W. at 1199 ("We have found no subsequent case that has commented upon [*Erck*], or has questioned the distinction there taken between an accidental possession held by actual inclosure, and an accidental possession of a part of a large tract, and a claim of actual possession of the entire boundary under color of title. . . . *Erck v. Church* is reaffirmed, and will be followed in cases similar in their facts, in so far as it holds that an actual inclosure of lands, although taken and held by accident or mistake, if maintained for a period of more than seven years, will bar an action of ejectment.").

seem to be in tension with one of the purposes of the rule-of-property doctrine. The doctrine is animated not merely by a concern about finality in judgment or stability in rules generally, but also by a particular concern that the rules governing property must be stable, given that commercial transactions rely on them. It's the recurring motif in this book: it's better that the rules be settled than settled right, especially when they affect property rights. Bowing to principles governing property established in a single decision of a highest court, to long-standing dicta, or to repeated and long-standing principles established in the opinions of lower courts may serve this purpose. On the other hand, given concerns about judicial takings, stringent application of these standards for recognizing a rule as an established rule of property may be more prudent. In light of these considerations, an alternative way to understand the requirements we've discussed is to view them as governing the ambit of the rule so established and the degree of deference to which it is entitled—not its mere existence.

The presumption of reliance

Whether a rule constitutes a rule of property is determined by its content (governing property rights) and the extent to which it has become settled (as evidenced by its legal source and repetition). But once a rule of property has been established, reliance is presumed.[37] The underlying rationale for the doctrine isn't whether a particular litigant relied on the rule, but whether the rule is fixed and sturdy enough that reliance would be reasonable.[38] So

---

37   See *Bank of Philadelphia v. Posey*, 95 So. 134, 135 (Miss. 1923); *Shumaker v. Pearson*, 65 N.E. 1005, 1006–07 (Ohio 1902). *But see Bogle Farms, Inc. v. Baca*, 925 P.2d 1184, 1193 (N.M. 1996) (suggesting that "we must assess the extent to which a proposition cited as a rule of property has induced persons to enter into transactions in actual or demonstrable reliance thereon" because not every rule affecting vesting of rights, "however limited in extent or the number of persons claiming," is an irreversible rule of property) (quoting *Hart v. Burnett*, 15 Cal. 530, 609 (1860)); *cf. Kimble v. Marvel Entm't, LLC*, 135 S.Ct. 2401, 2410 (2015) (suggesting that even "a reasonable possibility that parties have structured their business in light of" a previous decision at the intersection of property and contract law provides reason to uphold it).

38   See, *e.g.*, *Hill v. Atlantic & N.C. R.R.*, 55 S.E. 854, 868–69 (N.C. 1906) (citing *Farrior v. New England Mortg. Sec. Co.*, 9 So. 532, 533–34 (Ala. 1891)).

evidence of reliance on a rule of property isn't necessary to invoke a rule of property or to argue that one has been established.[39]

But there is some disagreement about what happens when an old rule of property is uprooted. Must reliance on the old rule be shown in order to prevent retroactive application of the new rule? One view is that because reliance is presumed, no such showing is necessary.[40] The views expressed in 1906 by the North Carolina Supreme Court are entirely conventional on this point:

> We hold the doctrine to be sound and firmly established that rights to property and the benefits of investments acquired by contract, in reliance upon a statute as construed by the Supreme Court of the state, and which were valid contracts under the statute as thus interpreted, when the contracts or investments were made, cannot be annulled or divested by subsequent decisions of the same court overruling the former decisions: that, as to such contracts or investments, it will be held that the decisions which were in force when the contracts were made had established a rule of property, upon which the parties *had a right to rely*, and that subsequent decisions cannot retroact so as to impair rights acquired in good faith under a statute as construed by the former decisions.[41]

Jurisdictions adhering to this principle further split between those that permit the presumption to be overcome and those that don't.[42] The courts presuming reliance reason that when property

---

39 *Bank of Philadelphia*, 95 So. at 135 ("If the decisions [invoked] announce a rule of property, reliance thereon in the acquisition of property will be presumed.").

40 *See id.*; *see also Holden v. Circleville Light & Power Co.*, 216 F. 490, 494 (6th Cir. 1914); *Hill*, 55 S.E. at 867–68; *Shumaker*, 65 N.E. at 1006 ("It is a conclusive presumption that every instrument is executed with regard to every valid statute by which it may be affected, and, ordinarily, intentions are more likely to be ascertained and rights to be enforced if a like presumption is indulged with respect to judicial decisions by which statutes have been interpreted.").

41 *Hill*, 55 S.E. at 869 (quoting *Farrior*, 9 So. at 533–34) (emphasis added).

42 *Compare Bank of Philadelphia*, 95 So. at 135 (permitting litigants to invoke rule of property even though it "d[id] not appear" that they had relied on it), *with Nickoll v. Racine Cloak & Suit Co.*, 216 N.W. 502, 504–05 (Wis. 1927) ("Perhaps such reliance on the decision of the court may be presumed in the absence of proof to the contrary, but as in the instant case, where the fact affirmatively appears that plaintiff did not rely upon such decisions . . . it is difficult to see how plaintiff secured any vested rights in the common-law rule of quantum meruit.").

rights "have been acquired in accordance with the law as declared by a decision of a court of last resort, a subsequent decision, overruling the prior decision and reversing the rule of law thereby established, will not be allowed to retroact so as to destroy such rights."[43] When making this statement, the Mississippi Supreme Court overruled previous decisions that affected whether a disputed parcel had been unencumbered or subject to liens.[44] But the court declined to apply the new rule retroactively.[45] The parties had acquired the property rights "in accordance with the law as declared by a decision of a court of last resort," and so were permitted to invoke the rule of property even though "it d[id] not appear that [they] had relied upon the decisions" establishing it.[46]

A competing view is that reliance on a particular decision as a rule of property "may be a factual issue with respect to . . . the interests in question."[47] The analysis begins with the notion that although judicial decisions do function retroactively, they permit exemptions "when considerations of fairness and public policy preclude full retroactivity."[48] That is, they treat an exemption from the retroactive application of a decision overruling a rule of property as "depend[ing] upon the equities in each case."[49] Hence some jurisdictions may require a litigant to prove reliance to obtain the equitable benefit of a rule of property.[50]

---

43   *Bank of Philadelphia*, 95 So. at 135.
44   *Id.* at 134.
45   *Id.* at 135.
46   *Id.*
47   *Bogle Farms*, 925 P.2d at 1194 ("Absent reliance, any effect of [a previous case] as a rule of property is hereby overruled."); *see also Kreisher v. Mobil Oil Corp.*, 243 Cal. Rptr. 662, 668 (Ct. App. 1988).
48   *Kreisher*, 243 Cal. Rptr. at 668 (quoting *Peterson v. Superior Court*, 642 P.2d 1305, 1307 (Cal. 1982)) (internal quotation marks omitted); *see also Jackson v. Harris*, 43 F.2d 513, 516–17 (10th Cir. 1930) (collecting cases).
49   *Kreisher*, 243 Cal. Rptr. at 668 (quoting *County of Los Angeles v. Faus*, 312 P.2d 680, 685 (Cal. 1957) (in bank)).
50   *Id.* at 668–69, 672–73 (applying overruled decision governing "a lessor's contractual right to refuse consent to an assignment of the contract" because lessor had acted in reliance on old rule).

Overturning a rule of property

Even if a former decision does create a rule of property, it is subject to overruling when necessary to correct a palpable error or to prevent a continued injustice. But a decision or series of decisions constituting a rule of property won't be overruled merely because the court later becomes convinced that the decision was wrong as a matter of principle. As we have suggested, a court that overturns a rule of property must then decide to what extent the new decision ought to be given retroactive effect.

Courts have consistently stressed that if a rule of property is involved, stare decisis applies with extra force. As the Arkansas Supreme Court once wrote: "It is with a great deal of trepidation that any court should overrule a previous decision. Rarely, if ever, should this be done when the decision is a rule of property."[51] But courts *have* been willing to overrule a previous rule of property in certain circumstances. One of these arises when the reasons for overruling are so overwhelming that the benefits greatly outweigh the costs of change.[52] Another occurs when the costs of change are low because the rule of property has faded.[53]

The threshold for overruling a rule of property remains high. Courts generally won't overturn a rule of property even if they believe that the previous decisions were wrongly decided or don't suit the modern world—unless the reasons for doing so are overwhelming.[54] Rather, when litigants urge that a rule of property should be overturned, many courts will direct them to the legislature as the appropriate governmental entity to effect the requested

---

[51] *Gibson v. Talley*, 174 S.W.2d 551, 554 (Ark. 1943); *see also Kimble v. Marvel Entm't, LLC*, 135 S.Ct. 2401, 2410 (2015) (noting that "we have often recognized that in . . . 'cases involving property and contract rights' . . . considerations favoring stare decisis are 'at their acme'") (quoting *Payne v. Tennessee*, 501 U.S. 808, 828 (1991)).

[52] *See, e.g., City of Berkeley v. Superior Court*, 606 P.2d 362, 372–73 (Cal. 1980).

[53] *See, e.g., In re Propst*, 788 P.2d 628, 633–34 (Cal. 1990) (in bank); *City of Memphis v. Overton*, 392 S.W.2d 98, 101 (Tenn. 1965).

[54] *See, e.g., Brown v. Wall*, 176 S.W.2d 707, 708 (Ark. 1944) (declining to review decisions that had become rules of property even though they seemed incorrect); *Grandjean v. Beyl*, 114 N.W. 414, 414–15 (Neb. 1907); *see also Oklahoma Cnty. v. Queen City Lodge No. 197*, 156 P.2d 340, 345–46 (Okla. 1945) (stating the rule).

change.[55] For example, in a 1907 case,[56] the Nebraska Supreme Court declined to overturn rules governing the rights of a dower as against heirs, even though the position sought to be upended was "wholly indefensible upon reason," because the mere fact that the erroneous decisions had become a rule of property itself provided a strong reason for adhering to that rule: in light of the extensive reliance on the rule of property, overruling would penalize many and introduce uncertainty.[57]

But sometimes decisions are so wrongly decided—and the cost of continuing to enforce the established rule so great—that courts may jettison them. For example, in 1980 the California Supreme Court reconsidered its decision that an 1870 statute governing conveyances of tidelands to private parties permitted the conveyances to be made free of the public trust, that is, not kept open to the public for "commerce, navigation, fishing, and related uses."[58] The court recognized "the special role of the 'rule of property' in the application of the doctrine of stare decisis," but ultimately concluded that there were "most cogent reasons" to overturn it.[59] The court explained:

> We do not divest anyone of title to property; the consequence of our decision will be only that some landowners whose predecessors in interest acquired property under the 1870 act will ... hold it subject to the public trust. The *Knudson*[60] decision in 1915 and [another decision] 53 years later were the only cases holding that the grants in issue were free of the public trust, and it was apparent from the face of the *Knudson* opinion that although the public's right to large tracts of tidelands in the Bay was at

---

[55] *See, e.g., Brown*, 176 S.W.2d at 708 (noting that the argument that a rule of property creates impossible demands "should be addressed to the Legislature rather than the courts"); *see also, e.g., Kimble*, 135 S.Ct. at 2405 ("Critics of the *Brulotte* rule[, concerning royalties for an invention after its patent has expired,] must seek relief not from this Court but from Congress.") (citing *Brulotte v. Thys Co.*, 379 U.S. 29 (1964)).

[56] *Grandjean*, 114 N.W. at 414.

[57] *Id.* at 415 (noting that the rule's "apparent absurdity ... derived from some supposed technical definitions of the common law").

[58] *City of Berkeley v. Superior Court*, 606 P.2d 362, 368–69 (Cal. 1980).

[59] *Id.* at 372.

[60] *Knudson v. Kearney*, 152 P. 541 (Cal. 1915) (in bank).

stake, the state as trustee of those rights was not a party to the action. The summary and conclusory nature of the decision of the issues in *Knudson*, virtually devoid of reasoning, undermines its status as substantial authority. Finally, these decisions have not been overturned on some minor technicality: to the contrary, our conclusion is based on a studied analysis revealing that they are wholly in error, failed to follow prior law on the subject, and misinterpreted the Legislature's intention.[61]

That is, the court found that the previous construction of a statute was both erroneous and harmful, that the relevant parties hadn't been able to protect their interests in the initial proceedings, and that the cost of overruling amounted merely to subjecting title to new restrictions, not divesting anyone of title.[62] This, the court concluded, satisfied the heightened standard for overruling a rule of property.[63]

In addition to cases in which the positive reasons for overruling are irresistable, courts may also overturn a rule of property when the considerations that ordinarily counsel against disturbing a rule of property have faded. They may do so even if the positive reasons in favor of overruling, like legal error or harm, aren't themselves overpowering.[64] For example, in a 1965 case,[65] the Tennessee Supreme Court reconsidered whether Memphis held a fee or easement in an area of the city that had been dedicated to the city by the city's original proprietors to be used as a public promenade.[66] An earlier decision[67] had held that as a rule of property, "the city is the owner of the property, and has the right to make any disposition of it authorized by its charter."[68]

---

61 *City of Berkeley*, 606 P.2d at 372.

62 *Id.* at 372–73.

63 *Id.*

64 *See, e.g., In re Propst*, 788 P.2d at 633–34; *City of Memphis*, 392 S.W.2d at 101 ("[A]ssuming the existence of an erroneous judicial rule of property, so long as no restraining consideration is present, *e.g.*, vesting of property rights thereunder, a court should reexamine its prior statement(s) and revise same where necessary to preserve the character of the law.").

65 *City of Memphis*, 392 S.W.2d 98.

66 *Id.* at 99–100.

67 *Wilkins v. Chicago, St. Louis & New Orleans R.R.*, 75 S.W. 1026 (Tenn. 1903).

68 *Id.* at 1035.

But 62 years later, in 1965, the court declined to repeat that holding, instead reasoning that with one insignificant exception, the city had never tried to convey a fee title to the property, and so no "intervening rights" had vested that necessitated adherence to the rule.[69] As the California Supreme Court put it: "[J]udicially formulated rules of property carry special weight only because of the reliance placed upon them in property transactions."[70] Finding "no widespread reliance" on a rule governing the severance of a joint tenancy between the city and the original proprietors' heirs, the court overturned its earlier rule even though admitting that it had been considered "a binding 'rule of property.'"[71]

In these cases, as in the cases having insuperably powerful reasons to overturn a rule of property, the loss or injury from overruling is small in comparison to the expected benefit of overruling. So they are analyzed as ordinary cases of stare decisis. Indeed, the language of such decisions may be ambiguous between overruling a rule of property or rejecting that one exists.[72]

Effects of an overruling

The primary question to be decided when a rule of property is overruled is whether to give the decision "full retroactive effect."[73] Although court decisions are usually retroactive, decisions overturning a rule of property are sometimes held to be much more limited in their application. Some courts have declined to give the new decision full retroactive effect in the interests of fairness; others have done so to sidestep potential takings problems.[74] Whether

---

69 *City of Memphis*, 392 S.W.2d at 102.
70 *In re Propst*, 788 P.2d at 633.
71 *Id.*
72 *See, e.g., City of Memphis*, 392 S.W.2d at 103 ("[T]he previous decisions . . . do not establish a rule of property whereby fee simple title was vested in the City. To so hold would be to ignore the accepted rule of law in this State concerning the effect of a common law dedication, and in addition, the rule of stare decisis would be vitiated.").
73 *See, e.g., City of Berkeley v. Superior Court*, 606 P.2d 362, 373 (Cal. 1980).
74 *See, e.g., id.* at 373–74 (adopting an "intermediate course").

the decision itself might constitute a "judicial taking" if given retroactive effect remains largely contested.[75]

Decisions to overturn previous decisions, like most other judicial decisions, are generally given full retroactive effect[76] (see § 37). This retroactivity principle derives from "the ancient dogma that the law declared by . . . courts had a Platonic or ideal existence before the act of declaration, in which event the discredited declaration will be viewed as if it had never been, and the reconsidered declaration as law from the beginning."[77] Because of this, parties are assumed to recognize that future transactions may be governed by a different rule.[78]

The difficulty is that the doctrine of the rule of property directly undermines this assumption: the purpose of the doctrine is to permit parties to assume that rules of property, once fixed, will so remain, and to act in reliance on them.[79] That is, under the rule of property, parties aren't presumed to recognize that the rule might change; instead, they are presumed to act in reliance on the stability of established rules.[80] So overturning a previous rule of property may raise both reliance-based hardship and takings concerns that are not present (or not as strongly present) in the run-of-the-mill case.

---

75 See generally *Stop the Beach Renourishment, Inc. v. Florida Dep't of Envtl. Prot.*, 560 U.S. 702 (2010).

76 See, e.g., *Massaglia v. Commissioner*, 286 F.2d 258, 260 (10th Cir. 1961) ("Historically the decisional law of New Mexico strongly indicates that an overruling decision has retroactive as well as prospective effect, and for that reason has overruled decisions involving rules of property only for the most compelling reasons.") (collecting cases).

77 *Great Northern Ry. v. Sunburst Oil & Ref. Co.*, 287 U.S. 358, 365 (1932) (Cardozo J.); *Massaglia*, 286 F.2d at 261 ("In effect, [an overruling decision] declares that the former decision never was the law.") (quoting *Jackson v. Harris*, 43 F.2d 513, 516 (10th Cir. 1930)); see also *In re Will of Allis*, 94 N.W.2d 226, 230–31 & n.3 (Wis. 1959).

78 See, e.g., *Great Northern Ry.*, 287 U.S. at 366 ("Accompanying the recognition is a prophecy, which may or may not be realized in conduct, that transactions arising in the future will be governed by a different rule.").

79 *Minnesota Mining Co. v. National Mining Co.*, 70 U.S. (3 Wall.) 332, 334 (1865); *Bogle Farms, Inc. v. Baca*, 925 P.2d 1184, 1192–93 (N.M. 1996) (collecting cases).

80 See, e.g., *Bank of Philadelphia v. Posey*, 95 So. 134, 135 (Miss. 1923); *Shumaker v. Pearson*, 65 N.E. 1005, 1006–07 (Ohio 1902).

For this reason, some courts have carved out exceptions from the application of the new rule—in the case in which it is announced—when required by "considerations of fairness and public policy."[81] Here, the rule-of-property doctrine has an embedded equitable doctrine in addition to that of stare decisis: a litigant may obtain the equitable benefit of a rule of property, even though it has been overruled.[82] This feature of the doctrine of the rule of property distinguishes it from the genus of the doctrine of stare decisis of which it is generally believed to be a part. The availability of this "equitable doctrine" application of the rule of property allows courts to alter the path of the law to establish a sounder and fairer basis for future rulings, while limiting the negative impact that the alteration might have on the reliance interests that the rule-of-property doctrine was designed to both engender and protect.[83]

Yet as with other equitable doctrines, the rule-of-property doctrine isn't always available. General restraints on equitable actions, including limits on equitable actions against the government, may apply.[84] Parties aren't generally required to show reliance to invoke the stare decisis application of the rule of property in arguing against overturning a previous decision. But once the decision is made to overturn a rule of property, the court may require parties to show reliance to invoke the equitable aspect of

---

81 *Kreisher v. Mobil Oil Corp.*, 243 Cal. Rptr. 662, 668 (Ct. App. 1988) (quoting *Peterson v. Superior Court*, 642 P.2d 1305, 1307 (Cal. 1982)); *see, e.g., Bogle Farms*, 925 P.2d at 1194; *In re Propst*, 788 P.2d 628, 636–37 (Cal. 1990) (in bank); *see also Great Northern Ry.*, 287 U.S. at 364 (recognizing that a state court may decline to apply a decision retroactively "whenever injustice or hardship will thereby be averted") (collecting cases).

82 *See, e.g., Bank of Philadelphia*, 95 So. at 135.

83 *See Minnesota Mining*, 70 U.S. at 334; *Bank of Philadelphia*, 95 So. at 135; *see also Sutter Basin Corp. v. Brown*, 253 P.2d 649, 657 (Cal. 1953) (in bank) (Traynor J. concurring) ("This court could provide a sound rule for the future by declaring that although those cases [establishing a rule of property] govern past bond issues, they are to be deemed overruled as applied to future bond issues.").

84 *Massaglia*, 286 F.2d at 261–62 (refusing to equitably estop government agent from retroactively applying a new decision that overturned a rule of property because the "nature of government" requires that estoppel be applied with caution).

the doctrine to avoid retroactive application.[85] Other jurisdictions apply the equitable aspect of the rule-of-property doctrine as a matter of course and will not apply a decision overturning a rule of property retroactively[86] (see § 37). This equitable doctrine may raise considerable *Erie* concerns for federal courts, which must decide how they are bound by the state-court decisions (see § 70). Before *Erie*,[87] federal courts generally held that when a state high court overturned a rule of property, federal courts were not bound to apply the new decision retroactively.[88]

Takings Clause considerations

Finally, although it is well settled that judicial impairment of contractual obligations isn't prohibited by the Contracts Clause,[89] there remains an open question whether this "equitable" application of the rule of property may be necessary to avoid constitutional

---

85 *See, e.g., Bogle Farms*, 925 P.2d at 1194 (remanding for determination of actual reliance on overturned rule of property); *In re Propst*, 788 P.2d at 638 (same).

86 *See, e.g., Powers v. Wilkinson*, 506 N.E.2d 842, 848–49 (Mass. 1987) (noting that as a general rule, Massachusetts courts do not apply changes to property rules retroactively out of "concern for litigants") (quoting *Payton v. Abbott Labs*, 437 N.E.2d 171, 185 (Mass. 1982)); *In re Estate of Kern*, 274 N.W.2d 325, 328 (Iowa 1979) (en banc) ("The worthier title doctrine is a rule of property, and we abrogate it prospectively only."); *Hare v. General Contract Purchase Corp.*, 249 S.W.2d 973, 977 (Ark. 1952) ("In the case at bar, the parties dealt on the strength of the aforesaid holdings, which have become a rule of property, and we must not overrule these cases retroactively.").

87 304 U.S. 64 (1938).

88 *See, e.g., Kuhn v. Fairmont Coal Co.*, 215 U.S. 349, 360 (1910) ("Where, *before the rights of the parties accrued*, certain rules relating to real estates have been so established by state decisions as to become rules of property and action in the state, those rules are accepted by the Federal courts as authoritative declarations of the law of the state.").

89 *See, e.g., Fleming v. Fleming*, 264 U.S. 29, 31 (1924) (rejecting the argument that the overturning of a former state high court's rulings, under which a contract would have been valid, violated the Contracts Clause) (citing U.S. Const. art. I, § 10); *see also Tidal Oil Co. v. Flanagan*, 263 U.S. 444, 451 (1924) ("It has been settled by a long line of decisions, that the provision of section 10, article 1, of the federal Constitution protecting the obligation of contracts against state action, is directed only against impairment by legislation and not by judgments of courts.") (footnote omitted) (collecting cases); *but see Douglass v. County of Pike*, 101 U.S. 677, 687 (1879) (suggesting that once "a statute has been settled by judicial construction, the construction becomes . . . as much a part of the statute as the text itself" so that a "change of decision is . . . the same in its effect on contracts as an amendment . . . by means of a legislative enactment"

difficulties under the Takings Clause.[90] In particular, it appears to have been assumed for some time that judicial decisions overturning previous decisions governing property rights don't raise constitutional issues.

The origin of this line of cases seems traceable to the debate over whether judicial impairment of contractual obligations is prohibited by the Contracts Clause. When the Supreme Court finally held that it was not, the Court's expansive language suggested the lack of any violation.[91] Some courts have construed this language broadly to conclude that "the mere fact, that a state supreme court decides against a party's claim of property . . . by reversing its earlier decision of the law applicable to such cases, does not deprive him of his property without due process of law."[92] Other courts based their reasoning on the nature of judicial decisions: "There is no vested right in the decisions of a court and [so] a change of decision does not deprive one of equal protection of the laws or property without due process of law."[93] The Hawaii Supreme Court explains this view: "[W]e are convinced that an action which alleged that all applications of [a decision overturning a rule of property] would constitute takings must inevitably fail. For a change in rules of law governing property does not, in itself, provide the basis for an alleged constitutional violation."[94] Indeed, although some early opinions continued to recognize the possibility of a takings vulnerability, they emphasized that merely

---

and so may be applied only prospectively to avoid "impairing the obligation of contracts").

90 U.S. Const. amend. V. *See generally Stop the Beach Renourishment, Inc. v. Florida Dep't of Envtl. Prot.*, 560 U.S. 702 (2010).

91 *See Tidal Oil*, 263 U.S. at 455 ("The mere reversal by a state court of its previous decision, . . . whatever its effect upon contracts, does not . . . violate *any* clause of the federal Constitution.") (emphasis added).

92 *See, e.g., In re Will of Allis*, 94 N.W.2d at 230 (discussing *Tidal Oil*).

93 *Baumann v. Smrha*, 145 F. Supp. 617, 625 & n.4 (D. Kan. 1956) (collecting cases). *But see Stevens v. City of Cannon Beach*, 510 U.S. 1207, 1213–14 (1994) (Scalia J. dissenting from denial of certiorari) (suggesting that there may be a due process problem when the judicial decision is pretextual).

94 *Robinson v. Ariyoshi*, 658 P.2d 287, 305 n.24 (Haw. 1982).

being "take[n] by surprise" by the new decision is insufficient to establish a takings claim.[95]

This assumption seems to have been called into question in recent years, and the Supreme Court expressly left open the possibility of judicial takings in its 2010 decision *Stop the Beach Renourishment v. Florida Department of Environmental Protection*.[96] In that case, a unanimous Court agreed that a Florida Supreme Court decision upholding Florida's restoration of eroded beach didn't constitute a judicial taking of beachfront-property owners' littoral rights.[97] But the Court divided over whether a judicial taking was even possible: four Justices argued in favor of the possibility, and the remaining declined to decide the issue.[98] Scalia J., writing for the judicial-takings proponents, reasoned that the Takings Clause—unlike the Contracts Clause—"is not addressed to the action of a specific branch or branches" but rather "is concerned simply with the act" of taking.[99] Hence "[t]here is no textual justification for saying that the existence or the scope of a State's power to expropriate private property without just compensation varies according to the branch of government effecting the expropriation."[100] Although some other members of the Court believe the question isn't quite so straightforward—in part because they believe it isn't clear, "as a historical matter," that the Takings Clause was "understood . . . to apply to judicial decisions"[101]—the resolution of the question may have ramifications for the rule-of-property doctrine.

---

95 *O'Neil v. Northern Colo. Irrigation Co.*, 242 U.S. 20, 26–27 (1916) (Holmes J.); *see also Robinson*, 658 P.2d at 305 n.24 ("[T]he fact that [the challenged decision] departed from the parties' understanding of pre-existing common law and may have extinguished theretofore unexercised usufructory rights under that system does not provide a grounds for a takings action.") (collecting cases).

96 560 U.S. 702 (2010).

97 *Id.* at 733.

98 *See id.* at 713–33 (plurality opinion); *id.* at 733–42 (Kennedy J. concurring); *id.* at 742–45 (Breyer J. concurring).

99 *Id.* at 713–14.

100 *Id.* at 714.

101 *Id.* at 739 (Kennedy J. concurring).

In particular, Scalia J.'s reasoning in rejecting a predictability-of-change test for determining when a judicial taking has occurred suggests that the rule of property might have an important role to play if judicial takings should come to be recognized: "[A] judicial property decision need not be predictable, so long as it does not declare that what had been private property under established law no longer is."[102] For example, a ruling that merely clears up a muddy question touching on property rights might not be predictable, but it wouldn't necessarily detract from those rights, Scalia J. said. "[T]he predictability test covers too little," he wrote, "because a judicial elimination of established private-property rights that is foreshadowed by dicta or even by holdings years in advance is nonetheless a taking."[103] On this reasoning, a decision overturning an established rule of property *would* constitute a taking precisely because established rules of property are generally taken to settle property rights. Indeed, some courts have expressly linked the standard governing the existence of a rule of property with whether overturning it would amount to a taking.[104] Hence if reliance is shown, the "equitable" application of the rule-of-property doctrine, unlike other forms of equitable relief, isn't discretionary.

---

102 *Id.* at 728 (plurality opinion).
103 *Id.*
104 *See, e.g., United States v. Standard Oil Co.*, 20 F. Supp. 427, 458 (S.D. Cal. 1937) ("[B]efore setting up a judicial declaration as a rule of property, we should require, at least, that it be fixed, long-continued, and relied upon by persons acquiring property, so that its repudiation would amount to a denial of due process.").

D. The Law of the Case

52. The Doctrine Generally

When a point or question arising in the course of litigation has been finally decided, the legal rule or principle announced as applicable to the facts presented becomes the law of that case in all its later stages or developments. It is binding on the parties, their privies, and the courts.

Once a court finally decides a contested point, that decision governs later stages of the dispute. That is, courts should treat the same litigants in the same case the same way throughout the same dispute. They have created a law of the case.

As it is most commonly depicted, the law-of-the-case doctrine commands that when a court has ruled, its decision "should continue to govern the same issues in subsequent stages in the same case."[1] Those stages may take place in the trial court before an appeal, after the case has been remanded to the trial court by an appellate court, or in a later appeal.[2] For example, a criminal defendant appeals a conviction on the grounds that a certain document was incorrectly admitted and that the trial court incorrectly instructed the jury on the burden of proof. The appellate court might decide that the evidence was correctly admitted but remand the case on the second issue. If the defendant appeals again after a second trial, any argument on the evidentiary issue is barred by the law of the case.

This rule of practice "promotes the finality and efficiency of the judicial process by 'protecting against the agitation of settled

---

[1] *Arizona v. California*, 460 U.S. 605, 618 (1983), *decision supplemented*, 466 U.S. 144 (1984).

[2] *See Great Western Tel. Co. v. Burnham*, 162 U.S. 339, 343–44 (1896) (stating that the law-of-the-case doctrine is "necessary to enable an appellate court to perform its duties satisfactorily and efficiently, which would be impossible if a question once considered and decided by it were to be litigated anew in the same case upon any and every subsequent appeal").

issues.'"[3] The doctrine shares the stability functions of stare decisis and claim and issue preclusion but differs from both. It doesn't have the same mandatory qualities of the preclusion rules after a final judgment ends a case, and it is less flexible than the admonition to follow precedents established by earlier cases.

Surrounding the core of the doctrine is an intricate set of exceptions and applications. The law-of-the-case doctrine is commonly described as "amorphous,"[4] in part because it touches on the relationship between trial and appellate courts across multiple decisions in the same case. The doctrine also closely parallels the preclusion rules that similarly bar relitigation of issues in later cases. Thanks to its complexity, the doctrine is amenable to disagreement and confusion over its details.

The law-of-the-case doctrine is said to come in at least two forms. One form, also called the *mandate rule*, forestalls "relitigation in the trial court of matters that were explicitly or implicitly decided by an early appellate decision in the same case."[5] Once an appellate court decides an issue, then it is settled in further proceedings in the trial court and controls the case (see § 55).

The other form generally binds a court to its own earlier rulings in the same case—in the absence of an intervening ruling by a higher court on the same issue.[6] This form of the doctrine can occur in either the trial court or an appellate court. The law of the case controls even if a different trial judge takes over the case or if a later appeal comes before a different panel of the appellate court (see § 57).

The following sections explore both forms of the law-of-the-case doctrine. We also consider the three major exceptions to the law of the case: to address new evidence, to deal with a change in controlling legal authority, and to prevent a miscarriage of justice (see § 59).

---

3   *Christianson v. Colt Indus. Operating Corp.*, 486 U.S. 800, 816 (1988) (quoting 1B James W. Moore et al., *Moore's Federal Practice* § 0.404[1] (1984) [now § 134.20[2] in vol. 18 of *Moore's* (3d ed. 2016)]).

4   *Arizona*, 460 U.S. at 618.

5   *United States v. Moran*, 393 F.3d 1, 7 (1st Cir. 2004).

6   *United States v. Quintieri*, 306 F.3d 1217, 1225 (2d Cir. 2002).

Throughout, an animating principle can be discerned: once a court decides an issue, it should not reopen that issue without good reason. This principle supports the traditional values of consistency and finality, giving litigants stability and predictability over the course of litigation. It enhances comity both within and between courts. And it preserves judicial economy, as judges decide issues conclusively. It does all this without blunting the sense of fairness for litigants, since the court must render a final decision on the issue for it to become law of the case. A prudential rule, the law of the case doesn't limit a court's jurisdiction: courts generally retain discretion to reopen a decided issue.[7]

In the 1912 case of *Messinger v. Anderson*,[8] Holmes J. offered an early discussion of the law-of-the-case doctrine and its limits. That case concerned the interpretation of a will that governed the disposition of property in Toledo, Ohio.[9] If the will gave absolute title to the testator's son, then the property passed by that son's action to another landowner.[10] But if the will gave the son a life estate, the son couldn't assign the property, and the grandson owned the land.[11] The circuit court first held that the will gave the son a life estate.[12] In a case involving the same litigants, the same will, and other pieces of land, the Ohio Supreme Court held that the will passed a greater interest to the son.[13] The court of appeals again held that the son received only a life estate because it was "not at liberty to reverse the judgment" under the law of the case.[14]

The U.S. Supreme Court reversed: "the phrase 'law of the case,'" Holmes J. wrote, "as applied to the effect of previous orders on the later action of the court rendering them in the same case, merely expresses the practice of courts generally to refuse to

---

7   See, e.g., *King v. West Virginia*, 216 U.S. 92, 100 (1910).
8   225 U.S. 436 (1912).
9   *Id.* at 441.
10 *Id.* at 442.
11 *Id.*
12 *Id.* at 443.
13 *Id.*
14 *Id.* at 444.

reopen what has been decided, not a limit to their power."[15] At a minimum, a higher appellate court isn't bound by a lower court's ruling in the same case. So the U.S. Supreme Court was free to take a different path, and it chose to follow the Ohio Supreme Court because "it was right."[16]

For a more modern example, consider a 2009 First Circuit case[17] in which a jury convicted the defendant of crimes related to a September 2000 armed robbery.[18] He was sentenced to 25 years in prison. On appeal, when he challenged his conviction and sentence, the court of appeals remanded for resentencing. After the district court resentenced him to 24 years and six months in prison, he appealed again.

The court of appeals dismissed two sets of the defendant's arguments by applying different forms of the law-of-the-case doctrine. First, the defendant argued that the district court had improperly applied sentencing enhancements for use of a stolen firearm and obstruction of justice. The district court had applied both of those enhancements at sentencing as well as at resentencing, but the defendant didn't challenge their application in his first appeal. The court of appeals found that "[w]hen [the defendant] failed to challenge the . . . enhancement[s] the first time around, [they] became the law of the case," so his later challenge was barred.[19] The defendant also renewed challenges to two grounds on which the district court departed upward from the sentencing guidelines. Having rejected those challenges in his first appeal, the court of appeals declined to reconsider that determination in his second appeal, since the law of the case governed.

The law-of-the-case doctrine has practical and discretionary qualities as well as legal and mandatory qualities. Practically speaking, no court wants to reopen rulings or reargue positions over and over but instead wants to display disciplined

---

15 *Id.*
16 *Id.*
17 *United States v. Wallace*, 573 F.3d 82 (1st Cir. 2009).
18 *Id.* at 84.
19 *Id.* at 90.

"self-consistency" throughout a case.[20] That is the only way to achieve, in the words of Federal Rule of Civil Procedure 1, "the just, speedy, and inexpensive" resolution of every action. This component of the doctrine channels discretion and expresses typical judicial practice but doesn't limit the court's authority.[21] "In the absence of statute"[22] (and no such state or federal statute to our knowledge exists), this feature of the doctrine doesn't confine power. Nor does the United States Constitution require or limit this common-law doctrine in its basic contours. More than a century ago, the Supreme Court confirmed the point when it held that a state court's failure to stand by a prior decision doesn't violate the Fourteenth Amendment's Due Process Clause.[23] Nothing in the Due Process Clause or any other part of the Fourteenth Amendment, the Court held, "prevents a state from permitting an appellate court to alter or correct its interlocutory decision upon a first appeal when the same case, with the same parties, comes before it again."[24] Whether to impose law-of-the-case requirements in a given case and when to exempt them "is a question of local law, upon which the decision of the highest court of the state is controlling."[25]

The occasional necessity of rethinking a decision

To say that a trial court or appellate court generally won't rethink a prior ruling isn't to say that it can't. As long as the court hasn't entered a final judgment and the case hasn't left its jurisdiction, the court may have the obligation in some settings, and the discretion in others, to reconsider the ruling. Why would a court be *obligated* to rethink an earlier ruling before an appeal has been filed? Perhaps an appellate court in another case within the same circuit has issued a controlling interpretation of the statute

---

20   18B Charles Alan Wright, Arthur R. Miller et al., *Federal Practice and Procedure* § 4478, at 637 (2d ed. 2002 & Supp. 2015).
21   *Messinger v. Anderson*, 225 U.S. 436, 444 (1912) (Holmes J.).
22   *Id.*
23   *Moss v. Ramey*, 239 U.S. 538, 546–47 (1916).
24   *Id.*
25   *Id.* at 547.

contrary to the trial court's earlier ruling. Or perhaps the statute at issue is a state law and the state high court in the interim has issued a controlling ruling in another case (see § 71). Then the trial court has no choice but to follow the superior federal court's ruling or the state high court's controlling state-law ruling.

Other factors might influence the trial court's *discretion* to rethink its ruling. Perhaps several noncontrolling decisions have come out the other way in the interim and have done so on persuasive grounds. In this context, when the law-of-the-case doctrine directs a court's discretion, not its power,[26] the doctrine doesn't restrict a court's authority to review its own prior decision if the court is persuaded that its earlier decision is "clearly erroneous and would work a manifest injustice."[27]

State and federal administrative agencies have considerable freedom to change earlier interpretations of statutes or other policies under a statute. The relevant agency may have discretion to change its position—perhaps because of a change in control of the agency by a new President or governor, perhaps because of a change of heart by the same agency about the policy issue. Such a change in position is typically thought permissible and indeed is entitled to respect by the courts, as long as it turns on a reasonable interpretation of the statute.[28] The *Chevron* doctrine applies to federal statutes and has been embraced by many, if not most, state courts in construing state statutes.[29] Of critical import for law-of-the-case purposes, the doctrine allows an agency to alter its position after a binding court decision. Hence an ongoing

---

26 *Arizona v. California*, 460 U.S. 605, 618 (1983), *decision supplemented*, 466 U.S. 144 (1984).

27 *Agostini v. Felton*, 521 U.S. 203, 236 (1997) (quoting *Arizona*, 460 U.S. at 618 n.8); *see, e.g., FMC Corp. v. EPA*, 557 F. Supp. 2d 105, 109 (D.D.C. 2008) (declining to reexamine an earlier ruling because the alleged deficiencies didn't rise to the level of clear error that produced a manifest injustice); *Van Horn v. Van Horn*, 393 F. Supp. 2d 730, 740 (N.D. Iowa 2005) (concluding that the law-of-the-case doctrine applied because the court's prior holding would not work a manifest injustice).

28 *Chevron, U.S.A., Inc. v. Natural Res. Def. Council, Inc.*, 467 U.S. 837, 844 (1984).

29 *See, e.g., Agricultural Labor Relations Bd. v. Laflin & Laflin*, 152 Cal. Rptr. 800, 818 (Ct. App. 1979); *State v. New York Movers Tariff Bureau, Inc.*, 264 N.Y.S.2d 931, 955 (Sup. Ct. 1965).

agency proceeding, independent of the court case, might prompt a trial court to determine that the clear-error and manifest-injustice exceptions permit the court to apply a new—and presumably permissible—agency decision to the case.

One other point. When it comes to a court's *discretion* to change its mind about an earlier ruling, it is fair to ask how often courts insist on clear error and manifest injustice before reconsidering a prior ruling. It is a rare court, it seems to us, that concedes its prior ruling to have been wrong—not clearly wrong, just wrong—yet is unwilling to correct the earlier ruling. It would be a particularly strange admission for a trial court to make because its second ruling—now admitted to be wrong—remains eligible for appeal. What appellate court on direct review is going to uphold a mistaken first decision on the ground that it was later shown only to be wrong but not clearly wrong? None, to our knowledge. After all, it isn't an abuse of discretion under the law-of-the-case doctrine to put aright an erroneous prior ruling.[30]

The same is true for an intermediate appellate court. Why would an appellate court admit its decision to be wrong yet not correct it? What appellant/petitioner would not appreciate, indeed salivate over, the possibility of opening a petition for discretionary review (or better yet, mandatory review) to a high court by pointing out that the decision under review was admittedly wrong—admitted so by the very court under review? That gift is theoretically possible given the difference between error and clear error and between error and manifest injustice. Yet as the caselaw shows, it is a gift rarely given.

---

30 *Pacific Emp'rs Ins. Co. v. Sav-a-Lot of Winchester*, 291 F.3d 392, 398 (6th Cir. 2002).

53. Final Rulings and Decisions

For a ruling or decision to become the law of the case, it must issue from a court with jurisdiction over the dispute and be final as to the matters involved—and it must be part of the same case.

Because the law of the case is a rule of practice—one "based upon sound policy that when an issue is once litigated and decided, that should be the end of the matter"[1]—it isn't a general bar to the relitigation of issues that arise during the life of a case. A ruling qualifies as the law of the case only if it meets two conditions: there must be a decision on a particular legal issue, and that decision must be final.

As to the first condition, the court must have actually considered and decided the issue.[2] The doctrine applies to decisions made explicitly or by necessary implication.[3]

The doctrine doesn't cover a matter never decided, including a matter assumed for the sake of argument: "Omissions do not constitute a part of a decision and become the law of the case, nor does a contention of counsel not responded to."[4] Unless and until a court addresses a point implicated by the dispute, whether raised by the parties or not, there is no *law* of the *case* to apply. Once such judicial action exists, it takes a final decision on the point at hand to implicate law-of-the-case requirements.[5] On top of that, any final decision must be issued by a court with subject-matter jurisdiction over the matter. In the absence of a prior decision on

---

1   *United States v. United States Smelting Ref. & Mining Co.*, 339 U.S. 186, 198 (1950).
2   *See Quern v. Jordan*, 440 U.S. 332, 346 n.18 (1979).
3   *United States v. Jordan*, 429 F.3d 1032, 1035 (11th Cir. 2005); *Alpha/Omega Ins. Servs., Inc. v. Prudential Ins. Co.*, 272 F.3d 276, 279 (5th Cir. 2001).
4   *Hartford Life Ins. Co. v. Blincoe*, 255 U.S. 129, 136 (1921); *see* Henry Campbell Black, *Handbook on the Law of Judicial Precedents* § 87, at 283–86 (1912).
5   Black, *Handbook on the Law of Judicial Precedents* § 85, at 277; *see* David F. Herr et al., *Motion Practice* § 16.06, at 16–58 (6th ed. 2015).

the merits, the doctrine doesn't apply.[6] If it turns out that the court lacked jurisdiction over the dispute when it issued the ruling, the proper remedy is to vacate the earlier ruling, making it no longer final, much less a form of action eligible for law-of-the-case treatment.

The most difficult part of this analysis is often determining whether a previous court decided an issue by necessary implication or avoided deciding the issue. In the context of the mandate rule, the Tenth Circuit has identified three grounds under the law-of-the-case doctrine "by which we might conclude an issue was implicitly resolved in a prior appeal":

> (1) resolution of the issue was a necessary step in resolving the earlier appeal; (2) resolution of the issue would abrogate the prior decision and so must have been considered in the prior appeal; and (3) the issue is so closely related to the earlier appeal its resolution involves no additional consideration and so might have been resolved but unstated.[7]

Though these factors aren't exhaustive, they provide some guidance to the inquiry.[8]

Whether an issue was implicitly decided in an earlier appeal was central to a 2013 federal appellate decision.[9] The district court had seriously reduced a plaintiff's fee award for two reasons.[10] First, three of the plaintiff Diaz's six claims were voluntarily dismissed, and she lost a fourth on a motion for summary judgment.[11] Second, Diaz "had rejected a settlement offer that would have left [her] counsel with a $25,000 contingent fee and Diaz with an

---

6   *United States v. Hatter*, 532 U.S. 557, 566 (2001) (refusing to apply the law of the case to an earlier request for review when the Supreme Court lacked a quorum to consider it); *State v. Pratt*, 766 N.W.2d 111, 116 (Neb. 2009) (refusing to apply the law of the case to a matter that it didn't decide and over which it didn't have jurisdiction).

7   *Guidry v. Sheet Metal Workers Int'l Ass'n, Local No. 9*, 10 F.3d 700, 707 (10th Cir. 1993), *abrogated in part on other grounds on reh'g*, 39 F.3d 1078 (10th Cir. 1994) (en banc); *see Copart, Inc. v. Administrative Review Bd., U.S. Dep't of Labor*, 495 F.3d 1197, 1201–02 (10th Cir. 2007) (quoting *Guidry*, 10 F.3d at 707).

8   *Guidry*, 10 F.3d at 707 n.5.

9   *Diaz v. Jiten Hotel Mgmt., Inc.*, 741 F.3d 170 (1st Cir. 2013).

10 *Id.* at 172–73.

11 *Id.* at 172.

amount in excess of what the jury awarded."[12] Diaz challenged both reductions on appeal. The appellate court found no abuse of discretion as to the first basis for reduction, but held that the district court had erred as to the second basis for reduction. On remand, the district court altered the way in which it had calculated the reduction for the unsuccessful claims under Rule 60(a), resulting in an increased fee award for Diaz. This time, the defendant appealed and argued that the upward adjustment was precluded by the appellate court's prior decision. Given the lack of express language in the first opinion, the defendant argued that "[the] mandate implicitly precluded any increase in the fee award other than what [the appellate court] expressly ordered."[13] The court held that "[o]ur opinion . . . cannot plausibly be read to have conclusively determined the correctness of the formula used to calculate the proportional award, particularly when the propriety of that formula was neither challenged nor briefed on appeal."[14] Further, the court explained, "this is not a case in which the logic of our prior opinion implied any judgment that the amount of the award exhausted the maximum reach of the district court's discretion."[15] The court affirmed the district court's increase in the fee award.

Second, the prior court's decision or ruling must have been final. This requirement has been attributed to the Supreme Court's decision in *United States v. United States Smelting Refining & Mining Co.*[16] In that case, a three-judge district-court panel had reversed and remanded a decision to the Interstate Commerce Commission, finding that the decision wasn't supported by the evidence. On remand, the Commission took no additional evidence and restated its original decision. The decision was appealed to the district court, which again held the orders unlawful, and then to the Supreme Court, which reversed. The Supreme Court held that the law-of-the-case doctrine didn't apply to the original

---

12 *Id.* at 173.
13 *Id.* at 175.
14 *Id.* at 176.
15 *Id.*
16 339 U.S. 186 (1950).

district-court decision "because when the case was first remanded, nothing was finally decided."[17] In this context, the Supreme Court stated that the law-of-the-case doctrine "requires a final judgment."[18]

Despite the language in *United States Smelting*, courts often assume that a technical final judgment is unnecessary as long as an order was intended to finally resolve an issue.[19] The Fifth Circuit has explained that "[f]inality in this sense does not refer to technical concepts of finality but rather is a functional finality which 'seeks to identify a determination intended to put a matter to rest.'"[20]

Based on this requirement, a district court's decision on a preliminary injunction or some other interlocutory order doesn't ordinarily become the law of the case. These are prototypical preliminary decisions made before a full and final consideration on the merits: they aren't intended to conclusively resolve an issue. Hence a district court's decision to grant a preliminary injunction would not normally foreclose a later decision by the district court to dismiss the case on summary judgment.[21] Likewise, a state court's denial of a motion to dismiss would not preclude a later federal district court's granting the same motion in a case removed to federal court[22] (see § 57). Yet issues involved in these preliminary decisions can become the law of the case if decided on appeal after a consideration of the merits.[23]

---

17 *Id.* at 198.

18 *Id.* at 199.

19 *See also* 18B Charles Alan Wright, Arthur R. Miller et al., *Federal Practice and Procedure* § 4478, at 637–45 (2d ed. 2002 & Supp. 2015) (suggesting that the law-of-the-case doctrine "regulate[s] judicial affairs before final judgment," while preclusion rules apply after a final judgment).

20 *In re Evangeline Ref. Co.*, 890 F.2d 1312, 1322 (5th Cir. 1989) (quoting 18 Charles Alan Wright, Arthur R. Miller et al., *Federal Practice and Procedure* § 4478 (1981 & Supp. 1989)) (finding that the law-of-the-case doctrine doesn't apply to interim fee awards).

21 *See, e.g., Southern Or. Barter Fair v. Jackson Cnty.*, 372 F.3d 1128, 1136 (9th Cir. 2004).

22 *See, e.g., Harlow v. Children's Hosp.*, 432 F.3d 50, 55–56 (1st Cir. 2005).

23 *United States v. Turtle Mountain Band of Chippewa Indians*, 612 F.2d 517, 520–21 (Ct. Cl. 1979) (stating "[t]he general rule . . . that 'once affirmed on appeal, . . .

In the end, what matters is that the court issue a dispositive ruling on the point at hand. A court that merely suggests that it will deny a motion for summary judgment doesn't trigger the doctrine, and the doctrine will not apply until the court formally and finally denies the motion. Once the court denies (or grants) the motion, the law-of-the-case doctrine applies to holdings in that final ruling. One qualification to the final action requirement is that a waived or forfeited issue—a decision by inaction—may become the law of the case.[24]

No requirement of a final judgment

By contrast, the final-action requirement isn't a final-judgment requirement in the sense that the doctrine applies only after the relevant court finally decides everything in the case and makes the case eligible for appeal. Nor is it accurate to think of the finality requirement as akin to whatever it takes to make an interlocutory decision eligible for appeal. The law of the case may apply to interlocutory rulings ineligible for appeal, and it is here that the discretionary nature of the doctrine often comes into view. Although a court has "no duty to reconsider a case, an issue, or a question of fact or law, once decided, the power to do so remains in the court until final judgment or decree"—and "so long as the case has not passed beyond the power of the court."[25] The trial court need not

---

an (interlocutory) order loses its interlocutory character and becomes the law of the case'") (quoting *United States ex rel. Greenhalgh v. F.D. Rich Co.*, 520 F.2d 886, 889 (9th Cir. 1975)); *see also Naser Jewelers, Inc. v. City of Concord*, 538 F.3d 17, 20 (1st Cir. 2008) (preliminary injunction); *In re Oil Spill by Amoco Cadiz Off Coast of France on March 16, 1978*, 954 F.2d 1279, 1291 (7th Cir. 1992) (per curiam) (interlocutory appeal).

24 *See Medical Ctr. Pharmacy v. Holder*, 634 F.3d 830, 834 (5th Cir. 2011); *Liccardi v. Stolt Terminals, Inc.*, 687 N.E.2d 968, 972 (Ill. 1997) ("[A]s a general rule, the failure of a party to challenge a legal decision when it has the opportunity to do so renders that decision the law of the case for future stages of the same litigation, and [that party is] deemed to have waived the right to challenge that decision at a later time.") (internal quotation marks and citations omitted). *But see In re Trans Union Corp. Privacy Litig.*, 741 F.3d 811, 817 (7th Cir. 2014) (holding that the appellate court had jurisdication over issues even if they could have been raised in an interlocutory appeal but were not).

25 *Peterson v. Hopson*, 29 N.E.2d 140, 144 (Mass. 1940).

issue an appealable final judgment or for that matter a ruling eligible for interlocutory appeal for the doctrine to apply.

In this respect, the doctrine is distinct from the kindred rules of issue and claim preclusion.[26] As a general guide, the law-of-the-case doctrine applies to decisions of a trial court *before* it issues a final judgment that brings the trial-level phase of the case to a close, while preclusion rules apply only *after* a final judgment and, if appealed, only after a finally appealed judgment.[27] In the context of a prior ruling issued by the same court, the law-of-the-case doctrine directs discretion while issue and claim preclusion compel judgment.[28] The first permits informed choice; the others require submission.[29]

The requirement of a final decision is less apt to cause confusion when it comes to applying the doctrine to a junior court after a decision by a senior court. Appellate courts rarely issue anything but final decisions. Even an appellate court's decision to stay (or not) a lower-court decision or to reverse (or affirm) a preliminary injunction amounts to a final decision for purposes of the doctrine. It may be that the senior appellate decision in such settings doesn't establish a holding on point. The stay decision might, for example, turn on a balancing of harms to the parties rather than a ruling of law. The same could be true in a mandamus setting.[30] But that is a different problem. It doesn't make stay decisions, preliminary

---

26 *United States v. United States Smelting Ref. & Mining Co.*, 339 U.S. 186, 199 (1950).

27 *Mendenhall v. Barber-Greene Co.*, 26 F.3d 1573, 1582 (Fed. Cir. 1994) (citing 18 Charles Alan Wright, Arthur R. Miller et al., *Federal Practice and Procedure* § 4478 (1981)) ("The law of the case does not involve preclusion after final judgment, but rather it regulates judicial affairs before final judgment."); *People v. Evans*, 727 N.E.2d 1232, 1234 (N.Y. 2000) ("As distinguished from issue preclusion and claim preclusion, however, law of the case addresses the potentially preclusive effect of judicial determinations made in the course of a single litigation *before* final judgment.") (internal citations omitted).

28 *Southern Ry. v. Clift*, 260 U.S. 316, 319 (1922).

29 *Id.*

30 See *Kennedy v. Lubar*, 273 F.3d 1293, 1299 (10th Cir. 2001) ("Because orders denying a petition for mandamus are most frequently denied as a result of the special limitations inherent in the writ itself, and not on the merits, such denials are not ordinarily given 'law of the case' effect, and the parties are not precluded from raising the issue in a subsequent appeal.").

decisions, or mandamus decisions categorically ineligible for law-of-the-case treatment in the first instance.[31] All that the lower court must do to trigger the doctrine is to determine whether the higher court has issued a relevant holding. If so, the lower court must follow it.

Unlike the doctrine of stare decisis, the law-of-the-case doctrine doesn't apply to distinct lawsuits. The point of the doctrine is to limit a court's discretion, and in some instances its power, to alter rulings in the same case, but not in others.[32]

---

[31] See *Ex parte King*, 821 So. 2d 205, 209 (Ala. 2001) ("[A]lthough the denial of a petition for a writ of mandamus does not have res judicata effect, the grant of the writ becomes the law of the case. Therefore, in the absence of changed circumstances resulting from subsequent events, relitigation of a previously determined issue is contrary to the mandate of [the earlier case].") (internal citation omitted).

[32] *Arizona v. California*, 460 U.S. 605, 618 (1983), *decision supplemented*, 466 U.S. 144 (1984); *Quern v. Jordan*, 440 U.S. 332, 347 n.18 (1979); *Lange v. Nelson-Ryan Flight Serv., Inc.*, 116 N.W.2d 266, 269 (Minn. 1962) ("There exists a well-established rule that issues considered and adjudicated on a first appeal become the law of the case and will not be reexamined or readjudicated on a second appeal of the *same case*.") (emphasis added).

54. Incidental and Collateral Decisions

The law-of-the-case doctrine applies to decisions necessary to resolve the dispute as opposed to decisions collateral or incidental to its resolution. The doctrine requires a holding on the relevant issue before it can be closed to its further consideration.

The law-of-the-case doctrine applies only to issues necessarily decided at an earlier phase of the lawsuit. Prior holdings, as opposed to dicta, measure the rule's reach.[1] A holding remains eligible for law-of-the-case treatment even if the decision doesn't explain its rationale. In the words of the U.S. Supreme Court, that a court "did not explicate its rationale is irrelevant, for the law of the case turns on whether a court previously 'decide[d] upon a rule of law'—which the [court] necessarily did—not on whether, or how well, it explained the decision."[2]

Inferior courts doubtless frequently follow the dicta, even the suggestions, of higher courts.[3] But that's not a function of the law-of-the-case doctrine. Rather, it's a function of the natural (but still discretionary) inclination of most lower-court judges to heed the utterances of the higher court. Although lower courts by and large follow dicta almost as tenaciously as they follow the holdings of superior courts, this habit follows from the customs that one would expect to see in a hierarchical system of vertical precedent—not from the requirements of the law-of-the-case doctrine.

---

[1] *United States v. Bloate*, 655 F.3d 750, 755 (8th Cir. 2011) ("The doctrine applies only to actual decisions—not dicta—in prior stages of the case."); *State v. Odom*, 336 S.W.3d 541, 563 (Tenn. 2011) ("This doctrine 'applies to issues that were actually before the appellate court in the first appeal and to issues that were necessarily decided by implication,' but it is inapplicable to dicta.") (quoting *Memphis Publ'g Co. v. Tennessee Petroleum Underground Storage Tank Bd.*, 975 S.W.2d 303, 306 (Tenn. 1998)).

[2] *Christianson v. Colt Indus. Operating Corp.*, 486 U.S. 800, 817 (1988); *see State v. Stuart*, 664 N.W.2d 82, 90 (Wis. 2003) (quoting *Christianson*, 486 U.S. at 817).

[3] *See, e.g., Awuah v. Coverall N. Am., Inc.*, 985 F. Supp. 2d 185, 190 n.3 (D. Mass. 2013); *Doe v. Friendfinder Network, Inc.*, 540 F. Supp. 2d 288, 299 (D.N.H. 2008).

When an appellate court reverses the lower court's judgment, remands the case for further proceedings, and states in its opinion the legal rules and principles that are to be applied to the questions likely to arise in the new trial, those statements aren't to be regarded as dicta even if they are additional to the determination of the precise point that caused the reversal.[4]

This aspect of the holding/dictum dichotomy often arises in criminal cases. A criminal defendant may appeal many claimed errors, such as evidentiary errors and instructional errors. Let's say that the court reverses and remands the case for a new trial because of an instructional error. The appellate court's decision may also point out an evidentiary ruling that wasn't sufficiently prejudicial to justify reversal by itself, but that on retrial should be avoided. The appellate court's instruction on the correct solution to the evidentiary issue should not be treated as dicta by the trial

---

[4] *Harris v. Sentry Title Co.*, 806 F.2d 1278, 1280 n.1 (5th Cir. 1987) (per curiam) ("[T]his Court often addresses issues for the guidance of the parties and the district court on remand. It cannot be said that such considered statements should be dismissed as dictum simply because the Court was not absolutely required to raise and address such an issue."); *Cole Energy Dev. Co. v. Ingersoll-Rand Co.*, 8 F.3d 607, 609 (7th Cir. 1993) (explaining that "explicit directives by that court to the lower court concerning proceedings on remand are not dicta" and that even if the appellate court calls its directives "useful comments" or the like, that doesn't "authorize the judge to ignore them"); *Karen Kane Inc. v. Reliance Ins. Co.*, 202 F.3d 1180, 1186 (9th Cir. 2000) (noting that an appellate court's statements "cannot be dismissed as mere dicta" if its disposition of the case requires the district court to follow those statements on remand); *Morales v. Zenith Ins. Co.*, 714 F.3d 1220, 1225 n.9 (11th Cir. 2013) (disagreeing with the district court's characterization of language in an applicable case as dicta, and explaining that "[s]pecific instructions to a trial court, which limit what it may consider or hold on remand, are not dicta"); *Sonic-Calabasas A, Inc. v. Moreno*, 311 P.3d 184, 212 (Cal. 2013) (clarifying that "[s]tatements by appellate courts 'responsive to the issues raised on appeal and . . . intended to guide the parties and the trial court in resolving the matter following . . . remand' are not dicta"); *State v. Hussein*, 229 P.3d 313, 333 (Haw. 2010) (approving of the statement that "this court's discussion of an issue is not dicta when it is 'closely connected with the question upon which the case was decided, and the opinion [is] expressed with a view to settling a question that would in all probability have to be decided before the litigation was ended'").

court on remand,[5] or by another appellate panel.[6] The rationale is that the harmless-error rules "are not a license to disregard procedural constraints announced by an appellate court."[7]

Yet the dichotomy is hardly limited to criminal cases. On a second appeal to the California Court of Appeal in a case challenging the State of California's title in property around the shores of Lake Tahoe, the plaintiffs argued that an instruction from the California Supreme Court to the trial court was dictum and could be disregarded.[8] The Court of Appeal disagreed, saying that even if some part of the opinion isn't relevant to the material facts presented in the case, "if it is responsive to an argument raised by counsel and intended for guidance of the court and attorneys upon a new hearing, it probably constitutes the basis of the decision and cannot be disregarded by a lower court as mere dictum."[9] The court noted that the Supreme Court had issued the writ directing the lower court to rule "consistent with the views expressed above." Even if the guidance was dicta, the Court of Appeal held itself bound to follow it.[10]

Lower courts have been known to characterize the appellate court's statements as "mere dicta" rather than guidance on remand.[11] If those characterizations correctly state the law—and we doubt their soundness—the jurisdiction's general rules on dicta still apply. On remand from the U.S. Supreme Court, the Seventh Circuit made this distinction when it held that a statement made by the Court was "mere dicta touching upon issues not formally

---

5   *See generally State v. Timberlake*, 744 N.W.2d 390, 395 n.7 (Minn. 2008) (en banc) (noting that language in an order that guides a new trial isn't dictum); Michael Abramowicz & Maxwell Stearns, *Defining Dicta*, 57 Stan. L. Rev. 953, 1065 (2005) (positing that finding an error, though the court ultimately finds it harmless, isn't dictum and thus is a holding binding on the lower court).

6   *See United States v. Oshatz*, 912 F.2d 534, 540 (2d Cir. 1990).

7   *Id.*

8   *Fogerty v. State*, 231 Cal. Rptr. 810, 815 (Ct. App. 1986).

9   *Id.*

10 *Id.* at 815 & n.7 (holding that if the statement wasn't dictum, it was a holding that represented the law of the case).

11 *See Cole Energy*, 8 F.3d at 609 (holding that lower courts aren't bound by a higher court's dicta, but that explicit directives to the lower court regarding proceedings on remand aren't dicta and cannot be ignored).

before the Court" and didn't constitute binding determinations on remand.[12] (For a discussion of the effect of Supreme Court dicta generally, see § 4, pp. 69–72.) But even if the lower court followed "mere dicta" in an appellate decision on remand, failure of the parties to object to the use of the dicta results in invited error.[13] When the parties do object, whether the later appellate court may reverse the lower court's judgment for having relied on the remanding appellate court's dictum depends on how the jurisdiction treats dicta. For example, in the Third Circuit a later panel isn't bound by a prior panel's dicta,[14] but in the Ninth Circuit later panels are bound by well-reasoned dicta.[15]

---

12   *Gertz v. Robert Welch, Inc.*, 680 F.2d 527, 533 (7th Cir. 1982).

13   *Dedham Water Co. v. Cumberland Farms Dairy, Inc.*, 972 F.2d 453, 459 (1st Cir. 1992) ("When, as here, the district court, on remand, proposed to act upon dicta contained in the appeals court's earlier opinion in the same case, and no one demurred, it is especially important that we toe the mark and hold the parties to the usual consequence of invited error.").

14   *ACLU of N.J. ex rel. Lander v. Schundler*, 168 F.3d 92, 98 (3d Cir. 1999) ("Not unreasonably, the District Court interpreted certain statements in the prior panel opinion to mean that the panel viewed the modified display as constitutionally dubious. We conclude, however, that the statements on which the District Court relied were merely dicta, that the prior panel did not render a decision regarding the constitutionality of the modified display, and that we are therefore obligated to analyze that question in accordance with our own best independent judgment.").

15   *United States v. Johnson*, 256 F.3d 895, 914 (9th Cir. 2001) (en banc) (per Kozinski J.); *Miller v. Gammie*, 335 F.3d 889, 899 (9th Cir. 2003) (en banc).

55. Cases Remanded to Trial Courts

When a case has been heard and determined by an appellate court, the legal rules and principles laid down as applicable to it bind the trial court in all further proceedings in the same lawsuit. They cannot be reviewed, ignored, or departed from.

Appellate courts usually don't implement or execute their own rulings. Instead, whether an appellate court is affirming or reversing the trial-court ruling, it will remand the case to the trial court to carry out the ruling. At this stage, the trial court's discretion has evaporated. The trial court "is bound by the decree as the law of the case, and must carry it into execution according to the mandate."[1] The trial court has no authority to vary the ruling or even to examine it except by way of executing it.[2] Essentially, it must genuflect.

This proposition of law is known as the "mandate rule."[3] The mandate of a court of appeals is "[t]echnically . . . a certified copy of [the court's] judgment, a copy of the opinion, and any direction as to costs."[4] The mandate rule derives from the structure of the court system. For appellate review to be meaningful, the decisions of the appellate court must bind the lower court on remand. Even if the appellate court may be incorrect, finality and the structure of the system require adherence to its decisions. The rule applies to issues decided by the appellate court, as well as to instructions from the appellate court. For example, if the appellate court remands and instructs the lower court to decide an issue or dismiss the case, the failure to do so violates the mandate rule.

---

1   *In re Sanford Fork & Tool Co.*, 160 U.S. 247, 255 (1895).
2   *Id.*; *see Black's Law Dictionary* 1106 (Bryan A. Garner ed., 10th ed. 2014) (defining *mandate rule* as "[t]he doctrine that, after an appellate court has remanded a case to a lower court, the lower court must follow the decision that the appellate court has made in the case, unless new evidence or an intervening change in the law dictates a different result").
3   *United States v. Quintieri*, 306 F.3d 1217, 1225 (2d Cir. 2002) (quoting *United States v. Reyes*, 49 F.3d 63, 66 (2d Cir. 1995)) (internal quotation marks omitted).
4   *Id.* at 1225 n.5.

This structural basis for the mandate rule has several important implications. The mandate rule applies whether it is a high court that has reviewed an intermediate appellate court's decision or an intermediate appellate court that has reviewed a trial court's decision. The mandate rule typically trumps the other branch of the law-of-the-case doctrine: if an appellate court reverses a trial court's judgment on an issue, the trial court on remand must follow the appellate court's decision in accordance with the mandate rule—not the trial court's earlier decision in accordance with the law of the case. As the Fourth Circuit put it, "Few legal precepts are as firmly established as the doctrine that the mandate of a higher court is controlling as to matters within its compass."[5] Hence a trial court isn't free to depart from the appellate court's mandate unless an exception to the law-of-the-case doctrine applies—for example, if controlling legal authority changes in the interim.[6]

One federal circuit court discussed the scope of the mandate rule in a 2008 case[7] in which a jury convicted the defendant of three drug and firearm counts arising from an incident that resulted in death.[8] In accordance with the sentencing guidelines, the district court sentenced the defendant to three concurrent life sentences. On appeal, the court found that evidence had been wrongly admitted and issued the following mandate: "For the foregoing reasons, we VACATE Genao's convictions on counts two and three of the second superseding indictment and REMAND to the district court for a new trial on those charges if the government wishes to so proceed, and for resentencing. We AFFIRM Genao's conviction on count one."[9]

---

5   *United States v. Bell*, 5 F.3d 64, 66 (4th Cir. 1993) (quoting *Sprague v. Ticonic Nat'l Bank*, 307 U.S. 161, 168 (1939)). *See* 18B Charles Alan Wright, Arthur R. Miller et al., *Federal Practice and Procedure* § 4478.3, at 734–45 (2d ed. 2002 & Supp. 2015).

6   *See* 36 C.J.S. *Federal Courts* § 744 (2014).

7   *United States v. Genao-Sánchez*, 525 F.3d 67 (1st Cir. 2008).

8   *Id.* at 68.

9   *Id.* at 69.

On remand, the government asked the district court to let the life sentence on count one stand without resentencing, without retrying the defendant on counts two and three, and without conducting a new sentencing hearing. The district court agreed, and the defendant appealed, arguing in part that the district court had violated the mandate rule because the appellate court's mandate required that the district court conduct a resentencing. The appellate court reversed and required resentencing: "This language clearly conveys two distinct commands. First, it instructs the district court to wipe out the judgments on counts two and three and to retry those counts if the government elects to press forward. Second, it independently instructs the district court to 'resentenc[e]' the appellant."[10] The court continued: "A mandate, like a statute, should be read so that to the maximum extent practicable every word and phrase has meaning; and any other reading of [the earlier opinion] would render superfluous our instruction to 'resentenc[e]' the appellant."[11]

Two features of the mandate rule are illustrated by a 2007 decision of the Fourth Circuit.[12] The case concerned a series of lawsuits by black-lung-benefit claimants against the Secretary of Labor under the Privacy Act. The plaintiffs moved in district court for attorneys' fees under the Privacy Act and the Equal Access to Justice Act. The district court denied all attorneys' fees claims except for fees to plaintiff Buck Doe under the Privacy Act for work performed at summary judgment. The Secretary appealed, and the Fourth Circuit vacated because the district court had failed to consider that Doe had recovered no damages in setting the fee. On remand, the district court eliminated its original fee award, but it also reversed itself and awarded Doe attorney's fees for two other phases of the litigation—a contempt motion and an earlier appeal. The Secretary appealed again.

The Fourth Circuit found that the district court had violated the mandate rule in two respects. First, the district court

---

10   *Id.* at 70 (alteration in original).
11   *Id.* (alteration in original).
12   *Doe v. Chao*, 511 F.3d 461 (4th Cir. 2007).

had originally decided against awarding attorney's fees to Doe for work performed on the contempt motion, and Doe didn't appeal. "Because the mandate rule forecloses litigation of issues decided by the district court but [forgone] on appeal or otherwise waived," the Fourth Circuit held, "the district court was not free to deviate from this court's mandate by reconsidering Buck Doe's claims for attorney's fees."[13] Second, the remand order from the Fourth Circuit instructed the district court to reconsider the award of fees under the Privacy Act only for work performed on the motion for summary judgment. The scope of the remand didn't permit the district court to broach the entirely new issue whether Buck Doe was entitled to an award of attorneys' fees for work performed on the earlier appellate phase of the merits litigation.[14] In the Fourth Circuit's view, the district court's actions prolonged a course of litigation that should have ended after decision of the sole issue remanded by the court of appeals.[15]

Corrective measures

A trial court that fails to adhere to appellate decisions subjects itself to at least two forms of correction. The aggrieved party may appeal the new decision anew and obtain relief that way.[16] Or, in one of the classic explanations for a writ of mandamus, the litigant may obtain a writ of mandamus from the appellate court directing the lower court to adhere to the decision and mandate of the superior court.[17]

It isn't just trial courts (or for that matter intermediate appellate courts) that must adhere to the directions of their superiors. Agency decisions are often appealable to trial courts and in some instances directly to appellate courts. The same rule applies. Just as a lower court is bound to follow a higher court's final decision,

---

13   *Id.* at 466 (quoting *United States v. Bell*, 5 F.3d 64, 66 (4th Cir. 1993)).
14   *Id.*
15   *Id.* at 468.
16   *Sanford Fork*, 160 U.S. at 255.
17   *Id.*

so too an agency is bound to follow a reviewing court's final decision.[18]

All these rules generally apply to civil and criminal cases alike. One area in which criminal cases have generated unique law-of-the-case disputes on remand is sentencing. Ever since the U.S. Supreme Court determined that the sentencing guidelines were not mandatory in *United States v. Booker*,[19] the lower federal courts have faced an avalanche of sentencing challenges by criminal defendants—many of them successful. A frequent point of disagreement after a successful challenge to a sentence is whether the trial court should undertake a full resentencing or merely address the problem or problems identified by the appellate court. The choice turns in legal parlance on whether the appellate court issued a "general remand" (permitting a full resentencing) or a "limited remand" (permitting a resentencing focused on the specific errors identified by the appellate court).[20] The distinction makes a difference. A limited remand requires far less of the trial court than a general remand and narrows the defendant's options for lowering the sentence. Given the stakes, it isn't unusual to see considerable litigation over the nature of the remand. Most courts assume, in the absence of direction, that the remand is general in nature.[21] None of these complications arises if the appellate court states its intentions explicitly—that the remand is general and

---

18   *Industrial TurnAround Corp. v. NLRB*, 115 F.3d 248, 254 (4th Cir. 1997); *Carey v. Federal Election Comm'n*, 864 F. Supp. 2d 57, 63 (D.D.C. 2012).

19   543 U.S. 220 (2005).

20   *Pepper v. United States*, 562 U.S. 476, 505 n.17 (2011); *State ex rel. Frazier & Oxley, L.C. v. Cummings*, 591 S.E.2d 728, 735 (W. Va. 2003) ("Limited remands explicitly outline the issues to be addressed by the circuit court and create a narrow framework within which the [trial] court must operate. General remands, in contrast, give [trial] courts authority to address all matters as long as remaining consistent with the remand.").

21   *See United States v. West*, 646 F.3d 745, 749 (10th Cir. 2011) ("[T]he district court is to look to the mandate for any limitations on the scope of remand and, in the absence of such limitations, exercise discretion in determining the appropriate scope."); *United States v. Matthews*, 278 F.3d 880, 885–86 (9th Cir. 2002) (en banc) ("On remand, the district court generally should be free to consider any matters relevant to sentencing . . . as if it were sentencing de novo."); *United States v. Moore*, 131 F.3d 595, 598 (6th Cir. 1997) ("In the absence of an explicit limitation, the remand order is presumptively a general one.").

permits a full resentencing, or limited and permits resentencing only to address whether the error identified by the appellate court requires a different sentence.

Pepper v. United States[22] illustrates this distinction. At the original sentencing hearing, the trial judge granted the defendant a 40% downward departure from his proposed sentence under the sentencing guidelines for assisting the government. After the court of appeals twice vacated that sentence in two appeals, the case was reassigned to a new trial judge. On remand, the new trial judge concluded that he wasn't bound by the 40% reduction and gave Pepper a 20% reduction instead.[23] At the U.S. Supreme Court, Pepper argued that the trial judge was bound by the earlier 40% reduction as the law of the case because neither the court of appeals nor the Supreme Court had ever overruled that reduction and because the trial judge had never identified a "compelling justification" for overturning it.[24] No such luck, the Court responded. The first problem was that the court of appeals had "set aside Pepper's entire sentence" and "remanded for *de novo* resentencing"—a general, not a limited, remand.[25] The general remand thus "wiped the slate clean" and gave the trial judge authority to sentence Pepper anew without being required to show that the earlier departure was clearly wrong or would work a manifest injustice.[26] The second problem concerned the holistic nature of sentencing: "Because a district court's 'original sentencing intent may be undermined by altering one portion of the calculus,'" an appellate court may vacate the entire sentence in order to give the district court authority to reassess the relevant sentencing factors as a whole.[27]

---

22   562 U.S. at 476.
23   *Id.* at 485.
24   *Id.* at 507.
25   *Id.*
26   *Id.*
27   *Id.* (quoting *United States v. White*, 406 F.3d 827, 832 (7th Cir. 2005)).

56. Subsequent Appeals

When an appellate court decides a case that later returns there by appeal or writ of error, only questions that were not determined in the previous decision will be considered. A point of law already adjudicated becomes the law of the case and may not be reversed or departed from at any later stage without a relevant exception to the doctrine.

A corollary to the mandate rule is that a court is generally bound by its own earlier decisions on an issue in the absence of an intervening ruling by a higher court. For appellate courts, this means that "one panel of an appellate court will not as a general rule reconsider questions which another panel has decided on a prior appeal in the same case."[1] The law of the case binds a successive appellate panel only if the earlier panel considered and decided the particular issue.

Once an appellate court resolves a matter, its ruling binds all lower courts within its jurisdiction unless or until that appellate court alters its ruling en banc or a superior court reverses it. Case after case at the U.S. Supreme Court makes the point. Says one decision: "When matters are decided by an appellate court, its rulings, unless reversed by it or a superior court, bind the lower court. Thus a cause proceeds to final determination."[2] Says another:

> Whatever was before the Court, and is disposed of, is considered as finally settled. The inferior court is bound by the decree as the law of the case; and must carry it into execution, according to the mandate. They cannot vary it, or examine it for any other purpose than execution; or give any other or further relief; or review it upon any matter decided on appeal for error apparent; or intermeddle with it, further than to settle so much as has been remanded.[3]

---

[1] *Merritt v. Mackey*, 932 F.2d 1317, 1320 (9th Cir. 1991) (quoting *Kimball v. Callahan*, 590 F.2d 768, 771 (9th Cir. 1979)); *see also United States v. Moran*, 393 F.3d 1, 7 (1st Cir. 2004) (noting that this branch of the doctrine "binds . . . a successor appellate panel in a second appeal in the same case").

[2] *Insurance Grp. Comm. v. Denver & Rio Grande Western R.R.*, 329 U.S. 607, 612 (1947).

[3] *Sibbald v. United States*, 37 U.S. (12 Pet.) 488, 492 (1838).

Says still another: "In its earliest days this Court consistently held that an inferior court has no power or authority to deviate from the mandate issued by an appellate court. The rule . . . has been uniformly followed in later days."[4]

Not only has the Court adhered to the doctrine since "its earliest days," but some of its earliest and most influential Justices have written decisions following it. Marshall C.J. applied the doctrine to prevent a litigant from obtaining interest not identified in the mandate.[5] Story J. expounded on the doctrine and clung to it.[6]

The Court has gone so far as to say that the law-of-the-case doctrine is "something of a misnomer" in this setting.[7] For it is "not counsel[ing] a court to abide by its own prior decision in a given case, but goes rather to an appellate court's relationship to the court of trial."[8] In this context, the doctrine merely enforces a fundamental necessity of a system of state and federal courts that have a ladder of successively greater authority.

For like reason, the law-of-the-case doctrine doesn't dictate the rule of decision from a junior court to a senior court. It thus doesn't "bind" the U.S. Supreme Court as it reviews decisions: "Just as a district court's adherence to law of the case cannot insulate an issue from appellate review, a court of appeals' adherence to the law of the case cannot insulate an issue from this Court's review."[9]

---

4   *Briggs v. Pennsylvania R.R.*, 334 U.S. 304, 306 (1948) (internal citations omitted).

5   *Himely v. Rose*, 9 U.S. (5 Cranch) 313, 314 (1809) ("Nothing is before this court but what is subsequent to the mandate.").

6   See *The Santa Maria*, 23 U.S. (10 Wheat.) 431, 434–35 (1825); *Boyce's Ex'rs v. Grundy*, 34 U.S. (9 Pet.) 275, 281–82 (1835) ("Though it be generally true, that when a cause comes up to this court a second time, the court will not look behind its mandate, yet the prior proceedings will be examined so far as it is necessary to an investigation of new points of controversy, between the parties, not disposed of by the first decree.").

7   *United States v. Wells*, 519 U.S. 482, 487 n.4 (1997).

8   *Id.*

9   *Christianson v. Colt Indus. Operating Corp.*, 486 U.S. 800, 817 (1988); see also *F. Enters., Inc. v. Kentucky Fried Chicken Corp.*, 351 N.E.2d 121, 126–27 (Ohio 1976) ("[A] prior erroneous unappealed decision of a Court of Appeals which established the law of the case for a subsequent trial . . . does not bind this court upon a further appeal.").

Nor does the doctrine prohibit a court of appeals from rethinking an earlier decision when there is a later change in the law of the circuit. In *Davis v. United States*,[10] the U.S. Supreme Court held that "the Court of Appeals erred in holding that 'the law of the case,' as determined in the earlier appeal from the petitioner's conviction, precluded him from securing relief under § 2255 on the basis of an intervening change in law."[11]

The doctrine may interact with the final-judgment rule in the context of an appeal in another respect. Even if a state high court adheres to a decision on federal law on law-of-the-case grounds, and even if the law-of-the-case ruling turns on state law, that doesn't preclude a discretionary court of last review from reviewing the federal question in a later appeal from a final judgment. That is just what the Court held in 1997: "If a state court judgment is not final for purposes of Supreme Court review, the federal questions it determines will . . . be open in the Supreme Court on later review of the final judgment, whether or not under state law the initial adjudication is the law of the case."[12] Because the U.S. Supreme Court "cannot review a state court judgment until it is final, a contrary rule would insulate interlocutory state court rulings on important federal questions from [its] consideration."[13] The Supreme Court's prior denial of a writ of certiorari—a decision not to review a lower-court decision—likewise doesn't preclude the Court "from examining questions decided during the first state appeal."[14]

Nor, again, does the doctrine prohibit a motion under Federal Rule of Civil Procedure 60(b)(5) to alter a judgment based on intervening law. In one case, a district court had enjoined the New York Board of Education from sending public-school teachers into parochial schools to provide remedial education

---

10   417 U.S. 333 (1974).

11   *Id.* at 342.

12   *Jefferson v. City of Tarrant*, 522 U.S. 75, 83 (1997) (quoting Richard H. Fallon Jr. et al., *Hart & Wechsler's The Federal Courts and the Federal System* 642 (4th ed. 1996)).

13   *Hathorn v. Lovorn*, 457 U.S. 255, 262 (1982).

14   *Id.* at 262 n.11.

to disadvantaged children.[15] Twelve years later, the same Board and several affected children filed a Civil Rule 60(b)(5) motion to obtain relief from the injunction based on intervening changes in the Supreme Court's Establishment Clause jurisprudence. The Supreme Court permitted the motion and ended the injunction. In doing so, it reminded litigants and lower courts that only the Supreme Court may overrule its own decisions.[16] Said the Court: "We do not acknowledge, and we do not hold, that other courts should conclude our more recent cases have, by implication, overruled an earlier precedent."[17] It therefore concluded that the trial court had the right to entertain the motion and that it had properly "recognize[d] that the motion had to be denied unless and until this Court reinterpreted the binding precedent."[18] That the trial court had no right to assume authority to overrule a superior court's precedents, however, said nothing about the Court's authority to do so under a Rule 60(b)(5) motion. Nor did the law-of-the-case doctrine stand in the way of the Court's overruling an earlier Establishment Clause precedent—established in that same case—in response to a Rule 60(b)(5) motion. Acknowledging that "a court should not reopen issues decided in earlier stages of the same litigation," it concluded that the doctrine didn't apply there because *Aguilar*—the earlier decision in the case—"would be decided differently under our current Establishment Clause law" and that outcome "would undoubtedly work a 'manifest injustice,'" so that the law-of-the-case doctrine did not apply.[19]

Forfeiting law-of-the-case issues

The Supreme Court has suggested that the law-of-the-case doctrine can be forfeited if not raised. In *Salazar v. Buono*,[20] the Court considered a question of standing in a case with many iterations. The district court had originally entered a permanent

---

15 *Agostini v. Felton*, 521 U.S. 203, 208 (1997).
16 Id. at 235.
17 Id. at 237.
18 Id. at 238.
19 Id. at 236.
20 559 U.S. 700 (2010).

injunction against the government's display of a cross on federal land, and the Ninth Circuit affirmed on appeal. The district court later enjoined the government from conveying the land on which the cross stood to a private party, and the Ninth Circuit again affirmed. This second decision was appealed to the Supreme Court. In a concurrence, Scalia J. concluded that the plaintiff lacked standing and that the merits need not be reached.[21] He explained that the first, unappealed Ninth Circuit decision, which had found standing, didn't control as law of the case, since the later suit concerned a different issue. Significantly, Scalia J. continued, the plaintiff "failed to raise the issue in his brief in opposition to certiorari."[22] Hence the Court treated it as having been forfeited.[23]

Yet even if the litigants don't raise the law-of-the-case doctrine, the court may address the doctrine on its own. As the Eighth Circuit has explained, "[b]ecause the court has a strong interest in avoiding repetitive litigation, we may raise [the] doctrine[] *sua sponte*."[24]

Jurisdictional issues relating to the doctrine prove interesting at the appellate level. The Supreme Court has held that there is no "jurisdiction exception" to the law-of-the-case doctrine, noting that "[p]erpetual litigation of any issue—jurisdictional or nonjurisdictional—delays, and therefore threatens to deny, justice."[25]

The Fifth Circuit analyzed this issue in a 2011 case[26] in which the district court had dismissed a plaintiff's state-law claims of fraud and breach of fiduciary duty in connection with a patent application as time-barred.[27] The first panel reversed and remanded for further factual development in an unpublished opinion that cursorily stated that the case was based on diversity

---

21   *Id.* at 729.
22   *Id.* at 729 n.1 (Scalia J. concurring).
23   *Id.*
24   *Maxfield v. Cintas Corp., No. 2*, 487 F.3d 1132, 1135 (8th Cir. 2007).
25   *See Christianson v. Colt Indus. Operating Corp.*, 486 U.S. 800, 816 n.5 (1988); *see also Free v. Abbott Labs., Inc.*, 164 F.3d 270, 272–73 (5th Cir. 1999); *LaShawn A. v. Barry*, 87 F.3d 1389, 1393–94 (D.C. Cir. 1996) (en banc).
26   *USPPS, Ltd. v. Avery Dennison Corp.*, 647 F.3d 274 (5th Cir. 2011).
27   *Id.* at 275.

of citizenship.[28] In a later appeal, the Fifth Circuit was asked to determine whether the Federal Circuit had exclusive jurisdiction over the case.[29] Addressing the question "whether jurisdiction was 'decided by necessary implication' simply by the prior panel hearing and deciding the earlier appeal," the Fifth Circuit drew a distinction based on whether jurisdiction "was actually raised and argued before the prior panel."[30] If the parties had raised a jurisdictional argument before the panel and the panel later exercised jurisdiction without explanation, "it is clear enough that 'the necessary assumption is that the prior panel found subject matter jurisdiction present,' and the ruling constitutes law of the case."[31] But if the issue wasn't briefed or addressed by the prior panel, the Fifth Circuit held, the law-of-the-case doctrine would not apply to the prior panel's exercise of jurisdiction.

It's unclear how literally courts will interpret the requirement that the law of the case applies only in the same case. Suppose, for example, that between appellate panels the district court entered a judgment of acquittal and the government filed a new, substantially similar indictment. Or suppose that the district court dismissed a complaint without prejudice and the plaintiff sued anew on a related complaint.

The first of these fact patterns actually arose in a 2015 federal appellate case.[32] There, a defendant appealed after being convicted of a broadly defined conspiracy. The original appellate panel held that there was insufficient evidence to support the existence of a single conspiracy. Rather, the panel believed that the evidence actually suggested the existence of two separate conspiracies—one sweeping in scope and one much narrower. The panel held that there was insufficient evidence to tie the defendant to the larger conspiracy, and that although there might be sufficient evidence

---

28 *USPPS, Ltd. v. Avery Dennison Corp.*, 326 F. App'x 842, 843 (5th Cir. 2009) (per curiam).

29 *USPPS*, 647 F.3d at 275–76.

30 *Id.* at 283 (quoting *Morrow v. Dillard*, 580 F.2d 1284, 1290 (5th Cir. 1978)).

31 *Id.* (quoting *Trans World Airlines, Inc. v. Morales*, 949 F.2d 141, 144 (5th Cir. 1991) (per curiam)).

32 *United States v. Szpyt*, 785 F.3d 31 (1st Cir. 2015).

of the smaller conspiracy, the defendant had been unfairly prejudiced by the difference between the larger conspiracy alleged and the smaller conspiracy arguably proved. After the appellate court vacated the conviction, the district court entered a judgment of acquittal. The government then obtained a new indictment alleging the smaller conspiracy, which had been squarely at issue in the earlier appeal. The question thus arose whether the earlier panel's decisions on the indictment now charged constituted the law of the case in a technically distinct case.

The three-judge panel was unable to agree on whether the law-of-the-case doctrine governed, with each judge writing a separate opinion. The lead opinion suggested that, as a practical matter, the case was "no different than had the government on remand moved . . . to amend the indictment," so issue preclusion required adopting the previous panel's findings.[33] But the concurring judge found that this position implied that the appeal was a "new, discrete matter," when in fact it was the same as "any other that follows a remand and subsequent proceeding for law of the case purposes."[34] The dissent persuasively declared that the doctrine had no place in this appeal because for the doctrine to apply, the appeal must be in the *same* case as before.[35] But "[a]s the docket numbers and common sense evidence, it is clearly not."[36] The opinions stake out positions that may someday be authoritatively resolved in future iterations of this question. Then again, the precise circumstances may have been unique.

---

33   *Id.* at 39.
34   *Id.* at 43 (Howard J. concurring).
35   *Id.* at 45 (Kayatta J. dissenting).
36   *Id.*

57. Transferred Decisions, Newly Assigned Judges, and Removed Actions

When a case has been transferred from one venue to another in the same court system, reassigned to new judges within the same court system, or removed from one court system to another, the rulings and decisions previously made by the prior court and judges are generally binding on the later court and judges—except on questions of law within the special expertise of the transferee court.

Trial-court rulings and decisions can become the law of the case, binding even a different trial judge who assumes responsibility for the case. This is so for the same pragmatic reasons that motivate the doctrine in other contexts.

A judge within the same court should not overrule another judge's appealable decision unless there are exceptional reasons to do so.[1] This aspect of the doctrine came to the fore in a 1963 case, in which a car-rental agency and a licensee of the agency disputed who had the rights to rent cars in a certain territory under the car-rental agency's name.[2] The case was filed in a federal district court and assigned to Clarke J., who went on an extended vacation. He was temporarily replaced by Hall C.J. The licensee sought a preliminary injunction to prevent the car-rental agency from interfering with its business, which Hall C.J. granted. He made and filed his findings of fact and conclusions of law and entered the preliminary injunction. Later, after Clarke J. returned, the car-rental agency asked for a preliminary injunction against the licensee, and it was granted; Hall C.J.'s preliminary injunction was dissolved.[3] The Ninth Circuit reversed on the basis of abuse of discretion. Because Hall C.J.'s order granting the preliminary injunction was appealable as of right by statute and the car-rental agency did not appeal it, another judge of the same court could reconsider the order only if the car-rental agency showed that exceptional

---

1 *Fairbank v. Wunderman Cato Johnson*, 212 F.3d 528, 532 (9th Cir. 2000).
2 *Tanner Motor Livery, Ltd. v. Avis, Inc.*, 316 F.2d 804 (9th Cir. 1963).
3 *Id.* at 806–08.

circumstances existed or presented "the most cogent reasons" for reconsideration.[4] The court emphasized the order's appealability because the car-rental agency could have sought an appellate court's review if the agency believed that Hall C.J. had erred. It was not necessary to seek review by a different judge in the district court.[5] The court held that because the car-rental agency hadn't shown any reason why Hall C.J. couldn't or shouldn't review his order and no special circumstances existed, Clarke J. had no authority to change the order.[6]

The law-of-the-case doctrine applies to lawsuits transferred from one court to another, whether for lack of venue, inconvenient venue, the requirements of multidistrict litigation, or other reasons.[7] Under core law-of-the-case principles, a transferee court must respect the earlier decisions by the transferor court. Otherwise, a change in venue would come with the potential windfall of a change in law, prompting all manner of sharp-elbowed skirmishing in which the losing litigant in early rulings might seek to change venue. The doctrine thus "applies as much to the decisions of a coordinate court in the same case as to a court's own decisions."[8] These considerations demand special attention when it comes to the transfer decision itself. As the U.S. Supreme Court has pointed out, "the policies supporting the doctrine apply with even greater force to transfer decisions than to decisions of substantive law; transferee courts that feel entirely free to revisit transfer decisions of a coordinate court threaten to send litigants into a vicious circle of litigation."[9]

A dramatic application of the law-of-the-case doctrine occurred in a 2008 lawsuit[10] that FMC Corporation filed in the

---

4   *Id.* at 809–10.
5   *Id.* at 810.
6   *Id.*
7   *See* 28 U.S.C. § 1404(a) (venue); 28 U.S.C. § 1407 (multidistrict litigation).
8   *Christianson v. Colt Indus. Operating Corp.*, 486 U.S. 800, 816 (1988); *see Commonwealth v. Starr*, 664 A.2d 1326, 1333 (Pa. 1995) (applying the law of the case to "coordinate" state courts).
9   *Christianson*, 486 U.S. at 816.
10 *FMC Corp. v. EPA*, 557 F. Supp. 2d 105 (D.D.C. 2008).

United States District Court for the Eastern District of Virginia, seeking review of an EPA regulation.[11] After briefing, a judge of the Eastern District of Virginia ordered the case transferred to a federal trial court in the District of Columbia.[12] FMC then filed for transfer back to the Eastern District of Virginia or to the District of Delaware.[13] A District of Columbia judge denied the motion, finding that the first judge's decision to transfer the case to federal court in D.C. was the law of the case and that no exception to the doctrine applied.[14] In addition to the traditional justifications of finality and efficiency, comity counseled against "reconsideration of one judge's ruling by a different judge."[15] In the context of transfer decisions, the law-of-the-case doctrine is "especially salient" to prevent circuitous litigation if "transferee courts . . . feel entirely free"[16] to rethink a coordinate court's transfer decisions: "The proper forum for challenging a transfer order," the D.C. judge observed, "is in the appellate court of the transferor's circuit"[17]—where the law-of-the-case doctrine would not apply.

Just as the law of the case applies to transferred lawsuits, so too do its exceptions. Even with transferred lawsuits, the law of the case remains anything but an ironclad rule when applied to decisions by coordinate courts at the same level in the state or federal courts. When the Supreme Court confirmed in 1988 that the doctrine applied to transferred cases, it explained that the coordinate court "did not exceed its power in revisiting the jurisdictional issue" and was "obliged to decline jurisdiction" once it realized that the earlier decision was "clearly wrong."[18] The Court found no reason to apply law-of-the-case principles less rigorously to transfer decisions that involve the transferee court's jurisdiction: "Perpetual

---

11   *Id.* at 107.
12   *Id.* at 108.
13   *Id.*
14   *Id.* at 109–10.
15   *Id.* at 109.
16   *Id.* (quoting *Christianson*, 486 U.S. at 816).
17   *Id.* at 110.
18   *Christianson*, 486 U.S. at 817.

litigation of any issue—jurisdictional or nonjurisdictional—delays, and therefore threatens to deny, justice."[19]

Even when a case hasn't been transferred to another court (and a different judge), similar issues may arise in a related setting. From time to time, new judges take over pending cases. The trial judge handling a case may retire. A court may reassign the case to a different trial judge. A second appeal in the same case may come before a different panel of appellate judges from the same court. Or all the judges on an appellate court may have to recuse themselves, requiring judges from another court to handle the case.[20] All these settings raise law-of-the-case considerations when the new judge or judges decide disputes that involve prior rulings by the same court. May the new judges give a fresh look at the case and ignore or effectively overturn rulings by their predecessors with which they disagree? No. The key reason is that courts, not judges, issue rulings. That is why all judges wear the same black robes—to signify that the one institution defines the rule of law, not the varied people behind it. Each court and each judge is bound by prior judgments and holdings of *that court*, no matter which judge or group of judges issued the earlier ruling.[21]

Law-of-the-case application on removal

Cases removed from one court to another present a variation on this theme. Under the removal statute, a litigant may remove a case filed in state court to federal court because the case raises a federal question or implicates the diversity jurisdiction of the federal courts.[22] Sometimes the federal court will remand the case to state court. In either setting, the case may bring with it prior rulings of the relevant state or federal court. Assuming that the earlier court had jurisdiction over the case at the time of its rulings,

---

19 *Id.* at 816 n.5.
20 *See United States v. Nettles*, 476 F.3d 508 (7th Cir. 2007).
21 *See* Daniel J. Meador et al., *Appellate Courts: Structures, Functions, Processes, and Personnel* 456 (2d ed. 2006) ("[I]n all the U.S. courts of appeals the practice is to consider the decision of any three-judge panel to be the decision of the court and hence binding on all other subsequent three-judge panels.").
22 28 U.S.C. § 1441; *see* 18 U.S.C. § 1446.

the law of the case applies with full force to those rulings when the case reaches its ultimate judicial domicile.[23]

This proposition is the corollary of 28 U.S.C. § 1450, which continues the effect of state-court injunctions, orders, and other proceedings after removal—until the federal court instructs otherwise.[24] The statute supports law-of-the-case policies in removed cases, but two concerns weigh especially heavily in this setting. First, the comity concerns underlying the doctrine are strong, since they are influenced by federalism. Second, application of the doctrine after removal prevents removal from being used as a strategic device to obtain reconsideration of a state-court ruling.

Despite the stronger policy justifications for applying the doctrine in removed cases, in practice the doctrine applies only infrequently. Since removal often occurs early in a lawsuit, any state-court orders before removal are interlocutory. As discussed in § 24, interlocutory orders typically aren't subject to law of the case because they remain open for reconsideration by the same court. For example, in a 2005 federal appellate case,[25] the plaintiff had sued the hospital and four doctors for medical malpractice in Maine state court. The defendants moved to dismiss for lack of personal jurisdiction, and the Maine state court denied the motion as to the hospital. The hospital then removed the case to federal court and moved again to dismiss for lack of personal jurisdiction. The plaintiff argued that the Maine court's personal jurisdiction over the hospital was settled as law of the case. The district court granted the motion, dismissed, and was affirmed. As the appellate panel observed, if the federal court had originally denied the motion to dismiss, it could still have reconsidered

---

23 *Pacific Emp'rs Ins. Co. v. Sav-a-Lot of Winchester*, 291 F.3d 392, 398 (6th Cir. 2002) ("The doctrine also has relevance to rulings made by state courts prior to removal."); *Redfield v. Continental Cas. Corp.*, 818 F.2d 596, 605 (7th Cir. 1987) ("Although the law of the case doctrine is most commonly applied to govern the conduct of litigation on remand after an appeal, the doctrine also applies when a state court action is removed to federal court.").

24 *See In re Diet Drugs*, 282 F.3d 220, 231–32 (3d Cir. 2002) ("After removal, interlocutory orders of the state court are transformed into orders of the court to which the case is removed.").

25 *Harlow v. Children's Hosp.*, 432 F.3d 50 (1st Cir. 2005).

the motion—after all, it was an interlocutory order: "[F]ederalism does not require more deferential treatment of a state-court interlocutory order in a case removed to federal court than it would have required had the order originated in federal court."[26]

Some federal courts have found that they needn't follow prior state-court decisions on federal issues. This position typically arises with procedural issues: the law-of-the-case doctrine "may come into conflict with the Federal Rules of Civil Procedure which govern procedural matters in the federal courts."[27] In such cases, state procedural determinations yield to federal procedural law.[28] For example, in a 1987 Seventh Circuit case,[29] the plaintiffs sued an insurance company in Illinois state court to require its performance on three insurance contracts.[30] The Illinois court granted the insurer's motion to dismiss because the plaintiffs were not parties to the contracts, but it gave the plaintiffs leave to amend the complaint. The plaintiffs removed the case to federal court and amended their complaint, but the federal district court granted a new motion to dismiss under the law of the case, holding that by state-law pleading standards, the amended complaint still failed to state a claim. The Seventh Circuit reversed, explaining that although Illinois pleading standards applied in state court, federal pleading standards applied in federal court. The federal court was not bound by the earlier state-court ruling but rather was obliged to assess the adequacy of pleading under the federal rules.[31]

---

26 *Id.* at 56; *see also Pacific Emp'rs*, 291 F.3d at 398 ("[I]t is not an abuse of discretion [for a federal court] to revisit a prior [state] ruling that is found to be erroneous.").

27 *Redfield*, 818 F.2d at 605.

28 *See id.*; *see also Gasperini v. Center for Humanities, Inc.*, 518 U.S. 415, 427 (1996).

29 *Redfield*, 818 F.2d at 596.

30 *Id.* at 599.

31 *Id.* at 605.

58. Original-Jurisdiction Actions

The law-of-the-case doctrine is relaxed in original actions before the U.S. Supreme Court.

With original actions in the U.S. Supreme Court, the law-of-the-case doctrine has a diminished force. At issue in *Arizona v. California*[1] was whether the rights to the waters of the Colorado River established by an earlier decree could be modified by reason of changed circumstances. "Unlike the more precise requirements of res judicata," White J. noted, the law-of-the-case doctrine has few unbending restrictions.[2] Even those strictures, he added, have less relevance to original actions because the doctrine

> proceeds through preliminary stages, generally matures at trial, and produces a judgment, to which, after appeal, the binding finality of res judicata and collateral estoppel will attach. To extrapolate wholesale law of the case into the situation of our original jurisdiction, where jurisdiction to accommodate changed circumstances is often retained, would weaken to an intolerable extent the finality of our decrees in original actions.[3]

An allied question of moment is whether the law-of-the-case doctrine applies with equal vigor to a *jurisdictional* ruling—a point that could arise at any stage of litigation but perhaps involves special considerations in an original action before the Supreme Court. Given the unflagging obligation of federal courts to ensure that they have jurisdiction over a dispute at all stages of the case, one might think that the law of the case doesn't apply with as much clout in that setting, or that the doctrine perhaps doesn't apply at all in that setting. Undoubtedly if a superior court determines that jurisdiction over a dispute is proper, and if no legal or factual development alters the premises of that ruling, the inferior court must adhere to it. But what if the same court that issued the relevant jurisdictional ruling has second thoughts about the ruling even though nothing has changed factually or legally, while any

---

[1] 460 U.S. 605 (1983), *decision supplemented*, 466 U.S. 144 (1984).
[2] *Id.* at 618.
[3] *Id.* at 618–19.

error in the prior ruling wasn't a clear one? That issue arose in an original action in *Wyoming v. Oklahoma*.[4] The majority acknowledged that the Court had "been reluctant to import wholesale law-of-the-case principles into original actions," but added that "prior rulings . . . 'should be subject to the general principles of finality and repose, absent changed circumstances or unforeseen issues not previously litigated.'"[5] It then noted that there was no changed factual or legal circumstance. Even so, it added, the Court might change its mind at that late date if it became "convinced" that its earlier jurisdictional ruling had been "clearly wrong," after which the Court concluded that this standard had not been met.[6] The Court didn't mention the "manifest injustice" requirement, presumably because it had no work to do in the absence of subject-matter jurisdiction.

In dissent, Scalia J., joined by Rehnquist C.J. and Thomas J., questioned whether the doctrine applied to an earlier jurisdictional ruling. Law-of-the-case requirements had "never to [his] knowledge," he wrote, "been applied to jurisdictional issues raised (or reraised) before final judgment."[7] Because "it is a court's *obligation* to dismiss a case *whenever* it becomes convinced that it has no proper jurisdiction," the law-of-the-case doctrine—including the clearly-erroneous requirement—should not "impede" that assessment "no matter how late that wisdom may arrive."[8]

---

4   502 U.S. 437 (1992).
5   *Id.* at 446 (quoting *Arizona v. California*, 460 U.S. at 619).
6   *Id.*
7   *Id.* at 462 (Scalia J. dissenting).
8   *Id.*

59. Exceptions to Law of the Case

A court may reconsider legal questions previously decided during the same case if materially new facts are presented at a later stage of the case, if controlling legal authority has changed significantly since the prior decision, or if reconsideration is necessary to prevent a miscarriage of justice.

The law-of-the-case doctrine is hardly absolute. In three particular situations, it can be appropriate to veer from a prior decision that had otherwise finally settled an issue within the lawsuit.

New evidence

The first in the trio of exceptions to the law-of-the-case doctrine applies when new evidence is introduced at a later stage of a case. A court isn't bound by a former decision made either by itself or by an appellate court if the court is presented with new evidence that undermines the rationale for the earlier decision. As the Third Circuit has explained, this exception "makes sense because when the record contains new evidence, the question has not really been decided earlier and is posed for the first time."[1] But the court made clear that "this is so only if the new evidence differs materially from the evidence of record when the issue was first decided and if it provides less support for that decision."[2] These statements assume that the evidence is admissible and isn't barred by some other rule—as when the evidence is new but could have been discussed and used at the earlier proceedings.

The Eleventh Circuit relied on this exception in a 2005 case.[3] To establish that he was fired in violation of the First Amendment under the *Pickering* test, the plaintiff had to show that the following balance of competing interests weighed in his favor: the "balance between the interests of the teacher, as

---

1 *Hamilton v. Leavy*, 322 F.3d 776, 787 (3d Cir. 2003) (quoting *Bridge v. United States Parole Comm'n*, 981 F.2d 97, 103 (3d Cir. 1992)).
2 *Id.*
3 *Jackson v. Alabama State Tenure Comm'n*, 405 F.3d 1276 (11th Cir. 2005).

a citizen, in commenting upon matters of public concern, and the interest of the State, as an employer, in promoting the efficiency of the public services it performs through its employees."[4] The district court had granted the defendants' motion for summary judgment on the plaintiff's First Amendment claim after finding that the necessary *Pickering* balance weighed in favor of the plaintiff,[5] but that the defendants had properly asserted a defense by showing that they "would have made the same decision to fire [the plaintiff] regardless of his speech."[6] On appeal, the Eleventh Circuit reversed the district court's decision on the defense and remanded. A different district judge granted judgment as a matter of law to the defendants after finding that the necessary *Pickering* balance actually weighed in favor of the defendants. On appeal for the second time, one of the questions presented was whether the prior appellate decision implicitly affirmed the original district court's *Pickering* decision when it reversed on the second ground. The Eleventh Circuit held that the law of the case didn't apply, since "substantially different" evidence had been presented after the appeal.[7] The Eleventh Circuit noted the difference in how well the evidence had been developed at different stages in the litigation, saying that "[t]wo different sets of facts framed two different issues and permitted two different rulings."[8] Even if the law-of-the-case doctrine held that the *Pickering* balance favored the plaintiff on the summary-judgment record in the first district court, the court held, "the law of the case is not that the *Pickering* balance favored him on the record as it stood when [the second district court] entered judgment as a matter of law for the [defendants]."[9]

For this first exception to apply, the evidence must be "new," which courts have interpreted to mean both (1) "substantially

---

4   *Id.* at 1282 (quoting *Pickering v. Board of Educ.*, 391 U.S. 563, 568 (1968)).
5   *Id.*
6   *Id.* at 1280 (citing *Mt. Healthy City Sch. Dist. Bd. of Educ. v. Doyle*, 429 U.S. 274, 285–86 (1977)).
7   *Id.* at 1283.
8   *Id.* at 1284.
9   *Id.* at 1284–85.

different" from the evidence previously presented and (2) previously unavailable or unknown. For example, a court could reject a defendant's attempt to relitigate a suppression issue if the evidence presented at trial isn't substantially different from that presented at the suppression hearing. Likewise, a court could reject a defendant's attempt to invoke this exception to the law-of-the-case doctrine when "[i]t is not clear that any of the defendant['s] evidence was truly 'new' in the sense that it could not have reasonably been developed and presented in earlier stages of this litigation."[10]

The substantially new and previously unavailable evidence must undermine the earlier decision. In a 2000 case,[11] for example, the Second Circuit required the new evidence to "shed[] substantial doubt" on its previous decision to warrant reconsideration.[12] Finding that the new evidence didn't undermine its previous decision, the Second Circuit adhered to the law of the case.

Even so, the new-evidence exception cannot be used to reopen issues outside the scope of the mandate. In a 1991 case,[13] the First Circuit explained how this limitation works after a remand. The appellate court had considered and affirmed the district court's refusal to allow a defendant to withdraw his guilty plea but had remanded to allow a psychologist to perform testing at the defendant's expense before sentencing.[14] On remand, and contrary to the appellate court's express instructions, the district court considered anew the defendant's request to withdraw his guilty plea based on evidence gleaned from the psychological testing. The appellate court held that the new-evidence exception to the law-of-the-case doctrine "does not apply when a trial court gratuitously jettisons the rule in order to address an issue explicitly

---

10 *Yankton Sioux Tribe v. Podhradsky*, 606 F.3d 994, 1005 (8th Cir. 2010); *see also United States v. Bell*, 5 F.3d 64, 67 (4th Cir. 1993) (phrasing exception as requiring "significant new evidence, not earlier obtainable in the exercise of due diligence") (quoting *United States v. Bell*, 988 F.2d 247, 250 (1st Cir. 1993)).

11 *United States v. Tenzer*, 213 F.3d 34 (2d Cir. 2000).

12 *Id.* at 40.

13 *United States v. Rivera-Martinez*, 931 F.2d 148 (1st Cir. 1991).

14 *Id.* at 149.

decided, and foreclosed, in an earlier appeal in the same case."[15] The efficacy of the law-of-the-case doctrine would be undermined if the outcome were otherwise, the court reasoned. If a trial court could flout the law of the case instead of deferring to the appellate court's resolution, the court said, "the doctrine would disappear into thin air. Federal jurisprudence wisely prohibits trial judges from orchestrating self-fulfilling prophecies of that sort."[16]

Change in authority

A second exception to the law-of-the-case doctrine—a narrow exception—allows a court to rethink an earlier decision if controlling legal authority has changed significantly since the earlier decision and now compels a different outcome.[17] Suppose that a district court has sentenced a defendant under the then-binding sentencing guidelines based on an upward departure. Finding the upward departure unwarranted, the court of appeals remands for sentencing within the relevant guidelines range. Under the normal application of the mandate rule, the district court would be bound to sentence the defendant within the guidelines' range, and a later appellate panel would likewise be bound by the decision that the upward departure was unwarranted. But if the Supreme Court decided *United States v. Booker*[18] after the first appellate decision, the guidelines would then have become advisory rather than mandatory. With this intervening change in controlling authority, the district court would be able to sentence above the guidelines range without violating the mandate rule.[19]

For this second exception to apply, the new authority must amount to "an intervening change in the law."[20] The change must postdate the decision that would otherwise constitute the law of the case. To continue the example above, *Booker* would not be a

---

15 *Id.* at 151.
16 *Id.*
17 *See, e.g., United States v. Rivera-Martinez*, 931 F.2d 148, 151 (1st Cir. 1991); *Hsu v. County of Clark*, 173 P.3d 724, 730 (Nev. 2007) (en banc).
18 543 U.S. 220 (2005).
19 *See, e.g., United States v. Bad Marriage*, 439 F.3d 534, 537–38 (9th Cir. 2006).
20 *United States v. Matthews*, 643 F.3d 9, 14–15 (1st Cir. 2011) (emphasis omitted).

basis to avoid the mandate rule if it had been decided before the appellate decision. It would not then constitute a change in the relevant law.

The timing can be crucial. In a Ninth Circuit case,[21] a plaintiff sued two officials for alleged due-process violations.[22] The appellate panel affirmed the grant of summary judgment for the defendants on the plaintiff's claims of liberty deprivation but reversed and remanded on the plaintiff's claims of property deprivation. In its decision, the panel held that the officials were not entitled to qualified immunity. On remand, the claims went to a bench trial in the absence of qualified immunity, and the officials were found liable. One of the officials appealed, asking the appellate panel to reconsider the issue of his qualified immunity, in part because of the Supreme Court's decision in *Anderson v. Creighton*,[23] which considered the standard for qualified immunity. The court rejected this argument, saying that *Anderson* "did not change controlling authority on this issue so as to require us to reconsider the merits of [the appellant's] qualified immunity defense."[24] The Ninth Circuit reasoned: "*Anderson* was decided three months prior to *Merritt*, so there was no *intervening* change of law. More important, *Anderson* did not *change* the controlling standard as [the appellant] suggests. *Anderson* clarified and refined the law articulated in *Harlow v. Fitzgerald*."[25] The court had relied on *Harlow*[26] in its previous opinion in a way that "complie[d] with the *Anderson* 'clarification.'"[27] Given the lack of an intervening change, the law-of-the-case doctrine applied with full force.

But in exceptional circumstances involving a dramatic change in controlling legal authority, a court may deviate from the law of the case.[28] The question is often just how dramatic the change

---

21 *Merritt v. Mackey*, 932 F.2d 1317 (9th Cir. 1991).
22 *Id.* at 1319.
23 483 U.S. 635 (1987).
24 *Merritt*, 932 F.2d at 1320.
25 *Id.* at 1320–21 (citations omitted).
26 *Harlow v. Fitzgerald*, 457 U.S. 800 (1982).
27 *Merritt*, 932 F.2d at 1321.
28 *See, e.g.*, *Nkihtaqmikon v. Impson*, 585 F.3d 495, 498 (1st Cir. 2009).

must be. The petitioner in a 2011 Tenth Circuit case[29] focused on the word *dramatic* when arguing that a new BIA decision "did not embody a dramatic change in the controlling authority, because it was merely one in a line of published BIA cases that followed a similar rationale."[30] That rationale, the petitioner continued, had been known to the prior panel and rejected by it. But the BIA in fact departed from the law of the case. Although the Tenth Circuit conceded that it had not mentioned the cases on which the petitioner relied in its previous decision, it rejected the petitioner's argument that the BIA's new decision "did not constitute a sufficient departure from the controlling law to justify a departure from the law of the case."[31] Still, this argument that a predictable change doesn't qualify for the exception may one day prove tenable.

For this second exception to apply, the intervening change in controlling legal authority must also undermine a relevant issue in the earlier decision. Later legal authority need not directly contradict the earlier decision to undermine it.[32] In one case, the appellate court acknowledged that an intervening Supreme Court decision didn't specifically address the issue decided in an earlier appeal. Even so, the court concluded that "[a] close inspection" of the Supreme Court's analysis "reveal[ed] a significant tension" between the reasoning of the Supreme Court's decision and the reasoning relied on in the first appeal.[33]

Miscarriage of justice

The third and final exception to the law-of-the-case doctrine emerges from the rule's discretionary nature. If applying the doctrine would lead to a clearly erroneous result and, if uncorrected, would work a serious injustice, the policy justifications of the

---

29 *Padilla-Caldera v. Holder*, 637 F.3d 1140, 1145 (10th Cir. 2011), as corrected.
30 *Id.* at 1145.
31 *Id.* at 1146.
32 *United States v. Holloway*, 630 F.3d 252, 254 (1st Cir. 2011).
33 *Id.* at 259.

doctrine yield to interests of justice, and courts decline to apply the former decision.[34]

For example, in *Dobbs v. Zant*,[35] an inmate claimed that he had received ineffective assistance at his criminal trial. Because no one could track down the trial transcript, the inmate had to rely on the testimony of his counsel as to what had happened during the trial. After the federal courts rejected his claim, he found the trial transcript, and it contradicted his trial lawyer's testimony. The Eleventh Circuit refused to reopen the proceeding to consider the new evidence on law-of-the-case grounds. The U.S. Supreme Court reversed, reasoning that without examining the transcript, the lower courts couldn't apply the manifest-injustice exception to the law-of-the-case doctrine, and hence were "unable to determine whether its prior decision should be reconsidered."[36] Whether this ruling would apply outside the context of a capital sentence or in the aftermath of the later-enacted Anti-Terrorism and Effective Death Penalty Act of 1996 remains to be seen. But the ruling confirms that courts take law-of-the-case requirements *and* exceptions seriously, whether due to new facts or new law.

As another example, in a 2009 First Circuit case,[37] the plaintiffs sued two state officials, one in her personal capacity, and one in both his personal and official capacities, for injunctive relief under 42 U.S.C. § 1983.[38] Early in the case, the district court entered partial summary judgment against the plaintiffs, dismissing the official-capacity claim as barred by sovereign immunity. After entry of the final judgment, the plaintiffs appealed, but didn't appeal the partial-summary-judgment ruling. On remand, the district court revised the partial-summary-judgment order. On a later appeal, an intervenor asserted that the district court's original partial-summary-judgment order was the law of the case. The appellate court disagreed, applying the miscarriage-of-justice

---

34 *See United States v. Rivera-Martinez*, 931 F.2d 148, 151 (1st Cir. 1991) (collecting cases).

35 506 U.S. 357 (1993) (per curiam).

36 *Id.* at 359.

37 *Negrón-Almeda v. Santiago*, 579 F.3d 45 (1st Cir. 2009).

38 *Id.* at 48.

exception. First, the court reasoned that the lower court's original decision was "obviously wrong": "[t]he very authority on which the district court relied in granting summary judgment" expressly barred damage suits against state officials in their official capacities, not equitable relief.[39] Second, the grant of summary judgment "was highly prejudicial to the plaintiffs[:] It prevented them from obtaining the equitable relief they sought and to which the district court determined they were otherwise entitled after hearing objections."[40] So the court applied the miscarriage-of-justice exception to the law-of-the-case doctrine and affirmed.[41]

The miscarriage-of-justice exception presents a high bar for those opposing application of an otherwise valid earlier decision as law of the case. Some courts impose two separate requirements: the earlier decision must be clearly erroneous, and it must create a manifest injustice.[42] The court doesn't inquire simply into whether the earlier view was incorrect; it must be "so *clearly* incorrect that [the court is] justified in refusing to regard it as law of the case."[43] A case doesn't involve a manifest injustice when the earlier conclusion finds adequate support in the record.[44]

Despite this roster of three exceptions to the law-of-the-case doctrine, it bears repeating that the doctrine is a prudential one. These rules and exceptions are meant to be a "guide to discretion," and not "a set of categorical rules, mechanically applied."[45] For example, in a 2001 Tenth Circuit case,[46] the district court had remanded a case to state court, finding that it lacked jurisdiction over the claims.[47] The defendant then filed both a petition for a

---

39   *Id.* at 52.
40   *Id.*
41   *Id.* at 52, 54.
42   See, e.g., *Jeffries v. Wood*, 114 F.3d 1484, 1489, 1492 (9th Cir. 1997) (en banc), *overruled on other grounds by Gonzalez v. Arizona*, 677 F.3d 383 (9th Cir. 2012) (en banc).
43   *Merritt v. Mackey*, 932 F.2d 1317, 1321 (9th Cir. 1991).
44   See *United States v. Ticchiarelli*, 171 F.3d 24, 29 (1st Cir. 1999).
45   *Jeffries*, 114 F.3d at 1492 (quoting *United States v. Alexander*, 106 F.3d 874, 876 (9th Cir. 1997)).
46   *Kennedy v. Lubar*, 273 F.3d 1293 (10th Cir. 2001).
47   *Id.* at 1296.

writ of mandamus and a notice of appeal. The mandamus panel of the Tenth Circuit denied the writ, finding that it had jurisdiction over the appeal but that the appropriate form of relief was through a direct appeal.

In the direct appeal, the defendant argued that the mandamus panel's jurisdictional holding was law of the case. The merits panel emphasized that the law-of-the-case doctrine is discretionary, and it "exercise[d] [its] discretion to reexamine the mandamus panel's prior jurisdictional determination."[48] Because the merits panel found that the mandamus panel's conclusion was clearly erroneous, it dismissed the appeal for lack of jurisdiction.

What about the application of the miscarriage-of-justice exception by high courts? How often do they admit that they erred in an earlier appeal of the case but decline to correct the error during a later appeal on law-of-the-case grounds? As between the competing goals of correctness and stability, we suspect that correctness usually prevails. Except for the law-of-the-case requirement that lower courts adhere to superior-court judgments and directives, the law-of-the-case doctrine, as this discussion suggests, is indeed a discretionary custom, not a rigid law. In this respect, there is something to the Supreme Court's observation that the doctrine is "amorphous" in nature[49] and has more bark than bite. Perhaps a better way to put all this is that for reasons of practicality and efficiency, all courts, whether trial or appellate, generally refrain from reconsidering close calls—particularly close calls arising in the context of difficult issues. But they will be willing to reconsider rulings later shown for one reason or another not to be close after all.

The discerning reader may wonder how a court's reluctance to let an acknowledged error go uncorrected jibes with other areas in which courts correct errors. When appellate courts uphold mistaken decisions because a litigant has forfeited or waived a winning argument, that raises a different problem. In that type of

---

48 *Id.* at 1299–1300 & 1300 n.9.

49 *Arizona v. California*, 460 U.S. 605, 618 (1983), *decision supplemented*, 466 U.S. 144 (1984).

circumstance, someone else—a lawyer, not the judge presiding over the case and whose ruling is on appeal—made the mistake. And there, the victim of the mistake has other recourse: an ineffective-assistance claim in criminal cases or a malpractice action in civil cases.

E. Federal Doctrine and Practice

60. Law of the Circuit

A federal district court or (with rare exceptions) a circuit panel must follow decisions of the court of appeals in the same circuit in preference to the decisions of all other courts, state or national, unless there is a contrary decision by the U.S. Supreme Court.

As a matter of vertical precedent, federal district courts, including three-judge district courts, must defer to their circuit court.[1] But they owe no deference whatsoever to their own precedents. In *Camreta v. Greene*,[2] the U.S. Supreme Court stated that "a decision of a federal district court judge is not binding precedent in either a different judicial district, the same judicial district, or even upon the same judge in a different case."[3] While district courts generally agree that opinions of judges of coordinate jurisdiction should be respected and followed when possible, it is settled that the decisions in those opinions aren't binding.[4]

---

1 *See In re Korean Air Lines Disaster*, 829 F.2d 1171, 1176 (D.C. Cir. 1987) (per Ginsburg J.) ("Binding precedent for all is set only by the Supreme Court, and for the district courts within a circuit, only by the court of appeals for that circuit."), *aff'd sub nom. Chan v. Korean Air Lines, Ltd.*, 490 U.S. 122 (1989); *Alabama NAACP v. Wallace*, 269 F. Supp. 346, 350 (M.D. Ala. 1967) ("It is the clear duty of this district court to follow the decision of our Court of Appeals."). *But see Jehovah's Witnesses in Wash. v. King Cnty. Hosp.*, 278 F. Supp. 488, 504–05 (W.D. Wash. 1967) (per curiam) ("In this special three-judge court case we are not bound by any judicial decisions other than those of the United States Supreme Court."), *aff'd*, 398 U.S. 598 (1968) (per curiam).

2 563 U.S. 692 (2011).

3 *Id.* at 709 n.7 (quoting 18 James W. Moore et al., *Moore's Federal Practice* § 134.02[1][d], at 134-26 (3d ed. 2011)).

4 *Bluebeard's Castle, Inc. v. Delmar Mktg., Inc.*, 886 F. Supp. 1204, 1211 n.1 (D.V.I. 1995) (noting that while the ruling of a judge of a district court deserves respect, it is "nonetheless only persuasive to another judge of the same court"); *State Farm Mut. Auto. Ins. Co. v. Bates*, 542 F. Supp. 807, 816 (N.D. Ga. 1982) (explaining that while the court gives another judge's decision "serious consideration," it undertakes its own analysis); *White v. Baltic Conveyor Co.*, 209 F. Supp. 716, 722 (D.N.J. 1962) (holding that even though "brother judges" in same district follow each other's decisions out of comity and professional courtesy, the judge's reasoning in this case leads to a different ruling).

But for panels of a circuit court, horizontal precedent does apply: the traditional view is that one circuit panel cannot overrule another.[5] Generally speaking, a panel decision may be overruled only by (1) the court of that circuit sitting en banc; (2) a contrary opinion of the Supreme Court; or (3) statutory amendment.[6] In the case of intracircuit conflict, the rule is that the "earlier opinion controls and is binding precedent."[7] (See §§ 36, 60.)

The rule about intracircuit adherence to earlier decisions is an old one. A respected 1904 legal encyclopedia stated the proposition clearly, that "a federal circuit court will abide by decisions made in its circuit even though it considers the decision inconsistent with principle and though it would not take the same view were the question a new one."[8]

Yet the traditional rule has undergone erosion in some circuits. The First Circuit has allowed a circuit panel to depart from stare decisis when noncontrolling but persuasive caselaw, as from another circuit, suggests that an earlier panel decision should be overruled.[9] Still, this watered-down law-of-the-circuit doctrine arises only "in extremely rare circumstances."[10] The First Circuit also uses an informal procedure in lieu of an en banc sitting: with "extreme caution" in "special circumstances," the panel may overrule a horizontal precedent by circulating the overruling opinion to all the active judges for prepublication comment—and if a

---

5   18 James W. Moore et al., *Moore's Federal Practice* § 134.02[1][c], at 134-16 (3d ed. 2015); *see Bonner v. City of Prichard*, 661 F.2d 1206, 1208 (11th Cir. 1981) (en banc).

6   *Jacobs v. National Drug Intelligence Ctr.*, 548 F.3d 375, 378 (5th Cir. 2008).

7   *United States v. Jackson*, 220 F.3d 635, 639 (5th Cir. 2000) (noting that "where two previous holdings or lines of precedent conflict, the earlier opinion controls and is the binding precedent") (quoting *Billiot v. Puckett*, 135 F.3d 311, 316 (5th Cir. 1998)), *overruled on other grounds by United States v. Charles*, 301 F.3d 309 (5th Cir. 2002).

8   Basil Jones, "Stare Decisis," 26 *The American and English Encyclopaedia of Law* 158, 165–66 (David S. Garland & Lucius P. McGehee eds., 2d ed. 1904).

9   *United States v. Lewko*, 269 F.3d 64, 66 (1st Cir. 2001) ("'[A] prior panel decision shall not be disturbed "absent either the occurrence of a controlling intervening event (e.g., a Supreme Court opinion on the point; a ruling of the circuit, sitting en banc; or a statutory overruling) or, in extremely rare circumstances, where non-controlling but persuasive case law suggests such a course."'") (quoting *United States v. Chhien*, 266 F.3d 1, 11 (1st Cir. 2001)).

10 *Id.*

majority of them do not object, the horizontal precedent is overruled.[11] The Second Circuit has a similar procedure, except that it appears that a single judge might be able to prevent the overruling by objecting.[12] Likewise, the D.C. Circuit has a similar informal procedure.[13]

The Seventh Circuit has gone furthest: there *is* no binding law of the circuit. An appellate panel may overturn the circuit precedent for "compelling reasons,"[14] such as when other circuits reject the Seventh Circuit's position. The Seventh Circuit has further distinguished itself by codifying a panel's ability to overrule horizontal precedent—which no other circuit has done—and by

---

[11] See *United States v. Dowdell*, 595 F.3d 50, 62 n.8 (1st Cir. 2010) ("Following the procedure described in cases such as *Crowe v. Bolduc*, 365 F.3d 86, 89 n.1 (1st Cir. 2004) and *Carpenters Local Union No. 26 v. U.S. Fid. & Guar. Co.*, 215 F.3d 136, 138 n.1 (1st Cir. 2000), the proposed panel opinion in this case was circulated to all active judges of the court, a majority of whom posed no objection."); *Gallagher v. Wilton Enters., Inc.*, 962 F.2d 120, 124 n.4 (1st Cir. 1992) (per curiam) ("[W]e would ordinarily have convened the en banc court. We have, however, in rare instances, where it has become reasonably clear that a prior precedent of this court was erroneously decided or is no longer good law, achieved the same result more informally by circulating the proposed panel opinion to all the active judges of the court for pre-publication comment. . . . While this practice is to be used sparingly and with extreme caution, we have employed it in the special circumstances of this case, with the result that the entire court has approved the overruling.").

[12] *Shipping Corp. of India v. Jaldhi Overseas Pte Ltd.*, 585 F.3d 58, 67 & n.9 (2d Cir. 2009) ("[I]t would ordinarily be neither appropriate nor possible for us to reverse an existing Circuit precedent. In this case, however, we have circulated this opinion to all active members of this Court prior to filing and have received no objection. . . . We refer to this process as a 'mini-*en banc*.'").

[13] *In re Sealed Case No. 97-3112*, 181 F.3d 128, 145 (D.C. Cir. 1999) (en banc) (Henderson J. concurring) ("Under the *Irons* footnote procedure, a panel decision departing from precedent is circulated to the full court for endorsement before issuance and issued with a footnote indicating the endorsement.").

[14] *United States v. Reyes-Hernandez*, 624 F.3d 405, 413–14 (7th Cir. 2010) ("This ongoing debate and current circuit split are compelling reasons to revisit our precedent."); *Glaser v. Wound Care Consultants, Inc.*, 570 F.3d 907, 915 (7th Cir. 2009) ("We have overruled our prior decisions when our position remains a minority one among other circuits."); *Russ v. Watts*, 414 F.3d 783, 788 (7th Cir. 2005) ("Although we must give considerable weight to our prior decisions, we are not bound by them absolutely and may overturn Circuit precedent for compelling reasons. Other circuits' rejection of our position provides one such compelling reason."). *See United States v. Wolfe*, 701 F.3d 1206, 1217 (7th Cir. 2012) ("[A] 'compelling reason' is required . . . . Being in the minority is not enough.").

holding informal hearings with unabashed frequency.[15] That rule was invoked, for example, in a 2016 case,[16] when a circuit panel overruled a 1992 panel decision holding that a lawyer couldn't appeal a formal, nonmonetary sanction.[17] When the overruling was announced to the other circuit judges, none asked that the case be reheard en banc.

---

[15] *See* 7th Cir. R. 40(e) ("Rehearing Sua Sponte Before Decision. A proposed opinion approved by a panel of this court adopting a position which would overrule a prior decision of this court or create a conflict between or among circuits shall not be published unless it is first circulated among the active members of this court and a majority of them do not vote to rehear en banc the issue of whether the position should be adopted."); *see also* Michael S. Kanne, *The "Non-Banc En Banc": Seventh Circuit Rule 40(e) and the Law of the Circuit*, 32 S. Ill. U. L.J. 611, 611 (2008) (in which Kanne J. of the Seventh Circuit highlights "the merits of Circuit Rule 40(e)[,] a Rule that provides an opportunity for each judge to weigh in on important issues, regardless of whether a case is heard en banc"); Amy E. Sloan, *The Dog That Didn't Bark: Stealth Procedures and the Erosion of Stare Decisis in the Federal Courts of Appeals*, 78 Fordham L. Rev. 713, 728 (2009) (stating that a review of formal and informal en banc hearings found that the Seventh Circuit held 272 informal en banc hearings through 2007, compared to the Second Circuit, which had held 71 through 2007—the second most).

[16] *Martinez v. City of Chicago*, 823 F.3d 1050, 1057 (7th Cir. 2016).

[17] *Id.* (overruling *Clark Equip. Co. v. Lift Parts Mfg. Co.*, 972 F.2d 817, 820 (7th Cir. 1992)).

61. En Banc Review

Although a decision of a three-judge panel of a federal circuit is binding precedent within the circuit, a circuit court may hear or rehear a case en banc to consider an issue of exceptional importance, to resolve a conflict in the court's precedents, or to ensure that the court's decisions conform to Supreme Court precedent. An en banc decision is especially authoritative.

The federal circuit courts normally sit in three-judge panels.[1] As we've already seen, a holding by a three-judge panel is binding precedent within the circuit. Apart from the few anomalies noted in § 60, a panel decision can be abrogated only by an intervening Supreme Court decision, an en banc decision to overturn, or a statutory amendment.[2]

In 1948, Congress enacted legislation authorizing courts of appeals to hear or rehear cases en banc. The current version provides that cases "shall be heard and determined by a court or panel of not more than three judges (except that the United States Court of Appeals for the Federal Circuit may sit in panels of more than three judges if its rules so provide), unless a hearing or rehearing before the court in banc is ordered by a majority of the circuit judges of the circuit who are in regular active service."[3] Only active circuit judges may vote on a petition to hear or rehear a case en banc.[4] Yet a senior circuit judge may participate in an en banc

---

1 *See* 28 U.S.C. § 46.

2 *See, e.g., Rutherford v. Columbia Gas,* 575 F.3d 616, 619 (6th Cir. 2009) ("A published prior panel decision remains controlling authority unless an inconsistent decision of the United States Supreme Court requires modification of the decision or this Court sitting en banc overrules the prior decision.") (internal quotation marks and citation omitted); *see also, e.g., Tokoph v. United States,* 774 F.3d 1300, 1303 (10th Cir. 2014); *Lair v. Bullock,* 697 F.3d 1200, 1202 (9th Cir. 2012); *United States v. Martinez,* 606 F.3d 1303, 1305 (11th Cir. 2010); *Gochicoa v. Johnson,* 238 F.3d 278, 286 n.11 (5th Cir. 2000); *ACLU of N.J. ex rel. Lander v. Schundler,* 168 F.3d 92, 98 n.6 (3d Cir. 1999).

3 28 U.S.C. § 46(c) (using the spelling *in banc* rather than the predominant form—*see Garner's Dictionary of Legal Usage* 315 (3d ed. 2011)).

4 28 U.S.C. § 46(c).

rehearing if the judge sat on the panel that decided the case.[5] Apart from the requirements set forth in 28 U.S.C. § 46(c) and Federal Rule of Appellate Procedure 35, the courts of appeals "are largely free to devise whatever procedures they choose to initiate the process of decision" to hear or rehear a case en banc.[6] Some courts permit the overruling of horizontal precedent without oral argument or separate briefing, subject to the agreement of the full court.[7]

The decision to grant a petition for hearing or rehearing en banc, or to initiate en banc review on the court's own motion, is discretionary.[8] Although a court of appeals is almost never required to grant en banc consideration, it cannot eliminate en banc review. The Supreme Court has stated that it is "essential" that litigants have the opportunity to suggest "that a particular case is appropriate for consideration by all the judges. A court may take steps to use the en banc power sparingly, but it may not take steps to curtail its use indiscriminately."[9]

Litigants must submit a petition for an initial hearing en banc by the date when the appellee's brief is due and a petition for rehearing en banc within 14 days after entry of judgment.[10]

---

5   *Id.*

6   *Moody v. Albemarle Paper Co.*, 417 U.S. 622, 626 (1974) (per curiam).

7   *See, e.g., Gallagher v. Wilton Enters., Inc.*, 962 F.2d 120, 124 n.4 (1st Cir. 1992) (per curiam) ("Because this case required us to reexamine *Olin*, we would ordinarily have convened the en banc court. We have, however, in rare instances, where it has become reasonably clear that a prior precedent of this court was erroneously decided or is no longer good law, achieved the same result more informally by circulating the proposed panel opinion to all the active judges of the court."); *Irons v. Diamond*, 670 F.2d 265, 268 n.11 (D.C. Cir. 1981) ("The foregoing part of the division's decision, because it resolves an apparent conflict between two prior decisions, has been separately considered and approved by the full court, and thus constitutes the law of the circuit."); 7th Cir. R. 40(e) (authorizing procedure akin to that set forth in *Gallagher*, 962 F.2d at 124 n.4, and *Irons*, 670 F.2d at 268 n.11).

8   *See Western Pac. R.R. Corp. v. Western Pac. R.R. Co.*, 345 U.S. 247, 250, 262 (1953); *see also Moody*, 417 U.S. at 625.

9   *Western Pac.*, 345 U.S. at 261 (italics omitted).

10 Fed. R. App. P. 35(c), 40(a)(1).

When is a decision enbancworthy?[11] Some federal statutes provide for automatic en banc appellate review.[12] When en banc review isn't required by statute, Federal Rule of Appellate Procedure 35 provides guidance: "An en banc hearing or rehearing is not favored and ordinarily will not be ordered unless: (1) en banc consideration is necessary to secure or maintain uniformity of the court's decisions; or (2) the proceeding involves a question of exceptional importance."[13] The Supreme Court has cautioned that en banc courts should be "the exception, not the rule. They are convened only when extraordinary circumstances exist that call for authoritative consideration and decision by those charged with the administration and development of the law of the circuit."[14]

The first category in Rule 35—uniformity—is fairly easy to identify. En banc review is necessary to maintain uniformity of a court's decisions when a panel's decision conflicts with past decisions in the circuit.[15] Consideration of a decision en banc may also be appropriate to resolve a conflict with Supreme Court precedent, especially when a later Supreme Court decision has undermined an earlier circuit precedent.[16]

---

11   See *Garner's Dictionary of Legal Usage* 315–16 (3d ed. 2011) (noting the Fifth Circuit origins of the words *enbancworthy* and *enbancworthiness*); *see also Black's Law Dictionary* 643 (Bryan A. Garner ed., 10th ed. 2014).

12   See, e.g., Federal Election Campaign Act of 1971, 52 U.S.C. § 30110.

13   Fed. R. App. P. 35(a).

14   *United States v. American-Foreign S.S.*, 363 U.S. 685, 689 (1960).

15   See, e.g., *United States v. Hardman*, 297 F.3d 1116, 1118 (10th Cir. 2002) (en banc) ("Because of the conflicting panel outcomes [of three separate panels] and the factual and legal similarities among the cases, we simultaneously issued and vacated the panel opinions, and then sua sponte ordered that the cases be reheard en banc.").

16   See, e.g., *Day v. Bond*, 511 F.3d 1030, 1032 (10th Cir. 2007) (order denying petition for panel rehearing and rehearing en banc) ("Plaintiffs' arguments do not justify rehearing because our decision does not conflict with prior decisions of the Supreme Court, the Tenth Circuit, or our sister circuits."); *Miller v. Gammie*, 335 F.3d 889, 892 (9th Cir. 2003) (en banc) ("We took this case en banc to clarify the narrow scope of absolute immunity after Supreme Court decisions have taken an approach that is fundamentally inconsistent with the reasoning of our earlier circuit authority."); *United States v. Hill*, 53 F.3d 1151, 1152 (10th Cir. 1995) (en banc) ("We *sua sponte* ordered *en banc* consideration of this case in order to resolve an apparent conflict between our decision in *Hill* and prior circuit precedent."); *United States v. Nixon*, 827 F.2d 1019, 1023 (5th Cir. 1987)

The second category—exceptional importance—is harder to nail down. Judges have their own ideas. As Judge Douglas Ginsburg and Donald Falk have explained, "'[e]xceptional importance' is in the eye of the beholder."[17]

Eight categories of enbancworthiness

Judges have given as many as eight distinct reasons for viewing an issue as exceptionally important in a given case:[18]

(1) The panel's decision creates new law or addresses a novel legal issue likely to recur.

(2) The panel's decision creates an intercircuit conflict.

(3) The panel's decision is governed by older circuit precedent that merits reconsideration.

(4) The case involves an issue of law that requires clarification.

(5) The panel's decision misapplies Supreme Court precedent.

(6) The case poses a question pertaining to the court's jurisdiction or standards governing justiciability in a particular case.

(7) The case affects the administration of justice within the circuit.

(8) The case addresses a recurring issue that will affect many cases or individuals in the circuit.

Yet courts often give no reason for voting to consider a case en banc, not even in the en banc opinion itself. Often, the clearest explanation for why an en banc petition was granted or denied appears in a judge's separate opinion concurring in or dissenting

---

(per curiam) (denying en banc consideration when panel opinion was "not in direct conflict with any prior Supreme Court or Fifth Circuit precedent").

[17] Douglas H. Ginsburg & Donald Falk, *The Court En Banc: 1981–1990*, 59 Geo. Wash. L. Rev. 1008, 1022 (1991) (shedding helpful light on the meaning of "exceptional importance" in the D.C. Circuit's en banc process); *see* Mayer Brown LLP, *Federal Appellate Practice* § 13.3(b)(3), at 485–86 (Philip Allen Lacovara ed., 2008) (elucidating the exceptional-importance criterion).

[18] *See, e.g., Defenders of Wildlife v. EPA*, 450 F.3d 394, 395 (9th Cir. 2006) (Kozinski J., joined by five other judges, dissenting from denial of rehearing en banc) (arguing that a panel decision not only presents an issue "of considerable importance to the federal government and the states of our circuit" but also "deliberately creates a square inter-circuit conflict with the Fifth and D.C. Circuits, and ignores at least six prior opinions of our own court").

from the denial of the en banc petition.

Let's consider each of the eight rationales.

First, an issue of exceptional importance may be presented when a panel decision creates new law on an issue that will recur often—a landmark or pathbreaking decision of sorts.[19]

Second, a question of exceptional importance may arise if a panel decision creates a conflict with other circuits' precedents.[20]

---

19 See, e.g., *Narragansett Indian Tribe v. Rhode Island*, 449 F.3d 16, 18 (1st Cir. 2006) (en banc) (finding that this case poses "a challenging question of first impression: May officers of the State, acting pursuant to an otherwise valid search warrant, enter upon tribal lands and seize contraband . . . owned by the Tribe and held by it for sale to the general public?"); *Wallace v. City of Chicago*, 440 F.3d 421, 430 (7th Cir. 2006) (Posner J. dissenting from denial of rehearing en banc) ("The panel decision creates an intercircuit conflict on a recurrent issue: when does a claim for damages arising out of a false arrest or other search or seizure forbidden by the Fourth Amendment, or a coerced confession forbidden by the due process clause of the Fifth Amendment, accrue . . . ?"); *Tchoukhrova v. Gonzales*, 430 F.3d 1222, 1223, 1225 (9th Cir. 2005) (Kozinski J., joined by six other judges, dissenting from denial of rehearing en banc) (stating that the panel's decision has "profound implications for our nation's immigration laws" and creates "very new law"); *United States v. Michael*, 645 F.2d 252, 254 (5th Cir. 1981) (en banc) ("[T]he appropriate standard for the warrantless installation of an electronic tracking device" poses a question "of first impression for this circuit" and is of "exceptional importance."); *Narenji v. Civiletti*, 617 F.2d 745, 754 (D.C. Cir. 1979) (joint statement of Wright C.J. and Robinson, Wald, and Mikva JJ. in support of rehearing en banc) (noting that selective enforcement of immigration statute "poses a novel and serious question implicating an equal protection component of Fifth Amendment due process").

20 See, e.g., *United States v. Ressam*, 491 F.3d 997, 1001 (9th Cir. 2007) (O'Scannlain J., joined by five other judges, dissenting from denial of rehearing en banc) ("Because the panel's decision . . . is in square conflict with the reasoning of our sister circuits and with the cautionary pronouncements of the Supreme Court, we should have reheard this case en banc."); *Moran v. Rush Prudential HMO, Inc.*, 230 F.3d 959, 973 (7th Cir. 2000) (Posner J., joined by three judges, dissenting from denial of rehearing en banc) ("This case is well worth the attention of the full court. The panel's decision creates a square conflict with another circuit, is very probably unsound, and will affect an enormous number of cases."); *United States v. Hurtado*, 899 F.2d 371, 375 (5th Cir. 1990) ("In light of the Supreme Court authority noted above and the conflicts among the Circuits in legally similar situations, en banc reconsideration of the government's burden of proof would appear to be warranted."); *Air Line Pilots Ass'n, Int'l v. Eastern Air Lines, Inc.*, 863 F.2d 891, 927 n.2 (D.C. Cir. 1988) (Silberman J. concurring in denial of rehearing en banc) ("[A]n inter-circuit conflict is ordinarily an important factor to consider in determining whether a case is *en banc*-worthy.").

In a 1988 case,[21] Starr J. of the D.C. Circuit gave the following rationale for hesitating to create intercircuit conflict: "The reason is not only one of respect for our judicial colleagues elsewhere; equally fundamental is the Supreme Court's manifest lack of capacity to address all significant conflicts of law within the ever growing circuits."[22] Ultimately in that case, Starr J. concurred in the denial of rehearing en banc, concluding that the panel's decision was "much more likely than not, entirely correct."[23]

Third, a case may present an issue of exceptional importance when it is controlled by older precedent that merits reconsideration. Because one panel cannot overrule or depart from the decision of another panel, the court must hear or rehear the case en banc in order to overrule the governing precedent.[24] The First Circuit did this in a 2005 case,[25] with Selya J. writing for the full court and explaining that members of the panel that initially heard the case "advocated that the en banc court reexamine" an older precedent.[26] A majority of the First Circuit's active judges voted sua sponte to take the case en banc and overruled the earlier decision.[27]

Fourth, a matter of exceptional importance may arise from a need to clarify a confusing point of law within the circuit. A Ninth Circuit en banc decision in 2003 provides a case in point.[28] The court explained that it had taken the case en banc "to clarify the important role that magistrate judges play in conducting plea colloquies" under Federal Rule of Criminal Procedure 11 and "to

---

21 *Air Line Pilots Ass'n, Int'l*, 863 F.2d at 891.
22 *Id.* at 925 (Starr J. concurring in denial of rehearing en banc).
23 *Id.* at 926.
24 But see discussion about Seventh Circuit *supra* pp. 493–94.
25 *United States v. Padilla*, 415 F.3d 211 (1st Cir. 2005) (en banc).
26 *Id.* at 215.
27 *Id.*; *see also, e.g., Cyr v. Reliance Standard Life Ins. Co.*, 642 F.3d 1202, 1203 (9th Cir. 2011) (en banc) ("We agreed to hear this case en banc in order to reconsider our precedent as to which parties may be sued as defendants in actions for benefits."); *United States v. Palmer*, 380 F.3d 395, 396 (8th Cir. 2004) (en banc) ("We vacated our prior panel opinion in this case, . . . and granted rehearing *en banc* to reconsider the interpretation of 18 U.S.C. § 3583 advanced in *United States v. St. John*.").
28 *United States v. Reyna-Tapia*, 328 F.3d 1114 (9th Cir. 2003) (en banc).

clarify the circumstances under which the district court must conduct a de novo review of the magistrate judge's findings and recommendations."[29]

Fifth, courts have considered a panel's perceived misapplication of Supreme Court precedent to be an issue of exceptional importance. Perhaps the panel's decision doesn't squarely conflict with a Supreme Court case but instead misinterprets or misapplies Supreme Court precedent in a specific context. In 2001, the Fifth Circuit took a case en banc for this reason.[30] That case presented the question whether a district court had properly enjoined a Louisiana tort statute that gave patients a right of action against abortion providers.[31] Some providers sued the governor and other state officials in federal court. They won there before a three-judge circuit panel. But the en banc court reversed, holding that the panel had erred "in finding that this case presents an *Ex parte Young* exception to the Eleventh Amendment immunity from suit in federal court."[32]

---

29   *Id.* at 1116, 1121; *see also, e.g., United States v. Phillips*, 731 F.3d 649, 650 (7th Cir. 2013) (en banc) ("The full court granted rehearing en banc to clarify the elements of the crime and their application to charges of mortgage fraud."); *Fisher v. City of San Jose*, 558 F.3d 1069, 1071 (9th Cir. 2009) (en banc) ("We consider whether sufficient evidence supports the jury's verdict. We believe so, and in reaching this conclusion, we take the opportunity to clarify our jurisprudence relating to the Fourth Amendment's application to armed standoffs."); *United States v. Calverley*, 37 F.3d 160, 161 (5th Cir. 1994) (en banc) ("This appeal provides the occasion for our *en banc* court to revisit and clarify the issue of plain error in criminal cases in this circuit.").

30   *Okpalobi v. Foster*, 244 F.3d 405 (5th Cir. 2001) (en banc).

31   *Id.* at 409.

32   *Id.*; *see also id.* at 410 ("[T]he panel opinion erroneously applied established Eleventh Amendment jurisprudence."); *Rattigan v. Holder*, 689 F.3d 764, 773 (D.C. Cir. 2012) (Kavanaugh J. dissenting) (rehearing en banc appropriate if "the majority opinion's conclusion cannot be squared with the Supreme Court's decision in *Department of the Navy v. Egan* [484 U.S. 518 (1988)]"); *United States v. Rodriguez*, 406 F.3d 1261, 1298 (11th Cir. 2005) (Barkett J. dissenting from denial of rehearing en banc) ("I believe that the panel erroneously applies *Jones v. United States*, 527 U.S. 373 (1999), instead of *United States v. Dominguez Benitez*, 542 U.S. 74 (2004)."); *Cardtoons, L.C. v. Major League Baseball Players Ass'n*, 208 F.3d 885, 888 (10th Cir. 2000) (en banc) (granting rehearing en banc to consider whether "panel majority misapplied the *Noerr-Pennington* doctrine").

Sixth, an issue pertaining to the court's jurisdiction or to the standards governing justiciability in a specific case may pose questions of exceptional importance.[33] The issue addressed by the 2001 en banc decision of the Fifth Circuit mentioned in the preceding paragraph concerned the court's "Article III jurisdiction to decide this case."[34] Similarly, in a 2011 case,[35] eight judges of the Ninth Circuit dissented from the denial of rehearing en banc. The case involved a suit against a German corporation for its Argentinian subsidiary's activities in Argentina.[36] Writing for the dissenters, O'Scannlain J. opined that the panel's decision had extended "the reach of general personal jurisdiction far beyond its breaking point."[37]

Seventh, questions about appellate standards of review or other issues of judicial administration within a circuit have been considered issues of exceptional importance.[38] Questions of this nature might involve the standards governing analysis of a specific claim. In 2005, for example, the First Circuit sat en banc to consider whether plain-error review or automatic reversal applies when a district court improperly delegates sentencing authority to

---

[33] *See* Douglas H. Ginsburg & Donald Falk, *The Court En Banc: 1981–1990*, 59 Geo. Wash. L. Rev. 1008, 1028–29 (1991) (explaining that matters "concerning the jurisdiction of the court or the standards for determining the justiciability of a particular case" are often considered enbancworthy because "it is exceptionally important that the court remain within its constitutional competence").

[34] *Okpalobi*, 244 F.3d at 409.

[35] *Bauman v. DaimlerChrysler Corp.*, 676 F.3d 774 (9th Cir. 2011) (O'Scannlain J., joined by seven other judges, dissenting from denial of rehearing en banc).

[36] *Id.* at 775.

[37] *Id.* at 774–75; *see also, e.g., Amnesty Int'l USA v. Clapper*, 667 F.3d 163, 172 (2d Cir. 2011) (Raggi J., joined by four other judges, dissenting from denial of rehearing en banc on question of standing); *El-Shifa Pharm. Indus. Co. v. United States*, 607 F.3d 836, 837–38 (D.C. Cir. 2010) (en banc) (political-question doctrine); *Thomas v. Anchorage Equal Rights Comm'n*, 220 F.3d 1134, 1137 (9th Cir. 2000) (en banc) (justiciability of preenforcement challenge); *In re Hen House Interstate, Inc.*, 177 F.3d 719, 720 (8th Cir. 1999) (en banc) (statutory standing); *Hotel & Rest. Emps. Union, Local 25 v. Smith*, 846 F.2d 1499, 1501 (D.C. Cir. 1988) (en banc) (per curiam) (standing and ripeness).

[38] *See* Sarah J. Berkus, *A Critique and Comparison of En Banc Review in the Tenth and D.C. Circuits and* United States v. Nacchio, 86 Denv. U. L. Rev. 1069, 1086 (2009).

a probation officer.[39] A year later, the Ninth Circuit gave en banc consideration to the standard of review governing ERISA cases in which a conflict of interest exists.[40]

And eighth, a question may be of exceptional importance if its determination will affect many cases or people. The recurring nature of a legal question or the considerable segment of the populace affected by its determination is a common reason for considering an issue enbancworthy.[41]

---

39 *United States v. Padilla*, 415 F.3d 211, 215 (1st Cir. 2005) (en banc).

40 *Abatie v. Alta Health & Life Ins. Co.*, 458 F.3d 955, 959 (9th Cir. 2006) (en banc); see also, e.g., *United States v. Flores-Mejia*, 759 F.3d 253, 254 (3d Cir. 2014) (en banc) (granting en banc petition to "develop a new rule which is applicable in those situations in which a party has an objection based upon a procedural error in sentencing but, after that error has become evident, has not stated that objection on the record"); *Lighting Ballast Control LLC v. Philips Elecs. N. Am. Corp.*, 744 F.3d 1272, 1276 (Fed. Cir. 2014) (en banc) (granting en banc petition to reconsider standard of appellate review of district-court decisions concerning claim construction), *vacated sub nom. Lighting Ballast Control LLC v. Universal Lighting Techs., Inc.*, 135 S.Ct. 1173 (2015); *Grand Isle Shipyard, Inc. v. Seacor Marine, LLC*, 589 F.3d 778, 780 (5th Cir. 2009) (en banc) ("The question presented by this appeal is what law governs the resolution of a contractual dispute" when the act triggering the claim occurred on navigable water on the outer continental shelf but the contract calls for the majority of work to be performed on stationary platforms.); *Cortez v. McCauley*, 478 F.3d 1108, 1112 (10th Cir. 2007) (en banc) (court "granted rehearing en banc primarily to consider under what circumstances, if any, an excessive force claim is subsumed in an unlawful arrest claim"); *Chatman-Bey v. Thornburgh*, 864 F.2d 804, 805 (D.C. Cir. 1988) (en banc) ("We agreed to hear this case *en banc* to consider a recurring issue in the administration of justice in this district, namely whether a federal prisoner, incarcerated outside the jurisdictional limits of the District of Columbia, can properly maintain an action in this district challenging his or her parole eligibility date.").

41 *See, e.g., Wexler v. White's Fine Furniture, Inc.*, 317 F.3d 564, 569 (6th Cir. 2003) (en banc) (granting petition for rehearing en banc "to clarify several important, recurring issues in employment discrimination law"); *United States v. Ruiz*, 257 F.3d 1030, 1032 (9th Cir. 2001) (en banc) ("We granted en banc review and vacated the panel decision to clarify the appropriate standard for this recurring issue in criminal procedure" pertaining to presentence plea withdrawals.); *Chatman-Bey*, 864 F.2d at 805; *Ford v. Strickland*, 696 F.2d 804, 808 (11th Cir. 1983) (en banc) (per curiam) (separate opinion of Roney J.) ("A rehearing *en banc* was granted to examine several important recurring issues in habeas corpus petitions filed by Florida death row inmates."); *Pigrenet v. Boland Marine & Mfg. Co.*, 656 F.2d 1091, 1092 (5th Cir. 1981) (en banc) (per curiam) ("Because [the panel's] holding could be said to apply to the making of credibility choices in a wide range of forums, we took this case en banc.").

An issue that has one or more of the eight features just discussed will be a strong candidate for en banc consideration because of its exceptional importance. But judges have also drawn on other considerations that might not reflect a consensus view. For example, some judges have suggested that cases of particular relevance to the work or litigants of that circuit merit en banc consideration.[42] During his tenure on the D.C. Circuit, Scalia J. cited the court's "leading role in formulating banking law, and administrative law generally," as a ground for en banc consideration of a case that "squarely presents important questions in both areas."[43] In a similar vein, six Ninth Circuit judges dissented from the denial of rehearing en banc in *Defenders of Wildlife v. EPA*, noting (among other reasons) that the question presented was "one of considerable importance to the federal government and the states of our circuit."[44]

Less commonly, an issue has been found to be exceptionally important because it involves matters of public policy affecting the nation at large. This view of exceptional importance is exemplified in Tatel J.'s dissent from the denial of rehearing en banc in a 2005 case[45] in which a three-judge panel of the D.C. Circuit had held that the EPA properly exercised its discretion in declining to regulate greenhouse gases under the Clean Air Act.[46] Tatel J. acknowledged that because the panel didn't address the EPA's authority to regulate greenhouse-gas emissions, its decision had "no precedential effect" on that question.[47] Still, because the case involved "the threat of global warming and its attendant consequences for human health and the environment," Tatel J. considered en banc

---

42 *See* Michael E. Solimine, *Ideology and En Banc Review*, 67 N.C. L. Rev. 29, 58 (1988).

43 *Securities Indus. Ass'n v. Comptroller of Currency*, 765 F.2d 1196, 1198 (D.C. Cir. 1985) (Scalia J. dissenting from denial of rehearing en banc).

44 *Defenders of Wildlife v. EPA*, 450 F.3d 394, 395 (9th Cir. 2006) (Kozinski J. dissenting from denial of rehearing en banc).

45 *Massachusetts v. EPA*, 433 F.3d 66, 67 (D.C. Cir. 2005) (Tatel J., joined by one other judge, dissenting from denial of rehearing en banc).

46 *Massachusetts v. EPA*, 415 F.3d 50, 58 (D.C. Cir. 2005), *rev'd*, 549 U.S. 497 (2007).

47 *Massachusetts v. EPA*, 433 F.3d at 67.

review appropriate: "Indeed, if global warming is not a matter of exceptional importance, then those words have no meaning."[48]

Other factors at play

Beyond the general category of "exceptional importance" set forth in Rule 35, a circuit's local rules may elaborate on the criteria for en banc consideration, even though Rule 47 requires that local rules be consistent with the Federal Rules.[49] The local rules or internal operating procedures of the Fifth, Sixth, and Tenth Circuits, for example, call for "an issue of exceptional *public* importance."[50] The Ninth Circuit rules provide that en banc consideration is appropriate for a panel decision that both "directly conflicts with an existing opinion by another court of appeals" and "substantially affects a rule of national application in which there is an overriding need for national uniformity."[51] When a court decides to consider a case en banc, it is free to limit its consideration in advance to a specific issue.[52]

What if the question is of exceptional importance but the three-judge panel decision is correct? Most judges, it seems, will vote to deny en banc review in those circumstances.[53] Although

---

48 *Id.*

49 Fed. R. App. P. 47(a).

50 5th Cir. I.O.P. (accompanying 5th Cir. R. 35) (emphasis added); 6th Cir. I.O.P. 35(a) (accompanying 6th Cir. R. 35) (emphasis added); 10th Cir. R. 35.1(A) (emphasis added).

51 9th Cir. R. 35-1.

52 *See, e.g., United States v. Padilla*, 415 F.3d 211, 217 (1st Cir. 2005) (en banc) ("The scope of en banc review ordinarily is delimited by the order convening the en banc court."); *Melton v. City of Oklahoma City*, 928 F.2d 920, 932 (10th Cir. 1991) (en banc) (Logan J. dissenting) ("This court granted en banc review limited to four issues.").

53 *See, e.g., United States v. Taylor*, 752 F.3d 254, 255 (2d Cir. 2014) (Pooler J. concurring in denial of rehearing en banc) ("I voted to deny rehearing en banc because I believe that the panel's decision in this case is substantively correct."); *Young v. Conway*, 715 F.3d 79, 79–80 (2d Cir. 2013) (Parker J., joined by one other judge, concurring in denial of rehearing en banc) ("I concur fully in the panel's decision and write separately to emphasize why the panel's decision was correct."); *Planes v. Holder*, 686 F.3d 1033, 1036 (9th Cir. 2012) (Ikuta J., joined by three other judges, concurring in denial of rehearing en banc) ("The panel's approach and conclusion were correct, as was the decision of the court not to rehear the case en banc."); *Biotechnology Indus. Org. v. District of Columbia*, 505 F.3d 1343, 1344 (Fed. Cir. 2007) (per curiam) (Gajarsa J. concurring in

that consideration isn't written into the rule, it's a matter of common sense. The wheels of the courts of appeals would grind to a halt if every exceptionally important three-judge panel decision were reheard en banc even though a majority of judges agreed with the panel decision. There are occasional exceptions to this reality, but only occasional.

Is en banc review limited to federal questions, or is it also appropriate for state-law issues? The courts of appeals have taken different approaches to that question. The Sixth Circuit's internal operating procedures and the Eleventh Circuit's rules provide that an alleged error in the determination of state law is a matter for panel rehearing only.[54] The Fifth Circuit's internal operating procedures, by contrast, permit en banc review of state-law issues.[55] But even if a circuit's rules would permit en banc consideration of a state-law question, that might not be the best use of judicial resources. Sentelle J. of the D.C. Circuit took that position in a 1991 case[56] involving the application of the res ipsa loquitur doctrine, "a matter of District of Columbia law."[57] Despite his view that the panel's decision conflicted with a previous D.C. Circuit

---

denial of rehearing en banc) ("The panel decision reached the correct result on the proper legal basis."); *Hamdi v. Rumsfeld*, 337 F.3d 335, 341 (4th Cir. 2003) (Wilkinson J. concurring in denial of rehearing en banc) ("I concur in the denial of the rehearing en banc. The panel opinion . . . has already properly resolved this case."); *Liberty Mut. Ins. Co. v. Elgin Warehouse & Equip.*, 4 F.3d 567, 573 (8th Cir. 1993) (Hansen J., joined by two other judges, concurring in denial of rehearing en banc) ("Because I agree with the panel's disposition of this case I decline to vote to rehear it en banc."); *Air Line Pilots Ass'n, Int'l v. Eastern Air Lines, Inc.*, 863 F.2d 891, 926 (D.C. Cir. 1988) (Starr J. concurring in denial of rehearing en banc) ("I am firmly persuaded that my colleagues on the panel are, much more likely than not, entirely correct."); Douglas H. Ginsburg & Donald Falk, *The Court En Banc: 1981–1990*, 59 Geo. Wash. L. Rev. 1008, 1032 (1991) ("Even if a panel decision resolves an issue of exceptional importance or creates an apparent inconsistency with the law of this or of another circuit, it may not be an economical use of the court's time to rehear the case if a majority of the judges do not believe that the panel erred.").

54 *See* 6th Cir. I.O.P. 35 (accompanying 6th Cir. R. 35); 11th Cir. R. 35-3.

55 5th Cir. I.O.P. (accompanying 5th Cir. R. 35).

56 *Barwick v. Department of Interior*, No. 89-5478, 1991 WL 65477 (D.C. Cir. 21 Mar. 1991) (Sentelle J., joined by one other judge, concurring in denial of rehearing en banc).

57 *Id.* at *1.

opinion, Sentelle J. concluded that the cost of an en banc review wasn't justified: "Because the answer to this question is a matter of District law, and because the District of Columbia Court of Appeals could, at any time, speak to the exact issue presented here, anything this Court could decide through the *en banc* process could be voided immediately."[58]

When a court decides to rehear a case en banc, it isn't limited to reviewing the three-judge panel's most recent decision. Most courts of appeals have determined that an en banc court may consider issues decided by panels of the court in earlier appeals in the same litigation.[59] In a 1998 case,[60] for example, the First Circuit provided the following rationale: "The authority to overrule the decision of a prior panel in the same case flows logically from the error-correcting function of the full court."[61] When sitting en banc, the court said, concerns about past resolution of issues and the doctrines of law of the case and law of the circuit "must give way to the institutional interest in correcting a precedent-setting error of great public import or a panel opinion that conflicts with Supreme Court precedent."[62]

In sum, en banc review is an important mechanism for reconsidering earlier decisions and examining exceptionally important issues in the federal circuit courts. En banc decisions allow a majority of circuit judges to secure continuity and uniformity of circuit decisions—while still enabling the court to issue most decisions through three-judge panels.[63]

---

58 *Id.*
59 *See, e.g., Cottier v. City of Martin,* 604 F.3d 553, 557 (8th Cir. 2010) (en banc) (collecting cases); *Irving v. United States,* 162 F.3d 154, 161 (1st Cir. 1998) (en banc); *Watkins v. U.S. Army,* 875 F.2d 699, 704 n.8 (9th Cir. 1989) (en banc); *Shimman v. International Union of Operating Eng'rs, Local 18,* 744 F.2d 1226, 1229 n.3 (6th Cir. 1984) (en banc); *Van Gemert v. Boeing Co.,* 590 F.2d 433, 436 n.9 (2d Cir. 1978) (en banc); *In re Central R.R. of N.J.,* 485 F.2d 208, 210–11 (3d Cir. 1973) (en banc).
60 *Irving v. United States,* 162 F.3d 154 (1st Cir. 1998) (en banc).
61 *Id.* at 161.
62 *Id.*
63 *United States v. American-Foreign S.S.,* 363 U.S. 685, 689–90 (1960).

Unsurprisingly, an en banc decision carries great weight within a court that ordinarily sits in panels: it represents not merely the view set forth by a subset of judges who sit on a court, but the most authoritative consideration by the full bench.[64]

---

64 Joshua A. Douglas, *The Procedure of Election Law in Federal Courts*, 2011 Utah L. Rev. 433, 474 ("When a case goes en banc, the lawyers hone their arguments, the judges refocus their energies, and the public is told, 'This is an important one.' En banc cases have greater weight than decisions of a three-judge panel because the decision speaks for the entire court. The nature of en banc review thus signals the importance of the issues to all involved.") (citing for support, *Brown v. First Nat'l Bank in Lenox*, 844 F.2d 580, 582 (8th Cir. 1988) ("[O]ne panel of this Court is not at liberty to overrule an opinion filed by another panel. Only the Court en banc may take such a step.")).

62. Federal Courts of Coordinate Jurisdiction

Although ordinarily a decision of a coordinate court has no stare decisis effect, a federal court will treat a decision of a federal court of equal rank respectfully and may be persuaded by it. A federal court may decide to treat as binding the decisions of its parent court issued before the court's own creation. On appeal from a federal district court, the Federal Circuit will follow the law of the district court's regional circuit on matters outside its specific statutory jurisdiction.

How much, if at all, should a federal court defer to a horizontal precedent established by a court of coordinate jurisdiction—that is, a federal court of equal rank? Story J. took a humble approach. Sitting as a circuit justice in 1844, he adopted the rulings of fellow justices acting in the same capacity, writing:

> As to the points, which had been ruled by my brethren on other circuits, and which I adopted from that just comity, which belongs to their learning and ability, and which has long been adopted as a fit rule to govern me in my circuits, since I know of no higher authority except that of the [S]upreme [C]ourt of the United States, I shall continue to adhere to their doctrine, as I have not the presumption to suppose my own judgment entitled to more weight than theirs.[1]

The appropriateness of such deference to a coordinate authority appears to have been the common understanding in the 19th century. An oft-cited 1885 essay on stare decisis—the winner of a prize from the New York State Bar Association—treated coordinate courts the same as the court of decision for purposes of the doctrine. It stated the doctrine as follows:

> That a deliberate or solemn decision of a court or judge, made after argument on a question of law fairly arising in a case and necessary to its determination, is an authority or binding precedent, *in the same court or in other courts of equal or lower rank*, in subsequent cases where "the very point" is again in controversy; but that the degree of authority belonging to such a precedent depends, of necessity, on its agreement with the spirit of the

---

1 *Washburn v. Gould*, 29 F. Cas. 312, 325 (C.C.D. Mass. 1844) (No. 17,214).

times or the judgment of subsequent tribunals upon its correctness as a statement of the existing or actual law; and that the compulsion or exigency of the doctrine is, in the last analysis, moral and intellectual, rather than arbitrary or inflexible.[2]

The author assumed that there was no need to explain why the doctrine applied to "courts of equal . . . rank." The point is never discussed in the essay.

A Third Circuit decision[3] in 1898 couldn't have been blunter in adopting a decision by the First Circuit. Holding that it lacked jurisdiction to review the trial court's remand of a removed case back to the state court, it followed the earlier decision, writing that contentions about the judgment being unsound are not relevant to the court's "duty to follow that judgment, not for the reasons assigned in its support, which it is not necessary either to adopt or to reject, but because uniformity of decision amongst the several courts of appeals upon such a jurisdictional question seems to us to be of paramount importance."[4] Concerns that such a result would perpetuate error are unfounded, the court said: "It will not result from acceptance of this view of the subject that an error once committed would be indefinitely perpetuated, for the supreme court may at any time settle such questions for all the courts of appeals alike."[5]

This view didn't survive the turn of the 20th century. In the 1900 case of *Mast, Foos & Co. v. Stover Manufacturing Co.*,[6] the Supreme Court considered a petition to review a Seventh Circuit decision rejecting Mast's patent-infringement claim on the ground that the patent was invalid. Mast complained that the Seventh Circuit had refused to follow the Eighth Circuit, which had upheld Mast's infringement claim under the same patent. Before going on to say that the Supreme Court itself would not be influenced by whether the court below had given sufficient weight

---

2 Daniel H. Chamberlain, *The Doctrine of Stare Decisis: Its Reasons and Its Extent* 19 (1885) (emphasis added).
3 *In re Aspinwall's Estate*, 90 F. 675 (3d Cir. 1898).
4 *Id.* at 676.
5 *Id.*
6 177 U.S. 485 (1900).

to the doctrine of comity,[7] it expounded its view of what comity required. The Court noted the virtue of uniformity in decisions but recognized that comity plays a role only when the judge is in doubt: "Comity is not a rule of law, but one of practice, convenience, and expediency. It is something more than mere courtesy, which implies only deference to the opinion of others, since it has a substantial value in securing uniformity of decision, and discouraging repeated litigation of the same question."[8] But it's not obligatory, the Court said. "If it were, the indiscreet action of one court might become a precedent, increasing in weight with each successive adjudication, until the whole country was tied down to an unsound principle."[9] Instead, comity shows "not how a case shall be decided, but how it may with propriety be decided. It recognizes the fact that the primary duty of every court is to dispose of cases according to the law and the facts; in a word, to decide them right."[10] It's the judge's job to decide outcomes, the Court said, "according to his own convictions. . . . It is only in cases where, in his own mind, there may be a doubt as to the soundness of his views that comity comes in play and suggests a uniformity of ruling to avoid confusion, until a higher court has settled the law."[11]

This comity-light approach didn't lead to disparity among the circuits as long as the Supreme Court aggressively reviewed circuit splits. So routine was the Court's practice through the first half of the 20th century of granting certiorari whenever there was a circuit split that in 1953 the *Harvard Law Review* published a comment entitled "Denial of Certiorari Despite a Conflict,"[12] which reported the surprising discovery of several such denials during that term of the Court.

For decades now, the number of circuit splits has been far too great for the Supreme Court to resolve them all, or even a

---

7   *Id.* at 488.
8   *Id.*
9   *Id.*
10 *Id.*
11 *Id.* at 488–89.
12 66 Harv. L. Rev. 465 (1953).

substantial fraction. But comity-light has been embedded in the culture of the circuit courts of appeals. Aside from the few circumstances discussed below in which one federal appellate court will give stare decisis effect to an opinion by another, comity's role is limited. In opinions addressing a matter of first impression in a circuit, the court will ordinarily set forth the relevant law in the other circuits. It may well find the reasoning of other circuits' opinions to be persuasive and follow their lead. It will not, however, adopt a view contrary to its own. It will display its respect simply by discussing other circuits' opinions, distinguishing them or explaining why it isn't persuaded by their reasoning. When a court writes that it is "always chary to create a circuit split, absent a persuasive reason for doing so,"[13] it is implying that it will feel free to create a split if it finds the contrary view persuasive. The Seventh Circuit expressed the general view as follows: "[W]hile we carefully consider the opinions of our sister circuits, we certainly do not defer to them. Our duty is to independently decide our own cases, which sometimes results in disagreements with decisions of the other circuits."[14]

In a 2010 case,[15] the Sixth Circuit expressed somewhat more strongly the desirability of uniformity: "[W]hile we recognize that we are not bound by the law of other Circuits, this court has also routinely looked to the majority position of other Circuits in resolving undecided issues of law."[16] Naturally, "each [federal court] has an obligation to engage independently in reasoned analysis."[17]

The closest that a court will come to true deference occurs when the court is late to address a question that many other circuits have already addressed and resolved in the same way. Rather

---

[13] *United States v. Kebodeaux*, 647 F.3d 137, 141 (5th Cir. 2011) (internal quotation marks and citation omitted).

[14] *Atchison, Topeka & Santa Fe Ry. v. Pena*, 44 F.3d 437, 443 (7th Cir. 1994) (citation omitted).

[15] *Terry v. Tyson Farms, Inc.*, 604 F.3d 272 (6th Cir. 2010).

[16] *Id.* at 278 (quoting *Wong v. PartyGaming Ltd.*, 589 F.3d 821, 827–28 (6th Cir. 2009)).

[17] *Id.* (quoting *In re Korean Air Lines Disaster*, 829 F.2d 1171, 1176 (D.C. Cir. 1987), aff'd sub nom. *Chan v. Korean Air Lines Ltd.*, 490 U.S. 122 (1989)).

than looking for a fight with its sibling circuits, the court may decide to go along without examining the issue too closely. But even then, if a litigant's brief, the court's own research, or the court's independent reasoning suggests a contrary result, the court may well create a circuit split.[18]

Similarly, when the court has already established precedent on a point, it may decide to reconsider the matter through en banc review when the issue arises later and the court discovers that in the interim a number of other circuits have rejected the precedent. For example, in a 2009 case,[19] the Tenth Circuit "granted en banc rehearing to reconsider [its] precedent concerning the scope and application of federally mandated insurance for interstate commercial motor carriers."[20] It noted that its precedent had become the minority view, only one other circuit having followed its lead, thereby "imped[ing] the uniform regulation of interstate trucking."[21] The en banc court decided to adopt the majority view.[22]

Received precedents

Yet there are special circumstances in which a circuit court will treat another circuit's decision as having stare decisis effect. Most notably, a newly created circuit court may decide to treat as binding the precedents of the court or courts that had previously exercised the same jurisdiction. When the Eleventh Circuit was carved from the Fifth Circuit, it chose to treat as binding horizontal precedent all Fifth Circuit decisions antedating the split (1 October 1981).[23] (See § 50.) The Federal Circuit adopted the same approach when it assumed the jurisdiction of the Court

---

18 *See, e.g., DeBoer v. Snyder*, 772 F.3d 388, 402 (6th Cir. 2014) (rejecting views of four other circuits on same-sex marriage), *rev'd sub nom. Obergefell v. Hodges*, 135 S.Ct. 2584 (2015).
19 *Carolina Cas. Ins. Co. v. Yeates*, 584 F.3d 868 (10th Cir. 2009).
20 *Id.* at 870.
21 *Id.* at 871.
22 *Id.*; *see also United States v. Reyes-Hernandez*, 624 F.3d 405, 414, 419 n.1 (7th Cir. 2010) (considering "ongoing debate and current circuit split [] compelling reasons to revisit our precedent," and letting off-panel judges give court panel permission to overturn precedent without an en banc hearing).
23 *Bonner v. City of Prichard*, 661 F.2d 1206, 1209 (11th Cir. 1981) (en banc).

of Claims and the Court of Customs and Patent Appeals.[24] The Tenth Circuit, on the other hand, has never held that the decisions of its mother circuit, the Eighth, are controlling.[25]

The Federal Circuit defers also to the regional circuits on certain issues for reasons unique to that circuit. Appeals to the Federal Circuit are often from a district court that is otherwise bound to follow the law of its regional circuit. On appeal from a district court, the Federal Circuit will follow the law of the regional circuit on issues "not specific to [its] statutory jurisdiction,"[26] such as evidentiary rulings and the standard of review for denial of a motion for new trial.[27]

On the assumption that a regional circuit court has a special understanding of state law within its circuit, a circuit court that must determine the law of a state may give extra weight to an interpretation by the state's "home" circuit.[28] The court may even feel bound unless a home-circuit decision "has disregarded clear signals emanating from the state's highest court pointing toward a different rule."[29]

A Seventh Circuit opinion once suggested that special deference to another circuit's decision is appropriate "[w]here different outcomes would place the defendant under inconsistent legal duties."[30] But in our federal system, where state law often reigns, legal duties often depend on one's location, so this suggestion hasn't gained support.[31]

---

24 *South Corp. v. United States*, 690 F.2d 1368, 1370–71 (Fed. Cir. 1982) (en banc).
25 *Estate of McMorris v. Commissioner*, 243 F.3d 1254, 1258 (10th Cir. 2001).
26 *Registration Control Sys., Inc. v. Compusystems, Inc.*, 922 F.2d 805, 807 (Fed. Cir. 1990).
27 *Sulzer Textil A.G. v. Picanol N.V.*, 358 F.3d 1356, 1363 (Fed. Cir. 2004).
28 *Independent Petrochemical Corp. v. Aetna Cas. & Sur. Co.*, 944 F.2d 940, 944 (D.C. Cir. 1991).
29 *Factors Etc., Inc. v. Pro Arts, Inc.*, 652 F.2d 278, 283 (2d Cir. 1981).
30 *Colby v. J.C. Penney Co.*, 811 F.2d 1119, 1124 (7th Cir. 1987).
31 See *United States v. Cinemark USA, Inc.*, 348 F.3d 569, 579 n.7 (6th Cir. 2003).

Although district courts are bound to follow only vertical precedents,[32] they often—on a question of first impression within the circuit—defer to outside circuit courts in order to maintain "a reasonable uniformity of federal law."[33]

The stare decisis effect of federal district-court decisions on other trial courts is nil. True, it hasn't been uncommon for district courts to say that they will follow an earlier ruling by a court within the same district[34] or will follow district precedent "absent unusual or exceptional circumstances."[35] But the U.S. Supreme Court made it clear in 2011 that on the federal level, a district judge's decision isn't binding on any other judge—including (in a different case) the very judge who made the decision.[36] This proposition also holds even when the district court sits as a three-judge court.[37] But in those rare instances when the judges of a federal district court sit en banc, the resulting opinion presumably does bind those judges, even dissenters.[38]

Do federal district-court decisions have stare decisis effect on bankruptcy courts within the same district? The courts are divided on this point. Some say yes,[39] others no.[40] But note that the district-court opinions on this point have no precedential

---

32 *In re Korean Air Lines Disaster*, 829 F.2d 1171, 1176 (D.C. Cir. 1987) (explaining that district courts within a circuit are bound only by decisions of Court of Appeals for that circuit), *aff'd sub nom. Chan v. Korean Air Lines, Ltd.*, 490 U.S. 122 (1989).

33 *Colby*, 811 F.2d at 1123.

34 *E.g., Peterson v. BASF Corp.*, 12 F. Supp. 2d 964, 970 (D. Minn. 1998).

35 *Kelly v. Wehrum*, 956 F. Supp. 1369, 1372–73 (S.D. Ohio 1997) (citing *Fricker v. Town of Foster*, 596 F. Supp. 1353, 1356 (D.R.I. 1984)).

36 *Camreta v. Greene*, 563 U.S. 692, 709 n.7 (2011).

37 *San Diego Unified Port Dist. v. Gianturco*, 651 F.2d 1306, 1315 n.24 (9th Cir. 1981) (per curiam) (noting that the decision of a three-judge district court has same precedential weight as any other district-court decision); *Farley v. Farley*, 481 F.2d 1009, 1012 (3d Cir. 1973).

38 *See United States v. Anaya*, 509 F. Supp. 289 (S.D. Fla. 1980).

39 *Bryant v. Smith*, 165 B.R. 176, 180–81 (W.D. Va. 1994) (holding that bankruptcy courts are bound by district-court precedent from within the district).

40 *In re KAR Dev. Assocs., L.P.*, 180 B.R. 629, 640 (D. Kan. 1995) (holding that bankruptcy courts aren't bound by district-court precedent within the district).

effect themselves. Indeed, the one circuit court to have raised the question abstained from answering it.[41]

---

41 *In re Hillsborough Holdings Corp.*, 127 F.3d 1398, 1402 n.3 (11th Cir. 1997) (raising but not deciding the issue: "We have been presented with no Supreme Court or court of appeals precedent on whether decisions by a district court will constitute binding precedent for the bankruptcy courts in the same district, and the few district courts to consider the issue are split.").

63. Certworthiness

A federal circuit-court or state high-court decision is considered certworthy—that is, a serious candidate for U.S. Supreme Court review—if it (1) involves a federal question that has split the federal circuits or state high courts, or (2) has great practical significance or importance to federal jurisprudence.

Each year, the federal circuit courts decide some 50,000 appeals.[1] State high courts also decide legions of cases involving federal questions. For most litigants, the road ends in those courts. Although "I'll take this all the way to the Supreme Court!" may be a trusted Hollywood cliché, in the real world—and by federal statute—disappointed litigants ordinarily have no automatic right to further review by the U.S. Supreme Court. Instead, the Supreme Court has nearly complete discretion to choose which cases it will hear.[2]

Although the writ of certiorari is the primary mechanism for Supreme Court review today, that wasn't always the case. For its first 135 years, the Supreme Court had little discretion over its caseload.[3] In fact, from 1789 to 1891, the Supreme Court had *no* discretion to decline to review cases appealed to it under statute; it heard appeals as a matter of the appellant's right. In 1891, Congress first instituted the writ of certiorari—which gave the Court discretion to deny review of certain cases—because the Court's caseload had

---

[1] *See* Admin. Off. of the U.S. Cts., *U.S. Courts of Appeals—Judicial Business 2014*, U.S. Cts. (2014), http://www.uscourts.gov/statistics-reports/us-courts-appeals-judicial-business-2014 (noting that 55,216 appeals were decided by federal circuit courts in 2014—a 20% reduction since 2005).

[2] *See* 28 U.S.C. §§ 1254–1260 (providing for review by writ of certiorari).

[3] *See* Margaret Meriwether Cordray & Richard Cordray, *The Philosophy of Certiorari: Jurisprudential Considerations in Supreme Court Case Selection*, 82 Wash. U. L.Q. 389, 389 (2004) (quoting Marshall C.J. as declaring that "the Court has 'no more right to decline the exercise of jurisdiction which is given than to usurp that which is not given'" and that "the Court 'must take jurisdiction if it should'").

grown "beyond its capacity."[4] In 1925, Congress made more cases subject to discretionary review rather than appeal as of right. At that point, certiorari became the dominant course by which cases reach the Supreme Court.[5] In 1988, Congress further tightened the categories of cases that receive appeal as of right[6] (surviving examples including certain voting-rights and campaign-finance cases[7]). In very rare circumstances, the courts of appeals may also certify questions to the Supreme Court.[8]

The size of the Supreme Court's docket has diminished over time. In the early 1980s, the Supreme Court regularly decided more than 150 cases a year.[9] Now, each October term, the Court winnows its pool of some 9,000 petitions for a writ of certiorari to what in recent years has been fewer than 100 cases.[10]

By custom, to grant certiorari, four Justices must vote to grant review. How does the Supreme Court separate the wheat from the

---

[4] William Howard Taft, *The Jurisdiction of the Supreme Court Under the Act of February 13, 1925*, 35 Yale L.J. 1, 1–2 (1925) (noting that by the time Congress instituted the writ of certiorari, the Court had fallen three years behind on its docket); *see* Stephen M. Shapiro et al., *Supreme Court Practice* 235 n.2 (10th ed. 2013); *Dick v. New York Life Ins. Co.*, 359 U.S. 437, 448–55 (1959) (Frankfurter J. dissenting).

[5] Shapiro et al., *Supreme Court Practice* at 235 n.2.

[6] *See* Supreme Court Case Selections Act of 1988, Pub. L. No. 100-352, 102 Stat. 662 (codified as amended in 28 U.S.C. §§ 1257, 1258); Cordray & Cordray, *The Philosophy of Certiorari*, 82 Wash. U. L.Q. at 394.

[7] *See, e.g.*, 26 U.S.C. § 9010(c) ("any appeal" from a three-judge district-court decision concerning the Presidential Election Campaign Fund Act of 1971 "shall lie to the Supreme Court"); 52 U.S.C. § 10306(c) ("any appeal" from a three-judge district-court decision granting or denying declaratory or injunctive relief against enforcement of a poll tax as a precondition to voting "shall lie to the Supreme Court"); 52 U.S.C. § 30110 note ("A final decision" in certain constitutional challenges to a provision of the Bipartisan Campaign Reform Act "shall be reviewable only by appeal directly to the Supreme Court of the United States."). *See generally* Sup. Ct. R. 18 (establishing procedures for direct appeals); Shapiro et al., *Supreme Court Practice* at 92–119, 526–29.

[8] 28 U.S.C. § 1254(2); *see United States v. Seale*, 558 U.S. 985, 986 (2009) (statement of Stevens J.) ("The certification process has all but disappeared in recent decades. The Court has accepted only a handful of certified cases since the 1940s and none since 1981."); *Iran Nat'l Airlines Corp. v. Marschalk Co.*, 453 U.S. 919 (1981) (deciding certified questions from the Second Circuit).

[9] *See* Adam Liptak, *The Case of the Plummeting Supreme Court Docket*, New York Times, 28 Sept. 2009, http://www.nytimes.com/2009/09/29/us/29bar.html.

[10] *Frequently Asked Questions (FAQ)*, Supreme Court of the United States (18 July 2015), http://www.supremecourt.gov/faq.aspx.

chaff? The answer lies in the concept of certworthiness, a term of art that has come to describe the standard for when a case is at least a serious candidate for Supreme Court review.[11]

What makes a case certworthy? There is no hard-and-fast answer. As one Justice described the certiorari process, "It is really hard to know what makes up this broth of the cert. process. Some cases are ones you can just smell as grants."[12] As another Justice stated, "frequently the question whether a case is 'certworthy' is more a matter of 'feel' than of precisely ascertainable rules."[13]

The natural starting point for an investigation of certworthiness is the Supreme Court's own statement on the subject: Supreme Court of the United States Rule 10. It provides:

> Review on a writ of certiorari is not a matter of right, but of judicial discretion. A petition for a writ of certiorari will be granted only for compelling reasons. The following, although neither controlling nor fully measuring the Court's discretion, indicate the character of the reasons the Court considers:
> (a) a United States court of appeals has entered a decision in conflict with the decision of another United States court of appeals on the same important matter; has decided an important federal question in a way that conflicts with a decision by a state court of last resort; or has so far departed from the accepted and usual course of judicial proceedings, or sanctioned such a departure by a lower court, as to call for an exercise of this Court's supervisory power;
> (b) a state court of last resort has decided an important federal question in a way that conflicts with the decision of another state court of last resort or of a United States court of appeals;

---

11 See *Garner's Dictionary of Legal Usage* 145 (3d ed. 2011) ("*Certworthy* = (of a case) meriting Supreme Court review by grant of a writ of certiorari."); *see also* David J. Sharpe, *The Maritime Origin of the Word "Certworthiness,"* 24 J. Mar. L. & Com. 667 (1993) (offering etymological account of *certworthiness*).

12 H.W. Perry Jr., *Deciding to Decide: Agenda Setting in the United States Supreme Court* 216 (paperback ed. 1994) (alteration omitted) (quoting personal interview with unnamed Supreme Court Justice).

13 Margaret Meriwether Cordray & Richard Cordray, *Strategy in Supreme Court Case Selection: The Relationship Between Certiorari and the Merits*, 69 Ohio St. L.J. 1, 7 (2008) (quoting John M. Harlan, *Manning the Dikes*, 13 Rec. Ass'n of the Bar of City of N.Y. 541, 549 (1958)) (alterations omitted).

(c) a state court or a United States court of appeals has decided an important question of federal law that has not been, but should be, settled by this Court, or has decided an important federal question in a way that conflicts with relevant decisions of this Court.

A petition for a writ of certiorari is rarely granted when the asserted error consists of erroneous factual findings or the misapplication of a properly stated rule of law.[14]

An additional requirement applies when a litigant petitions for review by the Supreme Court before the circuit court has entered judgment. The Court will grant the petition "only upon a showing that the case is of such imperative public importance as to justify deviation from normal appellate practice and to require immediate determination in this Court."[15]

Certain principles about certworthiness can be distilled from Rule 10, from the Supreme Court's cases discussing the certiorari process, and from public comments made by the Justices. Two broad categories emerge. First, a case is certworthy if it involves a conflict among the federal circuit courts or state high courts on a federal question. Second, a case is certworthy even without such a conflict if it presents a particularly important question of federal law or has great practical significance.

The existence of conflict among the federal circuit courts or the state high courts ordinarily makes a case certworthy.[16] Although conflicts carry "less than decisive weight," they still weigh heavily in favor of granting certiorari.[17] Indeed, most cases in which certiorari is granted do involve such conflicts.[18] To be

---

14 Sup. Ct. R. 10.

15 Sup. Ct. R. 11.

16 *E.g.*, *United States v. Woods*, 134 S.Ct. 557, 562 (2013) (granting certiorari to resolve "[c]ircuit split over whether the valuation-misstatement penalty is applicable in these circumstances"); *United States v. Hughes Props., Inc.*, 476 U.S. 593, 599 (1986) (granting certiorari because "of the clear conflict between the two Circuits"). *See generally* Shapiro et al., *Supreme Court Practice* at 241–63.

17 Shapiro et al., *Supreme Court Practice* at 245.

18 *See id.* at 241.

sure, not every conflict is certworthy: a conflict on a trivial or relatively unimportant question rarely makes a case certworthy.[19]

Grant of certiorari for importance of the issue

Even without a circuit split, a case may be certworthy if it raises a sufficiently important question. As a leading treatise on Supreme Court practice states, importance depends on "the type of issue involved, the way in which it was decided below, the status of the law on the matter, the correctness of the decision below, and the nature and number of persons who may be affected by the case."[20] The so-called important cases fall into seven discernible categories.

First, decisions holding federal or state laws or practices invalid under the federal Constitution are certworthy[21]—as are cases holding state laws to be preempted by federal statutes.[22] Examples abound. In *Gonzales v. Raich*,[23] the Ninth Circuit concluded that the federal Controlled Substances Act was likely an unconstitutional exercise of Congress's Commerce Clause authority.[24] The Supreme Court granted certiorari based on the "obvious importance of the case."[25] In *United States v. Windsor*,[26] the lower court had held unconstitutional a provision of an important federal statute, the Defense of Marriage Act.[27] And in *Oneok, Inc. v. Learjet, Inc.*,[28] the Court granted certiorari to resolve whether the federal Natural Gas Act preempts certain state antitrust-law challenges.[29]

---

19 See id. at 246–47.
20 Id. at 263.
21 See, e.g., *Hollingsworth v. Perry*, 133 S.Ct. 2652, 2661 (2013) (granting certiorari to review determination that state ban on same-sex marriage violated federal Constitution). See generally Shapiro et al., *Supreme Court Practice* at 264–65.
22 See Shapiro et al., *Supreme Court Practice* at 271–72.
23 545 U.S. 1 (2005).
24 Id. at 8.
25 Id. at 9.
26 133 S.Ct. 2675 (2013).
27 Id. at 2682.
28 135 S.Ct. 1591 (2015).
29 Id. at 1599.

Second, cases that substantially affect American foreign policy or national security often qualify as certworthy.[30] In *Christopher v. Harbury*,[31] for instance, the Court addressed a *Bivens* claim against State Department and National Security Council officials who had allegedly prevented the plaintiff from accessing the courts.[32] The Supreme Court granted certiorari "because of the importance of this issue to the Government in its conduct of the Nation's foreign affairs."[33] Another recent example is *Boumediene v. Bush*,[34] in which the Court granted certiorari to determine whether aliens designated as enemy combatants and detained at Guantanamo Bay had the constitutional privilege of habeas corpus.[35] And in *Zivotofsky v. Clinton*,[36] the Court granted certiorari to resolve whether the courts had authority to decide whether Congress, over the President's objection, could require the State Department to issue passports that listed "Jerusalem, Israel" as the birthplace of those born in Jerusalem.[37]

Third, cases of substantial importance to the operations of the federal government or the states are certworthy. In a particularly dramatic example, the Supreme Court granted certiorari in *United States v. Nixon*[38] even before the D.C. Circuit had rendered judgment.[39] The case concerned a subpoena duces tecum issued to President Richard Nixon for tapes of his Oval Office

---

30 *See, e.g., Christopher v. Harbury*, 536 U.S. 403, 412 (2002); *Bank Markazi v. Peterson*, 136 S.Ct. 1310, 1317 (2016); *Forsyth v. City of Hammond*, 166 U.S. 506, 514 (1897) (considering a question "affecting the relations of this country to foreign nations"); *see also* Shapiro et al., *Supreme Court Practice* at 266.

31 536 U.S. 403 (2002).

32 *Id.* at 412.

33 *Id.*

34 553 U.S. 723 (2008).

35 *Id.* at 732; *see also Youngstown Sheet & Tube Co. v. Sawyer*, 343 U.S. 579, 582–84 (1952) (granting certiorari to consider whether President had authority to seize steel mills necessary to national defense because Court deemed "it best that the issues raised be promptly decided by this Court").

36 *Zivotofsky ex rel. Zivotofsky v. Clinton*, 132 S.Ct. 1421 (2012).

37 *Id.* at 1424.

38 *United States v. Nixon*, 418 U.S. 683 (1974).

39 *Id.* at 686–87.

conversations that he claimed were privileged.[40] The Court took that unusual step "because of the public importance of the issues presented and the need for their prompt resolution."[41] And in *Bush v. Gore*,[42] the Court granted certiorari to resolve disputes concerning Florida's vote-counting processes in the 2000 presidential election.

Fourth, cases that have significant impact on a large number of people are also often certworthy, particularly if a delay in review would cause extraordinary hardship or make it difficult to undo the effects of the current law.[43] *King v. Burwell*[44] is one such example. There, the Court resolved a critical question of statutory interpretation involving the Affordable Care Act. The case involved one of the "Act's key reforms," which affected "the price of health insurance for millions of people."[45]

The obvious corollary to this principle is that a case is unlikely to be important enough (and thus unlikely to be certworthy) if its outcome matters only to the affected parties. Instead of "seeking only to resolve a dispute between two parties, the Supreme Court is primarily interested in deciding questions of law."[46] The Court therefore rarely grants certiorari in cases that serve only to remedy "a particular litigant's wrong."[47]

---

40 *Id.* at 686.

41 *Id.* at 687.

42 531 U.S. 98 (2000) (per curiam).

43 *See, e.g., Barber v. Thomas*, 560 U.S. 474, 480 (2010) ("Because the . . . administration of good time credits affects the interests of a large number of federal prisoners, we granted the consolidated petition for certiorari.").

44 135 S.Ct. 2480 (2015).

45 *Id.* at 2489.

46 Stephen Breyer, *Reflections on the Role of Appellate Courts: A View from the Supreme Court*, 8 J. App. Prac. & Process 91, 93 (2006).

47 William Howard Taft, *The Jurisdiction of the Supreme Court Under the Act of February 13, 1925*, 35 Yale L.J. 1, 2 (1925); *see Tolan v. Cotton*, 134 S.Ct. 1861, 1869 (2014) (per curiam) (Alito J. concurring in the judgment) (asserting that the question whether evidence sufficed to support summary judgment was "important for the parties" but nevertheless "utterly routine" and therefore not certworthy); *Butz v. Glover Livestock Comm'n Co.*, 411 U.S. 182, 189 (1973) (Stewart J. dissenting) ("The only remarkable thing about this case is its presence in this Court. For the case involves no more than the application of well-settled principles to a familiar situation, and has little significance except for

Fifth, decisions that involve especially large sums of money may be certworthy.[48] The size of the "potential liability" faced by a petitioner "is a strong factor in deciding whether to grant certiorari."[49] In *United States v. Mitchell*,[50] for example, the federal government faced damages of up to $100 million.[51] The Court granted certiorari "[b]ecause the decision of the Court of Claims raises issues of substantial importance concerning the liability of the United States."[52] Similarly, in *Exxon Shipping Co. v. Baker*,[53] the Court granted certiorari to review a $2.5 billion punitive-damages award,[54] acting in part to determine "whether the punitive damages ... were excessive as a matter of maritime common law."[55]

Sixth, the Supreme Court occasionally grants certiorari in cases—particularly death-penalty cases—that could result in great injustice if the lower-court decision were left undisturbed.[56] In *Montana v. Kennedy*,[57] the petitioner—the foreign-born son of a native-born American citizen—claimed American citizenship but faced deportation as an alien.[58] The Court granted certiorari "in view of the apparent harshness of the result entailed" by the lower court's denial of relief.[59] And in *Herrera v. Collins*,[60] the Court

---

the respondent. Why certiorari was granted is a mystery to me."); *Rice v. Sioux City Mem'l Park Cemetery*, 349 U.S. 70, 74 (1955) (maintaining that the Supreme Court does not "sit for the benefit of the particular litigants").

48   *See, e.g., Pennzoil Co. v. Texaco, Inc.*, 481 U.S. 1 (1987) ($11 billion state-court judgment). *See generally* Shapiro et al., *Supreme Court Practice* at 269–70.

49   *Fidelity Fed. Bank & Trust v. Kehoe*, 547 U.S. 1051, 1051 (2006) (Scalia J. concurring in denial of certiorari).

50   463 U.S. 206 (1983).

51   *Id.* at 211 n.7.

52   *Id.* at 211.

53   554 U.S. 471 (2008).

54   *Id.* at 481.

55   *Id.*

56   *See, e.g., Glossip v. Gross*, 135 S.Ct. 2726 (2015) (upholding method of execution).

57   366 U.S. 308 (1961).

58   *Id.* at 309.

59   *Id.*

60   506 U.S. 390 (1993).

granted certiorari after the Fifth Circuit held that a death-row habeas petitioner's claim of actual innocence wasn't cognizable.[61]

Seventh, a case may be certworthy for reasons based on policy, new developments, or egregious legal error, as discussed below.

Grant of certiorari over legal error or bad policy

The Court doesn't ordinarily grant review simply because of perceived error in the lower court. It isn't "primarily concerned with the correction of errors in lower court decisions."[62] In the words of Rehnquist C.J., it "would be a useless duplication of [lower-court] functions if the Supreme Court of the United States were to serve simply as an even higher court for the correction of errors in cases involving no generally important principle of law."[63] In practice, that means that when the law governing a particular area is already well established, the Court seldom takes cases merely because the lower courts erred in applying that law. Remember Rule 10: a "petition for a writ of certiorari is rarely granted when the asserted error consists of . . . the misapplication of a properly stated rule of law."[64] Many questions presented in petitions for a writ of certiorari "have undoubtedly been decided wrongly."[65] But the Supreme Court nevertheless usually declines to review those cases.[66]

The Supreme Court sometimes considers it appropriate to grant certiorari to consider whether to overrule its own precedent. In *Kimble v. Marvel Entertainment*, for example, recent developments in the field of economics indicated that an earlier case may

---

61 *Id.* at 397–98.
62 Shapiro et al., *Supreme Court Practice* at 236 (quoting Vinson C.J.); *see City & Cnty. of San Francisco v. Sheehan*, 135 S.Ct. 1765, 1780 (2015) (Scalia J. concurring in part and dissenting in part) ("[W]e are not, and for well over a century have not been, a court of error correction."); Breyer, *Reflections on the Role of Appellate Courts*, 8 J. App. Prac. & Process at 92 ("Rather than correcting errors, then, the Supreme Court is charged with providing a uniform rule of federal law in areas that require one.").
63 William H. Rehnquist, *The Supreme Court* 269 (1987).
64 Sup. Ct. R. 10.
65 *Sheehan*, 135 S.Ct. at 1780 (Scalia J. concurring in part and dissenting in part).
66 *See id.*

have been incorrectly decided.[67] The Court therefore granted certiorari "to decide whether, as some courts and commentators have suggested," the Court should overrule that case.[68]

Still, cases in which the Court believes the lower court erred egregiously may be certworthy. The Court sometimes appears to grant certiorari in such cases in order to prevent a grossly wrong legal interpretation from taking root, or in order to "enforce the Court's supremacy over recalcitrant lower courts."[69] Hence Rule 10 provides that the Court will grant certiorari when a lower court "has so far departed from the accepted and usual course of judicial proceedings . . . as to call for an exercise of this Court's supervisory power" or "has decided an important federal question in a way that conflicts with relevant decisions of this Court."[70]

For example, several times the Supreme Court has corrected lower courts "when they wrongly subject [police] officers to liability" in violation of the Court's qualified-immunity precedent.[71] In the space of four years, the Court has issued a remarkable ten decisions reversing federal circuit courts in such cases, often on purely error-correcting grounds.[72] The Court has exercised similarly

---

67 *Kimble v. Marvel Entm't, LLC*, 135 S.Ct. 2401, 2412 (2015).

68 *Id.* at 2406; *see also Lawrence v. Texas*, 539 U.S. 558, 564 (2003) (granting certiorari in part to determine whether *Bowers v. Hardwick*, 478 U.S. 186 (1986), "should be overruled").

69 William Baude, *Foreword: The Supreme Court's Shadow Docket*, 9 N.Y.U. J.L. & Liberty 1, 2 (2015) (discussing the Supreme Court's use of summary reversals to ensure that lower courts follow Supreme Court precedent, among other things).

70 Sup. Ct. R. 10; *see, e.g., Elmbrook Sch. Dist. v. Doe 3*, 134 S.Ct. 2283, 2283–84 (2014) (Scalia J. dissenting from denial of certiorari) (encouraging Court to "grant certiorari, vacate the judgment, and remand for reconsideration" because court of appeals issued a decision that was "fundamentally inconsistent" with Supreme Court precedent).

71 *Sheehan*, 135 S.Ct. at 1774 n.3.

72 *See Taylor v. Barkes*, 135 S.Ct. 2042 (2015) (per curiam) (summary reversal); *Sheehan*, 135 S.Ct. 1765; *Carroll v. Carman*, 135 S.Ct. 348 (2014) (per curiam) (summary reversal); *Plumhoff v. Rickard*, 134 S.Ct. 2012 (2014); *Wood v. Moss*, 134 S.Ct. 2056 (2014); *Stanton v. Sims*, 134 S.Ct. 3 (2013) (per curiam) (summary reversal); *Reichle v. Howards*, 132 S.Ct. 2088 (2012); *Ryburn v. Huff*, 132 S.Ct. 987 (2012) (per curiam) (summary reversal); *Messerschmidt v. Millender*, 132 S.Ct. 1235 (2012); *Ashcroft v. al-Kidd*, 563 U.S. 731 (2011).

close review of lower courts' misapplication of the habeas corpus statute.[73]

The Court appears particularly likely to grant certiorari to correct lower-court error if a recalcitrant court has repeatedly ignored precedent.[74] In *Cavazos v. Smith*,[75] the Court granted certiorari after the Ninth Circuit erred for the third time in the same case.[76] "The decision below cannot be allowed to stand," the Court said,[77] adding that each time it had vacated and remanded the case, "the panel persisted in its course, reinstating its judgment without seriously confronting the significance of the cases called to its attention. Its refusal to do so necessitates this Court's action today."[78]

Further, a case is also certworthy—though only in a limited sense—if the lower-court decision at issue conflicts with a later-decided Supreme Court decision or another intervening development. In those cases, the Court often employs a practice known as *GVR*, in which the Court simultaneously *grants* certiorari, *vacates* the decision below, and *remands* the case without issuing an opinion on the merits.[79] A case is a suitable candidate for a GVR order when "intervening developments, or recent developments that... the court below did not fully consider, reveal a reasonable probability that the decision below rests upon a premise that the lower court would reject if given the opportunity for further consideration, and where it appears that such a redetermination may

---

73 See, e.g., *Glebe v. Frost*, 135 S.Ct. 429 (2014) (per curiam) (summary reversal).

74 See Shapiro et al., *Supreme Court Practice* at 281–82 (noting that in recent years the Supreme Court has paid particularly close attention to the Ninth Circuit and Federal Circuit); Mark Walsh, *A Sixth Sense: 6th Circuit Has Surpassed 9th as the Most Reversed Appeals Court*, ABA Journal (1 Dec. 2012), http://www.abajournal.com/magazine/article/a_sixth_sense_6th_circuit_has_surpassed_the_9th_as_the_most_reversed_appeal/ (indicating that the Court has reversed the Sixth Circuit a disproportionate number of times).

75 132 S.Ct. 2 (2011) (per curiam).

76 *Id.* at 8.

77 *Id.* (citations omitted).

78 *Id.* (citations omitted).

79 See generally *Lawrence ex rel. Lawrence v. Chater*, 516 U.S. 163 (1996) (per curiam) (explaining at length the purposes animating GVR orders and guidelines for determining whether GVR order is appropriate).

determine the ultimate outcome of the litigation."[80] The equities of the case must also favor remand.[81]

After the Supreme Court issued its decision in *Burwell v. Hobby Lobby*,[82] the Court issued a GVR order in a case that touched on similar issues[83] but that had been decided before *Hobby Lobby*.[84] In the GVR order, the Court granted the petition for a writ of certiorari, vacated the judgment, and remanded the case to the United States Court of Appeals for the Seventh Circuit "for further consideration in light of [*Hobby Lobby*]."[85]

As the above descriptions suggest, several kinds of cases are rarely certworthy. For instance, unless other weighty factors counsel in favor of review, the Court doesn't usually grant certiorari in cases turning on factual disputes.[86] When the Court grants certiorari and later discovers that a case primarily presents a question of fact, the Court may dismiss that case as improvidently granted.[87]

Moreover, cases that can be expected to have little lasting legal significance are rarely certworthy. In *Rice v. Sioux City Memorial Park Cemetery*,[88] for example, the Court learned—after

---

80   *Id.* at 167.
81   *Id.* at 167–68.
82   *Burwell v. Hobby Lobby Stores, Inc.*, 134 S.Ct. 2751 (2014).
83   *University of Notre Dame v. Burwell*, 135 S.Ct. 1528 (2015) (mem.).
84   *University of Notre Dame v. Sebelius*, 743 F.3d 547 (7th Cir. 2014) (decided 21 Feb. 2014, months before the Supreme Court issued its decision in *Hobby Lobby* on 30 June 2014).
85   *University of Notre Dame v. Burwell*, 135 S.Ct. at 1528.
86   *See, e.g., Sheehan*, 135 S.Ct. at 1779 (Scalia J. concurring in part and dissenting in part) (noting that there is normally "little chance" that Court will take case presenting "fact-bound" question); *United States v. Johnston*, 268 U.S. 220, 227 (1925) ("We do not grant a certiorari to review evidence and discuss specific facts."). *See generally* Shapiro et al., *Supreme Court Practice* at 272–75.
87   *See, e.g., NLRB v. Hendricks Cnty. Rural Elec. Membership Corp.*, 454 U.S. 170, 176 n.8 (1981) (dismissing cross-petition as improvidently granted because cross-petition presented "primarily . . . a question of fact, which does not merit Court review"); *Rudolph v. United States*, 370 U.S. 269, 270 (1962) (per curiam) (dismissing as improvidently granted case turning entirely on factual determination); *see also Sheehan*, 135 S.Ct. at 1779–80 (Scalia J. concurring in part and dissenting in part) (advocating dismissal of case as improvidently granted because question presented was fact-bound).
88   349 U.S. 70 (1955).

granting certiorari and conducting oral argument—that a state law made it unlikely that the federal question presented would ever arise again.[89] Had the Court been aware of the state law from the outset, "the case would have assumed such an isolated significance" that the Court would not have granted certiorari in the first place.[90] The Court explained that it "does not sit to satisfy a scholarly interest" in legal issues, and that cases are certworthy only when they reach "a problem beyond the academic or the episodic."[91] The Court therefore dismissed the case as improvidently granted, despite having already heard oral argument.[92]

There are exceptions. For example, in 2015 the Supreme Court decided a statutory-interpretation case[93] even though Congress had recently made changes to the statute that might "limit the future significance of our interpretation of the Act."[94] But the Court soldiered on, noting in passing that "[w]e express no view on these statutory and regulatory changes."[95]

Choice of cases for Supreme Court decision

Certworthiness merely makes a case a serious candidate for Supreme Court review. It doesn't guarantee certiorari. Of all the certworthy cases the Court receives, it will grant only a small fraction.

How does the Supreme Court decide which of the many certworthy cases to grant? That is also a hard question, in part because nine individual Justices have different views.[96] No hard-and-fast rules bind the Court or explain its decisions. One commentator summarized the state of affairs this way: "[N]o one can predict

---

89 *Id.* at 73.
90 *Id.* at 76–77.
91 *Id.* at 74.
92 *Id.* at 77–78.
93 See *Young v. United Parcel Serv., Inc.*, 135 S.Ct. 1338, 1348 (2015).
94 *Id.*
95 *Id.*
96 See William H. Rehnquist, *The Supreme Court* 265 (1987) ("Whether or not to vote to grant certiorari strikes me as a rather subjective decision, made up in part of intuition and in part of legal judgment.").

with much certainty whether or not a certain case will be taken. One can predict in a trivial sense. Since so few cases are granted, one can predict denial and be right 95 percent of the time. ... But for most cases, meaningful prediction is a faulty enterprise."[97]

Three general principles help us determine whether a certworthy case is likely to be granted.

First, if a case presents a certworthy question, it must also provide a suitable vehicle for deciding that question. The importance of the questions before the Court "demand[s] that such questions be presented in a context conducive to the most searching analysis possible."[98] For example, only in rare circumstances will the Court grant certiorari to review an interlocutory judgment, particularly if the ultimate outcome of the case remains unclear.[99] Or if there is a lurking antecedent jurisdictional issue—standing or ripeness, for example—the Court may be more reluctant to grant certiorari.

Even so, cases that present these types of "vehicle" problems do sometimes slip through the cracks and end up on the Court's docket. The Court, having granted certiorari, may then dismiss the case as improvidently granted. In *New York v. Uplinger*,[100] for instance, the Court determined that the court of appeals' decision was "fairly subject to varying interpretations," making the case "an inappropriate vehicle for resolving the important constitutional issues raised by the parties."[101] The Court therefore dismissed the case as improvidently granted.[102] Similarly, the Court dismissed *Public Employees' Retirement System of Mississippi v.*

---

97 H.W. Perry Jr., *Deciding to Decide: Agenda Setting in the United States Supreme Court* 216 (paperback ed. 1994).

98 *New York v. Uplinger*, 467 U.S. 246, 251 (1984) (Stevens J. concurring) (discussing need for appropriate vehicle before deciding constitutional questions).

99 *See* Sup. Ct. R. 11; *see also Mount Soledad Mem'l Ass'n v. Trunk*, 132 S.Ct. 2535, 2536 (2012) (statement of Alito J. respecting denial of petitions for writs of certiorari) ("Because no final judgment has been rendered and it remains unclear precisely what action the Federal Government will be required to take, I agree with the Court's decision to deny the petitions for certiorari.").

100 467 U.S. 246 (1984) (per curiam).

101 *Id.* at 248–49.

102 *Id.* at 249.

IndyMac MBS[103] as improvidently granted after the existence of a proposed settlement emerged.[104] In dismissing the case, the Court relinquished an opportunity to resolve a significant circuit split.[105]

Second, the timing of a petition for a writ of certiorari matters. Petitions are sometimes denied "because, even though serious constitutional questions were raised, it seemed to at least six members of the Court that the issue was either not ripe enough or too moribund for adjudication; that the question had better await the perspective of time or that time would soon bury the question or, for one reason or another, it was desirable to wait and see."[106] In other words, the Court may allow certain otherwise certworthy issues to work their way through the lower courts in order to benefit from those courts' expertise. The Court has recognized that "when frontier legal problems are presented, periods of 'percolation' in, and diverse opinions from, state and federal appellate courts may yield a better informed and more enduring final pronouncement."[107]

Third, some Justices may have strong views on the merits of the issue. An individual Justice may vote to grant or deny a case based on whether its facts, its timing, and the Court's current composition are likely to lead to a favorable outcome from that Justice's perspective. Although Justices rarely publicly discuss these factors, they often want to prevail on issues they care about and may assess the likelihood that their view on a particular issue will prevail if certiorari is granted.

---

103   135 S.Ct. 42 (2014).

104   *Id.* (dismissing case as improvidently granted); *see Public Emps. Ret. Sys. of Miss. v. IndyMac MBS, Inc.*, No. 13-640 (U.S. 23 Sept. 2014) (order directing parties to file briefs on effect of proposed settlement agreement).

105   *See* Lyle Denniston, *Securities Case Dropped; Split on Legal Issue Remains*, SCOTUSblog (29 Sept. 2014), http://www.scotusblog.com/2014/09/securities-case-dropped-split-on-legal-issue-remains/.

106   *Darr v. Burford*, 339 U.S. 200, 227 (1950) (Frankfurter J. dissenting), *overruled in part by Fay v. Noia*, 372 U.S. 391 (1963).

107   *Arizona v. Evans*, 514 U.S. 1, 23 n.1 (1995) (Ginsburg J. dissenting).

Blackmun J. once implied that the Court might not want to hear cases "devoid of glamour and emotion."[108] Stevens J. contemporaneously dismissed that notion and disdained giving reasons for or against denials of certiorari.[109]

Commentators have noted that in the 21st century the Court has granted certiorari in only half as many cases as it did in the 1960s and 1970s. The quality and types of cases resolved in the lower state and federal courts haven't changed radically over that time.[110] But individual Justices have higher or lower tolerances for leaving issues unresolved, so it's likely that the changing composition of Justices on the Court affects what they consider certworthy. For example, White J. in 1989 dissented from a denial of certiorari because he perceived a conflict in the circuits about the necessity of a profit-making motive in a RICO prosecution.[111] He noted that a week earlier the Supreme Court had denied certiorari in a dozen cases in which he identified intercircuit conflicts that needed to be resolved or raised important issues related to the administration of federal programs.[112]

Judges themselves may attempt to influence the likelihood that the Supreme Court will grant certiorari. Lower courts may urge that an issue is of sufficient importance for Supreme Court resolution—citing reasons.[113] When a case heard or reheard en banc by a federal circuit court results in a vigorous split, the exten-

---

108 *Singleton v. Commissioner*, 439 U.S. 940, 942 (1978) (Blackmun J. dissenting from denial of certiorari).

109 *Id.* at 945 (statement of Stevens J.).

110 *See* Kenneth W. Starr, *The Supreme Court and Its Shrinking Docket: The Ghost of William Howard Taft*, 90 Minn. L. Rev. 1363, 1368 (2006) ("[T]he number of cases coming before the Supreme Court grew steadily since 1925, while the number of cases the Court decides has been in steady decline."); Ryan J. Owens & David A. Simon, *Explaining the Supreme Court's Shrinking Docket*, 53 Wm. & Mary L. Rev. 1219, 1228 (2012) (graphically depicting the Supreme Court's shrinking docket from 1940 to 2008 and noting "the contemporary Court decides fewer cases than any Supreme Court in modern times").

111 *McMonagle v. Northeast Women's Ctr., Inc.*, 493 U.S. 901 (1989) (White J. dissenting from denial of certiorari) (an issue later resolved by *Scheidler v. National Org. for Women, Inc.*, 537 U.S. 393 (2003)).

112 *Id.* at 901–05.

113 *See* Tracey E. George & Michael E. Solimine, *Supreme Court Monitoring of the United States Courts of Appeals En Banc*, 9 Sup. Ct. Econ. Rev. 171 (2001).

sive and controverted judicial positions may be designed to attract the Supreme Court's attention. Finally, the increasingly common practice of writing dissentals—that is, opinions dissenting from a circuit's refusal to hear a case en banc and giving reasons that should attract the Supreme Court's attention—may be designed (often successfully) to influence a grant of certiorari.[114]

---

114 Alex Kozinski & James Burnham, *I Say Dissental, You Say Concurral*, 121 Yale L.J. Online 601, 610 (2012), http://yalelawjournal.org/forum/i-say-dissental-you-say-concurral ("Dissentals and concurrals fall comfortably within Bryan Garner's definition of persuasive precedent. In addition to enriching the law, dissentals give judges an opportunity to focus public scrutiny on a particular case. The fact that a number of appellate judges took pains to voice their public disagreement with an opinion of their court is significant. It no doubt increases the likelihood of certiorari review and stimulates changes through the political process."); *see* Scott Graham, *9th Circuit's Clarion Calls Are Being Heard*, The Recorder (Cal.), 31 Aug. 2012 (suggesting that there is statistical support for the notion that cases with dissentals are disproportionately likely to be granted certiorari: 32% of cases were granted when five or more Ninth Circuit judges joined in dissent from denial of rehearing en banc).

64. Federal Courts Bound Only by Federal Precedents on Federal Questions

In interpreting and applying the U.S. Constitution, a treaty, or a federal statute, federal courts are not bound to follow the decisions of any state court—only relevant federal decisions. State-court precedents construing federal law are persuasive only.

The role of state precedents on federal issues in federal courts is rooted in the Constitution. Under Article III, the judicial power of the federal courts extends "to all Cases, in Law and Equity, arising under this Constitution, the Laws of the United States, and Treaties made, or [to] be made, under their Authority."[1] This judicial power is referred to as federal-question jurisdiction. Yet state courts also have authority to interpret and apply the U.S. Constitution, federal statutes, and federal treaties.[2] If a state court decides a federal question, federal courts are not bound to follow that precedent. Under Article III of the Constitution and judicial practice as it has evolved from the founding, federal courts must independently interpret and apply the U.S. Constitution, federal statutes, and federal treaties.

The relationship between the lower federal courts and the state courts was hotly debated at the Constitutional Convention. There was consensus about creating the U.S. Supreme Court. But there was disagreement about creating the lower federal courts. James Madison, a delegate from Virginia, favored a system of lower federal courts.[3] John Rutledge—a delegate from South Carolina who would become the second Chief Justice of the United States—argued against the creation of the lower federal

---

[1] U.S. Const. art. III, § 2, cl. 1.

[2] *See Tafflin v. Levitt*, 493 U.S. 455, 458–59 (1990); *see also Mims v. Arrow Fin. Servs., LLC*, 132 S.Ct. 740, 748 (2012); *Lockhart v. Fretwell*, 506 U.S. 364, 376 (1993) (Thomas J. concurring); *Howlett v. Rose*, 496 U.S. 356, 367 (1990); *Steffel v. Thompson*, 415 U.S. 452, 482 n.3 (1974) (Rehnquist J. concurring); *ASARCO Inc. v. Kadish*, 490 U.S. 605, 617 (1989); *Claflin v. Houseman*, 93 U.S. 130, 136 (1876).

[3] 1 *The Records of the Federal Convention of 1787*, at 124 (Max Farrand ed., Yale Univ. Press 1911) (5 June 1787) (statement of James Madison).

courts. According to Rutledge, state courts could adjudicate all cases, both federal-law and state-law cases.[4] James Madison and James Wilson (later a Justice of the Supreme Court) suggested a compromise: leave it up to Congress to decide whether to establish the lower federal courts.[5]

This Madisonian Compromise is reflected in the text of the Constitution, which gives Congress the power to vest judicial power "in such inferior Courts as the Congress may from time to time ordain and establish."[6] In 1789, the First Congress established a system of lower federal courts.[7] But the Madisonian Compromise didn't prohibit state courts from adjudicating federal questions. As Alexander Hamilton explained in *The Federalist* No. 82, "the inference seems to be conclusive that the State courts would have a concurrent jurisdiction in all cases arising under the laws of the Union where it was not expressly prohibited."[8] Under this system, the U.S. Supreme Court retains authority to review state courts' federal-law decisions to ensure uniformity.

The question then arises whether federal courts are bound by state-court interpretations of federal law. The answer is no.[9] As Alexander Hamilton colorfully explained in *The Federalist* No. 80, if state courts were permitted to have the last word on federal law,

---

4   *Id.* at 124 (statement of John Rutledge).
5   *Id.* at 125 (statement of James Madison and James Wilson).
6   U.S. Const. art. III, § 1, cl. 1.
7   Judiciary Act of 1789, ch. 20, §§ 2–4, 1 Stat. 73, 73–75.
8   *The Federalist* No. 82, at 493 (Alexander Hamilton) (Clinton Rossiter ed., 1961).
9   *See, e.g., Hucul Advert., LLC v. Charter Twp. of Gaines*, 748 F.3d 273, 279 (6th Cir. 2014) ("[A] state court's interpretation and application of the First Amendment of the United States Constitution are not binding on this court."); *Waugh Chapel S., LLC v. United Food & Commercial Workers Union Local 27*, 728 F.3d 354, 366 (4th Cir. 2013); *William Jefferson & Co. v. Board of Assessment & Appeals No. 3 for Orange Cnty.*, 695 F.3d 960, 963 (9th Cir. 2012) ("The California court's resolution of a federal constitutional question is persuasive but is not binding on us."); *Streit v. County of Los Angeles*, 236 F.3d 552, 560 (9th Cir. 2001) ("[S]tate law does not control our interpretation of a federal statute."); *United States v. Collazo*, 117 F.3d 793, 795 (5th Cir. 1997); *Noel v. Linea Aeropostal Venezolana*, 247 F.2d 677, 679 (2d Cir. 1957) (stating that "in interpreting a federal treaty, the federal courts are certainly not bound by state court interpretations"), *overruled on other grounds by Benjamins v. British European Airways*, 572 F.2d 913 (2d Cir. 1978).

it would create a many-headed "hydra in government from which nothing but contradiction and confusion can proceed."[10]

So although state courts have concurrent authority to decide federal questions, federal courts needn't follow state precedents on federal questions.[11] According to the conventional view, although state courts aren't bound by federal judicial precedents on federal questions, some state courts give significant weight to federal-court interpretations of federal law.[12] According to one scholar, the courts of at least 46 states and the District of Columbia regard federal-court precedent as not binding on the state court—though Delaware state courts appear to take the opposite view.[13]

It is firmly established that federal courts "are not bound by a state court's interpretation of federal law,"[14] any more than one federal circuit would be bound by another's interpretation of federal

---

10   *The Federalist* No. 80, at 476 (Alexander Hamilton) (Clinton Rossiter ed., 1961).

11   See *Tafflin*, 493 U.S. at 465 (maintaining that federal courts aren't bound by a state court's interpretation of a federal statute).

12   See *Johnson v. Williams*, 133 S.Ct. 1088, 1098 (2013) (stating that "the views of the federal courts of appeals do not bind the California Supreme Court when it decides a federal constitutional question"); see also *Lockhart*, 506 U.S. at 376 (Thomas J. concurring); *Steffel*, 415 U.S. at 482 n.3 (Rehnquist J. concurring). But see *Tafflin*, 493 U.S. at 465 ("State courts adjudicating civil RICO claims will, in addition, be guided by federal court interpretations of the relevant federal criminal statutes, just as federal courts sitting in diversity are guided by state court interpretations of state law."); *Yniguez v. Arizona*, 939 F.2d 727, 736 (9th Cir. 1991) ("Despite the authorities that take the view that the state courts are free to ignore decisions of the lower federal courts on federal questions, we have serious doubts as to the wisdom of this view."); Amanda Frost, *Inferiority Complex: Should State Courts Follow Lower Federal Court Precedent on the Meaning of Federal Law?*, 68 Vand. L. Rev. 53, 66–67 (2015) (noting that whether state courts are bound by federal precedents on federal law is an open question even after *Johnson*).

13   See Wayne A. Logan, *A House Divided: When State and Lower Federal Courts Disagree on Federal Constitutional Rights*, 90 Notre Dame L. Rev. 235, 251 & n.111, 280–81 (2014) (collecting cases).

14   *Grantham v. Avondale Indus., Inc.*, 964 F.2d 471, 473 (5th Cir. 1992); see also *Wilder v. Turner*, 490 F.3d 810, 814 (10th Cir. 2007); *Oja v. U.S. Army Corps of Eng'rs*, 440 F.3d 1122, 1129 n.4 (9th Cir. 2006); *RAR, Inc. v. Turner Diesel, Ltd.*, 107 F.3d 1272, 1276 (7th Cir. 1997); *In re Asbestos Litig.*, 829 F.2d 1233, 1237 (3d Cir. 1987); *Pauk v. Board of Trs. of City Univ. of New York*, 654 F.2d 856, 865–66 & n.6 (2d Cir. 1981).

law.[15] Instead, federal courts must interpret the Constitution, federal laws, and treaties based on their independent judgment, guided by the precedent of their circuit court of appeals and the Supreme Court. As the Third Circuit has aptly explained, when it comes to federal questions, the "state trial court is bound by its judicial hierarchical organization to follow the state supreme court's rulings"; yet the federal district court takes as its authority "decisions of the United States Courts of Appeals and the United States Supreme Court, rather than those of the state supreme court."[16] If a case involves both state-law and federal-law questions, a federal court may be required to apply state precedents on questions of state law but federal precedents on questions of federal law (see §§ 65–67, 70–75).

Doctrinal conflicts between state and federal courts

The existence of two parallel court systems, both with authority to hear cases involving federal questions, inevitably leads to conflicts.[17] A controversy over marriage in Alabama illustrates that point. After a federal district judge in Alabama held that two Alabama laws banning same-sex marriage violated the U.S. Constitution,[18] the Alabama Supreme Court reached the opposite conclusion.[19] Stating that it had an independent duty to interpret federal law, the court concluded that the Alabama laws banning same-sex marriage were constitutional under the U.S. Constitution.[20] At the end of its 2014–2015 term, of course, the

---

15 See, e.g., *Cheng Lin v. Board of Immigration Appeals*, 177 F. App'x 162, 163 (2d Cir. 2006) (unreported) ("Third Circuit law is not controlling in this jurisdiction."); *United States v. Sykes*, 598 F.3d 334, 337 (7th Cir. 2010) (stating that decisions of other circuits are entitled to careful consideration but not to outright deference).

16 *In re Asbestos Litig.*, 829 F.2d at 1237.

17 See Logan, *A House Divided*, 90 Notre Dame L. Rev. at 254–58 (surveying conflicts between federal and state courts); Frost, *Inferiority Complex*, 68 Vand. L. Rev. at 59–60 (same).

18 *Searcy v. Strange*, 81 F. Supp. 3d 1285 (S.D. Ala. 2015).

19 *Ex parte Alabama ex rel. Ala. Policy Inst.*, No. 1140460, 2015 WL 892752, at *28 (Ala. 3 Mar. 2015), *abrogated by Obergefell v. Hodges*, 135 S.Ct. 2584 (2015).

20 *Ex parte Alabama*, 2015 WL 892752, at *26–30.

U.S. Supreme Court announced a constitutional right to same-sex marriage[21]—or "marriage equality," as it is sometimes called.

Consider other federal–state conflicts. The Ninth Circuit held that a police officer may frisk someone for weapons without a warrant even if the officer has no reasonable suspicion that the person committed a crime.[22] The Supreme Court of Arizona—a state within the Ninth Circuit—took the opposite position.[23] In another example, the Virginia Supreme Court upheld the constitutionality of a Virginia statute criminalizing sodomy between adults and minors.[24] The Fourth Circuit, which encompasses Virginia, then held that the same statute was unconstitutional under *Lawrence v. Texas*[25] as applied to conduct between adults and minors.[26]

As the Third Circuit correctly explained, "there is nothing inherently offensive" about having state and federal courts reach different legal conclusions: "[S]uch results were contemplated by our federal system, and neither sovereign is required to, nor expected to, yield to the other."[27] That isn't to say that federal courts should ignore state precedents on federal questions. State precedents, like those of other federal courts, may be persuasive even if they aren't binding.[28] Consistency between state and federal courts "promotes respect for the law and prevents litigants from forum-shopping."[29]

When a decision of a state high court rests on "adequate and independent state grounds," the Supreme Court will set aside the state-law ruling to reach a federal question only when the

---

21   *Obergefell*, 135 S.Ct. 2584.
22   *United States v. Orman*, 486 F.3d 1170, 1173–74 (9th Cir. 2007).
23   *Arizona v. Serna*, 331 P.3d 405, 410 (Ariz. 2014).
24   *See McDonald v. Virginia*, 645 S.E.2d 918, 924 (Va. 2007).
25   539 U.S. 558 (2003).
26   *See MacDonald v. Moose*, 710 F.3d 154, 163–66 (4th Cir. 2013).
27   *Surrick v. Killion*, 449 F.3d 520, 535 (3d Cir. 2006); *see also Johnson*, 133 S.Ct. at 1098); *United States ex rel. Lawrence v. Woods*, 432 F.2d 1072, 1075 (7th Cir. 1970); *State v. Coleman*, 214 A.2d 393, 403 (N.J. 1965).
28   *See, e.g.*, *Oja*, 440 F.3d at 1129 n.4; *RAR*, 107 F.3d at 1276; *United States v. Collazo*, 117 F.3d 793, 795 (5th Cir. 1997).
29   *Surrick*, 449 F.3d at 535.

state-law ruling lacks "fair or substantial" support.[30] But when the decision raises a federal question, the state high court's decision is reviewable by the U.S. Supreme Court: "To this extent, at least, the judicial power of a state is subordinate to that of the United States."[31] But for any lower federal court, the reported decisions of the state supreme or intermediate appellate courts construing the Constitution and any federal laws within their jurisdiction are persuasive only: "[T]here is no . . . subordination on the part of any federal court to any state court."[32]

When state high courts resolve federal questions, the U.S. Supreme Court has the final say. For example, in the 1921 case of *Missouri Pacific Railroad v. Ault*,[33] a railroad employee sued under state law to recover damages for his discharge without just cause. The state court awarded him both his past wages of $50 and any future wages that accrued from the date of his discharge to the date his employer paid the damages.[34] While the employee's lawsuit was pending, the President took possession of the railroad company under the Federal Control Act,[35] and the Director General of Railroads was substituted for the employer as the defendant.[36] Under the Act, the Director General assumed the same "liabilities as common carriers, whether arising under State or Federal laws or at common law," unless those liabilities were "inconsistent" with federal law.[37] Although the Director General didn't dispute that he could be liable for the employee's unpaid past wages, he insisted that Congress never "intended to authorize suit against the government for a penalty" under the Act.[38]

---

30 See *NAACP v. Alabama ex rel. Patterson*, 357 U.S. 449 (1958); *Murdock v. City of Memphis*, 87 U.S. (20 Wall.) 590 (1874).

31 *Central Trust Co. of N.Y. v. Citizens' St. Ry. of Indianapolis*, 82 F. 1, 4 (C.C.D. Ind. 1897).

32 *Id.*

33 256 U.S. 554 (1921).

34 *Id.* at 556.

35 Federal Control Act of 21 March 1918, ch. 25, 40 Stat. 451 (1918).

36 *Ault*, 256 U.S. at 556.

37 Federal Control Act, ch. 25, § 10, 40 Stat. at 456.

38 *Ault*, 256 U.S. at 563 ("The government undertook as carrier to observe all existing laws; it undertook to compensate any person injured through a departure by

The Supreme Court agreed, even though the Arkansas Supreme Court had earlier held that the award of future wages under state law wasn't merely a penalty, but instead served "a double purpose[]—as a compensation for the delay, and as a punishment for the failure to pay" and "serves all the purposes of exemplary damages."[39] The Supreme Court refused to defer to that state ruling, concluding that "whether in a proceeding against the Director General it shall be deemed compensation or a penalty presents a question not of state, but of federal law."[40] Under its interpretation of federal law, any "recovery of the penalty was erroneous."[41]

More recently, in *Nitro-Lift Technologies, LLC v. Howard*,[42] the U.S. Supreme Court rejected, as contrary to federal law, a decision of the Oklahoma Supreme Court that would have avoided the arbitration of an employment dispute involving noncompetition agreements. Instead of submitting the dispute to arbitration, the state high court held the agreements void and unenforceable under Oklahoma law.[43] The court also declared that its decision rested on adequate and independent state grounds. But the U.S. Supreme Court decided otherwise,[44] ruling that, under the Federal Arbitration Act, the state high court had committed "precisely th[e] type of 'judicial hostility towards arbitration'" foreclosed by federal precedents.[45]

When state statutes are judged against federal law

If the validity of a state statute is assailed on the ground that it conflicts with the U.S. Constitution or federal laws, a decision of the state court on the compatibility of state law with federal law

---

its agents or servants from their duty under such law; but it did not undertake to punish itself for any departure by the imposition upon itself of fines and penalties or to permit any other sovereignty to punish it.").

39 *Leep v. St. Louis, Iron Mountain & Southern Ry.*, 25 S.W. 75, 85 (Ark. 1894).
40 *Ault*, 256 U.S. at 565.
41 *Id.*
42 133 S.Ct. 500 (2012) (per curiam).
43 *Id.* at 502.
44 *Id.* at 502–03.
45 *Id.* at 503 (quoting *AT&T Mobility LLC v. Concepcion*, 563 U.S. 333, 342 (2011)).

does not bind the federal court. As we have seen, the Supremacy Clause of the United States Constitution makes the Constitution and the laws of the United States the "supreme Law of the Land."[46] Relying on this provision, federal courts often evaluate the constitutionality of state laws. But state courts can also be called on to decide whether a state statute conflicts with a federal law or the Constitution. Indeed, as the U.S. Supreme Court makes clear, it's the responsibility of state courts as much as federal courts "when the question of the validity of a state statute is necessarily involved, as being in alleged violation of any provision of the federal constitution, to decide that question, and to hold the law void if it violate that instrument."[47] Although the U.S. Supreme Court will give a state statute the construction the state's courts give it[48] (see § 77), it is federal law that determines the statute's conformity to the Constitution or other federal law.

For example, in the seminal case of *Missouri v. Hunter*,[49] the U.S. Supreme Court deferred to a state decision construing two state criminal statutes as defining the same crime.[50] But the Supreme Court rejected "the Missouri Supreme Court's legal conclusion that th[ose] two statutes violate[d] the Double Jeopardy Clause"[51] because their provision for cumulative punishments after a single trial was found to be federally permissible.[52] Similarly, in a 1972 case[53] the Third Circuit considered a relator's claim that the state statute creating the New Jersey State Commission of Investigation—responsible for ferreting out public corruption—failed to provide sufficient due process for witnesses who

---

46 U.S. Const. art. VI, cl. 2.
47 *Baker v. Grice*, 169 U.S. 284, 291 (1898).
48 See *Elmendorf v. Taylor*, 23 U.S. (10 Wheat.) 152, 159–60 (1825) (observing that the U.S. Supreme Court will "adopt the construction which the Courts of the State have given to" the "laws of a particular state").
49 459 U.S. 359 (1983).
50 *Id.* at 368.
51 *Id.*
52 *Id.*
53 *United States ex rel. Catena v. Elias*, 465 F.2d 765 (3d Cir. 1972).

appeared before it.[54] The New Jersey Supreme Court had ruled that the commission acted well within the bounds of the Due Process Clause.[55] But the Third Circuit correctly observed that it was "not bound by the resolution of the federal constitutional questions by the Supreme Court of New Jersey," and was instead bound only "by that court's construction of the statute creating the commission."[56]

Yet the principle has even earlier roots. A 1941 Iowa case[57] involved the constitutionality, under the U.S. Constitution, of Iowa's sales-tax regime. Sears, Roebuck & Co., a New York corporation, had retail stores in the state of Iowa. As required by state law, it collected use taxes on sales made in those stores. It also accepted and filled mail orders from Iowa residents sent to its out-of-state branches but refused to collect Iowa use taxes on those purchases.[58] The state's law defined *use* as "the exercise by any person of any right or power over tangible personal property incident to the ownership of that property"[59] and required that a "retailer maintaining a place of business in this state and making sales of tangible personal property for use in this state . . . shall at the time of making such sales, whether within or without the state, collect the tax imposed by this chapter from the purchaser."[60] Sears contended that these tax laws as applied discriminated against interstate commerce and were therefore unconstitutional.[61] The Iowa Supreme Court agreed, finding that the mail-order sales were distinct from sales made in retail outlets, so the state had no power to regulate the corporation's out-of-state activities and could not

---

54 *Id.* at 767.

55 *See Zicarelli v. New Jersey State Comm'n of Investigation*, 261 A.2d 129, 135 (N.J. 1970).

56 *Elias*, 465 F.2d at 769; *see also Helton v. Fauver*, 930 F.2d 1040, 1044 (3d Cir. 1991) ("We are not, however, bound by the state court's determination as to whether its construction offends the federal Constitution.").

57 *Nelson v. Sears, Roebuck & Co.*, 312 U.S. 359, 364 (1941).

58 *Id.* at 363.

59 Iowa Code § 6943.102.

60 *Id.* § 6943.109.

61 *Nelson*, 312 U.S. at 362.

levy use taxes on mail-order sales.[62] The United States Supreme Court reversed.[63]

Soon after that decision, the Utah Supreme Court was faced with a similar case involving the constitutionality of Utah's sales-tax statutes.[64] Utah's tax commission had applied the state's use-tax laws to sales made by Montgomery Ward—a company located in Denver, Colorado—to residents of Utah, and required Montgomery Ward to collect the tax.[65] The Utah Supreme Court addressed the narrow issue "whether a retailer who does business within this state can constitutionally be required to collect a use tax in connection with its mail order business conducted wholly from outside the state with customers within the state."[66] Montgomery Ward argued that it couldn't be required to collect the tax for mail-order sales because its part of the business was conducted wholly outside Utah.[67] The Utah Supreme Court concluded that the use-tax statute was indistinguishable from the Iowa use-tax statute that the U.S. Supreme Court had upheld.[68]

State courts commonly construe their state's statutes and common law so as not to violate the U.S. Constitution. In a 1996 case,[69] for example, the Texas Supreme Court considered the extent to which the federal Airline Deregulation Act preempted personal-injury negligence claims under state common law—specifically, one passenger's claim for being hit on the back of the head by a briefcase falling from an overhead storage bin, and a mentally ill passenger's claim that because an airline attendant had failed to meet him at the gate, he had wandered off and wound up in an altercation for which he was arrested.[70] The court noted that although it was obliged to follow U.S. Supreme Court precedent,

---

62 *Id.* at 362–63.
63 *Id.* at 366.
64 *Montgomery Ward & Co. v. State Tax Comm'n*, 112 P.2d 152 (Utah 1941).
65 *Id.* at 152.
66 *Id.*
67 *Id.* at 153.
68 *Nelson*, 312 U.S. at 363.
69 *Continental Airlines v. Kiefer*, 920 S.W.2d 274 (Tex. 1996).
70 *Id.*

that Court's two decisions on the subject had not spoken directly to personal-injury claims.[71] After a careful analysis, the Texas court concluded that the federal statute's purpose wasn't to absolve airlines of all liability under state law but instead to prohibit state regulation of air carriers, whether direct or indirect.[72] The court reasoned that when a state's law doesn't have a regulatory effect on an airline, the state may enforce the state law. So the federal statute did not preempt a negligence-based personal-injury claim under Texas common law or a contract-based claim for failure to perform promised meet-and-assist services.[73]

When the Supreme Court has not spoken, how should a federal court handle state precedent regarding the validity of a state statute under federal law or the Constitution? Federal courts are required to accept the state court's construction of its own statutes, but not its conclusion about the statute's validity under federal law.[74]

For example, in *St. Louis Southwestern Railway v. Arkansas ex rel. Norwood*,[75] the Supreme Court reviewed an Arkansas tax imposed on businesses that operated within the state. A Missouri railroad argued that the tax violated the Constitution. The Arkansas Supreme Court held that it didn't.[76] Reviewing that

---

71 *Id.* at 278–82.
72 *Id.* at 282.
73 *Id.* at 284.
74 See *St. Louis SW Ry. v. Arkansas ex rel. Norwood*, 235 U.S. 350 (1914); *RAR, Inc. v. Turner Diesel, Ltd.*, 107 F.3d 1272, 1276 n.1 (7th Cir. 1997) (calling it "beyond cavil that we are not bound by a state court's interpretation of federal law regardless of whether our jurisdiction is based on diversity of citizenship or a federal question") (internal quotation marks and citations omitted); *cf. Grantham v. Avondale Indus., Inc.*, 964 F.2d 471, 473 (5th Cir. 1992) ("The *Erie* doctrine does not apply . . . in matters governed by the federal Constitution or by acts of Congress."); *In re Asbestos Litig.*, 829 F.2d 1233, 1237 (3d Cir. 1987) ("The federal district court . . . takes as its authority on federal constitutional issues decisions of the United States Courts of Appeals and the United States Supreme Court, rather than those of the state supreme court."); *cf. Exxon-Mobil Corp. v. Saudi Basic Indus. Corp.*, 544 U.S. 280, 291–93 (2005) (clarifying that the role of the *Rooker-Feldman* doctrine is to prevent federal district courts from exercising appellate review over state-court judgments).
75 235 U.S. 350 (1914).
76 *Id.* at 361.

decision, the Supreme Court first noted that on "the mere question of construction we are, of course, concluded by the decision of the state court of last resort."[77] But it added that when the question is whether a state tax deprives a party of a right secured by the U.S. Constitution, the decision doesn't depend on "the characterization of that scheme as adopted by the state court."[78] Rather, federal courts must decide for themselves whether the state statute comports with the federal Constitution.[79]

The Supreme Court routinely applies this bedrock principle.[80] Lower federal courts similarly make independent judgments regarding whether state statutes are preempted by federal law or invalid under the Constitution.[81]

Federal legislation sometimes requires federal courts to review state-court decisions on federal law in a particular way.

---

77 *Id.* at 362.

78 *Id.*

79 *See also Hanover Fire Ins. Co. v. Carr*, 272 U.S. 494, 509 (1926) ("It is true that the interpretation put upon such a tax law of a state by its Supreme Court is binding upon this court as to its meaning; but it is not true that this court, in accepting the meaning thus given, may not exercise its independent judgment in determining whether, with the meaning given, its effect would not involve a violation of the federal Constitution."); *Truax v. Corrigan*, 257 U.S. 312, 325 (1921) ("[W]here the issue is whether a state statute in its application to facts ... violates the federal Constitution, this court must analyze the facts as averred and draw its own inferences as to their ultimate effect, and is not bound by the conclusion of the state Supreme Court in this regard.").

80 *See, e.g., Virginia v. Black*, 538 U.S. 343 (2003) (reversing the Virginia Supreme Court's determination that flag-burning statute was facially invalid under the First Amendment of the United States Constitution); *Minnesota v. Clover Leaf Creamery Co.*, 449 U.S. 456 (1981) (reversing Minnesota Supreme Court's conclusion that Minnesota milk-distribution statute violated the Equal Protection Clause of the United States Constitution); *North Dakota State Bd. of Pharmacy v. Snyder's Drug Stores, Inc.*, 414 U.S. 156 (1973) (reversing North Dakota Supreme Court decision invalidating a North Dakota statute regulating pharmacies under the United States Constitution); *Wisconsin v. Yoder*, 406 U.S. 205 (1972) (affirming a Wisconsin Supreme Court decision finding a compulsory education law to be invalid under the First Amendment, but relying on reasoning independent of that in the Wisconsin Supreme Court decision).

81 *See, e.g., Jackson v. Builders Transp., Inc.*, No. 95-2983, 1996 WL 431992, at *3 (4th Cir. 2 Aug. 1996) (unpublished opinion) ("[F]ederal courts are not bound by state court determinations regarding federal preemption."); *United States v. Flynn*, 709 F. Supp. 2d 737, 741 (D.S.D. 2010) ("[T]his Court is not bound by state court determinations on the issue of federal preemption."); *Montgomery v. Bank of Am. Corp.*, 515 F. Supp. 2d 1106, 1113 (C.D. Cal. 2007) (same).

For instance, the Antiterrorism and Effective Death Penalty Act of 1996 governs how federal courts review habeas petitions.[82] This statute requires federal courts to defer to a state decision on federal constitutional violations unless the decision "was contrary to, or involved an unreasonable application of, clearly established Federal law, as determined by the Supreme Court of the United States."[83]

When federal questions involve state law in other ways

A caveat is in order when a federal statute refers to state law. That can happen in a variety of contexts, such as bankruptcy, criminal law, family law, and taxation. The Supreme Court will "generally assume, in the absence of a plain indication to the contrary, that Congress when it enacts a statute is not making the application of the federal act dependent on state law."[84] But when a federal statute makes reference to a state law, federal courts follow the state precedents about the meaning of those state laws, though not about the scope and meaning of the federal statutes that refer to them. For example, in *Johnson v. United States*, the Court was asked to decide whether the term *physical force* in the Armed Career Criminal Act included any kind of unwanted physical touching.[85] The Florida Supreme Court having interpreted a similar Florida law, Johnson argued that the Court was bound by the state court's conclusion that unwanted touching didn't constitute "physical force."[86] The Court rejected his contention: "We are . . . bound by the Florida Supreme Court's interpretation of state law, including its determination of the elements of [the state crime]."[87] But "[t]he meaning of 'physical force' . . . is a question of federal law, not state law. And in answering that question we are

---

82   Pub. L. No. 104-132, § 104, 110 Stat. 1214, 1218–19 (codified as amended at 28 U.S.C. § 2254).
83   28 U.S.C. § 2254(d)(1).
84   *Jerome v. United States*, 318 U.S. 101, 104 (1943).
85   559 U.S. 133, 138 (2010).
86   *Id.*
87   *Id.*

not bound by a state court's interpretation of a similar—or even identical—state statute."[88]

Similarly, in a 2014 case,[89] the Eleventh Circuit looked to Florida law, including caselaw, to determine that a prior state conviction for fleeing a police officer in a marked patrol vehicle[90] qualified as a "violent felony" that could enhance a federal sentence under the Armed Career Criminal Act.[91] The Eleventh Circuit determined the elements of the Florida offense, as interpreted by Florida courts, before deciding the federal question whether the offense "involve[d] conduct that presents a serious potential risk of physical injury to another."[92] But in a 1995 case,[93] the Eleventh Circuit held that the meaning of the term "conviction" in a federal statute[94] is a question of federal law, not state law, when determining whether a plea of nolo contendere followed by a withholding of adjudication in a Florida court supported a sentencing enhancement under the federal statute.[95]

Occasionally, interpretation or application of the Constitution, a federal statute, or a federal treaty does involve issues of state law. When that is so, state precedents may be binding on federal courts with regard to those state-law issues.[96]

Although federal courts aren't bound by state-court precedents, they may rely on them in two situations. The first is that the best *evidence* of what a federal constitutional guarantee means

---

88 *Id.*
89 *United States v. Smith*, 742 F.3d 949, 953–54 (11th Cir. 2014).
90 Fla. Stat. § 316.1935(2).
91 18 U.S.C. § 924(e).
92 18 U.S.C. § 924(e)(2)(B)(ii), *invalidated by Johnson v. United States*, 135 S.Ct. 2551 (2015).
93 *United States v. Mejias*, 47 F.3d 401 (11th Cir. 1995) (per curiam).
94 21 U.S.C. § 841(b)(1)(B).
95 *Mejias*, 47 F.3d at 403; *see also United States v. Medina*, 718 F.3d 364, 367 (4th Cir. 2013) ("Although some Guidelines provisions may incorporate definitions from state law, it is clear that federal law controls our interpretation of the Guidelines absent a specific indication to the contrary. We may therefore rely on Maryland law in defining the term 'conviction' only if the Guidelines direct us to look to state law for interpretive guidance.") (citation omitted).
96 *See NLRB v. Natural Gas Util. Dist. of Hawkins Cnty.*, 402 U.S. 600, 603 (1971).

will sometimes come from state-court decisions construing the same language. As we will see later (§ 77), most of the individual rights contained in the United States Constitution appeared in the pre-1789 state constitutions, and many originated there. That makes state-court decisions of the founding era relevant to the interpreter who seeks to understand what a federal guarantee (modeled after the state guarantees) meant and means.

The Supreme Court's decision in *District of Columbia v. Heller*[97] confirms the point. At issue was whether the Second Amendment of the United States Constitution protects an individual's right to bear arms.[98] The Court divided 5–4 over whether the Amendment guaranteed an individual's right to bear arms, the majority holding that it did. As a matter of methodology, the Court spoke as one in looking to state-court decisions of the founding era to decipher what the terms of the Second Amendment mean. The majority thought its interpretation was "confirmed by analogous arms-bearing rights in state constitutions that preceded and immediately followed adoption of the Second Amendment."[99] Over several pages, it then analyzed the language of the state guarantees and the preratification and postratification decisions of state courts interpreting their guarantees.[100] The dissent didn't disagree with the inquiry. It, too, looked to the state constitutional guarantees from the founding era and state-court decisions construing them; it simply drew a different conclusion from the record.[101] Other decisions confirm the role of state precedents in interpreting the federal Constitution.[102]

---

97   554 U.S. 570 (2008).
98   *Id.* at 573–76.
99   *Id.* at 600–01.
100 *Id.* at 600–14.
101 *Id.* at 639–42, 648 n.10, 662 n.29 (Stevens J. dissenting).
102 See *Crawford v. Washington*, 541 U.S. 36, 49–50 (2004) (relying on early state-court common law and state constitutional decisions in deciphering the meaning of the right to confrontation under the Sixth Amendment); *Wilson v. Arkansas*, 514 U.S. 927, 933–34 (1995) (relying on early state-court decisions in determining that the Fourth Amendment contains a knock-and-announce requirement before serving a warrant); *Griffin v. United States*, 502 U.S. 46, 50–51 (1991) (considering state-court practices in determining the meaning of federal due process); *Harmelin v. Michigan*, 501 U.S. 957, 982–85 (1991) ("Perhaps the most

State-court decisions may play a role in federal constitutional debates in another way: they may provide evidence of the kinds of evolving norms that the U.S. Supreme Court has recognized from time to time in expanding the guarantees beyond their original understanding.[103] In overruling *Bowers v. Hardwick*[104] to declare sodomy statutes unconstitutional under the liberty guarantee of the Fourteenth Amendment, the Supreme Court relied in part on the fact that "[t]he courts of five different States have declined to follow [*Bowers*] in interpreting provisions in their own state constitutions parallel to the Due Process Clause of the Fourteenth Amendment."[105] The Court has done so in other settings.[106] Relatedly, nothing prevents Justices of the U.S. Supreme Court—or, for that matter, all judges looking vertically down the judicial hierarchy or horizontally to sister courts—from relying on precedents from a state court based on persuasiveness of reasoning.[107]

In sum, federal courts aren't bound by state precedents on federal questions. When conflicts arise between state courts and

---

persuasive evidence of what 'cruel and unusual' meant, however, is found in early judicial constructions of the Eighth Amendment and its state counterparts. . . . Throughout the 19th century, state courts interpreting state constitutional provisions with identical or more expansive wording (*i.e.*, 'cruel *or* unusual') concluded that these provisions did not proscribe disproportionality but only certain modes of punishment.").

103 *United States v. Virginia*, 518 U.S. 515, 557 (1996) ("A prime part of the history of our Constitution . . . is the story of the extension of constitutional rights . . . to people once ignored or excluded.").

104 478 U.S. 186 (1986).

105 *Lawrence v. Texas*, 539 U.S. 558, 576 (2003).

106 *See, e.g., Caldwell v. Mississippi*, 472 U.S. 320, 333–34 & nn.4–5 (1985) (relying on "the view of almost all of the State Supreme Courts" in holding improper under the Eighth Amendment a prosecutorial comment to the jury that responsibility for a death sentence rests with the appellate court that will review the case).

107 *See Lynch v. Donnelly*, 465 U.S. 668, 701 n.7 (1984) (Brennan J. dissenting) (finding, in a case deciding the effect of a nativity scene, that "the views expressed by the California Supreme Court in considering a similar issue are particularly relevant"); *id.* (citing a decision of the Oregon Supreme Court for the same reason).

federal courts with respect to federal questions, the Supreme Court has authority to resolve them.[108]

---

108 See *Tafflin v. Levitt*, 493 U.S. 455, 465 (1990) ("State court judgments misinterpreting federal criminal law would, of course, also be subject to direct review by this Court.").

65. Jurisdiction and Powers of Federal Courts

Questions concerning the jurisdiction and powers of federal courts are to be decided exclusively by those courts. The statutes and judicial decisions of a state are not controlling authority.

What does a federal court consider in delineating the boundaries of its jurisdiction and powers? It looks to the U.S. Constitution, federal statutes, U.S. Supreme Court precedent, and the precedent of the relevant federal circuit court—but not to state statutes or state precedents.

Under Article III of the Constitution, Congress has the power to establish the lower federal courts and to determine their jurisdiction and powers.[1] By that constitutional authority, Congress has adopted statutes defining the jurisdiction and powers of the federal courts.[2] The Supreme Court's jurisdiction is fixed by the Constitution, but Congress has the power to make exceptions to the Court's appellate jurisdiction.[3]

Although Congress writes the statutes defining the jurisdiction and powers of the federal courts, federal courts *interpret* those statutes. As the Supreme Court declared in *Marbury v. Madison*, "It is emphatically the province and duty of the judicial department to say what the law is."[4] In *Marbury* itself, the Supreme Court interpreted the Constitution to hold that the Court didn't have the power to issue a writ of mandamus under the Court's original jurisdiction.[5] From the founding era, then, federal courts have had the authority to interpret the Constitution and federal statutes so as to determine their own jurisdiction and powers.

---

1 *See* U.S. Const. art. III, § 1; *see also Palmore v. United States*, 411 U.S. 389, 400–01 (1973); *Sheldon v. Sill*, 49 U.S. (8 How.) 441, 448–49 (1850).

2 *See, e.g.*, 28 U.S.C. § 1331 (conferring general federal-question jurisdiction on the federal district courts); 28 U.S.C. § 1291 (conferring appellate jurisdiction on the federal circuit courts); 28 U.S.C. § 1651 (conferring power to issue writs on the federal courts).

3 *See* U.S. Const. art. III, § 2.

4 5 U.S. (1 Cranch) 137, 177 (1803).

5 *See id.* at 173–76.

The federal courts are not only empowered but also required to ascertain their jurisdiction and powers. As the Supreme Court has held, the "federal courts are under an independent obligation to examine their own jurisdiction."[6] *Jurisdiction* "is power to declare the law, and when it ceases to exist, the only function remaining to the court is that of announcing the fact and dismissing the cause."[7] Federal district courts must determine their own jurisdiction and powers, and federal circuit courts must determine both their own jurisdiction and powers and those of the lower court whose judgment is under review.[8]

Given this independent obligation, state and federal courts may reach different conclusions on jurisdiction-related issues[9]—particularly because state courts aren't bound by Article III's case-or-controversy requirement. This difference usually reveals itself when the U.S. Supreme Court considers a federal issue decided by a state court.[10] In such cases, the U.S. Supreme Court ensures that Article III's case-or-controversy requirement is met.[11] The decision doesn't rest on the state law's stricter or looser case-or-controversy requirement.

Many cases illustrate that only federal courts have the authority to decide whether they have jurisdiction. For example, in *Liner v. Jafco, Inc.*,[12] a Tennessee court had enjoined a union from picketing at a construction site, and a state appellate court had then ruled that the case was moot because construction at the site had been completed.[13] The Supreme Court rejected the notion that it was bound by the state court's determination: "We think . . . that in this case the question of mootness is itself a question of federal

---

6   *FW/PBS, Inc. v. City of Dallas*, 493 U.S. 215, 231 (1990).
7   *Ex parte McCardle*, 74 U.S. (7 Wall.) 506, 514 (1868).
8   *See Steel Co. v. Citizens for a Better Env't*, 523 U.S. 83, 95 (1998).
9   *See ASARCO Inc. v. Kadish*, 490 U.S. 605, 617 (1989); *New York State Club Ass'n v. City of New York*, 487 U.S. 1, 8 n.2 (1988).
10 *See ASARCO*, 490 U.S. at 617; *see also Virginia v. Hicks*, 539 U.S. 113, 120–21 (2003); *Doremus v. Board of Educ.*, 342 U.S. 429, 434 (1952).
11 *See ASARCO*, 490 U.S. at 623–24.
12 375 U.S. 301 (1964).
13 *Id.* at 302–04.

law upon which we must pronounce final judgment."[14] Likewise, in *Doremus v. Board of Education*,[15] the New Jersey Supreme Court had ruled that a state law providing for the reading of "five verses of the Old Testament at the opening of each public school day"[16] didn't offend the United States Constitution. On review, the U.S. Supreme Court made "an independent examination of the record"[17] to determine whether the "facts amount to a justifiable case or controversy"[18] and concluded that the plaintiffs—a taxpayer and a parent—lacked standing. The Court reasoned that "because our own jurisdiction is cast in terms of 'case or controversy,' we cannot accept as the basis for review, nor as the basis for conclusive disposition of an issue of federal law without review, any procedure which does not constitute such."[19] In *Tileston v. Ullman*,[20] the Supreme Court ruled that a physician lacked standing to complain that a Connecticut law forbidding the use of contraceptives endangered the lives of his patients. The state high court had upheld the state law without addressing whether it had jurisdiction to decide the case on the merits.

The broader grants of jurisdiction to state courts in state constitutions and laws don't ordinarily affect the more limited jurisdiction of federal courts under Article III. In *Hollingsworth v. Perry*,[21] the U.S. Supreme Court refused to defer to a ruling by the California Supreme Court that the sponsors of a ballot initiative had suffered a particularized grievance sufficient to establish standing.[22] The Ninth Circuit had certified to the California Supreme Court the question whether under California law "the official proponents of an initiative measure possess either a particularized interest in the initiative's validity or the authority to

---

14   *Id.* at 304.
15   342 U.S. 429 (1952).
16   *Id.* at 430.
17   *Id.* at 432.
18   *Id.* at 433.
19   *Id.* at 434.
20   318 U.S. 44, 45–46 (1943) (per curiam).
21   133 S.Ct. 2652 (2013).
22   *Id.* at 2667–68.

assert the State's interest in the initiative's validity."[23] After the California Supreme Court answered yes, the Ninth Circuit decided the merits of the appeal.[24] But the U.S. Supreme Court refused to allow the state ruling to alter the circumscribed role of the federal courts "simply by issuing to private parties who otherwise lack standing a ticket to the federal courthouse."[25] In the words of the Supreme Court, "The Article III requirement that a party invoking the jurisdiction of a federal court seek relief for a personal, particularized injury serves vital interests going to the role of the Judiciary in our system of separated powers"—namely, the "properly limited . . . role of the [federal] courts in a democratic society."[26]

Although the Supreme Court acknowledges that "state courts are not bound by the limitations of a case or controversy or other federal rules of justiciability even when they address issues of federal law,"[27] a state judgment against a litigant might make an otherwise nonjusticiable case reviewable by the Supreme Court. In *ASARCO Inc. v. Kadish*, the Supreme Court considered an appeal from an Arizona Supreme Court decision.[28] In the state-court case, a group of Arizona taxpayers and an organization representing public-school teachers sued the Arizona Land Department and others to challenge an Arizona statute permitting mineral leases on state lands. ASARCO, a mining company, and other state mineral leaseholders intervened as defendants. The Arizona Supreme Court held that the statute was void under federal law.[29] ASARCO and the mineral leaseholders appealed to the U.S. Supreme Court. Before reaching the merits, the U.S. Supreme Court considered whether the requirements of Article III standing were met.

---

23 *Perry v. Schwarzenegger*, 628 F.3d 1191, 1193 (9th Cir. 2011).
24 *Hollingsworth v. Perry*, 133 S.Ct. at 2660–61.
25 *Id.* at 2667.
26 *Id.*
27 *ASARCO Inc. v. Kadish*, 490 U.S. 605, 617 (1989).
28 *See id.* at 610.
29 *See Kadish v. Arizona State Land Dep't*, 747 P.2d 1183, 1196 (Ariz. 1987).

Because the case was filed in an Arizona state court, the Arizona state court "took no account of federal standing rules," as was its right.[30] As the U.S. Supreme Court recognized, "the constraints of Article III do not apply to state courts, and accordingly the state courts are not bound by the limitations of a case or controversy or other federal rules of justiciability even when they address issues of federal law, as when they are called upon to interpret the Constitution or, in this case, a federal statute."[31]

Whose procedural rules?

Even so, the U.S. Supreme Court is bound by Article III's standing requirements. In *ASARCO*, the Supreme Court found that the taxpayer and schoolteacher plaintiffs had not suffered an injury in fact and therefore didn't satisfy the Article III standing requirements.[32] Yet the Court concluded that ASARCO and the mineral leaseholders had suffered a "direct, specific, and concrete injury" under the Arizona Supreme Court decision. That injury posed "a serious and immediate threat to the continuing validity" of their mineral leases, the Court found,[33] so the standing requirements of Article III were met.[34]

Relatedly, neither state precedents nor state laws limit the enforcement of a state-created right to the jurisdiction of its courts if a federal court otherwise has jurisdiction over the litigants. In *Railway Co. v. Whitton's Administrator*,[35] for example, a Wisconsin law required an action for wrongful death to be brought in a Wisconsin court, but the U.S. Supreme Court ruled that the removal jurisdiction of a federal court, based on diversity of citizenship, "is not subject to State limitation."[36] The Court declared: "In all cases, where a general right is thus conferred, it can be

---

30 *ASARCO*, 490 U.S. at 617.
31 *Id.*
32 *See id.* at 616–17.
33 *Id.* at 618.
34 *See id.* at 619.
35 80 U.S. (13 Wall.) 270 (1871).
36 *Id.* at 285–86.

enforced in any Federal court within the State having jurisdiction of the parties."[37]

A different rule applies when the state itself is sued. A state can limit a waiver of its sovereign immunity to its own courts without waiving its Eleventh Amendment immunity from suit in federal court. In *Smith v. Reeves*,[38] the Supreme Court ruled that California could permit its treasurer to be sued in a state court for a tax refund without waiving its immunity from the same kind of lawsuit in a federal court. The Supreme Court reaffirmed that holding in *Great Northern Life Insurance Co. v. Read*.[39] As the Supreme Court explained more recently: "Whether [a State] permits such a suit to be brought against the State in its own courts is not determinative of whether [it] has relinquished its Eleventh Amendment immunity from suit in the federal courts."[40]

The lower federal courts must similarly determine their jurisdiction and powers without regard to state law. In a 2001 case,[41] the Ninth Circuit recognized that under California law, a plaintiff has authority to challenge a company's allegedly unfair business practices even if the plaintiff hasn't suffered an injury in fact.[42] Yet in federal court, a plaintiff must demonstrate just such an injury to have standing under Article III.[43] As a result, a plaintiff whose claim is "perfectly viable in state court under state law may nonetheless be foreclosed from litigating the same [claim] in federal court, if he cannot demonstrate the requisite injury."[44] The Ninth Circuit concluded that under federal law, the plaintiff had no standing because he hadn't suffered an injury in fact.

---

37   *Id.* at 286.
38   178 U.S. 436 (1900).
39   322 U.S. 47 (1944).
40   *Edelman v. Jordan*, 415 U.S. 651, 677 n.19 (1974).
41   *Lee v. American Nat'l Ins. Co.*, 260 F.3d 997 (9th Cir. 2001).
42   *Id.* at 1001.
43   *See Phillips Petroleum Co. v. Shutts*, 472 U.S 797, 804 (1985) ("Standing to sue in any Article III court is, of course, a federal question which does not depend on the party's prior standing in state court.").
44   *Lee*, 260 F.3d at 1001–02.

In cases that involve both state and federal jurisdictional issues, state precedents don't bind federal courts with respect to the federal-law issues. In a 1997 breach-of-contract case, the Seventh Circuit addressed whether the district court had personal jurisdiction over the defendant.[45] The Seventh Circuit noted that there were three distinct obstacles to personal jurisdiction: (1) state statutory law, (2) state constitutional law, and (3) federal law. The Seventh Circuit looked first to state precedent to determine whether the district court had personal jurisdiction over the defendant under state law. When that analysis was inconclusive, the Seventh Circuit then examined U.S. Supreme Court and Seventh Circuit precedent to determine whether the district court had personal jurisdiction over the defendant under federal law. As the Seventh Circuit explained, although "state court precedent is binding upon us regarding issues of state law, it is only persuasive authority on matters of federal law."[46] The Seventh Circuit concluded that under federal law, the district court lacked personal jurisdiction over the defendant.

In sum, federal courts have both the authority and the obligation to determine their own jurisdiction and powers, including their jurisdiction under Article III. On all such issues, the statutes and judicial precedents of a state are nugatory.

---

45   *RAR, Inc. v. Turner Diesel, Ltd.*, 107 F.3d 1272, 1274 (7th Cir. 1997).
46   *Id.* at 1276.

66. Federal Common Law

Although there is no general federal common law, federal courts fashion common law in limited circumstances and sometimes borrow state law to supply a legal rule.

Generally speaking, federal courts don't fashion common-law rules to decide cases and controversies. As early as 1812, in *United States v. Hudson & Goodwin*,[1] the Supreme Court held that federal courts lack the power to create common-law crimes against the United States. Meanwhile, the Rules of Decision Act provides that "[t]he laws of the several states, except where the Constitution or treaties of the United States or Acts of Congress otherwise require or provide, shall be regarded as rules of decision in civil actions in the courts of the United States, in cases where they apply."[2] And in *Erie Railroad v. Tompkins*,[3] the U.S. Supreme Court declared that the Act requires the application of state common law in addition to state statutes in civil cases because "[t]here is no federal general common law."[4] (See § 70.)

Yet there are exceptions to the general rule. In civil actions, federal courts sometimes fashion federal common law to protect federal interests, especially when the federal government, as a litigant, seeks to protect a proprietary interest. In *Clearfield Trust Co. v. United States*,[5] the U.S. Supreme Court ruled that federal common law, not state law, governed the rights and duties of the United States in its suit for theft and forgery of a check drawn by the Treasurer on a Federal Reserve Bank. And in *United States v. Little Lake Misere Land Co.*,[6] the Supreme Court ruled that federal common law governed federal contracts to acquire lands. The same was true in *United States v. 93.970 Acres of Land*,[7] in which

---

[1] 11 U.S. (7 Cranch) 32 (1812).
[2] 28 U.S.C. § 1652.
[3] 304 U.S. 64 (1938).
[4] *Id.* at 78.
[5] 318 U.S. 363 (1943).
[6] 412 U.S. 580 (1973).
[7] 360 U.S. 328 (1959).

the Court ruled that a state law about election of remedies couldn't govern the authority of the Army to choose whether to revoke a lease of an airfield or condemn the private lessee's remaining interest. But in *United States v. Kimbell Foods, Inc.*,[8] the Supreme Court ruled that state law should be applied to determine the priority of a government lien. The Court explained that "when there is little need for a nationally uniform body of law, state law may be incorporated as the federal rule of decision," but that a court also must consider whether applying state law "would frustrate [federal] objectives" and whether applying federal law "would disrupt commercial relationships predicated on state law."[9]

Although state law ordinarily governs civil disputes between private litigants, a rule of federal common law may govern when necessary to protect a federal interest. For example, the Supreme Court rejected the application of federal common law in a suit for conversion of a federal bond because the "litigation [wa]s purely between private parties and d[id] not touch the rights and duties of the United States."[10] But in *Boyle v. United Technologies Corp.*,[11] the Supreme Court fashioned a military-contractor defense, as a matter of federal common law, in a product-liability suit filed by the father of a deceased Marine pilot against the manufacturer of a military helicopter. In *Miree v. DeKalb County*,[12] the Supreme Court explained that federal common law will govern a dispute between private litigants only when there will be a "significant conflict between some federal policy or interest and the use of state law."[13]

Federal courts also fashion federal common law to resolve disputes between states. State law is unsuited to this task. Article III, § 2, of the Constitution grants the U.S. Supreme Court original and exclusive jurisdiction over cases between two or more states,[14]

---

8   440 U.S. 715 (1979).
9   *Id.* at 728–29.
10 *Bank of Am. Nat'l Trust & Sav. Ass'n v. Parnell*, 352 U.S. 29, 33 (1956).
11 487 U.S. 500 (1988).
12 433 U.S. 25 (1977).
13 *Id.* at 31.
14 U.S. Const. art. III, § 2.

and the Supreme Court has exercised that jurisdiction in boundary disputes,[15] cases about interstate waters,[16] and commercial[17] and tax disputes,[18] among others. In each case, the "[C]ourt is called upon to settle that dispute in such a way as will recognize the equal rights of both and at the same time establish justice between them."[19] In this circumstance, the law of each state is unsuited to an impartial resolution, and the Court has developed "what may not improperly be called interstate common law."[20]

Interstate disputes involving private litigants and not within the original jurisdiction of the Supreme Court may also require the application of federal common law. For example, in *Hinderlider v. La Plata River & Cherry Creek Ditch Co.*,[21] decided the same day and written by the same author, Brandeis J., as *Erie*, a private company sued state officials regarding water rights regulated by an interstate compact, and the Supreme Court ruled that "whether the water of an interstate stream must be apportioned between the two States is a question of 'federal common law' upon which neither the statutes nor the decisions of either State can be conclusive."[22] The *Hinderlider* litigation commenced and remained in state courts before the Supreme Court reviewed the matter, and its decision means that both state courts and inferior federal courts must adhere to federal common law in interstate disputes, when applicable.

Federal common law may also exist in fields in which Congress has "empowered [federal courts] to create governing rules of law."[23] For example, in *Textile Workers Union of America v. Lincoln Mills of Alabama*,[24] the U.S. Supreme Court held that the

---

15 *See, e.g., Rhode Island v. Massachusetts*, 37 U.S. (12 Pet.) 657 (1838).
16 *See, e.g., Colorado v. New Mexico*, 467 U.S. 310 (1984).
17 *See, e.g., South Dakota v. North Carolina*, 192 U.S. 286 (1904).
18 *See, e.g., Maryland v. Louisiana*, 451 U.S. 725 (1981).
19 *Kansas v. Colorado*, 206 U.S. 46, 98 (1907).
20 *Id.*
21 304 U.S. 92 (1938).
22 *Id.* at 110.
23 *Texas Indus., Inc. v. Radcliff Materials, Inc.*, 451 U.S. 630, 642 (1981).
24 353 U.S. 448 (1957).

statutory grant of federal jurisdiction in § 301 of the Taft–Hartley Act[25] requires federal courts to develop their own common law to enforce collective-bargaining agreements. The Supreme Court later explained that "Congress . . . did not intend the text of the Sherman [Antitrust] Act to delineate the full meaning of the statute or its application in concrete situations."[26] Rather, Congress "expected the courts to give shape to the statute's broad mandate by drawing on common-law tradition."[27] Similarly, in relation to employee pension and benefit plans, the Supreme Court has ruled that "courts are to develop a federal common law of rights and obligations."[28]

---

25 29 U.S.C. § 185; 9 U.S.C. § 301.
26 *National Soc'y Prof'l Eng'rs v. United States*, 435 U.S. 679, 688 (1978).
27 *Id.*
28 *Firestone Tire & Rubber Co. v. Bruch*, 489 U.S. 101, 110 (1989) (finding that ERISA's legislative history requires courts to incorporate the evolving law of trusts into interpretations of fiduciary responsibilities under the Act); *see also* 29 U.S.C. §§ 1101–1114 (ERISA's fiduciary-responsibility provisions).

67. Treaties and Interstate Compacts

Because treaties and interstate compacts are federal law, federal courts are not bound by state-court interpretations of them.

As we saw in § 64, federal courts ruling on questions of federal law aren't bound by state-court decisions. This fundamental precept applies to questions arising under interstate compacts and treaties with foreign powers. Federal courts decide such questions guided by their own precedent and principles of federal law. State precedents govern neither type of legal instrument. We'll consider them both here.

First, federal law governs questions arising under compacts between states. Under Article I of the Constitution, "No State shall, without the Consent of Congress," enter "into any Agreement or Compact with another State."[1] The U.S. Supreme Court has explained that when Congress approves an interstate compact under Article I, "congressional consent transforms an interstate compact within this Clause into a law of the United States."[2] As a result, "the construction of an interstate agreement sanctioned by Congress under the Compact Clause presents a federal question."[3] Hence a state-court determination of a question arising under a congressionally sanctioned interstate compact doesn't bind a federal court.

The Supreme Court's decision in *Petty v. Tennessee-Missouri Bridge Commission*[4] illustrates this principle. The question in that case was whether Tennessee and Missouri had waived their sovereign immunity under the terms of an interstate compact.[5] The Court acknowledged that under the state-court decisions of both states, the relevant language in the compact would not

---

1   U.S. Const. art. I, § 10, cl. 3.
2   *Cuyler v. Adams*, 449 U.S. 433, 438 (1981).
3   *Id.*
4   359 U.S. 275 (1959).
5   *Id.* at 276–77.

amount to a waiver of sovereign immunity.[6] But it concluded that Congress had intended the clause to waive sovereign immunity.[7] Because the waiver arose from a congressionally approved interstate compact, the Court was "called on to interpret not unilateral state action but the terms of a consensual agreement, the meaning of which, because made by different States acting under the Constitution and with congressional approval, is a question of federal law."[8] State-court decisions do not control the construction of an interstate compact even when "the matter in dispute concerns a question of state law on which the courts or other agencies of the State have spoken."[9] Although the Court would "show deference to state law in construing a compact, state law as pronounced in prior adjudications and rulings is not binding."[10] The Court therefore held that the state-court decisions regarding sovereign immunity were not controlling: the states were subject to suit under the compact.

Second, federal law governs questions arising under treaties with foreign nations. The Constitution vests jurisdiction in the federal courts over "all Cases, in Law and Equity, arising under this Constitution, the Laws of the United States, and Treaties made, or which shall be made, under their Authority."[11] The Supremacy Clause, meanwhile, provides that "all Treaties made,

---

6 *Id.* at 279–80; *see also League to Save Lake Tahoe v. Tahoe Reg'l Planning Agency*, 507 F.2d 517, 523 n.13 (9th Cir. 1974).

7 *Petty*, 359 U.S. at 280–82.

8 *Id.* at 279.

9 *Id.* at 278 n.4.

10 *Id.*; *see also West Virginia ex rel. Dyer v. Sims*, 341 U.S. 22, 28 (1951) ("Of course every deference will be shown to what the highest court of a State deems to be the law and policy of its State, particularly when recondite or unique features of local law are urged. Deference is one thing; submission to a State's own determination of whether it has undertaken an obligation, what that obligation is, and whether it conflicts with a disability of the State to undertake it is quite another."); *Pievsky v. Ridge*, 98 F.3d 730, 733 (3d Cir. 1996) ("Though state law is not binding, federal courts show deference to prior state adjudications and rulings in construing an interstate compact."); *League to Save Lake Tahoe*, 507 F.2d at 523 ("The Supreme Court has made it clear that the construction of an interstate compact is a matter of federal law, not the law of the party states.").

11 U.S. Const. art. III, § 2, cl. 1.

or which shall be made, under the Authority of the United States, shall be the supreme Law of the Land; and the Judges in every State shall be bound thereby, any Thing in the Constitution or Laws of any State to the Contrary notwithstanding."[12] Treaties therefore constitute federal law. State-court determinations of questions arising under treaties don't control in federal court.

The 1812 case of *Fairfax's Devisee v. Hunter's Lessee*[13] exemplifies the rule that federal courts aren't bound by state-court treaty interpretations. That case involved a British subject's title to land in Virginia under a treaty concluded between the United States and Great Britain. The Virginia Court of Appeals had already determined that the treaty didn't apply. The Supreme Court rejected the state court's conclusion, "well satisfied that the treaty of 1794 completely protects and confirms the title" of the British subject.[14]

In a similar vein, the Second Circuit rejected the argument that it was bound by a New York state court's interpretation of a federal treaty. Although the suit in *Noel v. Linea Aeropostal Venezolana*[15] was brought in diversity, the Second Circuit concluded that "the law to be applied in this case is not state law but a federal treaty. It is applied in the state courts not because it expresses a state policy which a federal court must follow, but because it expresses federal policy which a state court must follow. And in interpreting a federal treaty, the federal courts are certainly not bound by state court interpretations."[16]

---

12 U.S. Const. art. VI, cl. 2.

13 11 U.S. (7 Cranch) 603 (1812).

14 *Id.* at 627.

15 247 F.2d 677 (2d Cir. 1957), *overruled on other grounds by Benjamins v. British European Airways*, 572 F.2d 913 (2d Cir. 1978).

16 *Id.* at 679; *see also Mitchell v. Theriault*, 516 F. Supp. 2d 450, 453 (M.D. Pa. 2007) (noting that "a state court's interpretation of a federal treaty is not binding on a federal court, even if the federal court's jurisdiction is based on diversity") (internal quotes & cite omitted); *In re Air Crash in Bali*, 462 F. Supp. 1114, 1122 (C.D. Cal. 1978) (explaining that "this court is interpreting a document which is allegedly a federal treaty, and is not bound by state court interpretations"), *rev'd on other grounds*, 684 F.2d 1301 (9th Cir. 1982); *cf. Ademodi v. State*, 616 N.W.2d 716, 717 n.2 (Minn. 2000) ("State courts have jurisdiction to enforce rights arising under federal law. We are reluctant, however, to interpret the provisions of the Vienna Convention where the federal courts have not definitively interpreted its requirements.").

68. Federal Law and International Law

Questions of international law and international comity, like those arising under treaties with foreign nations, are decided by federal courts in the exercise of their independent judgment. The decisions of the state courts are not controlling.

When necessary to respect the constitutional powers of Congress and the President to conduct foreign affairs, federal courts interpret and apply some international law as a species of federal common law. (Scholars debate whether customary international law is itself a species of federal common law.[1]) State laws and judicial decisions "must give way if they impair the effective exercise of the Nation's foreign policy."[2]

For example, in *Republic of Philippines v. Marcos*,[3] the Second Circuit reviewed a property dispute in which the President of the Philippines had issued an executive order freezing all assets of a former head of state and his associates as beneficial owners of several properties.[4] Even though the foreign nation stated a claim for relief akin to a state claim for conversion, the Second Circuit ruled that the district court had subject-matter jurisdiction because the controversy with the former head of state presented "a federal question to be decided with uniformity as a matter of federal law,

---

[1] *Compare* Anthony J. Bellia Jr. & Bradford R. Clark, *The Federal Common Law of Nations*, 109 Colum. L. Rev. 1 (2009) (arguing that customary international law is neither state nor federal law), *and* Curtis A. Bradley & Jack L. Goldsmith, *Customary International Law as Federal Common Law: A Critique of the Modern Position*, 110 Harv. L. Rev. 815 (1997) (arguing that customary international law isn't federal common law), *with* Harold Hongju Koh, *Is International Law Really State Law?*, 111 Harv. L. Rev. 1824 (1998) (arguing the modern position that customary international law is federal common law). *See also Sosa v. Alvarez-Machain*, 542 U.S. 692, 726 (2004) ("And although we have even assumed competence to make judicial rules of decision of particular importance to foreign relations, . . . the general practice has been to look for legislative guidance before exercising innovative authority over substantive law."); Ernest A. Young, *Sorting Out the Debate over Customary International Law*, 42 Va. J. Int'l L. 365 (2002) (providing an overview of the debate).

[2] *Zschernig v. Miller*, 389 U.S. 429, 440 (1968).

[3] 806 F.2d 344 (2d Cir. 1986).

[4] *Id.* at 347.

and not separately in each state regardless of whether the overall claim is viewed as one of federal or state common law."[5] In deciding the merits of the plaintiffs' motion for a preliminary injunction, the Second Circuit first applied state law, but then in the alternative—assuming that "the claim is one under federal common law"—applied federal common law, which included both federal decisions and state law that did "not conflict with federal policy."[6]

---

5   *Id.* at 354 (internal citation omitted).
6   *Id.* at 355–56.

69. Maritime Law

In exercising their jurisdiction in admiralty and maritime cases, federal courts are governed by federal statutes and the general principles of maritime law. In some instances, however, federal courts may borrow state rules or allow state law to supplement general maritime law.

The Constitution extends the federal judicial power "to all Cases of admiralty and maritime Jurisdiction."[1] This sweeping grant of jurisdiction empowers the federal judiciary, in the absence of federal statutory authority, to fashion the general maritime law of the United States as a species of federal common law. At the founding, there was little debate about this grant of national authority. Alexander Hamilton wrote in *The Federalist* No. 80 that the "most bigoted idolizers of State authority have not thus far shown a disposition to deny the national judiciary the cognizance of maritime causes."[2] He further explained that the principles of the general maritime law "so generally depend on the laws of nations, and so commonly affect the rights of foreigners, that they fall within the considerations which are relative to the public peace."[3] Even before the ratification of the Constitution, Congress had the authority, under the Articles of Confederation, to appoint "courts for the trial of piracie and felonies committed on the high seas."[4] Under the Constitution, § 8 of Article I empowers Congress "to define and punish Piracies and Felonies committed on the high Seas."[5]

Federal courts exercise broad judicial power in the realm of admiralty and maritime jurisdiction. Riding circuit in 1815, Story J. discussed his understanding of federal maritime jurisdiction.[6] He explained that although many English statutes had

---

1 U.S. Const. art. III, § 2, cl. 1.
2 *The Federalist* No. 80, at 478 (Alexander Hamilton) (Clinton Rossiter ed., 1961).
3 *Id.*
4 Articles of Confederation of 1781, art. IX, para. 1.
5 U.S. Const. art. I, § 8, cl. 10.
6 *DeLovio v. Boit*, 7 F. Cas. 418, 443 (C.C.D. Mass. 1815).

undercut the "former splendor... [and] ancient foundations of the admiralty before the reign of Richard II," that hasn't been true in the United States.[7] His views have been borne out in later decisions of the U.S. Supreme Court, which in 1870 wrote that "the admiralty and maritime jurisdiction of the United States is not limited... by the restraining statutes or the judicial prohibitions of England."[8] Instead, the Court held, "[it] is to be interpreted by a more enlarged view of its essential nature and objects, and with reference to analogous jurisdictions in other countries constituting the maritime commercial world, as well as to that of England."[9]

Even though Congress has "paramount power to determine the maritime law which shall prevail throughout the country,"[10] the federal courts' broad jurisdiction cannot be infringed. As Story J. explained in the early circuit case, that jurisdiction includes maritime contracts on the one hand, and torts and injuries on the other: "The latter branch is necessarily bounded by locality; the former extends over all contracts (wheresoever they may be made or executed, or whatsoever may be the form of the stipulations), which relate to the navigation, business, or commerce of the sea."[11]

Two decisions by the U.S. Supreme Court in the early 20th century, both written by McReynolds J., established the now-settled hierarchy of authority for maritime law. In *Southern Pacific Co. v. Jensen*,[12] the Court acknowledged that "Congress has paramount power to fix and determine the maritime law which shall prevail throughout the country."[13] But federal common law fills the legislative interstices: "in the absence of some controlling statute, the general maritime law, as accepted by the Federal courts, constitutes part of our national law, applicable to matters within the admiralty and maritime jurisdiction."[14]

---

7   *See id.*
8   *New England Mut. Marine Ins. Co. v. Dunham*, 78 U.S. (11 Wall.) 1, 15 (1870).
9   *Id.*
10 *Detroit Trust Co. v. Barlum S.S. (The Thomas Barlum)*, 293 U.S. 21, 43–44 (1934).
11 *DeLovio*, 7 F. Cas. at 444.
12 244 U.S. 205 (1917).
13 *Id.* at 215.
14 *Id.*

The Court ruled that the relatives of a longshoreman killed while loading a vessel in the port of New York couldn't obtain workers' compensation under a New York statute when it "works material prejudice to the characteristic features of the general maritime law, or interferes with the proper harmony and uniformity of that law in its international and interstate relations."[15] A year later, in *Chelentis v. Luckenbach S.S.*,[16] the Court held that a seaman injured aboard a vessel at sea couldn't maintain an action for the negligence of his superior officer under the common law of New York. Citing the doctrine established in *Jensen*, the Court explained that "no state has power to abolish the well-recognized maritime rule concerning measure of recovery and substitute therefor the full indemnity rule of the common law."[17] The seaman's rights were governed instead by the principles of unseaworthiness and maintenance and cure under the general maritime law.

Federal courts remain free to borrow state rules or allow state laws to supplement the general maritime law when a uniform rule isn't required. The Supreme Court put it this way:

> Although the corpus of admiralty law is federal in the sense that it derives from the implications of Article III evolved by the courts, to claim that all enforced rights pertaining to matters maritime are rooted in federal law is a destructive oversimplification of the highly intricate interplay of the States and the National Government in their regulation of maritime commerce. It is true that state law must yield to the needs of a uniform federal maritime law when this Court finds inroads on a harmonious system. But this limitation still leaves the States a wide scope.[18]

The Court provided a list of examples ranging from wrongful-death statutes and survival actions to laws for the partition and sale of ships.[19]

---

15 *Id.* at 216.
16 247 U.S. 372 (1918).
17 *Id.* at 382.
18 *Romero v. International Terminal Operating Co.*, 358 U.S. 354, 373 (1959) (internal footnote omitted).
19 *Id.*

The Supreme Court has made it clear that some areas, like the regulation of marine insurance, have been left entirely to the states. For example, in *Wilburn Boat Co. v. Fireman's Fund Insurance Co.*,[20] the Supreme Court concluded (Black J. writing): "The whole judicial and legislative history of insurance regulation in the United States warns us against the judicial creation of admiralty rules to govern marine policy terms and warranties."[21] For that reason, the Court, like Congress, left "the regulation of marine insurance where it has been—with the States."[22] But other areas, like the fundamental choice between doctrines of comparative and contributory negligence in cases of torts, have not been left to the states. For example, when a carpenter sued a shipowner for injuries sustained in repairs to the ship, in *Pope & Talbot, Inc. v. Hawn*,[23] Black J. explained for the Court that the "harsh rule of the common law"[24] of contributory negligence, which would have barred recovery, couldn't supersede or supplement the federal maritime law of comparative negligence. So federal law, as determined by the federal judiciary, controls when state rules and laws should be borrowed or allowed to supplement the general maritime law.

---

20 348 U.S. 310 (1955).
21 *Id.* at 316.
22 *Id.* at 321.
23 346 U.S. 406 (1953).
24 *Id.* at 408–09.

F. State Law in Federal Court

70. *Erie* Doctrine

Common-law claims that came to the federal courts under diversity jurisdiction were once typically decided as matters of federal law. But in *Erie Railroad v. Tompkins* (1938), the U.S. Supreme Court overruled a century of precedent to hold that such claims must be decided under state law. Even so, federal procedural rules apply in federal litigation.

Federal courts are often called on to apply state law. Within some of the most heavily litigated federal statutes, Congress has directed that state law governs. For example, under the Federal Tort Claims Act, the liability of the United States depends on state tort law. The Act states that the government is liable "for injury or loss of property, or personal injury or death caused by the negligent or wrongful act or omission of any employee of the Government while acting within the scope of his office or employment, under circumstances where the United States, if a private person, would be liable to the claimant *in accordance with the law of the place where the act or omission occurred.*"[1] The Price–Anderson Act similarly authorizes public-liability actions in the event of a nuclear disaster and provides that "the substantive rules for decision in such action shall be derived from the law of the State in which the nuclear incident involved occurs."[2] As another example, the Internal Revenue Code incorporates state property law into provisions imposing tax liability.[3]

Some other federal statutes don't explicitly incorporate state law but instead provide that state law should be used to fill perceived gaps in the statutes. For example, the federal civil-rights statutes have engendered a good deal of litigation regarding incorporation of state law. Under 42 U.S.C. § 1983, the federal court's

---

1   28 U.S.C. § 1346(b)(1) (emphasis added).
2   42 U.S.C. § 2014(hh).
3   *See Commissioner v. Estate of Bosch*, 387 U.S. 456, 462–65 (1967).

jurisdiction in civil-rights cases "shall be exercised and enforced in conformity with the laws of the United States, so far as such laws are suitable to carry the same into effect."[4] But it goes on to say that "in all cases where they are not adapted to the object, or are deficient in the provisions necessary to furnish suitable remedies and punish offenses against law, the common law, as modified and changed by the constitution and statutes of the State wherein the court having jurisdiction of such civil or criminal cause is held, . . . shall be extended to and govern the said courts in the trial and disposition of the cause."[5] So because there was no federal statute of limitations for claims under 42 U.S.C. § 1983, the U.S. Supreme Court in *Wilson v. Garcia*[6] had to apply the gap-filling provision of § 1988. It held that the applicable limitations period for personal-injury claims is the one in the state where the § 1983 claim was to be tried.[7]

Even without a statutory directive to do so, federal courts may look to state law to fill a perceived gap in a federal statute. In *O'Melveny & Myers v. FDIC*,[8] the Supreme Court stated that if Congress has adopted a "federal statutory regulation that is comprehensive and detailed[,] matters left unaddressed in such a scheme are presumably left subject to the disposition provided by state law."[9] In that case the FDIC, acting as the receiver of a failed savings-and-loan, sued the O'Melveny & Myers law firm, alleging breach of fiduciary duty. The firm defended on the ground that under California law, knowledge of the savings-and-loan's officers was imputed to the receiver, estopping the FDIC from pursuing its claims against the firm. The Supreme Court said that if the federal Financial Institutions Reform, Recovery, and Enforcement Act of 1989 governed the case (the Court had doubts), the inclusion in that statute of various special rules benefiting the FDIC in

---

[4] 42 U.S.C. § 1988(a).
[5] *Id.*
[6] 471 U.S. 261 (1985).
[7] *See id.* at 279–80.
[8] 512 U.S. 79 (1994).
[9] *Id.* at 85.

litigation implied that aside from those rules, FDIC litigation was subject to the same state law as litigation by any other receiver.[10]

One statutory gap that the Supreme Court has routinely filled with state law has been the absence of a statute of limitations in a federal statute creating a right of action.[11] The Supreme Court said in *North Star Steel Co. v. Thomas*[12] that a state's limitations period applies unless it would "stymie the policies" underlying the federal claim.[13] The Court will "decline to follow a state limitations period only when a rule from elsewhere in federal law clearly provides a closer analogy than available state statutes, and when the federal policies at stake and the practicalities of litigation make that rule a significantly more appropriate vehicle for interstitial lawmaking."[14] But there are now only rare instances for such incorporation because of the 1990 enactment of a catchall federal statute of limitations.[15]

State law may also be incorporated into federal common law, which has a limited compass. The Supreme Court explained in *Texas Industries v. Radcliff Materials* that federal common law applies "only in such narrow areas as those concerned with the rights and obligations of the United States, interstate and international disputes implicating the conflicting rights of States or our relations with foreign nations, and admiralty cases."[16] Those are all areas of the law in which "our federal system does not permit the controversy to be resolved under state law, either because the authority and duties of the United States as sovereign are intimately involved or because the interstate or international nature of

---

10   *See id.* at 86–87.
11   *See International Union, UAW v. Hoosier Cardinal Corp.*, 383 U.S. 696, 703–05 (1966).
12   515 U.S. 29 (1995).
13   *Id.* at 34.
14   *Id.* at 35 (internal quotation marks omitted); *see also DelCostello v. International Bhd. of Teamsters*, 462 U.S. 151, 165–72 (1983) (holding state statute of limitations inadequate).
15   28 U.S.C. § 1658; *see generally Jones v. Railroad Donnelley & Sons Co.*, 541 U.S. 369 (2004).
16   *Texas Indus., Inc. v. Radcliff Materials, Inc.*, 451 U.S. 630, 641 (1981) (citations omitted).

the controversy makes it inappropriate for state law to control."[17] Yet the mere recognition that a given subject should be governed by federal law doesn't "necessarily mean that the federal courts should create th[at] controlling law."[18] The Supreme Court provided an example in *United States v. Kimbell Foods, Inc.*:

> Controversies directly affecting the operations of federal programs, although governed by federal law, do not inevitably require resort to uniform federal rules. Whether to adopt state law or to fashion a nationwide federal rule is a matter of judicial policy "dependent upon a variety of considerations always relevant to the nature of the specific governmental interests and to the effects upon them of applying state law."
>
> Undoubtedly, federal programs that "by their nature are and must be uniform in character throughout the Nation" necessitate formulation of controlling federal rules. Conversely, when there is little need for a nationally uniform body of law, state law may be incorporated as the federal rule of decision. Apart from considerations of uniformity, we must also determine whether application of state law would frustrate specific objectives of the federal programs. If so, we must fashion special rules solicitous of those federal interests. Finally, our choice-of-law inquiry must consider the extent to which application of a federal rule would disrupt commercial relationships predicated on state law.[19]

The Court has even more recently summarized its position in *American Electric Power v. Connecticut*: "Absent a demonstrated need for a federal rule of decision, the Court has taken the prudent course of adopting the ready-made body of state law as the federal rule of decision until Congress strikes a different accommodation."[20]

A federal court must also apply state law when there is a federal constitutional challenge to state action. How the state's law is interpreted will affect the analysis of the federal issue, and may

---

17 *Id.*
18 *American Elec. Power Co. v. Connecticut*, 564 U.S. 410, 422 (2011).
19 440 U.S. 715, 727–29 (1979) (quoting, respectively, *United States v. Standard Oil Co. of Cal.*, 332 U.S. 301, 310 (1947), and *United States v. Yazell*, 382 U.S. 341, 354 (1966)).
20 564 U.S. at 422 (brackets and internal quotation marks omitted).

even moot it. A state law itself may be challenged as unconstitutional, as in *Arizonans for Official English v. Arizona*,[21] in which a Spanish-speaking Arizona government employee claimed that her civil rights were violated when English was declared the state's official language.[22] Or the constitutional claim may be based on an alleged substantive right created by state law, as in *Town of Castle Rock v. Gonzales*,[23] in which the Supreme Court addressed whether the Due Process Clause applies to enforcement of a restraining order issued under state law.[24]

Background on jurisdictional questions

Historically, the greatest difficulty in determining whether to apply state law or federal law arose in common-law disputes arising in federal litigation because of the parties' diversity of citizenship. The matter was addressed by the first Congress in § 34 of the Federal Judiciary Act of September 24, 1789, which stated: "The laws of the several states, except where the constitution, treaties or statutes of the United States shall otherwise require or provide, shall be regarded as rules of decision in trials at common law in the courts of the United States in cases where they apply."[25] This statute is now commonly referred to as the Rules of Decision Act.

Writing for the Supreme Court in the 1842 decision of *Swift v. Tyson*,[26] Story J. adopted a relatively straitened view of the role of state law under the Act, leaving most issues to federal law. The Court later described *Swift* as holding "that federal courts exercising jurisdiction on the ground of diversity of citizenship need not, in matters of general jurisprudence, apply the unwritten law of the state as declared by its highest court; that they are free to exercise

---

21 520 U.S. 43 (1997).
22 *Id.* at 48, 49, 75–80 (1997) (explaining that federal courts had no jurisdiction).
23 545 U.S. 748 (2005).
24 *Id.* at 748, 757–66 (explaining why a person who obtains a restraining order under state law doesn't have a constitutionally protected property interest in its enforcement by the police).
25 1 Stat. 73, 92 (current version at 28 U.S.C. § 1652).
26 41 U.S. (1 Pet.) 1 (1842).

an independent judgment as to what the common law of the state is—or should be."[27] In Story J.'s own words:

> In the ordinary use of language, it will hardly be contended, that the decisions of courts constitute laws. They are, at most, only evidence of what the laws are, and are not, of themselves, laws. They are often re-examined, reversed and qualified by the courts themselves, whenever they are found to be either defective, or ill-founded, or otherwise incorrect. The laws of a state are more usually understood to mean the rules and enactments promulgated by the legislative authority thereof, or long-established local customs having the force of laws.[28]

The consequences would be far-reaching:

> In all the various cases, which have hitherto come before us for decision, this court have uniformly supposed, that the true interpretation of the [Rules of Decision Act] limited its application to state laws, strictly local, that is to say, to the positive statutes of the state, and the construction thereof adopted by the local tribunals, and to rights and titles to things having a permanent locality, such as the rights and titles to real estate, and other matters immovable and intra-territorial in their nature and character. It never has been supposed by us, that the section did apply, or was designed to apply, to questions of a more general nature, not at all dependent upon local statutes or local usages of a fixed and permanent operation.... And we have not now the slightest difficulty in holding, that this section, upon its true intendment and construction, is strictly limited to local statutes and local usages ... and does not extend to contracts and other instruments of a commercial nature, the true interpretation and effect whereof are to be sought, not in the decisions of the local tribunals, but in the general principles and doctrines of commercial jurisprudence.[29]

Note from this statement that the decision held that federal courts must apply state law to real-property matters and other local issues

---

27   *Erie R.R. v. Tompkins*, 304 U.S. 64, 71 (1938).
28   *Swift*, 41 U.S. at 18.
29   *Id.* at 18–19.

but not to matters relating to commerce, contracts, and "general jurisprudence" (such as torts, damages, and conflicts of law).[30]

In the wake of *Swift*, a body of law developed to determine whether an issue was a matter of general law or local law, only the latter being governed by state law. The federal courts were not shy in deciding that an issue was governed by general law that they could determine for themselves. As later summarized in *Erie*:

> In addition to questions of purely commercial law, "general law" was held to include the obligations under contracts entered into and to be performed within the state, the extent to which a carrier operating within a state may stipulate for exemption from liability for his own negligence or that of his employee; the liability for torts committed within the state upon persons resident or property located there, even where the question of liability depended upon the scope of a property right conferred by the state; and the right to exemplary or punitive damages. Furthermore, state decisions construing local deeds, mineral conveyances, and even devises of real estate, were disregarded.[31]

Before *Erie*, there were occasional animadversions against *Swift*, perhaps the most eloquent being that of Holmes J.'s dissent in *Black & White Taxicab & Transfer Co. v. Brown & Yellow Taxicab & Transfer Co.*[32] He argued that the doctrine rested on the false assumption that there is "a transcendental body of law outside of any particular State but obligatory within it unless and until changed by statute" and that in federal court "the parties are entitled to an independent judgment on matters of general law."[33]

Perhaps academic research turned the tide against *Swift*. Brandeis J. relied on what he described in *Erie* as "the more recent research of a competent scholar,[34] who examined the original

---

30   17A James W. Moore et al., *Moore's Federal Practice* § 124.01[1], at 124-28 (3d ed. 2015).

31   304 U.S. at 75–76 (internal footnotes omitted).

32   276 U.S. 518 (1928).

33   *Id.* at 533.

34   *See Erie*, 304 U.S. at 73 n.5 (citing Charles Warren, *New Light on the History of the Federal Judiciary Act of 1789*, 37 Harv. L. Rev. 49, 51–52, 81–88, 108 (1923)).

document, which established that the construction given to [the Rules of Decision Act] was erroneous."[35] This scholar had opined that

> the purpose of the section was merely to make certain that, in all matters except those in which some federal law is controlling, the federal courts exercising jurisdiction in diversity of citizenship cases would apply as their rules of decision the law of the state, unwritten as well as written.[36]

But even with the intervening scholarship (which, by the way, isn't held in high esteem by some scholars today[37]), any court would ordinarily resist overturning the interpretation of a statute that had survived for almost a century.

Rejecting the Swift *doctrine*

Erie noted the substantial difficulties that had arisen in determining whether law was general or local and, most important, the discrimination against a state's citizens caused by the *Swift* doctrine. The discrimination arose because "[i]t made rights enjoyed under the unwritten 'general law' vary according to whether enforcement was sought in the state or in the federal court; and the privilege of selecting the court in which the right should be determined was conferred upon the noncitizen."[38] That is, a citizen of the state could rely on the state's law in litigation in state court; but if the opposing party was a noncitizen, that party could sue in federal court (or remove the suit to federal court) if federal law might be more favorable to that party than state law. The Supreme Court held that such a doctrine "rendered impossible equal protection of the law."[39] It further noted that the federal courts had

---

35   *Id.* at 72.

36   *Id.* at 72–73; *see* 28 U.S.C. § 1652 (the current version of the Rules of Decision Act, which reads: "The laws of the several states, except where the Constitution or treaties of the United States or Acts of Congress otherwise require or provide, shall be regarded as rules of decision in civil actions in the courts of the United States, in cases where they apply.").

37   *See, e.g.*, Ernest A. Young, *A General Defense of* Erie Railroad Co. v. Tompkins, 10 J.L. Econ. & Pol'y 17, 25–27 (2013).

38   *Erie*, 304 U.S. at 74–75.

39   *Id.* at 75.

no authority under the Constitution to impose their view of the law, "invad[ing] rights which in our opinion are reserved by the Constitution to the several states."[40] By rejecting the *Swift* doctrine, *Erie* established that a federal court in a diversity case will apply the common law of the state in which it sits.[41] The same is true if a state-law claim is before a federal court under pendent or supplemental jurisdiction.[42]

The *Erie* Court announced its holding in three key sentences:

> Except in matters governed by the Federal Constitution or by Acts of Congress, the law to be applied in any case is the law of the State. And whether the law of the State shall be declared by its Legislature in a statute or by its highest court in a decision is not a matter of federal concern. There is no federal general common law.[43]

In other words, as the Court explained in a later case, the "broad command" of *Erie* is that "federal courts are to apply state substantive law and federal procedural law."[44] (The District of Columbia is treated as a state for *Erie* purposes.[45])

Sometimes, the federal court must decide whether to apply a federal rule of civil procedure or to apply a state law that addresses the same question. If no federal rule of civil procedure applies, then the federal court must make the "relatively unguided"[46] *Erie* determination whether the state law should be the rule of decision. Sometimes a state law is so obviously substantive that no further analysis is required to conclude that, under *Erie*, it must apply in

---

40 *Id.* at 80.

41 *See, e.g., Gasperini v. Center for Humanities, Inc.*, 518 U.S. 415, 427 (1996) ("Under the *Erie* doctrine, federal courts sitting in diversity apply state substantive law and federal procedural law.").

42 *In re ZAGG, Inc.*, 826 F.3d 1222 (10th Cir. 2016); *Timmerman v. Modern Indus., Inc.*, 960 F.2d 692, 696 (7th Cir. 1992).

43 304 U.S. at 78.

44 *Hanna v. Plumer*, 380 U.S. 460, 465 (1965).

45 *See Burke v. Air Serv Int'l, Inc.*, 685 F.3d 1102, 1107 n.4 (D.C. Cir. 2012).

46 *Shady Grove Orthopedic Assocs., P.A. v. Allstate Ins. Co.*, 559 U.S. 393, 417 (2010) (Stevens J. concurring in part & concurring in the judgment).

federal proceedings. But at other times, classifying a state law as either substantive or procedural is "a challenging endeavor."[47]

To decide this point, federal courts must consider whether it would significantly affect the result of a lawsuit "for a federal court to disregard a law of a State that would be controlling in an action upon the same claim by the same parties in a State court."[48] That "outcome-determination" test isn't absolute; it must be read with "reference to the twin aims of the *Erie* rule: discouragement of forum-shopping and avoidance of inequitable administration of the laws."[49] The potential for disparate outcomes must be balanced against important countervailing federal interests, such as the independence of the federal system.[50]

Rules of Decision Act

As interpreted in *Erie*, the Rules of Decision Act requires federal courts in diversity cases—and other cases presenting state-law issues[51]—to apply state substantive law to resolve claims.[52] When no federal statute or rule of procedure directly addresses an outcome-determinative issue[53] in a diversity case, a federal court will apply state law. For example, a federal court will apply state statutes of limitation[54] and state laws about the commencement or

---

47 *Gasperini*, 518 U.S. at 427.
48 *Id.* (quoting *Guaranty Trust Co. v. York*, 326 U.S. 99, 109 (1945)).
49 *Hanna*, 380 U.S. at 468 (internal quotation marks omitted).
50 *See Byrd v. Blue Ridge Rural Elec. Coop.*, 356 U.S. 525, 537–38 (1958).
51 *See* Abbe R. Gluck, *Intersystemic Statutory Interpretation: Methodology as "Law" and the* Erie *Doctrine*, 120 Yale L.J. 1898, 1926 & n.87 (2011) ("It is important to remember that the *Erie* doctrine applies in federal-question and federal constitutional cases, just as it does in diversity cases, provided that an analytically separate question of state law is presented.").
52 *Guaranty Trust Co. v. York*, 326 U.S. 99 (1945).
53 *Id.* at 109 ("In essence, the intent of [*Erie*] was to insure that, in all cases where a federal court is exercising jurisdiction solely because of the diversity of citizenship of the parties, the outcome of the litigation in the federal court should be substantially the same, so far as legal rules determine the outcome of a litigation, as it would be if tried in a State court.").
54 *Id.* at 110.

tolling of limitations periods.[55] The federal courts will also defer to some state gatekeeping rules in diversity suits. For example, in a 1950 case,[56] the Seventh Circuit reviewed a diversity suit involving a claim for the wrongful death of an Illinois citizen who had been fatally injured in Indiana but died in Ohio.[57] The plaintiff sued under an Illinois statute, which barred wrongful-death actions for out-of-state deaths if the law of the state where the death occurred allowed suit for wrongful death.[58] The defendant urged dismissal because the plaintiff had a claim under Indiana law. The plaintiff responded that the defense was improperly raised as a matter of Illinois law even if the federal court was required to defer to it.[59] The district court rejected the defense.[60] After a careful review of the Illinois Supreme Court's precedents, the Seventh Circuit remanded the case to the district court to consider the state-law defense.[61]

A federal court will apply state law regarding burdens of proof for claims and defenses,[62] as well as state choice-of-law rules.[63] Most notably, federal courts will follow the state law of contributory negligence.[64] But a federal court will not apply a state's law or procedure that conflicts with an overriding federal interest, such as the right to trial by jury guaranteed by the Seventh Amendment.[65]

---

55 *Walker v. Armco Steel Corp.*, 446 U.S. 740, 750–53 (1980); *Ragan v. Merchants Transfer & Warehouse Co.*, 337 U.S. 530, 532–34 (1949).
56 *Trust Co. of Chicago v. Pennsylvania R.R.*, 183 F.2d 640 (7th Cir. 1950).
57 *Id.* at 641.
58 *Id.* at 641–42.
59 *Id.* at 645.
60 *Id.* at 644.
61 *Id.* at 645–46.
62 *Palmer v. Hoffman*, 318 U.S. 109, 117 (1943).
63 *Klaxon Co. v. Stentor Elec. Mfg. Co.*, 313 U.S. 487, 496 (1941).
64 *Palmer*, 318 U.S. at 117.
65 *Gasperini*, 518 U.S. at 426; *Byrd v. Blue Ridge Rural Elec. Coop.*, 356 U.S. 525, 537–40 (1958).

Rules Enabling Act

The Rules Enabling Act[66] authorizes the Supreme Court to "prescribe general rules of practice and procedure and rules of evidence for cases" in the federal courts so long as those rules do not "abridge, enlarge or modify any substantive right."[67] When both a federal rule of civil procedure and a state law address the same matter, the federal rule governs as long as it is valid under the Act.

Relying on the Act, the Supreme Court has promulgated the well-known Federal Rules of Civil Procedure, Federal Rules of Criminal Procedure, and Federal Rules of Appellate Procedure. Procedural rules become effective unless Congress enacts contrary legislation within a short time limit. Although the Supreme Court also promulgates the Federal Rules of Evidence, rules relating to evidentiary privileges must be ratified by federal legislation.[68]

Some federal rules incorporate state laws and procedures. For example, Federal Rule of Civil Procedure 4(e)(1) allows service of process on some people by following state law, and Rule 4(n)(2) governs the exercise of personal jurisdiction by seizing assets as allowed by state law. In addition, Federal Rule of Evidence 501 states that, in a civil case in which state law provides the rule of decision, state law governs a privilege.[69]

In a case involving state-law claims, what happens when a rule promulgated under the Rules Enabling Act—such as a federal rule of civil procedure—conflicts with a state rule or precedent? In most cases, the federal court easily determines that state law, rather than federal law, applies. Then the federal court must perform two further tasks. First, it must decide which state's laws

---

66 *See* 28 U.S.C. § 2072.

67 28 U.S.C. § 2072.

68 *Id.*

69 *See, e.g., In re Avantel, S.A.*, 343 F.3d 311, 323–24 (5th Cir. 2003) (reviewing the law of Texas regarding attorney–client privilege and the inadvertent publishing of confidential documents); *Patterson v. Caterpillar, Inc.*, 70 F.3d 503, 506–07 (7th Cir. 1995) (reviewing the law of Wisconsin, including interpretations from the Supreme Court of Wisconsin, to reject the plaintiff's claim of a physician–patient privilege).

govern (see § 72). Second, it must determine what the relevant law of that state is (see § 73).

These questions raise the forum-shopping problem that concerned the *Erie* Court. If the outcome depends on whether the case is conducted in state or federal court, the litigant with an advantage in federal court will file in that court or have the case removed to it. This prospect has arisen in many different contexts. Often the issue is resolved by narrowly construing the scope of the federal rule to avoid any conflict. In the 1943 case of *Palmer v. Hoffman*,[70] Federal Rule 8(c), which requires responsive pleadings to set forth affirmative defenses, was read to govern only the manner of pleading, not the burden of persuasion, which is governed by state law.[71] In 1949, the Court in *Ragan v. Merchants Transfer & Warehouse Co.*[72] held that state law governs when a diversity suit commences for purposes of tolling the state's statutory limitations period, despite the declaration in Federal Rule 3 that a civil action is commenced when the complaint is filed.[73] *Ragan* was reaffirmed in 1980 in *Walker v. Armco Steel Corp.*[74] In *Cohen v. Beneficial Industrial Loan Corp.*,[75] the Court upheld imposition of a state rule requiring posting a bond as security for costs in a stockholder's derivative action even though the federal rule (now Rule 23.1) did not require a bond in a derivative action in federal court.[76] And in the 2001 case of *Semtek International Inc. v. Lockheed Martin Corp.*,[77] the Court said that although Federal Rule 41(b) provides that with a few specified exceptions, a dismissal is "an adjudication on the merits," a term commonly denoting that a judgment has res judicata effect,[78] the dismissal of a federal diversity claim in

---

70   318 U.S. 109 (1943).
71   *Id.* at 117.
72   337 U.S. 530 (1949).
73   *Id.* at 533–34.
74   446 U.S. 740, 752–53 (1980).
75   337 U.S. 541 (1949).
76   *Id.* at 555–57.
77   531 U.S. 497 (2001).
78   *See* Restatement (Second) of Judgments § 19 cmt. e (1982) (stating that "such dismissals shall not operate as an adjudication 'on the merits' (i.e., shall not

a California federal court based on a California statute of limitations didn't preclude the plaintiff from bringing the same claim in a diversity action in Maryland, which had a longer limitations period.[79]

For procedural matters, the federal rule may prevail. In *Hanna v. Plumer*,[80] the Supreme Court upheld service that accorded with the federal rule, but not the Massachusetts rule—even though applying the state rule would have barred the suit and the lower courts had said that the Massachusetts rule reflected a state substantive policy.[81] In the wake of *Hanna*, the Supreme Court developed a two-part test to guide federal courts in resolving apparent conflicts between state law and the Federal Rules of Civil Procedure.[82] Specifically, a "federal court exercising diversity jurisdiction should not apply a state law or rule if (1) a Federal Rule of Civil Procedure 'answer[s] the same question' as the state law or rule and (2) the Federal Rule does not violate the Rules Enabling Act."[83]

In the 2010 case of *Shady Grove Orthopedic Associates, P.A. v. Allstate Insurance Co.*, the Supreme Court applied the *Hanna* framework.[84] The Supreme Court considered whether a New York statute prohibiting certain class actions precluded a federal court sitting in diversity from entertaining a class action under Federal Rule of Civil Procedure 23.[85] Under New York law, a statutory penalty couldn't be imposed in a class action. But Shady Grove brought a diversity case in federal court on behalf of a class of

---

operate as a bar)").

79 *Semtek*, 531 U.S. at 503–04, 509.
80 380 U.S. 460 (1965).
81 *Id.* at 468, 473–74.
82 *See id.*; *see also Gasperini v. Center for Humanities, Inc.*, 518 U.S. 415 (1996); *Burlington Northern R.R. v. Woods*, 480 U.S. 1 (1987); *Walker v. Armco Steel Corp.*, 446 U.S. 740 (1980).
83 *Abbas v. Foreign Policy Grp., LLC*, 783 F.3d 1328, 1333 (D.C. Cir. 2015) (quoting *Shady Grove Orthopedic Assocs., P.A. v. Allstate Ins. Co.*, 559 U.S. 393, 398–99 (2010)). *See generally* John Hart Ely, *The Irrepressible Myth of Erie*, 87 Harv. L. Rev. 693 (1974).
84 *Shady Grove*, 559 U.S. at 398 (majority opinion).
85 *Id.* at 396.

some 1,000 members seeking a statutory penalty of about $500 for each member. Noting that each class member could have brought a separate action for the penalty, the Supreme Court held that the federal rules permitted such a class action, despite the prospect that the defendant could suffer a total statutory penalty of $5 million.

Applying the *Hanna* test's first prong, the *Shady Grove* majority agreed that Federal Rule 23 "answer[ed] the question in dispute" and provided "a one-size-fits-all formula for deciding" the question before the Court.[86] On its face, the state statute attempted "to answer the same question."[87]

As for *Hanna*'s second prong, a plurality of the *Shady Grove* Court concluded that Rule 23 didn't violate the Rules Enabling Act or the Constitution.[88] The plurality applied the test first established in *Sibbach v. Wilson & Co.*[89] *Sibbach* held that the test of a federal rule's validity under the Rules Enabling Act is whether the rule "really regulates procedure"—that is, "the judicial process for enforcing rights and duties recognized by substantive law and for justly administering remedy and redress for disregard or infraction of them."[90] The plurality explained that "it is not the substantive or procedural nature or purpose of the affected state law that matters, but the substantive or procedural nature of the Federal Rule. We have held since *Sibbach*, and reaffirmed repeatedly, that the validity of a Federal Rule depends entirely upon whether it regulates procedure."[91] If it's procedural, the Court said, the Rules Enabling Act applies and the rule is "valid in all jurisdictions, with respect to all claims, regardless of its incidental effect upon state-created rights."[92]

---

86   *Id.* at 398–99.
87   *Id.* at 399.
88   *Id.* at 410, 416 (plurality opinion of Scalia J.).
89   *Id.* at 407 (quoting *Sibbach v. Wilson & Co.*, 312 U.S. 1, 14 (1941)).
90   *Sibbach*, 312 U.S. at 14.
91   *Shady Grove*, 559 U.S. at 410 (plurality opinion) (citations omitted).
92   *Id.*

On the second prong, Stevens J. concurred only in the judgment. He would have distinguished and limited *Sibbach*.[93] In his view, if a federal rule would displace a state rule that is "so intertwined with a state right or remedy that it functions to define the scope of the state-created right," then that federal rule violates the Rules Enabling Act.[94] In other words, Stevens J. sought to give greater effect to the Rules Enabling Act's requirement that no federal rule "abridge, enlarge or modify any substantive right."[95]

When analyzing the second prong—whether a federal rule violates the Rules Enabling Act or Constitution—the courts of appeals have divided over whether to follow the plurality opinion's *Sibbach*-based approach or Stevens J.'s reasoning.[96] We believe that the most prudential resolution of the problem was announced by the D.C. Circuit in a case in which it applied *Shady Grove*:

> So four Justices adopted one formulation. One Justice adopted a different formulation. And four Justices did not address the question. What should we do in the face of such an unresolved 4–1 disagreement? Neither the 4-Justice view nor the 1-Justice view on its own is binding in these unusual circumstances. Moreover, neither opinion can be considered the *Marks* middle ground or narrowest opinion, as the four Justices in dissent simply did not address the issue. *See generally Marks v. United States*, 430 U.S. 188 (1977); *cf. United States v. Duvall*, 740 F.3d 604, 609–11 (D.C. Cir. 2013) (Kavanaugh, J., concurring). In addition, on the precise question before us—whether the governing standard is still the *Sibbach* standard of "really regulates procedure" or instead something else—no common conclusion was articulated by the 4-Justice opinion and the 1-Justice opinion. Therefore, the answer for us, in these particular circumstances, is to follow the Supreme Court's pre-existing precedent

---

93 *Id.* at 427–28 (Stevens J. concurring in part & concurring in the judgment); *cf. id.* at 412 (plurality opinion) ("In reality, the concurrence seeks not to apply *Sibbach*, but to overrule it (or, what is the same, to rewrite it).").

94 *Id.* at 423 (Stevens J. concurring in part & concurring in the judgment).

95 28 U.S.C. § 2072(b).

96 *See, e.g., Knepper v. Rite Aid Corp.*, 675 F.3d 249, 265 (3d Cir. 2012) (applying both *Shady Grove* tests); *Godin v. Schencks*, 629 F.3d 79, 87–90 (1st Cir. 2010) (suggesting that Stevens J.'s concurrence would govern); *Retained Realty, Inc. v. McCabe*, 376 F. App'x 52, 55 n.1 (2d Cir. 2010) (applying both *Shady Grove* tests).

in *Sibbach*. Unless and until the Supreme Court overrules or narrows its decision in *Sibbach*, that case remains good law and is binding on lower courts.[97]

Applications in penal law

Incorporating state law into federal statutes isn't limited to civil matters. The Assimilative Crimes Act, which governs the "special maritime and territorial jurisdiction of the United States,"[98] provides that a person "guilty of any act or omission which . . . would be punishable if committed or omitted within the jurisdiction of the State . . . in which such place is situated, by the laws thereof in force at the time of such act or omission, shall be guilty of a like offense and subject to a like punishment."[99] A similar statute applies to some offenses by "Indian[s]" in "Indian Country."[100] The Racketeer Influenced and Corrupt Organizations Act (RICO) imposes criminal (and civil) liability on those who engage in "racketeering activity," which includes various offenses "chargeable under State law and punishable by imprisonment for more than one year."[101]

State law is often the focus of litigation under the Armed Career Criminal Act[102] and similar sentencing guidelines promulgated by the U.S. Sentencing Commission,[103] which enhance penalties for those with histories of committing certain state crimes. Determining whether a state crime qualifies for enhancement often requires resolving the state-law issue of what the elements of the crime are.[104]

---

97 *Abbas*, 783 F.3d at 1336–37.
98 18 U.S.C. § 7 (internal quotation marks omitted).
99 *Id.* § 13(a).
100 *Id.* § 1153(b).
101 *Id.* § 1961(1)(A).
102 *Id.* § 924(e).
103 *See, e.g.*, U.S. Sentencing Guidelines Manual § 4B1.2(a).
104 *See, e.g.*, *Descamps v. United States*, 133 S.Ct. 2276, 2291–93 (2013).

An oddity explained

One result of *Erie* may seem peculiar. The same federal court (generally a circuit court of appeals) may state different legal rules in cases involving indistinguishable facts just because they arose in different states. A Florida contract may be construed differently from a Georgia contract with identical language. But before *Erie*, the identical Florida contract might be interpreted differently by two courts within that state—one federal and one state court. *Erie*, in the interest of federalism, chose vertical uniformity (among the courts in the same state) over horizontal uniformity (among federal courts in various states).

71. Superseding State Decisions

When a state-law question has been decided by a federal court in the preliminary stages of a lawsuit, and a contrary ruling is made by the state's high court on the same question before the federal court finally disposes of the case, the federal court will reverse its decision and conform to the judgment of the state court.

As we saw in the preceding section, the Supreme Court's *Erie* decision requires federal courts to resolve diversity cases (and other cases presenting state-law questions) by using state law rather than federal common law. But in *Erie*, there was no occasion "for discussing at what step in the cause the state law would be finally determined."[1] Most important, it was unclear how federal courts should treat changes to state law arising in their proceedings.

This ambiguity didn't long persist. Three years after *Erie*, in the 1941 case of *Vandenbark v. Owens-Illinois Glass Co.*, the Supreme Court held that federal circuit courts must "conform their orders to the state law *as of the time of the entry*."[2] If a state clarifies, alters, or overrules an earlier holding while a federal proceeding is ongoing, the federal court must change its ruling to conform to the transformed state-law landscape.[3]

In essence, the *Vandenbark* rule creates a commonsense exception to the law-of-the-case doctrine, which "posits that when a court decides upon a rule of law, that decision should continue to govern the same issues in subsequent stages in the same case."[4] The law-of-the-case doctrine generally requires district and appellate courts to follow their own legal conclusions in later stages of

---

1 *Vandenbark v. Owens-Illinois Glass Co.*, 311 U.S. 538, 540 (1941).
2 *Id.* at 543 (emphasis added).
3 *E.g., Harrow Prods., Inc. v. Liberty Mut. Ins. Co.*, 64 F.3d 1015, 1025–26 (6th Cir. 1995) (reversing a district-court holding based on earlier circuit interpretation of Michigan law in light of intervening and contrary decision of the Michigan Supreme Court); *see Michigan Millers Mut. Ins. Co. v. Bronson Plating Co.*, 519 N.W.2d 864 (Mich. 1994).
4 *Pepper v. United States*, 562 U.S. 476, 506 (2011) (quoting *Arizona v. California*, 460 U.S. 605, 618 (1983), *decision supplemented*, 466 U.S. 144 (1984)).

the same litigation (see §§ 52–59). But when that doctrine would force a federal court to bind itself to a defunct interpretation of state law, *Vandenbark* instructs the court not to follow the law of the case. It instead requires the federal court to alter its legal conclusions to comply with the most recent articulation of state law.

The *Vandenbark* rule isn't a matter of discretion. The Supreme Court has stated that federal courts have a "duty" to revise decisions "in accordance with the then controlling" state law.[5] This duty extends "until such time as a case is no longer" under judicial consideration.[6]

A change in state law need not be dramatic or definitive to warrant reconsideration. In 1944, the Supreme Court vacated and remanded a decision of the Tenth Circuit when the Oklahoma Supreme Court issued an intervening decision that "at least raised . . . doubt as to the applicable Oklahoma law."[7]

Federal circuit courts most often apply *Vandenbark* when reviewing district-court determinations of state law that were correct when entered, but were superseded before appellate review.[8] But it can also be invoked in a variety of other procedural postures. For instance, federal circuit courts apply *Vandenbark* when new state law arises between separate phases of the appellate proceeding. In a 1970 case,[9] for example, the Second Circuit suspended several rules of its own procedure to accommodate a revision in state law.[10] It granted petitioners' motion for rehearing even after the time to file such a petition had run and even after petitioners

---

5   *Vandenbark*, 311 U.S. at 543.

6   *Id.*

7   *Huddleston v. Dwyer*, 322 U.S. 232, 236 (1944) (per curiam).

8   *See, e.g., Air Prods. & Chems., Inc. v. Hartford Accident & Indem. Co.*, 25 F.3d 177, 181 (3d Cir. 1994) (reversing because the Supreme Court of Pennsylvania altered the law relied on by the district court); *Riley v. Brown & Root, Inc.*, 896 F.2d 474, 477 (10th Cir. 1990) (finding it "incumbent on us to remand the case for reconsideration in light of" a recent state high-court case); *Baker v. Outboard Marine Corp.*, 595 F.2d 176, 182 (3d Cir. 1979) (finding that "the district court committed reversible error when it employed" a state-law proposition that was correct at the time but that was later overruled by the state high court).

9   *Braniff Airways, Inc. v. Curtiss-Wright Corp.*, 424 F.2d 427 (2d Cir. 1970).

10 *See id.* at 429–30.

had sought and been denied certiorari from the Supreme Court.[11] Hence courts of appeals must at times exercise procedural flexibility to ensure that cases within their jurisdiction reflect all relevant state law.

What if the state's high court declares the applicable state law after the federal judgment has become final? Ordinarily, the federal judgment stands. The general rule is that after the expiration of appellate review, a judgment cannot be corrected simply because it was based on an error of law. That applies also under *Erie*. As the Fifth Circuit stated: "[T]he fact that federal courts must follow state law when deciding a diversity case does not mean that a subsequent change in the law of the state will provide grounds for relief under Rule 60(b)(6)."[12] At least one circuit, however, has recognized a very narrow exception. The Tenth Circuit allowed a final judgment to be reopened when the intervening decision by the Oklahoma Supreme Court involved the very same motor-vehicle accident as the one before the federal court.[13] At least the Seventh Circuit has declined to follow the Tenth.[14]

Federal district courts also sometimes have occasion to apply *Vandenbark*. For example, in a lawsuit in the late 1970s,[15] a district court in Michigan, hearing a case on remand, modified an appellate ruling in light of an intervening state high-court decision.[16] The case involved a product-liability suit under Michigan law. The district court dismissed the suit because, in the absence of a definitive ruling from the Michigan Supreme Court, it predicted that Michigan would apply a three-year statute of limitations to the plaintiff's claim. The Sixth Circuit reversed. It predicted that Michigan would instead apply a four-year statute of limitations. After remand, but before the trial, the Michigan Supreme Court stated that a three-year statute of limitations applied to claims

---

11   *Id.* at 429.
12   *Batts v. Tow-Motor Forklift Co.*, 66 F.3d 743, 750 (5th Cir. 1995) (quoting *DeWeerth v. Baldinger*, 38 F.3d 1266, 1272–73 (2d Cir. 1994)).
13   *Pierce v. Cook & Co.*, 518 F.2d 720 (10th Cir. 1975).
14   *See Norgaard v. DePuy Orthopedics, Inc.*, 121 F.3d 1074, 1078 (7th Cir. 1997).
15   *Reid v. Volkswagen of Am., Inc.*, 575 F.2d 1175 (6th Cir. 1978) (per curiam).
16   *Id.* at 1176.

like the one at bar. On that basis, the district court dismissed the plaintiff's claim again, even though doing so required it to depart from the Sixth Circuit's ruling. The Sixth Circuit affirmed that second dismissal.[17]

As this case illustrates, if state law shifts after a federal circuit court has issued its decision, a district court on remand must still conform its interpretation to the law of the state.

Although the *Vandenbark* rule has been applied across the courts of appeals for decades, criticism has occasionally bubbled up, at least for certain applications of it. *Erie* typically requires federal courts to apply state law as a state court would. But Fifth and Ninth Circuit judges have pointed out that *Vandenbark* makes state-court judgments retroactive for litigants in federal court, even if they would not apply retroactively within the state's own courts. Because *Vandenbark* doesn't "contemplate an independent determination of whether the state will apply a change" retroactively,[18] its application can lead to the "anomalous result of giving a state court decision retroactive effect in federal court when the decision would be given only prospective application in the state's own courts."[19] Courts have resolved this tension with *Erie* in favor of *Vandenbark* and applied that case as a bright-line rule.[20]

---

17   *Id.*

18   *Nelson v. Brunswick Corp.*, 503 F.2d 376, 381 n.12 (9th Cir. 1974).

19   *Downs v. J.M. Huber Corp.*, 580 F.2d 794, 796 (5th Cir. 1978); *see also Nelson*, 503 F.2d at 381 n.12 (In cases in which a state would not retroactively apply its own rule, "the federal appellate court's application of the new rule will lead to a different result than would have resulted in a case pending in the state appellate courts.").

20   *Downs*, 580 F.2d at 796; *see also Nelson*, 503 F.2d at 381 n.12 (commenting that "we apply *Vandenbark* as a 'hard-and-fast' rule").

72. Which State's Law Governs

A federal court in a diversity case must follow the conflict-of-laws doctrine of the forum state to determine which state's substantive law applies to a state-law issue in the case. The same rule applies to a state-law claim before the federal court under supplemental jurisdiction. There is no clear rule, however, to determine which state's laws should govern when a state-law question comes before the federal court under its federal-question jurisdiction.

A state court doesn't necessarily apply the law of its own state when a dispute comes before it. If the dispute concerns a matter that it is appropriate to decide under the law of another state—such as the state where an accident occurred or a contract was signed or performed—the state court will apply the law of that state. The question whether to apply the law of another state falls under the doctrine of conflict of laws. Each state has its own doctrine, as does the federal judiciary. When a federal court must apply state law, it must first decide which state's law to apply. But what conflict-of-laws doctrine should it use?

In a diversity case, the established rule is that the federal court should apply the law of the state whose law would apply in the courts of the forum state (the state in which the federal court sits). That is, the federal court must apply the forum state's conflict-of-laws rules in deciding which state's substantive law governs the case. For example, if the federal court in Ohio has diversity jurisdiction over a contract dispute between two private litigants, it will apply the contract law of the state selected under Ohio's conflict-of-laws rules for contract cases. Depending on the specifics of the contract dispute, the federal court may end up applying Ohio contract law or the contract law of another state. This proposition was settled by the U.S. Supreme Court in *Klaxon Co. v. Stentor Electric Manufacturing Co.*[1] Stentor successfully sued Klaxon in the federal district court of Delaware for breaching a contract that had been executed and largely performed in New York. The district

---

[1] 313 U.S. 487 (1941).

court then awarded prejudgment interest under a New York statute. The circuit court, affirming the district court, applied the Restatement of Conflict of Laws in holding that the award of interest is part of the damages for breach of contract and should be assessed under the law of the place of the contract's performance. The Supreme Court, noting that the circuit court's decision had not cited or discussed any Delaware law on the subject, reversed and remanded for consideration of what law Delaware would have selected. Stating that *Erie*[2] controlled, the Court wrote: "The conflict of laws rules to be applied by the federal court in Delaware must conform to those prevailing in Delaware's state courts."[3] It explained that "any other ruling would do violence to the principle of uniformity within a state upon which the [*Erie*] decision is based."[4]

The *Klaxon* rule also applies to a state-law claim before the federal court under pendent or supplemental jurisdiction.[5]

The Supreme Court has announced an exception to the *Klaxon* rule. When the court trying a case has received it from a transferor court under 28 U.S.C. § 1404(a), which permits such a transfer "[f]or the convenience of parties and witnesses, in the interest of justice," the transferee court must apply the conflict-of-laws rules of the state of the transferor court.[6] The Supreme Court explained in *Atlantic Marine Construction Co. v. United States District Court*[7] that this exception is "necessary to prevent defendants, properly subjected to suit in the transferor State, from invoking § 1404(a) to gain the benefits of the laws of another jurisdiction."[8] Yet there's an exception to the exception when the transfer is required to enforce a valid contractual forum-selection clause. In that circumstance,

---

2   *Erie R.R. v. Tompkins*, 304 U.S. 64 (1938).

3   313 U.S. at 496.

4   *Id.*

5   *See Baltimore Orioles, Inc. v. Major League Baseball Players Ass'n*, 805 F.2d 663 (7th Cir. 1986) (collecting cases from the D.C., First, Second, Third, and Fourth Circuits).

6   *See Van Dusen v. Barrack*, 376 U.S. 612, 639 (1964).

7   134 S.Ct. 568 (2012).

8   *Id.* at 582 (quoting *Van Dusen*, 376 U.S. at 638) (brackets omitted).

the plaintiff who filed in the improper forum cannot benefit from breaching the contractual requirement.[9]

Less clear is whose conflict-of-laws rules apply when state substantive law governs in a case before the federal court under federal-question jurisdiction. The Supreme Court addressed the issue in *Richards v. United States*.[10] The issue was "what law a Federal District Court should apply in an action brought under the Federal Tort Claims Act [FTCA] where an act of negligence occurs in one state and results in an injury and death in another state."[11] A plane had departed from Tulsa, Oklahoma, and crashed in Missouri. The government's alleged negligence occurred in Tulsa. Under the FTCA, the government can be liable "if a private person would be liable to the claimant in accordance with the law of the place where the act or omission occurred."[12] The Court held that the "law" governing the claim must be the law of the state where the negligence occurred (Oklahoma, in that case) and that the "law" included that state's conflict-of-laws conflict-of-laws doctrine. Therefore, rather than applying Oklahoma's substantive law, the federal district court rightly applied Oklahoma's conflict-of-laws doctrine to determine which state's substantive laws governed the action (in that case, Missouri, where the injury and death had occurred).[13] Because the Court's analysis was based on the specific language of the FTCA, this rule should almost certainly be limited to litigation under that statute.

Lacking additional guidance from the Supreme Court, the circuit courts have arrived at varying formulations for determining which jurisdiction's conflict-of-laws rules to apply. The First, Sixth, and Eleventh Circuits consider the question a matter of federal common law.[14] Although a Fifth Circuit panel stated the

---

9   *See id.* at 583.
10 369 U.S. 1 (1962).
11 *Id.* at 2.
12 28 U.S.C. § 1346(b).
13 *See Richards*, 369 U.S. at 11–12, 15–16.
14 *See Edelmann v. Chase Manhattan Bank*, 861 F.2d 1291, 1294 n.14 (1st Cir. 1988); *Boggio v. USAA Fed. Sav. Bank*, 696 F.3d 611, 620–21 (6th Cir. 2012); *Medical*

same proposition,[15] the en banc court vacated the decision on other grounds.[16] By contrast, the Tenth Circuit has said in an ERISA case that "[a] federal court adjudicating state law claims must apply the forum state's choice of law principles."[17] The Eighth Circuit, meanwhile, has said: "The bankruptcy court applies the choice of law rules of the state in which it sits."[18] The Fourth Circuit had adopted an intermediate position, writing that "in the absence of a compelling federal interest which dictates otherwise, the *Klaxon* rule should prevail where the federal bankruptcy court seeks to determine the extent of a debtor's property interest."[19]

The Second, Third, Seventh, and Ninth Circuits appear inconsistent on the matter. The Second Circuit decided to apply the forum state's conflict-of-laws rules after deciding that doing so best accords with congressional purpose in the Foreign Sovereign Immunities Act.[20] But a decade earlier it had written: "This is a federal question case, . . . and it is appropriate that we apply a federal common law choice of law rule in order to decide which of the concerned jurisdiction's substantive law of fraud . . . should govern."[21] The Third Circuit said in 2000 that "[t]he appropriate choice-of-law rule to be applied is controlled by the basis for federal jurisdiction" and applied the federal rule in an admiralty case.[22] But in 1987, the circuit had applied the forum state's choice-of-law rules for a third-party action for contribution arising out

---

Mut. of Ohio v. deSoto, 245 F.3d 561, 570 (6th Cir. 2001); *Nguyen v. J.P. Morgan Chase Bank*, 709 F.3d 1342, 1345 (11th Cir. 2013) (per curiam).

15 *Halkias v. General Dynamics Corp.*, 31 F.3d 224, 236–37 (5th Cir. 1994).

16 *Halkias v. General Dynamics Corp.*, 56 F.3d 27 (5th Cir. 1995) (per curiam).

17 *Dang v. UNUM Life Ins. Co.*, 175 F.3d 1186, 1190 (10th Cir. 1999).

18 *In re Payless Cashways*, 203 F.3d 1081, 1084 (8th Cir. 2000).

19 *In re Merritt Dredging Co.*, 839 F.2d 203, 206 (4th Cir. 1988).

20 *Barkanic v. General Admin. of Civil Aviation of the People's Republic of China*, 923 F.2d 957, 959 (2d Cir. 1991); *accord Bank of N.Y. v. Yugoimport*, 745 F.3d 599, 608–09 (2d Cir. 2014).

21 *Corporacion Venezolana de Fomento v. Vintero Sales Corp.*, 629 F.2d 786, 795 (2d Cir. 1980).

22 *Calhoun v. Yamaha Motor Corp. U.S.A.*, 216 F.3d 338, 343–45 (3d Cir. 2000); *see also Gluck v. Unisys Corp.*, 960 F.2d 1168, 1179 n.8 (3d Cir. 1992).

of a claim under the Federal Employers' Liability Act.[23] The Seventh Circuit said in a § 1983 case that the federal district court in Wisconsin should use that state's choice-of-law rules to decide which state's personal-injury statute of limitations to apply.[24] But three years earlier it had repeated the "general maxim that, when state law is borrowed in a *federal* question suit, the choice of which state law to select is itself a question of *federal* law."[25] As for the Ninth Circuit, in 2011 it wrote that "[a] federal court applying state substantive law is bound to follow the choice-of-law rules of the forum state" when addressing claims under the federal Real Estate Settlement Procedures Act and the Fair Credit Reporting Act.[26] But in an earlier case, it had said that "[i]n federal question cases with exclusive jurisdiction in federal court, such as bankruptcy, the court should apply federal, not forum state, choice of law rules," because there is no possibility of forum-shopping between state and federal courts.[27] Lawyers should be alert to the issue.

---

23 *Shields v. Consolidated Rail Corp.*, 810 F.2d 397, 399 (3d Cir. 1987).
24 *Malone v. Corrections Corp. of Am.*, 553 F.3d 540, 542–43 (7th Cir. 2009).
25 *Berger v. AXA Network LLC*, 459 F.3d 804, 810 (7th Cir. 2006) (quoting *Resolution Trust Corp. v. Chapman*, 29 F.3d 1120, 1124 (7th Cir. 1994)) (brackets omitted).
26 *Johnson v. Wells Fargo Home Mortg., Inc.*, 635 F.3d 401, 420 n.16 (9th Cir. 2011).
27 *In re Lindsay*, 59 F.3d 942, 948 (9th Cir. 1995). *See generally* Note, *Applicability of State Conflicts Rules When Issues of State Law Arise in Federal Question Cases*, 68 Harv. L. Rev. 1212 (1955).

73. Predicting State Law

When a question of state law must be resolved by a federal court, and there is no decision by the highest state court, the federal court must predict how the high court would decide the issue, relying on the same clues that would be used by the state's lower courts and following decisions of the state's intermediate appellate courts unless there is good reason to believe that the high court would not agree.

Once the federal court has determined which state's substantive law governs the case before it, how does it determine what that law is? *Erie* itself didn't resolve the issue. In that seminal case, the U.S. Supreme Court declared that "[e]xcept in matters governed by the Federal Constitution or by acts of Congress, the law to be applied in any case is the law of the state" as set by state statute or a state high-court decision.[1] We're informed only that a decision by the state's high court settles state law.

The Supreme Court has repeatedly emphasized the primacy of state high courts in construing state statutes. As early as 1879, the Supreme Court explained that if its own earlier opinion "is at variance with the decision" of a state court "construing her own statute, we must follow the latter."[2] If no authoritative state-high-court construction of a state statute exists, federal courts may use all the tools for ascertaining state law that the following chapters describe (see §§ 74–75).

The Supreme Court has reiterated on many occasions that "the highest court of the state is the final arbiter of what is state law," adding: "When it has spoken, its pronouncement is to be accepted by federal courts as defining state law unless it has later given clear and persuasive indication that its pronouncement will be modified, limited or restricted."[3]

---

1   *Erie R.R. v. Tompkins*, 304 U.S. 64, 78 (1938).
2   *Brooks v. Railway Co.*, 101 U.S. 443, 452 (1879).
3   *West v. AT&T Co.*, 311 U.S. 223, 236 (1940); *see, e.g.*, *Montana v. Wyoming*, 563 U.S. 368, 377 n.5 (2011) (quoting *West*); *Commissioner v. Estate of Bosch*, 387 U.S. 456, 465 (1967) (principle, frequently stated in diversity cases, that federal courts must follow "state law as announced by the highest court of the State"

Federal courts must occasionally interpret ambiguous state statutes or constitutional provisions before the state high court has done so. If the applicable state high court hasn't yet spoken, federal courts may use the state's certification procedure to ask for an authoritative construction[4] (see § 74). Or the federal court may instead predict how the state high court would rule, using the range of interpretive tools discussed in this section.[5]

Before turning to how the state's law should be determined in the absence of a holding by the state's high court, we mention the few, and relatively uncommon, issues concerning decisions of the state's high court itself.

First, there may be more than one high court in a state. In Texas and Oklahoma the last step in review for criminal cases is the court of criminal appeals rather than the state supreme court,

---

applies in federal-question cases in which "the underlying substantive rule involved is based on state law"); *Alabama State Fed'n of Labor v. McAdory*, 325 U.S. 450, 460 (1945) (Supreme Court lacked "any authoritative construction of the [state] statute by the state courts" and had no "authority to give such a controlling construction" itself); *City of Chicago v. Fieldcrest Dairies, Inc.*, 316 U.S. 168, 171–72 (1942) (state high court "has the final word" on state statutory question); *Union Pac. R.R. v. Board of Cnty. Comm'rs*, 247 U.S. 282, 287 (1918) ("The question is purely one of state law, and, so far as we are advised, the supreme court of the state has not passed on or considered it. A ruling by us on the question would neither settle it for that court nor be binding in an action to recover the tax if paid.").

[4] See, e.g., *Arizonans for Official English v. Arizona*, 520 U.S. 43, 76 (1997) (state certification statutes allow federal courts to put novel state-law questions directly to the state's high court).

[5] See, e.g., *Stenberg v. Carhart*, 530 U.S. 914, 945–46 (2000) (Supreme Court relied on its own interpretation of state law because certification wasn't appropriate); *Grayned v. City of Rockford*, 408 U.S. 104, 109–10 (1972) (if state high court failed to "elaborate on the meaning" of local ordinance, federal court must "extrapolate its allowable meaning" using statutory text and state high court's interpretations of analogous statutes) (quoting *Garner v. Louisiana*, 368 U.S. 157, 174 (1961)); *Fidelity Union Trust Co. v. Field*, 311 U.S. 169, 177 (1940) ("[I]t is still the duty of the federal courts, where the state law supplies the rule of decision, to ascertain and apply that law even though it has not been expounded by the highest court of the State.") (footnote omitted); *State Auto Prop. & Cas. Ins. Co. v. Hargis*, 785 F.3d 189, 195 (6th Cir. 2015) ("When the state's highest court has not spoken on the issue, the federal court is called upon to predict what that court would do if confronted with the question."); *Berrington v. Wal-Mart Stores, Inc.*, 696 F.3d 604, 608 (6th Cir. 2012) (if Michigan Supreme Court hasn't addressed issue, federal court must predict how it would rule).

so federal courts look to the courts of criminal appeals for the definitive construction of state criminal laws.[6]

Second, as we discussed in detail in § 71, the timing of the high-court decision can be important. The applicable state law may change before judgment is rendered by the federal district court. If the state's high court issues a decision changing the law while the case is still on direct review, the appellate court must apply the new law.[7]

Third, what is the effect of a decision by the state's high court to deny review? If the longtime rule of the U.S. Supreme Court is followed, the "denial of a writ of certiorari imports no expression of opinion upon the merits of the case."[8] Yet one must be alert to whether the same is true in state courts. In *West v. AT&T Co.*,[9] the Supreme Court thought it significant that "the highest court has refused to review the lower court's decision rendered in one phase of the very litigation which is now prosecuted by the same parties before the federal court."[10] The Third Circuit appeared to endorse that view in a case arising in Pennsylvania.[11] But a year later it expressed a different view, quoting a decision of the Pennsylvania Supreme Court to the effect that denial of review has no precedential value and simply lets "the lower tribunal's opinion and order stand as a decision of that court."[12] Similarly, the Eighth Circuit noted that a denial of review by the Minnesota Supreme Court had no effect on its analysis of Minnesota law.[13] But the

---

6   See, e.g., *United States v. Najera-Mendoza*, 683 F.3d 627, 633 n.10 (5th Cir. 2012) (looking to Oklahoma Court of Criminal Appeals); *United States v. Miranda-Ortegon*, 670 F.3d 661, 663 (5th Cir. 2012) (same); *United States v. Rose*, 587 F.3d 695, 704 (5th Cir. 2009) (per curiam) (looking to Texas Court of Criminal Appeals); *United States v. Smith*, 652 F.3d 1244, 1247 (10th Cir. 2011) (looking to Oklahoma Court of Criminal Appeals).

7   See *Vandenbark v. Owens-Illinois Glass Co.*, 311 U.S. 538 (1941).

8   *United States v. Carver*, 260 U.S. 482, 490 (1923); accord *Missouri v. Jenkins*, 515 U.S. 70, 85 (1995).

9   311 U.S. 223 (1949).

10   *Id.* at 237.

11   See *Sheridan v. NGK Metals Corp.*, 609 F.3d 239, 254 (3d Cir. 2010).

12   *Covell v. Bell Sports, Inc.*, 651 F.3d 357, 364 (3d Cir. 2011) (quoting *Commonwealth v. Tilghman*, 673 A.2d 898, 904 (Pa. 1996)).

13   *Haugen v. Total Petroleum, Inc.*, 971 F.2d 124, 126 n.2 (8th Cir. 1992).

Fifth Circuit in 1966 explained that under what was referred to as "rule certiorari" in Florida, the denial of a petition "was an affirmance of the [lower-court] order."[14] As for a grant of a petition for review, if the federal court doesn't deem it appropriate to await the decision by the state's high court, it may do as the Fourth Circuit has done and, by looking to the high court's affirmance rate, decide that the grant doesn't affect the precedential weight of the lower court's decision.[15]

Finally, even when there is a holding on point by the state's high court, the federal court may decline to follow it if it is confident that the state's high court will overrule its own precedent. The Supreme Court wrote in *Meredith v. City of Winter Haven*[16] that the rulings of the state's high court aren't controlling if "it can be said with some assurance that the [court] will not follow them in the future."[17] A decision by the Third Circuit exemplifies that exception to the general rule. In a 1980 case, the Third Circuit predicted that the Ohio Supreme Court would adopt the discovery rule for accrual of a medical-malpractice claim even though it had rejected the rule nine years earlier.[18] The prediction proved accurate.[19] But the exemption is rarely used. The Supreme Court has never applied or even repeated the "some assurance" standard in *Meredith*, and for the most part the federal circuits haven't been as adventurous as *McKenna*. The Tenth Circuit has written: "We do not believe that it is our position to predict that the New Mexico Supreme Court would overrule its precedent in the complete absence of any indication *from that court* of its inclination to do so."[20] Other circuits have also expressed reluctance to be too bold in predicting adoption of novel jurisprudence. The Fourth Circuit has admonished that "the federal courts sitting in diversity rule

---

14 *Miami Parts & Spring, Inc. v. Champion Spark Plug Co.*, 364 F.2d 957, 965–66 (5th Cir. 1966).
15 *See Assicurazioni Generali, S.p.A. v. Neil*, 160 F.3d 997, 1003–04 (4th Cir. 1998).
16 320 U.S. 228 (1943).
17 *Id.* at 234.
18 *McKenna v. Ortho Pharm. Corp.*, 622 F.2d 657, 666–67 (3d Cir. 1980).
19 *See Oliver v. Kaiser Cmty. Health Found.*, 449 N.E.2d 438, 438–39 (Ohio 1983).
20 *AG Servs. of Am., Inc. v. Nielsen*, 231 F.3d 726, 735–36 (10th Cir. 2000).

upon state law as it exists and do not surmise or suggest its expansion."[21] The Fifth Circuit has repeatedly declared that its role is "not to create or modify" state law.[22] The Sixth Circuit has stated: "[F]ederal courts must be cautious when making pronouncements about state law and when given a choice between an interpretation of state law which reasonably restricts liability, and one which greatly expands liability, we should choose the narrower and more reasonable path."[23] The Seventh Circuit expressed a similar attitude when it wrote: "We take state law as it is rather than predicting novel developments."[24] And the Eighth Circuit warns itself: "As a federal court, our role in diversity cases is to interpret state law, not to fashion it."[25] Of course, a decision by the state high court interpreting a statute may no longer be binding after the legislature has amended the statute.[26]

When there's no case on point

The much more common problem in determining state law arises when there is no holding on point by the state's high court. In that circumstance, as the Supreme Court said in *Commissioner v. Estate of Bosch*,[27] the federal court proceeds in the same manner whether the state-law issue arises in a diversity case or in a case under federal law.[28] Although *Erie* didn't say how to proceed in the absence of a holding by the state's high court, in *King v. Order of United Commercial Travelers*,[29] the Supreme Court approved the

---

21 *Burris Chem., Inc. v. USX Corp.*, 10 F.3d 243, 247 (4th Cir. 1993).

22 *GE Capital Commercial, Inc. v. Worthington Nat'l Bank*, 754 F.3d 297, 303 (5th Cir. 2014) (quoting *Memorial Herman Healthcare Sys., Inc. v. Eurocopter Deutschland, GMBH*, 524 F.3d 676, 678 (5th Cir. 2008)).

23 *In re Darvocet, Darvon & Propoxyphene Prods. Liab. Litig.*, 756 F.3d 917, 937 (6th Cir. 2014) (quoting *Combs v. International Ins.*, 354 F.3d 568, 577 (6th Cir. 2004)) (second brackets and internal quotation marks omitted).

24 *Knight v. Enbridge Pipelines (FSP) LLC*, 759 F.3d 675, 678 (7th Cir. 2014).

25 *Wivell v. Wells Fargo Bank*, 773 F.3d 887, 896 (8th Cir. 2014) (quoting *Dannix Painting, LLC v. Sherwin–Williams Co.*, 732 F.3d 902, 905 (8th Cir. 2013)).

26 *See, e.g., Warner v. Gregory*, 415 F.2d 1345, 1346–47 (7th Cir. 1969).

27 387 U.S. 456 (1967).

28 *Id.* at 465.

29 333 U.S. 153 (1948).

approach of the federal circuit court "in proceeding to make its own determination of what the Supreme Court of South Carolina would probably rule in a similar case."[30] Every regional circuit court has now stated that when there is no decision on point by the state's high court, its task is "predicting" what that court would do.[31] This rule applies in criminal and civil contexts.[32] The lower federal courts lack the authority to expand state law.[33]

In large part the role of the federal court in "predicting" state law is similar to the role of an inferior appellate court in the state. As the Supreme Court stated in *Commissioner v. Estate of Bosch*,[34] a federal court predicting state law "may be said to be, in effect, sitting as a state court."[35] But there are differences. As we'll see, the federal court isn't bound by a decision of a lower state appellate court, even if stare decisis would bind that lower court.

One obvious source for predicting the decisions of the state's high court is its dicta. Wisdom J. of the Fifth Circuit stated the point memorably: "[The appellant] characterizes the [Mississippi

---

30   *Id.* at 160–61.

31   *See Showtime Entm't, LLC v. Town of Mendon*, 769 F.3d 61, 79 (1st Cir. 2014); *Giuffre Hyundai, Ltd. v. Hyundai Motor Am.*, 756 F.3d 204, 209 (2d Cir. 2014); *McKenna v. Ortho Pharm. Corp.*, 622 F.2d 657, 661 n.15 (3d Cir. 1980); *AGI Assocs., LLC v. City of Hickory*, 773 F.3d 576, 579 (4th Cir. 2014); *Wisznia Co. v. General Star Indem. Co.*, 759 F.3d 446, 448 (5th Cir. 2014); *In re Darvocet, Darvon & Propoxyphene Prods. Liab. Litig.*, 756 F.3d 917, 937 (6th Cir. 2014); *Cannon v. Burge*, 752 F.3d 1079, 1091 (7th Cir. 2014); *Hudson Specialty Ins. Co. v. Brash Tygr, LLC*, 769 F.3d 586, 591 (8th Cir. 2014); *Sinibaldi v. Redbox Automated Retail, LLC*, 754 F.3d 703, 706 (9th Cir. 2014); *Daitom, Inc. v. Pennwalt Corp.*, 741 F.2d 1569, 1574 (10th Cir. 1984); *Molinos Valle Del Cibao, C. por A. v. Lama*, 633 F.3d 1330, 1348 (11th Cir. 2011).

32   *See United States v. DeGasso*, 369 F.3d 1139, 1145 n.5 (10th Cir. 2004).

33   *Proctor & Gamble Co. v. Haugen*, 222 F.3d 1262, 1280 (10th Cir. 2000) (noting that "it is not our place to expand Utah state law beyond the bounds set by the Utah Supreme Court or, in the absence of Utah Supreme Court precedent, by the lower Utah courts") (citing *Sellers v. Allstate Ins. Co.*, 82 F.3d 350, 352 (10th Cir. 1996) ("Our duty [as a federal court sitting in diversity jurisdiction] is . . . to ascertain and 'apply the most recent statement of state law by the state's highest court.'")) (with *Sellers* quoting *Wood v. Eli Lilly & Co.*, 38 F.3d 510, 513 (10th Cir. 1994)); *Taylor v. Phelan*, 9 F.3d 882, 887 (10th Cir. 1993) ("As a federal court, we are generally reticent to expand state law without clear guidance from [the state's] highest court.").

34   387 U.S. 456 (1967).

35   *Id.* at 465.

Supreme Court's] statement as dictum and urges us to ignore it. We cannot do so. Under diversity jurisdiction, considered dictum stating how an issue is to be resolved is evidence we must consider in determining the most likely result to be reached" by the state's highest court.[36] With no other Mississippi decision on point, the court said, "we consider this plain and unconditioned statement by the [Mississippi] Court to be convincing evidence of the likely result under Mississippi law."[37] But as we know, not all dicta are equal (see § 4).

Another factor high on the list should be intermediate appellate-court decisions from the state, as the Supreme Court wrote just two years after deciding *Erie*: "Where an intermediate appellate state court rests its considered judgment upon the rule of law which it announces, that is a datum for ascertaining state law which is not to be disregarded by a federal court unless it is convinced by other persuasive data that the highest court of the state would decide otherwise."[38] But in a case in which the only decision or decisions squarely on point are from lower appellate courts (or, worse, trial courts) and seem to point in an arguably different direction from what the high court would take on the matter, the federal court may take a different view, based on its own analysis of why the high court would disagree with its own lower courts.[39]

---

36 *Thomas v. Hoffman-LaRoche, Inc.*, 949 F.2d 806, 812 (5th Cir. 1992).

37 *Id.*

38 *West v. AT&T Co.*, 311 U.S. 223, 237 (1940).

39 *See, e.g., Ray Indus., Inc. v. Liberty Mut. Ins. Co.*, 974 F.2d 754, 763–64 (6th Cir. 1992) (federal court convinced that Michigan Supreme Court would not follow intermediate-court decision on meaning of *suit* in insurance contract); *R.W. Murray Co. v. Shatterproof Glass Corp.*, 697 F.2d 818, 828–29 (8th Cir. 1983) (declining to follow a Missouri Court of Appeals decision because other Missouri state-court decisions, including a Missouri Supreme Court decision on a similar matter, provided "persuasive data that the highest court of the state would decide otherwise") (quoting *West*, 311 U.S. at 236–37) (internal citations omitted); *Safeco Ins. Co. of Am. v. Wetherill*, 622 F.2d 685, 690–91 (3d Cir. 1980) (declining to follow a decision of the Superior Court of Pennsylvania and instead "mak[ing] an independent judgment as to what the decision of the highest court in Pennsylvania would be"). *But see Assicurazioni Generali, S.p.A. v. Neil*, 160 F.3d 997, 1003 (4th Cir. 1998) ("Generally, only if the decision of a state's intermediate court cannot be reconciled with state statutes, or decisions of the state's highest court, or both, may a federal court sitting in diversity refuse to follow it.").

Federal courts have also noted many other means of predicting what a state's high court would do. For example, the First Circuit advised that "the federal court should consult the types of sources that the state's highest court would be apt to consult, including analogous opinions of that court, decisions of lower courts in the state, precedents and trends in other jurisdictions, learned treatises, and considerations of sound public policy."[40] In addition, the federal court should "pay particular attention to sources cited approvingly by the state's highest court in other opinions."[41] In deciding that the state court would enforce a contract to negotiate, the court noted that the clear majority of other jurisdictions had "recognized the enforceability of contracts to negotiate" and that "the trend line appear[ed] to be moving steadily" in that direction.[42]

Similarly, the Third Circuit says about making its prediction: "[W]e are not inflexibly confined by dicta or by lower state court decisions, although we should look to such statements as indicia of how the state's highest court might decide."[43] Rather, "[t]he policies underlying the applicable legal doctrines, the doctrinal trends indicated by these policies, and the decisions of other courts may also inform our analysis. In addition, we may consult treatises, the Restatement, and the works of scholarly commentators."[44]

And in predicting Mississippi law, the Fifth Circuit will rely on (1) Mississippi Supreme Court decisions in analogous cases, (2) the reasoning supporting those decisions, (3) the court's dicta relevant to the issue, (4) lower Mississippi state-court decisions,

---

40 *Butler v. Balolia*, 736 F.3d 609, 613 (1st Cir. 2013) (citations omitted).

41 *Id.*

42 *Id.* at 614.

43 *Pennsylvania Glass Sand Corp. v. Caterpillar Tractor Co.*, 652 F.2d 1165, 1167 (3d Cir. 1981) (citation omitted); *cf. Spence v. ESAB Grp., Inc.*, 623 F.3d 212, 216–17 (3d Cir. 2010) (stating that the court looks to "decisions of state intermediate appellate courts, of federal courts interpreting that state's law, and of other state supreme courts that have addressed the issue," as well as to "analogous decisions, considered dicta, scholarly works, and any other reliable data tending convincingly to show how the highest court in the state would decide the issue at hand") (quoting *Norfolk Southern Ry. v. Basell USA Inc.*, 512 F.3d 86, 92 (3d Cir. 2008)).

44 *Pennsylvania Glass Sand Corp.*, 652 F.2d at 1167.

(5) general rules on the issue, (6) rulings from other states that Mississippi courts historically look to when formulating substantive law, and (7) treatises, legal commentaries, and other available sources.[45]

In one decision, the Sixth Circuit appears to ascribe a greater degree of importance to decisions by intermediate state appellate courts: "[I]f . . . the only precedent is from the state's intermediate appellate courts, the intermediate court's decision should be followed absent a strong showing that the state supreme court would act in a different manner."[46]

The Ninth Circuit makes its prediction "using intermediate appellate court decisions, decisions from other jurisdictions, statutes, treatises and restatements for guidance."[47] In the absence of any of those sources, the court "focuses on the language of the statute itself."[48] When there is no pertinent law from the legislature or courts of the state, the Ninth Circuit looks to general legal principles.[49] The Tenth Circuit "seek[s] guidance from decisions rendered by lower courts in the relevant state, appellate decisions in other states with similar legal principles, district court decisions interpreting the law of the state in question, and the general weight and trend of authority in the relevant area of law."[50] When the courts of Colorado had repeatedly relied on an earlier version of the Restatement of Restitution and the rule stated in the present version had been adopted by a substantial majority of jurisdictions, the Tenth Circuit predicted that Colorado would follow the present version of the Restatement.[51]

---

45 *Avakian v. Citibank, N.A.*, 773 F.3d 647, 650 (5th Cir. 2014) (quoting *Centennial Ins. Co. v. Ryder Truck Rental, Inc.*, 149 F.3d 378, 382 (5th Cir. 1998)).
46 *Derungs v. Wal-Mart Stores, Inc.*, 374 F.3d 428, 433 (6th Cir. 2004).
47 See *Sinibaldi v. Redbox Automated Retail, LLC*, 754 F.3d 703, 706 (9th Cir. 2014) (quoting *Alliance for Prop. Rights & Fiscal Responsibility v. City of Idaho Falls*, 742 F.3d 1100, 1102 (9th Cir. 2013)).
48 *Id.*
49 See *American Triticale, Inc. v. Nytco Servs., Inc.*, 664 F.2d 1136, 1142 (9th Cir. 1981) (citing the Restatement (Second) of Conflict of Laws).
50 *Wade v. EMCASCO Ins.*, 483 F.3d 657, 666 (10th Cir. 2007) (citations and internal quotation marks omitted).
51 *Van Zanen v. Qwest Wireless, LLC*, 522 F.3d 1127, 1132 (10th Cir. 2008).

Deference to state agencies, intermediate courts

One source of authority may be decisions of state administrative agencies. Federal courts regularly defer to an administrative agency's interpretation of a statute that it administers,[52] and state courts may do the same. When they do, a federal court should also defer to an agency decision. For example, noting that New York's high court had said "that the construction given statutes and regulations by the agency responsible for their administration, if not irrational or unreasonable, should be upheld," the Second Circuit showed the same deference in interpreting New York law.[53] Other federal circuits have done the same.[54] Similarly, an authoritative opinion by the state attorney general may be persuasive.[55]

A federal court may look to how federal courts, circuit and district, interpret a state's law. The Sixth Circuit has stated: "While not binding, this Court may turn to decisions of its sister circuits and lower federal courts interpreting state law for guidance."[56]

One permissible and often-used source when there is no high-court precedent is decisions by the state's intermediate appellate courts. These provide data that a federal court should consider closely unless there is good reason to believe that the state's high court would embark on a different course.[57] The Supreme Court

---

52 *See generally Chevron, U.S.A., Inc. v. Natural Res. Def. Council, Inc.*, 467 U.S. 837 (1984).

53 *Ramos v. SimplexGrinnell LP*, 740 F.3d 852, 856 (2d Cir. 2014) (quoting *Samiento v. World Yacht Inc.*, 883 N.E.2d 990, 995 (N.Y. 2008)).

54 *See, e.g., Knuth v. Erie-Crawford Dairy Co-op*, 463 F.2d 470, 483 (3d Cir. 1972); *Estate of Dancy v. Commissioner*, 872 F.2d 84, 85 (4th Cir. 1989); *Dickinson v. First Nat'l Bank*, 400 F.2d 548, 557–58 (5th Cir. 1968); *Ernie Haire Ford, Inc. v. Ford Motor Co.*, 260 F.3d 1285, 1293 n.7 (11th Cir. 2001).

55 *See, e.g., Harris Cnty. Comm'rs Court v. Moore*, 420 U.S. 77, 87 n.10 (1975); *FDIC v. Municipality of Ponce*, 904 F.2d 740, 746–47 (1st Cir. 1990); *Huggins v. Isenbarger*, 798 F.2d 203, 209 (7th Cir. 1986) (per curiam); *Barks v. Armontrout*, 872 F.2d 237, 239 (8th Cir. 1989).

56 *In re Darvocet, Darvon & Propoxyphene Prods. Liab. Litig.*, 756 F.3d 917, 937 (6th Cir. 2014).

57 *West v. AT&T Co.*, 311 U.S. 223, 237 (1940).

originated and affirmed this principle in 1940 over four back-to-back cases.[58] It remains good law today.[59]

Federal courts tend to presume that a state's high court would agree with decisions of the intermediate appellate courts.[60] A federal court may find the decision by an intermediate appellate court dispositive even when it isn't on all fours but is closely on point.[61] The Fourth Circuit has suggested that deference is particularly appropriate in jurisdictions such as North Carolina because the North Carolina Court of Appeals is a court of statewide jurisdiction in which the panel opinions bind all other panels and its decisions are binding on the state trial courts when they don't conflict with North Carolina Supreme Court decisions.[62]

But if the court has good reason to believe that the state high court would adopt a different rule, the federal court may do so as

---

58 *See id.*; *Six Companies of Cal. v. Joint Highway Dist. No. 13*, 311 U.S. 180, 188 (1940); *Stoner v. New York Life Ins. Co.*, 311 U.S. 464, 467 (1940); *Fidelity Union Trust Co. v. Field*, 311 U.S. 169, 177–78 (1940).

59 *See, e.g., Schoenefeld v. New York*, 748 F.3d 464, 469 (2d Cir. 2014) (quoting *Statharos v. New York City Taxi & Limousine Comm'n*, 198 F.3d 317, 321 (2d Cir. 1999)); *Pacific Emp'rs Ins. Co. v. Global Reinsurance Corp.*, 693 F.3d 417, 433 (3d Cir. 2012) (same); *Hayes v. County of San Diego*, 658 F.3d 867, 872 (9th Cir. 2011) (same); *Commonwealth Prop. Advocates, LLC v. Mortgage Elec. Registration Sys., Inc.*, 680 F.3d 1194, 1204 (10th Cir. 2011) (same); *Bravo v. United States*, 577 F.3d 1324, 1325–26 (11th Cir. 2009) (per curiam) (same); *MRCO, Inc. v. Juarbe-Jimenez*, 521 F.3d 88, 95 n.5 (1st Cir. 2008) (same); *Waremart Foods v. NLRB*, 354 F.3d 870, 876 (D.C. Cir. 2004) (same).

60 *See Waremart Foods*, 354 F.3d at 876; *Candelario Del Moral v. UBS Fin. Servs. Inc.*, 699 F.3d 93, 103 n.7 (1st Cir. 2012); *Licci ex rel. Licci v. Lebanese Canadian Bank, SAL*, 739 F.3d 45, 48 (2d Cir. 2013) (per curiam); *In re Makowka*, 754 F.3d 143, 148 (3d Cir. 2014); *AGI Assocs., LLC v. City of Hickory*, 773 F.3d 576, 579 (4th Cir. 2014); *Coastal Agric. Supply, Inc. v. J.P. Morgan Chase Bank*, 759 F.3d 498, 509–10 (5th Cir. 2014); *Standard Fire Ins. v. Ford Motor Co.*, 723 F.3d 690, 694 (6th Cir. 2013); *Wilson v. City of Chicago*, 758 F.3d 875, 880 (7th Cir. 2014); *First Tenn. Bank Nat'l Ass'n v. Pathfinder Expl., LLC*, 754 F.3d 489, 490–91 (8th Cir. 2014); *Muniz v. United Parcel Serv.*, 738 F.3d 214, 219 (9th Cir. 2013); *Commonwealth Prop. Advocates, LLC*, 680 F.3d at 1204; *Winn-Dixie Stores, Inc. v. Dolgencorp, LLC*, 746 F.3d 1008, 1021 (11th Cir. 2014).

61 *See, e.g., American Triticale, Inc. v. Nytco Servs., Inc.*, 664 F.2d 1136, 1143 (9th Cir. 1981).

62 *See Lynch v. Universal Life Church*, 775 F.2d 576, 580 (4th Cir. 1985); *see also United States v. Vann*, 660 F.3d 771, 777 (4th Cir. 2011) (en banc) (per curiam) (King J. concurring).

well.⁶³ What counts as "persuasive data" for declining to follow an intermediate court's ruling? Federal courts have considered a variety of factors in determining whether to reject a particular opinion as not indicating how the state's high court would rule.

When a state's intermediate courts disagree among themselves, the federal court must reject at least one opinion. When the Fourth Circuit confronted a conflict between decisions issued by two different panels of the North Carolina Court of Appeals, the court considered other authorities to reconstruct how it thought the North Carolina Supreme Court would resolve that conflict.⁶⁴ Similarly, when faced with conflicting opinions in Texas, the Fifth Circuit chose the opinion that was the most thorough and well reasoned in applying an asserted statutory defense: it accorded with many other persuasive authorities.⁶⁵ The Ninth Circuit felt itself bound by an interpretation adopted by a majority of California courts and noted that the majority view was the one adopted in most other states.⁶⁶ In another case, the Ninth Circuit rejected three recent opinions by California's intermediate appellate courts because (1) they departed from an earlier appellate decision considered the seminal authority on the subject; (2) two of the three decisions were critical of the first one but felt bound to follow it; and (3) the decisions were contrary to general principles established by the California Supreme Court.⁶⁷

Occasionally, even when an opinion by a state intermediate appellate court isn't contradicted by a coequal court, a federal court refuses to follow it. For example, in a lawsuit by shareholders who dissented from a corporate merger and sought evaluation of their shares, the Eighth Circuit in a 2001 case⁶⁸ declined to follow the precedents of Missouri intermediate appellate courts that

---

63   *West*, 311 U.S. at 237.
64   *See Sanderson v. Rice*, 777 F.2d 902, 907 (4th Cir. 1985).
65   *See GE Capital Commercial, Inc. v. Worthington Nat'l Bank*, 754 F.3d 297, 313 (5th Cir. 2014).
66   *See In re Kirkland*, 915 F.2d 1236, 1239–40 (9th Cir. 1990).
67   *Owen v. United States*, 713 F.2d 1461, 1465–66 (9th Cir. 1983).
68   *Swope v. Siegel-Robert, Inc.*, 243 F.3d 486 (8th Cir. 2001).

had permitted minority and marketability discounts in valuing shares.[69] The court explained that it found Delaware's decisions persuasive because of that state's judicial expertise in the field, and specifically the Delaware Supreme Court's reasoning in a seminal case on the specific subject of minority and marketability discounts. It noted also that only one contrary decision had issued in another state and concluded that the Missouri Supreme Court would follow the current trend of disallowing discounts.[70]

When a federal court rejects an erroneous decision

A federal court may also reject what it finds to be a flawed opinion. The Second Circuit refused to follow a lower appellate court because it thought that the court had misinterpreted a precedent of the state's high court.[71] The Seventh Circuit was unpersuaded by an intermediate-appellate-court decision because, in its view, the decision was "contrary to the clear intent of the statute."[72] The Third Circuit ruled that a recent opinion of a Pennsylvania intermediate appellate court interpreting a statute wasn't binding because it was internally inconsistent, conflicted with the statute's text and structure, and "contraven[ed] a fundamental precept of Pennsylvania law."[73] It also declined to follow an intermediate appellate court's guidance that appeared in dictum because it had no foundation in New Jersey caselaw.[74] The Third Circuit had declared that an intermediate court's articulation of a statute's interpretation in dictum wasn't alone sufficient justification to depart from the court's judgment,[75] but that dictum without solid reasoning behind it can be sufficient.[76] The Ninth Circuit did the same, on the ground that "the text of the statute is 'persuasive

---

69   *Id.* at 496–97.

70   *Id.*

71   *Licci ex rel. Licci v. Lebanese Canadian Bank, SAL*, 739 F.3d 45, 48–51 (2d Cir. 2013).

72   *McGeshick v. Choucair*, 9 F.3d 1229, 1234 (7th Cir. 1993).

73   *In re Makowka*, 754 F.3d 143, 148 (3d Cir. 2014).

74   *National Sur. Corp. v. Midland Bank*, 551 F.2d 21, 31 (3d Cir. 1977).

75   *See Metropolitan Life Ins. v. Chase*, 294 F.2d 500, 505 (3d Cir. 1961).

76   *National Sur. Corp.*, 551 F.2d at 31.

data' that the California Court of Appeal misinterpreted [the statute]."[77] It also refused to follow dictum of an intermediate appellate court because it thought the court's analysis to be ill-considered.[78] Likewise, the Tenth Circuit departed somewhat from a decision by the Colorado Court of Appeals because of the prevailing view in other jurisdictions, the purposes of the insurance-policy provision at issue, and the law expressed by Colorado courts on related issues.[79]

The Supreme Court has provided guidance on using the decisions of lower state courts other than intermediate appellate courts. In *Fidelity Union Trust Co. v. Field*,[80] the Court held that the Third Circuit ordinarily had to follow the decisions of the New Jersey Court of Chancery, a court of original jurisdiction, in determining what the New Jersey Supreme Court would do.[81] It pointed out that the chancery court had statewide jurisdiction and standing (in equity cases) comparable to that of the state's intermediate appellate courts, its uniform rulings were seldom set aside by a higher court, and its decrees were ordinarily treated as binding in chancery cases.[82] In short, the chancery court's decisions had significant authority in New Jersey law.

Not all state courts have such status. In *King v. Order of United Commercial Travelers*,[83] the Supreme Court expressed skepticism about extending deference to the decisions of state trial courts. The only relevant case was from the South Carolina Court of Common Pleas, and the Fourth Circuit had declined to follow the decision. The Supreme Court agreed—the ruling of the court of common pleas wasn't binding on other trial courts and wasn't

---

77 *American Tower Corp. v. City of San Diego*, 763 F.3d 1035, 1047 (9th Cir. 2014).
78 *Doggett v. United States*, 858 F.2d 555, 562 n.4 (9th Cir. 1988).
79 *Greystone Constr., Inc. v. National Fire & Marine Ins.*, 661 F.3d 1272, 1282–90 (10th Cir. 2011).
80 311 U.S. 169 (1940).
81 *Id.* at 177–79.
82 *Id.* at 178–79; *see also King v. Order of United Commercial Travelers*, 333 U.S. 153, 159 (1948).
83 333 U.S. 153.

a final expression of South Carolina law.[84] Trial-court decisions were not published or digested and were filed only in the county of the trial, or were indexed only by the litigants' names, so they were not readily available to the bench and bar. The South Carolina Chief Justice had submitted a certificate that decisions of the trial courts were not precedent.[85] The Court explained that a federal court "adjudicating a matter of state law" is "'in effect only another court of the State,' [and] it would be incongruous indeed to hold the federal court bound by a decision which would not be binding on any state court."[86]

Similarly, in *Commissioner v. Estate of Bosch*,[87] the Supreme Court refused to make the decision of a state trial court regarding property rights and interests under state law binding authority in a federal estate-tax controversy.[88] The Court wrote that under some circumstances, an intermediate state-appellate-court ruling doesn't bind federal courts. "It follows here then, that when the application of a federal statute is involved, the decision of a state trial court as to an underlying issue of state law should *a fortiori* not be controlling."[89]

King and *Estate of Bosch* are generally followed for trial courts. As stated by the Tenth Circuit: "A federal court need not follow state decisions which are not precedents in the state itself."[90] Similarly, the Second Circuit has said that "two unreported decisions by trial courts of general jurisdictions are not binding on us,"

---

84   *Id.* at 156–57.
85   *Id.* at 160.
86   *Id.* at 161 (quoting *Guaranty Trust Co. v. York*, 326 U.S. 99, 108 (1945)).
87   387 U.S. 456 (1967).
88   *Id.* at 456–57.
89   *Id.* at 465; *see also King*, 333 U.S. at 160–61; *Twin City Fire Ins. Co. v. Ben Arnold-Sunbelt Beverage Co.*, 433 F.3d 365, 370 (4th Cir. 2005); *Bryant v. Civiletti*, 663 F.2d 286, 292 n.15 (D.C. Cir. 1981).
90   *United States v. Wyoming Nat'l Bank*, 505 F.2d 1064, 1067 (10th Cir. 1974).

noting that the "decisions were not necessarily binding on other Connecticut courts."[91] Other circuits agree.[92]

What about a state's principles of interpretation, such as the state's rules of statutory construction? Those principles and rules may be set forth in state statutes or state-court decisions. A few (but not all) federal courts apply those state interpretive principles and rules when interpreting a state constitution or statutory decision.[93] Interpreting a Texas statute, the Fifth Circuit has said that it must "follow the same rules of construction that a Texas court would apply."[94] In that case, it applied the Texas Supreme Court's practice of using the "plain language of the statute" as the "starting point of [its] analysis."[95] The Ninth Circuit has similarly said that a federal court's obligation to "determine what meaning the state's high court would give to the law" requires only that a court "follow the state's rules of statutory interpretation."[96] The Fourth Circuit has stated the same.[97]

---

91 *Connecticut State Fed'n of Teachers v. Board of Educ. Members*, 538 F.2d 471, 485 (2d Cir. 1976).

92 *See Houbigant, Inc. v. Federal Ins.*, 374 F.3d 192, 199 (3d Cir. 2004); *Twin City Fire Ins. Co. v. Ben Arnold-Sunbelt Beverage Co.*, 433 F.3d 365, 370 (4th Cir. 2005); *Backar v. Western States Producing Co.*, 547 F.2d 876, 882 (5th Cir. 1977); *Bradley v. General Motors Corp.*, 512 F.2d 602, 605 (6th Cir. 1975); *Weisberg v. Powell*, 417 F.2d 388, 393 (7th Cir. 1969) (per curiam); *Hove v. Atchison*, 238 F.2d 819, 823 (8th Cir. 1956); *MGM Grand Hotel, Inc. v. Imperial Glass Co.*, 533 F.2d 486, 489 n.5 (9th Cir. 1976).

93 *See generally* Abbe R. Gluck, *Intersystemic Statutory Interpretation: Methodology as "Law" and the* Erie *Doctrine*, 120 Yale L.J. 1898 (2011).

94 *Forte v. Wal-Mart Stores, Inc.*, 780 F.3d 272, 277 (5th Cir. 2015) (quoting *Wright v. Ford Motor Co.*, 508 F.3d 263, 264 (5th Cir. 2007)).

95 *Id.*

96 *See Bass v. County of Butte*, 458 F.3d 978, 981 (9th Cir. 2006) (internal citations omitted). *But see Golden W. Ref. Co. v. SunTrust Bank*, 538 F.3d 1233, 1239 (9th Cir. 2008) (citing both federal and state precedent when applying the canon disfavoring surplusage in the interpretation of a state statute).

97 *See, e.g., Carolina Trucks & Equip., Inc. v. Volvo Trucks of N. Am., Inc.*, 492 F.3d 484, 489 (4th Cir. 2007) ("In construing a state law, we look to the rules of construction applied by the enacting state's highest court.").

Levels of deference

For several decades, federal circuit courts maintained different views regarding the level of deference to give to predictive judgments of district courts within the circuit regarding the content of state law. District-court judges sit in one state, whereas court-of-appeals judges are in circuits with numerous states. So some might think that district judges are better positioned to make predictions about what that state's high court might do. Some circuits therefore reviewed district-court predictions of state law using a deferential standard.[98] Others treated predictive judgments as core questions of law and reviewed them de novo.[99] In 1991, the Supreme Court resolved this circuit split, determining that a circuit court "should review de novo a district court's determination of state law."[100] In so holding, the Supreme Court rejected the idea that "district judges are better arbiters of unsettled state law because they have exposure to the judicial system of the State in which they sit."[101] Yet even when exercising de novo review, a circuit judge is likely to be cautious before overruling a decision on state law by a judge who draws on considerable experience with that state's law.

The Supreme Court will also review de novo a state-law determination by a federal circuit court. Reversing a ruling that a state statute wasn't severable, the Court wrote: "Our general presumption that courts of appeals correctly decide questions of state law reflects a judgment as to the utility of reviewing them in most

---

98   See, e.g., *Weiss v. United States*, 787 F.2d 518, 525 (10th Cir. 1986) ("Generally, we apply the clearly erroneous standard in reviewing a district court's grant of summary judgment on a legal question upon which the state's highest court has not ruled.").

99   See, e.g., *Craig v. Lake Asbestos of Quebec, Ltd.*, 843 F.2d 145, 148 (3d Cir. 1988).

100 *Salve Regina Coll. v. Russell*, 499 U.S. 225, 231 (1991) (italics omitted).

101 *Id.* at 235. *But see id.* at 241 (Rehnquist C.J. dissenting) (arguing that a "judge attempting to predict how a state court would rule must use not only his legal reasoning skills, but also his experiences and perceptions of judicial behavior in that State," which are better known to federal judges who live and sit in the state).

cases, not a belief that the courts of appeals have some natural advantage in this domain."[102]

The circuit courts remain divided about whether they should defer to another circuit that has already ruled on the state law of a state within the jurisdiction of that other circuit. In a 1981 case,[103] the Second Circuit said that when the circuit that covers the state in question "has essayed its own prediction of the course of state law on a question of first impression within that state, the federal courts of other circuits should defer to that holding" except in "the rare instance when it can be said with conviction that the pertinent court of appeals has disregarded clear signals emanating from the state's highest court."[104] Since that time, the circuits have debated the validity of that principle. The Second Circuit continues to defer to predictions of state law made by that state's federal circuit court.[105] But this approach (again, dating from 1981) hasn't gained favor elsewhere, perhaps because of the Supreme Court's 1991 decision[106] requiring de novo review of federal district courts' determinations of state law. The Seventh Circuit has urged caution. Because "federal court pronouncements on the content of state law inherently involve a significant intrusion on the prerogative of the state courts to control that development,"[107] the court noted, "conservatism is in order in relying on the practice of other jurisdictions, even in analogous cases."[108]

Sometimes the federal court cannot do much more than assume the role of the state's high court and make the soundest decision it can. Yet there is an alternative path. When the federal court has too much doubt about the proper course, it can often

---

102 *Leavitt v. Jane L.*, 518 U.S. 137, 145 (1996) (per curiam) (citation omitted).
103 *Factors Etc., Inc. v. Pro Arts, Inc.*, 652 F.2d 278 (2d Cir. 1981).
104 *Id.* at 283.
105 *See, e.g., Liberty Synergistics Inc. v. Microflo Ltd.*, 718 F.3d 138, 148 (2d Cir. 2013) (citing *Factors* to defer to Ninth Circuit's interpretation of California Anti-SLAPP statute).
106 *Salve Regina Coll. v. Russell*, 499 U.S. 225 (1991).
107 *Lexington Ins. v. Rugg & Knopp, Inc.*, 165 F.3d 1087, 1092 (7th Cir. 1999) (quoting *Todd v. Societe Bic, S.A.*, 21 F.3d 1402, 1416 (7th Cir. 1994) (Ripple J. dissenting)).
108 *Id.* at 1093.

simply ask the state's high court for help. Most states have now adopted laws permitting certification of questions of law. We turn to that practice now.

74. Certified Questions

If a federal court must rule on a question of unclear state law, and the state has a procedure in place for ruling on certified questions received from federal courts, the federal court has the option of certifying the question directly to the state high court.

When a federal court is presented with a tricky or nettlesome question of state law, the court may be tempted to ease its burden and avoid a conflict with the state courts by asking a state court to answer. But how and when should this be done?

Certification entails a formal request from the federal court to the state high court to resolve a specific question of state law. When the answer to a certified question is returned to a federal court, the federal court applies that answer as it would any binding state-high-court precedent.[1]

In our system of dual federalism, certification requires a reciprocal willingness. A state is under no obligation to accept a certified question. But most states now have a certification procedure. That is a relatively recent development. In 1945, Florida was the only state with a law authorizing its high court to accept certification.[2]

In the 1960s, some courts refused to answer questions certified to them by a federal court, whereas others responded.[3] Yet many states have since enacted statutes expressly allowing the high court of the state to answer certified questions from a federal

---

1 *Reinkemeyer v. SAFECO Ins. Co. of Am.*, 166 F.3d 982, 984 (9th Cir. 1999) (per curiam) ("We are bound by the answers of state supreme courts to certified questions just as we are bound by state supreme court interpretations of state law in other contexts.").

2 Rebecca A. Cochran, *Federal Court Certification of Questions of State Law to State Courts: A Theoretical and Empirical Study*, 29 J. Legis. 157, 159 n.12 (2003).

3 *Compare Leiter Minerals, Inc. v. California Co.*, 132 So. 2d 845, 849–50 (La. 1961), and *In re Richards*, 223 A.2d 827, 832 (Me. 1966), *with United Servs. Life Ins. Co. v. Delaney*, 396 S.W.2d 855, 861 (Tex. 1965).

court.[4] Almost all states now accept certification under at least some circumstances.[5]

The U.S. Supreme Court has endorsed the practice of certifying difficult questions of state law to the high court of the state when the state authorizes the practice. But for some time states didn't have certification laws, and the Supreme Court struggled with balancing the responsibility of the federal judiciary to exercise its jurisdiction with dispatch against the federalism interest in avoiding unnecessary conflicts with state courts.

Some history is in order. The Court's first venture into the arena was a brief opinion in *Railroad Commission of Texas v. Pullman Co.*,[6] a 1941 case the Court has since referred to as "generative."[7] The Commission had issued an order requiring that each railroad sleeping car be under the charge of a Pullman conductor. At the time, all conductors were white. Pullman had placed porters, who were all black, in charge of sleeping cars when there was only one such car on the train. Pullman, some railroads, and the porters sought an injunction against the order in federal court. They argued that the Commission had exceeded its state statutory authority and that the order violated several provisions of the federal Constitution. The three-judge district court enjoined the order's enforcement. The Supreme Court reversed and remanded, noting that the porters' claim of unconstitutional discrimination

---

4   *E.g.*, Ariz. Rev. Stat. Ann. § 12-1861 (1993) ("The supreme court may answer questions of law certified to it by [a federal court]."); Ga. Code Ann. § 15-2-9 (2005) ("[F]ederal court[s] may certify . . . questions of the laws of this state to the Supreme Court . . . , which certificate the Supreme Court of this state may answer by written opinion."); Tenn. Sup. Ct. R. 23, § 1 ("The Supreme Court may, at its discretion, answer questions of law certified to it by the Supreme Court of the United States."); Wash. Rev. Code § 2.60.020 (1965) ("[A] federal court may certify to the supreme court for answer the question of local law involved and the supreme court shall render its opinion in answer thereto.").

5   *See* Cochran, *Federal Court Certification*, 29 J. Legis. at 59 n.13 (listing state statutes and rules of procedure authorizing certification). North Carolina doesn't accept certification and Missouri has a certification statute, Mo. Rev. Stat. § 477.004, but that statute has been deemed unconstitutional under the Missouri Constitution; *Grantham v. Missouri Dep't of Corr.*, No. 72576, 1990 WL 602159 (Mo. 13 July 1990) (en banc).

6   312 U.S. 496 (1941).

7   *Arizonans for Official English v. Arizona*, 520 U.S. 43, 75–76 (1997).

was "a substantial constitutional issue" that "touche[d] a sensitive area of social policy upon which the federal courts ought not to enter unless no alternative to its adjudication is open."[8] Because "[s]uch constitutional adjudication plainly [could] be avoided if a definitive ruling on the state issue would terminate the controversy[, it was] therefore [the Court's] duty to turn to a consideration of questions under Texas law."[9] The Court recognized that the three-judge lower court, whose members were knowledgeable about Texas law, had ruled that the Commission had exceeded its authority. But the issue wasn't without doubt, and a Texas court might later rule to the contrary. The Court wrote: "The reign of law is hardly promoted if an unnecessary ruling of a federal court is thus supplanted by a controlling decision of a state court. The resources of equity are equal to an adjustment that will avoid the waste of a tentative decision as well as the friction of a premature constitutional adjudication."[10] Applying equitable principles, the Court ordered the district court to stay its hand while the litigants "with reasonable promptness" pursued state-court proceedings to resolve the state-law issue.[11] Hence was born the *Pullman* Abstention Doctrine.

The doctrine was hardly a panacea, though. For one thing, its scope was limited. In the 1943 U.S. Supreme Court case of *Meredith v. City of Winter Haven*,[12] the Fifth Circuit had reversed the district court's decision because it had resolved an uncertain issue of Florida law (regarding municipal bonds) rather than directing the plaintiffs to proceed in state court. The Supreme Court reversed the circuit-court opinion, saying that *Pullman* didn't apply—it was limited to stays of proceedings "to enable the parties to litigate first in the state courts questions of state law, decision of which is preliminary to, and may render unnecessary,

---

8   312 U.S. at 498.
9   *Id.*
10 *Id.* at 500.
11 *Id.* at 501–02.
12 320 U.S. 228, 230–31 (1943).

decision of the constitutional questions presented."[13] *Meredith* presented no federal constitutional question.

Further, proceeding in state court after abstention could be tricky. As a unanimous per curiam Court held in *Government & Civic Employees Organizing Committee v. Windsor*,[14] it wasn't enough for the plaintiff union to present only the state-law issues to the state court. The union had brought federal constitutional challenges to a state law providing that public employees who joined a labor union forfeited the rights and benefits of public employment. The three-judge federal district court abstained to permit the pursuit of state remedies. In state court, the union argued that the statute didn't apply to it or its members, but it didn't mention the federal constitutional arguments that it would raise if the statute did apply. The state high court ruled that the statute applied, and the federal district court then upheld its constitutionality. The Supreme Court reversed. Noting that the state court "was not asked to interpret the statute in light of the constitutional objections," it observed that if the union's constitutional arguments "had been presented to the state court, it might have construed the statute in a different manner."[15] The Court told the union to try again. It remanded the case "with directions to retain jurisdiction until efforts to obtain an appropriate adjudication in the state courts have been exhausted."[16]

Windsor created confusion. Some read the opinion as requiring the plaintiff to present the federal issues for decision by the state court. Proceeding in that manner, however, could jeopardize the plaintiff's right to obtain a decision on the federal issue by the federal court because a state-court decision on the federal issue would likely have res judicata consequences. That is what happened in *England v. Louisiana State Board of Medical Examiners*.[17] The three-judge federal district court first abstained so that the

---

13 *Id.* at 236.
14 353 U.S. 364 (1957) (per curiam).
15 *Id.* at 366.
16 *Id.* at 367.
17 375 U.S. 411 (1964).

plaintiffs could obtain a definitive ruling on state law in state court. But when the plaintiffs returned after receiving adverse decisions by the state court on the state and federal issues, the federal court dismissed the suit because the state court had passed judgment on all the issues. The Supreme Court reversed. It provided directions to litigants for navigating abstention procedures: They could decide to waive their right to return to the federal court and let the state court decide all the state and federal issues. But they might instead preserve their right of return while still complying with *Windsor*. This option, the Court explained, required the plaintiff only to "inform [the state] courts what his federal claims are, so that the state statute may be construed in light of those claims."[18] The plaintiff wasn't required by *Windsor* to litigate the federal issues. But because *Windsor* had been unclear on the point, the Court ruled that the *England* plaintiffs (but not later plaintiffs) would be allowed to pursue their federal claims in federal court despite having litigated them in state court.

The difficulty of compliance with *Windsor* and *England*, however, wasn't the chief concern raised by the *Pullman* process. As Douglas J. wrote in his concurrence in *England*, "I was a member of the Court that launched *Pullman* and sent it on its way. But if I had realized the creature it was to become, my doubts would have been far deeper than they were."[19] He complained of the expense and delay resulting from requiring the plaintiff to proceed with a new suit in state court, quoting an earlier dissent:

> Some litigants have long purses. Many, however, can hardly afford one lawsuit, let alone two. Shuttling the parties between state and federal tribunals is a sure way of defeating the ends of justice. The pursuit of justice is not an academic exercise. There are no foundations to finance the resolution of nice state law questions involved in federal court litigation. The parties are entitled—absent unique and rare situations—to adjudication of their rights in the tribunals which Congress has empowered to act.[20]

---

18   *Id.* at 420 (internal quotation marks omitted).
19   *Id.* at 425 (Douglas J. concurring).
20   *Id.* (quoting *Clay v. Sun Ins. Office*, 363 U.S. 207, 228 (1960) (Douglas J. dissenting)).

He also quoted law-review articles stating that having litigants go to and fro between state and federal courts had sometimes consumed eight to ten years and that in one case there had been no decision on the merits of a state statute for five years, despite two trips to the U.S. Supreme Court and two to the state's high court.

Certification as an alternative to litigation

Fortunately, in the two decades between *Pullman* and *England*, a remedy, or at least a palliative, to the problems of cost and delay had emerged. Florida and a few other states had enacted legislation allowing courts in other jurisdictions to certify questions of state law to the state's high court, making it unnecessary to file a new lawsuit and then proceed through the lower courts before, perhaps, obtaining a definitive decision from that court. The Supreme Court hinted at employing this technique in the 1960 case of *Clay v. Sun Insurance Office*.[21] The Fifth Circuit had held that it would be a violation of due process for Florida to apply its statute invalidating contractual limitations periods to a contract formed in Illinois—without first determining whether Florida would actually apply the statute to the contract. The Supreme Court vacated the decision and remanded, criticizing the circuit court for reaching the federal constitutional issue without first determining whether there were state-law grounds for denying relief, which would have mooted the constitutional issue. The Court didn't issue directions to the circuit court on whether to decide the state-law issues or to abstain, but it noted that the Florida legislature had acted "with rare foresight" in creating a certification procedure.[22] (Three Justices dissented on the ground that the Court itself should proceed to decide the state-law issues because they "border[ed] on the frivolous."[23])

Three years later, the Supreme Court twice decided to invoke the certification procedure itself. On both occasions it was reviewing state-court decisions. The federal-law issue in *Aldrich v.*

---

[21] 363 U.S. 207 (1960).
[22] *Id.* at 212.
[23] *Id.* at 213–14 (Black J. dissenting).

Aldrich[24] was whether the Full Faith and Credit Clause required the West Virginia courts to enforce a provision in a Florida divorce decree. The West Virginia courts had refused to enforce the provision on the ground that it was invalid under Florida law. The Supreme Court certified to the Florida Supreme Court several questions, including whether the provision was proper under Florida law and, if not, whether it could be collaterally challenged. After the Florida Supreme Court responded that the provision was improper but couldn't be collaterally challenged, the Supreme Court reversed the West Virginia court's opinion, ordering it to enforce the provision.[25] The other case, *Dresner v. City of Tallahassee*,[26] was a criminal prosecution. The defendant had been convicted in Tallahassee municipal court, lost an appeal to a state circuit court, and then petitioned the U.S. Supreme Court for a writ of certiorari. The Court was uncertain of its jurisdiction under 28 U.S.C. § 1257 (now 1257(a)), which restricts its review to judgments "rendered by the highest court of a State in which a decision could be had." It certified to the Florida Supreme Court several questions concerning whether a court higher than the state circuit court could have reviewed the issues presented to the Supreme Court. Once the Florida court responded that review could have been obtained in a higher state court, the Supreme Court dismissed its writ of certiorari as having been improvidently granted.[27] Douglas J. referred to *Aldrich* and *Dresner* in his *England* concurrence, commending certification as preferable to *Pullman* abstention and suggesting that the federal courts would encourage state adoption of the procedure by limiting the occasions on which they would delay adjudication by abstaining.[28]

---

24 375 U.S. 75 (1963) (per curiam) (certifying four questions to the Supreme Court of Florida).

25 *Aldrich v. Aldrich*, 378 U.S. 540 (1964) (per curiam) (reversing the Supreme Court of West Virginia based on the Supreme Court of Florida's answers to the certification request).

26 375 U.S. 136 (1963) (per curiam).

27 *Dresner v. City of Tallahassee*, 378 U.S. 539 (1964) (per curiam) (mem.).

28 See *England*, 375 U.S. at 433–34 (Douglas J. concurring).

Within ten years of *England*, at least nine states had joined Florida in adopting certification procedures.[29] This trend may have encouraged the Supreme Court in the 1974 case of *Lehman Brothers v. Schein*[30] to give its first emphatic (if not peremptory) endorsement to the practice of certifying state-law issues to state high courts. The endorsement was all the stronger because certification wasn't an alternative to abstention in that case, no ground having been present for *Pullman* abstention. Certification was simply an alternative to the federal court's deciding the state-law issue itself. The lawsuits in *Lehman Brothers* were shareholder-derivative actions filed in federal district court in New York under diversity jurisdiction. The central question was the scope of liability for insider trading. There was no dispute that Florida law governed. The Second Circuit, recognizing the uncertainty of Florida law on the point, looked to the law of other jurisdictions, particularly New York, and found enough support in Florida law to decide that Florida would hold that there would be liability for the alleged misconduct. One judge dissented, suggesting that certification would be appropriate. The defendants requested certification for the first time in a petition for rehearing. The request was rejected. The Supreme Court vacated the judgment of the Second Circuit and remanded "so that the court may consider whether the controlling issue of Florida law should be certified to the Florida Supreme Court."[31] The Court declined to insist that certification is always mandatory: "We do not suggest that where there is doubt as to local law and where the certification procedure is available, resort to it is obligatory."[32] But it revealed where its heart was: "[Certification] does, of course, in the long run save time, energy, and resources and helps build a cooperative judicial federalism."[33] Even so, "[i]ts use in a given case rests in the sound discretion of the federal court."[34] Although the Court expressed

---

29 *See Lehman Bros. v. Schein*, 416 U.S. 386, 391 n.7 (1974).
30 *Id.* at 386.
31 *Id.* at 391–92.
32 *Id.* at 390–91.
33 *Id.* at 391.
34 *Id.*

its view that certification seemed "particularly appropriate" in that case because of "the novelty of the question and the great unsettlement of Florida law," as well as the Second Circuit's unfamiliarity with Florida law,[35] it didn't order certification. After remand, the Second Circuit certified questions to the Florida Supreme Court, that court disagreed with the panel majority's prediction of Florida law,[36] and the Second Circuit acted accordingly.[37]

Certification of state-law questions is now commonplace in the federal courts. The District of Columbia and all the states but Missouri and North Carolina have adopted statutes or rules allowing the state's high court to respond to requests for certification, but not all take questions from federal district courts.[38] Although some have argued that answering a certified question amounts to issuing an improper advisory opinion, courts have rejected this argument on various grounds.[39] Some state high courts have held that the state constitution doesn't give the court original jurisdiction to consider certified questions from federal courts,[40] but that the problem can be cured by a constitutional amendment.[41] Meanwhile, although the Fifth Circuit in an early

---

35 *Id.*

36 *See Schein v. Chasen*, 313 So. 2d 739 (Fla. 1975).

37 *See Schein v. Chasen*, 519 F.2d 453 (2d Cir. 1975) (per curiam).

38 *See, e.g.*, Miss. R. App. P. 20; N.J. Rules of Court 2:12A-1; Pa. R. App. P. 3341.

39 *See, e.g., Los Angeles All. for Survival v. City of Los Angeles*, 993 P.2d 334, 338–39 (Cal. 2000) ("[O]ur sister-state high courts overwhelmingly have rejected contentions that in answering a certified question a court issues an improper advisory opinion."); *Wolner v. Mahaska Indus., Inc.*, 325 N.W.2d 39, 41 (Minn. 1982) (en banc) (opinion in response to request for certification isn't advisory); *In re Elliott*, 446 P.2d 347, 354–58 (Wash. 1968) (en banc) (answer to certified question isn't an advisory opinion, and state Supreme Court has discretion to render advisory opinions when doing so is in the public interest); *cf. Leiter Minerals, Inc. v. California Co.*, 132 So. 2d 845, 849–50 (La. 1961) (in declaratory action instituted at direction of U.S. Supreme Court to obtain determination of state property-law question, Louisiana Supreme Court states that the litigation improperly called on court to render advisory opinion but court issues opinion "out of respect for, and as a courtesy to," the highest court in the land). *See generally* Ira Robbins, *Interjurisdictional Certification and Choice of Law*, 41 Vand. L. Rev. 411, 419–24 (1988).

40 *See Grantham v. Missouri Dep't of Corr.*, No. 72576, 1990 WL 602159 (Mo. 13 July 1990) (en banc); *Holden v. NL Indus., Inc.*, 629 P.2d 428, 432 (Utah 1981).

41 *See In re West Side Prop. Assocs.*, 13 P.3d 168, 170 (Utah 2000).

case (the remand from the U.S. Supreme Court in *Clay*[42]) suggested that a state-court opinion on certification may simply be dictum (persuasive but not binding),[43] the court later had a change of heart.[44] Those opinions are now universally considered binding on the certifying court.[45]

Diversity of state practice on certification

States differ in their certification procedures. But the usual considerations can be illustrated by summarizing the provisions regarding the acceptance of certifications from federal courts in the 1995 Uniform Certification of Questions of Law Act, which has been adopted in eight states.[46]

Section 3 of the uniform act provides that the state's high court "may answer a question of law certified to it by a court of the United States ... if the answer may be determinative of an issue in pending litigation in the certifying court and there is no controlling appellate decision, constitutional provision, or statute of this State."[47] The term *court of the United States* includes all federal courts from the Tax Court to the bankruptcy courts to courts of appeals and the Supreme Court. Despite the number of such courts, states haven't been overwhelmed by requests for certification; and in any event, accepting a request is discretionary. The requirement that there be "no controlling appellate decision, constitutional provision, or statute of this State" may seem unnecessary because there would be no reason to certify a question on which there is controlling law. But it could be unnecessarily limiting. If, for example,

---

42 363 U.S. 207.

43 See *Sun Ins. Office, Ltd. v. Clay*, 319 F.2d 505, 509 (5th Cir. 1963), *rev'd on other grounds*, 377 U.S. 179 (1964).

44 See, e.g., *Hopkins v. Lockheed Aircraft Corp.*, 394 F.2d 656, 657 (5th Cir. 1968).

45 See *Engel v. CBS, Inc.*, 182 F.3d 124, 125–26 (2d Cir. 1999) (per curiam) (binding even though state court reformulated the question); *Grover v. Eli Lilly & Co.*, 33 F.3d 716, 719 (6th Cir. 1994) (binding even though the state-high-court decision was on a 4–3 vote); *Richardson ex rel. Richardson v. Navistar Int'l Transp. Corp.*, 231 F.3d 740, 743 (10th Cir. 2000).

46 Another 22 states and the District of Columbia adopted the 1967 uniform act. The discussion here addresses the newer statute.

47 Uniform Certification of Questions of Law Act, § 3 (1995).

the federal court is concerned that an ancient decision of the state high court would no longer be followed, the request for certification might be rejected on the ground that the decision is still "controlling." At least one state high court has rejected a request for certification on the ground that a decision by the state's lower appellate court was controlling precedent.[48] On the other hand, the request might provide the state high court with the opportunity to explain why it no longer feels bound by an earlier decision (so that the earlier decision isn't "controlling").

The requirement that the answer "may be determinative of an issue in pending litigation in the certifying court" is more likely to come into play. State courts have differed a bit on the requirement's meaning. The high court in Nebraska has suggested that the requirement isn't satisfied if one of the potential answers to the certified question would not resolve the federal case. A federal district court apparently facing a constitutional challenge to a city ordinance had certified to the state high court the question whether the ordinance was invalid under state law. The Nebraska court said that "if this court held that the ordinance did not violate a state statute or the state Constitution, that holding would not be determinative of a federal constitutional challenge to the ordinance."[49]

An early decision of the Wyoming Supreme Court has occasionally been cited as adopting a very restrictive interpretation when it stated that "it will not consider a reserved constitutional question until there is nothing left for the trial court to do but apply our answer to the question or questions and enter judgment consistent with the answer or answers."[50] But that decision was based on a state procedural rule rather than the language of the uniform act. Under the present Wyoming Rule of Appellate Procedure 11, the court has been very accommodating to the federal courts. For example, in a 2002 case,[51] it answered a question

---

48 See *Western Helicopter Servs. v. Rogerson Aircraft Corp.*, 811 P.2d 627, 635 (Or. 1991).
49 *Keller v. City of Fremont*, 790 N.W.2d 711, 712 (Neb. 2010) (per curiam).
50 *In re Certified Question from U.S. Dist. Ct.*, 549 P.2d 1310, 1311 (Wyo. 1976).
51 *Miech v. Sheridan Cnty.*, 59 P.3d 143 (Wyo. 2002).

from the federal district court—a question that served only as a predicate for jury instructions at the federal trial.[52]

Some states will accept a certified question if one possible answer would resolve a federal claim.[53] Others appear to have a more liberal standard. The New Mexico Supreme Court has said that its answer is determinative if "it resolves the issue in the case out of which the question arose, and the resolution of [the] issue materially advances the ultimate termination of the litigation."[54] The Arkansas Supreme Court will accept a request for certification if the question certified "concern[s] an unsettled issue of the construction of a statute."[55] The Arizona Supreme Court will not "second-guess the Court of Appeals on whether the question certified will be case-determinative."[56]

State courts sometimes refuse a request for certification on the ground that the state-law question would not be determinative. The Maine Supreme Court has demurred on answering a certified question from a federal district court because it couldn't tell whether its answer would be determinative: the federal court had not made findings of fact, and the litigants disputed the facts.[57] The Nevada Supreme Court has declined to answer a federal district court's question whether evidence of compliance with government standards or industry practices was admissible in a product-liability case. The court said that its answers would not be determinative because they "would resolve only a discrete evidentiary issue" and that "essentially to resolve a motion in limine before the federal trial . . . would not promote judicial efficiency

---

52   See *Miech v. Sheridan Cnty.*, 109 F. App'x 280, 282 (10th Cir. 2004).

53   See *White v. Edgar*, 320 A.2d 668, 677 (Me. 1974) ("question of state law 'may be determinative of the cause' [under state certification statute]" if it "is susceptible of an answer in one alternative which, if it be the answer given by this Court, will produce a final disposition of the federal cause"); *Western Helicopter*, 811 P.2d at 630 ("[O]ur decision must, in one or more of the forms it could take, have the potential to determine at least one claim in the case.").

54   *Schlieter v. Carlos*, 775 P.2d 709, 710 (N.M. 1989) (per curiam).

55   *Longview Prod. Co. v. Dubberly*, 99 S.W.3d 427, 429 (Ark. 2003) (per curiam).

56   *Scheehle v. Justices of Supreme Court of Ariz.*, 57 P.3d 379, 381 (Ariz. 2002).

57   *In re Richards*, 223 A.2d 827, 833 (Me. 1966).

either for this court or for the federal courts."[58] Declining to answer a question regarding the scope of a provision of the state long-arm statute, the New York Court of Appeals expressed uncertainty about whether the answer was "likely to be dispositive of the matter" because of the possibility of other grounds, both federal and state, for obtaining personal jurisdiction.[59] In a case before the federal district court in New Mexico, the plaintiff in a medical-malpractice case opposed a motion to sever defendants covered by the state medical-malpractice statute on the issue of future medical expenses, arguing that the statute was unconstitutional. The federal district court certified questions regarding the statute's validity under the state constitution. The state court said that answers to the certified questions would not be determinative because "the trial court could properly decide whether to sever the future medical expenses issue on other bases, regardless of how we were to resolve the constitutional questions presented."[60]

Section 4 of the uniform act authorizes the state court to "reformulate a question of law certified to it." This provision gives the state court the flexibility needed when its analysis leads to conclusions that cannot be expressed in the terms of the certification request. Even without the explicit authorization of § 4, state courts have found it appropriate to restate the questions to be answered. Before the 1995 uniform act was promulgated, the Oregon Supreme Court stated that "the majority rule, . . . agreeable to us, is that this court (the deciding court) has the discretion to reframe questions and is not bound to answer the question as certified."[61] In one instructive example, a court even answered its own follow-on question to the one posed by the certifying court. After answering affirmatively that a statute violated the state

---

58 *Volvo Cars of N. Am., Inc. v. Ricci*, 137 P.3d 1161, 1164 (Nev. 2006) (en banc).
59 *Yesil v. Reno*, 705 N.E.2d 655, 656 (N.Y. 1998) (per curiam).
60 *Schlieter*, 775 P.2d at 712.
61 *Western Helicopter*, 811 P.2d at 633 (stating, however, that the court would ordinarily consult with the certifying court about a possible reformulation); *see Walters v. Inexco Oil Co.*, 440 So. 2d 268, 272 (Miss. 1983) (noting that certification from circuit court had said that state court should not consider itself limited by the phrasing of the questions); *Lenhardt v. Ford Motor Co.*, 683 P.2d 1097, 1098 (Wash. 1984) (en banc) (same).

constitution, the West Virginia high court proceeded to decide that its ruling would not apply retroactively—an issue briefed in the state court but not certified.[62]

Section 5 provides that the certifying court must issue a certification order that is forwarded to the state high court and must, upon request, deliver all or part of its record. The record can be important not only in resolving the legal issue presented but also in helping the state court determine whether to exercise its discretion to honor the request. For example, if the state court discovers that the federal court hasn't yet resolved a jurisdictional question, it will probably reject the request until it knows that the federal court must rule on the certified question.

Section 6 requires the certification order to contain

> (1) the question of law to be answered; (2) the facts relevant to the question, showing fully the nature of the controversy out of which the question arose; (3) a statement acknowledging that the [state high court], acting as the receiving court, may reformulate the question; and (4) the names and addresses of counsel of record and parties appearing without counsel.

It also provides that the certifying court should determine and state the relevant facts if the litigants cannot agree. Section 7 requires the state court to notify the certifying court whether it accepts or rejects the request and, if it accepts, to decide the question promptly. Section 9 requires the state court to issue a written opinion and send it to the certifying court, counsel, and unrepresented parties.

State discretion under the uniform act

Even when all the requirements of the uniform act have been satisfied, the state high court retains discretion to deny a certification request. Some reasons for denial are obvious. In a 1998 case,[63] the New Mexico Supreme Court declined to answer a question about city condemnation power because a newly enacted statute

---

62   See *Kincaid v. Mangum*, 432 S.E.2d 74, 82–86 (W. Va. 1993).
63   *City of Las Cruces v. El Paso Elec. Co.*, 954 P.2d 72 (N.M. 1998).

had mooted the question.[64] Other common themes in declining certification are that the facts haven't been sufficiently developed, the question is too abstract, or the question did not merit the state court's attention. In a 1993 Iowa case,[65] for example, a resident of a house across the street from a Pizza Hut restaurant was struck by a rock thrown from an unknown member of a crowd near the Pizza Hut.[66] The issue was whether Pizza Hut owed a duty of care to the victim. The Iowa Supreme Court declined to answer the questions certified by the federal district court. The court explained that although a request to expand the common law might be reasonable, "[t]he problem we have with attempting to accommodate the parties in this case is that we do not have the specificity in the facts presented to us that we would have in the course of normal appeal to our court . . . , or at least a clear factual record."[67] In addition, the court said, such a request to plow new ground when it comes to state common law should be viewed with some skepticism: "The discretion to choose a more appropriate vehicle for developing our law has been cited by one authority as a strong reason for allowing discretion on the part of the answering court to deny answers to certified questions."[68]

In a 1998 case,[69] the New York Court of Appeals declined to answer the question whether personal jurisdiction over the district director of the federal Immigration and Naturalization Service was proper under the state's long-arm statute because the answer wasn't likely to be "determinative." The court also added two further reasons for declining: (1) the case "present[ed] a fact pattern that most likely would not arise in any State court proceeding," and (2) the questions were too theoretical, a feature that could "curb this Court's ability to promulgate a precedentially prudent

---

64 *Id.* at 74.
65 *Eley v. Pizza Hut of Am., Inc.*, 500 N.W.2d 61 (Iowa 1993).
66 *Id.* at 61.
67 *Id.* at 63.
68 *Id.*
69 *Yesil*, 705 N.E.2d at 655.

and definitive answer to a law question."[70] In a 1991 case,[71] the Oregon Supreme Court declined to answer a question certified by a federal district court that had previously been resolved by the Oregon Court of Appeals.[72] It said that it would "review the request for certification in much the same way [it] would review a petition for review of the Court of Appeals decision,"[73] and the issue in the case wasn't "one of such general importance that we now believe that we should address it, nor is this a *Pullman*-type case in which a decision from this court will facilitate the functioning of the federal courts."[74] The New Mexico Supreme Court denied a request to answer a federal district court's question about a state statute's validity under the state constitution, in part because the factual record necessary for determining constitutionality had not been adequately developed.[75] For future guidance, it indicated that it would ordinarily consider pretrial certifications with the same disfavor it gives interlocutory appeals and that a certified issue "should present a significant question of law under the New Mexico Constitution or be one of such substantial public interest that it should be determined by this Court."[76]

Notably, the federal court may sometimes go too far in resolving issues before certifying a question. In a 1996 case,[77] the Oklahoma Supreme Court expressed its reluctance to answer a question already decided by the federal court. The district court granted summary judgment on the ground that the defendant owed no duty of care to the plaintiff. But when the plaintiff filed a motion to reconsider and, in the alternative, a request that the duty question be certified to the state court, the district court denied the motion to reconsider but certified the question.[78] The

---

70 *Id.* at 656.
71 *Western Helicopter*, 811 P.2d at 627.
72 *Id.* at 635.
73 *Id.* at 631.
74 *Id.* at 635.
75 *Schlieter v. Carlos*, 775 P.2d 709, 712 (N.M. 1989) (per curiam).
76 *Id.* at 713.
77 *Cray v. Deloitte Haskins & Sells*, 925 P.2d 60 (Okla. 1996).
78 *See id.* at 62.

Oklahoma court stated: "We decline to afford appellate review of a ruling made by a federal judge under the guise of a certified question of law. We are without judicial authority to either affirm or reverse the judgment of a federal court."[79]

The state court isn't the only one vested with discretion in certification. The certifying court must first exercise its discretion to determine whether to make a request in the first place. The U.S. Supreme Court regularly certifies cases to state high courts. Although the Court hasn't attempted to set forth an exhaustive list of factors that guide its certification decisions, a few guidelines emerge. To begin with, the Court now favors certification in cases that it would have abstained from in the past.[80] As the Court said in 1997, "Certification today covers territory once dominated by . . . *Pullman* abstention."[81] Hence in cases "[w]here resolution of [a] federal constitutional question is dependent upon, or may be materially altered by, the determination of an uncertain issue of state law,"[82] the Court frequently certifies issues.[83] The Supreme Court's reasons for certifying such questions were vigorously expressed in the *Arizonans* case.[84] Although the Court vacated the court of appeals' judgment on the ground of mootness, it provided significant instruction to the lower courts on the benefits of certification when a state law is challenged as violating the federal

---

79 *Id.*
80 See *Arizonans for Official English v. Arizona*, 520 U.S. 43, 75–76 (1997). See also *Brockett v. Spokane Arcades, Inc.*, 472 U.S. 491, 510 (1985) (O'Connor J. concurring) (writing in favor of abstention and noting that it is "particularly gratuitous" to speculate on state law when "the state courts stand willing to address questions of state law on certification from a federal court").
81 *Arizonans*, 520 U.S. at 75–76. See pp. 618–19.
82 *Harman v. Forssenius*, 380 U.S. 528, 534 (1965) (discussing requirements of *Pullman* abstention).
83 See, e.g., *Fiore v. White*, 531 U.S. 225 (2001) (per curiam) (to resolve whether a Pennsylvania Supreme Court decision was a new interpretation or a correct interpretation at the time when Fiore's conviction became final, because the decision made it clear that Fiore's conduct wasn't within the scope of the statute); *Virginia v. American Booksellers Ass'n*, 484 U.S. 383, 393–98 (1988) (certifying construction of state statute restricting access of minors to pornography because narrowing construction would change the analysis of First Amendment claim).
84 520 U.S. at 75–76.

Constitution: "Given the novelty of the question and its potential importance to the conduct of Arizona's business, plus the views of the Attorney General and those of [the state constitutional provision's] sponsors, the certification requests merited more respectful consideration than they received in the proceedings below."[85]

In general, the Court said, a federal court facing a challenge to the constitutionality of a federal statute should first try to reconcile any conflicts, if possible: "They will first ascertain whether a construction is fairly possible that will contain the statute within constitutional bounds. State courts, when interpreting state statutes, are similarly equipped to apply that cardinal principle."[86] Caution is especially important when a state's highest court hasn't yet addressed the issue, the Court added: "Warnings against premature adjudication of constitutional questions bear heightened attention when a federal court is asked to invalidate a State's law, for the federal tribunal risks friction-generating error when it endeavors to construe a novel state Act not yet reviewed by the State's highest court."[87] And this is especially so when the state seems willing to address the issue in a certified question: "Speculation by a federal court about the meaning of a state statute in the absence of prior state court adjudication is particularly gratuitous when the state courts stand willing to address questions of state law on certification from a federal court."[88]

The Court also noted that the district court and the court of appeals had set too high a standard for certification on the construction of the Arizona constitutional provision whose federal constitutionality had been successfully challenged in those courts: "Blending abstention with certification, the Ninth Circuit found 'no unique circumstances in this case militating in favor of certification.' Novel, unsettled questions of state law, however, not 'unique circumstances,' are necessary before federal courts may

---

85 *Id.* at 78.
86 *Id.* at 79 (ellipses, internal quotation marks, and citations omitted).
87 *Id.*
88 *Id.* (ellipses, internal quotation marks, and citations omitted).

avail themselves of state certification procedures."[89] Certification avoids "the delays, expense, and procedural complexity that generally attend abstention decisions," the Court said, and can greatly simplify the federal court's job in resolving the matter.[90] "The complexity [of this case] might have been avoided had the District Court, more than eight years ago, accepted the certification suggestion made by Arizona's Attorney General," the Court concluded.[91] "The Arizona Supreme Court was not asked by the District Court or the Court of Appeals to say what [the challenged provision] means."[92]

This isn't to say that when the constitutionality of state action is challenged, the Supreme Court now invariably uses the certification process to obtain a construction of the state law at issue. Several times it has declined to certify because the state law was clear. In *City of Houston v. Hill*,[93] the Court explained that a federal court isn't free to "ask a state court if it would care in effect to rewrite a statute."[94] And in *Stenberg v. Carhart*,[95] the Court refused to certify the question whether the Nebraska Supreme Court would adopt a narrow interpretation of a state abortion statute—an interpretation urged by the state attorney general. The Court explained that the statute wasn't "'fairly susceptible' to a narrowing construction."[96] The attorney general had not sought certification in the lower courts, and the certified question would not be "determinative of the cause," as required by Nebraska's certification statute, because the Court had found the statute to be unconstitutional on other grounds as well.[97] In *Town of Castle Rock v. Gonzales*,[98] the failure of any litigant to seek certification, either

---

89   *Id.* (citation omitted).
90   *Id.*
91   *Id.*
92   *Id.*
93   482 U.S. 451 (1987).
94   *Id.* at 471.
95   530 U.S. 914 (2000).
96   *Id.* at 945.
97   *Id.*
98   545 U.S. 748 (2005).

by the lower courts or by the Supreme Court itself, was apparently also a compelling reason for the Supreme Court not to certify a state-law question that might have affected the Court's analysis of a federal constitutional challenge to state action (actually, inaction).[99] Nor, presumably, would certification be required when the Court has said that *Pullman* abstention wouldn't be proper, as when time is of the essence (for example, in an election case),[100] or when a state-court interpretation of state law in a single case cannot resolve the federal question (for example, a vagueness challenge to a statute).[101]

Unsurprisingly, the Supreme Court has continued its practice, initiated in *Aldrich* and *Dresner*, of certifying questions for important reasons that don't come under the *Pullman* doctrine. Two examples will suffice. In *Stewart v. Smith*,[102] the Court certified a question to the Arizona Supreme Court to determine whether the lower federal courts had properly reviewed a habeas claim of ineffective assistance of counsel in his state prosecution. The issue was whether the federal courts had to recognize a state-court determination that the ineffectiveness claim was procedurally barred. That depended on whether the state procedural bar was independent of federal law. The Court certified to the Arizona Supreme Court the question whether the state courts could determine that a claim was procedurally barred without first assessing the merits of the ineffectiveness claim—and soon learned that they could.[103] In *United States v. Juvenile Male*,[104] the juvenile had challenged the constitutionality of the requirement imposed by a federal court

---

99   *Id.* at 758 n.5.

100 *See Harman v. Forssenius*, 380 U.S. 528, 537 (1965) (district court didn't abuse its discretion in declining to abstain in federal-voting-rights challenge to state restrictions on the franchise); *Afran v. McGreevey*, 115 F. App'x 539, 543 (3d Cir. 2004) (per curiam).

101 *See Baggett v. Bullitt*, 377 U.S. 360, 378 (1964) (rejecting suggestion of abstention in case raising vagueness challenge to state mandatory oath because "[i]t is fictional to believe that anything less than extensive [state] adjudications, under the impact of a variety of factual situations, would bring the oath within the bounds of permissible constitutional certainty").

102 534 U.S. 157 (2001) (per curiam).

103 *Stewart v. Smith*, 46 P.3d 1067, 1071 (Ariz. 2002) (en banc).

104 560 U.S. 558 (2010) (per curiam).

that he register as a sex offender. The Court was concerned about whether the challenge had been mooted when the term of his juvenile supervision had expired and he was no longer required to register. Mootness would depend on whether there were still collateral consequences flowing from the federal-court requirement, and "the most likely potential collateral consequence" was that the juvenile was still required to register as a sex offender under Montana law.[105] The Court certified to the Montana Supreme Court the question whether the state registration requirement was conditional on the validity of the expired federally imposed registration requirement—a question that, in the end, was mooted.[106]

Certification sought by lower federal courts

As for the lower federal courts, their marching orders from the Supreme Court are fairly clear in cases that would come under the *Pullman* abstention doctrine: when a federal constitutional challenge to state action turns on the interpretation of an ambiguous state law, the court should try to resolve the ambiguity by certifying the question to the state's high court. The question whether to certify an issue, however, arises much more often when the federal court must interpret state law to resolve a state-law claim arising under the federal court's diversity jurisdiction. In general, as the Supreme Court said in *Lehman Brothers v. Schein*,[107] the decision whether to certify an issue "rests in the sound discretion of the federal court."[108] A litigant may request certification, or the court may act sua sponte.[109] What factors influenced the decision?

One crucial factor is whether the question to be certified to a state high court satisfies the requirements of the state—generally, that the question be unsettled and that the answer to the question

---

105 *Id.* at 560 (brackets and internal quotation marks omitted).
106 *United States v. Juvenile Male*, 564 U.S. 932, 937–38 (2011).
107 416 U.S. 386 (1974).
108 *Id.* at 391.
109 *See Queen Anne Park Homeowners Ass'n v. State Farm Fire & Cas. Co.*, 763 F.3d 1232, 1235 (9th Cir. 2014); *Easthampton Sav. Bank v. City of Springfield*, 736 F.3d 46, 50 n.4 (1st Cir. 2013); *Brown v. Argosy Gaming Co.*, 384 F.3d 413, 415 (7th Cir. 2004).

may be determinative of an issue (or a claim) in federal litigation.[110] Some states have additional requirements.[111]

Occasionally the certifying federal court doesn't discuss any other factors.[112] But usually it will. The most restrictive court of appeals, at least in its language, is the Fifth Circuit, which has stated that a "court should exercise [its] discretion sparingly, certifying only in exceptional cases,"[113] and that it does "not use certification as a panacea for resolution of those complex or difficult state law questions which have not been answered by the highest court of the state."[114]

Several factors are characteristically mentioned by the federal courts of appeals as supporting the use of certification. Most commonly, they include these: (1) that the certified issue is important

---

110 *See, e.g., Metz v. Bae Sys. Tech. Sols. & Servs. Inc.*, 774 F.3d 18, 22 (D.C. Cir. 2014) ("The most important consideration is that the question upon which [the plaintiff] seeks certification is not genuinely uncertain.") (internal quotation marks omitted); *Castagnaro v. Bank of N.Y. Mellon*, 772 F.3d 734, 736 (1st Cir. 2014); *Queen Anne Park Homeowners Ass'n*, 763 F.3d at 1235; *Antonio v. SSA Sec., Inc.*, 749 F.3d 227, 234 (4th Cir. 2014); *Nguyen v. Holder*, 743 F.3d 311, 316 (2d Cir. 2014); *FDIC v. Skow*, 741 F.3d 1342, 1346 (11th Cir. 2013) (per curiam); *Bernstein v. Bankert*, 733 F.3d 190, 221 (7th Cir. 2013); *Pino v. United States*, 507 F.3d 1233, 1236 (10th Cir. 2007); *Hatfield v. Bishop Clarkson Mem'l Hosp.*, 701 F.2d 1266, 1267 (8th Cir. 1983) (en banc).

111 *See Wirth v. Aetna U.S. Healthcare*, 137 F. App'x 455, 461 (3d Cir. 2005) (setting forth Pennsylvania requirements).

112 *See, e.g., Antonio*, 749 F.3d at 234–37; *Skow*, 741 F.3d at 1346–47; *Nuveen Mun. Trust v. WithumSmith Brown, P.C.*, 692 F.3d 283, 312 (3d Cir. 2012); *Kulinski v. Medtronic Bio-Medicus, Inc.*, 112 F.3d 368, 372 (8th Cir. 1997).

113 *In re FEMA Trailer Formaldehyde Prods. Liab. Litig.*, 668 F.3d 281, 290 (5th Cir. 2012) (brackets and internal quotation marks omitted).

114 *Patterson v. Mobil Oil Corp.*, 335 F.3d 476, 487 (5th Cir. 2003) (internal quotation marks omitted).

to the state,[115] (2) that a considerable sum of money is at stake,[116] (3) that resolution of the certified question will depend on policy or value judgments by the court,[117] and (4) that the issue recurs with some frequency.[118] One factor that is often influential but rarely expressed is that the panel of the court of appeals is divided in interpreting the state law. In one of the early decisions certifying a question, the court wasn't so coy about the matter: it certified a question in response to a petition for rehearing both because the issue raised was important and "in especial consideration of the fact that one of the Judges of this Court dissented from this Court's disposition of that question on original hearing, and that the Judges of this Court, on petition for rehearing, remained of the same views as expressed in their opinions on original hearing."[119]

---

115 See *Metz*, 774 F.3d at 24 (noting that the court previously granted certification in a case raising an issue of "public importance in which the District of Columbia has a substantial interest") (internal quotation marks omitted); *Castagnaro*, 772 F.3d at 739 (issue "is one with significant implications for the state of New Hampshire"); *Queen Anne Park Homeowners Ass'n*, 763 F.3d at 1235 ("[T]he answer to the question may have far-reaching effects on individuals and entities insured under residential and commercial property insurance policies subject to Washington law."); *Nguyen*, 743 F.3d at 316 ("the question must be important to the state"); *Easthampton Sav. Bank*, 736 F.3d at 53 (case "involves an area of traditional state authority"); *Bernstein*, 733 F.3d at 221 (including as factors that "the case concerns a matter of vital public concern" and "is of interest to the state supreme court in its development of state law") (internal quotation marks omitted); *Doyle v. City of Medford*, 565 F.3d 536, 543 (9th Cir. 2009) (issue "is one of exceptional importance to citizens of the State of Oregon and to local governments within the state"); *Wirth*, 137 F. App'x at 461 (question "implicate[s] an issue of substantial public importance heretofore unresolved"); *Ward v. State Farm Mut. Auto. Ins. Co.*, 539 F.2d 1044, 1049-50 (5th Cir. 1976).

116 See *Easthampton Sav. Bank*, 736 F.3d at 53.

117 See *Austin v. Kroger Texas L.P.*, 746 F.3d 191, 204 (5th Cir. 2014) (per curiam); *Nguyen*, 743 F.3d at 316 (resolving the question "must require value-laden judgments or public policy choices"); *Pino*, 507 F.3d at 1236 ("the judicial policy of a state should be decided when possible by state, not federal, courts").

118 See *Easthampton Sav. Bank*, 736 F.3d at 52 (considering "the likely effects of a decision on future cases"); *Bernstein*, 733 F.3d at 221; *Hatfield*, 701 F.2d at 1268; *Florida ex rel. Shevin v. Exxon Corp.*, 526 F.2d 266, 275 n.29 (5th Cir. 1976); *but see RAR, Inc. v. Turner Diesel, Ltd.*, 107 F.3d 1272, 1277 (7th Cir. 1997) (appearing to suggest that when each recurrence of the issue has a unique factual context, certification is inappropriate).

119 *Green v. American Tobacco Co.*, 304 F.2d 70, 86 (5th Cir. 1962).

Surprisingly, one certification-supporting factor mentioned by the Supreme Court in *Lehman Brothers*—that the disputed law is that of a "distant State," so that the certifying judges are "'outsiders' lacking the common exposure to local law which comes from sitting in the jurisdiction"[120]—is only occasionally relied on by certifying courts.[121]

Among the reasons courts give for declining to certify a question is that the litigant requesting certification had the option of suing in state court but instead sued in a federal forum. As the Seventh Circuit has written: "[I]f the plaintiff had wanted to know only whether the Indiana courts would support her cause of action, she had the option of bringing her case there in the first instance."[122] Similarly, circuit courts have expressed distaste for a litigant's seeking certification only after suffering an adverse judgment in the district court. The Eighth Circuit has said: "The practice of requesting certification after an adverse judgment has been entered should be discouraged. Otherwise, the initial federal court decision will be nothing but a gamble with certification sought only after an adverse decision."[123]

---

120 *Lehman Bros. v. Schein*, 416 U.S. 386, 391 (1974).

121 *See, e.g., Schroeder v. United States*, 66 Fed. Cl. 508, 518 (2005); *Collins v. Straight, Inc.*, 748 F.2d 916, 922, 924-25 (4th Cir. 1984) (Miller J. dissenting).

122 *Brown v. Argosy Gaming Co.*, 384 F.3d 413, 417 (7th Cir. 2004); *see also Metz v. 774 F.3d* at 24; *Afran v. McGreevey*, 115 F. App'x 539, 543 (3d Cir. 2004) (per curiam); *Jefferson v. Lead Indus. Ass'n*, 106 F.3d 1245, 1248 (5th Cir. 1997) (per curiam); *Powell v. U.S. Fid. & Guar. Co.*, 88 F.3d 271, 273 n.3 (4th Cir. 1996) (per curiam); *Seaboard Sur. Co. v. Garrison, Webb & Stanaland, P.A.*, 823 F.2d 434, 438 (11th Cir. 1987) (per curiam); *Colonial Park Country Club v. Joan of Arc*, 746 F.2d 1425, 1429 (10th Cir. 1984) (quoting with approval *Cantwell v. University of Mass.*, 551 F.2d 879, 880 (1st Cir. 1977)).

123 *Perkins v. Clark Equip. Co.*, 823 F.2d 207, 210 (8th Cir. 1987). *See also City of Columbus v. Hotels.com L.P.*, 693 F.3d 642, 654 (6th Cir. 2012); *Thompson v. Paul*, 547 F.3d 1055, 1065 (9th Cir. 2008); *Afran*, 115 F. App'x at 543; *Enfield ex rel. Enfield v. A.B. Chance Co.*, 228 F.3d 1245, 1255 (10th Cir. 2000) ("Although the issues raised by the City are novel and somewhat difficult, the City did not seek certification until after it received an adverse decision from the district court. That fact alone persuades us that certification is inappropriate."); *Tidler v. Eli Lilly & Co.*, 851 F.2d 418, 426 (D.C. Cir. 1988) ("[P]laintiffs pursued discovery and pre-trial motions for several years, filed and opposed dispositive motions grounded upon Maryland and District of Columbia law, and when they saw the result, thought better of the state after all."); *Harris v. Karri-On*

Despite these statements of hostility to certifying questions after the district court has ruled, especially when the litigant requesting certification chose the federal forum, circuit courts commonly certify without discussing whether there was a request for certification in the district court, or whether the litigant seeking certification was the one that chose the federal forum.

A court may also deny certification because the evidentiary record is insufficiently clear to frame a lucid question[124] or because the circuit court itself has previously decided the state-law issue.[125] One consideration unlikely to repeat itself influenced the Second Circuit's decision not to certify to the New York Court of Appeals the question whether New York would recognize same-sex marriages entered into in other jurisdictions. The circuit court declined because it thought that "the [New York] Court of Appeals ha[d] signaled its disinclination to decide this very question."[126]

When the Supreme Court stated in 1974 that the decision whether to certify is committed to the "sound discretion" of the certifying court, it didn't distinguish between trial and appellate courts.[127] The factors guiding the district court "are more or less the same as those that [a circuit court] considers."[128] But as noted in the above discussion of state certification laws, the district court must be careful not to make a certification request until the case has reached the stage of development that will assure the state court that the certified question will be dispositive of an issue or claim and that will make the question sufficiently fact-bound that it will not be rejected as too abstract. (Appellate courts, naturally,

---

Campers, Inc., 640 F.2d 65, 68 (7th Cir. 1981). *But see Castagnaro*, 772 F.3d at 736 (issue certified even though not requested until appeal).

124 See *Tidler*, 851 F.2d at 427 ("[T]he record before us is so lacking in concreteness that to certify plaintiffs' questions of law would merely be to invite our state court colleagues to an exercise in speculation."); *Florida ex rel. Shevin*, 526 F.2d at 275. *But see Doyle v. City of Medford*, 565 F.3d 536, 544 (9th Cir. 2009) (noting that developing the full factual record isn't necessary to resolve a purely legal issue).

125 See *Rutherford v. Columbia Gas*, 575 F.3d 616, 618–19 (6th Cir. 2009); *Jefferson*, 106 F.3d at 1247–48.

126 *Windsor v. United States*, 699 F.3d 169, 177 (2d Cir. 2012).

127 *Lehman Bros.*, 416 U.S. at 391.

128 *Brown*, 384 F.3d at 417–18.

are far less likely to have such difficulties.) The circuit court will review the district court's decision for abuse of discretion,[129] although it may decide to certify the question while still affirming the district court's refusal to do so.[130] The district court's decision to certify a question or to reject a request for certification cannot be reviewed on an interlocutory appeal under the collateral-order doctrine of *Cohen v. Beneficial Industrial Loan Corp.*[131] But if a litigant fails to request certification from the district court and loses on the state-law issue, the circuit court may be reluctant to grant a certfication request on appeal.[132] Otherwise, a litigant would have two bites at the apple, which would encourage the litigant to delay seeking a resolution of the issue.

Problems arising from certified questions

Once the federal court decides to certify a question to the state court, the rest of the process ordinarily flows smoothly. At one time the Fifth Circuit would ask the litigants to take the first stab at formulating the request for certification to the state court.[133] But the other circuits generally prepare their own requests, and this appears to be the Fifth Circuit's practice now.[134] If the state court grants the request to decide the certified issue, the federal court is bound by the state court's decision and proceeds to apply it. But occasionally hindrances beset the process. For example, one of the litigants may fail to comply with the state court's procedures on certification, as by failing to submit a brief. If the state court dismisses its proceeding for that reason, the federal court could

---

129 See, e.g., *City of Columbus*, 693 F.3d at 654; *Thompson*, 547 F.3d at 1064–65; *Brown*, 384 F.3d at 417.

130 *Antonio v. SSA Sec., Inc.*, 749 F.3d 227, 234 (4th Cir. 2014).

131 337 U.S. 541 (1949); see *Nemours Found. v. Manganaro Corp.*, 878 F.2d 98 (3d Cir. 1989) (refusing to hear appeal of certification order).

132 See, e.g., *Perkins v. Clark Equip. Co.*, 823 F.2d 207, 209–10 (8th Cir. 1987) ("The practice of requesting certification after an adverse judgment has been entered should be discouraged. Otherwise, the initial federal court decision will be nothing but a gamble.").

133 See, e.g., *Ward v. State Farm Mut. Auto. Ins. Co.*, 539 F.2d 1044, 1050 n.3 (5th Cir. 1976); *Green*, 304 F.2d at 86.

134 See, e.g., *Austin v. Kroger Texas L.P.*, 746 F.3d 191, 204 (5th Cir. 2014) (per curiam); *DeCarlo v. Bonus Stores, Inc.*, 512 F.3d 173, 177 (5th Cir. 2007).

dismiss the case.[135] Or if a litigant fails to make a ripe state-law argument to the state court regarding the certified issue, that litigant won't ordinarily be permitted to make the argument after the case returns to the federal court.

A 1986 D.C. Circuit case[136] is illustrative. The district court interpreted Indiana law and granted summary judgment in favor of the plaintiff. When the defendant appealed to the D.C. Circuit, that court certified the question of interpretation to the Indiana Supreme Court, which confirmed the district court's interpretation. The appellant hadn't challenged the constitutionality of the state-law interpretation in its original briefing to the district court, or on its initial appeal to the circuit court, or in the state-court proceedings that resulted in the opinion on the certified question. Upon returning to the D.C. Circuit, the appellant argued that the issue hadn't been ripe when the state court provided its interpretation.[137] Rejecting this view, the D.C. Circuit found that the issue had clearly been ripe after the federal district court interpreted the state law (as the state court later would), so the challenge had been forfeited.[138]

A litigant need not, however, submit to the state court a federal-law issue presented to the federal court.[139] The Supreme Court averred in *City of Houston v. Hill*[140] that "certified questions should be confined to uncertain questions of state law."[141] If the state court's opinion on certification were to address an issue of federal law, the federal court wouldn't be bound on the issue.[142] The same is true of the state court's opinion on an uncertified

---

135 *See Diamond Club v. Insurance Co. of N. Am.*, 984 F.2d 746, 748 (6th Cir. 1993) (noting that one member of the panel was in favor of dismissal).
136 *Eli Lilly & Co. v. Home Ins. Co.*, 794 F.2d 710 (D.C. Cir. 1986).
137 *Id.* at 716–17.
138 *Id.* at 717.
139 *See Burdick v. Takushi*, 937 F.2d 415, 422 (9th Cir. 1991).
140 482 U.S. 451 (1987).
141 *Id.* at 471 n.23.
142 *See Allison v. UNUM Life Ins. Co.*, 381 F.3d 1015, 1027 n.1 (10th Cir. 2004).

state-law issue.[143] Yet a circuit-court decision dating from 1976 appears to say that if a litigant believes that the state court has answered an uncertified question, it must timely seek rehearing in the state court or else be bound by the court's authoritative answer.[144]

Certification has benefits and drawbacks. The Supreme Court has noted some important benefits: "in the long run," certification can "save time, energy, and resources" and can "help build a cooperative judicial federalism."[145] But some judges have warned against its overuse.[146] In dissent from a Ninth Circuit certification case, Kozinski J. noted some of the drawbacks of the practice. First, certification imposes burdens on state high courts, which have their own important work to complete and have only limited time to address questions posed by federal courts. Kozinski J. showed, for instance, that the California Supreme Court had rejected one-third of the Ninth Circuit's certification requests at the time of his writing.[147] Against this backdrop, when "a federal court certifies a case to a state supreme court, it draws from a limited reservoir of comity."[148] Second, certification imposes burdens on litigants, "forcing them to reargue the case in a different forum—a process that is costly."[149] Third, certification almost certainly entails delay because the process often takes many months.

---

143 See *Roe v. Alabama*, 68 F.3d 404, 406, 409 n.8 (11th Cir. 1995) (per curiam) (factual statement by state court wasn't binding when extraneous to certified issue and contradicted by evidence at later district-court hearing); *Shebester v. Triple Crown Insurers*, 974 F.2d 135, 139 n.3 (10th Cir. 1992) (statement by state court was "not binding on the district court on remand as this question was not certified to the [state] court and it is unclear whether the [state] court had an adequate record to make this determination").

144 See *Tarr v. Manchester Ins. Corp.*, 544 F.2d 14, 15 (1st Cir. 1976) (per curiam).

145 *Lehman Bros.*, 416 U.S. at 391.

146 See generally Bruce M. Selya, *Certified Madness: Ask a Silly Question . . .*, 29 Suffolk U. L. Rev. 677 (1995).

147 *Kremen v. Cohen*, 325 F.3d 1035, 1051 (9th Cir. 2003) (Kozinski J. dissenting).

148 *Id.* at 1043.

149 *Id.* at 1044.

Hence certification should not be sought unreflectively, but should instead be a considered and deliberate choice.[150]

---

[150] *See Chang v. Michiana Telecasting Corp.*, 900 F.2d 1085, 1087 (7th Cir. 1990) ("We do not reflexively certify when parties dispute the meaning of the state's rules.").

75. Controlling State Precedents That Raise a Federal Question

In a federal-question case, a federal court is ordinarily bound to follow the precedents established by state-court decisions on the interpretation of the state constitution and state statutes.

Federal-question cases often raise important issues of state law.[1] For example, a federal statute may expressly borrow from state law to define statutory terms or supply remedies.[2] Or the availability of a federal right or claim may be contingent on state-law-based conditions. The Federal Tort Claims Act, for example, waives federal sovereign immunity only "where the United States, if a private person, would be liable to the claimant in accordance with the law of the place where the act or omission occurred."[3] Or the merits of a federal constitutional challenge to a state law may depend on the scope and meaning of the state law. In due-process claims under 42 U.S.C. § 1983, courts must determine whether a state actor has improperly deprived the plaintiff of a property interest.[4] But these property interests don't arise from the Constitution. Instead, "they are created and their dimensions

---

1   Abbe R. Gluck, *Intersystemic Statutory Interpretation: Methodology as "Law" and the* Erie *Doctrine*, 120 Yale L.J. 1898, 1940 (2011) (observing that cases arising under federal law frequently contain "embedded and often preliminary question[s] of state law" that federal courts must answer en route to resolving the ultimate federal question); *see also* 19 Charles Alan Wright, Arthur R. Miller et al., *Federal Practice and Procedure* § 4520, at 636 (2d ed. 1996 & Supp. 2015) (noting that federal courts commonly apply state law in federal-question cases).

2   *See, e.g.*, 42 U.S.C. § 1988 (When federal law is inadequate to protect civil rights, "the common law, as modified and changed by the constitution and statutes of the State wherein the court having jurisdiction of such civil or criminal cause is held, so far as the same is not inconsistent with the Constitution and laws of the United States, shall be extended to and govern the said courts in the trial and disposition of the cause."); *Astrue v. Capato ex rel. B.N.C.*, 132 S.Ct. 2021, 2031–32 (2012) (noting that the Social Security Act "commonly refers to state law on matters of family status").

3   28 U.S.C. § 1346(b)(1).

4   *See, e.g., Town of Castle Rock v. Gonzales*, 545 U.S. 748, 755 (2005) (plaintiff alleged deprivation of right to enforcement of restraining order); *Memphis Light, Gas & Water Div. v. Craft*, 436 U.S. 1, 3 (1978) (plaintiffs alleged deprivation of right

are defined by existing rules or understandings that stem from an independent source such as state law."[5]

In federal-question cases, therefore, "[r]esolution of the federal issue begins . . . with a determination of what it is that state law provides."[6] Federal courts find themselves in the delicate position of having to interpret state statutory and constitutional provisions without offending important "principles of federalism and comity"[7] or creating inconsistencies in state law.[8]

A litigant may claim that a state statute is invalid under the United States Constitution or is preempted by a federal statute. In such a case, the federal court must determine what the state statute means.[9] How should a federal court navigate those choppy waters when the meaning of the state statute or state constitutional provision is contested? The answer is straightforward: in federal-question cases, as in diversity cases, federal courts look to the decisions of state courts to properly understand state law.[10]

When a state's high court has interpreted a state statute or state constitutional provision, federal courts will not disturb that interpretation.[11] Three representative cases from the civil-rights era illustrate this rule.

---

to continued utility service); *Goss v. Lopez*, 419 U.S. 565, 568–69 (1975) (plaintiffs alleged deprivation of right to public education).

5   *Town of Castle Rock*, 545 U.S. at 756 (quoting *Paul v. Davis*, 424 U.S. 693, 709 (1976)).

6   *Id.* at 757.

7   *Id.* at 777 (Stevens J. dissenting).

8   *See Arizonans for Official English v. Arizona*, 520 U.S. 43, 79 (1997) (holding that when federal court construes state statute without benefit of guidance from state high court, federal court "risks friction-generating error").

9   *See, e.g., Stenberg v. Carhart*, 530 U.S. 914, 938–46 (2000) (Supreme Court determined scope of Nebraska law banning partial-birth abortion before determining whether law, as construed, violated Constitution); *Grayned v. City of Rockford*, 408 U.S. 104, 109–14 (1972) (Supreme Court interpreted meaning of municipal anti-noise ordinance before evaluating validity under First Amendment).

10 *See Commissioner v. Estate of Bosch*, 387 U.S. 456, 465 (1967) (stating the principle that federal courts must follow "state law as announced by the highest court of the State" in both diversity and federal-question cases in which "the underlying substantive rule involved is based on state law").

11 *West v. AT&T Co.*, 311 U.S. 223, 236 (1940).

First, in the classic First Amendment case *Cox v. Louisiana*,[12] a minister who led a peaceable demonstration against segregation was convicted of violating a state statute that prohibited disturbing the peace.[13] The state high court had previously interpreted the statute to "allow persons to be punished merely for peacefully expressing unpopular views."[14] The U.S. Supreme Court—rather than interpreting the state statute from scratch—accepted the state high court's interpretation of the statute as authoritative.[15] The Supreme Court ultimately concluded that the statute, as construed by the state's high court, was unconstitutionally vague.[16]

Garner v. Louisiana[17] provides a second illustration of the point. In *Garner*, several students had been arrested and convicted after participating in a sit-in at a Louisiana lunch counter.[18] The students challenged their convictions under a variety of constitutional theories.[19] But before reaching the constitutional issues, the Supreme Court sought to pinpoint "the type of conduct proscribed" by the state statute under which the students were convicted.[20] To answer that question, the Supreme Court relied on state high-court precedent interpreting an earlier version of the relevant state statute.[21] As the Court explained: "We of course are bound by a State's interpretation of its own statute and will not substitute our judgment for that of the State's."[22] In other words, "Louisiana courts have the final authority to interpret, and, where

---

12 379 U.S. 536 (1965).

13 *Id.* at 537.

14 *Id.* at 551.

15 *Id.*

16 *Id.* at 552; *cf. Shuttlesworth v. City of Birmingham*, 382 U.S. 87, 90–91 (1965) (finding that the municipal ordinance wasn't unconstitutionally overbroad, despite being expansively written, because that state appeals court had issued a narrowing construction).

17 368 U.S. 157 (1961).

18 *Id.* at 158.

19 *Id.* at 162–63.

20 *Id.* at 165.

21 *Id.* at 165–69.

22 *Id.* at 166.

they see fit, to reinterpret that State's legislation."[23] Only after fully understanding the state high court's interpretation of the relevant statute did the Court analyze the federal constitutional issues in the case.[24]

Third, in *Shaw v. Delta Air Lines, Inc.*,[25] the Supreme Court confronted the question whether the federal Employee Retirement Income Security Act of 1974 preempted New York's Human Rights Law.[26] The Human Rights Law made discrimination on the basis of sex unlawful.[27] Interpreting that broad statutory proscription, the New York Court of Appeals had earlier held that "a private employer whose employee benefit plan treats pregnancy differently from other nonoccupational disabilities engages in sex discrimination within the meaning of the Human Rights Law."[28] In analyzing the preemption question, the Supreme Court didn't construe the Human Rights Law on its own. Instead, it accepted without question the New York Court of Appeals' construction of that statute.[29]

Faced with a serious federal constitutional challenge to a federal statute, federal courts usually "ascertain whether a construction of the statute is fairly possible by which the question may be avoided."[30] Many state courts do the same when evaluating state constitutional attacks on state statutes.[31] Federal courts only sometimes use the constitutional-avoidance canon to construe

---

23 *Id.* at 169.
24 *See id.* at 170.
25 463 U.S. 85 (1983).
26 *Id.* at 88.
27 *Id.*
28 *Id.*
29 *See id.* at 96–97.
30 *Crowell v. Benson*, 285 U.S. 22, 62 (1932); *see, e.g., Rodriguez v. Robbins*, 715 F.3d 1127, 1133–34 (9th Cir. 2013) (applying constitutional-avoidance doctrine).
31 *See, e.g., Beaufort Cnty. Bd. of Educ. v. Beaufort Cnty. Bd. of Comm'rs*, 681 S.E.2d 278, 282 (N.C. 2009) (When "one of two reasonable constructions will raise a serious constitutional question, the construction which avoids this question should be adopted.") (quoting *In re Arthur*, 231 S.E.2d 614, 616 (N.C. 1977)).

state statutes if the state in question employs the canon.[32] But the option of adopting a narrowing construction is unavailable when federal courts hear constitutional challenges to state statutes that have *already* been authoritatively interpreted by the state high court.

In the 1972 Supreme Court case of *Gooding v. Wilson*,[33] for example, a defendant challenged his misdemeanor conviction under a Georgia statute that prohibited the use of "opprobrious words or abusive language, tending to cause a breach of the peace."[34] The Supreme Court noted that the statute could withstand his challenge "upon its facial constitutionality only if, as authoritatively construed by the Georgia courts, it is not susceptible of application to speech, although vulgar or offensive, that is protected by the First and Fourteenth Amendments."[35] But when construing the statute, the Georgia courts had not so narrowed it.[36] The Supreme Court therefore concluded that the statute, as written and as interpreted by the state courts, was unconstitutionally vague and overbroad.[37]

An age-old principle of interpretation—the presumption of validity, known also as *ut res magis valeat quam pereat*[38]—holds that if a statute can be read two ways, one upholding it as valid and the other vitiating it as unconstitutional or otherwise invalid, the interpretation leading to validity controls. That is the rule if all other things are equal. But sometimes they aren't equal: a state high court may have interpreted a state statute in a way that forecloses the valid reading. If that is so, the state interpretation persists and the statute fails.

---

32   *See* Abbe R. Gluck, *Intersystemic Statutory Interpretation: Methodology as "Law" and the* Erie *Doctrine*, 120 Yale L.J. 1898, 1950 (2011) (arguing that the federal courts too rarely consider whether state courts apply constitutional avoidance).

33   405 U.S. 518 (1972).

34   *Id.* at 519 (quoting Ga. Code Ann. § 26–6303).

35   *Id.* at 520.

36   *Id.* at 524.

37   *Id.* at 528.

38   Antonin Scalia & Bryan A. Garner, *Reading Law: The Interpretation of Legal Texts* 66–68 (2012).

76. Fictitious-Case and Test-Case Decisions

A federal court will not entertain a suggestion that a decision of a state's high court was rendered in a fictitious or test case—and is therefore not binding—unless the facts underlying the decision show that it was made solely for the purpose of anticipating and influencing the judgment of the federal court in an already-pending action.

The Constitution circumscribes the judicial power of the federal courts to the adjudication of cases and controversies.[1] Under Article III's case-or-controversy requirement, federal courts may hear only cases that involve an actual conflict between adverse parties.

Unlike federal courts, state courts aren't bound by Article III.[2] As a result, state courts may hear cases that would not satisfy the case-or-controversy requirement. In practice, though, many state courts prohibit nonadversarial lawsuits.[3]

As a general matter, federal courts are bound to follow state-court decisions on state law.[4] That is true even if those decisions were rendered in a case that would not meet Article III's case-or-controversy requirement, in what might be called a *fictitious case* or *test case*.

An 1895 Sixth Circuit decision[5] illustrates this principle. That case involved a challenge to an Ohio state law under the Ohio

---

[1] U.S. Const. art. III, § 2, cl. 1.

[2] *See ASARCO Inc. v. Kadish*, 490 U.S. 605, 617 (1989) ("We have recognized often that the constraints of Article III do not apply to state courts, and accordingly the state courts are not bound by the limitations of a case or controversy."); *New York State Club Ass'n v. City of New York*, 487 U.S. 1, 8 n.2 (1988) ("The States are thus left free as a matter of their own procedural law to determine whether their courts may issue advisory opinions or to determine matters that would not satisfy the more stringent requirement in the federal courts that an actual 'case' or 'controversy' be presented for resolution.").

[3] *See* F. Andrew Hessick, *Cases, Controversies, and Diversity*, 109 Nw. U. L. Rev. 57, 72 & n.110 (2015) (collecting state-court cases).

[4] *See West v. AT&T Co.*, 311 U.S. 223, 236 (1940); *see also Montana v. Wyoming*, 563 U.S. 368, 377 n.5 (2011).

[5] *Sanford v. Poe*, 69 F. 546 (6th Cir. 1895), *abrogated in part by Quill Corp. v. North Dakota*, 504 U.S. 298, 309 (1992).

Constitution. The Sixth Circuit concluded that the state constitutional question "must be regarded as conclusively settled for this court by the opinion of the highest court of the state."[6] The case in which that decision was made "had many features of a moot-court case,"[7] the court said. But even though "[t]he facts do show that a case was made up for the purpose of obtaining the opinion of that court in as summary a way as possible, and that it was intended as a test case,"[8] any suggestion that the holding should not be followed "cannot be seriously entertained."[9] The conclusion reached by the Ohio Supreme Court "was that the case was one fairly under its jurisdiction."[10] The fact that the case "was in reality a friendly suit does not detract from the weight of the court's opinion as an opinion."[11]

Yet there is one exception to this principle: When a state high court issues a decision in a nonadversarial case in order to anticipate and influence the judgment of a federal court in a pending action, the federal court may depart from the state court's decision. The Supreme Court alluded to this exception in *Pease v. Peck*.[12] The Court first stated the "general rule" that "the courts of the United States are bound to follow the decisions of the state courts on the construction of their own laws."[13] It then cautioned that the rule is not without exceptions; for example, cases "may exist also, when a cause is got up in a state court for the very purpose of anticipating our decision of a question known to be pending in this court."[14] In that circumstance, a federal court is not necessarily bound by the state court's decision.

More than a century after the Supreme Court's decision in *Pease*, the Fifth Circuit faced that exceptional situation in a 1975

---

6   69 F. at 548.
7   *Id.* at 549.
8   *Id.*
9   *Id.*
10 *Id.*
11 *Id.*
12 59 U.S. (18 How.) 595 (1855).
13 *Id.* at 598.
14 *Id.* at 599.

case.[15] In that case, a corporation sued in federal court to enforce a contract to purchase state land in Dade County, Florida.[16] The board of trustees of a Florida state agency and the state board of education held title to the land.[17] After the district court entered judgment in the corporation's favor, the county brought a mandamus action in the Florida Supreme Court to compel the state boards to convey the land.[18] The state boards consented to the entry of the writ of mandamus, and the Florida Supreme Court issued the writ.[19] The corporation then sought a federal injunction against the county's further prosecution of the mandamus action, on the ground that the earlier federal-court judgment was res judicata and barred the county's assertion of rights.[20] The state argued that the Florida Supreme Court's decision to issue the writ of mandamus "was the definitive statement of Florida law" on whether the earlier federal-court judgment in the corporation's favor was res judicata.[21] The Fifth Circuit concluded that it wasn't bound by the Florida Supreme Court's judgment issuing the writ of mandamus in the county's favor. Although the state-court judgment was "entitled to a presumption of regularity," that presumption was "overcome by evidence that the judgment" resulted from "a nonadversary proceeding."[22] Under those exceptional circumstances, the Fifth Circuit concluded that it wasn't obligated to follow the state court's decision.[23]

---

[15] *Aerojet-General Corp. v. Askew*, 511 F.2d 710 (5th Cir. 1975).

[16] *Id.* at 713.

[17] *Id.*

[18] *Id.* at 714.

[19] *Id.*

[20] *Id.*

[21] *Id.*

[22] *Id.* at 720.

[23] *Id.* at 721 ("Respect for the integrity of the courts of the states requires that the federal courts exercise great caution in questioning the nonadversary nature of a state court proceeding. In the present case, however, the Deputy Attorney General of Florida admitted to the District Judge that the relationship between the state boards and Dade County was not an adversary one in the state court mandamus action. Under the circumstances, we are not obliged to follow the state court decision in favor of Dade County.") (footnote omitted).

A state-court decision made for the sole purpose of influencing a pending federal-court judgment may not bind federal courts. But short of that exceptional situation, federal courts will follow state-court decisions on questions of state law without inquiring into whether the decision was rendered in a traditional adversarial setting.

G. State-Law Doctrine and Practice

77. Preeminence of State High Courts on State-Law Questions

Whether construing a state's constitution, statutes, or regulations, or for that matter developing common law, the state high court has the final say—and thus final authority— over the interpretation of its own state's laws.

Sitting at the apex of the third branch of independent sovereigns, the state high courts are free to interpret their own state laws however they see fit. In the absence of a federal question, the U.S. Supreme Court lacks jurisdiction to review those decisions. So the *required* impact of the U.S. Supreme Court's precedents on state high courts' decisions on state law is almost nil. As long as a state-court decision clearly rests on an independent and adequate state ground, the national Supreme Court has no power of review,[1] since Congress has granted it power to review only state-court decisions that turn on the meaning of federal law.[2]

The U.S. Supreme Court has occasionally looked beyond a state's interpretation of its own law when, as that Court explains, it appears that the state interpretation is a "subterfuge to evade consideration of a federal issue."[3] In one such case, *Ward v. Board of County Commissioners*,[4] American Indians sued to recover county taxes imposed on their federal allotments—land that was declared nontaxable by federal statute. The Oklahoma Supreme Court denied a refund based on adequate and independent state-law grounds—that the taxes had been paid voluntarily. Whether adequate and independent state grounds exist is a federal question, and the U.S. Supreme Court looked beyond the state court's

---

[1] *Michigan v. Long*, 463 U.S. 1032, 1040 (1983).
[2] 28 U.S.C. § 1257.
[3] *See Mullaney v. Wilbur*, 421 U.S. 684, 691 n.11 (1975) (quoting *Radio Station WOW v. Johnson*, 326 U.S. 120, 129 (1945)). *See also Terre Haute & Indianapolis R.R. v. Indiana ex rel. Ketcham*, 194 U.S. 579 (1904).
[4] 253 U.S. 17, 21 (1920).

determination that the taxes had been voluntarily paid, concluding that they were actually paid under compulsion and threats of seizure. Since the allotments were a vested property right, the county's collections had amounted to a taking without due process under the Fifth Amendment.[5]

A state high court's interpretations of state law are authoritative in all other jurisdictions. In 1815, the U.S. Supreme Court observed that "[i]n cases depending on the statutes of a state . . . this Court adopts the construction of the state where that construction is settled, and can be ascertained."[6] This rule applies to the courts of all other sovereigns: both federal and state courts are to follow the interpretation given to the constitution and laws of a state by that state's courts, following the authoritative rulings of the state's high court.[7] This rule derives from the fact that each state is a unique sovereign.[8]

The rule applies with particular force when the state's courts have passed upon the constitutionality, under the state constitution, of a state statute.[9] That state's courts are the final interpreters

---

5 *Id.* at 23–24.

6 *Polk's Lessee v. Wendal*, 13 U.S. (9 Cranch) 87, 98 (1815).

7 *See Glenn v. Field Packing Co.*, 290 U.S. 177, 178 (1933) (per curiam) (noting that "so far as the application of the state Constitution is concerned, the ultimate determination of the validity of the statute necessarily rests with [the state high] court"); *Walker v. State Harbor Comm'rs*, 84 U.S. (17 Wall.) 648, 651 (1873) (the interpretation of a California statute by the California Supreme Court "is accepted as the true interpretation, whatever may be our opinion of its original soundness"); *Elmendorf v. Taylor*, 23 U.S. (10 Wheat.) 152, 159–60 (1825) (recognizing that the Court "adopt[s] the construction which the Courts of the State have given to [its] laws"); *In re Cohen's Estate*, 269 N.Y.S. 235, 242 (Surr. Ct. 1933) (applying Illinois courts' interpretations of the Illinois Constitution); *Kwilecki v. Holman*, 167 S.W. 989, 990 (Mo. 1914) (recognizing that the decision of a sister state's courts as to "the validity of an act of [the] sister state as judged by its own Constitution" is binding on the courts of other states); *Crocker v. Scott*, 87 P. 102, 105 (Cal. 1906); *Fowler v. Lamson*, 34 N.E. 932, 933 (Ill. 1893); *Brown v. Phillipps*, 16 Iowa 210, 212 (1864) (following the Maryland Supreme Court's ruling under the Maryland Constitution); *cf. Ex Parte Francis*, 165 S.W. 147, 167 (Tex. Crim. App. 1914) (applying the same principle to the validity of a statute under the United States Constitution).

8 *See Redding v. City of Los Angeles*, 185 P.2d 430 (Cal. Dist. Ct. App. 1947).

9 *See Rietz v. California Camino Bank*, 154 Cal. Rptr. 3 (Ct. App. 1979) (unpublished).

of the statute and the final arbiters of its constitutionality under the state's own law.

The Supreme Court may sometimes express its understanding of state law in diversity cases, when interpretation of state law is incidental to a federal question, or when the validity of the law under the United States Constitution is challenged. When a state court later disagrees with the Court's reading of a state-law question, it is free to disregard it.[10]

In a 1912 case[11] before the Illinois Supreme Court, for example, a piano retailer sought to enforce an injunction prohibiting the use of its copyrighted tradename by a competitor.[12] The competitor and its agents were held in contempt and fined, and the individuals were given jail sentences.[13] They challenged these punishments under *Gompers v. Buck's Stove & Range Co.*,[14] a case in which the U.S. Supreme Court had held that a litigant found liable for civil contempt may be ordered to pay a fine to his opponent as compensation for the damages suffered, but that because imprisonment or a fine paid to the court does nothing to remedy the harm done, it is impermissible.[15] Illinois law had long been to the contrary, allowing a contemnor to be punished in both civil and criminal proceedings.[16] The Illinois court declined to alter its precedent to conform to *Gompers*, observing that when U.S. Supreme Court decisions "conflict with those of this court upon questions over which this court has complete and final jurisdiction, it is our plain

---

10   *See, e.g., Soehnlein v. Soehnlein*, 131 N.W. 739, 744 (Wis. 1911) (opining that the U.S. Supreme Court had "somehow[] got, it seems, a wrong idea of the authorities" and followed a minority rule regarding the law of corporations instead of the true majority rule).

11   *Rothschild & Co. v. Steger & Sons Piano Mfg. Co.*, 99 N.E. 920 (Ill. 1912).

12   *Id.* at 921.

13   *Id.*

14   221 U.S. 418 (1911).

15   *Id.* at 443–45.

16   *Rothschild*, 99 N.E. at 921–22; *see also Leopold v. People*, 30 N.E. 348, 350 (Ill. 1892) (recognizing the court's power to "imprison or fine the offender, or do both, as to it, under all the circumstances, seemed just, and best calculated to compel obedience").

duty, under the law, to adhere to our own decisions."[17] Of course, a federal decision may have res judicata effect in a state-court proceeding, and the state court must determine whether res judicata applies under federal principles.[18]

If a court's interpretation of the law of another state is superseded by a contrary interpretation by that state's courts, the later interpretation must be given precedence. In *Fairfield v. County of Gallatin*, the U.S. Supreme Court abandoned its earlier interpretation of the Illinois Constitution in favor of the interpretation given by the Illinois Supreme Court.[19] At issue was whether a constitutional provision allowed a county, under certain conditions, to make a donation to a railroad company in order to induce it to build a line through the county.[20] The question was whether bonds that had been approved in an election before the adoption of the provision could lawfully be issued.[21] The U.S. Supreme Court had previously decided that the Illinois constitutional provision barred issuing bonds in such circumstances.[22] But in doing so, it had not been aware that the Illinois Supreme Court had reached the opposite conclusion.[23] Recognizing the state precedent in *Fairfield*, the Court followed the state-court decision and observed that "it is the peculiar province of the Supreme Court of a State to interpret its organic law, as well as its statutes, and that it is the duty as well as the pleasure of this court to follow and adopt that court's interpretation."[24]

But when a state court must decide the validity of a sister state's statutes under the United States Constitution, the court is bound by the rulings of the U.S. Supreme Court. The court must

---

17 *Rothschild*, 99 N.E. at 923; *see also Round Lake Sanitary Dist. v. Basic Elecs. Mfg. Corp.*, 376 N.E.2d 436, 438–39 (Ill. App. Ct. 1978) (recognizing the distinctive Illinois rule).

18 *See VanDeWalle v. Albion Nat'l Bank*, 500 N.W.2d 566, 571 (Neb. 1993).

19 100 U.S. 47, 49–50 (1879).

20 *Id.* at 48–49.

21 *Id.*

22 *Town of Concord v. Portsmouth Sav. Bank*, 92 U.S. 625 (1875).

23 *Chicago & Iowa R.R. v. Pinckney*, 74 Ill. 277 (1874).

24 *Fairfield*, 100 U.S. at 50.

adopt the interpretation of the sister-state's statute given by the courts of that state (see § 84) but must decide for itself whether the statute, so interpreted, is constitutional by reference to the rulings of the U.S. Supreme Court.[25]

Courts sometimes erroneously conflate a sister state's binding authority in rulings on the constitutionality of its statutes under the United States Constitution with the state's authority to determine the statute's constitutionality under the state's own constitution. In a 1920 case[26] before the Utah Supreme Court, the constitutionality of the Wyoming workers' compensation act was challenged under the Fourteenth Amendment. The court correctly deferred to the Wyoming Supreme Court's interpretation of the statute as barring an employee from a common-law right of action.[27] But the Utah court incorrectly deferred to the Wyoming court's decision that the statute was valid under the Fourteenth Amendment.[28] As a matter of federal law, the Utah court should have decided that issue on its own.

The interpretation of state constitutions

As long as a state court doesn't violate another federal guarantee in the process, it may construe a provision in its own constitution more broadly than the U.S. Supreme Court has construed the analogous federal guarantee.[29] That is true even when the state constitutional guarantee parallels the federal guarantee word for word or resembles it closely.[30] When "[t]he Framers split the atom

---

25 *See, e.g., Kwilecki v. Holman*, 167 S.W. 989, 990 (Mo. 1914); *Stoddart v. Smith*, 5 Binn. 355 (Pa. 1812) (determining the constitutionality of a Maryland statute).

26 *Bozo v. Central Coal & Coke Co.*, 193 P. 1111 (Utah 1920).

27 *Id.* at 1112 (citing *Zancanelli v. Central Coal & Coke Co.*, 173 P. 981 (Wyo. 1918)).

28 *Id.*

29 *See State v. Santiago*, 492 P.2d 657, 664 (Haw. 1971); *Shelton v. Hamilton*, 23 Miss. 496, 498 (1852); *see also* Joseph Blocher, *Reverse Incorporation of State Constitutional Law*, 84 S. Cal. L. Rev. 323, 334 (2011); Robert F. Williams, *The Law of American State Constitutions* 113–14 (2009) (noting that the New Judicial Federalism, dating from the 1970s, means that state judges may "interpret[] their state constitutional rights provisions to provide *more* protection than the national minimum standard guaranteed by the federal Constitution").

30 *Compare South Dakota v. Opperman*, 428 U.S. 364, 372–76 (1976) (finding no Fourth Amendment violation), *with State v. Opperman*, 247 N.W.2d 673,

of sovereignty,"[31] they created a government that featured two sets of sovereigns over nearly every part of the country, enabling 51 constitutions that simultaneously empower and constrain. Hence all state and local laws have *two* potential constitutional limitations on their validity. Every state constitution is "a document of independent force."[32] As one state high court opined, "As long as state courts provide at least as much protection as the United States Supreme Court has provided in its interpretation of the federal Bill of Rights, state courts are unrestricted in according greater civil liberties and protections to individuals and groups" under their constitutions.[33] The U.S. Supreme Court has echoed this sentiment—for example, with regard to police activity—that "a State is free *as a matter of its own law* to impose greater restrictions on police activity than those this Court holds to be necessary upon federal constitutional standards."[34] The same holds for legislative activity.

Yet state courts may also construe identically worded state constitutional guarantees *less broadly* than their federal counterparts.[35] What may independently go up may independently go down. This last possibility, it is true, usually makes little difference in the outcome of a case given the omnipresent backstop of the federal guarantee. If the claimants (wisely) rely on the state *and* federal constitutional guarantees in filing a state-court action, they will never be at risk of losing a case on the independent and adequate state ground that the state constitutional guarantee covers less ground than the federal one. For if the state court rejects

---

674–75 (S.D. 1976) (finding violation of the state constitution on the same facts, although its language was "almost identical to the Fourth Amendment"). *See also* Blocher, *Reverse Incorporation*, 84 S. Cal. L. Rev. at 334.

31   *U.S. Term Limits, Inc. v. Thornton*, 514 U.S. 779, 838 (1995) (Kennedy J. concurring).

32   *See, e.g., Arnold v. Cleveland*, 616 N.E.2d 163, 169 (Ohio 1993).

33   *Id.*

34   *Oregon v. Hass*, 420 U.S. 714, 719 (1975); *cf. California v. Greenwood*, 486 U.S. 35, 43 (1988) (the scope of federal protection doesn't depend on state law).

35   *See State v. Smith*, 725 P.2d 894 (Or. 1986) (en banc) (plurality) (explaining that the Oregon Constitution doesn't require *Miranda* warnings); *State v. Walker*, 267 P.3d 210 (Utah 2011) (Lee J. concurring) (explaining that the Utah Constitution doesn't contain an exclusionary rule).

the claimant's request for relief on the state-law claim, it will be required to consider the independent request for relief under the more protective federal guarantee.

All this is prelude to a question of considerable practical importance and the main topic of this section: the precedential value of national Supreme Court constitutional decisions in litigation in the state high courts when the state courts must construe identically or similarly worded state constitutional guarantees. One might expect the state courts to take ownership over, indeed considerable pride in, construing their own guarantees independently and without regard to any shadow cast by related U.S. Supreme Court decisions on the matter. But the reality is more complicated. While the state courts' sovereign interest in construing their own constitutions independently tugs the state courts in one direction, the prominence of U.S. Supreme Court precedents tugs them in the other. That the state courts *may* construe their own constitutions differently from the federal Constitution isn't to say that they *will* or even *should*.

Some history puts the issue in context. Initially, the state courts had few federal constitutional precedents to consider. In the first 75 years of our history, there were just two U.S. Supreme Court decisions enforcing federal constitutional rights against the states or the national government.[36] The federal guarantees in the Bill of Rights applied only to the federal government, not to the states.[37] For much of our early history, then, the state courts were the primary enforcers of constitutional rights, and the states' constitutions together with the precedents developed under them were the primary vehicles for enforcing individual-rights guarantees.[38]

---

36 *See* John E. Nowak & Ronald D. Rotunda, *Constitutional Law* 136 n.13 (6th ed. 2000) ("In only two cases prior to the Civil War did the Court strike down federal legislation."); William B. Lockhart et al., *Constitutional Law: Cases, Comments, Questions* 8 n.f (5th ed. 1980); *see also Dred Scott v. Sandford*, 60 U.S. (19 How.) 393 (1856); *Marbury v. Madison*, 5 U.S. (1 Cranch) 137 (1803).

37 *See Barron v. City of Baltimore*, 32 U.S. (7 Pet.) 243, 248–49 (1833).

38 Paul M. Bator et al., *Hart & Wechsler's The Federal Courts and the Federal System* 359 (2d ed. 1973) (in which Hart, in dialogue, says: "In the scheme of the Constitution," the state courts "are the primary guarantors of constitutional rights.").

Two developments shifted the focus from the state guarantees to the federal guarantees. The U.S. Supreme Court eventually incorporated most provisions in the Bill of Rights through the Fourteenth Amendment to make them applicable to the states.[39] In so doing, the Supreme Court over time expanded the nature of these rights as well as the due-process and equal-protection rights of the Fourteenth Amendment. Before long, state courts faced federal and state constitutional claims in the same case—say a free-speech claim under the federal *and* state constitutions—and before long they faced an abundance of federal precedent to work with in considering both claims.

None of this history—whether incorporation or the growth of federal constitutional law—altered the *required* impact of federal precedents on state courts when they resolve similar state constitutional claims. As independent court systems, the state courts remain free to ignore federal precedents in construing their own constitutions. They remain free to use such precedents when they are persuasive and to ignore them when they aren't. But the state courts also remain free to follow federal precedents in construing their own guarantees.

Lockstepping with the U.S. Constitution

For many state courts (and for many litigants), the allure of U.S. Supreme Court precedents in the post-Warren Court era has been difficult to resist, giving the federal precedents a salience in state constitutional debates that is difficult to overstate. So it is that many state courts engage in lockstepping—of linking interpretations of some state guarantees to the federal-court interpretations of their federal counterparts, or of treating the federal precedents as presumptively "coextensive" in some areas,[40] or at least

---

39 *See, e.g., Cantwell v. Connecticut*, 310 U.S. 296, 303 (1940) (incorporating the free-exercise guarantee of the First Amendment into the due-process guarantee of the Fourteenth Amendment).

40 *See State v. Robinette*, 685 N.E.2d 762, 766 (Ohio 1997) (commenting that "where the provisions [of the federal and state constitutions] are similar and no persuasive reason for a differing interpretation is presented, this court has determined that protections afforded by Ohio's Constitution are coextensive with those provided by the United States Constitution").

of treating them as "very persuasive."[41] A few state constitutions indeed *require* lockstepping in some areas.[42] The "aura of correctness" of decisions by the U.S. Supreme Court,[43] together with the prestige of the federal high court and the resulting "glare" of its precedents, has heavily influenced many state courts in construing their own guarantees.[44] Any such linking of the two interpretations gives the federal precedents even more weight over time—whether because it creates a "poverty of state constitutional discourse" with which state judges can work[45] or because it prompts state-court litigants not to brief the state constitutional-law claims independently from the federal claims.[46]

Yet many state courts remain willing to resist the pull of the federal precedents and to construe their state constitutional guarantees independently.[47] As the Kentucky Supreme Court observed in expanding the right to privacy in the commonwealth, no such right is spelled out explicitly in either the U.S. or the Kentucky Constitution: "The Commonwealth recognizes [that] such rights exist, but takes the position that, since they are implicit rather than explicit, our Court should march in lock step with the United States Supreme Court in declaring when such rights exist."[48] To

---

41 *Id.* at 767.

42 *See* Cal. Const. art. I, § 24 (requiring that courts afford criminal defendants no greater rights than those afforded by the U.S. Constitution); Fla. Const. art. I, § 12 (prohibiting state exclusionary rule from being extended beyond what is required for violations of the Fourth Amendment).

43 Robert F. Williams, *State Constitutional Law: Cases and Materials* 194 (3d ed. 1999).

44 Robert F. Williams, *State Courts Adopting Federal Constitutional Doctrine: Case-by-Case Adoptionism or Prospective Lockstepping?*, 46 Wm. & Mary L. Rev. 1499, 1500–01 (2005).

45 James A. Gardner, *The Failed Discourse of State Constitutionalism*, 90 Mich. L. Rev. 761, 778, 788 (1992).

46 Jeffrey S. Sutton, *What Does—and Does Not—Ail State Constitutional Law*, 59 U. Kan. L. Rev. 687, 710 (2011).

47 *See, e.g., Hill-Murray Fed'n of Teachers v. Hill-Murray High Sch.*, 487 N.W.2d 857, 864–66 (Minn. 1992) (en banc) (construing the state's constitutional free-exercise guarantee more broadly than that in the First Amendment); *State v. Beauchesne*, 868 A.2d 972, 979–80 (N.H. 2005) (construing the state's constitutional search-and-seizure limitations more broadly than those in the Fourth Amendment).

48 *Commonwealth v. Wasson*, 842 S.W.2d 487, 492 (Ky. 1992).

do so, the court said, would be to shirk its duty: "Such is not the formulation of federalism. On the contrary, under our system of dual sovereignty, it is our responsibility to interpret and apply our constitution independently."[49]

There are many explanations for why a state court might construe its provisions differently from the federal guarantees.

First, remember that the original liberty and property protections in the United States Constitution primarily originated in the state constitutions.[50] Before ratifying the national Constitution in 1789, all the colonies but Rhode Island had written their own constitutions. Yet it may fairly be said that 13 American constitutions antedated the federal Constitution because Vermont—not yet an independent state but an ambitious territory—ratified its own constitution in 1777.[51] Those 13 original state constitutions all guaranteed a wide range of individual rights that became the prototypes for the federal Bill of Rights and other individual rights expressed in the federal Constitution.[52] So an inquiry into the meaning of a federal individual right most sensibly begins with the meaning of the state guarantee on which it was based—and the drafting history of the state constitutions on the point.[53]

Second, the state guarantees are often distinctively worded. They were ratified in—and continue to be interpreted in—unique historical and cultural contexts.[54] Different language often leads to

---

49 *Id.*

50 Sutton, *What Does—and Does Not—Ail State Constitutional Law*, 59 U. Kan. L. Rev. at 708; Randy J. Holland, *State Constitutions: Purpose and Function*, 69 Temple L. Rev. 989, 997 (1996); Harry G. Hutchison, Lochner, *Liberty of Contract, and Paternalism: Revising the Revisionists?*, 47 Ind. L. Rev. 421, 428–29 (2014).

51 Hans A. Linde, *The Bill of Rights: A Documentary History*, 52 Or. L. Rev. 325, 332 (1973) (book review).

52 Holland, *State Constitutions: Purpose and Function*, 69 Temple L. Rev. at 997.

53 *See generally* Gordon S. Wood, *The Creation of the American Republic, 1776–1787* (1969); Gordon S. Wood, *The Making of the Constitution* (1987).

54 *See Sitz v. Department of State Police*, 506 N.W.2d 209, 217 (Mich. 1993) ("As a matter of simple logic, because the [state and federal constitutional] texts were written at different times by different people, the protections afforded may be greater, lesser, or the same."); *Blum v. Merrell Dow Pharm., Inc.*, 626 A.2d 537, 549 (Pa. 1993) (concluding that the state's history and caselaw warrant a departure from the Supreme Court's constitutional interpretation).

a different meaning.[55] The local traditions of each state essentially do the same.[56] A free-exercise guarantee in the constitution of a state like Utah or Rhode Island, even if it mirrors or resembles the language of the federal guarantee, comes with a historical context apt to shape its meaning. The same is true for property-rights protections or gun-rights protections in rural states as opposed to states with significant urban populations.[57] And so on with other rights.

The Pennsylvania Supreme Court makes four inquiries in determining whether one of its constitutional guarantees should be construed differently from its federal counterpart: "(1) text of the Pennsylvania constitutional provision; (2) history of the provision, including Pennsylvania case law; (3) related case law from other states; (4) policy considerations, including unique issues of state and local concern, and applicability within modern Pennsylvania jurisprudence."[58] Guided by these factors, the court in one case held that the Pennsylvania and federal constitutional rights to

---

55 *See, e.g., Richardson v. State*, 717 N.E.2d 32 (Ind. 1999); *Commonwealth v. Ludwig*, 594 A.2d 281 (Pa. 1991) (noting that the Pennsylvania Constitution's confrontation clause, unlike the Sixth Amendment's, guarantees "face to face" confrontation); *Jensen ex rel. Jensen v. Cunningham*, 250 P.3d 465, 477 (Utah 2011) (noting that "the standards for state and federal constitutional claims are different because they are based on different constitutional language and different interpretive case law"); *Manufactured Hous. Cmtys. v. State*, 13 P.3d 183, 195 (Wash. 2000) (en banc) (noting that unlike the Fifth Amendment, "the Washington State Constitution explicitly prohibits taking private property solely for a private use—with or without compensation").

56 *Claudio v. State*, 585 A.2d 1278, 1289–90 (Del. 1991) (relying on unique drafting history and local traditions in construing the right to a jury trial in a criminal case under the Delaware Constitution more broadly than the Sixth Amendment's guarantee under the Federal Constitution).

57 *See Doe v. Wilmington Hous. Auth.*, 88 A.3d 654, 663 (Del. 2014) (en banc) (discussing the state's "long history, dating back to the Revolution," of allowing citizens to bear arms for protection against public and private violence, for membership in the militia, and for hunting); *compare Goldstein v. New York State Urban Dev. Corp.*, 921 N.E.2d 164 (N.Y. 2009) (rejecting property-rights claim and upholding "removal of urban blight" as proper), *with Board of Cnty. Comm'rs v. Lowery*, 136 P.3d 639, 651 (Okla. 2006) (granting property-rights claim and extending state guarantee beyond federal protection), *and City of Norwood v. Horney*, 853 N.E.2d 1115 (Ohio 2006) (granting property-rights claim and extending guarantee beyond U.S. Constitution).

58 *Commonwealth v. Edmunds*, 586 A.2d 887, 895 (Pa. 1991).

"trial by jury" in a civil case differ, since the federal guarantee permits six jurors,[59] while the state guarantee demands twelve.[60]

Third, the size of the two sets of jurisdictions—the federal on the one hand, the 50 states on the other—suggests ample room for state-court independence from Supreme Court interpretations of the federal guarantees. All else being equal, an interpreter of rights applicable to 51 jurisdictions and 322 million people—as opposed to one jurisdiction and, say, 10 million people—is less apt to take chances or innovate when presented with close questions about the meaning of language.[61] The far larger jurisdiction of the U.S. Supreme Court may lead that court to underenforce certain language—to apply a "federalism discount" to it[62]—while the state courts have no such concern in addressing a guarantee applicable to one state. Aware of the cultural and legal diversity within the nation, the U.S. Supreme Court has traditionally hesitated to impose far-reaching constitutional rules binding all the states.[63] Further, mistakes are more readily corrected at the state level, where most state constitutions can be amended by a majority vote. At the federal level, three-quarters of the states must ratify an amendment.[64] Meanwhile, the election of state-court judges means that the composition of the state courts changes far more often, creating greater possibilities for revising earlier decisions than at the Supreme Court, where life tenures are the norm.

Fourth, a state high court may simply disagree with the U.S. Supreme Court about the meaning of text.[65] The general, sometimes indeterminate, language of the text may legitimately support

---

59 *Colgrove v. Battin*, 413 U.S. 149, 158 (1973) (civil case); *Williams v. Florida*, 399 U.S. 78, 103 (1970) (criminal case).
60 *Blum*, 626 A.2d at 547.
61 *State v. Hempele*, 576 A.2d 793, 800 (N.J. 1990).
62 Sutton, *What Does—and Does Not—Ail State Constitutional Law*, 59 U. Kan. L. Rev. at 708.
63 *See, e.g., San Antonio Indep. Sch. Dist. v. Rodriguez*, 411 U.S. 1, 43 (1973).
64 U.S. Const. art. V.
65 William J. Brennan, *State Constitutions and the Protection of Individual Rights*, 90 Harv. L. Rev. 489 (1977).

two distinct interpretations.[66] All these considerations may lead state courts not to follow the U.S. Supreme Court when construing identical or similar language in their own constitutions.

One other exception and explanation are in order. As we've seen, U.S. Supreme Court decisions on issues of state law do not bind state high courts—and indeed do not even bind a state's lower courts. But what of a federal circuit court's decision interpreting state law? May the U.S. Supreme Court review such decisions, and if so, does the Court's decision control? Yes and yes. Although the Court has no authority to review state-court decisions turning on independent and adequate state-law grounds,[67] the same isn't true of a federal circuit court's decision turning on state law. The Supreme Court's supervisory power over the federal courts permits it to exercise certiorari jurisdiction over all such decisions, even those turning on state law.[68] To say that the Court has power to review such decisions, however, isn't to say that it does so much at all. To our knowledge, in the past 20 years the Supreme Court has not reviewed the merits of a decision premised on state law by any circuit other than the Tenth.[69] Despite the Supreme Court's authority to review all such state-law decisions in the many diversity cases filed in federal court, the reality is that a circuit court's decisions will generally represent the final word on such matters in that case and in all future federal cases filed within that circuit—unless the state high court issues a contrary decision either on its own or in a case certified to it from a federal trial or appellate court.

---

66 *See Hempele*, 576 A.2d at 814 (noting that its decision "does not follow the course set by the Supreme Court because 'we are persuaded that the equities so strongly favor protection of a person's privacy interest that we should apply our own standard rather than defer to the federal provision'") (quoting *State v. Hunt*, 450 A.2d 952, 954 (N.J. 1982)).

67 *Michigan v. Long*, 463 U.S. 1032 (1983).

68 *See Leavitt v. Jane L.*, 518 U.S. 137, 146 (1996) (per curiam).

69 *See Town of Castle Rock v. Gonzales*, 545 U.S. 748, 756–58 (2005).

Supremacy Clause implications

We say that the impact of Supreme Court precedents on matters of state law is almost nil because the state high courts must not violate the Supremacy Clause of the United States Constitution in the process of construing their own constitutions or state laws. They must not construe a state constitutional guarantee—or any other state or local law—in a way that conflicts with federal law. For example, a state court must not construe a state law in a way that triggers preemption by a federal statute.[70] Similarly, a state court's interpretation of its state constitution must not violate federal law—as by ruling on a state constitutional question in a way that forces a governmental actor to violate a federal guarantee.

Locke v. Davey[71] illustrates one way in which this last possibility *might* occur, though it didn't in fact occur there. The State of Washington offered scholarships to residents for postsecondary education but excluded theology students from those benefits.[72] The source of the exemption was a provision in the Washington Constitution, stating: "No [state] public money or property shall be appropriated for or applied to any religious worship, exercise or instruction."[73] The *Locke* majority held that the state's prohibition on giving scholarships to theology students didn't violate the free-exercise guarantee of the First Amendment.[74] In dissent, Scalia J. reasoned that the classification, even though grounded in the state constitution, discriminated against religion on its face and thus necessarily violated the federal free-exercise guarantee.[75] If Scalia J.'s view had prevailed, the state constitution would have run afoul of the federal one.

---

[70] *Ingersoll-Rand Co. v. McClendon*, 498 U.S. 133, 140 (1990) (holding that ERISA preempts the state wrongful-discharge claim recognized by the Texas Supreme Court under state law).

[71] 540 U.S. 712 (2004).

[72] *Id.* at 715–18.

[73] Wash. Const. art. I, § 11.

[74] *Locke*, 540 U.S. at 725–26.

[75] *Id.* (Scalia J. dissenting).

PruneYard Shopping Center v. Robins[76] illustrates another way in which this last possibility might occur. The California Supreme Court construed the free-speech guarantee in its state constitution to cover *private* restrictions on speech, constitutionalizing the right of individuals to speak or protest at a privately owned shopping center.[77] Even though the federal free-speech requirement requires state action before it applies, the U.S. Supreme Court had no trouble permitting the state courts to construe their own guarantees to give greater protection as long as they didn't violate *other* federal constitutional guarantees in the process.[78] The California Supreme Court's authorization of picketing at a privately owned shopping center, the federal high court held, raised concerns about (but ultimately didn't violate) the shopping center's property rights under the Takings Clause of the Fifth and Fourteenth Amendments.[79]

The principle that state courts aren't bound by the U.S. Supreme Court on questions of state law[80] applies to state courts' interpretation of their states' statutes, even a statute similar to or identical with one at issue in the Supreme Court precedent. So if a state court interprets its own state's statutes, it need not adopt the Supreme Court's construction of the statute, though it may consider the decision for its persuasive value.[81] The same is true

---

76 447 U.S. 74 (1980).

77 *Robins v. PruneYard Shopping Ctr.*, 592 P.2d 341, 347 (Cal. 1979).

78 *PruneYard*, 447 U.S. at 81 ("It is, of course, well established that a State in the exercise of its police power may adopt reasonable restrictions on private property so long as the restrictions do not amount to a taking without just compensation or contravene any other federal constitutional provision.").

79 *Id.* at 82, 85.

80 *See, e.g., Johnson v. Ruark Obstetrics & Gynecology Assocs., P.A.*, 395 S.E.2d 85, 92 (N.C. 1990) (rejecting U.S. Supreme Court's interpretation of North Carolina common law).

81 *See, e.g., People v. Spykstra*, 234 P.3d 662, 666–70 (Colo. 2010) (en banc) (considering precedent from federal and state courts considering analogous similar rules of criminal procedure because the Colorado rule was modeled after the federal rule); *Dejetley v. Kahóohalahala*, 226 P.3d 421, 440 (Haw. 2010) (relying on federal precedent to interpret a Hawaii rule of civil procedure that was "functionally identical" to the federal rule); *State v. Leach*, 370 N.W.2d 240, 252–53 (Wis. 1985) (considering federal precedent regarding Wisconsin rules of criminal procedure that were "taken from" the federal rules); *Clark v. Uniroyal*

when determining whether a state's statute conforms to the state's constitution rather than to the United States Constitution.[82]

Although state courts aren't bound by federal precedent, they often give it persuasive authority. Some courts cite the desirability of uniformity in following a federal precedent construing a procedural rule or statute similar to their own.[83] State courts may also follow federal interpretations of a statute or rules used as a model for the state rules under the canon of construction that the state legislature adopted the state statute with existing federal interpretations in mind.[84] Some states have simply turned to federal precedent because there is no precedent from their own courts.[85]

But this isn't always true. In the 2008 case of *Hall Street Associates v. Mattel, Inc.*, the U.S. Supreme Court held that the grounds for vacating or modifying an arbitration award under the Federal Arbitration Act are exclusive and cannot be supplemented by contract.[86] Hence the litigants' agreement for judicial review of an arbitration award for simple reversible error, as with appellate review of trial-court judgments, was held not to be enforceable.[87] Three years later, the Texas Supreme Court, interpreting essentially identical provisions of the Texas Arbitration Act, reached the

---

    Corp., 327 N.W.2d 372, 374 (Mich. 1982) (per curiam) (observing that federal precedent interpreting federal Civil Rights Act of 1964 is persuasive authority for the interpretation of Michigan analogous Fair Employment Practices Act, and following federal precedent).

82 *Louisville Gas & Elec. Co. v. Coleman*, 277 U.S. 32, 36 (1928) (accepting the state court's rejection of challenge to statute under the state constitution as conclusive, but going on to consider the challenge to the statute under the federal constitution); *Glenn v. Field Packing Co.*, 290 U.S. 177, 178 (1933) (per curiam) (recognizing that "so far as the application of the state Constitution is concerned, the ultimate determination of the validity of the statute necessarily rests with [the state's highest court]"); *Calder v. Bull*, 3 U.S. (3 Dall.) 386 (1798).

83 See *Orme Sch. v. Reeves*, 802 P.2d 1000, 1003 (Ariz. 1990) (in banc).

84 See, e.g., *Rollins Envtl. Servs., Inc. v. Superior Court*, 330 N.E.2d 814, 818 (Mass. 1975); *Wilson v. Great Northern Ry.*, 157 N.W.2d 19, 21 (S.D. 1968) (observing that summary judgment didn't exist in South Dakota until it adopted rules of procedure based on the Federal Rules of Civil Procedure).

85 See, e.g., *Warren, Little & Lund, Inc. v. Max J. Kuney Co.*, 796 P.2d 1263, 1265 (Wash. 1990) (en banc).

86 552 U.S. 576, 578 (2008).

87 *Id.*

opposite conclusion.[88] Noting that it was "of course" required to follow *Hall Street*'s interpretation of the federal statute, the Texas court stated that it was "obliged to examine *Hall Street*'s reasoning" and reach its own judgment in construing the Texas statute.[89] In the end, the Texas court concluded: "With great respect, we are unable to conclude that *Hall Street*'s analysis of the FAA provides a persuasive basis for construing the TAA the same way."[90]

This principle of independent interpretation—even when a state law is modeled on or identical to a federal statute or rule—is further illustrated by a 1990 decision of the Minnesota Supreme Court.[91] The question in that case was whether the filing of an amended complaint naming the proper defendant related back to the filing of the original complaint naming the wrong defendant.[92] In a similar case, *Schiavone v. Fortune*,[93] the U.S. Supreme Court had interpreted Federal Rule of Civil Procedure 15(c) to bar relation back unless the newly named defendant had received the notice required by Rule 15(c) within the limitations period, even though the rule allowed a reasonable time afterward for service.[94] The Minnesota Supreme Court noted that the U.S. Supreme Court's interpretation of Rule 15(c) didn't control its interpretation of its own identical Rule 15.03 in light of differences in other Minnesota rules.[95] The Minnesota rules provided that an action was "commenced" on the date when the complaint was delivered to the sheriff for service so long as it was served within 60 days.[96] So a complaint served outside the limitations period but within the additional 60-day grace period for service—naming a new defendant who had received the notice required by Rule 15.03 from the original complaint—related back to the date on which

---

88 *Nafta Traders, Inc. v. Quinn*, 339 S.W.3d 84, 87 (Tex. 2011).
89 *Id.* at 91.
90 *Id.*
91 *Johnson v. Soo Line R.R.*, 463 N.W.2d 894 (Minn. 1990) (en banc).
92 *Id.* at 895.
93 *Schiavone v. Fortune*, 477 U.S. 21, 29 (1986).
94 *Id.* at 30 (discussing the impact of Fed. R. Civ. P. 4).
95 *Johnson*, 463 N.W.2d at 899.
96 *Id.* at 898.

the original complaint was delivered to the sheriff.[97] The mere fact that *Schiavone* had rejected a similar argument didn't preclude the Minnesota Supreme Court from interpreting its own rules differently.

---

97   *Id.*

78. Validity Under the State's Constitution

A federal court should be reluctant to adjudge a state statute as consistent with or conflicting with the state constitution if the state courts have not addressed the statute's validity. Yet exceptional circumstances may arise in which the federal court may have to rule on a state statute's validity under the state constitution.

As we saw in the preceding section, when a state's high court construes a state statute or a state constitutional provision, even the U.S. Supreme Court must accept that court's authoritative pronouncement on state law.[1] But what if the state courts haven't passed on the validity—under the *state* constitution—of a state statute at issue in a federal proceeding? In general, federal courts are reluctant to address such state constitutional questions in the first instance, unless the answer is somehow unmistakable.

At least two reasons explain this reluctance. First, as one commentator has noted, state constitutional claims generally "raise issues both more fundamental to individual liberties and more central to state autonomy than the state-law claims typically asserted in federal litigation."[2] Letting state courts take the first crack at applying state constitutional provisions therefore serves "fundamental principles of federalism and comity."[3] Second, state courts often possess subject-matter expertise that federal courts lack. State constitutions encompass a range of matters beyond the federal judiciary's ken, from the management of public education

---

1 *See, e.g., Montana v. Wyoming*, 563 U.S. 368, 377 n.5 (2011) ("The highest court of each State, of course, remains 'the final arbiter of what is state law.'") (quoting *West v. AT&T Co.*, 311 U.S. 223, 236 (1940)).

2 Robert A. Schapiro, *Polyphonic Federalism: State Constitutions in the Federal Courts*, 87 Cal. L. Rev. 1409, 1413 (1999).

3 *Young v. New York City Transit Auth.*, 903 F.2d 146, 164 (2d Cir. 1990); *see, e.g., Doe v. Sundquist*, 106 F.3d 702, 708 (6th Cir. 1997) (consideration of comity supported decision not to exercise supplemental jurisdiction over state constitutional challenge to state statute); *Castellano v. Board of Trs. of Police Officers' Variable Supplements Fund*, 937 F.2d 752, 758 (2d Cir. 1991) (concern about comity supported decision not to assert supplemental jurisdiction over "state constitutional claim of first impression").

to the structure of local governments. The Alaska Constitution, for example, contains provisions governing the management of "fish resources, an asset unique in its abundance in Alaska" and "a matter of great state concern."[4]

Those considerations have led federal courts to develop three methods for funneling state constitutional challenges into the state courts for decisions there in the first instance.

First, federal courts have applied *Pullman* abstention to avoid reviewing state constitutional claims before state courts do so. Under that doctrine, federal courts abstain from deciding a federal constitutional challenge if allowing the state courts to resolve a predicate question of state law would more easily resolve the case.[5] In the mid-20th century, the Supreme Court extended *Pullman* abstention to cases in which plaintiffs challenged state statutes on state constitutional grounds.[6]

In *City of Meridian v. Southern Bell Telephone & Telegraph Co.*,[7] for instance, the Supreme Court reviewed the Fifth Circuit's decision that a Mississippi statute conflicted with both the United States and Mississippi Constitutions.[8] The Court vacated the Fifth Circuit's judgment and remanded the case "to the District Court with directions to hold the cause while the parties repair to a state tribunal for an authoritative declaration of applicable state law."[9] As explanation, the Court said that "[p]roper exercise of federal jurisdiction requires that controversies involving unsettled questions of state law be decided in the state tribunals."[10] The Supreme Court has since echoed that principle in other cases raising state constitutional claims.[11]

---

4   *Reetz v. Bozanich*, 397 U.S. 82, 87 (1970).
5   *Railroad Comm'n of Tex. v. Pullman Co.*, 312 U.S. 496, 501 (1941).
6   *See* Schapiro, *Polyphonic Federalism*, 87 Cal. L. Rev. at 1424–27.
7   358 U.S. 639 (1959) (per curiam).
8   *Id.* at 640.
9   *Id.*
10 *Id.*
11 *See, e.g., Harris Cnty. Comm'rs Court v. Moore*, 420 U.S. 77, 84 (1975) (*Pullman* abstention applies "where, as in this case, the uncertain status of local law

But today the issue of when *Pullman* abstention is available to resolve unsettled issues of state constitutional law is murkier.[12] In several cases, the Supreme Court has rejected invoking *Pullman* abstention despite an unresolved or potential state constitutional challenge.[13] The Court has touted other alternatives to the "protracted and expensive" *Pullman* abstention process.[14] In short, although *Pullman* abstention remains good law, it is no longer the Supreme Court's favored alternative.

Second, a federal court confronting a serious state constitutional challenge to a state statute may certify that question to the state courts[15] (see § 74). Certification, as the Supreme Court has explained, "today covers territory once dominated by . . . *Pullman* abstention."[16] Most states have enacted certification statutes, which generally provide that the state's high court will accept questions from the U.S. Supreme Court, the federal circuit courts, and often the federal district courts.

A 1998 Ninth Circuit case[17] illustrates how certification works in this context. The case involved a challenge to a Los Angeles anti-solicitation ordinance under the Liberty of Speech Clause of the California Constitution.[18] The California Supreme Court had not yet resolved the particular constitutional issue raised by the case. Complicating matters, a state appellate court (applying

---

stems from the unsettled relationship between the state constitution and a statute."); *Reetz*, 397 U.S. at 86–87.

12   See Richard H. Fallon Jr. et al., *Hart & Wechsler's The Federal Courts and the Federal System* 1067–68 (6th ed. 2009).

13   See *Hawaii Hous. Auth. v. Midkiff*, 467 U.S. 229, 237 n.4 (1984) (noting that the court could proceed to federal constitutional question rather than abstaining for resolution of state constitutional question because state constitutional provision paralleled federal constitutional provision); *Examining Bd. of Eng'rs, Architects & Surveyors v. Flores de Otero*, 426 U.S. 572, 598 (1976); *Wisconsin v. Constantineau*, 400 U.S. 433, 439 (1971).

14   *Arizonans for Official English v. Arizona*, 520 U.S. 43, 75–80 (1997).

15   See Fallon et al., *Hart & Wechsler's The Federal Courts and the Federal System* at 1072–75; 17A Charles Alan Wright, Arthur R. Miller et al., *Federal Practice and Procedure* § 4248, at 482–86 (3d ed. 2007 & Supp. 2015).

16   *Arizonans for Official English*, 520 U.S. at 75 (internal quotation marks omitted).

17   *Los Angeles All. for Survival v. City of Los Angeles*, 157 F.3d 1162 (9th Cir. 1998).

18   *Id.* at 1162–63.

the state Liberty of Speech Clause) and the U.S. Supreme Court (applying the federal First Amendment) had previously reached different conclusions on the validity of such ordinances.[19] The Ninth Circuit therefore sought guidance from the California Supreme Court on whether the Liberty of Speech Clause was more protective of the kind of speech at issue than was the First Amendment.[20] The California Supreme Court granted the certification request and eventually issued a definitive answer.[21]

Third, federal courts may decline to assert supplemental jurisdiction over novel state constitutional claims.[22] When a federal district court has original jurisdiction over a civil lawsuit, the court also has supplemental jurisdiction "over all other claims that are so related to claims in the action within such original jurisdiction that they form part of the same case or controversy."[23] But a district court may decline to exercise supplemental jurisdiction if "the claim raises a novel or complex issue of State law."[24]

In a 1991 Second Circuit case,[25] retired police officers mounted a constitutional challenge to certain state laws that governed eligibility for retirement benefits.[26] One of the claims required the district court "to interpret the Constitution of the State of New York."[27] The Second Circuit affirmed the district court's decision not to assert supplemental jurisdiction over that claim.[28] Why? The New York Court of Appeals—the state's high court—had never ruled on the particular state constitutional question at

---

19 *Id.* at 1164.

20 *Id.* at 1165.

21 *Los Angeles All. for Survival v. City of Los Angeles*, 993 P.2d 334 (Cal. 2000).

22 *See generally* Schapiro, *Polyphonic Federalism*, 87 Cal. L. Rev. at 1421–22; 13D Charles Alan Wright, Arthur R. Miller et al., *Federal Practice and Procedure* § 3567.3, at 399–400 (3d ed. 2008 & Supp. 2015).

23 28 U.S.C. § 1367(a).

24 *Id.* § 1367(c)(1).

25 *Castellano v. Board of Trs. of Police Officers' Variable Supplements Fund*, 937 F.2d 752 (2d Cir. 1991).

26 *Id.* at 753.

27 *Id.* at 758.

28 *Id.* at 758–59.

issue.[29] The Second Circuit concluded that "it would be, at the very least, imprudent for us to determine a state constitutional claim of first impression" and affirmed the district court's judgment of dismissal.[30]

Similarly, in a 1997 Sixth Circuit case,[31] the court declined to exercise supplemental jurisdiction over a claim that Tennessee's adoption-records disclosure statute violated the state constitution.[32] The court explained that the lawsuit "would have been better brought in state court in the first place, and we deem it prudent to allow the Tennessee courts to decide the purely state law issues."[33]

In sum, federal courts use these three mechanisms—*Pullman* abstention, certification, and declining the exercise of supplemental jurisdiction—to avoid addressing in the first instance the validity of a state statute under a state constitution.

At times, though, a federal court's waiting for a state court to resolve a state constitutional issue would be pointless. For example, some state constitutional provisions have been interpreted by state high courts as identical in every respect with the analogous federal constitutional provisions[34]—in which case review becomes straightforward. But other situations requiring review may occasionally arise. Say that a state constitutional argument is raised as a defense to a state-law claim over which the federal court has diversity jurisdiction, and the state doesn't have a certification

---

29 *Id.* at 758.

30 *Id.* at 758–59; *see also Chandler v. Miller*, 73 F.3d 1543, 1546 n.3 (11th Cir. 1996) (affirming denial of supplemental jurisdiction over claim that drug-testing statute violated Georgia Constitution), *rev'd on other grounds*, 520 U.S. 305 (1997).

31 *Doe v. Sundquist*, 106 F.3d 702 (6th Cir. 1997).

32 *Id.* at 708.

33 *Id.*

34 *See, e.g., State v. Neighbors*, 328 P.3d 1081, 1086 (Kan. 2014) ("Kansas courts interpret § 15 of the Kansas Constitution Bill of Rights to provide the same protection from unlawful government searches and seizures as the Fourth Amendment."); *Eastwood Mall, Inc. v. Slanco*, 626 N.E.2d 59, 61 (Ohio 1994) ("[The] free speech guarantees accorded by the Ohio Constitution are no broader than the First Amendment," and "the First Amendment is the proper basis for interpretation of Section 11, Article I of the Ohio Constitution.").

procedure. The court can't abstain, because this is a defense; there's no certification; and the court can't decline to exercise jurisdiction since diversity jurisdiction is mandatory, not discretionary. Yet if the statute is neither clearly valid nor clearly invalid, what is the federal court to do? We believe that the federal court should take its best shot at evaluating the state statute's constitutionality.

79. Federal Questions in State Courts

With a federal question—that is, one arising under the Constitution, statutes, or treaties of the United States—state courts must follow any applicable U.S. Supreme Court decisions, overruling if necessary their own previous decisions to the contrary.

Just as inferior state courts look to decisions of the state's high court for binding vertical authority on questions of state law, they look to the U.S. Supreme Court on questions of federal law.[1] If a conflict arises between state precedent on a federal question and Supreme Court precedent on the same question, the latter controls.[2]

The Constitution plainly provides that state courts must follow the decisions of the U.S. Supreme Court on matters of federal law: "The Constitution, and the Laws of the United States . . . shall be the supreme Law of the Land; and the Judges in every State shall be bound thereby."[3] The Minnesota Supreme Court summed up this mandate succinctly in 1943: "Where the decisions of the Supreme Court of the United States in matters of federal law arising under the constitution and laws of the United States

---

1 *Marmet Health Care Ctr., Inc. v. Brown*, 132 S.Ct. 1201, 1202 (2012) (per curiam) ("When this Court has fulfilled its duty to interpret federal law, a state court may not contradict or fail to implement the rule so established."); *Chesapeake & Ohio Ry. v. Martin*, 283 U.S. 209, 221 (1931) (explaining that "[t]he determination by this court of [a federal] question is binding upon the state courts, and must be followed, any state law, decision, or rule to the contrary notwithstanding").

2 *See, e.g., Truly Nolen of Am. v. Superior Court*, 145 Cal. Rptr. 3d 432, 446 (Ct. App. 2012) (observing that "[o]n federal statutory issues, intermediate appellate courts in California are absolutely bound to follow the decisions of the California Supreme Court, unless the United States Supreme Court has decided the same question differently") (emphasis omitted).

3 U.S. Const. art. VI, cl. 2. *See Mayor of Nashville v. Cooper*, 73 U.S. (6 Wall.) 247, 253 (1867) ("It is the right and duty of the national government to have its Constitution and laws interpreted and applied in its own judicial tribunals. In cases arising under them . . . this court is the final arbiter.").

are opposed to our prior decisions, it is our plain duty to disregard our decisions and to conform to [them]."[4]

A 1990 decision[5] of the Wisconsin Supreme Court illustrates the principle. The defendant, Pamela Weide, challenged the search of her purse as unreasonable under the Fourth Amendment.[6] An officer had given Ms. Weide a ride home because her car had become disabled, and she accidentally left her purse on the backseat of the car. After Ms. Weide called the police dispatcher to inquire about her purse, the dispatcher instructed the officer to bring the purse to the police station. Before returning the purse, the officer inventoried its contents, finding a vial of cocaine.[7] Ms. Weide was charged with the unlawful possession of the cocaine, and she moved to suppress the evidence on grounds that the search of her purse was unreasonable under the Fourth Amendment.[8]

The Wisconsin Supreme Court had previously held in a 1980 case[9] that a search of a purse found in the locked trunk of a car during an inventory search was unreasonable.[10] The court had recognized that inventory searches serve three valid interests: protecting the owner's property, protecting the police against claims of lost or stolen property, and protecting the police from danger.[11] These interests had all been recognized by the U.S. Supreme Court in *South Dakota v. Opperman*.[12] But the 1980 case had reasoned that one's privacy interest in a closed container such as a

---

4   *Glover v. Minneapolis Bldg. Trades Council*, 10 N.W.2d 481, 484 (Minn. 1943). See Basil Jones, "Stare Decisis," in 26 *The American and English Encyclopaedia of Law* 158, 172 (David S. Garland & Lucius P. McGehee eds., 2d ed. 1904) ("On all questions which involve the construction of the Constitution of the United States [or a federal statute], the Supreme Court of the United States is the ultimate tribunal. Its decision on such questions cannot be withstood or disregarded by the state court without a dereliction of duty and a violation of the cardinal principles of the federal government.").

5   *State v. Weide*, 455 N.W.2d 899 (Wis. 1990).

6   *Id.* at 900.

7   *Id.* at 900–01.

8   *Id.* at 901.

9   *State v. Prober*, 297 N.W.2d 1 (Wis. 1980).

10 *Id.*

11 *Id.* at 5.

12 *South Dakota v. Opperman*, 428 U.S. 364, 369 (1976).

purse or luggage warrants additional protection.[13] In that case, the purse could have been inventoried "as a closed unit" to protect more fully the privacy interests in closed containers.[14] So the court had held the search of the purse unreasonable even though the search of the vehicle and its trunk were reasonable as an inventory search.[15]

The *Weide* court observed that in *Colorado v. Bertine*, the U.S. Supreme Court had held that the search of a backpack during an inventory search didn't violate the Fourth Amendment because it had been conducted according to "reasonable police regulations relating to inventory procedures administered in good faith."[16] The Wisconsin court properly overruled its 1980 precedent as inconsistent with *Bertine* and concluded that the inventory search of Ms. Weide's purse was reasonable.[17]

Similarly, in a 2012 case,[18] the Washington Supreme Court, sitting en banc, overruled its own earlier decision in light of U.S. Supreme Court precedent interpreting the Confrontation Clause. After the landmark decision in *Crawford v. Washington*,[19] courts were faced with the question whether affidavits of certification, such as affidavits accompanying the defendant's driving record or interpreting forensic analysis, were testimonial statements subject to the Confrontation Clause. The Washington court had agreed with two federal circuit courts that certifications of driving records and similar records were not testimonial statements because although the certification itself was prepared for litigation, the underlying material wasn't.[20] Later the U.S. Supreme Court

---

13   *Prober*, 297 N.W.2d at 6–7; *see also State v. McDougal*, 228 N.W.2d 671, 678 (Wis. 1975) (holding that inventory search of contents of locked suitcases found in the trunk of an impounded car was unreasonable).
14   *Prober*, 297 N.W.2d at 7.
15   *Id.*
16   *State v. Weide*, 455 N.W.2d 899, 902, 903 (Wis. 1990) (citing *Colorado v. Bertine*, 479 U.S. 367, 368–69 (1987)).
17   *Id.* at 904–05.
18   *State v. Jasper*, 271 P.3d 876 (Wash. 2012) (en banc).
19   541 U.S. 36 (2004).
20   *Jasper*, 271 P.3d at 884–85.

decided *Melendez-Diaz v. Massachusetts*,[21] holding that forensic analyses are testimonial statements subject to the Confrontation Clause and observing that affidavits attesting to a record's absence were similarly testimonial.[22]

The Washington Supreme Court faced the question whether certifications of the absence of public records, including driving records and registration with the Washington Department of Labor and Industries, were testimonial statements subject to the Confrontation Clause.[23] Several defendants convicted of driving without a license and other crimes predicated on the record's absence challenged their convictions.[24] The Washington court recognized that in *Melendez-Diaz*, the Supreme Court had concluded that when an affidavit is used to establish a fact at trial, it takes the place of live testimony and is therefore testimonial.[25] The Supreme Court had observed that a clerk's affidavit about the absence of a record, such as a driving record, qualifies as testimonial because it involves analysis of the record and is used as substantive evidence against the defendant.[26] In light of *Melendez-Diaz*, the Washington court overruled its earlier decisions and held that a clerk's affidavit attesting to the defendants' driving records was subject to the Confrontation Clause.[27] The affidavits proved elements of the defendants' guilt—the absence of the license or registration—and were therefore testimonial under *Melendez-Diaz*.[28]

In a case involving a conflict between the U.S. Supreme Court's economic-due-process decisions and the First Amendment, the Minnesota Supreme Court had previously held that everyone has "a fundamental right to work unmolested in his own business .... [And] picketing to induce a person to forgo the right to work in

---

21 557 U.S. 305 (2009).
22 *Id.*
23 *Jasper*, 271 P.3d at 883.
24 *Id.* at 879–83.
25 *Melendez-Diaz*, 557 U.S. at 305.
26 *Id.* at 323.
27 *Jasper*, 271 P.3d at 883.
28 *Id.*

his own business is an invasion of the right."²⁹ The plaintiff sought to enjoin a union from picketing his construction sites based on his refusal to hire a unionized subcontractor to perform certain tile work that he usually performed himself. Observing that the U.S. Supreme Court had recently held that peaceful picketing is protected by the First Amendment (as incorporated against the states), the court concluded that the plaintiff's attempt to enjoin the union from picketing his place of business must be denied.³⁰

The same principle holds true for federal statutes: a U.S. Supreme Court decision sustaining or denying the constitutionality of a federal statute, or interpreting such a statute, binds the state courts as a precedent for determining all similar questions arising under the same statute. State courts aren't free to reconsider the constitutionality (under the U.S. Constitution) of a statute if the Supreme Court has already done so. This is so because the Supreme Court is the final authority on both the United States Constitution and the interpretation of federal statutes (see § 2). The state courts are bound by rulings on both.³¹ When an earlier decision of the state court is contrary to that of the Supreme Court on the constitutionality of a federal statute, it is no longer good law and must be overruled in favor of the binding federal precedent.

U.S. Supreme Court on federal questions

The U.S. Supreme Court's interpretation of a federal statute is binding on all state courts, their own contrary interpretation notwithstanding.³² In 1971, the New Mexico Supreme Court

---

29 *Glover v. Minneapolis Bldg. Trades Council*, 10 N.W.2d 481, 484 (Minn. 1943).

30 *Id.* at 482–44. *See also Thornhill v. Alabama*, 310 U.S. 88, 101 (1940) (recognizing that "the dissemination of information concerning the facts of a labor dispute must be regarded as within that area of free discussion that is guaranteed by the Constitution"); *Senn v. Tile Layers Protective Union*, 301 U.S. 468, 478 (1937) (holding that "[m]embers of a union might . . . make known the facts of a labor dispute" because "freedom of speech is guaranteed by the Federal Constitution").

31 *See Martin v. Hunter's Lessee*, 14 U.S. (1 Wheat.) 304 (1816) (upholding the constitutionality of the U.S. Supreme Court's appellate jurisdiction over decisions of the states' high courts on questions of federal law).

32 *Marmet Health Care Ctr., Inc. v. Brown*, 132 S.Ct. 1201, 1202 (2012) (per curiam) ("The decision of the state court found the [statute's] coverage to be more

addressed the question whether monzonite rock that had been taken from the surface of the landowner's property to be used as gravel was included in a reservation of all rights to "coal and other minerals."[33] The land had originally been patented to the landowner's predecessors in interest under the federal Stock-Raising Homestead Act.[34] The patents reserved to the United States "all the coal and other minerals in the lands so entered and patented."[35] The New Mexico state highway commission obtained permission from the Federal Bureau of Land Management to remove the gravel for use in a highway-construction project.[36] The highway commission refused to pay compensation to the landowners for taking the gravel from their land on grounds that it belonged to the federal government, not the landowners.[37] The New Mexico Supreme Court reasoned that the monzonite rock "had no rare or exceptional character and possessed no peculiar property giving it special value" because it was "useful only for road building purposes" and, further, had "been taken in its exposed state."[38] The court rejected the argument that the grant had entirely separated the subsurface estate from the surface estate and concluded that such rock wasn't reserved to the United States by a reservation of "coal and other minerals."[39]

But in *Watt v. Western Nuclear*,[40] decided just over a decade later, the U.S. Supreme Court determined that gravel was reserved to the United States by patents under the Stock-Raising Homestead Act.[41] The Court relied on the purposes of the statute: because

---

limited than mandated by this Court's previous cases. The decision ... must be vacated. When this Court has fulfilled its duty to interpret federal law, a state court may not contradict or fail to implement the rule so established.").

33 *State ex rel. State Highway Comm'n v. Trujillo*, 487 P.2d 122 (N.M. 1971), overruled by *Champlin Petroleum Co. v. Lyman*, 708 P.2d 319 (N.M. 1985).
34 43 U.S.C. §§ 291–302.
35 *Trujillo*, 487 P.2d at 123.
36 *Id.*
37 *Id.*
38 *Id.* at 124.
39 *Id.*
40 462 U.S. 36 (1983).
41 *Id.* at 60.

"Congress's underlying purpose in severing the surface estate from the mineral estate was to facilitate the concurrent development of both surface and subsurface resources," the Act should be construed to reserve even gravel to the United States.[42] Highlighting the fact that ranching and other agricultural uses aren't expected to exploit the mineral resources of the land, the Court reasoned that Congress must have intended the reservation to allow some other means for such exploitation.[43] The reservation of "coal and other minerals" was held to include "substances that are mineral in character (i.e., that are inorganic), that can be removed from the soil, that can be used for commercial purposes, and that there is no reason to suppose were intended to be included in the surface estate."[44] Four Justices dissented, arguing that the understanding of the term *minerals* in 1916 (the time of enactment) excluded gravel and other "commonplace substances."[45] They observed that the Department of Interior had long excluded such commonplace minerals from the mining laws, and that Congress would not have intended to depart only by implication from a long-standing interpretation of the agency administering the statute.[46]

Two years later, in 1985, the New Mexico Supreme Court was again presented with the interpretation of the Stock-Raising Homestead Act.[47] At issue was whether caliche rock to be used for road-building was reserved to the United States.[48] Observing that the U.S. Supreme Court had interpreted the reservation to include gravel, the court concluded that its contrary interpretation of the federal statute must yield: "We, of course, must adopt the classification that the majority of the Supreme Court has accorded to the meaning of a federal act, even though we may share the reservations of the dissenters that the majority's definition of a reserved

---

42   *Id.* at 46–47.
43   *Id.* at 52–53.
44   *Id.* at 53–54 (italics omitted).
45   *Id.* at 60–67 (Powell J. dissenting).
46   *Id.* at 65–66.
47   *Champlin Petroleum Co. v. Lyman*, 708 P.2d 319 (N.M. 1985).
48   *Id.* at 320.

mineral may be overly broad."[49] The state court correctly recognized that the interpretation of the Stock-Raising Homestead Act was a federal question controlled by U.S. Supreme Court authority.

State courts need not extend decisions of the U.S. Supreme Court beyond their precise holdings, express and necessarily implied. As the Supreme Court has observed, "[c]onstitutional rights are not defined by inferences from opinions which did not address the question at issue."[50] State courts may be particularly hesitant to extend a Supreme Court decision beyond its necessary results if doing so would conflict with existing state precedent.[51]

Take the following example. New Jersey's hate-crime law once allowed the imposition of a sentence beyond the statutory maximum if a judge found that the defendant, during the commission of a given crime, intended to intimidate another person because of race, color, gender, handicap, religion, sexual orientation, or ethnicity. In *Apprendi v. New Jersey*,[52] the Supreme Court invalidated this procedure, holding: "Other than . . . a prior conviction, any fact that increases the penalty for a crime beyond the prescribed statutory maximum must be submitted to a jury, and proved beyond a reasonable doubt."[53] The Court reasoned that judicial fact-finding in such circumstances would deprive juries of their traditional function of deciding "all facts necessary to constitute a statutory offense" and thus erode the right to trial by jury.[54]

---

49 *Id.* at 321–22; *see Watt*, 462 U.S. at 60–72 (Powell J. dissenting). *But see Bed-Roc Ltd., LLC v. United States*, 541 U.S. 176, 185–86 (2004) (plurality opinion) (declining to apply *Watt*'s interpretation of "other minerals" to the term "valuable minerals" in another federal statute, but not overruling the precedent); *id.* at 187–89 (Thomas J. concurring) (criticizing *Watt*).

50 *Texas v. Cobb*, 532 U.S. 162, 169 (2001).

51 *See, e.g.*, *People v. Wagener*, 752 N.E.2d 430, 442–43 (Ill. 2001) ("[W]e are not bound to extend the decisions of the [Supreme] Court to arenas which it did not purport to address, which indeed it specifically disavowed addressing, in order to find unconstitutional a law of this state. This is especially true where, as here, to do so would require us to overrule settled law in this state."); *State v. Allen*, 259 S.W.3d 671, 688 (Tenn. 2008) (quoting *Wagener*).

52 530 U.S. 466 (2000).

53 *Id.* at 490.

54 *Id.* at 483.

An Oregon intermediate appellate court later determined that *Apprendi* didn't apply to an Oregon statute[55] allowing a court to impose consecutive terms of imprisonment for separate convictions arising out of the same conduct if the accused's commission of separate crimes was intentional and not incidental.[56] The court reasoned that *Apprendi* applied only to a finding that affects the sentence for a particular crime, not to one that affects the relationship between the sentences for different crimes.[57] The traditional function of juries, important in *Apprendi*, had not generally extended to determining how sentences should be served.[58] The court observed that "while our court is bound to apply the constitution in the manner dictated by the [Supreme] Court, it is not bound to extend the decisions of the Court to arenas which it did not purport to address."[59]

The Oregon Supreme Court disagreed, concluding that it was "obvious" that *Apprendi* had to be read broadly.[60] The U.S. Supreme Court reversed, concluding that the Oregon Supreme Court had extended *Apprendi* beyond its moorings to historical jury functions and contrary to federal respect for state sovereignty in the administration of criminal justice.[61] The state intermediate appellate court had correctly refused to extend the Supreme Court's decision beyond the issue it narrowly addressed.

State lower courts may rightly hesitate to extend the reasoning of a U.S. Supreme Court precedent beyond its narrow holding when there is controlling state-high-court precedent to the contrary. For example, in a 2012 case,[62] the issue before the California Court of Appeal was whether the Federal Arbitration Act preempted an employee's class-action waiver in an arbitration provision. The California Supreme Court had held a few years earlier, in

---

55   Or. Rev. Stat. § 137.123(5)(a).
56   *State v. Tanner*, 150 P.3d 31, 39 (Or. Ct. App. 2006) (en banc).
57   *Id.* at 34.
58   *Id.* at 39.
59   *Id.* (quoting *Wagener*, 752 N.E.2d at 442) (internal quotation marks omitted).
60   *State v. Ice*, 170 P.3d 1049, 1058–59 (Or. 2007).
61   *Oregon v. Ice*, 555 U.S. 160, 167–68 (2009).
62   *Truly Nolen of Am. v. Superior Court*, 145 Cal. Rptr. 3d 432 (Ct. App. 2012).

a 2007 case,[63] that such waivers are unconscionable and thus unenforceable in certain circumstances. After that, the U.S. Supreme Court had held in *AT&T v. Concepcion*[64] that the Act preempted California's refusal to enforce class-action waivers in consumer contracts. The intermediate state court in the 2012 case acknowledged that "*Concepcion*'s expansive language and its clear mandate that arbitration agreements must be enforced according to their terms despite a state's policy reasons to the contrary" significantly undermined the continued validity of the 2007 case.[65] The court nevertheless concluded that it was "absolutely bound" to follow the 2007 case because the issues in the two cases were not precisely the same.[66] "[I]ntermediate appellate courts in California," the court stated, "are absolutely bound to follow the decisions of the California Supreme Court, unless [and until] the United States Supreme Court has decided the *same* question differently."[67]

A state court is certainly not expected to overrule its own prior decision based only on its anticipation of how the U.S. Supreme Court may rule in the future. Accurately divining the Court's future rulings is a precarious task.

U.S. Supreme Court decisions that undercut state precedent

Some state courts have mistakenly expressed the view that they must continue to follow state precedent on a federal question despite supervening U.S. Supreme Court authority until overturned by the state high court.[68] Although grounded in the principle that it is up to a higher court to overrule its own precedent if it has been undermined by other reasoning,[69] this approach

---

63   *Gentry v. Superior Court*, 165 P.3d 556 (Cal. 2007).

64   *AT&T Mobility LLC v. Concepcion*, 563 U.S. 333 (2011).

65   *Truly Nolen*, 145 Cal. Rptr. 3d at 445–46.

66   *Id.*

67   *Id.* at 446 (emphasis in original).

68   *See, e.g., State v. Weide*, 455 N.W.2d 899, 901 (Wis. 1990) ("The court of appeals reasoned that it is the role of this court to determine whether one of its decisions is valid in light of an intervening decision of the United States Supreme Court."); *State v. Manzanares*, 674 P.2d 511, 512 (N.M. 1983).

69   *See Rodriguez de Quijas v. Shearson/Am. Express, Inc.*, 490 U.S. 477, 484 (1989) ("If a precedent of this Court has direct application in a case, yet appears to

is flawed. The U.S. Supreme Court may have no authority over state courts on state-law questions, but state courts at all levels are subject to its authority on questions of federal law.[70] Just as a state trial court wouldn't continue to apply the vertical precedent of an intermediate state court that is no longer good law in light of a ruling of the state's high court, it shouldn't continue to apply state precedent—even the precedent of the state's high court—if it is superseded by U.S. Supreme Court precedent. State courts have independent authority to interpret and apply federal law.[71] If a state high court's decision has plainly been overruled by the U.S. Supreme Court, the lower courts fail to apply the law properly if they refuse to apply federal law as it has been set out by that Court.

A 2014 case[72] decided by a Wisconsin intermediate court of appeals illustrates the challenge of whether to follow precedent from the state's high court or a supervening decision of the U.S. Supreme Court.[73] The Wisconsin Supreme Court had held that the federal Constitution's Confrontation Clause isn't offended when evidence of forensic laboratory testing is presented at trial not by the expert who actually performed the testing, but by another who supervised or reviewed the original expert's work or is familiar with it.[74] The U.S. Supreme Court had later announced what the state court considered to be a new Confrontation Clause test for hearsay evidence, holding it "inadmissible unless the declarant is unavailable to testify and the defendant had a prior opportunity to cross-examine him or her."[75] Still later, the Wisconsin Supreme Court had reaffirmed its rule regarding test results, distinguishing

---

rest on reasons rejected in some other line of decisions, the Court of Appeals should follow the case which directly controls, leaving to this Court the prerogative of overruling its own decisions.").

70 *See Gulf Offshore Co. v. Mobil Oil Corp.*, 453 U.S. 473, 478 & n.4 (1981).

71 *See ASARCO Inc. v. Kadish*, 490 U.S. 605, 617 (1989); *United States ex rel. Lawrence v. Woods*, 432 F.2d 1072, 1075 (7th Cir. 1970); *State v. Ward*, 604 N.W.2d 517, 525 (Wis. 2000).

72 *State v. Griep*, 845 N.W.2d 24 (Wis. Ct. App. 2014).

73 *Id.* at 24–25.

74 *State v. Williams*, 644 N.W.2d 919, 926 (Wis. 2002).

75 *See Griep*, 845 N.W.2d at 28 (quoting *Crawford v. Washington*, 541 U.S. 36, 68 (2004)).

the U.S. Supreme Court's decision on grounds that it involved rules governing admissibility of hearsay, as opposed to those governing expert testimony.[76] The state court acknowledged that a U.S. Supreme Court decision could override state-high-court precedent "in such clear terms that the Supremacy Clause compels our adherence" to the Supreme Court decision.[77] But the court concluded that the state high court's rule had survived the intervening Supreme Court decision.[78]

---

76   Id.
77   Id.
78   Id.

80. Inferior Federal Courts' Decisions in State Court

Though entitled to respectful consideration in the state courts, the decisions of inferior federal courts are not controlling authority in state court unless their judgments operate by way of estoppel.

The inferior federal courts and the state courts can be seen as coordinate arbiters of federal law.[1] State courts, like the lower federal courts, are subject to the supervision of the U.S. Supreme Court on questions of federal law and are subject to its appellate jurisdiction. But the lower federal courts don't have appellate jurisdiction over state courts.[2] Hence their decisions aren't binding on the state courts, which have an independent duty to decide questions of federal law as presented.[3] One state's high court has guided its lower courts as follows: "While [state] courts may certainly draw upon the precedents of the Fifth Circuit, or any other federal or state court, in determining the appropriate federal rule of decision, they are obligated to follow only higher Texas courts and the United States Supreme Court."[4]

The U.S. Supreme Court affirmed this principle in 2013, observing that a state court isn't bound by the decisions of the federal circuit court exercising jurisdiction in the state.[5] Federal

---

1 See *United States ex rel. Lawrence v. Woods*, 432 F.2d 1072, 1075–76 (7th Cir. 1970) (discussing the relationship between state and federal courts on questions of federal law); *State v. Ward*, 604 N.W.2d 517, 525 (Wis. 2000) ("state courts exercise concurrent jurisdiction with the federal courts in cases arising under the Constitution of the United States"); *State v. Coleman*, 214 A.2d 393, 402, 403 (N.J. 1965).

2 28 U.S.C. § 1257; see *District of Columbia Ct. of Appeals v. Feldman*, 460 U.S. 462, 476 (1983); *Rooker v. Fidelity Trust Co.*, 263 U.S. 413, 415 (1923); *People v. Leavitt*, 22 N.E.3d 430, 444–45 (Ill. App. Ct. 2014).

3 *ASARCO Inc. v. Kadish*, 490 U.S. 605, 620 (1989) (recognizing the "established tradition[ ]" that "the state courts . . . have it within both their power and their proper role to render binding judgments on issues of federal law, subject only to review by this Court"). See *Woods*, 432 F.2d at 1075–76 ("[B]ecause lower federal courts exercise no appellate jurisdiction over state tribunals, decisions of lower federal courts are not conclusive on state courts.").

4 *Penrod Drilling Corp. v. Williams*, 868 S.W.2d 294, 296 (Tex. 1993) (per curiam).

5 *Johnson v. Williams*, 133 S.Ct. 1088, 1098 (2013).

statutory habeas corpus is recognized as a limited exception to this principle: when conducting collateral review of state proceedings under the federal habeas statutes, federal courts may conduct substantive review of the state courts' application of federal law.[6]

Courts have made a connection between a state court's inquiry into questions of federal law yet to be decided by the Supreme Court and a federal court's *Erie*[7] inquiry. One Florida court observed that the state court "must guess how the [Supreme Court] is likely to decide the issue" in much the same way that a federal court must determine how a state's high court would decide an uncertain question of state law.[8] Such an inquiry rightly takes into account the decisions of the lower federal courts, noting their reasoning and any disagreement on the issue. Indeed, most courts observe that the lower federal courts' decisions are entitled to "great weight"[9] or "respect."[10] But the decisions of no federal court except the Supreme Court are binding on the state courts.

Naturally, a state court considering whether to follow an inferior federal court's decision will consider the soundness of its reasoning.[11] Many courts also observe that an interest in maintaining uniformity in the law often militates in favor of agreement with the federal courts.[12] When the federal courts are uniform in their

---

6   *See generally* 17B Charles Alan Wright, Arthur R. Miller et al., *Federal Practice and Procedure* § 4261, at 139, 146–47 (3d ed. 2007 & Supp. 2015).

7   *Erie R.R. v. Tompkins*, 304 U.S. 64 (1938).

8   *Wylie v. Investment Mgmt. & Research Inc.*, 629 So. 2d 898, 900 (Fla. Dist. Ct. App. 1993) (en banc); *see also Tafflin v. Levitt*, 493 U.S. 455, 465 (1990) (observing that "State courts adjudicating civil RICO claims will, in addition, be guided by federal court interpretations of the relevant federal criminal statutes, just as federal courts sitting in diversity are guided by state court interpretations of state law"); *In re Morgan Stanley & Co.*, 293 S.W.3d 182, 189 (Tex. 2009) ("When deciding federal questions of first impression, we anticipate how the U.S. Supreme Court would decide the issue.").

9   *Venegas v. County of Los Angeles*, 87 P.3d 1, 8 (Cal. 2004); *People v. Bradley*, 460 P.2d 129, 132 (Cal. 1969) (in bank); *see Lomax v. Fiedler*, 554 N.W.2d 841, 849 (Wis. Ct. App. 1996).

10 *People ex rel. Ray v. Martin*, 60 N.E.2d 541, 547 (N.Y. 1945); *see Wimberly v. Labor & Indus. Relations Comm'n of Mo.*, 688 S.W.2d 344, 347–48 (Mo. 1985) (en banc).

11 *See State Bank of Cherry v. CGB Enters., Inc.*, 984 N.E.2d 449, 458 (Ill. 2013).

12 *See, e.g., id.* (observing that its earlier decisions had "overstate[d] the degree of deference" that state courts must pay to lower federal courts' decisions" and

interpretation of federal law or an interpretation is long-standing, a state court will almost certainly be more likely to follow it.[13]

This principle wasn't always universally accepted.[14] For example, in a 1935 decision[15] the Alabama Supreme Court treated a decision of the Fifth Circuit interpreting the National Industrial Recovery Act as binding because it "involved a construction and application of the federal statute."[16] Yet this view that federal decisions bind state courts gradually eroded, as it should have. In a 2004 case,[17] the Alabama Supreme Court rejected the implications of its earlier decision, observing that opinions of Justices of the Supreme Court had "suggested that state courts owe allegiance only to the United States Supreme Court and the state's own decisions interpreting federal law."[18] Similarly, the Illinois Supreme Court has rejected language from its earlier decisions as "overstat[ing] the degree of deference" that is due to lower federal decisions.[19]

---

that in earlier cases it had deferred to federal courts in the interest of "uniformity of decisions").

13   See Shaw ex rel. Zollner v. PACC Health Plan, Inc., 908 P.2d 308, 314 n.8 (Or. 1995) (en banc); Wimberly, 688 S.W.2d at 347–48.

14   For discussion of state courts' varying approaches to the question before Johnson, see Donald H. Zeigler, Gazing into the Crystal Ball: Reflections on the Standards State Judges Should Use to Ascertain Federal Law, 40 Wm. & Mary L. Rev. 1143, 1152–57 (1999).

15   Handy v. Goodyear Tire & Rubber Co., 160 So. 530 (Ala. 1935).

16   Id. at 530; see also Boyer v. Atchison, Topeka & Santa Fe Ry., 230 N.E.2d 173, 176 (Ill. 1967); Iowa Nat'l Bank v. Stewart, 232 N.W. 445, 454 (Iowa 1930), rev'd on other grounds sub nom. Iowa-Des Moines Nat'l Bank v. Bennett, 284 U.S. 239 (1931); Kuchenmeister v. Los Angeles & Salt Lake R.R., 172 P. 725, 725 (Utah 1918) ("If, therefore, there is a decision from a federal court which is decisive of the question here, . . . it is our duty to follow the federal court rather than the state court, since the question involved is one upon which the federal courts have the ultimate right to speak.").

17   Glass v. Birmingham Southern R.R., 905 So. 2d 789 (Ala. 2004).

18   Id. at 794 n.2 (citing Lockhart v. Fretwell, 506 U.S. 364, 376 (1993) (Thomas J. concurring); Steffel v. Thompson, 415 U.S. 452, 483 n.3 (1974) (Rehnquist J. concurring)).

19   State Bank of Cherry, 984 N.E.2d at 458.

81. Reverse *Erie* Doctrine

When state law is preempted by federal law, or federal law controls, state courts are bound by U.S. Supreme Court precedent.

Although in *Erie*[1] the U.S. Supreme Court disclaimed the existence of any "federal general common law," the Court has recognized instances in which the development of federal common law in certain specialized areas is necessary.[2] (See § 66.) On the very day when *Erie* was announced, the Court issued an opinion about water rights between Colorado and New Mexico, concluding that these rights were to be determined by federal law rather than the law of either state.[3] A few short years later, the Court held in *Clearfield Trust Co. v. United States* that federal law must govern "the rights and duties of the United States on commercial paper which it issues" because the disbursement of such instruments is an "exercis[e] [of] a constitutional function or power."[4]

The Supreme Court has recognized that various aspects of the states' control over navigable waters are subject to federal common law rather than the property law of the particular state.[5] Similarly, state courts must apply the federal maritime law to maritime claims brought in state court.[6] When such federal common law applies, the state courts are bound by U.S. Supreme Court

---

1 *Erie R.R. v. Tompkins*, 304 U.S. 64, 71 (1938).
2 *See* 19 Charles Alan Wright, Arthur R. Miller et al., *Federal Practice and Procedure* § 4515, at 451–54 (2d ed. 1996 & Supp. 2015).
3 *Hinderlider v. La Plata River & Cherry Creek Ditch Co.*, 304 U.S. 92, 110 (1938).
4 318 U.S. 363, 366 (1943).
5 *See, e.g.*, *Hinderlider*, 304 U.S. at 110 (concluding that apportionment of an interstate stream between two states is to be determined by federal common law, not by the law of either state); *United States v. Oregon*, 295 U.S. 1, 14 (1935) (whether particular waters are navigable, and therefore subject to federal ownership, or nonnavigable, is a question of federal law); *Wyoming v. Colorado*, 286 U.S. 494 (1932) (apportionment of water between Colorado and Wyoming governed by federal law rather than the law of either state).
6 *See Offshore Logistics, Inc. v. Tallentire*, 477 U.S. 207, 223 (1986).

precedent.[7] While states have concurrent jurisdiction to hear many maritime causes of action, states are, for the most part, to apply the federal common law to disputes involving such claims.[8]

Take a 2009 Georgia case.[9] The Georgia Ports Authority leased a crane to a stevedoring company to unload cargo from a ship.[10] When the crane fell over and was destroyed, the Authority sued for damages under the lease.[11] The court noted that under the saving-to-suitors clause of 28 U.S.C. § 1333(1), "state courts have concurrent jurisdiction with federal courts sitting in admiralty over in personam claims based on maritime causes of action."[12] But the trial court had applied only state law. The court reversed and remanded with directions to consider the application of state law and federal common law.[13]

Federal common law has also been developed through interpretation of federal statutes creating comprehensive regulatory schemes, as with the law of labor relations[14] or ERISA. Federal courts sometimes determine that although federal law must control because of a substantial federal interest or the need for uniformity in a federal governing scheme, the application of state law isn't inconsistent with federal interests. In such a case the federal courts may adopt state law not because it is intrinsically binding,

---

7   See Free v. Bland, 369 U.S. 663 (1962) (concluding that Texas courts were bound to apply federal regulation governing federal government bonds despite contrary state law); Hinderlider, 304 U.S. 92 (overturning a decision of the Colorado courts on the grounds that it violated federal law on interstate compacts).
8   See Norfolk Southern Ry. v. Kirby, 543 U.S. 14, 22–23 (2004); Garrett v. Moore-McCormack Co., 317 U.S. 239, 243 (1942) (discussing the obligation of state courts to apply federal admiralty law to suits brought in state court under the "savings to suitors" provision of the Jones Act).
9   Cooper/T. Smith Stevedoring Co. v. Georgia Ports Auth., 686 S.E.2d 844 (Ga. Ct. App. 2009).
10 Id. at 845–46.
11 Id.
12 Id. at 846.
13 Id. at 847.
14 See Local 174, Teamsters, Chauffeurs, Warehousemen & Helpers of Am. v. Lucas Flour Co., 369 U.S. 95, 103 (1962) (recognizing that § 301 of the Labor Management Act was intended to create a uniform federal labor law); Textile Workers Union of Am. v. Lincoln Mills of Alabama, 353 U.S. 448 (1957).

but as a matter of federal law.[15] Similarly, federal caselaw regarding the major federal civil-rights statutes, such as Title VII, is binding vertical precedent on state courts when a federal claim is adjudicated in state court.

---

[15] *See, e.g., Local 1416, Int'l Ass'n of Machinists v. Jostens, Inc.*, 250 F. Supp. 496, 499 (D. Minn. 1966) (recognizing that the Minnesota Uniform Arbitration Act may apply to a suit under the Labor Management Relations Act because it is "compatible with the purpose" of that Act).

82. State-Court Determinations Relating to Federalism

On a question relating to the jurisdiction, powers, and procedures of the various federal courts, the decisions of the U.S. Supreme Court are binding and conclusive on the state courts, and decisions of lower federal courts merit careful consideration.

A court's jurisdiction is determined by "the constitution and the laws of the sovereignty which created [the court]."[1] The U.S. Supreme Court is created by, and the federal courts are created under, the United States Constitution and are creatures of federal law. Their jurisdiction, powers, and procedures are therefore matters of federal law.[2] (See § 65.) When a state court is called on to ascertain issues regarding federalism, it is bound by federal caselaw just as on other federal questions.[3]

Of course, state courts are affirmatively bound on such questions only by the U.S. Supreme Court. Lower federal courts' decisions regarding federal procedure and jurisdiction are highly persuasive authority but not binding as vertical precedents.[4] Federal courts have exclusive jurisdiction over certain types of lawsuits,

---

[1] *Markham v. City of Newport News*, 292 F.2d 711, 716 (4th Cir. 1961).

[2] *Cf. Federal Home Loan Mortg. Corp. v. Matassino*, 911 F. Supp. 2d 1276, 1281–82 (N.D. Ga. 2012) (federal court must determine whether Georgia dispossessory action is a "civil action" over which it has jurisdiction under federal law; Georgia courts' determination that such an action isn't a civil action for purposes of Georgia law isn't binding on the federal court).

[3] *See Kramer v. Caribbean Mills, Inc.*, 394 U.S. 823, 829 (1969) (observing that "[t]he existence of federal jurisdiction is a matter of federal, not state law") (citing, *e.g.*, *Missouri Pac. Ry. v. Fitzgerald*, 160 U.S. 556, 582 (1896)); *Horton v. Liberty Mut. Ins. Co.*, 367 U.S. 348, 352 (1961) (stating that the "determination of the value of the matter in controversy for purposes of federal jurisdiction is a federal question to be decided under federal standards"); *Constant v. Pacific Nat'l Ins. Co.*, 201 A.2d 405, 410–11 (N.J. Super. Ct. Law Div. 1964) (concluding that "federal law determines whether a federal court can enter a declaratory judgment" even though state substantive law may govern the merits of the declaratory adjudication).

[4] *See, e.g., Minton v. Gunn*, 355 S.W.3d 634, 641 (Tex. 2011) (considering Federal Circuit precedent on a question of federal patent jurisdiction persuasive but not binding on the state courts), *rev'd*, 133 S.Ct. 1059 (2013).

such as those involving bankruptcy,[5] antitrust,[6] and patents.[7] State courts will never need to determine jurisdiction in most lawsuits of this kind, since federal jurisdiction will be clear and they will be filed in federal court in the first instance or promptly removed.

But some state-law cases may involve federal issues—such as bankruptcy, patent, and most antitrust issues—that are ordinarily heard only in federal court. Those state-law cases are nonetheless subject to exclusive federal jurisdiction if the claims "necessarily raise a stated federal issue, actually disputed and substantial, which a federal forum may entertain without disturbing any congressionally approved balance of federal and state judicial responsibilities."[8] A state court facing the argument that a suit before it is within this exclusive federal jurisdiction—and that therefore the state court lacks jurisdiction—will need to adjudicate the scope of exclusive federal jurisdiction.

Texas courts were called on to adjudicate the scope of the federal courts' exclusive jurisdiction over federal patent law in a 2011 case.[9] After a federal district court held that his patent was invalid based on the "on-sale bar" in the Patent Act, Minton hired new counsel and raised the experimental-use exception to the bar for the first time.[10] The district court held that the new argument came too late, and the Federal Circuit affirmed. Minton then sued his original counsel for legal malpractice in Texas court.[11] Under Texas law, Minton was required to show that but for counsel's negligence, he would have prevailed in his suit.[12] The Texas trial court granted summary judgment for the defendant-counsel, concluding that the experimental-use exception was neither factually

---

5 28 U.S.C. § 1334.
6 *Id.* § 1337.
7 *Id.* § 1338.
8 *Grable & Sons Metal Prods. v. Darue Eng'g & Mfg.*, 545 U.S. 308, 314 (2005).
9 *Minton v. Gunn*, 355 S.W.3d 634 (Tex. 2011).
10 *Id.* at 637–38.
11 *Id.* at 638–39.
12 *See Alexander v. Turtur & Assocs.*, 146 S.W.3d 113, 117 (Tex. 2004) (plaintiff must show that the alleged malpractice proximately caused him injury).

nor legally tenable at the time of the original litigation, and therefore that counsel wasn't negligent in failing to raise it.[13]

On appeal, Minton argued that under recent Federal Circuit precedent, federal courts have exclusive jurisdiction over legal-malpractice claims "stemming from alleged mishandling of . . . patent litigation."[14] Declining to follow the Federal Circuit, the Texas intermediate appellate court concluded that it had jurisdiction over the malpractice claim. Applying U.S. Supreme Court precedent, the court reasoned that the federal question—whether the experimental-use exception would have applied if raised—wasn't substantial to the malpractice claim because it involved a question of fact rather than a question of patent law. Hence it wasn't within the federal court's exclusive jurisdiction.[15] The intermediate court also concluded that exclusive federal jurisdiction would interfere with the state courts' ability to "regulate the practice of law" through legal malpractice, which is traditionally within the domain of the states.[16] The court correctly observed that it was bound by U.S. Supreme Court precedent on the federal question of federal jurisdiction, and that Federal Circuit precedent, while helpful and persuasive authority, isn't binding.[17] The court declined to follow the Federal Circuit's decisions, concluding that the circuit court had "misapplied United States Supreme Court precedent by disregarding the federalism analysis that the Supreme Court has applied to restrict the scope of federal 'arising under' jurisdiction to a 'small and special category' of cases where

---

13 *Minton*, 355 S.W.3d at 638–39.

14 *Id.* at 639 (quoting *Air Measurement Tech., Inc. v. Akin Gump Strauss Hauer & Feld, L.L.P.*, 504 F.3d 1262, 1273 (Fed. Cir. 2007)).

15 *Minton v. Gunn*, 301 S.W.3d 702, 708–09 (Tex. App.—Fort Worth 2009), *rev'd*, 355 S.W.3d 634 (Tex. 2011), *rev'd*, 133 S.Ct. 1059 (2013).

16 *Id.* (citing *Singh v. Duane Morris LLP*, 538 F.3d 334, 338 (5th Cir. 2008)). In *Singh*, the Fifth Circuit had applied *Grable* to conclude that federal courts didn't have exclusive jurisdiction over legal-malpractice claims arising from a matter of federal trademark law.

17 *Minton*, 301 S.W.3d at 709.

a substantial question of pure federal law is in dispute that has precedential value."[18]

The Texas Supreme Court found the Federal Circuit more persuasive, concluding that patent law *is* substantial in the adjudication of a malpractice claim when the court must interpret federal patent law as part of an element of the plaintiff's claim.[19] It also concluded that federal courts could decide such a case "without upsetting the jurisdictional balance between federal and state courts" because the federal government has a strong interest in the uniform application of patent law.[20] The court considered, as persuasive authority, that federal courts and other state courts had concluded that such a claim is subject to federal jurisdiction.[21]

The U.S. Supreme Court disagreed with both the Texas Supreme Court and the Federal Circuit, concluding that legal-malpractice claims requiring proof of a patent-law issue "are by their nature unlikely to have the sort of significance for the federal system necessary to establish [federal] jurisdiction."[22] The case aptly illustrates that a state court called on to determine an issue of federal jurisdiction is bound by U.S. Supreme Court precedent and must faithfully apply it but isn't bound by lower-federal-court precedent. State courts have an independent duty and ability to apply federal law on questions of federal jurisdiction and procedure.

State courts are commonly called on to decide questions of federal procedure in determining whether a federal judgment should be given preclusive effect. The U.S. Supreme Court has made it clear that the preclusive effect of a federal court's judgment is to be determined by federal common law.[23] A 2012 Pennsylvania

---

18 *Id.* (quoting *Empire Healthchoice Assurance, Inc. v. McVeigh*, 547 U.S. 677, 699–701 (2006)).

19 *Minton*, 355 S.W.3d at 643–44 (stating that "because the success of Minton's malpractice claim is reliant upon the viability of the experimental use exception as a defense to the on-sale bar, we hold that it is a substantial federal issue satisfying the third prong of the *Grable* inquiry").

20 *Id.* at 645.

21 *Id.* at 644–45.

22 *Gunn v. Minton*, 133 S.Ct. 1059, 1065 (2013).

23 *Taylor v. Sturgell*, 553 U.S. 880, 891 (2008) (citing *Semtek Int'l Inc. v. Lockheed Martin Corp.*, 531 U.S. 497, 507–08 (2001)).

case[24] involved a First Amendment challenge to a Pennsylvania statutory requirement that persons circulating the nomination petition papers of a candidate for office must be residents of the electoral district in which the candidate is running.[25] Several years earlier, the commonwealth had been involved in federal litigation involving this statutory requirement. The federal court had permanently enjoined the enforcement of the district-residency requirement, finding that it burdened core political speech and wasn't narrowly tailored to implement a compelling government interest.[26] The lower courts had declined to follow the federal court's judgment, on grounds that the judgments of inferior federal courts aren't binding on the state courts (see §§ 2, 80). The Pennsylvania Supreme Court concluded that although the federal district court's reasoning wasn't binding on the Pennsylvania courts, collateral estoppel barred the state courts from disregarding its judgment. The court relied on federal law, particularly federal precedent allowing a nonparty to the previous litigation to use issue preclusion offensively to bar an opponent from relitigating an issue resolved in the earlier litigation.[27] The Pennsylvania court may have stretched federal precedent by applying issue preclusion from an earlier decision against the commonwealth to the private litigants challenging the validity of the candidate's nomination papers.[28] Yet it correctly recognized that the federal judgment could have preclusive effect and that federal common law governs the question of issue preclusion.

Of course, state law governs the preclusive effect of a federal court's judgment in a diversity case unless state law is incompatible with federal interests.[29]

---

24 *In re Stevenson*, 40 A.3d 1212 (Pa. 2012).
25 *Id.* at 1214–15.
26 *Morrill v. Weaver*, 224 F. Supp. 2d 882 (E.D. Pa. 2002).
27 *In re Stevenson*, 40 A.3d at 1223 (citing *Allen v. McCurry*, 449 U.S. 90, 94–96 (1980)).
28 *See id.* at 1226 (Saylor J. concurring); *id.* at 1228–29 (Baer J. concurring).
29 *See Semtek Int'l Inc.*, 531 U.S. at 508; *Garcia v. Prudential Ins. Co.*, 293 P.3d 869, 872 (Nev. 2013) (en banc).

83. Interstate Uniformity of Decisions

For the sake of uniformity, as well as out of respect for authority, a state's high court deciding a new question should consider the general or current trend of judicial decisions in other states if unanimity is apparent and widely extended. If the matter is important and the general prevalence of the same legal rule is desirable, the state high court may pursue this course even though doing so requires overruling one or more horizontal precedents.

The desideratum of greater uniformity in the law—especially but not only business law—long predates the Uniform Commercial Code.[1] In 1851, the Louisiana Supreme Court observed that it "should adhere to the decision [of another court], for the sake of uniformity in commercial law with our sister States, unless prevented by the positive injunction of our own laws."[2] The law merchant developed at common law to govern the affairs of business across state and national borders. Uniformity between jurisdictions mitigates the uncertainty of cross-border contracting by letting parties plan their affairs under a single rule that will apply the same way across jurisdictions.[3]

---

[1] *See Piatt v. Eads*, 1 Blackf. 81, 82 (Ind. 1820) ("[T]he custom of merchants is and always has been regarded as a part of the common law of England. . . . It is a law of a general nature, and not local to that kingdom; and is there recognized and acknowledged by the Courts as a part of their system, from the circumstance of its universal application and use in all mercantile transactions throughout the commercial world; being in those cases a rule of decision to which all nations agree, and of which all Courts take notice.").

[2] *Dubuch v. Goudchaux*, 6 La. Ann. 780, 781 (1851).

[3] *See, e.g., Sudden & Christenson v. Industrial Accident Comm'n*, 188 P. 803, 806 (Cal. 1920) (in bank) (observing that adoption of disparate state laws governing foreign shipping "would be destructive to the very uniformity in respect to maritime matters which the *Constitution* was designed to establish" and that a "serious injury would result to commerce"). *But see Louisiana Bank v. Kenner's Succession*, 1 La. 384 (1830) (noting that it is "to be desired that an uniformity in [the laws and usages which govern commercial contracts] should prevail in commercial business carried on between the states of the Union" but concluding that "no general usage can destroy the force and effect of local regulations" and that therefore certain civil-law rules of partnership were not enforceable in Louisiana).

Although the decisions of state and federal courts in other jurisdictions aren't binding, state courts have long shown a willingness to follow these decisions in the interest of uniformity or comity.[4] Most courts note that they will do so only to the extent that the foreign court's reasoning is persuasive or doesn't contravene the state's public policy.[5]

Up until *Erie Railroad v. Tompkins*,[6] the federal courts participated directly in the common-law development of the law merchant (see § 70). Under today's law, even the U.S. Supreme Court decides most questions of commercial law as state-law matters under the principle of *Erie*. But before *Erie*, the Court participated substantively in developing this law.[7] The Court's role as a unifying agent was discussed by the North Dakota Supreme Court in an 1894 case.[8] Faced with a question whether certain bond coupons were negotiable instruments, the court stated: "There should be only one rule for the nation, and it is to be hoped that, whatever conclusion is ultimately reached [by the federal Supreme Court], it will be adopted in all of the states."[9]

At issue in the North Dakota case was whether a bond and its interest coupons were negotiable instruments. If so, the holder was a bona fide purchaser for value against whom a defense of failure

---

4   *See, e.g., McKim v. King*, 58 Md. 502, 504 (1882) (adopting the rule established by foreign courts, both state and federal, for whether coupons payable on bearer or order are negotiable instruments).

5   *See, e.g., Tillman Cnty. Bank of Grandfield v. Behringer*, 257 S.W. 206, 207 (Tex. 1923) ("It is very desirable that decisions of our state courts should conform to those of the United States Supreme Court in questions of commercial law, and we would feel inclined to follow said court, unless we thought the weight of better reasoning was decidedly in favor of the opposite holding.").

6   304 U.S. 64 (1938).

7   *See Hughitt v. Johnson*, 28 F. 865, 865 (C.C.E.D. Mo. 1886) (observing that on "a question of general commercial law," the "federal courts follow their own opinions, rather than necessarily the decisions of the state courts").

8   *Flagg v. School Dist. No. 70, Barnes Cnty.*, 58 N.W. 499, 502 (N.D. 1894).

9   *Id. See also Asmussen v. Post Printing & Publ'g Co.*, 143 P. 396, 400 (Colo. App. 1914) ("[W]e feel in duty bound to obtain light, if possible, upon the disputed issue, from the rulings of the supreme judicial tribunal of our country, the United States Supreme Court. The question involved is one of commercial importance, and that court has directly passed on the law, governing the situation we have before us.").

of consideration couldn't be raised.[10] The bond provided for payment "at St. Paul, Minn. with New York Exchange."[11] At the time (remember, the case was decided in 1894), *exchange* was an amount for the cost of transferring funds from the place of payment to where the money was desired. The amount was usually small and readily ascertainable at the time of payment, but not from the face of the bond, as required by the legal rule for negotiable instruments.[12] After deciding that the exchange requirement did make the amount due on the bond uncertain, the state court observed that the federal circuit court for North Dakota had held that such a requirement resulted in the instrument's not being negotiable.[13] "Had this suit been instituted in the United States circuit court for this district," the state court wrote, "that court would have applied and enforced this rule. Therefore, for us to establish a different doctrine would make the rights of the parties depend upon the court in which the action should be brought."[14] Though the state court agreed with the federal court, an important consideration in its decision was the interest of uniformity within the jurisdiction.[15]

The adoption of uniform laws

During the 20th century, many state legislatures adopted uniform legislation on matters relating to the law merchant. For example, many states adopted a uniform law governing negotiable instruments.[16] One court described this uniform law as "a compendium of established custom concerning negotiable instruments as construed and applied in the best-considered decisions of the courts."[17]

---

10 *Flagg*, 58 N.W. at 499.

11 *Id.*

12 *Id.* at 499–500.

13 *Id.* at 500, 502 (citing *Hughitt*, 28 F. at 866).

14 *Id.* at 502.

15 *Id.*

16 See, e.g., *First Nat'l Bank v. Yakey*, 253 Ill. App. 128, 133 (1929); *Utah State Nat'l Bank v. Smith*, 179 P. 160, 161 (Cal. 1919); *Felt v. Bush*, 126 P. 688, 690–91 (Utah 1912); *Foster's Adm'r v. Metcalfe*, 138 S.W. 314, 316 (Ky. 1911).

17 *Foster's*, 138 S.W. at 316.

Courts are often careful to adopt other state courts' interpretation of a uniform act.[18] Meanwhile, the Uniform Law Commission has been at pains for many decades to codify the creed of uniformity. Toward the end of every uniform act promulgated in recent years appears this provision (with its dangling participle): "In applying and construing this uniform act, consideration must be given to the need to promote uniformity of the law with respect to its subject matter among the states that enact it."[19]

The Tennessee Supreme Court summed up the rationale behind the development of a uniform commercial law as follows:

> It is axiomatic that a purpose in enacting uniform laws is to achieve conformity, not uniqueness. While opinions by courts of sister states construing a uniform act are not binding upon this court, we are mindful that the objective of uniformity cannot be achieved by ignoring utterances of other jurisdictions. This court should strive to maintain the standardization of construction of uniform acts to carry out the legislative intent of uniformity. This does not mean that this court will blindly follow decisions of other states interpreting uniform acts, but this court will seriously consider the constructions given to comparable statutes in other jurisdictions and will espouse them to maintain conformity when they are in harmony with the spirit of the statute and do not antagonize public policy of this state.[20]

First published in 1952, the Uniform Commercial Code has been enacted in some form in all 50 states and the District of Columbia. Because of this uniformity between jurisdictions on many issues of commercial law, courts are likely to consider

---

18 *See, e.g., Citizens State Bank Norwood Young Am. v. Brown*, 849 N.W.2d 55, 61 (Minn. 2014) (explaining that "uniform laws are interpreted to effect their general purpose to make uniform the laws of those states that enact them" and adopting the interpretation given to a statute by other states' highest courts); *People ex rel. LeGout v. Decker*, 586 N.E.2d 1257, 1260–61 (Ill. 1992); *Ohio Ins. Guar. Ass'n v. Simpson*, 439 N.E.2d 1257, 1258 (Ohio Ct. App. 1981); *State v. Hawkins*, 406 S.W.3d 121, 138 (Tenn. 2013) (declining to "adopt a standalone abandonment doctrine" in light of uniform caselaw from other states interpreting the Model Penal Code's evidence-tampering provision).

19 *See, e.g.*, Uniform Real Property Transfer on Death Act § 18 (2009) (verbatim as quoted above); Uniform Prudent Management of Institutional Funds Act § 10 (2006) (verbatim as quoted above); Uniform Athlete Agents Act § 18 (2000) (verbatim as quoted above except that *states* is capitalized).

20 *Holiday Inns, Inc. v. Olsen*, 692 S.W.2d 850, 853 (Tenn. 1985).

decisions from other jurisdictions in this area. The Oklahoma Supreme Court, for example, has observed that decisions from other jurisdictions aren't to be "brush[ed] aside" in light of the purpose of the Oklahoma Uniform Commercial Code: "making uniform the law among the various jurisdictions."[21] Further, it is now standard for model acts of the Uniform Law Commission to contain a rule of construction requiring the code to be liberally construed and applied to promote its underlying purpose and policies.[22]

State courts may be especially reluctant to disregard federal precedent in an area of commercial law when doing so would lead to inconsistencies within the jurisdiction. True, the pre-*Erie* forum-shopping concerns voiced by the North Dakota Supreme Court in 1894 have diminished under that doctrine. But when a federal court has predicted state law in a diversity case, state courts may be inclined to follow its reasoning for reasons of comity and to eliminate uncertainty in the law of the jurisdiction.

Beyond commercial law

As the blackletter of this section suggests, the preference for uniformity across jurisdictions transcends commercial law. A broad, though weak, policy favors avoiding conflict with the weight of authority on an issue of first impression, particularly when courts in other jurisdictions agree.[23]

Part of the rationale for this principle is that parties are likely to have planned their prelitigation affairs with established authority in mind. In a 1955 case,[24] an Indiana court considered, as a matter of first impression under Indiana law, whether a fire-insurance

---

21 *Reynolds-Wilson Lumber Co. v. Peoples Nat'l Bank*, 699 P.2d 146, 149 (Okla. 1985) (per curiam); *see Specialty Beverages, LLC v. Pabst Brewing Co.*, 537 F.3d 1165, 1174 n.7 (10th Cir. 2008) (observing that Oklahoma courts look to the law of other jurisdictions when applying the Uniform Commercial Code).

22 *See, e.g.*, U.C.C. § 1-103; Unif. Probate Code § 1-102.

23 *See, e.g., People v. Palomo*, 272 P.3d 1106, 1112 (Colo. App. 2011) (adopting the uniformly accepted rule that the costs incurred by the government in unsuccessfully prosecuting charges unrelated to the charge on which the defendant was convicted aren't chargeable to the defendant).

24 *Owens v. Milwaukee Ins. Co.*, 123 N.E.2d 645 (Ind. App. 1955) (in banc).

policy covered losses caused by "friendly fire"—fire that was "wholly confined to the place it was intended to be."[25] The insured sought coverage for the loss of her lower denture, which had accidentally been "thrown into a trash fire" at her home.[26] The insurance company denied coverage under the rule that "where a fire is intentionally kindled for a lawful purpose the insurer is not liable for the consequence thereof so long as the fire itself is confined as intended."[27] Although the language of the policy made no such exclusion explicit, the court recognized that nearly all states had long recognized it as the proper interpretation of the term *fire* within the meaning of a fire-insurance policy.[28] Further, the Indiana court noted that the friendly-fire doctrine had been announced in the English courts as early as 1815.[29] In light of this great weight of authority, the court concluded that "both insured and insurer" should be presumed to have "contracted with such definition in mind."[30]

Courts are also mindful of the need for decisional uniformity when other issues are likely to arise across jurisdictions. So if a particular contract form is used in several states, a court may rely heavily on the decisions of other state courts interpreting that contract.[31] For example, in a 1999 case,[32] the Texas Supreme Court was required to decide whether the unintentional discharge of a shotgun on a gun rack in a nearby pickup truck, causing injury, was an accident arising out of the truck's "use" within the meaning of a personal auto policy.[33] The court decided that it was, pointedly

---

25   *Id.* at 646.
26   *Id.* at 645.
27   *Id.*
28   *Id.* (citing *Mode, Ltd. v. Fireman's Fund Ins. Co.*, 110 P.2d 840, 842–43 (Idaho 1941) (collecting cases that recognize a distinction between "friendly fires" and "hostile fires" in fire-insurance contracts)).
29   *Owens*, 123 N.E.2d at 646.
30   *Id.* at 647 (quoting *Mode, Ltd.*, 110 P.2d at 843).
31   *See, e.g., Converting/Biophile Labs., Inc. v. Ludlow Composites Corp.*, 722 N.W.2d 633, 640–42 (Wis. Ct. App. 2006) (following other jurisdictions' interpretation of a forum-selection clause in a contract).
32   *Mid-Century Ins. Co. v. Lindsey*, 997 S.W.2d 153 (Tex. 1999).
33   *Id.* at 154.

noting that its conclusion was consistent with the majority of decisions in other jurisdictions in similar cases.[34]

A state court may even be persuaded to overrule its horizontal precedent when faced with a clear weight of contrary authority on an issue in which uniformity is particularly important. In a 1980 case,[35] the Tennessee Supreme Court explicitly recognized the availability of the entrapment defense in a criminal prosecution.[36] In doing so, the court recognized that it was the only state not to have recognized this defense: it "welcomed [the] opportunity to clarify, harmonize and modernize" the law of Tennessee.[37]

---

[34] *Id.* at 159–63.
[35] *State v. Jones*, 598 S.W.2d 209 (Tenn. 1980).
[36] *Id.* at 212.
[37] *Id.*

84. Statutory Interpretation of Governing Out-of-State Laws

When a pending issue is governed by the law of another state, or by some law other than that of the forum state, and authoritative expositions of the other state's law can be found from that state's courts, they will generally be accepted and followed as binding precedents.

Although out-of-state law is today treated by most state courts as a subject for legal interpretation, that hasn't always been so. Foreign law was once considered a question of fact to be pleaded and proved to the court.[1] If no foreign law was proved, many courts entertained a presumption that the common law of the foreign state was the same as the common law of the forum.[2] Some even refused to apply the statutory law of another state, choosing instead to apply the forum state's common law.[3] Although courts today generally take judicial notice of a sister state's laws, the burden may be on the litigant claiming the protection of those laws to bring them to the court's attention.[4]

A state's high court is the final interpreter of its statutes. The courts of other states as well as federal courts will accept its

---

1 *See, e.g., Askew v. Smith*, 246 S.W.2d 920, 922–23 (Tex. Civ. App.—Dallas 1952, no writ); *Keasler v. Mutual Life Ins. Co.*, 99 S.E. 97, 97 (N.C. 1919); *Midland Steel Co. v. Citizens' Nat'l Bank*, 72 N.E. 290, 292 (Ind. App. 1904). *See also* Roger M. Michalski, *Pleading and Proving Foreign Law in the Age of Plausibility Reading*, 59 Buff. L. Rev. 1207, 1216–36 (2011) (summarizing the shift from foreign law as fact to foreign law as law).

2 *See, e.g., Thomas v. Shepherd*, 156 S.E. 724, 725 (Ga. Ct. App. 1931); *Wade v. Boone*, 168 S.W. 360, 362 (Mo. Ct. App. 1914) (noting that "in the absence of any showing to the contrary, the presumption obtains that [the common law] is still in force respecting the matter in hand"); *Strout v. Burgess*, 68 A.2d 241, 251 (Me. 1949); *Jenness v. Simpson*, 78 A. 886, 894 (Vt. 1911).

3 *See, e.g., New Hampshire Fire Ins. Co. v. Curtis*, 85 So. 2d 441, 446 (Ala. 1955) (per curiam). *But see Lamb v. Hardy*, 211 S.W. 445, 446 (Tex. 1919); *Midland Steel Co.*, 72 N.E. at 292 (declining to distinguish between statute and common law, and applying applicable foreign law when either is at issue).

4 *See Leonard v. Johns-Manville Sales Corp.*, 305 S.E.2d 528, 531 (N.C. 1983) (North Carolina courts are authorized by statute to take judicial notice of foreign law "in the same manner as if the question arose under" North Carolina law); *Ferster v. Ferster*, 138 S.E.2d 674, 676 (Ga. 1964) ("No Maryland law appears in this record on this point, and in such case we apply Georgia law.").

interpretation as a correct and binding statement of the law of that state. In 1825, the U.S. Supreme Court recognized that "no Court which professed to be governed by principle" would presume that a foreign sovereign "had misunderstood [its] own statutes" and "therefore erect itself into a tribunal which should correct such misunderstanding."[5] The state courts are the "ultimate expositors of state law," and their interpretation is to be followed by courts in other jurisdictions.[6]

New York's high court described the rationale behind this rule in 1880, saying that if a New York statute, as interpreted by the state's highest court, could be construed differently in another state, people subject to the law would have "no security against a different construction elsewhere, and thus liabilities might be incurred which were never contemplated by the Legislature of the State which passed the statute, and great injustice done."[7] Enforcing the law that way, as the *lex loci*, "would be an infringement upon the rights of individuals and at war with the policy of the law that no man should be subject to liability at the same time by reason of different and conflicting constructions of the same law in different localities."[8]

Under common-law choice-of-law doctrines such as *lex loci delicti*—the common-law doctrine that the law applicable to an action in tort is the law of the state where the tort occurred[9]— courts may be called on to apply the law of a foreign state.

---

[5] *Elmendorf v. Taylor*, 23 U.S. (10 Wheat.) 152, 159–60 (1825).

[6] *Mullaney v. Wilbur*, 421 U.S. 684, 691 (1975); *see Hamilton v. Hannibal & St. Joseph R.R.*, 18 P. 57, 61 (Kan. 1888); *Gramercy Inv. Trust v. Lakemont Homes Nev., Inc.*, 130 Cal. Rptr. 3d 496, 502 (Ct. App. 2011); *Southern Ry. v. Decker*, 62 S.E. 678, 680 (Ga. Ct. App. 1908); *Cortes v. Ryder Truck Rental, Inc.*, 581 N.E.2d 1, 5 (Ill. App. Ct. 1991). *But see Gurley v. Rhoden*, 421 U.S. 200, 208 (1975) (suggesting that a state's interpretation of its statutes may not be given effect if it isn't "consistent with the statute's reasonable interpretation").

[7] *Jessup v. Carnegie*, 80 N.Y. 441, 446 (1880).

[8] *Id.*

[9] *See, e.g., Cousins v. Instrument Flyers, Inc.*, 376 N.E.2d 914, 915 (N.Y. 1978) (per curiam); *Jones v. Louisiana Western Ry.*, 243 S.W. 976, 978 (Tex. Comm'n App. 1922, judgm't adopted) (discussing application of Louisiana law to *lex loci delictus*); *Merrimac Mining Co. v. Levy*, 54 Pa. 227 (1867) (stocks of a Michigan corporation governed by Michigan law).

Similarly, choice-of-law provisions often lead to adjudication of a contract by a court outside the state whose law is to be applied.[10] When a court must apply the law of another state, it will generally follow decisions of that state's courts as binding statements of the state's law.[11] Some courts observe that this analysis is similar to a federal court's *Erie* analysis: the forum state must determine the law based on existing precedent from the state's courts, applying precedent from the state's highest court, if available, and weighing lower-court precedent if not.[12]

When applying a sister state's statute, a court must apply the statute as it has been interpreted by that state's courts, even if it would interpret the statute differently or if its own law is different on the matter. In a 1902 case,[13] the Mississippi Supreme Court addressed the liability of a telegraph company that had mistranscribed a "cipher" message—a message in code—sent from Massachusetts to Mississippi.[14] Because the message had been contracted for and sent in Massachusetts, law of that state applied to the contract.[15] A Massachusetts statute provided that a telegraph company was obliged to transmit messages "faithfully and impartially" upon payment of the usual charges.[16] The Supreme Judicial Court of Massachusetts had interpreted this statute to recognize "the rights of the owners and conductors of the telegraph companies to make rules and regulations by which to define and limit their duties and obligations in the transaction of the[ir]

---

10 *See, e.g., Young v. Baltimore & Ohio R.R.*, 146 S.E.2d 441 (N.C. 1966); *Bayer Corp. v. DX Terminals, Ltd.*, 214 S.W.3d 586 (Tex. App.—Houston [14th Dist.] 2006, pet. denied); *Schaffert ex rel. Schaffert v. Jackson Nat'l Life Ins. Co.*, 687 N.E.2d 230, 232–33 (Ind. Ct. App. 1997).

11 *See, e.g., Gramercy Inv. Trust*, 130 Cal. Rptr. 3d at 502; *Cortes*, 581 N.E.2d at 5.

12 *See, e.g., Fantis Foods, Inc. v. North River Ins. Co.*, 753 A.2d 176, 183 (N.J. Super. Ct. App. Div. 2000); *Wilmington Trust Co. v. Clark*, 424 A.2d 744, 753 (Md. 1981); *Highland Crusader Offshore Partners, L.P. v. Andrews & Kurth, L.L.P.*, 248 S.W.3d 887, 892 n.4 (Tex. App.—Dallas 2008, no pet.); *Ragan v. AT&T Corp.*, 824 N.E.2d 1183, 1193 (Ill. App. Ct. 2005).

13 *Shaw v. Postal Tel. Cable Co.*, 31 So. 222 (Miss. 1902).

14 *Id.* at 223.

15 *Id.*

16 *Id.* (quoting Mass. Gen. Stat. 1860, § 10, at 373).

business."[17] The defendant telegraph company disclaimed liability for mistakes in the transmission of "obscure or cipher messages" unless the sender paid an additional "trifling sum" for insurance.[18] The plaintiff had not paid for such insurance, and the substitution of a "t" for an "r" in his coded telegraph message, involving a transaction in cotton, resulted in a loss to him of just over $1,000.[19] He sued in Mississippi, arguing that the court should disregard the Massachusetts court's interpretation of that state's statute and determine under the common law that he was entitled to recover for the telegraph company's mistake.[20] Under Mississippi law, a telegraph company was unable to contract out of its negligence, and the plaintiff argued that this rule should be applied to his action. The Mississippi Supreme Court correctly rejected this contention, recognizing that the Massachusetts court's interpretation of its own statute, which the plaintiff conceded applied to the contract, controlled.[21] Because the Massachusetts court had held that a surcharge to insure accuracy in the transcription of a message was permissible as a reasonable regulation of the telegraph company's business, the plaintiff couldn't recover.[22]

Some courts describe this rule as an exercise of comity or of the court's discretion.[23] But the better view is that judicial interpretation is as much the binding law of the state as the text of the statute, and the courts of another sovereign aren't empowered to disregard the state's law when they are called on to apply it unless its enforcement violates their state's public policy.

In a 1927 case,[24] a California appellate court was asked to interpret the Oregon divorce laws. The defendant had been convicted

---

17 *Ellis v. American Tel. Co.*, 95 Mass. (13 Allen) 226, 235 (1866).
18 *Shaw*, 31 So. at 223.
19 *Id.*
20 *Id.*
21 *Id.* at 223–24.
22 *Id.* at 224.
23 *See, e.g., Nesbit v. Clark*, 116 A. 404, 406 (Pa. 1922); *Stevers v. Walker*, 125 S.W.2d 920, 924 (Mo. Ct. App. 1939) (describing its application of another state's interpretation of its statutes as in "the spirit of the 'good faith and credit clause' and as a privilege rather than as a right").
24 *People v. Goddard*, 258 P. 447 (Cal. Dist. Ct. App. 1927).

of bigamy based on his marriage to one Audrey Hargranf in 1926. The evidence showed that he had already married Marjorie Roys in 1923.[25] The defendant argued that the earlier marriage should be considered void because under Oregon law Ms. Roys's Oregon divorce from her previous husband had not become final when she married the defendant.[26] If the divorce wasn't final, then Ms. Roys *couldn't* have remarried. Therefore her marriage to the defendant was void, and the defendant's later marriage to Ms. Hargranf couldn't be bigamous.[27] The California court correctly referred to Oregon courts in determining the effect of that state's divorce laws, concluding that because the Oregon courts had not treated their statutes as having extraterritorial effect, the statute disallowing an Oregon divorcée from marrying until at least six months after the entry of judgment didn't affect the validity of Ms. Roys's later California marriage to the defendant.[28] The defendant's conviction was affirmed.[29]

Years later, the same Oregon statute was considered by another California court. In that case, the court interpreted Oregon caselaw differently, holding that a marriage entered into in California within the six-month limitation required by Oregon law voided the California marriage.[30]

When there isn't any law in the relevant jurisdiction, the forum court must use its own general principles to decide the issue. For example, the court may refer to the enacting state's decisions regarding tools of statutory construction.[31] Although such an interpretation will not be binding on the courts of the enacting

---

25 *Id.* at 447.
26 *Id.* at 448.
27 *Id.*
28 *Id.*
29 *Id.* at 449.
30 *Jones v. Jones*, 5 Cal. Rptr. 803, 808 (Dist. Ct. App. 1960).
31 *See, e.g., Magee v. Huppin-Fleck*, 664 N.E.2d 246, 251 (Ill. App. Ct. 1996) (observing that the "rules for statutory construction" used "in the enacting state are most relevant" to an independent interpretation of its statute); *Brock v. Blackwood*, 143 S.W.3d 47, 68 (Mo. Ct. App. 2004) (applying Oklahoma rules of statutory interpretation to construe an Oklahoma statute that had not been addressed by any Oklahoma court).

state, it may (as with any pertinent foreign decision) serve as persuasive authority.

In a 2008 case,[32] a Texas appellate court was asked to determine the validity of stock shares issued by a Delaware corporation.[33] The corporation's charter disallowed issuing "nonvoting stock," and the plaintiffs contended that the stock at issue was nonvoting because it wasn't entitled to vote with the common stock but could vote only "as required by law."[34] The corporation proposed to modify stockholders' rights adversely. The court observed that the litigants had not cited, and it had not found, Delaware authority construing the phrase *nonvoting stock*.[35] The court therefore relied on "general principles" of interpretation to determine whether a Delaware court would treat the stock as nonvoting.[36] Because Delaware law treats a charter as a contract, ordinary principles of contractual interpretation applied.[37] When a term isn't defined in a contract, Delaware courts consult dictionaries to determine what meaning a reasonable person in the position of the parties would have given the term.[38] The plain meaning of *nonvoting* is "not entitling the holder to vote."[39] The court found that because the holders of the stock at issue could sometimes vote under the charter's terms, the stock wasn't nonvoting[40] and therefore was not forbidden by the charter.[41]

The forum state's courts may disagree about the meaning of a foreign state's law or its applicability, just as they may disagree

---

32   *Highland Crusader Offshore Partners, L.P. v. Andrews & Kurth, L.L.P.*, 248 S.W.3d 887 (Tex. App.—Dallas 2008, no pet.).
33   *Id.* at 890–91.
34   *Id.*
35   *Id.*
36   *Id.*
37   *Id.*
38   *Id.*
39   *Id.*
40   *Id.*
41   *Id.* at 892.

about their own state's law. In a 2013 case,[42] a New York intermediate appellate court was called on to decide whether the New Jersey Workers' Compensation Act provided the exclusive remedy to an employee injured on the job when his hand was crushed by a hot leather-stamping machine.[43] The Act provided an exclusive remedy "except for intentional wrong."[44] The employee argued that the employer's removal of a safety guard from the machine was an intentional wrong.[45] The New Jersey Supreme Court had decided that whether the removal of a safety guard is an intentional wrong depends on whether, as a matter of fact, the employer knew that removal of the guard was "substantially certain" to cause injury.[46] The New York court's majority concluded that the employer in its case had no reason to know that injury would result because none ever had, and in any event the injury was caused by the employee's misjudgment, not the missing guard.[47] The dissenting judge agreed about the applicable legal test under the New Jersey statute but disagreed about whether the facts conclusively favored the employer.[48]

Each state is entitled to decide for itself whether a sister state's laws are penal (see § 87) and, if so, whether to enforce them in its own courts. The source state's characterization of its own statute as penal or not penal isn't binding under these circumstances even though the meaning of the statute is fixed by the courts of the source state.

---

42   *Lebron v. SML Veteran Leather, LLC*, 971 N.Y.S.2d 82 (App. Div. 2013), *aff'd*, 5 N.E.3d 999 (N.Y. 2014).

43   *Id.* at 83.

44   N.J. Stat. Ann. § 34:15-8.

45   *Lebron*, 971 N.Y.S.2d at 85.

46   *Id.* at 84–85 (the following facts create a fact question: "the defendant's admission the guard was removed to expedite processing of work and increase profits; the number of close calls involving the machine; the repeated requests by employees to reactivate the guards, particularly those in close temporal proximity to the incident in question; and the employer's actions in systematically deceiv[ing] OSHA into believing that the machine was guarded") (citing *Laidlow v. Hariton Mach. Co.*, 790 A.2d 884, 897 (N.J. 2002)).

47   *Lebron*, 971 N.Y.S.2d at 85.

48   *Id.* at 86–88 (Manzanet-Daniels J. dissenting).

85. Borrowed-Statute Doctrine

When one state enacts another state's statutory language that has a settled judicial interpretation, it is sometimes presumed that the settled interpretation is adopted with the statute. But this overstates the matter: properly viewed, the decisions of the source state's high court on a point concerning the statute are merely persuasive precedents and are not binding on the courts of the borrowing state.

It has often been said that when one state adopts a statute already in place in another, the adopting state also imports the extant judicial interpretations of the statute. This idea derives from the presumption that the adopting state's legislature is aware of how the statute has already been interpreted and intends to have that interpretation applied in the future.[1] The principle applies to conclusive constructions of the statute by the source state's highest court—if made before the borrowing state's adoption.[2]

Often referred to as the "borrowed-statute doctrine,"[3] the principle is sometimes described in quite strong terms, as if the courts considered themselves affirmatively bound by preexisting interpretations as part of the adopted law.[4] This strong view of the principle is most often endorsed when the court finds direct evidence that the statute was adopted from a particular sister state; mere similarity between the two statutes is not sufficient. In

---

1   See *Randolph v. Hudson*, 74 P. 946, 950 (Okla. 1903) (quoting an unnamed opinion by Marshall C.J.); *State v. Klein*, 224 S.W.2d 250, 243 (Tex. Crim. App. 1949); *Elliott v. Clement*, 151 P.2d 739, 740 (Or. 1944) (stating that "it is only a construction announced before the adoption of the statute that is ever considered controlling").

2   *Given v. Owen*, 175 P. 345, 346 (Okla. 1918) (declining to follow a decision of the Kansas intermediate appellate court on a statute adopted from Kansas because the decision was rendered after the statute's adoption and because the decision wasn't from Kansas's high court).

3   *Pope v. Brock*, 912 So. 2d 935, 938 (Miss. 2005) (en banc).

4   See, e.g., *State v. Tower*, 881 P.2d 1317, 1319 (Mont. 1994) ("When Montana's legislature adopts a statute from a sister state, Montana courts follow the general rule of also adopting the construction which has been placed upon that statute by the highest court of the sister state.").

deciding an 1898 case,[5] for example, the D.C. Circuit considered itself affirmatively bound by an interpretation given to a statute adopted from Illinois. The court reasoned that to go "beyond the interpretation that has been given this statute by the Supreme Court of Illinois . . . would savor too much of judicial legislation" because "if Congress had intended to repudiate the construction that the statute had received in the State from which it was adopted, it would have made some corresponding changes in the language used, so as to remove all doubt in respect of its intention."[6]

More recently, the Oklahoma Supreme Court expressed this view in interpreting a statute expressly adopted from Kansas: "The text came to us encumbered by the meaning accorded it in Kansas. Judicial interpretation by a court of last resort impressed on adopted legislation before its reception cannot be changed by jurisprudence of the receiving state."[7]

We believe that this strong position—in truth a weak position for the writing court to impose upon itself—is erroneous. The better, more circumspect view is that the borrowed-statute doctrine is actually a tenuous canon of construction that typically requires an extensive use of legislative history (which is hardly a recommendation for it in the eyes of traditionalists).[8] Although some will consider the doctrine helpful as an occasional aid in statutory construction,[9] it should never bind the courts when

---

5   *Strasburger v. Dodge*, 12 App. D.C. 37 (1898).

6   *Id.* at 49–50. *But see Texas & Pac. Ry. v. Humble*, 181 U.S. 57, 65–66 (1901) (declining to apply interpretations from the courts of a state with a "nearly identical" statute because there was no indication that the statute at issue was derived from that state's statute rather than some other state's similarly worded statute).

7   *In re Estate of Speake*, 743 P.2d 648 (Okla. 1987).

8   *See* Book Notice, 7 Am. L. Rev. 154, 155 (1872) (stating that the borrowed-statute doctrine "must be taken with a good deal of caution"—possibly written by Holmes J. as editor of the journal). *See also* Antonin Scalia & Bryan A. Garner, *Reading Law: The Interpretation of Legal Texts* 325 (2012) (casting doubt on this canon of interpretation).

9   *See, e.g., Spratt v. Toft*, 324 P.3d 707, 712 (Wash. Ct. App. 2014) (noting that California precedent is helpful in interpreting Washington's anti-SLAPP statute, which was "patterned" after California's); *Holiday Inns, Inc. v. Olsen*, 692 S.W.2d 850, 853 (Tenn. 1985) ("This does not mean that this court will blindly

other interpretive tools indicate a better interpretation. The U.S. Supreme Court has viewed the principle this way, observing that it is a canon of statutory construction.[10] As such, this presumption is only a tool toward interpretation and isn't strictly binding on the courts. At bottom, this principle is like any other soft canon of construction: it is an aid to interpretation, not a hard-and-fast rule. It must often be subordinated to other interpretive tools. Courts applying the doctrine in this way may also observe that the source state's judicial decisions will not be followed if they are contrary to public policy or existing law in the borrowing state.[11] Most courts refer to the doctrine as simply a form of persuasive authority: other courts' interpretations of the same statutory language can be persuasive, but only that.[12]

For the doctrine to have any persuasive force, the statute in the adopting state must be precisely the same as the one in the source state. If the borrowing state's legislature has changed the statute, it can no longer be presumed to have adopted earlier interpretations, particularly those related to the changes.

A 1902 Nebraska Supreme Court decision[13] provides a case in point. Nebraska had borrowed an Ohio statute defining *murder* as killing someone "purposely, and of deliberate and premeditated

---

follow decisions of other states interpreting uniform acts but[] this court will seriously consider the constructions given to comparable statutes in other jurisdictions and will espouse them to maintain conformity when they are in harmony with the spirit of the statute and do not antagonize public policy of this state.").

10 *Shannon v. United States*, 512 U.S. 573, 582 n.8 (1994) (characterizing the rule as one of statutory construction). *See also State v. Brooks*, 232 N.W. 331, 266 (Minn. 1930) (observing that the doctrine doesn't apply as to another state's determination that the statute is constitutional when applied to the validity of the statute under Minnesota's constitution).

11 *See Elliott v. Clement*, 151 P.2d 739, 740 (Or. 1944).

12 *See, e.g., Cacho v. Superior Court ex rel. Cnty. of Maricopa*, 821 P.2d 721, 724 (Ariz. 1991) (in banc) (observing that source state's interpretations of a statute are "of particular interest"); *Hunter-Hayes Elevator Co. v. Petroleum Club Inn Co.*, 419 P.2d 465, 467 (N.M. 1966) ("Although not binding on this court, the interpretation of the Illinois statute by Illinois courts is persuasive."); *Kortum v. Johnson*, 755 N.W.2d 432, 441 (N.D. 2008) (observing that "[w]hen our statute is derived from and substantially identical to a statute from another state, the judicial decisions interpreting the foreign statute are highly persuasive").

13 *Rhea v. State*, 88 N.W. 789 (Neb. 1902).

malice, or in the perpetration, or attempt to perpetrate any rape, arson, robbery, or burglary, or by administering poison, or causing the same to be done."[14] The issue before the court was whether a killing during the commission of one of the other stated crimes was murder if it wasn't the purpose of the defendant's action but merely a consequence—in other words, whether any killing during the commission of one of the listed crimes was serious enough to be treated as murder rather than manslaughter.[15] The Ohio Supreme Court had interpreted the statute, emphasizing the comma after *purposely*, to require purpose and, in addition, either malice, another crime, or poisoning.[16] But after borrowing the statute, the Nebraska legislature had amended it to omit the comma after *purposely*.[17] The Nebraska court concluded that "a purpose to alter the section by amendment, and thereby avoid the force of the [borrowed-statute doctrine,] . . . is inferable, because the modification is regarding a point on which, in a marked degree, [the Ohio] decision rested."[18] The court therefore correctly declined to follow the Ohio decision. The court also noted that no other state court had followed the Ohio court's interpretation, and that Ohio had itself changed its own statute.[19] The Nebraska court interpreted the statute as not always requiring a purposeful killing for murder.[20]

Exceptions to the borrowed-statute doctrine

Courts have long recognized wide exceptions to the doctrine.[21] For example, a statute's earlier interpretation isn't to be imported if it would be against the public policy of the adopting state. In a

---

14 *Id.* at 796.
15 *Id.* at 793–94.
16 *Id.* at 797.
17 *Id.*
18 *Id.*
19 *Id.*
20 *Id.* at 797–98.
21 *See Kraus v. Chicago, Burlington & Quincy R.R.*, 16 F.2d 79, 82 (8th Cir. 1926) ("There is no absolute rule which requires the adoption of the construction of a statute which is taken from another state, and the rule that the adopting state

1927 case,[22] the Arizona Supreme Court observed that the doctrine "is not an absolute rule, and if [the court] think[s] the construction" given by the sister state's courts "is not consonant with common sense, reason, and our public policy, we are not absolutely bound to accept it."[23] And in a 2012 case,[24] the Montana Supreme Court observed that although Montana's criminal code is "modeled after" the Illinois code, the court wasn't bound to "blindly follow the interpretations of the criminal code provided by the courts in Illinois without taking into consideration Montana's unique character and history."[25] The application of a public-policy exception indicates that the court is of the view that the doctrine is no more than a canon of construction, helpful in aid of interpretation but hardly binding. Were earlier interpretations binding, they would embody the public policy of the adopting state and therefore couldn't be contrary to its public policy.

Some courts have recognized another exception to this principle when a statute exists in some form in various states and the actual source state's interpretation is contrary to the weight of authority.[26] Even if such courts don't say so expressly, they reinforce the view that the borrowed-statute doctrine is only a tenuous principle of statutory construction. If the source state's interpretations were truly binding as part of the adopted law, courts would not be free to disregard them even in the face of contrary authority. But when the doctrine is used as an interpretive tool, it is appropriate to give the source state's interpretations less weight if there was disagreement about the proper interpretation when the statute was adopted. In such a situation, it is difficult to say which interpretation the adopting legislature had in mind. More important, since the aim of statutory interpretation isn't to ascertain the subjective intent of the legislature but to determine the

---

will lean to the construction which has been placed upon the statute by the courts of the state from which it was taken is subject to many exceptions.").

22   *Lewis v. State*, 256 P. 1048 (Ariz. 1927).
23   *Id.* at 1049–50.
24   *City of Missoula v. Paffhausen*, 289 P.3d 141 (Mont. 2012).
25   *Id.* at 149.
26   *See, e.g.*, *State v. Campbell*, 85 P. 784, 790 (Kan. 1906).

plain meaning of the words it used, a court rightly hesitates to say that the words were adopted with one interpretation in mind when they have been given various interpretations. A court facing this situation is likely to give little weight to the borrowed-statute doctrine, choosing instead to apply stronger canons of construction to come to its own judgment about the statute's meaning.

Even some courts that say the doctrine isn't binding end up misapplying it. The Mississippi Supreme Court did so in a 2005 case[27] involving limitations and statutory notice requirements in medical-negligence claims.[28] A Mississippi statute provided that "[i]f notice is served within sixty (60) days prior to the expiration of the applicable statute of limitations, the time for the commencement of the action shall be extended sixty (60) days from the service of the notice."[29] The plaintiff had provided notice within 60 days of the end of the limitations period and then filed the complaint 61 days after providing the required notice. Literally speaking, limitations ran on the 60th day after notice, and the claim was barred. But the plaintiff argued that the extended "time" was the original limitations period, and that in effect the statute tolled limitations for 60 days, so that her claim wasn't barred. The court considered a related statute to support the tolling interpretation and observed that California courts had long interpreted California's nearly identical statute that way.[30] The Mississippi court stated the borrowed-statute doctrine as follows: "While statutory interpretation by another state's supreme court is not binding upon this Court, . . . we may consider a sister state's interpretation of its statutes where there is clear evidence that our Legislature consciously borrowed statutory language from that state's enactment."[31] Although there was no textual indication that the Mississippi legislature had borrowed the statute from

---

27   *Pope v. Brock*, 912 So. 2d 935 (Miss. 2005) (en banc).
28   *Id.*
29   *Id.* at 937 (quoting Miss. Code Ann. § 15-1-36(15) (2003)).
30   *Id.* at 938–39.
31   *Id.* at 938.

California, and although the wording wasn't identical, the court somehow found the doctrine applicable.[32]

The doctrine should never apply to judicial interpretations of the source statute occurring after its adoption. Because the new interpretation didn't yet exist when the legislature adopted the statute, it cannot be presumed that the legislature adopted the statute with that interpretation in mind. In a 1912 decision of the Michigan Supreme Court,[33] a litigant argued that a Massachusetts decision interpreting a statute adopted from Michigan was binding on the court.[34] The court correctly rejected this contention because the Massachusetts decision postdated the Michigan adoption by eight years.[35]

Nor will the doctrine be applied to the decisions of lower courts in the source state at the time of adoption.[36] Neither final nor authoritative, they cannot be said to have been embodied in the statute when the borrowing state's legislature adopted it.

Borrowed constitutional provisions

An allied principle is the supposed "borrowed-constitutional-provision doctrine," espoused perhaps too boldly by Henry Campbell Black in 1912:

> [W]here a clause or provision in a constitution, which has received a settled judicial construction, is adopted in the same words by the framers of another constitution, it will be presumed that the construction thereof was likewise adopted, and the decisions in which that construction was announced will be regarded as binding precedents.[37]

---

32 *Id.* at 939.
33 *Goodell v. Yezerski*, 136 N.W. 451 (Mich. 1912).
34 *Id.* at 452; *see also McIlroy v. Fugitt*, 33 S.W.2d 719, 721–22 (Ark. 1930).
35 *Goodell*, 136 N.W. at 452.
36 *See Lewis v. State*, 256 P. 1048, 1050 (Ariz. 1927).
37 Henry Campbell Black, *Handbook on the Law of Judicial Precedents* § 119, at 395–96 (1912) ("[W]here a clause or provision in a constitution, which has received a settled judicial construction, is adopted in the same words by the framers of another constitution, it will be presumed that the construction thereof was likewise adopted, and the decisions in which that construction was announced will be regarded as binding precedents.").

We believe that the better view is that when a state high court has interpreted a state constitutional provision that is identical to one in another state's constitution, the decision may be considered persuasive only—not controlling.

Some older authorities support the stronger position that Black advocated. At issue in an 1872 Mississippi case[38] was the meaning of the "equal and uniform" requirement for exercising the taxing power under the Mississippi Constitution. In resolving the issue, the Mississippi Supreme Court observed: "We must suppose also, that the convention were conversant with the interpretation which had been put upon a similar provision in other state constitutions; and that they meant also to adopt, with the words, the judicial construction of them in other states."[39] Having thus suggested something in the nature of binding authority, the court surveyed the state-court decisions and found them informative and persuasive.[40]

Modern precedents tend toward the more moderate stance that the source state's precedents are merely persuasive.[41]

---

38 *Daily v. Swope*, 47 Miss. 367 (1872).

39 *Id.* at 385.

40 *Id.* at 385–86; *see* Black, *Handbook on the Law of Judicial Precedents* § 119, at 395–96.

41 *State v. Wheeler*, 175 P.3d 438 (Or. 2007) (en banc) ("We turn to the Indiana Constitution, which draws our attention in part because many provisions of the Oregon Constitution were taken from it."); *Blum v. Merrell Dow Pharm., Inc.*, 626 A.2d 537 (Pa. 1993) (looking to related caselaw from other states in construing the Pennsylvania right to a jury trial in a civil case); *McHugh v. Santa Monica Rent Control Bd.*, 777 P.2d 91, 108 (Cal. 1989) (in bank) (adopting the approach of sister supreme court's reflecting "a practical and reasoned understanding of the judicial powers doctrine").

86. Out-of-State Precedents as Persuasive Authority

On a question of general jurisprudence or the interpretation of a domestic statute, a decision made in a similar legal system is not binding as precedent. Yet it may be cited as persuasive authority, respected for its reasoning and judgment, and followed if approved.

A state court interpreting its own state's law isn't bound by the decisions of courts in other states—even if a sister state's courts have interpreted identical constitutional or statutory language.[1] Yet state courts will often refer to such decisions as persuasive authority, particularly on questions of first impression.[2] For example, in a 2012 case,[3] the Nevada Supreme Court considered analyses from other state courts regarding the novel question of how to authenticate text messages as evidence.[4]

Courts are likely to consult foreign precedent when addressing a common-law question of first impression,[5] particularly because the development of the common law naturally depends on judicial

---

1   See *State v. Chenoweth*, 158 P.3d 595, 605 (Wash. 2007) (en banc) (rejecting California and Montana decisions); *State v. Muckerheide*, 725 N.W.2d 930, 939 (Wis. 2007) (lower courts do not err by failing to follow foreign precedent, without more, since foreign precedent may be considered but isn't binding); *Union Leader Corp. v. New Hampshire Hous. Fin. Auth.*, 705 A.2d 725, 730 (N.H. 1997); *City of Montgomery v. Zgouvas*, 953 So. 2d 434, 443 n.2 (Ala. Crim. App. 2006) (declining to follow Colorado precedent interpreting similar statutory language as unconstitutionally overbroad because the Colorado court didn't consider the effect of a specific intent requirement).

2   See *Strozinsky v. School Dist. of Brown Deer*, 614 N.W.2d 443, 461 (Wis. 2000) ("Because this is an issue of first impression, we turn to the persuasive authority from other jurisdictions in the course of this analysis."); *see also August Entm't, Inc. v. Philadelphia Indem. Ins. Co.*, 52 Cal. Rptr. 3d 908, 915–16 (Ct. App. 2007) (referring to foreign precedent when there is a dearth of California precedent).

3   *Rodriguez v. State*, 273 P.3d 845 (Nev. 2012).

4   *Id.* at 849.

5   See *Holton v. Ward*, 847 N.W.2d 1, 7 (Mich. Ct. App. 2014) (noting that sister states agreed on the nature of riparian rights, which originate "in the most ancient property right: the right to exclude"); *State v. Courchesne*, 998 A.2d 1, 43 (Conn. 2010) (citing *Rogers v. Tennessee*, 532 U.S. 451, 464 (2001)).

reasoning rather than textual interpretation. Consider a 2010 case[6] in which the Connecticut Supreme Court had to decide, as a matter of first impression, whether the "born-alive rule" applied to allow a defendant's conviction for murder of both a mother and her child.[7] The defendant had repeatedly stabbed the mother, who was eight months pregnant. She was pronounced dead at the hospital, and her daughter was delivered by cesarean section, surviving for 45 days in the intensive-care unit.[8] The Connecticut court relied on precedent from other states recognizing the born-alive rule, under which a person who injures a fetus commits murder if the child is born alive and dies of the injury, but not if the fetus dies in utero.[9]

In another case of first-impression, the Idaho Supreme Court marshaled a number of sister-state decisions supporting its determination that parimutuel betting on horse racing isn't a "lottery" prohibited by the Idaho Constitution.[10] Under the parimutuel system, bettors have information about the horses, trainers, and jockeys before betting on the horse they think most likely to win. The amount they win depends on how many others bet on the same horse, which cannot be determined until all betting is closed. Challengers argued that parimutuel betting is a game of chance and therefore a lottery. Idaho law mirrored a common-law definition of *lottery*: "a species of gaming, wherein prizes are distributed by chance among persons paying a consideration for the chance to win; a game of hazard in which sums are paid for the chance to obtain a larger value in money or articles."[11] The court held that parimutuel betting isn't a lottery because the outcome isn't determined solely by chance. The opinion discussed, in detail, many state-court common-law decisions,[12] concluding:

---

6   *Courchesne*, 998 A.2d 1.
7   *Id.* at 33–68.
8   *Id.* at 102.
9   *Id.* at 14.
10 *Oneida Cnty. Fair Bd. v. Smylie*, 386 P.2d 374 (Idaho 1963).
11 *Id.* at 376 (quoting *State v. Village of Garden City*, 265 P.2d 328, 330 (Idaho 1953)).
12 *Id.* at 377–91.

"If skill plays any part in determining the distribution there is no lottery as prohibited by our Constitution."[13] A dissenting justice marshaled his own authority for the opposite conclusion—also citing opinions from a number of sister states.[14]

Courts often cite precedent from other jurisdictions as support for a conclusion reached based on independent reasoning.[15] In those cases, the court's decision is independent of foreign precedent, but foreign precedent does serve to buttress its reasoning or conclusion. For instance, in a 1973 case[16] the Michigan Supreme Court analyzed the origins of Michigan law regarding limitations on the use of juvenile-court records in criminal court.[17] At issue was whether such records could be brought to a sentencing judge's attention despite a statute barring their use as evidence.[18] Although the court conducted its own review of the history of the statute and Michigan's sentencing scheme when it was enacted, it also cited sister-state precedent to support its decision that use of juvenile-court records wasn't barred at the sentencing stage of an adult's criminal trial.[19] The court concluded that "the clear weight of judicial authority is in favor of full disclosure of the defendant's past, including his juvenile court history, to the sentencing judge."[20]

Courts will not follow authority from other jurisdictions deciding an issue if the law of the sister state is materially inconsistent with the forum state's law. For example, in a 2010 case,[21]

---

13 *Id.* at 374.

14 *Id.* at 392–95 (Taylor J. dissenting).

15 *See, e.g., Lambert v. Belknap Cnty. Convention,* 949 A.2d 709, 715 (N.H. 2008) (citing Connecticut authority in support of its reasoning); *K & K Constr., Inc. v. Department of Envtl. Quality,* 705 N.W.2d 365, 385 (Mich. Ct. App. 2005) (citing *R & Y, Inc. v. Municipality of Anchorage,* 34 P.3d 289, 298 (Alaska 2001)); *Martinez v. Enterprise Rent-A-Car Co.,* 13 Cal. Rptr. 3d 857, 862 (Ct. App. 2004); *Brown v. Commonwealth,* 40 S.W.3d 873, 877 (Ky. Ct. App. 1999).

16 *People v. McFarlin,* 208 N.W.2d 504 (Mich. 1973).

17 *Id.* at 507.

18 *Id.*

19 *Id.* at 509–10.

20 *Id.* at 510.

21 *People v. Campbell,* 798 N.W.2d 514 (Mich. Ct. App. 2010) (per curiam).

a Michigan appellate court declined to follow a California decision on the retroactive application of its medical-marijuana statute, which provided an affirmative defense to prosecution for marijuana-related charges.[22] California precedent established that amendments to criminal laws could be applied retroactively to pending cases when the punishment for a particular crime was lessened or "criminal sanctions have been completely repealed before a criminal conviction becomes final."[23] The California court allowed a defendant convicted of transporting marijuana to assert the medical-use immunity added by statute after his arrest.[24] But the Michigan court declined to follow in California's footsteps, referring to its own precedent establishing that new statutes affecting substantive rights are to be applied only prospectively.[25] Because the Michigan defendant's conduct had not been subject to a medical-use affirmative defense at the time it took place, he wasn't entitled to apply the defense retroactively.[26] By contrast, if the foreign state's law had been materially the same, the court might have been more likely to follow its precedent.[27]

By the same token, a court that *has* followed foreign precedent on an issue may well cease to do so if relevant considerations change. In a 1992 case,[28] the Kansas Supreme Court noted that its state law, like California's, defined *aggravated kidnapping* as causing bodily harm to the victim, and it had at one point followed

---

22 *Id.* at 515–16.

23 *People v. Wright*, 146 P.3d 531, 539–40 (Cal. 2006) (quoting *People v. Rossi*, 555 P.2d 1313, 1316 (Cal. 1976) (in bank)).

24 *Id.* at 540–42.

25 *Campbell*, 798 N.W.2d at 535–36 (citing *People v. Conyer*, 762 N.W.2d 198 (Mich. Ct. App. 2008) (per curiam)).

26 *Id.* at 536. But quaere whether this wasn't a misapplication of both the retroactivity canon and the pending-action canon. *See* Antonin Scalia & Bryan A. Garner, *Reading Law: The Interpretation of Legal Texts* §§ 41–42, at 261–67 (2012).

27 *See, e.g., Catlett v. State*, 336 S.W.2d 8, 10 (Tenn. 1960) (citing *Commonwealth ex rel. Tinder v. Werner*, 280 S.W.2d 214, 216 (Ky. 1955)) (observing that the Kentucky decision interpreted a similar constitutional provision and relied on Kentucky precedent "almost identical" with existing Tennessee precedent).

28 *State v. Mason*, 827 P.2d 748 (Kan. 1992).

the California Supreme Court's definition of *bodily harm*:[29] "any touching of the person of another against his will with physical force in an intentional, hostile and aggravated manner, or projecting of such force against his person."[30] But California had later changed the definition in its pattern jury instructions to "substantial bodily injury or damage,"[31] and the defendant in the Kansas case argued that Kansas law should follow suit.[32] The Kansas court rightly rejected this contention, since the earlier California definition had been embodied in Kansas law and controlled under stare decisis just as it was formulated when Kansas adopted it.[33] The change in California's definition wasn't reason in itself for the Kansas court to overrule its own existing precedent.

Only in the absence of binding precedent on an issue is foreign precedent to be treated as persuasive.[34] This doesn't mean that foreign cases can't be cited. Rather, it's a reflection of the principle that the courts of a state are bound by their own state's precedent. If foreign precedent conflicts with binding precedent, of course the latter controls. A foreign case reflecting similar facts and decided under a similar legal rule might still prove helpful to a litigant seeking to argue by analogy that its position does or doesn't fall under the rule set by binding precedent.

---

29 *Id.* at 751–52.

30 *People v. Tanner*, 44 P.2d 324, 332 (Cal. 1935) (in bank).

31 *Mason*, 827 P.2d at 752 (quoting *People v. Schoenfeld*, 168 Cal. Rptr. 762, 770 n.14 (Ct. App. 1980)).

32 *Id.*

33 See *Twinco Romax Auto. Warehouse, Inc. v. Olson Gen. Contractors, Inc.*, 643 N.W.2d 338, 343 (Minn. Ct. App. 2002) (stating—in a case involving the interpretation of a statute modeled after a Virginia statute—that when "a Minnesota court in a particular case chooses to follow a Virginia case, . . . then the Virginia case has the same precedential value of the Minnesota case that adopted it").

34 See, e.g., *Egleston ex rel. Chesapeake Energy Corp. v. McClendon*, 318 P.3d 210, 215 (Okla. Civ. App. 2013); *McGill v. Garza*, 881 N.E.2d 419, 423 (Ill. App. Ct. 2007).

87. Comity with Penal or Criminal Provisions

A state trial court will determine for itself, not necessarily following another state's decisions, whether a sister state's legislation is penal or criminal, and therefore unenforceable in the state where the lawsuit is filed, or whether it is either contrary to the laws and policy of that state or injurious to its own citizens.

The rule that state courts needn't enforce the penal laws or judgments of a foreign sovereign is an exception to the Full Faith and Credit Clause.[1] It flows from the principle of international law that "the courts of no country execute the penal laws of another."[2] In *Huntington v. Attrill*,[3] the U.S. Supreme Court recognized that this principle applies to the state courts with respect to the laws of other states.[4] And because a state court asked to enforce the law of another state determines for itself whether the law is penal or criminal, it wouldn't be bound by the other state's determination to the contrary.[5]

Huntington sets out the basic test for whether a law is penal: the issue is "whether the wrong sought to be redressed is a wrong to the public or a wrong to the individual,"[6] which in many cases

---

1 U.S. Const. art. IV, § 1.
2 *The Antelope*, 23 U.S. (10 Wheat.) 66, 123 (1825); *see also United States v. Federative Republic of Brazil*, 748 F.3d 86, 93–95 (2d Cir. 2014) (concluding that U.S. courts would not transfer funds held in the United States under a criminal-forfeiture judgment rendered in Brazil).
3 146 U.S. 657 (1892).
4 *Id.* at 669; *see also Nelson v. George*, 399 U.S. 224, 229 (1970) (noting that "the Full Faith and Credit Clause does not require that sister States enforce a foreign penal judgment"); *City of Oakland v. Desert Outdoor Advert., Inc.*, 267 P.3d 48, 53 (Nev. 2011) (*Huntington* recognized an exception to the Full Faith and Credit Clause).
5 *See, e.g., Terenzio v. Nelson*, 258 A.2d 20, 23 (N.J. Super. Ct. App. Div. 1969) (observing that "[r]eference by a trial court of another state in its opinion to one of its statutes as 'penal in nature' . . . does not make the characterization binding upon our State if, in fact and substance, the statute is not a penal law"); *Rein v. Koons Ford, Inc.*, 567 A.2d 101, 105 (Md. 1989) (reasoning that even if Virginia courts would classify a statute as penal, "that conclusion would not control" its own decision whether the Virginia statute at issue were penal).
6 *Huntington*, 146 U.S. at 668.

can be determined by whether it is the state or a private individual seeking to enforce the law and collect any damages.[7] This test has been followed by state courts as a correct statement of the common-law rule.

In a 2011 Nevada case,[8] the City of Oakland, California, had sued Desert Outdoor in California state court for erecting an outdoor billboard within the city in violation of its municipal code.[9] The court had rendered judgment against Desert Outdoor for civil penalties for violating California's unlawful-business-practices statute, as well as for disgorgement of profits, costs, and attorneys' fees.[10] The City of Oakland then sued Desert Outdoor in Nevada, where it was incorporated, to enforce the California judgment.[11] Desert Outdoor argued to the Nevada court that the California judgment was penal and unenforceable in Nevada. The City of Oakland argued that the unfair-business-practices penalties were not penal but were imposed under unfair-competition laws to protect private rights.[12] The court concluded that the City had sued to enforce its zoning ordinances in a way that a private party couldn't have done under the unfair-business-practices act and therefore that the action was penal.[13] The court refused to enforce the California judgment in Nevada.[14]

But the Nevada court failed to consider whether it should nevertheless have enforced the California judgment as a matter of comity.[15] State courts have the discretion to enforce sister states' penal laws, even though not required to do so by the Constitution. In making that decision, state courts look to their own states' public policy. For example, the Tennessee Supreme Court was asked in 1953 to enforce an Arkansas statute that made a corporation's

---

7   *Id.* at 668–70.
8   *City of Oakland*, 267 P.3d at 48.
9   *Id.* at 49.
10 *Id.* at 50.
11 *Id.*
12 *Id.* at 54.
13 *Id.*
14 *Id.*
15 *Id.* at 54 n.10.

stockholders personally liable for the corporation's debts if the corporation's charter wasn't filed with the clerk of the Arkansas county where it was to have its principal place of business.[16] The court observed that under Tennessee law, stockholders were not liable for a corporation's debts if they had made a bona fide effort to comply with the law but had inadvertently failed to do so.[17] The court concluded that stricter Arkansas law prescribed a penalty by Tennessee standards.[18] The court also noted on rehearing that the failure to file a corporate charter properly wasn't a wrong against any individual, and hence the imposition of liability was penal in nature and unenforceable.[19]

---

16   *Paper Prods. Co. v. Doggrell*, 261 S.W.2d 127, 128 (Tenn. 1953).
17   *Id.* at 129 (quoting *Cunnyngham v. Shelby*, 188 S.W. 1147, 1149 (Tenn. 1916)).
18   *Id.*
19   *Id.* at 131–32 (opinion on rehearing).

88. Territorial Courts

The courts of a territory will follow the decisions of the U.S. Supreme Court, and of the U.S. circuit court having appellate jurisdiction, on all questions of law with one exception: on questions about the interpretation of a statute adopted from a state, they will follow the decisions of that state's courts.

Each territorial court today is under the direct appellate jurisdiction of a federal circuit court, and that court's rulings are binding on the territorial court just as they are binding on an Article III district court. For example, Congress established a court for the territory of Guam under Article IV, § 3, which provides: "The Congress shall have the power to . . . make needful Rules and Regulations respecting the Territory or other Property belonging to the United States."[1] The territorial courts are part of the federal system even though some territories are served by Article IV courts or by Article I judges.[2] Hence under the doctrine of stare decisis, they are bound by the vertical precedent of the circuit court having jurisdiction over the territory. They are similar to the lower federal courts in that they are part of the federal judicial system and are therefore bound by circuit precedent in the same way that a federal district court is bound.

But Congress has used different court structures in the territories over the years. The distinction between the state courts and territorial courts was recognized in 1890 by the Supreme Court of the Territory of Arizona.[3] The courts of the Arizona Territory were organized so that there was direct appeal from all decisions of the territorial Supreme Court of Arizona to the U.S. Supreme Court on all questions, both federal and local.[4] The territorial court recognized that "[t]he state courts are subordinate to the United States Supreme Court only in cases involving federal

---

[1] U.S. Const. art. IV, § 3.
[2] *See, e.g.*, 48 U.S.C. §§ 1424-2, 1424-3(c) (establishing appellate jurisdiction over the District Court of Guam in the Ninth Circuit).
[3] *Richards v. Green*, 32 P. 266 (Ariz. 1890).
[4] *Id.* at 267–68.

questions, and not in those involving only local questions. The territorial courts are completely subordinate to the United States court."[5] The court correctly concluded that the U.S. Supreme Court would not defer to its interpretation of local law in the way it would defer to a state court on a question of state law.[6]

Yet territorial courts follow state precedent when legislation has been adopted from another state's statutes.[7] This is an application of the borrowed-statute doctrine, a weak canon of construction regarding the adoption of a statute from another jurisdiction (see § 85). Its proponents presume that the legislature adopted, along with the statute itself, any then-existing judicial interpretations of it.[8] This presumption is based on another: that existing constructions of statutory text are "in the legislative mind" when the language is adopted.[9] Although the doctrine is ordinarily applied (if at all) as a canon of construction,[10] in territorial courts it has been elevated to the status of legal rule.

When the territorial legislature makes clear that it has adopted a statute from a state's existing law, one may safely presume that the legislature also adopted that statute's judicial interpretation.[11] This presumption is harder to justify when based on similarity of language alone. Some territorial courts have presumed that the

---

5   *Id.* at 268.

6   *Id.*

7   *See, e.g., Randolph v. Hudson*, 74 P. 946, 950 (Okla. 1903) (recognizing the presumption when a North Dakota statute had been adopted by the territory).

8   *See Stutsman Cnty. v. Wallace*, 142 U.S. 293, 312 (1892) (recognizing "the rule that the known and settled construction of a statute of one state will be regarded as accompanying its adoption by another"); *Connecticut Gen. Life Ins. Co. v. Speer*, 48 S.W.2d 553, 554 (Ark. 1932); *Randolph*, 74 P. at 950.

9   *Randolph*, 74 P. at 950 (quoting an unnamed opinion by Marshall C.J.); *see State v. Klein*, 224 S.W.2d 250, 253 (Tex. Crim. App. 1949) (observing that when a statute from another jurisdiction is adopted, "the presumption follows that the legislature knew of and intended to adopt the construction placed upon the . . . statute by the [jurisdiction's] courts").

10 *See Shannon v. United States*, 512 U.S. 573, 582 n.8 (1994) (emphasizing that the rule is one of statutory construction); *Hunter-Hayes Elevator Co. v. Petroleum Club Inn Co.*, 419 P.2d 465, 467 (N.M. 1966) (observing that the Illinois courts' interpretation of a statute adopted from that state by the New Mexico legislature is "persuasive" but "not binding").

11 *See, e.g., Richards*, 32 P. at 267.

legislature adopted a statute from a state's identical laws because the two were identically worded. The Supreme Court of the Territory of Oklahoma addressed the application of a negotiable-instrument statute that, the court observed, seemed to have been adopted from an identical statute in force in South Dakota.[12] In construing the statute, the court relied on precedent from the South Dakota Supreme Court rendered before the adoption of the statute in the Oklahoma Territory.[13] Yet when the identical statute can be found in the laws of several states, this practice leads to unclarity. The constructions placed on the statute in each state are unlikely to be uniform, and it is difficult to presume that the legislature had one state's construction in mind but not another's.

Only interpretations antedating the territory's adoption of a state statute are binding in the territorial courts. Later judicial interpretations by the state court cannot be said to have been "in the mind" of the territorial legislature when it adopted the statute. In a 1973 case,[14] the district court of the Virgin Islands recognized this distinction. Although it was plain that the Virgin Islands had enacted a statute from the laws of Alaska and there was a relevant opinion from an Alaska territorial court on the question, that decision postdated the enactment of the statute by the Virgin Islands and was held inapplicable.[15]

Over the course of time, Congress has occasionally made the law of a state applicable to a territory before that territory entered statehood.[16] When this occurs, precedent of the source state becomes truly binding authority over the territorial courts. A 1914 Oklahoma case[17] is illustrative. The case involved the law of Arkansas as applied to Indian Territory and as heard by the

---

12 *Randolph*, 74 P. at 949.
13 *Id.* at 949–50 (citing *Hegeler v. Comstock*, 45 N.W. 331 (S.D. 1890)).
14 *Cirino v. Hess Oil Virgin Islands Corp.*, 384 F. Supp. 621 (D.V.I. 1973).
15 *Id.* at 623.
16 *See, e.g., Pitman v. City of El Reno*, 37 P. 851, 854 (Okla. 1894) (applying Indiana law that had been in place at the time of the events at issue); *see also Marlin v. Lewallen*, 276 U.S. 58, 61–62 (1928) (discussing Congress's application of the law of Arkansas to Indian Territory, subject to any agreements with the tribes).
17 *Johnson v. Simpson*, 139 P. 129 (Okla. 1914).

Oklahoma Supreme Court. The court faced the question whether the right of curtesy existed in Indian Territory. That question turned on whether that right existed at common law in Arkansas and whether it had been made applicable to the litigants by the adoption of Arkansas law. The court properly considered Arkansas caselaw in deciding that the estate of curtesy consummate had been extended to Indian Territory as part of Arkansas common law.

H. Foreign Precedents

89. Precedential Effect of English Common Law

Most states have adopted English common law antedating the American Revolution as binding judicial precedent as long as it is not repugnant to the laws of those states or the laws of the United States. States often treat later English precedents as persuasive authority.

In the wake of the first American settlement at Jamestown, colonial charters generally imported the laws of England into local law.[1] As the colonies developed, their legal systems adopted English common law in varying degrees.[2] As the 17th and 18th centuries progressed, the influence of English common law grew for myriad reasons, including the spread of the British Empire and the increased access to legal training and legal texts.[3] But law was by no means the same in all the colonies. English common law had slightly less influence in Rhode Island, Connecticut, and New Hampshire[4] than in other colonies—and even less in Massachusetts.[5] It was more revered in New York, where beginning in 1761 it was held to bind the New York colonists,[6] and in New Jersey, which followed English precedents to a high degree.[7] In Maryland, English common law governed only when no

---

1 *See generally* William B. Stoebuck, *Reception of English Common Law in the American Colonies*, 10 Wm. & Mary L. Rev. 393, 396–98 (1968); Ford W. Hall, *The Common Law: An Account of Its Reception in the United States*, 4 Vand. L. Rev. 791, 791–93 (1951).

2 Stoebuck, *Reception*, 10 Wm. & Mary L. Rev. at 401. *See* L. Kinvin Wroth, "Common Law: United States Law," in 2 *The Oxford International Encyclopedia of Legal History* 82, 83 (Stanley N. Katz ed., 2009) ("After about 1750, English law reports and digests were regularly cited and accepted in the Colonial courts, with deviations from English authority based on prior Colonial practice or the Colonial situation.").

3 Stoebuck, *Reception*, 10 Wm. & Mary L. Rev. at 409–10.

4 *Id.* at 403.

5 *Id.* at 398–401.

6 *Id.* at 401.

7 *Id.* at 403.

colonial statute controlled.[8] Virginia expressly sought to "imitate and follow" the laws, customs, manner of trial, and administration of justice of England "as near as may be."[9] Pennsylvania also adopted the common law but departed from specific common-law rules when they didn't apply to extraordinary colonial situations.[10]

By the time of the founding, the colonies had adopted the common law of England, not in all respects but certainly in "its general principles."[11] As Story J. explained in *Van Ness v. Pacard*: "Our ancestors brought with them its general principles, and claimed it as their birthright; but they brought with them and adopted only that portion which was applicable to their situation."[12] After the founding, the states passed "reception statutes" to adopt English common law as judicial precedent.[13] These statutes made it easier for state courts to cite English cases and secondary authorities without need to explain their applicability to American cases.[14]

States expressly adopted English common law in their constitutions or by reception statute to the extent that it wasn't repugnant to the laws of the state or the United States. Those constitutional provisions and reception statutes remain in effect today and bind state and federal courts in applying state law, but their precise operation varies among the states—especially on the question of timing. A handful of states adopted the common law of England as of 1607, "the fourth year of James the First," when colonists established Jamestown.[15] In Vermont, 1 October 1760, "for convenience," was "arbitrarily selected" as the effective date.[16] New York chose 19 April 1775—the date on which the American Revolution

---

8   *Id.* at 402.
9   *Id.* at 403 (quoting 9 *English Historical Documents* 185 (Merrill Jensen ed., 1955)).
10 *Id.*
11 *Van Ness v. Pacard*, 27 U.S. (2 Pet.) 137, 144 (1829) (per Story J.).
12 *Id.*
13 Stoebuck, *Reception*, 10 Wm. & Mary L. Rev. at 423.
14 *Id.*
15 Colo. Rev. Stat. § 2-4-211; *see also* Ark. Code Ann. § 1-2-119; 5 Ill. Comp. Stat. 50/1; Ind. Code § 1-1-2-1; Mo. Rev. Stat. § 1.010; Va. Code Ann. § 1-200; Wyo. Stat. Ann. § 8-1-101. See *Commonwealth v. Morris*, 705 S.E.2d 503, 508–09 (Va. 2011).
16 *Comstock's Adm'r v. Jacobs*, 96 A. 4, 5 (Vt. 1915).

began with the "shot heard around the world"—as the effective date for its adoption of English common law.[17] Other states—including Delaware,[18] Florida,[19] Georgia,[20] Maryland,[21] New Jersey,[22] Oregon,[23] Pennsylvania,[24] Rhode Island,[25] Washington,[26] and Wisconsin[27]—chose 1776, when America declared its independence from England. In Kentucky, North Carolina, and West Virginia, the adoption became effective as of the time when those states achieved statehood.[28] Many other states, including Alabama, Michigan, and South Carolina, adopted the common law but didn't specify an effective date.[29]

Louisiana, with its civil-law system, is exceptional. By statute, Louisiana adopted the common law in 1805 for criminal-law matters. The state adopted the English definitions of certain offenses and certain modes of procedure for criminal prosecutions, but it didn't go so far as to "adopt the whole criminal law of England as it existed in 1805."[30] Nor did it include later changes in English common law, even those that changed the adopted definitions and

---

17 N.Y. Const. art. I, § 14.
18 Del. Const. sched. § 18.
19 Fla. Stat. § 2.01.
20 Ga. Code Ann. § 1-1-10(c)(1).
21 Md. Const. Declaration of Rights, art. 5.
22 N.J. Const. art. XI, § 1.
23 Or. Const. art. XVIII, § 7; see *Smothers v. Gresham Transfer, Inc.*, 23 P.3d 333, 359 (Or. 2001); *Peery v. Fletcher*, 182 P. 143, 146-47 (Or. 1919).
24 1 Pa. Cons. Stat. § 1503(a).
25 43 R.I. Gen. Laws § 43-3-1.
26 Wash. Rev. Code § 4.04.010.
27 Wis. Const. art. 14, § 13; see *State v. Picotte*, 661 N.W.2d 381, 387 (Wis. 2003).
28 Ky. Const. § 233 (adopting the laws—including the English common law—of Virginia); N.C. Gen. Stat. § 4-1; W. Va. Code § 2-1-1; D.C. Code § 49-301.
29 *See, e.g.*, Ala. Code § 1-3-1; Alaska Stat. § 01.10.010; Ariz. Rev. Stat. § 1-201; Cal. Civ. Code § 22.2; Conn. Const. art. I, § 10; Haw. Rev. Stat. § 1-1; Idaho Code § 73-116; Kan. Stat. Ann. § 77-109; Me. Const. art. X, § 3; Mass. Const. pt. 2, ch. VI, art. VI; Mich. Const. art. III, § 7; Miss. Const. art. 15, § 274; Neb. Rev. Stat. § 49-101; Nev. Rev. Stat. § 1.030; N.H. Const. pt. 2, art. 90; N.M. Stat. Ann. § 38-1-3; N.D. Cent. Code §§ 1-01-04 to -06; Okla. Stat. tit. 12, § 2; S.C. Code Ann. § 14-1-50; Tenn. Const. art. XI, § 1; Tex. Civ. Prac. & Rem. Code Ann. § 5.001; Utah Code Ann. § 68-3-1.
30 *State v. Smith*, 30 La. Ann. 846, 847 (1878).

modes.[31] Although Louisiana never adopted English common law for other matters, its courts will apply that law when choice-of-law principles so require. For example, in a pre-Civil War dispute about the ownership of slaves,[32] the Louisiana Supreme Court looked to the common law of England to resolve the dispute brought by Mississippi plaintiffs and arising out of a contract entered into in Mississippi because "the principles of equity jurisprudence which prevail[ed] in England are those which prevail in ... Mississippi."[33]

The reception statutes and constitutional provisions didn't adopt all the English common law but instead only those rules "suited to the habits and conditions of the colonies, and in harmony with the genius, spirit, and objects of American institutions."[34] Two cases illustrate the point.

First, in a 1952 case,[35] the Mississippi Supreme Court acknowledged the common-law rule that "an owner of cattle was bound to prevent them from entering upon the premises of another."[36] But the court explained that this English rule "did not prevail" in Mississippi and that "an owner of cattle may rightfully suffer [allow] his animals to go at large for pasture upon the neighboring range."[37] The Mississippi court's rejection of this English common-law rule was later abrogated by statute.[38]

Second, in a 1954 case,[39] the New Mexico Supreme Court ruled on a lawsuit for money damages for a funeral director's interference with the corpse of the plaintiff's spouse. The court considered "the early common law of England," which "recognized no property or property rights in the body of a deceased

---

31 *See State v. Davis*, 22 La. Ann. 77, 77–78 (1870).
32 *Young v. Templeton*, 4 La. Ann. 254 (1849).
33 *Id.* at 256–57.
34 *Peery*, 182 P. at 146.
35 *Pongetti v. Spraggins*, 61 So. 2d 158 (Miss. 1952).
36 *Id.* at 160.
37 *Id.*
38 *See Carpenter v. Nobile*, 620 So. 2d 961, 963 (Miss. 1993).
39 *Infield v. Cope*, 270 P.2d 716, 718–20 (N.M. 1954).

person."[40] But the court explained that this English common-law rule was undoubtedly based on "the fact that the ecclesiastical courts exercised jurisdiction over the affairs of decedents."[41] The court deemed the rule unfit for New Mexico, just as other states had done: "[T]here is a quasiproperty right in a dead body vesting in the nearest relatives of the deceased and arising out of their duty to bury their dead" in the United States.[42]

In states with constitutional provisions or reception statutes, the dates of the reception statutes are starting points for common-law actions in the states' histories. They preserve English common law while keeping it subject to development, rather than making it controlling or immutable.[43] Delaware, for instance, expressly stated that English common law would remain in force until the state legislature altered it.[44] The same rule applied in New Jersey.[45]

English common law antedating a state's reception

English common law that antedates the effective date of a state's reception statute is binding as long as it isn't repugnant to state or federal law and isn't supplanted by state common law or statute.[46] For example, the Indiana Supreme Court reasoned that it was bound by the English common-law rule that contracts entered into on Sundays are null and void.[47] The court acknowledged that a conflicting rule applied in Vermont but concluded that "[t]he common law rule binds us, as we have adopted the common law by statute."[48]

---

40 *Id.*
41 *Id.*
42 *Id.*
43 *See, e.g., Williams v. Miles,* 94 N.W. 705, 708 (Neb. 1903) (per curiam); *Ketelson v. Stilz,* 111 N.E. 423, 424–25 (Ind. 1916); *State v. Pearl,* 1 P.2d 315, 317 (Wash. 1931).
44 *See Turnbull v. Fink,* 668 A.2d 1370, 1373–74 (Del. 1995) (en banc).
45 *See State v. Smith,* 426 A.2d 38, 41 (N.J. 1981).
46 *See* Stoebuck, *Reception,* 10 Wm. & Mary L. Rev. 393, 425 (1968); *see, e.g., Moses v. Boston & Maine R.R.,* 24 N.H. 71, 87–88 (1951); *Gwathmey v. State,* 464 S.E.2d 674, 679 (N.C. 1995).
47 *Perkins v. Jones,* 26 Ind. 499, 502–03 (1866).
48 *Id.*

Similarly, in 2011 the Virginia Court of Appeals considered whether a state trial court had the power to acquit a defendant who had been convicted of grand larceny and to instead adjudge her guilty of petit larceny, a lesser crime.[49] Even though she didn't contest her guilt for grand larceny, the defendant urged the court to lessen her offense because she had helped law enforcement in another matter.[50] Relying on "the inherent common law authority inherited from England at the time of [the] Commonwealth's founding," the court ruled that the state trial court would exceed its judicial power if it acquitted the convicted defendant of grand larceny.[51] The court explained that common-law courts lacked the power to suspend any portion of a criminal sentence without express statutory authority to do so: "Under English common law, only the crown had the prerogative power of pardon. There simply was no such thing as a judicial pardon."[52] The court concluded, "[I]t is inconceivable the common law would nonetheless authorize courts to refuse to convict a criminal defendant (for reasons wholly unrelated to guilt or innocence)."[53]

The Missouri Supreme Court also relied on English common law to decide that sovereign immunity applied and an injured student wrestler couldn't sue a school district for his coach's negligence during a high-school wrestling practice.[54] Tracing the origins of sovereign immunity back to 16th-century England, the court held that "the common law adopted in Missouri when it came into the Union of states was that an action cannot be maintained for negligence against the public."[55]

The *absence* of English common-law precedent before a state's reception may also bind its courts. For example, in 2012 the Court

---

49 *Taylor v. Commonwealth*, 710 S.E.2d 518, 519–20 (Va. Ct. App. 2011).
50 *Id.*
51 *Id.* at 520.
52 *Id.* at 523.
53 *Id.*; *see also Roach v. Commonwealth*, 162 S.E. 50, 51–52 (Va. 1932) (holding that English common law barred a state court from accepting a plea of nolo contendere in a felony case).
54 *O'Dell v. School Dist. of Independence*, 521 S.W.2d 403, 407 (Mo. 1975) (en banc).
55 *Id.*

of Appeals of Maryland considered whether an evicted tenant had a civil remedy against a landlord who had entered the tenant's home while he was away and disposed of all his belongings before he returned.[56] No common-law doctrine supported the tenant's suit. To the contrary, English common-law doctrines of forcible entry and self-help led the Maryland high court to decide that the landlord, the rightful property owner, could lawfully enter the tenant's home without prior notice and remove his belongings.[57] Another ubiquitous example is the recent disagreement among state and federal courts about whether English common law barred a claim for wrongful death in 1776.[58] During the 19th century, state legislatures across the country enacted statutes providing for a wrongful-death claim based on the understanding that such a claim was unavailable under English common law, but in recent decades courts and commentators have criticized that understanding of founding-era common law.[59]

English common law postdating a state's reception

Although English authorities after the founding aren't binding, they are persuasive, "much as a sister state's decision would be today."[60] The systems are, after all, kindred: "Where the English decisions are consulted as persuasive evidence of the doctrines of

---

56 *Nickens v. Mount Vernon Realty Grp., LLC*, 54 A.3d 742, 751–52 (Md. 2012).

57 *Id.*

58 *See, e.g., LaFage v. Jani*, 766 A.2d 1066, 1076 (N.J. 2001) (discussing *Baker v. Bolton* [1808] 170 Eng. Rep. 1033 (Nisi Prius)); *Summerfield v. Superior Court*, 698 P.2d 712, 716–17 (Ariz. 1985) (in banc); *cf. Khalifa v. Shannon*, 945 A.2d 1244, 1248–62 (Md. 2008).

59 *See, e.g., LaFage*, 766 A.2d at 1076; *Moreno v. Sterling Drug, Inc.*, 787 S.W.2d 348, 365 & n.16 (Tex. 1990) (Doggett J. dissenting).

60 William B. Stoebuck, *Reception of English Common Law in the American Colonies*, 10 Wm. & Mary L. Rev. 393, 425 (1968); *see, e.g., In re Heaton's Estate*, 96 A. 21, 29 (Vt. 1915) (explaining that English decisions after 1760 are persuasive but not precedential). *See also* Thomas M. Cooley, *A Treatise on the Constitutional Limitations Which Rest upon the Legislative Power of the States of the American Union* 52 (1868) ("[A] decision now by one of the higher courts of Great Britain as to what the common law is upon any point is certainly entitled to great respect in any of the States, though not necessarily to be accepted as binding authority any more than the decisions in any one of the other States upon the same point.").

the common law or the general principles of jurisprudence, not as binding authorities to be followed whether right or wrong, their value is of course to be determined by those considerations which ordinarily affect the force of judicial precedents."[61] For example, in a 1987 case,[62] the Court of Appeals of Maryland considered English authorities to decide that a defendant convicted of misdemeanor assault and battery could be imprisoned. The court first reviewed binding pre-1776 English authorities, which permitted imprisonment, a fine, or both without limitation.[63] The court then considered "the explicit guidance of the House of Lords" from 1966, in which the House of Lords decided that a convicted batterer could be imprisoned for up to two years.[64] The defendant invoked this 1966 authority as support for his contention that imprisonment for misdemeanor assault and battery must be limited to a term of two years.[65] The court deemed the post-1776 authority helpful, distinguished it, and then rejected the defendant's contention: "We have no history of a similar practice in this country, and we would not be bound by a change in the common law of England occurring after 1776."[66]

Other American courts have also treated post-reception English common law as persuasive but not binding. In a 1945 case,[67] the Massachusetts Supreme Judicial Court decided that withholding information about a murder wasn't punishable under Massachusetts law, even though it would have been punishable as misprision of felony under the early common law of England.[68] One justification for the court's rejection of that notion was that "[t]he offence of misprision of felony has been said to be 'practically

---

61 Henry Campbell Black, *Handbook on the Law of Judicial Precedents* § 126, at 430–31 (1912).

62 *Ireland v. State*, 529 A.2d 365 (Md. 1987).

63 *Id.* at 368–69.

64 *Id.* at 370–71 (quoting *Verrier v. Director of Pub. Prosecutions* [1966] 3 All ER 568).

65 *Id.* at 371.

66 *Id.*

67 *Commonwealth v. Lopes*, 61 N.E.2d 849 (Mass. 1945).

68 *Id.* at 850–51.

obsolete' in England" since the late 19th century.[69] Similarly, in a 1993 case[70] the Colorado high court discussed English common law from the "early 19th century" regarding the defense of "settled insanity" caused by the defendant's drug addiction,[71] explaining that this "action by English courts [after 1607] . . . may have persuasive value but has no precedential value for our interpretation."[72] The court decided that the defense was barred by a state law that prohibited intoxication as a defense to criminal charges.[73]

American courts often decline to adopt changes that were made in English common law after the state's reception. For example, in an 1851 case,[74] the New Hampshire Supreme Court confronted a post-Revolution change that allowed common carriers to limit their liability if they notified the passengers of those limitations.[75] The high court opted not to incorporate that change in New Hampshire, choosing to adhere to the "fixed and simple rule of the common law."[76] Likewise, in a 1941 case,[77] the Court of Chancery of New Jersey decided that a testator couldn't condition gifts in his will on the requirement that the beneficiaries couldn't live with or communicate with a hated brother and sister of the testator, despite dictum from an 1844 English authority to the contrary.[78]

Federal courts exercising diversity jurisdiction will apply English common law. For example, in a 1956 case,[79] the Seventh Circuit considered an employment dispute involving the California-owned State Belt Railroad and two unions of railway

---

69   *Id.* at 851.
70   *Bieber v. People*, 856 P.2d 811 (Colo. 1993) (en banc).
71   *Id.* at 815.
72   *Id.*
73   *Id.* at 815–16.
74   *Moses v. Boston & Maine R.R.*, 24 N.H. 71 (1851).
75   *Id.* at 88.
76   *Id.* at 87.
77   *Girard Trust Co. v. Schmitz*, 20 A.2d 21 (N.J. Ch. 1941).
78   *Id.* at 35.
79   *Taylor v. Fee*, 233 F.2d 251 (7th Cir. 1956), *aff'd sub nom. California v. Taylor*, 353 U.S. 553 (1957).

employees. The court had to decide first whether the state had approved one of the collective-bargaining agreements.[80] To decide that preliminary question, the court explained: "If the constitution, statutes and court decisions of California furnish no rule by which to determine the question before us, we are required to determine it by resort, in that effort, to any authoritative court decisions enunciating the common law of England in this respect."[81]

Reception of English statutory law

Most American states impliedly adopted English statutory law when they adopted common law[82]—some even expressly

---

80   *Id.* at 256.

81   *Id.*

82   *See Doe ex dem. Patterson v. Winn*, 30 U.S. (5 Pet.) 233, 241–42 (1831) ("These statutes being passed before the emigration of our ancestors, being applicable to our situation, and in amendment of the law, constitute a part of our common law."); *Commonwealth v. Leach*, 1 Mass. 59, 60 (1804) ("In *this* act, the term *common law* cannot mean the common law of *England*[.]. . . [I]t must, therefore, mean *our* common law; and on *this* subject, *our* common law must be precisely what the *statute* law of *England* was at the time of the emigration of our ancestors from that country."); *id.* at 61 ("The term *common law* ought not to be construed so strictly as is contended for by the counsel for the defendant. Generally when an *English statute* has been made in amendment of the common law of *England*, it is *here* to be considered as part of *our* common law.") (emphasis in original); *Sackett v. Sackett*, 25 Mass. (8 Pick.) 309, 324–25 (1829) ("Then the question is, whether the law by which they would be governed in relation to waste committed by tenants, was the ancient common law, as it stood before the statute of Marlebridge, or as modified by that statute, or the law which was in force in England at the time of their emigration and for centuries before; and we think it very clear that it was the latter. It would seem exceedingly strange that their coming over to this country should operate as a repeal of either of those ancient statutes, so as to reinstate the law as it existed in the time of Henry 3, which had been abrogated three or four centuries, and was found inconvenient in the reign of that prince."); *Paschal v. Acklin*, 27 Tex. 173, 185–86 (1863) ("The current of decisions in the old states of the Union is to the effect that all English statutes passed previous to 1776, and suitable to their condition, are part of the common law of the land. By parity of reasoning, it may be alleged that all English statutes enacted previous to 1840, the time of the adoption of the common law in Texas, and suitable to our condition, are a part of the common law of Texas."); *John W. Masury & Son v. Bisbee Lumber Co.*, 68 P.2d 679, 688 (Ariz. 1937) ("We agree that the rule laid down by the Supreme Court of New Mexico is the one applicable to Arizona, and hold that the 'common law' referred to by our Legislature at various times means the unwritten or common law of England, together with the acts of parliament of a general nature, and not local to Great Britain, which had been passed and

providing for the adoption of English statutes.[83] In the words of James Kent, whose *Commentaries on American Law* became singularly authoritative: "It is . . . the established doctrine that English statutes passed before the emigration of our ancestors, and applicable to our situation, and in the amendment of our law, constitute a part of the common law of this country."[84] But only those laws suitable to the American jurisdiction came into force.[85] A state

> were enforced at the time of our separation from the mother country so far, of course, as they are suitable to our wants, conditions, and circumstances."). *But see Clark v. Luvel Dairy Prods., Inc.*, 731 So. 2d 1098, 1105 (Miss. 1998) ("[T]he common law of Mississippi does not include the statutes of England in existence at the time of the Revolution, but was adopted independently of such statutes, as the law of this state.") (quoting *City of Jackson v. McFadden*, 177 So. 755, 758 (Miss. 1937)); *Brooks v. Kimball Cnty.*, 256 N.W. 501, 504 (Neb. 1934) ("[T]his state adopted the 'common law of England' and not the statutory law of England.").

83 *See, e.g.*, Md. Const. Declaration of Rights, art. 5 ("That the Inhabitants of Maryland are entitled to the Common Law of England, and the trial by Jury, according to the course of that Law, and to the benefit of such of the English statutes as existed on the Fourth day of July, seventeen hundred and seventy-six."). *See Browning v. Browning*, 9 P. 677, 683–84 (N.M. 1886) ("[I]t is clear that there are three classes of 'common law as recognized in the United States of America:' First, in those states which were a part of the original colonies, and which have not by legislation adopted statutes passed prior to a particular date, the unwritten law, and such general British statutes, applicable to their condition, as were in force at the time of the formation of the colonial governments, and such as were afterwards adopted, expressly or tacitly, constituted the common law; second, in those states which have adopted the common law, and the British statutes passed and in force prior to the date fixed in the act of adoption, and were of a general nature, and suitable to their situation, such common law and statutes constitute their common law; and, third, in those states and territories which were not of the original colonies, and which have not in terms adopted any English statutes, but have adopted the common law, the unwritten or common law of England, and the acts of parliament of a general nature, not local to Great Britain, which had been passed and were in force at the date of the war of the Revolution, and not in conflict with the constitution or laws of the United States, nor of the state or territory, and which were suitable to the wants and condition of the people, are the common law of such states and territories.").

84 1 James Kent, *Commentaries on American Law* *473 (Charles M. Barnes ed., 13th ed. 1884) (punctuation lightly updated); *cf.* Gwen Morris et al., *Laying Down the Law* 6–7 (2d ed. 1988) ("The term 'common law,' as well as meaning the system of law which developed in the King's courts, has been extended to mean the system of law which developed in England. In this context it comprises both statute law and case law.").

85 *See Winn*, 30 U.S. at 241–42; *Morris' Lessee v. Vanderen*, 1 U.S. (1 Dall.) 64, 67 (1782) ("It is the opinion of the court, however, that the common law of England has always been in force in Pennsylvania; that all statutes made in

will disregard an English statute if it is contrary to the state's practices and statutory scheme.[86]

To determine whether a particular English statute applies in the United States, "the courts have used about the same approach as they have adopted in determining whether English common-law doctrines are suited to the situation on this side of the Atlantic."[87] For example, the Supreme Court of New Mexico refused to adopt the "harsh rule" of the ancient statute of Gloucester granting landlords a right to treble damages in a suit against a tenant for waste of leased premises.[88] And the Supreme Court of Oregon ruled that the English statutes of mortmain, "as far as they inhibited public corporations from taking real property by devise, were local in character, and intended to remedy a mischief in England."[89] Therefore, the Oregon court ruled, "[t]hey were not applicable to the conditions of our people, and were incompatible with the nature of our political institutions."[90] But the Supreme Court of Nevada declared the antigambling Statute of Anne severable and enforceable in a suit for damages by a loser who had already paid a winner on a gambling debt.[91]

Magna Carta also deserves special mention. Although they were mistaken, "American writers of the Revolutionary period often used the terms 'common law' and 'Magna Carta' as synonymous terms."[92] As Story J. explained, Massachusetts and New York identified Magna Carta as the starting point for their colonial

---

Great-Britain before the settlement of Pennsylvania, have no force here, unless they are convenient and adapted to the circumstances of the country.").

86 *See, e.g., Farmers' & Merchants' Ins. Co. v. Jensen*, 78 N.W. 1054, 1056 (Neb. 1899) (holding that the statute of uses wasn't in effect in Nebraska); *cf. Horton v. Sledge*, 29 Ala. 478, 496 (1856) (finding that the statute of uses was in effect until repealed).

87 Ford W. Hall, *The Common Law: An Account of Its Reception in the United States*, 4 Vand. L. Rev. 791, 818 (1951).

88 *Blake v. Hoover Motor Co.*, 212 P. 738, 739 (N.M. 1923).

89 *In re Moore's Estate*, 223 P.2d 393, 396 (Or. 1950).

90 *Id.*

91 *West Indies, Inc. v. First Nat'l Bank of Nev.*, 214 P.2d 144 (Nev. 1950).

92 Hall, *The Common Law*, 4 Vand. L. Rev. at 797–98.

legal systems.[93] Later, in 1780, the Massachusetts Constitution drew on Magna Carta to forbid any subject from being "deprived of his life, liberty, or estate, but by the judgment of his peers, or the law of the land."[94] This early American homage to Magna Carta was likely influenced by Sir Edward Coke, who viewed common law as including Magna Carta.[95] Story J. reported that after the Revolution, the rights secured by Magna Carta provided examples "as clear perhaps as any" of common law "presumptively adopted, or applicable" in the United States.[96] But Story J. also recognized that some protections of Magna Carta, like other provisions of English common law, "may be in fact inapplicable, or inconvenient and impolitic" in a state.[97] Note well: the Magna Carta that became part of the common law was the version that took effect in 1225—not the original one signed by King John in 1215.[98]

When an American state adopts an English statute, it is presumed to also adopt the English caselaw interpreting that statute.[99] Courts naturally give less weight to English cases

---

93 1 Joseph Story, *Commentaries on the Constitution of the United States* § 68, at 114 (2d ed. 1858).

94 Mass. Const. pt. 1, art. XII.

95 Bernadette Meyler, *Towards a Common Law Originalism*, 59 Stan. L. Rev. 551, 587 & n.171 (2006); *see also id.* at 568–69 (discussing Thomas Jefferson's inclusion of Magna Carta as part of English common law).

96 1 Story, *Commentaries on the Constitution of the United States* § 149.

97 *Id.*

98 *See* Bryan A. Garner, "A Lexicographic Look at Magna Carta," in *Magna Carta: Muse and Mentor* 85, 92–93 (Randy J. Holland ed., 2014).

99 *See Cathcart v. Robinson*, 30 U.S. (5 Pet.) 264, 280 (1831) ("The rule, which has been uniformly observed by this court in construing statutes, is to adopt the construction made by the courts of the country by whose legislature the statute was enacted. This rule may be susceptible of some modification, when applied to British statutes which are adopted in any of these states. By adopting them they become our own as entirely as if they had been enacted by the legislature of the state. The received construction in England at the time they are admitted to operate in this country, indeed to the time of our separation from the British empire, may very properly be considered as accompanying the statutes themselves, and forming an integral part of them."); *Pennock v. Dialogue*, 27 U.S. (2 Pet.) 1, 18 (1829) ("It is doubtless true, as has been suggested at the bar, that where English statutes, such for instance, as the statute of frauds, and the statute of limitations; have been adopted into our own legislation; the known and settled construction of those statutes by courts of law, has been considered as silently incorporated into the acts, or has been received with all the weight

interpreting the statute after it has been adopted and enacted in America; in fact, most courts will not consider English caselaw from after the Revolutionary War.[100]

This rule regarding English statutes has also been cited to support the inheritance of interpretive caselaw from another state when one state adopts a statute from another—the "borrowed-statute doctrine"[101] (see § 85). But the connection is a weak one, given that the reception of English statutes was almost uniformly concomitant with the reception of English caselaw.[102]

---

of authority."). *See also Barney v. State*, 42 Md. 480, 484–85 (1875) ("The plain language of the statute . . . expressly re-enacted in our Code, ought necessarily to have been construed and applied as it was construed and applied by the Courts in England prior to the Revolution and the ruling of the English Courts, prior to the Revolution, ought to have been taken as conclusive upon the question.") (internal citations omitted); *Kirkpatrick v. Gibson*, 14 F. Cas. 683, 684 (C.C.D. Va. 1828) ("I am the more inclined to this opinion, because it is reasonable to suppose, that where a British statute is re-enacted in this country, we adopt the settled construction it has received, as well as the statute itself; and such, I believe, has been the course of every court in the Union.").

[100] *See Cathcart*, 30 U.S. at 280 ("The received construction in England at the time they are admitted to operate in this country, indeed to the time of our separation from the British empire, may very properly be considered as accompanying the statutes themselves, and forming an integral part of them. But however we may respect subsequent decisions, and certainly they are entitled to great respect, we do not admit their absolute authority. If the English courts vary their construction of a statute which is common to the two countries, we do not hold ourselves bound to fluctuate with them.").

[101] *J.M. Robinson & Co. v. Belt*, 187 U.S. 41, 48 (1902) ("The same rule has been applied in the state courts in the construction of statutes adopted from other states.") (citing *Commonwealth v. Hartnett*, 69 Mass. (3 Gray) 450, 451 (1855)); *Commonwealth v. Hartnett*, 69 Mass. (3 Gray) 450, 451 (1855) ("[I]t has always been held that the construction previously given to the same terms, by the English courts, is the construction to be given to them by our courts. It is a common learning, that the adjudged construction of the terms of a statute is enacted, as well as the terms themselves, when an act, which has been passed by the legislature of one state or country, is afterwards passed by the legislature of another. So when the same legislature, in a later statute, use the terms of an earlier one which has received a judicial construction, that construction is to be given to the later statute. And this is manifestly right. For if it were intended to exclude any known construction of a previous statute, the legal presumption is, that its terms would be so changed as to effect that intention.").

[102] *See* Antonin Scalia & Bryan A. Garner, *Reading Law: The Interpretation of Legal Texts* 325 (2012) (casting doubt on this canon of interpretation).

90. Value of Foreign Precedents

The value of a foreign precedent is increased by its relevance to the issue at hand, but is diminished to the extent that it is based on conditions—geographic, climatic, social, economic, or political—peculiar to the foreign state or country. U.S. courts generally do not apply the law of a foreign country unless it gives rise to the claim or applies through choice-of-law principles. But a U.S. court will apply foreign law when the litigants' rights depend on it and the circumstances favor keeping the case in an American forum.

When we speak of a "foreign precedent," what does the adjective *foreign* mean? It's a term of art in law, and it simply describes any institution that was established by a different government. It can be used in an international sense, to refer to any political entity that isn't part of the United States, or it can be used in a more legalistic sense to refer to any jurisdiction apart from the one of which the court is a part. State courts commonly refer to corporations from other U.S. states as "foreign" corporations; likewise, they consider the law of sister states to be "foreign" law. This approach has a distinguished lineage: at the time of the founding, the states constituting the union retained part of their status as international bodies.

This viewpoint pervades the Supreme Court's decision in *Pennoyer v. Neff*,[1] which dealt with the power of an Oregon court to serve process on, and ultimately to issue a binding judgment against, a noncitizen of Oregon who never appeared before the tribunal. Field J. made the point plainly:

> The several States of the Union are not, it is true, in every respect independent, many of the rights and powers which originally belonged to them being now vested in the government created by the Constitution. But except as restrained and limited by that instrument, they possess and exercise the authority of independent States, and the principles of public law to which we have referred are applicable to them. . . . The

---

1   95 U.S. (5 Otto) 714 (1877).

other principle of public law referred to follows from the one mentioned; that is, that no State can exercise direct jurisdiction and authority over persons or property without its territory.²

State high courts regard themselves as free to take or leave precedents from their sister states, based on the kinds of factors listed in the blackletter rule.³ These foreign holdings are always persuasive rather than binding. It surprises those new to law to learn that even a holding by the U.S. Supreme Court on a strictly state-law issue can't be binding on the high court of that state.

The more difficult, and controversial, situation arises when the proposed ruling comes from a court that is "foreign" in the international sense. In fact though, when a U.S. court is asked to consider foreign law, the occasion is ordinarily a mundane one. Federal Rule of Civil Procedure 44.1 instructs litigants who intend to raise an issue of foreign law about how to do so. It allows the court to consult "any relevant material or source, including testimony" to resolve the question, and (disapproving an earlier line of authority) it states that the court's determination is a "question of law" and hence fully reviewable by an appellate court. It's not a question for a jury to decide. Foreign-law issues may arise in many situations, including cases in which (1) choice-of-law rules

---

2   *Id.* at 722.

3   E.g., *Rhoades v. State*, 233 P.3d 61, 67 (Idaho 2010) ("[W]e follow the lead of the Minnesota Supreme Court and hold that Idaho courts must independently review requests for retroactive application of newly-announced principles of law under the *Teague* standard."); *State v. Murray*, 169 P.3d 955, 972 n.14 (Haw. 2007) ("We decline to follow the Minnesota Supreme Court's holding inasmuch as the reasoning underlying the decision in *Berkelman* was not clearly stated."); *Alaska Native Tribal Health Consortium v. Settlement Funds*, 84 P.3d 418, 431 (Alaska 2004) ("[W]e follow the approach of *Cooper* [*v. Argonaut*] and the New Mexico Supreme Court and apply equitable considerations."); *Dunlavey v. Economy Fire & Cas. Co.*, 526 N.W.2d 845, 855 (Iowa 1995) ("[W]e adopt an 'unusual stress' standard but decline to follow the Wisconsin supreme court's characterization of it. Rather, we adopt the 'unusual stress' standard as formulated by the Wyoming supreme court."); *Sudheimer v. Cheatham*, 443 P.2d 951, 954 (Okla. 1968) (per curiam) ("We follow the reasoning of the Supreme Court of Oregon."); *Meade v. State*, 85 So. 2d 613, 616 (Fla. 1956) (en banc) ("[W]e do not adopt the ruling indicated in the decision of the Pennsylvania Supreme Court in *Commonwealth v. Valotta*."); *Foshay v. Town of Glen Haven*, 25 Wis. 288, 290 (1870) ("We adopt upon this subject the rule established by the supreme courts of Vermont, New Hampshire and Connecticut.").

in private law point to foreign law;[4] (2) foreign law plays a role,[5] as with international taxation cases[6] or criminal statutes that make commission of a foreign crime relevant; or (3) a foreign court has faced a similar problem and its resolution is presented as persuasive authority.[7]

In each of these circumstances, a U.S. court might find itself confronted with a foreign judicial ruling. Many foreign judicial decisions cannot sensibly be regarded as "precedent" for anything. For instance, not all criminal statutes extend to foreign convictions. In *Small v. United States*,[8] the Supreme Court held (6–3) that the statute prohibiting felons from possessing firearms excluded convictions entered in foreign courts. In doing so, the court applied "the legal presumption that Congress ordinarily intends

---

4   *E.g., Day & Zimmerman, Inc. v. Challoner*, 423 U.S. 3, 3–5 (1975) (per curiam) (in diversity case, state-court choice-of-law rule pointed to Cambodian law); *Bodum USA, Inc. v. La Cafetiere, Inc.*, 621 F.3d 624, 630–31 (7th Cir. 2010); *Yavuz v. 61 MM, Ltd.*, 576 F.3d 1166, 1178–79 (10th Cir. 2009) (Oklahoma choice-of-law principles dictated that Swiss law governed fraud and contract claims); *Foster Wheeler Energy Corp. v. An Ning Jiang MV*, 383 F.3d 349, 357 (5th Cir. 2004) (deciding that Spain's Hague–Visby Rules applied to certain cargo and maritime claims); *Curran v. Kwon*, 153 F.3d 481, 488–89 (7th Cir. 1998) (affirming application of law of France considering Illinois's abandonment of *lex loci contractus* rule in favor of most-significant-contacts test); *In re Bankers Trust Co.*, 752 F.2d 874, 883 (3d Cir. 1984) (district court should have applied substantive law of India rather than Pennsylvania law); *Franklin Supply Co. v. Tolman*, 454 F.2d 1059, 1076 (9th Cir. 1971) (Venezuela's law, not Colorado's, governed tort claims); *McDermott Inc. v. Lewis*, 531 A.2d 206, 209 (Del. 1987) ("We conclude that the trial court erred in refusing to apply the law of Panama to the internal affairs of International.").

5   *E.g., Pasquantino v. United States*, 544 U.S. 349 (2005) (element of federal wire-fraud scheme involved avoidance of liquor taxes payable under Canadian law).

6   *E.g., Amoco Corp. v. Commissioner*, 138 F.3d 1139 (7th Cir. 1998) (application of foreign tax credit to entities created by Egyptian government).

7   *See, e.g., Roper v. Simmons*, 543 U.S. 551, 575–78 (2005) (after reviewing reasons based in U.S. law for imposing the death penalty on a person who was under 18 when the crime was committed, the Court "finds confirmation" for its determination "in the stark reality that the United States is the only country in the world that continues to give official sanction to the juvenile death penalty"). *See also Lawrence v. Texas*, 539 U.S. 558, 572–73 (2003) (looking to authorities and developments outside the United States, including a decision of the European Court of Human Rights, to support the argument that prevailing moral standards do not condemn consensual, adult same-sex relationships).

8   544 U.S. 385, 388–89 (2005).

its statutes to have domestic, not extraterritorial, application."[9] It's worth remembering that the legal systems derived from the English common law represent only one of the major world systems; legal systems derived from English law exist, roughly, wherever the British Empire reached—hence, in addition to the United States, in Canada, Australia, New Zealand, India, South Africa, and some of the other Anglophone African countries. The other broad model, the civil-law system (derived ultimately from Roman law but mediated in Francophone countries by the Napoleonic Code), doesn't recognize judicial pronouncements as precedent.[10] A U.S. federal or state court would have no reason to give broader precedential value to the decision of a foreign court than the courts in the rendering country would have assigned to it, and so the question of "following" a decision from a civil-law jurisdiction should never arise. The same limitation is true for countries whose legal system is based on Islam.

Foreign judicial rulings can be of immediate importance in cases in which a U.S. court is construing a multilateral treaty, as it is important that all states that are parties to the treaty maintain a common understanding of its terms. So for example, in construing the Warsaw Convention, the Supreme Court has relied on the decisions of courts in other signatory countries.[11] It has also listed the "practical construction adopted by the parties" as among the tools the court should use in construing a treaty.[12] International conventions may also incorporate domestic legal standards. The Hague Convention on the Civil Aspects of

---

9   *Id.* at 388–89.

10 *See generally* "The Common Law and Civil Law Traditions," Univ. of Cal. at Berkeley Sch. of Law, https://www.law.berkeley.edu/library/robbins/CommonLawCivilLawTraditions.html (last visited 2 June 2015).

11 *See, e.g., El Al Israel Airlines, Ltd. v. Tsui Yuan Tseng,* 525 U.S. 155, 175 (1999) (looking to a decision of the House of Lords in the United Kingdom for guidance and reaffirming the importance of the views of sister signatories); *Air France v. Saks,* 470 U.S. 392, 403–04 (1985) (relying on the interpretations of other signatories).

12 *See Volkswagenwerk AG v. Schlunk,* 486 U.S. 694, 700 (1988) (construing the Convention on Service Abroad of Judicial and Extrajudicial Documents, known as the Hague Service Convention).

International Child Abduction[13]—which gives the country of the child's habitual residence the authority to adjudicate issues arising out of an alleged abduction—is such a treaty. In *Abbott v. Abbott*,[14] the Supreme Court had to decide whether a child's father had removed the child from Chile in violation of a custody right. That question in turn required the Court to decide whether the rights that Chilean law had conferred on the father amounted to "custody" for purposes of the Convention. The Court therefore had to delve into Chilean law to answer that question. After doing so, it consulted the U.S. State Department's views on the issue, and it noted that its conclusion (in favor of custody) was "further informed by the views of other contracting states."[15] It mentioned specifically in this connection rulings of the English High Court of Justice and the House of Lords, the Supreme Court of Israel, the High Courts of Austria, South Africa, and Germany, and appellate courts in Australia and Scotland.[16] The Court also noted that the Canadian courts took a more restrictive view of the issue, and that French courts were divided.[17] Perhaps that isn't quite the same as saying that the views of those other states and their tribunals had "precedential" weight in the U.S. judicial proceeding, but it is close.

In the broadest group of cases, in which the foreign legal ruling is of interest only because the issue touches on individual rights, there are differences of opinion on how useful it is to cite the foreign case.[18] As the blackletter rule indicates, conditions prevailing

---

13   24 Oct. 1980, T.I.A.S. No. 11670, S. Treaty Doc. No. 99-11, implemented through the International Child Abduction Remedies Act, 22 U.S.C. §§ 9001–9011.
14   560 U.S. 1 (2010).
15   *Id.* at 15–16.
16   *Id.* at 16–17.
17   *Id.* at 17–18.
18   *See, e.g.*, *Lawrence v. Texas*, 539 U.S. 558, 573 (2003) (Kennedy J.) (relying in part on precedent from the European Court of Human Rights); *id.* at 598 (Scalia J. dissenting) (denouncing the Court's reliance on foreign precedent); *Atkins v. Virginia*, 536 U.S. 304, 316 n.21 (2002) (Stevens J.) (relying in part on the disapproval of the "world community"); *id.* at 322 (Rehnquist J. dissenting) (noting "the defects in the Court's decision to place weight on foreign laws"); *id.* at 347–48 (Scalia J. dissenting) (stating that the world community's practices are "irrelevant").

in the foreign country may be quite different from those in the United States. Even if the conditions are similar and the principle seems clear, effectiveness of enforcement varies considerably across the globe. If a country purports to follow a rule but in practice ignores it, its approach should carry little weight outside its borders.

It's not just the lack of authority that diminishes the force of an opinion dealing with another government's law. It's common sense, too. A court that is dealing with the law of another government rarely has the broad familiarity and intuitive understanding needed for a sure-footed ruling. So there are good reasons why in these circumstances you can't get as much advantage from a favorable opinion issued by a foreign court, or suffer as much disadvantage from an unfavorable one. On the whole, we are inclined to believe that decisions from other countries should be accorded little if any consideration.

The Supreme Court has said that the necessity to apply foreign law counsels in favor of dismissing the plaintiff's action without prejudice, so that the suit may be filed in the more convenient foreign forum.[19] But when the balance of factors counsels in favor of keeping the case in an American court and the rights of the parties depend on foreign law, the domestic court must apply foreign law.

This issue arises most often in disputes over contracts including a choice-of-law provision. Such a provision will be given effect "[a]bsent a strong showing that it should be set aside," such as proof that it was effected by "fraud, undue influence, or overweening bargaining power."[20] In the tort context, foreign law becomes applicable when the choice-of-law regime mandates it. A good example is the Ninth Circuit case of *Arno v. Club Med Inc.*[21] There, California resident Carolyn Arno had formerly been employed by

---

19 *Gulf Oil Corp. v. Gilbert*, 330 U.S. 501, 509 (1947). *But see Piper Aircraft Co. v. Reyno*, 454 U.S. 235, 260 n.29 (1981) (explaining that while "the need to apply foreign law favors dismissal, . . . this factor alone is not sufficient to warrant dismissal when a balancing of all relevant factors shows that the plaintiff's chosen forum is appropriate").

20 *Trans-Tec Asia v. M/V Harmony Container*, 518 F.3d 1120, 1126 (9th Cir. 2008) (quoting *M/S Bremen v. Zapata Off-Shore Co.*, 407 U.S. 1, 12–13 (1972)).

21 22 F.3d 1464 (9th Cir. 1994).

Club Med at its French resort. Arno brought a tort claim in federal district court in California against Club Med's New York office, based on her alleged rape by her supervisor at the French location. The federal district court granted summary judgment to Club Med, and Arno appealed to the Ninth Circuit. Because the Ninth Circuit was sitting in diversity, it applied California's choice-of-law regime,[22] which it concluded required it to apply French tort law. The court examined the text of the French Civil Code and opinions of France's highest court, the Cour de Cassation, and concluded that an employer is vicariously liable under French law for torts arising from an employee's abuse of a job function.[23] Since Arno alleged that her supervisor had used his job function as Arno's supervisor to rape her, there was a genuine question of material fact whether the supervisor had been acting within the scope of his employment, requiring reversal of the grant of summary judgment.

Determining the content of foreign law

When a federal court must apply foreign law, it begins by determining the content of that law. Federal Rule of Civil Procedure 44.1 governs this process. The rule directs the litigant raising a question of foreign law to give notice to the district court "by a pleading or other writing." (A litigant who fails to notify the court that foreign law is relevant to the suit may be considered to have forfeited the issue, meaning that the claim will be subject to the law of the forum state.[24]) Once notice is given, "the court may consider any relevant material or source, including testimony, whether or not submitted by a party or admissible under the Federal Rules of Evidence." This rule was intended to end the earlier practice of treating the content of foreign law as a question of fact—but it has had only limited success.[25]

---

22   *Id.* at 1467.
23   *Id.* at 1469–70.
24   *Whirlpool Fin. Corp. v. Sevaux*, 96 F.3d 216, 221 (7th Cir. 1996).
25   *See generally* Matthew J. Ahn, Note, *44.1 Luftballons: The Communication Breakdown of Foreign Law in the Federal Courts*, 89 N.Y.U. L. Rev. 1343 (2014). As Ahn notes, the Second Circuit has declined to apply foreign law in some cases even though "the forum's choice of law rules would have called for the

Once the court has decided to apply foreign law, which sources should guide its inquiry? The answer varies based on the nation whose law is to be applied. The cases discussed below reveal that American courts will follow the decision of a country's highest court as binding only when that country's own courts would treat that decision as precedential.

So for example, in a tax case turning on whether property obtained during marriage was joint or separate property, the First Circuit applied an English case that held such property to be separately owned. This despite arguments (in the form of treatises and policy arguments) explaining that the doctrine applied by the First Circuit was flawed and likely to be discarded when the House of Lords (the highest court in England at the time) next took up the issue.[26] The First Circuit explained that it was bound to follow the rule espoused by binding English precedent "absent a compelling showing that the English courts would scuttle that rule."[27] Since there had been no doctrinal developments to support such a showing, the First Circuit found itself obligated to apply the contemporary English rule.

By contrast, when the Fifth Circuit was asked to decide whether a maritime lien against two ships owned by a Spanish company was valid under Spanish law, it noted that in Spain, a civil-law country, "the role of positive legislation is emphasized at the expense of stare decisis."[28] Thus the court looked "first to the text of the legislation, and then to any customs which have developed with respect to its application."[29] Only after considering those, the court said, would it "turn to judicial decisions to the extent that they fill in gaps left by law or custom."[30]

---

application of foreign law." *Id.* at 1364 (quoting *Vishipco Line v. Chase Manhattan Bank, N.A.*, 660 F.2d 854, 860 (2d Cir. 1981)). Meanwhile, the Fifth Circuit has resurrected the old notion that the substance of foreign law is a question of fact to be proved by the parties. *Id.* at 1365–68 (quoting *Banque Libanaise Pour le Commerce v. Khreich*, 915 F.2d 1000, 1006 (5th Cir. 1990)).

26   *Estate of Charania v. Shulman*, 608 F.3d 67, 71–74 (1st Cir. 2010).
27   *Id.* at 75.
28   *Banco de Credito Indus., S.A. v. Tesoreria Gen.*, 990 F.2d 827, 833 (5th Cir. 1993).
29   *Id.*
30   *Id.*

Indeed, courts have gone further still, refusing to obey decisions of foreign courts on the grounds that those decisions would not be given precedential effect in their own country. In *Phoenix Canada Oil Co. v. Texaco, Inc.*, the Third Circuit was faced with a situation in which interest rates in Ecuador rose from 8% to 23% while the litigation was pending and until the Ecuadorian Monetary Board fixed the rate at 8%.[31] The question before the court was whether the prejudgment interest rate to be applied to a breach-of-contract dispute should be the newly enacted maximum of 8% or a segmented interest rate reflecting the actual increases in the Ecuadorian rate. In identical factual circumstances, the Supreme Court of Ecuador had applied the new maximum rate of 8% to the entire period. Nonetheless, the district court granted the plaintiffs a substantially higher segmented rate, and the Third Circuit affirmed, explaining that "[t]he district court observed correctly the lack of precedential effect of judicial decisions in civil law jurisdictions," meaning that the American courts could ignore the Ecuadorian decisions.[32]

So unless the parties' rights turn on a question of foreign law and that country treats its own decisions as precedential, American courts do not consider themselves obligated to follow the decisions of foreign courts.

In some contexts, foreign decisions are persuasive to an American tribunal. In maritime law, for example, the Ninth Circuit has noted that "[a]lthough Canadian law has no precedential value here, the [Canadian] decision is instructive, particularly in light of the relatively uncharted waters presented by this appeal."[33] And in *Roper v. Simmons*,[34] the Supreme Court found "confirmation" for its conclusion that "the death penalty is disproportionate punishment for offenders under 18 [years of age]" in "the stark reality that the United States is the only country in the world that continues to give official sanction to the juvenile death

---

31   842 F.2d 1466, 1479–80 (3d Cir. 1988).
32   *Id.*
33   *Trans-Tec Asia v. M/V Harmony Container*, 518 F.3d 1120, 1127 (9th Cir. 2008).
34   543 U.S. 551 (2005).

penalty."[35] Though this survey of the decisions of foreign courts wasn't controlling, the Court concluded that it was instructive for the Eighth Amendment question.[36]

More commonly, however, foreign precedents are simply dismissed out of hand. So when a criminal defendant sought a "familial privilege" to avoid giving evidence against his father—relying on "the rule in continental Europe where such a privilege obtains"—the Fourth Circuit dismissed the claim, explaining: "Our law, of course, derives from England, which does not lie within the confines of 'continental' Europe. The differences between Roman law and the common law are sufficient to reduce such authority to a status of practical irrelevance."[37]

The Supreme Court phrased its rejection of international precedent (from the International Court of Justice) more politely. A Honduran national, Mario Bustillo, was arrested and charged in Virginia with first-degree murder.[38] When a national of one country is detained by authorities of another, Article 36 of the Vienna Convention requires those authorities, upon the detainee's request, to notify the consular officers of the detainee's country. Bustillo was never informed of his Article 36 right. His case proceeded to a jury trial in Virginia state court, where he was convicted. On state habeas review, Bustillo for the first time raised his argument that because his Article 36 right had been violated, the court had to vacate his conviction. The Virginia court of appeals dismissed the claim as procedurally barred for Bustillo's failure to raise it on direct appeal. The Supreme Court of Virginia affirmed.[39]

---

35   *Id.* at 575–76.

36   The Supreme Court majority's analysis of international law was met with significant criticism from the dissenters, rendering unclear the future vitality of such application of foreign law. *See Roper*, 543 U.S. at 604 (O'Connor J. dissenting) ("In short, the evidence of an international consensus does not alter my determination that the Eighth Amendment does not, at this time, forbid capital punishment of 17-year-old murderers in all cases."); *id.* at 624 (Scalia J. dissenting) ("[T]he basic premise of the Court's argument—that American law should conform to the laws of the rest of the world—ought to be rejected out of hand.").

37   *United States v. Jones*, 683 F.2d 817, 819 (4th Cir. 1982).

38   *Sanchez-Llamas v. Oregon*, 548 U.S. 331 (2006).

39   *Id.* at 340–42.

The International Court of Justice has interpreted the Vienna Convention as precluding the application of domestic procedural-default rules to criminal defendants' Vienna Convention claims under Article 36. The Supreme Court said that the ICJ's interpretation deserved "respectful consideration" but wasn't conclusive on American courts.[40]

Hence the Court took the contrary approach and held that a Vienna Convention claim could be barred by state procedural rules requiring a defendant to raise all claims for relief on direct appeal.[41]

Two years later, when a petitioner pointed out that the ICJ had held that the United States was in violation of the Vienna Convention because of the Court's application of state procedural rules to Article 36 claims, the Supreme Court held firm.[42] The Court explained that while an ICJ decision could constitute "an international law obligation on the part of the United States," that decision didn't "automatically constitute binding federal law enforceable in United States courts."[43] So even though the ICJ had specifically held that petitioner Medellin, a Mexican national, was being held by Texas authorities in violation of international law, there was no federal-law obligation imposed on Texas to comply with that judgment.[44]

In short, American courts treat the decisions of foreign courts much as they do any other persuasive authority: not binding, but helpful if the reasoning is sound and applicable to the case at hand. The exception to this rule occurs when the rights of the litigants depend on a question of foreign law and the nation at issue treats decisions of its highest court as precedential. In such a context, American courts will follow those decisions as binding precedent.

---

40 *Id.* at 352–56.
41 *Id.*
42 *Medellin v. Texas*, 552 U.S. 491 (2008).
43 *Id.* at 504.
44 *Id.* at 510–12.

91. Precedents in International Law

In international law, precedents are never treated as binding; they are often considered persuasive, sometimes highly so.

Because international law involves no hierarchical system of courts in which vertical precedent could apply,[1] it is commonly understood that the doctrine of stare decisis "does not apply as such to international law."[2] This is so whether the reference is to public international law[3] or to private international law.[4]

The traditional aversion to stare decisis is attributable in part to the governing rules of the International Court of Justice.[5] The statute establishing that court is commonly cited as precluding stare decisis.[6] Meanwhile, there may be some reluctance for international courts to acknowledge the role of precedent in their

---

[1] 3 Shabtai Rosenne, *The Law and Practice of the International Court, 1920–2005* 1553 (4th ed. 2006) ("While there is no formal hierarchy of international courts and tribunals, the pre-eminence of the . . . International Court is today generally accepted."); Frédéric G. Sourgens, *Law's Laboratory: Developing International Law on Investment Protection as Common Law*, 34 Nw. J. Int'l L. & Bus. 181, 240–41 (2014) ("There is no hierarchy of international courts and tribunals—they operate alongside, and in competition with, each other."). *But see, e.g.*, WTO Organization Chart, www.WTO.org (2016) (showing the hierarchy of the World Trade Organization, including the Dispute Settlement Panels and the Appellate Body).

[2] Guido Acquaviva & Fausto Pocar, "Stare Decisis," in 9 *The Max Planck Encyclopedia of Public International Law* 469, 469 (Rüdriger Wolfrum ed., 2012). *See* Mohamed Shahabuddeen, *Precedent in the World Court* 97 (1996) ("It is not in dispute that the doctrine does not apply in relation to the [World] Court.").

[3] Acquaviva & Pocar, "Stare Decisis" at 469.

[4] Stefan Vogenauer, "Precedent, Rule of," in 2 *The Max Planck Encyclopedia of European Private Law* 1304, 1304 (Jürgen Basedow et al. eds., 2012).

[5] *See* Raj Bhala, *The Myth About Stare Decisis and International Trade Law (Part One of a Trilogy)*, 14 Am. U. Int'l L. Rev. 845, 864–65 (1999) ("The doctrine of stare decisis is not simply foreign to international law, it is expressly disavowed by the near-sacred sources of the foundational field, public international law.").

[6] *See* Statute of the International Court of Justice art. 38 (1945) ("[J]udicial decisions . . . [are] subsidiary means for the determination of rules of law."); *id.* art. 59 ("The decision of the Court has no binding force except between the parties and in respect of that particular case."). *But see* 3 Rosenne, *The Law and Practice of the International Court* at 1553 (discussing the original understanding of the statute to preclude the enforcement of a judgment against nonparties, not to preclude the use of precedent); Manley O. Hudson, *The Permanent Court of International Justice*, 36 Harv. L. Rev. 245, 256–57 (1922) ("The object of the

decision-making because there are no coordinate governmental branches that can easily alter the effect of a judicial decision.[7]

Yet paradoxically, it is also said that as a practical matter, "all international judicial bodies follow their previous decisions, except where departure is considered necessary."[8] Whole volumes could be written on the definition of *necessary* in this context. Essentially, precedents in international law are persuasive authority only—yet the degree of persuasiveness seems to grow stronger as litigation is being resorted to more and more often in resolving international disputes.[9]

Doubtless a kind of horizontal stare decisis exists in international law, despite the drumbeat of assertions to the contrary. That is, the essence of stare decisis and the rationales supporting it are spreading. Although there is no "de jure" stare decisis, there is "de facto" stare decisis,[10] and a common-law lawyer would mostly be at home with the decisional methods of international law.[11] In

---

framers of this clause was to obviate the necessity of a third state's intervening whenever its interest might be involved in a case.").

[7] *See* Jenny S. Martinez, *Towards an International Judicial System*, 56 Stan. L. Rev. 429, 486 (2003).

[8] Acquaviva & Pocar, "Stare Decisis" at 469.

[9] *Id.*

[10] *See* Bhala, *The Myth About Stare Decisis*, 14 Am. U. Int'l L. Rev. at 937–38 ("[I]n a de jure stare decisis regime, there is a legal obligation incumbent on the adjudicator to accord due respect to its prior decisions and the prior decisions of a higher authority. . . . [T]hese earlier decisions are officially recognized as a source of law for future disputes . . . . In contrast, . . . a 'de facto' doctrine of stare decisis is one that exists in fact. We may . . . see the adjudicator referring to and citing cases repeatedly in ways that suggest it feels bound, . . . struggling mightily to distinguish prior cases from the case at bar . . . . [And] we may even see lines of precedent spawned by leading cases, on certain issues that do indeed appear to bind future disputants.").

[11] *Id.* at 890 ("A common-law lawyer would find himself very much at home in GATT legal discussions."). *See* Raj Bhala, *The Precedent Setters: De Facto Stare Decisis in WTO Adjudication (Part Two of a Trilogy)*, 9 J. Transnat'l L. & Pol'y 1, 4 (1999) ("[I]n the present context, the WTO Appellate Body behaves very much like a high court (or the highest court) in a common law jurisdiction."); Sourgens, *Law's Laboratory*, 34 Nw. J. Int'l L. & Bus. at 241–42 ("The common law treatment of precedent better reflects current practices in investor-state arbitration because even a single decision by an out-of-state court can be highly persuasive, and perhaps even binding, if it is convincing."). See also Introduction (discussing the increasing commonality of civil- and common-law jurisdictions and how stare decisis is "not so much a doctrine as a method").

particular, the following characteristics of international law suggest the presence of stare decisis:
- International courts often cite precedent in their decisions.[12]
- There is a growing body of international caselaw.[13]

---

12   *See* 3 Rosenne, *The Law and Practice of International Court* at 1553 ("[W]e find the Court habitually referring to its own decisions and those of the Permanent Court."); Marc Jacob, *Precedents and Case-Based Reasoning in the European Court of Justice* 87–125 (2014) (discussing studies of the frequency and types of use of precedent in the European Court of Justice); Bhala, *The Myth About Stare Decisis*, 14 Am. U. Int'l L. Rev. at 849 ("[T]here is now a de facto doctrine of stare decisis in international trade law."); Gleider I. Hernandéz, *The International Court of Justice and the Judicial Function* 157 (2014) (discussing the World Court's "declared strict adherence" to precedent in its cases regarding Yugoslavia); Bhala, *The Precedent Setters*, 9 J. Transnat'l L. & Pol'y at 7–8 ("Any careful reader of WTO Appellate Body and, indeed, Panel reports must be struck by the extensive citations to prior Panel and Appellate Body reports."); Joseph Lookofsky, *Digesting CISG Case Law: How Much Regard Should We Have?*, 8 Vindobona J. Int'l L. & Com. Arb. 181, 184 (2004) ("These traditional distinctions notwithstanding, UNCITRAL (an organ designed to serve the interests of all legal systems) regularly refers to CISG 'case law.'"). *See also* Yusuf Aksar, *Implementing International Economic Law* 107 (2011) ("There is no binding precedent for Appellate Body reports. . . . However, the Appellate Body attempts to follow its own decisions to achieve consistency and coherence, and this has been an important stabilizer.").

13   *See* United States Diplomatic and Consular Staff in Tehran (*U.S. v. Iran*), Judgment, 1980 I.C.J. 3 (May 24) (discussing "its settled jurisprudence"); Statute of the International Court of Justice art. 38 ("The Court, whose function is to decide in accordance with international law such disputes as are submitted to it, shall apply: . . . international custom, as evidence of a general practice accepted as law."). *See also* Andrew T. Guzman & Timothy L. Meyer, *International Common Law: The Soft Law of International Tribunals*, 9 Chi. J. Int'l L. 515, 525 (2009) ("One cannot . . . discuss the international law governing intervention in another state's internal conflict without considering the ICJ's *Nicaragua* case. Similarly, understanding World Trade Organization law relating to health and safety measures requires analysis of the *EC-Hormones* ruling."); David Palmeter & Petros C. Mavroidis, *The WTO Legal System: Sources of Law*, 92 Am. J. Int'l L. 398, 400 (1998) ("Other than the texts of the WTO Agreements themselves, no source of law is as important in WTO dispute settlement as the reported decisions of prior dispute settlement panels."); Shahabuddeen, *Precedent in the World Court* at 13 ("The prospect of the [Permanent] Court building up its own case law and the practical implications of this for the international community had been the subject of early notice, going back to the period leading up to the establishment of the first Court."). *See further* Bhala, *The Precedent Setters*, 9 J. Transnat'l L. & Pol'y at 9 ("For all practical purposes, the reports of the Appellate Body do have a precedential effect on non-party Members in the future, they are a *binding* source of law for these parties, and taken together they represent an emerging body of common law for international trade."); Sourgens, *Law's Laboratory*, 34 Nw. J. Int'l L. & Bus. at 183 ("The resulting explosion of international law in the form of judgments, arbitral awards, and tribunal decisions under crisscrossing treaties has given an unprecedented concreteness to international legal rights

- International courts are careful to distinguish earlier cases.[14]
- International courts are recognized as having some law-making function.[15]

The existence of stare decisis doesn't imply that one tribunal's decision will forever settle an issue. But as a distinguished scholar has amply demonstrated, much of the terminology about international precedent is more confusing than useful—and some form of stare decisis does indeed exist.

---

and obligations."); Aksar, *Implementing International Economic Law* at 148–49 (referring to "landmark" and "fundamental" precedent).

14 Jacob, *Precedents and Case-Based Reasoning in the European Court of Justice* at 145 (discussing how the European Court of Justice carefully distinguishes earlier cases so that it can coherently state the law); Shahabuddeen, *Precedent in the World Court* at 2–3 ("[T]he Court seeks guidance from its previous decisions, . . . [and] it regards them as reliable expositions of the law. . . . [T]hough having the power to depart from them, it will not lightly exercise that power.").

15 *See* Jacob, *Precedents and Case-Based Reasoning in the European Court of Justice* at 24, 60; Shahabuddeen, *Precedent in the World Court* at 90 ("There is a general agreement that the Court has power, and indeed responsibility, to develop the law.").

I. Arbitrations

92. The Use of Precedents in Arbitrations

Ordinary principles of stare decisis generally do not apply in arbitration proceedings, or in court review and enforcement of arbitration awards.

Strictly speaking, stare decisis doesn't apply in arbitrations. For one thing, arbitral awards aren't reviewable for legal error. If an arbitrator misinterprets or misapplies a case through a lack of understanding, the arbitral award will stand as is even though a court would have reached a different conclusion if following precedents. Some jurisdictions—but by no means all—do permit review to determine whether the arbitrator understood but disregarded the applicable law. So even though arbitrators might be ethically bound to follow the law of the chosen jurisdiction and might be liable for willful failure to do so, mistakes of law are generally not corrected. Because many arbitrators aren't lawyers and have no legal training, only the clearest rules in caselaw could possibly have a binding effect. Hence many jurisdictions don't recognize claims of manifest disregard of the law: the parties select the arbitrator, and if they choose a nonlawyer, they can't reasonably demand expert interpretations or applications of caselaw.

Arbitration proceedings are governed by contractual provisions. The general rule is that no one is obligated to arbitrate without first agreeing to do so.[1] But when one has so agreed, courts may force arbitration and refuse to hear any lawsuit that the

---

[1] *Granite Rock Co. v. International Bhd. of Teamsters*, 561 U.S. 287, 299 (2010) ("[T]he first principle that underscores all of our arbitration decisions" is that "[a]rbitration is strictly a matter of consent, and thus is a way to resolve those disputes—but only those disputes—that the parties have agreed to submit to arbitration.") (internal quotation marks and citations omitted); *Volt Info. Sciences, Inc. v. Board of Trs. of Leland Stanford Junior Univ.*, 489 U.S. 468, 479 (1989) ("Arbitration under the [Federal Arbitration] Act is a matter of consent, not coercion, and parties are generally free to structure their arbitration agreements as they see fit.").

arbitration would preclude.[2] Those matters can still reach courts, though, and especially federal courts, if a prevailing party seeks to enforce an arbitration award when the losing party doesn't comply with it.[3] Federal jurisdiction over arbitration enforcement generally falls under the Federal Arbitration Act[4] or, with labor arbitration, § 301 of the Taft–Hartley Act.[5]

The general concept of arbitration is that the parties have bargained for an arbitrator's award, not a court's view of the matter. Hence an arbitrator's award will be upheld as long as it plausibly draws "its essence from the [contract]."[6] The Supreme Court has emphatically declared that the arbitrator's judgment will be upheld if the arbitrator is "even arguably construing or applying the contract," despite the arbitrator's "improvident, even silly, factfinding."[7]

Traditionally, courts won't set aside an arbitral award for a garden-variety error of law.[8] But courts will not enforce a manifest departure from the law.[9] Moreover, courts may decline to enforce

---

2   *Dean Witter Reynolds, Inc. v. Byrd*, 470 U.S. 213, 217 (1985).

3   *D.H. Blair & Co. v. Gottdiener*, 462 F.3d 95, 110 (2d Cir. 2006) ("[C]onfirmation of an arbitration award is a summary proceeding that merely makes what is already a final arbitration award a judgment of the court, and the court must grant the award unless the award is vacated, modified, or corrected.").

4   9 U.S.C. § 1 et seq.

5   29 U.S.C. § 185.

6   *Steelworkers Trilogy* (*United Steelworkers of Am. v. Enterprise Wheel & Car Corp.*), 363 U.S. 593, 597 (1960).

7   *United Paperworkers Int'l Union v. Misco, Inc.*, 484 U.S. 29, 38, 39 (1987); *Major League Baseball Players Ass'n v. Garvey*, 532 U.S. 504, 509–10 (2001) (per curiam).

8   *Major League Baseball Players*, 532 U.S. at 509.

9   *See, e.g., MCI Constructors, LLC v. City of Greensboro*, 610 F.3d 849, 857 (4th Cir. 2010) ("The permissible common law grounds for vacating such an award include those circumstances where an award fails to draw its essence from the contract, or the award evidences a manifest disregard of the law.") (internal quotation marks omitted); *Schwartz v. Merrill Lynch & Co.*, 665 F.3d 444, 452 (2d Cir. 2011) ("[M]anifest disregard remains a valid ground for vacating arbitration awards . . . . [T]he court must consider, first, whether the governing law alleged to have been ignored by the arbitrators was well defined, explicit, and clearly applicable, and, second, whether the arbitrator knew about the existence of a clearly governing legal principle but decided to ignore it or pay no attention to it.") (internal quotation marks omitted).

arbitral awards that grossly deviate from a clear public policy.[10] It's said that "arbitrators cannot direct a violation of the law,"[11] so in this sense an arbitrator's discretion *is* bounded by the law. Still, an arbitrator isn't required to follow precedents.

Yet arbitrators do follow the law and precedent to the extent that the parties wish. Typically, parties regulate an arbitrator's use of law.[12] The law specified in a choice-of-law provision should be considered informally binding on the arbitrator.[13] An arbitrator should follow the law to instill predictability and consistency for the parties.[14] Sometimes a federal statute or regulation will require an arbitrator to consider statutes and precedent for federal public arbitrations.[15] For example, in arbitrations relating to federal employees and water-and-power agencies, arbitrators are required to consider legal precedents.[16]

Otherwise, according to one authority, the majority view is that when an agreement doesn't conflict with a law, the arbitrator may consider the law in interpreting the agreement.[17] Arbitrators

---

10   *W.R. Grace & Co. v. Local 759, Int'l Union of Rubber Workers*, 461 U.S. 757, 766 (1983) ("If the contract as interpreted by [an arbitrator] violates some explicit public policy, we are obliged to refrain from enforcing it.") (per Blackmun J.).

11   Frank Elkouri & Edna Asper Elkouri, *How Arbitration Works* 519 (Marlin M. Volz & Edward P. Goggin eds., 5th ed. 1997). *See also Titan Tire Corp. v. United Steel Workers Int'l Union*, 734 F.3d 708, 716 (7th Cir. 2013) ("A violation of a statute or some other positive law is the clearest example of a violation of public policy and no arbitrator is entitled to direct a violation of positive law.") (internal quotation marks omitted).

12   *See* Elkouri & Elkouri, *How Arbitration Works* at 516.

13   *See* 2 Gary B. Born, *International Commercial Arbitration* 2963 (2009) ("Judicial precedent applying a state's laws should have the same binding effects in international arbitral proceedings as it possesses in national court proceedings. . . . [O]ne of the fundamental objectives of businesses in entering into international commercial arbitration agreements, coupled with choice-of-law provisions, is to obtain predicable results.").

14   *See* Klaus Peter Berger, *The International Arbitrator's Application of Precedents*, 9 J. Int'l Arb. 11 (1992).

15   *See* Elkouri & Elkouri, *How Arbitration Works* at 541.

16   *See* Government Organization and Employees, 5 U.S.C. § 579(c)(5) (2012) ("The arbitrator shall interpret and apply relevant statutory and regulatory requirements, legal precedents, and policy directives."); Conservation of Water and Power Resources, 18 C.F.R. § 385.605(v) (2015) (same).

17   Elkouri & Elkouri, *How Arbitration Works* at 524 ("(1) [W]here the contractual provision being interpreted or applied has been formulated loosely, the arbitrator

are more divided when the law is inconsistent with the arbitration agreement. For example, one authority urges that "where there is clear conflict between the agreement and law, the arbitrator 'should respect the agreement and ignore the law.'"[18]

One arbitrator believes consideration of the law to be appropriate when:

(1) the agreement incorporates the law;

(2) the parties agree to apply the law; or

(3) the law might help interpret an agreement.[19]

But the arbitrator was disinclined to consider outside law when the effect would be "to amend the contract by adding or subtracting."[20]

The U.S. Supreme Court has even said that the arbitrator's role is to effectuate the intent of the parties.[21] An arbitrator isn't meant to impose public law in an arbitration.[22] And going beyond the parties' submission can cause an award to be reversed.[23]

In addition, parties may give an arbitrator even greater flexibility through the equitable doctrines of *ex aequo et bono*[24] and

---

may consider all relevant factors, including relevant law; (2) where a contractual provision is susceptible to two interpretations, one compatible with and the other repugnant to an applicable statute, the statute is a relevant factor—arbitrators should seek to avoid a construction that would make the agreement invalid; and (3) where the submission makes it clear that the parties want an advisory opinion as to the law, such opinion would be within the arbitrator's role.").

18   *Id.* at 527.

19   *See id.* at 531.

20   *Id.*

21   *Alexander v. Gardner-Denver Co.*, 415 U.S. 36, 52–57 (1974) ("The arbitrator . . . has no general authority to invoke public laws that conflict with the bargain between the parties . . . . [The arbitrator's task] is to effectuate the intent of the parties rather than the requirements of enacted legislation. Where the collective-bargaining agreement conflicts with Title VII, the arbitrator must follow the agreement.").

22   *See* Elkouri & Elkouri, *How Arbitration Works* at 535.

23   *See id.* at 542 ("[I]f the agreement and external law do conflict, and if the award is based . . . 'solely upon the arbitrator's view of the requirements of enacted legislation, which would mean that he exceeded the scope of the submission,' the award would not withstand court review.").

24   *See Black's Law Dictionary* 679 (Bryan A. Garner ed., 10th ed. 2014) (defining *ex aequo et bono* as "[a]ccording to what is equitable and good" and stating: "A decision-maker (esp. in international law) who is authorized to decide *ex*

amiable compositeur.[25] Both doctrines mean that "the tribunal does not have to strictly apply the law, but can render a decision based on reasonableness and fairness."[26] These powers may require the parties' express agreement.[27]

Beyond mere flexibility, there may be good reasons to disregard the law. Three have been proposed:

(1) the parties may have chosen incomplete law that doesn't provide a sufficient basis for the decision;

(2) international trade usages may more properly reflect the intent of the agreement; or

(3) some international rules may be considered superseding.[28]

Although judicial precedent may well be part of the body of law that an arbitrator applies,[29] precedent isn't given stare decisis effect. That is, in the United States, arbitrators will strongly consider Supreme Court decisions, but they may be dismissive of lower-court opinions.[30] And in civil-law countries such as Germany,

---

aequo et bono is not bound by legal rules and may instead follow equitable principles.").

25 *See* 2 Gary B. Born, *International Commercial Arbitration* 2963 (2009) ("[S]ave when parties have agreed to arbitration *ex aequo et bono* or *amiable compositeur*, the arbitrators' mandate is to resolve the parties' dispute in an adjudicative manner, in accordance with the applicable law."); *see also Black's Law Dictionary* at 102 (defining the anglicized *amiable compositor* as "[a]n arbitrator empowered, by agreement of the parties, to settle a dispute on the basis of what is equitable and good (*ex aequo et bono*), subject to procedural fairness and the terms of the arbitration agreement as opposed to the settled substantive rules of a given legal system").

26 Margaret L. Moses, *The Principles and Practice of International Commercial Arbitration* 77–78 (2012).

27 *See* Yves Derains & Eric A. Schwartz, *A Guide to the ICC Rules of Arbitration* 245–46 (2d ed. 2005) ("[B]oth terms are products of the civil law and have to do with an arbitrator deciding a case on the basis of fairness and equitable considerations. . . . [The Arbitral Tribunal] may assume such authority 'only if the parties have agreed' to grant it this power.").

28 *See* Fouchard, Gaillard, Goldman *on International Commercial Arbitration* 842–51 (Emmanuel Gaillard & John Savage eds., 1999).

29 *See generally* Elkouri & Elkouri, *How Arbitration Works* at 558.

30 *See id.* ("An arbitrator's willingness to follow judicial precedent . . . will depend to a large extent upon the level of the court rendering the decision and upon the unanimity of the decisions. . . . [I]f an arbitrator does not agree with a

where stare decisis isn't strictly applied within the court system, arbitrators rarely follow court decisions.[31]

The parties' choice of law is normally juxtaposed against the arbitrator's discretionary application of it. Treatises about arbitration routinely dedicate chapters to the importance of choice-of-law provisions. Meanwhile, treatises also abound with references to an arbitrator's discretion and the importance of flexibility in arbitration.

Although at first glance the juxtaposition seems muddled, the two positions are reconcilable. The parties' choice of law reflects their intentions and expectations regarding their agreement. Importantly, so does their choice to resolve their dispute through arbitration. That is, a choice-of-law provision within an arbitration agreement includes an implied term for the arbitrator to reach what he or she believes is the best result under the particular circumstances of the dispute.

Most parties to an arbitration are aware of how arbitrators employ substantive laws. So unless the parties can agree on an express statement of a specific law, the arbitrator's flexible application is part of their bargain.

One premise of this argument is that the parties are aware of how arbitrators make decisions. Some consistency in arbitral awards is necessary for the parties to reach an informed bargain. If arbitrators fail to apply principles consistently across decisions, the parties will not be able to rely on prior awards to manifest their intent in future agreements.

---

decision handed down by a court other than one of last resort, he or she may refuse to follow it.").

31 *See* Rolf A. Schütze, *The Precedential Effect of Arbitration Decisions*, 11 J. Int'l Arb. 3, 69 (1994) ("[A]rbitration decisions do not follow the judgements of the courts which, at least in a narrow sense, are not a binding source of German law. Yet . . . the opinions of German courts, and in particular Germany's higher Federal courts, have a considerable and real effect upon the decisions of other courts.").

93. The Precedential Effect of Arbitral Awards

Although arbitral awards have no binding precedential value, they may be considered persuasive.

As a means of settling disputes privately—a means generally not open to the public—arbitrations usually result in decisions that are neither published nor collected. If trial-court decisions aren't considered precedential, it only makes sense that arbitral decisions wouldn't be. Even when arbitrators cite earlier arbitral decisions—as with those involving environmental or investment issues—those earlier decisions are persuasive only, not binding.

The prevailing view is that cases decided before different arbitrators or even the same arbitrator at different times will be upheld even if they would conflict—or would violate precedent or stare decisis if they were court cases—as long as the conflicting decisions draw their essence from the governing contract.[1] Parties can contract if they choose to for particular arbitral decisions to have preclusive effect on later decisions.[2] But an arbitration ruling under a contract cannot estop a plaintiff from later litigating the same issue under a federal antidiscrimination statute.[3]

---

[1] *Consolidation Coal Co. v. UMWA Local 1545*, 213 F.3d 404, 406 (7th Cir. 2000) (noting that enforcing inconsistent decisions "is not a happy" result, yet that when the parties have simply agreed to be bound by a proper arbitrator's decision, "arbitral awards based on diametrically opposed interpretations of the identical contract can all withstand judicial review").

[2] *See id.* at 407. *See also Connecticut Light & Power Co. v. Local 420, IBEW*, 718 F.2d 14, 20 (2d Cir. 1983) ("Courts reviewing inconsistent arbitration awards have generally concluded that arbitrators are not bound by the rationale of earlier decisions and that inconsistency with another award is not enough by itself to justify vacating an award. Principles of stare decisis and res judicata do not have the same doctrinal force in arbitration proceedings as they do in judicial proceedings.") (citation omitted) (collecting cases).

[3] *Nance v. Goodyear Tire & Rubber Co.*, 527 F.3d 539, 548 (6th Cir. 2008).

Most circuits have held that arbitrators needn't give preclusive effect to earlier arbitral decisions.[4] An arbitrator can decide inconsistently with earlier arbitration results in similar cases.[5]

Even so, earlier arbitral awards are generally given about as much weight as cases are in a civil-law jurisdiction. Although the use of precedent in arbitrations can vary dramatically,[6] it can be analogized to the civil-law concept of *jurisprudence constante*.[7] Not bound by precedent,[8] arbitrators have frequently relied on earlier

---

4   *International Union, UAW v. Dana Corp.*, 278 F.3d 548, 555–56 (6th Cir. 2002). *But see* possible disagreement in *Trailways Lines Inc. v. Trailways, Inc. Joint Council*, 807 F.2d 1416, 1422–23 (8th Cir. 1986), *and Oil Workers Int'l Union v. Ethyl Corp.*, 644 F.2d 1044, 1050 (5th Cir. 1981).

5   *Hotel Ass'n of Washington, D.C., Inc. v. Hotel & Rest. Emps. Union*, 963 F.2d 388, 390 (D.C. Cir. 1992) ("[W]here the agreement is silent, the 'arbitrator may decline to follow arbitral precedent . . . .'") (quoting *Fournelle v. NLRB*, 670 F.2d 331, 344 n.22 (D.C. Cir. 1982)); *id.* ("Of course, the parties may make an arbitral decision binding in a future dispute by so providing in their [contract].").

6   Frank Elkouri & Edna Asper Elkouri, *How Arbitration Works* 600 (Marlin M. Volz & Edward P. Goggin eds., 5th ed. 1997) ("Diverse views exist concerning the use of prior awards as precedents in the arbitration of labor-management controversies."); Thomas Schultz, *Transnational Legality: Stateless Law and International Arbitration* 177 (2014) ("Various studies have converged in their findings: the practice of following arbitral precedents is almost inexistent in the field of international commercial arbitration . . . , commonplace and increasingly frequent in investment arbitration . . . , and routine in sports arbitrations.").

7   *See* Andrea K. Bjorklund, "Investment Treaty Arbitral Decisions as *Jurisprudence Constante*," in *International Economic Law: The State and Future of the Discipline* 265, 272 (Colin B. Picker et al. eds., 2008) ("A better analogy is to the '*jurisprudence constante*' of the French civil law tradition."); Elkouri & Elkouri, *How Arbitration Works* at 621 (analogizing arbitration to civil-law cases in which lines of precedent gain force); *see also Black's Law Dictionary* 985 (Bryan A. Garner ed., 10th ed. 2014) (defining *jurisprudence constante* as "[t]he doctrine that a court should give great weight to a rule of law that is accepted and applied in a long line of cases, and should not overrule or modify its own decisions unless clear error is shown and injustice will arise from continuation of a particular rule of law").

8   Jackson H. Ralston, *International Arbitration from Athens to Locarno* 84 (1929) ("[M]any arbitral tribunals have decided expressly that they did not consider themselves bound by the prior decisions of other arbitrators and have acted accordingly; nor are they bound, as they have repeatedly declared, by their own decisions.").

awards to guide their own.[9] For many years now, the trend has been toward a greater use of precedent.[10]

The real issue is the weight to be accorded to precedent.[11] Arbitrators may be likely to use precedent—and just not under a version of stare decisis. Essentially, weight is ascribed to the principle and reasoning within an award, not to the award itself.[12] That is, arbitrators may rely on the principle of the award, without considering the award itself as being inherently valuable.[13] So it isn't uncommon for a line of precedents to be transformed into a "substantive principle."[14] As one commentator notes, "precedent is not used in labor arbitrations, but there is frequent reliance on

---

9 *Id.* ("Notwithstanding the foregoing, the arbitrators have frequently referred for their rules of action to the decisions of prior international tribunals."); Gabrielle Kaufmann-Kohler, "Is Consistency a Myth?," in *Precedent in International Arbitration* 137, 147 (Emmanuel Gaillard & Yas Banifatemi eds., 2008) (discussing international investment arbitration and the role of precedent: "Consistency is not a myth. Consistency is a reality and a necessary objective at the same time.").

10 Jeffery P. Commission, *Precedent in Investment Treaty Arbitration: A Citation Analysis of a Developing Jurisprudence*, 24 J. Int'l Arb. 2, 149–51 (2007) (discussing multiple studies and figures showing a trend toward more frequent citations and reliance on precedent).

11 Andrés Rigo Sureda, "Precedent in Investment Treaty Arbitration," in *International Investment Law for the 21st Century: Essays in Honour of Christoph Schreuer* 830, 835–36 (Christina Binder et al. eds., 2009) ("A review of decisions and awards shows that the practice of tribunals varies and that it could be classified in four categories depending on the weight attributed to precedent in their reasoning.").

12 Jan Paulsson, "The Role of Precedent in Investment Arbitration," in *Arbitration Under International Investment Agreements* 699, 710 (Katia Yannaca-Small ed., 2010) ("It might be said that precedents command respect only when the propositions they uphold are so clear that they would have carried the day in any event."); Bjorklund, "Investment Treaty Arbitral Decisions" at 272 (While discussing her analogy to French jurisprudence *constante*, she states: "[D]ecisions of other tribunals construing identical or similar treaty provisions would be viewed as persuasive to the extent they were well reasoned.").

13 Elkouri & Elkouri, *How Arbitration Works* at 625 ("[A] substantive principle might be revealed through a single well-reasoned decision, which becomes the 'leading case' on the point.").

14 *See id.* at 623–25 ("The controversy over use of awards as precedents is accompanied by a related and integrated controversy regarding development of substantive principles through arbitration.").

embedded principles."[15] One survey of labor arbitrators showed that 77% favored giving "some weight" to precedent.[16]

As the use of precedent in whatever form becomes expected in arbitral awards, it may eventually be required to support the reasoning.[17] But today, an arbitral award based solely on precedent might be annulled.[18]

Although most arbitrators are quick to disclaim that they apply any version of stare decisis, it is unclear how meaningful any distinction between judicial stare decisis and their own use of precedent is.[19] Sometimes precedent, under the guise of a substantive principle, ends up becoming law.[20]

---

15   Timothy J. Heinsz, *Grieve It Again: Of Stare Decisis, Res Judicata and Collateral Estoppel in Labor Arbitration*, 38 B.C. L. Rev. 275, 277 (1997) ("Some views have become so embedded in labor arbitration jurisprudence that, although not technically binding precedents, arbitrators almost universally apply these principles.").

16   Elkouri & Elkouri, *How Arbitration Works* at 605 ("An extensive survey of labor arbitration disclosed that 77% of the 238 responding arbitrators believed that precedents, even under other contracts, should be given 'some weight.'").

17   Bjorklund, "Investment Treaty Arbitral Decisions" at 278 (A "requirement is often that arbitrators find adequate reasons for their awards. Thus, an arbitral tribunal that does not take into account prior decisions risks its decision being set-aside, vacated, or not enforced.").

18   *The Oxford Handbook of International Investment Law* 1195 (Peter Muchlinski et al. eds., 2008) ("[A]n application for annulment that alleges an excess of powers or a failure to state reasons because the tribunal has simply relied on earlier decisions without making an independent decision or developing its own reasons is entirely possible.").

19   Ralston, *International Arbitration from Athens to Locarno* at 84 ("[A] certain weight is given to judicial decisions, and a certain law-establishing force, whether the principle of stare decisis be or be not accepted as an obligatory rule. Students of jurisprudence know that the difference is not so great as is commonly supposed.") (quoting John Bassett Moore, *International Law and Some Current Illusions and Other Essays* 118 (1924)); Gabrielle Kaufmann-Kohler, "Interpretation of Treaties: How Do Arbitral Tribunals Interpret Dispute Settlement Provisions Embodied in Investment Treaties?," in *Pervasive Problems in International Arbitration* 257, 274 (Loukas A. Mistelis & Julian D.M. Lew eds., 2006) ("[I]ntroducing a doctrine of precedent or stare decisis. . . . would not serve much of a purpose . . . . [A]rbitrators are indeed rather deferential.").

20   Gabrielle Kaufmann-Kohler, *Arbitral Precedent: Dream, Necessity or Excuse? The 2006 Freshfields Lecture*, 23 Arb. Int'l 357, 361 (2007) ("A series of CAS awards consistently has upheld this principle. The World Anti-Doping Code codified this arbitral practice."); Commission, *Precedent in Investment Treaty Arbitration*, 24 J. Int'l Arb. at 132 ("Given that international law develops principally

Practices vary in given fields. For example, although reliance on precedent is rare in commercial arbitrations, it's the norm in the specialized field of sports law.[21] Nearly every sports-law decision now cites earlier awards.[22] And when these decisions relate to the World Anti-Doping Code, the awards have created rules: one such rule was subsequently even codified.[23] One learned commentator has concluded that "true stare decisis" exists "within the field of sports arbitrations."[24]

Prior awards are effectively the law of certain fields—often those with permanent arbitrators.[25] In hosiery, prior awards are said to be the "common law" of the industry.[26] And the United States Postal Service model for arbitration has expressly adopted stare decisis for decisions by a national-level arbitrator.[27] One NAFTA award declared that an arbitrator should state a reason for departing from precedent—despite language in NAFTA restricting the precedential value of an award.[28]

---

through case law, the precedential value of each decision, award, and order, is, rightly or wrongly, tremendously significant."); Paulsson, "The Role of Precedent in Investment Arbitration" at 704 ("Numerous arbitral awards have made a distinct contribution to international law by reason of their scope, their elaboration, and the conscientiousness with which they have examined the issue before them.").

21 Schultz, *Transnational Legality* at 177 ("Various studies have converged in their findings: the practice of following arbitral precedents is almost inexistent in the field of international commercial arbitration . . . , commonplace and increasingly frequent in investment arbitration . . . , and routine in sports arbitrations.").

22 Kaufmann-Kohler, *Arbitral Precedent*, 23 Arb. Int'l at 365.

23 See id.

24 Id.

25 Elkouri & Elkouri, *How Arbitration Works* at 605 ("An extensive survey of labor arbitration disclosed that 77% of the 238 responding arbitrators believed that precedents, even under other contracts, should be given 'some weight.'").

26 Id. at 611.

27 See Gamble v. U.S. Postal Serv., 48 M.S.P.R. 228 (M.S.P.B. 1991) ("The Postal Service model of national arbitration follows the principle of *stare decisis*, in which the decision of one national-level arbitrator regarding an interpretive issue binds all other arbitrations considering the issue within the context of the same fact pattern.").

28 *Contemporary Issues in International Arbitration and Mediation: The Fordham Papers 2011* 51 (Arthur W. Rovine ed., 2011) ("While not discussing the issue of precedent in terms of a duty, the tribunal articulated its view that a NAFTA tribunal 'should indicate its reasons for departing from a major

The modern tendency of arbitrators toward using stare decisis was probably inevitable. All the parties involved in arbitration have an interest in consistency.[29] Therefore, when serving as arbitrators, lawyers and nonlawyers alike gravitate toward the notion of precedent.[30]

Still, obstacles remain. For some arbitrators, merely having different parties to the same contract will change the nature of the dispute and require a new application.[31] For arbitral awards to serve effectively as precedent, some kind of organized system is required.[32] As long as publication remains the exception rather than the rule in arbitrations, most might-be precedents remain buried, diminishing the value of the remainder.[33] But conversely, as one commentator has aptly said, "the only conceivable way of preventing a body of caselaw from developing in . . . arbitration would have involved a total ban on publication."[34]

---

trend of previous reasoning.'") (quoting an arbitral decision); North American Free Trade Agreement art. 1136(1) ("An award made by a Tribunal shall have no binding force except between the disputing parties and in respect of the particular case.").

29   Sureda, "Precedent in Investment Treaty Arbitration" at 835–36 ("As noted at the beginning, precedents have been the subject of attention because of the need for consistency in developing a jurisprudence *constante*.").

30   Roger A. Shiner, *Legal Institutions and the Sources of Law* 89 (2005); Elkouri & Elkouri, *How Arbitration Works* at 605 ("[I]t is important to note that many of the arbitrators who give precedential force to prior awards are not lawyers.").

31   Elkouri & Elkouri, *How Arbitration Works* at 620 ("[D]espite the great similarity of contract provisions and their apparent common origin and despite the fact of similarity of parties . . . [t]he parties are not the same parties. Their practices are not identical.").

32   Commission, *Precedent in Investment Treaty Arbitration*, 24 J. Int'l Arb. at 157 ("[I]t would be useful to organize the burgeoning corpus of precedents in an orderly system to ensure that the right awards and decisions flourish. Given the similarity of terms of investment treaties, and the related claims brought in investment arbitrations, a form of 'head note' and 'key number' system is both appropriate and fitting."); Bjorklund, "Investment Treaty Arbitral Decisions" at 275 ("The public availability of decisions in investment treaty arbitrations is crucial to the development of a jurisprudence *constante*.").

33   Elkouri & Elkouri, *How Arbitration Works* at 622 ("[T]he vast body of arbitration decisions by the most experienced arbitrators have never been published and . . . if there is a body of arbitral law it may be likened to an iceberg, of which only the tip is perceptible.").

34   Commission, *Precedent in Investment Treaty Arbitration*, 24 J. Int'l Arb. at 136 (quoting Fabien Gelinas, "Investment Tribunals and the Commercial

Then again, there's the analogous issue of why certain court decisions are precedential while others aren't. Multijudge appellate decisions are given precedential effect, while multijudge trial-court decisions aren't—much less single-judge trial-court decisions. Doubtless arbitrations are more akin to trials than they are to appeals. Hence despite the practice in some specialties of heeding what prior arbitrators have done, it seems unlikely that arbitral awards will ever be formally recognized as having binding status.

Arbitration Model: Mixed Procedures and Creeping Instiutionalism," in *Sustainable Development in World Trade Law* 475, 585 (Markus W. Gehring & Marie-Claire Cordonier Segger eds., 2005)). *See* Elkouri & Elkouri, *How Arbitration Works* at 604 ("The effects of publishing domestic arbitration awards are inevitable . . . . The fact of publication itself creates the atmosphere of precedent.") (quoting Leo Cherne, *Should Arbitration Awards Be Published?*, 1 Arb. J. 75 (1946)).

Epilogue

You may well have concluded by now that the law of judicial precedent is a dizzying matrix of doctrines and subdoctrines. That it is. And it's an ever-expanding matrix, as legal disputes grow ever more diverse—and therefore so do the decisions disposing of them.

In this book, we've provided a compendium of the law as it stands in 2016. A century from now, there will doubtless exist several additional doctrines and subdoctrines—which could never be guessed at today. Yet we feel confident that if history teaches us anything, the essence of most of the law we've discussed here will remain valid a century hence. Only because change is gradual do we have stability in the law. That idea is at the root of precedent.

Writing the book has prompted your coauthors to think about both the art of writing opinions and the task, and occasional joy, of reading them. A few closing observations come to mind.

Consider why judges must write at all. Given the power that courts exercise over people and institutions, our legal system has long insisted that judges, especially appellate judges, must explain in writing why they exercise their power as they do in a particular matter. Does the reason lie in a contract? In a statute? In a state or federal constitution? In an earlier judicial decision? Why, to take the usual dichotomy, does one side win and the other lose? The first objective of opinion-writing should be to answer these questions—to explain the result to the litigants, especially the losing side.

Opinion-writing forces judges not only to explain publicly why they decide as they do today but also to embrace reasoning that will apply to different litigants at a future time. That's the essence of equal justice under law: decisions that articulate a legal principle uniformly applicable to known litigants today and unknown litigants of the future. It's one thing to say that justice is blind; it's quite another to show as much in a later case.

Hence the vexing challenge of opinion-writing and a central theme of the book: how and when do judges decide whether to follow a precedent or to distinguish it? Stated differently, when should a principle of decision be fixed, and when mutable? This is no small matter. The questions raise the issue that justice isn't always blind—that courts sometimes announce a principle before one set of litigants but later vary it for newly seen litigants based on distinctions that seem more gossamer than substantial.

Opinion-writing minimizes the risk by promoting transparency. If a fair-minded reading of a certain precedent suggests problems in applying the law, the opinion should be criticized. Fair criticism encourages courts to deal with problems in any of several ways—to acknowledge a defect while standing by the principle on stare decisis grounds, to marginalize a questionable precedent so that it might rarely if ever be used again, or, if need be, to overrule the decision.

Long-serving judges acquire respect both for the difficulty of the immediate contest and for the decisional labors of their judicial forerunners. Judges accord respect to other branches of government in resolving constitutional claims against them. They should also accord respect to their predecessors' opinions. Appellate judges in particular have another source of assistance. They don't work alone: when current colleagues have insights of their own and bring different perspectives to the question to be decided, the decisions benefit from being a collective enterprise.

All judges have experienced rereading their own earlier opinions only to realize that what once seemed clear no longer seems so in light of new developments, new facts, and a new dispute. While judicial tenure tends to increase one's knowledge of law, it also increases one's humility about predicting the future and one's understanding of the perils of overwriting. Stare decisis quite properly rests on an assumption of judicial fallibility—both in its stability-seeking norm of standing by past mistakes and in its occasional allowance for overruling those mistakes. That's as it should be in this quintessentially human endeavor.

Shorter opinions, we tend to think, are often better than long ones. Overwriting often adds grounds for distinction, exacerbates the potential for confusion among future lawyers interpreting the decision for clients, and runs the risk of extending to unanticipated disputes that might better warrant a different rule. That isn't to say that judges should always be parsimonious with their insights along the way, even when expressing these amounts to doing more than deciding the case at hand. Separate opinions may usefully suggest how a doctrine should bend this way or that, or for that matter be reconsidered altogether.

In hard cases, judges rarely have binding precedents, or four-square holdings, to dictate the outcome. That's what makes hard cases hard. Good judges, like good lawyers, must mine relevant sources for guidance—and ought to be grateful whenever they find it.

Glossary

abstract question. See **hypothetical question.**

adjudicative law. See **caselaw.**

adverse authority. See **authority.**

advisory opinion. See **opinion.**

affirm, *vb.* To confirm, ratify, or approve (a lower court's judgment) on appeal. Cf. **overrule; vacate; reverse.**

affirmance, *n.* The formal confirmation by an appellate court of a lower court's judgment, order, or decree. Cf. **reversal.**

American common law. See **common law (2).**

amicable action. See *test case* under **case.**

analogy. A corresponding similarity or likeness. In logic, an inference that if two or more things are similar in some ways, they must be alike in others.—**analogical,** *adj.*

ancient decision. See **decision.**

Anglo-American common law. See *American common law* under **common law (2).**

antiformalism. An interpretive method that permits, or even encourages, a judge to consider nontextual sources such as abstract purpose, legislative intent, and public policy when interpreting a statute, thereby giving the courts more discretion to make or create law. Cf. **formalism; purposivism; consequentialism; textualism.**—**antiformalist,** *n.*

appellate court. See **court.**

authoritative precedent. See *binding precedent* under **precedent.**

authority. A legal writing taken as definitive or decisive; esp., a judicial or administrative decision cited as a precedent <this case is good authority in Massachusetts>. • The term includes not only the decisions of tribunals but also statutes, ordinances, and administrative rulings.

▸ **adverse authority.** Authority that is unfavorable to an advocate's position. • Most ethical codes require counsel to disclose adverse authority in the controlling jurisdiction even if the opposing counsel has not cited it.

- **binding authority.** See *imperative authority.*
- **imperative authority.** Authority that is absolutely binding on a court.—Also termed *binding authority.* See *binding precedent* under **precedent.**
- **persuasive authority.** Authority that carries some weight but is not binding on a court, often from a court in a different jurisdiction.
- **primary authority.** Authority that issues directly from a lawmaking body; legislation and the reports of litigated cases.
- **secondary authority.** Authority that explains the law but does not itself establish it, such as a treatise, annotation, or law-review article.

binding authority. See *imperative authority* under **authority.**

binding precedent. See **precedent.**

borrowed-constitutional-provision doctrine. The principle that if a state has adopted a constitutional provision identical to one in another state's constitution, an interpretation of it by the other state's high court may be considered as persuasive authority.

borrowed-statute doctrine. The proposition that if a legislature enacts a statute copied (borrowed) from another jurisdiction, the courts of the borrowing state are bound by any settled judicial construction of the statute in the lending state. *See Cathcart v. Robinson,* 30 U.S. (5 Pet.) 264, 264–65 (1831).—Also termed *borrowed-statutes doctrine.* Cf. **prior-construction canon.**

case. A civil or criminal proceeding, action, suit, or controversy at law or in equity <the parties settled the case>.
- **case of first impression.** A case that presents the court with an issue of law that has not previously been decided by any controlling legal authority in that jurisdiction.
- **hypothetical case.** A supposititious case posed merely to test a standard or principle as it might apply to the fabricated fact situation.
- **test case. 1.** A lawsuit brought to establish an important legal principle or right. • Such an action is frequently brought by the parties' mutual consent on agreed facts—when that is so, a test case is also sometimes termed *amicable action* or *amicable suit.*

The lawyer must have a good-faith basis for believing that the law or ruling challenged can be argued to be invalid on constitutional or other legal grounds. 2. An action selected from several suits that are based on the same facts and evidence, raise the same question of law, and have a common plaintiff or a common defendant. • Sometimes, when all parties agree, the court orders a consolidation and all parties are bound by the decision in the test case.—Also termed *test action*.

caselaw. The law to be found in the collection of reported cases that form all or part of the body of law within a given jurisdiction.—Also written *case law*; *case-law*.—Also termed *decisional law*; *adjudicative law*; *jurisprudence*; *organic law*. See **common law (1)**; *unwritten law* under **law**.

case of first impression. See **case**.

case-or-controversy requirement. The constitutional requirement that, for a federal court to hear a case, the case must involve an actual dispute. See *advisory opinion* under **opinion**.

certification. A procedure by which a federal appellate court asks the U.S. Supreme Court or the highest state court to review a question of law arising in a case pending before the appellate court and on which it needs guidance. • Certification is commonly used with state courts, but the U.S. Supreme Court has steadily restricted the number of cases it reviews by certification. *See* 28 U.S.C. § 1254(2). Cf. **certiorari**.

certiorari (sər-shee-ə-rair-ı *or* -rair-ee *or* -rah-ree). An extraordinary writ issued by an appellate court, at its discretion, directing a lower court to deliver the record in the case for review. • The writ evolved from one of the prerogative writs of the English Court of King's Bench, and in the United States it became a general appellate remedy. The U.S. Supreme Court uses certiorari to review most of the cases that it decides to hear.—Abbr. cert.—Also termed *writ of certiorari*. Cf. **certification**.

certworthy, *adj.* (Of a case or issue) deserving of review by writ of certiorari.—**certworthiness,** *n.*

circuit court. See **United States Court of Appeals**.

civil law. 1. (*usu. cap.*) One of the two prominent legal systems in the Western world, originally administered in the Roman Empire and still influential in continental Europe, Latin America, Scotland, and Louisiana, among other parts of the world; Roman law. Cf. **common law (2). 2.** The body of law imposed by the state, as opposed to moral law. **3.** The law of civil or private rights, as opposed to criminal law or administrative law.—Abbr. CL.

claim preclusion. See **res judicata.**

coercive precedent. See *binding precedent* under **precedent.**

collateral estoppel. 1. The binding effect of a judgment as to matters actually litigated and determined in one action on later controversies between the parties involving a different claim from that on which the original judgment was based. **2.** A doctrine barring a party from relitigating an issue determined against that party in an earlier action, even if the second action differs significantly from the first one.—Also termed *issue preclusion.* Cf. **res judicata.**

comity (kom-ə-tee). A principle or practice among political entities (as countries, states, or courts of different jurisdictions) whereby legislative, executive, and judicial acts are mutually recognized. See **federal-comity doctrine.**

common law. 1. The body of law derived from judicial decisions, rather than from statutes or constitutions; **caselaw** <federal common law>. Cf. *statutory law* under **law.**

▸ **federal common law.** The body of decisional law derived from federal courts when adjudicating federal questions and other matters of federal concern, such as disputes between the states and foreign relations, but excluding all cases governed by state law. • An example is the nonstatutory law applying to interstate streams of commerce.

▸ **general federal common law.** In the period before *Erie Railroad v. Tompkins*, 304 U.S. 64 (1938), the judge-made law developed by federal courts in deciding disputes in diversity-of-citizenship cases. • Since *Erie*, a federal court has been bound to apply the substantive law of the state in which it sits.

So even though there is a "federal common law," there is no longer a *general* federal common law applicable to all disputes heard in federal court.

2. The body of law based on the English legal system, as distinct from a civil-law system; the general Anglo-American system of legal concepts, together with the techniques of applying them, that form the basis of the law in jurisdictions where the system applies <all states except Louisiana have the common law as their legal system>. Cf. **civil law (1)**.

▸ **American common law.** 1. The body of English law that was adopted as the law of the American colonies and supplemented with local enactments and judgments. 2. The body of judge-made law that developed during and after the United States' colonial period, esp. since independence.—Also termed *Anglo-American common law*.

conclusion of law. 1. An inference on a question of law, made as a result of a factual showing, no further evidence being required; a legal inference. 2. A judge's final decision on a legal point raised in a trial or hearing, particularly one that is vital to reaching a judgment. Cf. **finding of fact**.

concurral, *n.* A judicial opinion expressing agreement with a court's denial of rehearing en banc or appellate review. Cf. **dissental**.

concurrence. See *concurring opinion* under **opinion**.

concurrent jurisdiction. See **coordinate jurisdiction**.

concurring opinion. See **opinion**.

consequentialism. An interpretive theory that judges the rightness or wrongness of a judge-interpreter's reading according to its extratextual consequences. Cf. **antiformalism; formalism; textualism; purposivism**.—**consequentialist,** *adj.*

controlling law. See **law**.

converse-*Erie* doctrine. See **reverse *Erie* doctrine**.

coordinate jurisdiction. 1. Jurisdiction that might be exercised simultaneously by more than one court over the same subject matter and within the same territory, a litigant having the right to choose the court in which to file the action. 2. Jurisdiction shared by two or more states, esp. over the physical boundaries (such as rivers or other bodies of water) between them.—Also termed *concurrent jurisdiction*.

court. 1. A tribunal constituted to administer justice; esp., a governmental body consisting of one or more judges who sit to adjudicate disputes <a question of law for the court to decide>. 2. The judge or judges who sit on such a tribunal <the court asked the parties to approach the bench>. 3. A legislative assembly <in Massachusetts, the General Court is the legislature>. 4. A place where justice is judicially administered; the locale for legal proceedings <an out-of-court statement>. 5. The building where the judge or judges convene to adjudicate disputes and administer justice <the lawyers agreed to meet at the court at 8:00 a.m.>.— Also termed (in senses 1 & 2) *law court*; (in sense 5) *courthouse*.

- **appellate court.** A court with jurisdiction to review decisions of lower courts or administrative agencies.—Also termed *appeals court*; *appeal court*; *court of appeals*; *court of appeal*; *court of review*. See *court of appeals*.
- **circuit court.** See **United States Court of Appeals.**
- **court not of record.** An inferior court that is not required to routinely make a record of each proceeding and usu. does not.
- **court of appeals.** 1. An intermediate appellate court.—Also termed (as in California and England) *court of appeal*. See *appellate court*. Cf. **United States Court of Appeals.** 2. In New York and Maryland, the highest appellate court within the jurisdiction.
- **court of first instance.** See *trial court*.
- **court of last resort.** The court having the authority to handle the final appeal of a case, such as the U.S. Supreme Court.
- **court of record.** A court that is required to keep a record of its proceedings. • The court's records are presumed accurate and cannot be collaterally impeached.
- **divided court.** An appellate court whose opinion or decision in a particular case is not unanimous, esp. when the majority is slim, as in a 5-to-4 decision of the U.S. Supreme Court.
- **federal circuit court.** See **United States Court of Appeals.**

- **full court.** A court session that is attended by all the court's judges; an en banc court.
- **high court.** The court of last resort in a particular jurisdiction; a court whose decision is final and cannot be appealed because no higher court exists to consider the matter. • The U.S. Supreme Court, for example, is the highest federal court.
- **inferior court. 1.** Any court that is subordinate to the chief appellate tribunal within a judicial system. **2.** A court of special, limited, or statutory jurisdiction, whose record must show the existence of jurisdiction in any given case to give its ruling presumptive validity.—Also termed *lower court*.
- **intermediate court.** An appellate court that is below a court of last resort.
- **lower court.** See *inferior court*.
- **superior court. 1.** In some states, a trial court of general jurisdiction. **2.** In Pennsylvania, an intermediate court between the trial court and the chief appellate court.
- **territorial court.** A U.S. court established in a U.S. territory (such as the Virgin Islands) and serving as both a federal and state court. • The Constitution authorizes Congress to create such a court. U.S. Const. art. IV, § 3, cl. 2.
- **trial court.** A court of original jurisdiction where the evidence is first received and considered.—Also termed *court of first instance*.

decision. A judicial or agency determination of a particular issue after consideration of the facts and the law; esp., a ruling, order, or judgment pronounced by a court when considering or disposing of a case. Cf. **judgment; opinion; decree.**—**decisional,** *adj.*
- **ancient decision. 1.** *Archaic.* In the 19th century, a judicial determination from 1688 or before. **2.** Modernly, a judicial determination antedating the 20th century.
- **nonjudicial decision.** A legal determination rendered by a special tribunal or a quasi-judicial body.
- **solitary decision.** An isolated decision that has never been followed in any later decision.

- **split decision.** A decision in which not all the members of a multimember panel agree.
- **unanimous decision.** A decision in which all the members of a multimember panel agree.

decisional law. See **caselaw**.

declaratory precedent. See **precedent**.

decree. 1. Traditionally, a judicial decision in a court of equity, admiralty, divorce, or probate—similar to a judgment of a court of law <the judge's decree in favor of the will's beneficiary>. 2. A court's final judgment. Cf. **judgment; decision; opinion.**

deductive reasoning. See **reasoning**.

dictum. A judicial comment made while delivering a judicial opinion, but one that is unnecessary to the decision in the case and therefore not precedential (although it may be considered persuasive).—Also termed *obiter dictum*. Cf. **holding.** Pl. **dicta.**

- *dictum proprium* (dik-təm proh-pree-əm). A personal or individual dictum that is given by the judge who delivers an opinion but that is not necessarily concurred in by the whole court and is not essential to the disposition of the case.—Also termed (loosely) *dictum propria*.
- *gratis dictum* (gray-tis dik-təm). 1. A voluntary statement; an assertion that a person makes without being obligated to do so. 2. A court's stating of a legal principle more broadly than is necessary to decide the case. 3. A court's discussion of points or questions not raised by the record or its suggestion of rules not applicable in the case at bar.
- **judicial dictum.** An opinion by a court on a question that is directly involved, briefed, and argued by counsel, and even passed on by the court, but that is not essential to the decision and therefore not binding even if it may later be accorded some weight.

disposition. A final settlement or determination <the court's disposition of the case>.

dissent, *n.* See *dissenting opinion* under **opinion**.

dissental, *n.* A judicial opinion expressing disagreement with a court's denial of rehearing en banc or appellate review. Cf. **concurral.**

dissenting opinion. See **opinion.**

distinguish, *vb.* **1.** To note a significant factual, procedural, or legal difference in (an earlier case), usu. to minimize the case's precedential effect or to show that it is inapplicable <the lawyer distinguished the cited case from the case at bar>. **2.** To make a distinction <the court distinguished between willful and reckless conduct>.—**distinction,** *n.*

distinguishable, *adj.* (Of a case or law) different from, and thereby not controlling or applicable in, a given case or situation.

divided court. See **court.**

doctrine of precedent. 1. The rule that precedents not only have persuasive authority but also must be followed when similar circumstances arise. • This rule developed in the 19th century and prevails today. See **precedent; stare decisis. 2.** A rule that precedents are reported, may be cited, and will probably be followed by courts. • This is the rule that prevailed in England until the 19th century.

en banc (on **bongk** *or* en **bangk**), *adv.* & *adj.* With all judges present and participating; in full court <the court heard the case en banc> <an en banc rehearing>. Also spelled (in some states) *in banc*; *in bank.*

enbancworthy, *adj.* (Of an appellate case) worthy of being considered en banc <the Fifth Circuit concluded that two of the four issues are truly enbancworthy>.—**enbancworthiness,** *n.*

enthymeme (en-thə-meem). A syllogism in which one of the premises is suppressed; specif., an argument in which a legal or factual premise is unexpressed but implied. Cf. **syllogism.**

Erie **doctrine** (eer-ee). The principle that a federal court exercising diversity jurisdiction over a case that does not involve a federal question must apply the substantive law of the state where the court sits. *Erie Railroad v. Tompkins*, 304 U.S. 64 (1938). Cf. **reverse *Erie* doctrine.**

failure of justice. See **miscarriage of justice.**

federal circuit court. See **United States Court of Appeals.**

federal-comity doctrine. The principle encouraging federal district courts to refrain from interfering in each other's affairs. • Under this doctrine, a federal court has the discretion to transfer, stay, or dismiss a case that is duplicative of a case filed in another federal court. See **comity.**

federal common law. See **common law (1).**

federal law. See **law.**

finding of fact. A determination by a judge, jury, or administrative agency of a fact supported by the evidence in the record, usu. presented at the trial or hearing <he agreed with the jury's finding of fact that the driver did not stop before proceeding into the intersection>.—Often shortened to *finding.* Cf. **conclusion of law.**

follow, *vb.* To conform to or comply with; to accept as authority <the lawyer assumed that the Supreme Court would follow its own precedent>.

foreign law. See **law.**

foreign precedent. See **precedent.**

formalism (for-mə-liz-əm), *n.* **1.** An approach to law, and esp. to constitutional and statutory interpretation, holding that (1) when an authoritative text governs, meaning is to be derived from its words, (2) the meaning so derived can be applied to particular facts, (3) some situations are governed by that meaning, and some are not, and (4) the standards for deciding what constitutes following the rules are objectively ascertainable. **2.** Decision-making on the basis of form rather than substance; specif., an interpretive method whereby the judge adheres to the words rather than pursuing the text's unexpressed purposes (purposivism) or evaluating its consequences (consequentialism). Cf. **textualism; antiformalism; purposivism; consequentialism.**—**formalist,** *n.*

former adjudication. See **res judicata.**

full court. See **court.**

general federal common law. See **common law (1).**

gratis dictum. See **dictum.**

high court. See **court.**

holding, *n.* A court's determination of a matter of law pivotal to its decision; a principle drawn from such a decision. Cf. **dictum;** *ratio decidendi.*

horizontal precedent. See **precedent.**

horizontal stare decisis. See **stare decisis.**

hypothetical case. See **case.**

hypothetical question. A question posed on assumed facts, usu. changed facts, to discover or test how a given principle or rule would apply in one of several possible situations; esp., a judge's query posed to counsel to see what result a posited legal rule would yield under circumstances different from those in the case to be decided.—Also termed *abstract question.*

imperative authority. See **authority.**

in banc. See **en banc.**

in bank. See **en banc.**

inductive reasoning. See **reasoning.**

inferior court. See **court.**

institutional stare decisis. See **stare decisis.**

intermediate court. See **court.**

inverse-*Erie* doctrine. See **reverse** *Erie* **doctrine.**

inviolable (in-vi-ə-lə-bəl), *adj.* Safe from violation; incapable of being violated.—**inviolability,** *n.*

issue preclusion. See **collateral estoppel.**

judge-made law. See *unwritten law* under **law.**

judgment. A court's final determination of the rights and obligations of the parties in a case. • The term *judgment* includes an equitable decree and any order from which an appeal lies.—Also spelled (esp. BrE) *judgement.*—Abbr. J. Cf. **opinion; decision; decree.**

judicial dictum. See **dictum.**

judicial opinion. See **opinion.**

judicial policy. An established course of action often followed by courts as a matter of prudence and expeditious decision-making.

judiciary law. See *unwritten law* under **law**.

jurisprudence. Judicial precedents considered collectively; **caselaw**.

- *jurisprudence constante* (kən-**stan**-tee). The doctrine that a court should give great weight to a legal rule that is accepted and applied in a long line of cases, and should not overrule or modify its own decisions unless clear error is shown and injustice will arise from continuation of a particular legal rule. • Civil-law courts are not bound by the common-law doctrine of stare decisis. But they do recognize the doctrine of *jurisprudence constante*, which is similar to stare decisis, one exception being that *jurisprudence constante* does not command strict adherence to a legal principle applied on one occasion in the past. Cf. **stare decisis**.

law. 1. The regime that orders human activities and relations through systematic application of the force of politically organized society, or through social pressure, backed by force, in such a society; the legal system <respect and obey the law>. 2. The aggregate of legislation, judicial precedents, and accepted legal principles; the body of authoritative grounds of judicial and administrative action; esp., the body of rules, standards, and principles that the courts of a particular jurisdiction apply in deciding controversies brought before them <the law of the land>. 3. The set of rules or principles dealing with a specific area of a legal system <copyright law>. 4. The judicial and administrative process; legal action and proceedings <when settlement negotiations failed, they submitted their dispute to the law>. 5. A statute <Congress passed a law>.

- **caselaw.** See **caselaw**.
- **civil law.** See **civil law**.
- **common law.** See **common law**.
- **controlling law.** Law that governs a disposition because it has been issued by a court whose decisions must be followed and because the facts make the earlier decision indistinguishable from the case now to be decided.

- **federal law.** 1. The body of law consisting of the U.S. Constitution, federal statutes and regulations, U.S. treaties, and federal common law. See *statutory law*. Cf. *state law*. 2. A federal statute.
- **foreign law.** The law of another state or of a foreign country.
- **judge-made law.** See *unwritten law*.
- **judiciary law.** See *unwritten law*.
- **prospective law.** Law that applies to future events.
- **retroactive law.** A statute that looks backward or contemplates the past, affecting acts or facts that existed before the act came into effect. • A retroactive law is not unconstitutional unless it (1) is in the nature of an ex post facto law or a bill of attainder, (2) impairs the obligation of contracts, (3) divests vested rights, or (4) is constitutionally forbidden.—Also termed *retrospective law*.
- **state law.** 1. A body of law in a particular state consisting of the state's constitution, statutes, regulations, and common law. Cf. *federal law* (1). 2. A state statute.
- **statutory law.** The body of law derived from statutes rather than from constitutions or judicial decisions. See *federal law* (1). Cf. **common law (1).**
- **unwritten law.** A rule, custom, or practice that has not been enacted in the form of a statute or ordinance. • The term traditionally includes caselaw. Hence there certainly is a written memorial of the "unwritten law." The phrase simply denotes that this law does not originate in a writing such as a statute.—Also termed *judiciary law*; *judge-made law*. See **caselaw.** Cf. *written law*.
- **written law.** Statutory law, together with constitutions and treaties, as opposed to judge-made law. See *statutory law*. Cf. *unwritten law*.

law of the case. 1. The doctrine holding that a decision rendered in a former appeal of a case is binding in a later appeal. 2. An earlier decision giving rise to the application of this doctrine. Cf. **res judicata; stare decisis.**

law of the circuit. 1. The law as announced and followed by a U.S. Circuit Court of Appeals. **2.** The rule that one panel of judges on a U.S. circuit court of appeals should not overrule a decision of another panel of judges on the same court. **3.** The rule that an opinion of one U.S. circuit court of appeals is not binding on another circuit but may be considered persuasive.

legal principle. A background concept that may influence a court's decision despite not being outcome-determinative. (See pp. 77–78.)

legal reasoning. See **reasoning.**

local stare decisis. See **stare decisis.**

loose stare decisis. See **stare decisis.**

lower court. See *inferior court* under **court.**

main opinion. See *majority opinion* under **opinion.**

majority opinion. See **opinion.**

mandate rule. The principle that if matters have been explicitly or implicitly ruled on by an appellate court in a given case, they cannot later be relitigated in the trial court after a remand.

***Marks* rule.** The doctrine that when the U.S. Supreme Court issues a fractured, plurality opinion, the opinion of the justices concurring in the judgment on the narrowest grounds—that is, the legal standard with which a majority of the Court would agree—is considered the Court's holding. *Marks v. United States*, 430 U.S. 188 (1977).

memorandum opinion. See **opinion.**

minority opinion. See *dissenting opinion* under **opinion.**

miscarriage of justice. A grossly unfair outcome in a judicial proceeding, as when a defendant is convicted despite a lack of evidence on an essential element of the crime.—Also termed *failure of justice.*

mode of analysis. A conceptual tool that may influence a court when scrutinizing statutes or judicial decisions. • The canons of statutory construction are one significant mode of analysis. (See p. 79.)

nonjudicial decision. See **decision.**

obiter dictum (ob-i-tər dik-təm). See **dictum**.

official report. See **report**.

on all fours. (Of a law case) squarely on point (with a precedent) on both facts and law; nearly identical in all material ways <our client's case is on all fours with the Supreme Court's most recent opinion>.

opinion. A court's written statement explaining its decision in a given case, usu. including the statement of facts, points of law, rationale, and dicta.—Abbr. op.—Also termed *judicial opinion*. Cf. **judgment; decision; decree**.

> **advisory opinion.** A nonbinding statement by a court of its interpretation of the law on a matter submitted for that purpose. • Federal courts are constitutionally prohibited from issuing advisory opinions by the case-or-controversy requirement, but other courts, such as the International Court of Justice, render them routinely. See **case-or-controversy requirement**.

> **concurring opinion.** A separate written opinion explaining a vote cast by a judge in favor of the judgment reached, often on grounds differing from those expressed in the opinion or opinions explaining the judgment.—Also termed *concurrence*.

> **dissenting opinion.** An opinion by one or more judges who disagree with the decision reached by the majority.—Often shortened to *dissent*.—Also termed *minority opinion*.

> **majority opinion.** An opinion joined in by more than half the judges considering a given case.—Also termed *main opinion*.

> **memorandum opinion.** A unanimous appellate opinion that succinctly states the decision of the court; an opinion that briefly reports the court's conclusion, usu. without elaboration because the decision follows a well-established legal principle or does not relate to any point of law.—Also termed *memorandum decision; memorandum disposition*.

> **minority opinion.** See *dissenting opinion*.

> **per curiam opinion** (pər kyoor-ee-əm). An opinion handed down by an appellate court without identifying the individual

judge who wrote the opinion.—Sometimes shortened to *per curiam* (*per cur.*).

- **plurality opinion.** An opinion lacking enough judges' votes to constitute a majority, but receiving more votes than any other opinion.
- **seriatim opinions** (seer-ee-**ay**-tim). A series of opinions written individually by each judge on the bench, as opposed to a single opinion speaking for the court as a whole.
- **unpublished opinion.** An opinion that the court has specifically designated as not for publication. • Court rules usually prohibit citing an unpublished opinion as authority. Such an opinion is considered binding only on the parties to the particular case in which it is issued.
- **unwritten opinion.** An opinion delivered orally from the bench and not reduced to writing by the judge (though it may have been transcribed by someone present).

organic law. See **caselaw.**

original precedent. See **precedent.**

orthodox stare decisis. See *strict stare decisis* under **stare decisis.**

overrule, *vb.* **1.** To rule against; to reject <the judge overruled all of the defendant's objections>. **2.** (Of a court) to overturn or set aside (a precedent) by expressly deciding that it should no longer be controlling law <in *Brown v. Board of Education*, the Supreme Court overruled *Plessy v. Ferguson*>. Cf. **vacate; affirm; reverse.**

per curiam, *adv.* & *adj.* By the court as a whole. See *per curiam opinion* under **opinion.**

per curiam opinion. See **opinion.**

per incuriam (pər in-**kyoor**-ee-əm), *adj.* (Of a judicial decision) wrongly decided, usu. because the judge or judges were ill-informed about the applicable law.

personal stare decisis. See **stare decisis.**

persuasive authority. See **authority.**

persuasive precedent. See **precedent.**

plurality. The greatest number (esp. of votes), regardless of whether it is a simple or an absolute majority <a four-member plurality of

the Supreme Court agreed with this view, which received more votes than any other>.—Also termed *plural majority*.

plurality opinion. See opinion.

plural majority. See plurality.

positivism. 1. The doctrine that all true knowledge is derived from observable phenomena, rather than speculation or reasoning. 2. An approach to philosophy grounded in empirical facts that can be scientifically verified, as opposed to unverifiable assumptions.—positivist, *adj.* & *n.*

precedent (pres-ə-dənt), *n.* 1. Something of the same type that has occurred or existed before. 2. An action or official decision that can be used as support for later actions or decisions; esp., a decided case that furnishes a basis for determining later cases involving similar facts or issues. See **stare decisis; doctrine of precedent.**

▸ **binding precedent.** A precedent that a court must follow. • For example, a lower court is bound by an applicable holding of a higher court in the same jurisdiction.—Also termed *authoritative precedent; coercive precedent; binding authority.* See *imperative authority* under **authority.**

▸ **declaratory precedent.** A precedent that is merely the application of an already-existing legal rule.

▸ **foreign precedent.** 1. A precedent established in some other domestic jurisdiction from the one in which it is being considered. 2. A precedent established in some other country from the one in which it is being considered.

▸ **horizontal precedent.** A precedent established at an earlier sitting of the same court. See *horizontal stare decisis* under **stare decisis.**

▸ **original precedent.** A precedent that creates and applies a new legal rule. • An original precedent is usually created when the court distinguishes the matter to be decided from older cases.

▸ **persuasive precedent.** A precedent that is not binding on a court, but that is entitled to respect and careful consideration. • For example, if the case was decided in a neighboring jurisdiction, the court might evaluate the earlier court's reasoning without being bound to decide the same way.

- **precedent sub silentio** (səb sə-**len**-shee-oh). A legal question that was neither argued nor explicitly discussed in a judicial decision but that seems to have been silently ruled on and might therefore be treated as a precedent.
- **superprecedent. 1.** A precedent that defines the law and its requirements so effectively that it prevents divergent holdings in later legal decisions on similar facts or induces disputants to settle their claims without litigation. • This sense was posited by W. Landes and Richard A. Posner in *Legal Precedent: A Theoretical and Empirical Analysis*, 19 J. Law & Econ. 249, 251 (1976). **2.** A precedent that has become so well established in the law by a long line of reaffirmations that it is very difficult to overturn it; specif., a precedent that has been reaffirmed many times and whose rationale has been extended to cover cases in which the facts are dissimilar, even wholly unrelated, to those of the precedent. • For example, *Roe v. Wade* has been called a superprecedent because it has survived more than three dozen attempts to overturn it and has been relied on in decisions protecting gay rights and the right to die. Cf. *super stare decisis* under **stare decisis**.
- **vertical precedent.** A precedent established by a higher court within the same jurisdiction. See *vertical stare decisis* under **stare decisis**.

primary authority. See **authority**.

prior-construction canon. The doctrine that if a statute uses words or phrases that have already received authoritative construction by the jurisdiction's court of last resort, or even uniform construction by inferior courts or a responsible administrative agency, they are to be understood according to that construction. Cf. **borrowed-statute doctrine.**

prospective law. See **law**.

prospectivity. The quality, state, or condition of being concerned with or having reference to the future; esp., a statute's or legal ruling's effectiveness in the future. Cf. **retroactivity.**

▶ **selective prospectivity.** A court's decision to apply a new legal rule in the particular case in which the new rule is announced, but to apply the old rule in all other cases pending when the new rule is announced or cases in which the facts antedate the new rule's announcement.

purposivism (pər-pəs-iv-izm). The doctrine that texts are to be interpreted to achieve the broad purposes that their drafters had in mind; specif., the idea that a judge-interpreter should seek an answer not only in the words of the text but also in its social, economic, and political objectives. Cf. **antiformalism; formalism; textualism; consequentialism.**—**purposivist,** *adj.* & *n.*

ratio decidendi (ray-shee-oh des-ə-den-dı), *n.* **1.** The principle or legal rule on which a court's decision is founded <many poorly written judicial opinions do not contain a clearly ascertainable *ratio decidendi*>. **2.** The legal rule on which a later court thinks that a previous court founded its decision; a general rule without which a case must have been decided otherwise <this opinion recognizes the Supreme Court's *ratio decidendi* in the school desegregation cases>. • In this book, we avoid this expression in favor of the word *holding*.—Often shortened to *ratio*. Pl. *rationes decidendi* (ray-shee-oh-neez des-ə-den-dı). Cf. **dictum; holding.**

rationale (rash-ə-nal), *n.* **1.** A statement of reasons; specif., a reasoned explanation or exposition of principles that underlie an art, science, procedure, opinion, etc. <the rationale for osteopathy>. **2.** The logical basis for a procedure, fact, position, etc.; a foundation <the rationale for removing the case to federal court>.

reason, *n.* **1.** An expression or statement given by way of explanation or justification; whatever is supposed or affirmed to support a conclusion, inference, or plan of action <he proffered several reasons for the relief he requested>. **2.** A ground or cause that explains or accounts for something <weakened by reason of chronic illness>. **3.** The power of comprehending and inferring; collectively, the faculties that enable someone to think and draw conclusions; the normal exercise of rationality <reason itself

distinguishes humans from brutes>. **4.** A sound mind; sanity <he lost his reason>. **5.** Correct thinking; the mature consensus of informed thought within a community <listen to reason>. **6.** A premise, esp. a minor premise—that is, a factual statement that implicates the principle used in a syllogism <What is the reason for that conclusion?>. **7.** A reasonable act; whatever is right or befitting <she ought within reason to be excused>.

reason, *vb.* **1.** To attempt to arrive at a conclusion through close examination, inference, and thought; to form a specific judgment about a situation after carefully considering the facts <the ability to reason>. **2.** To examine or deduce by means of close analysis and thought; to infer or conclude <to reason why it happened>. **3.** To persuade or dissuade by marshaling grounds for proving; to influence by argument <she reasoned with him for two hours>. **4.** To present or discuss (pros and cons); to debate <to reason the point with the judge>.

reasoning. 1. The drawing of inferences or conclusions through a logical process. **2.** Ideas and opinions that are based on logical thinking.

- **deductive reasoning.** Reasoning that begins with a general statement or hypothesis and examines the possibilities before drawing a specific, logical conclusion. • Deductive reasoning can be expressed as a syllogism with a major premise ("All men are mortal"), a minor premise ("Socrates is a man"), and a conclusion ("Therefore, Socrates is mortal"). If the premises are true, the conclusion will be true.—Also termed *syllogistic reasoning.* See **syllogism.**

- **inductive reasoning.** Reasoning that begins with specific observations from which broad generalizations are drawn. • Even if the premises are true, the conclusion may be false.

- **legal reasoning.** A mode of thought typical of lawyers and judges, who in their work seek to apply legal rules to specific fact patterns to arrive at enforceable decisions.

reenactment. A legislature's passing a statute again for some purpose (such as codification) in substantially the same form as it has previously been in effect.

reenactment canon. 1. In statutory construction, the principle that when reenacting a law, the legislature implicitly adopts well-settled judicial or administrative interpretations of the law. **2.** The doctrine that if the legislature amends or reenacts a provision other than by way of a consolidating statute or restyling project, a significant change in language is presumed to entail a change in meaning.

remand, *n.* The act or an instance of sending a case or claim back to the court from which it came.

removal, *n.* The transfer of an action from state to federal court. • In removing a case to federal court, a litigant must timely file the removal papers and show a valid basis for federal jurisdiction.

render, *vb.* (Of a judge) to deliver formally (a judgment).

report. 1. A written account of a court proceeding and judicial decision. **2.** (*usu. pl.*) A published volume of judicial decisions by a particular court or group of courts.—Also termed *reporter.*

▸ **official report.** (usu. pl.) The governmentally approved set of reported cases within a given jurisdiction.

reporter. 1. The person responsible for publishing a court's opinion.—Also termed *reporter of decisions.* **2.** See **report.**

res judicata (rays joo-di-**kay**-tə or -**kah**-tə). **1.** An issue that has been definitively settled by judicial decision. **2.** An affirmative defense barring the same parties from litigating a second lawsuit on the same claim, or any other claim arising from the same transaction or series of transactions and that could have been—but was not—raised in the first suit. • The three essential elements are (1) an earlier decision on the issue, (2) a final judgment on the merits, and (3) the involvement of the same parties, or parties in privity with the original parties. Restatement (Second) of Judgments §§ 17, 24 (1982).—Also termed *claim preclusion*; *former adjudication*; *res adjudicata*; *doctrine of res judicata.* Cf. **collateral estoppel; law of the case; stare decisis.**

retroactive law. See **law.**

retroactivity. The quality, state, or condition of having relation or reference to, or effect in, a prior time; specif., (of a statute, regulation, ruling, etc.) the quality of becoming effective at some time before the enactment, promulgation, imposition, or the like, and of having application to acts that occurred earlier.— Also termed *retrospectivity*. Cf. **prospectivity**.

retrospective law. See *retroactive law* under **law**.

retrospectivity. See **retroactivity**.

reversal, *n*. An annulling or setting aside; esp., an appellate court's overturning of a lower court's decision. Cf. **affirmance**.

reverse, *vb*. To overturn (a judgment or ruling), esp. on appeal. Cf. **affirm; overrule; vacate**.

reverse *Erie* doctrine. The rule that a state court must apply federal law when state law is preempted by federal law or federal law prevails by an *Erie*-like balancing of the facts in situations not already regulated by Congress or the Constitution.—Often shortened to *reverse Erie*.—Also termed *converse-Erie doctrine*; *inverse-Erie doctrine*. Cf. ***Erie* doctrine**.

rule, *n*. **1.** A specific norm with a clear delineation; a norm that mandates or guides conduct or action in a specified type of situation. Cf. **standard**. **2.** A regulation governing a court's or agency's procedures.

rule of property. A general principle of law established by a judicial decision or series of decisions relating to the acquisition or devolution of title to real or personal property, or to the nature, incidents, or extent of a title, or to its encumbrance that has been relied on by the people as part of the law governing their transactions, and the reversal of which would destroy or impair existing titles or rights.

SCOTUS. *abbr.* Supreme Court of the United States. See **United States Supreme Court**.

secondary authority. See **authority**.

selective prospectivity. See **prospectivity**.

seriatim opinions. See **opinion**.

solitary decision. See **decision**.

split decision. See **decision**.

standard, *n*. A general norm for assessing quality, accuracy, or acceptability. Cf. **rule (1)**.

stare decisis (stahr-ee di-sɪ-sis or stair-ee), *n.* The doctrine of precedent, under which a court must follow earlier judicial decisions when the same points arise again in litigation.—Also termed *traditional stare decisis*; *institutional stare decisis.* See **precedent; doctrine of precedent (1).** Cf. **res judicata; law of the case;** (in civil law) *jurisprudence constante* under **jurisprudence.**
- **horizontal stare decisis.** The doctrine that a court, esp. an appellate court, must adhere to its own prior decisions, unless it finds compelling reasons to overrule itself. See *horizontal precedent* under **precedent.**
- **local stare decisis.** The doctrine that a group of judges making up a current court (as of a regional court of appeals or a subregional trial bench) should adhere to the previous exercises of judicial discretion within the group, so as to lead to greater consistency in judgments or voting patterns.
- **loose stare decisis.** The doctrine that a court will adhere to nonessential holdings that are adequately reasoned and germane to the case decided.
- **orthodox stare decisis.** See **strict stare decisis.**
- **personal stare decisis.** The doctrine that a judge will adhere to his or her own previous exercises of judicial discretion, so as to lead to a consistency in judgments or voting patterns.
- **strict stare decisis.** The doctrine that a court need adhere only to holdings necessary to the decision, not to nonessential holdings of any kind.—Also termed *orthodox stare decisis.*
- **super stare decisis.** The supposed doctrine that courts must follow earlier court decisions without considering whether those decisions were correct. • Critics argue that strict adherence to old decisions can result in grave injustices and cite as an example the repudiation of *Plessy v. Ferguson*, 163 U.S. 537 (1896), by *Brown v. Board of Education*, 347 U.S. 483 (1954). Cf. *superprecedent* under **precedent.**
- **vertical stare decisis.** The doctrine that a court must strictly follow the decisions handed down by higher courts within the same jurisdiction. See *vertical precedent* under **precedent.**

state law. See **law.**

statutory construction. 1. The act or process of interpreting a statute. 2. Collectively, the principles developed by courts for interpreting statutes. —Also termed *statutory interpretation.*

statutory law. See **law.**

strict stare decisis. See **stare decisis.**

superior court. See **court.**

superprecedent. See **precedent.**

super stare decisis. See **stare decisis.**

Supreme Court of the United States. See **United States Supreme Court.**

syllogism (sil-ə-jiz-əm), *n.* A three-part statement of a formal argument consisting of a major premise (an established rule), a minor premise (a factual statement showing the applicability or inapplicability of the rule to the present circumstance), and a conclusion (the application of the rule to the present circumstance). • Hence: *Every virtue is praiseworthy. Kindness is a virtue. Therefore, kindness is praiseworthy.* The two premises are related by a middle term (in that example *virtue*) that disappears in the conclusion. The truth of a syllogism depends on the truth of its premises. See *deductive reasoning* under **reasoning.** Cf. **enthymeme.**—**syllogistic,** *adj.*—**syllogize,** *vb.*

syllogistic reasoning. See *deductive reasoning* under **reasoning.**

territorial court. See **court.**

test action. See *test case* under **case.**

test case. See **case.**

textualism. The doctrine that the words of a governing text are of paramount concern and that what they fairly convey in their context is what the text means.—Also termed *verbal-meaning theory; textual interpretation.* Cf. **antiformalism; consequentialism; formalism; purposivism.**—**textualist,** *adj. & n.*

traditional stare decisis. See **stare decisis.**

trial court. See **court.**

unanimous decision. See **decision.**

United States Court of Appeals. A federal appellate court having jurisdiction to hear cases in one of the 13 judicial circuits of the United States (the First Circuit through the Eleventh Circuit, plus the District of Columbia Circuit and the Federal Circuit).—Also termed *circuit court*; *federal circuit court*. Cf. *court of appeals* under **court.**

United States Supreme Court. The court of last resort in the federal system, whose members are appointed by the President and approved by the Senate. • The Court was established in 1789 by Article III of the U.S. Constitution, which vests the Court with the "judicial power of the United States."—Abbr. SCOTUS.—Often shortened to *Supreme Court.*—Also termed *Supreme Court of the United States.*

unpublished opinion. See **opinion.**

unwritten law. See **law.**

unwritten opinion. See **opinion.**

vacate, *vb.* To nullify or cancel; make void; invalidate <the court vacated the judgment>. Cf. **overrule; affirm; reverse.**

verbal-meaning theory. See **textualism.**

vertical precedent. See **precedent.**

vertical stare decisis. See **stare decisis.**

writ of certiorari. See **certiorari.**

written law. See **law.**

Table of Cases

Abatie v. Alta Health & Life Ins. Co., 503
Abbas v. Foreign Policy Grp., 584, 586–87
Abbott v. Abbott, 755
Abbott v. City of Los Angeles, 421, 423
ACLU of Ky. v. McCreary Cnty., 70–71
ACLU of N.J. ex rel. Lander v. Schundler, 458, 495
Acosta v. Master Maint. & Constr. Inc., 71
Acute Care Specialists II v. United States, 168
Adams Outdoor Advert., L.P. v. Cnty. of Dane, 284
Ademodi v. State, 564
Adkins v. Children's Hosp., 367
Advisory Ops. re Constitutionality of 1972 PA 294, 276
Advisory Op. to Governor re Judicial Vacancy Due to Mandatory Ret., 134
Advisory Op. to the Governor, 135
Aerojet-General Corp. v. Askew, 653
Afran v. McGreevey, 636, 640
Afroyim v. Rusk, 190–91
AGI Assocs., LLC v. City of Hickory, 603, 608
Agostini v. Felton, 6, 29, 302, 330, 331, 391, 446, 468
Agricultural Labor Relations Bd. v. Laflin & Laflin, 446
AG Servs. of Am., Inc. v. Nielsen, 601
Air France v. Saks, 754
Air Line Pilots Ass'n, Int'l v. Eastern Air Lines, Inc., 499, 500, 506
Air Measurement Tech., Inc. v. Akin Gump Strauss Hauer & Feld, L.L.P., 699
Air Prods. & Chems., Inc. v. Hartford Accident & Indem. Co., 590
Ake v. Birnbaum, 384
Alabama Dep't of Pub. Safety v. Barbour, 284
Alabama NAACP v. Wallace, 491
Alabama State Fed'n of Labor v. McAdory, 599
Alabama-Tenn. Nat. Gas Co. v. Southern Nat. Gas Co., 278
Alaska Native Tribal Health Consortium v. Settlement Funds, 752
Albers v. Great Cent. Transp. Corp., 234
Albrecht v. Herald Co., 29, 302, 303, 323

Aldrich v. Aldrich (S.Ct. 1963), 622–23, 636
Aldrich v. Aldrich (S.Ct. 1964), 623, 636
Alexander v. Choate, 210–11
Alexander v. Gardner–Denver Co., 770
Alexander v. Gladden, 279, 283
Alexander v. Sandoval, 213
Alexander v. Turtur & Assocs., 698
Al–Harbi v. INS, 90
Al–Kidd v. Ashcroft, 33
Allaithi v. Rumsfeld, 38
Allen v. McCurry, 330, 373, 701
Alleyne v. United States, 31, 352
Alliance for Prop. Rights & Fiscal Responsibility v. City of Idaho Falls, 606
Allison v. UNUM Life Ins. Co., 643
Almendarez–Torres v. United States, 30, 31, 359
Alonso v. Blackstone Fin. Grp. LLC, 169
Alpha/Omega Ins. Servs., Inc. v. Prudential Ins. Co., 448
Al–Sharif v. U.S. Citizenship & Immigration Servs., 39
Alvarez v. Smith, 271
American Elec. Power Co. v. Connecticut, 574
American Home Prods. Corp. v. Lockwood Mfg. Co., 379–80
American Nat'l Prop. & Cas. Co. v. Julie R., 170
American Tower Corp. v. City of San Diego, 610–11
American Triticale, Inc. v. Nytco Servs., Inc., 606, 608
Amnesty Int'l USA v. Clapper, 502
Amoco Corp. v. Commissioner, 753
Anastasoff v. United States, 8, 148, 149
Anderson v. Creighton, 109, 484
Anker Energy Corp. v. Consolidation Coal Co., 201
Answer of the Justices to the Governor, 134–35, 273
Antelope, The, 221–22, 729
Antonio v. SSA Sec., Inc., 638, 642
Apprendi v. New Jersey, 30, 31, 359, 686, 687
Arizona v. California, 232, 441, 446, 454, 478, 479, 488, 589
Arizona v. Evans, 531

Arizona v. Gant, 237
Arizona v. Serna, 538
Arizona Christian Sch. Tuition Org. v. Winn, 87
Arizona Citizens Clean Elections Comm'n v. Brain, 294
Arizonans for Official English v. Arizona, 575, 599, 618, 633–35, 647, 675
Arizona State Legislature v. Arizona Indep. Redistricting Comm'n, 116
Arkansas Game & Fish Comm'n v. United States, 119–20
Arkansas Prof'l Bail Bondsman Licensing Bd. v. Oudin, 285
Armour & Co. v. Wantock, 82
Armstrong v. Exceptional Child Ctr., Inc., 346
Arno v. Club Med Inc., 756–57
Arnold v. Cleveland, 660
Aron v. United States, 126–27
ASARCO Inc. v. Kadish, 534, 552, 554, 555, 651, 689, 691
Ashcroft v. al-Kidd, 33, 109, 526
Ashcroft v. Iqbal, 187
Ashwander v. Tennessee Valley Auth., 79, 410
Askew v. Smith, 709
Asmussen v. Post Printing & Publ'g Co., 703
Assicurazioni Generali, S.p.A. v. Neil, 601, 604
Association of Bituminous Contractors, Inc. v. Apfel, 209
Association of Data Processing Serv. Orgs. v. Camp, 166
Astrue v. Capato ex rel. B.N.C., 646
AT&T Mobility LLC v. Concepcion, 540, 688
Atchison, Topeka & Santa Fe Ry. v. Pena, 37, 512
Atkins v. Virginia, 755
Atlantic Marine Constr. Co. v. United States Dist. Ct., 594–95
A.T. Massey Coal Co., Inc. v. Massanari, 201
ATSI Commc'ns, Inc. v. Shaar Fund, Ltd., 40
Attorney Gen. v. PowerPick Club of Mich., 284
Attorney Gen. of U.S. v. Covington & Burling, 131

August Entm't, Inc. v. Philadelphia Indem. Ins. Co., 724
Austin v. Kroger Texas L.P., 639, 642
Austin v. Michigan Chamber of Commerce, 354
Auto Equity Sales, Inc. v. Superior Court of Santa Clara Cnty., 33–34, 307
Avakian v. Citibank, N.A., 606
Awuah v. Coverall N. Am., Inc., 455
Ayrshire Collieries Corp. v. United States, 229
Babb v. Lozowsky, 304
Babbitt v. Sweet Home Chapter of Cmtys. for a Great Or., 4
Babcock v. Whatmore, 241
Backar v. Western States Producing Co., 613
Baggett v. Bullitt, 636
Bailey v. Federal Land Bank, 320
Bailey v. Lewis Farm, Inc., 224
Bakala v. Town of Stonington, 293
Baker v. Bolton, 743
Baker v. Grice, 541
Baker v. Nelson, 218, 354
Baker v. Outboard Marine Corp., 590
Baker v. Pataki, 223
Baker v. Town of Goshen, 134
Bakewell v. United States, 28
Baldasar v. Illinois, 206
Balmer v. Elan Corp., 375
Baltimore Orioles, Inc. v. Major League Baseball Players Ass'n, 594
Banco de Credito Indus., S.A. v. Tesoreria Gen., 758
Bank v. Fellowes, 191
Bank Markazi v. Peterson, 522
Bank of Am., N.A. v. Moglia, 40
Bank of Am. Nat'l Trust & Sav. Ass'n v. Parnell, 559
Bank of N.Y. v. Yugoimport, 596
Bank of Philadelphia v. Posey, 427, 428, 429, 434, 435
Banque Libanaise Pour le Commerce v. Khreich, 758
Barapind v. Enomoto, 116
Barber v. Thomas, 523
Barden v. Northern Pac. R.R., 391
Barkanic v. General Admin. of Civil Aviation of the People's Republic of China, 596
Barker v. Kallash, 77

TABLE OF CASES 813

Barks v. Armontrout, 607
Barland v. Eau Claire Cnty., 233
Barley v. South Fla. Water Mgmt. Dist., 276
Barney v. State, 750
Barnhart v. Sigmon Coal Co., 291
Barnhart v. Thomas, 228
Barron v. City of Baltimore, 661
Barwick v. Department of Interior, 506–07
Bass v. County of Butte, 613
Batson v. Kentucky, 385
Batts v. Tow-Motor Forklift Co., 591
Bauman v. DaimlerChrysler Corp., 502
Baumann v. Smrha, 437
Bayer Corp. v. DX Terminals, Ltd., 711
Beacon Oil Co. v. O'Leary, 376
Beaufort Cnty. Bd. of Educ. v. Beaufort Cnty. Bd. of Comm'rs, 649
Beck v. Shelton, 279, 282
BedRoc Ltd., LLC v. United States, 686
Behrendt v. Gulf Underwriters Ins. Co., 175
Bell v. Johnson, 37
Bell v. Presbytery of Boise, 180
Beneficial Consumer Disc. Co. v. Vukman, 165
Benjamins v. British European Airways, 535, 564
Bennett v. MIS Corp., 304, 386
Berger v. AXA Network LLC, 597
Bernstein v. Bankert, 638, 639
Berrington v. Wal–Mart Stores, Inc., 599
Berry v. Labor & Indus. Review Comm'n, 288
Best Life Assurance Co. v. Commissioner, 127, 128
Betts v. Brady, 191, 363
Beverly v. Division of Beverage of Dep't of Bus. Regulation, 278, 283
Bieber v. People, 745
Billigmeier v. County of Hennepin, 278, 281, 282
Billiot v. Puckett, 303–04, 492
Bingham v. United States, 87
Biotechnology Indus. Org. v. District of Columbia, 505
Birr v. State, 191
Bisso v. Inland Waterways Corp., 150

Black & White Taxicab & Transfer Co. v. Brown & Yellow Taxicab & Transfer Co., 577
Blackjack Bonding v. City of Las Vegas Mun. Court, 279
Blackwell v. Mississippi Bd. of Animal Health, 278
Blake v. Baker, 71
Blake v. Hoover Motor Co., 748
Blount v. Rizzi, 25
Blount v. Stroud, 293
Bluebeard's Castle, Inc. v. Delmar Mktg., Inc., 491
Blum v. Merrell Dow Pharm., Inc., 664–65, 666, 723
Board of Cnty. Comm'rs v. Lowery, 665
Board of Educ. of Louisville v. County Bd. of Educ. for Jefferson Cnty., 118
Board of Educ. Lands & Funds v. Gillett, 374, 375
Bocanegra v. City of Chicago Electoral Bd., 284
Bodum USA, Inc. v. La Cafetiere, Inc., 753
Boggio v. USAA Fed. Sav. Bank, 595
Bogle Farms, Inc. v. Baca, 422, 423, 425, 427, 429, 434, 435, 436
Bonanza, Inc. v. McLean, 151
Bond v. United States, 410
Bonito Partners, LLC v. City of Flagstaff, 284
Bonn v. City of Omaha, 279
Bonner v. City of Prichard, 5, 39, 244, 417, 492, 513
Booth v. Maryland, 190, 398
Boschetto v. Hansing, 172
Boston Tpk. Co. v. Town of Pomfret, 130
Boumediene v. Bush, 187, 522
Bowers v. Hardwick, 190, 353, 526, 549
Boyce's Ex'rs v. Grundy, 466
Boyd v. Alabama, 229
Boyer v. Atchison, Topeka & Santa Fe Ry., 693
Boyett v. Redland Ins. Co., 79
Boyle v. United Techs. Corp., 559
Boys Mkts., Inc. v. Retail Clerks Union, Local 770, 347, 348, 355
Bozo v. Central Coal & Coke Co., 659
Braden v. 30th Judicial City Court of Ky., 86
Bradley v. General Motors Corp., 613

Bradley v. Iowa Dep't of Pers., 278
Bradley v. Richmond Sch. Bd., 328
Bragdon v. Abbott, 346
Braniff Airways, Inc. v. Curtiss–Wright Corp., 590–91
Bravo v. United States, 608
Breaux v. Diamond M. Drilling Co., 52
Brewer v. Valk, 101
Brewster v. Commissioner, 380
Briggs v. Pennsylvania R.R., 466
Broad River Power Co. v. South Carolina ex rel. Daniel, 216
Brock v. Blackwood, 713
Brockett v. Spokane Arcades, Inc., 633
Brooks v. Central Bank of Birmingham, 418
Brooks v. Kimball Cnty., 747
Brooks v. Railway Co., 598
Brower v. State, 158
Brown v. Allen, 28, 219
Brown v. Argosy Gaming Co., 637, 640, 641, 642
Brown v. Board of Educ., 36, 177, 184, 323, 353, 356, 800, 807
Brown v. Commonwealth, 726
Brown v. Edwards Transfer Co., 250
Brown v. Felsen, 376
Brown v. First Nat'l Bank in Lenox, 508
Brown v. Hartlage, 57
Brown v. Phillipps, 656
Brown v. Wall, 430, 431
Browning v. Browning, 747
Browning v. Florida Prosecuting Attorneys Ass'n, 284
Browning–Ferris, Inc. v. Commonwealth, 282
Brownlow v. Schwartz, 133
Brulotte v. Thys Co., 337, 349, 350, 351, 431
Bruner v. Automobile Ins. Co. of Hartford, 301
Bruzas v. Richardson, 289
Bryant v. Civiletti, 612
Bryant v. Smith, 515
Buck v. Bell, 99, 100
Buckley v. Valeo, 215, 227
Bunting v. Mellen, 123
Burdick v. Takushi, 643
Burke v. Air Serv Int'l, Inc., 579
Burke v. Lewis, 289
Burkett v. Schwendiman, 138–39

Burlington N. R.R. v. Woods, 584
Burnet v. Coronado Oil & Gas Co., 9, 353
Burns v. Lukens, 118
Burns v. Pennsylvania Dep't of Corr., 109
Burns v. Wilson, 86
Burns Mfg. Co. v. Boehm, 308
Burr v. Boone, 134
Burris v. White, 278, 284
Burris Chem., Inc. v. USX Corp., 601–02
Burwell v. Hobby Lobby Stores, Inc., 83, 85, 86, 156, 359, 528
Buscaglia v. Ballester, 365
Busey v. District of Columbia, 419
Bush v. Gore, 216, 217, 523
Butler v. Balolia, 605
Butler v. Eaton, 329
Butler v. WinCo Foods, LLC, 136
Butterworth v. United States ex rel. Hoe, 54
Butz v. Glover Livestock Comm'n Co., 523–24
Byrd v. Blue Ridge Rural Elec. Coop., 580, 581
Cable Holdings of Ga., Inc. v. McNeil Real Estate Fund VI, Ltd., 382
Cacho v. Superior Court ex rel. Cnty. of Maricopa, 718
Calaf v. Gonzalez, 424, 425
Calder v. Bull, 670
Caldwell v. Mississippi, 549
Calhoun v. Yamaha Motor Corp., U.S.A., 596
California v. Greenwood, 660
California v. San Pablo & T.R. Co., 133–34
California v. Taylor, 745–46
California v. Thompson, 11
California Canning Peach Growers v. Myers, 134
Callins v. Collins, 359
Campbell v. Reynolds, 135
Campbell–Ewald Co. v. Gomez, 138
Camreta v. Greene, 40, 123, 491, 515
Candelario Del Moral v. UBS Fin. Servs. Inc., 608
Cannon v. Burge, 603
Cantwell v. Connecticut, 662
Cantwell v. University of Mass., 640
CAO Holdings, Inc. v. Trost, 284
Cardon v. Cotton Lane Holdings, Inc., 169

TABLE OF CASES 815

Cardtoons, L.C. v. Major League Baseball Players Ass'n, 501
Carey v. Federal Election Comm'n, 463
Carey v. Musladin, 107
Carlson v. McLyman, 131
Carolina Cas. Ins. Co. v. Yeates, 513
Carolina Trucks & Equip., Inc. v. Volvo Trucks of N. Am., Inc., 613
Carpenter v. Nobile, 740
Carpenters Local Union No. 26 v. U.S. Fid. & Guar. Co., 493
Carpentier v. Montgomery, 47
Carroll v. Carman, 33, 526
Carroll v. Kittle, 179
Carroll v. President & Comm'rs of Princess Anne, 139
Carstairs v. Cochran, 117
Carter v. Smith, 278
Castagnaro v. Bank of N.Y. Mellon, 638, 639, 641
Castañeda v. Souza, 223
Castellano v. Board of Trs. of Police Officers' Variable Supplements Fund, 673, 676–77
Castillo v. Industrial Comm'n, 306
Catalina Mktg. Sales Corp. v. Department of Treasury, 376
Cathcart v. Robinson, 749, 750, 786
Catlett v. State, 727
Catudal v. Browne, 166
Cavazos v. Smith, 527
Cayuga Indian Nation v. Cuomo, 412–13
Cedar Shake & Shingle Bureau v. City of Los Angeles, 280
Centennial Ins. Co. v. Ryder Truck Rental, Inc., 606
Central Bank of Denver, N.A. v. First Interstate Bank of Denver, N.A., 349
Central Green Co. v. United States (9th Cir. 1999), 68
Central Green Co. v. United States (S.Ct. 2001), 62, 67, 68–69
Central Trust Co. of N.Y. v. Citizens' St. Ry. of Indianapolis, 539
Central Va. Cmty. Coll. v. Katz, 71–72, 228
Cerro Wire & Cable Co. v. FERC, 136
Chadbourne & Parke LLP v. Troice, 106
Chamberlin v. State Farm Mut. Auto. Ins. Co., 389
Chambers v. O'Quinn, 267

Champlin Petroleum Co. v. Lyman, 684, 685–86
Chan v. Korean Air Lines Ltd., 491, 512, 515
Chandler v. Deaton, 49
Chandler v. Miller, 677
Chang v. Michiana Telecasting Co., 645
Chapman v. Pinellas Cnty., 34
Charleston Cnty. Sch. Dist. v. Harrell, 279
Chase v. American Cartage Co., 117
Chatman–Bey v. Thornburgh, 503
Chelentis v. Luckenbach S.S., 569
Chen v. Allstate Ins. Co., 138
Cheng Lin v. Board of Immigration Appeals, 537
Cherokee Nation of Okla. v. Leavitt, 25
Chesapeake & Ohio Ry. v. Martin, 679
Chester ex rel. NLRB v. Grane Healthcare Co., 38
Chevron Oil Co. v. Huson, 312
Chevron, U.S.A., Inc. v. Natural Res. Def. Council, Inc., 82, 163, 286–87, 288, 289, 446, 607, 854, 858, 860
Chicago & Iowa R.R. v. Pinckney, 658
Chicago, Burlington & Quincy Ry. v. Williams, 216
Chicago, Rock Island & Pac. Ry. v. Cobbs, 94
Chicago, Rock Island & Pac. Ry. v. National Fire Ins. Co., 95
Children's Hosp. of Birmingham, Inc. v. Kelley, 308
Chrismon v. Brown, 263–65
Christensen v. Harris Cnty., 287
Christianson v. Colt Indus. Operating Corp., 441–42, 455, 466, 469, 473, 474–75
Christopher v. Harbury, 522
Chrysler Credit Corp. v. Country Chrysler, Inc., 167
Church Point Wholesale Beverage Co. v. Tarver, 134
Cirino v. Hess Oil Virgin Islands Corp., 734
Citizens State Bank Norwood Young Am. v. Brown, 705
Citizens United v. Federal Election Comm'n, 36, 41, 187, 353, 354, 356, 399, 407
City & Cnty. of San Francisco v. Sheehan, 525, 526, 528
City of Berkeley v. Superior Court, 430, 431, 432, 433

City of Brainerd v. Brainerd Inv. P'ship, 281
City of Chicago v. Fieldcrest Dairies, Inc., 599
City of Columbus v. Hotels.com L.P., 640, 642
City of Corsicana v. Wren, 191
City of Dallas v. Abbott, 280
City of Detroit v. Public Utils. Comm'n, 117
City of Fort Worth v. Abbott, 283
City of Houston v. Hill, 635, 643
City of Jackson v. McFadden, 747
City of Las Cruces v. El Paso Elec. Co., 630–31
City of Los Angeles v. Lyons, 84, 85, 86, 88, 89, 90
City of Memphis v. Overton, 421, 423, 430, 432, 433
City of Meridian v. Southern Bell Tel. & Tel. Co., 674
City of Missoula v. Paffhausen, 720
City of Monterey v. Del Monte Dunes at Monterey, Ltd., 178
City of Montgomery v. Zgouvas, 724
City of North Wildwood v. Board of Comm'rs, 399
City of Norwood v. Horney, 665
City of Oakland v. Desert Outdoor Advert., Inc., 729, 730
City of Prescott v. Town of Chino Valley, 280
City of Roswell v. Jones, 191
City of San Jose v. Commissioner of Baseball, 335
Claflin v. Houseman, 534
Clark v. Luvel Dairy Prods., Inc., 747
Clark v. Uniroyal Corp., 669–70
Clark v. United States, 228
Clark Equip. Co. v. Lift Parts Mfg. Co., 494
Claudio v. State, 665
Clay v. Sun Ins. Office, 621, 622, 626
Clearfield Trust Co. v. United States, 558, 694
Clinton v. Jones, 186–87
Clohessy v. Bachelor, 164
Coastal Agric. Supply, Inc. v. J.P. Morgan Chase Bank, 608
Coca–Cola Co. v. Standard Bottling Co., 331–32

Coeur D'Alene Tribe of Idaho v. Hammond, 55
Coffey v. United States, 242
Cohen v. Alliant Enters., Inc., 52
Cohen v. Beneficial Indus. Loan Corp., 583, 642
Cohens v. Virginia, 58, 82, 120
Coito v. Superior Court, 242
Colby v. J.C. Penney Co., 376, 514, 515
Cold Metal Process Co. v. Republic Steel Corp., 380
Cole v. Rush, 307
Cole Energy Dev. Co. v. Ingersoll–Rand Co., 456, 457
Coleman v. Donahoe, 108
Coleman v. Johnson, 183–84
Colgrove v. Battin, 666
College Sports Council v. Department of Educ., 375
Collins v. Straight, Inc., 640
Colonial Park Country Club v. Joan of Arc, 640
Colorado v. Bertine, 681
Colorado v. New Mexico, 560
Colorado Ass'n of Pub. Emps. v. Lamm, 278
Colorado River Water Conservation Dist. v. United States, 211–12
Commerce Bank of St. Joseph, N.A. v. State, 179
Commissioner v. Estate of Bosch, 571, 598, 602, 603, 612, 647
Commonwealth v. Edmunds, 665
Commonwealth v. Hartnett, 750
Commonwealth v. Highhawk, 292
Commonwealth v. Jordan, 170
Commonwealth v. Leach, 746
Commonwealth v. LeClair, 262
Commonwealth v. Lopes, 744–45
Commonwealth v. Ludwig, 665
Commonwealth v. Mavredakis, 297
Commonwealth v. Morris, 738
Commonwealth v. Murdock, 418
Commonwealth v. Nole, 221
Commonwealth v. Starr, 473
Commonwealth v. Tilghman, 263, 600
Commonwealth v. Wasson, 663–64
Commonwealth ex rel. Berman v. Berman, 243

Commonwealth ex rel. Pappert v. Coy, 279, 280
Commonwealth ex rel. Tinder v. Werner, 727
Commonwealth Prop. Advocates, LLC v. Mortgage Elec. Registration Sys., Inc., 608
Compucredit Holdings Corp. v. Akanthos Capital Mgmt., LLC, 223
Comstock's Adm'r v. Jacobs, 738
Connally v. Georgia, 184
Connecticut Gen. Life Ins. Co. v. Speer, 733
Connecticut Light & Power Co. v. Local 420, IBEW, 773
Connecticut Nat'l Bank v. Germain, 292
Connecticut State Fed'n of Teachers v. Board of Educ. Members, 612–13
Consolidation Coal Co. v. UMWA Local 1545, 773
Constant v. Pacific Nat'l Ins. Co., 697
Continental Airlines v. Kiefer, 543–44
Converting/Biophile Labs., Inc. v. Ludlow Composites Corp., 707
Cook v. State, 191
Cooper v. Aaron, 34, 185
Cooper/T. Smith Stevedoring Co. v. Georgia Ports Auth., 695
Copart, Inc. v. Administrative Review Bd., U.S. Dep't of Labor, 449
Corporacion Venezolana de Fomento v. Vintero Sales Corp., 596
Cortes v. Ryder Truck Rental, Inc., 710, 711
Cortez v. McCauley, 503
Cottier v. City of Martin, 39, 507
Council 81 v. State, 278
Counselman v. Hitchcock, 104
County of Los Angeles v. Faus, 313, 316, 429
County of Washington v. Gunther, 84
Cousins v. Instrument Flyers, Inc., 710
Covell v. Bell Sports, Inc., 601
Covington v. Continental Gen. Tire, Inc., 64
Cox v. Hickman, 270
Cox v. Louisiana, 648
Craig v. Lake Asbestos of Quebec, Ltd., 278
Crawford v. Coleman ex rel. Shoaf (Tex. App.—Fort Worth 1985), 394
Crawford v. Coleman ex rel. Shoaf (Tex. 1987), 392, 394–95
Crawford v. Washington, 314–15, 548, 681, 689
Cray v. Deloitte Haskins & Sells, 632–33
Critical Mass Energy Project v. NRC, 39
Crocker v. Scott, 656
Croton Chem. Corp. v. Birkenwald, Inc., 221
Crowe v. Bolduc, 493
Crowell v. Benson, 649
Crump v. Lafler, 142
Cuevas v. United States, 122
Cunningham v. California, 261
Cunnyngham v. Shelby, 731
Curran v. Kwon, 753
Cuyler v. Adams, 562
Cyr v. Reliance Standard Life Ins. Co., 40, 500
Dagel v. Resident News, LLC, 162
Daily v. Swope, 723
DaimlerChrysler Corp. v. Cuno, 271
Daitom, Inc. v. Pennwalt Corp., 603
Danforth v. Minnesota, 313, 315
Danforth v. United States, 111
Dang v. UNUM Life Ins. Co., 596
Dannix Painting, LLC v. Sherwin–Williams Co., 602
Danse Corp. v. City of Madison Heights, 280
Darr v. Burford, 531
Dasher v. Stripling, 224
Data Tree, LLC v. Meek, 278
Davis v. Georgia, 227
Davis v. Greer, 264
Davis v. United States, 467
Davis v. Zoning Bd. of Adjustment, 241
Day v. Bond, 497
Day & Zimmerman, Inc. v. Challoner, 753
Dean Witter Reynolds, Inc. v. Byrd, 768
DeBoer v. Snyder, 218, 513
DeCarlo v. Bonus Stores, Inc., 642
Deckers Corp. v. United States, 39, 382
Dedham Water Co. v. Cumberland Farms Dairy, Inc., 458
DeElche v. Jacobsen, 391
Defenders of Wildlife v. EPA, 498, 504
De Herrera v. Gonzales, 107
Dejetley v. Kaho'ohalahala, 669
Delconte v. State, 279

DelCostello v. International Bhd. of Teamsters, 573
DeLovio v. Boit, 567–68
DeMartino v. Zurich Ins. Co., 317
Department of Revenue v. Kuhnlein, 273
Department of Transp. v. Kendricks, 301
Derungs v. Wal–Mart Stores, Inc., 606
Descamps v. United States, 587
Desist v. United States, 311
Detroit Trust Co. v. Barlum S.S. (The Thomas Barlum), 568
Deutsche Bank Nat'l Trust Co. v. Matthews, 190
Deveroex v. Nelson (Tex. Civ. App.—Houston [14th Dist.] 1974), 393–94
Deveroex v. Nelson (Tex. 1975), 392–94
DeWeerth v. Baldinger, 591
D.H. Blair & Co. v. Gottdiener, 768
Diamond Club v. Insurance Co. of N. Am., 643
Diaz v. Jiten Hotel Mgmt., Inc., 449–50
Dibella v. Hopkins, 64
DiCenzo v. A-Best Prods. Co., 313
Dick v. New York Life Ins. Co., 518
Dickens v. Brewer, 202
Dickerson v. United States, 7, 36, 236, 340, 361–62, 391
Dickinson v. First Nat'l Bank, 607
Diggins v. Jackson, 352
Dillon v. Legg, 164, 170–72
Dillon v. Medellin, 134
Dini v. Naiditch, 400
Direct Mktg. Ass'n v. Brohl, 365
Di Santo v. Pennsylvania, 11
District of Columbia v. Beretta, U.S.A., Corp., 117
District of Columbia v. Heller, 134, 356, 548
District of Columbia Ct. of Appeals v. Feldman, 691
Dobbs v. Zant, 486
Dodds v. Shamer, 278
Doe v. Chao, 461–62
Doe v. Friendfinder Network, Inc., 455
Doe v. Sundquist, 673, 677
Doe v. Wilmington Hous. Auth., 665
Doe ex dem. Patterson v. Winn, 746, 748
Doggett v. United States, 611
Doll v. Major Muffler Ctrs., Inc., 220
Doremus v. Board of Educ., 552, 553

Dorosh v. Ashcroft, 167
Douglass v. County of Pike, 436
Downs v. J.M. Huber Corp., 592
Doyle v. City of Medford, 639, 641
Dred Scott v. Sandford, 13, 661
Dresner v. City of Tallahassee (S.Ct. 1963), 623, 636
Dresner v. City of Tallahassee (S.Ct. 1964), 623, 636
Driggs v. Rockwell, 417
Dr. Miles Med. Co. v. John D. Park & Sons Co., 338–39
Dubuch v. Goudchaux, 702
Dunlavey v. Economy Fire & Cas. Co., 752
DuPree v. Carroll, 284
Dupree v. Hiraga, 284
Durant v. Essex Co., 220, 221, 223
Dyer v. Calderon, 74
Dyer v. SEC, 139
East Carroll Parish Sch. Bd. v. Marshall, 102–03
Eastern R.R. Presidents Conference v. Noerr Motor Freight, Inc., 25, 501
Easthampton Sav. Bank v. City of Springfield, 637, 639
Eastwood Mall, Inc. v. Slanco, 677
Edelman v. Jordan, 227, 353, 556
Edelmann v. Chase Manhattan Bank, 595
Edney v. State, 285
EEOC v. Trabucco, 375, 378
Egleston ex rel. Chesapeake Energy Corp. v. McClendon, 728
Ehrenzweig v. Ehrenzweig, 298
El Al Israel Airlines, Ltd. v. Tsui Yuan Tseng, 754
Elane v. St. Bernard Hosp., 289
Eley v. Pizza Hut of Am., Inc., 631
Eli Lilly & Co. v. Home Ins. Co., 643
Elk Grove Unified Sch. Dist. v. Newdow, 55–56, 84
Elliott v. Clement, 716, 718
Ellis v. American Tel. Co., 712
Elmbrook Sch. Dist. v. Doe 3, 526
Elmendorf v. Taylor, 541, 656, 710
El Paso Pipe & Supply Co. v. Mountain States Leasing, Inc., 240
El–Shifa Pharm. Indus. Co. v. United States, 502
Empire Healthchoice Assurance, Inc. v. McVeigh, 700

TABLE OF CASES

Enfield ex rel. Enfield v. A.B. Chance Co., 640
Engel v. CBS, Inc., 626
England v. Louisiana State Bd. of Med. Exam'rs, 620–24
Ennabe v. Manosa, 280
Entergy Gulf States, Inc. v. Traxler, 387
Erck v. Church, 426
Erie R.R. v. Tompkins, 163, 226, 234, 323, 335, 353, 363, 436, 544, 558, 560, 571–88, 589–92, 594, 598, 602, 604, 613, 646, 650, 692, 694, 703, 706, 711, 788–89, 793, 806
Ernie Haire Ford, Inc. v. Ford Motor Co., 607
Estate of Charania v. Shulman, 758
Estate of Dancy v. Commissioner, 607
Estate of McMorris v. Commissioner, 514
Estelle v. Williams, 107
Etcheverry v. Tri-Ag Serv., Inc., 235
Etting v. Bank of the U.S., 221–22
Eulitt ex rel. Eulitt v. Maine Dep't of Educ., 368
Evans v. Commonwealth, 110
Evans v. Secretary, Fla. Dep't of Corrections, 302
Examining Bd. of Eng'rs, Architects & Surveyors v. Flores de Otero, 675
Ex parte Alabama ex rel. Ala. Policy Inst., 537
Ex parte Crane, 415
Ex parte Francis, 656
Ex parte Jim Walter Res., Inc., 284
Ex parte King, 454
Ex parte Lewis, 399
Ex parte McCardle, 553
Ex parte Rathmell, 69
Ex parte Young, 501
Export Grp. v. Reef Indus., Inc., 116
Exxon–Mobil Corp. v. Saudi Basic Indus. Corp., 544
Exxon Shipping Co. v. Baker, 524
Factors Etc., Inc. v. Pro Arts, Inc., 514, 615
Fairbank v. Wunderman Cato Johnson, 472
Fairfax's Devisee v. Hunter's Lessee, 564
Fairfield v. County of Gallatin, 658
Fantis Foods, Inc. v. North River Ins. Co., 298, 711
Farley v. Farley, 515
Farmers' & Merchants' Ins. Co. v. Jensen, 748

Farrior v. New England Mortg. Sec. Co., 427, 428
Fay v. Noia, 531
FDIC v. Municipality of Ponce, 607
FDIC v. Skow, 638
Federal Baseball Club of Baltimore v. National League of Prof'l Baseball Clubs, 4, 335–36
Federal Home Loan Mortg. Corp. v. Matassino, 697
Felt v. Bush, 704
F. Enters., Inc. v. Kentucky Fried Chicken Corp., 466
Ferris v. United States, 25
Ferster v. Ferster, 709
F. Hoffmann–La Roche Ltd. v. Empagran S.A., 251
Fidelity Fed. Bank & Trust v. Kehoe, 524
Fidelity–Phenix Ins. Co. v. Mauldin, 301
Fidelity Union Trust Co. v. Field, 599, 608, 611
Findlay v. Lendermon, 109
Fiore v. White, 633
Firestone Tire & Rubber Co. v. Bruch, 561
First Merit Bank v. Angelini, 262
First Nat'l Bank v. Yakey, 704
First Tenn. Bank Nat'l Ass'n v. Pathfinder Expl., LLC, 608
First Thrift & Loan Ass'n v. State ex rel. Robinson, 279
Fishburn v. Indiana Pub. Ret. Sys., 288
Fisher v. City of San Jose, 501
Fishman & Tobin, Inc. v. Tropical Shipping & Constr. Co., 40, 106
Fiswick v. United States, 137
Flagg v. School Dist. No. 70, Barnes Cnty., 703–04
Flagiello v. Pennsylvania Hosp., 179
Fleming v. Fleming, 424, 436
Flood v. Kuhn, 4, 336
Florida v. Jardines, 174
Florida v. Royer, 131
Florida Dep't of Revenue v. Florida Mun. Power Agency, 288
Florida ex rel. Shevin v. Exxon Corp., 639, 641
Fluor W., Inc. v. G & H Offshore Towing Co., 234
FMC Corp. v. EPA, 446, 473–74
Fogerty v. State, 457

Ford v. Dilley, 397
Ford v. Strickland, 503
Forest Grove Sch. Dist. v. T.A., 348
Forsyth v. City of Hammond, 522
Forte v. Wal–Mart Stores, Inc., 613
Foshay v. Town of Glen Haven, 752
Foster v. Bowen, 318
Foster's Adm'r v. Metcalfe, 704
Foster Wheeler Energy Corp. v. An Ning Jiang MV, 753
Fournelle v. NLRB, 774
Fowler v. Lamson, 656
Fox v. State, 301
Fox Film Corp. v. Doyal, 322
Francis v. Southern Pac. Co., 346
Franklin Supply Co. v. Tolman, 753
Frank M. Hall & Co. v. Newsom, 293
Free v. Abbott Labs., Inc., 469
Free v. Bland, 695
Freedman v. Maryland, 25
Freeman v. Board of Med. Exam'rs for S. Dist. of Indian Territory, 134
Freeman v. United States, 203–06
Fricker v. Town of Foster, 515
Friends of the Earth v. Laidlaw Envtl. Servs. (TOC), Inc., 136–37
Frisk v. Superior Court, 295
Froud v. Celotex Corp., 334
Fuentes v. Shevin, 199
Fulmer v. Southern Ry., 165
Furman v. Georgia, 216–17
Fusari v. Steinberg, 158
FW/PBS, Inc. v. City of Dallas, 552
Galesburg Constr. Co. v. Board of Trs. of Mem'l Hosp., 278–79, 282
Gallagher v. Wilton Enters., Inc., 493, 496
Gamble v. U.S. Postal Serv., 777
Garcia v. Prudential Ins. Co., 701
Garcia v. San Antonio Metro. Transit Auth., 159, 190, 356
Garcia v. Tyson Foods, Inc., 40
Garner v. Louisiana, 599, 648
Garrett v. Moore–McCormack Co., 695
Garrett v. State, 416
Garrison v. Louisiana, 56
Gasperini v. Center for Humanities, Inc., 108, 477, 579–80, 581, 584
Gately v. Massachusetts, 27

Gawry v. Countrywide Home Loans, 138
Gaylor v. United States, 71
Gaynor Constr. Co. v. Board of Trs., Ector Cnty. Indep. Sch. Dist., 282
GE Capital Commercial, Inc. v. Worthington Nat'l Bank, 602, 609
Gelman v. Ashcroft, 38
General Dynamics Land Sys., Inc. v. Tracy, 284
Genesee Chief, The, 407
Genesis Healthcare Corp. v. Symczyk, 133
Gentry v. Superior Court, 688
German Alliance Ins. Co. v. Home Water Supply Co., 82
German Gymnastic Ass'n v. City of Louisville, 319
Gershman Inv. Corp. v. Danforth, 280
Gertz v. Robert Welch, Inc. (7th Cir. 1982), 458
Gertz v. Robert Welch, Inc. (S.Ct. 1974), 56
GE Solid State, Inc. v. Director, Div. of Taxation, 288
Gibson v. American Cyanamid Co., 201, 208
Gibson v. Talley, 430
Gideon v. Wainwright, 174, 191, 314, 363
Gilman v. Philadelphia, 11
Gilstrap v. Amtrak, 234
Ginzburg v. United States, 200
Girard Trust Co. v. Schmitz, 745
Girouard v. United States, 348, 350
Giuffre Hyundai, Ltd. v. Hyundai Motor Am., 603
Given v. Owen, 716
Glaser v. Wound Care Consultants, Inc., 493
Glass v. Birmingham Southern R.R., 693
Glebe v. Frost, 527
Glenn v. Field Packing Co., 656, 670
Glossip v. Gross, 524
Glover v. Minneapolis Bldg. Trades Council, 680, 683
Gluck v. Unisys Corp., 596
Gochicoa v. Johnson, 38, 53, 495
Godbout v. WLB Holding, Inc., 406
Godin v. Schencks, 586
Golden W. Ref. Co. v. SunTrust Bank, 613
Goldstein v. New York State Urban Dev. Corp., 665
Gompers v. Buck's Stove & Range Co., 657–58

TABLE OF CASES 821

Gonzales v. Carhart, 187, 367
Gonzales v. O Centro Espirita Beneficente Uniao do Vegetal, 156
Gonzales v. Raich, 521
Gonzalez v. Arizona, 487
Goodell v. Yezerski, 722
Gooding v. Wilson, 650
Goodwin v. State, 241
Goss v. Lopez, 647
Gottschalk v. Sueppel, 281
Government & Civic Emps. Org. Comm. v. Windsor, 620–22
Grable & Sons Metal Prods. v. Darue Eng'g & Mfg., 698, 699, 700
Grady v. Corbin, 241
Graffeo v. U.S. Fid. & Guar. Co., 298
Graham Cnty. Soil & Water Conservation Dist. v. United States ex rel. Wilson, 293
Gramercy Inv. Trust v. Lakemont Homes Nev., Inc., 710, 711
Grand Isle Shipyard, Inc. v. Seacor Marine, LLC, 503
Grandjean v. Beyl, 430, 431
Granite Rock Co. v. International Bhd. of Teamsters, 767
Grantham v. Avondale Indus., Inc., 536, 544
Grantham v. Missouri Dep't of Corr., 618, 625
Grant Smith-Porter Ship Co. v. Rohde, 214
Graves v. New York ex rel. O'Keefe, 198
Gray v. Mississippi, 227
Gray v. Mitchell, 278
Grayned v. City of Rockford, 599, 647
Great N. Life Ins. Co. v. Read, 556
Great Northern Ry. v. Sunburst Oil & Ref. Co., 310, 422, 434, 435
Great Western Tel. Co. v. Burnham, 441
Green v. American Tobacco Co., 639, 642
Green Bay Educ. Ass'n v. State Dep't of Pub. Instruction, 280
Greenwood v. Estes, 285
Gregg v. Georgia, 200
Gregory Constr. Co. v. Blanchard, 366
Greystone Constr., Inc. v. National Fire & Marine Ins., 611
Griffin v. United States, 548
Griffin Indus., Inc. v. Irvin, 109
Griffith v. Kentucky, 311–12
Grillot v. State, 166

Gross Coal Co. v. City of Milwaukee, 384
Grover v. Eli Lilly & Co., 626
Grutter v. Bollinger (E.D. Mich. 2001), 197
Grutter v. Bollinger (6th Cir. 2002), 197
Grutter v. Bollinger (S.Ct. 2003), 196–97, 202
Guaranty Trust Co. v. York, 580, 612
Guardians Ass'n v. Civil Serv. Comm'n of the City of N.Y., 210–11, 213
Guardiola v. Oakwood Hosp., 383
Guelfi v. Marin Cnty. Emps. Ret. Ass'n, 317
Guidry v. Sheet Metal Workers Int'l Ass'n, Local No. 9, 449
Gulf Offshore Co. v. Mobil Oil Corp., 689
Gulf Oil Corp. v. Gilbert, 756
Gunn v. Minton, 700
Gurley v. Rhoden, 710
Gwathmey v. State, 741
Hack v. Hack, 389
Haddock v. Haddock, 132
Hadley v. Baxendale, 153–54
Hagans v. Lavine, 72, 87
Halkias v. General Dynamics Corp. (5th Cir. 1994), 596
Halkias v. General Dynamics Corp. (5th Cir. 1995), 596
Hall v. Hopper, 301
Hall v. Pennsylvania Bd. of Prob. & Parole, 245
Halliburton Co. v. Erica P. John Fund, Inc., 41, 42, 334, 391
Hall St. Assocs., L.L.C. v. Mattel, Inc., 670–71
Halsell v. Dehoyos, 241
Hamdi v. Rumsfeld, 505
Hamilton v. Hannibal & St. Joseph R.R., 710
Hamilton v. Leavy, 480
Hamilton Watch Co. v. Benrus Watch Co., 230
Hammer v. Dagenhart, 191
Handy v. Goodyear Tire & Rubber Co., 693
Haney v. City of Lexington, 400
Hanna v. Plumer, 579, 580, 584–87
Hanover Fire Ins. Co. v. Carr, 545
Hans v. Louisiana, 364
Hardy Salt Co. v. Illinois, 381
Hare v. General Contract Purchase Corp., 436

Harlow v. Children's Hosp., 451, 476
Harlow v. Fitzgerald, 108–09, 484
Harman v. Forssenius, 633, 636
Harmelin v. Michigan, 237, 548
Harper v. Virginia Dep't of Taxation, 310, 312
Harpole v. Arkansas Dep't of Human Servs., 71
Harris v. Karri-On Campers, Inc., 640–41
Harris v. Martin, 329, 330
Harris v. Sentry Title Co., 456
Harris Cnty. Comm'rs Court v. Moore, 283, 607, 674–75
Harrow Prods., Inc. v. Liberty Mut. Ins. Co., 589
Hart v. Burnett, 425, 427
Hart v. Massanari, 8, 23, 37, 106, 148, 149, 243
Hartford Life Ins. Co. v. Blincoe, 448
Hatfield v. Bishop Clarkson Mem'l Hosp., 638, 639
Hathorn v. Lovorn, 467
Haugen v. Total Petroleum, Inc., 600
Hawaii Hous. Auth. v. Midkiff, 675
Hayes v. County of San Diego, 608
Hayes v. Fessenden, 191
Hayes v. Hayes, 233
Haynes v. Williams, 304
Haynie v. State, 396
Heaney v. Northeast Park Dist. of Evanston, 229
Heartland Bank v. National City Bank, 262
Hegeler v. Comstock, 734
Hein v. Freedom from Religion Found., Inc., 372
Heinlein v. Stefan, 59
Helmerich & Payne Int'l Drilling Co. v. Bolivarian Republic of Venezuela, 37
Helton v. Fauver, 542
Helvering v. Hallock, 11, 390
Helvering v. Proctor, 367
Hemphill v. Montgomery, 282
Henderson v. Fort Worth Indep. Sch. Dist., 223
Henderson v. Los Angeles City Bd. of Educ., 281
Henslee v. Union Planters Nat'l Bank & Trust Co., 355
Hentzner v. State, 251

Hepburn v. Griswold, 398
Herbert v. Lando, 57
Heritage Farms, Inc. v. Markel Ins. Co., 310
Herrera v. Collins, 524
Herrera v. Quality Pontiac, 398, 400
Herrera v. United States, 291
Herring v. Warwick, 234
Hertz v. Industrial Comm'n, 189
Hess v. Pawloski, 172
Heyert v. Orange & Rockland Utils., Inc., 397, 409, 422–24, 425
Hicks v. Miranda, 218
Higby v. Mahoney, 390, 408, 410
Highland Crusader Offshore Partners, L.P. v. Andrews & Kurth, L.L.P., 711, 714
Hill v. Atlantic & N.C. R.R., 335, 427, 428
Hill–Murray Fed'n of Teachers v. Hill–Murray High Sch., 663
Himely v. Rose, 466
Hinderlider v. La Plata River & Cherry Creek Ditch Co., 560, 694, 695
Hines v. Winters, 291
Hinton v. Alabama, 183
Hodges v. United States, 160–61
Hoffman v. Jones, 401
Hofman Ranch v. Yuba Cnty. Local Agency Formation Comm'n, 284
Hohn v. United States, 227, 308, 368, 371
Holden v. Circleville Light & Power Co., 428
Holden v. N L Indus., Inc., 625
Hole v. Rittenhouse (Pa. 1852), 419–20
Hole v. Rittenhouse (Pa. 1855), 420
Hole v. Rittenhouse (Pa. 1860), 419–20
Holiday Inns, Inc. v. Olsen, 705, 717–18
Holley v. Plum Creek Timber Co., 278
Hollingsworth v. Perry, 521, 553–54
Holly Care Ctr. v. State, Dep't of Emp't, 278
Hollywood Television Serv., Inc. v. Picture Waves, Inc., 165
Holmes v. City of Atlanta, 356
Holmes v. Morales, 279
Holmstrom v. Mutual Benefit Health & Accident Ass'n, 296
Holton v. Ward, 724
Honig v. Doe, 89
Hoover v. Blankenship, 279
Hope v. Pelzer, 109
Hopkins v. Lockheed Aircraft Corp., 626

TABLE OF CASES

Hornback v. Archdiocese of Milwaukee, 221
Hornsby v. State, 301
Horton v. Liberty Mut. Ins. Co., 697
Horton v. Sledge, 748
Hotel & Rest. Emps. Union, Local 25 v. Smith, 502
Hotel Ass'n of Washington D.C., Inc. v. Hotel & Rest. Emps. Union, 774
Houbigant, Inc. v. Federal Ins. Co., 613
Houston v. Lowes of Savannah, Inc., 301
Hove v. Atchison, 613
Howard v. Veazie, 191
Howard v. Wal–Mart Stores, Inc., 106
Howard Frank, M.D., P.C. v. Superior Court, 171
Howlett v. Rose, 534
H.P. Hood & Sons, Inc. v. Du Mond, 101
Hsu v. County of Clark, 483
Hubbard v. United States, 11, 341
Hucul Advert., LLC v. Charter Twp. of Gaines, 535
Huddleston v. Dwyer, 590
Hudson Specialty Ins. Co. v. Brash Tygr, LLC, 603
Huggins v. Isenbarger, 607
Hughitt v. Johnson, 703–04
Humphrey's Executor v. United States, 58, 62, 67
Hunter v. Underwood, 330
Hunter–Hayes Elevator Co. v. Petroleum Club Inn Co., 718, 733
Huntington v. Attrill, 729–30
Hustler Magazine, Inc. v. Falwell, 56
Hutto v. Davis, 27, 28
Hyundai Motor Co. v. Vasquez, 263
Ianni v. Loram Maint. of Way, Inc., 265, 266
IBP, Inc. v. Alvarez, 406, 409
Igartua v. United States, 304–05
Illinois Brick Co. v. Illinois, 335
Illinois State Bd. of Elections v. Socialist Workers Party, 218
Illinois Tool Works, Inc. v. Foster Grant Co., 379
Independent Petrochemical Corp. v. Aetna Cas. & Sur. Co., 514
Indian Oasis–Baboquivari Unified Sch. Dist. No. 40 v. Kirk, 87
Industrial TurnAround Corp. v. NLRB, 463

Infield v. Cope, 740–41
Ingersoll–Rand Co. v. McClendon, 668
Ingram v. State, 166
In re Adoption of L.O., 134
In re Advisory Op. to the Governor (N.C. 1950), 271
In re Advisory Op. to the Governor (R.I. 1999), 135
In re Air Crash in Bali, 564
In re Alfred H.H., 137
In re American Cont'l Corp./Lincoln Sav. & Loan Sec. Litig., 162
In re Arthur, 649
In re Asbestos Litig., 536–37, 544
In re Aspinwall's Estate, 510
In re Avantel, S.A., 582
In re Bankers Trust Co., 753
In re Barakat, 243, 244–45
In re Barnwell Cnty. Hosp., 284
In re Bartell v. State, 283
In re Cavalry Constr., Inc., 70
In re Central R.R. of N.J., 40, 507
In re Certified Question from U.S. Ct. App. for the Sixth Cir., 292
In re Certified Question from U.S. Dist. Ct., 627
In re Cohen's Estate, 656
In re Cummings, 137
In re Custody of Hernandez, 243
In re Darvocet, Darvon & Propoxyphene Prods. Liab. Litig., 602, 603, 607
In re Diet Drugs, 476
In re Dixon, 279, 282
In re Elliott, 625
In re Estate of Kern, 436
In re Estate of McFarland, 179, 409
In re Estate of Speake, 717
In re Evangeline Ref. Co., 232, 451
In re Exec. Office of President, 40
In re FEMA Trailer Formaldehyde Prods. Liab. Litig., 638
In re Ford, 40
In re Fretter, Inc., 169
In re Gerling, 294
In re Glen Rock, 399
In re Godoshian's Estate, 224
In re Grant, 304
In re Hearn, 53, 129
In re Heaton's Estate, 743

In re Hendrickson, 101
In re Hen House Interstate, Inc., 502
In re Hillsborough Holdings Corp., 516
In re International Nutronics, Inc., 373
In re Isserman, 222
In re J.Y., 383–84
In re Jones' Estate, 233
In re KAR Dev. Assocs., L.P., 515
In re Kirkland, 609
In re Korean Air Lines Disaster, 491, 512, 515
In re Lietz Constr. Co., 280
In re Lindsay, 597
In re Makowka, 608, 610
In re McKinney, 240
In re Merritt Dredging Co., 596
In re Mersmann, 312
In re Moody's Estate, 117
In re Moore's Estate, 748
In re Morgan Stanley & Co., 692
In re Muskin, Inc., 243
In re Oil Spill by Amoco Cadiz Off Coast of France on March 16, 1978, 452
In re Opinion of the Justices (Ala. 1935), 101
In re Opinion of the Justices (Mass. 1917), 275
In re Opinion of the Justices (Me. 1840), 274
In re Opinion of the Justices (Me. 1923), 276
In re Opinions of the Justices (Ala. 1923), 273, 274
In re Opinions of the Justices (Del. 1952), 274
In re Osborne, 5
In re Payless Cashways, 596
In re People, by Beha, 383
In re Propst, 430, 432, 433, 435, 436
In re Request for Advisory Op. from Governor, 274
In re Retirement Cases, 317
In re Richards, 617, 628
In re Sanford Fork & Tool Co., 459, 462
In re Sealed Case No. 97-3112, 493
In re Selden, 244
In re Shelby R., 138
In re Staff Mortg. & Inv. Corp. (9th Cir. 1980), 380
In re Staff Mortg. & Inv. Corp. (9th Cir. 1981), 380
In re Stevenson, 263, 701
In re Surrick, 137

In re Swanson, 244
In re Texas Dep't of State Health Servs., 284
In re Texas Grand Prairie Hotel Realty, L.L.C., 305
In re Trans Union Corp. Privacy Litig., 452
In re Tug Helen B. Moran, Inc., 382
In re Watts, 38
In re West Side Prop. Assocs., 625
In re Will of Allis, 434, 437
In re Workmen's Comp. Fund, 273
In re ZAGG Inc., 579
INS v. Cardoza–Fonseca, 90
Insurance Grp. Comm. v. Denver & Rio Grande Western R.R., 465
International Truck & Engine Corp. v. Bray, 53
International Union, UAW v. Dana Corp., 774
International Union, UAW v. Hoosier Cardinal Corp., 573
Iowa–Des Moines Nat'l Bank v. Bennett, 693
Iowa Nat'l Bank v. Stewart, 693
Iran Nat'l Airlines Corp. v. Marschalk Co., 518
Ireland v. State, 744
Irons v. Diamond, 496
Irvin v. Dowd, 112–13
Irving v. United States, 39, 507
Irwin v. Simmons, 58–59
Jackson v. Alabama State Tenure Comm'n, 480–81
Jackson v. Builders Transp., Inc., 545
Jackson v. Danberg, 202
Jackson v. Harris, 429, 434
Jackson v. King, 233
Jacobs v. National Drug Intelligence Ctr., 492
Jacobson v. Massachusetts, 99
Jaffree v. Board of Sch. Comm'rs (S.D. Ala. 1983), 32
Jaffree v. Board of Sch. Comm'rs (S.Ct. 1983), 32
Jaffree v. Wallace, 32
James v. United States, 320
James B. Beam Distilling Co. v. Georgia, 312
Jankowiak v. Allstate Prop. & Cas. Ins. Co., 387
Jansen v. City of Atchison, 406

TABLE OF CASES

J.E. Bernard & Co. v. United States, 377
Jefferson v. City of Tarrant, 467
Jefferson v. Lead Indus. Ass'n, Inc., 640, 641
Jeffries v. Wood, 487
Jehovah's Witnesses in Wash. v. King Cnty. Hosp., 491
Jenness v. Simpson, 709
Jensen ex rel. Jensen v. Cunningham, 665
Jerome v. United States, 546
Jesinoski v. Countrywide Home Loans, Inc., 386
Jessup v. Carnegie, 710
Jewett v. United States, 107
J.M. Robinson & Co. v. Belt, 750
John Baizley Iron Works v. Span, 215
John R. Sand & Gravel Co. v. United States, 334, 335, 336–37
Johnson v. Chicago, Burlington & Qunicy R.R., 409
Johnson v. City of Shelby, 183
Johnson v. Ruark Obstetrics & Gynecology Assocs., P.A., 669
Johnson v. Simpson, 734–35
Johnson v. Soo Line R.R., 671–72
Johnson v. State, 410
Johnson v. Transportation Agency, Santa Clara Cnty., 410
Johnson v. United States (S.Ct. 2010), 546–47
Johnson v. United States (S.Ct. 2015), 367–68, 547
Johnson v. Wells Fargo Home Mortg., Inc., 597
Johnson v. Williams, 536, 538, 691
John W. Masury & Son v. Bisbee Lumber Co., 746–47
Jolley v. Clemens, 301
Jones v. Alfred H. Mayer Co., 160–61
Jones v. City of Opelika (S.Ct. 1942), 357–58, 418
Jones v. City of Opelika (S.Ct. 1943), 358, 418–19
Jones v. Head, 223
Jones v. Jones, 713
Jones v. Louisiana Western Ry., 710
Jones v. Railroad Donnelley & Sons Co., 573
Jones v. United States, 501
Jones Cnty. Sch. Dist. v. Department of Revenue, 288
Kadish v. Arizona State Land Dep't, 554

Kaley v. United States, 106–07
K & K Constr., Inc. v. Department of Envtl. Quality, 726
Kansas v. Colorado, 560
Kansas City Southern Ry. v. Anderson, 367
Kansas City Southern Ry. v. Beaty, 96
Kappos v. Hyatt, 54
Karen Kane Inc. v. Reliance Ins. Co., 456
Karl v. City of Mountlake Terrace, 109
Kastigar v. United States, 104, 120
Katz v. United States, 174, 182, 190
Keasler v. Mutual Life Ins. Co., 709
Kehoe v. Fidelity Fed. Bank & Trust, 71
Keller v. City of Fremont, 627
Kelly v. Wehrum, 515
Keltner v. Washington Cnty., 405
Kennedy v. Lubar, 453, 487–88
Kentucky v. Whorton, 130
Ketelson v. Stilz, 741
Keystone Bituminous Coal Ass'n v. DeBenedictis, 250
Khalifa v. Shannon, 743
Khan v. Attorney Gen., 167
Khan v. State Oil Co., 29, 302–03, 323
Kimball v. Callahan, 465
Kimble v. Marvel Entm't, LLC, 115–16, 337–38, 340, 349–51, 422, 427, 430, 431, 525–26
Kincaid v. Mangum, 630
King v. Burwell, 523
King v. Order of United Commercial Travelers, 255, 602–03, 611–12
King v. Palmer, 201, 202, 205, 208, 209
King v. West Virginia, 443
Kiowa Tribe of Okla. v. Manufacturing Techs., Inc., 7
Kirkpatrick v. Gibson, 750
Klaxon Co. v. Stentor Elec. Mfg. Co., 581, 593–94, 596
Knepper v. Rite Aid Corp., 586
Knight v. Enbridge Pipelines (FSP) LLC, 602
Know v. Service Emps., 133
Knox v. Lee, 236
Knudson v. Kearney, 431–32
Knuth v. Erie–Crawford Dairy Co-op, 607
Koonce v. Doolittle, 152
Kopp v. Fair Political Practices Comm'n, 254

Kortum v. Johnson, 718
Kortyna v. Lafayette Coll., 169
Kramer v. Caribbean Mills, Inc., 697
Kraus v. Chicago, Burlington & Quincy R.R., 719–20
Kreisher v. Mobil Oil Corp., 429, 435
Kremen v. Cohen, 644
Krentz v. Consolidated Rail Corp., 245
Kruzel v. Podell, 280
Kuchenmeister v. Los Angeles & Salt Lake R.R., 693
Kuhn v. Fairmont Coal Co., 308–09, 312, 436
Kulinski v. Medtronic Bio-Medicus, Inc., 638
Kurczi v. Eli Lilly & Co., 69
KVUE, Inc. v. Moore, 279
Kwilecki v. Holman, 656, 659
Kyocera Corp. v. Prudential–Bache Trade Servs., Inc., 304
LaBarbera v. Batsch, 377
LaFage v. Jani, 743
LaFountain v. Attorney Gen., 277
Laidlow v. Hariton Mach. Co., 715
Lair v. Bullock, 201, 206, 305–06, 495
Lake Valley Assocs., LLC v. Township of Pemberton, 189
Lamb v. Hardy, 709
Lambert v. Belknap Cnty. Convention, 726
Landgraf v. USI Film Prods., 309
Landress v. Phoenix Mut. Life Ins. Co., 252
Lange v. Nelson–Ryan Flight Serv., Inc., 454
Lansing Sch. Educ. Ass'n v. Lansing Bd. of Educ., 372
Lanvale Props., LLC v. County of Cabarrus, 189–90
La Reunion Francaise SA v. Barnes, 107
LaShawn A. v. Barry, 469
Lawrence v. Texas, 36, 166, 190, 353, 526, 538, 549, 753, 755, 854
Lawrence ex rel. Lawrence v. Chater, 527–28
Lawton v. Commissioner, 382
L.D.G., Inc. v. Brown, 224
League of Or. Cities v. State, 221
League of United Latin Am. Citizens v. Perry, 213
League to Save Lake Tahoe v. Tahoe Reg'l Planning Agency, 563

Leavitt v. Jane L., 614–15, 667
Lebron v. SML Veteran Leather, LLC, 715
Leddy v. Cornell, 284–85
Lee v. American Nat'l Ins. Co., 556
Lee v. Dowda, 276
Leegin Creative Leather Prods., Inc. v. PSKS, Inc., 338–40
Leep v. St. Louis, Iron Mountain & Southern Ry., 540
Legal Servs. Corp. v. Velazquez, 229
Legal Tender Cases, 235–36, 398–99
LeGendre v. Monroe Cnty., 240
Lehman Bros. v. Schein, 624–25, 637, 640, 641, 644
Leiter Minerals, Inc. v. California Co., 617, 625
Lenhardt v. Ford Motor Co., 629
Leonard v. Johns–Manville Sales Corp., 709
Leong v. Takasaki, 171
Leopold v. People, 657
Lewis v. Casey, 121
Lewis v. State, 720, 722
Lexecon Inc. v. Milberg Weiss Bershad Hynes & Lerach, 162
Lexington Ins. v. Rugg & Knopp, Inc., 615
Li v. Yellow Cab Co., 401
Liberto v. Steele, 425–26
Liberty Mut. Ins. Co. v. Elgin Warehouse & Equip., 505–06
Liberty Synergistics Inc. v. Microflo Ltd., 615
Liccardi v. Stolt Terminals, Inc., 452
Licci ex rel. Licci v. Lebanese Canadian Bank, SAL, 608, 610
Lighting Ballast Control LLC v. Philips Elecs. N. Am. Corp., 503
Lincoln Cnty. Fiscal Court v. Department of Pub. Advocacy, 291–92
Lindahl v. Howe, 342
Liner v. Jafco, Inc., 552–53
Linkletter v. Walker, 260, 309
Lisbon v. Lyman, 388
Local 174, Teamsters, Chauffeurs, Warehousemen & Helpers of Am. v. Lucas Flour Co., 695
Local 1416, Int'l Ass'n of Machinists v. Jostens, Inc., 696
Local No. 6167, United Mine Workers of Am. v. Jewell Ridge Coal Corp., 123

TABLE OF CASES 827

Lochner v. New York, 182, 367
Locke v. Davey, 668
Lockhart v. Attorney Gen., 228
Lockhart v. Fretwell, 534, 536, 693
Logan v. Forever Living Prods. Int'l, Inc., 278
Logan v. Logan, 249–50
Lomax v. Fiedler, 692
London St. Tramways Ltd. v. London City Council, 35
Long v. Rockwood, 322
Longview Prod. Co. v. Dubberly, 628
Lopez–Fernandez v. Holder, 168
Loram Maint. of Way, Inc. v. Ianni (Tex. App.—El Paso 2004), 266
Loram Maint. of Way, Inc. v. Ianni (Tex. 2006), 262, 265–66
Lord v. Veazie, 139–40, 141
Lorillard v. Pons, 346–47
Los Angeles All. for Survival v. City of Los Angeles (Cal. 2000), 625, 676
Los Angeles All. for Survival v. City of Los Angeles (9th Cir. 1998), 675–76
Los Angeles Title Ins. Co. v. City of Los Angeles, 234
Louisiana Bank v. Kenner's Succession, 702
Louisiana Bd. of Ethics v. Holden, 289
Louisville Gas & Elec. Co. v. Coleman, 670
Louisville Metro Dep't of Corr. v. Commonwealth, 284
Luhman v. Beecher, 117, 301
Lunsford v. Saberhagen Holdings, Inc., 323
Lynch v. Donnelly, 549
Lynch v. Universal Life Church, 608
Lyons v. City of Xenia, 29
MacDonald v. Moose, 538
MacDonald v. University of N.C., 316
MacFee v. Horan, 111
Mackey v. United States, 311, 314
MacPherson v. Buick Motor Co., 172, 179
Mader v. United States, 305
Madison Square Garden Boxing, Inc. v. Shavers, 230
Magee v. Huppin-Fleck, 713
Mahan v. Howell, 130
Mahoney v. Babbitt, 382
Major League Baseball Players Ass'n v. Garvey, 768
Malone v. Corrections Corp. of Am., 597

Maloney v. Conroy, 164
Management Council of Wyo. Legislature v. Geringer, 291
Mansfield State Bank v. Cohn, 258
Manufactured Hous. Cmtys. v. State, 665
Mapp v. Ohio, 36
Marbury v. Madison, 160, 173, 235, 309, 357, 415, 551, 661
Marine Ins. Co. of Alexandria v. Tucker, 421
Markham v. City of Newport News, 697
Marks v. United States, 188, 196, 197, 199–213, 586, 798
Marlin v. Lewallen, 734
Marlin v. State, 189
Marmet Health Care Ctr., Inc. v. Brown, 679, 683–84
Marquez-Ramos v. Reno, 291
Marsh v. Chambers, 359
Martin v. Blessing, 268
Martin v. Commonwealth, 228
Martin v. Francis, 141
Martin v. Hunter's Lessee, 255, 683
Martin v. Lavender Radio & Supply, Inc., 251–52
Martinez v. City of Chicago, 494
Martinez v. City of Oxnard, 70
Martinez v. Enterprise Rent-A-Car Co., 297, 726
Maryland v. Baltimore Radio Show, 261–62
Maryland v. Louisiana, 560
Massachusetts v. EPA, 504
Massachusetts v. United States, 359
Massaglia v. Commissioner, 321–22, 434, 435
Massey v. Butts Cnty., 301
Massey v. Fulks, 229
Massie v. Enyart, 233
Mast, Foos & Co. v. Stover Mfg. Co., 510–11
Matheney v. Commonwealth, 390
Maxfield v. Cintas Corp., No. 2, 469
Mayhew v. Burwell, 203
Mayor & City Council of Baltimore v. Dawson, 356
Mayor of Nashville v. Cooper, 679
McCallum v. McCallum, 307
McCarthy v. Olin Corp., 243
McConnell v. Federal Election Comm'n, 354

McCoy v. Massachusetts Inst. of Tech., 70, 122
McCulloch v. Maryland, 34
McCutcheon v. Federal Election Comm'n, 227, 356
McDaid v. Oklahoma ex rel. Smith, 344–45
McDaniel v. Sanchez, 102–03
McDermott Inc. v. Lewis, 753
McDonald v. Brown, 110
McDonald v. City of Chicago, 356
McDonald v. Virginia, 538
McDonald's Corp. v. Robertson, 69
McDonnell Douglas Corp. v. Green, 88
McDuffie v. Estelle, 378
McElroy v. State, 388
McElroy v. United States ex rel. Guagliardo, 278
McGeshick v. Choucair, 610
McGill v. Garza, 728
McGraw v. Merryman, 412
McHugh v. Santa Monica Rent Control Bd., 723
MCI Commc'ns Corp. v. AT&T Co., 228
MCI Constructors, LLC v. City of Greensboro, 768
McIlroy v. Fugitt, 722
McKenna v. Ortho Pharm. Corp., 601, 603
McKim v. King, 703
McKinney v. McKinney, 101
McMahon v. Presidential Airways, Inc., 418
McMellon v. United States, 38, 303, 386
McMillan v. Live Nation Entm't, Inc., 291
McMonagle v. Northeast Women's Ctr., Inc., 532
Meade v. Commonwealth, 301
Meade v. State, 752
Medellin v. Texas, 761
Medical Ctr. Pharmacy v. Holder, 452
Medical Mut. of Ohio v. deSoto, 595–96
Melendez–Diaz v. Massachusetts, 682
Melton v. City of Oklahoma City, 505
Memorial Herman Healthcare Sys., Inc. v. Eurocopter Deutschland, GMBH, 602
Memphis Light, Gas & Water Div. v. Craft, 646–47
Memphis Publ'g Co. v. Tennessee Petroleum Underground Storage Tank Bd., 455
Mendenhall v. Barber–Greene Co., 453

Mennen Co. v. Atlantic Mut. Ins. Co., 304
Meredith v. Beech Aircraft Corp., 382
Meredith v. City of Winter Haven, 601, 619–20
Meridian Mut. Ins. Co. v. Kellman, 256
Merrill v. Preston, 92
Merrimac Mining Co. v. Levy, 710
Merritt v. Mackey, 465, 484, 487
Mertens v. Hewitt Assocs., 66
Mesker Bros. Indus., Inc. v. Leachman, 278
Messerschmidt v. Millender, 526
Messinger v. Anderson, 443–44, 445
Metropolitan Life Ins. v. Chase, 610
Metz v. Bae Sys. Tech. Sols. & Servs. Inc., 638, 639, 640
Meyer v. Board of Trs. of San Dieguito Union High Sch. Dist., 281
Meyer v. Schnucks Mkts., Inc., 305
MGM Grand Hotel, Inc. v. Imperial Glass Co., 613
Miami Parts & Spring, Inc. v. Champion Spark Plug Co., 601
Michigan v. Bay Mills Indian Cmty., 7, 334, 370, 407–08
Michigan v. Jackson, 178, 237, 400
Michigan v. Long, 655, 667
Michigan v. Morton Salt Co., 381
Michigan Millers Mut. Ins. Co. v. Bronson Plating Co., 589
Mid-Century Ins. Co. v. Lindsey, 707–08
Midland Steel Co. v. Citizens' Nat'l Bank, 709
Midlock v. Apple Vacations W., Inc., 40
Midway Airlines, Inc. v. Department of Revenue, 243
Miech v. Sheridan Cnty. (Wyo. 2002), 627–28
Miech v. Sheridan Cnty. (10th Cir. 2004), 628
Migra v. Warren City Sch. Dist. Bd. of Educ., 373, 375
Miller v. Burley, 259
Miller v. Gammie, 304, 305, 306, 323, 386, 458, 497
Miller v. Johnson, 25
Miller v. Westfield Ins. Co., 342–43
Miller Brewing Co. v. Bartholemew Cnty. Beverage Co., 278
Millers' Indem. Underwriters v. Braud, 214
Mills v. Green, 133

Mills v. Woods, 296
Mims v. Arrow Fin. Servs., LLC, 534
Minersville Sch. Dist. v. Gobitis, 357–58
Minn-Chem, Inc. v. Agrium, Inc., 39
Minnesota v. Clover Leaf Creamery Co., 545
Minnesota Mining Co. v. National Mining Co., 370, 407, 422, 434, 435
Minor v. Bostwick Labs., Inc., 37, 142
Minton v. Gunn (Tex. App.—Fort Worth 2009), 699–700
Minton v. Gunn (Tex. 2011), 697, 698–700
Miranda v. Arizona, 7, 61, 88, 174–75, 236, 361–62, 660, 856, 857
Miranda B. v. Kitzhaber, 104
Miree v. DeKalb Cnty., 559
Missouri v. Hunter, 541
Missouri v. Jenkins, 600
Missouri & Arkansas Ry. v. Treece, 95
Missouri & North Arkansas R.R. v. Phillips, 94
Missouri Pac. R.R. v. Ault, 539–40
Missouri Pac. R.R. v. Campbell, 94–95
Missouri Pac. Ry. v. Fitzgerald, 697
Mitchell v. Theriault, 564
Mitchell v. W.T. Grant Co., 199
M'Naghten's Case, 270
Mode, Ltd. v. Fireman's Fund Ins. Co., 707
Molinos Valle Del Cibao, C. por A. v. Lama, 603
Moncrief v. Wyoming State Bd. of Equalization, 294
Monsanto Co. v. Geertson Seed Farms, 116
Montana v. Kennedy, 524
Montana v. United States, 327
Montana v. Wyoming, 598, 651, 673
Montejo v. Louisiana, 41, 178, 236, 237, 397, 400
Montgomery v. Bank of Am. Corp., 545
Montgomery v. Louisiana, 315
Montgomery Ward & Co. v. State Tax Comm'n, 543
Moody v. Albemarle Paper Co., 496
Mooney v. Edwards, 130
Moore v. Barnhart, 37
Moore v. City of Creedmoor, 220
Moore v. Helling, 304
Moore v. Magrath, 50–51
Moore v. Ray, 278

Morales v. Zenith Ins. Co., 456
Moran v. Burbine, 297
Moran v. Rush Prudential HMO, Inc., 499
Moreno v. Sterling Drug, Inc., 743
Morgan v. Carillon Invs., Inc., 262
Morgan v. United States, 341
Morrill v. Weaver, 701
Morris v. Stifel, Nicolaus & Co., 372
Morris' Lessee v. Vanderen, 747
Morrissey v. Brewer, 311
Morrow v. Balaski, 39
Morrow v. Corbin, 272
Morrow v. Dillard, 470
Moses v. Boston & Maine R.R., 741, 745
Moses H. Cone Mem'l Hosp. v. Mercury Constr. Corp., 210–13
Moss v. Ramey, 445
Moulton Niguel Water Dist. v. Colombo, 189
Mountain View Coach Lines, Inc. v. Storms, 34, 387
Mount Soledad Mem'l Ass'n v. Trunk, 530
MRCO, Inc. v. Juarbe-Jimenez, 608
M/S Bremen v. Zapata Off-Shore Co., 756
Mt. Healthy City Sch. Dist. Bd. of Educ. v. Doyle, 481
Mullaney v. Wilbur, 33, 655, 710
Multnomah Cnty. v. Sliker, 366
Muniz v. Sabol, 167
Muniz v. United Parcel Serv., 608
Murdock v. City of Memphis, 539
Murdock v. Pennsylvania, 419
Murfreesboro Bank & Trust Co. v. Evans, 282
Murphy v. State, 241
Mutual Benefit Health & Accident Ass'n v. Cohen, 123
Myers v. Loudoun Cnty. Pub. Schs., 55
NAACP v. Alabama ex rel. Patterson, 539
Nafta Traders, Inc. v. Quinn, 671
Nance v. Goodyear Tire & Rubber Co., 773
Napa Valley Educators Ass'n v. Napa Valley Unified Sch. Dist., 281
Narenji v. Civiletti, 499
Narragansett Indian Tribe v. Rhode Island, 499
Naser Jewelers, Inc. v. City of Concord, 452
National Advert. Co. v. City of Miami, 134

National Bellas Hess, Inc. v. Department of Revenue of Ill., 365
National Carbide Corp. v. Commissioner, 228
National Classification Comm. v. United States, 149
National Educ. Ass'n Topeka, Inc. v. U.S.D. 501, 273
National Fed'n of Indep. Bus. v. Sebelius, 187, 203
National League of Cities v. Usery, 159, 190, 356
National Soc'y Prof'l Eng'rs v. United States, 561
National Sur. Corp. v. Midland Bank, 610
Nebraska Press Ass'n v. Stuart, 214
Negrón-Almeda v. Santiago, 486
Neil v. Biggers, 224
Nelson v. Brunswick Corp., 592
Nelson v. George, 729
Nelson v. New York State Civil Serv. Comm'n, 279
Nelson v. Sears, Roebuck & Co., 542
Nemours Found. v. Manganaro Corp., 642
Nesbit v. Clark, 712
Newdow v. Peterson, 70, 71
Newdow v. Rio Linda Union Sch. Dist., 56, 415
New England Health Care Emps. Union, Dist. 1199, SEIU AFL-CIO v. Mt. Sinai Hosp., 137
New England Mut. Marine Ins. Co. v. Dunham, 568
New Hampshire Fire Ins. Co. v. Curtis, 709
New Haven, Middletown & Willimantic R.R. v. Town of Chatham, 130
Newport Beach Country Club, Inc. v. Founding Members of the Newport Beach Country Club, 234
Newton v. Mann, 189
New York v. Quarles, 362
New York v. United States, 25
New York v. Uplinger, 530
New York Life Ins. Co. v. Ware, 244
New York State Club Ass'n v. City of New York, 552, 651
New York Times Co. v. United States, 214, 217
Nguyen v. Holder, 638, 639
Nguyen v. J.P. Morgan Chase Bank, 596

Niagara Falls Urban Renewal Agency v. O'Hara, 292
Nichol v. Pullman Standard, Inc., 55
Nichols v. United States, 197, 202, 206, 400
Nickens v. Mount Vernon Realty Grp., LLC, 743
Nickoll v. Racine Cloak & Suit Co., 428
Nitro-Lift Techs., LLC v. Howard, 184, 217, 540
Nkihtaqmikon v. Impson, 484
NLRB v. Hendricks Cnty. Rural Elec. Membership Corp., 119, 528
NLRB v. Natural Gas Util. Dist. of Hawkins Cnty., 547
Nobrega v. Nobrega, 118
Noel v. Linea Aeropostal Venezolana, 535, 564
Nored v. City of Tempe, 242
Norfolk Southern Ry. v. Basell USA Inc., 605
Norfolk Southern Ry. v. Kirby, 695
Norgaard v. DePuy Orthopedics, Inc., 591
Norma Fay Pyles Lynch Family Purpose LLC v. Putnam Cnty., 139
North Dakota State Bd. of Pharmacy v. Snyder's Drug Stores, Inc., 545
North Georgia Finishing, Inc. v. Di-Chem, Inc., 199
Northland Family Planning Clinic, Inc. v. Cox, 280
North Star Steel Co. v. Thomas, 573
Northwest Youth Servs., Inc. v. Commonwealth Dep't of Pub. Welfare, 288
Not In Montana: Citizens Against CI-97 v. State ex rel. McGrath, 134
Nuveen Mun. Trust v. WithumSmith Brown, P.C., 638
Obergefell v. Hodges, 218, 354, 513, 537
Obral v. Fairview Gen. Hosp., 318
O'Connor v. City of Rutland, 389
O'Dell v. School Dist. of Independence, 742
Of Course, Inc. v. Commissioner, 320
Offshore Logistics, Inc. v. Tallentire, 694
Ohio v. Clark, 120
Ohio v. Robinette, 131
Ohio Civil Serv. Emps. Ass'n v. Seiter, 109
Ohio ex rel. Eaton v. Price, 224
Ohio Ins. Guar. Ass'n v. Simpson, 705
Oil Workers Int'l Union v. Ethyl Corp., 774

TABLE OF CASES 831

Oja v. U.S. Army Corps of Eng'rs, 536, 538
Oklahoma Cnty. v. Queen City Lodge No. 197, 430
Okpalobi v. Foster, 501–02
Olcott v. Tioga R.R., 416
Oliver v. Kaiser Cmty. Health Found., 601
Olmstead v. United States, 190
Olympic Airways v. Husain, 166
O'Melveny & Myers v. FDIC, 572–73
Oneida Cnty. Fair Bd. v. Smylie, 725
O'Neil v. Northern Colo. Irrigation Co., 438
Oneok, Inc. v. Learjet, Inc., 521
Operating Eng'rs Pension Trust v. Charles Minor Equip. Rental, 126
Opinion of the Justices (Ala. 1967), 274
Opinion of the Justices (Ala. 1980), 135
Opinion of the Justices (Ala. 2005), 275
Opinion of the Justices (Del. 1980), 274, 276
Opinion of the Justices (Del. 2003), 275
Opinion of the Justices (Me. 2002), 273
Opinion of the Justices (N.H. 1852), 274
Opinion of the Justices to the Senate, 274
Opinions of the Justices, 272
Orca Commc'ns Unlimited, LLC v. Noder, 295
Oregon v. Hass, 660
Oregon v. Ice, 687
Oregon ex rel. State Land Bd. v. Corvallis Sand & Gravel Co., 407
Orme Sch. v. Reeves, 670
Oscanyan v. Arms Co., 111
Otis Eng'g Corp. v. Clark, 266
Owen v. Jim Allee Imps., Inc., 243
Owen v. United States, 609
Owens v. Milwaukee Ins. Co., 295, 706
Pacific Emp'rs Ins. Co. v. Global Reinsurance Corp., 608
Pacific Emp'rs Ins. Co. v. Sav-a-Lot of Winchester, 447, 476, 477
Padilla-Caldera v. Holder, 485
Paige v. City of Sterling Heights, 412, 413–14
Palmer v. Hoffman, 581, 583
Palmore v. United States, 551
Palsgraf v. Long Island R.R., 174, 175, 250
Panetti v. Quarterman, 200
Paper Prods. Co. v. Doggrell, 731
Parents Involved in Cmty. Sch. v. Seattle Sch. Dist. No. 1, 187

Parker v. Brown, 25
Parker v. Davis, 236
Parker v. K&L Gates, LLP, 119, 122
Parker v. Plympton, 301
Parklane Hosiery Co. v. Shore, 373
Parsons v. Federal Realty Corp., 123
Partos v. Pacific Coast S.S. (The Diamond Cement), 384
Pasadena City Bd. of Educ. v. Spangler, 332
Paschal v. Acklin, 746
Pasquantino v. United States, 753
Patterson v. Caterpillar, Inc., 582
Patterson v. Hays, 330
Patterson v. McLean Credit Union, 21, 341, 398, 399
Patterson v. Mobil Oil Corp., 638
Pattisson v. Cavanagh, 241
Pauk v. Board of Trs. of City Univ. of New York, 536
Paul v. Davis, 647
Paul v. State, 241
Paul Revere Variable Annuity Ins. Co. v. Zang, 330
Payne v. Tennessee, 6, 35, 40–41, 161, 190, 237, 352, 368, 370, 398, 399, 407, 422, 430
Payton v. Abbott Labs, 436
Pearson v. Callahan, 29, 42, 103, 109, 125, 370, 371, 409
Pease v. Peck, 652
Peerless Elec. Co. v. Bowers, 321
Peerless Indem. Ins. Co. v. Frost, 64
Peery v. Fletcher, 739, 740
Pendleton v. Pendleton, 233
Pennington v. Coxe, 140
Pennock v. Dialogue, 749–50
Pennoyer v. Neff, 751–52
Pennsylvania v. Brown, 87
Pennsylvania v. Delaware Valley Citizens' Council for Clean Air, 196, 210
Pennsylvania v. Union Gas Co., 190, 363–64
Pennsylvania Coal Co. v. Mahon, 235
Pennsylvania Glass Sand Corp. v. Caterpillar Tractor Co., 605
Pennzoil Co. v. Texaco, Inc., 524
Penrod Drilling Corp. v. Williams, 691
People v. Barrow, 416
People v. Bing, 258, 390
People v. Black, 261

People v. Bneses, 244
People v. Bonnetta, 293
People v. Bradley, 692
People v. Campbell (Colo. 1978), 273
People v. Campbell (Mich. Ct. App. 2010), 726
People v. Collins, 292
People v. Conyer, 727
People v. Evans, 453
People v. Foote, 34
People v. Goddard, 712
People v. Hernandez, 400
People v. Kidd, 377
People v. Lammers, 261
People v. Leavitt, 691
People v. MacShane, 289
People v. Maxson, 315
People v. McFarlin, 726
People v. Palomo, 706
People v. Petit, 402
People v. Petrenko, 390
People v. Rossi, 727
People v. Schoenfeld, 728
People v. Spykstra, 669
People v. Tanner, 728
People v. Thoro Prods. Co., 165
People v. Wagener, 686
People v. Wright, 727
People v. Yeats, 387
People ex rel. Birkett v. Bakilis, 267
People ex rel. Breuning v. Berry, 277
People ex rel. Daley v. Strayhorn, 237
People ex rel. Daley v. Suria, 267
People ex rel. LeGout v. Decker, 705
People ex rel. Madigan v. Illinois Commerce Comm'n, 267
People ex rel. Ray v. Martin, 692
People ex rel. Rice v. Graves, 322
People for the Ethical Treatment of Animals, Inc. v. Gittens, 136
Peoples v. CCA Detention Ctrs., 224
Pepper v. United States, 463, 464, 589
Peralta v. United States, 131
Peregoy v. Amoco Prod. Co., 374
Perez v. Brownell, 190–91
Perez v. Volvo Car Corp., 378
Perkins v. Clark Equip. Co., 640, 642
Perkins v. Jones, 741

Perry v. Schwarzenegger, 554
Peschel v. City of Missoula, 245
Peterson v. BASF Corp., 515
Peterson v. Hopson, 452
Peterson v. Superior Court, 429, 435
Petty v. Tennessee–Missouri Bridge Comm'n, 562–63
Petway v. Hoover, 141
Phi Delta Theta Co. v. Moore, 264
Philadelphia Trust, Safe Deposit & Ins. Co. v. Allison, 110
Phillips v. Larry's Drive-In Pharmacy, Inc., 292
Phillips Petroleum Co. v. Shutts, 556
Phoenix Canada Oil Co. v. Texaco, Inc., 759
Piatt v. Eads, 702
Pickering v. Board of Educ., 480–83
Pierce v. Cook & Co., 331, 591
Pierce v. Pierce, 220
Pierce v. Woods, 282
Pierce Cnty. v. State, 294
Pievsky v. Ridge, 563
Pigrenet v. Boland Marine & Mfg. Co., 503
Pino v. United States, 638, 639
Piper Aircraft Co. v. Reyno, 756
Pitcock v. State, 401
Pitman v. City of El Reno, 734
Pittsburgh Press Co. v. Pittsburgh Comm'n on Human Relations, 214
Planes v. Holder, 505
Planned Parenthood Affiliates of Cal. v. Van de Kamp, 278
Planned Parenthood of SE Pa. v. Casey (3d Cir. 1991), 31, 201, 205
Planned Parenthood of SE Pa. v. Casey (S.Ct. 1992), 5, 21, 36, 42, 179, 190, 360–61, 408
Plessy v. Ferguson, 177, 182, 323, 353, 800, 807
Plumhoff v. Rickard, 526
Plumley v. Austin, 149
Polk's Lessee v. Wendal, 656
Pollock v. Farmers' Loan & Trust Co., 343–44, 415
Pongetti v. Spraggins, 740
Pope v. Brock, 716, 721–22
Pope & Talbot, Inc. v. Hawn, 570
Potvin v. Lincoln Serv. & Equip. Co., 262
Powell v. Anderson, 262

TABLE OF CASES 833

Powell v. U.S. Fid. & Guar. Co., 640
Powers v. Wilkinson, 436
Prack v. Weissinger, 385
President of Georgetown Coll. v. Hughes, 180
Priesmeyer v. Pacific SW Bank, F.S.B., 169
Pritchard v. State, 240
Proctor & Gamble Co. v. Haugen, 603
Progressive N. Ins. Co. v. Romanshek, 391, 409
PruneYard Shopping Ctr. v. Robins, 669
Public Emps. Ret. Sys. of Miss. v. IndyMac MBS, Inc., 530–31
Public, Inc. v. County of Galveston, 387
Public Serv. Ry. v. Matteucci, 405
Puryear v. State, 324, 397, 400
Quarto v. Adams, 279
Queen Anne Park Homeowners Ass'n v. State Farm Fire & Cas. Co., 637, 638, 639
Quern v. Jordan, 448, 454
Quill Corp. v. North Dakota, 365, 651
Quinn v. Leathem, 82
Radio Station WOW v. Johnson, 655
Radovich v. National Football League, 100
Raffles v. Wichelhaus, 153
Ragan v. AT&T Corp., 711
Ragan v. Merchants Transfer & Warehouse Co., 581, 583
Railroad Comm'n of Tex. v. Pullman Co., 618–19, 674
Railway Co. v. Whitton's Administrator, 555–56
Raines v. Byrd, 271
Raley v. Life & Cas. Ins. Co. of Tenn., 252
Ramos v. SimplexGrinnell LP, 607
Randall v. Sorrell, 234
Randolph v. Hudson, 716, 733, 734
R & Y, Inc. v. Municipality of Anchorage, 726
Ranger Cellular v. FCC, 386
Ransom v. S&S Food Ctr., Inc., 380
Rantz v. Kaufman, 258
Rapanos v. United States, 209–10
Rappa v. New Castle Cnty., 202
RAR, Inc. v. Turner Diesel, Ltd., 536, 538, 544, 557, 639
Rattigan v. Holder, 501
Ray v. Mortham, 276

Ray Indus., Inc. v. Liberty Mut. Ins. Co., 604
Redding v. City of Los Angeles, 656
Redfield v. Continental Cas. Corp., 476, 477
Reed v. Allen, 326
Reed v. Breton, 289
Reetz v. Bozanich, 674, 675
Regents of Univ. of Cal. v. Bakke, 196–97, 211
Registration Control Sys., Inc. v. Compusystems, Inc., 514
Rehberg v. Paulk, 177
Reich v. Continental Cas. Co., 65
Reich v. D.M. Sabia Co., 386
Reichle v. Howards, 526
Reid v. Volkswagen of Am., Inc., 591
Rein v. Koons Ford, Inc., 729
Reinkemeyer v. SAFECO Ins. Co. of Am., 617
Rendon v. Holder, 38
Renn v. Utah State Bd. of Pardons, 243
Republic of Philippines v. Marcos, 565–66
Resolution Trust Corp. v. Camp, 169
Resolution Trust Corp. v. Chapman, 597
Restifo v. McDonald, 396
Retained Realty, Inc. v. McCabe, 586
Reynolds v. Sims, 158
Reynolds-Wilson Lumber Co. v. Peoples Nat'l Bank, 706
Rhea v. State, 718–19
Rhoades v. State, 752
Rhode Island v. Massachusetts, 560
Rhoten v. Dickson, 258
Rice v. Sioux City Mem'l Park Cemetery, 524, 528–29
Richards v. Green, 732
Richards v. United States, 595
Richardson v. State, 665
Richardson ex rel. Richardson v. Navistar Int'l Transp. Corp., 626
Richland Cnty. Water Res. Bd. v. Pribbernow, 134
Richmond Screw Anchor Co. v. United States, 123
Riemers v. City of Grand Forks, 279, 281
Rietz v. California Camino Bank, 656–57
Riggs v. Palmer, 77
Riley v. Brown & Root, Inc., 590
Riley v. Kennedy, 33

Ring v. Arizona, 314, 355
Rios v. City of Del Rio, 304
Riverisland Cold Storage, Inc. v. Fresno-Madera Prod. Credit Ass'n, 390
Roach v. Commonwealth, 742
Roark v. Macoupin Creek Drainage Dist., 208
Robbins v. Arizona Dep't of Econ. Sec., 288
Robert L. v. Superior Court, 294
Roberts v. Tishman Speyer Props., L.P., 294
Roberts v. United States, 278
Robidoux v. Celani, 138
Robins v. PruneYard Shopping Ctr., 669
Robinson v. Ariyoshi, 117, 437
Robinson v. City of Detroit, 180
Robinson v. Neil, 310
Rodrigue v. Rodrigue, 161–62
Rodriguez v. Robbins, 649
Rodriguez v. State, 724
Rodriguez de Quijas v. Shearson/Am. Express, Inc., 29, 302, 688
Rodriguez de Quijas v. Shearson/Lehman Bros., Inc., 29
Roe v. Alabama, 644
Roe v. Flores-Ortega, 121
Roe v. Wade, 136, 179, 360–61, 802
Rogers v. Tennessee, 724
Rollins Envtl. Servs., Inc. v. Superior Ct., 330, 670
Romero v. International Terminal Operating Co., 569
Roofing Wholesale Co. v. Palmer, 199
Rooker v. Fidelity Trust Co., 691
Roper v. Simmons, 166, 190, 753, 759–60
Rosengrant v. Havard, 214
Rosenzweig v. Thompson, 130
Rosnick v. Zoning Comm'n of Southbury, 273
Ross v. Policemen's Relief & Pension Fund of Pittsburgh, 240
Ross v. Reed, 39
Rossiter v. Potter, 119
Rotemi Realty, Inc. v. Act Realty Co., 179
Rothschild & Co. v. Steger & Sons Piano Mfg. Co., 657–58
Round Lake Sanitary Dist. v. Basic Elecs. Mfg. Corp., 658
Royston, Rayzor, Vickery & Williams, LLP v. Lopez, 289

Rudolph v. United States, 528
Rufo v. Inmates of Suffolk Cnty. Jail, 330, 332
Runyon v. McCrary, 41
Russ v. Watts, 493
Rutherford v. Columbia Gas, 38, 495, 641
R.W. Murray Co. v. Shatterproof Glass Corp., 604
Ryburn v. Huff, 526
Sackett v. Sackett, 746
Saefke v. Stenehjem, 277
Safeco Ins. Co. of Am. v. Wetherill, 604
Salazar v. Buono, 468–69
Salazar v. Ramah Navajo Chapter, 25
Salve Regina Coll. v. Russell, 614, 615
Samiento v. World Yacht Inc., 607
San Antonio Indep. Sch. Dist. v. Rodriguez, 666
Sanchez v. Forster, 233
Sanchez-Llamas v. Oregon, 760
Sandell v. Des Moines City Ry., 384
Sanderson v. Rice, 609
San Diego Unified Port Dist. v. Gianturco, 515
Sanford v. Poe, 651
Sanguinetti v. United States, 119–20
San Juan Cable LLC v. Puerto Rico Tel. Co., 386
Santa Maria, The, 466
Santow v. Ullman, 158, 424
Sarnoff v. American Home Prods. Corp., 47
Sarti v. Salt Creek Ltd., 387
Saucier v. Katz, 42, 103, 125, 371
Sawyer v. Smith, 315
Scappaticci v. Southwest Sav. & Loan Ass'n, 306
Schaffert ex rel. Schaffert v. Jackson Nat'l Life Ins. Co., 711
Scheehle v. Justices of Supreme Court of Ariz., 628
Scheidler v. National Org. for Women, Inc., 532
Schein v. Chasen (Fla. 1975), 625
Schein v. Chasen (2d Cir. 1975), 625
Schiavone v. Fortune, 671–72
Schill v. Wisconsin Rapids Sch. Dist., 279, 282
Schiro v. Farley, 373
Schiro v. Indiana, 262

Schlaefer v. Schlaefer, 191
Schlieter v. Carlos, 628, 629, 632
Schmaltz v. York Mfg. Co., 256
Schmidt v. Prince George's Hosp., 117
Schoenefeld v. New York, 608
Schooley v. Schooley, 191
Schrader v. Hamilton, 166
Schriro v. Summerlin, 314
Schroeder v. United States, 640
Schuette v. Coalition to Defend Affirmative Action, 117
Schultz v. Harrison Radiator Div. Gen. Motors Corp., 292
Schultze v. Alamo Ice & Brewing Co., 191
Schumann v. Fisher, 233
Schwab v. Crosby, 122
Schwartz v. Merrill Lynch & Co., 768
Scibilia v. City of Philadelphia, 191
Scott v. Ashland Healthcare Ctr., Inc., 279
Scott v. Gossett, 374
Scott v. State, 255
Seaboard Sur. Co. v. Garrison, Webb & Stanaland, P.A., 640
Searcy v. Strange, 537
Seay v. Hutto, 382
SEC v. Okin, 136
SEC v. Sloan, 136
Securities Indus. Ass'n v. Comptroller of Currency, 504
Self v. Bennett, 355
Sellers v. Allstate Ins. Co., 603
Seminole Tribe of Fla. v. Florida, 6, 27, 31, 35, 45, 71, 74, 119, 190, 364, 410
Semtek Int'l Inc. v. Lockheed Martin Corp., 375, 583–84, 700, 701
Senn v. Tile Layers Protective Union, 683
Septer v. Boyles, 234
Service Emps. Int'l, Inc. v. Director, Office of Workers' Comp. Program, 168
SGC Land, LLC v. Louisiana Midstream Gas Servs., 381
Shady Grove Orthopedic Assocs., P.A. v. Allstate Ins. Co., 108, 579, 584–86
Shannon v. United States, 718, 733
Shaw v. Delta Air Lines, Inc., 649
Shaw v. Postal Tel. Cable Co., 711, 712
Shaw v. Reno, 25
Shaw ex rel. Zollner v. PACC Health Plan, Inc., 693

Shebester v. Triple Crown Insurers, 644
Sheldon v. Sill, 551
Shelton v. Hamilton, 659
Sheridan v. NGK Metals Corp., 600
Shields v. Consolidated Rail Corp., 597
Shimman v. International Union of Operating Eng'rs, Local 18, 40, 507
Shipping Corp. of India Ltd. v. Jaldhi Overseas Pte Ltd., 493
Shook v. State, 387
Showtime Entm't, LLC v. Town of Mendon, 603
Shumaker v. Pearson, 427, 428, 434
Shuttlesworth v. City of Birmingham, 648
Sibbach v. Wilson & Co., 585, 586, 587
Sibbald v. United States, 465
Sibron v. New York, 137
Siefferman v. Johnson, 135
Siers v. Weber, 315
Sinclair Ref. Co. v. Atkinson, 347, 348
Singer Mfg. Co. v. Wright, 134
Singh v. Duane Morris LLP, 699
Singleton v. Commissioner, 268, 532
Sinibaldi v. Redbox Automated Retail, LLC, 603, 606
Sitz v. Department of State Police, 664
Six Companies of Cal. v. Joint Highway Dist. No. 13, 608
Skidmore v. Swift & Co., 286, 287, 288
Skilling v. United States, 60, 111–13
Skinner v. Oklahoma ex rel. Williamson, 101
Small v. United States, 753–54
Smallwood v. Jeter, 118
Smith v. Alabama Dry Dock & Shipbuilding Co., 273
Smith v. Allwright, 84
Smith v. GTE Corp., 386
Smith v. Klem, 152
Smith v. Municipal Court of Glendale Judicial Dist., 282
Smith v. North Carolina, 268
Smith v. Overstreet's Adm'r, 301
Smith v. Reeves, 556
Smith v. Russo Asiatic Bank, 383
Smith v. State, 405
Smith & Spidahl Enters., Inc. v. Lee, 165
Smothers v. Gresham Transfer, Inc., 739
Soehnlein v. Soehnlein, 295, 657

Sonic-Calabasas A, Inc. v. Moreno, 456
Sosa v. Alvarez-Machain, 251, 565
South Carolina v. Gathers, 190, 237–38, 398
South Corp. v. United States, 514
South Dakota v. North Carolina, 560
South Dakota v. Opperman, 659–60, 680
Southern Or. Barter Fair v. Jackson Cnty., 451
Southern Pac. Co. v. Jensen, 568–69
Southern Pac. Terminal Co. v. ICC, 136
Southern Ry. v. Clift, 453
Southern Ry. v. Decker, 710
Southern Star Lightning Rod Co. v. Duvall, 411
Specialty Beverages, LLC v. Pabst Brewing Co., 706
Spector v. United States, 382
Spence v. ESAB Grp., Inc., 605
Spencer v. Kemna, 137
Sprague v. Ticonic Nat'l Bank, 460
Spratt v. Toft, 717
Squeo v. Norwalk Hosp. Ass'n, 164
Standard Fire Ins. v. Ford Motor Co., 608
Standley v. Sansom, 284
Stanford v. Kentucky, 190
Stanton v. Sims, 33, 526
Staples ex rel. Staples v. Glienke, 282
Star Tribune Co. v. University of Minn. Bd. of Regents, 283
Starzenski v. City of Elkhart, 258
State v. Allen, 686
State v. Beauchesne, 663
State v. Brooks (Minn. 1930), 718
State v. Brooks (Wash. Ct. App. 2010), 189
State v. Brown, 284
State v. California Co., 158
State v. Campbell, 720
State v. Chapman, 170
State v. Chenoweth, 724
State v. Coleman, 538, 691
State v. Constantine, 210
State v. Courchesne, 724, 725
State v. Davis, 740
State v. Gore, 254
State v. Griep (Wis. Ct. App. 2014), 689–90
State v. Griep (Wis. 2015), 208
State v. Guthrie, 158

State v. Hall, 241
State v. Harris, 169
State v. Hawkins, 705
State v. Hayes, 34
State v. Hempele, 666, 667
State v. Hickman, 391
State v. Honeycutt, 324, 376–77
State v. Hunt, 667
State v. Hussein, 456
State v. Ice, 687
State v. Jasper, 681, 682
State v. Jones (N.M. 1940), 191
State v. Jones (Tenn. 1980), 708
State v. Kenaitze Indian Tribe, 278
State v. Ketterer, 327
State v. Klein, 716, 733
State v. Leach, 669
State v. Lewis, 131
State v. Manzanares, 688
State v. Mason, 727–28
State v. McCullough, 141
State v. McDougal, 681
State v. McKinley, 152
State v. Means, 384
State v. Miranda, 391–92
State v. Muckerheide, 724
State v. Mueller, 228
State v. Murray, 752
State v. Neighbors, 677
State v. New York Movers Tariff Bureau, Inc., 446
State v. Niemeyer, 189
State v. Odom, 455
State v. Opperman, 659–60
State v. Outagamie Cnty. Bd. of Adjustment, 398
State v. Patterson, 306–07
State v. Pearl, 741
State v. Picotte, 739
State v. Pratt, 449
State v. Prober, 680, 681
State v. Quintero, 398
State v. Rascon, 257
State v. Roache, 296, 297
State v. Robinette, 662
State v. Sanders, 52
State v. Santiago, 659
State v. Smith (La. 1878), 739

TABLE OF CASES   837

State v. Smith (N.C. 1900), 233
State v. Smith (N.J. 1981), 741
State v. Smith (N.M. Ct. App. 2013), 260
State v. Smith (Or. 1986), 660
State v. Stuart, 455
State v. Surma, 397
State v. Tanner, 687
State v. Timberlake, 457
State v. Tower, 716
State v. Varner, 241
State v. Village of Garden City, 725–26
State v. Walker, 660
State v. Ward, 689, 691
State v. Warmington, 135
State v. Weide, 680, 681, 688
State v. Wheeler, 723
State v. Williams (La. 2001), 262
State v. Williams (Mo. Ct. App. 1999), 301
State v. Williams (N.C. 2009), 262
State v. Williams (Wis. 2002), 689
State v. Wilson, 152
State Auto Prop. & Cas. Ins. Co. v. Hargis, 599
State Bank of Cherry v. CGB Enters., Inc., 692, 693
State Bd. of Equalization v. Courtesy Motors, Inc., 376
State Commercial Fisheries Entry Comm'n v. Carlson, 400
State ex rel. Citizens for Responsible Dev. v. City of Milton, 285
State ex rel. Clayburgh v. American W. Cmty. Promotions, Inc., 288
State ex rel. Clifton v. Reeser, 279
State ex rel. Data Trace Info. Servs., LLC v. Cuyahoga Cnty. Fiscal Officer, 284
State ex rel. Dep't of Fin. Insts. of Ind. v. Sonntag, 301, 302
State ex rel. Dep't of Nat. Res. & Envtl. Control v. Phillips, 374
State ex rel. Fent v. State ex rel. Okla. Water Res. Bd., 281
State ex rel. Foster v. Naftalin, 405
State ex rel. Frazier & Oxley, L.C. v. Cummings, 463
State ex rel. Gardner v. Holm, 291
State ex rel. Howard Elec. Coop. v. Riney, 293
State ex rel. Jenkins v. Carisch Theatres, Inc., 278–79

State ex rel. Martinez v. City of Las Vegas, 376
State ex rel. Moore v. Molpus, 391, 401
State ex rel. Morrison v. Sebelius, 134
State ex rel. North Olmsted Fire Fighters Ass'n v. City of North Olmsted, 279
State ex rel. State Highway Comm'n v. Trujillo, 684
State ex rel. Utils. Comm'n v. Thornburg, 258
State ex rel. Van Dyke v. Public Emps. Ret. Bd., 280
State ex rel. Walker v. Harrington, 253
State ex rel. Weast v. Moore, 117
State Farm Ins. Co. v. Edwards, 260
State Farm Mut. Auto. Ins. Co. v. Bates, 491
State Hosp. for Criminal Insane v. Consolidated Water Supply Co., 374
State Oil Co. v. Khan, 303, 323, 338, 390, 408
Statharos v. New York City Taxi & Limousine Comm'n, 608
Steel Co. v. Citizens for a Better Env't, 121, 552
Steelworkers Trilogy (United Steelworkers of Am. v. Enterprise Wheel & Car Corp.), 768
Steffel v. Thompson, 534, 536, 693
Stein v. New York, 47
Stein Enters., Inc. v. Golla, 397
Stenberg v. Carhart, 599, 635, 647
Stevens v. City of Cannon Beach, 437
Stevers v. Walker, 712
Stewart v. Smith, 636
St. Louis & San Francisco Ry. v. Dodd, 93, 95
St. Louis, Iron Mountain & Southern Ry. v. Coombs, 94
St. Louis, Iron Mountain & Southern Ry. v. Dawson, 95
St. Louis SW Ry. v. Arkansas ex rel. Norwood, 544–45
Stoddart v. Smith, 659
Stone v. Mellon Mortg. Co., 244
Stoner v. New York Life Ins. Co., 256, 608
Stop the Beach Renourishment, Inc. v. Florida Dep't of Envtl. Prot., 422, 434, 437, 438–39
Stowik v. Sirker, 233
St. Pierre v. United States, 137

Strasburger v. Dodge, 717
Strawn v. State Tax Comm'n, 131
Street Emps. Div. 998 v. Wisconsin Emp't Relations Bd., 139
Streit v. County of Los Angeles, 535
Strickland v. Washington, 159–60
Strout v. Albanese, 368
Strout v. Burgess, 709
Strozinsky v. School Dist. of Brown Deer, 724
Stuart v. Pilgrim, 343
Student Pub. Interest Research Grp. of N.J., Inc. v. AT&T Bell Labs., 210
Stumes v. Delano, 279
Stupak-Thrall v. United States, 223
Stutsman Cnty. v. Wallace, 733
Sudden & Christenson v. Industrial Accident Comm'n, 702
Sudheimer v. Cheatham, 752
Sulzer Textil A.G. v. Picanol N.V., 514
Summerfield v. Superior Court, 743
Sun Ins. Office, Ltd. v. Clay, 626
Surrick v. Killion, 538
Sutter Basin Corp. v. Brown, 435
Sutton v. Leib, 375
Swann v. Charlotte-Mecklenburg Bd. of Educ., 185, 332
Sweet Home Chapter of Cmtys. for a Great Or. v. Babbitt, 4
Swift v. Tyson, 226, 234, 323, 353, 363, 575–80
Swiss Oil Corp. v. Shanks, 123
Swope v. Siegel-Robert, Inc., 609–10
Sykes v. Perry, 151
Synanon Church v. United States, 374
System Fed'n No. 91 Ry. Emps. v. Wright, 332

Tafflin v. Levitt, 534, 536, 550, 692
Taniguchi v. Association of Apartment Owners of King Manor, Inc., 278
Tanner Motor Livery, Ltd. v. Avis, Inc., 472–73
Taomae v. Lingle, 291
Tarr v. Manchester Ins. Corp., 644
Tate v. Showboat Marina Casino P'ship, 39
Taylor v. Barkes, 526
Taylor v. Commonwealth, 742
Taylor v. Fee, 745–46
Taylor v. Kentucky, 130

Taylor v. Phelan, 603
Taylor v. Sturgell, 700
Tchoukhrova v. Gonzales, 499
Teague v. Lane, 113, 163, 219, 261, 313–14, 315, 752, 857
Tebo v. Havlik, 243
Tennessee Bd. of Dispensing Opticians v. Eyear Corp., 283
Terenzio v. Nelson, 729
Terre Haute & Indianapolis R.R. v. Indiana ex rel. Ketcham, 655
Terry v. Edgin, 282
Terry v. Tyson Farms, Inc., 512
Texas v. Cobb, 686
Texas v. Johnson, 55
Texas & Pac. Ry. v. Humble, 717
Texas Co. v. Oklahoma Tax Comm'n, 322
Texas Indus., Inc. v. Radcliff Materials, Inc., 339, 560, 573–74
Texas Instruments, Inc. v. Linear Techs. Corp., 381, 385
Textile Workers Union of Am. v. Lincoln Mills of Alabama, 560–61, 695
Thomas v. Anchorage Equal Rights Comm'n (Alaska 2004), 402
Thomas v. Anchorage Equal Rights Comm'n (9th Cir. 2000), 502
Thomas v. Hoffman-LaRoche, Inc., 603–04
Thomas v. Shepherd, 709
Thomas v. State, 416
Thomas Phillips Co. v. Dover Mach. Prods., 220–21
Thompson v. Paul, 640, 642
Thompson v. Sanford, 392, 412
Thornhill v. Alabama, 683
Thorpe v. District of Columbia, 138
Threadgill v. Armstrong World Indus., Inc., 40
Thurston Cnty. ex rel. Bd. of Cnty. Comm'rs v. City of Olympia, 279
Thurston Motor Lines, Inc. v. Jordan K. Rand, Ltd., 29
Tidal Oil Co. v. Flanagan, 436, 437
Tidler v. Eli Lilly & Co., 640, 641
Tileston v. Ullman, 553
Tillman Cnty. Bank of Grandfield v. Behringer, 703
Timmerman v. Modern Indus., Inc., 579
Titan Tire Corp. v. United Steel Workers Int'l Union, 769

T.L. ex rel. Ingram v. United States, 305
TMF Tool Co. v. Muller, 385–86
Todd v. Societe Bic, S.A., 615
Tokoph v. United States, 495
Tolan v. Cotton, 523
Toolson v. New York Yankees, Inc., 4, 335–36
Toucey v. New York Life Ins. Co., 227
Town of Bloomfield v. Charter Oak Nat'l Bank, 130
Town of Castle Rock v. Gonzales, 575, 635–36, 646–47, 667
Town of Concord v. Portsmouth Sav. Bank, 658
Toyosaburo Korematsu v. United States, 130
Trailer Marine Transp. Corp. v. Rivera Vazquez, 365, 366
Trailways Lines, Inc. v. Trailways, Inc. Joint Council, 774
Trans-Tec Asia v. M/V Harmony Container, 756, 759
Trans World Airlines, Inc. v. Morales, 470
Travelers Indem. Co. v. DiBartolo, 244
Travieso v. Travieso, 47
Treme v. Thomas, 301
Trigalet v. Young, 109
Trombetta v. Conkling, 171
Trope v. Katz, 389–90
Truax v. Corrigan, 545
Truly Nolen of Am. v. Superior Court, 679, 687, 688
Trust Co. of Chicago v. Pennsylvania R.R., 581
Tully v. Griffin, Inc., 218
Tumey v. Ohio, 184
Tunik v. Merit Sys. Prots. Bd., 387
Turnbull v. Fink, 741
Turner v. Beneficial Corp., 380
Turner v. Elliott, 384
Turner v. Mellon, 384
Twin City Fire Ins. Co. v. Ben Arnold-Sunbelt Beverage Co., 612, 613
Twinco Romax Auto. Warehouse, Inc. v. Olson Gen. Contractors, Inc., 728
Tyler v. Bethlehem Steel Corp., 209
Underwriters Nat'l Assurance Co. v. North Carolina Life & Accident & Health Ins. Guar. Ass'n, 375
Union Asset Mgmt. Holding A.G. v. Dell, Inc., 168
Union Ink Co. v. AT&T Corp., 296

Union Leader Corp. v. New Hampshire Hous. Fin. Auth., 724
Union Pac. R.R. v. Board of Cnty. Comm'rs, 599
Union Pac. R.R. v. Mason City & Fort Dodge R.R., 103
Union Trust Co. v. Williamson Cnty. Bd. of Zoning Appeals, 382, 421, 425
United Egg Producers v. Standard Brands, Inc., 166
United Food & Commercial Workers Union, Local 72 v. Borough of Dunmore, 224–25
United Paperworkers Int'l Union v. Misco, Inc., 768
United Servs. Life Ins. Co. v. Delaney, 273, 617
United States v. 93.970 Acres of Land, 558
United States v. 177.51 Acres of Land, 379
United States v. Abuagla, 291
United States v. Alcan Aluminum Corp., 201
United States v. Alexander (9th Cir. 1997), 487
United States v. Alexander (9th Cir. 2002), 167
United States v. Alvarez, 56–57
United States v. American-Foreign S.S., 497, 507
United States v. Anaya, 515
United States v. Articles of Drug Consisting of 203 Paper Bags, 376
United States v. Asad, 120–21
United States v. Auginash, 106
United States v. Austin (9th Cir. 2012), 204
United States v. Austin (10th Cir. 2005), 69
United States v. Bad Marriage, 483
United States v. Bailey, 201, 210
United States v. Banks, 204
United States v. Barton, 134
United States v. Bell (1st Cir. 1993), 482
United States v. Bell (2d Cir. 1975), 64
United States v. Bell (4th Cir. 1993), 460, 462, 482
United States v. Bennett, 228
United States v. Bettenhausen, 232
United States v. Bibbins, 284
United States v. Bloate, 455
United States v. Bloom, 60–61
United States v. Board of Comm'rs of Sheffield, 347

United States v. Booker (1st Cir. 2011), 366
United States v. Booker (S.Ct. 2005), 463, 483
United States v. Bowling, 39
United States v. Bramblett, 341, 342
United States v. Brooks, 123
United States v. Brown (3d Cir. 2011), 382
United States v. Brown (4th Cir. 2011), 204
United States v. Browne, 204
United States v. California, 378
United States v. Calverley, 501
United States v. Carolene Prods., 117
United States v. Caro-Muñiz, 120
United States v. Carrizales-Toledo, 201
United States v. Carter, 366
United States v. Carver, 219, 261, 600
United States v. Charles, 492
United States v. Chhien, 492
United States v. Cinemark USA, Inc., 514
United States v. Collazo, 535, 538
United States v. Crawley, 66–67, 74, 129, 228
United States v. Curtiss-Wright Exp. Corp., 120
United States v. Darby, 191
United States v. Davenport, 168
United States v. Davis, 205–06, 209
United States v. DeGasso, 603
United States v. Detroit Timber & Lumber Co., 151
United States v. Dickinson, 111
United States v. Dixon (7th Cir. 2012), 204
United States v. Dixon (S.Ct. 1993), 240–41
United States v. Dominguez Benitez, 501
United States v. Donovan, 210
United States v. Dow, 111
United States v. Dowdell, 493
United States v. Duarte-Acero, 291
United States v. Duron-Caldera, 201
United States v. Duvall, 202, 205, 206, 211, 586
United States v. Epps, 204, 205
United States v. Falk & Brother, 278
United States v. Fareed, 71
United States v. Federative Republic of Brazil, 729
United States v. Ferreira, 140
United States v. Flores-Mejia, 503

United States v. Flynn, 545
United States v. Fortner, 147
United States v. Franz, 38
United States v. Freedman Farms, Inc., 208
United States v. Gallo, 308
United States v. Games-Perez, 167
United States v. Garcia, 224
United States v. Gaudin, 371
United States v. Genao-Sánchez, 460–61
United States v. Gerke Excavating, Inc., 210
United States v. Goff, 37
United States v. Graham, 204
United States v. Hardman, 497
United States v. Hatter, 449
United States v. Hawes, 366
United States v. Heredia, 39
United States v. Hill, 497
United States v. Hogan, 300
United States v. Holloway, 485
United States v. Hoover, 380
United States v. Hudson & Goodwin, 558
United States v. Hughes Props., Inc., 520
United States v. Hurtado, 499
United States v. Husted, 291
United States v. International Boxing Club of N.Y., 100
United States v. Jackson, 492
United States v. Jacobsen, 211
United States v. James, 68
United States v. Jenkins, 159
United States v. Johnson (1st Cir. 2006), 201, 203, 206, 208, 209, 210, 213
United States v. Johnson (9th Cir. 2000), 63
United States v. Johnson (9th Cir. 2001), 45, 46, 62, 63–64, 104, 116, 129, 458
United States v. Johnson (S.Ct. 1982), 311
United States v. Johnston, 528
United States v. Jones (E.D. Mich. 2000), 166
United States v. Jones (4th Cir. 1982), 760
United States v. Jordan, 448
United States v. Juvenile Male, 636–37
United States v. Kebodeaux, 512
United States v. Kimbell Foods, Inc., 559, 574
United States v. Koenig, 385
United States v. Kratt, 201

TABLE OF CASES

United States v. *Kwai Fun Wong*, 337, 347
United States v. *Lara-Unzueta*, 168
United States v. *Lawson*, 204
United States v. *Leija-Sanchez*, 302
United States v. *Lewko*, 492
United States v. *Little Lake Misere Land Co.*, 558
United States v. *Los Angeles Tucker Truck Lines, Inc.*, 229
United States v. *Louisiana*, 378
United States v. *Madden*, 237, 304
United States v. *Magnesium Corp. of Am.*, 168–69
United States v. *Maine*, 362, 378–79
United States v. *Martinez*, 38, 495
United States v. *Master*, 37
United States v. *Matthews* (1st Cir. 2011), 483
United States v. *Matthews* (9th Cir. 2002), 463
United States v. *Mead Corp.*, 287
United States v. *Medina*, 547
United States v. *Mejias*, 547
United States v. *Meyers*, 386
United States v. *Michael*, 499
United States v. *Miranda-Ortegon*, 600
United States v. *Mitchell*, 524
United States v. *Moore*, 463
United States v. *Moran*, 442, 465
United States v. *More*, 229
United States v. *Najera-Mendoza*, 600
United States v. *Nettles*, 475
United States v. *Nixon* (5th Cir. 1987), 497–98
United States v. *Nixon* (S.Ct. 1974), 186, 522–23
United States v. *Occidental Life Ins. Co.*, 127–28
United States v. *One 1959 Buick 4-Door Sedan*, 250
United States v. *One Assortment of 89 Firearms*, 242
United States v. *Oregon*, 694
United States v. *Orman*, 538
United States v. *Oshatz*, 64, 457
United States v. *Padilla*, 40, 500, 502, 505
United States v. *Page*, 278
United States v. *Palmer*, 40, 500
United States v. *Pate*, 28

United States v. *Philip Morris USA Inc.*, 167
United States v. *Phillips*, 501
United States v. *Quinn*, 71
United States v. *Quintieri*, 442, 459
United States v. *Rentz*, 168
United States v. *Ressam*, 499
United States v. *Reveron Martinez*, 381, 382
United States v. *Reyes*, 459
United States v. *Reyes-Hernandez*, 493, 513
United States v. *Reyna-Tapia*, 500–01
United States v. *Rivera*, 224
United States v. *Rivera-Martinez* (1st Cir. 1991), 482–83, 486
United States v. *Rivera-Martínez* (1st Cir. 2011), 204–05
United States v. *Robison* (11th Cir. 2007), 210
United States v. *Robison* (11th Cir. 2008), 201
United States v. *Rocha*, 204
United States v. *Rodriguez*, 122–23, 501
United States v. *Rodriguez-Pacheco*, 38, 365
United States v. *Rose*, 600
United States v. *Rubin*, 89, 119
United States v. *Ruiz*, 503
United States v. *Santiago*, 302
United States v. *Santos*, 200
United States v. *Sauseda*, 37
United States v. *Scott*, 159
United States v. *Seale*, 518
United States v. *Short*, 386
United States v. *Shubert*, 4, 100
United States v. *Si*, 116, 123
United States v. *Singletary*, 302
United States v. *Smith* (6th Cir. 2011), 204
United States v. *Smith* (10th Cir. 2011), 600
United States v. *Smith* (11th Cir. 2014), 547
United States v. *Snyder*, 38
United States v. *South-Eastern Underwriters Ass'n*, 401–02
United States v. *Standard Oil Co.*, 422, 424, 425, 439
United States v. *Standard Oil Co. of Cal.*, 574
United States v. *Swift & Co.*, 332
United States v. *Sykes*, 37, 537
United States v. *Szpyt*, 470–71

United States v. Tapp, 121
United States v. Taylor, 505
United States v. Tenzer, 482
United States v. Texas, 378
United States v. Thompson, 204–05
United States v. Ticchiarelli, 487
United States v. Tisdale, 168
United States v. Title Ins. & Trust Co., 122, 407
United States v. Townsend, 37
United States v. Turtle Mountain Band of Chippewa Indians, 451–52
United States v. United States Smelting Ref. & Mining Co., 232, 448, 450–51, 453
United States v. Vann, 608
United States v. Virginia, 549
United States v. Voisine, 366
United States v. Wallace, 444
United States v. Wells, 466
United States v. West, 463
United States v. White (2d Cir. 2011), 204
United States v. White (7th Cir. 2005), 464
United States v. White (10th Cir. 2015), 38
United States v. Wilkerson, 386
United States v. Williams (7th Cir. 1999), 387
United States v. Williams (9th Cir. 2006), 200–01, 202
United States v. Windsor, 116, 521
United States v. Winnie, 131
United States v. Wolfe, 493
United States v. Woods, 520
United States v. W.T. Grant Co., 136
United States v. Wyoming Nat'l Bank, 612
United States v. Yale Todd, 140
United States v. Yazell, 574
United States v. Zhang, 115
United States ex rel. Catena v. Elias, 541–42
United States ex rel. Greenhalgh v. F.D. Rich Co., 451–52
United States ex rel. Lawrence v. Woods, 538, 689, 691
Unity Real Estate Co. v. Hudson, 198
University of Notre Dame v. Burwell, 528
University of Notre Dame v. Sebelius, 528
University of Tex. v. Camenisch, 156, 230
USPPS, Ltd. v. Avery Dennison Corp. (5th Cir. 2009), 470

USPPS, Ltd. v. Avery Dennison Corp. (5th Cir. 2011), 469–70
U.S. Term Limits, Inc. v. Thornton, 659–60
Utah State Nat'l Bank v. Smith, 704
Valdez v. Applegate, 230
Valentine v. Francis, 142
Valladolid v. Pacific Operations Offshore LLP, 70
Vallandigham v. Clover Park Sch. Dist. No. 400, 241
Vandenbark v. Owens-Illinois Glass Co., 589–92, 600
Vanderhoef v. Silver, 387
VanDeWalle v. Albion Nat'l Bank, 658
Van Dusen v. Barrack, 594
Van Gemert v. Boeing Co., 40, 507
Van Horn v. Van Horn, 446
Van Ness v. Pacard, 738
Vantrease v. Commissioner of Soc. Sec., 169
Van Zanen v. Qwest Wireless, LLC, 606
Vega v. Morris, 257
Velez v. Commissioner of Corr., 278
Venegas v. County of Los Angeles, 692
Veneklase v. City of Fargo, 109
Ventura Cnty. Deputy Sheriffs' Ass'n v. Board of Ret., 317
Verba v. Ghaphery, 366
Verrier v. Director of Pub. Prosecutions, 744
Vesely v. Sager, 307
Victor v. Nebraska, 359
Vieth v. Jubelirer, 213
Virginia v. American Booksellers Ass'n, 633
Virginia v. Black, 545
Virginia v. Hicks, 552
Virginia State Bd. of Pharmacy v. Virginia Citizens Consumer Council, Inc., 57
Vishipco Line v. Chase Manhattan Bank, N.A., 758
Vitro v. Mihelcic, 402
Volkswagenwerk AG v. Schlunk, 754
Volt Info. Sciences, Inc. v. Board of Trs. of Leland Stanford Junior Univ., 767
Volvo Cars of N. Am., Inc. v. Ricci, 628–29
Wade v. Boone, 709
Wade v. EMCASCO Ins., 606
Waggoner v. Hastings, 419–20
Waldrop v. State, 111
Walker v. Armco Steel Corp., 581, 583, 584
Walker v. Astrue, 168

TABLE OF CASES 843

Walker v. Doe, 214
Walker v. State Harbor Comm'rs, 656
Wallace v. City of Chicago, 499
Walling v. Shenandoah-Dives Mining Co., 134
Wal-Mart Stores, Inc. v. Dukes, 174
Wal-Mart Stores, Inc. v. Samara Bros., Inc., 110–11
Walter v. United States, 211
Walters v. Inexco Oil Co., 629
Ward v. Board of Cnty. Comm'rs, 655–56
Ward v. State Farm Mut. Auto. Ins. Co., 639, 642
Ward v. Utah, 366
Waremart Foods v. NLRB, 608
Warhurst v. Morgan, 135
Warner v. Gregory, 602
Warren, Little & Lund, Inc. v. Max J. Kuney Co., 670
Washburn v. Gould, 509
Waters v. Churchill, 213
Watervale Mining Co. v. Leach, 250
Water Works & Sewer Bd. of Talladega v. Consolidated Publ'g, Inc., 280
Watkins v. U.S. Army, 39–40, 507
Watt v. Western Nuclear, 684–85, 686
Waugh Chapel S., LLC v. United Food & Commercial Workers Union Local 27, 535
Webster v. Fall, 6, 87, 229
Weiley v. Albert Einstein Med. Ctr., 224–25
Weinberger v. Salfi, 47
Weinstein v. Bradford, 136
Weisberg v. Powell, 613
Weiss v. Home Ins. Co., 298
Weiss v. United States, 614
Welk v. GMAC Mortg., LLC, 115
Wells v. Davis, 223
Wendell v. Ameritrust Co., 316
Wenke v. Gehl Co., 410
West v. AT&T Co., 598, 600, 604, 607, 647, 651, 673
West Coast Hotel Co. v. Parrish, 367
Western Helicopter Servs. v. Rogerson Aircraft Corp., 627, 628, 629, 632
Western Pac. R.R. Corp. v. Western Pac. R.R. Co., 496
Westfield Ins. Co. v. Galatis, 181
West Indies, Inc. v. First Nat'l Bank of Nev., 748

West Virginia ex rel. Dyer v. Sims, 563
West Virginia Health Care Cost Review Auth. v. Boone Mem'l Hosp., 289
West Virginia State Bd. of Educ. v. Barnette, 36, 357–59
Wexler v. White's Fine Furniture, Inc., 503
Wheeler v. Pilgrim's Pride Corp., 351
Whetsel v. Network Prop. Servs., LLC, 53
Whirlpool Fin. Corp. v. Sevaux, 757
White v. Baltic Conveyor Co., 491
White v. Denman, 411
White v. Edgar, 628
White v. United States Pipe & Foundry Co., 418
White v. White, 233
Whorton v. Bockting, 314–15
Wibben v. Iowa Dep't of Transp., Motor Vehicle Div., 284
Wilburn Boat Co. v. Fireman's Fund Ins. Co., 570
Wilder v. Turner, 536
Wilkins v. Chicago, St. Louis & New Orleans R.R., 432
Wilkinson v. Wallace, 316
Wilko v. Swan, 29
Will v. Calvert Fire Ins. Co., 211–12
William Jefferson & Co. v. Board of Assessment & Appeals No. 3 for Orange Cnty., 535
Williams v. Ashland Eng'g Co., 365
Williams v. City of Rochester Hills, 278
Williams v. Florida, 666
Williams v. Hewitt, 426
Williams v. Johnson, 217
Williams v. Miles, 741
Williams v. State, 219
Williams v. Williams, 394
Wilmington Trust Co. v. Clark, 711
Wilson v. Arkansas, 548
Wilson v. City of Chicago, 608
Wilson v. Garcia, 572
Wilson v. Gordon, 138
Wilson v. Great Northern Ry., 670
Wilson v. Simpson, 132
Wimberly v. Labor & Indus. Relations Comm'n of Mo., 692, 693
Windsor v. United States, 218, 641
Winn-Dixie Stores, Inc. v. Dolgencorp, LLC, 608

Winston Bros. Co. v. Galloway, 374
Wirth v. Aetna U.S. Healthcare, 638, 639
Wisconsin v. Constantineau, 675
Wisconsin v. Yoder, 545
Wisconsin Dep't of Indus. v. Gould, Inc., 136
Wisconsin Dep't of Revenue v. William Wrigley Jr., Co., 218
Wisconsin Right to Life, Inc. v. Barland, 71
Wisznia Co. v. General Star Indem. Co., 603
Wivell v. Wells Fargo Bank, 602
Wolf v. Meister-Neiberg, Inc., 62
Wolner v. Mahaska Indus., Inc., 625
Wong v. PartyGaming Ltd., 512
Wood v. Eli Lilly & Co., 603
Wood v. Moss, 526
Woods v. Carey, 167
Woods v. Interstate Realty Co., 53, 122, 124
Workman v. United Methodist Comm. on Relief of Gen. Bd. of Glob. Ministries of United Methodist Church, 107
W.R. Grace & Co. v. Local 759, Int'l Union of the United Rubber Workers, 769
Wright v. Cordesville Pentecostal Holiness Church, 327, 329
Wright v. Ford Motor Co., 613
Wright v. General Elec. Co., 302
Wright v. Tatham, 270
Wyatt v. Pennsylvania R.R., 382
Wylie v. Investment Mgmt. & Research Inc., 692

Wyoming v. Colorado, 694
Wyoming v. Oklahoma, 111, 479
Yanez-Marquez v. Lynch, 122
Yankton Sioux Tribe v. Podhradsky, 482
Yarbrough v. Oklahoma Tax Comm'n, 319
Yavuz v. 61 MM, Ltd., 753
Yesil v. Reno, 629, 631–32
Yniguez v. Arizona, 536
Young v. Baltimore & Ohio R.R., 711
Young v. Conway, 505
Young v. New York City Transit Auth., 673
Young v. Templeton, 740
Young v. United Parcel Serv., Inc., 529
Youngstown Sheet & Tube Co. v. Sawyer, 522
Zancanelli v. Central Coal & Coke Co., 659
Zheng v. Ashcroft, 242
Zicarelli v. New Jersey State Comm'n of Investigation, 542
Zigan v. State, 405
Zivotofsky ex rel. Zivotofsky v. Clinton, 522
Zivotofsky ex rel. Zivotofsky v. Kerry, 120
Zschernig v. Miller, 565
Zubik v. Burwell, 86
Zubulake v. UBS Warburg LLC, 172
Zuni Pub. Sch. Dist. No. 89 v. United States Dep't of Educ., 224
Zygowski v. Erie Morning Telegram, Inc., 131

Bibliography

Books

Abraham, Henry J. *The Judicial Process: An Introductory Analysis of the Courts of the United States, England, and France.* 6th ed. New York: Oxford Univ. Press, 1993.

Abraham, Henry J. *The Judiciary: The Supreme Court in the Governmental Process.* 5th ed. Boston: Allyn & Bacon, Inc., 1980.

Aksar, Yusuf. *Implementing International Economic Law.* Boston: Martinus Nijhoff, 2011.

Alexander, Larry; and Emily Sherwin. *Demystifying Legal Reasoning.* N.Y.: Cambridge Univ. Press, 2008.

Alexy, Robert. *A Theory of Legal Argumentation: The Theory of Rational Discourse as Theory of Legal Justification.* Ruth Adler & Neil MacCormick, trans. Oxford Univ. Press, 2011.

Allen, Carleton Kemp. *Law in the Making.* 7th ed. Oxford: Clarendon Press, 1964.

American and English Encyclopaedia of Law, The. 32 vols. David S. Garland & Lucius P. McGehee, eds. 2d ed. N.Y.: Edward Thompson, 1896–1905.

American Law and Procedure. 13 vols. Rev. ed. Chicago: LaSalle Extension Univ., 1950.

Aristotle. *Nicomachean Ethics.* Trans. Terence Irwin. Indianapolis: Hackett Pub. Co., 1985.

Atiyah, P.S.; and R.S. Summers. *Form and Substance in Anglo-American Law: A Comparative Study in Legal Reasoning, Legal Theory and Legal Institutions.* Oxford: Clarendon Press, 1987.

Atiyah, P.S. *Law and Modern Society.* Oxford: Oxford Univ. Press, 1983.

Austin, John. *Lectures on Jurisprudence, or the Philosophy of Positive Law.* Robert Campbell, ed. 2 vols. London: John Murray, 1885.

Austin, John. *The Province of Jurisprudence Determined.* [1832.] H.L.A. Hart, ed. N.Y.: Noonday Press, 1954.

Bacon, Francis. *The Works of Francis Bacon, Lord Chancellor of England.* Basil Montagu, ed. 3 vols. Philadelphia: M. Murphy, 1887.

Baker, J.H. *An Introduction to English Legal History.* 4th ed. London: Butterworths LexisNexis, 2002.

Basedow, Jürgen et al. (eds.). *The Max Planck Encyclopedia of European Private Law.* 2 vols. Oxford: Oxford Univ. Press, 2012.

Bellia, Anthony J., Jr. *Federalism.* N.Y.: Aspen Pubs., 2011.

Berch, Michael A.; Rebecca White Berch; Ralph S. Spritzer; and Jessica J. Berch. *Introduction to Legal Method and Process: Cases and Materials.* 5th ed. St. Paul: Thomson Reuters/West, 2010.

Black, Henry Campbell. *Handbook of American Constitutional Law.* 4th ed. St. Paul: West, 1927.

Black, Henry Campbell. *Handbook on the Construction and Interpretation of the Laws.* 2d ed. St. Paul: West, 1911.

Black, Henry Campbell. *Handbook on the Law of Judicial Precedents, or the Science of Case Law.* St. Paul: West, 1912.

Black, Henry Campbell. *A Treatise on the Law of Judgments.* 2d ed. 2 vols. St. Paul: West Pub. Co., 1902.

Black's Law Dictionary. Bryan A. Garner, ed. 10th ed. St. Paul: Thomson Reuters, 2014.

Blackstone, William. *Commentaries on the Laws of England.* 4th ed. 4 vols. Oxford: Clarendon Press, 1770.

Blom-Cooper, Louis; Brice Dickson; and Gavin Drewry (eds.). *The Judicial House of Lords 1876–2009.* Oxford: Oxford Univ. Press, 2009.

Bodenheimer, Edgar. *Jurisprudence: The Philosophy and Method of the Law.* Rev. ed. Cambridge, Mass.: Harvard Univ. Press, 1974.

Born, Gary B. *International Commercial Arbitration.* 2 vols. The Netherlands: Wolters Kluwer Law & Business, 2009.

Bracton, Henry de. *On the Laws and Customs of England.* [ca. 1250.] Trans. Samuel E. Thorne. 4 vols. Cambridge, Mass.: Harvard Univ. Press, 1968–1977.

Branch, Thomas. *Principia Legis et Aequitatis.* London: Henry Lintot, 1753.

Brenner, Saul; and Harold J. Spaeth. *Stare Indecisis: The Alteration of Precedent on the Supreme Court, 1946–1992.* N.Y.: Cambridge Univ. Press, 1995.

Breyer, Stephen. *Active Liberty: Interpreting Our Democratic Constitution.* N.Y.: Random House, 2007.

Breyer, Stephen. *Making Our Democracy Work: A Judge's View.* N.Y.: Random House, 2010.

Brumbaugh, Jesse Franklin. *Legal Reasoning and Briefing.* Indianapolis: Bobbs-Merrill, 1917.

Bryce, James. *The American Commonwealth.* [1888.] Repr. Indianapolis: Liberty Fund, 1995.

Buckland, W.W. *A Text-book of Roman Law from Augustus to Justinian*. Peter Stein, ed. 3d ed. Cambridge: Cambridge Univ. Press, 1963.

Buckland, W.W.; and Arnold D. McNair. *Roman Law and Common Law*. 2d ed. F.H. Lawson, ed. Cambridge: Cambridge Univ. Press, 1952.

Burke, Edmund. *Reflections on the Revolution in France*. [1790.] L.G. Mitchell, ed. N.Y.: Oxford Univ. Press, 1999.

Burton, Steven J. *Elements of Contract Interpretation*. N.Y.: Oxford Univ. Press, 2009.

Burton, Steven J. *An Introduction to Law and Legal Reasoning*. 2d ed. Boston: Aspen Law & Bus., 1995.

Cane, Peter; and Joanne Conaghan. *The New Oxford Companion to Law*. Oxford: Oxford Univ. Press, 2008.

Cappalli, Richard B. *The American Common Law Method*. Irvington-on-Hudson, N.Y.: Transnational Pubs., Inc., 1997.

Cardozo, Benjamin N. *The Nature of the Judicial Process*. New Haven: Yale Univ. Press, 1921.

Cardozo, Benjamin N. *The Paradoxes of Legal Science*. N.Y.: Columbia Univ. Press, 1928.

Carter, Lief H.; and Thomas F. Burke. *Reason in Law*. 6th ed. N.Y.: Longman, 2002. 8th ed. N.Y.: Longman, 2010.

Chamberlain, Daniel H. *The Doctrine of Stare Decisis: Its Reasons and Its Extent*. N.Y.: Baker, Voorhis, 1885.

Chemerinsky, Erwin. *Federal Jurisdiction*. 6th ed. N.Y.: Wolters Kluwer Law & Business, 2012.

Cohen, Felix S. *Ethical Systems and Legal Ideals*. N.Y.: Falcon Press, 1933. Repr., Westport, Conn.: Greenwood Press, 1976.

Columbia Law Review. *Essays on Jurisprudence from the Columbia Law Review*. N.Y.: Columbia Univ. Press, 1963.

Cooley, Roger W. (ed.). *Brief Making and the Use of Law Books*. 5th ed. St. Paul: West Pub. Co., 1926.

Cooley, Thomas M. *A Treatise on the Constitutional Limitations Which Rest upon the Legislative Power of the States of the American Union*. Boston: Little, Brown & Co., 1868.

Corley, Pamela C.; Amy Steigerwalt; and Artemus Ward. *The Puzzle of Unanimity: Consensus on the United States Supreme Court*. Stanford, Cal.: Stanford Law Books, 2013.

Coudert, Frederic R. *Certainty and Justice*. N.Y.: D. Appleton & Co., 1914.

Cross, Rupert. *Precedent in English Law*. Oxford: Clarendon Press, 1961. 2d ed. Oxford: Clarendon Press, 1968. 3d ed. Oxford: Clarendon Press, 1977. 4th ed. With J.W. Harris. Oxford: Clarendon Press, 1991.

Cueto-Rua, Julio C. *Judicial Methods of Interpretation of the Law*. Baton Rouge, La.: Paul M. Hebert Law Center Pubs. Institute, 1981.

Curtis, Charles P. *It's Your Law*. Cambridge, Mass.: Harvard Univ. Press, 1954.

Denning, Lord. *The Discipline of Law*. London: Butterworth, 1979.

Derains, Yves; and Eric A. Schwartz. *A Guide to the ICC Rules of Arbitration*. 2d ed. The Hague: Kluwer Law Int'l, 2005.

Devlin, Patrick. *The Judge*. Oxford: Oxford Univ. Press, 1979.

Devlin, Patrick. *Samples of Lawmaking*. London: Oxford Univ. Press, 1962.

Dias, R.W.M.; and G.B.J. Hughes. *Jurisprudence*. London: Butterworth, 1957.

Dicey, A.V. *Lectures on the Relation Between Law and Public Opinion in England During the Nineteenth Century*. London: Macmillan & Co., 1905.

Dillon, John F. *The Laws and Jurisprudence of England and America*. Boston: Little, Brown & Co., 1894.

Douglas, William O. *We the Judges: Studies in American and Indian Constitutional Law from Marshall to Mukherjea*. Garden City, N.Y.: Doubleday & Co., 1956.

Dowling, Noel T.; Edwin W. Patterson; and Richard R.B. Powell. *Materials for Legal Method*. 2d ed. Harry Willmer Jones, ed. Brooklyn: Foundation Press, 1952.

Dudley, Robert J. *Think Like a Lawyer*. Chicago: Nelson-Hall, 1980.

Duxbury, Neil. *The Nature and Authority of Precedent*. Cambridge: Cambridge Univ. Press, 2008.

Dworkin, Ronald. *Law's Empire*. Cambridge, Mass: Harvard Univ. Press, 1986.

Ehrenzweig, Albert A. *Psychoanalytic Jurisprudence*. Dobbs Ferry, N.Y.: Oceana Pubs., 1971.

Eisenberg, Melvin Aron. *The Nature of the Common Law*. Cambridge: Harvard Univ. Press, 1988.

Elkouri, Frank; and Edna Asper Elkouri. *How Arbitration Works*. Marlin M. Volz & Edward P. Goggin, eds. 5th ed. Washington, D.C.: Bureau of Nat'l Affairs, 1997.

Epstein, Lee; Jeffrey A. Segal; Harold J. Spaeth; and Thomas G. Walker. *The Supreme Court Compendium: Data, Decisions, and Developments*. 5th ed. Thousand Oaks, Cal.: CQ Press, 2012.

Erskine, John. *An Institute of the Law of Scotland*. [1773.] James Baldenach Nicolson, ed. 2 vols. Edinburgh: Bell & Bradfute, 1871.

BIBLIOGRAPHY: BOOKS 847

Fallon, Richard H., Jr.; John F. Manning; Daniel J. Meltzer; and David L. Shapiro. *Hart & Wechsler's The Federal Courts and the Federal System.* 6th ed. N.Y.: ThomsonReuters/Foundation Press, 2009.

Farnsworth, Ward. *The Legal Analyst: A Toolkit for Thinking About the Law.* Chicago: Univ. of Chicago Press, 2007.

Farrar, John H.; and Anthony M. Dugdale. *Introduction to Legal Method.* 2d ed. London: Sweet & Maxwell, 1984.

Fidel, Gary; and Linda Cantoni. *Think Like a Lawyer.* N.Y.: Xlibris Corp., 2004.

Finch, Henry. *Law, or, A Discourse Thereof.* London: Henry Lintot, 1759.

Fortescue, John. *De Laudibus Legum Angliæ: A Treatise in Commendation of the Laws of England.* [ca. 1470.] Andrew Amos, ed. Francis Gregor, trans. Cincinnati: Robert Clarke & Co., 1874.

Frank, Jerome. *Courts on Trial: Myth and Reality in American Justice.* Princeton: Princeton Univ. Press, 1950.

Frank, Jerome. *Law and the Modern Mind.* N.Y.: Brentano's, 1930.

Frank, W.F. *The General Principles of English Law.* 3d ed. London: George G. Harrap & Co., 1964.

Freeman, A.C. *A Treatise of the Law of Judgments.* 5th ed. 3 vols. San Francisco: Bancroft-Whitney Co., 1925.

Friedman, Lawrence M. *A History of American Law.* New York: Simon & Schuster, 1973.

Friedmann, Wolfgang. *Legal Theory.* 5th ed. London: Stevens & Sons, 1967.

Gaillard, Emmanuel; and John Savage (eds.). *Fouchard, Gaillard, Goldman on International Commercial Arbitration.* The Hague: Kluwer Law Int'l, 1999.

Gaillard, Emmanuel; and Yas Banifatemi (eds.). *Precedent in International Arbitration.* Huntington, N.Y.: Juris Pub., 2008.

Garber, Lyman A. *Of Men, and Not of Law: How the Courts Are Usurping the Political Function.* New York: Devin-Adair Co., 1966.

Gardner, John C. *Judicial Precedent in Scots Law.* Edinburgh: W. Green & Son, 1936.

Garner, Bryan A. *Garner's Dictionary of Legal Usage.* 3d ed. N.Y.: Oxford Univ. Press, 2011.

Garner, Bryan A. *The Winning Brief.* 3d ed. N.Y.: Oxford Univ. Press, 2014.

Gehring, Markus W.; Marie-Claire Cordonier Segger (eds.). *Sustainable Development in World Trade Law.* The Hague: Kluwer Law Int'l, 2005.

Gerhardt, Michael J. *The Power of Precedent.* N.Y.: Oxford Univ. Press, 2008.

Goldstein, Laurence (ed.). *Precedent in Law.* Oxford: Clarendon Press, 1987.

Goodhart, A.L. *Precedent in English and Continental Law.* London: Stevens, 1934.

Gray, John Chipman. *The Nature and Sources of the Law.* Roland Gray, ed. 2d ed. N.Y.: Macmillan, 1921.

Gross, Hyman; and Ross Harrison (eds.). *Jurisprudence: Cambridge Essays.* Oxford: Clarendon Press, 1992.

Guest, A.G. (ed.) *Oxford Essays in Jurisprudence.* Oxford: Oxford Univ. Press, 1961.

Hage, Jaap. *Studies in Legal Logic.* The Netherlands: Springer, 2005.

Hall, Kermit L. (ed.). *The Oxford Companion to American Law.* N.Y.: Oxford Univ. Press, 2002.

Hall, Kermit L. (ed.). *The Oxford Companion to the Supreme Court of the United States.* 2d ed. N.Y.: Oxford Univ. Press, 2005.

Hamilton, Alexander; James Madison; and John Jay. *The Federalist.* [1788.] Clinton Rossiter, ed. N.Y.: New American Library, 1961.

Hanks, Eva H.; Michael E. Herz; and Steven S. Nemerson. *Elements of Law.* Cincinnati: Anderson Pub. Co., 1994.

Hansford, Thomas G.; and James F. Spriggs II. *The Politics of Precedent on the U.S. Supreme Court.* Princeton: Princeton Univ. Press, 2006.

Hart, H.L.A. *The Concept of Law.* Oxford: Clarendon Press, 1961. 2d ed. N.Y.: Oxford Univ. Press, 1994. 3d ed. Oxford: Oxford Univ. Press, 2012.

Hernandéz, Gleider I. *The International Court of Justice and the Judicial Function.* Oxford: Oxford Univ. Press, 2014.

Holdsworth, William. *A History of English Law.* 2d ed. 16 vols. London: Methuen & Co., 1937.

Holdsworth, William. *Some Makers of English Law.* Cambridge: Cambridge Univ. Press, 1966.

Holdsworth, William. *Sources and Literature of English Law.* Oxford: Clarendon Press, 1925.

Holland, Randy J. (ed.). *Magna Carta: Muse and Mentor.* St. Paul: Thomson Reuters, 2014.

Holland, Thomas Erskine. *The Elements of Jurisprudence.* 7th ed. Oxford: Clarendon Press, 1895.

Holmes, Oliver Wendell. *Collected Legal Papers.* Boston: Harcourt, Brace & Howe, 1920.

Holmes, Oliver Wendell. *The Common Law.* Boston: Little, Brown & Co., 1881.

Honoré, Tony. *About Law: An Introduction.* Oxford: Clarendon Press, 1995.

Hughes, William T. *The Law Restated: The Roots of the Law.* Wash., D.C.: William T. Hughes & A.E.L. Leckie, 1915.

Huscroft, Grant (ed.). *Expounding the Constitution: Essays in Constitutional Theory.* N.Y.: Cambridge Univ. Press, 2008.

Jackson, Percival E. *Dissent in the Supreme Court: A Chronology.* Norman, Okla.: Univ. of Oklahoma Press, 1969.

Jackson, Robert H. *The Supreme Court in the American System of Government.* Cambridge: Harvard Univ. Press, 1955.

Jacob, Marc. *Precedents and Case-Based Reasoning in the European Court of Justice.* Cambridge: Cambridge Univ. Press, 2014.

Janosik, Robert J. (ed.). *Encyclopedia of the American Judicial System.* 3 vols. N.Y.: Charles Scribner's Sons, 1987.

Jolowicz, H.F. *Historical Introduction to the Study of Roman Law.* Cambridge: Cambridge Univ. Press, 1952.

Katz, Stanley N. (ed.). *The Oxford International Encyclopedia of Legal History.* 6 vols. N.Y.: Oxford Univ. Press, 2009.

Katzmann, Robert A. *Judging Statutes.* Oxford: Oxford Univ. Press, 2014.

Keeton, G.W. *The Elementary Principles of Jurisprudence.* 2d ed. London: Pitman, 1949.

Keeton, Robert E. *Keeton on Judging in the American Legal System.* Charlottesville, Va.: Lexis Law Pub., 1999.

Keeton, Robert E. *Venturing to Do Justice: Reforming Private Law.* Cambridge, Mass.: Harvard Univ. Press, 1969.

Kennedy, Duncan. *A Critique of Adjudication.* Cambridge, Mass.: Harvard Univ. Press, 1997.

Kent, James. *Commentaries on American Law.* [1826.] 4 vols. Oliver Wendell Holmes, ed. 12th ed. [1873.] Charles M. Barnes, ed. 13th ed. Boston: Little, Brown & Co., 1884.

Klafter, Craig Evan. *Reason over Precedents: Origins of American Legal Thought.* Westport, Conn.: Greenwood Press, 1993.

Klein, David E. *Making Law in the United States Courts of Appeals.* Cambridge: Cambridge Univ. Press, 2002.

Kocourek, Albert. *An Introduction to Science of Law*: Boston: Little, Brown & Co., 1930.

Korkunov, N.M. *General Theory of Law.* W.G. Hastings, trans. Rev. ed. N.Y.: Macmillan, 1922.

Lakshminath, A. *Precedent in Indian Law.* 3d ed. Lucknow: Eastern Book Co., 2009.

Law Books and Their Use. 3d ed. Rochester, N.Y.: Lawyers Co-operative Pub. Co., 1925.

Levi, Edward H. *An Introduction to Legal Reasoning.* Chicago: Univ. of Chicago Press, 1949.

Levy, Leonard W.; Kenneth L. Karst; and Dennis J. Mahoney (eds.). *Encyclopedia of the American Constitution.* 4 vols. N.Y.: Macmillan, 1986.

Lévy-Ullmann, Henri. *The English Legal Tradition: Its Sources and History.* M. Mitchell, trans. Frederic M. Goadby, ed. London: Macmillan, 1935.

Lieber, Francis. *Legal and Political Hermeneutics.* 3d ed. William G. Hammond, ed. St. Louis: F.H. Thomas & Co., 1880.

Lieber, Francis. *On Civil Liberty and Self-Government.* 3d ed. Theodore D. Woolsey, ed. Philadelphia: J.B. Lippincott & Co., 1883.

Lind, Douglas. *Logic and Legal Reasoning.* Reno, Nev.: Nat'l Judicial College, 2001.

Llewellyn, Karl. *The Bramble Bush.* [1930.] Dobbs Ferry, N.Y.: Oceana, 1960. Steve Sheppard, ed. N.Y.: Oxford Univ. Press, 2008.

Llewellyn, Karl. *The Case Law System in America.* Paul Gewirtz, ed. Chicago: Univ. of Chicago Press, 1989.

Llewellyn, Karl. *The Common Law Tradition: Deciding Appeals.* Boston: Little, Brown & Co., 1960.

Llewellyn, Karl. *Jurisprudence: Realism in Theory and Practice.* Chicago: Univ. of Chicago Press, 1962.

Lloyd, Dennis. *Introduction to Jurisprudence.* Rev. ed. N.Y.: Frederick A. Praeger, 1965.

Lobban, Michael. *The Common Law and English Jurisprudence 1760–1850.* Oxford: Clarendon Press, 1991.

Lockhart, William B.; Yale Kamisar; and Jesse H. Choper. *Constitutional Law: Cases, Comments, Questions.* 5th ed. St. Paul: West, 1980.

Lusky, Louis. *By What Right? A Commentary on the Supreme Court's Power to Revise the Constitution.* Charlottesville, Va.: Michie Co., 1975.

MacCormick, Neil. *Legal Reasoning and Legal Theory.* Oxford: Clarendon Press, 1978.

MacCormick, Neil. *Legal Right and Social Democracy: Essays in Legal and Political Philosophy.* Oxford: Clarendon Press, 1982.

MacCormick, Neil. *Rhetoric and the Rule of Law: A Theory of Legal Reasoning.* N.Y.: Oxford Univ. Press, 2005.

MacCormick, Neil; and Peter Birks (eds.). *The Legal Mind: Essays for Tony Honoré.* Oxford: Clarendon Press, 1986.

MacCormick, Neil; and Robert S. Summers. *Interpreting Precedents: A Comparative Study.* Aldershot: Dartmouth/Ashgate, 1997.

Maine, Henry Sumner. *Ancient Law.* Frederick Pollock, ed. 4th Am. ed. fr. 10th London ed. N.Y.: Henry Holt & Co., 1906.

Manchester, Colin; David Salter; Peter Moodie; and Bernadette Lynch. *Exploring the Law: The Dynamics of Precedent and Statutory Interpretation.* Sydney: Law Book Co., 1996.

BIBLIOGRAPHY: BOOKS 849

Marvell, Thomas B. *Appellate Courts and Lawyers: Information Gathering in the Adversary System.* Westport, Conn.: Greenwood Press, 1978.

Mayer Brown LLP. *Federal Appellate Practice.* Philip Allen Lacovara, ed. Arlington, Va.: BNA Books, 2008.

Mayers, Lewis. *The American Legal System.* Rev. ed. N.Y.: Harper & Row, 1964.

McKinney, Ruth Ann. *Reading Like a Lawyer: Time-Saving Strategies for Reading Law Like an Expert.* Durham, N.C.: Carolina Academic Press, 2005.

Meador, Daniel J.; Thomas E. Baker; and Joan E. Steinman. *Appellate Courts: Structures, Functions, Processes, and Personnel.* 2d ed. Newark, N.J.: LexisNexis, 2006.

Merryman, John Henry. *The Civil Law Tradition.* Stanford: Stanford Univ. Press, 1969.

Mertz, Elizabeth. *The Language of Law School.* N.Y.: Oxford Univ. Press, 2007.

Mistelis, Loukas A.; and Julian D.M. Lew (eds.). *Pervasive Problems in International Arbitration.* The Hague: Kluwer Law Int'l, 2006.

Monahan, James H. *The Method of Law: An Essay on the Statement and Arrangement of the Legal Standard of Conduct.* London: Macmillan, 1878.

Montrose, James Louis. *Precedent in English Law and Other Essays.* Harold Greville Hanbury, ed. Shannon, Ireland: Irish Univ. Press, 1968.

Moore, James W.; et al. *Moore's Federal Practice.* 3d ed. 33 vols. N.Y.: Matthew Bender, 2016.

Moore, Russell F. *Stare Decisis: Some Trends in British and American Application of the Doctrine.* N.Y.: Simmons-Boardman Pub. Corp., 1958.

Morgan, Edmund M. *Introduction to the Study of Law.* Chicago: Callaghan & Co., 1926.

Morris, Clarence. *How Lawyers Think.* Cambridge, Mass.: Harvard Univ. Press, 1937.

Morris, Gwen; Catriona Cook; Robin Creyke; and Robert Geddes. *Laying Down the Law.* 2d ed. Sydney: Butterworths, 1988.

Moses, Margaret L. *The Principles and Practice of International Commercial Arbitration.* 2d ed. N.Y.: Cambridge Univ. Press, 2012.

Muchlinski, Peter; Federico Ortino; and Christoph Schreuer (eds.). *The Oxford Handbook of International Investment Law.* N.Y.: Oxford Univ. Press, 2008.

Murphy, J. David; and Robert Rueter. *Stare Decisis in Commonwealth Appellate Courts.* Toronto: Butterworths, 1981.

Nowak, John E.; and Ronald D. Rotunda. *Constitutional Law.* 6th ed. St. Paul: West, 2000.

Paton, George Whitecross. *A Textbook of Jurisprudence.* 4th ed. G.W. Paton & David P. Derham, eds. Oxford: Oxford Univ. Press, 1972.

Patterson, Edwin W. *Jurisprudence: Men and Ideas of the Law.* Brooklyn: Foundation Press, 1953.

Paulsen, Monrad G. (ed.). *Legal Institutions Today and Tomorrow.* N.Y.: Columbia Univ. Press, 1959.

Perry, H.W., Jr. *Deciding to Decide: Agenda Setting in the United States Supreme Court.* Paperback ed. Cambridge, Mass.: Harvard Univ. Press, 1994.

Peters, Christopher J. (ed.). *Precedent in the United States Supreme Court.* N.Y.: Springer, 2013.

Pollock, Frederick. *A First Book of Jurisprudence for Students of the Common Law.* London: Macmillan, 1896.

Pollock, Frederick. *Jurisprudence and Legal Essays.* A.L. Goodhart, ed. London: Macmillan & Co., 1961.

Popkin, William D. *Evolution of the Judicial Opinion.* N.Y.: N.Y.U. Press, 2007.

Posner, Richard A. *Overcoming Law.* Cambridge, Mass.: Harvard Univ. Press, 1995.

Posner, Richard A. *The Problems of Jurisprudence.* Cambridge, Mass: Harvard Univ. Press, 1990.

Pound, Roscoe. *The Formative Era of American Law.* Boston: Little, Brown & Co., 1938.

Pound, Roscoe. *Interpretations of Legal History.* N.Y.: Macmillan, 1923.

Pound, Roscoe. *Justice According to Law.* New Haven: Yale Univ. Press, 1951.

Pound, Roscoe. *The Spirit of the Common Law.* Francestown, N.H.: Marshall Jones Co., 1921.

Ralston, Jackson H. *International Arbitration from Athens to Locarno.* Stanford, Cal.: Stanford Univ. Press, 1929.

Ram, James. *The Science of Legal Judgment.* London: A. Maxwell, 1834. Am. ed. John Townshend, ed. N.Y.: Baker, Voorhis & Co., 1871.

Raz, Joseph. *The Authority of Law: Essays on Law and Morality.* 2d ed. Oxford: Oxford Univ. Press, 2009.

Re, Edward D. *Stare Decisis.* Washington, D.C.: Federal Judicial Center, 1975.

Re, Edward D.; and Joseph R. Re. *Brief Writing and Oral Argument.* 8th ed. Dobbs Ferry, N.Y.: Oceana Pubs., 1999.

Rehnquist, William H. *The Supreme Court.* Rev. ed. N.Y.: Knopf, 2004.

Restatement (Second) of Judgments. St. Paul: American Law Institute, 1982.

Romantz, David S.; and Kathleen Elliott Vinson. *Legal Analysis: The Fundamental Skill.* 2d ed. Durham, N.C.: Carolina Academic Press, 2009.

Rosenne, Shabtai. *The Law and Practice of the International Court, 1920–2005.* 4 vols. 4th ed. Boston: Martinus Nijhoff, 2006.

Ross, Alf. *On Law and Justice.* Berkeley: Univ. of California Press, 1959.

Rovine, Arthur W. (ed.). *Contemporary Issues in International Arbitration and Mediation: The Fordham Papers 2011.* Leiden, The Netherlands: Martinus Nijhoff Pub., 2012.

Salmond, John. *Jurisprudence.* Glanville L. Williams, ed. 10th ed. London: Sweet & Maxwell, 1947.

Sampford, Charles. *Retrospectivity and the Rule of Law.* N.Y.: Oxford Univ. Press, 2006.

Scalia, Antonin; and Bryan A. Garner. *Reading Law: The Interpretation of Legal Texts.* St. Paul: Thomson/West, 2012.

Schauer, Frederick. *Thinking Like a Lawyer: A New Introduction to Legal Reasoning.* Cambridge, Mass.: Harvard Univ. Press, 2009.

Schoenbaum, Thomas J. *Admiralty and Maritime Law.* 5th ed. St. Paul: West, 2012.

Schubert, Glendon (ed.). *Judicial Decision-Making.* N.Y.: Free Press of Glencoe, 1963.

Schultz, Thomas. *Transnational Legality: Stateless Law and International Arbitration.* Oxford: Oxford Univ. Press, 2014.

Shahabuddeen, Mohamed. *Precedent in the World Court.* Cambridge: Cambridge Univ. Press, 1996.

Shapiro, Stephen M.; Kenneth Geller; Timothy S. Bishop; Edward A. Hartnett; and Dan Himmelfarb. *Supreme Court Practice.* 10th ed. Arlington, Va.: Bloomberg BNA, 2013.

Shartel, Burke. *Our Legal System and How It Operates.* Ann Arbor: Univ. of Michigan Press, 1951. Repr., N.Y.: Da Capo Press, 1971.

Shiner, Roger A. *Legal Institutions and the Sources of Law.* Amsterdam: Springer, 2005.

Siltata, Raimo. *A Theory of Precedent: From Analytical Positivism to a Post-Analytical Philosophy of Law.* Oxford: Hart Pub., 2000.

Simpson, A.W.B. *Invitation to Law.* N.Y.: Blackwell Pub., 1988.

Slapper, Gary. *How the Law Works.* 2d ed. London: Routledge, 2011.

Smith, John William. *A Selection of Leading Cases on Various Branches of the Law.* 2 vols. Thomas Willes Chitty, John Herbert Williams & Herbert Chitty, eds. 11th ed. London: Sweet & Maxwell, 1903.

Smith, Walter Denton. *A Manual of Elementary Law.* St. Paul: West, 1896.

Spaeth, Harold J.; and Jeffrey A. Segal. *Majority Rule or Minority Will: Adherence to Precedent on the U.S. Supreme Court.* N.Y.: Cambridge Univ. Press, 1999.

Stone, Ferdinand F. *Handbook of Law Study.* N.Y.: Prentice-Hall, Inc., 1952.

Stone, Julius. *Precedent and Law: Dynamics of Common Law Growth.* Sydney: Butterworths, 1985.

Story, Joseph. *Commentaries on the Constitution of the United States.* 3 vols. Boston: Hilliard, Gray & Company, 1833. 2d ed. 2 vols. Boston: Little, Brown & Co., 1858.

Sunstein, Cass R. *Legal Reasoning and Political Conflict.* N.Y.: Oxford Univ. Press, 1996.

Sunstein, Cass R. *One Case at a Time: Judicial Minimalism on the Supreme Court.* Cambridge, Mass.: Harvard Univ. Press, 1999.

Tamanaha, Brian Z. *Beyond the Formalist–Realist Divide.* Princeton: Princeton Univ. Press, 2010.

Tribe, Laurence H. *American Constitutional Law.* 3d ed. Vol. 1. N.Y.: Foundation Press, 2000.

Tribe, Laurence H. *The Invisible Constitution.* N.Y.: Oxford Univ. Press, 2008.

Twining, William. *General Jurisprudence: Understanding Law from a Global Perspective.* Cambridge: Cambridge Univ. Press, 2009.

Twining, William; and David Miers. *How to Do Things with Rules.* 4th ed. Cambridge: Cambridge Univ. Press, 1999.

Vinogradoff, Paul. *Common-Sense in Law.* London: Williams & Norgate, 1925.

von Moschzisker, Robert. *Stare Decisis, Res Judicata and Other Selected Essays.* Philadelphia: Cyrus M. Dixon, 1929.

Walker, David M. *The Oxford Companion to Law.* Oxford: Oxford Univ. Press, 1980.

Walker, David M. *The Scottish Legal System.* 6th ed. Edinburgh: W. Green/Sweet & Maxwell, 1992.

Walker, James M. *The Theory of the Common Law.* Boston: Little Brown, 1852.

Walker, Timothy. *Introduction to American Law.* Clement Bates, ed. 10th ed. Boston: Little Brown, 1895.

Wambaugh, Eugene. *The Study of Cases: A Course of Instruction.* 2d ed. Boston: Little Brown, 1894.

Warren, Samuel. *Popular and Practical Introduction to Law Studies.* N.Y.: Law Press, 1837.

Wasserstrom, Richard A. *The Judicial Decision: Toward a Theory of Legal Justification.* Stanford, Cal.: Stanford Univ. Press, 1961.

Weinreb, Lloyd L. *Legal Reason: The Use of Analogy in Legal Argument.* Cambridge: Cambridge Univ. Press, 2005.

Wigmore, John Henry. *Problems of Law: Its Past, Present, and Future*. N.Y.: Charles Scribner's Sons, 1920.

Williams, Glanville L. *Learning the Law*. A.T.H. Smith, ed. 15th ed. London: Sweet & Maxwell, 2013.

Williams, Robert F. *The Law of American State Constitutions*. Oxford Univ. Press, 2009.

Williams, Robert F. *State Constitutional Law: Cases and Materials*. 3d ed. Charlottesville, Va.: Lexis Law, 1999.

Williston, Samuel. *Some Modern Tendencies in the Law*. N.Y.: Baker, Voorhis & Co., 1929.

Windeyer, W.J.V. *Lectures in Legal History*. 2d ed. Sydney: Law Book Co. of Australasia, 1949.

Winfield, Percy H. *The Chief Sources of English Legal History*. Cambridge, Mass.: Harvard Univ. Press, 1925.

Wolfrum, Rüdiger (ed.). *The Max Planck Encyclopedia of Public International Law*. 10 vols. Oxford: Oxford Univ. Press, 2012.

Wood, Gordon S. *The Creation of the American Republic, 1776–1787*. Chapel Hill, N.C.: Univ. of North Carolina Press, 1969.

Wood, Gordon S. *The Making of the Constitution*. Waco, Tex.: Baylor Univ. Press, 1987.

Woodruff, Edwin H. *Introduction to the Study of Law*. N.Y.: Baker, Voorhis & Co., 1922.

Wortley, B.A. *Jurisprudence*. Manchester: Manchester Univ. Press, 1967.

Wright, Charles Alan; Arthur R. Miller; and Edward H. Cooper. *Federal Practice and Procedure*. 31 vols. St. Paul: West Pub. Co., 1969–2016.

Articles

Abramowicz, Michael; and Maxwell Stearns. *Defining Dicta.* 57 Stan. L. Rev. 953 (2005).

Acquaviva, Guido; and Fausto Pocar, "Stare Decisis." In 9 *The Max Planck Encyclopedia of Public International Law.* Rüdriger Wolfrum, ed. Oxford: Oxford Univ. Press, 2012.

Ahn, Matthew J. Note, *44.1 Luftbaloons: The Communication Breakdown of Foreign Law in the Federal Courts.* 89 N.Y.U. L. Rev. 1343 (2014).

Aldisert, Ruggero J. *Precedent: What It Is and What It Isn't; When Do We Kiss It and When Do We Kill It?* 17 Pepp. L. Rev. 605 (1990).

Alexander, Larry. *The Objectivity of Morality, Rules, and Law: A Conceptual Map.* 65 Ala. L. Rev. 501 (2013).

American Law Institute and American Bar Association Continuing Legal Education. *Eminent Domain and Land Valuation Litigation Appellate Practice.* C709 ALI-ABA 149 (1992).

Amos, Maurice S. *The Legal Mind.* 49 L.Q. Rev. 27 (1933).

Andrews, James DeWitt. "Jurisprudence and Legal Institutions." In 13 *American Law and Procedure.* Rev. ed. Chicago: LaSalle Extension Univ., 1950.

Asquith, Lord. *Some Aspects of the Work of the Court of Appeal.* 1 J. Soc'y Pub. Tchrs. L. 350 (1950).

Bacon, Francis. "The Lord Keeper's Speech in the Exchequer" (1617). In 2 *The Works of Francis Bacon.* Basil Montagu, ed. Philadelphia: M. Murphy, 1887.

Barfield, Daniel A. *Better to Give Than to Receive: Should Nonprofit Corporations and Charities Pay Punitive Damages?* 29 Val. U. L. Rev. 1193 (1995).

Barnett, Randy E. *It's a Bird, It's a Plane, No, It's Super Precedent: A Response to Farber and Gerhardt.* 90 Minn. L. Rev. 1232 (2006).

Barnett, Randy E. *Trumping Precedent with Original Meaning: Not as Radical as It Sounds.* 22 Const. Comment. 257 (2005).

Barrett, Amy Coney. *Stare Decisis and Due Process.* 74 U. Colo. L. Rev. 1011 (2003).

Barrett, Amy Coney. *Statutory Stare Decisis in the Courts of Appeals.* 73 Geo. Wash. L. Rev. 317 (2005).

Baude, William. *Foreword: The Supreme Court's Shadow Docket.* 9 N.Y.U. J.L. & Liberty 1 (2015).

Beck, Randy. *Transtemporal Separation of Powers in the Law of Precedent.* 87 Notre Dame L. Rev. 1405 (2012).

Bell, John. "Precedent." In *The New Oxford Companion to Law.* Peter Cane & Joanne Conaghan, eds. Oxford: Oxford Univ. Press, 2008.

Bellia, Anthony J., Jr.; and Bradford R. Clark. *The Federal Common Law of Nations.* 109 Colum. L. Rev. 1 (2009).

Berch, Michael A. *Analysis of Arizona's Depublication Rule and Practice.* 32 Ariz. St. L.J. 175 (2000).

Berger, Klaus Peter. *The International Arbitrator's Application of Precedents.* 9 J. Int'l Arb. 11 (1992).

Berkus, Sarah J. *A Critique and Comparison of En Banc Review in the Tenth and D.C. Circuits and* United States v. Nacchio. 86 Denv. U. L. Rev. 1069 (2009).

Bhagwat, Ashutosh. *Separate but Equal? The Supreme Court, The Lower Federal Courts, and the Nature of the "Judicial Power."* 80 B.U. L. Rev. 967 (2000).

Bhala, Raj. *The Myth About Stare Decisis and International Trade Law (Part One of a Trilogy).* 14 Am. U. Int'l L. Rev. 845 (1999).

Bhala, Raj. *Power of the Past: Towards De Jure Stare Decisis in WTO Adjudication (Part Three of a Trilogy).* 33 Geo. Wash. Int'l L. Rev. 873 (2001).

Bhala, Raj. *The Precedent Setters: De Facto Stare Decisis in WTO Adjudication (Part Two of a Trilogy).* 9 J. Transnat'l L. & Pol'y 1 (1999).

Bjorklund, Andrea K. "Investment Treaty Arbitral Decisions as *Jurisprudence Constante.*" In *International Economic Law: The State and Future of the Discipline.* Colin B. Picker; Isabella D. Bunn; and Douglas W. Arner, eds. Portland, Or.: Hart Pub., 2008.

Black, Ryan; and Lee Epstein. *Recusals and the "Problem" of an Equally Divided Supreme Court.* 7 J. App. Prac. & Process 75 (2005).

Bleich, Jeff. *The Reversed Circuit.* 57 Or. St. B. Bull. 17 (1997).

Blocher, Joseph. *Reverse Incorporation of State Constitutional Law.* 84 S. Cal. L. Rev. 323 (2011).

Blom-Cooper, Louis. "1966 and All That: The Story of the Practice Statement." In *The Judicial House of Lords 1876–2009.* Louis Blom-Cooper; Brice Dickson; and Gavin Drewry, eds. Oxford: Oxford Univ. Press, 2009.

Boggs, Danny J.; and Brian P. Brooks. *Unpublished Opinions and the Nature of Precedent.* 4 Green Bag 2d 17 (2000).

Bradford, C. Steven. *Following Dead Precedent: The Supreme Court's Ill-Advised Rejection of Anticipatory Overruling.* 59 Fordham L. Rev. 39 (1990).

Bradley, Curtis A.; and Jack L. Goldsmith. *Customary International Law as Federal Common Law: A Critique of the Modern Position.* 110 Harv. L. Rev. 815 (1997).

BIBLIOGRAPHY: ARTICLES

Brennan, William J. *State Constitutions and the Protection of Individual Rights.* 90 Harv. L. Rev. 489 (1977).

Brewer, Scott. *Exemplary Reasoning: Semantics, Pragmatics, and the Rational Force of Legal Argument by Analogy.* 109 Harv. L. Rev. 923 (1996).

Breyer, Stephen. *Reflections on the Role of Appellate Courts: A View from the Supreme Court.* 8 J. App. Prac. & Process 91 (2006).

Calogero, Pascal F., Jr. *Advisory Opinions: A Wise Change for Louisiana and Its Judiciary?* 38 Loy. L. Rev. 329 (1992).

Caminker, Evan H. *Precedent and Prediction: The Forward-Looking Aspects of Inferior Court Decisionmaking.* 73 Tex. L. Rev. 1 (1994).

Caminker, Evan H. *Why Must Inferior Courts Obey Superior Court Precedents?* 46 Stan. L. Rev. 817 (1994).

Carpenter, Charles E. *Court Decisions and the Common Law.* 17 Colum. L. Rev. 593 (1917).

Coale, David; and Wendy Couture. *Loud Rules.* 34 Pepp. L. Rev. 715 (2007).

Cochran, Rebecca A. *Federal Court Certification of Questions of State Law to State Courts: A Theoretical and Empirical Study.* 29 J. Legis. 157 (2003).

Collier, Charles W. *Precedent and Legal Authority: A Critical History.* 1988 Wis. L. Rev. 771.

Comment. *Supreme Court No-Clear-Majority Decisions: A Study in Stare Decisis.* 24 U. Chi. L. Rev. 99 (1956).

Commission, Jeffery P. *Precedent in Investment Treaty Arbitration: A Citation Analysis of a Developing Jurisprudence.* 24 J. Int'l Arb. 2 (2007).

Consovoy, William S. *The Rehnquist Court and the End of Constitutional Stare Decisis:* Casey, Dickerson *and the Consequences of Pragmatic Adjudication.* 2002 Utah L. Rev. 53 (2002).

Cooper, Charles J. *Stare Decisis: Precedent and Principle in Constitutional Adjudication.* 73 Cornell L. Rev. 401 (1988).

Corbin, Arthur L. *The Law and the Judges.* 3 Yale Rev. 234 (1914).

Corbin, Arthur L. *What Is the Common Law?* 3 Am. L. Sch. Rev. 73 (1911).

Cordray, Margaret Meriwether; and Richard Cordray. *The Philosophy of Certiorari: Jurisprudential Considerations in Supreme Court Case Selection.* 82 Wash. U. L.Q. 389 (2004).

Cordray, Margaret Meriwether; and Richard Cordray. *Strategy in Supreme Court Case Selection: The Relationship Between Certiorari and the Merits.* 69 Ohio St. L.J. 1 (2008).

Cotropia, Christopher A. *Determining Uniformity Within the Federal Circuit by Measuring Dissent and En Banc Review.* 43 Loy. L.A. L. Rev. 801 (2010).

Coudert, Frederic R. *Certainty and Justice.* 14 Yale L.J. 361 (1905).

Dennis, James L. *Interpretation and Application of the Civil Code and the Evaluation of Judicial Precedent.* 54 La. L. Rev. 1 (1993).

Dickinson, John. *Legal Rules: Their Function in the Process of Decision.* 79 U. Penn. L. Rev. 833 (1931).

Dobbins, Jeffrey C. *Structure and Precedent.* 108 Mich. L. Rev. 1453 (2010).

Dorf, Michael C. *Dicta and Article III.* 142 U. Pa. L. Rev. 1997 (1994).

Dorf, Michael C. *Prediction and the Rule of Law.* 42 UCLA L. Rev. 651 (1995).

Douglas, Joshua A. *The Procedure of Election Law in Federal Courts.* 2011 Utah L. Rev. 433.

Douglas, William O. "The Decline of Stare Decisis." In *An Autobiography of the Supreme Court.* Alan F. Westin, ed. N.Y.: Macmillan, 1963.

Douglas, William O. "Stare Decisis." In *Essays on Jurisprudence from the Columbia Law Review.* N.Y.: Columbia Univ. Press, 1963.

Dragich, Martha J. *Uniformity, Inferiority, and the Law of the Circuit Doctrine.* 56 Loy. L. Rev. 535 (2010).

Dragich, Martha J. *Will the Federal Courts of Appeals Perish if They Publish? Or Does the Declining Use of Opinions to Explain and Justify Judicial Decisions Pose a Greater Threat?* 44 Am. U. L. Rev. 757 (1995).

Easterbrook, Frank H. *Judicial Discretion in Statutory Interpretation.* 57 Okla. L. Rev. 1 (2004).

Easterbrook, Frank H. *Stability and Reliability in Judicial Decisions.* 73 Cornell L. Rev. 422 (1988).

Eber, Michael L. Comment, *When the Dissent Creates the Law: Cross-Cutting Majorities and the Prediction Model of Precedent.* 58 Emory L.J. 207 (2008).

Eisenberg, Theodore; and Geoffrey P. Miller. *Reversal, Dissent, and Variability in State Supreme Courts: The Centrality of Jurisdictional Source.* 89 B.U. L. Rev. 1451 (2009).

Ely, John Hart. *The Irrepressible Myth of* Erie. 87 Harv. L. Rev. 693 (1974).

Eskridge, William N., Jr. *The Case of the Amorous Defendant: Criticizing Absolute Stare Decisis for Statutory Cases.* 88 Mich. L. Rev. 2450 (1990).

Eskridge, William N., Jr. *Overruling Statutory Precedents.* 76 Geo. L.J. 1361 (1988).

Fallon, Richard H., Jr. *Stare Decisis and the Constitution: An Essay on Constitutional Methodology.* 76 N.Y.U. L. Rev. 570 (2001).

Fallon, Richard H., Jr.; and Daniel J. Meltzer. *New Law, Non-Retroactivity, and Constitutional Remedies.* 104 Harv. L. Rev. 1731 (1991).

Farber, Daniel A. *The Rule of Law and the Law of Precedents*. 90 Minn. L. Rev. 1173 (2006).

Feldman, Stephen M. "History and Law." In *The Oxford Companion to American Law*. Kermit L. Hall, ed. N.Y.: Oxford Univ. Press, 2002.

Finkelstein, Maurice. *Judicial Self-Limitation*. 37 Harv. L. Rev. 338 (1924).

Flanders, Chad. *Toward a Theory of Persuasive Authority*. 62 Okla. L. Rev. 55 (2009).

Fleming, Elizabeth; and Rebecca Clawson. *Fraud Counterclaims in the Court of Federal Claims: Not So Fast, My Friend*. 46 Procurement Law. 3 (2011).

Fon, Vincy; and Francesco Parisi. *Judicial Precedents in Civil Law Systems: A Dynamic Analysis*. 26 Int'l Rev. L. & Econ. 519 (2007).

Foster, Sydney. *Should Courts Give Stare Decisis Effect to Statutory Interpretation Methodology?* 96 Geo. L.J. 1863 (2008).

Fowler, Thomas L. *Holding, Dictum... Whatever*. 25 N.C. Cent. L.J. 139 (2003).

Fox, Lawrence J. *Those Unpublished Opinions: An Appropriate Expedience or an Abdication of Responsibility*. 32 Hofstra L. Rev. 1215 (2004).

Frankfurter, Felix. *A Note on Advisory Opinions*. 37 Harv. L. Rev. 1002 (1924).

Friendly, Henry J. *In Praise of* Erie—*and of the New Federal Common Law*. 39 N.Y.U. L. Rev. 383 (1964).

Friendly, Henry J. *Is Innocence Irrelevant? Collateral Attacks on Criminal Judgments*. 38 U. Chi. L. Rev. 142 (1970).

Frost, Amanda. *Inferiority Complex: Should State Courts Follow Lower Federal Court Precedent on the Meaning of Federal Law?* 68 Vand. L. Rev. 53 (2015).

Fuller, Lon L. *Reason and Fiat in Case Law*. 59 Harv. L. Rev. 376 (1946).

Gardner, James A. *The Failed Discourse of State Constitutionalism*. 90 Mich. L. Rev. 761 (1992).

Garner, Bryan A. "A Lexicographic Look at Magna Carta." In *Magna Carta: Muse and Mentor*. Randy J. Holland, ed. St. Paul: Thomson Reuters, 2014.

Garner, Bryan A. "Opinions, Style of." In *The Oxford Companion to the Supreme Court of the United States*. 2d ed. Kermit Hall, ed. N.Y.: Oxford Univ. Press, 2005.

George, Tracey E.; and Michael E. Solimine. *Supreme Court Monitoring of the United States Courts of Appeals En Banc*. 9 Sup. Ct. Econ. Rev. 171 (2001).

Gelinas, Fabian. "Investment Tribunals and the Commercial Arbitration Model: Mixed Procedures and Creeping Instiutionalism." In *Sustainable Development in World Trade Law*. Markus W. Gehring & Marie-Claire Cordonier Segger, eds. The Hague: Kluwer Law Int'l, 2005.

George, Tracey E.; and Michael E. Solimine. *Supreme Court Monitoring of the United States Courts of Appeals En Banc*. 9 Sup. Ct. Econ. Rev. 171 (2001).

Gerhardt, Michael J. *Super Precedent*. 90 Minn. L. Rev. 1204 (2006).

Gilmore, Grant. *Legal Realism: Its Cause and Cure*. 70 Yale L.J. 1037 (1961).

Ginsburg, Douglas H.; and Donald Falk. *The Court En Banc: 1981–1990*. 59 Geo. Wash. L. Rev. 1008 (1991).

Glensy, Rex D. *Which Countries Count?* Lawrence v. Texas *and the Selection of Foreign Persuasive Authority*. 45 Va. J. Int'l L. 357 (2005).

Gluck, Abbe R. *Intersystemic Statutory Interpretation: Methodology as "Law" and the* Erie *Doctrine*. 120 Yale L.J. 1898 (2011).

Goodhart, Arthur L. *Case Law—A Short Replication*. 50 L.Q. Rev. 196 (1934).

Goodhart, Arthur L. *Case Law in England and America*. 15 Cornell L.Q. 173 (1930).

Goodhart, Arthur L. *Determining the* Ratio Decidendi *of a Case*. 40 Yale L.J. 161 (1930).

Goodhart, Arthur. "The *Ratio Decidendi* of a Case." In *Essays in Jurisprudence and the Common Law*. Cambridge: Cambridge Univ. Press, 1931.

Goodhart, Arthur L. *The* Ratio Decidendi *of a Case*. 22 Mod. L. Rev. 117 (1959).

Gorsuch, Neil M. *Of Lions and Bears, Judges and Legislators, and the Legacy of Justice Scalia*. 66 Case W. Res. L. Rev. 905 (2016).

Gossett, David M. Chevron, *Take Two: Deference to Revised Agency Interpretations of Statutes*. 64 U. Chi. L. Rev. 681 (1997).

Graham, Scott. *9th Circuit's Clarion Calls Are Being Heard*. The Recorder (Cal.), 31 Aug. 2012.

Grantmore, Gil [pseudonym]. *The Headnote*. 5 Green Bag 2d 157 (2002).

Gray, John Chipman. *Judicial Precedents—A Short Study in Comparative Jurisprudence*. 9 Harv. L. Rev. 27 (1895).

Greenawalt, Kent. *Reflections on Holding and Dictum*. 39 J. Legal Educ. 431 (1989).

Greenberg, Harold M. *Why Agency Interpretations of Ambiguous Statutes Should Be Subject to Stare Decisis*. 79 Tenn. L. Rev. 573 (2012).

Guest, A.G. "Logic in the Law." In *Oxford Essays in Jurisprudence*. A.G. Guest, ed. Oxford: Oxford Univ. Press, 1961.

Gulati, Mitu; and Veronica Sanchez. *Giants in a World of Pygmies? Testing the Superstar Hypothesis with Judicial Opinions in Casebooks*. 87 Iowa L. Rev. 1141 (2002).

Gunderson, Joan R. "Advisory Opinions." In *The Oxford Companion to the Supreme Court of the United States*. 2d ed. Kermit L. Hall, ed. N.Y.: Oxford Univ. Press, 2005.

Guzman, Andrew T.; and Timothy L. Meyer. *International Common Law: The Soft Law of International Tribunals*. 9 Chi. J. Int'l L. 515 (2009).

Hall, Ford W. *The Common Law: An Account of Its Reception in the United States*, 4 Vand. L. Rev. 791 (1951).

Hamilton, Clyde H. *Effective Appellate Brief Writing*. 50 S.C. L. Rev. 581 (1999).

Hardisty, James. *Reflections on Stare Decisis*. 55 Ind. L.J. 41 (1979).

Harlan, John M. *Manning the Dikes*. 13 Rec. Ass'n of the Bar of City of N.Y. 541 (1958).

Hartnett, Edward A. *Ties in the Supreme Court of the United States*. 44 Wm. & Mary L. Rev. 643 (2002).

Hasen, David M. *The Ambiguous Basis of Judicial Deference to Administrative Rules*. 17 Yale J. on Reg. 327 (2000).

Healy, Thomas. *The Rise of Unnecessary Constitutional Rulings*. 83 N.C. L. Rev. 847 (2005).

Healy, Thomas. *Stare Decisis as a Constitutional Requirement*. 104 W. Va. L. Rev. 43 (2001).

Heinsz, Timothy J. *Grieve It Again: Of Stare Decisis, Res Judicata and Collateral Estoppel in Labor Arbitration*. 38 B.C. L. Rev. 275 (1997).

Henderson, M. Todd. *From Seriatim to Consensus and Back Again: A Theory of Dissent*. 2007 Sup. Ct. Rev. 283 (2007).

Hensley, Thomas R.; and Scott P. Johnson. *Unanimity on the Rehnquist Court*. 31 Akron L. Rev. 387 (1998).

Hessick, F. Andrew. *Cases, Controversies, and Diversity*. 109 Nw. U. L. Rev. 57 (2015).

Hickman, Kristin E.; and Matthew D. Krueger. *In Search of the Modern* Skidmore *Standard*. 107 Colum. L. Rev. 1235 (2007).

Hilyerd, William A. *Using the Law Library: A Guide for Educators Part VI: Working with Judicial Opinions and Other Primary Sources*. 35 J.L. & Educ. 67 (2006).

Holdsworth, William S. *Case Law*. 50 L.Q. Rev. 180 (1934).

Holdsworth, William S. "The Case-Law System: Historical Factors Which Controlled Its Development." In *The Life of the Law*. John Honnold, ed. N.Y.: Free Press of Glencoe, 1964.

Holland, Randy J. *State Constitutions: Purpose and Function*. 69 Temple L. Rev. 989 (1996).

Holmes, Oliver Wendell. "Holdsworth's English Law." In *Collected Legal Papers*. Boston: Harcourt, Brace & Howe, 1920.

Holmes, Oliver Wendell. *The Path of the Law*. 10 Harv. L. Rev. 457 (1897).

Hoover, Craig A. *Deference to Federal Circuit Court Interpretations of Unsettled State Law: Factors, Etc., Inc. v. Pro Arts, Inc.* 1982 Duke L.J. 704.

Hopenfeld, James E. Festo: *A Jurisprudential Test for the Supreme Court?* 1 J. Marshall Rev. Intell. Prop. L. 69 (2001).

Hornblower, William B. *A Century of "Judge-Made" Law*. 7 Colum. L. Rev. 453 (1907).

Hudson, Manley O. *Advisory Opinions of National and International Courts*. 37 Harv. L. Rev. 970 (1924).

Hudson, Manley O. *The Permanent Court of International Justice*. 36 Harv. L. Rev. 245 (1922).

Hunter, Dan. *Reason Is Too Large: Analogy and Precedent in Law*. 50 Emory L.J. 1197 (2001).

Hutchinson, Dennis J. *Unanimity and Desegregation: Decisionmaking in the Supreme Court, 1948–1958*. 68 Geo. L.J. 1 (1979).

Hutchison, Harry G. Lochner, *Liberty of Contract, and Paternalism: Revising the Revisionists?* 47 Ind. L. Rev. 421 (2014).

Ibbetson, David. "Doctrine of Precedent." In 4 *The Oxford International Encyclopedia of Legal History*. Stanley N. Katz, ed. N.Y.: Oxford Univ. Press, 2009.

Jackson, Robert H. *Decisional Law and Stare Decisis*. 30 A.B.A. J. 334 (1944).

Jay, Stewart. *Most Humble Servants: The Advisory Role of Early Judges*. New Haven: Yale Univ. Press, 1997.

Jessup, Philip C. *The Doctrine of* Erie Railroad v. Tompkins *Applied to International Law*. 33 Am. J. Int'l L. 740 (1939).

Johnson, Foster Calhoun. *Judicial Magic: The Use of Dicta as Equitable Remedy*. 46 U.S.F. L. Rev. 883 (2012).

Kadens, Emily. *Justice Blackstone's Common Law Orthodoxy*. 103 Nw. U. L. Rev. 1553 (2009).

Kanne, Michael S. *The "Non-Banc En Banc": Seventh Circuit Rule 40(e) and the Law of the Circuit*. 32 S. Ill. U. L.J. 611 (2008).

Karst, Kenneth L. "Precedent." In 3 *Encyclopedia of the American Constitution*. Leonard W. Levy et al., eds. N.Y.: Macmillan, 1986.

Kaufmann-Kohler, Gabrielle. *Arbitral Precedent: Dream, Necessity or Excuse? The 2006 Freshfields Lecture*. 23 Arb. Int'l 357 (2007).

Kaufmann-Kohler, Gabrielle. "Interpretation of Treaties: How Do Arbitral Tribunals Interpret Dispute Settlement Provisions Embodied in Investment Treaties?" In *Pervasive Problems in International Arbitration*. Loukas A. Mistelis & Julian D.M. Lew, eds. The Hague: Kluwer Law Int'l, 2006.

Kaufmann-Kohler, Gabrielle. "Is Consistency a Myth?" In *Precedent in International Arbitration.* Emmanuel Gaillard & Yas Banifatemi, eds. Huntington, N.Y.: Juris Pub., 2008.

Keckler, Charles N.W. *The Hazards of Precedent: A Parameterization of Legal Change.* 80 Miss. L.J. 105 (2010).

Kempin, Frederick G., Jr. *Precedent and Stare Decisis: The Critical Years, 1800 to 1850.* 3 Am. J. Legal Hist. 28 (1959).

Killian, Ryan S. *Dicta and the Rule of Law.* 2013 Pepp. L. Rev. 1 (2013).

Kimura, Ken. Note, *A Legitimacy Model for the Interpretation of Plurality Decisions.* 77 Cornell L. Rev. 1593 (1992).

Kinports, Kit. *The Supreme Court's Love–Hate Relationship with Miranda.* 101 J. Crim L. & Criminology 375 (2011).

Kirman, Igor. *Standing Apart to Be a Part: The Precedential Value of Supreme Court Concurring Opinions,* 95 Colum. L. Rev. 2083 (1995).

Klein, David E.; and Neal Devins. *Dicta, Schmicta: Theory Versus Practice in Lower Court Decision Making.* 54 Wm. & Mary L. Rev. 2021 (2013).

Kocourek, Albert. *Retrospective Decisions and Stare Decisis and a Proposal.* 17 A.B.A. J. 180 (1931).

Kocourek, Albert; and Harold Koven. *Renovation of the Common Law Through Stare Decisis.* 29 Ill. L. Rev. 971 (1935).

Koh, Harold Hongju. *Is International Law Really State Law?* 111 Harv. L. Rev. 1824 (1998).

Kornhauser, Lewis A. *Adjudication by a Resource-Constrained Team: Hierarchy and Precedent in a Judicial System.* 68 S. Cal. L. Rev. 1605 (1995).

Kornhauser, Lewis A. *An Economic Perspective on Stare Decisis.* 65 Chi.-Kent L. Rev. 63 (1989).

Kort, Fred. "Content Analysis of Judicial Opinions and Rules of Law." In *Judicial Decision-Making.* Glendon Schubert, ed. N.Y.: Free Press of Glencoe, 1963.

Kozel, Randy J. *The Scope of Precedent.* 113 Mich. L. Rev. 179 (2014).

Kozel, Randy J. *Stare Decisis as Judicial Doctrine.* 67 Wash. & Lee L. Rev. 411 (2010).

Kozinski, Alex; and James Burnham. *I Say Dissental, You Say Concurral.* 121 Yale L.J. 601 (2012).

Kozinski, Alex; and Stephen Reinhardt. *Please Don't Cite This.* Cal. Law. June 2000, at 44.

Kress, Ken. *Legal Indeterminacy,* 77 Cal. L. Rev. 283 (1989).

Krishnakumar, Anita S. *Longstanding Agency Interpretations.* 83 Fordham L. Rev. 1823 (2015).

Kroger, John R. *Supreme Court Equity, 1789–1835, and the History of American Judging.* 34 Hous. L. Rev. 1425 (1998).

Kronman, Anthony T. *Precedent and Tradition.* 99 Yale L.J. 1029 (1990).

Landes, W.; and Richard A. Posner. *Legal Precedent: A Theoretical and Empirical Analysis.* 19 J. Law & Econ. 249 (1976).

Larson, Robert L. *Importance and Value of Attorney General Opinions.* 41 Iowa L. Rev. 351 (1955).

Lash, Kurt T. *Originalism, Popular Sovereignty, and Reverse Stare Decisis.* 93 Va. L. Rev. 1437 (2007).

Lawson, Gary. *Controlling Precedent: Congressional Regulation of Judicial Decision-Making.* 18 Const. Comment. 191 (2001).

Lawson, Gary. *Stare Decisis and Constitutional Meaning: Panel II—The Constitutional Case Against Precedent.* 17 Harv. J. L. & Pub. Pol'y 23 (1994).

Lebovits, Gerald. *Technique: A Legal Method to the Madness.* N.Y. St. B. Ass'n J., June 2003, at 64.

Ledebur, Linas E. Comment, *Plurality Rule: Concurring Opinions and a Divided Supreme Court.* 113 Penn St. L. Rev. 899 (2009).

Lee, Thomas R. *Stare Decisis in Historical Perspective: From the Founding Era to the Rehnquist Court.* 52 Vand. L. Rev. 647 (1999).

Lefstin, Jeffrey A. *The Measure of the Doubt: Dissent, Indeterminacy, and Interpretation at the Federal Circuit.* 58 Hastings L.J. 1025 (2007).

Leonard, James. *An Analysis of Citations to Authority in Ohio Appellate Decisions Published in 1990.* 86 Law Libr. J. 129 (1994).

LeRoy, Michael H. *Death of a Precedent: Should Justices Rethink Their Consensus Norms?* 43 Hofstra L. Rev. 377 (2014).

LeRoy, Michael H. *Overruling Precedent: "A Derelict in the Stream of the Law."* 66 SMU L. Rev. 711 (2013).

Leval, Pierre N. *Judging Under the Constitution: Dicta About Dicta.* 81 N.Y.U. L. Rev. 1249 (2006).

Levy, Beryl Harold. *Realist Jurisprudence and Prospective Overruling.* 109 U. Pa. L. Rev. 1 (1960).

Lewis, T. Ellis. *The History of Judicial Precedent,* 1930–32. 46 L.Q. Rev. 207, 341 (1930); 47 L.Q. Rev. 411 (1931); 48 L.Q. Rev. 230 (1932).

Lieber, Francis. *Legal and Political Hermeneutics, or Principles of Interpretation and Construction in Law and Politics, with Remarks on Precedents and Authorities Note G: On Analogy and the Ratio Legis.* 16 Cardozo L. Rev. 2079 (1995).

Lile, W.M. *Some Views on the Rule of Stare Decisis.* 4 Va. L. Rev. 95 (1916).

Lincoln, Alexander. *The Relation of Judicial Decisions to the Law.* 21 Harv. L. Rev. 120 (1907).

Logan, Wayne A. *A House Divided: When State and Lower Federal Courts Disagree on Federal Constitutional Rights.* 90 Notre Dame L. Rev. 235 (2014).

Lookofsky, Joseph. *Digesting CISG Case Law: How Much Regard Should We Have?* 8 Vindobona J. Int'l L. & Com. Arb. 181 (2004).

Lucy, William. "Judges, Distinguished." In *The New Oxford Companion to Law.* Peter Cane & Joanne Conaghan, eds. Oxford: Oxford Univ. Press, 2008.

Lunney, Leslie A. *The Erosion of* Miranda: *Stare Decisis Consequences.* 48 Cath. U. L. Rev. 727 (1999).

Lyons, David. *Formal Justice and Judicial Precedent.* 38 Vand. L. Rev. 495 (1985).

Macey, Jonathan R. *The Internal and External Costs and Benefits of Stare Decisis.* 65 Chi.-Kent L. Rev. 93 (1989).

Maltz, Earl. *The Nature of Precedent.* 66 N.C. L. Rev. 367 (1988).

Maltz, Earl. *Some Thoughts on the Death of Stare Decisis in Constitutional Law.* 1980 Wis. L. Rev. 467.

Marshall, Lawrence C. *"Let Congress Do It": The Case for an Absolute Rule of Statutory Stare Decisis.* 88 Mich. L. Rev. 177 (1989).

Martin, Peter W. *Reconfiguring Law Reports and the Concept of Precedent for a Digital Age.* 53 Vill. L. Rev. 1 (2008).

Martinez, Jenny S. *Towards an International Judicial System.* 56 Stan. L. Rev. 429 (2003).

Masur, Jonathan. *Judicial Deference and the Credibility of Agency Commitments.* 60 Vand. L. Rev. 1021 (2007).

McAllister, Marc. *Dicta Redefined.* 47 Willamette L. Rev. 161 (2011).

McClain, Emlin. *Dissenting Opinions.* 14 Yale L.J. 191 (1905).

McGinnis, John O.; and Michael B. Rappaport. *Reconciling Originalism and Precedent.* 103 Nw. U. L. Rev. 803 (2009).

McGowan, Daniel. *Judicial Writing and the Ethics of the Judicial Office*, 14 Geo. J. Legal Ethics 509 (2001).

McKean, Frederick G., Jr. *The Rule of Precedents.* 76 U. Pa. L. Rev. 481 (1928).

McKnight, H. Brent. *How Shall We Then Reason? The Historical Setting of Equity.* 45 Mercer L. Rev. 919 (1994).

Mead, Joseph. *Stare Decisis in the Inferior Courts of the United States.* 12 Nev. L.J. 787 (2012).

Merrill, Thomas W. *Judicial Deference to Executive Precedent.* 101 Yale L.J. 969 (1992).

Merrill, Thomas W. *Originalism, Stare Decisis and the Promotion of Judicial Restraint.* 22 Const. Comment. 271 (2005).

Meyer, Linda. *"Nothing We Say Matters":* Teague *and New Rules.* 61 U. Chi. L. Rev. 423 (1994).

Meyler, Bernadette. *Towards a Common Law Originalism*, 59 Stan. L. Rev. 551 (2006).

Michalski, Roger M. *Pleading and Proving Foreign Law in the Age of Plausibility Reading.* 59 Buff. L. Rev. 1207 (2011).

Miguel, Alfonso Ruiz. *Equality Before the Law and Precedent.* 10 Ratio Juris 372 (1997).

Miller, Samuel F. *The Use and Value of Authorities.* 23 Am. L. Rev. 165 (1889).

Mitchell, Jonathan F. *Stare Decisis and Constitutional Text.* 110 Mich. L. Rev. 1 (2011).

Molot, Jonathan T. *The Judicial Perspective in the Administrative State: Reconciling Modern Doctrines of Deference with the Judiciary's Structural Role.* 53 Stan. L. Rev. 1 (2000).

Monaghan, Henry Paul. *Stare Decisis and Constitutional Adjudication.* 88 Colum. L. Rev. 723 (1988).

Moore, James W.; and Robert Stephen Oglebay. *The Supreme Court, Stare Decisis and Law of the Case.* 21 Tex. L. Rev. 514 (1943).

Morrison, Trevor W. *Stare Decisis in the Office of Legal Counsel.* 110 Colum. L. Rev. 1448 (2010).

Nelson, Caleb. *Stare Decisis and Demonstrably Erroneous Precedents.* 87 Va. L. Rev. 1 (2001).

Note. *Advisory Opinions on the Constitutionality of Statutes.* 69 Harv. L. Rev. 1302 (1956).

Note. *Applicability of State Conflicts Rules When Issues of State Law Arise in Federal Question Cases.* 68 Harv. L. Rev. 1212 (1955).

Note. *Constitutional Stare Decisis.* 103 Harv. L. Rev. 1344 (1990).

Note. *Developments in the Law of Res Judicata.* 65 Harv. L. Rev. 818 (1952).

Note. *The Law of the Case.* 42 Harv. L. Rev. 938 (1929).

Note. *Stare Decisis.* 34 Harv. L. Rev. 74 (1920).

Note. *Stare Decisis and the Lower Courts: Two Recent Cases.* 59 Colum. L. Rev. 504 (1959).

Novak, Linda. Note, *The Precedential Value of Supreme Court Plurality Decisions.* 80 Colum. L. Rev. 756 (1980).

Nygaard, Richard Lowell. *The Maligned Per Curiam: A Fresh Look at an Old Colleague.* 5 Scribes J. Legal Writing 41 (1996).

O'Connor, Sandra Day. *William Howard Taft and the Importance of Unanimity.* 28 J. Sup. Ct. History 157 (2003).

O'Hara, Erin. *Social Constraint or Implicit Collusion? Toward a Game Theoretic Analysis of Stare Decisis.* 24 Seton Hall L. Rev. 736 (1993).

Ohrenschall, John C. *Diverse Views of What Constitutes the Principle of Law of a Case.* 36 U. Colo. L. Rev. 377 (1964).

Oliphant, Herman. *A Return to Stare Decisis.* 14 A.B.A. J. 71 (1928).

Oliphant, Herman. *Stare Decisis—Continued.* 14 A.B.A. J. 159 (1928).

O'Neill, Paul T. *Charitable Immunity: The Time to End Laissez-Faire Health Care in Massachusetts Has Come.* 82 Mass. L. Rev. 223 (1997).

Owens, Ryan J.; and David A. Simon. *Explaining the Supreme Court's Shrinking Docket.* 53 Wm. & Mary L. Rev. 1219 (2012).

Padden, Amy L. *Overruling Decisions in the Supreme Court: The Role of a Decision's Vote, Age, and Subject Matter in the Application of Stare Decisis After* Payne v. Tennessee. 82 Geo. L.J. 1689 (1994).

Palmeter, David; and Petros C. Mavroidis. *The WTO Legal System: Sources of Law.* 92 Am. J. Int'l L. 398 (1998).

Paulsen, Michael Stokes. *Abrogating Stare Decisis by Statute: May Congress Remove the Precedential Effect of* Roe *and* Casey? 109 Yale L.J. 1535 (2000).

Paulsson, Jan. "The Role of Precedent in Investment Arbitration." In *Arbitration Under International Investment Agreements.* Katia Yannaca-Small, ed. N.Y.: Oxford Univ. Press, 2010.

Persky, Jonathan D. *"Ghosts That Slay": A Contemporary Look at State Advisory Opinions.* 37 Conn. L. Rev. 1155 (2005).

Peters, Christopher J. *Foolish Consistency: On Equality, Integrity, and Justice in Stare Decisis.* 105 Yale L.J. 2031 (1996).

Peterson, G.L., et al. *Recollections of* West Virginia State Board of Education v. Barnette. 81 St. John's L. Rev. 755 (2007).

Pfander, James E. *Federal Supremacy, State Court Inferiority, and the Constitutionality of Jurisdiction-Stripping Legislation.* 101 Nw. U. L. Rev. 191 (2007).

Pierce, Richard J., Jr. *Reconciling* Chevron *and Stare Decisis.* 85 Geo. L.J. 2225 (1997).

Pittman, Larry J. *The Federal Arbitration Act: The Supreme Court's Erroneous Statutory Interpretation, Stare Decisis, and a Proposal for Change.* 53 Ala. L. Rev. 789 (2002).

Pollock, Frederick. "Judicial Caution and Valour" (1929). In *Jurisprudence in Action: A Pleader's Anthology.* N.Y.: Baker, Voorhis & Co., 1953.

Ponzetto, Giacomo A.M.; and Patricio A. Fernandez. *Case Law Versus Statute Law: An Evolutionary Comparison.* 37 J. Legal Stud. 379 (2008).

Posner, Richard A. *The Meaning of Judicial Self-Restraint.* 59 Ind. L.J. 1 (1984).

Pound, Roscoe. *Common Law and Legislation.* 21 Harv. L. Rev. 383 (1908).

Pound, Roscoe. *Juristic Science and Law.* 31 Harv. L. Rev. 1047 (1918).

Pound, Roscoe. *The Theory of Judicial Decision.* 36 Harv. L. Rev. 641 (1923).

Pound, Roscoe. *What of Stare Decisis?* 10 Fordham L. Rev. 1 (1941).

Powell, Lewis F., Jr. *Stare Decisis and Judicial Restraint.* 47 Wash. & Lee L. Rev. 281 (1990).

Price, Polly J. *Precedent and Judicial Power After the Founding.* 42 B.C. L. Rev. 81 (2000).

Radin, Max. "Case Law and Stare Decisis: Concerning *Präjudizienrecht in Amerika.*" In *Essays on Jurisprudence from the Columbia Law Review.* N.Y.: Columbia Univ. Press, 1963.

Radin, Max. *The Method of Law.* 1950 Wash. U. L.Q. 471.

Radin, Max. *The Trail of the Calf.* 32 Cornell L.Q. 137 (1946).

Ray, Laura Krugman. *The History of the Per Curiam Opinion: Consensus and Individual Expression on the Supreme Court.* 27 J. Sup. Ct. Hist. 176 (2002).

Ray, Laura Krugman. *The Road to* Bush v. Gore: *The History of the Supreme Court's Use of the Per Curiam Opinion.* 79 Neb. L. Rev. 517 (2000).

Raz, Joseph. *Legal Principles and the Limits of Law.* 81 Yale L.J. 823 (1972).

Re, Edward D. *Stare Decisis.* 79 F.R.D. 509 (1979).

Re, Richard M. *On "A Ticket Good for One Day Only."* 16 Green Bag 2d 155 (2013).

Rehnquist, James C. *The Power That Shall Be Vested in a Precedent: Stare Decisis, the Constitution and the Supreme Court.* 66 B.U. L. Rev. 345 (1986).

Reid, Charles J., Jr. *The Creativity of the Common-Law Judge: The Jurisprudence of William Mitchell.* 30 Wm. Mitchell L. Rev. 213 (2003).

Reynolds, William L.; and William M. Richman. *The Non-Precedential Precedent—Limited Publication and No-Citation Rules in the United States Courts of Appeals.* 78 Colum. L. Rev. 1167 (1978).

Rihani, A. Ferris. *Stare Decisis.* 57 Alb. L.J. 392 (1898).

Robbins, Ira. *Interjurisdictional Certification and Choice of Law.* 41 Vand. L. Rev. 411 (1988).

Robel, Lauren K. *The Myth of the Disposable Opinion: Unpublished Opinions and Government Litigants in the United States Courts of Appeals.* 87 Mich. L. Rev. 940 (1989).

Ross, William G. *The Ratings Game: Factors That Influence Judicial Reputation.* 79 Marq. L. Rev. 401 (1996).

Sachs, Margaret V. *Judge Friendly and the Law of Securities Regulation: The Creation of a Judicial Reputation.* 50 SMU L. Rev. 777 (1997).

Salmond, John W. *The Theory of Judicial Precedents.* 16 L.Q. Rev. 376 (1900).

Scalia, Antonin. *The Rule of Law as a Law of Rules.* 56 U. Chi. L. Rev. 1175 (1989).

Schaefer, Walter V. *Precedent and Policy.* 34 U. Chi. L. Rev. 3 (1966).

Schapiro, Robert A. *Polyphonic Federalism: State Constitutions in the Federal Courts.* 87 Cal. L. Rev. 1409 (1999).

Schauer, Frederick. *Authority and Authorities.* 94 Va. L. Rev. 1931 (2008).

Schauer, Frederick. *Has Precedent Ever Really Mattered in the Supreme Court?* 24 Ga. St. U. L. Rev. 381 (2007).

Schauer, Frederick. *Precedent.* 39 Stan. L. Rev. 571 (1987).

Schauer, Frederick. "Precedent." In *The Routledge Companion to Philosophy of Law.* Andrei Marmor, ed. N.Y.: Routledge, 2012.

Schroeder, James C.; and Robert M. Dow Jr. *Arguing for Changes in the Law.* 25 No. 2 Litig. 37 (1999).

Schuckers, Daniel R.; and Kyle Appelgate. *The Rise of Pennsylvania's Administrative Agencies and Legislative and Judicial Attempts to Constrain Them.* 81 Pa. B. Ass'n Q. 124 (2010).

Schütze, Rolf A. *The Precedential Effect of Arbitration Decisions.* 11 J. Int'l Arb. 3 (1994).

Schwartz, Bernard. *Supreme Court Superstars: The Ten Greatest Justices.* 31 Tulsa L.J. 93 (1995).

Schwarz, Timothy. Comment, *Cases Time Forgot: Why Judges Can Sometimes Ignore Controlling Precedent.* 56 Emory L.J. 1475 (2007).

Selya, Bruce M. *Certified Madness: Ask a Silly Question....* 29 Suffolk U. L. Rev. 677 (1995).

Shapiro, S.R. *Prospective or Retroactive Operation of Overruling Decision.* 10 A.L.R.3d 1371 (1966).

Sharpe, David J. *The Maritime Origin of the Word "Certworthiness."* 24 J. Mar. L. & Com. 667 (1993).

Sheppard, John S., Jr. *The Decadence of the System of Precedent.* 24 Harv. L. Rev. 298 (1911).

Sherwin, Emily. *A Defense of Analogical Reasoning in Law.* 66 U. Chi. L. Rev. 1179 (1999).

Sherwin, Emily. *Judges as Rulemakers.* 73 U. Chi. L. Rev. 919 (2006).

Shroder, William J. *The Doctrine of Stare Decisis—Its Application to Decisions Involving Constitutional Interpretation*, 58 Cent. L.J. 23 (1904).

Shuldberg, Kirt. *Digital Influence: Technology and Unpublished Opinions in the Federal Courts of Appeals.* 85 Cal. L. Rev. 541 (1997).

Simpson, A.W.B. "The *Ratio Decidendi* of a Case and the Doctrine of Binding Precedent." In *Oxford Essays in Jurisprudence.* A.G. Guest, ed. Oxford: Oxford Univ. Press, 1961.

Sinclair, Michael. *Precedent, Super-Precedent.* 14 Geo. Mason L. Rev. 363 (2007).

Sloan, Amy E. *The Dog That Didn't Bark: Stealth Procedures and the Erosion of Stare Decisis in the Federal Courts of Appeals.* 78 Fordham L. Rev. 713 (2009).

Smith, Bryant. *Cumulative Reasons and Legal Method.* 27 Tex. L. Rev. 454 (1949).

Solimine, Michael E. *Ideology and En Banc Review.* 67 N.C. L. Rev. 29 (1988).

Solimine, Michael E. *Judicial Stratification and the Reputations of the United States Courts of Appeals.* 32 Fla. St. U. L. Rev. 1331 (2005).

Solum, Lawrence B. *The Supreme Court in Bondage: Constitutional Stare Decisis, Legal Formalism, and the Future of Unenumerated Rights.* 9 U. Pa. J. Const. L. 155 (2006).

Sourgens, Frédéric G. *Law's Laboratory: Developing International Law on Investment Protection as Common Law.* 34 Nw. J. Int'l L. & Bus. 181 (2014).

Southwick, Christian F. *Unprecedented: The Eighth Circuit Repaves Antiquas Vias with a New Constitutional Doctrine.* 21 Rev. Litig. 191 (2002).

Sparling, Steven C. Note, *Cutting the Gordian Knot: Resolution of the Sentencing Dispute Over Dismissed Charges After* United States v. Watts. 6 Geo. Mason L. Rev. 1079 (1998).

Sprecher, Robert A. *The Development of the Doctrine of Stare Decisis and the Extent to Which It Should Be Applied.* 31 A.B.A. J. 501 (1945).

Spriggs, James F., II; and David R. Stras. *Explaining Plurality Decisions.* 99 Geo. L.J. 515 (2011).

Starr, Kenneth W. *The Supreme Court and Its Shrinking Docket: The Ghost of William Howard Taft.* 90 Minn. L. Rev. 1363 (2006).

Stevens, John Paul. *The Life Span of a Judge-Made Rule.* 58 N.Y.U. L. Rev. 1 (1983).

Stewart, Richard B. *The Reformation of American Administrative Law.* 88 Harv. L. Rev. 1669 (1975).

Stinson, Judith M. *Why Dicta Becomes [sic] Holding and Why It Matters.* 76 Brook. L. Rev. 219 (2010).

Stoebuck, William B. *Reception of English Common Law in the American Colonies.* 10 Wm. & Mary L. Rev. 393 (1968).

Stone, Harlan F. *The Common Law in the United States.* 50 Harv. L. Rev. 4 (1936).

Stone, Julius. *The Ratio of the Ratio Decidendi.* 22 Mod. L. Rev. 597 (1959).

Sunstein, Cass R. *On Analogical Reasoning.* 106 Harv. L. Rev. 741 (1993).

Sureda, Andrés Rigo. "Precedent in Investment Treaty Arbitration." In *International Investment Law for the 21st Century: Essays in Honour of Christoph Schreuer.* Christina Binder; Ursula Kriebaum; August Reinisch; and Stephan Wittich, eds. Oxford: Oxford Univ. Press, 2009.

Surrency, Erwin C. *Legal Opinions of the Attorney General of the United States: Their Application in the Courts,* 29 Temple L.Q. 26 (1955).

Sutton, Jeffrey S. *Barnette, Frankfurter, and Judicial Review.* 96 Marq. L. Rev. 133 (2012).

Sutton, Jeffrey S. *What Does—and Does Not—Ail State Constitutional Law.* 59 U. Kan. L. Rev. 687 (2011).

Symposium. *The Status of the Rule of Judicial Precedent.* 14 U. Cin. L. Rev. 203 (1940).

Taft, William Howard. *The Jurisdiction of the Supreme Court Under the Act of February 13, 1925,* 35 Yale L.J. 1 (1925).

Teisen, Axel. *The False Theory of the Binding Force of Precedent.* 76 Cent. L.J. 147 (1913).

Tetley, William. *Mixed Jurisdictions: Common Law v. Civil Law (Codified and Uncodified).* 60 La. L. Rev. 677 (2000).

Thayer, Damon. *Learning to Differentiate Between Judicial and Obiter Dicta.* 35 L.A. Law. 10 (Apr. 2012).

Thayer, Ezra R. *Judicial Legislation: Its Legitimate Function in the Development of the Common Law.* 5 Harv. L. Rev. 172 (1891).

Thurmon, Mark Alan. Note, *When the Court Divides: Reconsidering the Precedential Value of Supreme Court Plurality Decisions.* 42 Duke L.J. 419 (1992).

Topf, Mel A. *State Supreme Court Advisory Opinions as Illegitimate Judicial Review.* 2001 Mich. St. L. Rev. 101.

Traynor, Roger J. *Badlands in an Appellate Judge's Realm of Reason.* 7 Utah L. Rev. 157 (1960).

Traynor, Roger J. *No Magic Words Could Do It Justice.* 49 Cal. L. Rev. 615 (1961).

Ulmer, S. Sidney. *An Empirical Analysis of Selected Aspects of Lawmaking of the United States Supreme Court.* 8 J. Pub. L. 414 (1959).

Vogenauer, Stefan. "Precedent, Rule of." In 2 *The Max Planck Encyclopedia of European Private Law.* Jürgen Basedow et al., eds. Oxford: Oxford Univ. Press, 2012.

Vong, David. *Binding Precedent and English Judicial Law-Making.* 21 Jura Falconis 318 (1985). https://www.law.kuleuven.be/jura/art/21n3/vong.pdf.

von Moschzisker, Robert. *Stare Decisis in Courts of Last Resort.* 37 Harv. L. Rev. 409 (1924).

Walbolt, Sylvia H.; and Stephanie C. Zimmerman. *"I Must Dissent." Why?* Fla. B.J., Nov. 2008, at 36.

Waldron, Jeremy. *Stare Decisis and the Rule of Law: A Layered Approach.* 111 Mich. L. Rev. 1 (2012).

Warren, Charles. *New Light on the History of the Federal Judiciary Act of 1789.* 37 Harv. L. Rev. 49 (1923).

Wasby, Stephen L.; et al. *The Per Curiam Opinion: Its Nature and Functions.* 76 Judicature 29 (1992).

Weisgerber, Erica S. *Unpublished Opinions: A Convenient Means to an Unconstitutional End.* 97 Geo. L.J. 621 (2009).

Whitney, Edward B. *The Doctrine of Stare Decisis.* 3 Mich. L. Rev. 89 (1904).

Williams, Glanville L. *The Origin and Logical Implications of the* Ejusdem Generis *Rule.* 7 Conv. & Prop. Law. 119 (1943).

Williams, Robert F. *State Courts Adopting Federal Constitutional Doctrine: Case-by-Case Adoptionism or Prospective Lockstepping?* 46 Wm. & Mary L. Rev. 1499 (2005).

Womack, Eric R. *Into the Third Era of Administrative Law: An Empirical Study of the Supreme Court's Retreat from* Chevron *Principles in* United States v. Mead. 107 Dick. L. Rev. 289 (2002).

Wood, Diane P. *Legal Scholarship for Judges.* 124 Yale L.J. 2592 (2015).

Wood, Diane P. *When to Hold, When to Fold, and When to Reshuffle: The Art of Decisionmaking on a Multi-member Court.* 100 Cal. L. Rev. 1445 (2012).

Wroth, L. Kinvin. "Common Law: United States Law." In 2 *The Oxford International Encyclopedia of Legal History.* Stanley N. Katz, ed. N.Y.: Oxford Univ. Press, 2009.

Young, Ernest A. *A General Defense of* Erie Railroad Co. v. Tompkins. 10 J.L. Econ. & Pol'y 17 (2013).

Young, Ernest A. *Sorting Out the Debate over Customary International Law.* 42 Va. J. Int'l L. 365 (2002).

Zeigler, Donald H. *Gazing into the Crystal Ball: Reflections on the Standards State Judges Should Use to Ascertain Federal Law.* 40 Wm. & Mary L. Rev. 1143 (1999).

ZoBell, Karl M. *Division of Opinion in the Supreme Court: A History of Judicial Disintegration.* 44 Cornell L.Q. 186 (1959).

Acknowledgments

We are grateful to all the following people, among others, who contributed in various ways to our enterprise:

John S. Adams	Karen Magnuson
Ryden McComas Anderson	Taylor Meehan
Aditya Bamzai	Becky R. Moler
Danny J. Boggs	Elizabeth Nanez
Edward H. Cooper	Jeff Newman
Ross E. Davies	Kevin Newsom
Mike DeBow	Richard M. Re
Ward Farnsworth	Lee H. Rosenthal
Ira Feinberg	Victoria L. Spickler
Karolyne H.C. Garner	Mia Taylor
Christina Gigliotti	Peter Tiersma
Stephen A. Higginson	Eugene Volokh
Tiger Jackson	Justin Walker

Index

About Law (Honoré), 847
Abraham, Henry J. (b. 1921), 176, 845
Abramowicz, Michael, 44, 53, 73, 104, 115, 135, 457, 852
"Abrogating Stare Decisis by Statute" (M.S. Paulsen), 7, 8, 858
Ackerman, Bruce A. (b. 1943), 251
Acquaviva, Guido, 762, 763, 852
Active Liberty (Breyer), 845
"Adjudication by a Resource-Constrained Team" (Kornhauser), 856
Adler, Ruth, 17, 845
administrative law, 285–89
Admiralty and Maritime Law (Schoenbaum), 850
admiralty law, 567–70, 694–95, 759
adverse authority, defined, 785
adverse possession, 419–20
advisory opinions, 134, 140, 269–76, 799
"Advisory Opinions" (Calogero), 270, 271, 853
"Advisory Opinions" (Gunderson), 269, 855
"Advisory Opinions of National and International Courts" (Hudson), 272, 855
"Advisory Opinions on the Constitutionality of Statutes" (unsigned note), 270, 272, 275, 857
affirm, defined, 785
affirmance,
 defined, 785
 judgment of, 262
 rule of, 220–25, 227
 summary, 158, 217–20, 227
 without opinion, 147–48
agency interpretations, 285–89, 446–47, 607
AG opinions, 277–85, 289, 290, 607
Ahn, Matthew J., 757–58, 852
Airline Deregulation Act, 543
Aksar, Yusuf, 764, 765, 845
Alabama Court of Civil Appeals, 284, 301, 308

Alabama Court of Criminal Appeals, 724
Alabama Supreme Court, 32, 101, 135, 244, 250, 273, 274, 275, 278, 280, 284, 330, 355, 427, 454, 537, 693, 709, 748
Alaska Constitution, 674
Alaska Supreme Court, 224, 251, 278, 331, 352, 400, 402, 726, 752
Aldisert, Ruggero J. (1919–2014), 21, 45, 852
Alexander, Larry, 77–78, 106, 845, 852
Alexy, Robert, 17, 845
Alito, Samuel (b. 1950), 178, 237, 268, 350, 368, 523, 530
Allen, Carleton Kemp (1887–1966), 845
ambiguity, 27, 46, 174, 291–94, 599, 637
"Ambiguous Basis of Judicial Deference to Administrative Rules" (Hasen), 286, 855
American and English Encyclopaedia of Law, The (Garland & McGehee eds.), 27, 123, 415, 492, 680, 845
American Bar Association Continuing Legal Education, 165, 852
American common law, 737–50, 789
American Common Law Method, The (Cappalli), 846
American Commonwealth, The (Bryce), 269, 845
American Constitutional Law (Tribe), 850
American Indians, 655–56
American Law and Procedure, 46, 845, 852
American Law Institute, 36, 165, 852
American Legal System, The (Mayers), 849
amiable compositeur, 770–71
amicable action, 133, 139–41, 786–87
Amos, Andrew (1791–1860), 847
Amos, Maurice S. (1872–1940), 852
analogical reasoning, 24, 105–14
analogy, defined, 785

863

"Analysis of Arizona's Depublication Rule and Practice" (M. Berch), 255, 852
"Analysis of Citations to Authority in Ohio Appellate Decisions Published in 1990, An" (Leonard), 167, 856
ancient decisions, 176–78, 236–38, 626–27, 791
Ancient Law (Maine), 848
Andrews, James DeWitt (1856–1928), 114, 852
Anglo-American law, 1, 9, 15, 16, 36, 114, 333, 789
antiformalism, defined, 785
Antiterrorism and Effective Death Penalty Act, 32, 546
Appelgate, Kyle, 285, 859
Appellate Courts (Meador et al.), 475, 849
Appellate Courts and Lawyers (Marvell), 849
"Applicability of State Conflicts Rules When Issues of State Law Arise in Federal Question Cases" (unsigned note), 597, 857
arbitral awards, 767–72, 773–79
"Arbitral Precedent" (Kaufmann-Kohler), 776, 777, 855
arbitrations, 767–79
Arbitration Under International Investment Agreements (Yannaca-Small ed.), 775, 858
"Arguing for Changes in the Law" (Schroeder & Dow), 250, 859
argument,
  generally, 226–29
  printed after headnotes, 153
  winning argument forfeited or waived, 488–89
Aristotle (384–322 B.C.), 18, 845
Aristotle at Afternoon Tea (Wilde), 300
Arizona Court of Appeals, 262, 284, 288, 306
Arizona Supreme Court, 169, 171, 198–99, 240, 250, 257, 278, 280, 294, 295, 306, 391, 538, 554, 555, 628, 635, 636, 670, 718, 720, 722, 732, 743, 746
Arkansas Constitution, 401

Arkansas Supreme Court, 93–96, 101, 166, 229, 233, 251–52, 278, 285, 291, 389, 392, 401, 412, 430, 436, 450, 540, 544–45, 624, 628, 722, 733
Armed Career Criminal Act, 368, 546, 547, 587
Arner, Douglas W., 852
Article I, 562, 567, 732
Article III, 7, 28, 87, 133–34, 502, 534, 551, 552, 553, 554, 555, 556, 557, 559–60, 569, 650, 651, 732
Article IV, 732
Articles of Confederation (1781), 567
Asquith, Lord (Cyril) (1890–1954), 74, 852
Assimilative Crimes Act, 587
Atiyah, P.S. (b. 1931), 845
attorney-general opinions, 277–85, 289, 290, 607
Austin, John (1790–1859), 44, 45, 845
Australia, 754, 755
Austria, 755
authority, various types defined, 785–86
"Authority and Authorities" (Schauer), 164, 170, 859
Authority of Law, The (Raz), 10, 13, 48, 73, 97, 98, 99, 849
Autobiography of the Supreme Court, An (Westin ed.), 853

Bacon, Francis (1561–1626), iii, 44, 845, 852
"Badlands in an Appellate Judge's Realm of Reason" (Traynor), 860
Baer, Max (b. 1947), 701
Baker, J.H. (b. 1944), 35, 845
Baker, Thomas E. (b. 1953), 849
Baldwin, Henry (1780–1844), 415
Bamzai, Aditya, 861
Banifatemi, Yas, 775, 847, 856
Barfield, Daniel A., 179, 180, 852
Barkett, Rosemary (b. 1939), 501
Barnes, Charles M., 8, 110, 176, 421, 747, 848
Barnett, Randy E. (b. 1952), 6, 7, 334, 852

"Barnette, Frankfurter, and Judicial Review" (Sutton), 357, 860
Barrett, Amy Coney, 852
baseball decisions, 3–5, 13, 100–01, 335–36
Basedow, Jürgen (b. 1949), 762, 845, 860
Bates, Clement (1836–1913), 1, 850
Bator, Paul M. (1929–1989), 661
Baude, William, 526, 852
Beck, Randy, 113, 852
Bell, John, 46, 852
Bell, John C. (1892–1974), 396
Bellia, Anthony J., Jr., 565, 845, 852
Berch, Jessica J., 845
Berch, Michael A., 199, 255, 287, 845, 852
Berch, Rebecca White (b. 1955), 845
Berger, Klaus Peter (b. 1961), 769, 852
Berkus, Sarah J., 502, 852
"Better to Give Than to Receive" (Barfield), 179, 180, 852
Beyond the Formalist–Realist Divide (Tamanaha), 850
Bhagwat, Ashutosh (b. 1964), 30, 852
Bhala, Raj (b. 1962), 762, 763, 764, 852
Bill of Rights (1791), 352, 358
"Bill of Rights, The" (Linde), 664
Binder, Christina, 775, 860
"Binding Precedent and English Judicial Law-Making" (Vong), 238, 860
binding precedents, 27–34, 801
Birks, Peter (1941–2004), 848
Bishop, Timothy S., 850
Bjorklund, Andrea K., 774, 775, 776, 778, 852
Black, Henry Campbell (1860–1927), xiii, 22, 76, 77, 82, 83, 146, 147, 150, 156, 189, 309, 317–18, 326, 333, 354, 417, 418, 448, 722, 723, 744, 845
Black, Hugo (1886–1971), 101, 200, 201, 358–59, 420, 570, 622
Black, Jeremiah S. (1810–1883), 420
Black, Ryan, 220, 221, 225, 852
Blackmun, Harry (1908–1999), 199, 211, 212, 359, 532, 769

Black's Law Dictionary (Garner ed.), xiii, 5, 22, 24, 44, 47, 62, 164, 173, 230, 235, 270, 333, 346, 382, 387, 423, 459, 497, 770–71, 774, 845
Blackstone, William (1723–1780), 7, 309, 845
Bleckley, Logan (1827–1907), 411
Bleich, Jeff, 247, 852
Blocher, Joseph, 659, 660, 852
Blom-Cooper, Louis (b. 1926), 35, 354, 845, 852
Bloom, Lackland H., Jr. (b. 1949), 74
Bodenheimer, Edgar (1908–1991), 845
Boggs, Danny J. (b. 1944), 852, 861
Born, Gary B., 769, 771, 845
borrowed-constitutional-provision doctrine, 722–23, 786
borrowed-statute doctrine, 296, 716–23, 733, 750, 786
Bracton, Henry de (1210–1268), 7, 8, 105, 845
Bradford, C. Steven, 30, 852
Bradley, Curtis A., 565, 852
Bradley, Joseph P. (1813–1892), 398–99
Bramble Bush, The (Llewellyn), 116, 129, 848
Branch, Thomas (fl. 1738–1753), 333, 845
Brandeis, Louis (1856–1941), 9, 11, 79, 248, 342, 353, 410, 560, 577–78
Brennan, William J., Jr. (1906–1997), 47, 130, 200, 359, 549, 666, 853
Brenner, Saul (b. 1962), 355, 845
Brewer, Scott, 113, 853
Breyer, Stephen (b. 1938), xi, 187, 339–40, 355, 438, 523, 525, 845, 853
Brief Making and the Use of Law Books (R. Cooley ed.), 65, 123, 133, 153, 846
Brief Writing and Oral Argument (E. Re & J. Re), 849
Brooks, Brian P., 852
Brown, Richard (b. 1946), 52
Brumbaugh, Jesse Franklin (ca. 1875–1958), 845
Bryce, James (1838–1922), 269, 845
Buckland, W.W. (1859–1946), 1, 16, 18, 846
Bunn, Isabella D., 852

Burger, Warren E. (1907–1995), 102, 158, 185, 186, 190
Burke, Edmund (1729–1797), 9, 846
Burke, Thomas F., 10, 846
Burnham, James, 268, 533, 856
Burton, Harold Hitz (1888–1964), 336
Burton, Steven J., 44, 846
Butler, Pierce (1866–1939), 234
Byrnes, James F. (1882–1972), 418, 419
By What Right? (Lusky), 848

Calabresi, Guido (b. 1932), 18
California Constitution, 675
California Court of Appeal, 170, 189, 233, 234, 261, 277, 278, 281, 282–83, 284, 295, 297, 301, 307, 317, 384, 387, 429, 435, 446, 457, 656, 687–88, 710, 711, 712, 713, 724, 726, 728
California Procedure (Witkin), 387
California Supreme Court, 33, 164, 170–71, 233, 235, 241–42, 254, 261, 280, 293–94, 307, 313, 316, 317, 384, 387, 389, 390, 401, 421, 425, 427, 429, 430, 431–32, 433, 435, 456, 457, 536, 549, 553–54, 609, 625, 644, 656, 669, 675–76, 679, 687–88, 692, 702, 704, 723, 727, 728
Calogero, Pascal F., Jr. (b. 1931), 131, 270, 271, 853
Caminker, Evan H. (b. 1961), 28, 30, 256–57, 853
Campbell, Charles Franklin (b. 1944), 416
Campbell, Robert, 44, 45, 845
Canada, 754
Cane, Peter (b. 1950), 46, 248, 846, 852, 857
canons of construction,
 borrowed-constitutional-provision doctrine, 722–23, 786
 borrowed-statute doctrine, 296, 716–23, 733, 750, 786
 constitutional-avoidance canon, 79, 649–50
 ordinary-meaning canon, 79, 90, 291
 presumption-of-validity canon, 379–80, 650
 prior-construction canon, 346–47, 348, 392, 802
 reenactment canon, 346–49, 351, 805

canons of construction (*cont'd*)
 related-statutes canon, 79
Cantoni, Linda, 847
Cappalli, Richard B., 846
Cardozo, Benjamin N. (1870–1938), iii, 10, 41, 113, 179, 248, 250, 252, 273, 388, 416, 422, 434, 846
Carnes, Edward E. (b. 1950), 69, 122, 127
Carpenter, Charles E., 853
Carter, Lief H., 1, 10, 846
case, defined, 786–87
caselaw, defined, 787
"Case Law" (Goodhart), 854
"Case Law" (Holdsworth), 855
"Case Law and Stare Decisis" (Radin), 6, 334, 858
"Case Law in England and America" (Goodhart), 37, 854
"Case-Law System, The" (Holdsworth), 855
Case Law System in America, The (Llewellyn), 67, 98–99, 848
"Case Law Versus Statute Law" (Ponzetto & Fernandez), 19, 858
"Case of the Amorous Defendant, The" (Eskridge), 853
"Case of the Plummeting Supreme Court Docket, The" (Liptak), 518
case or controversy, 133, 552, 554, 555, 651, 676
case-or-controversy requirement, defined, 787
cases,
 age of, 23–24, 70–71, 175–78, 236–38, 355–56, 626–27, 791
 amicable, 133, 139–41
 analogous, 100, 105–14, 394, 605, 615
 ancient, 176–78, 236–38, 626–27, 791
 conflicting, 155, 158, 257, 300–07, 609
 distinguishing, 97–104, 111–13, 242
 diversity, 285, 571–88, 589, 591, 593–94, 657–58, 701
 fictitious, 651–54
 first impression, of, 101, 295, 499, 512, 515, 706–07, 724–25, 786
 friendly, 652
 hardships, 130–32, 411–14, 523
 hypothetical, 133, 786
 leading, 160, 173–75, 176–77

cases (cont'd)
  moot, 133–41, 228, 552–53, 652
  narrow, 130–32
  obsolete, 178–81
  outlier, 100, 160–63, 172, 173, 418–20
  out-of-state, 724–28
  remanded, 459–64
  reversed, as authority, 308–24
  test, 133, 139–40, 651–54, 786–87
  various types defined, 786–87
"Cases, Controversies, and Diversity" (Hessick), 651, 855
"Cases Time Forgot" (Schwarz), 240, 859
Cavanaugh, Michael F. (b. 1940), 414
"Century of 'Judge-Made' Law, A" (Hornblower), 855
Certainty and Justice (Coudert), 15, 846
certification, defined, 787
"Certified Madness" (Selya), 644, 859
certified questions,
  abstention, 618–22, 623–24, 633, 634–35, 636, 637, 674–75, 677
  benefits, 644
  certification, defined, 787
  drawbacks, 644–45
  generally, 599, 617–18, 625–26, 637–38, 675–76
  historically, 622–25
  procedure, 626–27, 629, 631, 637–40, 642–43
  rejecting or declining, 627, 628–29, 630–33, 640–42
  to state courts from federal courts, generally, 272, 276, 617–18
certiorari,
  cases chosen for, 529–33
  certworthiness, generally, 517–33, 787
  circuit splits, 517, 520–21, 531–33
  defined, 787
  dissentals, 267–69, 533, 793
  historically, 511, 517–18
  issues, 521–23, 531–32
  legal errors and bad policy, 520, 525–27
  significance of denial of writ, 219, 261–68, 467, 531–32, 600–01
  unworthiness of, generally, 523, 525, 528–29, 530–31
Chamberlain, Daniel H. (1835–1907), 510, 846
change in law, 442, 445–46

charitable immunity, 179–80, 383
"Charitable Immunity" (O'Neill), 180, 858
Chemerinsky, Erwin (b. 1953), 846
Cherne, Leo (1912–1999), 779
Chevron deference, 287–89, 446–47
"*Chevron*, Take Two" (Gossett), 854
Chief Sources of English Legal History, The (Winfield), 851
Chile, 755
Chitty, Herbert (1863–1949), 850
Chitty, Thomas Willes (1855–1930), 173, 850
choice of law, 574, 581, 596–97, 710–11, 752–53, 756–57, 769, 772
Choper, Jesse H. (b. 1935), 287, 848
civil law, 15, 16–18, 739–40, 754, 758, 759, 771–72, 774, 788
Civil Law Tradition, The (Merryman), 17, 849
claim preclusion, 326, 327, 373–74, 376, 442, 453
Clark, Bradford R., 565, 852
Clark, Tom C. (1899–1977), 200, 222
Clarke, Thurmond (1902–1971), 472–73
Clawson, Rebecca, 854
Clean Air Act, 504
Clean Water Act, 209
Clinton, Bill (b. 1946), 186–87, 522
Coale, David S. (b. 1968), 853
Cochran, Rebecca A., 617, 618, 853
Cohen, Felix S. (1907–1953), 92, 846
Coke, Sir Edward (1552–1634), 749
collateral estoppel, 327, 375, 376, 379, 380, 478, 691, 701, 788
collateral review, 308, 313–15
Collected Legal Papers (Holmes), 16, 847, 855
Collier, Charles W., 18, 48, 102, 853
Colorado Constitution, 275
Colorado Court of Appeals, 703, 706
Colorado Supreme Court, 165, 189, 258, 273, 275, 278, 284, 293, 301, 669, 745
comity,
  defined, 788
  federal comity doctrine, 510–11, 794
  federal courts, 476, 509–12, 647, 794
  generally, 443, 474, 644, 703, 706, 712

comity (cont'd)
  international, 565
  state courts, 34, 79, 313, 673
  state penal or criminal provisions, 729–31
Commentaries on American Law (Kent), 8, 22, 110, 176, 421, 747, 848
Commentaries on the Constitution of the United States (Story), 8, 749, 850
Commentaries on the Laws of England (Blackstone), 7, 309, 845
Commerce Clause, 82, 159, 336, 356, 365, 651
Commission, Jeffery P., 775, 776–77, 778, 853
common law,
  American, defined, 789
  defined, 788–89
  English, 254, 270, 737–50, 754, 760
  Erie doctrine, 226, 234, 323, 353, 363, 436, 544, 558, 571–88, 589–92, 598, 692, 703, 788–89, 793, 806
  federal. See FEDERAL COMMON LAW.
  foreign law, 709, 712, 724–26
  general federal, 226, 234, 323, 353, 363, 558, 575–80, 788–89
  generally, 19, 105, 177–78, 309, 310, 313, 333, 339, 389, 445, 543,
  Louisiana, 739–40
  origin of system, 15–18
  stare decisis with, 333–35, 338, 389
  state, 175, 631, 655
  statutes, 334, 338, 389
  test for whether a law is penal, 729–30
"Common Law" (Ibbetson), 15
"Common Law" (Wroth), 737, 860
"Common Law, The" (F. Hall), 737, 748, 855
Common Law, The (Holmes), 12, 97, 98, 847
Common Law and English Jurisprudence 1760–1850, The (Lobban), 848
"Common Law and Legislation" (Pound), 858
Common Law for the Age of Statutes, A (Calabresi), 18
"Common Law in the United States, The" (H. Stone), 859

Common Law Tradition, The (Llewellyn), 848
Common-Sense in Law (Vinogradoff), 13, 173, 309, 850
Conaghan, Joanne, 46, 248, 846, 852, 857
Concept of Law, The (Hart), 21, 48, 847
conclusion of law, defined, 789
concurral, defined, 789
concurrences,
  defined (under *concurring opinion*), 799
  generally, 239, 783
  plurality decisions, 195, 197–98, 204–05, 209
  split decisions, 182–83, 185, 191, 192, 193, 194
conflict-of-laws doctrine, 593–97
Confrontation Clause, 314, 681–82, 689
Congress, 7, 30, 71–72, 159, 160, 185, 236, 286–87, 309, 334, 335–36, 339, 340, 342, 344, 348, 349–51, 356, 361–62, 363–64, 409, 417, 495, 517–18, 521, 522, 529, 535, 539, 546, 551, 558, 560, 561, 562–63, 565, 567, 568, 570, 571, 572, 574, 575, 582, 598, 655, 685, 698, 717, 732, 734, 753–54
Connecticut Appellate Court, 189
Connecticut Supreme Court, 130, 164, 262, 273, 278, 391, 724
consequentialism, defined, 789
consideration, 226–29, 360
consistency,
  arbitration, 769, 772, 778
  judicial opinions, 10–11, 13, 21, 114, 286, 300, 336, 360, 391, 443–45, 538, 702
Consovoy, William S., 853
Constitution, U.S.,
  Article I, 562, 567, 732
  Article III, 7, 28, 87, 133–34, 502, 534, 551, 552, 553, 554, 555, 556, 557, 559–60, 569, 650, 651, 732
  Article IV, 732
  Commerce Clause, 82, 159, 336, 356, 365, 651
  Confrontation Clause, 314, 681–82, 689
  Contracts Clause, 436–37, 438
  Dormant Commerce Clause, 365
  Double Jeopardy Clause, 541

INDEX 869

Constitution, U.S. (cont'd)
  Due Process Clause, 83, 367, 368, 445, 542, 549, 575
  Equal Protection Clause, 83, 106
  Establishment Clause, 55, 330, 468
  Fifth Amendment, 297, 367, 656, 669
  First Amendment, 25, 56–57, 132, 217, 357, 359, 480–81, 648, 668, 676, 682–83, 701
  Fourteenth Amendment, 30–31, 360, 363, 445, 549, 650, 659, 662, 669
  Fourth Amendment, 63, 89, 130–31, 174, 680, 681
  Free Exercise Clause, 359
  Full Faith and Credit Clause, 623, 729
  generally, 6, 7, 8, 28, 32, 34, 36, 271, 297, 309, 312–13, 315, 352, 353, 358–59, 361, 375, 381, 445, 521, 548, 558, 559–60, 563–64, 567, 598, 633–34, 697
  interpretation and application, 534–50, 551, 553, 646–47, 651, 658, 664, 679
  Second Amendment, 366, 548
  Seventh Amendment, 177–78, 581
  Sixth Amendment, 30–31, 160, 314, 359
  Spending Clause, 203
  Supremacy Clause, 34, 541, 563–64, 668–72, 690
  Takings Clause, 119–20, 436–39, 669
  Thirteenth Amendment, 160
constitutional-avoidance canon, 79, 649–50
Constitutional Convention, 270, 534
Constitutional Law (Lockhart et al.), 661, 848
Constitutional Law (Nowak & Rotunda), 661, 849
"Constitutional Stare Decisis" (unsigned note), 857
constitutions,
  federal. See CONSTITUTION, U.S.
  generally, 1, 277, 290, 291–92, 354, 553
  stare decisis with, 352–69
  state. See CONSTITUTIONS, STATE.
constitutions, state,
  Alaska, 674
  Arkansas, 401
  California, 675
  Colorado, 275

constitutions, state (cont'd)
  generally, 296, 301, 352, 549, 553, 613, 625, 646, 655, 656, 659–62, 663, 664–67, 673–78, 722–23, 738, 740, 741
  Idaho, 725–26
  Illinois, 658
  Kentucky, 663
  Massachusetts, 296–97, 749
  Mississippi, 674, 723
  New Hampshire, 296–97
  New Mexico, 632
  New York, 676
  Ohio, 651–52
  South Dakota, 275
  Texas, 272
construction, statutory. See STATUTORY INTERPRETATION.
Contemporary Issues in International Arbitration and Mediation (Rovine ed.), 777, 850
"Content Analysis of Judicial Opinions and Rules of Law" (Kort), 856
Contracts Clause, 436–37, 438
Controlled Substances Act, 521
controlling law, defined, 796
"Controlling Precedent" (G. Lawson), 856
Cook, Catriona, 849
Cooley, Roger W. (1824–1898), 65, 123, 133, 153, 846
Cooley, Thomas M. (1824–1898), 310, 743, 846
Cooper, Charles J. (b. 1952), 853
Cooper, Edward H. (b. 1941), 851, 861
coordinate jurisdiction, defined, 789–90
Copyright Act, 161–62
Corbin, Arthur L. (1874–1967), 853
Cordray, Margaret Meriwether, 517, 518, 519, 853
Cordray, Richard (b. 1959), 517, 518, 519, 853
Corley, Pamela C., 188, 846
Cotropia, Christopher A., 188, 853
Coudert, Frederic R. (1832–1903), 15, 846, 853
Cour de Cassation, 757

"Court Decisions and the Common Law" (Carpenter), 853
"Court En Banc, The" (D. Ginsburg & Falk), 498, 502, 506, 854
Court for the Correction of Errors of New York, 417
court not of record, defined, 790
court of appeals, defined, 790
Court of Claims, 513, 524
Court of Customs and Patent Appeals, 513–14
court of last resort, defined, 790
court of record, defined, 790
courts,
   administrative role, 267
   appellate, discretionary review, 260–68
   change in membership or organization, 416–21, 442, 475
   coordinate, 473–76, 789–90
   coordinate, conflicting decisions, 306–07
   doctrinal conflicts between, 537–40
   federal. See FEDERAL COURTS.
   horizontal conflicts in decisions, 300–01, 303–06
   inferior, decisions of, 253–57
   inferior and superior, 254
   not of record, defined, 790
   of last resort, defined, 790
   of record, defined, 790
   parallel systems and flexibility, 14
   particular types defined, 790–91
   rank and status of, 243–45
   reliability, 245–46
   reputation of, 245–47
   specialized, 165, 245–46, 253–54
   state. See STATE COURTS.
   trial vs. appellate in the creation of precedent, 32–34, 106, 243–45, 255–57, 385–86, 424–25, 491–92, 515, 779
   vertical conflicts in decisions, 301–03, 305–06
Courts on Trial (J. Frank), 13, 14, 46, 93, 847
Couture, Wendy, 853
Creation of the American Republic, The (G. Wood), 664, 851
"Creativity of the Common-Law Judge, The" (Reid), 858
Creyke, Robin, 849

"Critique and Comparison of En Banc Review in the Tenth and D.C. Circuits and *United States v. Nacchio*, A" (Berkus), 502, 852
Critique of Adjudication, A (D. Kennedy), 848
Cross, Rupert (1912–1980), 5, 17, 19, 41, 74, 846
Cueto-Rua, Julio C. (1920–2007), 46, 846
"Cumulative Reasons and Legal Method" (B. Smith), 859
Curtis, Charles P. (1891–1959), 846
"Customary International Law as Federal Common Law" (C. Bradley & Goldsmith), 565, 852
"Cutting the Gordian Knot" (Sparling), 214, 859

Davies, Ross E. (b. 1962), 861
D.C. Circuit. See UNITED STATES COURTS OF APPEALS.
"dead hand," precedent as, 67
"Death of a Precedent" (LeRoy), 355, 856
"Decadence of the System of Precedent, The" (J. Sheppard), 859
Deciding to Decide (Perry), 519, 530, 849
decision, 76, 791–92
"Decisional Law and Stare Decisis" (R. Jackson), 855
decisions,
   acceptance of, 233, 234–36
   age of, 236–38, 355–56, 357
   alternative grounds for, 103–04,
   ancient, 176–78, 236–38, 626–27, 791
   approval of, 233–34, 263–66, 404, 406
   assumed rules or principles underlying, 84–88
   breadth of, 45, 57–62, 157
   change in court's membership or organization, 415–20, 442
   collateral, 455
   common-law, 309, 389
   conflicting, 300–07
   contract rights, 340, 370, 407
   contrary to legal principles, 396, 397
   criticism of, 239, 241, 399, 400–01
   disapproval of, 239, 240–42, 265, 399
   discordant, 300–07

decisions (cont'd)
  dismissal, 217
  dispositive, 231
  distinguished from *opinion* (as a term), 76
  doubt about, 239, 396, 398–99, 404
  erroneous, 610–11
  exceptions to new rules, 435–36
  ex parte, 230
  finality of, 324–31
  implicit, 86–88, 449–50
  incidental, 455
  interlocutory, 452, 453–54, 476–77, 530
  interpreting statutes, 333–34, 389, 404, 409–10
  isolated, 396, 397–98
  law-of-the-case doctrine with final decisions, 328–29, 448–51, 452–54
  law-of-the-case doctrine with nonfinal decisions, 231–32, 448–49, 451–52, 453
  matters of practice, 370
  no-clear-majority, 195
  nonbinding, 164–72
  nonfinal, 230–32
  nonjudicial, 277–89, 791
  on the merits, 230
  overruling or reversal. See OVERRULING OR REVERSAL OF DECISIONS.
  pending appeal, 258–59
  plenary, 157
  preliminary, 92, 230, 451, 453–54
  procedural matters, 370–72
  property rights, 337, 370
  prospective effect of, 308, 309, 310, 316, 329–30
  recognition of, 233, 404, 406
  reconsidered, 497–508
  rehearing or pending appeal of, 258–59
  reliance interests, 41, 67, 100, 156, 159, 161, 312, 337, 339, 340, 341, 357, 366, 371–72, 405, 407, 412, 413–14, 421–22, 435
  rethinking, 445–47
  retroactive effect of, 308, 309–15
  rule of property, 404, 407–08, 422–25
  solitary, defined, 791
  split, 182–83, 187, 792
  statutory interpretation, 334, 404, 409–10
  summary disposition, 157, 214, 217–19
  transferred, 472

decisions (cont'd)
  unanimous, 182–87, 188–89, 792
  unchallenged, 404, 405
  various types defined, 791–92
  wrong, 5, 9, 101, 325–26
  See also HOLDINGS.
declaratory precedents, 333–34, 801
"Decline of Stare Decisis, The" (W.O. Douglas), 853
decree, defined, 77, 792
deductive reasoning, 23–24, 804
"Defense of Analogical Reasoning in Law, A" (Sherwin), 113, 859
Defense of Marriage Act, 521
deference,
  agency, 285, 286–89, 446–47, 607
  basis for, 6–7, 9
  breadth, 54
  Chevron, 287–89, 446–47
  degree of, 44, 61, 64, 614–16, 693
  generally, 5, 427, 511
  problems with, 12
  to courts, 243, 399, 509, 512–13, 514, 608–10, 611
  to state law, 563, 607–10
  to statutes, 333–34
"Deference to Federal Circuit Court Interpretations of Unsettled State Law" (Hoover), 855
"Defining Dicta" (Abramowicz & Stearns), 44, 53, 73, 104, 115, 135, 457, 852
De Laudibus Legum Angliæ (Fortescue), 847
Delaware Court of Chancery, 278, 374
Delaware Supreme Court, 158, 253, 274, 275, 276, 374, 424, 610, 665, 741, 753
De Legibus et Consuetudinibus Angliæ (Bracton), 7, 105
Democracy in America (de Tocqueville), 269
Demystifying Legal Reasoning (Alexander & Sherwin), 106, 845
Denning, Lord (Alfred Thompson) (1899–1999), 76, 846
Dennis, James L. (b. 1936), 853
Denniston, Lyle (b. 1931), 531
Department of Interior, 685
Department of Justice, 210
Department of Labor, 331

Derains, Yves (b. 1945), 771, 846
Derham, David P. (1920–1985), 47, 105, 849
desegregation, 332, 356
"Determining the *Ratio Decidendi* of a Case" (Goodhart), 48, 854
"Determining Uniformity Within the Federal Circuit by Measuring Dissent and En Banc Review" (Cotropia), 188, 853
de Tocqueville, Alexis (1805–1859), 269
"Development of the Doctrine of Stare Decisis and the Extent to Which It Should Be Applied, The" (Sprecher), 859
"Developments in the Law of Res Judicata" (unsigned note), 857
Devins, Neal (b. 1957), 55, 856
Devlin, Patrick (1905–1992), 388, 846
Dias, R.W.M. (1921–2009), 74, 846
Dicey, A.V. (1835–1922), iii, 846
Dickinson, John, 19, 853
Dickson, Brice (b. 1953), 845, 853
"Dicta and Article III" (Dorf), 54, 67, 70, 97, 100, 853
"Dicta and the Rule of Law" (Killian), 135, 856
"Dicta Redefined" (McAllister), 857
"Dicta, Schmicta" (Klein & Devins), 55, 856
dictum,
  as predictive tool, 603–04, 605
  binding statements that are not dicta, 456–58
  close calls in identifying, 50–51, 53–54, 126–29
  compared to holding, 44–45, 114
  creating rule of property, 425–26
  deference merited to, 44
  different types defined, 47, 792
  distinguishing from holdings, 116, 121–22, 125–28
  gratis dictum, 792
  headnotes, in, 153
  holding/dictum dichotomy, 47–54, 66–67, 74–75, 456–58
  invited error, 458
  judicial, 54, 62–65, 129, 792
  law of the case and, 455
  law of the circuit and, 63–64
  moot or hypothetical questions, 135

dictum (*cont'd*)
  necessary-to-the-result test, 119–20
  obiter/judicial dichotomy, 62, 65
  persuasive value of, 164
  rule of property, 425–26
  utility of, 66–69
  vertical, 70–72
  vertical precedent and, 55, 244
  weight of, 55, 62–63, 66, 70, 244
dictum propium, defined, 792
"Digesting CISG Case Law" (Lookofsky), 764, 857
"Digital Influence" (Shuldberg), 143, 859
Dillon, John F. (1831–1914), 101, 155, 226, 249, 846
direct precedents, 21–22, 24–25, 801
Discipline of Law, The (Denning), 846
discretionary review, 260–68, 517–18
disposition, defined, 792
dissentals, 267–68, 793
dissenting opinions, 182, 188–89, 191, 192, 193, 194, 195, 197, 216, 239–40, 799
"Dissenting Opinions" (McClain), 182, 183, 189, 857
Dissent in the Supreme Court (P. Jackson), 848
dissents, 182, 188–89, 191, 192, 193, 194, 195, 197, 216, 239–40, 799
distinguishing cases,
  defined generally, 793
  techniques for, 96–104, 242
"Diverse Views of What Constitutes the Principle of Law of a Case" (Ohrenschall), 858
divided court, defined, 790
"Division of Opinion in the Supreme Court" (ZoBell), 183, 860
Dobbins, Jeffrey C., 22, 30, 853
"Doctrine of *Erie Railroad v. Tompkins* Applied to International Law, The" (Jessup), 855
"Doctrine of Precedent" (Ibbetson), 105, 855
Doctrine of Stare Decisis, The (Chamberlain), 510, 846
"Doctrine of Stare Decisis, The" (Shroder), 859

"Doctrine of Stare Decisis, The" (Whitney), 17, 860
Documentary History of the Supreme Court of the United States, The (Marcus ed.), 140
Doe, Charles Cogswell (1830–1896), 388
Doggett, Lloyd (b. 1946), 743
"Dog That Didn't Bark, The" (Sloan), 144, 494, 859
Dorf, Michael C., 54, 67, 70, 97, 100, 853
Dormant Commerce Clause, 365
Dorsen, Norman (b. 1930), 74
Douglas, Joshua A., 508, 853
Douglas, William O. (1898–1980), 101, 200, 201, 354, 358–59, 621, 623, 846, 853
Dow, Robert M., Jr. (b. 1965), 250, 859
Dowling, Noel T., 846
Dragich, Martha J., 149, 253, 254, 853
Drewry, Gavin, 845, 852
dual-majority opinions, 207, 211–13
Dudley, Robert J., 846
due process, 7, 82–83, 184, 274, 381, 422, 424, 437, 484, 541–42, 622, 646, 656, 662, 682–83
Due Process Clause, 83, 367, 368, 445, 542, 549, 575
Dugdale, Anthony M., 54, 847
Duxbury, Neil (b. 1945), 14, 47, 73, 97, 98, 102, 182, 846
Dworkin, Ronald (1931–2013), 846

Easterbrook, Frank H. (b. 1948), 9, 10, 14, 18, 61, 252, 335, 354, 853
Eber, Michael L., 207, 208, 210, 212, 213, 853
"Economic Perspective on Stare Decisis, An" (Kornhauser), 856
Ecuador, 759
Edelman, Richard, 264
"Effective Appellate Brief Writing" (C. Hamilton), 166, 855
Ehrenzweig, Albert A. (1906–1974), 17, 846
18 U.S.C. § 1001, 341

Eighth Circuit. See UNITED STATES COURTS OF APPEALS.
Eisenberg, Melvin Aron (b. 1934), 846
Eisenberg, Theodore (1947–2014), 260, 853
ejusdem generis rule, 50
Elementary Principles of Jurisprudence, The (G.W. Keeton), 8, 15, 80, 848
Elements of Contract Interpretation (S. Burton), 846
Elements of Jurisprudence, The (T. Holland), 16, 333, 847
Elements of Law (Hanks et al.), 847
Eleventh Circuit. See UNITED STATES COURTS OF APPEALS.
Elkouri, Edna Asper (1922–2014), 769–70, 771–72, 774, 775, 776, 777, 778, 779, 846
Elkouri, Frank (1921–2013), 769–70, 771–72, 774, 775, 776, 777, 778, 779, 846
Ely, John Hart (1938–2003), 584, 853
Embattled Constitution, The (Dorsen), 74
Embry, T. Eric (1921–1992), 355
Emerson, Ralph Waldo (1803–1882), xi
Emerson's Essays, xi
"Eminent Domain and Land Valuation Litigation Appellate Practice" (ALI & ABA CLE), 165, 852
"Empirical Analysis of Selected Aspects of Lawmaking of the United States Supreme Court, An" (Ulmer), 355, 860
Employee Retirement Income Security Act (ERISA), 65, 166, 503, 561, 596, 649, 668, 695
en banc review,
 defined, 793
 enbancworthiness, generally, 497–98, 793
 generally, 495–508
Encyclopedia of the American Constitution (L. Levy et al. eds.), 352, 848, 855, 858
Encyclopedia of the American Judicial System (Janosik ed.), 1, 848
Endangered Species Act, 3–4
England, 15, 176

England, Arthur J. (1932–2013), 416
English common and statutory law,
    15, 19, 35, 221, 254–55, 333, 568, 702,
    737–50, 758, 760, 793
English Historical Documents (Jensen ed.), 738
English Legal Tradition, The (Lévy-Ullmann), 15, 848
Enoch, Craig T. (b. 1950), 264
enthymemes, 51, 793
Environmental Protection Agency, 210, 473–74, 504
Epstein, Lee (b. 1958), 220, 221, 225, 260, 846, 852
"Equality Before the Law and Precedent" (Miguel), 21, 857
Equal Protection Clause, 83, 106
equitable doctrines, 435–35, 770–71
Erie doctrine, 226, 234, 323, 353, 363, 436, 544, 558, 571–88, 589–92, 598, 692, 703, 788–89, 793, 806
ERISA, 65, 166, 503, 561, 596, 649, 668, 695
"Erosion of *Miranda*, The" (Lunney), 857
errors and inefficiency,
    claims of, 116, 123, 124, 125, 126–27, 380, 384, 456, 457, 506, 670
    in decisions, 41, 64, 93, 339, 342–43, 352, 353, 355, 358, 367–68, 377, 388, 390–91, 397, 401, 404, 416, 446–47, 463–64, 478–79, 485–86, 487, 488–89, 507, 510, 520, 526–29, 591, 610–13, 634, 659, 768
    invited error, 458
    rule of property, 430–32
Erskine, John (1695–1768), 846
Eskridge, William N., Jr. (b. 1951), 853
Essays in Jurisprudence and the Common Law, 37, 854
Essays on Jurisprudence from the Columbia Law Review, 6, 334, 354, 846, 853, 858
Establishment Clause, 55, 330, 468
Ethical Systems and Legal Ideals (Cohen), 92, 846
Evolution of the Judicial Opinion (Popkin), 146, 147, 849
ex aequo et bono, 770–71
executive agencies, 285–89, 607

executive opinions and decisions, 277–79
"Exemplary Reasoning" (Brewer), 113, 853
"Explaining Plurality Decisions" (Spriggs & Stras), 195, 859
"Explaining the Supreme Court's Shrinking Docket" (Owens & Simon), 532, 858
Exploring the Law (Manchester et al.), 848
Expounding the Constitution (Huscroft ed.), 848
"Extract from the Minutes of the Supreme Court, February 17, 1794," 140

FAA. See FEDERAL ARBITRATION ACT.
facts,
    analyzing to extract rule or standard, 80–84
    statements of, 153
    substantially similar, 92–96
    technology and, 172
    weight given to, 92
"Failed Discourse of State Constitutionalism, The" (James Gardner), 663, 854
Fair Credit Reporting Act, 597
Fair Labor Standards Act, 159, 346–47, 356
Falk, Donald M. (b. 1957), 498, 502, 506, 854
Fallon, Richard H., Jr., 7, 8, 313, 467, 675, 847, 853
"False Theory of the Binding Force of Precedent, The" (Teisen), 860
Farber, Daniel A. (b. 1950), 7, 852, 854
Farnsworth, Ward (b. 1967), 847, 861
Farrand, Max (1869–1945), 270, 534
Farrar, John H., 54, 847
FDIC, 572–73
Federal Appellate Practice (Mayer Brown LLP), 498, 849
Federal Appellate Practice Guide, 384
Federal Appendix (Thomson Reuters), 144
Federal Arbitration Act (FAA), 211, 540, 670, 671, 687, 768

"Federal Arbitration Act, The" (Pittman), 858
Federal Bureau of Land Management, 684
Federal Circuit. See UNITED STATES COURTS OF APPEALS.
federal comity doctrine, 510–11, 794
federal common law,
  defined, 788
  Erie doctrine, 226, 234, 323, 353, 363, 436, 544, 558, 571–88, 589–92, 598, 692, 703, 788–89, 793, 806
  "general" federal common law (*Swift* doctrine), 226, 234, 323, 353, 363, 558, 575–80, 788–89
  generally, 558–61, 695–96, 700
  international law, 565–66
  law merchant, 701, 703
  maritime law, 567–70, 694–95
  state law, and, 573
"Federal Common Law of Nations, The" (Bellia & B. Clark), 565, 852
Federal Control Act, 539
"Federal Court Certification of Questions of State Law to State Courts" (Cochran), 617, 618, 853
federal courts,
  abstention, 618–22, 633, 634, 636, 637, 674–76
  advisory opinions, 269–71, 799
  change in state law, 589–92, 600
  circuit courts and stare decisis, 515–16
  circuit splits, 351, 498–500, 511–12, 517, 520–21, 532
  collateral review, 313–15
  comity, 510–11
  coordinate jurisdiction, 509–16
  deference, 285–87, 512–14, 563, 607–08, 611–16
  district courts, 28, 32, 40, 86, 158, 162, 196–97, 203–04, 223, 244–45, 253, 259, 304, 329–30, 332, 376, 424, 451, 466, 470, 483, 491–94, 509, 514, 515–16, 537, 552, 591, 592, 600, 606, 614, 615, 625, 641, 642, 676, 732
  diversity cases, 571–88, 591, 593–94, 657–58
  doctrinal conflicts, 537–38
  en banc hearing or review, 495–508, 513
  English common law, 745–46

federal courts (*cont'd*)
  Erie doctrine, 226, 234, 323, 353, 363, 436, 544, 558, 571–88, 589–92, 598, 692, 703, 788–89, 793, 806
  federal common law. See FEDERAL COMMON LAW.
  horizontal precedent, 37–42, 202, 465, 491–94, 495, 509
  inferior federal courts, generally, 254
  judicial unity, 385–86
  jurisdiction, 475, 534, 551–57, 563, 565, 593, 595–97, 655, 676–87, 697–98, 745–46
  jurisdiction and powers, 534, 552–57
  law-of-the-case doctrine, 465–67, 589–90
  law-of-the-circuit rule, 37–38, 491–94
  newly created circuit court, 513–14
  powers, 551–52, 565–66, 567–71
  predicting state law, 598–99, 601–10, 613, 633
  retroactivity of decisions, 312–15
  state constitutions and statutes in, 673–78
  state-court precedent in, 534, 535–37
  trial courts, 28, 32, 40, 86, 158, 162, 196–97, 203–04, 223, 244–45, 253, 259, 304, 329–30, 332, 376, 424, 451, 466, 470, 483, 491–94, 509, 514, 515–16, 537, 552, 591, 592, 600, 606, 614, 615, 625, 641, 642, 676, 732
  vertical precedent in, 27–34, 38, 40, 202, 244–45, 465–66, 491
Federal Deposit Insurance Corporation (FDIC), 572–73
Federal Employers' Liability Act, 596–97
federalism,
  generally, 25, 476, 571–654, 666, 673
  state-court decisions relating to, 697–701
Federalism (Bellia), 845
Federalist, The (A. Hamilton et al.), xi, 7, 21, 309, 535–36, 567, 847
Federal Judiciary Act, 575
Federal Jurisdiction (Chemerinsky), 846
federal law, defined, 796–97
Federal Practice and Procedure (Wright et al.), 65, 133, 135–36, 231, 232, 269, 271, 328, 329, 379, 445, 451, 453, 460, 646, 675, 676, 692, 694, 851

federal questions, 217, 235, 467, 475,
    506, 517, 519–20, 526, 529, 534–50,
    556, 562, 565, 580, 593, 636, 646–50,
    655–56, 657, 679–90, 692, 697, 699,
    733, 788, 793
Federal Reporter, 13–14, 144–45
Federal Rules of Appellate Procedure,
    Rule 8, 259
    Rule 32.1, 144, 145, 148
    Rule 35, 39, 497, 505
    Rule 35(b)(1)(A), 300
    Rule 47, 505
    Rule 60(a), 450
Federal Rules of Civil Procedure,
    Erie decision, 579
    Rule 1, 445
    Rule 3, 583
    Rule 4(e)(1), 582
    Rule 4(n)(2), 582
    Rule 8(c), 583
    Rule 15(c), 671
    Rule 23, 108, 584–85
    Rule 23.1, 583
    Rule 41(b), 583
    Rule 44.1, 752, 757
    Rule 60(b), 327–29
    Rule 60(b)(5), 329–30, 467
    Rule 60(b)(6), 330–31
    Rule 62, 259
    Rules Enabling Act, 108, 582–87
Federal Rules of Criminal Procedure,
    generally, 582
    Rule 11, 500
    Rule 11(c)(1)(C), 201
Federal Rules of Evidence,
    generally, 582, 757
    Rule 501, 582
federal statutes,
    18 U.S.C. § 1001, 341
    28 U.S.C. § 46(c), 495–96
    28 U.S.C. § 1257, 623, 655, 691
    28 U.S.C. § 1333, 695
    28 U.S.C. § 1404, 473, 594
    28 U.S.C. § 1450, 476
    28 U.S.C. § 2255, 126–27, 219, 467
    42 U.S.C. § 1983, 89, 166, 177, 486,
        571–72, 597, 646
    Airline Deregulation Act, 543
    Antiterrorism and Effective Death
        Penalty Act, 32, 546
    Armed Career Criminal Act, 368,
        546, 547, 587
    Assimilative Crimes Act, 587

federal statutes (*cont'd*)
    Clean Air Act, 504
    Clean Water Act, 209
    Controlled Substances Act, 521
    Copyright Act, 161–62
    Defense of Marriage Act, 521
    Employee Retirement Income
        Security Act (ERISA), 65, 166,
        503, 561, 596, 649, 668, 695
    Endangered Species Act, 3–4
    Fair Credit Reporting Act, 597
    Fair Labor Standards Act, 159,
        346–47, 356
    Federal Arbitration Act (FAA), 211,
        540, 670, 671, 687, 768
    Federal Control Act, 539
    Federal Employers' Liability Act,
        596–97
    Federal Judiciary Act, 575
    Federal Tort Claims Act, 68, 347, 571,
        595, 646
    Financial Institutions Reform,
        Recovery, and Enforcement Act,
        572
    Flood Control Act, 68–69
    Foreign Sovereign Immunities Act,
        596
    Individuals with Disabilities
        Education Act, 348
    Internal Revenue Code, 127, 571
    Lanham Act, 110
    Longshoreman's and Harbor
        Workers' Compensation Act, 331
    National Industrial Recovery Act,
        693
    Natural Gas Act, 521
    Norris–LaGuardia Act, 347–48
    Patent Act, 350, 698
    Price–Anderson Act, 571
    Racketeer Influenced and Corrupt
        Organizations Act (RICO), 532,
        587
    Real Estate Settlement Procedures
        Act, 597
    Religious Freedom Restoration Act,
        83, 85–86
    Rules Enabling Act, 108, 582–87
    Rules of Decision Act, 558, 575, 576,
        578, 580–81
    Securities Exchange Act of 1934,
        29, 349
    Sherman Act, 334, 335–36, 338–39,
        561
    Stock-Raising Homestead Act,
        684–86

federal statutes (*cont'd*)
  Stolen Valor Act, 56–57
  Taft–Hartley Act, 561, 768
  Tucker Act, 336, 347
  Uniform Certification of Questions of Law Act, 626
  Voting Rights Act, 102
"Federal Supremacy, State Court Inferiority, and the Constitutionality of Jurisdiction-Stripping Legislation" (Pfander), 254–55, 858
Federal Tort Claims Act, 68, 347, 571, 595, 646
Feinberg, Ira, 861
Feldman, Stephen M., 92, 854
Fernandez, Patricio A., 19, 858
Ferren, John M. (b. 1937), 119
"*Festo*: A Jurisprudential Test for the Supreme Court?" (Hopenfeld), 855
fictitious cases, 133, 139–40, 651–54, 786–87
Fidel, Gary, 847
Field, Stephen Johnson (1816–1899), 223, 751–52
Fifth Amendment, 297, 367, 656, 669
Fifth Circuit. See UNITED STATES COURTS OF APPEALS.
finality, 41, 185, 231, 313, 324–31, 427, 441–42, 443, 451, 452, 459, 474, 479
final-judgment rule, 467
Financial Institutions Reform, Recovery, and Enforcement Act, 572
Finch, Henry (d. 1625), 11–12, 847
finding, 77, 794
findings of fact,
  defined, 794
  stare decisis and, 382–84
First Amendment, 25, 56–57, 132, 217, 357, 359, 480–81, 648, 668, 676, 682–83, 701
First Book of Jurisprudence for Students of the Common Law, A (Pollock), 27, 35–36, 421, 849
First Circuit. See UNITED STATES COURTS OF APPEALS.
Flanders, Chad, 166, 854
Fleming, Elizabeth, 854

Fletcher, William A. (b. 1945), 126
Flood Control Act, 68–69
Florida District Court of Appeal, 34, 219, 233, 241, 278, 283, 284, 285, 692
Florida Supreme Court, 47, 123, 134, 179, 223, 241, 273, 274, 276, 288, 324, 384, 397, 400, 401, 410, 416, 438, 546–47, 623–25, 653, 752
"Following Dead Precedent" (Bradford), 30, 852
Fon, Vincy, 19, 854
"Foolish Consistency" (Peters), 21, 858
foreign (as a term of art), 751
foreign law and precedent,
  English common and statutory law, 15, 19, 35, 221, 254–55, 333, 568, 702, 737–50, 758, 760, 793
  foreign law, defined, 797
  foreign precedents, 724–28, 751–61, 801
  other nations, 751, 752–61
  penal or criminal provisions, 729–31
  sister states, 709–15, 724–31, 751
  treaties, 562–64, 754–55, 759–61
Foreign Sovereign Immunities Act, 596
"Foreword: The Supreme Court's Shadow Docket" (Baude), 526, 852
formalism, defined, 794
"Formal Justice and Judicial Precedent" (Lyons), 857
Form and Substance in Anglo-American Law (Atiyah et al.), 845
Formative Era of American Law, The (Pound), 849
Fortas, Abe (1910–1982), 200
Fortescue, John (1394–1480), 847
"44.1 Luftballoons" (Ahn), 757–58, 852
42 U.S.C. § 1983, 89, 166, 177, 486, 571–72, 597, 646
forum-shopping, 385, 538, 580, 583, 597, 706
Foster, Sydney, 854
Fouchard, Gaillard, Goldman on International Commercial Arbitration (Gaillard & Savage eds.), 771, 847
Fourteenth Amendment, 30–31, 360, 363, 445, 549, 650, 659, 662, 669

Fourth Amendment, 63, 89, 130–31, 174, 680, 681
Fourth Circuit. See UNITED STATES COURTS OF APPEALS.
Fowler, Thomas L., 854
Fox, Lawrence J. (b. 1943), 149, 854
France, 269, 757
Franco-American Treaty of Alliance (1778), 269, 270
Frank, Jerome (1889–1957), 12, 13, 14, 46, 48, 93, 245, 367, 847
Frank, W.F., 303, 847
Frankfurter, Felix (1882–1965), 150, 185, 197–98, 248, 261–62, 269, 275, 355, 357, 518, 531, 854, 860
"Fraud Counterclaims in the Court of Federal Claims" (Fleming & Clawson), 854
Free Exercise Clause, 359
Freeman, A.C. (1843–1911), 76–77, 847
Freeman, Charles E. (b. 1933), 416
Friedman, Lawrence M. (b. 1930), 847
Friedmann, Wolfgang (1907–1972), 99, 847
Friendly, Henry J. (1903–1986), 89, 119, 245, 251, 854, 859
"friendly-fire" doctrine, 706–07
"From Seriatim to Consensus and Back Again" (M. Henderson), 183, 197, 855
Frost, Amanda, 536, 537, 854
Fuller, Lon L. (1902–1978), 854
Full Faith and Credit Clause, 623, 729

Gaillard, Emmanuel, 771, 775, 847, 856
Garber, Lyman A., 847
Gardner, James A., 663, 854
Gardner, John C., 847
Garland, David S., 27, 123, 415, 492, 680, 845
Garner, Bryan A. (b. 1958), 22, 44, 46, 47, 51, 62, 68, 79, 162, 164, 173, 178, 183, 230, 235, 270, 290, 292, 293, 294, 333, 346, 382, 387, 459, 497, 533, 650, 717, 727, 749, 750, 770–71, 774, 845, 847, 850, 854

Garner's Dictionary of Legal Usage (Garner), 5, 46, 62, 195, 495, 497, 519, 847
Garza, Emilio (b. 1938), 351
"Gazing into the Crystal Ball" (Zeigler), 693, 860
Geddes, Robert, 849
Gehring, Markus W., 779, 847, 854
Gelinas, Fabien, 778–79, 854
Geller, Kenneth S. (b. 1947), 850
"General Defense of *Erie Railroad Co. v. Tompkins*, A" (Young), 578, 860
general federal common law (*Swift* doctrine), 226, 234, 323, 353, 363, 558, 575–80, 788–89
General Jurisprudence (Twining), 850
General Principles of English Law, The (W. Frank), 303, 847
General Theory of Law (Korkunov), 848
George, Tracey E., 532, 854
Georgia Court of Appeals, 301, 695, 709, 710
Georgia Supreme Court, 223, 278, 301, 318, 375, 405, 411, 709
Gerhardt, Michael J. (b. 1956), 7, 235, 236, 847, 852, 854
Germany, 755, 771–72
Gewirtz, Paul (b. 1947), 67, 98, 848
"'Ghosts That Slay'" (Persky), 270, 271, 858
"Giants in a World of Pygmies?" (Gulati & Sanchez), 252, 854
Gilmore, Grant (1910–1982), 854
Ginsburg, Douglas H. (b. 1946), 498, 502, 506, 854
Ginsburg, Ruth Bader (b. 1933), 359, 491, 531
Glensy, Rex D. (b. 1969), 166, 854
Glorious Revolution, 176
Gluck, Abbe R., 580, 613, 646, 650, 854
Goadby, Frederic M. (1876–1956), 15, 848
Goggin, Edward P., 769, 774, 846
Goldsmith, Jack L., 565, 852
Goldstein, Laurence, 847
Gonzalez, Raul A. (b. 1940), 264
Goodhart, Arthur L. (1891–1978), 37, 48, 847, 849, 854

Gorsuch, Neil M. (b. 1967), 309, 854
Gossett, David M., 854
Graham, Scott, 533, 854
Grantmore, Gil (pseudonym), 152, 854
gratis dictum, defined, 792
Gray, John Chipman (1839–1915), 15, 16, 18, 847, 854
Gray, Roland, 15, 16, 18, 847
Greenawalt, Kent (b. 1936), 854
Greenberg, Harold M., 854
Gregor, Francis (1760–1815), 847
"Grieve It Again" (Heinsz), 776, 855
Gross, Hyman, 847
Guam, 732
Guest, A.G. (b. 1930), 2, 35, 44, 51, 54, 73, 847, 854, 859
Guide to the ICC Rules of Arbitration, A (Derains & E. Schwartz), 771, 846
Gulati, Mitu, 252, 854
Gulliver's Travels and Other Writings (Swift), 5
Gunderson, Joan R., 269, 855
Guzman, Andrew T., 764, 855
GVR order, 527–28

habeas corpus, 61, 219, 314, 522, 527, 691–92
Hage, Jaap, 847
Hague Convention on the Civil Aspects of International Child Abduction (1980), 754–55
Hall, Ford W., 737, 748, 855
Hall, Kermit L. (1944–2006), 28, 92, 183, 269, 847, 854, 855
Hall, Peirson M. (1894–1979), 472–73
Hallett, Moses (1834–1913), 250
Hamilton, Alexander (1755–1804), xi, 7, 21, 309, 535–36, 567, 847
Hamilton, Clyde H. (b. 1934), 166, 855
Hammond, William G. (1829–1894), 11, 13, 19, 848
Hanbury, Harold Greville (1898–1993), 849
Hand, Learned (1872–1961), 250
Handbook of American Constitutional Law (H.C. Black), 354, 845
Handbook of Law Study (F. Stone), 850

Handbook on the Construction and Interpretation of the Laws (H.C. Black), 333, 845
Handbook on the Law of Judicial Precedents (H.C. Black), xiii, 22, 82, 83, 146, 150, 156, 189, 309, 317, 326, 417, 418, 448, 722, 723, 744, 845
Hanks, Eva H., 847
Hansford, Thomas G., 847
Hardisty, James, 855
hardship, 130, 131–32, 322, 360, 411–14, 434, 523
Harlan, John Marshall (1833–1911), 182
Harlan, John Marshall, II (1899–1971), 182, 200, 311, 313–14, 363, 519, 855
Harris, J.W. (b. 1940), 5, 17, 19, 41, 74, 846
Harrison, Ross, 847
Hart, H.L.A. (1907–1992), 21, 48, 845, 847
Hart & Wechsler's The Federal Courts and the Federal System (Bator et al.), 661
Hart & Wechsler's The Federal Courts and the Federal System (Fallon et al.), 467, 675, 847
Hartnett, Edward A., 221, 222–23, 850, 855
Hasen, David M., 286, 855
"Has Precedent Ever Really Mattered in the Supreme Court?" (Schauer), 859
Hastings, W.G. (1853–1937), 848
Hawaii Supreme Court, 117, 118, 171, 278, 284, 291, 437, 456, 659, 669, 752
"Hazards of Precedent, The" (Keckler), 237, 239, 856
"Headnote, The" (Grantmore), 152, 854
headnotes, 150, 151, 152–53
Healy, Thomas, 125, 855
Heinsz, Timothy J. (1947–2004), 776, 855
Henderson, Karen L. (b. 1944), 493
Henderson, M. Todd, 183, 197, 855
Henry IV (1367–1413), 12, 390
Hensley, Thomas R. (b. 1943), 188, 855
Hernandéz, Gleider I., 764, 847
Herr, David F., 448
Herz, Michael E., 847

Hessick, F. Andrew, 651, 855
Hickman, Kristin E., 287, 855
Higginson, Stephen A., 861
high court, defined, 791
High Court of Justice (England), 755
Hilyerd, William A., 150, 855
Himmelfarb, Dan, 850
Historical Introduction to the Study of Roman Law (Jolowicz), 16, 848
"History and Law" (Feldman), 92, 854
History of American Law, A (Friedman), 847
History of English Law, A (Holdsworth), 8, 847
"History of Judicial Precedent, 1930-32, The" (Lewis), 856
"History of the Per Curiam Opinion, The" (Ray), 215, 216, 217, 858
"Holding, Dictum . . . Whatever" (Fowler), 854
holdings,
  alternative, 115, 122-29
  ascertaining, 45
  breadth of, 45, 57-62
  close calls in identifying, 50-51, 53-54, 126-29
  compared to dictum, 44-45, 125
  context and, 53-54
  defined, 2, 44-46, 795
  distinguishing from dictum, 116, 121-22, 125-28
  enthymemes, 51, 793
  explicit, 57-59
  factual, and stare decisis, 382-83
  findings distinguished, 57-62, 114-15
  holding/dictum dichotomy, 47-54, 66-67, 74-75, 456-58
  implicit, 86-88, 119-22
  inductive reasoning and, 45, 804
  language indicating, 48-52
  law of the case, 455
  limited to facts, 130-33
  loose or strict doctrines of precedent, 115, 122-24, 128
  multiple, 115-22
  necessary-to-the-result test, 45, 119-20, 122
  plurality opinions and, 196
  prior, 455
  rules or principles in, 2, 59, 86, 88, 110, 173, 308, 326, 382, 423, 441
  sub silentio, 72, 87, 229, 324, 802

holdings (*cont'd*)
  syllogisms and, 23, 51, 793, 804, 808
  vertical and horizontal precedent, 117-22
Holdsworth, William S. (1871-1944), 8, 847, 855
"Holdsworth's English Law" (Holmes), 16, 855
Holland, Randy J. (b. 1947), 664, 749, 847, 854, 855
Holland, Thomas Erskine (1835-1926), 16, 333, 847
Holmes, Oliver Wendell, Jr. (1841-1935), 4, 11, 12, 15-16, 92, 97-98, 99, 132, 182, 191, 216, 248, 250, 308-09, 312, 390, 438, 443-44, 445, 577, 717, 847, 848, 855
Honnold, John (1915-2011), 855
Honoré, Tony (b. 1921), 847
Hoover, Craig A., 855
Hopenfeld, James E., 855
horizontal precedent,
  American law, 35-37
  change of venue, 474
  change in court personnel, 472-73
  conflicting decisions, 300-01, 303-07
  defined, 35-36, 801
  dictum and, 57
  distinguishing cases and, 101
  English law, 35-37, 41
  evaluating, 155, 156-63, 180
  federal circuit courts, in, 37-40, 303-05, 418, 492-94, 495-96, 509-16
  generally, 27, 33, 35-43, 243, 385, 465
  holdings and, 116-21
  international law, in, 763-64
  law-of-the-circuit rule, 491-94
  Marks rule, 202, 205
  multiple questions involved, in, 115-25
  overruling, generally, 388-95, 411-13
  overruling, reasons disfavoring, 404-10, 414
  overruling, reasons favoring, 396-403
  principles summarized, in, 42-43
  property rights and, 423-24
  stare decisis, 35, 513-14
  summary affirmation, 227
  vertical precedent. See VERTICAL PRECEDENT.

horizontal stare decisis, defined, 807
Hornblower, William B. (1851–1914), 855
"House Divided, A" (W. Logan), 536, 537, 857
House of Lords, 270, 744, 755, 758
How Arbitration Works (F. Elkouri & E. Elkouri), 769–70, 771–72, 774, 775, 776, 777, 778, 779, 846
Howard, Jeffrey R. (b. 1955), 471
How Lawyers Think (C. Morris), 5, 849
"How Shall We Then Reason?" (McKnight), 132, 857
How the Law Works (Slapper), 850
How to Do Things with Rules (Twining & Miers), 43, 850
Hudson, Manley O. (1886–1960), 272, 762–63, 855
Hughes, G.B.J., 74, 846
Hughes, William T., 47, 847
Hunter, Dan, 113, 855
Hurst, James Willard (1910–1997), 18
Huscroft, Grant, 848
Hutchinson, Dennis J. (b. 1946), 184, 855
Hutchison, Harry G., 664, 855
hypothetical cases, 133, 786
hypothetical questions, 132, 134, 795

Ibbetson, David, 15, 105, 855
Idaho Constitution, 725–26
Idaho Supreme Court, 118, 180, 278, 374, 707, 725–26, 752
"Ideology and En Banc Review" (Solimine), 504, 859
Illinois Appellate Court, 34, 62, 208, 243, 267, 284, 289, 383, 658, 691, 704, 710, 711, 713, 728
Illinois Constitution, 658
Illinois Supreme Court, 62, 135, 137, 138, 229, 237, 267, 278, 284, 292, 293, 334, 377, 390, 400, 402, 416, 452, 581, 656, 657–58, 686, 692, 693, 705, 717
Immigration and Naturalization Service (1933–2003), 631
Implementing International Economic Law (Aksar), 764, 765, 845

"Importance and Value of Attorney General Opinions" (Larson), 277, 856
"'I Must Dissent'" (Walbolt & Zimmerman), 239, 240, 860
Indiana Court of Appeals, 278, 288, 295, 301, 302, 706, 709, 711
Indiana Supreme Court, 643, 665, 702, 741
Indian Territory, 734–35
Individuals with Disabilities Education Act, 348
ineffective-assistance claims, 120–21, 126, 486, 489, 636
"Inferiority Complex" (Frost), 536, 537, 854
injunctions, 331–32
"In Memoriam: Henry J. Friendly" (Ackerman et al.), 251
"In Praise of *Erie*" (Friendly), 854
"In Search of the Modern *Skidmore* Standard" (Hickman & Krueger), 287, 855
"Inside Agency Statutory Interpretation" (C. Walker), 288
Institute of the Law of Scotland, An (Erskine), 846
insurance, 79, 180, 252, 296, 298, 317–18, 342–43, 392–95, 412, 477, 513, 523, 570, 611, 706–07, 712
intercircuit conflicts, 351, 498–500, 532
"Interjurisdictional Certification and Choice of Law" (Robbins), 625, 858
interlocutory orders, 156, 230–32, 451–53, 476–77, 530
intermediate court, defined, 791
"Internal and External Costs and Benefits of Stare Decisis, The" (Macey), 857
Internal Revenue Code, 127, 571
International Arbitration from Athens to Locarno (Ralston), 774–75, 776, 849
"International Arbitrator's Application of Precedents, The" (Berger), 769, 852
International Commercial Arbitration (Born), 769, 771, 845

"International Common Law" (Guzman & T. Meyer), 764, 855
International Court of Justice, 760–61, 762
International Court of Justice and the Judicial Function, The (Hernandéz), 764, 847
International Economic Law (Picker et al. eds.), 774, 852
International Investment Law for the 21st Century (Binder et al. eds.), 775, 860
international law, 565–66, 762–65
International Law and Some Current Illusions and Other Essays (J.B. Moore), 776
interpretation,
  administrative agency, of, 285–89, 290
  attorney-general opinions, in, 277–85, 289, 290, 607
  basics of analyzing caselaw, 2–9
  constitutional, 352–69
  legislature, of, 290–94
  statutory. See STATUTORY INTERPRETATION.
"Interpretation and Application of the Civil Code and the Evaluation of Judicial Precedent" (Dennis), 853
"Interpretation of Treaties" (Kaufmann-Kohler), 776, 855
Interpretations of Legal History (Pound), 41, 849
Interpreting Precedents (MacCormick & Summers), 848
"Interpretive Issues in *Seminole* and *Alden*" (Bloom), 74
interstate commerce, 3, 4–5, 336, 542–43
Interstate Commerce Commission (1887–1996), 450
interstate compacts, 562–63
interstate disputes, 560
"Intersystemic Statutory Interpretation" (Gluck), 580, 613, 646, 650, 854
"Into the Third Era of Administrative Law" (Womack), 287, 860
intracircuit splits, 167–68, 244–45, 300, 387, 493, 511–13, 517, 520–21, 531, 614

Introduction to American Law (Timothy Walker), 1
Introduction to English Legal History, An (J. Baker), 35, 845
Introduction to Jurisprudence (Lloyd), 54, 58, 73, 848
Introduction to Law and Legal Reasoning, An (S. Burton), 44, 846
Introduction to Legal Method (Farrar & Dugdale), 54, 847
Introduction to Legal Method and Process (M. Berch et al.), 199, 287, 845
Introduction to Legal Reasoning, An (Levi), 848
Introduction to Science of Law, An (Kocourek), 848
Introduction to the Study of Law (Morgan), 124, 125, 849
Introduction to the Study of Law (Woodruff), 851
"Investment Treaty Arbitral Decisions as *Jurisprudence Constante*" (Bjorklund), 774, 775, 776, 778, 852
"Investment Tribunals and the Commercial Arbitration Model" (Gelinas), 778–79, 854
Invisible Constitution, The (Tribe), 5, 850
Invitation to Law (Simpson), 850
invited error, 458
Iowa Supreme Court, 191, 278, 281, 282, 284, 342–43, 384, 388, 394, 397, 436, 542–43, 631, 656, 693
"Irrepressible Myth of *Erie*" (Ely), 584, 853
Irwin, Terence (b. 1947), 18, 845
"I Say Dissental, You Say Concurral" (Kozinski & Burnham), 268, 533, 856
"Is Consistency a Myth?" (Kaufmann-Kohler), 775, 856
"Is Innocence Irrelevant?" (Friendly), 854
"Is International Law Really State Law?" (Koh), 565, 856
Islam, 754
Israel, 522, 755
issue preclusion, 373, 374, 379, 442, 453

issues,
  certworthiness, 521–23, 531–32
  constitutional questions, 521, 572–73
  exceptional importance, 495–506, 521–23, 524–25
  foreign policy or national security, 522
  government functions, 522–23
  jurisdictional, 72, 87, 121, 228–29, 469–70, 474–75, 478–79, 530, 557
  multiple, decided, 115–29
  ripeness, 531
  uncertworthiness, 523, 525, 528–29, 530–31
"It's a Bird, It's a Plane, No, It's Super Precedent" (Barnett), 7, 852
It's Your Law (Curtis), 846

Jackson, John Wyse, 300
Jackson, Percival E. (1891–1970), 848
Jackson, Robert H. (1892–1954), 28, 358, 359, 848, 855
Jacob, Marc, 764, 765, 848
Janosik, Robert J. (1946–1992), 1, 848
Jay, John (1745–1829), 847
Jay, Stewart, 271, 855
Jefferson, Thomas (1743–1826), 270–71
Jensen, Merrill (1905–1980), 738
Jessup, Philip C. (1897–1986), 855
Johnson, Foster Calhoun, 855
Johnson, Scott P., 188, 855
Johnstone, Edward Huggins (1922–2013), 52
Jolowicz, H.F. (1890–1954), 16, 848
Jones, Basil, 27, 123, 415, 492, 680
Jones, Harry Willmer (1912–1993), 846
Judge, The (Devlin), 388, 846
"Judge Friendly and the Law of Securities Regulation" (Sachs), 245–46, 251, 859
judges,
  deference to other judges, 385
  newly assigned to case, 472–73,
  new to court, 358, 475
  reputation of, 245, 248–52
  trial vs. appellate in the creation of precedent, 32–34, 106, 243–45, 255–57, 385–86, 424–25, 491–92, 515, 779

"Judges as Rulemakers" (Sherwin), 859
"Judges, Distinguished" (Lucy), 248, 857
Judging Statutes (Katzmann), 290, 848
"Judging Under the Constitution" (Leval), 46, 47, 55, 856
judgment, 76–77, 795
"Judicial Caution and Valour" (Pollock), 858
Judicial Decision, The (Wasserstrom), 9, 850
Judicial Decision-Making (Schubert ed.), 850, 856
"Judicial Deference and the Credibility of Agency Commitments" (Masur), 857
"Judicial Deference to Executive Precedent" (Merrill), 285–86, 857
judicial dictum, 54, 62–65, 129, 792
"Judicial Discretion in Statutory Interpretation" (Easterbrook), 853
judicial economy, 443, 628–29
Judicial House of Lords 1876–2009, The (Blom-Cooper et al. eds.), 35, 354, 845, 852
"Judicial Legislation" (E. Thayer), 860
"Judicial Magic" (F. Johnson), 855
Judicial Methods of Interpretation of the Law (Cueto-Rua), 46, 846
"Judicial Perspective in the Administrative State, The" (Molot), 285, 857
judicial policy, defined, 79–80, 796
Judicial Precedent in Scots Law (John Gardner), 847
"Judicial Precedents" (J. Gray), 854
"Judicial Precedents in Civil Law Systems" (Fon & Parisi), 19, 854
Judicial Process, The (Abraham), 176, 845
judicial restraint, 248, 216
"Judicial Stratification and the Reputations of the United States Courts of Appeals" (Solimine), 245, 246, 251, 859
judicial takings, 427, 433–34, 437–39
judicial unity, 385–87

"Judicial Writing and the Ethics of the Judicial Office" (McGowan), 268, 857
Judiciary, The (Abraham), 845
jurisdiction,
 coordinate, 34, 306–07, 789–90
 defined, 552
 effects of change in court's membership or organization, 417–19
 federal courts, 475, 534, 551–57, 563, 565, 593, 595–97, 655, 676–87, 697–98, 745–46
 federal-question, 534, 551, 565, 593, 595–97, 655
 law of the case, 448–49, 478–79
 original, 478–79
 supplemental, 676–77
jurisdictional questions, 87, 121, 190, 510, 551–57, 575–78, 630
"Jurisdiction of the Supreme Court Under the Act of February 13, 1925, The" (Taft), 518, 523, 860
jurisprudence, defined, 796
Jurisprudence (Bodenheimer), 845
Jurisprudence (Dias & G. Hughes), 74, 846
Jurisprudence (Gross & Harrison eds.), 847
Jurisprudence (Llewellyn), 52, 848
Jurisprudence (Patterson), 16, 19, 37, 849
Jurisprudence (Salmond), 2, 35, 176, 269, 333, 392, 850
Jurisprudence (Wortley), 9, 851
Jurisprudence and Legal Essays (Pollock), 849
"Jurisprudence and Legal Institutions" (Andrews), 114, 852
jurisprudence constante, 774, 796
Jurisprudence in Action, 858
"Juristic Science and Law" (Pound), 858
justice, miscarriage of, 442, 485–89, 798
Justice According to Law (Pound), 849
"Justice Blackstone's Common Law Orthodoxy" (Kadens), 7, 855
Justices of the United States Supreme Court,
 Alito, Samuel (b. 1950), 178, 237, 268, 350, 368, 523, 530
 Baldwin, Henry (1780–1844), 415

Justices of the U.S. Sup. Ct. (*cont'd*)
 Black, Hugo (1886–1971), 101, 200, 201, 358–59, 420, 570, 622
 Blackmun, Harry (1908–1999), 199, 211, 212, 359, 532, 769
 Bradley, Joseph P. (1813–1892), 398–99
 Brandeis, Louis (1856–1941), 9, 11, 79, 248, 342, 353, 410, 560, 577–78
 Brennan, William J., Jr. (1906–1997), 47, 130, 200, 359, 549, 666, 853
 Breyer, Stephen (b. 1938), xi, 187, 339–40, 355, 438, 523, 525, 845, 853
 Burger, Warren E. (1907–1995), 102, 158, 185, 186, 190
 Burton, Harold Hitz (1888–1964), 336
 Butler, Pierce (1866–1939), 234
 Byrnes, James F. (1882–1972), 418, 419
 Cardozo, Benjamin N. (1870–1938), iii, 10, 41, 113, 179, 248, 250, 252, 273, 388, 416, 422, 434, 846
 Clark, Tom C. (1899–1977), 200, 222
 Douglas, William O. (1898–1980), 101, 200, 201, 354, 358–59, 621, 623, 846, 853
 Field, Stephen Johnson (1816–1899), 223, 751–52
 Fortas, Abe (1910–1982), 200
 Frankfurter, Felix (1882–1965), 150, 185, 197–98, 248, 261–62, 269, 275, 355, 357, 518, 531, 854, 860
 Ginsburg, Ruth Bader (b. 1933), 359, 491, 531
 Harlan, John Marshall (1833–1911), 182
 Harlan, John Marshall, II (1899–1971), 182, 200, 311, 313–14, 363, 519, 855
 Holmes, Oliver Wendell, Jr. (1841–1935), 4, 11, 12, 15–16, 76, 92, 97–98, 99, 132, 182, 191, 216, 248, 250, 308–09, 390, 438, 443–44, 445, 577, 717, 847, 848, 855
 Jackson, Robert H. (1892–1954), 28, 358, 359, 848, 855
 Jay, John (1745–1829), 847
 Kennedy, Anthony (b. 1936), 204, 205, 209–10, 237, 341, 364–65, 438, 660, 755
 Marshall, John (1755–1835), 58, 120, 140, 176, 183, 197, 249, 415, 466, 517, 716, 733

Justices of the U.S. Sup. Ct. (*cont'd*)
   McReynolds, James Clark (1862–1946), 568
   Miller, Samuel F. (1816–1890), 102, 155, 249, 857
   Murphy, Frank (1890–1949), 358
   O'Connor, Sandra Day (b. 1930), 183, 196, 210, 633, 760, 857
   Powell, Lewis F., Jr. (1907–1998), 21, 32, 190, 196–97, 685, 686, 858
   Rehnquist, William H. (1924–2005), 5, 11, 84, 186, 188, 196, 212, 341–42, 362, 479, 525, 529, 534, 536, 614, 693, 755, 849, 853, 855, 856
   Roberts, John (b. 1955), 42, 183, 204, 353, 399
   Roberts, Owen (1875–1955), 84
   Rutledge, John (1739–1800), 534–35
   Rutledge, Wiley B. (1894–1949), 358, 419
   Scalia, Antonin (1936–2016), xi, 11, 68, 79, 117, 120, 123, 162, 166, 178, 196, 210, 220, 229, 237, 238, 290, 292, 293, 294, 309, 310, 341–42, 346, 362, 372, 410, 437, 438, 439, 469, 479, 504, 524, 525, 526, 528, 585, 650, 668, 717, 727, 750, 755, 760, 850, 854, 859
   Sotomayor, Sonia (b. 1954), 204–05
   Souter, David (b. 1939), 213
   Stevens, John Paul (b. 1920), 29, 41, 178, 210, 237, 262, 268, 341, 518, 530, 532, 548, 579, 586, 647, 755, 859
   Stewart, Potter (1915–1985), 200, 355, 523
   Stone, Harlan Fiske (1872–1946), 215, 248, 358, 401–02, 859
   Story, Joseph (1779–1845), 7–8, 248, 466, 509, 567–68, 575–76, 738, 748–49, 850
   Swayne, Noah (1804–1884), 11
   Taft, William Howard (1857–1930), 183, 518, 523, 532, 561, 768, 857, 859, 860
   Taney, Roger B. (1777–1864), 139–40, 249
   Thomas, Clarence (b. 1948), 41, 149, 334, 359, 479, 534, 536, 686, 693
   Vinson, Fred M. (1890–1953), 525
   Warren, Earl (1891–1974), 184–85, 200, 662
   Washington, Bushrod (1762–1829), 421
   White, Byron (1917–2002), 190, 196, 200, 478, 532

Justices of the U.S. Sup. Ct. (*cont'd*)
   Wilson, James (1742–1798), 535

Kadens, Emily, 7, 855
Kamisar, Yale (b. 1929), 848
Kane, Mary Kay, 65
Kanne, Michael S. (b. 1938), 494, 855
Kansas Court of Appeals, 233
Kansas Supreme Court, 134, 141, 151, 179, 220, 233, 234, 258, 273, 278, 280, 285, 406, 677, 710, 720, 727–28
Karst, Kenneth L. (b. 1929), 352, 848, 855
Katz, Stanley N. (b. 1934), 15, 105, 737, 848, 855, 860
Katzmann, Robert A. (b. 1953), 290, 848
Kaufmann-Kohler, Gabrielle (b. 1952), 775, 776, 777, 855, 856
Kavanaugh, Brett (b. 1965), 202, 205, 206, 211, 501, 586
Kayatta, William J. (b. 1953), 471
Keating, Kenneth Barnard (1900–1975), 423
Keckler, Charles N.W., 237, 239, 856
Keeton, G.W. (1902–1989), 8, 15, 80, 848
Keeton, Robert E. (1919–2007), 396, 404, 848
Keeton on Judging in the American Legal System (R. Keeton), 848
Kempin, Frederick G., Jr., 856
Kennedy, Anthony (b. 1936), 204, 205, 209–10, 237, 341, 364–65, 438, 660, 755
Kennedy, Duncan (b. 1942), 848
Kent, James (1763–1847), 8, 22, 110, 176, 249, 421, 747, 848
Kentucky Constitution, 663
Kentucky Court of Appeals, 284, 302, 726
Kentucky Supreme Court, 52, 118, 123, 260, 278, 291, 301, 319, 390, 400, 663, 704, 727
Killian, Ryan S. (b. 1985), 135, 856
Kimura, Ken, 207, 212, 213, 856
King, Robert B. (b. 1940), 608
King's Bench, 270
Kinports, Kit, 236, 856

Kirman, Igor, 183, 856
Klafter, Craig Evan, 848
Klaxon rule, 593–95, 596
Klein, David E., 55, 251, 848, 856
Kocourek, Albert (1875–1952), 848, 856
Koh, Harold Hongju (b. 1954), 565, 856
Korkunov, N.M. (1853–1904), 848
Kornhauser, Lewis A., 856
Kort, Fred, 856
Koven, Harold, 856
Kozel, Randy J., 54, 83, 234, 237, 238, 396, 404, 413, 856
Kozinski, Alex (b. 1950), 45, 104, 116, 129, 162, 268, 498, 499, 533, 644, 856
Krajick, Ruby J., 231
Kress, Ken, 124, 856
Kriebaum, Ursula, 860
Krishnakumar, Anita S., 856
Kroger, John R., 132, 856
Kronman, Anthony T. (b. 1945), 9, 856
Krueger, Matthew D., 287, 855

Lacovara, Philip Allen (b. 1943), 498, 849
Lakshminath, A., 848
Landes, William M. (b. 1939), 802, 856
Langdell, Christopher Columbus (1826–1906), 48
Language of Law School, The (Mertz), 72, 849
Lanham Act, 110
Larson, Robert L. (1898–1986), 277, 856
Lash, Kurt T., 856
law, various types defined, 796–97
Law and Modern Society (Atiyah), 845
Law and Practice of the International Court, The (Rosenne), 762, 764, 850
Law and Social Order in the United States (Hurst), 18
"Law and the Judges, The" (Corbin), 853
Law and the Modern Mind (J. Frank), 12, 13, 48, 847
Law Books and How to Use Them (Townes), 45, 49, 248
Law Books and Their Use, 150, 848

"Law in Science and Science in Law" (Holmes), 12
Law in the Making (Allen), 845
law merchant, 703
Law of American State Constitutions, The (R. Williams), 659, 851
"Law of the Case, The" (unsigned note), 857
law-of-the-case doctrine, 231–32, 328, 441–89, 797
law-of-the-circuit rule, 37–38, 491–94, 798
Law, or, A Discourse Thereof (Finch), 11–12, 847
Law Restated, The (W. Hughes), 47, 847
Laws and Jurisprudence of England and America, The (Dillon), 101, 155, 226, 249, 846
Law's Empire (Dworkin), 846
"Law's Laboratory" (Sourgens), 762, 763, 764–65, 859
Lawson, F.H. (1897–1983), 1, 18, 846
Lawson, Gary (b. 1958), 7, 856
Laying Down the Law (G. Morris et al.), 747, 849
Learning the Law (G. Williams), 92, 303, 851
"Learning to Differentiate Between Judicial and Obiter Dicta" (D. Thayer), 860
Lebovits, Gerald (b. 1955), 239, 856
Lectures on Jurisprudence (Austin), 44, 45, 845
Lectures on Legal History (Windeyer), 5, 851
Lectures on the Relation Between Law and Public Opinion in England During the Nineteenth Century (Dicey), 846
Ledebur, Linas E., 197, 198, 856
Lee, Thomas Rex (b. 1964), 660, 856
Lefstin, Jeffrey A., 239, 856
Legal Analysis (Romantz & K. Vinson), 850
Legal Analyst, The (Farnsworth), 847
Legal and Political Hermeneutics (Lieber), 11, 13, 19, 848

"Legal and Political Hermeneutics" (Lieber), 113, 856
"Legal Indeterminacy" (Kress), 124, 856
Legal Institutions and the Sources of Law (Shiner), 778, 850
Legal Institutions Today and Tomorrow (M.G. Paulsen ed.), 849
"Legal Mind, The" (M. Amos), 852
Legal Mind, The (MacCormick & Birks eds.), 848
"Legal Opinions of the Attorney General of the United States" (Surrency), 277, 860
"Legal Precedent" (Landes & Posner), 802, 856
legal principle, defined, 77, 798
"Legal Principles and the Limits of Law" (Raz), 77, 78, 858
"Legal Realism" (Gilmore), 854
Legal Reason (Weinreb), 850
legal reasoning, defined, 804
"Legal Reasoning" (Carter), 1
Legal Reasoning and Briefing (Brumbaugh), 845
Legal Reasoning and Legal Theory (MacCormick), 52, 848
Legal Reasoning and Political Conflict (Sunstein), 850
Legal Right and Social Democracy (MacCormick), 848
legal rule, defined, 77–78, 806
"Legal Rules" (Dickinson), 19, 853
"Legal Scholarship for Judges" (D. Wood), 114, 860
legal standards, defined, 78, 806
Legal Theory (Friedmann), 99, 847
legis interpretatio legis vim obtinet, 333
legislative history, 290–94, 570, 717
"Legitimacy Model for the Interpretation of Plurality Decisions, A" (Kimura), 207, 212, 213, 856
Leonard, James, 167, 856
LeRoy, Michael H., 240, 355, 856
"'Let Congress Do It'" (L. Marshall), 334, 857
Leval, Pierre N. (b. 1936), 46, 47, 55, 856

Levi, Edward H. (1911–2000), 848
Levin, Charles (b. 1926), 276
Levy, Beryl Harold (1908–1995), 311, 856
Levy, Leonard W. (1923–2006), 352, 848, 855, 858
Lévy-Ullmann, Henri (1870–1947), 15, 848
Lew, Julian D.M., 776, 849, 855
Lewis, T. Ellis, 856
"Lexicographic Look at Magna Carta, A" (Garner), 749, 854
lex loci delicti, 710
Lieber, Francis (1800–1872), 1, 10, 11, 13, 19, 22, 113, 392, 397, 848, 856
Life of the Law, The (Honnold ed.), 855
"Life Span of a Judge-Made Rule, The" (Stevens), 859
Lile, W.M. (1893–1932), 856
limited-duty rule, 263–64
Lincoln, Alexander, 857
Lind, Douglas, 105, 848
Linde, Hans A. (b. 1924), 664
Liptak, Adam (b. 1960), 518
Llewellyn, Karl (1893–1962), 52, 67, 98–99, 116, 129, 848
Lloyd, Dennis, 54, 58, 73, 848
Lobban, Michael (b. 1962), 848
"*Lochner*, Liberty of Contract, and Paternalism" (Hutchison), 664, 855
Lockhart, William B. (1906–1995), 661, 848
Lodge, H., 21
Logan, James K. (b. 1929), 505
Logan, Wayne A., 536, 537, 857
Logic and Legal Reasoning (Lind), 105, 848
"Logic in the Law" (Guest), 51, 854
Longshoreman's and Harbor Workers' Compensation Act, 331
"Longstanding Agency Interpretations" (Krishnakumar), 856
Lookofsky, Joseph, 764, 857
"Lord Keeper's Speech in the Exchequer, The" (Bacon), 44, 852
"Loud Rules" (Coale & Couture), 853

Louisiana Court of Appeal, 278, 289
Louisiana Supreme Court, 131, 134, 262, 617, 625, 702
Lowrie, Walter Hoge (1807–1876), 419–20
Lucy, William, 248, 857
Lunney, Leslie A., 857
Lusky, Louis (1915–2001), 848
Lynch, Bernadette, 848
Lyons, David, 857

MacCormick, Neil (1941–2009), 17, 52, 65, 845, 848
Macey, Jonathan R. (b. 1955), 857
Madison, James (1751–1836), 131, 309, 534–35, 847
Magna Carta (1225, not 1215), 748–49, 847, 854
Magna Carta (R. Holland ed.), 749, 847
Mahoney, Dennis J., 848
Maine, Henry Sumner (1822–1888), 848
Maine Supreme Court, 110, 273, 274, 276, 293, 406, 617, 628–29, 709
Majority Rule or Minority Will (Spaeth & Segal), 850
Making Law in the United States Courts of Appeals (Klein), 251, 848
"Making Motions and Opposing Motions" (Krajick), 231
Making of the Constitution, The (G. Wood), 664, 851
Making Our Democracy Work (Breyer), 845
Making Your Case (Scalia & Garner), 162, 290
"Maligned Per Curiam, The" (Nygaard), 215, 857
malpractice claims,
 legal, 489, 698–99, 700
 medical, 318, 383, 476, 601, 629
Maltz, Earl (b. 1950), 335, 857
Manchester, Colin, 848
mandamus, 267, 453–54, 462, 487–88, 551, 653
mandate, 77

mandate rule, 442, 449, 459–62, 465, 483–84, 798
Manning, John F. (b. 1961), 847
"Manning the Dikes" (Harlan II), 519, 855
Mansfield, Lord (William Murray) (1705–1793), 50, 51, 421
Manual of Elementary Law, A (W. Smith), 44, 850
Manzanet-Daniels, Sallie, 715
Marcus, Maeva, 140
maritime law, 567–70, 694–95, 759
"Maritime Origin of the Word 'Certworthiness,' The" (Sharpe), 519, 859
Marks rule, 188, 199–213, 798
Marmor, Andrei, 24, 859
Marshall, John (1755–1835), 58, 120, 140, 176, 183, 197, 249, 415, 466, 517, 716, 733
Marshall, Lawrence C., 334, 857
Martin, Peter W., 13, 152, 857
Martinez, Jenny S. (b. 1971), 763, 857
Marvell, Thomas B., 849
Maryland Court of Appeals, 117, 130, 166, 278, 412, 703, 711, 729, 743, 744, 750
Maryland Court of Special Appeals, 59, 189, 255
Massachusetts Constitution, 296–97, 749
Massachusetts Supreme Judicial Court, 12 (by allusion), 92, 134, 170, 228, 262, 272, 273, 274, 275, 296–97, 330, 390, 436, 452, 644, 670, 711–12, 744–45, 746, 750
Masur, Jonathan, 857
Materials for Legal Method (Dowling et al.), 846
Mavroidis, Petros C., 764, 858
Max Planck Encyclopedia of European Private Law, The (Basedow et al. eds.), 762, 845, 860
Max Planck Encyclopedia of Public International Law, The (Wolfrum ed.), 762, 851, 852
Mayer Brown LLP, 498, 849
Mayers, Lewis, 849
McAllister, Marc, 857

McClain, Emlin (1851–1915), 182, 183, 189, 857
McGehee, Lucius P. (1868–1923), 27, 123, 415, 492, 680, 845
McGinnis, John O., 7, 857
McGowan, Daniel (b. 1974), 268, 857
McKean, Frederick G., Jr., 857
McKinney, Ruth Ann, 849
McKnight, H. Brent (1952–2004), 132, 857
McLeese, Roy W., III, 119, 122
McNair, Arnold D. (1885–1975), 1, 18, 846
McReynolds, James Clark (1862–1946), 568
Mead, Joseph, 258, 857
Meador, Daniel J. (1926–2013), 475, 849
"Meaning of Judicial Self-Restraint, The" (Posner), 78, 858
"Measure of the Doubt, The" (Lefstin), 239, 856
Megarry, R.E. (1910–2006), 420
Meltzer, Daniel J. (1951–2015), 313, 847, 853
memorandum opinions, 147, 799
Merchant of Venice, The (Shakespeare), iii
Merrill, Thomas W. (b. 1949), 285, 857
Merryman, John Henry (1920–2015), 17, 849
Mertz, Elizabeth, 72, 849
Method of Law, The (Monahan), 849
"Method of Law, The" (Radin), 6, 334, 858
Meyer, Linda, 113, 857
Meyer, Timothy L., 764, 855
Meyler, Bernadette, 749, 857
Michalski, Roger M., 709, 857
Michigan Court of Appeals, 224, 240, 258, 277, 278, 284, 289, 383, 724, 726, 727
Michigan Supreme Court, 117, 180, 243, 276, 280, 292, 315, 372, 376, 396, 402–03, 412, 413–14, 589, 591–92, 599, 604, 664, 670, 722, 726
Miers, David, 43, 850
Miguel, Alfonso Ruiz, 21, 857

Miller, Arthur R. (b. 1934), 133, 135, 231, 269, 271, 328, 329, 379, 445, 451, 453, 460, 646, 675, 676, 692, 694, 851
Miller, Geoffrey P., 260, 853
Miller, James R., Jr. (1931–2014), 640
Miller, Samuel F. (1816–1890), 102, 155, 249, 857
Minnesota Court of Appeals, 281, 728
Minnesota Supreme Court, 111, 115, 262, 278, 281, 282, 283, 291, 405, 409, 454, 457, 564, 600, 625, 663, 671–72, 679–80, 682–83, 705, 718, 752
miscarriage of justice, 442, 485–89, 798
Mississippi Constitution, 674, 723
Mississippi Court of Appeals, 278
Mississippi Supreme Court, 111, 244, 284, 288, 320, 330, 391, 401, 427, 429, 434, 605–06, 629, 659, 711–12, 716, 721–22, 723, 740, 747
Missouri Court of Appeals, 117, 301, 709, 712, 713
Missouri Supreme Court, 278, 280, 293, 294, 324, 376, 604, 610, 617, 625, 656, 659, 692, 742
Mistelis, Loukas A., 776, 849, 855
Mitchell, Jonathan F., 7, 857
Mitchell, L.G., 9, 846
Mitchell, M., 15, 848
"Mixed Jurisdictions" (Tetley), 860
model acts, construction of, 706
modes of analysis, defined, 79, 798
Molot, Jonathan T., 285, 857
Monaghan, Henry Paul, 857
Monahan, James H., 849
Montagu, Basil (1770–1851), 44, 845, 852
Montana Supreme Court, 134, 220, 245, 279, 296, 637, 716, 720
Montrose, James Louis, 849
Moodie, Peter, 848
Moore, James William (1905–1994), 27, 40, 62, 70, 136, 442, 491, 492, 577, 849, 857
Moore, John Bassett (1860–1947), 776
Moore, Russell F., 849
Moore's Federal Practice (J.W. Moore et al.), 27, 40, 62, 70, 136, 442, 491, 492, 577, 849

mootness,
  doctrine and exceptions, 135–39
  federal question, 552–53
Morgan, Edmund M. (1878–1966), 124, 125, 849
Morris, Clarence, 5, 849
Morris, Gwen, 747, 849
Morrison, Trevor W. (b. 1972), 857
mortmain, 316, 748
Moschzisker, Robert von (1870–1939), 10, 850, 860
Moses, Margaret L., 771, 849
Most Humble Servants (S. Jay), 271, 855
Motion Practice (Herr et al.), 448
motions to dismiss, 231, 451, 476–77
Muchlinski, Peter, 776, 849
Murphy, Frank (1890–1949), 358
Murphy, J. David, 849
Murphy, Michael R. (b. 1947), 167
Murray, William (Lord Mansfield) (1705–1793), 50, 51, 421
"Myth About Stare Decisis and International Trade Law, The" (Bhala), 762, 763, 764, 852
"Myth of the Disposable Opinion, The" (Robel), 148, 858

NAFTA, 777
Napoleonic Code (1804), 17, 754
National Industrial Recovery Act, 693
Native Americans, 655–56
Natural Gas Act, 521
Nature and Authority of Precedent, The (Duxbury), 14, 47, 73, 97, 98, 102, 182, 846
Nature and Sources of the Law, The (J. Gray), 15, 16, 18, 847
"Nature of Precedent, The" (Maltz), 335, 857
Nature of the Common Law, The (M. Eisenberg), 846
Nature of the Judicial Process, The (Cardozo), 10, 41, 338, 416, 846
Nebraska Court of Appeals, 279
Nebraska Supreme Court, 374, 430, 431, 449, 627, 635, 658, 718–19, 741, 747, 748
Nelson, Caleb (b. 1966), 857

Nemerson, Steven S. (b. 1947), 847
Nevada Supreme Court, 135, 141, 279, 483, 628–29, 701, 724, 729, 748
New Hampshire Constitution, 296–97
New Hampshire Supreme Court, 274, 296, 388, 398, 663, 724, 726, 741, 745
New Jersey Court of Chancery, 745
New Jersey Superior Court, 189, 279, 296, 298, 697, 711, 729
New Jersey Supreme Court, 130, 256, 288, 399, 405, 538, 542, 553, 611, 666, 667, 691, 715, 741, 743
"New Law, Non-Retroactivity, and Constitutional Remedies" (Fallon & Meltzer), 313, 853
"New Light on the History of the Federal Judiciary Act of 1789" (C. Warren), 577, 860
New Mexico Constitution, 632
New Mexico Court of Appeals, 260
New Mexico Supreme Court, 191, 279, 321, 376, 398, 400, 422, 425, 427, 434, 601, 628, 630–31, 632, 683–84, 685–86, 688, 718, 733, 740–41, 747, 748, 752
New Oxford Companion to Law, The (Cane & Conaghan eds.), 46, 248, 846, 852, 857
New York Constitution, 676
New York Court of Appeals, 77, 171, 172, 174, 179, 239, 250, 252, 258, 273, 292, 294, 298, 383, 390, 397, 408, 409, 417, 422, 425, 453, 607, 629, 631–32, 641, 649, 665, 676–77, 692, 710, 715
New York State Bar Association, 509–10
New York Supreme Court Appellate Division, 34, 233, 279, 289, 292, 298, 322, 387, 715
New York Surrogate's Court, 656
Nicolson, James Baldenach, 846
Nicomachean Ethics (Aristotle), 18, 845
"1966 and All That" (Blom-Cooper), 35, 354, 852
Ninth Circuit. See UNITED STATES COURTS OF APPEALS.
"9th Circuit's Clarion Calls Are Being Heard" (Graham), 533, 854

Nixon, Richard (1913–1994), 185–86, 522–23
Nolla, Eduardo, 269
"No Magic Words Could Do It Justice" (Traynor), 860
"'Non-Banc En Banc,' The" (Kanne), 494, 855
"Non-Precedential Precedent, The" (Reynolds & Richman), 148–49, 858
Norris–LaGuardia Act, 347–48
North American Fair Trade Agreement (NAFTA) (1994), 777
North Carolina Supreme Court, 101, 189, 220, 233, 234, 258, 262, 271, 279, 316, 335, 427, 428, 608, 609, 649, 669, 709, 711, 741
North Dakota Supreme Court, 134, 158, 277, 279, 281, 284, 288, 545, 703–04, 706, 718
"Note on Advisory Opinions, A" (Frankfurter), 269, 275, 854
"'Nothing We Say Matters'" (L. Meyer), 113, 857
Novak, Linda, 195, 199, 207, 857
Nowak, John E. (b. 1947), 661, 849
Nygaard, Richard Lowell (b. 1940), 215, 857

obiter dictum. See DICTUM.
"Objectivity of Morality, Rules, and Law, The" (Alexander), 77, 852
obsolescence,
 charitable-immunity rule, 179–80
 conditions causing, 176, 178–81, 295, 364–65, 744–45
 rejuvenation, 233
O'Connor, Sandra Day (b. 1930), 183, 196, 210, 633, 760, 857
"Of Lions and Bears, Judges and Legislators, and the Legacy of Justice Scalia" (Gorsuch), 309, 854
Of Men, and Not of Law (Garber), 847
Oglebay, Robert Stephen, 857
O'Hara, Erin, 857
Ohio Constitution, 651–52, 677
Ohio Court of Appeals, 165, 189, 233–34, 262, 301, 318, 705

Ohio Supreme Court, 152, 167, 181, 220, 224, 263, 279, 280, 284, 313, 316, 318, 321, 327, 377, 411, 427, 434, 443–44, 446, 601, 652, 660, 662, 665, 677, 719
Ohrenschall, John C., 858
Oklahoma Court of Civil Appeals, 728
Oklahoma Court of Criminal Appeals, 599–600
Oklahoma Supreme Court, 134–35, 190, 217, 279, 281, 282, 291, 319, 322, 430, 540, 590, 591, 632, 655, 665, 706, 716, 717, 733–35, 752
Oliphant, Herman (1884–1939), 59, 858
"On Analogical Reasoning" (Sunstein), 10, 48, 99, 113, 114, 860
"On 'A Ticket Good for One Day Only'" (R. Re), 84, 858
On Civil Liberty and Self Government (Lieber), 1, 10, 22, 392, 397, 848
One Case at a Time (Sunstein), 850
O'Neill, Paul T., 180, 858
On Law and Justice (A. Ross), 8, 16, 850
On the Laws and Customs of England (Bracton), 845
opinions,
 advisory, 134, 140, 269–76, 799
 affirmance without, 147–48
 attorney general's, 277–85, 290
 concurring. See CONCURRENCES.
 decisions distinguished from, 76
 defined, 76, 799–800
 dissenting, 182, 188–89, 191, 192, 193, 194, 195, 197, 216, 239–40, 799
 dual majority, 207–09, 210–13
 equally divided, 220–25
 factors affecting precedential value, 243–47
 majority, 188–89, 193, 194, 799
 memorandum, 147, 799
 minority, 183
 narrowest ground, 188, 195, 196, 199–202, 205–210, 212
 nonprecedential, 144, 145, 148
 officially published, 142–43
 per curiam, 214–17, 799–800
 plurality, 192–94, 195–213, 364, 585, 800
 published, 6, 37, 63–64, 142, 143–44
 separate, 61–62, 185, 191–92, 216–17, 358, 471, 498–99
 seriatim, 183, 192, 197, 800

opinions (cont'd)
　syllabus of, 23, 51, 150–54
　unanimous, 182, 183, 185
　underlying assumptions of, 84–87
　unpublished, 37, 69, 142–43, 144–45, 148–49, 800
　unwritten, defined, 800
"Opinions, Style of" (Garner), 183, 854
ordinary-meaning canon, 79, 90, 291
Oregon Court of Appeals, 687
Oregon Supreme Court, 131, 221, 224, 283, 366, 374, 405, 549, 627, 629, 632, 660, 687, 693, 716, 718, 723, 739, 748
"Originalism, Popular Sovereignty, and Reverse Stare Decisis" (Lash), 856
"Originalism, Stare Decisis and the Promotion of Judicial Restraint" (Merrill), 857
original precedents, 334–35, 801
"Origin and Logical Implications of the *Ejusdem Generis* Rule, The" (G. Williams), 50, 860
Ortino, Federico, 849
Our Legal System and How It Operates (Shartel), 2, 850
Overcoming Law (Posner), 849
overrule, defined, 800
"Overruling Decisions in the Supreme Court" (Padden), 858
overruling or reversal of decisions,
　certiorari, 525–26
　constitutional precedents, 352–69
　defined, 800, 806
　factors considered, 338–40, 360–61, 388–89, 396–403, 411–12, 525–26
　generally, 30–33, 158–59, 181, 189–90, 242, 301, 308–09, 311, 316, 318–32, 388–439
　horizontal precedent, 388–96, 411–12
　judicial deference, 385
　reasons against, 404–10
　reasons favoring, 396–403
　rule of property, 430–34
　stare decisis and statutes, 337–45
　statutory precedents, 333–45, 409–10
　superseding, overruled, 323–24
"Overruling Precedent" (LeRoy), 240, 856

"Overruling Statutory Precedents" (Eskridge), 853
Owens, Ryan J., 532, 858
Oxford Companion to American Law, The (K. Hall ed.), 92, 847, 854
Oxford Companion to Law, The (D. Walker), 850
Oxford Companion to Law, The New (Cane & Conaghan eds.), 46, 248, 846, 852, 857
Oxford Companion to the Supreme Court of the United States, The (K. Hall ed.), 28, 183, 269, 847, 854, 855
Oxford Essays in Jurisprudence (Guest ed.), 2, 35, 44, 51, 54, 73, 847, 854, 859
Oxford Handbook of International Investment Law, The (Muchlinski et al. eds.), 776, 849
Oxford International Encyclopedia of Legal History, The (Katz ed.), 15, 105, 737, 848, 855, 860

Padden, Amy L., 858
Palmeter, David (b. 1938), 764, 858
Paradoxes of Legal Science, The (Cardozo), 846
Parisi, Francesco (b. 1962), 19, 854
Patent Act, 350, 698
"Path of the Law, The" (Holmes), 11, 390, 855
Paton, George Whitecross (1902–1985), 47, 105, 849
Patterson, Edwin W. (1889–1965), 16, 19, 37, 846, 849
Paulsen, Michael Stokes, 7, 8, 858
Paulsen, Monrad G. (1918–1980), 849
Paulsson, Jan (b. 1949), 775, 777, 858
Pennsylvania Commonwealth Court, 240, 279, 280
Pennsylvania Superior Court, 224, 243, 292, 418
Pennsylvania Supreme Court, 87, 165, 179, 191, 221, 224, 245, 256, 263, 288, 308, 317, 374, 389, 396, 397, 419–20, 473, 600, 633, 659, 664–65, 701, 710, 712, 723, 752
"Per Curiam Opinion, The" (Wasby et al.), 214, 215, 216, 860

per curiam opinions, 214–17, 799, 800–01
per incuriam, 303, 800
"Permanent Court of International Justice, The" (Hudson), 762–63, 855
Perry, H.W., Jr., 519, 530, 849
Persky, Jonathan D., 270, 271, 858
personal stare decisis, defined, 807
persuasive authority,
  advisory opinions, of, 269–76, 799
  arbitral awards as, 773–79
  defined, 786, 801–02
  English common law, 737
  English statutory law, 746–50
  foreign law, of, 752, 759–60
  generally, 162–72, 191, 244, 245, 257, 289
  international law, of, 762
  out-of-state opinions, of, 724–28
Pervasive Problems in International Arbitration (Mistelis & Lew eds.), 776, 849, 855
Peters, Christopher J., 21, 849, 858
Peterson, G.L., 357, 858
Pfander, James E., 140, 254–55, 858
"Philosophy of Certiorari, The" (M. Cordray & R. Cordray), 517, 518, 853
Picker, Colin B. (b. 1965), 774, 852
Pierce, Richard J., Jr., 858
Pittman, Larry J., 858
"Pleading and Proving Foreign Law in the Age of Plausibility Reading" (Michalski), 709, 857
"Please Don't Cite This" (Kozinski & Reinhardt), 856
Pledge of Allegiance, 55–56, 357–59
plurality, 193, 195–213, 634, 800–01
plurality opinions, 192–94, 195–213, 364, 585, 800
"Plurality Rule" (Ledebur), 197–98, 856
Pocar, Fausto (b. 1939), 762, 763, 852
Politics of Precedent on the U.S. Supreme Court, The (Hansford & Spriggs), 847
Pollock, Frederick (1845–1937), 27, 35–36, 48, 421–22, 848, 849, 858
"Polyphonic Federalism" (Schapiro), 673, 674, 676, 859

Ponzetto, Giacomo A.M., 19, 858
Popkin, William D. (b. 1937), 146, 147, 849
Popular and Practical Introduction to Law Studies (S. Warren), 850
positivism, defined, 801
Posner, Richard A. (b. 1939), 46–47, 66–67, 78, 129, 252, 499, 802, 849, 856, 858
Pound, Roscoe (1870–1964), iii, 41, 849, 858
Powell, Lewis F., Jr. (1907–1998), 21, 32, 190, 196–97, 685, 686, 858
Powell, Richard R.B. (1890–1982), 846
Power of Precedent, The (Gerhardt), 847
"Power of the Past" (Bhala), 852
"Power That Shall Be Vested in a Precedent, The" (J. Rehnquist), 858
precedent,
  binding, defined, 27–34, 801
  declaratory, 333–34, 801
  defined, 21–22, 24–25, 801–02
  direct, 105, 290
  doctrine of, defined, 6, 793
  foreign, 724–28, 801. See also FOREIGN LAW AND PRECEDENT.
  horizontal. See HORIZONTAL PRECEDENT.
  loose doctrine of, 115, 122–24, 128
  novelty of, 23–24, 159–60
  original, 334–35, 801
  persuasive. See PERSUASIVE AUTHORITY.
  prevalence of, 23–24
  rationales for, 9–12
  rationales sometimes urged against, 12–14
  related terminology, 76–79
  source of, 23–24
  strict or orthodox doctrine of, 115, 122–24
  sub silentio, 324, 802
  superprecedents, 235–36, 802
  taxation, 318–22
  trial vs. appellate courts in the creation of precedent, 32–34, 106, 243–45, 255–57, 385–86, 424–25, 491–92, 515, 779
  vertical. See VERTICAL PRECEDENT.
  weightiness of. See WEIGHTINESS OF PRECEDENTS.

"Precedent" (Aldisert), 21, 45, 852
"Precedent" (John Bell), 46, 852
"Precedent" (Karst), 352, 855
"Precedent" (Schauer), 11, 24, 859
"Precedent" (Thomas Walker), 28
"Precedent, Rule of" (Vogenauer), 762, 860
"Precedent and Judicial Power After the Founding" (Price), 858
Precedent and Law (J. Stone), 850
"Precedent and Legal Authority" (Collier), 18, 48, 102, 853
"Precedent and Policy" (Schaefer), 859
"Precedent and Prediction" (Caminker), 30, 256–57, 853
"Precedent and Stare Decisis" (Kempin), 856
"Precedent and Tradition" (Kronman), 9, 856
"Precedential Effect of Arbitration Decisions, The" (Schütze), 772, 859
"Precedential Value of Supreme Court Plurality Decisions, The" (Novak), 195, 199, 207, 857
Precedent in English and Continental Law (Goodhart), 847
Precedent in English Law (Cross & Harris), 5, 17, 19, 41, 74, 846
Precedent in English Law and Other Essays (Montrose), 849
Precedent in Indian Law (Lakshminath), 848
Precedent in International Arbitration (Gaillard & Banifatemi eds.), 775, 847, 856
"Precedent in Investment Treaty Arbitration" (Commission), 775, 776–77, 778, 853
"Precedent in Investment Treaty Arbitration" (Sureda), 775, 778, 860
Precedent in Law (Goldstein ed.), 847
Precedent in the United States Supreme Court (Peters ed.), 849
Precedent in the World Court (Shahabuddeen), 762, 764, 765, 850

"Precedent Setters, The" (Bhala), 763, 764, 852
Precedents and Case-Based Reasoning in the European Court of Justice (Jacob), 764, 765, 848
"Precedent, Super-Precedent" (Sinclair), 48, 859
preclusion doctrine, 373–74, 378
preclusion rules, 442, 453
predictability, 13–14, 21, 30, 67, 162, 368, 389–90, 439, 443, 769
"Prediction and the Rule of Law" (Dorf), 853
presidents, U.S.,
  Clinton, Bill (b. 1946), 186–87, 522
  Jefferson, Thomas (1743–1826), 270–71
  Madison, James (1751–1836), 131, 309, 534–35, 847
  Nixon, Richard (1913–1994), 185–86, 522–23
  Taft, William Howard (1857–1930), 183, 518, 523, 532, 561, 768, 857, 859, 860
  Washington, George (1732–1799), 269, 270
presumption-of-validity canon, 379–80, 650
Price, Polly J., 858
Price–Anderson Act, 571
primary authority, defined, 786
Principia Legis et Aequitatis (Branch), 333, 845
Principles and Practice of International Commercial Arbitration, The (Moses), 771, 849
principles of law, 77–78, 105, 798
prior-construction canon, 346–47, 348, 392, 802
private international law, 762
private rights, 401–02
Problems of Jurisprudence, The (Posner), 849
Problems of Law (Wigmore), 851
"Procedure of Election Law in Federal Courts, The" (J. Douglas), 508, 853
property,
  adverse possession, 419–20
  definitions of "rule of property," 422–23

property (*cont'd*)
　dicta creating rule of, 425–26
　inviolability of a rule of property, 424–27
　overruling a rule of property, 422, 430–36. See also TAKINGS.
　reliance interests, 421
　rights, 646–47
　rule-of-property doctrine, 404, 407–08, 421–29
　stare decisis, 425–26, 435–37
prospective law, defined, 308–09, 797
"Prospective or Retroactive Operation of Overruling Decision" (S.R. Shapiro), 859
prospectivity, 308, 311, 316, 318–19, 328, 329–30, 592, 727, 802–03
Province of Jurisprudence Determined, The (Austin), 845
Psychoanalytic Jurisprudence (Ehrenzweig), 17, 846
public international law, 762
Puerto Rico, 365–66
Pullman abstention doctrine, 618–20, 621, 622, 623, 624, 632, 633, 636, 637, 674–75, 677
purposivism, defined, 803
Puzzle of Unanimity, The (Corley et al.), 188, 846

qualified immunity, 108–10
quasi-judicial bodies, 277
questions,
　certified. See CERTIFIED QUESTIONS.
　distinguishing dicta and holdings, 116, 121–22, 125–28
　federal, 217, 235, 467, 475, 506, 517, 519–20, 526, 529, 534–50, 556, 562, 565, 580, 593, 636, 646–50, 655–56, 657, 679–90, 692, 697, 699, 733, 788, 793
　hypothetical, 132, 134, 795
　multiple decided, 122–25

racial segregation, 184–85
Racketeer Influenced and Corrupt Organizations Act (RICO), 532, 587
Radin, Max (1880–1950), 6, 334, 858

Ralston, Jackson H. (1857–1945), 774, 776, 849
Ram, James (1793–1870), 849
Rappaport, Michael B. (b. 1970), 7, 857
"Ratings Game, The" (W. Ross), 248, 858
ratio decidendi (as a term), 46, 50, 803
"*Ratio Decidendi* of a Case, The" (Goodhart), 854
"*Ratio Decidendi* of a Case and the Doctrine of Binding Precedent, The" (Simpson), 2, 35, 44, 53–54, 73, 859
rationale,
　defined, 803
　discerning, 44–75
"*Ratio* of the *Ratio Decidendi*, The" (J. Stone), 860
Ray, Laura Krugman, 215, 216, 217, 858
Raz, Joseph (b. 1939), 10, 13, 48, 73, 77, 97, 98, 99, 849, 858
Re, Edward D. (1920–2006), 849, 858
Re, Joseph R. (b. 1960), 849
Re, Richard M. (b. 1982), 84, 858, 861
Reading Law (Scalia & Garner), 68, 79, 178, 290, 292, 293, 294, 346, 650, 717, 727, 750, 850
Reading Like a Lawyer (McKinney), 849
Real Estate Settlement Procedures Act, 597
"Realist Jurisprudence and Prospective Overruling" (B. Levy), 311, 856
reason, defined, 803–04
"Reason and Fiat in Case Law" (Fuller), 854
reasoning, various types defined, 804
Reason in Law (Carter & T. Burke), 10, 846
"Reason Is Too Large" (Hunter), 113, 855
Reason over Precedents (Klafter), 848
"Reception of English Common Law in the American Colonies" (Stoebuck), 737–38, 741, 743, 859
reception of English law into American law, 737–50
reception statutes, 738

"Recollections of *West Virginia State Board of Education v. Barnette*" (Peterson et al.), 357, 858

"Reconciling *Chevron* and Stare Decisis" (Pierce), 858

"Reconciling Originalism and Precedent" (McGinnis & Rappaport), 7, 857

"Reconfiguring Law Reports and the Concept of Precedent for a Digital Age" (Martin), 13, 152, 857

Records of the Federal Convention of 1787, The (Farrand ed.), 270, 534

"Recusals and the 'Problem' of an Equally Divided Supreme Court" (R. Black & Epstein), 220, 221, 225, 852

reenactment, defined, 804

reenactment canon, 346–49, 351, 805

"Reflections on Holding and Dictum" (Greenawalt), 854

"Reflections on Stare Decisis" (Hardisty), 855

Reflections on the Revolution in France (E. Burke), 9, 846

"Reflections on the Role of Appellate Courts" (Breyer), 523, 525, 853

"Reformation of American Administrative Law, The" (R. Stewart), 285, 859

rehearings, 223, 258–59, 305, 419, 495–96

Rehnquist, James C., 858

Rehnquist, William H. (1924–2005), 5, 11, 84, 186, 188, 196, 212, 341–42, 362, 479, 525, 529, 534, 536, 614, 693, 755, 849, 853, 855, 856

"Rehnquist Court and the End of Constitutional Stare Decisis, The" (Consovoy), 853

Reid, Charles J., Jr. (b. 1953), 858

Reinhardt, Stephen (b. 1931), 415, 856

Reinisch, August, 860

related-statutes canon, 79

"Relation of Dress to Art, The" (Wilde), 300

"Relation of Judicial Decisions to the Law, The" (Lincoln), 857

reliance interests, 41, 67, 100, 156, 159, 161, 312, 337, 339, 340, 341, 357, 366, 371–72, 405, 407, 412, 413–14, 421–22, 435

Religious Freedom Restoration Act, 83, 85–86

remand, 459–64, 805

removal, 475–77, 555, 805

render, defined, 805

"Renovation of the Common Law Through Stare Decisis" (Kocourek & Koven), 856

report, defined, 805

reporter, defined, 805

reputation, role of, 245–52

res judicata,
  binding effects, 374–75,
  compared to stare decisis, 373–77
  defined, 805
  effects on other courts, 376–77
  error in decision or principle, 325–26
  final judgment on merits, 235
  goal of promoting stability in the law, 377
  hierarchical effect on courts, 376
  jurisdictional scope, 375
  law-of-the-case doctrine, 442
  preclusion doctrine, 373–74, 378
  prima facie rule compared, 381
  stability in the law, 377

Restatement of Conflict of Laws, 594

Restatement of Restitution, 606

Restatement (Second) of Judgments, 327, 583–84, 805, 849

retroactive law, defined, 797

retroactivity,
  contracts and, 316–18
  criminal procedure and, 313–15, 320
  defined, 805–06
  exception for injunctions, 331–32
  precedents as generally retroactive, 308–22
  rule of property and, 428–36
  tax precedents and, 318–22
  Vandenbark rule and state-court judgments, 375
  vested rights and, 316–18

"Retrospective Decisions and Stare Decisis and a Proposal" (Kocourek), 856

Retrospectivity and the Rule of Law (Sampford), 850
"Return to Stare Decisis, A" (Oliphant), 59, 858
reversal, defined, 806
"Reversal, Dissent, and Variability in State Supreme Courts" (T. Eisenberg & G. Miller), 260, 853
reverse, defined, 806
"Reversed Circuit, The" (Bleich), 247, 852
reverse *Erie* doctrine, 694–96, 806
"Reverse Incorporation of State Constitutional Law" (Blocher), 659, 660, 852
Reynolds, William L. (b. 1945), 148–49, 858
Rhetoric and the Rule of Law (MacCormick), 65, 848
Rhode Island Supreme Court, 110, 131, 135, 274
Richard II (1367–1400), 567–68
Richman, William M., 148–49, 858
RICO, 532, 587
rights, private, 401–02
Rihani, A. Ferris (1876–1940), 858
Ripple, Kenneth Francis (b. 1943), 615
"Rise of Pennsylvania's Administrative Agencies and Legislative and Judicial Attempts to Constrain Them, The" (Schuckers & Appelgate), 285, 859
"Rise of Unnecessary Constitutional Rulings, The" (Healy), 125, 855
"Road to *Bush v. Gore*, The" (Ray), 216, 217, 858
Robbins, Ira, 625, 858
Robel, Lauren K., 148, 858
Roberts, John (b. 1955), 42, 183, 204, 353, 399
Roberts, Owen (1875–1955), 84
"Roberts Touts Unanimity on Supreme Court" (Sherman), 183
"Role of Precedent in Investment Arbitration, The" (Paulsson), 775, 777, 858
Roman law, 16, 17, 754, 760
Roman Law and Common Law (Buckland & McNair), 1, 18, 846

Romantz, David S., 850
Roney, Paul Hitch (1921–2006), 503
Rosenne, Shabtai (1917–2010), 762, 764, 850
Rosenthal, Lee H., 861
Ross, Alf (1889–1979), 8, 16, 850
Ross, William G., 248, 858
Rossiter, Clinton (1917–1970), 7, 535, 536, 567, 847
Rotunda, Ronald D. (b. 1945), 661, 849
Routledge Companion to Philosophy of Law, The (Marmor ed.), 24, 859
Rovine, Arthur W. (b. 1937), 777–78, 850
Rueter, Robert, 849
rule, defined, 77–78, 806
"Rule of Law and the Law of Precedents, The" (Farber), 7, 852, 854
"Rule of Law as a Law of Rules, The" (Scalia), 859
"Rule of Precedents, The" (McKean), 857
rule of property (as a term of art), 422–23, 806
rule-of-property doctrine, 421–24, 435–36, 439, 806
rules and principles,
 adaptability of, 14
 adopting, 295–98
 assumed, 86, 87–88
 causing injustice, 401–03, 412
 deducing from opinion's logic, 45
 extracting from opinion, 80–91, 105
 of law, defined, 77–78, 798
 prudential, 443
 scope, 88–91
rules and standards, 76, 78, 806
Rules Enabling Act, 108, 582–87
Rules of Decision Act, 558, 575, 576, 578, 580–81
rules of evidence, 370
rules of property, 407–08, 421–39
Rutledge, John (1739–1800), 534–35
Rutledge, Wiley B. (1894–1949), 358, 419

Sachs, Margaret V., 245–46, 251, 859
Salmond, John W. (1862–1924), 2, 35, 176, 269, 333, 392, 850, 859
Salter, David, 848
Sampford, Charles, 850
Samples of Lawmaking (Devlin), 846
Sanchez, Veronica, 252, 854
Savage, John, 771, 847
saving-to-suitors clauses, 695
Saylor, Thomas G. (b. 1946), 701
Scalia, Antonin (1936–2016), xi, 11, 68, 79, 117, 120, 123, 162, 166, 178, 196, 210, 220, 229, 237, 238, 290, 292, 293, 294, 309, 310, 341–42, 346, 362, 372, 410, 437, 438, 439, 469, 479, 504, 524, 525, 526, 528, 585, 650, 668, 717, 727, 750, 755, 760, 850, 854, 859
Schaefer, Walter V. (1904–1986), 859
Schapiro, Robert A., 673, 674, 676, 859
Schauer, Frederick (b. 1946), 11, 24, 164, 170, 850, 859
Schoenbaum, Thomas J. (b. 1939), 850
Schreuer, Christoph (b. 1944), 775, 849, 860
Schroeder, James C., 250, 859
Schubert, Glendon A. (b. 1918), 850, 856
Schuckers, Daniel R., 285, 859
Schultz, Thomas, 774, 777, 850
Schütze, Rolf A. (b. 1934), 772, 859
Schwartz, Bernard (1923–1997), 248, 252, 859
Schwartz, Eric A., 771, 846
Schwarz, Timothy, 240, 859
Science of Legal Judgment, The (Ram), 849
"Scope of Precedent, The" (Kozel), 54, 83, 856
Scottish Legal System, The (D. Walker), 850
SCOTUS (Supreme Court of the United States), defined, 807
Second Amendment, 366, 548
secondary authority, defined, 786
Second Circuit. See UNITED STATES COURTS OF APPEALS.
Second Miscellany-at-Law, A (Megarry), 420

"Securities Case Dropped" (Denniston), 531
Securities Exchange Act of 1934, 29, 349
Segal, Jeffrey A., 846, 850
Segger, Marie-Claire Cordonier, 779, 847, 854
Selection of Leading Cases on Various Branches of the Law, A (J. Smith), 173, 850
"Self-Reliance" (Emerson), xi
Selya, Bruce M. (b. 1934), 644, 859
Sentelle, David B. (b. 1943), 4, 506–07
sentencing of criminal defendants, 463–64
"Separate but Equal?" (Bhagwat), 30, 852
separate-but-equal doctrine, 184–85, 323
separation of powers, 25, 311
seriatim opinions, 183, 192, 197, 800
Seventh Amendment, 177–78, 581
Seventh Circuit. See UNITED STATES COURTS OF APPEALS.
Shahabuddeen, Mohamed (b. 1931), 762, 764, 765, 850
Shakespeare, William (1564–1616), iii
Shapiro, David L., 847
Shapiro, S.R., 859
Shapiro, Stephen M. (b. 1946), 518, 520–21, 522, 524, 525, 527, 528, 850
Sharpe, David J., 519, 859
Shartel, Burke (1889–1967), 2, 850
Shaw, Lemuel (1781–1861), 249
Sheppard, John S., Jr., 859
Sheppard, Steve (b. 1963), 848
Sherman, Mark, 183
Sherman Act, 334, 335–36, 338–39, 561
Sherwin, Emily, 106, 113, 845, 859
Shiner, Roger A., 778, 850
"Should Arbitration Awards Be Published?" (Cherne), 779
"Should Courts Give Stare Decisis Effect to Statutory Interpretation Methodology?" (Foster), 854
Shroder, William J., 859
Shuldberg, Kirt, 143, 859
Siltata, Raimo, 850

Simon, David A., 532, 858
Simpson, A.W.B. (1931–2011), 2, 35, 44, 54, 73, 850, 859
Sinclair, Michael, 48, 859
Sixth Amendment, 30–31, 160, 314, 359
Sixth Circuit. See UNITED STATES COURTS OF APPEALS.
"Sixth Sense, A" (Walsh), 527
Slapper, Gary, 850
Sloan, Amy E., 144, 494, 859
Smith, A.T.H. (b. 1947), 92, 303, 851
Smith, Bryant, 859
Smith, D. Brooks (b. 1951), 39
Smith, John William, 173, 850
Smith, Walter Denton (1871–1896), 44–45, 850
"Social Constraint or Implicit Collusion?" (O'Hara), 857
Solimine, Michael E. (b. 1956), 245, 246, 251, 504, 532, 854, 859
Solum, Lawrence B., 859
"Some Aspects of the Work of the Court of Appeal" (Asquith), 852
Some Makers of English Law (Holdsworth), 847
Some Modern Tendencies in the Law (Williston), 851
"Some Thoughts on the Death of Stare Decisis in Constitutional Law" (Maltz), 857
"Some Views on the Rule of Stare Decisis" (Lile), 856
"Sorting Out the Debate over Customary International Law" (Young), 565, 860
Sotomayor, Sonia (b. 1954), 204–05
Sources and Literature of English Law (Holdsworth), 847
Sourgens, Frédéric G., 762, 763, 764–65, 859
Souter, David (b. 1939), 213
South Africa, 17, 754, 755
South Carolina Supreme Court, 165, 279, 301, 327, 329, 603
South Dakota Constitution, 275
South Dakota Supreme Court, 279, 315, 384, 660, 670, 734
Southwick, Christian F., 859

Spaeth, Harold J. (b. 1930), 355, 845, 846, 850
Spain, 758
Sparling, Steven C., 214, 859
Spending Clause, 203
Spirit of the Common Law, The (Pound), 849
split decisions, 182–83, 187, 194, 792
Sprecher, Robert A. (1917–1982), 859
Spriggs, James F., II, 195, 847, 859
Spritzer, Ralph S. (b. 1917), 845
"Stability and Reliability in Judicial Decisions" (Easterbrook), 9, 10, 14, 18, 335, 354, 853
stability in the law, iii, 10–11, 21–22, 161, 339–40, 352–53, 370–71, 377, 383, 389–91, 406–09, 421, 427, 441–42
standard, defined, 78, 806
"Standing Apart to Be a Part" (Kirman), 183, 856
stare decisis,
  admissibility of evidence, 383–84
  American three-tiered approach to, 334–35
  arbitration, in, 767–72
  arguments against, 12–15
  benefits of following precedent, 9–12
  binding effects of, 373, 374, 375, 376–77
  compared to issue preclusion, 374
  compared to res judicata, 373–77, 378
  constitutions and, 352–69
  continuity in law, 389
  defined, 5–6, 807
  de jure and de facto stare decisis, 763
  different dispute arising from same source, 378–81
  disadvantages of relying on precedent, 12–14
  due process and, 381
  facts, 373, 374
  findings of fact and, 382–84
  horizontal, defined, 807
  inapplicable to certain matters, 371–72, 383, 384
  international law, in, 762–65
  law, questions of, 374
  law-of-the-case doctrine and, 442
  legal basis for, 6–8
  local, defined, 807

stare decisis (cont'd)
  loose, defined, 807
  maxim, 388
  not absolutely binding or ineluctable, 389
  personal, defined, 807
  practical basis of, 9–12
  predictability in law and, 13–14, 21, 67, 389–90, 443
  principle of policy, 389
  rank of court and, 239
  rule of property's equitable doctrine, 435–37
  rules of property and, 407–08, 421–39
  stability in the law, iii, 10–11, 21–22, 377, 383, 389
  statutes and, 333–45
  strict, defined, 807
  super, defined, 807
  vertical, defined, 807
  vertical precedent, 27, 376, 381, 732, 807
  weakened, 354
"Stare Decisis" (Acquaviva & Pocar), 762, 763, 852
"Stare Decisis" (C. Cooper), 853
"Stare Decisis" (W.O. Douglas), 354, 853
"Stare Decisis" (B. Jones), 27, 123, 415, 492, 680
Stare Decisis (R. Moore), 849
Stare Decisis (E. Re), 849
"Stare Decisis" (Rihani), 858
"Stare Decisis" (unsigned note), 13, 35, 401, 857
"Stare Decisis and Constitutional Adjudication" (Monaghan), 857
"Stare Decisis and Constitutional Meaning" (G. Lawson), 7, 856
"Stare Decisis and Constitutional Text" (J. Mitchell), 7, 857
"Stare Decisis and Demonstrably Erroneous Precedents" (Nelson), 857
"Stare Decisis and Due Process" (Barrett), 852
"Stare Decisis and Judicial Restraint" (L. Powell), 21, 858
"Stare Decisis and the Constitution" (Fallon), 7, 8, 853

"Stare Decisis and the Lower Courts" (unsigned note), 857
"Stare Decisis and the Rule of Law" (Waldron), 860
"Stare Decisis as a Constitutional Requirement" (Healy), 855
"Stare Decisis as Judicial Doctrine" (Kozel), 234, 237, 238, 396, 404, 413, 856
"Stare Decisis—Continued" (Oliphant), 858
stare decisis et non quieta movere, 5, 417
Stare Decisis in Commonwealth Appellate Courts (J. Murphy & Rueter), 849
"Stare Decisis in Courts of Last Resort" (von Moschzisker), 10–11, 860
"Stare Decisis in Historical Perspective" (Lee), 856
"Stare Decisis in the Inferior Courts of the United States" (Mead), 258, 857
"Stare Decisis in the Office of Legal Counsel" (Morrison), 857
Stare Decisis, Res Judicata and Other Selected Essays (von Moschzisker), 850
Stare Indecisis (Brenner & Spaeth), 355, 845
Starr, Kenneth W. (b. 1946), 532, 859
State Constitutional Law (R. Williams), 663, 851
state constitutions. *See* CONSTITUTIONS, STATE.
"State Constitutions" (R. Holland), 664, 855
"State Constitutions and the Protection of Individual Rights" (Brennan), 666, 853
state courts,
  adopting rules, 295–98
  advisory opinions and, 269–70, 271–72, 274–76, 799
  approval of lower court's decision, 263–66
  borrowed-constitutional-provision doctrine, 723–24
  borrowed-statute doctrine, 716–23
  choice-of-law doctrine and, 710–11
  comity and, 34, 79, 313, 673

INDEX

state courts (*cont'd*)
  concurrent authority on federal questions, 534–35, 536, 537–38, 679–90, 691–92, 695
  coordinate, conflicting decisions of, 387
  decision in own state's lower courts, 295–99
  deference and, 288–89
  denial of review, 600–01
  determining federal jurisdiction, 697–701
  discretionary review of, 262–63
  doctrinal conflicts in, 537–38
  effects of federal precedent in, 688–92, 691–92, 697
  Erie doctrine, 226, 234, 323, 353, 363, 436, 544, 558, 571–88, 589–92, 598, 692, 703, 788–89, 793, 806
  horizontal and vertical precedent, 255
  inferior, 254, 297–98, 306–07
  interpreting state law, 656–57, 670–72, 709–10
  interstate compacts and, 562–63
  interstate decisions and uniformity, 702, 703, 705–08
  jurisdiction of, 552–57
  levels of, 253–54
  maritime law and, 570, 695
  persuasive authority, 256
  precedent in, 33–34
  precedent of, in federal courts, 534
  preeminence of highest, 655–72
  retroactivity of decisions, 312–13, 315
  reverse *Erie* doctrine, 694–96, 806
  sister-state precedent, 658–59, 709–10, 716–23, 724–28
  state constitution, 659–61, 673–78
  treaty interpretations, 534, 535, 547, 563–64, 565–66
  vertical precedent, 33–34, 244–45, 255, 679, 689, 696
"State Courts Adopting Federal Constitutional Doctrine" (R. Williams), 663, 860
state high courts,
  Alabama Supreme Court, 32, 101, 135, 244, 250, 273, 274, 275, 278, 280, 284, 330, 355, 427, 454, 537, 693, 709, 748
  Alaska Supreme Court, 224, 251, 278, 331, 352, 400, 402, 726, 752

state high courts (*cont'd*)
  Arizona Supreme Court, 169, 171, 198–99, 240, 250, 257, 278, 280, 294, 295, 306, 391, 538, 554, 555, 628, 635, 636, 670, 718, 720, 722, 732, 743, 746
  Arkansas Supreme Court, 93–96, 101, 166, 229, 233, 251–52, 278, 285, 291, 389, 392, 401, 412, 430, 436, 450, 540, 544–45, 624, 628, 722, 733
  California Supreme Court, 33, 164, 170–71, 233, 235, 241–42, 254, 261, 280, 293–94, 307, 313, 316, 317, 384, 387, 389, 390, 401, 421, 425, 427, 429, 430, 431–32, 433, 435, 456, 457, 536, 549, 553–54, 609, 625, 644, 656, 669, 675–76, 679, 687–88, 692, 702, 704, 723, 727, 728
  Colorado Supreme Court, 165, 189, 258, 273, 275, 278, 284, 293, 301, 669, 745
  Connecticut Supreme Court, 130, 164, 262, 273, 278, 391, 724–25
  Delaware Supreme Court, 158, 253, 274, 275, 276, 374, 424, 610, 665, 741, 753
  Florida Supreme Court, 47, 123, 134, 179, 223, 241, 273, 274, 276, 288, 324, 384, 397, 400, 401, 410, 416, 438, 546–47, 623–25, 653, 752
  Georgia Supreme Court, 223, 278, 301, 318, 375, 405, 411, 709
  Hawaii Supreme Court, 117, 118, 171, 278, 284, 291, 437, 456, 659, 669, 752
  Idaho Supreme Court, 118, 180, 278, 374, 707, 725–26, 752
  Illinois Supreme Court, 62, 135, 137, 138, 229, 237, 267, 278, 284, 292, 293, 334, 377, 390, 400, 402, 416, 452, 581, 656, 657–58, 686, 692, 693, 705, 717
  Indiana Supreme Court, 643, 665, 702, 741
  Iowa Supreme Court, 191, 278, 281, 282, 284, 342–43, 384, 388, 394, 397, 436, 542–43, 631, 656, 693
  Kansas Supreme Court, 134, 141, 151, 179, 220, 233, 234, 258, 273, 278, 280, 285, 406, 677, 710, 720, 727–28
  Kentucky Supreme Court, 52, 118, 123, 260, 278, 291, 301, 319, 390, 400, 663, 704, 727
  Louisiana Supreme Court, 131, 134, 262, 617, 625, 702
  Maine Supreme Court, 110, 273, 274, 276, 293, 406, 617, 628–29, 709

state high courts (*cont'd*)
Maryland Court of Appeals, 117, 130, 166, 278, 412, 703, 711, 729, 743, 744, 750
Massachusetts Supreme Judicial Court, 12 (by allusion), 92, 134, 170, 228, 262, 272, 273, 274, 275, 296–97, 330, 390, 436, 452, 644, 670, 711–12, 744–45, 746, 750
Michigan Supreme Court, 117, 180, 243, 276, 280, 292, 315, 372, 376, 396, 402–03, 412, 413–14, 589, 591–92, 599, 604, 664, 670, 722, 726
Minnesota Supreme Court, 111, 115, 262, 278, 281, 282, 283, 291, 405, 409, 454, 457, 564, 600, 625, 663, 671–72, 679–80, 682–83, 705, 718, 752
Mississippi Supreme Court, 111, 244, 284, 288, 320, 330, 391, 401, 427, 429, 434, 605–06, 629, 659, 711–12, 716, 721–22, 723, 740, 747
Missouri Supreme Court, 278, 280, 293, 294, 324, 376, 604, 610, 617, 625, 656, 659, 692, 742
Montana Supreme Court, 134, 220, 245, 279, 296, 637, 716, 720
Nebraska Supreme Court, 374, 430, 431, 449, 627, 635, 658, 718–19, 741, 747, 748
Nevada Supreme Court, 135, 141, 279, 483, 628–29, 701, 724, 729, 748
New Hampshire Supreme Court, 274, 296, 388, 398, 663, 724, 726, 741, 745
New Jersey Supreme Court, 130, 256, 288, 399, 405, 538, 542, 553, 611, 666, 667, 691, 715, 741, 743
New Mexico Supreme Court, 191, 279, 321, 376, 398, 400, 422, 425, 427, 434, 601, 628, 630–31, 632, 683–84, 685–86, 688, 718, 733, 740–41, 747, 748, 752
New York Court of Appeals, 77, 171, 172, 174, 179, 239, 250, 252, 258, 273, 292, 294, 298, 383, 390, 397, 408, 409, 417, 422, 425, 453, 607, 629, 631–32, 641, 649, 665, 676–77, 692, 710, 715
North Carolina Supreme Court, 101, 189, 220, 233, 234, 258, 262, 271, 279, 316, 335, 427, 428, 608, 609, 649, 669, 709, 711, 741

state high courts (*cont'd*)
North Dakota Supreme Court, 134, 158, 277, 279, 281, 284, 288, 545, 703–04, 706, 718
Ohio Supreme Court, 152, 167, 181, 220, 224, 263, 279, 280, 284, 313, 316, 318, 321, 327, 377, 411, 427, 434, 443–44, 446, 601, 652, 660, 662, 665, 677, 719
Oklahoma Court of Criminal Appeals, 599–600
Oklahoma Supreme Court, 134–35, 190, 217, 279, 281, 282, 291, 319, 322, 430, 540, 590, 591, 632, 655, 665, 706, 716, 717, 734–35, 752
Oregon Supreme Court, 131, 221, 224, 283, 366, 374, 405, 549, 627, 629, 632, 660, 687, 693, 716, 718, 723, 739, 748
Pennsylvania Supreme Court, 87, 165, 179, 191, 221, 224, 245, 256, 263, 288, 308, 317, 374, 389, 396, 397, 419–20, 473, 600, 633, 659, 664–65, 701, 710, 712, 723, 752
Rhode Island Supreme Court, 110, 131, 135, 274
South Carolina Supreme Court, 165, 279, 301, 327, 329, 603
South Dakota Supreme Court, 279, 315, 384, 660, 670, 734
Tennessee Supreme Court, 139, 179, 279, 282, 283, 284, 382, 409, 421, 425, 426, 430, 432–33, 455, 618, 686, 705, 708, 717, 727, 730–31
Territory of Arizona, Supreme Court of, 732–33
Territory of Oklahoma, Supreme Court of, 716, 733, 734
Texas Court of Criminal Appeals, 69, 387, 399, 416, 599–600, 656, 716, 733
Texas Supreme Court, 49, 137, 191, 240, 241, 243, 250, 262, 263–64, 265, 266, 267, 272, 273, 279, 280, 289, 387, 392, 394–95, 543, 617, 668, 670–71, 691, 692, 697, 698, 699–700, 703, 707, 709, 743, 746
Utah Supreme Court, 134, 138, 243, 289, 543, 603, 625, 659, 660, 665, 693, 704
Vermont Supreme Court, 134, 279, 282, 389, 709, 738, 743
Virginia Supreme Court, 110, 165, 279, 282, 538, 738, 742, 760

state high courts (*cont'd*)
  Washington Supreme Court, 101, 158, 221, 234, 241, 254, 279, 294, 323, 391, 625, 629, 665, 670, 681–82, 724, 741
  West Virginia Supreme Court of Appeals, 152, 158, 214, 259, 279, 289, 292, 296, 366, 463, 629–30, 739
  Wisconsin Supreme Court, 117, 175, 208, 221, 233, 279, 280, 282, 295, 310, 384, 391, 397, 398, 409, 410, 428, 434, 455, 545, 657, 669, 680–81, 688, 689–90, 691, 724, 739, 752
  Wyoming Supreme Court, 191, 279, 282, 291, 294, 376, 627–28, 659
state law,
  changes in, 589–92, 600
  conflict-of-laws doctrine, 593–97
  defined, 797
  filling gaps in federal law, 569–71
  high-court pronouncements, 598
  interpretive principles, 613
  precedent in federal courts, 534, 535–37
  predicting, 598–99, 601–10
  state-law doctrine and practice generally, 655–731
"State Supreme Court Advisory Opinions as Illegitimate Judicial Review" (Topf), 271–72, 275, 276, 860
"Status of the Rule of Judicial Precedent, The" (symposium), 860
Statute of Anne (1710), 748
Statute of Gloucester (1278), 748
statutes,
  canons of construction. See CANONS OF CONSTRUCTION.
  interpretation. See STATUTORY INTERPRETATION.
  reenacted, 346–49, 351, 805
  state, judged against federal laws, 540–46
statutes of limitations, 126, 318, 372, 572, 573, 583–84, 591–92, 597, 721
statutory construction, canons of. See CANONS OF CONSTRUCTION.
statutory construction, defined, 808
statutory interpretation,
  administrative agency's, 285–89, 290, 446–47
  ambiguity, resolving, 292–93, 599, 637

statutory interpretation (*cont'd*)
  antiformalism, defined, 785
  attorney general's, 281–82, 290
  canons. See CANONS OF CONSTRUCTION.
  choice-of-law doctrines, 613, 710–13
  foreign law, 709–15
  formalism, defined, 794
  generally, 75, 79
  independent, 670–71
  informal agency actions, 287
  legislative, 290–94
  legislative history, 290–92
  legislative silence, 281–82, 337, 348, 349–50
  prior, 337–38, 347, 348, 380
  purposivism, defined, 803
  resolving ambiguity in text, 292–93, 599, 637
  stare decisis, 333–45
  state's highest tribunal's, 256
  textualism, defined, 808
  title to real property, 407, 422
statutory law, defined, 797
statutory reenactment, 346–51
"Statutory Stare Decisis in the Courts of Appeals" (Barrett), 852
Stearns, Maxwell, 44, 53, 73, 104, 115, 135, 457, 852
Steigerwalt, Amy, 846
Stein, Peter (1926–2016), 16, 846
Steinman, Joan E. (b. 1947), 849
Stevens, John Paul (b. 1920), 29, 41, 178, 210, 237, 262, 268, 341, 518, 530, 532, 548, 579, 586, 647, 755, 859
Stewart, Potter (1915–1985), 200, 355, 523
Stewart, Richard B. (b. 1940), 285, 859
Stinson, Judith M., 135, 859
Stock-Raising Homestead Act, 684–86
Stoebuck, William B. (1929–2012), 737, 738, 741, 743, 859
Stolen Valor Act, 56–57
Stone, Ferdinand F. (1908–1989), 850
Stone, Harlan Fiske (1872–1946), 215, 248, 358, 401–02, 859
Stone, Julius (1907–1985), 850, 860
Story, Joseph (1779–1845), 7–8, 248, 466, 509, 567–68, 575–76, 738, 748–49, 850

Stras, David R. (b. 1974), 195, 859
"Strategy in Supreme Court Case Selection" (M. Cordray & R. Cordray), 519, 853
Straub, Chester J. (b. 1937), 218
"Structure and Precedent" (Dobbins), 22, 30, 853
Studies in Legal Logic (Hage), 847
Study of Cases, The (Wambaugh), 74, 269–70, 850
summary dispositions, 147–48, 157–58, 214, 217–19
Summers, Robert S. (b. 1933), 845, 848
Sunstein, Cass R. (b. 1954), 10, 48, 99, 113, 114, 850, 860
superior court, defined, 791
"Super Precedent" (Gerhardt), 7, 235, 236, 852, 854
superprecedents, 235–36, 802
super stare decisis, defined, 807
supervisory orders, 267
Supremacy Clause, 34, 541, 563–64, 668–72, 690
Supreme Court, The (W. Rehnquist), 525, 529, 849
"Supreme Court and Its Shrinking Docket, The" (Starr), 532, 859
Supreme Court Compendium, The (Epstein et al.), 260, 846
"Supreme Court Equity, 1789–1835, and the History of American Judging" (Kroger), 132, 856
"Supreme Court in Bondage, The" (Solum), 859
Supreme Court in the American System of Government, The (R. Jackson), 848
"Supreme Court Monitoring of the United States Courts of Appeals En Banc" (George & Solimine), 532, 854
"Supreme Court No-Clear-Majority Decisions" (unsigned comment), 853
Supreme Court of Ecuador, 759
Supreme Court of the Territory of Arizona, 732–33
Supreme Court of the Territory of Oklahoma, 716, 733, 734
Supreme Court of the United States, *passim*
Supreme Court of the United States Rule 10, 519
Supreme Court Practice (S.M. Shapiro et al.), 518, 520–21, 522, 524, 525, 527, 528, 850
Supreme Court Reporter, 143
"Supreme Court's Love–Hate Relationship with *Miranda*, The" (Kinports), 236, 856
"Supreme Court, Stare Decisis and Law of the Case, The" (J.W. Moore & Oglebay), 857
"Supreme Court Superstars" (B. Schwartz), 248, 252, 859
Sureda, Andrés Rigo (b. 1943), 775, 778, 860
Surrency, Erwin C. (1924–2012), 277, 860
Sustainable Development in World Trade Law and Jurisprudence (Gehring & Segger eds.), 779, 847, 854
Sutton, Jeffrey S. (b. 1960), 29, 357, 663, 664, 666, 860
Swayne, Noah (1804–1884), 11
Swift, Jonathan (1667–1745), 5
Swift doctrine, 226, 234, 323, 353, 363, 558, 575–80, 788–89
syllabus, 23, 51, 150–52
syllogisms, 23, 51, 793, 804, 808

Taft, William Howard (1857–1930), 183, 518, 523, 532, 561, 768, 857, 859, 860
Taft–Hartley Act (1947), 561, 768
takings,
 government, 119–20, 423–24
 judicial, 427, 433–34, 437–39
 Takings Clause, 119–20, 436–39, 669
 wildlife, 4
Tamanaha, Brian Z. (b. 1957), 850
Taney, Roger B. (1777–1864), 139–40, 249
Tashima, Wallace (b. 1934), 45, 46, 63, 116

taxation, 318–22, 343–44, 364–65, 542–43, 544–45, 546, 571, 612, 655–56, 758
Taylor, C.J., 726
"Technique" (Lebovits), 239, 856
Teisen, Axel, 860
temporary restraining orders, 230
Tennessee Court of Appeals, 141
Tennessee Supreme Court, 139, 179, 279, 282, 283, 284, 382, 409, 421, 425, 426, 430, 432–33, 455, 618, 686, 705, 708, 717, 727, 730–31
Tenth Circuit. See UNITED STATES COURTS OF APPEALS.
territorial courts, 732–35, 791
Territory of Arizona, Supreme Court of, 732–33
Territory of Oklahoma, Supreme Court of, 716, 733, 734
test cases, 133, 139–40, 651–54, 786–87
Tetley, William (1927–2014), 860
Texas Commission of Appeals, 710
Texas Constitution, 272
Texas Court of Appeals, 169, 191, 243, 263, 265, 266, 282, 283, 284, 289, 301, 387, 394, 699, 709, 711, 714
Texas Court of Criminal Appeals, 69, 387, 399, 416, 599–600, 656, 716, 733
Texas Supreme Court, 49, 137, 191, 240, 241, 243, 250, 262, 263–64, 265, 266, 267, 272, 273, 279, 280, 289, 387, 392, 394–95, 543, 617, 668, 670–71, 691, 692, 697, 698, 699–700, 703, 707, 709, 743, 746
Textbook of Jurisprudence, A (Paton), 47, 105, 849
Text-book of Roman Law from Augustus to Justinian, A (Buckland), 16, 846
textualism, defined, 808
Thayer, Damon, 860
Thayer, Ezra R. (1866–1915), 860
"Theory of Judicial Decision, The" (Pound), 858
"Theory of Judicial Precedents, The" (Salmond), 859
Theory of Legal Argumentation, A (Alexy), 17, 845

Theory of Precedent, A (Siltata), 850
Theory of the Common Law, The (J. Walker), 850
Thinking Like a Lawyer (Schauer), 850
Think Like a Lawyer (Dudley), 846
Think Like a Lawyer (Fidel & Cantoni), 847
Third Circuit. See UNITED STATES COURTS OF APPEALS.
Thirteenth Amendment, 160
Thomas, Clarence (b. 1948), 41, 149, 334, 359, 479, 534, 536, 686, 693
Thorne, Samuel E. (1908–1994), 845
"Those Unpublished Opinions" (Fox), 149, 854
Thurmon, Mark Alan, 196, 208, 212, 213, 860
Tiersma, Peter, 861
"Ties in the Supreme Court of the United States" (Hartnett), 221, 222–23, 855
Tjoflat, Gerald Bard (b. 1929), 382
Tocqueville, Alexis de (1805–1859), 269
Topf, Mel A., 271, 272, 275, 276, 860
"Toward a Theory of Persuasive Authority" (Flanders), 166, 854
"Towards a Common Law Originalism" (Meyler), 749, 857
"Towards an International Judicial System" (Martinez), 763, 857
Townes, John C. (1852–1923), 45, 49, 248
Townshend, John, 849
"Trail of the Calf, The" (Radin), 858
Transnational Legality (Schultz), 774, 777, 850
"Transtemporal Separation of Powers in the Law of Precedent" (Beck), 113, 852
Traynor, Roger J. (1900–1983), 171, 435, 860
treaties and conventions,
Franco-American Treaty of Alliance (1778), 269, 270
generally, 269–71, 277, 290–92, 534, 535, 537, 547, 558, 562–64, 565–66, 575, 578, 679, 754–55

treaties and conventions (*cont'd*)
   Hague Convention on the Civil
      Aspects of International Child
      Abduction (1980), 754–55
   North American Fair Trade
      Agreement (NAFTA) (1994), 777
   Vienna Convention, 760–61
   Warsaw Convention, 754
Treatise of the Law of Judgments, A (A. Freeman), 76–77, 847
Treatise on the Constitutional Limitations Which Rest upon the Legislative Power of the States of the American Union, A (T. Cooley), 743, 846
Treatise on the Law of Judgments, A (H.C. Black), 76, 77, 845
trial court, defined, 791
Tribe, Laurence H. (b. 1941), 5, 850
"Trumping Precedent with Original Meaning" (Barnett), 6, 334, 852
Tucker, St. George (1752–1827), 249
Tucker Act, 336, 347
Tuttle, Edward W., 76, 847
28 U.S.C. § 46(c), 495–96
28 U.S.C. § 1257, 623, 655, 691
28 U.S.C. § 1333, 695
28 U.S.C. § 1404, 473, 594
28 U.S.C. § 1450, 476
28 U.S.C. § 2255, 126–27, 219, 467
Twining, William (b. 1934), 43, 850
Twiss, Travers (1809–1897), 7

Ulmer, S. Sidney, 355, 860
unanimity, blackletter rule, 702
"Unanimity and Desegregation" (Hutchinson), 184, 855
"Unanimity on the Rehnquist Court" (Hensley & S. Johnson), 188, 855
unanimous decisions, 182–87, 188–89, 792
Uniform Certification of Questions of Law Act, 626
Uniform Commercial Code, 702, 705–06
"Uniformity, Inferiority, and the Law of the Circuit Doctrine" (Dragich), 253, 254, 853

uniformity of law,
   generally, 10–11, 13, 21, 114, 286, 300, 336, 360, 391, 443–45, 538, 702
   interstate decisions, 702, 703, 705–08
   uniform laws, 704–05
Uniform Law Commission, 705, 706
United States Courts of Appeals,
   D.C. Circuit, 4, 37, 38, 39, 40, 107, 136, 149, 167, 180, 191, 201, 202, 204, 205, 208, 209, 211, 245–46, 304, 341, 374, 375, 380, 382, 386, 419, 469, 491, 493, 496, 499, 500, 501, 502, 503, 504, 506–07, 512, 514, 515, 522, 579, 584, 586–87, 608, 612, 638, 640, 643, 717, 774
   Federal Circuit, 39, 188, 239, 376, 382, 387, 453, 470, 495, 503, 505, 509, 513–14, 527, 697–700, 809
   First Circuit, 27, 38, 39, 40, 64, 70, 107, 115, 119, 120, 122, 145, 167, 168, 201, 203, 204–05, 209–10, 223, 304–05, 327, 329, 330, 365–66, 368–69, 375, 378, 379, 381, 382, 386, 424, 442, 444, 449, 451, 452, 458, 460, 465, 470, 476, 482, 483, 484, 485, 486, 487, 492–93, 496, 499, 500, 502, 507, 510, 586, 595, 603, 605, 607, 608, 637, 638, 640, 644, 758
   Second Circuit, 38, 40, 58, 64, 70, 89, 119, 136, 138, 147, 148, 167, 168, 201, 204, 209, 218, 223, 230, 243, 245, 246, 250, 251, 302, 367, 382, 386, 442, 457, 459, 482, 483, 493, 494, 502, 505, 507, 514, 518, 535, 536, 537, 564, 565–66, 586, 590–91, 596, 603, 607, 608, 610, 612–13, 615, 624–25, 626, 638, 641, 673, 676–77, 729, 757–58, 768, 773
   Third Circuit, 31, 38, 39, 40, 64, 71, 87, 109, 131, 134, 137, 147, 167, 168, 198, 201, 202, 204, 205, 210, 228, 244, 302, 304, 317, 329, 330, 382, 386, 458, 476, 480, 495, 503, 507, 510, 515, 536, 537, 538, 541–42, 544, 563, 586, 590, 596–97, 600, 601, 603, 604, 605, 607, 610, 608, 610, 611, 613, 614, 636, 638, 640, 642, 753, 759
   Fourth Circuit, 37, 38, 39, 55, 71, 122, 123, 142, 147, 201, 204, 211, 291, 303, 320–21, 328, 331, 385, 386, 460, 461–62, 463, 482, 505, 535, 538, 545, 547, 596, 601–02, 603, 604, 607, 608, 609, 611, 612, 613, 638, 640, 642, 697, 760, 768

U.S. Courts of Appeals (*cont'd*)
Fifth Circuit, 29, 37, 38, 52, 53, 71, 79, 121, 129, 147, 161–62, 168, 169, 201, 204, 223, 224, 232, 234, 279, 304, 305–06, 331, 351, 366, 375, 378, 380, 382, 385, 386, 417–18, 448, 451, 452, 456, 469–70, 492, 495, 497–98, 499, 501, 502, 503, 506, 512, 513, 525, 535, 536, 538, 544, 582, 591, 592, 595–96, 600, 601, 602, 603, 604, 605–06, 607, 608, 609, 613, 619, 622, 625–26, 638, 639, 640, 642, 652–53, 674, 691, 693, 699, 753, 758, 774
Sixth Circuit, 29, 37, 38, 40, 69, 70–71, 109, 138, 142, 145, 167, 197, 201, 204, 218, 223, 256, 280, 304, 366, 379, 380, 382, 386, 408, 428, 447, 463, 476, 495, 503, 505, 506, 507, 512, 513, 514, 527, 535, 589, 591–92, 595, 596, 599, 602, 603, 604, 606, 607, 608, 613, 626, 640, 641, 643, 651–52, 673, 677, 773, 774
Seventh Circuit, 29, 37, 39, 40, 47, 53, 55, 60–61, 65–67, 71, 106, 108, 109, 129, 144–45, 147, 148, 167, 168, 201, 204, 208, 210, 228, 252, 258, 302–03, 305, 323, 376, 379, 380, 385–86, 387, 452, 456, 457–58, 464, 475, 476, 477, 493–94, 496, 499, 501, 510, 512, 513, 514, 528, 536, 537, 538, 544, 557, 579, 581, 582, 591, 594, 597, 602, 603, 607, 608, 610, 613, 615, 637, 638, 639, 640, 641, 645, 689, 691, 745–46, 753, 757, 769, 773
Eighth Circuit, 28, 38, 39, 40, 71, 106, 109, 123, 139, 148–49, 168, 201, 204, 210, 234, 305, 326, 328, 330, 372, 381, 386, 455, 469, 482, 500, 502, 506, 507, 508, 510, 596, 600, 602, 603, 604, 607, 608, 609–10, 613, 638, 640, 642, 719, 774

U.S. Courts of Appeals (*cont'd*)
Ninth Circuit, 5, 8, 23, 29–30, 33, 37, 38, 39, 40, 44, 55, 56, 62, 63–64, 68, 70, 71, 87, 90, 104, 106, 107, 109, 116, 123, 126, 127–28, 129, 134, 136, 137, 138, 147–48, 162, 167, 172, 200, 201, 202, 204, 205–06, 209, 242, 243, 280, 284, 304, 305–06, 323, 325, 333, 373, 380, 382, 384, 386, 415, 451, 452, 456, 458, 463, 465, 469, 472–73, 483, 484, 487, 495, 497, 498, 499, 500–01, 502–03, 504, 505, 507, 515, 521, 527, 535, 536, 538, 553–54, 556, 563, 564, 592, 596, 597, 603, 606, 608, 609, 610–11, 613, 617, 634–35, 637, 639, 640, 641, 643, 644, 649, 675–76, 753, 756–57, 759
Tenth Circuit, 37, 38, 39, 40, 69, 71, 109, 134, 145, 167, 168, 201, 204, 224, 230, 232, 291, 304, 309, 312, 321–22, 331, 332, 366, 382, 386, 429, 434, 449, 453, 463, 485, 487–88, 495, 497, 501, 503, 505, 513, 514, 536, 579, 590–91, 596, 600, 601, 603, 606, 608, 611, 612–13, 614, 626, 628, 638, 640, 643, 644, 706, 753
Eleventh Circuit, 5, 32, 37, 38, 39, 40, 69, 71, 106, 109, 122, 126, 134, 147, 166, 201, 204, 210, 223, 224, 237, 244, 291, 300, 302, 304, 308, 326, 380, 382, 386, 417–18, 448, 456, 480–81, 486, 492, 495, 501, 503, 506, 513, 516, 547, 595–96, 597, 603, 607, 608, 638, 640, 644, 677, 809

United States Postal Service, 777
United States Reports, 143
United States Supreme Court, defined, 807
"Unprecedented" (Southwick), 859
unpublished opinions, 37, 69, 142–43, 144–45, 148–49, 800
"Unpublished Opinions" (Weisgerber), 131, 860
"Unpublished Opinions and the Nature of Precedent" (Boggs & Brooks), 852
unwritten law, 1–2, 575, 578, 746, 747, 797
unwritten opinion, defined, 800
U.S. Constitution. See CONSTITUTION, U.S.
U.S. Court of Appeals for the Armed Forces, 253

U.S. Court of Appeals for Veteran Claims, 253
U.S. Court of Federal Claims, 253
U.S. Court of International Trade, 253
"Use and Value of Authorities, The" (S. Miller), 857
"Using the Law Library" (Hilyerd), 150, 855
U.S. Sentencing Commission, 587
U.S. Supreme Court Justices. See JUSTICES OF THE UNITED STATES SUPREME COURT.
U.S. Tax Court, 253
Utah Supreme Court, 134, 138, 243, 289, 543, 603, 625, 659, 660, 665, 693, 704
ut res magis valeat quam pereat, 650

vacate, defined, 809
Vandenbark rule, 592–95
Venturing to Do Justice (R. Keeton), 396, 404, 848
venue, change of, 473–74
Vermont Supreme Court, 134, 279, 282, 389, 709, 738, 743
vertical precedent,
 binding effect of, 155–56
 bright-line rule, 28–30
 conflicting decisions, 301–03, 305–06
 defined, 802
 dicta and, 55–57, 69–72
 disagreement with, 30
 distinguishing cases and, 101
 effect of grant of review on, 261
 generally, 27–34, 38, 40, 42–43, 455, 515, 565–66, 696, 802
 hierarchy, 28
 holdings and, 116, 121
 horizontal precedent. See HORIZONTAL PRECEDENT.
 international law, 762
 law-of-the-circuit rule, 491
 Marks rule, 202, 205–06
 multiple questions involved, 122
 overruling, 30–32
 principles summarized, 42–43
 rank of court, 28
 rule of property, 424
 stare decisis, 27, 376, 381, 732, 807
 state courts, 33–34, 244–45, 255, 679, 689, 696

vertical precedent (*cont'd*)
 Supremacy Clause, 34
vertical stare decisis, defined, 807
vested rights, 308, 316, 318
Vienna Convention, 760–61
Vinogradoff, Paul (1854–1925), 13, 173, 309, 850
Vinson, Fred M. (1890–1953), 525
Vinson, Kathleen Elliott, 850
Virginia Court of Appeals, 742
Virginia Supreme Court, 110, 165, 279, 282, 538, 738, 742, 760
Virgin Islands, 734
Vogenauer, Stefan (b. 1968), 762, 860
Volokh, Eugene (b. 1968), 861
Volz, Marlin M., 769, 774, 846
Vong, David, 238, 860
von Moschzisker, Robert (1870–1939), 10, 850, 860
Voting Rights Act, 102

Walbolt, Sylvia H., 239, 240, 860
Wald, Patricia (b. 1928), 149, 499
Waldron, Jeremy (b. 1953), 860
Walker, Christopher J., 288
Walker, David M. (1920–2014), 850
Walker, James M., 850
Walker, Thomas G., 28, 846
Walker, Timothy (1806–1856), 1, 850
Walsh, Mark, 527
Wambaugh, Eugene (1856–1940), 74, 269, 270, 850
Ward, Artemus, 846
Warren, Charles (1868–1954), 577, 860
Warren, Earl (1891–1974), 184–85, 200, 662
Warren, Samuel (1852–1910), 850
Warsaw Convention, 754
Wasby, Stephen L. (b. 1937), 214, 215, 216, 860
Washington, Bushrod (1762–1829), 421
Washington, George (1732–1799), 269, 270
Washington Court of Appeals, 169, 189, 210, 717

Washington Supreme Court, 101, 158, 221, 234, 241, 254, 279, 294, 323, 391, 625, 629, 665, 670, 681–82, 724, 741
Wasserstrom, Richard A. (b. 1936), 9, 850
Watergate, 185
weightiness of precedents,
  age of decision, 159–60, 176–81, 236–38, 355–56
  approval, 155, 240
  arbitration, 767–79
  concurrences, 239
  court's status, 243, 244, 245, 247
  dicta, 55, 62–63, 66, 70, 244
  disapproval, doubt, disagreement, 240, 242
  dissents, 188, 239
  dual majority, 210, 212
  equally divided court, 220–21, 223–24
  factors affecting, generally, 156–58, 228
  factual differences, 92
  horizontal precedents, 155, 156, 376, 507, 509
  hypothetical or moot cases, 133
  interlocutory orders, 156
  interpretations of law, 280, 281–83, 290, 536
  isolated decisions, 397, 406
  judge's reputation, 249, 251
  novel questions, 155, 159–60
  outlier cases, 160–63
  per curiam opinions, 214–15
  persuasive authority, 164–72, 280, 281–83, 290
  plurality, 198
  reliance interests, 159, 161
  rule of property, 423, 424, 433
  rulings, 116
  specialized courts, 243
  split decisions, 182
  summary disposition, 214, 227
  syllabus, 152
  thoroughness of consideration and reasoning, 226, 227, 286, 296, 374
  unanimous decisions, 182
  unpublished decisions, 142–49, 800
  vertical precedents, 155–56
Weinreb, Lloyd L. (b. 1936), 850
Weisgerber, Erica S., 131, 860
Westin, Alan F. (1929–2013), 853

West Virginia Supreme Court of Appeals, 152, 158, 214, 259, 279, 289, 292, 296, 366, 463, 629–30, 739
We the Judges (W.O. Douglas), 101, 354, 846
"What Does—and Does Not—Ail State Constitutional Law" (Sutton), 663, 664, 666, 860
"What Is the Common Law?" (Corbin), 853
"What of Stare Decisis?" (Pound), 858
"When the Court Divides" (Thurmon), 196, 208, 212, 213, 860
"When the Dissent Creates the Law" (Eber), 207, 208, 210, 212, 213, 853
"When to Hold, When to Fold, and When to Reshuffle" (D. Wood), 192, 860
"Which Countries Count?" (Glensy), 166, 854
White, Byron (1917–2002), 190, 196, 200, 478, 532
Whitney, Edward B. (1857–1911), 17, 860
"Why Agency Interpretations of Ambiguous Statutes Should Be Subject to Stare Decisis" (Greenberg), 854
"Why Dicta Becomes Holding and Why It Matters" (Stinson), 135, 859
"Why Must Inferior Courts Obey Superior Court Precedents?" (Caminker), 28, 30, 853
Wigmore, John Henry (1863–1943), 851
Wilde, Oscar (1854–1900), 300
"William Howard Taft and the Importance of Unanimity" (O'Connor), 183, 857
Williams, Glanville L. (1911–1997), 2, 35, 50, 92, 176, 269, 303, 333, 392, 850, 851, 860
Williams, John Herbert (1857–1917), 850
Williams, Robert F., 659, 663, 851, 860
Williston, Samuel (1861–1963), 851
Wills, Garry, xi
"Will the Federal Courts of Appeals Perish if They Publish?" (Dragich), 149, 853
Wilson, James (1742–1798), 535

Windeyer, W.J.V. (1900–1987), 5, 851
Winfield, Percy H. (1878–1953), 851
Winning Brief, The (Garner), 51, 847
Wisconsin Court of Appeals, 52, 117, 165, 228, 280, 282, 284, 285, 288, 301, 689, 692, 707, 724
Wisconsin Supreme Court, 117, 175, 208, 221, 233, 279, 280, 282, 295, 310, 384, 391, 397, 398, 409, 410, 428, 434, 455, 545, 657, 669, 680–81, 688, 689–90, 691, 724, 739, 752
Wisdom, John Minor (1905–1999), 603–04
Witkin, B.E. (1904–1995), 387
Wittich, Stephan, 860
Wolfrum, Rüdriger (b. 1941), 762, 851, 852
Womack, Eric R., 287, 860
Wood, Diane P. (b. 1950), 114, 192, 860
Wood, Gordon S. (b. 1933), 664, 851
Woodruff, Edwin H. (1862–1941), 851
Woolsey, Theodore D. (1801–1889), 1, 10, 22, 392, 397, 848
Works of Francis Bacon, The (Montagu ed.), 44, 845, 852

World Anti-Doping Code, 777
Wortley, Ben Atkinson (1907–1989), 9, 851
Wright, Charles Alan (1927–2000), 65, 133, 135, 136, 231, 232, 269, 271, 328, 329, 379, 445, 451, 453, 460, 646, 675, 676, 692, 694, 851
writ of certiorari. See CERTIORARI.
written law, defined, 1–2, 797
Wroth, L. Kinvin, 737, 860
"WTO Legal System, The" (Palmeter & Mavroidis), 764, 858
Wyoming Supreme Court, 191, 279, 282, 291, 294, 376, 627–28, 659

Yannaca-Small, Katia, 775, 858
Young, Ernest A., 565, 578, 860

Zeigler, Donald H., 693, 860
Zimmerman, Stephanie C., 239, 240, 860
ZoBell, Karl M., 183, 86
zone of danger, 170–71

Colophon

The pages of this book were laid out in the offices of LawProse Inc. in Dallas, Texas by Jeff Newman. The design draws on influences of classical law treatises. The body type, Caslon, was crafted by the English typefounder William Caslon (1692–1766) and was prevalent in England and America into the early 20th century. It was the face used for the first printed versions of the United States Declaration of Independence. The typeface used here is a modern cut, Adobe Caslon, designed by Carol Twombly and based on Caslon's mid-18th-century specimen pages.

Advance Praise for
The Law of Judicial Predecent

"A collective effort by some of the best judicial minds, coordinated by Bryan Garner, our leading authority on legal reasoning and writing, this amazing book is a signal accomplishment. Tackling the idea of precedent—a problem puzzled over by Holmes, Cardozo, and their intellectual heirs—in hornbook form, with a team of distinguished judicial thinkers, is a monumental achievement. The format and collaborative authorship make the book especially powerful. It's an essential read for anyone concerned with the state of the law."

—Robert C. Berring
University of California, Berkeley, School of Law

"What is the craft of judging? For as long as judges have judged, it is the end product that dominates. But Bryan Garner is our leading analyst of how judging is done and how it should be done. In his hands, the work of the judiciary is a learned skill, one that has masters and yeomen, one that rewards the high arts of the trade. Here he has enlisted a cast of judicial luminaries to examine the tools in the judicial toolbox. The result is both illuminating and, well, unprecedented."

—Samuel Issacharoff
New York University School of Law

"Don't let the size of this book scare you off! You'll keep dipping into it for wit and wisdom."

—Yale Kamisar
University of Michigan Law School

Advance Praise for *The Law of Judicial Precedent*

"No one is better than Bryan Garner at using direct and clear language to get at basic issues in the law. He displays that skill in abundance in his analysis of the meaning and uses of precedent. Drawing upon the vast experience of 13 professionals, mostly distinguished appellate-court judges, he nimbly explores the daunting world of precedent—surely the most distinguishing feature of the Anglo-American legal system. Precedents can be used in ways both helpful and harmful, yet the concept is ultimately intertwined with principles of reliance and due process of law. Indeed, precedent, rightly understood, helps keep the exercise of judicial power from being boundless and arbitrary. Bryan Garner draws upon history, theory, and a sense of the practical to steer the reader to a clearer understanding of the subject. This book should be at the elbow of judges, lawyers, and others who want a sure guide to the uses of precedent."

—A.E. Dick Howard
University of Virginia School of Law

"Clearly written, fully supported by caselaw, and impressively argued throughout, this book sheds new light on an important subject. Highly recommended for lawyers and students of American law."

—Richard Helmholz
University of Chicago Law School

Advance Praise for *The Law of Judicial Precedent*

"Garner and his stellar panel of judges have written the bible on the role of case decisions and precedent in law—an understanding of which is critical whatever the legal field. In one integrated narrative, they have given us a book that is both comprehensive and incredibly readable. Without it, the reader would have been required to research hundreds of disparate articles to get even a fraction of the information imparted here. Even then it would be without Garner and company's masterly insights and colorful modern examples. The table of contents alone (a list of concisely stated blackletter propositions in sentence form) is a font of information. The only faintly comparable book was written over 100 years ago, and it falls far short of this book. You don't understand law unless you understand the principles Garner and his group of judges explain, analyze, and illustrate so well. Their book is a must-read for absolutely every lawyer and law student, and I intend to assign it to my classes forthwith. I wish it had been available when I was in law school and in practice."

—Paul F. Rothstein
Georgetown University Law Center

"Garner and his coauthors have managed to corral an intimidatingly huge and complex topic. The result is an authoritative and comprehensive, yet comprehensible, treatise on judicial precedent. Perhaps even more remarkably, they have at the same time produced an admirable work of legal literature. This book is a pleasure to read, from page 1 to page 783."

—Ross E. Davies
George Mason University School of Law